RPG II AND RPG III STRUCTURED PROGRAMMING

RPG II AND RPG III STRUCTURED PROGRAMMING

2nd edition

Nancy Stern

Hofstra University

Robert A. Stern

Nassau Community College

Alden Sager

Nassau Community College

James Cooper

Lambton College

WILEY

John Wiley & Sons

New York   Chichester   Brisbane   Toronto   Singapore

Library of Congress Cataloging-in-Publication Data:

RPG II and RPG III structured programming.—2nd ed. / by Nancy Stern . . . [et al.]
   p. cm.
  Rev. ed. of: RPG II and RPG III programming / Nancy Stern, Alden Sager, Robert A. Stern. ©1984.
  Includes index.
  ISBN 0-471-52196-5 (paper)
  1. RPG (Computer program language) 2. Structured programming.
I. Stern, Nancy B. II. Title: RPG 2 and RPG 3 structured programming.
QA76.73.R2S7 1991
005.2'22—dc20

      90-23834
      CIP

Printed in the United States of America

10 9 8 7 6 5 4 3 2 1

To

Melanie Mara Stern
N.S. and R.A.S.

In memory of Alden and Myrtle Sager, and Joseph Perlman
Special appreciation to Nancy Sager.
A.S.

Liane Cooper
J.C.

PREFACE

Our text offers many advantages over the other RPG texts on the market today:

1. A step-by-step, proven and effective pedagogic approach that makes RPG relatively easy to learn. We include numerous illustrations, examples, and practice programs to help reinforce material presented. That is, the Stern & Stern approach, including chapter outlines, objectives, self-tests throughout each chapter and at the end of each chapter, summaries, practice programs, key terms lists, debugging exercises, and programming assignments is as effective here as in our other programming texts.

2. A focus on structured as well as traditional programming design features, with the former emphasized far more in this book than in any other RPG book. Our objective is to strike a proper balance between traditional programming and newer, structured design techniques.

   We focus not only on the four logical control constructs used in a structured program, but on top-down, modular programming concepts. We also include a discussion of planning tools such as pseudocode and hierarchy charts used to depict the logic in a top-down, modular, structured program.

3. A full discussion of interactive processing as well as the more traditional batch processing.

4. A discussion of RPG III and RPG/400 features. The basic elements of these versions of RPG are integrated throughout the text; the advanced features are explained in a full chapter—Chapter 12.

5. A focus on programming guidelines and documentation techniques that make programs easier to read, debug, maintain, and modify. More attention is given to proper coding style. For example, emphasis is placed on the use of prefixes for field names, the use of Data Structures for work areas, the use of comments in a program, and so on.

Several topics, such as fetch overflow, matching records, and TESTN, that are more characteristic of older, less structured uses of RPG have been de-emphasized or omitted entirely, since such methods are no longer the norm.

OCL for the System/36 is emphasized, while references to JCL and UNIVAC job control have been removed. The Source Entry Utility for interactive processing is also covered in detail. We have integrated, as well, features of processing RPG on an AS/400. Finally, the RPG Logic Cycle is explained in its entirety, as well as methods used to override the traditional sequence of operations.

Punched card references have been eliminated entirely from the text and references to magnetic tape have been minimized. Interactive processing and methods used for designing screen displays are emphasized in this edition.

Also, screen displays are used in place of coding sheets in numerous illustrations.

Several topics from the previous edition, like array and table handling, have been enhanced and new topics such as sorting, merging, and generating WORKSTN programs have been added.

The following is an Annotated Table of Contents listing the contents of all the chapters and how they differ from those in other RPG texts.

Annotated Table of Contents

1. Introduction to RPG Programming

This chapter provides a general overview of what a program is, why programs need to be translated, and the overall program development process. It then offers a full discussion of the techniques that should be used for producing a well-designed program. The focus here is on structured programming and on modular and top-down design.

We then focus on the nature of RPG and provide a full discussion of the basic RPG Coding Specifications and the RPG Logic Cycle. We include a full RPG program as an illustration so that students are exposed to RPG coding from the very beginning.

2. The Printing of Reports

We begin with a complete description of the elements that should be included in all well-designed reports and then provide a full discussion of how reports are generated in RPG. Edit words are discussed here so that they can be used by students in all their programs. After a student has completed Chapter 2, he or she will be ready to code full RPG programs in their entirety and will have learned the basic rules for producing effective reports.

3. Arithmetic Operations

This chapter focuses on the basic arithmetic operations. It also includes a full discussion of how numeric literals are used, how running totals are obtained, how to round results, how to use a counter, and so on. We also include a discussion of Data Structures and how they are effectively used in structured programs. This topic is either deemphasized or omitted in most RPG texts, which generally tend to minimize the importance of structured concepts.

4. Selection: Comparing Fields

This chapter provides a full discussion of the COMP instruction and introduces students to logical control procedures.

5. Structured Programming Design: Concepts and Tools

This chapter, unique to RPG texts, focuses on how to design programs, how to modularize programs, and how to use structured programming techniques. We illustrate how hierarchy charts are used for designing top-down programs. Subroutines are explained in far more detail and in a much earlier chapter than in any other RPG book.

Similarly, the IFxx/ELSE/END logical control structure and the CASE structure are also discussed in depth, whereas their importance tends to be minimized in other RPG texts.

6. Iteration and Looping

Ours is the only RPG book that not only explains looping in depth but illustrates how it is accomplished using the EXCPT and the DO structures, both of which are more modern, structured programming concepts. Most books focus on the GOTO for branching, which is really an outdated method of looping.

7. Control Break Processing

Our chapter on this important, but difficult topic continues to be clearer and more meaningful than similar chapters in other texts.

8. File Concepts and Sequential File Processing

We discuss file concepts in complete detail so that students learn the various ways in which files are created and organized. The chapter then considers sequential file processing concepts so that students learn how to create and update sequential files using a wide variety of techniques. Here, again, no other book provides such a comprehensive and pedagogically sound introduction to this important topic. We also focus on sort procedures and explain Tagalong and Address Out Sorts in far greater detail than any other book.

9. Indexed File Processing

We include a full discussion of why indexed files are so frequently used, how they are created and maintained, and how they are used for inquiry and reporting purposes. We discuss dynamic processing of indexed files, which is another topic omitted from most RPG texts.

10. Array Processing and Table Handling

This chapter discusses both dynamic and static arrays and tables as well as compile-time and pre-execution time arrays and tables. We focus on the use of arrays for accumulating totals and the use of tables for look-up purposes. Two-dimensional tables and arrays are discussed as well as parallel tables and arrays. Various array operations such as the SORTA are thoroughly discussed and illustrated in this chapter, whereas other RPG texts relegate this material to an appendix.

11. Interactive Processing

We explain the major differences between batch and interactive processing. Ours is the only RPG text to devote a full chapter to designing screen layouts and generating RPG WORKSTN programs for interactive processing.

12. Features of RPG III and RPG/400

While structured programming features of RPG III are integrated throughout the text, we devote this full chapter to advanced RPG III and RPG/400 techniques that are unique to the newer compilers. We include detailed discussions on externally described files, the CALL, DELET, EXFMT, UPDAT, and WRITE operations as well as many other operations. There is additional material here on processing inquiries from interactive workstations.

Appendixes

We have a full appendix on Communicating with Operating Systems, which includes an overview of Control Language commands for several RPG computers. We provide an appendix on the full RPG Logic Cycle, and a Glossary of all key terms defined in the text.

This book is written so that it can be used by introductory computer students as well as those with some previous programming background. It is also intended to be used with any computer, although special features of RPG for the IBM S/36 and AS/400 are emphasized.

We thank the following people for their review of the manuscript: Charles Biondi, Cumberland County College; Janet Dunford, Central Virginia Community College; Russel K. Lake, Parkland College; and Glenn F. Boswell, San Antonio College.

Finally, we would like to thank Carol L. Eisen for her assistance in manuscript preparation, Shelley Flannery for copyediting and proofreading, Edward A. Burke, Lorraine Burke, and Susan Posmentier of Hudson River Studio for the design and production of the book, Suzanne Ingrao and Joe Ford at Wiley for supervising the production process, Nancy Sager for her technical assistance with the manuscript, Carolyn Henderson at Wiley for her marketing plan, and Joseph Dougherty, our editor at Wiley, for his support and assistance.

We update and revise our books with some frequency and welcome your comments, suggestions, and even criticisms. We can be reached c/o Joseph Dougherty, John Wiley and Sons, Inc., 605 Third Avenue, New York, NY 10158, or via bitnet: ACSNNS@HOFSTRA.

CONTENTS

UNIT 1

THE BASICS

1

Introduction to RPG Programming

OBJECTIVES

To familiarize you with

1. Basic programming concepts and terms.
2. An overview of the RPG language and the coding forms used.
3. The concept of the RPG Logic Cycle.
4. The nature of a problem definition and how an RPG program is coded from it.

I. Computer Programming: An Overview

A. What Is a Program?

No matter how complex a computer is, its actions are directed by individual computer instructions that operate on **input** data and convert it to meaningful **output** information. The set of instructions is called a **program,** which is written by a computer professional called a **programmer**.

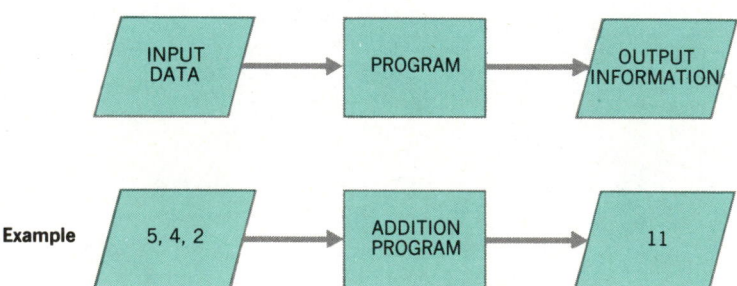

A computer, then, can process data only as efficiently and effectively as it is programmed.

B. Machine Language Programs

All instructions to be executed by the computer must be in **machine language.** It would be very tedious and cumbersome for the programmer to code instructions in this form. He or she would need to reference actual addresses or locations in memory and use complex instruction codes.

C. Symbolic Programs

Since programming in machine language is so difficult, programming languages were developed to enable the programmer to write English-like or symbolic instructions. However, before symbolic instructions can be executed or run, they must be translated or *compiled* into machine language. The computer itself uses a translator program or **compiler** to perform this conversion into machine language.

The output from the compiler consists of machine-level **object modules.** Most object modules are incomplete, however, containing references to other object modules such as access methods and prewritten subroutines; thus, they cannot be loaded and executed as is. Another program, called the **linkage editor,** is used to link these object modules together into one executable **load module** or **object program.** The load module can then be executed.

Most **RPG** compilers include the link-edit step as part of the compile process. That is, if the source program compiles without syntax errors the linkage-editor will automatically link the object modules into a load module ready for execution.

There are numerous **symbolic programming languages** that can be translated into machine language. RPG is one such language; it is the one used most extensively in the IBM mid-range environment. Other symbolic programming languages include COBOL, BASIC, and Pascal.

II. The Program Development Process for Application Programming

A. An Overview of the Program Development Process

Many people believe that computer programming begins with coding or writing program instructions and ends with program testing. Note, however, that programmers who begin coding without any prior planning often produce poorly designed or inadequate programs.

The steps involved in programming should be developmental, where coding is undertaken only *after* the program requirements have been fully specified and the logic to be used has been clearly designed.

In addition, there are steps required *after* a program has been coded and tested if it is to be used in regular production runs. Every program that is to be run on a regularly scheduled basis must be *documented*. This means that the program must be accompanied with a formal set of procedures and instructions that specify how it is to be used. This **documentation** is meant for (1) users who will be entering data and/or using the output and (2) maintenance programmers who will need to keep the program current.

An overview of the steps involved in the program development process follows. Each of these steps will then be discussed in detail.

PROGRAM DEVELOPMENT PROCESS

1. **Obtain Program Specifications**
   Programmers typically write programs for specific departments or users within a company. In large companies or in companies requiring long and complex programs, a programmer may work under the supervision of a systems analyst who designs the overall business systems and plans the requirements for each application. In small

companies, a programmer/analyst may be responsible for both the design of a system and the programs required.

Whether or not there is a systems analyst to supervise the job, the programmer should be certain he or she understands the precise requirements of the user.

2. **Plan the Program Using Planning Tools**
   Programmers use design tools such as *flowcharts*, *pseudocode*, and *hierarchy charts* to help map out the structure and logic of a program before the program is actually coded. We will illustrate the use of these planning tools throughout the text.

3. **Code and Enter the Program**
   After a program has been planned, the programmer writes the program and enters it into the computer system. Another term for "writing a program" is "coding a program." Most often, the program is keyed into the computer system using a keyboard and displayed on a screen.

4. **Compile and Link-Edit the Program into Machine Language**
   As noted, symbolic programs must be compiled and link-edited before they can be run. The compiler checks for rule violations or syntax errors when translating a program. If there are such errors, the compiler will list them and the program will need to be corrected and then recompiled before it can be run or tested.

5. **Test the Program**
   The program must be run or executed with test data to make certain that it reads input, processes it, and produces output that is correct. That is, a program is tested to eliminate any logic errors that may produce erroneous output. If there are any logic errors, the program will need to be corrected, recompiled, and then tested again.

6. **Document the Program**
   The programmer writes a manual or set of instructions so that users will be able to run the program and understand what it accomplishes.

B. A Detailed Look at the Steps Involved

1. Obtain Program Specifications

When a company decides to computerize a business application such as payroll or accounts receivable, a systems analyst is typically assigned the task of designing the entire computerized application. This systems analyst works closely with users in the specific business area to determine such factors as output needs, how many programs are required, and input requirements. A **user** is the person who, when the application is computerized, will depend on or work with the output.

When a systems analyst decides what programs are required, he or she prepares *program specifications* to be given to the programmers so that they can perform their tasks.

Typically, the program specifications consist of:

1. Record layout forms to describe the formats of the input and output data on disk or other storage medium. Figure 1.1 illustrates a sample record layout. It indicates:
   a. The data items or fields within each record.

Figure 1.1
Sample record layout.

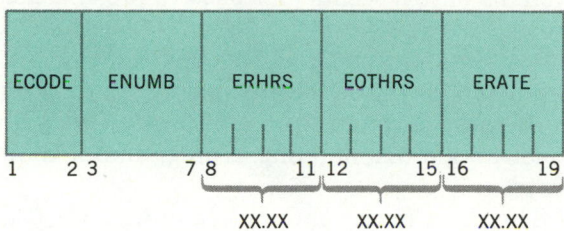

b. The location of each data item within the record.
c. The size of each data item.
d. For numeric data items, the number of decimal positions. For example, xxx.xx is a five-digit field with three integer and two decimal places. (Two decimal places are typically used in dollars and cents fields.)
e. In some organizations, standard names of the fields to be used in a program are specified on the record layouts. In other organizations, names of fields are assigned by the programmer.
2. Printer Spacing Charts for printed output. Printed output has special requirements not typically needed for other types of output:
   a. Headings are usually printed.
   b. Data must be spaced neatly across the page, allowing for margins.
   c. Sometimes additional lines for error messages or totals are required.

A **Printer Spacing Chart,** illustrated in Figure 1.2, is a tool used for determining the proper spacing of printed output. It specifies the print positions to be used in the output. It also includes all data items to be printed and their formats.

Thus, the analyst typically provides the programmer with record layout forms and/or a Printer Spacing Chart to indicate the precise format of the input and output. Along with these layout forms, a set of notes is provided by the systems analyst indicating the specific requirements of the program.

Illustrative programs and assignments in this text will include these same program specifications so that (1) you will become familiar with them as you read through the book and (2) you will know what you can expect to receive from a

Figure 1.2
Sample Printer Spacing Chart.

```
         6  PAYROLL LIST      XX/XX/XX    PAGE XX
H
         8  EMPLOYEE REGULAR   OVERTIME    GROSS
H
H        9  NUMBER   HOURS     HOURS       PAY
D       11  XXXXX    XX.XX     XX.XX      $X,XXX.XX
T       17  TOTAL GROSS PAY  $XX,XXX.XX
```

H = Heading line
D = Detail line
T = Total line

systems analyst if you work as a programmer. In addition, the more common systems design techniques used to prepare these forms will be explained.

2. Plan the Program Using Planning Tools

Before a programmer begins to code, he or she should *plan the logic* to be used in the program. Just as an architect draws a blueprint before undertaking the construction of a building, a programmer should use a planning tool before a program is coded.

The three most common planning tools used by programmers are:

1. Flowcharts.
2. Pseudocode.
3. Hierarchy charts.

A **flowchart** is a conventional block diagram providing a pictorial representation of the logic to be used in a program. **Pseudocode** uses written English-like expressions rather than diagrams and is specifically suited for depicting logic in a structured program. **Hierarchy** or **structure charts** are an excellent tool for showing the relationships among sections in a program. In Chapter 5 we provide an in-depth discussion of these tools.

3. Code and Enter the Program

The programmer writes a set of instructions, called the **source program,** in a symbolic programming language. This program cannot be executed or run by the computer until it has been compiled into machine language.

The source program is *keyed* into a computer using a keyboard of a terminal and then *stored* on a storage medium, usually a disk. A special program called a text editor is used for entering and making changes to a source program.

4. Compile and Link-Edit the Program into Machine Language

After the source program has been entered, the computer must translate it into a machine language executable module called the load module before execution can occur. The compiler program first translates the source program into an object module. Since the object module contains references to other object modules, it must be link-edited to form one executable module. The linkage-editor program is used to combine these object modules into a load module or object program ready for execution. Once this is complete, the load module can be saved and executed at any time, without the need for translation. This makes machine language load modules more efficient for regularly scheduled production runs.

5. Test the Program

a. Debugging Phases.

When the computer translates an RPG program, any errors detected by the compiler will be listed. That is, any violation of programming rules is noted as a **syntax error.** For example, if the RPG operation to add two numbers is spelled AD instead of ADD, the computer will print a message indicating that a syntax error has occurred. If such errors are very serious, then execution of the program cannot begin until the errors are corrected.

Note that the syntax errors detected during a compilation are just one type of programming error. A **logic error,** which is detected during program execution, is one in which the *sequence* of programming steps is not specified properly. Or it can be one in which the wrong instruction is coded; if you include an ADD instruction instead of a MULT (multiply), for example, this would result in a logic error.

Logic errors are detected by the programmer when the program is tested. To detect any logic errors, the program is run with **test data** to see if it will process the data correctly. The test run reads the test data as input, processes it, and produces output. The programmer then checks the output to be sure it is correct. If it is not correct, a logic error has occurred. The programmer must then find the error, correct it, recompile the program, and test it again. This procedure is repeated until the program is working properly. The process of eliminating all syntax and logic errors is called **debugging**.

Test data should be prepared carefully to ensure that all conditions in the program are actually tested. If not, a program that initially appears to be correct may eventually produce logic errors when run with more complete data or when run on a regular basis.

After a program has been compiled, the object program can be linked and executed immediately with test data, or it may be saved on disk for later use. If a program has been compiled, a saved object program may be loaded into the computer at any time, linked, and executed or run *without the necessity of recompiling the source program*. Figure 1.3 illustrates the steps involved in coding and testing a program.

b. Debugging Techniques.   We have seen that after a program has been planned and coded, it must be compiled and executed with test data. It is not unusual for errors to occur during either compilation or execution. Eliminating these errors is called debugging. Several methods of debugging should be used by the programmer.

(1) Desk Checking.   Programmers should carefully review their programs *before* they are keyed in, and again after they have been keyed. **Desk checking** will minimize syntax errors and execution or "run time" errors, and, in general, reduce the overall time it takes to debug a program. Frequently, inexperienced programmers fail to see the need for desk checking, on the assumption that it is better to let the computer find errors. Omitting the desk-checking phase, however, can result in undetected *logic errors* that could take hours or even days to find later on. Experienced programmers carefully review their programs after they have been coded and again after they have been keyed.

(2) Correcting Syntax Errors.   While a program is being compiled, the computer will print diagnostic messages that specify any rule violations or syntax errors. The programmer must then correct the errors and recompile the program before it can be run with test data. As we will see, the RPG compiler makes this process relatively easy not only by printing the error message, but by identifying the error's location within the program.

(3) Performing Structured Program Walkthroughs.   After a source program has been listed by the computer in a source listing, programmers test the logic by executing it with test data. It is best, however, to "walk through" the program first to see if it will produce the desired results. This is called a structured program **walkthrough**. During this process the programmer steps through the logic of the program by processing the test data manually to see if the correct results will be obtained. Walkthroughs are performed *before* machine execution, so that they can help the programmer find logic errors even before the program is run.

(4) Detecting Logic Errors by Executing the Program.   In many ways, detecting logic errors by executing the program is the most difficult and time-

Figure 1.3
Steps involved in coding and
testing a program.

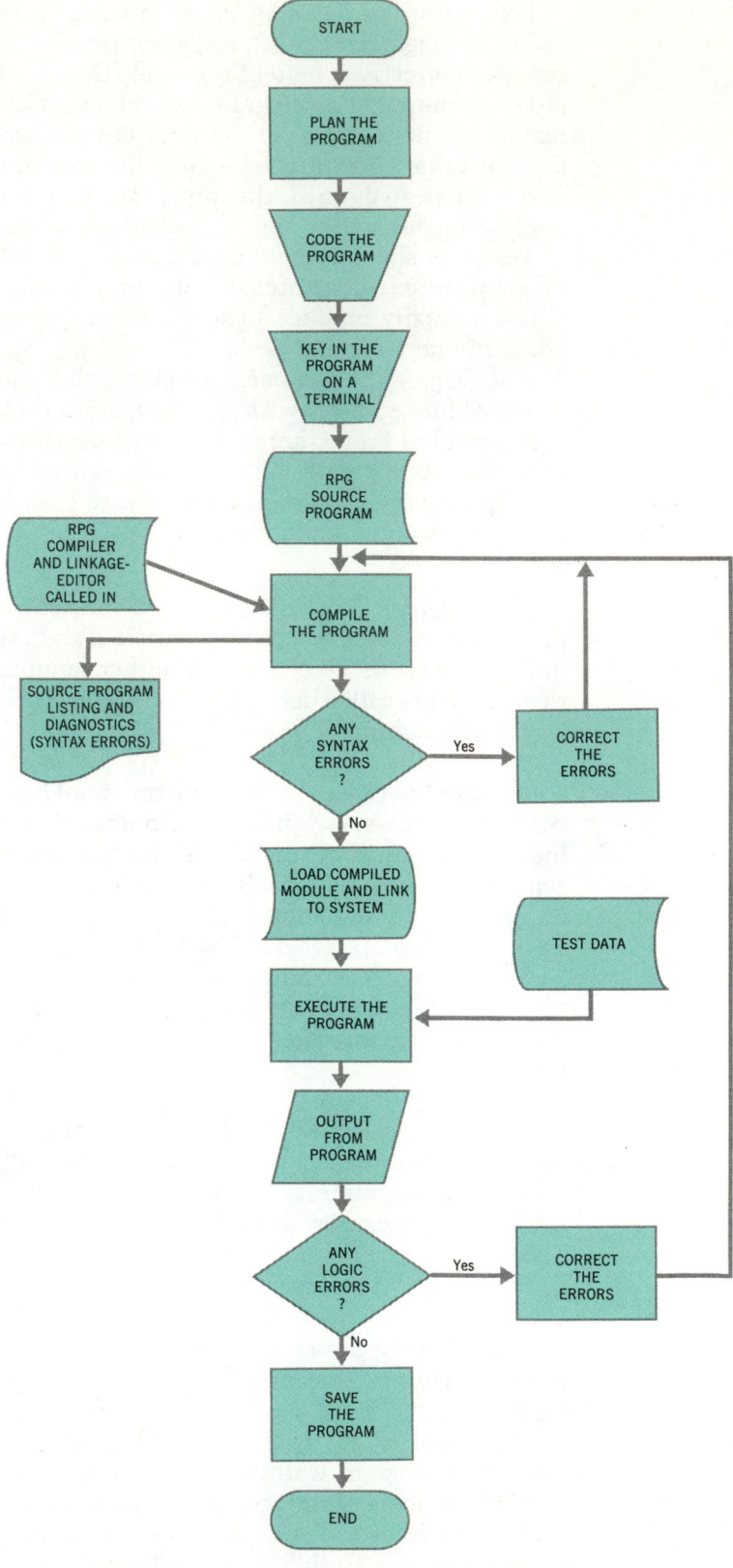

consuming aspect of debugging. If desk checking and structured program
walkthroughs are performed, the number of logic errors that are likely to occur
during program execution will be minimized.

(5) Testing Programs with Carefully Prepared Test Data. As noted, the preparation of test data is an extremely important aspect of debugging. The programmer should prepare data that will test *every possible condition* the program is likely to encounter under normal operating conditions. It is not uncommon for a program that has been thought to be fully tested and that has been operational for some time to suddenly produce errors. Most often, these problems arise because a specific condition not previously encountered has occurred for which the programmer did not adequately test.

6. Document the Program

The last element in the program development process is to prepare documentation so that the user and computer staff can run the program without the need for consulting the programmer. Documentation should provide instructions on how the program is to be run, what the program accomplishes, the type of error conditions that might occur, and so on. If the documentation is complete, then the program can be maintained and even modified without the original programmer's involvement.

III. The Nature of RPG

RPG is an abbreviation for Report Program Generator. It is a **high-level language** in which the programmer codes specifications for a problem and the computer generates a program. Since RPG consists of a series of specifications, it is considered very easy to code and is regarded as one of the highest level—or least machinelike—languages available.

RPG was developed by IBM in the 1960s. As originally conceived, and as the name implies, RPG was intended for applications that required report generation. Early RPG programs were written almost exclusively to read input data, perform a series of simple calculations, and print the results.

As the popularity of the language increased, its uses grew as well. In 1969, RPG II was introduced. It has far greater applicability than the original version and is well suited for handling high-level and complex input and output. This text considers RPG II in detail.

In 1980, RPG III was introduced. RPG III is designed for use in more sophisticated information processing environments where some of the more recent programming concepts and techniques have been implemented. RPG III is specifically designed to be used with two such techniques: structured programming and databases. Currently, RPG III is available on several IBM models such as the S/38 and AS/400 mid-range computers. Although this text focuses on RPG II, many RPG III enhancements are included in detail. In fact, many RPG II compilers have now been updated to include the RPG III enhancements discussed here.

Structured programming is a technique that results in more efficient and more standardized programs. By avoiding the use of branch instructions, each program can be modularized into a series of segments that can be written, evaluated, and debugged separately.

Database technology enables users to access one central store of data for all applications. The manner in which a database is manipulated, retrieved, and updated depends in large part on the programming languages used. RPG III has specific instructions and techniques designed to be used with databases.

Both RPG II and RPG III are used on mainframes, minicomputers, and even microcomputers. In addition to IBM, many other computer manufacturers and vendors have made RPG available.

IV. Techniques for Good Program Design

A. Structured Programming

1. An Overview

When programming became a major profession in the 1960s and 1970s, the primary goal of programmers was getting programs to work. Although this is still a programmer's main objective, writing programs so that they are easy to read, debug, modify, and maintain is now considered a very important goal as well. That is, as the computer field is developing, more and more attention is being given to *program design*, as well as to making programs operational.

The most important technique for coding well-designed programs *in any language* is called *structured programming*. Structured programming is an effort to standardize program design so that all programs, regardless of the language in which they are written, will have a similar form. In general, structured programs are easier to read than nonstructured programs. They are also easier to debug and modify if changes are required at a later date. Moreover, they are easier to evaluate so that programming managers and systems analysts are better able to assess programmers' skills and appraise the design elements in their programs.

In its earlier stages, RPG did not lend itself well to the more modern structured programming concepts. However, in recent years major improvements were added to RPG that allow the use of these newer, structured concepts. With these recent changes, RPG has become a very powerful structured programming language used on a wide variety of IBM mid-range computers.

In this book, we will discuss and illustrate the conventional methods of RPG programming. In addition, we will demonstrate the methods of writing more modern, structured RPG programs.

2. Structured Programming as GOTO-less Programming

For those of you who have previous programming experience, you may have encountered nonstructured techniques that include frequent use of GOTOs, which is another term for a branch. These GOTOs often make it very difficult to follow the logic of a program; similarly, they make debugging a program more difficult.

One major purpose of structured programming is to simplify debugging by reducing the number of entry and exit points or "GOTOs" in a program. For that reason, structured programming is sometimes referred to as GOTO-less programming. Using the techniques of structured programming, the GOTO statement is avoided entirely. In RPG this means writing programs where sequences are controlled by structured operations or some other logical control statement.

There are, however, thousands of existing RPG programs already written using the nonstructured GOTO technique; this book, therefore, will present both conventional, nonstructured programming techniques, as well as the more modern structured techniques.

B. Modular Programming

Long and complex structured programs are sometimes subdivided into **modules,** also called **subroutines.** These are separate sets of instructions that accomplish distinct functions. Programs that are subdivided into subroutines are called modular programs. In a modular program, the main body or module of the program calls in other subroutines as needed. That is, subroutines are written as separate sections and are *called into* the main body of a modular program when they are needed.

Modules of a program are not only written separately but can be tested separately as well. This makes it possible to segment a large or complex program into individual sections so that, if necessary, different programmers can code and debug these different sections. In summary, modular programs consist of individual sections that are executed under the control of a main module.

C. Top-Down Programming

Another important design technique that makes programs easier to read and more efficient is called **top-down programming.** Top-down programming implies that proper program design is best achieved by designing and coding major modules before minor ones. Thus, in a top-down program, the main routines are coded first, after which intermediate routines and then minor ones are coded. (We use the terms module, routine, and subroutine interchangeably in this text.)

By coding modules in this top-down manner, the *organization* or flow of the program is given primary attention. The main module is coded first; it includes references to minor modules that are to be called in. Detailed instructions are left to these minor modules, which are coded last.

Top-down programming is analogous to writing a term paper by developing an outline first that gets more detailed only after the main structure has been established. This standardized top-down technique provides an excellent complement to structured programming for achieving efficient and effective program design.

In this text, we will use a top-down approach in our more advanced programs so that you will learn to program using widely accepted, standardized, and effective techniques.

Chapter 5 discusses in depth the design features used in structured and top-down program design.

Self-Test

1. The major task of a computer programmer is to _____.
2. A set of instructions that will operate on input data and convert it to output is called a(n) _____.
3. To be executed by the computer, all instructions must be in _____ language.
4. Programs are written in _____ language. Why?
5. Programs written in a language other than machine language must be _____ before execution can occur.
6. _____ is an example of a high-level programming language.
7. _____ is the process of converting a source program into machine language.
8. The program written in a language such as RPG is called the _____ program.
9. The source program is the _____.
10. The object program is the _____.
11. A _____ converts a(n) _____ program into a(n) _____ program.
12. The errors that are detected during compilation denote _____ and are usually referred to as _____ errors.
13. The logic of a program can be checked by _____.
14. After a program has been compiled, it may be _____ or _____.
15. The two types of errors likely to be made by a programmer are _____ and _____.

Solutions

1. write and test computer instructions
2. program
3. machine

4. symbolic programming; machine language coding is tedious and cumbersome.
5. translated or compiled and link-edited
6. RPG
7. Compilation
8. source
9. set of instructions in a symbolic language such as RPG
10. set of instructions that has been converted into machine language
11. compiler; source; object
12. any violations of programming rules; syntax
13. testing it or executing it in a "test run" with sample data
14. executed; saved in translated form for future processing
15. syntax errors; logic errors

V. RPG Coding Requirements

A. The Six Basic Specifications Forms

Figure 1.4 shows the six basic RPG Specifications forms, which consist of the following:

1. Control and File Description Specifications	Lists the files to be used, the devices they will employ, and special features to be included.
2. Extension Specifications	Reserves storage for special types of data elements called tables and arrays. See Chapter 10.
3. Line Counter Specifications	Controls the length of forms for each application.
4. Input Specifications	Describes the format of input files.
5. Calculation Specifications	Describes arithmetic and logic operations to be performed.
6. Output Specifications	Describes the format of output files.

Typically, the Control and File Description Specifications form includes a single Control Specification line at the beginning of the program to provide information about program generation and execution.

The Control Specification must be the first entry of an RPG program followed in sequence by the other entries: File Description, Extension, Line Counter, Input, Calculation, and Output. The forms must be included in the order identified above.

The Extension Specifications will be discussed later in the text since this form is used with more advanced RPG programming problems. The Line Counter Specifications form, used for special printing applications, will be illustrated in Chapter 2.

The programs in the first few chapters of this text will focus exclusively on the four most important forms, namely the Control and File Description Specifications, Input, Calculation, and Output Specifications. The order of the forms is easy to remember if we remember the acronym of FICO.

B. The Basic Structure of an RPG Program

The six basic specifications forms are referred to as **RPG coding** or **program sheets**. All these forms have space for *80 columns* of information. Each line from a program sheet will be entered on one line of a terminal. Some computer

RPG CONTROL AND FILE DESCRIPTION SPECIFICATIONS

| Program | | Keying Instruction | Graphic | | | | Card Electro Number | | Page | 1 2 | of | Program Identification | 75 76 77 78 79 80 |
| Programmer | Date | | Key | | | | | | | | | | |

Control Specifications

For the valid entries for a system, refer to the RPG reference manual for that system.

H

Line | Form Type | Size to Compile | Object Output | Listing Options | Size to Execute | Debug | Reserved | Currency Symbol | Date Format | Date Edit | Inverted Print | Reserved | Number of Print Positions | Alternate Collating Sequence | Reserved | Inquiry | Reserved | Sign Handling | 1 P Forms Position | Indicator Setting | File Translation | Punch MFCU Zeros | Nonprint Characters | Reserved | Table Load Halt | Shared I/O | Field Print | Formatted Dump | RPG to RPG II Conversion | Number of Formats | S/3 Conversion | Subprogram | CICS/DL/I | Transparent Literal

File Description Specifications

For the valid entries for a system, refer to the RPG reference manual for that system.

F

Line | Filename | Form Type | I/O/U/C/D | P/S/C/R/T/D/F | E | A/D | F/V/S/M/D/E | Block Length | Record Length | L/R | A/P/I/K | U/X/D/T/R/ or 2 | Overflow Indicator | Key Field Starting Location | Extension Code E/L | Device | Symbolic Device | Labels S/N/E/M | K | Name of Label Exit | Option | Entry | Extent Exit for DAM | Storage Index | A/U | R/U/N | File Condition U1-U8, UC

RPG EXTENSION AND LINE COUNTER SPECIFICATIONS

| Program | | Keying Instruction | Graphic | | | | Card Electro Number | | Page | 1 2 | of __ | Program Identification | 75 76 77 78 79 80 |
| Programmer | Date | | Key | | | | | | | | | | |

Extension Specifications

E

Line | Form Type | Number of the Chaining Field | From Filename | To Filename | Table or Array Name | Number of Entries Per Record | Number of Entries Per Table or Array | Length of Entry | P/B/L/R | Decimal Positions | Sequence (A/D) | Table or Array Name (Alternating Format) | Length of Entry | P/B/L/R | Decimal Positions | Sequence (A/D) | Comments

Line Counter Specifications

L

Line | Form Type | Filename | 1 | 2 | 3 | 4 | 5 | 6 | 7 | 8 | 9 | 10 | 11 | 12

*Number of sheets per pad may vary slightly.

Figure 1.4
The six basic RPG
Specifications forms.

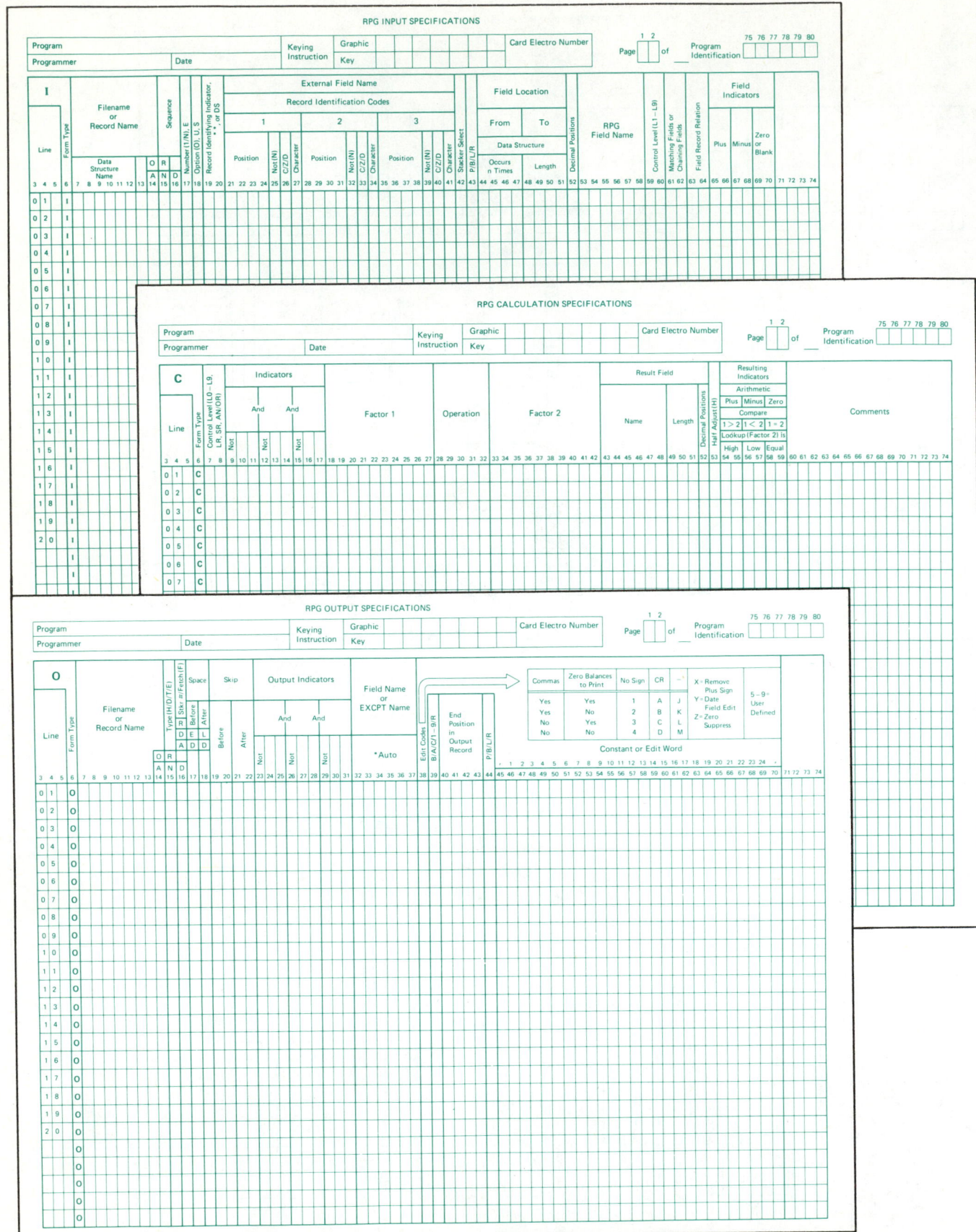

Figure 1.4
(*continued*)

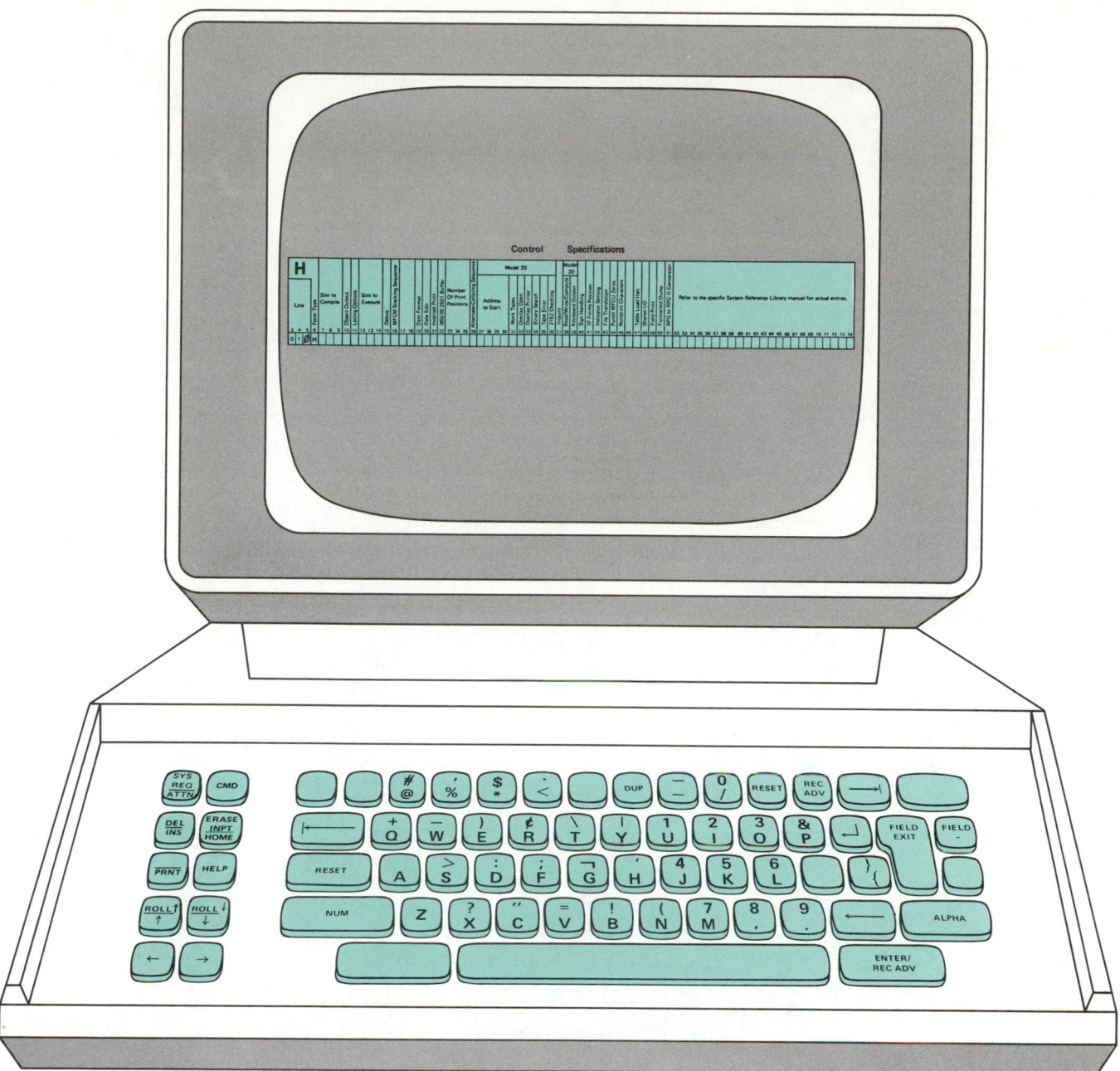

Figure 1.5
RPG coding form displayed on
a terminal screen.

systems will display the coding sheet format on a screen for ease of data entry (see Figure 1.5). Thus, for each line written on a coding sheet, you key one line of program specifications on a terminal or work station. The entire program keyed from coding sheets is called the RPG source program. See Figure 1.6 for a listing of an RPG source program.

Note that the date, program name, and programmer name at the top of each form may be used for identification purposes only since they are not keyed as part of the source program. See Figure 1.7, which describes these optional entries.

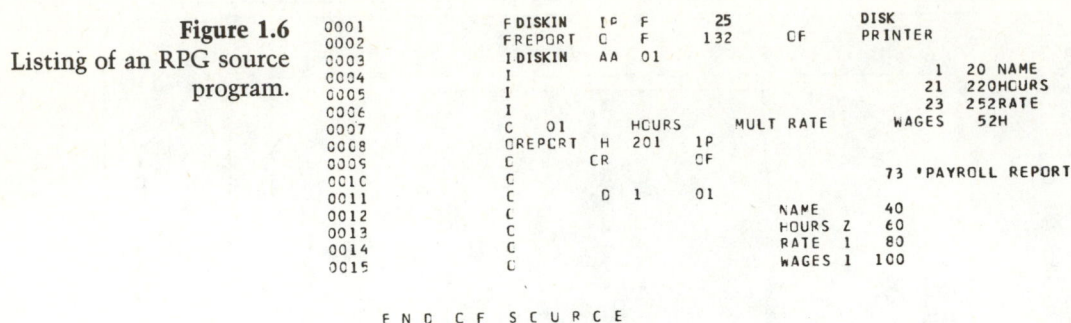

Figure 1.6
Listing of an RPG source
program.

```
0001        F DISKIN   IP  F       25            DISK
0002        FREPORT    O   F      132    OF      PRINTER
0003        I DISKIN   AA  01
0004        I                                        1   20 NAME
0005        I                                       21  220HOURS
0006        I                                       23  252RATE
0007        C   01         HOURS    MULT RATE     WAGES   52H
0008        OREPORT   H  201      1P
0009        C              OR      OF
0010        C                                       73 'PAYROLL REPORT'
0011        C              D  1     01
0012        C                                    NAME     40
0013        C                                    HOURS Z  60
0014        C                                    RATE  1  80
0015        C                                    WAGES 1 100
```

```
            E N D   O F   S O U R C E
```

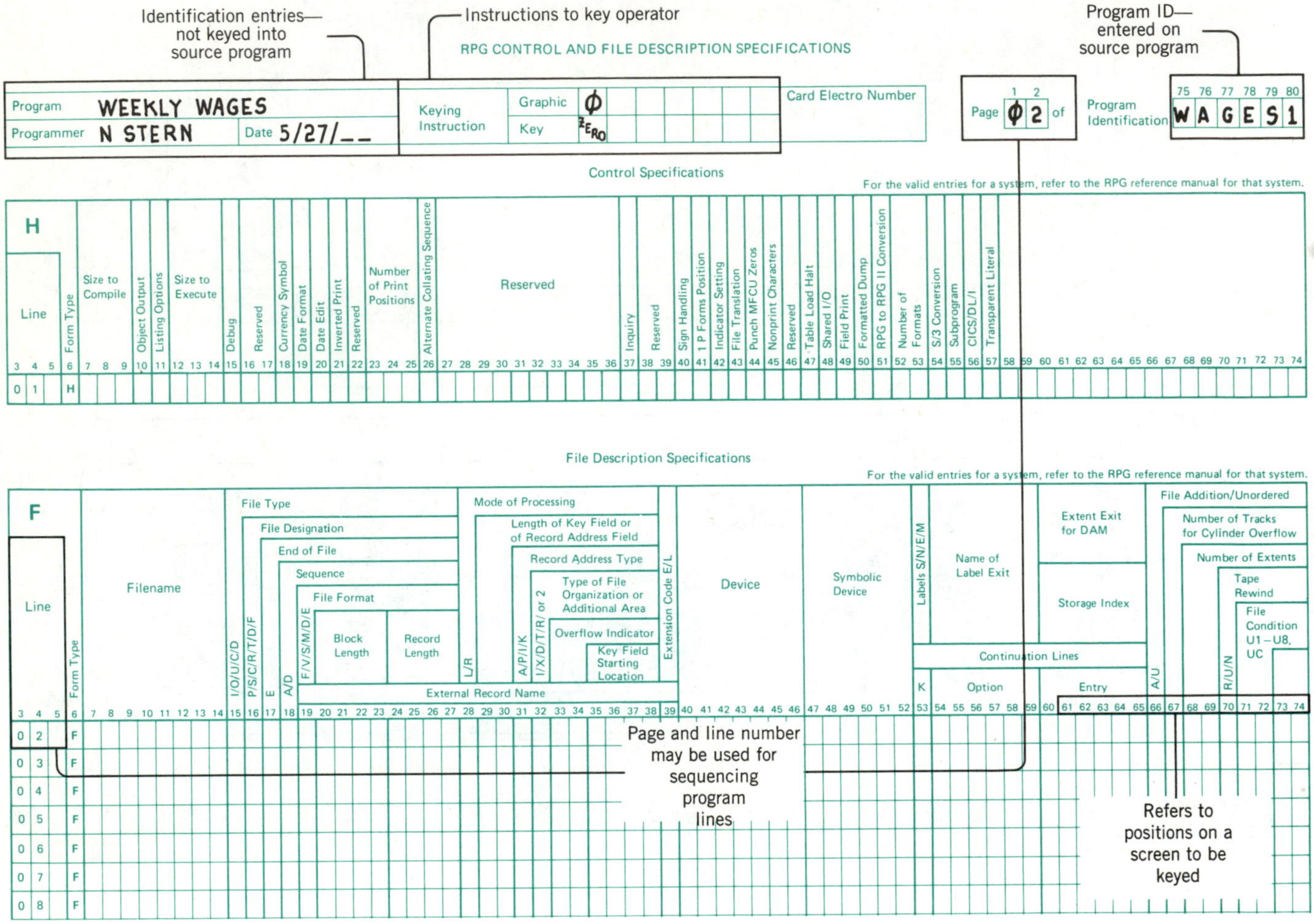

Program Identification, also on the top of the form, is used to identify the program and may be coded in columns 75–80 of each line. Again, this entry is optional, and if needed most modern text editors will provide this entry automatically.

If a data entry operator will be keying in the program for the programmer, *Keying Instructions* are used to explain which characters to enter, thereby eliminating any possible confusion. Since the letter O, for example, might be misinterpreted by a data entry operator as a zero, the programmer would use the convention of slashing zeros (Ø) to distinguish them from the letter O. The

Figure 1.7
Optional entries on the top of
each RPG form.

programmer might remind the operator of this convention by entering this information under Keying Instructions as shown in Figure 1.7.

This book uses the convention of slashing zeros (Ø) to distinguish them from the letter O.

Other characters that are sometimes confused by data entry operators are:

The letter I and the digit 1.
The letter Z and the digit 2.
The letter S and the digit 5.

Line Numbers (Columns 3–5)

The body of each form begins with a Line number field, columns 3–5, which is common to all the RPG specification forms. RPG coding forms were first used in a batch environment when data entry operators keyed RPG programs onto punched cards from coding sheets. Columns 1–2 were keyed with a page number (see the top of each form), while columns 3–5 contained line numbers. Keying the page numbers and line numbers insured that the program would be in proper sequence. If for some reason the program deck of cards got out of sequence, the program could be sorted into its correct sequence. The first entry would generally contain a line number 010, the next 020, and so on. The entries were numbered by tens, so that insertions could easily be made. That is, if a line was inadvertently omitted after line 010, it could be numbered as 015.

More recently, columns 1–4 are used for simply providing a sequence number for each line in the program (0001, 0002). Column 5 is usually left blank, but may be used if necessary. Keep in mind that these columns are used exclusively to enable a programmer to check the sequence of instructions; they do not affect the compiler. Modern text editors automatically provide sequence numbers for each line (0001, 0002, etc.). The advantages of new technology have greatly simplified the coding of RPG programs. We have included these older standards for completeness and to assist your understanding of the coding in the text. In the future, we will simply refer to each line in the program by its sequence number (0001, 0002, etc.), rather than page and line number, although some facilities may still use the older convention.

In summary, a line number is an optional entry and provides a means for a programmer to check the sequence of the program. Modern text editors, however, are capable of inserting sequence numbers and renumbering the program automatically whenever necessary.

Form Type (Column 6)

Each line of an RPG program must be identified by its specifications form type. Column 6 indicates the Form Type:

H for Control (Header) Specifications.
F for File Specifications.
E for Extension Specifications.
L for Line Counter Specifications.
I for Input Specifications.
C for Calculation Specifications.
O for Output Specifications.

Sequence numbers and Form Type are automatically entered by many computers when the program is keyed from a terminal.

Column 7 of all coding forms can be used to designate any line as a comment by coding an asterisk (*) in that column. Comments are very useful for providing documentary information about the coding. Because these comments are printed on the program, they can also help the programmer recall particular aspects of the coding during debugging.

All other coding requirements of the RPG specifications forms depend on the specific forms being used. This chapter provides coding rules for the File Description and Input forms in detail and indicates how the Calculation and Output forms are used as well.

The following will serve as a review of RPG coding rules:

	RPG CODING RULES	
Item	**Meaning**	**Columns into Which Data is Keyed**
Sequence number.	Provides identifying number for each line.	1–2 (Page number) 3–5 (Line number)
Form Type.	Indicates specifications sheet: H–Control (Header) Specifications. F–File Specifications. E–Extension Specifications. L–Line Counter Specifications. I–Input Specifications. C–Calculation Specifications. O–Output Specifications.	6
RPG statements.	These columns are coded according to the rules of the language.	7–74
Program Identification (upper right corner of form).	Identifies the program to the computer—an optional entry.	75–80 (of each line)

C. A Review of Data Organization

Data is processed by the computer in an organized way. Areas are set aside in memory for files, records, and fields. Each of these terms has special significance in RPG. If you are already familiar with these terms, you may skip this section.

1. Files

A **file** is the major classification of data pertaining to a specific application. An organization may have an *inventory file* containing all inventory information. A payroll file, accounts receivable file, and sales file are examples of commonly used business files. Each file is contained on a storage medium such as disk.

Most RPG programs use at least one input and one output file. Disk files are unique in that they can serve as both input and output during a single run. Changes can be made directly to a disk; thus it is possible to read from a disk and write back onto it. To use a disk in this way, however, requires a backup procedure to recreate the new disk each time it is outputted in case there is a problem with it. Sometimes disk files are designated as either "input only" or "output only."

In general, then, for each form of input and output used in a computer application, one file is designated.

Each file to be used in a program is defined and described on the File Description Specifications form along with the device to which it will be assigned.

Note that the overall collection of related files in an organization is referred to as a **database.** As we will see, this term has particular relevance when dealing with RPG III.

2. Records

A **record** is a collection of related fields of data stored as a unit within a file. A transaction file, for example, may consist of two types of records: credit records and sales records.

In RPG, each record could be designated with the use of a *coded field* that uniquely defines the record. For example, a "C" in position 1 might designate transaction records as credit records, and an "S" in position 1 might designate transaction records as sales records. On the Input Specifications form, record identifying indicators would be used to specify each record type. We use the term Input form and Input Specifications form interchangeably. Similarly Output form and Output Specifications form are used interchangeably.

3. Fields

A **field** is a group of consecutive storage positions reserved for a specific data item. A sales record, for example, may consist of the following fields: Account Number, Customer Name, Amount of Purchase, and Date of Purchase. Input fields are specified in RPG on the Input form, and output fields are specified on the Output form. In both cases, the relative positions of the field on either the input or the output record must be designated.

VI. Illustrative RPG Program

A. Problem Definition

A computer center of a large company is assigned the task of calculating weekly wages for all nonsalaried personnel. To process data, the input must be in a form that is acceptable or understandable to the computer. Magnetic disk, magnetic tape, and keyboarded data entered from a terminal are common forms of input to a computer system.

1. The Input

In this illustrative problem, the employee data will be received from the payroll department in the form of work records. These records will contain three fields, as indicated below:

Input Record Format for Sample Program

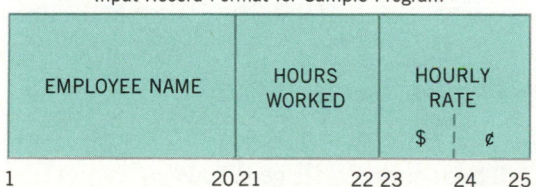

For each employee, the three fields of data will be keyed or entered into the information processing system.

Positions 1 to 20 of the input records are reserved for each NAME. If any name contains less than 20 characters, the low-order, or right-most, positions would be left blank. Similarly, HOURS will be placed in positions 21 and 22, and RATE in positions 23 to 25. The RATE field, as a dollars-and-cents amount, is to be interpreted as if it had two decimal positions. That is, 625 in positions 23 to 25 is to be interpreted by the computer as 6.25. The decimal point is not generally entered for commercial applications since it would waste a position in the record and a storage position in memory. As will be seen, this method of *implying* or assuming decimal points is easily handled in RPG.

A file of employee records, with the format just described, will be keyed and then read as input to the computer. WAGES will be calculated by the computer as follows:

$$WAGES = HOURS \times RATE$$

2. The Output

The output will be a printed report with the format illustrated in the following Printer Spacing Chart. The three input fields will be printed in addition to the WAGES field, which is calculated as HOURS times RATE:

Printer Spacing Chart for Sample Program

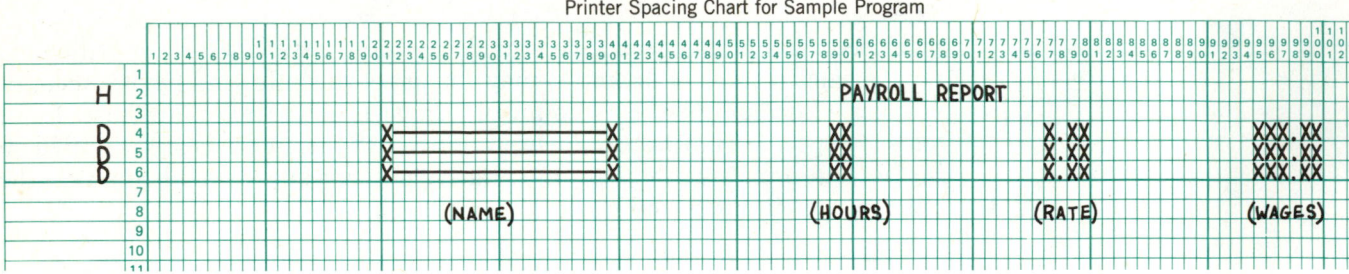

The Printer Spacing Chart indicates that a Heading (denoted by H) will appear on line 2 of each page. The Detail or D lines will consist of four fields: the first is a 20-character name field, followed by an hours worked field, followed by an edited rate field with a decimal point, and, finally, a six-position dollars-and-cents wages field edited to include the decimal point. All decimal points are implied on input but printed on output. The names in parentheses on the chart are *not* printed; they simply indicate what the output fields are.

Each problem definition in the text that describes the program to be written will consist of the following:

1. A brief narrative describing the problem.
2. An input layout form describing the input.
3. A Printer Spacing Chart or layout form describing the output.

These are standard elements in a problem definition.

B. The RPG Forms in Detail

Figure 1.8 illustrates the specifications forms required to code the program in RPG. These forms will be discussed in detail.

Simple RPG programs are generally written on the four specifications forms illustrated in Figure 1.8 in the order indicated. The Extension and Line Counter Specifications are discussed later in the text, and are required for specialized processing. Usually, however, the basic four forms in FICO order are sufficient.

Each specifications form has space for 80 columns or positions of information. Each *line* of a form is entered on one line of a terminal.

1. The Control and File Description Specifications Form

a. **The Control Specifications.** Consider the sample form in Figure 1.8*a*. In addition to the File Description Specifications, it includes the RPG Control Specifications. These specifications consist of a single line that provides information about program generation and execution. The one line of Control

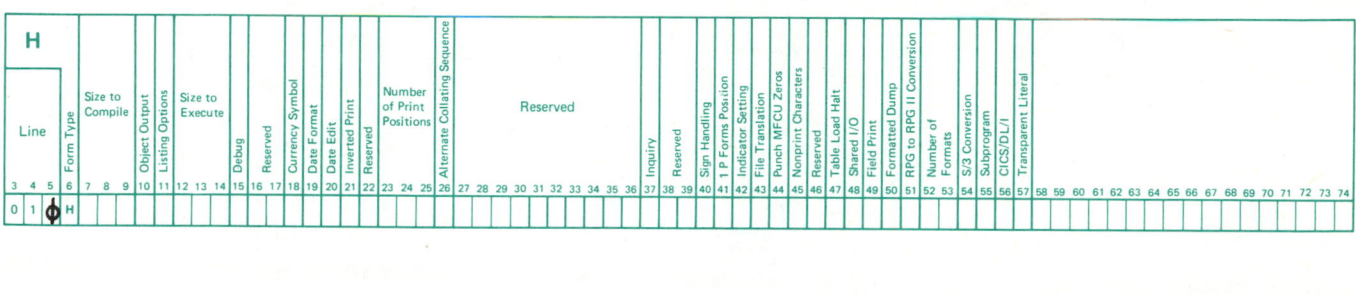

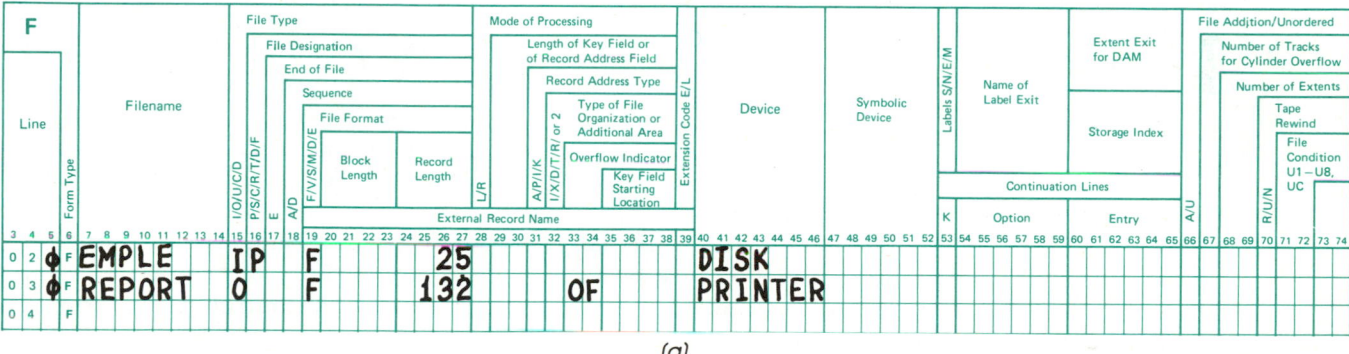

(a)

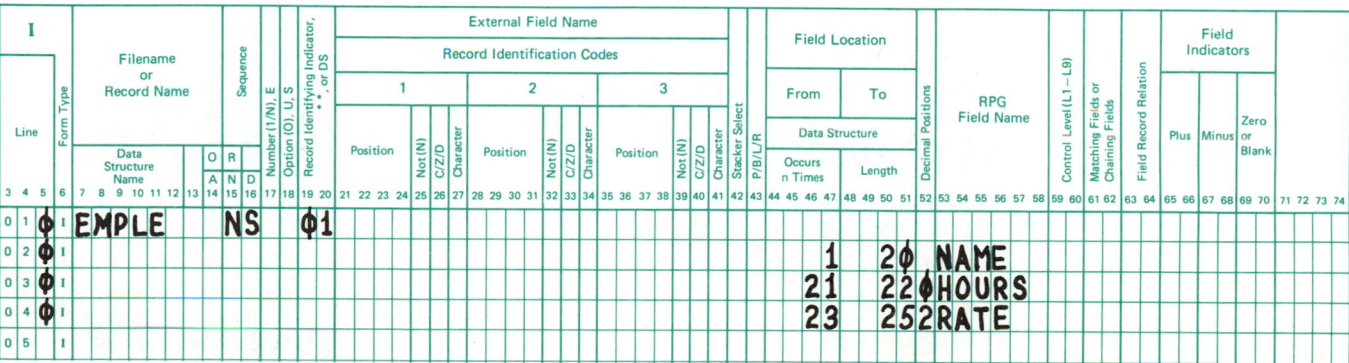

(b)

Figure 1.8
Specifications forms for the sample RPG program: (a) Control and File Description Specifications form; (b) Input Specifications form; (c) Calculation Specifications form; (d) Output Specifications form. (*Continued on next page.*)

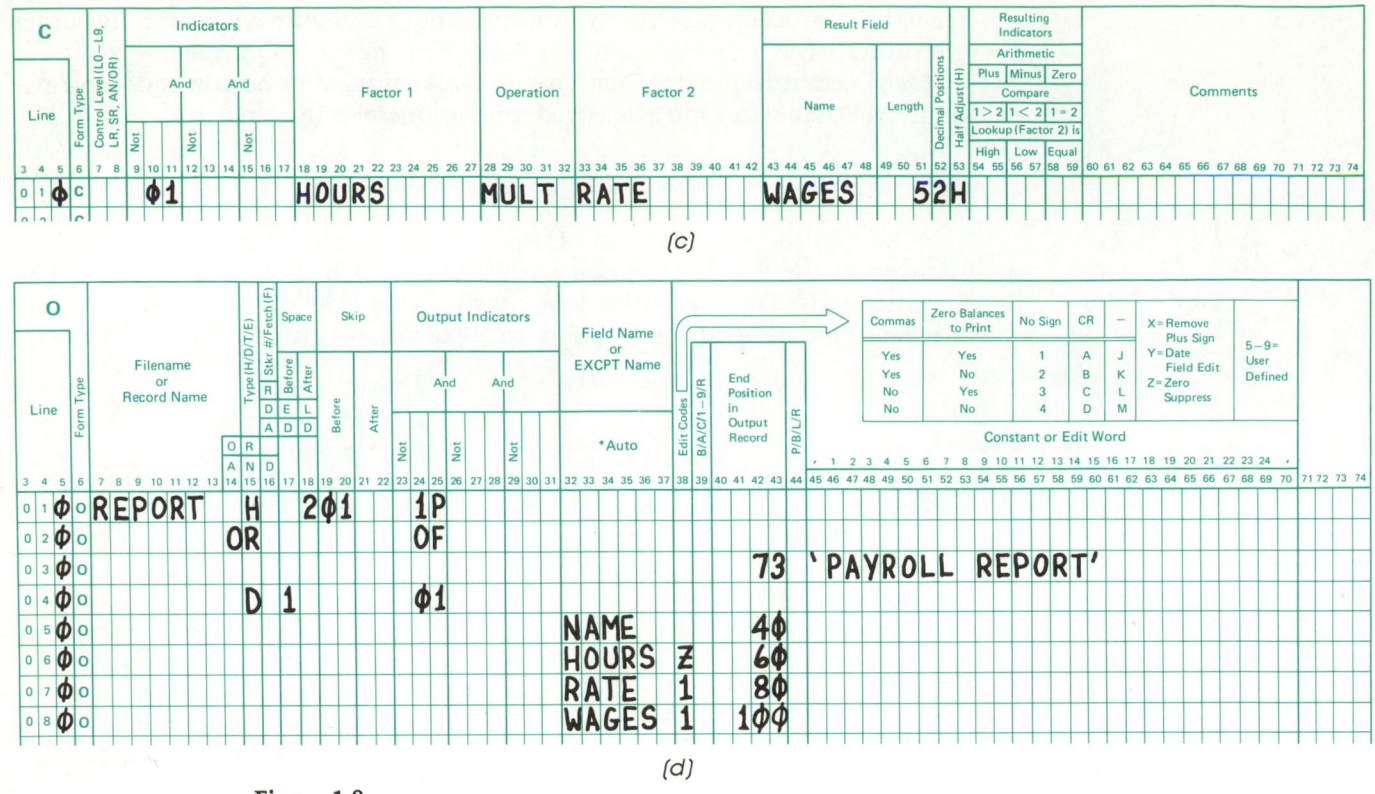

Figure 1.8
(continued)

Specifications is always the *first* entry in the program, and it contains an H in column 6. The RPG specifications manual provided by your computer manufacturer will indicate if any additional information on Control Specifications is required.

The remainder of this section focuses on the File Description Specifications.

b. The Purpose of the File Description Specifications. The File Description Specifications form performs several functions:

FUNCTIONS OF THE FILE DESCRIPTION SPECIFICATIONS

1. Defines the input and output files.
2. Describes these files.
3. Assigns the files to their respective devices.

Column 6 of the File Description Specifications form will always contain an F to denote its Form type.

The most important fields on this form will now be considered in depth. These are the fields used in the sample program in Figure 1.8. Other fields will be discussed throughout the text as the need arises.

FILENAME (Columns 7–14)

A file is a major grouping or collection of data for a specific application. For example, there are inventory files, accounts receivable files, and payroll files.

The FILENAME field of the File Description Specifications form defines each file to be used in the program and then associates it with a device.

Each file to be used in the program is identified by assigning a name in columns 7–14. One file is assigned on each line of this form.

RULES FOR FORMING FILENAMES

1. Must begin in column 7 (left-justified).
2. Must begin with an alphabetic character.
3. May include letters and digits but no embedded blanks or special characters except #, $, and @. (An embedded blank is a blank within the field.)
4. Must be eight characters or less.
5. Should be a meaningful name.

The input filenames are used again when describing the input on the Input Specifications form. The output filenames are used again when describing output on the Output Specifications form.

In the sample program, EMPLE, an abbreviation for Employee, is the name assigned to the input file of employee records, and REPORT is the name assigned to the output print file.

Self-Test

1. A file is a _____.
2. The three main purposes of the File Description Specifications are _____, _____, and _____.

Indicate what, if anything, is wrong with the following filenames (3–7):

3. FILE-4
4. FILE1233
5. FILE A
6. PAYROLLFILE
7. DISCT%
8. If FILE12 were a designated filename, it would appear in columns _____ through _____ in the FILENAME field.

Solutions

1. major group or collection of data
2. to define the files; to describe the files; to assign the files to specified devices
3. The hyphen is a special character that is not permitted in a filename.
4. OK
5. There is an embedded blank between FILE and A, which is not permitted in a filename.
6. A maximum of eight positions is permitted in a filename.
7. The percent sign, %, is a special character that is not permitted in a filename.
8. 7; 12

The main portion of the File Description Specifications form describes the file to the system. The entries necessary for disk or print files are relatively straightforward and standard. Specific disk concepts will be considered in Chapter 8.

FILE TYPE (Column 15)

A disk or print file is usually designated in column 15 as:

I for Input.
O for Output.

Print files are always output, but disk files can be either input or output.

Although other entries may be used, the discussion will be confined for now to I and O, the most frequently coded entries. In the sample program, the input file called EMPLE is designated with an I, and the output file called REPORT is designated with an O.

FILE DESIGNATION (Column 16)—For Input Files Only

The specification for column 16 is used for input files only. Column 16 must be blank for output files. Input files may be designated in column 16 as:

P for Primary.
S for Secondary.

One and only one primary file may be defined in a program. If there is more than one input file in a program, then one is defined as primary and the other(s) as secondary.

Since there is only one input file in the sample problem, it is designated with a P for primary. This position is left blank for the output file called REPORT.

FILE FORMAT (Column 19)

A file can have one of the following formats:

F   for Fixed-length records
V   for Variable-length records
E   for Externally defined file (RPG III and RPG/400 only—RPG/400 is the version of RPG used on the AS/400 computer).

When a file contains **fixed-length records,** all records in the file are the same length. **Variable-length records,** on the other hand, are records that are of different lengths within the same file.

Most disk files contain an F in column 19 because they are fixed in length; that is, each record contains the same number of bytes or characters. In addition to the file having fixed-length records, the F in column 19 indicates that the file's record format must be described within the program. That is, the record's data fields must be defined on the Input Specifications as we will see later in this chapter.

Some computers allow disk files to contain variable-length records, that is, records that can vary in length from record to record. The LNAME field of record 1, for example, could contain BROWN, which is five characters, and the same field in record 2 could be ANDREWS, which is seven characters. In a fixed-length file, the LNAME field would always be the same, large enough for the longest last name. Note that the newer releases of RPG do not support the V option and thus it will not be illustrated in this book.

An E in column 19 is used with RPG III and RPG/400 programs to identify **externally defined files.** The E indicates that the record description for the file is not defined as part of the program. The compiler obtains these descriptions at compilation time and includes them in the RPG source program. This option, which is only available with RPG III and RPG/400, is illustrated in Chapter 11.

BLOCK LENGTH (Columns 20–23) and RECORD LENGTH (Columns 24–27)

The BLOCK LENGTH is specified on the File Description Specifications only for files in which records are blocked. **Blocking** is a technique that increases the speed of input/output disk operations and makes more effective use of storage space for disk files. This is accomplished by grouping several logical records into one block to maximize the efficient use of disk space. That is, reading in a block of 10 records, for example, is more efficient than reading in each disk record separately. Even though a disk file may be blocked, the program processes records in the standard way, that is, one logical record at a time.

The RECORD LENGTH in columns 24–27 is used to specify the number of positions or **bytes** contained in a single record within the file. In general, RPG programmers are supplied with the record and block lengths for files by the systems analyst. If a record length and a blocking factor (the number of records per block) are given, then BLOCK LENGTH is determined by multiplying the blocking factor by the record length. The BLOCK LENGTH can be omitted, however, if it is the same length as the RECORD LENGTH.

The BLOCK LENGTH is *optional* for most RPG compilers *even when records are blocked.* This is because operating system commands can be used to indicate the blocking factor. With most computers used in the RPG environment, then, blocking is performed and specified external to the RPG program. Moreover, blocking is not specified with RPG III and RPG/400 programs, which are used primarily in database applications.

We will not include a BLOCK LENGTH in our illustrated programs.

The RECORD LENGTH requires a *numeric* value to denote the number of bytes in the record. Numeric specifications such as RECORD LENGTH are right-justified on RPG forms. That is, the numeric values are placed in the right-most positions, with nonfilled left-most positions remaining blank. Thus, 25 would be placed in columns 26–27 of the File Description Specifications for the RECORD LENGTH field of EMPLE as shown in the illustrated problem. Columns 24–25 would remain blank or contain zeros. The RECORD LENGTH of 132 is placed in columns 25–27 for REPORT, the sample output print file.

The RECORD LENGTH for input disk files will vary depending on the total accumulated length of all fields within the record. The RECORD LENGTH for print files will usually be 80, 100, 120, or 132 depending on the number of characters per line that the printer prints. Most of the illustrations in this book will use 132.

OVERFLOW INDICATOR (Columns 33–34)—For Print Output Files Only

The OVERFLOW INDICATOR, designated as OF, may be coded in this field for print files only. Use OF if you want the computer to test if the end of a page has been reached during processing so that you can advance the paper to the top of a new page.

DEVICE (Columns 40–46) and SYMBOLIC DEVICE (Columns 47–52)

DEVICE and SYMBOLIC DEVICE are machine-dependent entries that are provided to the programmer by the computer center. This book will use the following entries for DEVICE:

DEVICE (Columns 40–46)
DISK
PRINTER
CONSOLE (for terminal)
WORKSTN (for interactive work station)

SYMBOLIC DEVICE may be required on some non-IBM computers using RPG. If required, this information will be provided by the computer center.

SYMBOLIC DEVICE is not used with RPG III. We omit this entry in our illustrations.

In this sample program, then, there are two files: an input file of 25-character records assigned to a disk, and an output file of 132-character records assigned to the printer.

The remainder of the File Description Specifications is not required for elementary-level programs. See Figure 1.9 for a review.

Figure 1.9
Review of Control and File Description Specifications form.

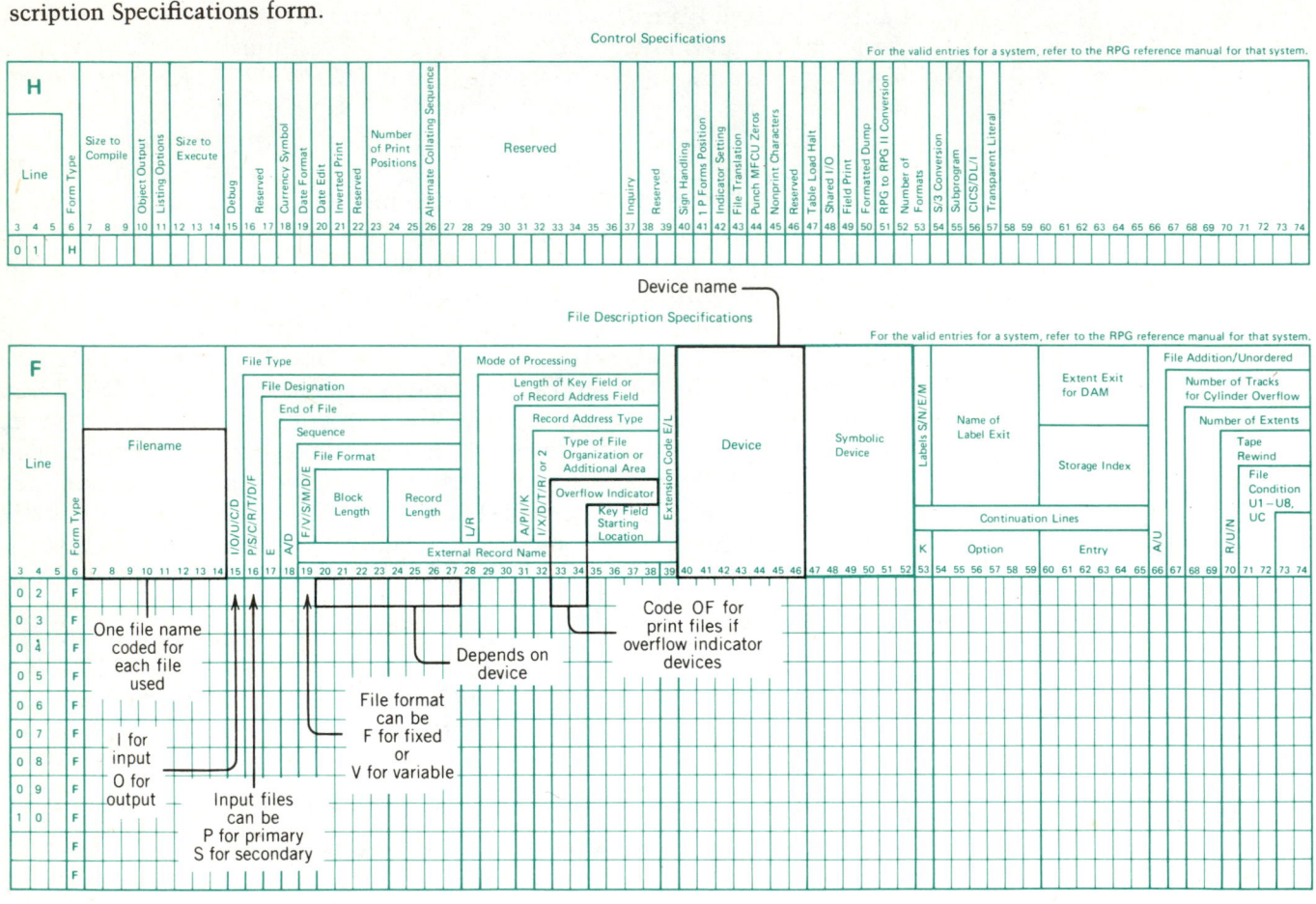

Self-Test For each of the following, assume that the input is a sequential disk file. Use the File Description Specifications form below to code the following:

1. Code the File Description Specifications entries for a program that reads a payroll disk file (282-character records) and produces a salary report on a 132-character-per-line printer.

2. Code the File Description entries for a program that reads data from a master inventory disk file (100-character records) and produces a summary report and an error file on disk. The printer is a 132-character-per-line printer and the error file has records that are also 100 characters long.

3. Code the File Description entries for an *update* program that reads a master payroll disk file (100-character records) and a salary change disk file, and produces a new, updated master payroll disk file.

4. In Question 3, the salary change disk file would be considered a secondary file because _____.

5. Code the File Description Specifications form for a program that reads disk input (100-character records) and produces a printed report (132-character records).

6. A standard sequential disk file always has a format of _____.

7. The P in column 16 is used to indicate _____.

8. (T or F) Output files must be coded with a P or S in column 16.

Solutions 1.

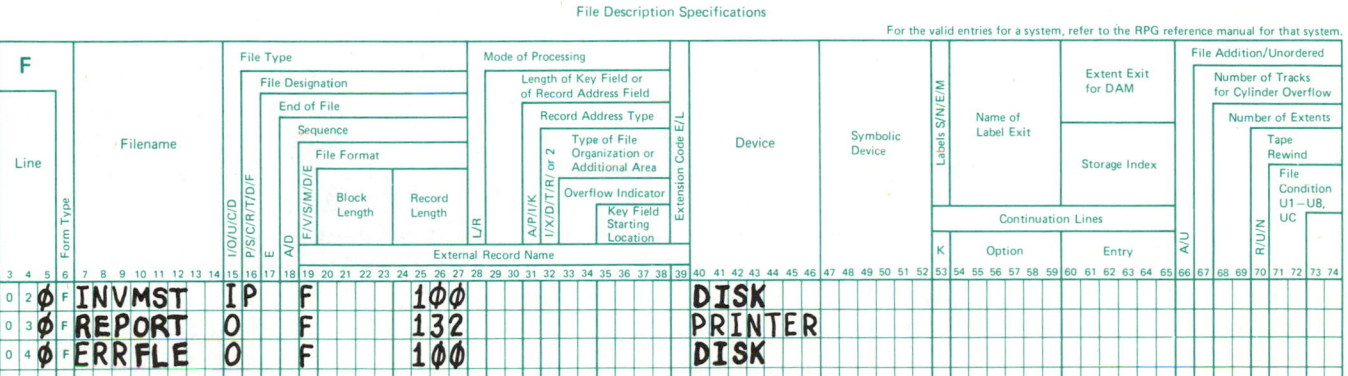

3.

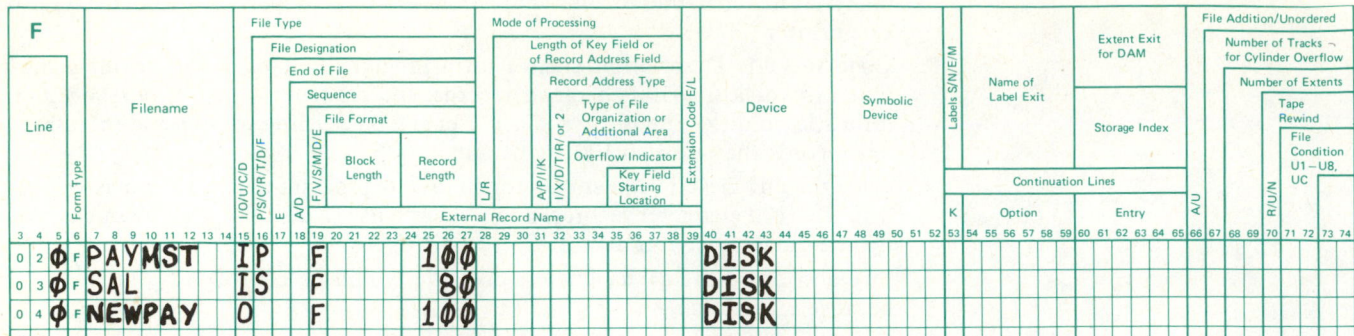

The table in the form shows:

Line		Filename	I/O/U/C/D P/S/C/R/T/D/F	E	A/D	F/V/S/M/D/E	Block Length	Record Length	L/R	External Record Name	Device
0 2	Ø F	PAYMST	IP	F			100				DISK
0 3	Ø F	SAL	IS	F			80				DISK
0 4	Ø F	NEWPAY	O	F			100				DISK

Note: There must be two master disk files, an old master and a new master, since information is not usually added to an existing sequential disk file (see Chapter 8).

4. its purpose is to alter the contents of the primary or most significant file, the master payroll disk file.

5.

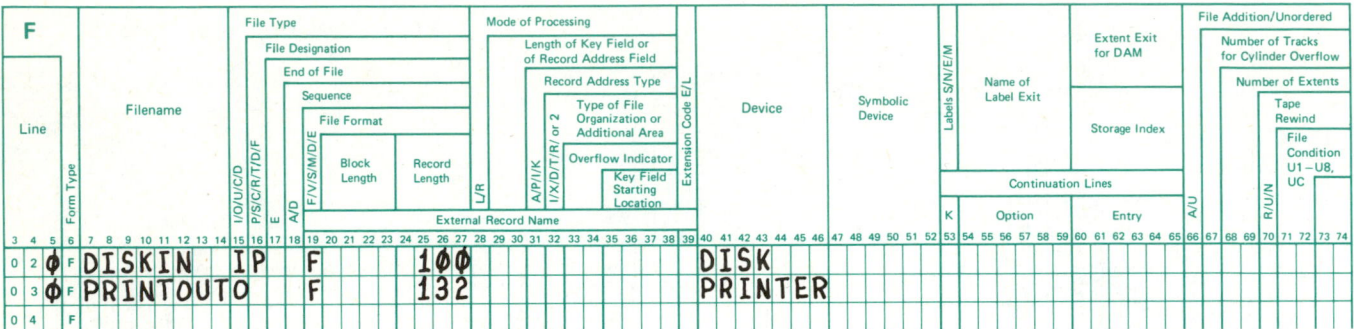

Line		Filename	I/O/U/C/D P/S/C/R/T/D/F	E	A/D	F/V/S/M/D/E	Block Length	Record Length	L/R	External Record Name	Device
0 2	Ø F	DISKIN	IP	F				100			DISK
0 3	Ø F	PRINTOUT	O	F				132			PRINTER
0 4	F										

6. F for Fixed
7. that the specific input file is the primary form of input
8. F—This field is only used for input.

2. The Input Specifications Form

Each input file defined on the File Description Specifications form must be described, in detail, on the Input Specifications form. This form is illustrated in Figure 1.8*b*. A record within the input file is defined on the first line followed by each field within that record. Each field is placed on a separate line. If there is more than one record for a file, then each additional record must follow with specific field identifiers. It is considered better programming form to describe the most frequently occurring records first, followed by those that occur less frequently.

This chapter will consider only those areas on the Input Specifications form that are necessary for coding elementary level programs. The other areas will be considered in subsequent chapters as needed.

FORM TYPE (Column 6)

The FORM TYPE field always contains a precoded I for Input Specifications in column 6. The Input Specifications form consists of entries that describe the overall record, called record description entries. A record is described on a single line of an Input Specifications form. Following the description of the record are field description entries on subsequent lines, with each field specified on a separate line.

a. Record Identification Entries

FILENAME (Columns 7–14)

For each input file specified in the File Description Specifications form, an entry is required on the Input Specifications form. The FILENAME for this input file must be exactly the same on both forms. This name appears only *once* on the Input Specifications form, on the *first* line defining a record for that file. Consider the sample Input Specifications form in Figure 1.8*b*. Note that the name of the file appears only once in the FILENAME field.

SEQUENCE (Columns 15–16)

The SEQUENCE field can be used for checking the sequence of records. Our programs will include NS in the sequence field for No Sequence to indicate that a sequence check is not required. Any two letters, however, would be permissible to indicate that no sequence checking is to be performed. In Figure 1.10, where there are numerous records and no sequence checking is required, AA, AB, and AC are coded in the SEQUENCE field for each record. NS for No Sequence, as indicated, is frequently coded for all records not requiring a sequence check.

RECORD IDENTIFYING INDICATOR (Columns 19–2Ø)

The purpose of the RECORD IDENTIFYING INDICATOR field is to uniquely identify the record. RPG uses indicators that serve as record identifiers. Indicators are nothing more than a series of on-off switches that can be used to indicate when a certain condition exists. In the sample problem, the record identifying indicator Ø1 is turned on for all input records.

Each record in a file can be identified by RECORD IDENTIFICATION CODES in columns 21–41 of the Input Specifications form. Since all records have the same format in the example, it is not necessary to provide for individual codes; thus the RECORD IDENTIFICATION CODES are not used.

Figure 1.10
Input Specifications form that describes an input file with three different types of records.

Line (3–5)	Form Type (6)	Filename or Record Name (7–14)	Sequence (15–16)	Record Identifying Indicator (19–20)	Code 1 Position (21–24)	Code 1 C/Z/D (26)	Code 1 Character (27)	Code 2 Position (28–31)	Code 2 C/Z/D (33)	Code 2 Character (34)	Field Location From (44–47)	Field Location To (48–51)	Decimal Positions (52)	RPG Field Name (53–58)
Ø1Ø	I	TRANSACT	AA	Ø1	8Ø	C	X							
Ø2Ø	I										1	5		ACCTNO
Ø3Ø	I										6	2Ø		NAME
Ø4Ø	I										21	4Ø		ITEM
Ø5Ø	I										41	45	Ø	UNPRIC
Ø6Ø	I										46	48	Ø	QTY
Ø7Ø	I										49	52	Ø	TAX
Ø8Ø	I		AB	Ø2	8Ø	C	Z	79	D	5				
Ø9Ø	I										1	6		DATE
1ØØ	I		AC	Ø3	8Ø	C	T							
11Ø	I										1	5		ACCTNO
12Ø	I										6	1Ø	Ø	CRAMT

Following the line that identifies a record, the fields are listed in sequence as they appear in the record. Figure 1.10 describes an input file with three different types of records. The first input record is defined by RECORD IDENTIFYING INDICATOR 01. This record is identified by the character X in position 80. The second record is defined by the letter Z in column 80 and the digit 5 in column 79. If 5Z appears in columns 79–80, then indicator 02 is turned on. Finally, a third record is described that turns on indicator 03 if column 80 has a character of a T.

A RECORD IDENTIFYING INDICATOR, then, can be used in conjunction with RECORD IDENTIFICATION CODES to uniquely identify a record. In both the Calculation and Output forms, the record to be processed is specified by its RECORD INDICATOR. Any number from 01–99 may be used as a RECORD INDICATOR, and the number may appear in any sequence.

RECORD IDENTIFICATION CODES (Columns 21–41)

As indicated, RECORD IDENTIFICATION CODES provide a method for identifying each type of record. Using a single line, a record can be uniquely identified by a maximum of *three* codes. This is indicated by a 1, 2, or 3 as a subheading under RECORD IDENTIFICATION CODES on the coding sheet. If more than three identifying codes are required for a single record, then *two* lines are required. Let us discuss the subfields for the RECORD IDENTIFICATION CODES.

POSITION (Columns 21–24)

This field refers to the single position on the input record that contains the code. This field, as all numeric fields, is right-justified.

NOT (Column 25)

If the *absence* of a specific character in a position is used to specify the code, then an N is placed here.

C/Z/D (Column 26)

C/Z/D stands for Character, Zone or Digit test, respectively, for the field. If a full character is to be tested, use C. If only the zone portion is to be tested, use Z. If the digit portion only is to be tested, use D.

CHARACTER (Column 27)

Any alphabetic, numeric, or special character may be used in column 27 to specify a record identification code.

Columns 28–34 and columns 35–41 are repetitions of the previous fields. Thus, when two or more characters in specified positions are required for record identification, these fields are used.

Columns 21–41 may be left blank if all records within a file are to be processed in the same way. If the following is the only entry for the record fields on the Input Specifications form, then all input records automatically turn on indicator 15:

I		Filename or Record Name		Sequence	Number (1/N), E	Option (O), U, S	Record Identifying Indicator, *, or DS	External Field Name													Stacker Select	P/B/L/R	Field Location			RPG Field Name	Control Level (L1–L9)	Matching Fields or Chaining Fields	Field Record Relation	Field Indicators		
								Record Identification Codes																From	To	Decimal Positions					Plus	Minus	Zero or Blank
								1			2			3																			
	Form Type		O R					Position	Not (N)	C/Z/D	Position	Not (N)	C/Z/D	Position	Not (N)	C/Z/D	Character						Data Structure									
Line		Data Structure Name	A N D							Character			Character				Character						Occurs n Times	Length								
3 4 5	6	7 8 9 10 11 12	13 14 15 16		17	18	19 20	21 22 23 24	25	26 27	28 29 30 31	32	33 34	35 36 37 38	39	40 41	42	43	44 45 46 47	48 49 50 51	52	53 54 55 56 57 58	59 60	61 62	63 64	65 66	67 68	69 70	71 72 73 74
0 1 0	I	FILE1	NS	15																													
0 2 0	I																		1	5		ACCTNO							
0 3 0	I																		6	10	0	AMT1							

If an input form describes a record with a 1 in position 80, we would have the following:

I		Filename or Record Name		Sequence	Number (1/N), E	Option (O), U, S	Record Identifying Indicator, *, or DS	External Field Name													Stacker Select	P/B/L/R	Field Location			RPG Field Name	Control Level (L1–L9)	Matching Fields or Chaining Fields	Field Record Relation	Field Indicators		
								Record Identification Codes																From	To	Decimal Positions					Plus	Minus	Zero or Blank
								1			2			3																			
	Form Type		O R					Position	Not (N)	C/Z/D	Position	Not (N)	C/Z/D	Position	Not (N)	C/Z/D	Character						Data Structure									
Line		Data Structure Name	A N D							Character			Character				Character						Occurs n Times	Length								
3 4 5	6	7 8 9 10 11 12	13 14 15 16		17	18	19 20	21 22 23 24	25	26 27	28 29 30 31	32	33 34	35 36 37 38	39	40 41	42	43	44 45 46 47	48 49 50 51	52	53 54 55 56 57 58	59 60	61 62	63 64	65 66	67 68	69 70	71 72 73 74
0 1 0	I	SAMPLE	NS	01				80		C1																							
0 2 0	I																				•								
0 3 0	I																				•	Field descriptions							
0 4 0	I																				•								
0 5	I																												

Processing will be performed correctly if position 80 contains a 1. Suppose a record does not have a 1 in position 80. Since there is no indicator turned on if position 80 does not have a 1, the computer will automatically turn on a halt indicator and, unless otherwise instructed, it will abort the job. To prevent this occurrence, add the following coding:

I		Filename or Record Name		Sequence	Number (1/N), E	Option (O), U, S	Record Identifying Indicator, *, or DS	External Field Name													Stacker Select	P/B/L/R	Field Location			RPG Field Name	Control Level (L1–L9)	Matching Fields or Chaining Fields	Field Record Relation	Field Indicators		
								Record Identification Codes																From	To	Decimal Positions					Plus	Minus	Zero or Blank
								1			2			3																			
	Form Type		O R					Position	Not (N)	C/Z/D	Position	Not (N)	C/Z/D	Position	Not (N)	C/Z/D	Character						Data Structure									
Line		Data Structure Name	A N D							Character			Character				Character						Occurs n Times	Length								
3 4 5	6	7 8 9 10 11 12	13 14 15 16		17	18	19 20	21 22 23 24	25	26 27	28 29 30 31	32	33 34	35 36 37 38	39	40 41	42	43	44 45 46 47	48 49 50 51	52	53 54 55 56 57 58	59 60	61 62	63 64	65 66	67 68	69 70	71 72 73 74
0 1 0	I	SAMPLE	NS	01				80		C1																							
0 2 0	I																				•								
0 3 0	I																				•	Field descriptions							
0 4 0	I																				•								
0 5 0	I			NS	02				80	N	C1																			
0 6	I																												

Recall that any two letters are permissible in the sequence field where no sequence checking is to be performed. In this way, indicator 02 will be turned on if the required code of 1 in column 80 is not present. Then the program can perform whatever error routines are appropriate if indicator 02 is on. It is recommended that this additional coding be included to avoid the possibility of the job aborting prematurely. When a job terminates because of an error, we call this a program interrupt or *abend*, an abbreviation for *ab*normal *end* of job.

Line (3–5)	Form Type (6)	Filename or Record Name / Data Structure Name (7–13)	Sequence / OR, AND (14–16)	Number (1/N), E (17)	Option (O), U, S (18)	Record Identifying Indicator, **, or DS (19–20)	1 Position (21–24)	Not (N) (25)	C/Z/D (26)	Character (27)	2 Position (28–31)	Not (N) (32)	C/Z/D (33)	Character (34)	3 Position (35–38)	Not (N) (39)	C/Z/D (40)	Character (41)	Stacker Select (42)	P/B/L/R (43)	Field Location / Data Structure: From / Occurs n Times (44–47)	To / Length (48–51)	Decimal Positions (52)	RPG Field Name (53–58)	Control Level (L1–L9) (59–60)	Matching Fields or Chaining Fields (61–62)	Field Record Relation (63–64)	Field Indicators: Plus (65–66)	Minus (67–68)	Zero or Blank (69–70)	71–74
01Ø	I	FILEIN	NS			Ø1	8Ø		C	6	79		C	5	78		C	4													
02Ø	I		AND				77		C	3	76		C	2	75		C	1													
03Ø	I																				1	5		ACCTNO							
04Ø	I																				6	1Ø		NAME							

Figure 1.11
Identifying a record with more than three identification codes.

AND or OR Relationships

If more than three conditions are required to identify a given record, then *two* coding lines are necessary. The first line would contain all the aforementioned data with record identification fields coded to include three conditions. The second line would contain the letters AND in columns 14–16 and the additional record identification codes required to identify the given record. If more than six conditions are required to identify a given record, then subsequent lines may be used with AND in columns 14–16. See Figure 1.11 for an illustration.

If the existence of *any one* of a series of possibilities is used to identify a record, these rules can be used with the OR qualifier. The condition or conditions are coded on individual lines with the word OR in columns 14–15 of all but the first line. See Figure 1.12 for an illustration. In this example, if positions 79–8Ø contain 56 *or* positions 77–78 contain 34, the Ø1 record identifying indicator is turned on.

b. Field Identification Entries (Columns 43–74). So far, the Input Specifications form has been used to define records within a file. Records are identified with identification codes and accessed by record indicators. One or more lines can be used to define a record.

Once a record has been defined and identified, subsequent lines are required to describe the *fields* within the record, in sequence as they appear in the

Figure 1.12
Identifying a record when any one of a series of codes exists.

Line (3–5)	Form Type (6)	Filename or Record Name / Data Structure Name (7–13)	Sequence / OR, AND (14–16)	Number (1/N), E (17)	Option (O), U, S (18)	Record Identifying Indicator, **, or DS (19–20)	1 Position (21–24)	Not (N) (25)	C/Z/D (26)	Character (27)	2 Position (28–31)	Not (N) (32)	C/Z/D (33)	Character (34)	3 Position (35–38)	Not (N) (39)	C/Z/D (40)	Character (41)	Stacker Select (42)	P/B/L/R (43)	Field Location / Data Structure: From / Occurs n Times (44–47)	To / Length (48–51)	Decimal Positions (52)	RPG Field Name (53–58)	Control Level (L1–L9) (59–60)	Matching Fields or Chaining Fields (61–62)	Field Record Relation (63–64)	Field Indicators: Plus (65–66)	Minus (67–68)	Zero or Blank (69–70)	71–74
01Ø	I	DISKIN	NS			Ø1	8Ø		C	6	79		C	5																	
02Ø	I		OR				77		C	3	78		C	4																	
03Ø	I																				1	5		ACCTNO							
04Ø	I																				6	1Ø	Ø	AMT							
05Ø	I																				11	3Ø		NAME							

record. Note that the field identifications appear on the lines *following* the record description. Note also that only those fields required for processing need be described. Unused input fields need not be identified.

FIELD LOCATION (Columns 44–51)

The FIELD LOCATION entry is used to indicate the *boundaries* of the field defined. In the FROM subfield (columns 44–47), enter the left-most or high-order position of the field. In the TO subfield (columns 48–51), enter the right-most or low-order position of the field. As with all numeric items, these entries are *right-justified*.

DECIMAL POSITIONS (Column 52)

The DECIMAL POSITIONS entry is coded for all numeric fields and remains blank for all other fields. It indicates the number of decimal positions in the numeric field. That is, the number of digits to the right of the decimal point is entered. If the field denoted contains integers only, then 0 is entered here; if it contains a dollars and cents amount, then a 2 would be entered.

FIELD NAME (Columns 53–58)

Each data item or field within a record must contain a user-defined field name. In RPG, field names must conform to the following rules:

Rules for Forming RPG Field Names

1. 1 to 6 characters.
2. First character must be A–Z, @, #, or $.
3. Can only contain letters, numbers, or the following special characters: @, #, and $.
4. Embedded blanks *are not* permitted.
5. If the field name is less than 6 characters, it is *left-justified* beginning in column 53.

Each field name within an RPG program must be unique.

Use Meaningful Names

The name should be meaningful, such as AMT, or DEPT, so it identifies the contents of the field. DEPT is a more meaningful field name than DT, for example, although both names are valid. Using field names that identify the contents of fields makes a program more readable and easier to debug. It also promotes the use of consistent programming and documentation standards.

Use Prefixes to Classify Data Items

RPG restricts data field names to six characters, which is a rather stringent limitation. As a result, uniform and distinct names must be described in concise terms. Programmers need to establish standards for identifying the unique fields within files used in RPG programs. *Prefixes* are commonly used to uniquely classify fields as part of a group. For example, all fields associated with one input record would be given the same prefix. Thus, SAMT and SDEPT might be used to designate fields as part of the same Sales file.

For field names, limit the actual name to four or five characters and use a unique one- or two-character prefix to associate the field name with a specific file. For example, the fields contained in a payroll file may be given a one-character prefix "P"—as in PNAME, PHOURS, and PRATE. This uniquely identifies those fields as being associated with the payroll file and distinguishes them from other fields that might be used in the program.

We will use prefixes throughout this text as one technique that makes programs easier to read and more standardized. Other uses for prefixes will be discussed in subsequent chapters as new categories of RPG specifications are introduced.

Types of Fields: Group and Elementary

There are two major categories of fields: **group items** and **elementary items.** A **group item** is a data field that is further subdivided; that is, it is a major field consisting of minor fields. A DATE field, for example, may be a group item consisting of MO, DAY, and YR. The data fields that are not further subdivided are called **elementary items.** In the example cited, MO, DAY, and YR would be elementary items within the group item DATE. They would be coded on the Input Specifications form as follows:

The field called DATE can be used to access the first six positions of the record. Similarly, MO can be used to access the first two positions, DAY can be used to access positions 3–4, and YR can be used to access positions 5–6.

Data Formats

In RPG there are several different formats in which data can be stored internally within the computer. The method used to represent data internally depends upon the type of processing to be performed on the data. The method used to define numeric data also affects the program's efficiency.

Fields can be classified as:

1. Character
2. Numeric
   a. Zoned Decimal
   b. Packed Decimal
   c. Binary

Before we begin to consider the different data formats, examine the record layout for the file called IA111 in Figure 1.13. This record structure will be used to illustrate RPG specifications throughout the remainder of this chapter.

Character Field

A **character field** is one that can contain any combination of letters, digits, and special characters such as $, %, @, or &. This is sometimes called an alphanu-

Figure 1.13
Record layout for sample file
IA111.

Record Description for File IA111				
Field Description	Field Type (C,N,P)	Width	Decimal Positions	RPG Field Name
Model Identification	C	7		AMODEL
Description	C	20		ADESC
Manufacturer's Code	N	5	0	AMFG
Date Manufactured	N	6	0	ADATEM
Quantity Sold	P	5	0	ASOLD
Returns	P	5	0	ARETNS
Unit Price	P	7	2	APRICE

Sample data for one record:

```
AMODEL    MW0480W
ADESC     MICROWAVE OVEN
AMFG      00480
ADATEM    910120
ASOLD     00042
ARETNS    00006
APRICE    0032550
```

IA111 Disk Record

AMODEL	ADESC	AMFG	ADATEM	ASOLD	ARETNS	APRICE
1 7	8 27	28 32	33 38	39 41	42 44	45 48

meric field. Simply, a character field is a field that contains any *printable* characters. In this format a single position of storage, or *byte*, is used to store one character of data.

Figure 1.14 identifies two character fields for the sample record. Here, the prefix "A" is used to help identify the fields as members of the same data file. All fields with the prefix A belong to the input file IA111.

The DECIMAL POSITIONS field (column 52) on the Input Specifications is used to distinguish between character and numeric fields. By leaving column 52 *blank* the computer will designate the field as a character field. Data defined in character format (no integer in the DECIMAL POSITIONS field)

Figure 1.14
Use of a prefix to identify
fields in the same file.

A prefix (A) is used to associate all fields in the file IA111.

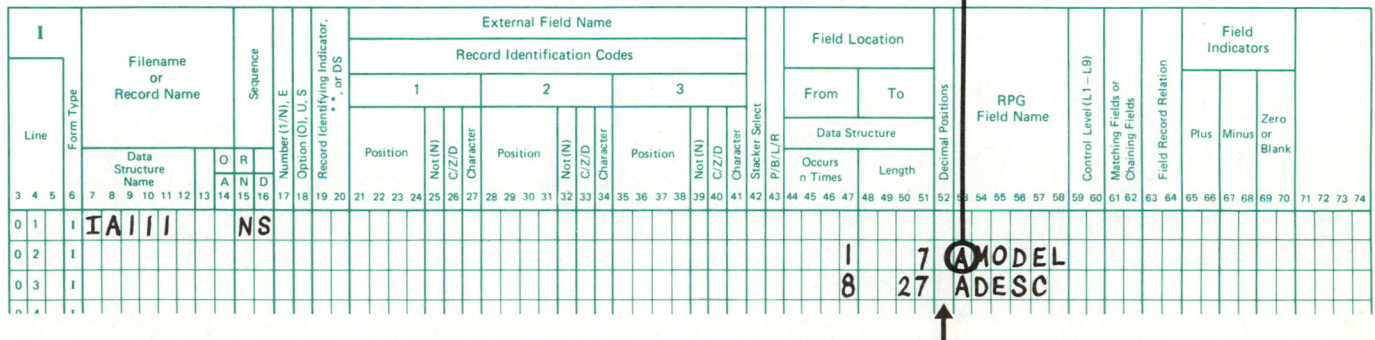

Must be BLANK for *character* fields.

cannot be used in arithmetic operations, even though it may contain only numeric digits.

As noted, the prefix A is used to associate all fields in the file IA111.

Numeric Fields

If a field is to be used in an arithmetic operation, it must be defined as a **numeric field**. The computer considers a field numeric if it is defined with an integer in the DECIMAL POSITIONS field (column 52) on the Input Specifications. An integer (1–9) in this column represents the number of *implied* decimal positions in the field. A "0" in this column means that this is a numeric field consisting of integers only; that is, it is a whole number field. Unless the programmer specifies the number of decimal positions, the data is always stored in *character* format.

Numeric data is stored in one of three formats (zoned decimal, packed decimal, or binary). The zoned decimal and packed decimal formats are explained below. The binary format, which is less widely used, will not be used in this text.

Zoned Decimal Format

A **zoned decimal** field stores one numeric digit in each byte of storage. Fields stored in zoned decimal format can be up to 15 bytes in length. Figure 1.15 illustrates the Input Specifications required to define the two zoned decimal fields AMFG and ADATEM.

Internally, the computer stores *character* and *zoned decimal* fields in the same format. IBM mid-range computers, mainframes, and some of their compatibles use EBCDIC (*Extended Binary-Coded Decimal Interchange Code*) as an internal machine code for representing data. The chart shown in Figure 1.16 illustrates the EBCDIC codes for letters, numbers, and a blank. It also displays the hexadecimal codes used by the computer to represent EBCDIC codes. You need not memorize this chart, but you should be familiar with these methods for representing data.

Each byte of a zoned decimal field is divided into two portions; the high-order, four-bit zone portion and the low-order, four-bit digit portion. The fol-

Figure 1.15
Defining AMFG and ADATEM as zoned decimal fields on the Input Specifications form.

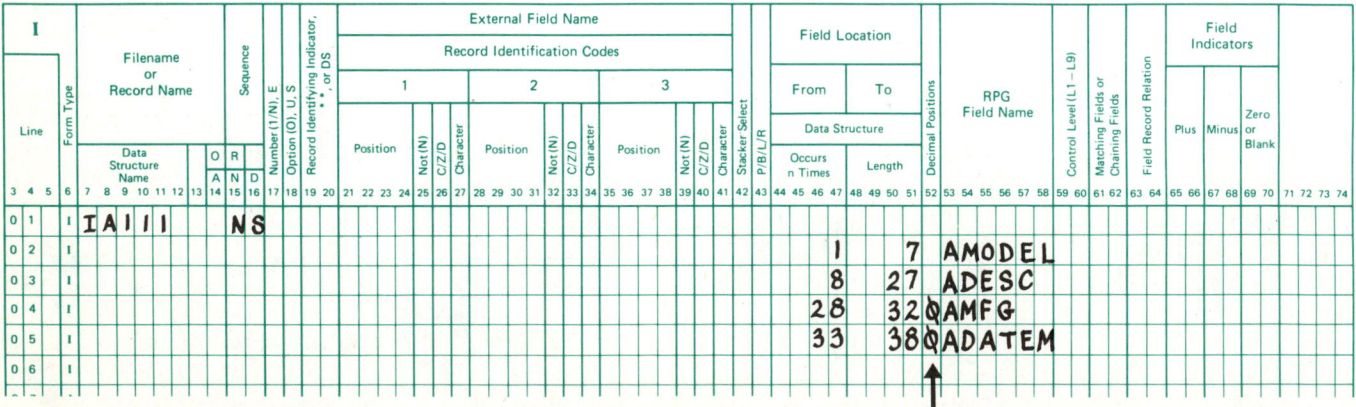

Decimal positions must contain an integer (0-9) for Zoned Decimal fields.

Figure 1.16
EBCDIC codes for letters, numbers, and a blank, and the corresponding hexadecimal codes.

| Character | EBCDIC | | Hexadecimal |
	Zone	Digit	
blank	0100	0000	40
A	1100	0001	C1
B	1100	0010	C2
C	1100	0011	C3
D	1100	0100	C4
E	1100	0101	C5
F	1100	0110	C6
G	1100	0111	C7
H	1100	1000	C8
I	1100	1001	C9
J	1101	0001	D1
K	1101	0010	D2
L	1101	0011	D3
M	1101	0100	D4
N	1101	0101	D5
O	1101	0110	D6
P	1101	0111	D7
Q	1101	1000	D8
R	1101	1001	D9
S	1110	0010	E2
T	1110	0011	E3
U	1110	0100	E4
V	1110	0101	E5
W	1110	0110	E6
X	1110	0111	E7
Y	1110	1000	E8
Z	1110	1001	E9
0	1111	0000	F0
1	1111	0001	F1
2	1111	0010	F2
3	1111	0011	F3
4	1111	0100	F4
5	1111	0101	F5
6	1111	0110	F6
7	1111	0111	F7
8	1111	1000	F8
9	1111	1001	F9

lowing shows how 5 is represented in EBCDIC in one byte of a zoned decimal field:

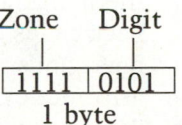

1 byte

Figure 1.17 illustrates a zoned decimal field in which each byte represents one number or digit. Thus, it takes five bytes to represent the number 68254 in zoned decimal format since 68254 consists of five characters.

Figure 1.17
Zoned decimal representation
of the number 68254 (5 bytes).

	6		8		2		5		4
Zone	Digit	Zone	Digit	Zone	Digit	Zone	Digit	Zone	Digit
1111	0110	1111	1000	1111	0010	1111	0101	1111	0100

↑
sign of field

The low-order or right-most byte of a zoned decimal field indicates whether the field is positive or negative; all other zone portions in the field are ignored.

The sign of a zoned decimal field can be represented as positive or negative as follows:

Bits		Hexadecimal	Result		
				F	5
				(+)	
1111	0101	F5	Positive	1111	0101	= +5
				D	5
				(−)	
1101	0101	D5	Negative	1101	0101	= −5

Thus far, we have seen how data may be represented in *zoned decimal format* using one byte or position of storage for each character. For numeric fields, we have seen how a byte can store one digit, where the zone portion is equivalent to "all bits on," and the digit portion is the binary equivalent of all decimal numbers 0 to 9. There is a method that can be utilized where the zone portion is stripped from each byte (except for the low-order byte) so that digits are *packed,* two per byte. In this way, the zone portion of each byte can be used to represent another digit. Thus, *two* digits can be represented in a single byte, which will save space. This technique is called *packing.* Let us now consider the **packed decimal format.**

Packed Decimal Format

Arithmetic operations are executed on data when stored in any of the three numeric formats. However, if a numeric field is not in packed decimal format, it will be converted by some computers to packed decimal format before any computations are performed. If numeric fields to be used in arithmetic are established in packed decimal form by the programmer, then this will result in a more efficient program.

NOTE:

The IBM System/34 and System/36, unlike other systems, execute arithmetic operations in zoned decimal format. Therefore, these systems unpack fields set up in packed decimal format before executing arithmetic operations. It is an industry standard to use packed decimal fields for arithmetic operations, except when operating on a System/34 or System/36.

Fields stored in packed decimal format can be up to eight bytes (15 digits) in length. To define an input numeric field as packed decimal, a P is placed in

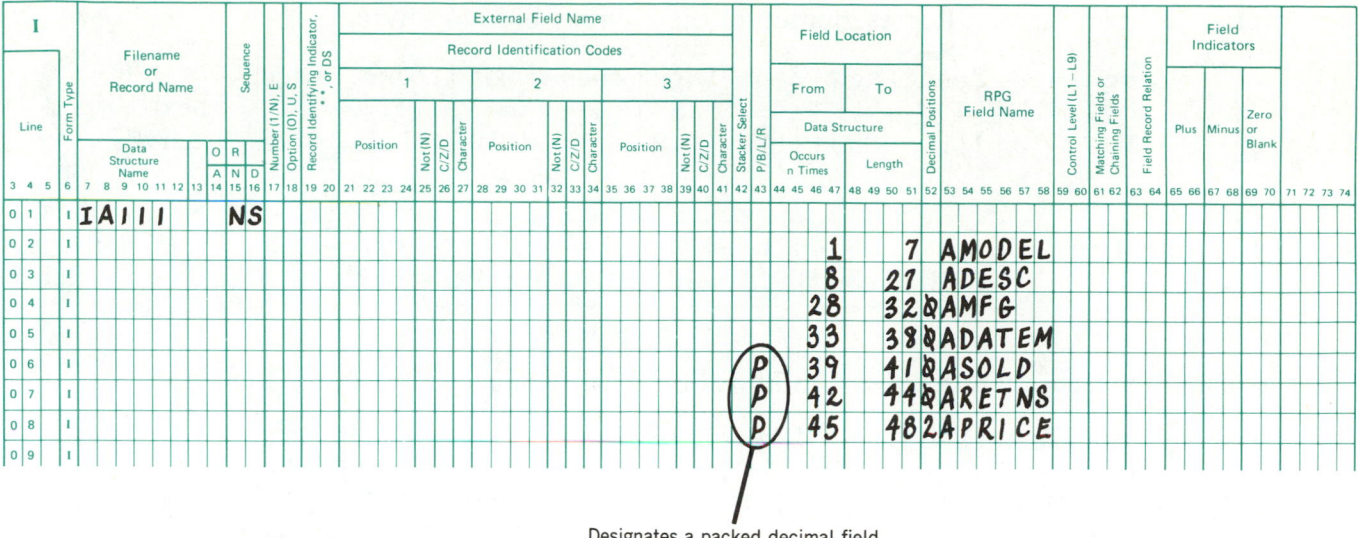

Figure 1.18
Designating packed decimal fields on the Input Specifications form.

column 43 of the Input Specifications. Remember, if you designate a field as packed decimal in the input record (Input Specifications), the field should have been created in packed decimal format. Figure 1.18 illustrates how packed decimal fields are specified on the Input Specifications form.

The packing of an output field is done as the field is written to a record from the Output Specifications. We will see later how to implement this packing operation when Output Specifications are discussed in detail. We should mention here that the packing procedure is automatically performed during output when the field is specified as a packed decimal field. Thus, no further action is required by the programmer to establish a field in packed decimal format.

Let us compare zoned decimal and packed decimal formats to see the result packing has on a field.

Packing Numeric Data

When a numeric field is packed:

1. The zone and digit portions of the *low-order* or right-most byte are switched. This designates the field as a packed field. The low-order four bits of the right-most byte of a packed field contain the sign (F = positive, D = negative).

2. All other zones are stripped, and two digits are *packed* into a single byte. See Figure 1.19.

Consider the number 68254 in Example 1 of Figure 1.19. When a five-position number is stored in the zone decimal format, it occupies five storage positions or bytes. When it is stored as packed decimal, however, it requires only three bytes. This is because the zone portion of each numeric digit (except the rightmost one) is removed, thereby permitting each byte to hold two digits. The low-order or rightmost byte only contains one digit as shown since it also contains the sign of the field. When a file contains a large number of numeric fields, a considerable savings in space and transfer time will be realized when

Example 1 Zoned Decimal Representation of the Number 68254 (5 Bytes)

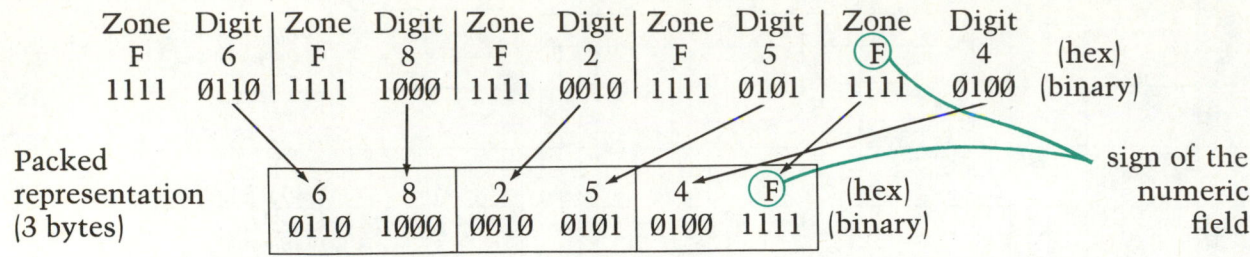

Example 2 Representation of 835674 in Zoned Decimal Format (6 Bytes)

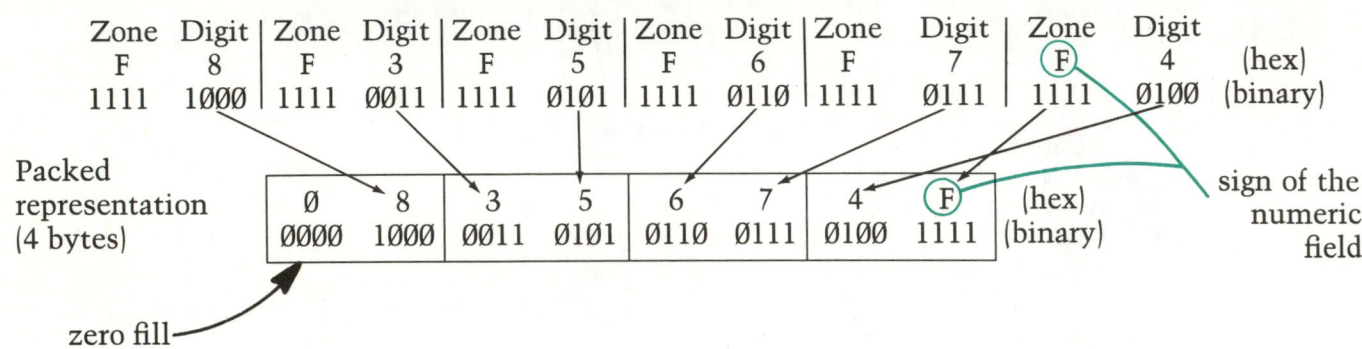

Figure 1.19
Packing of zoned
decimal fields.

using the packed decimal format. For example, if the price field (APRICE) consisting of seven bytes in zoned decimal format were converted to packed decimal format in a file of 100,000 records, 300,000 bytes of disk space would be saved.

In Example 2, the number 835674 occupies an even number of bytes (six bytes) when stored in the zoned decimal format. When converted to packed decimal format it requires four bytes. The computer must complete the packing operation by adding four zero bits to complete or "fill up" the high-order byte as shown. This occurs whenever the zoned decimal field contains an even number of bytes as in 835674 (six bytes).

When packing a field with an even number of digits, then, the leftmost or high-order four bits will be zero-filled.

To determine the number of bytes required when converting a zoned decimal field to a packed decimal field or vice versa, the following formulas can be used:

When converting Zoned Decimal Format to Packed Decimal Format, compute as follows:

1. Divide the number of digits in the zoned decimal field by 2.
2. If there is a decimal remainder of .5, drop it (e.g., round down).
3. Add 1 to the result.

Example 1

Convert 5 digits in zoned decimal format to packed format:

1. Divide by 2—2.5 is the quotient.
2. Round down to 2.
3. Add 1.

Result: 3 bytes are needed for the packed field.

Example 2

Convert 6 zoned decimal digits to packed format:

1. Divide by 2—3 is the quotient.
2. Add 1.

Result: 4 bytes are needed for the packed field.

Note: Since 6 is an even number, the high-order four bits will be zero-filled.

When converting Packed Decimal Format to Zoned Decimal Format, compute as follows:

number of bytes in the packed decimal field $\times$ 2 $-$ 1 =
number of bytes needed for zoned decimal field

Example 1

3 packed bytes: $3 \times 2 - 1 = 5$ bytes needed for the zoned decimal field

Example 2

4 packed bytes: $4 \times 2 - 1 = 7$ bytes needed for the zoned decimal field

---

If data is entered in zoned decimal format and you code an arithmetic operation, such as an ADD instruction, the computer must first pack the field, execute the ADD operation, and then unpack the field again. These conversions are performed automatically in RPG.

To print out or display numeric fields, they must be in zoned decimal format. Since packed decimal data is not in a readable form, we should never specify the packed decimal format in the Output Specifications for a print file. The computer will automatically handle the desired conversion from packed decimal to zoned decimal before printing since the system assumes zoned decimal is required. That is, unless specified otherwise, the computer system defaults to the zoned decimal format.

When *moving* a packed field to an unpacked zoned decimal field the computer automatically unpacks the sending field into the receiving field. In this way, packed fields stored on disk can be converted to zoned decimal format in order to be printed in readable form.

Let us consider the data record defined in Figure 1.18 to demonstrate how data is represented internally in character, zoned decimal, and packed decimal formats. We will show both the hexadecimal and character representations.

Sample data for one record:

Field	Data
AMODEL	MW0480W
ADESC	MICROWAVE OVEN
AMFG	00480
ADATEM	910120 (YY/MM/DD format)
ASOLD	00042
ARETNS	00006
APRICE	0032550

The actual data record is displayed below using the hexadecimal codes to represent the internal EBCDIC codes. In addition, the character representation is shown.

```
Hexadecimal {Zone   DEFFFFEDCCDDECEC4DECD444444FFFFFFFFFFF0020060350
            {Digit  46048064939661550655500000000048091012004F00F025F

Character              MW0480WMICROWAVE OVEN          00480910120
```

Note the following:

1. Blanks are represented as hexadecimal 40. When a value is stored in a character field the unused portion is padded with blanks, as shown in the ADESC field above.
2. The packed fields ASOLD, ARETNS, and APRICE each contain two digits per byte except for the last byte, which contains the sign (F = positive).
3. No characters are shown for the last three fields, which are packed decimal fields, since the individual bytes contain two digits and thus are not represented by characters.

See Figure 1.20 for a review of the Input Specifications form.

Self-Test

1. Code the Input Specifications form for a program that reads in disk records with a 4 in column 21 and a 5 in column 22. Account for all error conditions by turning on a second indicator if the conditions do not exist. This will be used to print an error.

Figure 1.20
Review of Input Specifications form.

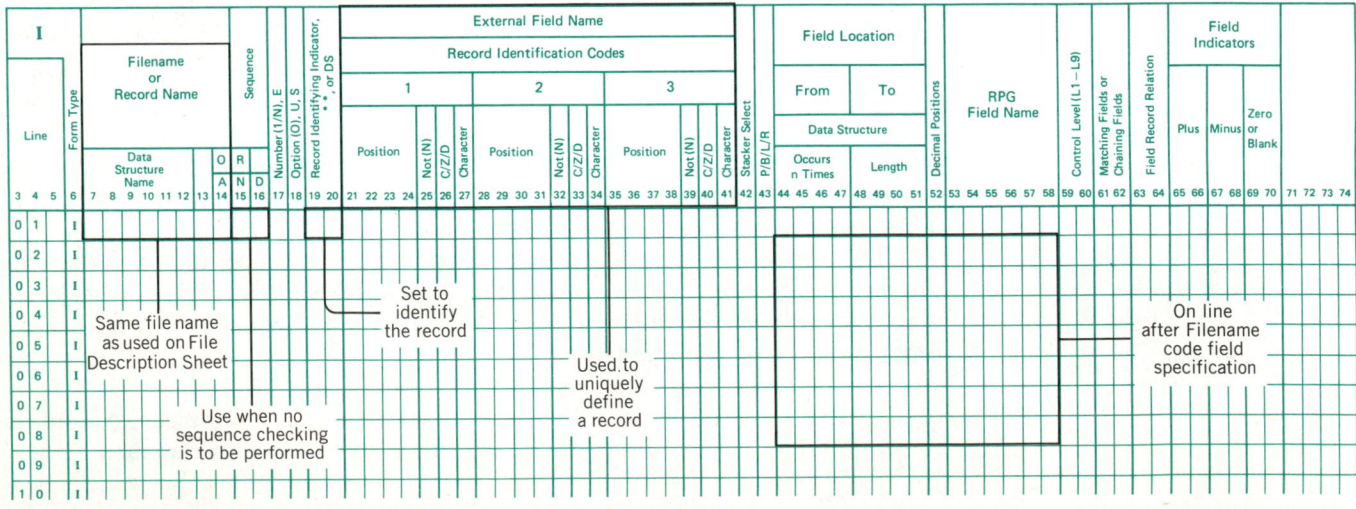

2. Code the Input Specifications form for a record, within the DISKIN file, with the following identifiers.

Column	Code
71	B
72	A
73	L
74	D
75	U
76	E

3. Code the Input Specifications form, insofar as you are able, for a file called TRANS that contains disk records. Credit records contain a C in column 1; debit records contain an S in column 1. No sequence checking is required.

4. The input file, INFILE, has two record formats. The first record, RECORD1, should have a 1 in column 80 and a minus sign in column 79. The second record, REC-ORD2, should have a 2 in column 78, a 6 in column 79, and an A in column 80. Write the Input Specifications for this problem.

5. (T or F) The RECORD IDENTIFYING INDICATORS used must be in numeric sequence.

6. (T or F) When three RECORD IDENTIFICATION CODES are coded on a single line, any one of the three conditions will turn on the RECORD IDENTIFYING INDICATOR.

7. The NOT subfield of the RECORD IDENTIFICATION CODES is used to denote _____. If column 80 is to be tested for a blank, then _____ is coded in the POSITION field, _____ is coded in the NOT field, _____ is coded in the C/Z/D field, and _____ is coded in the CHARACTER field.

8. Code the Input Specifications for a program that reads records from a file called DISKIN. The records are to be processed only if they contain a 7 in column 79 and a 4 in column 80.

9. (T or F) If all records are to be processed regardless of any format, then the record identifying indicator must be coded but the record identification codes may be left blank.

10. When defining fields on the Input Specifications both the _____ location and the _____ location of the field must be specified.

11. Numeric fields are identified by specifying _____ in column _____ of the Input Specifications.

12. Prefixes are used to _____.

13. The two major categories of data formats are _____ and _____.

14. A character field can contain _____.

15. If a field is to be used in an arithmetic operation, it must be defined as a _____ field.

16. A zoned decimal numeric field has a _____ in each byte that contains a(n) _____ for positive numbers.

17. An **advantage** of packing is that it _____.

18. Most computers execute arithmetic operations on numeric fields when they are in _____.

19. A nine-byte zoned decimal field when packed will require _____ bytes.

20. If a packed decimal field contains six bytes it can hold up to _____ digits.

21. The hexadecimal representation for the "blank" character is _____.

22. Indicate if the following coding is correct:

I — Input Specifications

Line	Form Type	Filename or Record Name / Data Structure Name	O/R AND	Sequence	Number (1/N), E	Option (O), U, S	Record Identifying Indicator, * or DS	Record Identification Codes 1 Position	Not(N)	C/Z/D	Character	2 Position	Not(N)	C/Z/D	Character	3 Position	Not(N)	C/Z/D	Character	Stacker Select	P/B/L/R	Field Location From / Occurs n Times	To / Length	Decimal Positions	RPG Field Name	Control Level (L1–L9)	Matching Fields or Chaining Fields	Field Record Relation	Field Indicators Plus	Minus	Zero or Blank
01	I	RECIN		NS			Ø1	8Ø		C	X																				
02	I																					1	6		CODE						
03	I																					7	2Ø		NAME						
04	I																					21	3Ø	Ø	BALANC						
05	I																					31	35		CUSTNO						
06	I																					36	5Ø		ADDRES						
07	I																					51	6Ø		CITY						
08	I																					61	65		STATE						
09	I																					66	8Ø		SHIPPR						
10	I																														

Solutions

1.

Line	Form Type	Filename or Record Name	O/R AND	Sequence	Number (1/N), E	Option (O), U, S	Record Identifying Indicator	1 Position	Not(N)	C/Z/D	Character	2 Position	Not(N)	C/Z/D	Character	3 Position	Not(N)	C/Z/D	Character	Stacker Select	P/B/L/R
01	I	DISKIN		NS			Ø1	21		C	4	22		C	5						
02	I																			•	
03	I																			•	
04	I																			•	
05	I			NS			Ø2	21	N	C	4										
06	I		OR					22	N	C	5										
07	I																				

2.

Line	Form Type	Filename or Record Name	O/R AND	Sequence	Number (1/N), E	Option (O), U, S	Record Identifying Indicator	1 Position	Not(N)	C/Z/D	Character	2 Position	Not(N)	C/Z/D	Character	3 Position	Not(N)	C/Z/D	Character
01	I	DISKIN		NS			Ø1	71		C	B	72		C	A	73		C	L
02	I		AND					74		C	D	75		C	U	76		C	E
03	I																		

3.

Line	Form Type	Filename or Record Name (Data Structure Name)	Sequence	Number (1/N), E	Option (O), U, S	Record Identifying Indicator, **, or DS	Position	Not(N)	C/Z/D	Character	Position	Not(N)	C/Z/D	Character	Position	Not(N)	C/Z/D	Character	
01	I	TRANS	NS			01	1		C	C									→ When position 1 has a 'C' indicator 01 is turned on
02	I																		
03	I																		
04	I																		
05	I																		
06	I																		
07	I																		
08	I		NS			02	1		C	S									→ When position 1 has an 'S' indicator 02 is turned on
09	I																		

4.

Line	Form Type	Filename or Record Name	Sequence	Record Identifying Indicator	Position	Not(N)	C/Z/D	Character	Position	Not(N)	C/Z/D	Character	Position	Not(N)	C/Z/D	Character
01	I	INFILE	NS	01	79		Z	-	80		D	1				
02	I		NS	02	78		D	2	79		D	6	80		C	A
03	I															

5. F

6. F—All three conditions must exist for the indicator to be turned on.

7. that a record identifying indicator should be turned on if a code does not exist; 80; blank; C; blank

8.

Line	Form Type	Filename or Record Name	Sequence	Record Identifying Indicator	Position	Not(N)	C/Z/D	Character	Position	Not(N)	C/Z/D	Character
01	I	DISKIN	NS	01	79		D	7	80		D	4
02	I		NS	99								
03	I											

9. F—When processing records regardless of the format, the record identifying indicator is not required because it would be set on for every record since no record identification codes are checked. This concept will be explained in more detail in Chapter 2.

10. beginning (high-order); ending (low-order)

11. 0–9 (any digit); 52

12. classify data fields as part of a group such as a record

13. character; numeric

14. any combination of printable characters—any combination of letters, digits, and special characters
15. numeric (with a digit in column 52 of the Input Specifications form)
16. four-bit zone portion; F
17. saves space and may be processed more efficiently
18. packed decimal format (except the S/34 and S/36)
19. five bytes; $9 \div 2 = 4 + 1 = 5$
20. 11 digits; $6 \times 2 = 12 - 1 = 11$
21. 40
22. Yes

3. Data Structures: An Introduction

RPG allows you to define a work area in storage and then subdivide that area into fields, called subfields.

A **data structure** can be used to:

1. Subdivide fields so that either the entire field or any of its subfields can be referenced.
2. Create new temporary work fields to be used during the processing stage.
3. Group noncontiguous fields together for easier reference.

Establishing data structures provides a method of confining all fields contained in a program to one central location, using the Input Specifications. This provides for better program documentation and facilitates debugging, since it is easier to locate and determine the attributes of not only input fields but work fields as well.

Data structures are defined on the Input Specifications using the same rules as we used for record definitions. Data structures must follow all input file descriptions; that is, they must be the last entries on the Input Specifications form.

To specify a data structure on the Input Specifications form, the following entries are coded:

FORM TYPE (Column 6)

Data structures are defined on the Input Specifications form, which always contains the precoded I.

DATA STRUCTURE NAME (Columns 7–12)

The name of the data structure is *optional* and, if specified, must meet the requirements of a field name (maximum of six characters). Data structure names *cannot* be used in the Calculation Specifications. However, subfields defined as members of the data structure may be used in calculations. As a coding guideline, begin each data structure with a unique prefix (e.g., WCTRS, WAMTS, etc.).

RECORD IDENTIFYING INDICATOR (Columns 19–20)

Code DS in columns 19–20 to identify an entry as a data structure. The first line of a data structure, then, would contain DS in columns 19–20 of an I-form (Input Specifications) and an optional data structure name.

To specify the subfields of a data structure, make the following entries starting on the line below the DS specification.

FROM FIELD LOCATION (Columns 44–47)

This entry is used to indicate the beginning or left-most (FROM) position of a subfield of the data structure.

TO FIELD LOCATION (Columns 48–51)

This entry is used to indicate the ending or right-most (TO) position of a subfield of the data structure.

DECIMAL POSITIONS (Column 52)

Enter 0–9 to specify the number of digits to the right of the decimal position if the subfield is numeric. This field remains blank if the subfield is alphanumeric.

SUBFIELD NAME (Columns 53–58)

This entry specifies the subfield name, which can be the same as an input field already defined on the Input Specifications or a new temporary work field name. RPG field name rules apply to subfield names. Subfields can be used in calculations or as an output field. The same subfield name cannot be specified as part of another data structure.

Subfield names, like data structure names, should begin with prefixes to help identify their association within a program.

Facts About Data Structures

1. Each data structure is considered an alphanumeric byte string.
2. Each data structure is initialized to blanks.
3. Data structures in System/34 and System/36 RPG cannot define packed decimal fields.

This chapter introduces the Input Specifications necessary for identifying and establishing data structures. Additional reasons for using data structures will be considered in subsequent chapters as they are needed.

Let us consider a data structure example by examining Figure 1.21. The data structure is stored in memory as a contiguous string. The data structure can be referenced by the field name AMODEL or by the subfields ATYPE, AIDENT, or ACOLOR. Each subfield occupies its own area relative to the beginning of the data structure. Note that data structures can be used to redefine input fields or can be used to establish work areas necessary for processing.

4. The COPY Statement

The COPY **statement** is used to insert into a program a series of prewritten RPG *source* statements. Normally, this series of prewritten specifications is stored as one module in a *source library*, which is a library built to hold just source statements or members. All programs and prewritten source specifications are entered into a library by using an editor, which is similar to a word processor. **SEU** or **Source Entry Utility** is the most widely used editor in the RPG environment. It is a utility program supplied along with the operating system that not only enables you to create source members but also to make changes to existing members easily and quickly. Among SEU's many features is its ability to display the different RPG specification formats on the screen, which makes source data entry and updating of programs much easier.

Copying source modules from a library, rather than coding them enables modules to be shared. Shared modules have the following advantages:

1. They increase programmer productivity by saving a considerable amount of coding and debugging time.
2. They assist in developing programming standards and improving documentation since modules copied from a library will have common file definitions and descriptions.

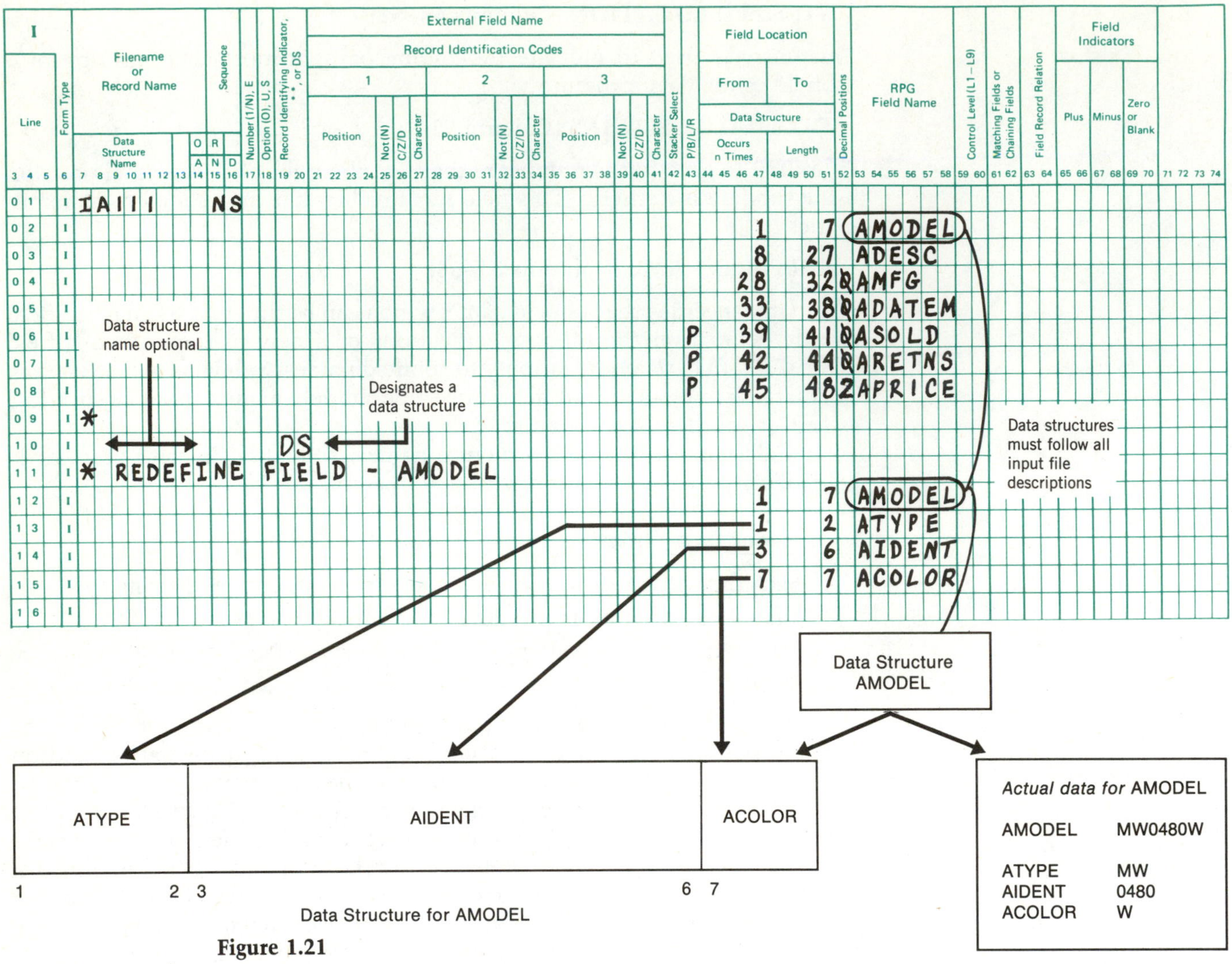

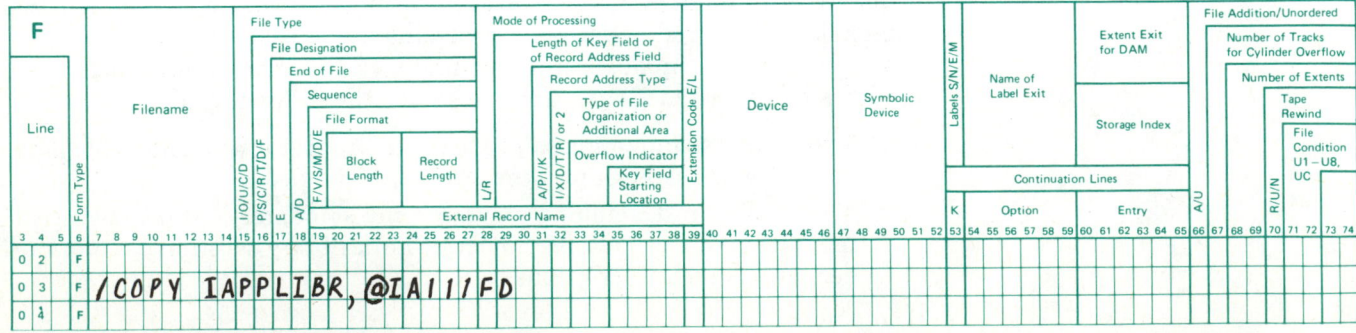

Figure 1.21
Using a data structure to
define subfields within a field.

3. They reduce the time it takes to make modifications. If a change needs to be made to a file definition, it can be made just once in the library without the need to alter the individual programs that use the file definitions.

4. They reduce the library space requirements for source programs since modules to be copied are stored only once, not in every program.

The format to copy stored source specifications using the /COPY statement is as follows:

```
/COPY IAPPLIBR, @IAIIIFD
```

Column 6

Because the COPY statement does not specifically relate to any one form, column 6 can contain any entry except H or U, or can be blank. Blank is recommended.

Columns 7–11

Must contain the characters /COPY

Column 12

Must be blank.

Columns 13–29

Identifies the module to be copied and its library name. Beginning in column 13, specify the library name containing the module. The source module name follows the library name separated by a comma. Both the library and module names can be up to eight characters in length.

Columns 30–49

Must be blank.

Columns 50–80

Comments. These columns are nonexecutable. They are for descriptive purposes only.

Most often, the COPY statement is used to copy file definitions that define and describe files and records. Thus the F, I, and E Specifications, which relate to files, can be copied from a library. In addition, standard *routines* to be used in the Calculation Specifications of several programs may also be stored in a library and copied as needed.

In this chapter we will focus on F and I Specifications of file definitions.

Prewritten specifications are included in a program during the first phase of the compile process. To merge a prewritten file definition into a program, a COPY statement is included in the File Description Specifications of the program. The compiler builds a complete source program by combining the programmer's source specifications with the prewritten specifications stored in the source library. Once the complete source program is intact the compiler completes the task by compiling the source program and producing a complete object module.

For example, suppose a programmer/analyst is working on an inventory application and has defined the product file and its record using File Description and Input Specifications. Suppose, too, that he or she has stored these source specifications in an RPG source library, as shown in Figure 1.22. The SEU in the figure refers to the Source Entry Utility, which is the RPG-specific text editor.

Once these source specifications are in the library, programmers can access them by inserting a COPY statement in the File Description Specifications of a program (Figure 1.23). As the RPG compiler scans the source program, it replaces COPY statements with the prewritten source specifications. These prewritten source statements (F and I Specifications) are automatically placed in the appropriate location of the program. Thus, the order of the RPG program is maintained in the required FICO sequence. Once the COPY statements have been expanded, the source module is complete, and compilation begins.

As noted, prewritten source statements other than file and record descriptions such as calculations and output specifications can also be copied.

It is especially important to uniquely identify fields that are inputted from an external source with the COPY statement because they will be common to several programs. As mentioned earlier, a prefix should be included as part of the field names to distinguish them from other input from files.

We focus on the COPY statement here because your instructor may use standard data file descriptions that he or she might want you to copy into your programs.

Figure 1.22
Storing source specifications in an RPG source library.

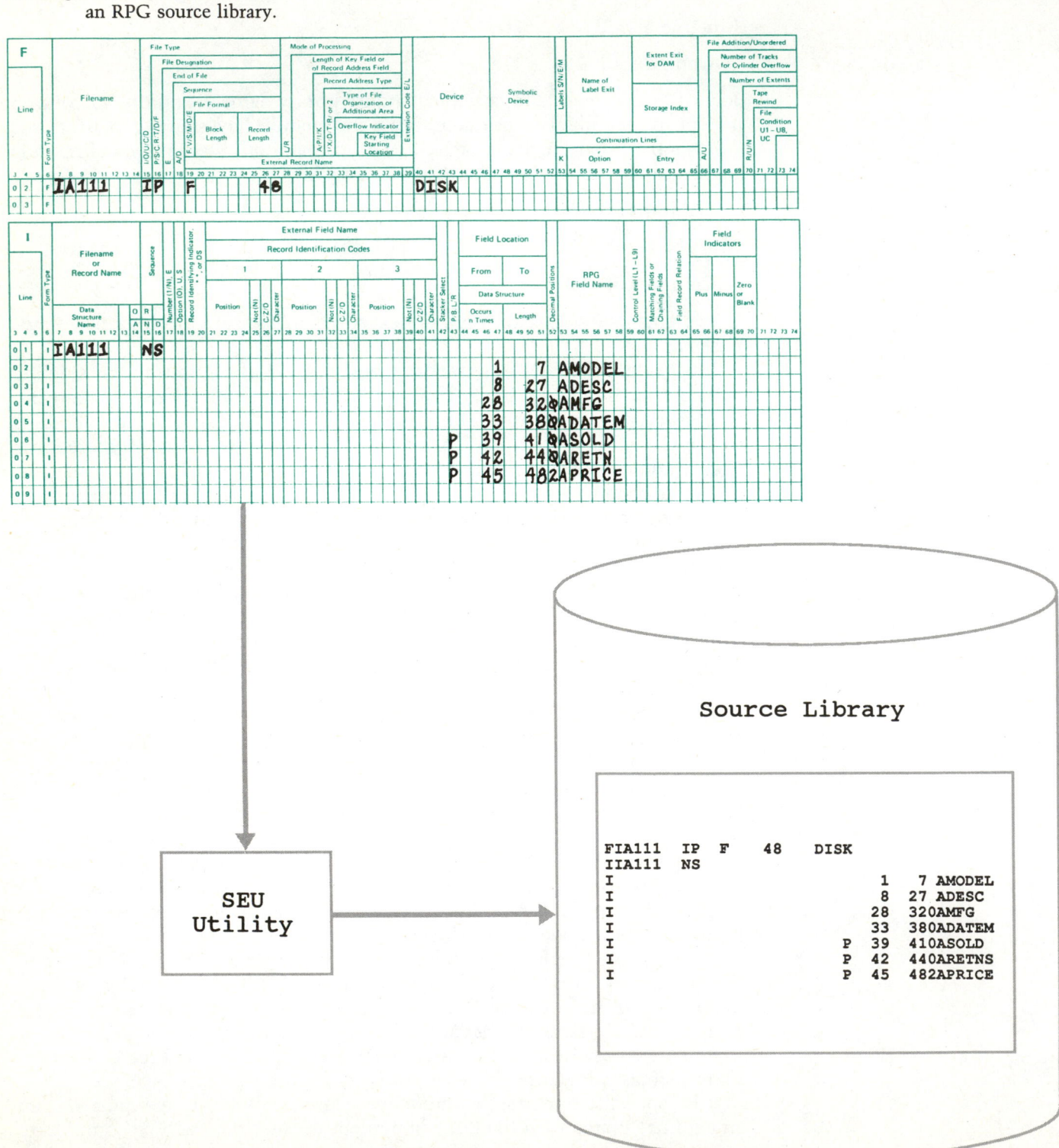

Source Program

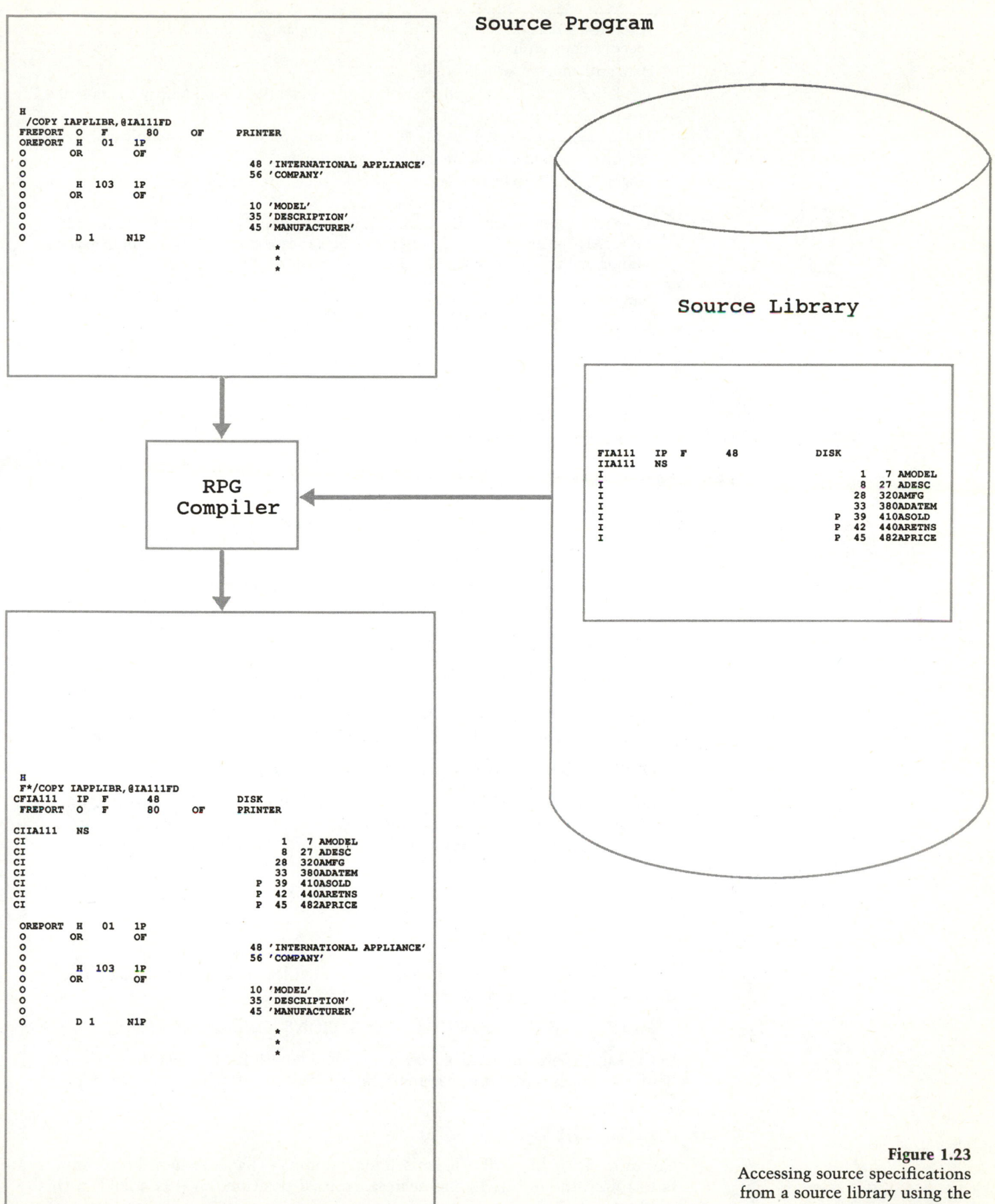

```
H
 /COPY IAPPLIBR,@IA111FD
FREPORT  O  F    80   OF    PRINTER
OREPORT  H  01  1P
O        OR      OF
O                              48 'INTERNATIONAL APPLIANCE'
O                              56 'COMPANY'
O        H 103  1P
O        OR      OF
O                              10 'MODEL'
O                              35 'DESCRIPTION'
O                              45 'MANUFACTURER'
O        D 1     N1P
                                *
                                *
                                *
```

Source Library

```
FIA111   IP F    48        DISK
IIA111   NS
I                          1   7 AMODEL
I                          8  27 ADESC
I                         28  320AMFG
I                         33  380ADATEM
I                       P 39  410ASOLD
I                       P 42  440ARETNS
I                       P 45  482APRICE
```

RPG
Compiler

```
H
 F*/COPY IAPPLIBR,@IA111FD
CFIA111  IP F    48        DISK
 FREPORT O  F    80   OF    PRINTER

CIIA111  NS
CI                         1   7 AMODEL
CI                         8  27 ADESC
CI                        28  320AMFG
CI                        33  380ADATEM
CI                      P 39  410ASOLD
CI                      P 42  440ARETNS
CI                      P 45  482APRICE

 OREPORT H  01  1P
O        OR      OF
O                              48 'INTERNATIONAL APPLIANCE'
O                              56 'COMPANY'
O        H 103  1P
O        OR      OF
O                              10 'MODEL'
O                              35 'DESCRIPTION'
O                              45 'MANUFACTURER'
O        D 1     N1P
                                *
                                *
                                *
```

Figure 1.23
Accessing source specifications
from a source library using the
COPY statement.

Self-Test
1. When using data structures, all fields in a program are defined on the _____ Specifications form.
2. Data structures must follow all _____.
3. The letters _____ must be specified in columns 19–20 to identify a data structure.
4. The _____ statement can be used to insert a prewritten file definition.
5. Prewritten specifications are normally stored in a _____ library.
6. Programs and prewritten source specifications are entered by means of a(n) _____.
7. To specify a COPY statement, _____ is placed starting in column 7, followed by a space. Then enter the _____ name where the member is located, followed by a comma and the name of the _____ to be copied.

Solutions
1. Input
2. input file definitions or input record descriptions
3. DS
4. COPY
5. source
6. line editor called the Source Entry Utility
7. /COPY; library; member or prewritten specifications

5. The Calculation Specifications Form

Figure 1.8c on page 24 shows a Calculation Specifications form. All arithmetic and logic operations are defined on the Calculation Specifications form.

CONTROL LEVELS (Columns 7–8)

Since no control fields are used in the sample program, columns 7 and 8 are blank. Control fields are discussed in Chapter 7.

INDICATORS (Columns 9–17)

Since a multiplication operation (HOURS × RATE) is to be performed for *all* input records, we use indicator Ø1, which is "turned on" for all input records. This is the only indicator required in the sample program. In general, the indicator fields are used to specify when calculations are to be performed.

OPERATION and RESULT FIELD (Columns 18–48)

In the sample program, Factor 1, HOURS, is multiplied (MULT) by Factor 2, RATE, to produce a resultant field called WAGES.
For other operations we may use:

```
ADD
SUB
DIV
COMP (compare)
```

The precise format for all calculations is provided in Chapter 3. Logic operations such as the compare are described in Chapter 4.

FIELD LENGTH and DECIMAL POSITIONS (Columns 49–52)

In the sample program in Figure 1.8, the field length for the resultant numeric field, WAGES, is 5 (column 51) including two decimal positions (2 in column 52).

HALF ADJUST (Column 53)

Column 53, HALF ADJUST, is used for rounding. That is, when the computer is to round the results to the nearest decimal position, an H is coded in this field.

RESULTING INDICATORS (Columns 54–59)

The RESULTING INDICATORS in columns 54–59 can be turned on as a result of a compare (COMP) operation. This will be discussed in Chapter 4.

COMMENTS (Columns 60–74)

Any comments may be included in columns 60 to 74. These are printed on the listing but do not affect processing. Entire lines may also be included as comments by using an asterisk (*) in column 7 of any line of any form.

6. The Output Specifications Form

Figure 1.8d on page 24 shows an Output Specifications form.

FILENAME (Columns 7–14)

For the sample program in Figure 1.8, the output file REPORT would be described using this form. The next chapter will discuss the output form in more detail. This chapter simply illustrates its use.

TYPE (Column 15)

There are four types of print output records:

Heading (H)
Detail (D)
Total (T)
Exception (E)

Since we only have Heading and Detail records here, only H and D types (column 15) have been included.

STACKER SELECT (Column 16)

This field is appropriate only for punched output. Since cards are rarely used, this column will be left blank in all our illustrations.

SPACE and SKIP (Columns 17–22)

These options are appropriate only for printed output. All printers can be made to space 1, 2, or 3 (and sometimes more) lines either *before* or *after* writing a line. The 2 in SPACE AFTER of the illustration (column 18) indicates that *after* the Heading line is printed, we wish to space the form two lines. Note, however, that *either* column 17 or 18 must include a 1, 2, or 3 to designate the type of spacing required. A 0 may be used in both columns 17 and 18 to suppress spacing entirely. A blank may also be used to indicate one line of spacing after printing. Some systems allow a number greater than three for spacing more than three lines; check your specifications manual.

The SKIP option for printed output is used to position the form at a specific line. An 01 in one of the SKIP fields (19–20 or 21–22) is a code for skipping to the beginning of a new page either before or after printing. In our illustration, we skip to a new page before printing the heading.

Thus the output file REPORT has a heading record (H), which requires the skipping to a new page *before* printing, and two lines of spacing *after* printing.

OUTPUT INDICATORS (Columns 23–31)

The OUTPUT INDICATOR 1P (columns 24 and 25) means that we wish to print the H record (Heading) on the first page (1P). If any other conditions also require the printing of a heading record, then we code OR on the next line in columns 14 and 15 along with the corresponding condition. The notation OF in columns 24 and 25 of the second line indicates that we also wish to print a heading on an overflow, or end-of-page, condition.

In short, we are indicating that we wish the H or heading type record to print on the first page *or* when the end of a page is reached. In either case, we skip to a new page, print the heading, and then advance the paper two lines.

In most print applications, we want headings to print on the first printed page. Also, when we have reached the end of a page, we want the program to skip to a new page and print new headings. In this way, each individual page of the continuous form has a heading so that when the report is separated into individual sheets, each page can be identified.

FIELD NAME, EDIT CODES, END POSITION and CONSTANT (Columns 32–70)

The heading PAYROLL REPORT is to print with the last character in print position 73 (see the Printer Spacing Chart on page 22).

The detail line, D, prints when indicator Ø1 is on, that is, for all input records. Each time a detail line prints, the form is spaced one line (before printing). Since each input record turns on indicator Ø1, a detail line will print for each input card.

There are four output fields to be printed:

PRINTING OF OUTPUT	
Field Name	**Print Positions**
NAME	21–4Ø
HOURS	59–6Ø
RATE	77–8Ø (A decimal point prints on output and therefore counts as a position)
WAGES	95–1ØØ (Here, too, a decimal point prints on output)

Note: On the Output form, indicate the low-order or right-most position for each field (e.g., 4Ø, 6Ø, 8Ø, 1ØØ for the above).

The first three fields are directly transmitted from the input record. Note that these input and output fields have the same names. See Figure 1.8*d*. NAME requires no editing. HOURS requires zero suppression (Z in column 38) to eliminate leading zeros. RATE requires a decimal point to print after the first integer position. You will recall that to save space in an input record, decimal points are often omitted. That is, they are *implied* or *assumed* in input records. The output document, however, must have these decimal points for readability. A 1 in column 38 will print a decimal point in the correct place. We will see later that the Edit Word, columns 45 to 7Ø, may be used in place of column 38.

The four specification forms in Figure 1.8 comprise a complete RPG program that performs the required operations outlined in our problem definition. Although there is no visible step-by-step logic displayed in the specifications, when the forms are coded so that they conform to the RPG rules, a program is compiled that contains the step-by-step logic.

VII. RPG Logic Cycle

As we have seen, RPG is coded using four basic specification forms that specify:

1. Files to be used.
2. Input formats.

3. Calculations to be performed.
4. Output formats.

The sequence in which RPG performs the required operations is relatively clear in simple programs such as the one discussed in this chapter. But this sequence becomes somewhat less obvious with more complex programming. The **RPG Logic Cycle** describes in detail the precise sequence in which RPG performs all operations.

In other programming languages, the programmer is in full control of the sequence in which instructions are executed. With the use of GOTO statements in most languages, FOR . . . NEXT statements in BASIC, PERFORM statements in COBOL, etc., the programmer can precisely specify logical control.

In RPG this logical control can be handled by the compiler, although there are methods to override the established structure. We will see in later chapters how structured programming concepts can be employed with RPG to control the sequence in which operations are performed. The programmer, then, must fully understand the logical control sequence provided by RPG in order to code programs accurately.

This RPG Logic Cycle is usually illustrated in pictorial form. Figure 1.24 illustrates the RPG Logic Cycle in flowchart or top-down form. All programs in RPG follow this fixed logic sequence:

1. Headings or H records are printed on the first page or if a page overflow occurs.
2. Detail or D records are printed if the specified indicators are satisfied.
3. If this is the first cycle, the 1P indicator is turned off.
4. All record identifying indicators are turned off.
5. A record is read.
6. The computer tests for the last record. If the last record has been processed, the LR indicator is turned on and may be used for performing end-of-job calculations or printing end-of-job summaries. After the end-of-job functions are completed, the program is terminated.
7. Record identifying indicators are turned on according to the specifications on the input form.
8. Calculations are performed using indicators to specify which calculations are required.
9. The process is repeated by returning to Step 1.

As our programs get more sophisticated, we will specify the sequence of execution by providing more detail in the RPG Logic Cycle illustrations.

VIII. Documentation

The beginning programmer should be aware of some of the reasons why computer systems have failed in the past, and sometimes continue to fail, in providing needed services to users. One main reason why users are often dissatisfied is because of inadequate documentation of programs. Documentation refers to the set of supporting specifications that are used to explain in detail how the program operates and what it is intended to accomplish.

All too frequently, programmers view their job as consisting *solely* of writing and debugging a program; they pay little or no attention to providing the user with a documentation package that adequately describes the program.

Figure 1.24
RPG Logic Cycle
in flowchart form.

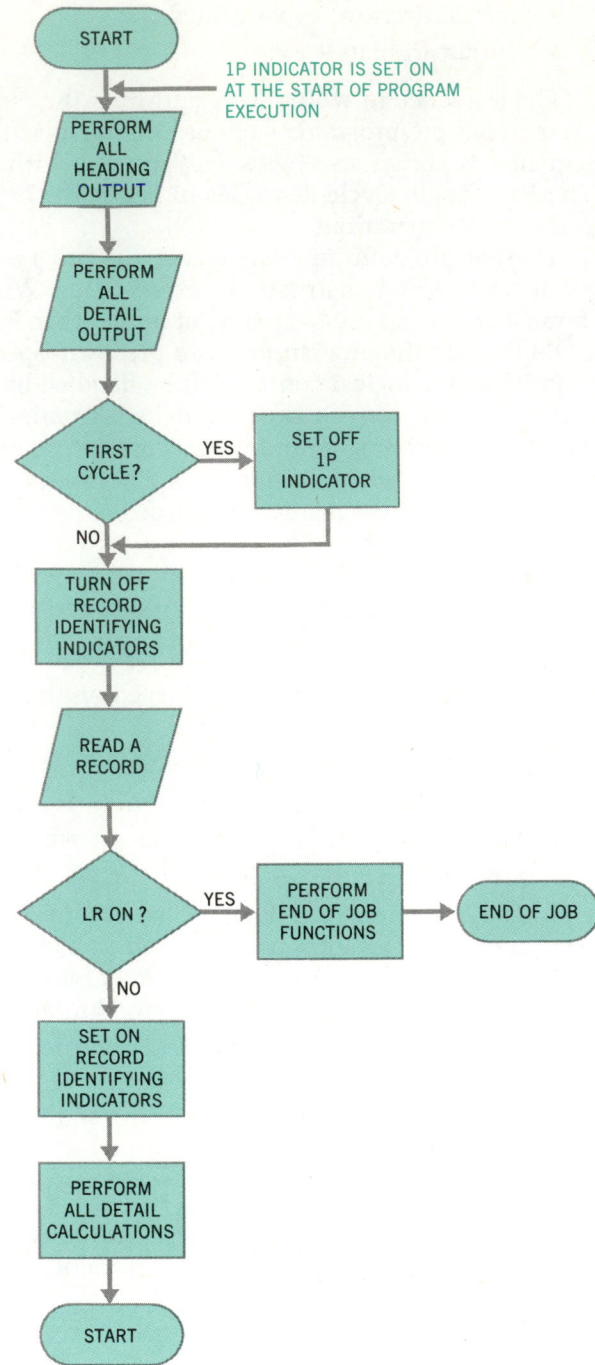

Without required documentation, the following problems are apt to occur:

1. Minor "bugs," which frequently occur only after a program has been running, would be difficult to locate and correct.

2. If programming modifications are required at a later date, they would be extremely difficult to make.

3. Users will have no written procedures to help them understand how the program functions.

Many computer centers now have established standards that require information processing professionals to supply specific documentation.

Typically, a programmer receives a program assignment from a systems analyst who is responsible for the overall design of the system (i.e., accounting system, inventory system, payroll system, etc.). The systems analyst should provide the programmer with a problem definition including standard specifications used for coding the problem:

1. A brief systems flowchart outlining the input, output, and processing required.
2. Record Layout forms describing all input and output.
3. Printer Spacing Charts describing all print output.

See Figure 1.25 for an illustration of a systems flowchart and an input layout for the program described in this chapter (Figure 1.8). The Printer Spacing Chart is illustrated on page 22. The programmer uses these forms in coding; they then become part of the documentation package.

These forms are standard within the information processing industry. Thus, every program discussed in this text will include the three documentation specifications: systems flowchart, input layout, and Printer Spacing Chart for print output, or output layout for disk output. These items are essential for providing the programmer with the problem definition. They can also be examined by users to ensure that all data is processed properly. At the end of the job, they become part of the documentation package.

The programmer also includes a source listing as part of documentation. Since users may wish to examine the source listing, or other programmers may need it if later modifications are desired, the following two points should be noted:

1. Field and file names should be as meaningful as possible. That is, AMT1 is a better description of the first amount field on a record, than A1, for example.

Figure 1.25
Systems flowchart and input layout for the sample program in Figure 1.8.

Systems Flowchart

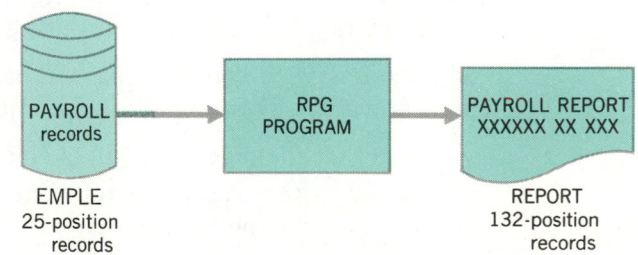

EMPLE Record Layout

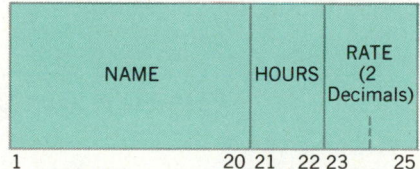

```
01-020    F*******************************************************************SSS01A
01-030    F* THIS PRCGRAM PRCLUCES A PAYRCLL REPCRT, CALCULATING WAGES EARNED *SSS01A
01-040    F* BY MULTIPLYING TCTAL NUMBER CF HOURS WCRKED BY THE RATE CF PAY   *SSS01A
01-050    F* FOR EACH EMPLOYEE.                                               *SSS01A
01-060    F*******************************************************************SSS01A
01-070    F*                                                                  SSS01A
0001   01-08C    FEMPLE      IP  F    25              DISK                     SSS01A
0002   01-09C    FREPORT     O   F    132     OF      PRINTER                  SSS01A
       01-1CC    F*                                                           SSS01A
       02-010    I********************** INPUT RECCRC *********************SSS01A
       02-02C    I*                                                           SSS01A
0003   02-030    IEMPLE      AA  01                                           SSS01A
0004   02-040    I                             1   20 NAME                    SSS01A
0005   02-050    I                            21   22CHOURS                   SSS01A
0006   02-060    I                            23   252RATE                    SSS01A
       02-070    I*                                                           SSS01A
       03-010    C********************** CALCULATICNS ********************SSS01A
       03-020    C*                                                           SSS01A
0007   03-030    C   01      HOURS     MULT RATE      WAGES     52H            SSS01A
       03-040    C*                                                           SSS01A
       04-010    C********************** HEADING LINE ********************SSS01A
       04-02C    C*                                                           SSS01A
0008   04-030    CREPORT   H 201      1P                                      SSS01A
0009   04-040    C        OR          CF                                      SSS01A
0010   04-050    C                                73 'PAYRCLL REPORT'         SSS01A
       04-06C    C*                                                           SSS01A
       04-070    O**********************-DETAIL LINE *********************SSS01A
       04-08C    C*                                                           SSS01A
0011   04-090    C        D 1         C1                                      SSS01A
0012   04-1CC    C                                NAME      40                SSS01A
0013   04-11C    C                                HCURS Z   60                SSS01A
0014   04-120    C                                RATE  1   8C                SSS01A
0015   04-130    C                                WAGES 1  1CO                SSS01A
       04-140    C*                                                           SSS01A
       04-150    O*******************************************************SSS01A
```

E N D   C F   S C U R C E

Figure 1.26
Source listing of sample program with comments.

2. Comments should be included on the listing as often as possible to help describe the processing. See Figure 1.26 for a source listing of our sample program, with comments. Note that such comments are also useful as reminders to the programmer during the debugging phase.

For programs with complex logic, it is best to plan the program using a *program flowchart*. Drawing a flowchart prior to coding will help to:

1. Ensure that the program logic is clear.
2. Verify with the user or systems analyst that the programmer's understanding of the job requirements is correct.

A program flowchart is not the only tool used for depicting program logic. Programs that use *structured* techniques are more apt to include *pseudocode* as a documentation tool. We will consider flowcharting, pseudocode, and structured programming in Chapter 5.

CHAPTER SUMMARY

A. Program considerations
1. Programs are written in a symbolic language that is relatively easy to learn. This program is called the source program.

2. Source programs must be translated into machine language programs before they can be run or executed. Machine language programs are called object programs.
3. Debugging a program is the process of finding and correcting any errors.
    a. Syntax errors—violations in the rules of the language; usually found when a program is compiled.
    b. Logic errors—mistakes in the structure or logic; usually found when testing the program during execution.
4. Methods of Debugging
    a. Desk checking—checking a program for typos and other errors before running it on a computer.
    b. Fixing syntax errors after compilation.
    c. Creating test data that will test all possible conditions.
    d. Program walkthroughs—checking the program by manually stepping through the logic with some sample test data.
    e. Executing the program with test data.

B. RPG language
1. RPG is an abbreviation for Report Program Generator.
2. RPG is useful for a wide variety of business applications including report writing and disk processing.
3. All RPG programs use the following forms in the sequence indicated:
    a. Control and File Description Specifications.
    b. Input Specifications.
    c. Calculation Specifications.
    d. Output Specifications.
        Other forms are also available, but these four are used for most programs.

C. RPG Logic Cycle
1. RPG has a specific sequence in which program statements are executed.
2. Unlike other languages, this sequence is not directly under the programmer's control.
3. Programmers must be familiar with this logic cycle to avoid program errors.

D. Documentation
1. Before coding, all programmers should be provided with the following problem definition:
    a. A systems flowchart describing the input, output, and processing required.
    b. A formal description of the files on Record Layout forms.
    c. A formal description of printed output on a Printer Spacing Chart.
2. These specifications help the programmer to better understand what is required and also provide users with needed information about the program.
3. All programs should contain meaningful field and file names.
4. Comments (∗ in column 7 of any form) should be included in an RPG program to help explain the processing.

CHAPTER SELF-TEST

1. RPG is called a (symbolic/machine) language.
2. (T or F) RPG can only be used on microcomputers.
3. (T or F) RPG is well suited for handling high-level and complex input and output.
4. (T or F) RPG can be used for writing structured programs.
5. (T or F) The Control and File Description Specifications form describes the format of input and output fields to be used.
6. The _____ Specification is the first entry of an RPG program.

7. RPG coding sheets have space for ___(no.)___ columns of information.

8. Column _____ on an RPG coding form is used to indicate the Form Type.

9. Column 7 of all RPG coding forms can be used to designate any line as a comment by coding a(n) _____ in that column.

10. Excluding sequence numbers and the program identification, RPG statements are coded in columns ___(no.)___ to ___(no.)___.

11. (T or F) On every RPG coding form, the program identification columns must be filled in.

12. (T or F) A decimal point is not generally entered in an input dollars-and-cents field.

13. The File Description Specifications form always has a(n) _____ in column 6 to denote its Form Type.

14. (T or F) On the File Description Specifications form, column 16 (Primary/Secondary) must be blank for output files.

15. (T or F) It is possible to define more than one primary file in an RPG program.

16. If there is more than one input file in a program, then one is defined as Primary and the other(s) as _____.

17. (T or F) A print file can contain variable-length records.

18. (T or F) If BLOCK LENGTH is omitted for a file, it is assumed to be the same as RECORD LENGTH.

19. An OVERFLOW INDICATOR designated as _____ can be coded for a print file in order to test for the end of a page.

20. (T or F) The SEQUENCE field on the Input Specifications form can contain any two letters to indicate that no sequence check is required.

21. (T or F) If all input records have the same format, then RECORD IDENTIFICATION CODES may be omitted.

22. (T or F) The DECIMAL POSITIONS field must be coded for all numeric fields that are to be used in arithmetic operations.

23. Field names are (left/right)-justified.

24. (T or F) All fields in an input record must be defined, even if they are not required for processing.

SOLUTIONS

1. symbolic
2. F
3. T
4. T
5. F—It lists the files to be used, the devices they will employ, and special features to be included.
6. Control or H
7. 80
8. 6
9. asterisk (*)
10. 6; 74
11. F—It is an optional entry.
12. T
13. F
14. T
15. F
16. Secondary
17. F
18. T
19. OF
20. T, but NS is recommended
21. T
22. T
23. left
24. F, but it is recommended that all fields be defined

KEY TERMS

Blocking	File	Object module	Source program
Byte	Fixed-length record	Object program	Structure chart
Character field	Flowchart	Output	Structured programming
Compiler	Group item	Packed decimal format	Subroutine
COPY statement	Hierarchy chart	Printer Spacing Chart	Symbolic programming language
Data structure	High-level language	Program	
Database	Input	Programmer	Syntax error
Debugging	Linkage-editor	Pseudocode	Test data
Desk checking	Load module	Record	Top-down programming
Documentation	Logic error	RPG	User
Elementary item	Machine language	RPG coding sheet	Variable-length record
Externally defined files	Module	RPG Logic Cycle	Walkthrough
Field	Numeric field	SEU (Source Entry Utility)	Zoned decimal format

REVIEW QUESTIONS

1. Code the Input Specifications form, for a record, within the MDISK file with the following codes:

Column	Code
71	B
or 71	D
or 71	W

2. Modify the solution to question 1 so that the test for B, D, or W records also includes a test for 73 in columns 79–80. That is, all B, D, and W records must contain a 73 in columns 79–80.

3. Code the Input Specifications form for a disk file with the record format denoted in Figure 1.27. Assume that no sequence-checking is required.

4. (T or F) A field identifier should always appear on a line with a record identifier.

5. Data fields that are further subdivided are called _____ items.

6. (T or F) Only numeric fields can contain an entry in column 52 of the Input Specifications form.

7. Indicate what, if anything, is wrong with the following RPG field names:
   a. 1RPG
   b. NAME 1
   c. NAMEFIELD
   d. NAME-A

Figure 1.27
DISKIN record format for Review Question 3.

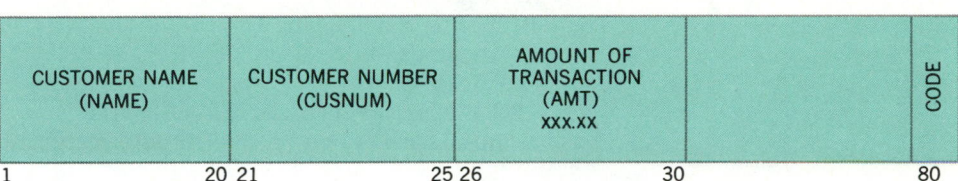

(1=Debit 2=Credit)

2

The Printing of Reports

OBJECTIVES

To familiarize you with

1. The characteristics of printed output.
2. The RPG coding specifications for printing reports.
3. The major types of editing performed with printed output and how RPG is used for editing.
4. The different types of reports typically generated in business organizations and how RPG is used to produce them.

I. Special Considerations for Printed Output

The printed report is the primary form of output for many computer applications. It is the type of output that will be used by management for decision-making purposes and by the operating staff to assist them in their day-to-day activities.

Disk output, created as intermediate products to be used for future reference or processing, is created with efficiency in mind. Fields within disk records are produced as concisely as possible to conserve space and decrease processing time.

The printed report, however, is written with the user in mind. It is designed to be **user-friendly,** that is, clear and easy to interpret. Several characteristics, not applicable to other forms of output, must be considered when printing reports.

A. Headings

Every printed report generated by the computer should have headings that describe the report. The initial **report heading** should contain:

ITEMS IN A REPORT HEADING
1. A clear and concise title of the report.
2. The date of the run.
3. Page numbers.

In addition to the report headings that describe the overall report, there are usually column headings that describe the fields to be printed. In Figure 2.1, for example, two lines were used for column headings; *both* lines must be described in the program.

	CUSTOMER REPORT		JULY, 19xx	PAGE 1	← Report Heading
NAME	AMOUNT OF PURCHASE	AMOUNT OF CREDIT	TOTAL DUE	}	Column Headings
L B JONES	$1,325.22	$21.10	$1,304.12	}	Detail Data

Figure 2.1
Illustration of printed output
with more than one
heading line.

B. Spacing and Skipping

Printed output is produced by a printer on **continuous forms** (see Figure 2.2) that will be separated into individual sheets after printing. Programs indicate how output data is to be aligned and what types of line spacing should be used. Moreover, the headings should begin on specific lines of each page of the continuous form so that each individual sheet will have the same identifying data on the same line of each page.

Advancing the paper a fixed number of lines is called **spacing.** In RPG, the programmer can space the form one, two, or three lines before or after a line is printed. In addition, the RPG programmer can advance the paper to a specific line. Advancing the paper to a specific line is called **skipping.**

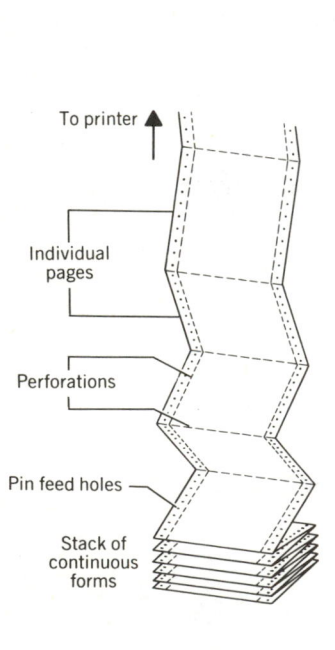

Figure 2.2
Continuous forms.
(Courtesy IBM.)

Consider the following excerpt from an RPG Output Specifications form:

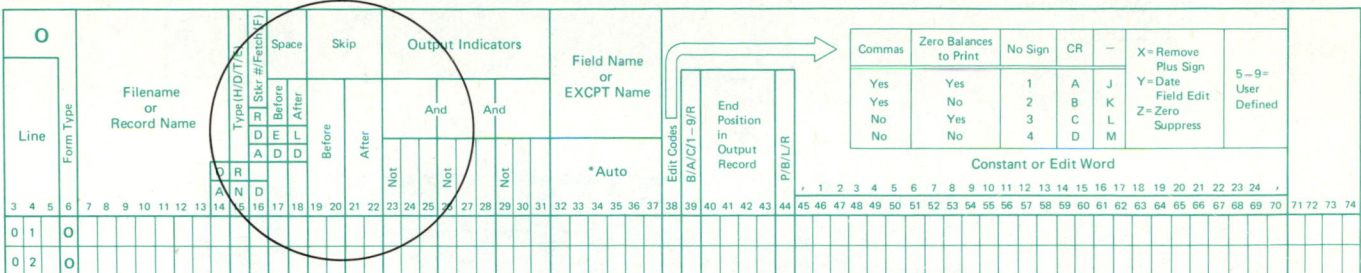

The SPACE fields, columns 17 and 18, can be coded with 1, 2, or 3 to denote single, double, or triple spacing. The numbers 1, 2, or 3 are the only acceptable entries. You can space *before* a line is printed by using column 17 or *after* a line is printed by using column 18. To advance the paper both before and after printing, use both columns 17 and 18.

The SKIP fields enable the output to print on a specific line. You usually skip to the beginning of a page to print the first heading or to the end of a page to print totals by coding the line number in the BEFORE or AFTER columns of the SKIP field.

Standard continuous forms have 66 lines, although there are numerous form sizes available. Typically, headings are printed on line 6 and the last output line is printed on line 60 to allow for top and bottom margins, but other conventions can be used.

If the programmer does not code the SPACE or SKIP fields on the Output Specifications, the computer will assume single spacing. An assumption of this type made by the system in the absence of specific coding is referred to as a **default.**

C. Alignment of Data

As previously illustrated, printed output is designed to be as easy to read as possible. Use of top and bottom margins and proper spacing between lines is one method to facilitate the reading of a document. Another is to align data evenly across the page.

The Printer Spacing Chart is used to map out where data will be placed to ensure proper alignment. It is prepared by the systems analyst or the programmer prior to any coding.

D. Editing

As noted, to maximize efficiency, data stored on disk is designed to be as concise as possible. For example, decimal points, dollar signs, and commas are always omitted from input records.

Printed output, on the other hand, should contain special symbols that will improve the readability of the data. The use of such symbols is called **editing.** Typically, editing consists of:

EDITING FEATURES

1. Insertion of dollar signs, commas, and decimal points.
2. Printing of a minus sign or CR for negative quantities.
3. Suppression of leading zeros.
4. Use of a floating dollar sign: i.e., $57.25 rather than $ 57.25.

Figure 2.3
Summary of the most common
items to be considered for
printed output.

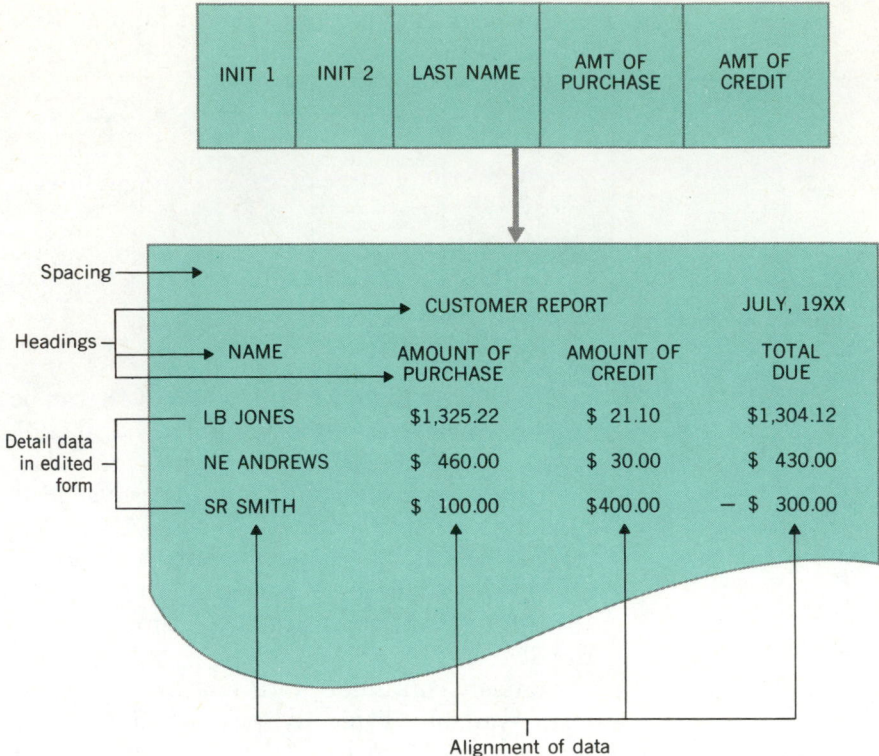

Figure 2.3
Summary of the most common items to be considered for printed output.

Figure 2.3 provides a summary of the most common items to be considered when preparing printed output.

II. RPG Coding for Printed Output

A. Initial Coding Line on the Output Specifications Form

Figure 2.4 identifies the fields that must be coded on the first line of the Output Specifications form.

These fields are discussed below.

1. Filename

This filename is the same name as defined for the output print file on the File Description Specifications form. It is only necessary to code the filename once on the Output Specifications form. This name, as all names in RPG, is coded beginning in the left-most position of the field. Unfilled right-most positions are left blank. Recall that a maximum of eight characters is permitted in a filename, and the name should be meaningful.

2. Type

The initial coding line must indicate whether the lines directly following this first one will be describing:

a Heading (H)—for report, page, and column headings.
a Detail line (D).
a Total line (T).
an Exception line (E).

Usually, the first group of lines will describe one or more headings, followed by

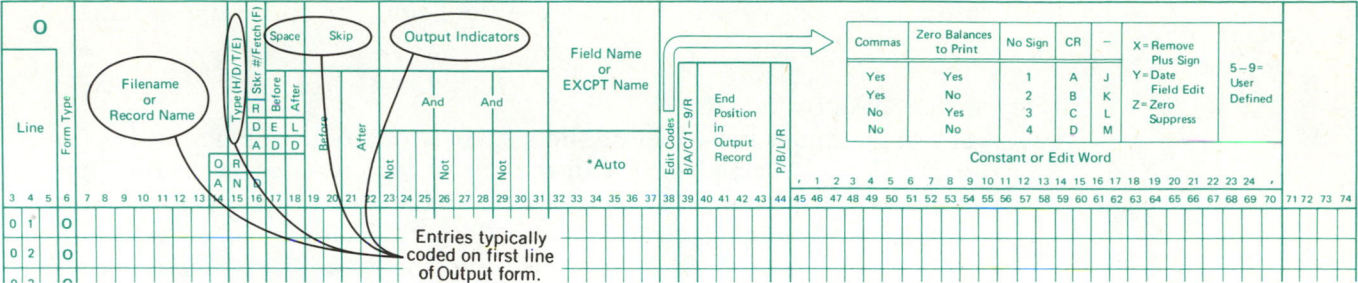

Figure 2.4
Entries coded on the first line of the Output Specifications form.

descriptions for detail lines and then total lines. Later on, we discuss Exception lines, which are printed in a sequence determined by the programmer, unlike H, D, and T lines, which are printed in the specified sequence by the RPG system.

3. Space or Skip

The programmer should indicate which paper-advancing options are desired:

1. Spacing one, two, or three lines before or after printing by coding 1, 2, or 3 in columns 17–18.
2. Skipping to a specific line before or after printing by coding the line number in columns 19–22. Note that to skip to line 3, for example, you must code 03, not 3 itself.

It is possible to use more than one of these Space and Skip options together. For example, you can skip to line 6 before printing and double space after printing by coding:

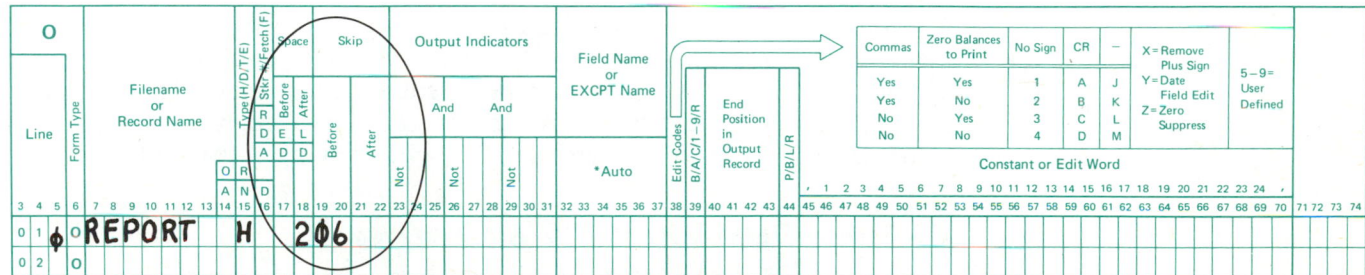

When using Space and Skip together, Skip takes precedence over Space; that is, the Skip operation will be executed first followed by the Space operation.

The purpose of the Space and Skip options is to control the form so that the paper will be on the proper line when printing is required. When you specify the Before option, the paper is first advanced to the desired line, the line is printed, and the form remains on the line just printed until another print operation is executed. With the After option, however, the line is printed first at the current position of the form and *then* the paper is advanced according to the Space or Skip-After requirements.

When the After option is specified what you are doing in effect is positioning the form for the *next* line to be printed. The Before option, on the other hand, positions the form to the desired line and *then* prints the line. We recommend that you use the Spacing or Skipping with the Before option because the paper is positioned on the desired line and printed *during the same print operation.* We will typically use the Before option for line spacing.

4. Output Indicators

The programmer must indicate under what conditions the output line is to print. This is accomplished with the use of indicators coded in the Output Indicator area (columns 23–31). The record indicators set on in the Input Specifications for incoming records are often used to determine when a detail line will print. Thus, if the Ø1 indicator is turned on for all input records, printing an input record would require the following coding:

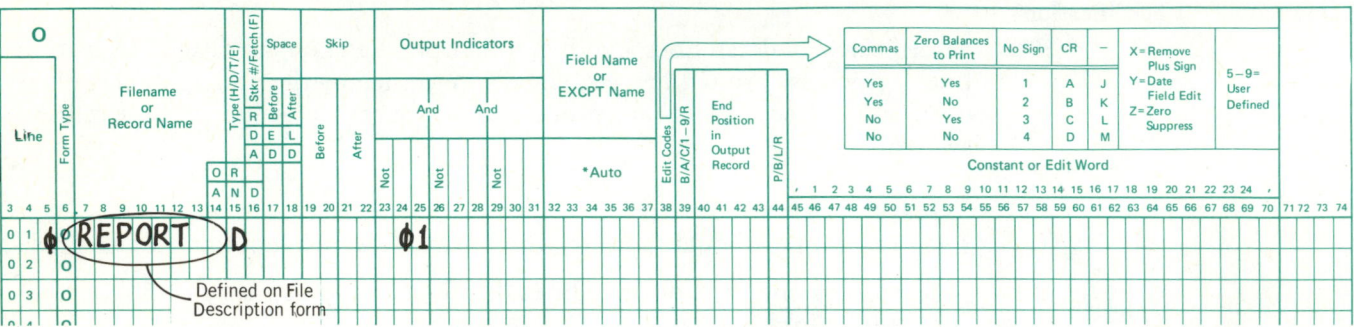

Note that the word REPORT appears only once on the first line. If there are headings, the first one would be described as an H type on the REPORT line itself. A D type would most likely not be coded on the REPORT line unless there are no headings.

Sometimes, indicators turned on during processing are used to control detail printing. You may, for example, wish to print a detail line only if the result of a specific computation is zero. Or you might wish to print a line only if the result is greater than a specified value. You can control printing by specifying that certain indicators should be on or off. A NOT condition in the indicator fields may also be used to test for the absence of an indicator. That is, by coding N in an indicator field (in columns 23, 26, or 29), printing will occur only if the indicator is off. Indicators are specified with two digits (Ø1–99).

B. Listing Detail Data in RPG: An Overview

Consider the problem definition in Figure 2.5. The RPG File Description and Input Specifications forms for the program that will list input data are given in Figure 2.6. When each record is printed on one or more lines of output, this is referred to as **detail printing.** An in-depth view of the Output Specifications form will be provided since this controls detail printing (see Figure 2.7 for an illustration).

1. Coding Output Specifications for Detail Lines

If the detail line is the first to be described on the Output Specifications form, the first line will indicate:

FILENAME—Same as on File Description form for the output file.
TYPE—D (for Detail).
SPACE—1, 2, or 3, either before or after printing.
INDICATORS—the indicator "turned on" by the input record is specified along with any others that should be on for printing to occur.

Figure 2.5
Problem definition
for sample problem.

Systems Flowchart.

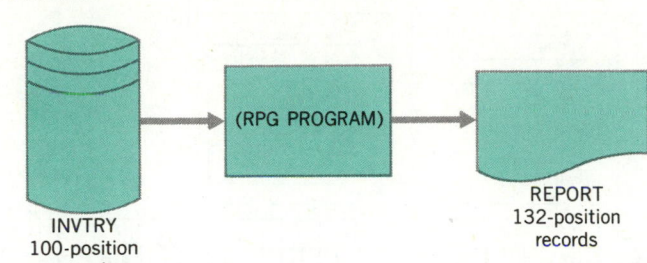

INVTRY
100-position
records

(RPG PROGRAM)

REPORT
132-position
records

INVTRY Record Layout

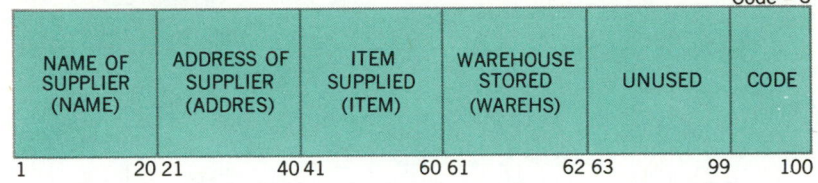

REPORT Printer Spacing Chart

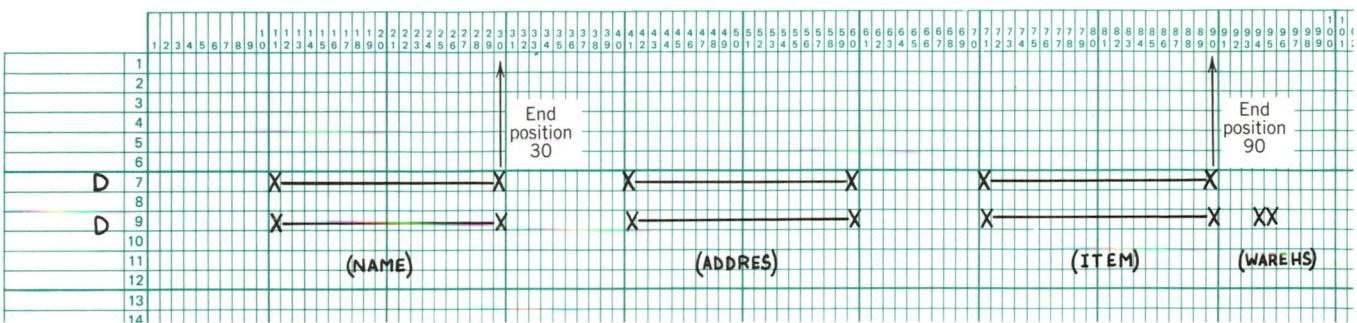

Note: 1. Field names in parentheses do not print; they just identify the data to be outputted.
2. Field names are those used in the RPG program.

Subsequent lines will indicate how the detail output line should appear.

Note that the only time detail lines will be described on line 1 of the Output Specifications form is if there are no headings.

2. Printing Fields and Constants

a. **Fields to be Printed.** Typically, detail lines print some of, or all, the data that has been read in from input records. The field names defined on the Input Specifications form are left-justified; that is, the field name is coded beginning in column 32. Result fields defined on the Calculation Specifications form or fields set up within data structures on the Input Specifications form may also be printed.

The END POSITION IN OUTPUT RECORD, columns 40–43 of the Output Specifications form, is always coded on the same line as the field name, to indicate the right-most print position in which the field should print. A Printer Spacing Chart is used to determine the actual end position of the field in the output record. This end position will have a numeric value, and, like all numeric entries, it must be right-justified.

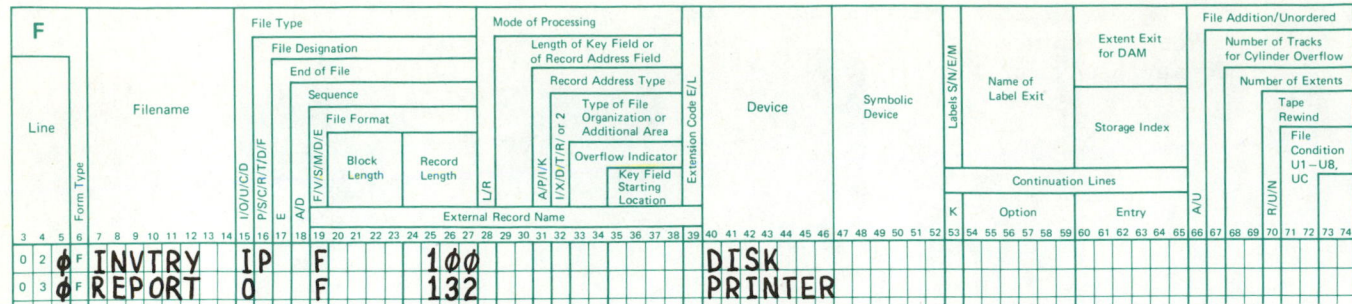

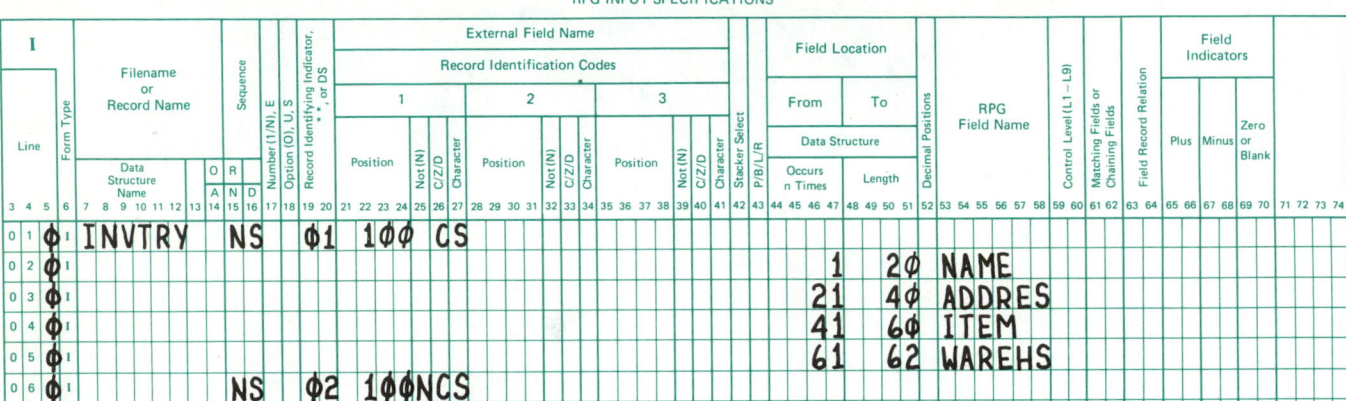

Note: 1. NS is used for no sequence; any alphabetic characters could be used.
2. Any number 01-99 could be used as a record identifying indicator.
3. The 02 indicator is turned on when a record without an S in position 100 is read. If we fail to set an indicator when this happens, the computer will halt the run.

Figure 2.6
File and Input Specifications forms for sample problem.

Figure 2.7
Output Specifications form for sample problem.

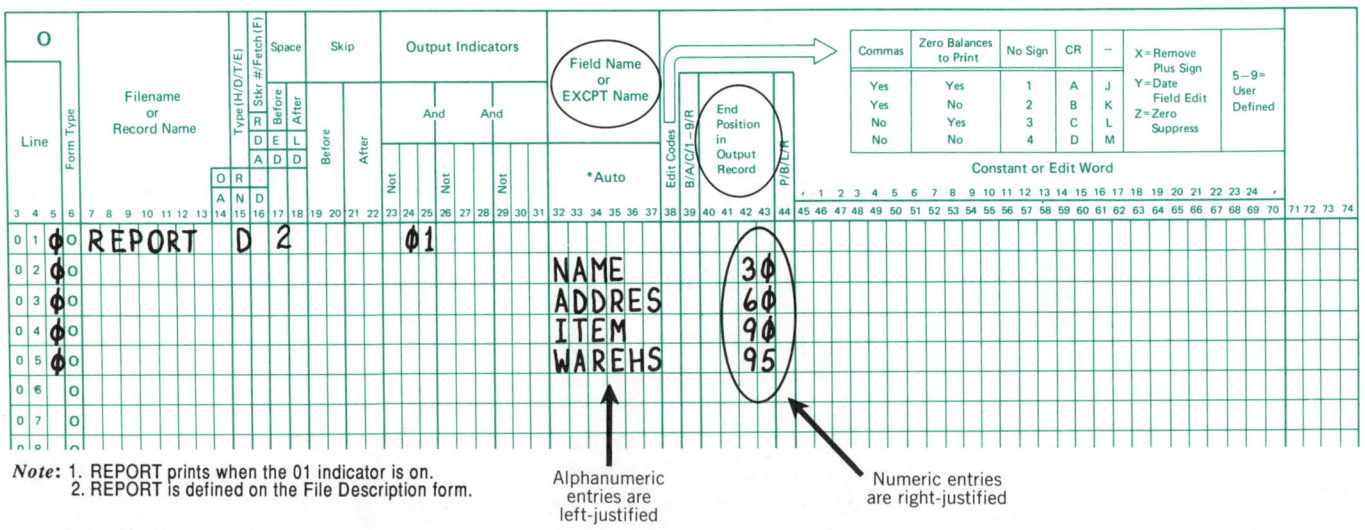

Note: 1. REPORT prints when the 01 indicator is on.
2. REPORT is defined on the File Description form.

Alphanumeric entries are left-justified

Numeric entries are right-justified

The first line in Figure 2.7 describes information about the *line* to be printed. Subsequent entries describe the fields within the line. Hence, the first line of *each* record description does *not* contain field description specifications. The description of each field begins on the line following the initial one for an H, D, or T line. Keep in mind that the field names used must be identical to the ones defined on the Input Specifications form and the Calculation Specifications form. The end positions must be identical to those specified on the Printer Spacing Chart.

As noted, only the END POSITION IN OUTPUT RECORD is needed for fields specified on the Output Specifications form. The RPG system, then, determines the length of all output fields. The length of a field is determined from the Input Specifications form where the starting and ending positions of the field are both indicated. In addition, editing symbols such as a dollar sign, commas, and a decimal point will increase the length of a numeric field to be printed. Thus, the size of a field as noted on the Input Specifications form, combined with any edit symbols that are needed, will determine the total length of an output field. Edit codes will be discussed later in this chapter.

b. Constants.   Input fields contain data that changes from record to record. Hence, we define an area of each record with a field name and we treat the data to be entered as **variable,** that is, it is unknown at execution time and it changes during every run.

Sometimes the data to be printed is **constant,** such as a message or note that is known initially and will always remain the same. Consider the following sample output:

```
SEX = M ROBERT REDFORD  111 NATURAL ST.    GARY, NY 11782
SEX = M PAUL NEWMAN      782 BLUEEYES AVE.  ST. PAUL, NJ 11825
SEX = F BROOKE SHIELDS   997 CALVIN ST.     NOME, NM 11828
```

The sex (M or F), names, and addresses are dependent on each input record and are therefore variable. But the phrase 'SEX =' is a constant that does not change. It is coded as a constant as follows:

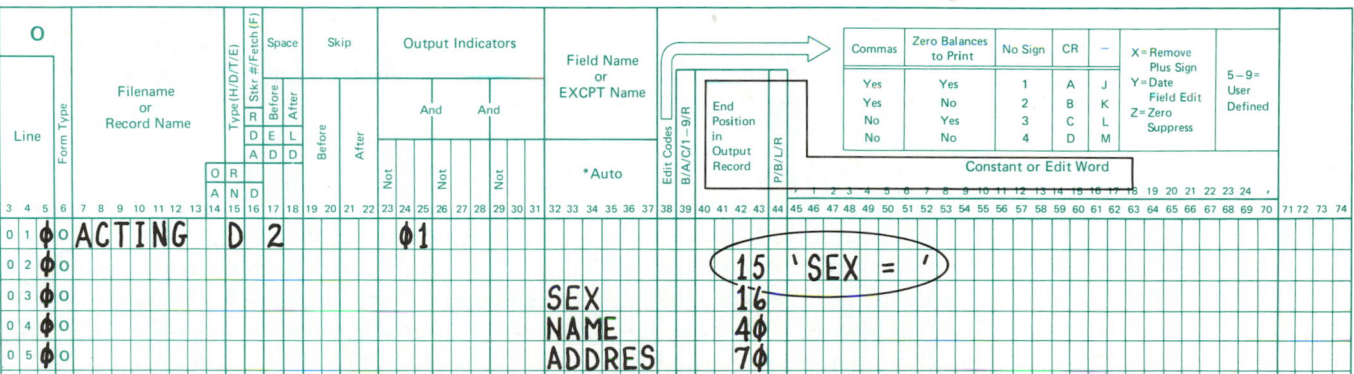

Single quotes (or apostrophes) are used to delimit a constant or **literal** in the Constant field.

Note that the word 'SEX =' as a constant should not be confused with the field name SEX. SEX is an input field that will contain variable data for each record—an M or F. The phrase 'SEX =' will always print as is.

Variable fields that are to print are coded in columns 32–37, along with the End Position in Output Record. *Constants* to print are coded in single quotes beginning in column 45 along with the End Position in Output Record. Including the quote marks, constants begin in column 45 and cannot go beyond column 70. Thus, any constant longer than 24 characters must be segmented so that it is coded on two or more lines.

C. Printing Headings

As previously noted, all output reports should contain headings to identify the report.

1. Denoting a Heading Line

Headings are denoted on the Output Specifications form with the use of H in the TYPE field. Typically, headings are printed on the first print line of a page. The first print line may, for example, be specified as line 6, thereby creating a margin with five blank lines at the top of the page. The following coding instructs the computer to skip to line 6 before printing:

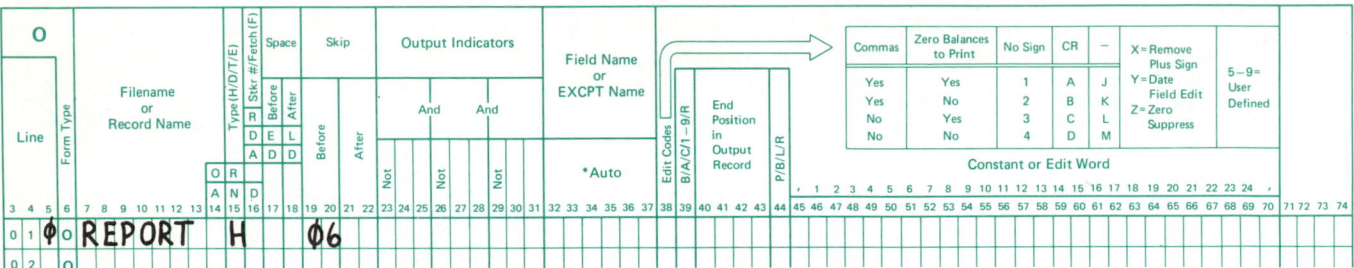

Since headings usually print first, they are typically coded on the same line as the Filename. The Filename need only be specified once, at the beginning; then the Filename field remains blank unless there is another Output file.

You will recall that the SKIP option is used when you wish to print on a specific line and the SPACE option is used to obtain single, double, or triple spacing. If you wish to skip to a specific line before or after printing the heading, or to space the form one, two, or three lines before or after printing, you would code the appropriate entry in the columns indicated. As noted, we typically use the Before option in our illustrations.

2. Indicators Used for Headings

Recall that the printing of output in RPG can be controlled by indicators.

To print headings, use two special indicators: 1P and OF. The 1P or **first page indicator** is automatically turned on at the beginning of execution of the RPG program and then turned off after the heading lines print on the first page. Thus the following will cause a heading to print at the very beginning of the run, that is, at the top of the first page:

O		Filename or Record Name	Type (H/D/T/E)	Stkr #/Fetch (F)	Space		Skip		Output Indicators			Field Name or EXCPT Name		End Position in Output Record		Commas	Zero Balances to Print	No Sign	CR	−	X = Remove Plus Sign Y = Date Field Edit Z = Zero Suppress	5 − 9 = User Defined
							Before	After	And	And				Edit Codes	B/A/C 1 − 9/R	Yes Yes No No	Yes No Yes No	1 2 3 4	A B C D	J K L M		
Line	Form Type			R D E L A D D	O R A N D	Before	After	Not	Not	Not	*Auto		P/B/L/R				Constant or Edit Word				
0 1	φ	O	REPORT	H		φ6			1P														
0 2		O																				

The Filename REPORT would be coded only once, on the first line of the Output Specifications form. Thus, it would usually be included with the heading description instead of with the detail description since the heading will print first.

Recall that printed output prints on continuous forms. If you have a very long report, and you specify the printing of headings on the first page only, you would have the following:

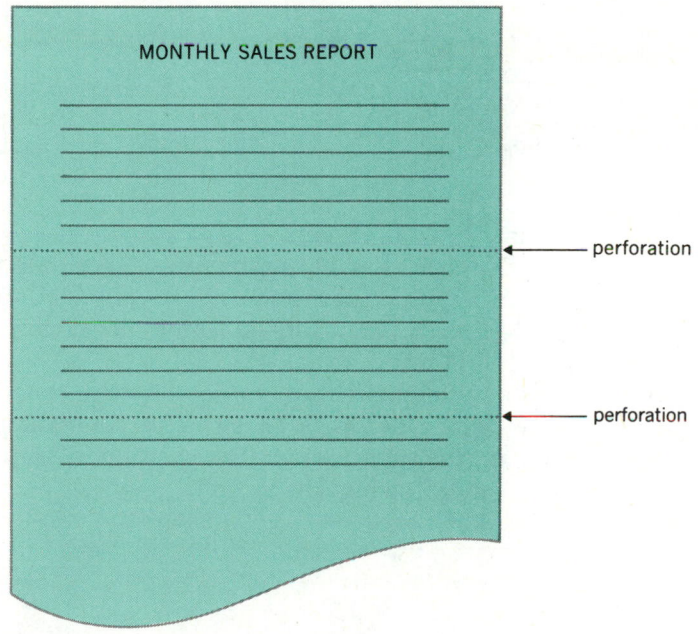

Most frequently, the report is split at the perforation into individual pages. By specifying the 1P indicator only, the first page would contain a heading; all subsequent pages would not be identified.

It would, of course, be better to print a heading on the top of each page. To obtain headings on the top of each page, use the **Overflow indicator, OF,** as well as 1P. On the Output Specifications form, then, you must specify that the headings should print if *either* the 1P indicator or the OF indicator is on.

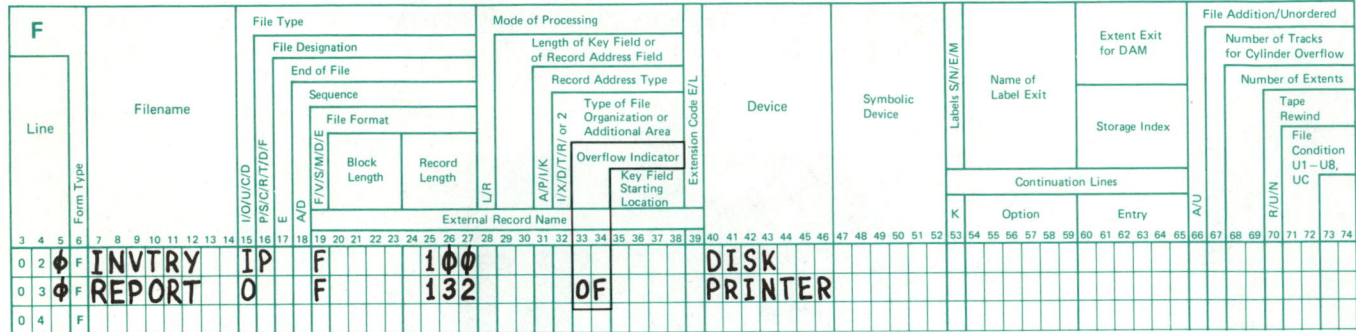

This means a heading will print at the beginning of the run and every time an end-of-page condition occurs.

The OF indicator is based on a hardware feature that keeps track of page overflow. You must indicate that your program will use this indicator by including it on the File Description Specifications form.

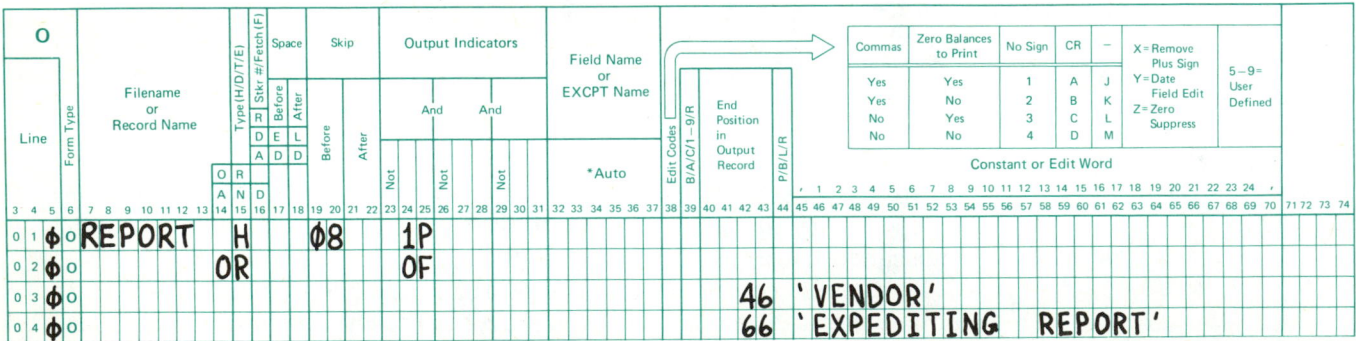

3. Printing the Constants

The first line of an output report, then, would typically include: (1) Filename, (2) H in Type, (3) Space and/or Skip option, (4) the 1P indicator. The second line would specify 'OR   OF', meaning that if the 1P or OF indicator is on, a heading should print.

On subsequent lines, you specify the exact format for your output. Typically, report headings consist of a constant that describes the report. You indicate the right-most or last position in which you want each field to print, as in the following illustration:

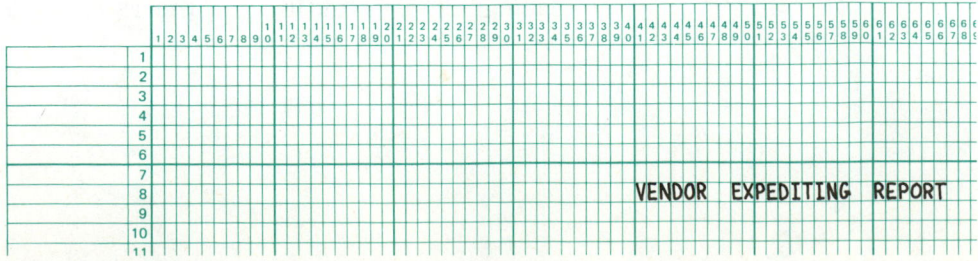

As with detail records, the specifications for each output line begin on the line following the indicator specification, in this instance, line 3.

4. Printing a Date with the Heading

It is usually desirable to include the date of the run as part of the heading. Accomplishing this in RPG is a simple matter: use the reserved word UDATE in the Field Name columns. UDATE refers to the system date, which is an internally stored entry. Coding UDATE will cause a date consisting of month, day, and year to print. To edit the date so that it prints with slashes as month/day/year, code a Y in the Edit Code column (column 38) of the line:

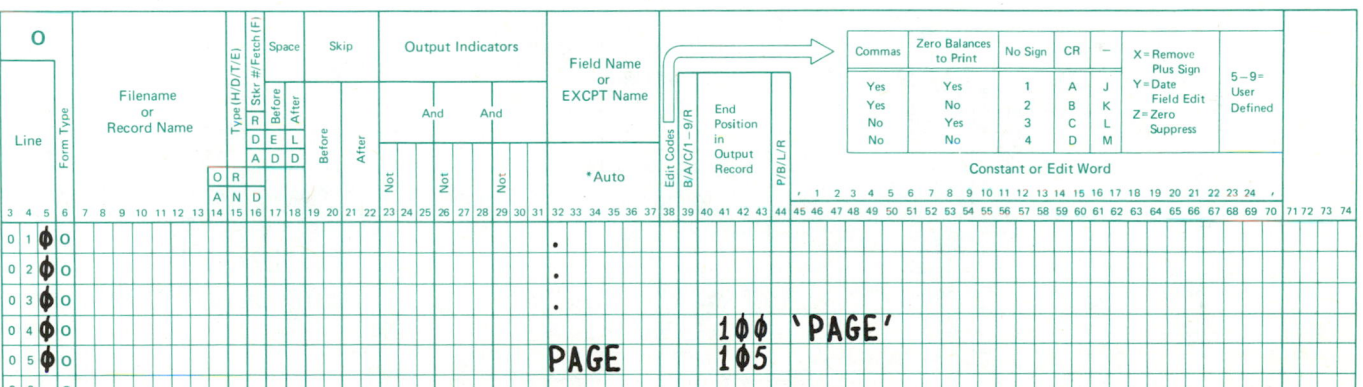

5. Printing a Page Number with the Heading

To instruct the computer to print page numbers, include the reserved word PAGE with the heading. The reserved word PAGE will print 1 on the first page, 2 on the second, and so on. To print the word or constant 'PAGE' along with the number, code:

When the constant PAGE prints it will appear in print positions 97–100. The actual page number will always be located in a four-position field, in this case positions 102–105. Leading zeros will automatically be replaced with blanks for PAGE. For example, 0001 will print as 1.

6. Printing Column Headings

Frequently one heading line is not sufficient to describe the report adequately. A second column heading line that indicates field names is often desirable. The following Output Specifications form illustrates the RPG coding for the Printer Spacing Chart specified in Figure 2.8:

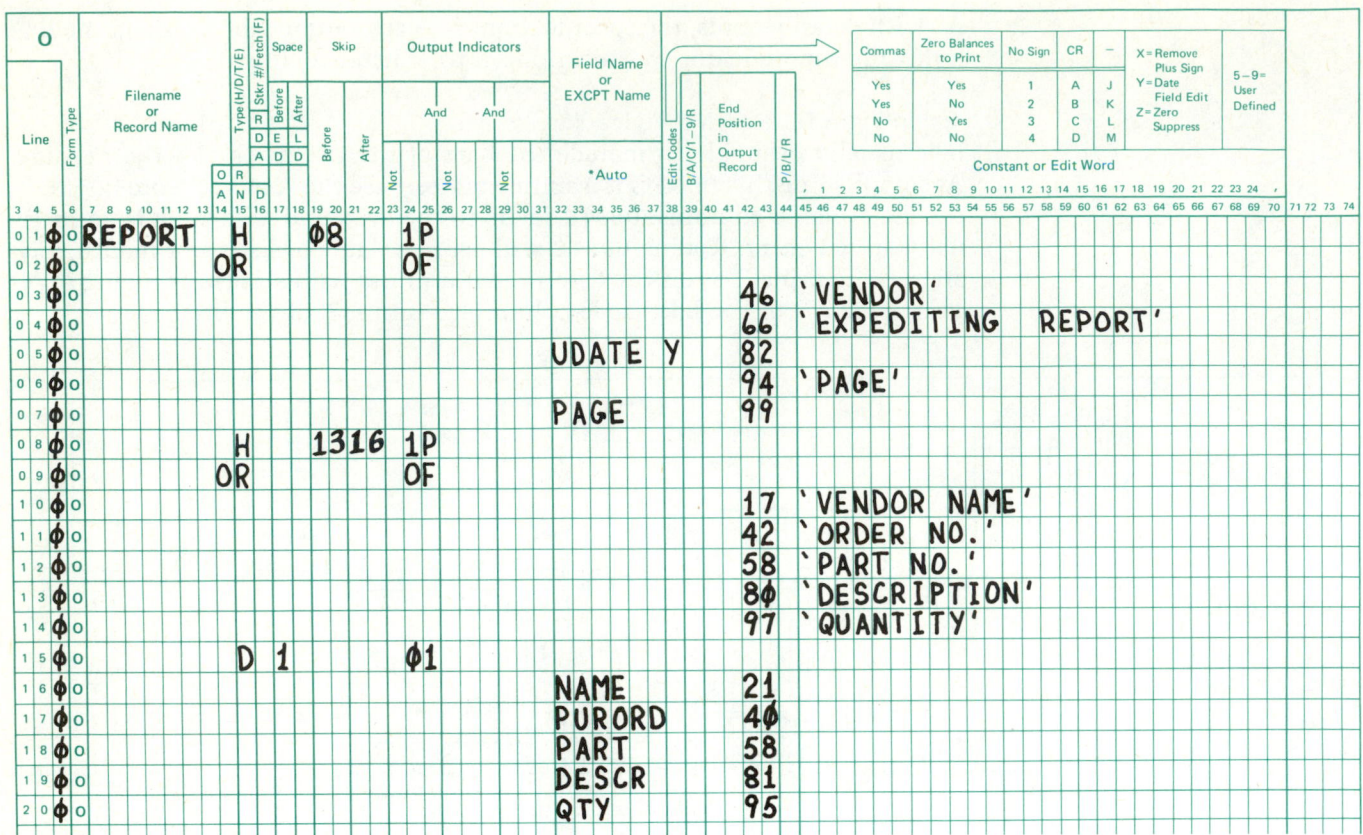

Figure 2.8
Sample Printer Spacing Chart.

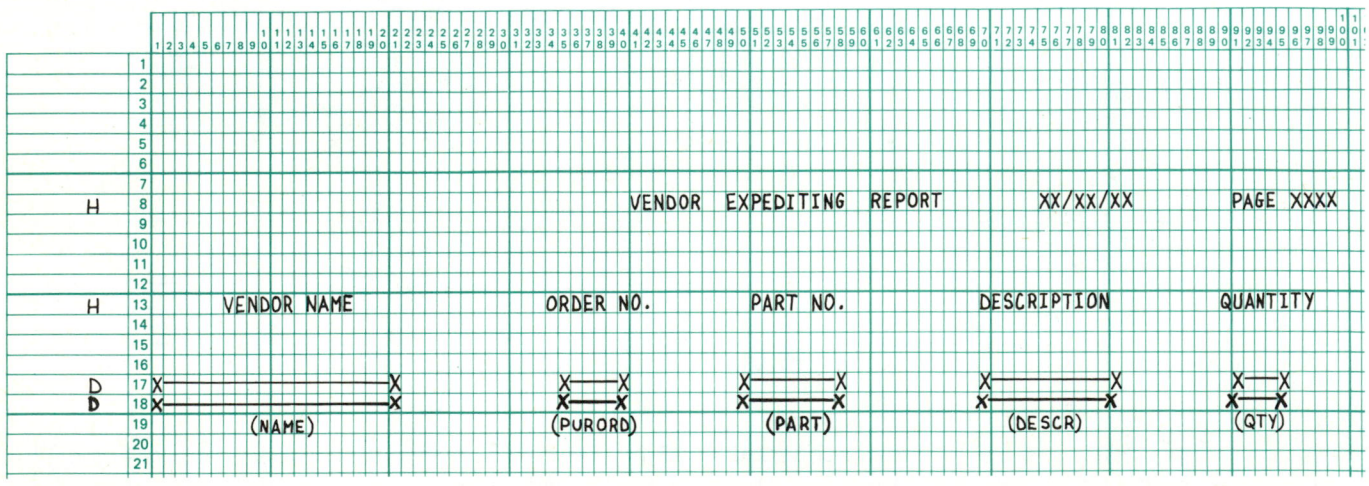

Note that headings print in sequence when the 1P or OF indicators are on. That is, the first heading coded is the first one printed.

Constants can be specified any way that is convenient for the programmer. Thus, the first heading could have specified VENDOR EXPEDITING REPORT as:

Output Specifications

Line	Filename or Record Name	Type(H/D/T/E)			Space	Skip	Output Indicators			Field Name or EXCPT Name	Edit Codes	End Position in Output Record		Constant or Edit Word
0 1	REPORT	H			08		1P							
0 2	OR						OF							
0 3												46		'VENDOR'
0 4												59		'EXPEDITING'
0 5												66		'REPORT'

D. Controlling Detail Output with the N1P Indicator

Earlier we described how Record Identification Indicators can be specified on the Input Specifications form to identify the record formats. In addition, we saw how the same indicators could be used to control printing of Output Specifications.

There are times, however, when these record indicators are not necessary. To illustrate this, let us consider the Vendor Expediting Report program illustrated in the previous section.

The purpose of this program is to print a detail report consisting of the vendor's name and information for each purchase order contained in the file called VMAST. In this program, every record is described using the same format or record description. Therefore, if the record indicator is used, it would be set on every time a record is read. Since it is unnecessary to distinguish between record types here, specifying a record indicator would serve no real purpose in this program. The following, then, are the Input Specifications required when no record format checking is to be performed:

Input Specifications

Line	Filename or Record Name	Sequence	Number(1/N)			Record Identification Codes			Field Location From	To		RPG Field Name		Field Indicators
0 1	VMAST	NS												
0 2									1	21		NAME		
0 3									22	27		PURORD		
0 4									28	36		PART		
0 5									37	48		DESCR		
0 6									49	53	0	QTY		

No record identification. All records contain the same format.

Here, the record indicator is *not* specified on the Input Specifications form since each record in the file has the same record format.

Let us consider what effect this has on detail output. If we are printing a detail report where one line is printed for each input record, there is also no need to control detail output with the record indicator.

However, one problem can occur. If there are no indicators for a detail line, extraneous lines can be printed particularly on the first cycle before any records have been read. This is because the RPG Logic Cycle outputs headings and detail lines on the same cycle; this can result in the erroneous printing of blank lines or lines with zero balances.

When the RPG program is executed, the 1P indicator is set on and heading and detail output, which print during the same cycle, are printed. During this *first cycle* however, we wish to print only the headings and not the detail lines because we have not yet read the first record. With no additional coding, the first data line printed on the first page would be a line containing no real data.

To eliminate this problem, the following specifications illustrate how to prevent detail output during the first page cycle.

The N1P (NOT first page) indicator is specified on the detail line to prevent the line from printing during 1P time. The detail line, then, will print each time detail output is written *except* when the 1P indicator is on.

E. Other Types of Print Lines

1. Total Lines
Totals can print under numerous conditions:

TYPES OF TOTALS

1. End of each page.
2. End of each group of records.
3. End of the report.

A T coded in TYPE on the Output Specifications form is used for specifying a total line. Testing for the end of a group of records is specified with control level indicators that will be considered in Chapter 7. Page totals can be printed using the OF indicator to indicate when an end-of-page condition has been reached. Report totals can be printed using the **Last Record** (LR) **indicator** to signal when the last record has been processed. Recall that the LR indicator will be turned on only after the last record has been read and processed. We will discuss the printing of summary totals in the next chapter.

You may also want to print messages at the end of the report. This type of line is called a report footing. Report footings would be considered Total Lines. Next, we focus on printing an end-of-job message.

2. Printing an End-of-Job Message as a Report Footing

Suppose you wish to print a total line at the end of a report that states:

> ***   END OF OUTPUT REPORT   ***

You would add the following to your description of the Output File Specifications for the output file:

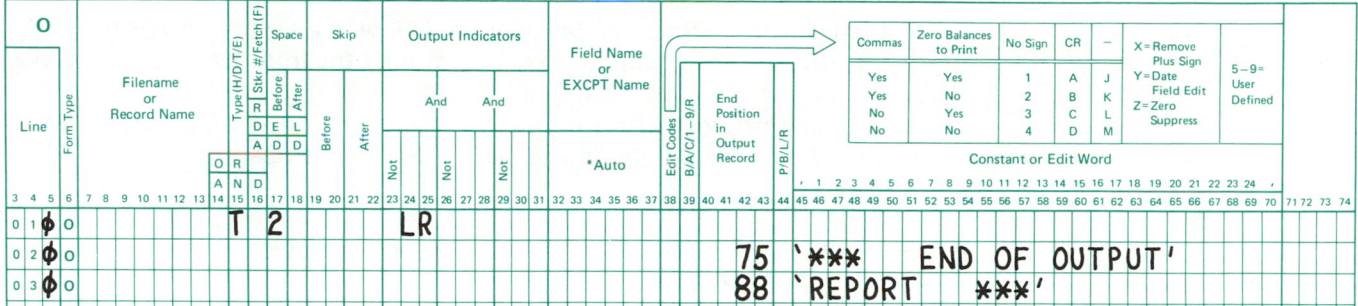

Self-Test

1. Headings are used to _____ .
2. The paper is advanced in the printer by using the _____ and _____ options.
3. The (before/after) option advances the paper prior to printing.
4. The (before/after) option allows the program to print the line first and then advance the paper.
5. When constants are to be printed, they are specified on the Output Specifications forms in the _____ section.
6. Headings are identified on the Output Specifications form by placing a(n) _____ in column 15.
7. To print the date in the headings, use the _____ RPG reserved word.
8. To print the page number on the report, use the _____ RPG reserved word.
9. When it is not necessary to check for record formats, only the _____ indicator need be used on detail output.
10. A total line is identified by a _____ in column 15 of the Output Specifications.

Solutions

1. describe a report
2. space; skip
3. before
4. after
5. constant or edit word
6. H
7. UDATE
8. PAGE
9. N1P
10. T

F. Basic Editing Considerations

As previously noted, printed output must be edited so that it is as easy to read as possible. Numeric fields are edited to include, for example:

BASIC EDITING

1. Decimal points.
2. Commas.
3. Dollar signs.
4. Suppression of leading zeros so that 0008, for example, prints as 8.
5. Printing of a minus sign or the letters CR for a negative amount.

Decimal points, commas, dollar signs, and CR take up space on a printed line of a report and must be counted when determining the number of positions in a field.

Most of the editing specified in the above box can be accomplished with the use of the **EDIT CODE** field on the Output Specifications form:

Example

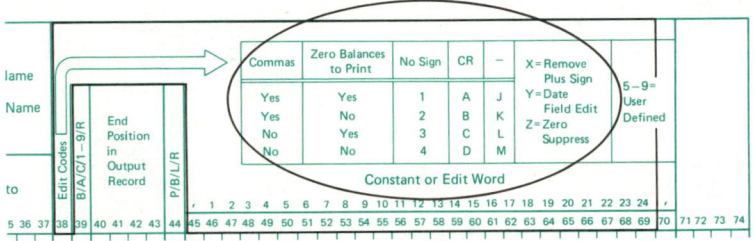

Suppose, for example, you wish to print an amount field so that:

1. Commas are included.
2. Zero balances do not print.
3. CR prints for negative amounts.

Use code B in column 38 to achieve this editing, as indicated by the instructions on the Output Specifications form.

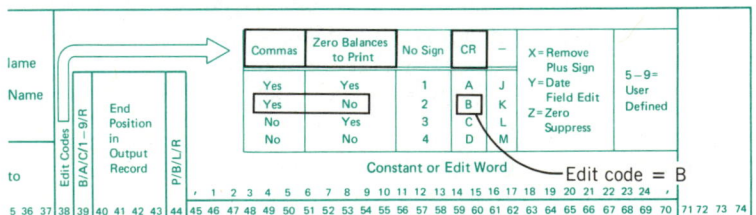

Similarly, suppose you wish to print an edited AMOUNT field without commas, with a zero to denote a zero balance, and no sign; you would use a 3 in column 38:

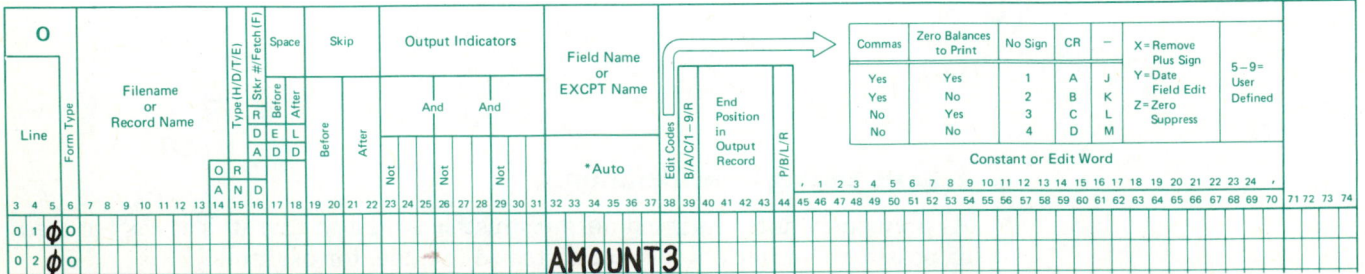

Editing of this type can be performed on *numeric* fields only. The RPG programmer indicates numeric input fields by including a digit in column 52, DECIMAL POSITIONS, of the Input Specifications form for incoming fields or data structures. If Result Fields are defined on the Calculation Specifications form, then the corresponding DECIMAL POSITIONS field of that form would be coded as well.

Note, too, that the use of any EDIT CODE automatically:

1. Suppresses leading zeros (so that 007 prints as 7). **Zero suppression** means that nonsignificant zeros are replaced with blanks.

2. Places a decimal point in the appropriate position on the printed line as indicated in the DECIMAL POSITIONS field of the Input or Calculation Specifications form.

Consider the following:

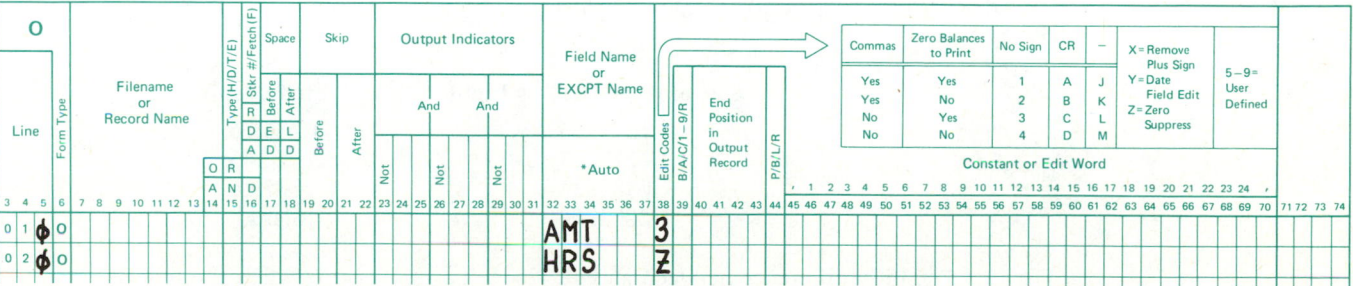

Since EMPNO has a blank in column 52 of the Input Specifications form, it is treated as an alphanumeric field and cannot be edited. AMT and HRS, however, are numeric fields. AMT is five positions long. The 2 in DECIMAL POSITIONS instructs the computer to treat AMT as a dollars-and-cents field, even though the actual decimal point does not appear within the input field; that is, it has an **implied decimal point**. For example, AMT with contents 12345 is stored as 123∧45 with the decimal point implied. Using any one of the EDIT CODES specified in the Output Specifications form will cause a decimal point to print in the appropriate place. Thus AMT will print as XXX.XX, where the Xs indicate the digits of the amount field.

If HRS is to print with zero suppression as well as with a decimal point, we put a Z in the EDIT CODE field of the Output Specifications form:

1. Using Edit Codes

We will now review the various Edit Codes used for numeric fields and illustrate how they affect printed output.

If any Edit Code is specified in column 38:

1. Leading zeros will be suppressed. For example, 008 will print as 8.
2. Decimal points will print where required.

We will now examine actual Edit Codes.

a. Edit Code = 1. An Edit Code of 1 results in the following:

1. Commas will print where appropriate.
2. Zeros, not blanks, will print for fields with contents of zero.

Example

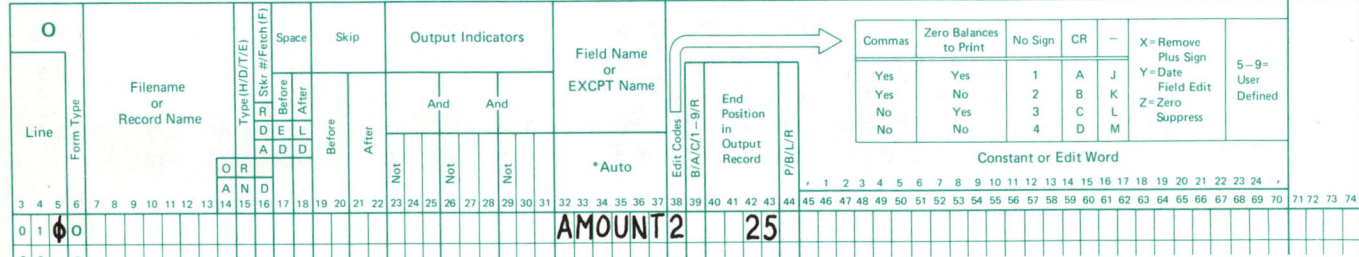

Value of AMOUNT as Input	Edited Result
1234∧56	1,234.56
0023∧45	23.45
0387∧24	387.24
0000∧00	.00

b. Edit Code = 2. An Edit Code of 2 results in the following:

1. Commas print where appropriate.
2. Blanks print if the field is zero.

Example

Value of AMOUNT as Input	Edited Result
1234∧56	1,234.56
0023∧45	23.45
0387∧24	387.24
0000∧00	(Blank)

The only difference between an Edit Code of 1 or 2 occurs when the field is zero.

c. Edit Code = 3. An Edit Code of 3 results in the following:

1. No commas are printed.
2. Zero balances will print.

Example

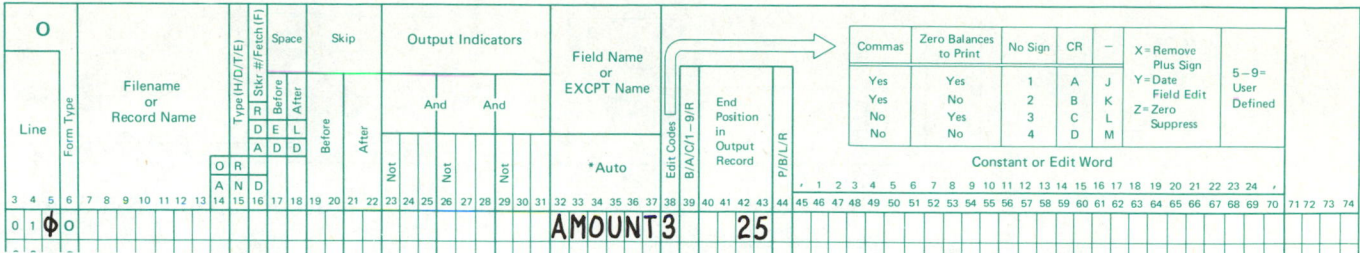

Value of AMOUNT as Input	Edited Result
1234∧56	1234.56
0023∧45	23.45
0387∧24	387.24
0000∧00	.00

d. **Edit Code = 4.** An Edit Code of 4 results in the following:

1. No commas are printed.
2. Blanks print if the field is zero.

Example

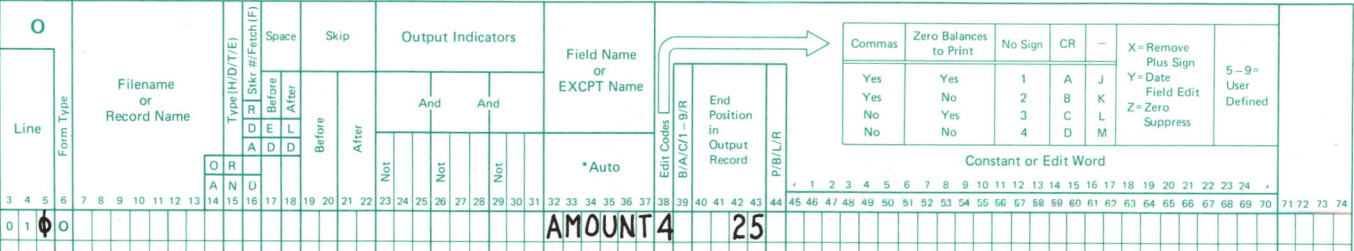

Value of AMOUNT as Input	Edited Result
1234∧56	1234.56
0023∧45	23.45
0387∧24	387.24
0000∧00	(blank)

e. **Other Edit Codes.** Codes A-D and J-M are used if a field can contain a negative amount. For conciseness, signed fields are designated in input records with a sign over the right-most position of a field. Hence 387̄ entered as input denotes −387. Only three positions are used to represent such a signed field.

A sign will not print on the output unless an appropriate edit code is used. To print a minus sign for negative quantities, use codes J-M in the EDIT CODE field. The sign will print to the right of the number. J will cause the same editing as Edit Code 1, but it will also print a minus sign for negative values; similarly, K, L, and M will result in the same editing as edit codes 2, 3, and 4, respectively, but minus signs will also be printed for negative amounts. An Edit Code of A-D is used just like 1-4 or J-M except that CR will print for negative amounts instead of a minus sign. CR stands for Credit. Minus signs and the letters CR use storage positions in the output.

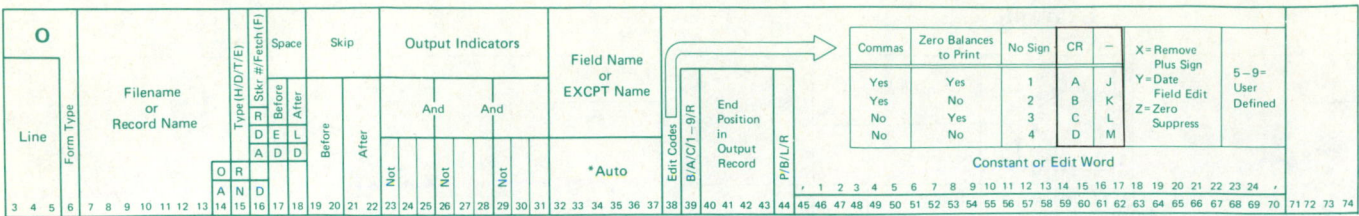

All Edit Codes perform zero suppression up to the decimal point in addition to the specified editing.

The following are samples of the type of editing that will be performed depending on the contents of the field and the Edit Code specified:

Edited Results

Unedited Contents of Field	Edit Code	1	2	3	4	A	B	C	D	J	K	L	M
000000		0	(Blank)	0	(Blank)	0	(Blank)	0	(Blank)	0	(Blank)	0	(Blank)
0000∧00ᵃ		.00	(Blank)	.00	(Blank)	.00	(Blank)	.00	(Blank)	.00	(Blank)	.00	(Blank)
000890ᵇ		890	890	890	890	890CR	890CR	890CR	890CR	890−	890−	890−	890−
000∧890		.890	.890	.890	.890	.890CR	.890CR	.890CR	.890CR	.890−	.890−	.890−	.890−
54321∧54		54,321.54	54,321.54	54 321.54	54 321.54	54,321.54CR	54,321.54CR	54 321.54CR	54 321.54CR	54,321.54−	54,321.54−	54 321.54−	54,321.54−

ᵃ ∧ is the implied decimal point. In this instance, the Decimal Position for the field was specified as 2.

ᵇ − 000890 is represented in a six-position field as 000890.

2. Printing Dollar Signs

If a dollar sign is desired in the left-most position of an edited field, the Output Specifications form could be coded as follows:

where AMT would be specified as having two decimal positions.

Suppose that AMT had the following content: 000∧84. Using the editing just presented, the output would print as:

$				.	8	4

Blanks between the $ and the first significant character are usually to be avoided. For one thing, if this output were to be a payment or check, some unscrupulous person could easily change the amount to $999.84.

To avoid this situation, it is best to have the dollar sign *float* with the field; that is, the dollar sign should print in the position directly to the left of the first significant digit. Thus 000∧84 should print as $.84; 00072∧64 should print as $72.64, and so forth, with no spaces between the dollar sign and the first significant digit.

To float a dollar sign in RPG, include the '$' constant on the *same* line as the edited field:

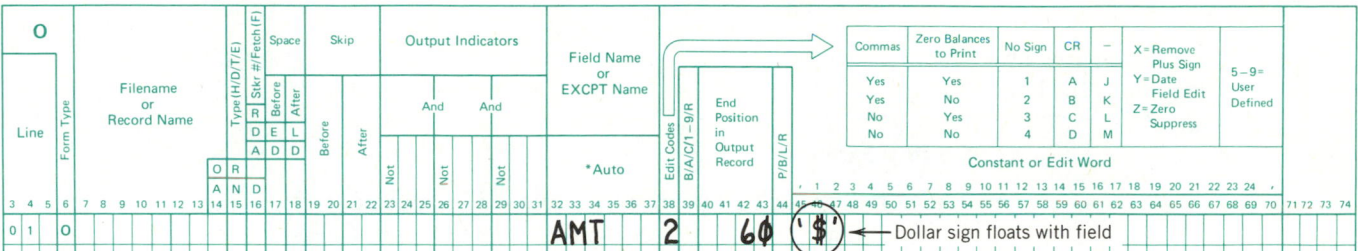

Where editing is to be performed and a **floating dollar sign** is to print:

1. Use the appropriate Edit Code.
2. Enter the '$' constant *on the same line* as the field to be edited.

Editing using Edit Codes just described is considered basic editing. More advanced editing options can be specified with the use of the Edit Word field (columns 45–70). Let us examine the use of edit words.

3. Using Edit Words

We will see that edit words, as well as edit codes, are useful means of editing printed output in RPG. If an editing operation can be performed by either an edit code or edit word, we recommend you use the edit code for the following reasons:

1. Edit codes are convenient to use and easy to understand.
2. The standard edit codes save coding time and keystrokes.
3. Edit codes reduce the need to plan and size edited fields.
4. Edit codes reduce the risk of editing errors.

However, certain editing operations cannot be performed with edit codes and we must therefore utilize the edit word to provide the necessary symbols desired in the finished report. Specifically, edit words permit us to perform the following operations not easily performed with edit codes:

1. Control the exact position where zero suppression is to stop.
2. Insert blanks, special characters, or dashes as found in social security and telephone numbers.
3. Insert asterisk fill characters (*) for check protection.
4. Print any combination of characters to the right of a field.

In order to define an edit word, the programmer must establish an edit pattern that is used to indicate the format of the printed output. The field to be edited is called the sending field. It interacts with the edit pattern by replacing the spaces in the pattern with the digits from the sending field. An example of coding an edit word appears in Figure 2.9.

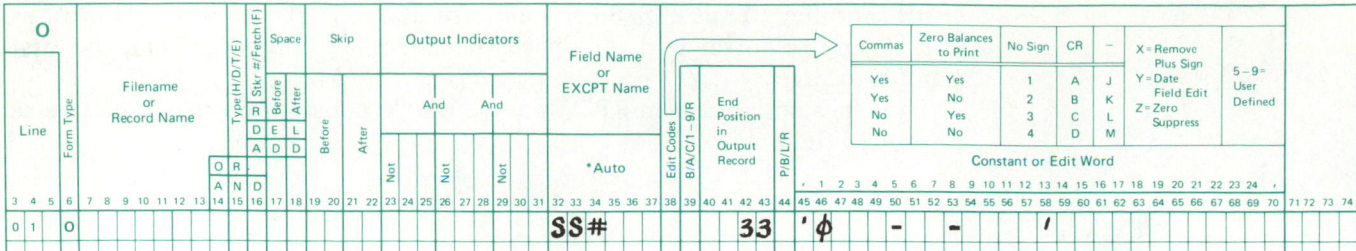

Figure 2.9
Example of coding
an edit word.

Coding Example

The edit word or edit pattern is enclosed in apostrophes or single quote marks and left-justified in positions 45–7Ø of the Output Specifications form; that is, the left apostrophe must be in position 45. The example in Figure 2.9 and Figure 2.10 illustrates how an edit word prints dashes or hyphens in a Social Security number. Note that the sending field consists of nine digits while the edit word occupies 12 print positions.

In an edit word, some of the characters occupy a position in the output and print exactly as shown in the edit pattern. They are called *insertion characters*. In our example we use the hyphen as an insertion character, but the dollar sign, decimal point, comma, and some others can also be used.

The blanks or spaces in the example (designated as ƀ) are called *replacement characters*, that is, they will be replaced by the digits in the field to be edited, or the sending field. Therefore, insertion characters print exactly as shown while the spaces are replaced by the digits stored in the sending field.

Blanks in the Edit Word

In Figure 2.10, the blanks in the edit word are replaced by the digits contained in the sending field. The number of replacement characters in the edit word must be equal to or greater than the number of digits contained in the field to be edited. If you specify an edit word that is too small to hold the results, high-order truncation, or loss of the high-order digit(s), will occur. For obvious reasons this type of error should be avoided.

Figure 2.10
Use of an edit word to print a
Social Security number.

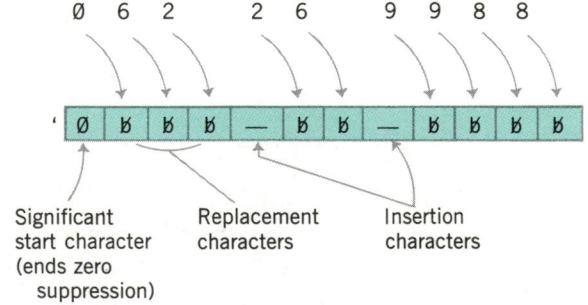

Result: 062-26-9988

Zero Suppression

If the sending field to be edited is a dollar-and-cents field, we would typically want the leading zeros to be suppressed, that is, to be replaced with blanks. But in this example, we are required to print *all* nine digits since the sending field is a Social Security number. We therefore want to *prevent* zero suppression in this instance. The *significant start character*, or zero in the left-most position of the edit pattern in Figure 2.9, enables us to print all nine digits, even if they are all zeros. If we wanted zero suppression, that zero would be changed to a blank and a zero placed where we want zero suppression to end. For example, ƀƀ,ƀ0ƀ terminates zero suppression at the tens position so that 00005 would print as 5. The high-order zero in the edit pattern of our illustration indicates that all characters *to the right* will be printed even if they are zeros. If the zero had been omitted and the first digit of the Social Security number is a zero, then the zero would be replaced with a blank and the printed results would be incorrect. Since the zero is used to terminate zero suppression, we call it a "significant start character." Remember, this means that everything to the right of the zero will always print in the output. That is, when no zero suppression is required, a 0 precedes the number of blanks needed as replacement characters.

Edit Word Format

There are three main parts to an edit word, namely the body, the status, and the expansion. The body is the area that receives the digits from the sending field. Each blank is replaced by a digit. Again, sufficient space must be allocated to accommodate all of the digits in the sending field. Consider the example in Figure 2.11:

Figure 2.11
Parts of an edit word.

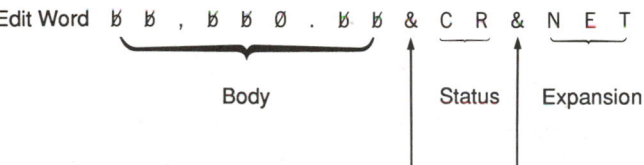

Results in the printing of a blank

The status is an optional entry used to indicate that a sending field could be *negative*. Thus, the status position may contain only the minus sign (−) or CR to denote CRedit. Hence these characters, the minus sign or CR, print only when the sending field contains a negative value. If the sending field is positive, the status positions will be filled with blanks. The status positions are coded when it is necessary to print negative values.

The expansion positions are also an optional entry and begin to the right of either the body or the status if the latter is included. The expansion is coded in the right-most positions of the edit word, and consists of insertion characters. This character string will always print and appear in the edited output as is.

An ampersand (&) in the edit word is used to print a blank. It can appear anywhere in the edit word.

Refer to Figure 2.12. In this example the sending field is negative. Only when the sending field is negative will the characters in the status (CR) be

Figure 2.12
How edit words actually
edit data.

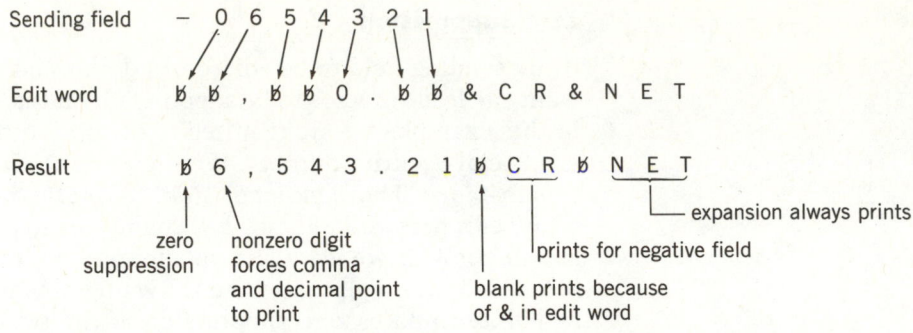

printed. In Figure 2.12, the negative value, −Ø654321 stored in the sending field is edited with the edit word and prints as 6,543.21 CR NET.

Recall that the high-order space is used because suppression of leading zeros is required (e.g., ƀƀ,ƀƀ0.ƀƀ suppresses all leading integers). The high-order spaces contained within the edit word indicate that leading zeros are simply replaced with blanks to improve readability. In the example, the leading zero in the sending field was replaced with a blank.

The zero preceding the decimal point in the above edit pattern forces all characters to the right to be printed regardless of their value. This means that a field with contents of all zeros will print as .00   NET. If the zero had been omitted in the edit pattern and the sending field actually contained a zero value, just NET would print with all blanks to the left of it. This is similar to "the blank when zero" option used with edit codes 2 and 4. We recommend that you always force zero values to print by including the zero (significant start character) in the edit pattern as shown.

Note that insertion characters such as commas print only when a significant character, meaning a nonzero character, is found in the sending field. Hence, in the following example, using the Edit word in Figure 2.12, the comma would not print because the sending value is less than one thousand dollars:

Sending Field   **Edited Result**

00345ʌ67   ƀƀƀ345.67ƀƀƀƀƀNET

Remember, the edited result will always occupy the same number of print positions as the number of characters in the edit pattern. Care should be taken to ensure that the edit pattern does not overlap any other printed fields.

As noted, the ampersand (&) is used for blank insertion in edit words. Any time we wish to insert blanks in numeric fields such as in dates or telephone numbers, we can insert the ampersand in the position where the space is to appear.

Again, the expansion is an optional entry and always prints as shown. In the example, the word NET will always appear in the printed output. The ability to print expansion characters when editing provides a great deal of flexibility in producing reports. A summary of the edit characters that may be used with the edit word is as follows:

Edit Characters for Edit Words

Character	Meaning
ƀ	Zero suppression and blank fill
.	Decimal point insertion
,	Comma insertion
0	Stops zero suppression. All characters to the right of the zero will print
$0	Prints a floating dollar sign
$	Fixed dollar sign insertion
*	Replaces the zero in the edit pattern and provides asterisk fill characters for check protection
&	Inserts a blank
CR	Inserts CR when field is negative
-	Inserts minus sign when field is negative

The above list contains the most commonly used edit characters. They will enable you to edit fields in a wide variety of ways that are useful for business applications. In Figure 2.13, a table of edit word applications is provided as a guide.

Self-Test

Indicate the printed result in each of the following. You may omit blanks resulting from zero suppression.

Sending Field	Edit Word
1. 00387∧52	ʹƀƀ,ƀƀ0.ƀƀ&AMT1ʹ
2. 00007∧52	ʹƀƀ.ƀ0ƀ.ƀƀ&CRʹ
3. -7	ʹƀ-ʹ
4. 123∧00	ʹ$ƀƀ0.00ʹ
5. 0012345	ʹ0ƀƀƀƀƀƀ&CODE1ʹ

Solutions

Printed Results

1. 387.52 AMT1
2. 7.52
3. 7-
4. $123.00
5. 0012345 CODE1 (no zero suppression)

Figure 2.13
Examples of edit words.

```
==============================================================
Edit Word              Use           Sending Field    Printed Result
==============================================================
ʹ0(bbb)&bbb-bbbbʹ   telephone #    5166211148     (516) 621-1148
ʹ0bbb-bb-bbbbʹ      soc sec #       082289987      082-28-9987
ʹbb&bb&bbʹ          date               012393           1 23 93
ʹbb&bb&bbʹ          date               000000          (blank)
ʹbb0.b&%ʹ           percent (XX.X)        216          21.6 %
ʹbb,bbb.bbʹ         dollars/cents     1234567       12,345.67
ʹbb,bbb.bbʹ         dollars/cents     0000000         (blank)
ʹbb,bb0.bbʹ         dollars/cents     1234567       12,345.67
ʹbb,bb0.bbʹ         dollars/cents     0000000             .00
ʹbb,b0b.bbʹ         dollars/cents     0000000            0.00
ʹbb,b0b.bbʹ         dollars/cents     0034567          345.67
ʹb,bb0.bb&CRʹ       dollars/cents      654321        6,543.21
ʹb,bb0.bb&CRʹ       dollars/cents     -654321        6,543.21 CR
ʹb,bb*.bb&-ʹ        asterisk fill      000000       *****.00
ʹb,bb*.bb&-ʹ        asterisk fill      -54321       **543.21 -
ʹbb,$0b.bbʹ         floating $         000000           $0.00
ʹbb,$0b.bbʹ         floating $         054321         $543.21
==============================================================
```

The Printer Spacing Chart should indicate the type of editing desired. We will use the following conventions:

Notation	Meaning
XXX.XX	Print a five-digit field with a decimal point.
XXØ.XX	Same as the preceding, but zero suppress only integers.
XØX.XX	Zero suppress only the left-most two digits (ØØØ.26 will print as Ø.26).
XX.XX	The dollar sign floats with the field.

G. Summary

H, D, and T type records can be processed using the Output Specifications form. They should be coded in the sequence shown. The filename need be specified only once, at the beginning. If there are two or more records of the same type that are to be printed when specific indicators are on, then these records will print in sequence as indicated on the Output form. Thus, if there are two headings that are to print if the 1P or OF indicator is on, the first one coded will print first.

III. Standard Forms, Nonstandard Forms, Preprinted Forms, and Forms Alignment

A. Standard Forms

Often forms to be printed by a computer will simply be blank, continuous forms. With these forms all report headings, page headings, and column headings are printed as specified in the program. Using blank stock forms is less expensive and eliminates the problem of keeping many different types of forms in inventory. Two *default assignments* are made by the computer for *standard continuous forms*. First, the form length is set to a default value of 66 lines. Second, the overflow indicator is automatically set on when line 60 has been reached, that is, six lines from the bottom. When the overflow indicator (OF) is specified in columns 33–34 on the File Description Specifications form for the printer file, the computer will automatically:

1. Set on the overflow (OF) indicator when the end of a printed page is reached, that is, when the overflow line has been printed on.
2. Enable the programmer to print headings on a new page when the overflow (OF) indicator is on.

B. Nonstandard Forms

If a specific application requires a different size form or the overflow indicator to be set on at some point other than line 60, a new specification form, the *Line Counter Specification*, is required.

C. Line Counter Specifications for Achieving Forms Alignment

The **Line Counter Specifications** form (Figure 2.14), employed with a nonstandard printer file, is used to:

1. Change the default setting for the *number of lines per page*.
2. Change the default setting for the *overflow line number*.

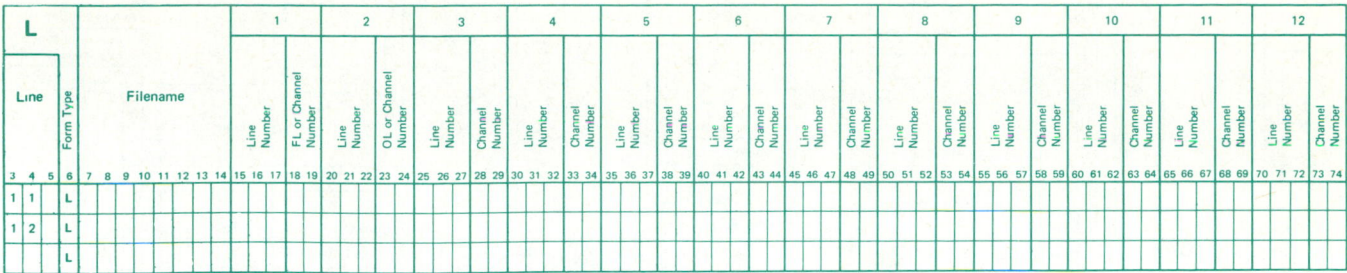

Figure 2.14
Line Counter Specifications
form.

The Line Counter Specifications form directly follows the File Description Specifications form in the sequence of an RPG program.

Rules for Using the Line Counter Specifications Form

1. The Line Counter Specifications form is only required if the length of the continuous form is not standard (66 lines) or the overflow line is not to be line 60.

2. The associated line on the File Description Specifications form for the printer file must contain an L in column 39 and OF in columns 33–34. The L indicates that a Line Counter Specification will follow the File Description Specifications form. The OF identifies the overflow indicator.

3. The *filename* (columns 7–14) field on the Line Counter Specifications form must be the same printer filename specified on the File Description Specifications form.

4. Columns 15–17 on the Line Counter Specifications form indicates the number of *lines per page* for the nonstandard form. When this entry is coded, the constant FL must be included in columns 18–19 to denote Form Length.

5. Columns 20–22 on the Line Counter Specifications form indicates the *overflow line number*. This is the line number that, when printed on, will result in the overflow indicator being set on, which will then cause page overflow. When this entry has been specified, the constant OL must be included in columns 23–24 to denote Overflow Line.

Figure 2.15 illustrates the File Description Specifications for a print file. Note the L in column 39. The corresponding Line Counter Specifications form in Figure 2.16 indicates that:

1. The form length is 44 lines.
2. The overflow line is 38.

Consider the following, which illustrates the RPG specifications for printing a report on nonstandard forms: The International Appliance Company wants to produce an Inventory Report printed on 8½ by 8½ paper, a nonstandard size. At six lines per inch (6 LPI), paper that is 8½ inches long would consist of 51 lines. To produce a one-inch bottom margin, the overflow line would have to be set at line 45. Using paper of nonstandard size requires the programmer to indicate to the computer the new form length and overflow line number. Figure 2.17 illustrates the program that will produce this report.

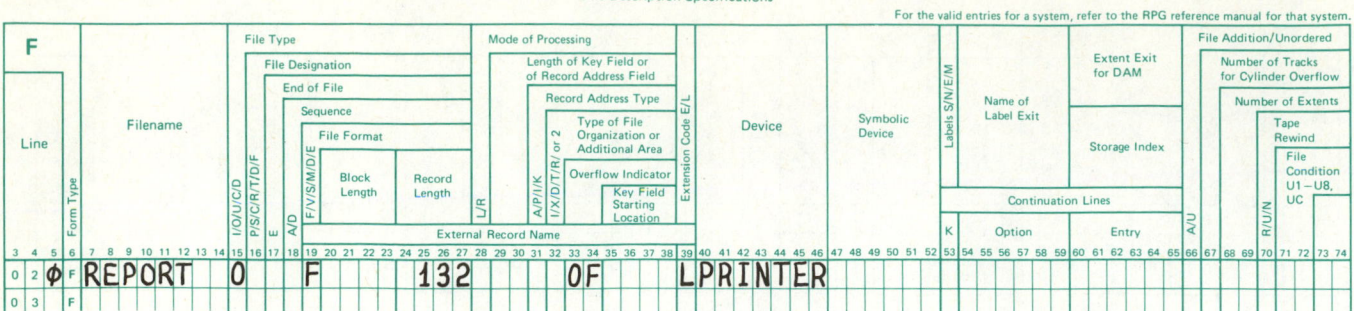

Figure 2.15
File Specifications for a print
file.

Figure 2.16
The corresponding Line
Counter Specifications for
Figure 2.15.

D. Preprinted Customized Forms

Preprinted forms are custom-designed by a forms manufacturer to meet the needs of a particular application. See Figure 2.18 for an example of a preprinted form. Preprinted forms are supplied with company logos, titles, headings, and dividing lines/boxes preprinted on the form by the forms manufacturer. Such forms are commonly used for payroll checks, purchase orders, and invoices.

Preprinted custom-designed forms provide some advantages:

1. Program and computer efficiency are increased because titles and headings are preprinted on the forms, thus requiring only the printing of detail information by the program and printer.
2. Titles and column headings can be much more flexible with a variety of sizes and styles of type.
3. Edit symbols such as decimal points may be preprinted on the form to separate dollars and cents.

The obvious disadvantages of preprinted forms are higher cost and the need to maintain a larger inventory of forms.

When printing on preprinted forms the function of the computer program is to print only the detail information in the spaces provided on the form. Normally, after preprinted forms are inserted into the printer they need to be properly aligned, that is, the first line to print must be aligned with the designated area on the form. To allow forms alignment by the operator an additional specification must be added to the program—the *forms alignment specification* on the Control Specifications form.

Figure 2.17
Printing a report on nonstandard forms.

```
....+....1....+....2....+....3....+....4....+....5....+....6....+....7...
0010 H
0020 F*/COPY IAPPLIBR,@IA111FD
0030CFIA111   IP  F      70         DISK
0040 FREPORT   O   F      110     OF  LPRINTER
0050 LREPORT    51FL  45OL
0060CIIA111   NS
0070CI                                    1   10 AWRHSE
0080CI                                   11   48 AMODEL
0090CI                                   49   530AMFG
0100CI                                   54   590ADATEM
0110CI                                  P 60   620ASOLD
0120CI                                  P 63   650ARETNS
0130CI                                  P 66   702APRICE
0140CI        DS
0150CI                                    1   38 AMODEL
0160CI                                    1   10 AMODL#
0170CI                                   11   30 ADESC
0180CI                                   31   38 ACOLOR

0190 OREPORT   H   01    1P
0200 O         OR        OF
0210 O                                    13 'IA254AXR'
0220 O                                    63 'INVENTORY REPORT'
0230 O                            UDATE Y  80
0240 O                                   100 'PAGE'
0250 O                            PAGE    105
0260 O         H   02    1P
0270 O         OR        OF
0280 O                                    25 'BRAND'
0290 O                                    40 'MODEL'
0300 O                                    91 'DATE'
0310 O                                   105 'LIST'
0320 O         H   103   1P
0330 O         OR        OF
0340 O                                    15 'WAREHOUSE'
0350 O                                    25 'NAME'
0360 O                                    40 'NUMBER'
0370 O                                    65 'DESCRIPTION'
0380 O                                    78 'COLOR'
0390 O                                    91 'MANUFACTURED'
0400 O                                   105 'PRICE'
0410 O         D 1       N1P
0420 O                             AWRHSE  15
0430 O                             AMFG    25
0440 O                             AMODL#  40
0450 O                             ADESC   65
0460 O                             ACOLOR  78
0470 O                             ADATEMY 91
0480 O                             APRICE1 105
```

indicates a Line Counter
Specification is used to change
the form defaults

51 lines per page

Overflow to be detected at line 45

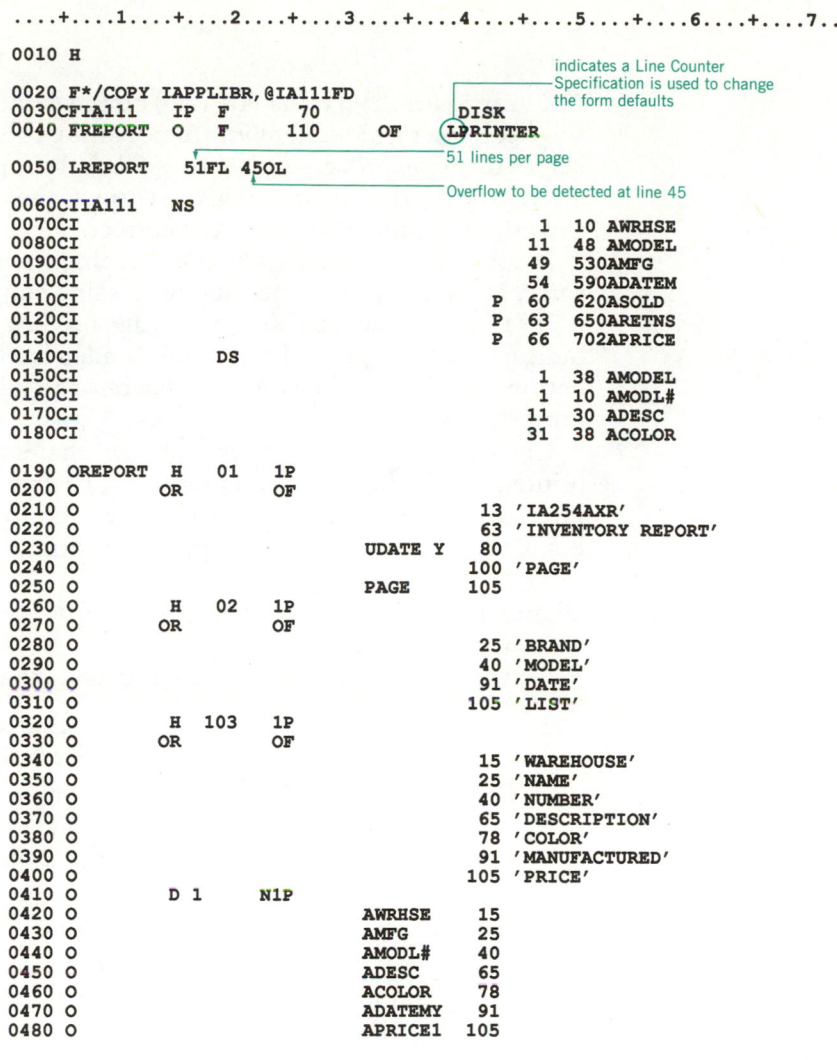

Figure 2.18
Example of a preprinted form.

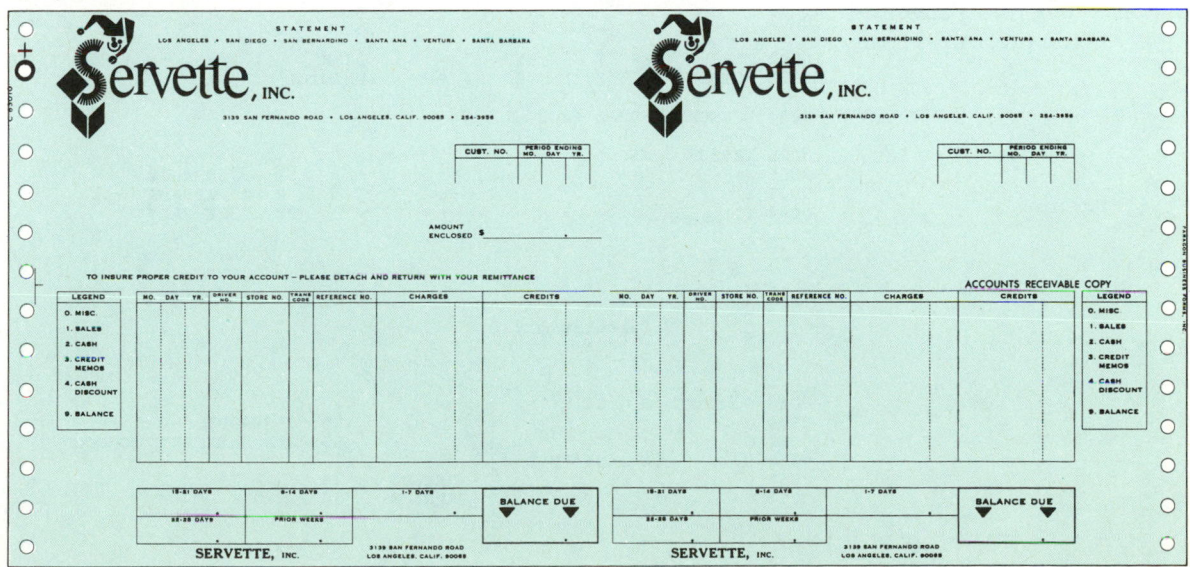

E. 1P Forms Alignment (Column 41) of the Control Specifications Form

Column 41 (the 1P Forms Position) on the Control Specifications form allows the operator to request *reprinting* of lines conditioned by the 1P indicator, before the main processing begins, so that the form may be aligned correctly. If, after printing, the alignment is not correct, the operator can adjust the form in the printer and reprint until it is correct.

If column 41 contains a *blank*, heading lines, conditioned by the 1P indicator, are printed only once and processing continues in the usual way.

If '1' is entered in column 41, the heading lines conditioned by the 1P indicator can be printed repeatedly under control of the operator. It is this option that allows the computer operator to adjust the positioning of a form until it is correct.

Consider the following example for enabling an operator to align a preprinted form before the main processing begins: The payroll department of the International Appliance Company wants to print paychecks for their employees. The paychecks, a custom-designed form preprinted by a forms manufacturer, are of a nonstandard size ($8\frac{1}{2}$ by 7). To provide the necessary forms alignment and print the paychecks, the program shown in Figure 2.19 was written.

Several features are incorporated to achieve the alignment required:

1. *"Dummy"* or sample headings are included on the Output Specifications form to allow the operator an opportunity to correctly align the preprinted forms before the main processing begins.

2. The 1P (first page) indicator is set on before the program begins processing and controls the alignment of the *dummy* headings on the first page.

3. Coding on the Line Counter Specifications form alters the default settings for form length and overflow line.

4. The '1' specified in column 41 on the Control Specifications form allows the operator to repeat the printing of the dummy headings until the forms are aligned.

Figure 2.19
Controlling forms alignment on preprinted forms.

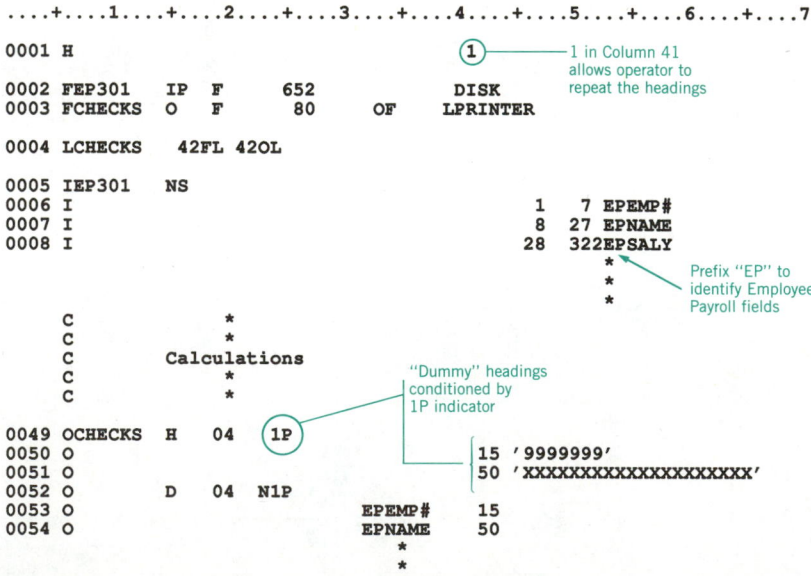

"Dummy" headings, that is, headings that resemble the actual report headings, are specified in the Output Specifications controlled by the 1P indicator. The program prints the dummy heading lines conditioned by the 1P indicator and the program halts. The system then prompts the operator with a message and waits for a response. This gives the operator an opportunity to examine the report to make sure that the form is properly aligned.

The computer prompts the operator to determine if processing should continue. The operator responds with either an upper- or lowercase Y for Yes or an upper- or lowercase N for No from the console keyboard. The response 'Y' indicates the form is aligned properly and the program continues. If the forms are not aligned properly, the operator would adjust the paper and enter an 'N'. An 'N' causes the program to reprint the heading lines (dummy lines) after performing the space/skip specifications for the line.

This process repeats until the operator types a 'Y' or 'y' to indicate that the program is to continue. If the RPG reserved field 'PAGE' is used in the program it will be reset after the forms are correctly aligned so that the page numbers are correct on the actual report.

Self-Test
1. Edit codes are used for editing (numeric/alphanumeric) fields.
2. To print a floating dollar sign, the $ must be specified as a _____ on the same line as the _____ field.
3. The _____ Specifications form is used to modify printer settings for nonstandard output forms.
4. The Line Counter Specifications form must be placed between the _____ Specifications form and the _____ Specifications form.
5. The _____ indicator allows the operator to request reprinting of lines so that the form may be aligned.

Solutions
1. numeric
2. constant; edited
3. Line Counter
4. File Description; Input
5. 1P

IV. Reporting Concepts Used in Business Systems

A. Categories of Reports

In general, output reports are categorized as follows:

CATEGORIES OF REPORTS
1. Detail.
2. Exception.
3. Group.

1. Detail Reports
Detail reports are those that generate lines of output for each input record read. A payroll program, for example, that produces a paycheck for each employee record is an example of a detail report.

The RPG programmer should be aware that producing detail reports requires more computer time than other reports and tends to be the most costly as well. Moreover, detail reports are sometimes wasteful. That is, users sometimes request detail reports when other types would serve just as well, or even better.

2. Exception Reports

One alternative to detail reporting is **exception reporting,** which is the printing of only that output that does not fall within established guidelines. Thus, we would be printing output that represents exceptions to some specified rule. For example, suppose a user requests a detail report that prints the names of all employees. After careful investigation, the programmer might discover that the purpose of this report is to identify all employees who are not full-time personnel, that is, contract employees only. An exception report, then, which lists only these individuals that are exceptions (e.g., not full-time) would be a more efficient and effective alternative to the detail listing. Figure 2.20 provides the specifications for such a program, and Figure 2.21 illustrates the RPG program that selects and prints contract employees only.

Figure 2.20
Problem definition for a program that produces an exception report.

Systems Flowchart

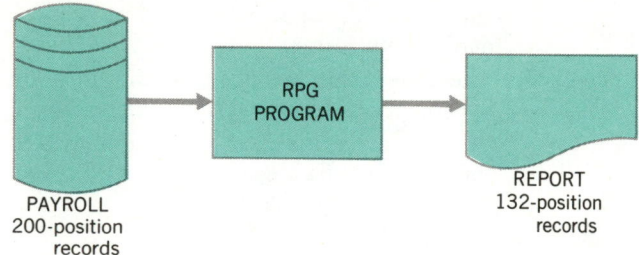

PAYROLL Record Layout

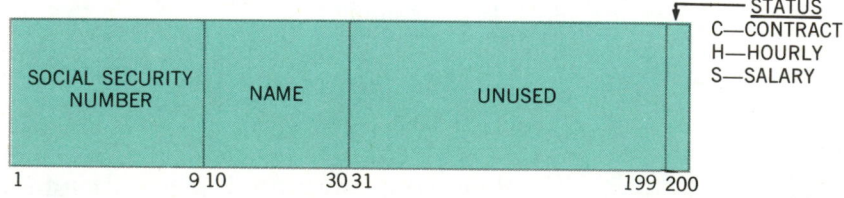

REPORT Printer Spacing Chart

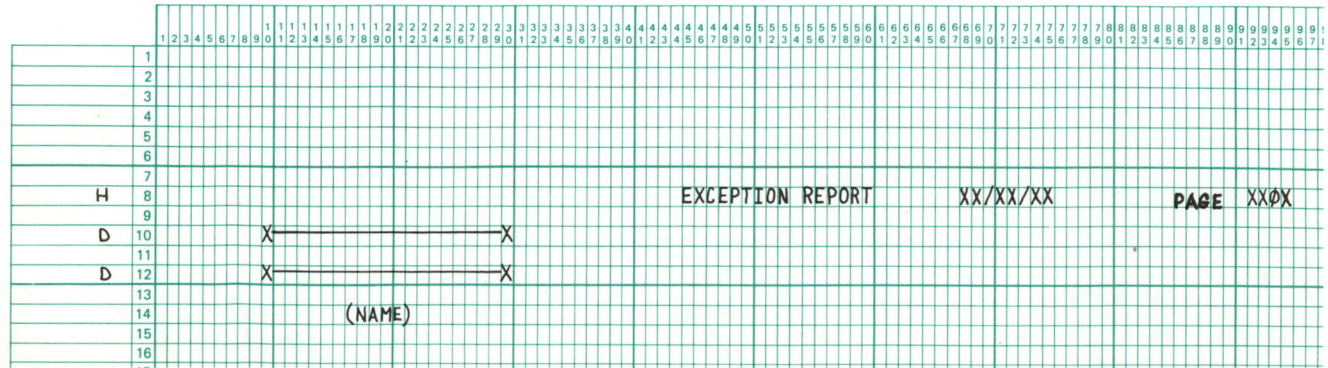

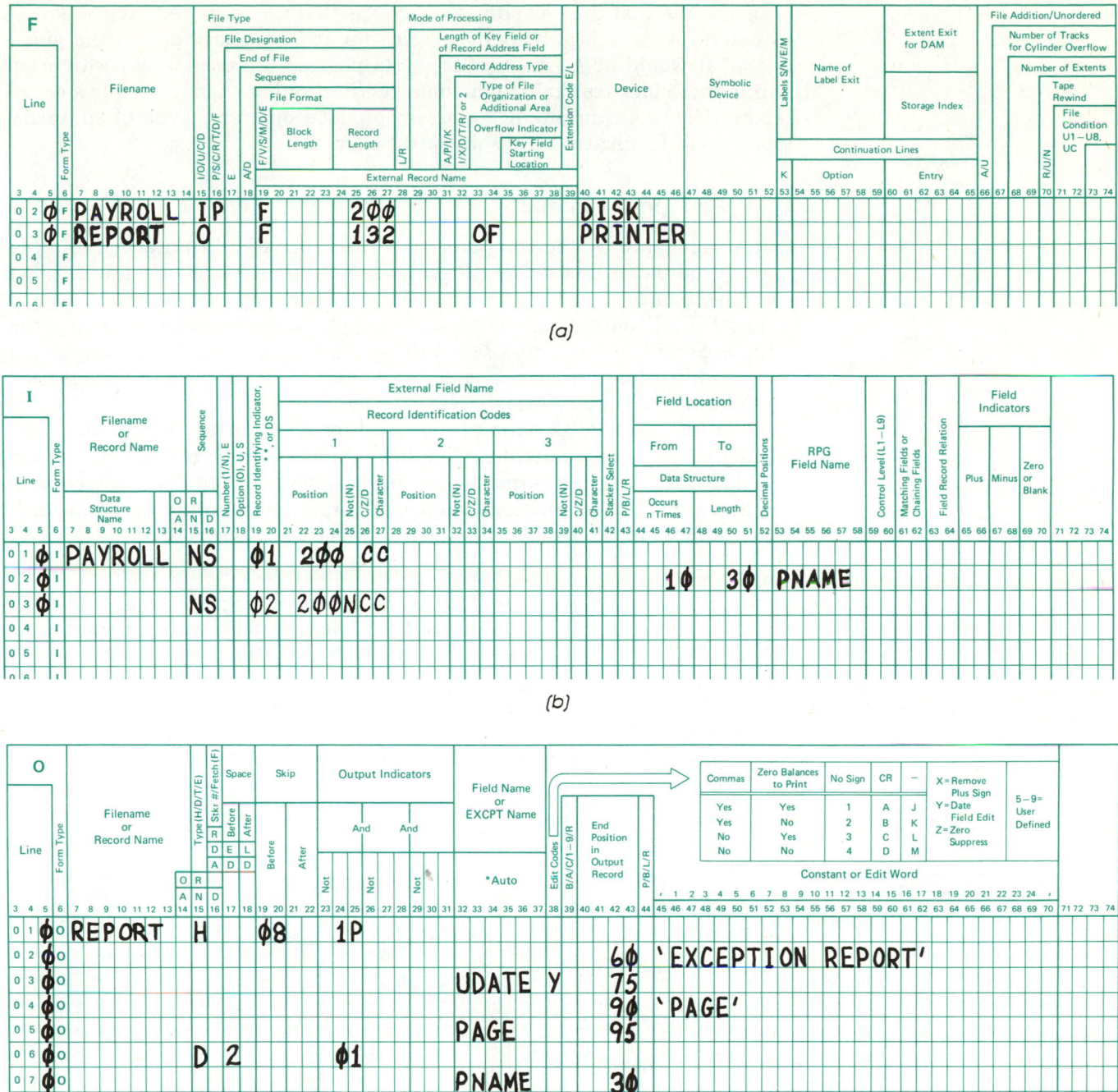

Figure 2.21
RPG program that produces an
exception report.

3. Group or Summary Reports

Another alternative to detail reports is summary or **group reports.** These print totals that can sometimes provide the user with enough information so that detail reports are not necessary at all.

Suppose a user asks for a list of all salespeople and the amount of sales they have brought in during a given period. If each input record contained the amount of sales for each salesperson, then this would be a detail report. Suppose, further, that the programmer discovers that the purpose of this report is to determine the total amount of sales for the company during the given period. It would be far more efficient to provide the user with a **summary listing** that indicates the total amount of sales, rather than providing a detail report. The programming necessary to produce different types of summary reports will be illustrated in subsequent chapters.

B. Other Types of Output

Output produced by the computer need not always be in printed form. Frequently, output will be a disk file that will need to be stored and processed at some later date.

In RPG, all output, including disk output, must be described using the Output Specifications form. Recall that a Printer Spacing Chart defines the output format for printed reports; for disk output, a record layout form is used for defining the output format.

Most frequently, disk output is designed to be as concise as possible. Thus editing symbols are omitted in disk files. A disk output record can contain detail data, that is, one output record for each input record. Or it can contain total or summary information, where one output record summarizes the data from several input records.

Example   The specifications for a problem that creates detail print output and disk output are indicated in Figure 2.22. The RPG File and Input Specifications forms are described in Figure 2.23. The output files would be described on an Output Specifications form as follows:

REVIEW OF RPG CODING RULES

1. Field names and Filenames
   a. Field names have 1 to 6 characters.
      Filenames have 1 to 8 characters.
   b. Names must begin with a letter.

Figure 2.22
Systems flowchart for a program that creates detail print output and disk output.

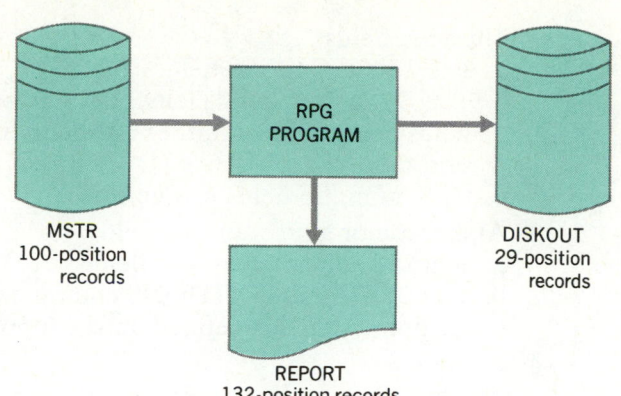

MSTR
100-position
records

RPG
PROGRAM

DISKOUT
29-position
records

REPORT
132-position records

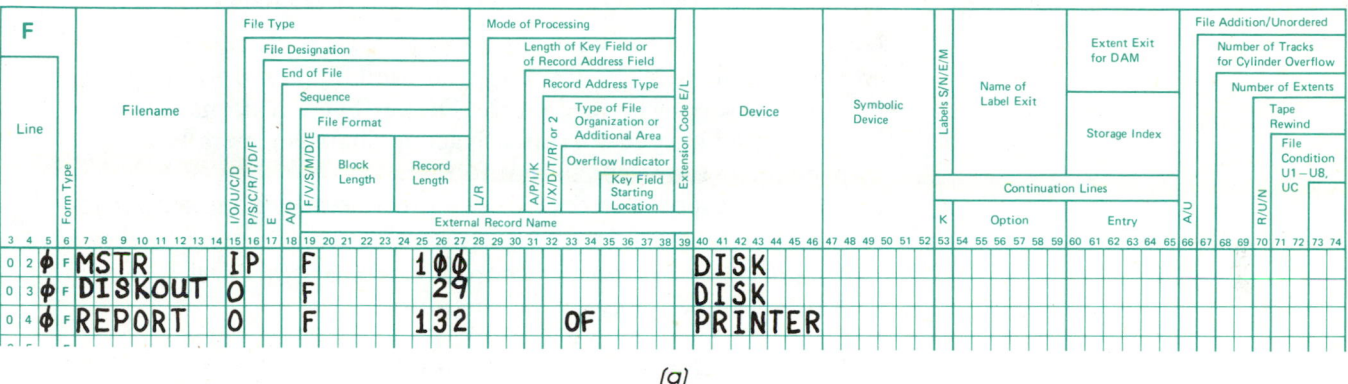

(a)

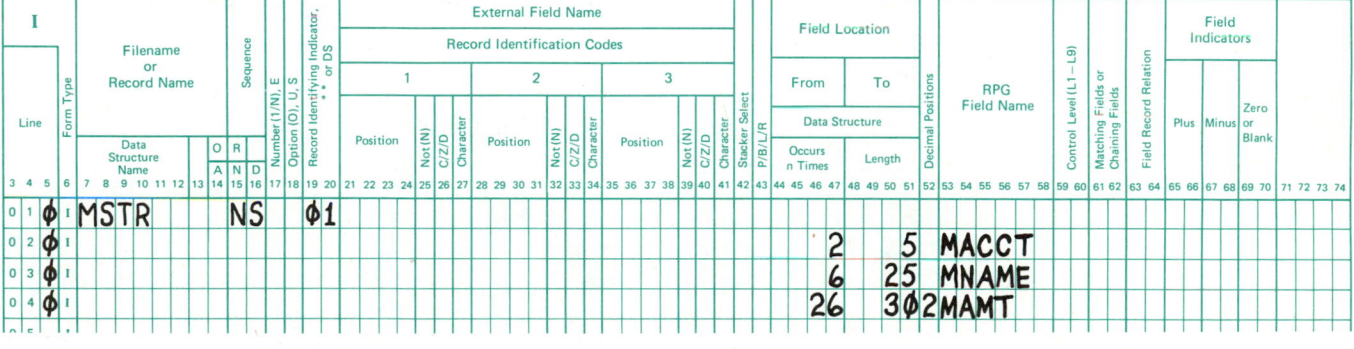

(b)

Figure 2.23
Coding to create detail print output and disk output.

c. When specified on a form, they are left-justified in the field—i.e.,

| A | B | C | ʙ | ʙ |

not

| ʙ | ʙ | A | B | C | .

d. No embedded blanks.

e. Letters, digits, and @, #, $ are permitted.

f. Names must be unique and should be meaningful.

g. We recommend that you begin a field name with a prefix that helps identify it as part of a record or data structure.

2. Numeric fields
   a. 1 to 15 digits in the field.
   b. The DECIMAL POSITIONS field must be coded for all numeric fields being defined, either on the Input form or on the Calculation form.
   c. Only numeric fields can be edited.
3. Alphabetic or alphanumeric fields
   a. 1 to 256 characters in the field.
   b. The DECIMAL POSITIONS columns must be blank for alphanumeric fields defined on the Input form.
4. Comments
   To designate any line in RPG as a comment, code an * in column 7.

REVIEW OF OUTPUT SPECIFICATIONS

1. How the Output Specifications are used
   a. Files coded with 'O' for output in the File Description Specifications must be described on the Output Specifications form.
   b. For printed output, a Printer Spacing Chart is generally used to plan and describe the output format.
   c. For disk output, a Record Layout form describes the output format.
2. Coding the First Line of the Output Specifications Form
   a. O in column 6 (precoded on the form).
   b. FILENAME begins in column 7.
      (1) Previously defined on the File Description Specifications form.
      (2) Coded only once at the beginning of the Output Specifications form.
   c. Record TYPE can be H, D, or T
      (1) Heading, detail, and total records are used for printed output.
      (2) Detail and total records are used for disk output.
   d. SPACE and SKIP
      (1) Can space the paper 1, 2, or 3 lines before or after printing.
      (2) Can skip to any specific print line.
   e. OUTPUT INDICATORS
      Include indicators that, when on, should result in printing or writing disk output. See Figure 2.24 for a review of indicators.
3. Coding Subsequent Lines of the Output Specifications Form
   The lines following an H, D, or T line are used for:
   a. Specifying fields to be printed.
   b. Specifying constants to be printed.
      (1) Begin each field or constant on the line following the entries mentioned above (a–e).
      (2) Each field to be printed must be defined on either the Input or Calculation form.
      (3) The END POSITION refers to the right-most print position for the field, as specified on the Printer Spacing Chart.
      (4) Field names are left-justified in columns 32–37 of the form. Any fixed data or constant to print is delimited with single quote marks.

Figure 2.24
Indicator summary.
(Courtesy IBM.)

Indicator	How Assigned	Turned on by	Turned off by	Usage
Record Identifying Indicator (can use 01-99)	Input Specifications	Conditions in records	RPG at end of cycle	For processing of input records; for printing detail output
1P	Automatically, at beginning of cycle	RPG	RPG after Heading and Detail output	1st-page heading at beginning of run
LR	Automatically in the cycle	After the last record has been processed	RPG	For obtaining total output, performing end-of-job processing, and printing end-of-job messages
OF	Automatically as an end-of-page or overflow indicator	RPG	RPG	To print headings at the beginning of each page

V. RPG Logic Cycle

Thus far we have seen RPG specifications that indicate:

1. Files to be used.
2. File definitions (input format) for input records.
3. Output Specifications for producing reports and other types of output.

The sequence in which RPG performs the required operations is relatively clear in simple programs. But this sequence becomes somewhat less obvious with more complex programming.

In other programming languages, the programmer is in full control of the sequence in which instructions are executed. That is, a programmer can precisely specify logical control. In RPG, programmers have a choice in program design. The Logic Cycle, a built-in function of RPG, can be used to control the sequence and operations of a program by default. The other approach is the Structured Programming technique, in which the programmer using structured programming concepts and new RPG operation codes controls the sequence and operations of the program. Structured concepts will be introduced in subsequent chapters. Let us now consider the RPG Logic Cycle.

The **RPG Logic Cycle** describes in detail the precise sequence in which RPG performs all operations. Using the RPG logic cycle, logical control of the program is handled by RPG. That is, functions such as reading files and writing records are performed automatically and in a specific sequence by the program. The programmer must fully understand the logical control sequence provided by RPG in order to write programs that are executed in the proper order.

The RPG Logic Cycle is usually illustrated in pictorial form. Figure 1.24 on page 58 illustrates the RPG Logic Cycle in flowchart form. All programs using the Logic Cycle approach follow this fixed logic sequence:

1. 1P indicator is set on by the program before processing begins.
2. Heading records (H) are printed.
3. Detail records (D) are written.
4. 1P indicator is set off by the program (for the first cycle only).

5. All record identifying indicators are set off.

6. A record is read.

7. The computer performs the last record test. If the last record has been processed, the LR indicator is set on and may be used for performing end-of-job or total time calculations or printing. Once the end-of-job functions are completed the program is terminated.

8. The record identifying indicator that identifies the input record just read is set on if the end of the file was not detected in the previous step.

9. Detail calculations are performed.

10. The process is repeated, starting with Step 2. (That is, 1P is not set on.)

As our programs get more sophisticated, we will provide more details about the RPG Logic Cycle.

CHAPTER SELF-TEST

Consider the following Output Specifications for Questions 1 through 5:

1. The filename HOURLY also appears on the _____ Specifications form.

2. Type D means that the record described is a(n) _____ record.

3. The line described in Question 2 will print when indicator _____ is on.

4. The fields specified on the Output Specifications form must be defined on either the _____ Specifications form or the _____ Specifications form.

5. If REGHRS is a three-digit field, it will print in print positions _____.

6. Using the Input Specifications form and Printer Spacing Chart in Figure 2.25, code the Output Specifications.

7. Only _____ fields can contain Edit Codes for editing.

8. If an input field is specified as having two decimal positions, then a decimal point (is, is not) part of the input record.

I	Filename or Record Name	Sequence	Number (1/N), E	Record Identifying Indicator	From	To	Decimal Positions	RPG Field Name
01 Ø I	PAYROLL	NS		Ø1				
02 Ø I					1	3		EMPNO
03 Ø I					4	16		NAME
04 Ø I					17	20	2	BLUE
05 Ø I					21	24	2	DUES
06 Ø I					25	28	2	HOSP

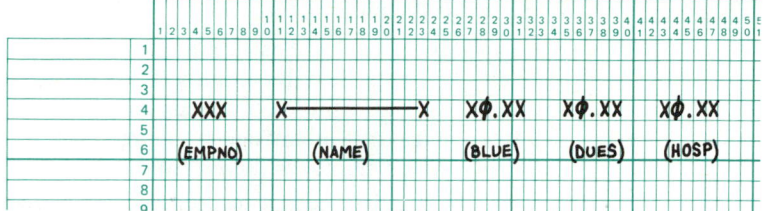

Figure 2.25
Input Specifications and Printer Spacing Chart for Question 6.

9. The use of any edit code will automatically cause
_____ and _____ where appropriate.

Indicate the results in each of the following cases (Questions 10 through 15):

Input Field	Edit Code	Result
10. ØØØ∧ØØ	2	
11. Ø234∧56	1	
12. 1234∧56	1	
13. ØØØ∧ØØ	1	
14. 1234∧56	4	
15. Ø234∧56	2	

16. Using the following Output Specifications, how would ØØØØ57 print, assuming the field is defined with two decimal positions?

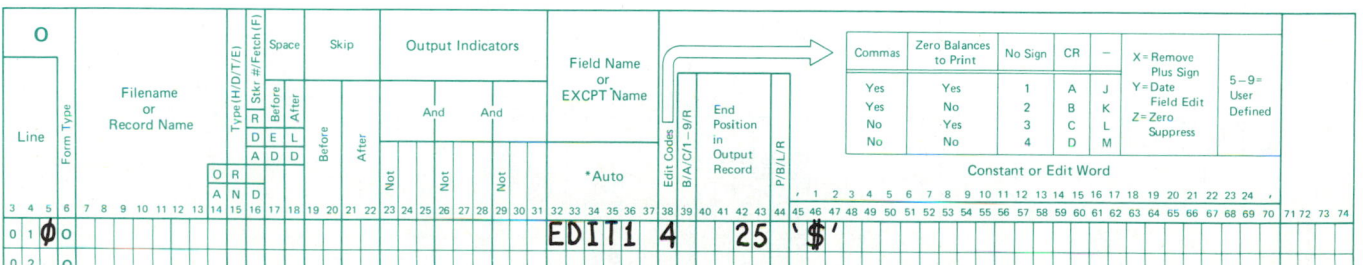

17. Using the following Output Specifications, how would ØØØØ57 print, assuming the field is defined with two decimal positions?

O	Line	Form Type	Filename or Record Name	Type (H/D/T/E)	R Stkr #/Fetch (F)	Space Before After	Skip Before After	Output Indicators And And Not Not Not	Field Name or EXCPT Name *Auto	Edit Codes B/A/C/1 – 9/R	End Position in Output Record	P/B/L/R	Commas Yes Yes No No	Zero Balances to Print Yes No Yes No	No Sign 1 2 3 4	CR A B C D	– J K L M	X = Remove Plus Sign Y = Date Field Edit Z = Zero Suppress	5 – 9 = User Defined	Constant or Edit Word
0 1 Ø O											19									'$'
0 2 Ø O									EDIT2 4		25									

18. In Question 16, the $ is said to _____ with the field.

19. In specifying a Field Name in RPG, the name is coded in the (right-, left-) most position of columns 32–37 of the Output form.

20. In specifying an End Position in RPG, the number is (right-, left-) justified in columns 40–43, which means that (left, right) unfilled positions are left blank.

21. (T or F) Negative quantities are represented on input with a minus sign over the right-most position.

22. (T or F) If Edit Codes 1-4 are used for a field that contains a minus sign, the field will print as if it did not have a sign.

23. To print CR along with any negative quantities, use Edit Codes _____.

24. To simply cause zero suppression, use the _____ in the Edit Code field.

25. A numeric field is denoted when the _____ field of either the Input Specifications or the Calculation Specifications is coded.

SOLUTIONS

1. File Description
2. detail
3. 19
4. Input; Calculation
5. 32–34
6.

O	Line	Form Type	Filename or Record Name	Type (H/D/T/E)	R Stkr #/Fetch (F)	Space Before After	Skip Before After	Output Indicators And And Not Not Not	Field Name or EXCPT Name *Auto	Edit Codes B/A/C/1 – 9/R	End Position in Output Record	P/B/L/R	Commas Yes Yes No No	Zero Balances to Print Yes No Yes No	No Sign 1 2 3 4	CR A B C D	– J K L M	X = Remove Plus Sign Y = Date Field Edit Z = Zero Suppress	5 – 9 = User Defined	Constant or Edit Word
0 1 Ø O			DEDUCT	D		2		Ø1												
0 2 Ø O									EMPNO		6									
0 3 Ø O									NAME		23									
0 4 Ø O									BLUE	1	31									
0 5 Ø O									DUES	1	39									
0 6 Ø O									HOSP	1	47									
0 7 O																				

7. numeric
8. is not
9. zero suppression; printing of decimal points

1Ø. blank	19. left
11. 234.56	2Ø. right-; left
12. 1,234.56	21. T
13. .ØØ	22. T
14. 1234.56	23. A-D
15. 234.56	24. Z
16. $.57	25. Decimal Positions
17. $ .57	(column 52)
18. float	

KEY TERMS

Constant	Exception reporting	Literal	Spacing
Continuous form	First page (1P) indicator	Overflow (OF) indicator	Summary listing
Default	Floating dollar sign	PAGE	UDATE
Detail printing	Group report	Preprinted form	User-friendly
Detail report	Implied decimal point	Report heading	Variable data
Edit Code	Last Record (LR) indi-	RPG Logic Cycle	Zero suppression
Editing	cator	Skipping	

REVIEW QUESTIONS

1. What, if anything, is wrong with the following field names?
   a. 5OUT
   b. AMT-OUT
   c. DESCRIPT
   d. QTY12
   e. AMTIN$

2. What is the purpose of the record identifying indicator and how is it used?

3. What is the purpose of headings? Indicate the items that are coded as part of a heading.

4. What is the meaning of editing? Indicate what symbols are used for editing.

5. State the meaning of the following:
   a. Detail reports
   b. Summary reports
   c. Exception reports

6. When is the Decimal Positions field used on the Input Specifications form?

7. Assume the field EDITFD is defined on the Output Specifications form with an Edit Code of 3. Indicate the edited result in each case.

Value in EDITFD	Edited Result
1234∧56	_____
ØØ34∧56	_____
ØØØØ∧25	_____
ØØØØ∧Ø6	_____
ØØØØ∧ØØ	_____

8. How are the following entries used in RPG?
   a. UDATE   c. 1P
   b. PAGE   d. OF

9. Indicate how numeric entries are coded on the RPG forms.

10. Indicate how nonnumeric entries are coded on the RPG forms.

DEBUGGING EXERCISES

As noted in Chapter 1, there are several types of errors that may occur in a program and there are several places where errors are likely to occur or to become evident.

1. *Coding the program.* The programmer may make *syntax errors*, which means that the rules of the language have been violated.

2. *Keying the program.* The programmer may make *keying or typographical errors* in entering the program.

3. *Compiling the program.* The computer will list any *syntax errors* or rule violations.

4. *Executing the program.* The computer will run the program and produce output that may indicate if *logic errors* have occurred.

Recall that *debugging a program* means eliminating all types of errors.

The first two types of errors—coding and keying errors—can be minimized by *desk checking* a program *before* it is compiled. Programmers, then, should review programs carefully at their desks to ensure their accuracy. In the end, it will save them a good deal of time if they make certain that the coding and keying of a program are as accurate as possible before compiling the program. There are likely to be programming errors that are not detected until a program is compiled or executed, but eliminating all obvious errors by desk checking will save computer time as well as the programmer's time.

Debugging exercises at the end of the chapters in the first half of the book will help identify common programming errors. Three types of exercises will be included.

1. *Debugging by Desk Checking.* These will include programs on coding sheets that contain errors that you must identify.
2. *Debugging Using a Source Listing.* These will include programs that have been compiled and that include compiler-generated error messages that you must identify.
3. *Debugging Using an Executed Program and the Output Generated.* These will include programs with logic errors that have been compiled and run. You must identify the logic errors by checking the computer-produced output against the program requirements.

Debugging Exercise

The problem definition for this exercise is shown in Figure 2.26. The coding sheets in Figure 2.27 contain syntax errors. Identify them and illustrate the corrections you would make to the program. The listing in Figure 2.28 includes the error diagnostics produced by running the program as coded. The syntax corrections are circled on the computer listing shown in Figure 2.29. There are, however, logic errors in the program. Your assignment is to desk check the program carefully, find the logic errors, and make the necessary corrections.

Figure 2.26
Problem definition for the debugging exercise.

Systems Flowchart

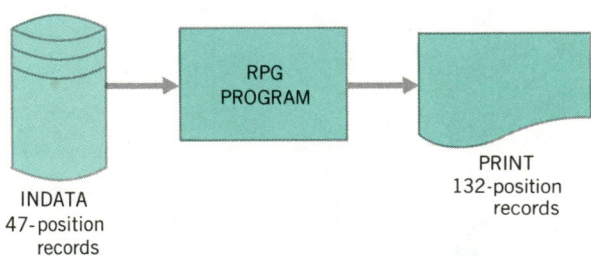

INDATA
47-position
records

PRINT
132-position
records

INDATA Record Layout

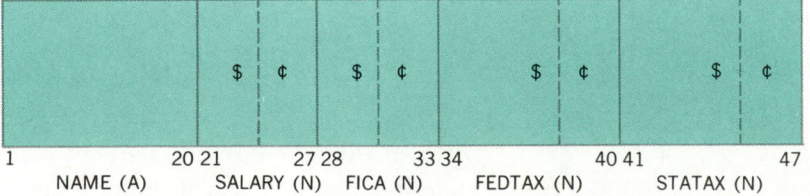

"A" denotes alphameric data; "N" denotes a numeric field containing two decimal positions.

Figure 2.26 PRINT Printer Spacing Chart
(continued)

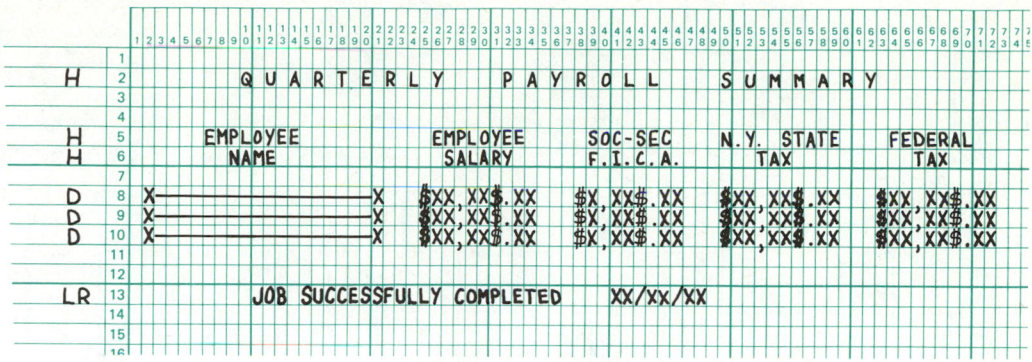

Figure 2.27
Coding sheets for the debugging exercise.

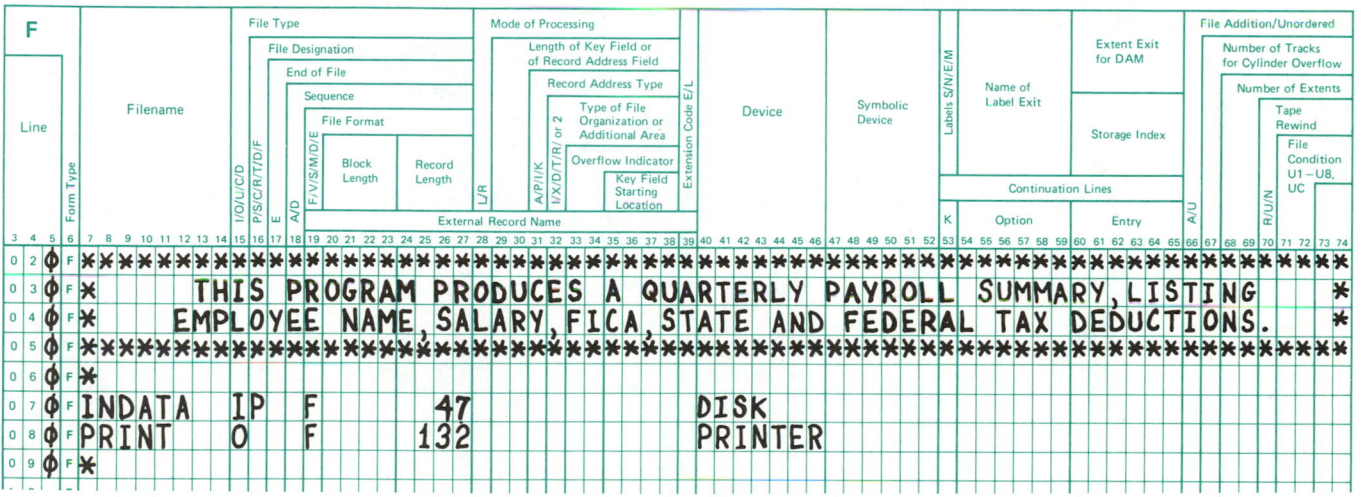

First output form (Heading Lines):

```
O  Line  FormType  Filename/RecordName  Type  Space  Skip  Output Indicators  Field Name or EXCPT Name  Edit Codes  End Position  Constant or Edit Word

01 0 O  ******************************** HEADING LINES ****************************************
02 0 O  *
03 0 O  PRINT          H  3      1P
04 0 O         OR             OF
05 0 O                                                    26  'QUARTERLY'
06 0 O                                                    44  'PAYROLL'
07 0 O                                                    62  'SUMMARY'
08 0 O          H  1      1P
09 0 O         OR             OF
10 0 O                                                    14  'EMPLOYEE'
11 0 O                                                    33  'EMPLOYEE'
12 0 O                                                    45  'SOC-SEC'
13 0 O                                                    59  'N.Y. STATE'
14 0 O                                                    70  'FEDERAL'
15 0 O          H  2      1P
16 0 O         OR             OF
17 0 O                                                    12  'NAME'
18 0 O                                                    32  'SALARY'
19 0 O                                                    46  'F.I.C.A.'
20 0 O                                                    55  'TAX'
21 0 O                                                    68  'TAX'
22 0 O  *
23 0 O  *********************** DETAIL LINE ****************************************
24 0 O  *
25 0 O          D  1      01
```

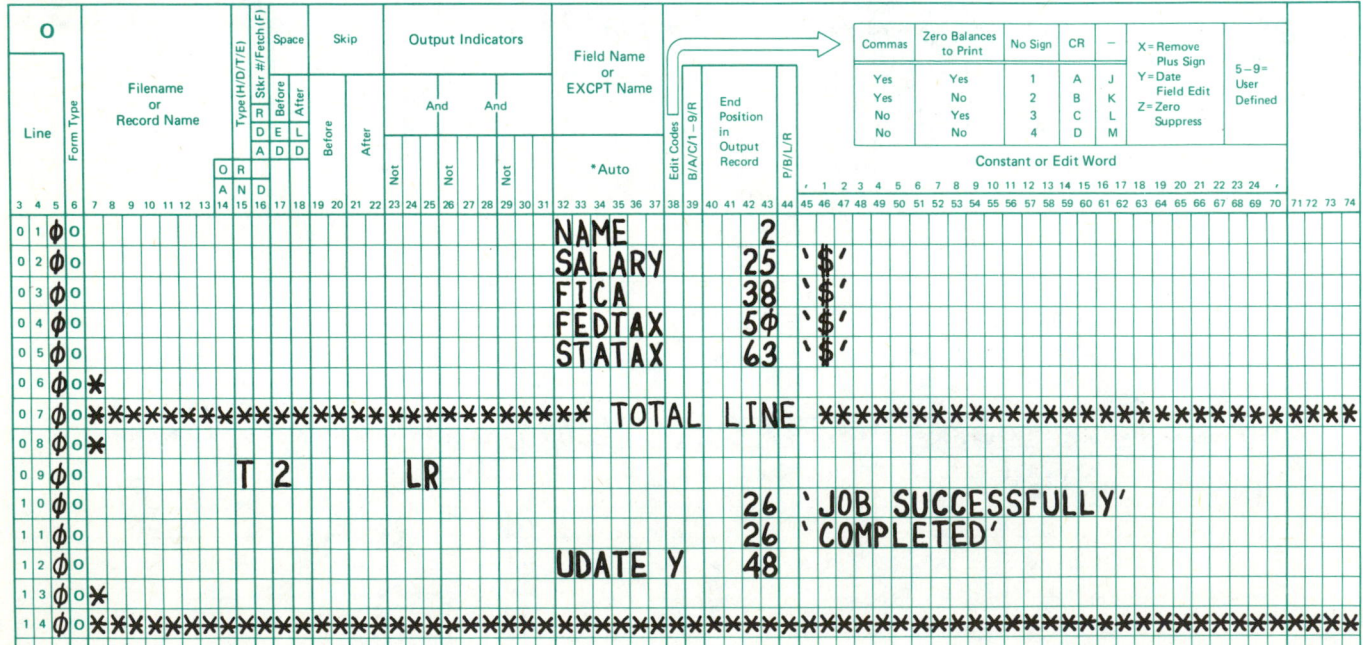

Second output form (Detail, Total Lines):

```
O  Line  FormType  ...  Field Name or EXCPT Name  Edit Codes  End Position  Constant or Edit Word

01 0 O                     NAME             2
02 0 O                     SALARY          25  '$'
03 0 O                     FICA            38  '$'
04 0 O                     FEDTAX          50  '$'
05 0 O                     STATAX          63  '$'
06 0 O  *
07 0 O  ********************** TOTAL LINE ****************************************
08 0 O  *
09 0 O          T  2      LR
10 0 O                                     26  'JOB SUCCESSFULLY'
11 0 O                                     26  'COMPLETED'
12 0 O                     UDATE Y         48
13 0 O  *
14 0 O  ****************************************************************************
```

Figure 2.27
(continued)

```
        01-020  F**********************************************************SSS02
        01-030  F*     THIS PROGRAM PRODUCES A QUARTERLY PAYROLL SUMMARY,LISTING  *SSS02
        01-04C  F*     EMPLCYEE NAME,SALARY,FICA,STATE AND FEDERAL TAX DEDUCTIONS.  *SSS02
        01-050  F**********************************************************SSS02
        01-06C  F*                                                          SSS02
0001    01-070  FINDATA IP F    47          DISK          SSS02
0002    01-08C  FPRINT  C  F    132         PRINTER       SSS02
        01-090  F*                                                          SSS02
        02-010  I**************************** INPUT RECCRD ****************************SSS02
        02-02C  I*                                                          SSS02
0003    02-030  IINDATA  NS  01                           SSS02
0004    02-04C  I                              1   20 NAME      SSS02
0005    02-05C  I                             21   272SALARY    SSS02
0006    02-060  I                             28   332FICA      SSS02
0007    02-07C  I                             34   402FEDTAX    SSS02
0008    02-08C  I                             41   472STATAX    SSS02
        02-090  I*                                                          SSS02
        03-010  C**************************** HEADING LINES ****************************SSS02
        03-02C  C*                                                          SSS02
0009    03-03C  CPRINT  H  3    1P                         SSS02
0010    03-04C  C       OR      CF                         SSS02                MSG  202
                                $
0011    03-050  C                              26 'C U A R T E R L Y'    SSS02
0012    03-060  C                              44 'P A Y R O L L'        SSS02
0013    03-07C  C                              62 'S U M M A R Y'        SSS02
0014    03-08C  C       H  1    1P                         SSS02
0015    03-09C  C       CR      CF                         SSS02                MSG  202
                                $
0016    03-100  C                              14 'EMPLCYEE'   SSS02
0017    03-110  C                              33 'EMPLCYEE'   SSS02
CC18    03-12C  C                              45 'SCC-SEC'    SSS02
0019    03-130  C                              59 'N.Y. STATE' SSS02
0020    03-140  C                              70 'FEDERAL'    SSS02
0021    03-15C  C       H  2    1P                         SSS02
0022    03-160  C       CR      CF                         SSS02                MSG  202
                                $
0023    03-170  C                              12 'NAME'      SSS02
0024    C3-18C  C                              32 'SALARY'    SSS02
0025    03-19C  C                              46 'F.I.C.A.'  SSS02
0026    03-2CC  C                              55 'TAX'       SSS02
0027    03-21C  C                              68 'TAX'       SSS02
        03-22C  C*                                                          SSS02
        03-230  C*********************** DETAIL LINE ***********************SSS02
        03-24C  C*                                                          SSS02
0028    03-250  C       D  1    01                         SSS02
0029    04-010  C                      NAME       2        SSS02
0030    04-020  C                      SALARY     25 '$'    SSS02                MSG  234
                                          $
0031    04-030  C                      FICA       38 '$'    SSS02                MSG  234
                                          $
0032    04-04C  C                      FEDTAX     50 '$'    SSS02                MSG  234
                                          $
0033    C4-05C  C                      STATAX     C3 '$'    SSS02                MSG  234
                                          $
        04-06C  C*                                                          SSS02
        04-070  O*********************** TOTAL LINE ***********************SSS02
        04-08C  C*                                                          SSS02
0034    04-09C  C       T  2    LR                         SSS02
0035    04-100  C                              26 'JOB SUCCESSFULLY'  SSS02
0036    04-11C  C                              26 'CCMPLETED'         SSS02
0037    04-120  C                      UDATE Y  48         SSS02
        04-13C  C*                                                          SSS02
        C4-140  O**********************************************************SSS02
```

E N D C F S C U R C E

C O M P I L E R D I A G N O S T I C S S U M M A R Y

ILN202   INDICATOR IS INVALID CR UNDEFINED. DROP ENTRY.

```
        C0010   C3-C4C
        00015   C3-09C
        00022   03-160
```

ILN234   INVALID NUMBER OF DIGIT PCSITICNS IN ECIT WCRD. CRCP EDITING.

```
        00030   C4-C2C    SALARY
        00031   C4-030    FICA
        00032   C4-040    FEDTAX
        00033   C4-C5C    STATAX
```

ILN432   FIELD LENGTH GREATER THAN END PCSITICN. LENGTH CF FIELD CR CORRECT END POSITION IS GIVEN. SPEC IS

ORCPPEC.

```
   D 00029   C4-C10
```

Figure 2.28
Program listing with error
diagnostics for the debugging
exercise.

Figure 2.29
Program listing that contains
logic errors for the debugging
exercise.

```
          01-020  F************************************************************SSS02
          01-030  F*      THIS PROGRAM PRODUCES A QUARTERLY PAYROLL SUMMARY,LISTING  *SSS02
          01-040  F*    EMPLOYEE NAME,SALARY,FICA,STATE AND FEDERAL TAX DEDUCTIONS.   *SSS02
          01-050  F************************************************************SSS02
          01-060  F*                                                               SSS02
   0001   01-070  FINDATA  IP  F      47            DISK              SSS02
   0002   01-080  FPRINT   O   F     132       CF   PRINTER           SSS02
          01-090  F*                                                               SSS02
          02-010  I************************* INPUT RECORD ************************SSS02
          02-020  I*                                                              SSS02
   0003   02-030  IINDATA   NS  01                                      SSS02
   0004   02-040  I                                    1   20 NAME      SSS02
   0005   02-050  I                                   21   272SALARY    SSS02
   0006   02-060  I                                   28   332FICA      SSS02
   0007   02-070  I                                   34   402FEDTAX    SSS02
   0008   02-080  I                                   41   472STATAX    SSS02
          02-090  I*                                                              SSS02
          03-010  O************************* HEADING LINES ***********************SSS02
          03-020  O*                                                              SSS02
   0009   03-030  OPRINT    H  3      1P                                SSS02
   0010   03-040  O         OR         CF                               SSS02
   0011   03-050  O                              26 'QUARTERLY'        SSS02
   0012   03-060  O                              44 'PAYROLL'          SSS02
   0013   03-070  O                              62 'SUMMARY'          SSS02
   0014   03-080  O         H  1      1P                                SSS02
   0015   03-090  O         OR         OF                               SSS02
   0016   03-100  O                              14 'EMPLOYEE'         SSS02
   0017   03-110  O                              33 'EMPLOYEE'         SSS02
   0018   03-120  O                              45 'SOC-SEC'          SSS02
   0019   03-130  O                              59 'N.Y. STATE'       SSS02
   0020   03-140  O                              70 'FEDERAL'          SSS02
   0021   03-150  O         H  2      1P                                SSS02
   0022   03-160  O         OR         CF                               SSS02
   0023   03-170  O                              12 'NAME'             SSS02
   0024   03-180  O                              32 'SALARY'           SSS02
   0025   03-190  O                              46 'F.I.C.A.'         SSS02
   0026   03-200  O                              55 'TAX'              SSS02
   0027   03-210  O                              68 'TAX'              SSS02
          03-220  O*                                                              SSS02
          03-230  O************************* DETAIL LINE ************************SSS02
          03-240  O*                                                              SSS02
   0028   03-250  O         D  1      01                                SSS02
   0029   04-010  O                      NAME      21                   SSS02
   0030   04-020  O                      SALARY1   34 '$'              SSS02
   0031   04-030  O                      FICA   1   46 '$'              SSS02
   0032   04-040  O                      FEDTAX1   73 '$'              SSS02
   0033   04-050  O                      STATAX1   59 '$'              SSS02
          04-060  O*                                                              SSS02
          04-070  O************************* TOTAL LINE ************************SSS02
          04-080  O*                                                              SSS02
   0034   04-090  O         T  2      LR                                SSS02
   0035   04-100  O                              26 'JOB SUCCESSFULLY'  SSS02
   0036   04-110  O                              26 'COMPLETED'         SSS02
   0037   04-120  O             UDATE Y          48                     SSS02
          04-130  O*                                                              SSS02
          04-140  O************************************************************SSS02
```

Required for overflow (annotation pointing to CF on line 01-080)

Required for editing (annotation pointing to line 04-070 area)

EMPLOYEE NAME		EMPLOYEE SALARY	SOC-SEC F.I.C.A.	N.Y. STATE TAX	FEDERAL TAX
BRONSON	DANIEL	$5,608.00	$429.01	$377.77	$1,055.73
CALHOUN	ROBERT A.	$7,896.00	$604.04	$531.89	$1,486.45
DIERCKS	GEORGE M.	$10,100.80	$772.71	$680.36	$1,901.51
FOO	LEON A.	$9,765.00	$747.02	$657.80	$1,838.29
FORTGANG	HANS	$13,450.88	$1,028.99	$906.10	$2,532.17
OEST	GILBERT U.	$12,917.17	$988.16	$870.12	$2,431.70
SAGER	WESLEY	$9,910.00	$758.12	$667.56	$1,865.60
STERN	MARILYN M.	$12,888.20	$985.95	$868.16	$2,462.47
VICTOR	VICTORIA	$11,917.00	$911.65	$802.76	$2,243.42

```
JOB SUCCOMPLETED                7/29/91
```

PROGRAMMING ASSIGNMENTS

1. Consider the following and write the RPG program to produce the desired results:

Systems Flowchart

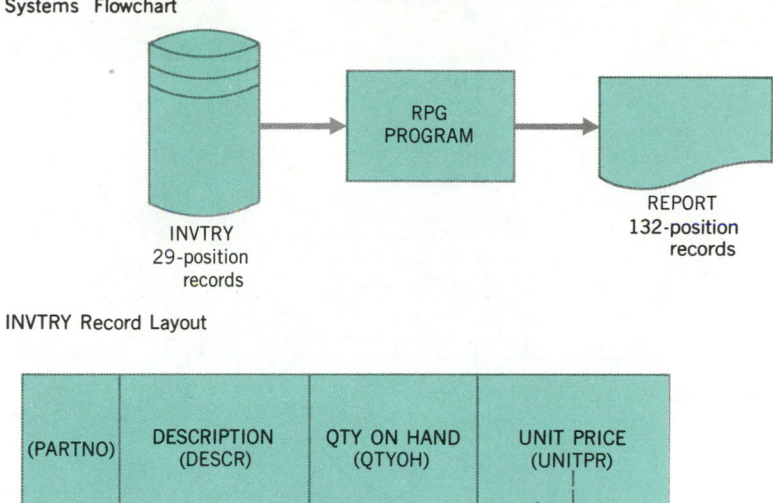

INVTRY
29-position
records

RPG
PROGRAM

REPORT
132-position
records

INVTRY Record Layout

(PARTNO)	DESCRIPTION (DESCR)	QTY ON HAND (QTYOH)	UNIT PRICE (UNITPR)
1 5 6	20 21	25 26	$ ¢ 29

REPORT Printer Spacing Chart

```
H    XX/XX/XX        P.J. GRADY DELOREAN PARTS          PAGE XXXX
H                      AMERICA'S MOST WANTED

H    PART NO  DESCRIPTION        QTY ON HAND   UNIT PRICE     TOTAL
D    XXXXX    X----------X        XXXXX         XX.XX        X,XXX,XXX.XX
     (PARTNO) (DESCR)             (QTYOH)       (UNITPR)     (TOTAL)
```

Note: All numeric fields are to be edited.

2. Consider the following and write the program to produce the desired output depicted in the Printer Spacing Chart:

Systems Flowchart

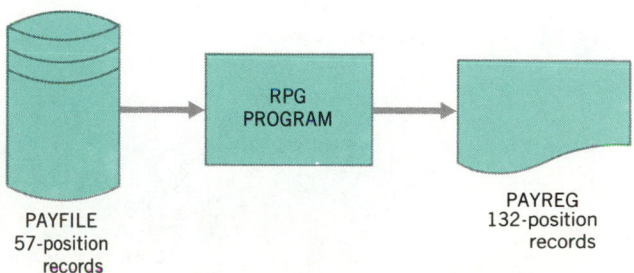

PAYFILE
57-position
records

RPG
PROGRAM

PAYREG
132-position
records

PAYFILE Record Layout

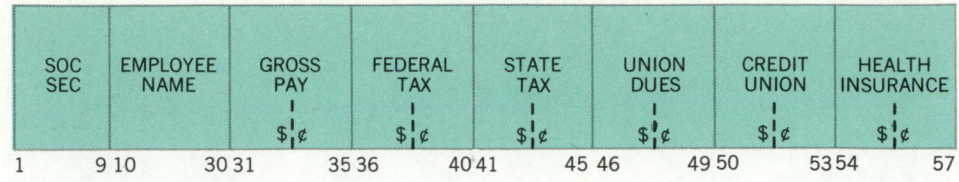

PAYREG Printer Spacing Chart

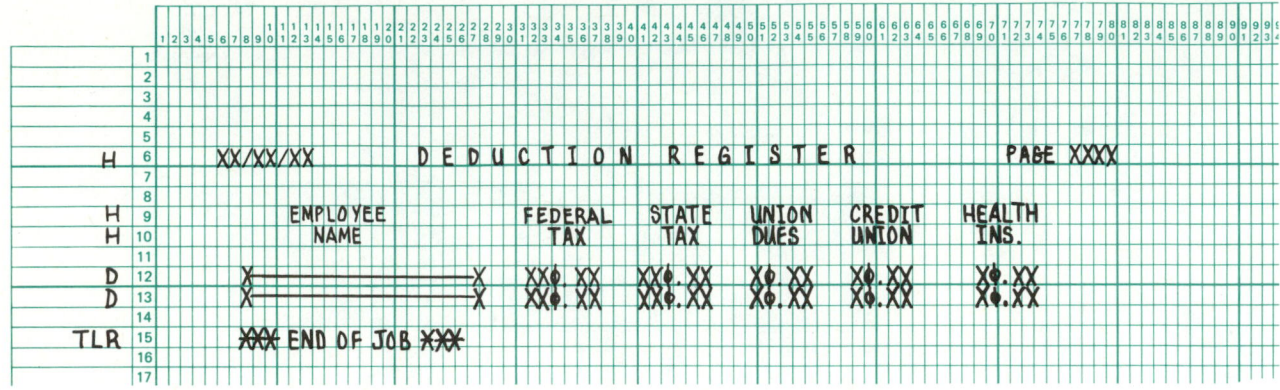

Notes
a. Edit all numeric fields.
b. Print *** END OF JOB *** after all records have been processed.
c. Be sure to include the embedded spaces in 'DEDUCTION REGISTER'

3. Consider the following and write the RPG program to produce the desired output:

Systems Flowchart

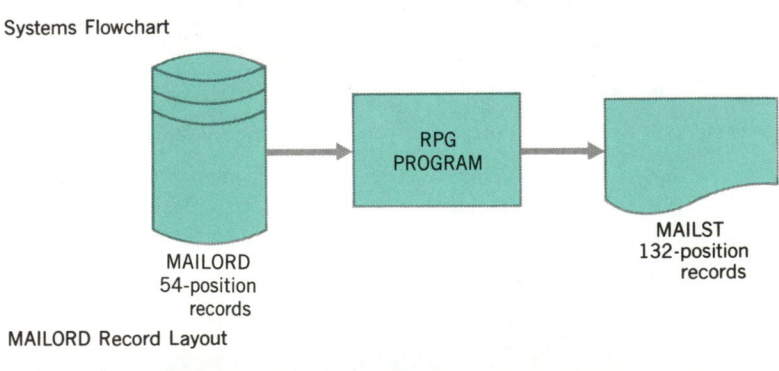

MAILORD Record Layout

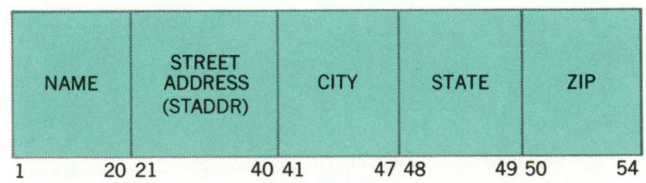

MAILST Printer Spacing Chart

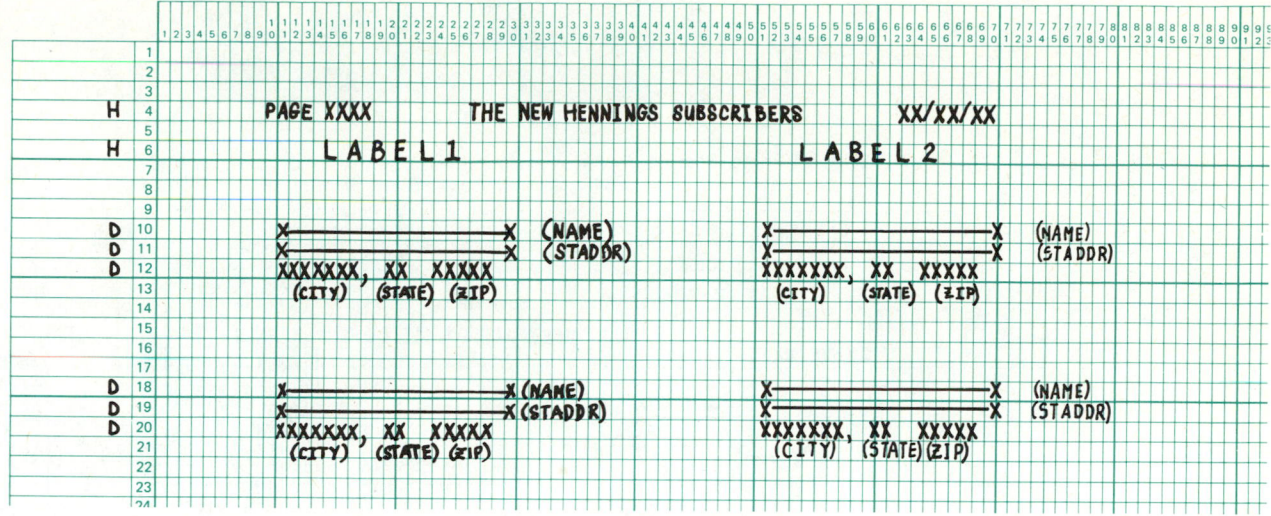

Notes

a. For every input record read, *three* lines of output will be generated.

b. Label 1 and Label 2 contain identical information.

c. Each input record produces three detail lines containing two labels.

4. Consider the following and write the RPG program to produce the desired results:

Systems Flowchart

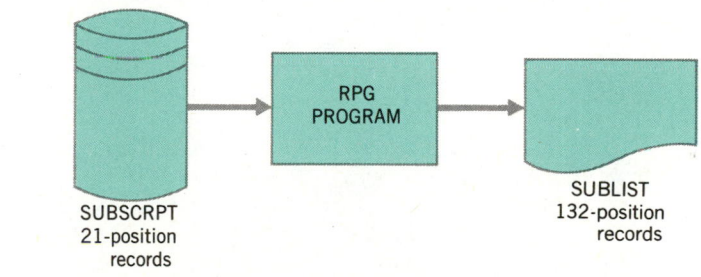

SUBSCRPT Record Layouts

Name record

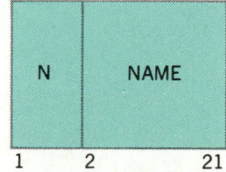

Street record

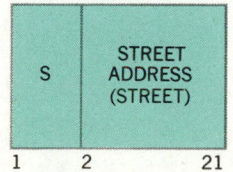

City, State, Zip
record

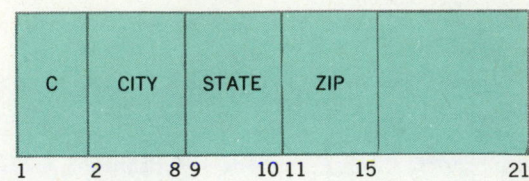

1   2   8 9   10 11   15   21

SUBLIST Printer Spacing Chart

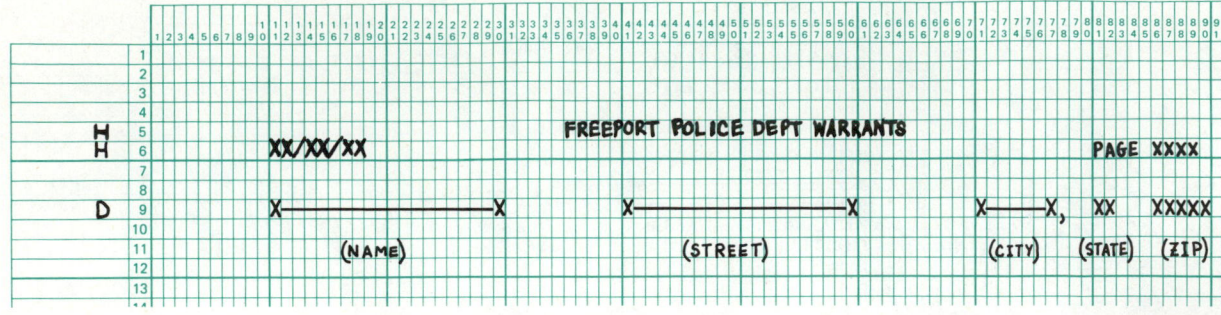

Notes

a. The Name record precedes the Street record, which precedes the City, State, and Zip record.

b. For every three input records read, one output line will print.

3

Arithmetic Operations

END-OF-CHAPTER AIDS
   Chapter Self-Test
   Key Terms
   Review Questions
   Debugging Exercises
   Programming Assignments

OBJECTIVES

To familiarize you with

1. The programming concepts related to arithmetic operations, counting, and accumulating totals.
2. How numeric fields are established in RPG for calculations and editing operations when totals are printed.
3. The ADD, SUBtract, MULTiply, and DIVide operations and their basic features.
4. Entering calculations correctly on the coding sheets for complex arithmetic operations.
5. How the correct size of Result Fields is determined for various arithmetic operations.
6. The differences between rounding and truncation.
7. How to move or copy data during calculations.
8. Structured concepts and the use of Data Structures.

I. Overview

A. Calculation Specifications

The Calculation Specifications form (Figure 3.1) performs the necessary arithmetic operations of adding (ADD), subtracting (SUB), multiplying (MULT), and dividing (DIV). The Calculation Specifications form is used to indicate:

1. Each calculation to be performed, which is coded on a separate line, in the sequence in which it is to be executed.
2. The fields or constants used in the calculations.
3. The Result Field names or receiving fields of the arithmetic operations.
4. Whether subsequent operations should or should not be executed depending on which indicators have been set.

The Calculation Specifications form is divided into three parts:

Conditions (Columns 7–17)

This area identifies the indicators controlling the conditions for which operations are to be performed. The area is subdivided into *total time conditions* (columns 7–8) and *detail time conditions* (columns 9–17). Detail calculations conditioned by detail indicators are always specified first, followed by total time calculations conditioned by total indicators.

Operation (Columns 18–53)

This area specifies the operation to be performed and identifies the data used in the operation. Only one operation may be specified per line on the Calculation Specifications form.

Tests (Columns 54–59)

This area sets indicators depending on the results of the arithmetic operation being performed.

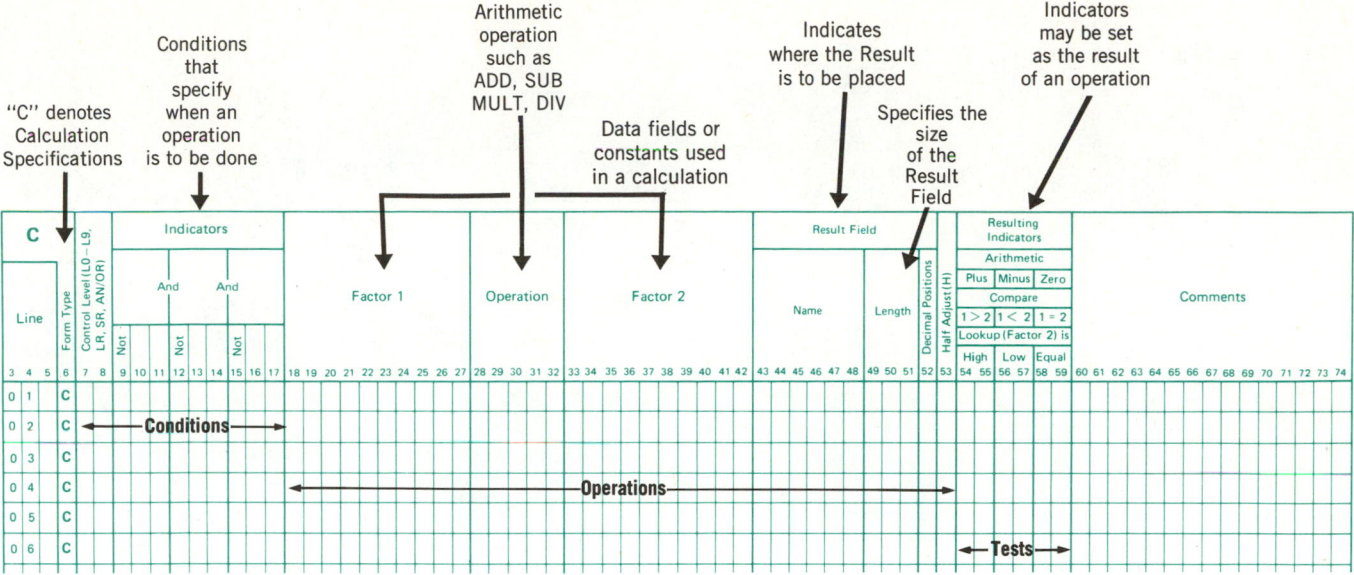

Figure 3.1
RPG Calculation
Specifications form.

B. Sample Program 1

The following sample program illustrates many of the concepts that will be taught in this chapter. The purpose of the program is to print from a payroll file the regular and overtime hours worked by each employee, as well as the total hours worked. The program consists of the File Description form, Input Specifications form, Calculation Specifications form, and Output Specifications form. When coded, the instructions on these forms must be entered into the computer system in the order indicated if a program is to function properly.

Moreover, an understanding of the RPG Logic Cycle is necessary in order for the programmer to arrange instructions in the proper sequence. The execution of the program occurs in time frames that correspond to the specific form being used. For instance, the traditional Input-Process-Output cycle may be thought of as being executed first by the coding on the Input Specifications form, then the Calculation Specifications form, and finally the Output Specifications form. Indicators are used during these different time frames to control the operations to be performed in RPG. The problem definition for the sample program is specified in Figure 3.2. The program itself is illustrated in Figure 3.3. Study this program before continuing.

C. Indicators

Calculations may be performed selectively depending on the setting of specific indicators. Indicators are "switches" that may be set "on" or "off" to check for (1) the presence of a particular condition such as a blank field on an input record, (2) the condition resulting from a comparison (high, low, or equal), or (3) the existence of a specific record type. Consider the Input Specifications in Figure 3.3. Note that indicator 10 is set on each time an input record is read. The Calculation and Output Specifications forms will use indicator 10 to indicate when operations on each input record are to be performed by the program.

Let us now consider the RPG Logic Cycle. Prior to reading a record from the file, indicator 10 is automatically set off by the RPG Logic Cycle. But whenever a new record is read, indicator 10 will be set on and the subsequent

Figure 3.2

Problem definition for Sample
Program 1

Systems Flowchart

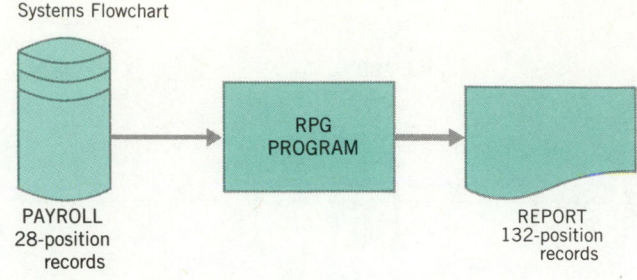

PAYROLL   REPORT
28-position   132-position
records   records

PAYROLL Record Layout

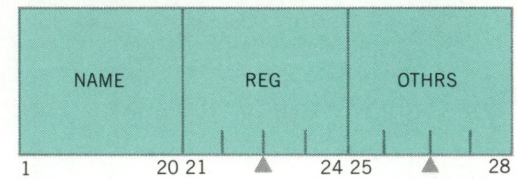

REPORT Printer Spacing Chart

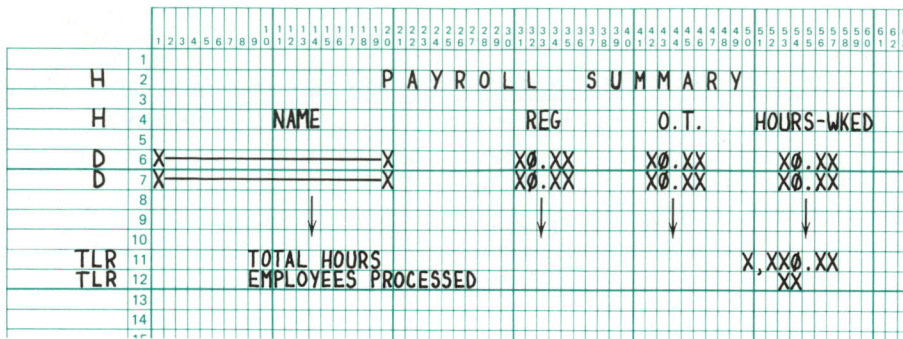

operations referencing this indicator will be executed as the program steps
through the different time frames.

In general, indicators are set on as the result of a test and used to specify
when calculations and output are to be performed. Misused indicators produce
unclear programs; therefore, care must be taken in the use of indicators. One
method for reducing errors is to use indicators sparingly and in the correct way.
A rule of thumb for indicators is "each indicator in a program should have only
one function." Using an indicator for two or more functions makes a program
difficult to follow and maintain. Proper indicator use is a key to better RPG
programs. Structured programming techniques illustrated in subsequent chapters will demonstrate ways in which the use of indicators can be limited.

Let us now turn our attention to the RPG Logic Cycle.

D. The RPG Logic Cycle

Figure 3.2 includes the Printer Spacing Chart as part of the problem definition.
The flowchart in Figure 3.4 depicts the steps necessary to produce the output
specified by the Printer Spacing Chart.

Examining the logic diagram in Figure 3.4, we find that calculations are
performed on each record being processed. Indicator 10 is turned on each time

Figure 3.3
Coding sheets for Sample
Program 1.

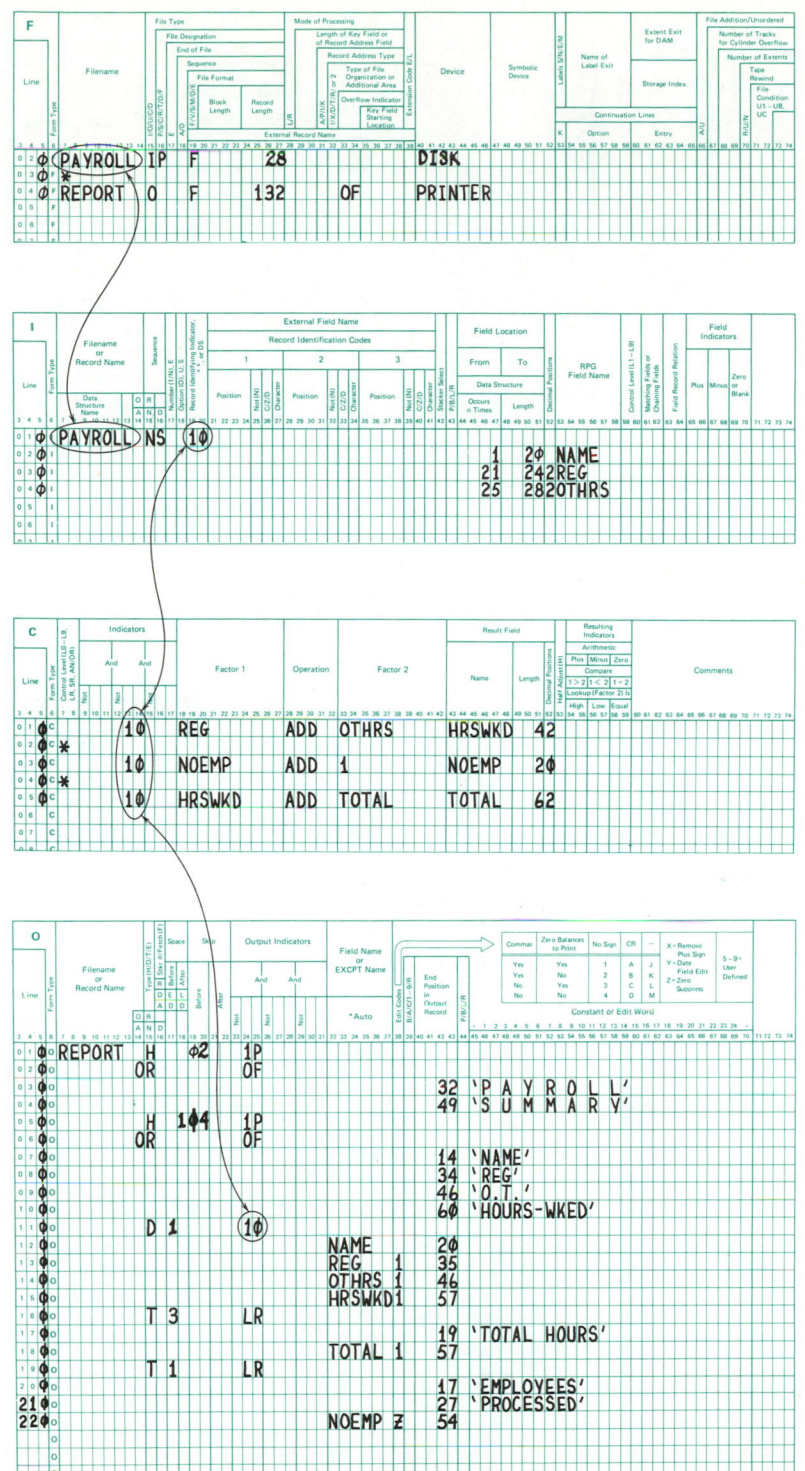

a record is read. Remember RPG uses indicators to determine if the calculation should be made. If a calculation was required only on records with a "B" in position 1, we would use an indicator to identify these records. The indicator (indicator 02) would then be used to execute the calculation (see Figure 3.5).

The sequence in which the instructions are executed in RPG is again dependent on the logic cycle. The correspondence between the operations to be performed, the indicators, and the coding forms used is illustrated here:

Indicators	Operation	Form
1. 1P or OF	Headings are printed on the first pass or when a page overflow condition exists.	Output form
2. Record Indicator (Ø1-99)	A data record is read into the computer.	Input form
3. (None)	Input data is moved to the respective input fields.	(Automatic)
4. Record or Resulting Indicator (Ø1-99)	Detail calculations are performed if the corresponding indicator is on.	Calculation form
5. Record or Resulting Indicator (Ø1-99)	Detail output is produced if the corresponding indicator is on.	Output form
6. (Repeat cycle)	Repeat step 2, using the next record.	(Repeat cycle)

Referring to the detail lines of the Printer Spacing Chart in Figure 3.2, note that the regular hours are added to the overtime hours to produce a third or Result Field containing total hours worked. This calculation is performed *as each record is processed*, since an indicator (indicator 1Ø) is set each time an input record is read. The total hours field prints on the same line as the input fields. Reviewing the RPG logic diagram in Figure 3.4, note that detail calculations and detail output will result for each record entered as input. As we have already learned, indicators such as LR are also used to control end-of-job routines and total line output, which are explained later in the chapter. For the present, however, we will focus on detail calculations.

Figure 3.4
Steps necessary to produce the output specified by the Printer Spacing Chart.

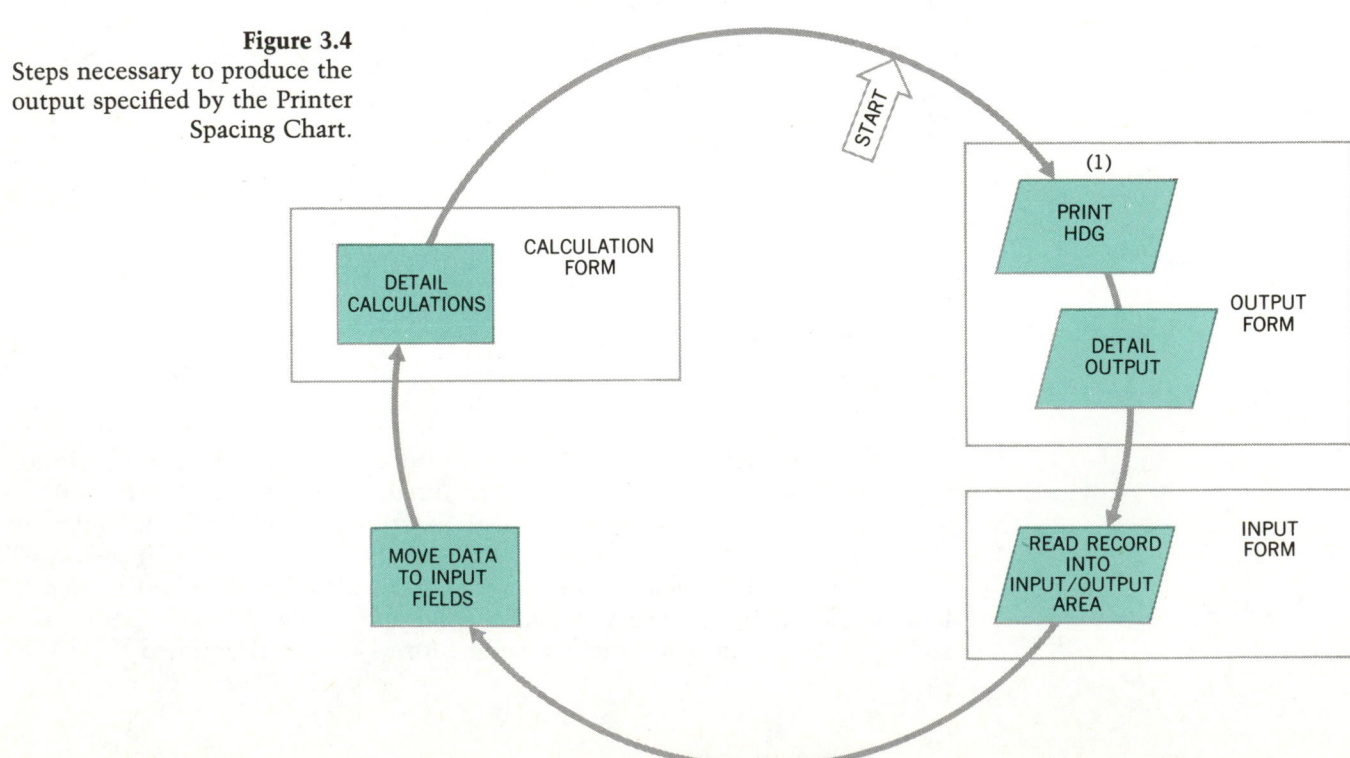

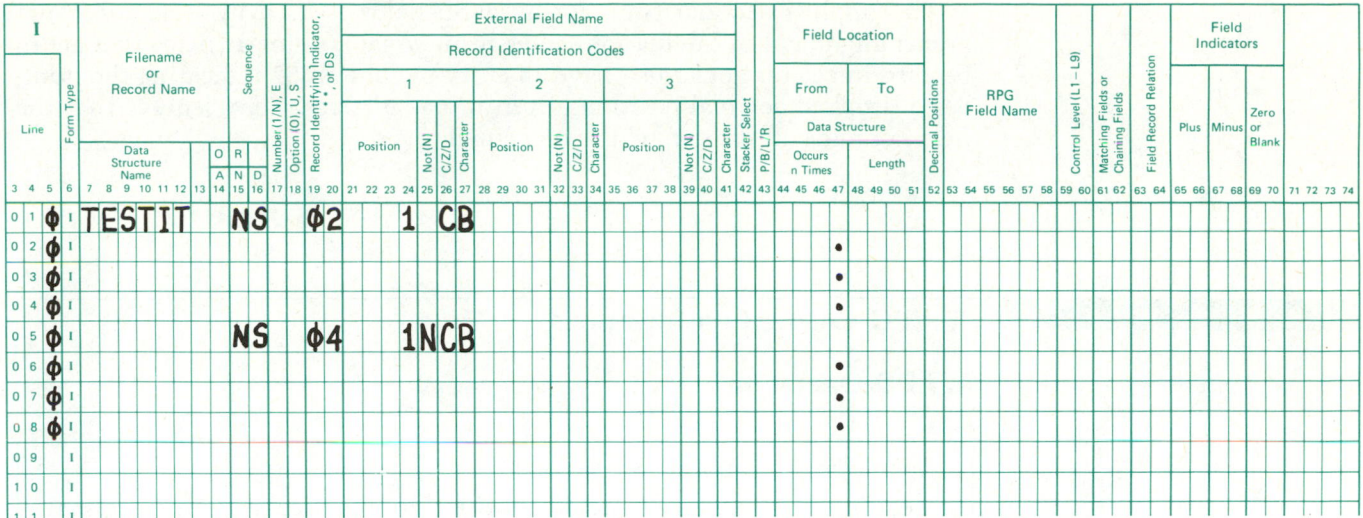

Record indicators

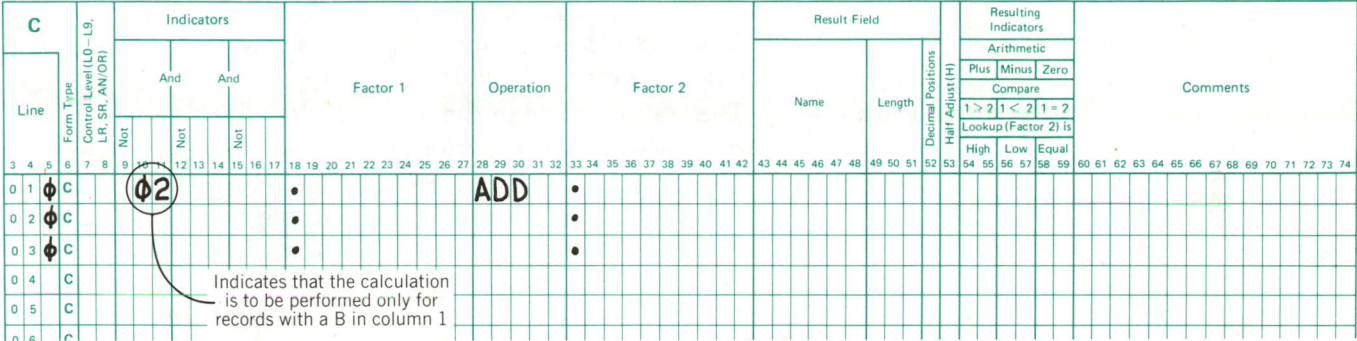

Indicates that the calculation
is to be performed only for
records with a B in column 1

Figure 3.5
The relationship between the
Input and Calculation
Specifications with respect to
Record Indicators.

E. Defining Numeric Fields

Calculations can be performed only on fields containing numeric data. Specifying an input field as numeric requires the programmer to enter a digit in column 52, Decimal Positions, on the Input Specifications form. If column 52 is left blank, the computer assumes the corresponding field to be alphameric, not numeric. Thus, calculations and editing will *not* be permitted on incoming fields that are specified on the Input Specifications form with a blank in column 52.

The Input form for the sample program is illustrated in Figure 3.3. In the sample program, the input records are contained in the PAYROLL file. In addition to the standard entries, column 52 contains a numeric entry for the number of decimal positions in those fields to be used in arithmetic operations. The fields named REG and OTHRS both contain a "2" in column 52, indicating that these fields are numeric and that two decimal positions are implied.

It is important to remember that the input record does not contain *actual* decimal points; rather, decimal points are implied. To include the decimal point would waste storage space. Recall that 12345 entered as input will be interpreted by the computer as $123_\wedge 45$ if a 2 is specified in column 52.

The implied decimal point for numeric fields is used by RPG to ensure proper alignment in calculations and editing. Again, numeric fields that are to be used in calculations *must* have an entry in column 52 indicating the number of implied decimal positions, even if it is 0 (zero). Zero denotes that the field contains all integers with no decimal places.

II. RPG Coding Considerations

A. ADD Operation

Operation:	ADD
Meaning:	Add two fields together to produce a sum. Decimal alignment will be maintained.
Factors:	Factor 1 and Factor 2 are added. The contents of these fields do not change unless one of the factors is also used in the Result Field. Factors 1 and 2 may be either numeric fields or numeric literals.
Result:	The sum is stored in the Result Field, which may be the same as Factor 1 or Factor 2.
Limitation:	Make certain the Result Field is large enough for the answer (usually at least one position longer than the larger field used in the ADD). Factor 1, Factor 2, and the Result Field must be numeric. Factor 1 or Factor 2 may be a numeric literal. The result must always be a field name, never a literal.

The **ADDition operation** has the following two instruction formats:

Format 1
(Use Factor 1, Factor 2, and
Result Field)

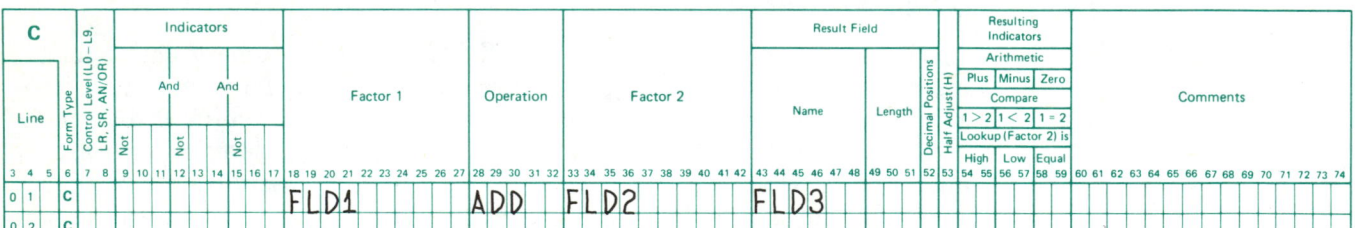

The contents of the field or literal in Factor 1 is added to the contents of the field or literal in Factor 2. The answer is stored in the Result Field. A numeric literal is a constant that is always fixed with the same value. Numeric literals will be discussed in more detail in the next section.

Another way of stating this instruction format is: ADD Factor 1 and Factor 2 *GIVING* the Result Field.

The following are examples of the ADD operation using Format 1:

Calculation Specifications — Form 1

Line	Form Type	Indicators	Factor 1	Operation	Factor 2	Result Name	Length	Dec
01	C*							
02	C	10	REG	ADD	OTHRS	TOTHRS	42	
03	C*							
04	C	10	NOEMP	ADD	1	NOEMP	20	
05	C*							
06	C	10	HRSWKD	ADD	TOTAL	TOTAL	62	
07	C							

Format 2
(Use Factor 2 and Result Field)

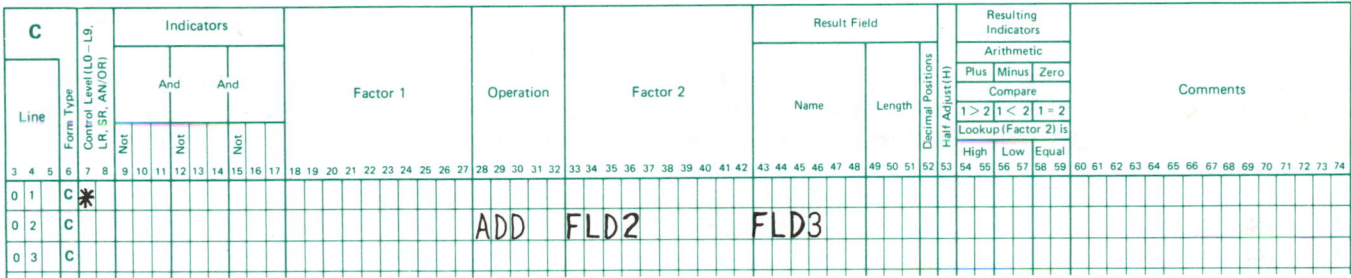

Line	Form Type	Factor 1	Operation	Factor 2	Result Name
01	C*				
02	C		ADD	FLD2	FLD3
03	C				

If Factor 1 is *not* present, Factor 2 is added to the Result Field, and the sum is placed in the Result Field. Hence, Format 2 should be used when a field is to be increased by the value of another field or literal. Format 2 is most often used for incrementing totals or counters. This instruction format can also be stated as ADD Factor 2 *TO* the Result Field. Note that Format 2 is not available with all RPG compilers.

The following are examples of the Format 2 ADD operation:

Line	Form Type	Indicators	Operation	Factor 2	Result Name	Length
01	C*					
02	C	10	ADD	1	NOEMP	20
03	C*					
04	C	10	ADD	HRSWKD	TOTAL	62
05	C					

In both formats, the result, or sum, of an ADD operation is always placed in the Result Field. The only field that is altered as a result of an ADD operation, regardless of the format used, is the Result Field.

Again, it should be noted that only one arithmetic operation can be performed on each line of the Calculation Specifications form.

B. Numeric Literals

Earlier, we discussed the organization of data as it is coded on the Input Specifications form. By defining files, records, and fields and assigning corresponding user-defined data-names in the Input Specifications, we reserve storage for data. These fields described on the Input Specifications form are said to contain *variable data*.

Variable data is the data that is entered into storage when the program reads a record. The contents of the fields containing variable data are not known until the program is actually executed. We say, then, that the contents of data fields coded on the Input Specifications form is *variable* because it changes each time a new record is read.

A **constant** or **literal,** on the other hand, is a form of data required for processing that is *not* dependent on input data. A constant, as opposed to variable data, may be coded directly on the Calculation Specifications form. Suppose, for example, that we wish to increase each commission field (ECOMM) of every input record by 100.00, a fixed bonus amount. The 100.00 bonus is *not* a variable amount in the input record but is nevertheless required for processing. We call 100.00 a *constant*, since it is a form of data required for processing that always has the same value.

We saw in Chapter 2 how a fixed value could be specified as an **alphanumeric constant** or **literal** on the Output Specifications form. Headings, end-of-job messages, and summary total messages are all examples of alphanumeric constants. We will see later how to use alphanumeric constants on the Calculation Specifications form. In this chapter, we will use numeric literals as constants in calculations.

A **numeric literal** is a constant used primarily for arithmetic operations. When actual numeric values are specified as one of the factors to be used in a calculation, they are referred to as numeric literals or constants.

A numeric literal entered on the Calculation Specifications form may be from 1 to 10 characters long and may contain a decimal point as well as a plus or minus sign. If the field is negative or signed positive, the sign must be the left-most character in the field. The decimal point, if used, must be included in the constant.

The rules for forming numeric literals are as follows:

Summary for Numeric Literals

1. A numeric literal may contain only the digits Ø-9, a decimal point, and a sign (+ or −).

2. The maximum length of a numeric literal is 1Ø digits, including a sign and a decimal point. This permits a maximum amount of 9,999,999.99 if dollars and cents were to be represented or 9,999,999,999 for integers. (Commas would *not* be specified in the numeric literals.)

3. Numeric literals are left-justified when entered in Factor 1 or Factor 2 of the Calculation Specifications form.

4. Numeric literals do not contain dollar signs, commas, blanks, or any other alphameric character.

> 5. Numeric literals may include a sign as the left-most character and a decimal point.
>
> 6. Unsigned literals are assumed positive. If the literal is negative, the minus sign must be the left-most character.

Typical examples of numeric literals are illustrated below:

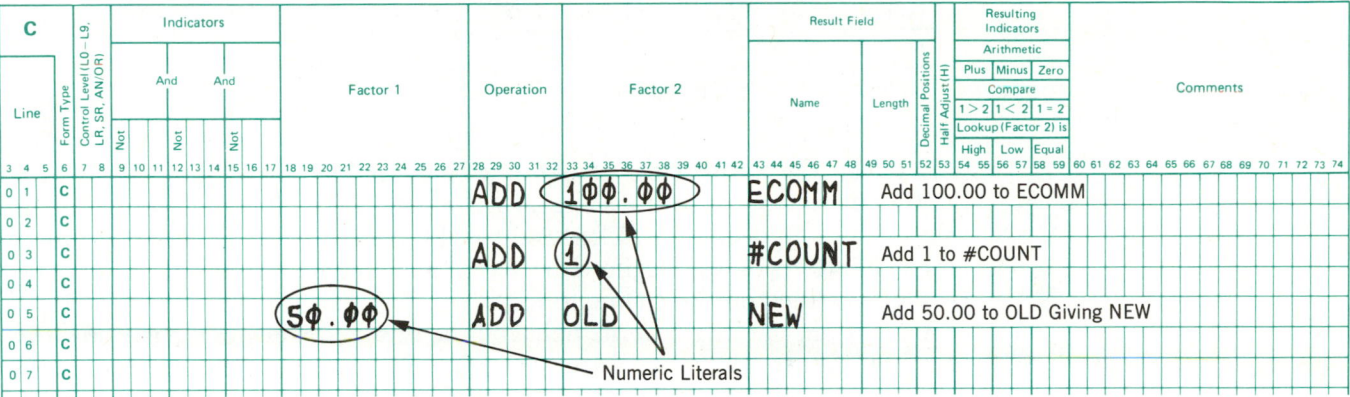

Numeric Literals

Again, the same rules apply when using numeric literals as with other numeric fields.

C. Typical ADDition Operations

Let us examine in detail the general types of ADDition operations that are typically used in RPG programs.

1. Finding the sum of two fields.
2. Adding to a counter.
3. Accumulating a running total.
4. Adding more than two fields.

1. Finding the Sum of Two Fields

In Figure 3.6, which is an excerpt from the sample program in Figure 3.3, Format 1 is used. The contents of Factor 1 and Factor 2 are added together, and the sum is placed in the Result Field. Thus, in this example, regular hours (REG) are added to the overtime hours (OTHRS) giving the Result Field, hours worked (HRSWKD). The fields REG and OTHRS remain unchanged, while the original contents of HRSWKD is replaced with the result or sum. The original content of HRSWKD does not in any way affect the arithmetic operation.

The addition takes place only when indicator 10 is "on." Recall that this indicator is set on each time an input record is read. The field names specified in **Factor 1, Factor 2,** and the Result Field are all left-justified. Decimal positions within the values of the fields are automatically aligned by RPG during calculations; therefore, result values are algebraically correct.

You must specify where the result of a calculation is to be stored by naming that field in positions 43 through 48 on the Calculation Specifications form. The field that is entered can be a new field or one already defined on the Input or Calculation Specifications form.

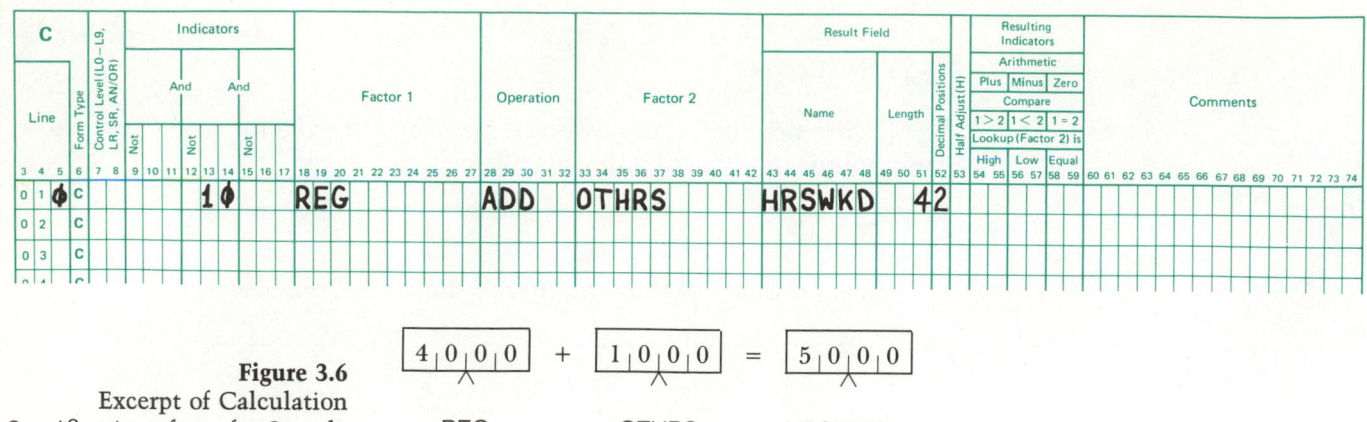

Figure 3.6
Excerpt of Calculation
Specifications form for Sample
Program 1.

In effect, the Result Field (HRSWKD) is being defined by the programmer on the Calculation Specifications form. Factor 1 and Factor 2 could be reversed in this and all ADD operations. The Result Field name, like all field names, must be six characters or less, begin with a letter, and contain letters and digits only. It is left-justified on the coding form.

In addition, the length of the field and the number of decimal positions it is to contain must also be specified. If the Result Field specifications for length and decimal positions have been previously defined on the Calculation or Input Specifications form, then they must *not* be repeated. To illustrate this point, the following Calculation Specifications form will compute a value for HRSWKD using a two-step process:

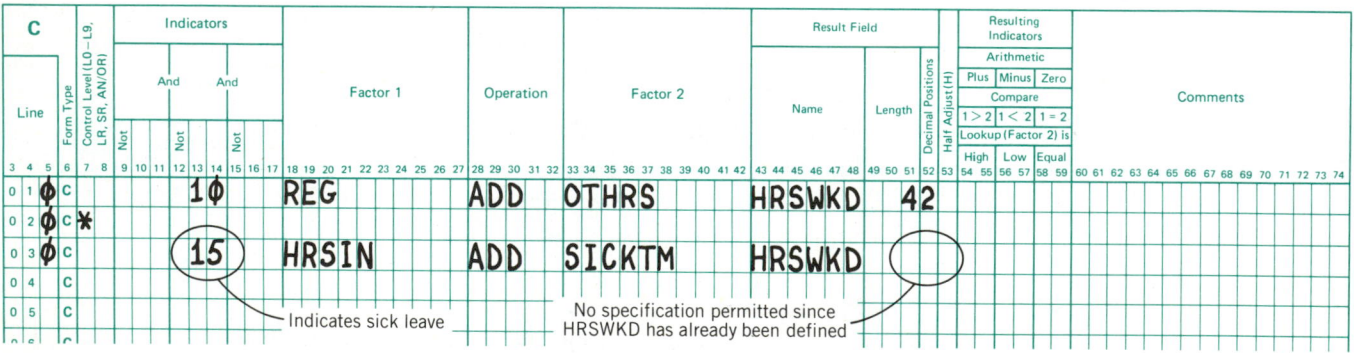

When indicator 10 is on, HRSWKD is calculated in the usual way by adding REG and OTHRS.

If indicator 15 is on, however, HRSWKD = SICKTM + HRSIN. Note that HRSWKD contains length and decimal specifications only *once*, the first time the field is referenced on the form. You can assume that the field called HRSWKD is initialized at zero, since RPG initially sets all fields to zero at the beginning of the program. Different indicators are being used by the different formulas; therefore, the calculation to be performed depends on whether indicator 10 or 15 is on. Remember:

> **Rule:** Fields may be defined only *once* in an RPG program. That is, the field length and the number of decimal positions are coded once for a Result Field.

Fields can be defined in only three places within an RPG program—as an input field or a Data Structure subfield on the Input Specifications form, or as a Result Field in the Calculation Specifications. If a field name does not appear in one of these three places, an undefined variable compile error will occur.

a. Result Fields: **The Problem of Truncation.** The Result Field must be of sufficient size to store the maximum value that can be obtained as a result of the calculation. When in doubt about how long to make a field, the programmer should add one position to the length of the field. This will ensure that **truncation,** or loss of significant digits, does not occur. Truncation may occur in two different ways.

High-Order Truncation

High-order truncation occurs when an insufficient number of integer positions are assigned to the left of the decimal point. If, for example, an attempt is made to store the number 123ʌ45 in a field consisting of four positions with two decimal positions, high-order truncation will occur. That is, the left-most digit, 1, would be lost.

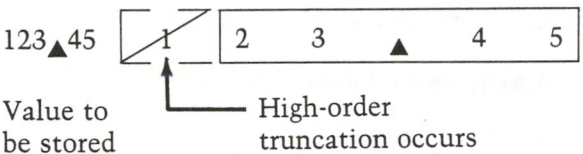

Value to   High-order
be stored   truncation occurs

To determine the size of a Result Field, perform the arithmetic operations required using the largest conceivable values for the factors. For example, if you assume that regular hours are 4Ø or less and that overtime hours may be as high as 99, then the largest result in HRSWKD would be 139, which is a three-digit integer field.

To determine the size of THRS (an abbreviation for total hours), or any running total field, you must know the approximate number of records to be processed for each run. If 139 is the maximum HRSWKD and you typically process 8Ø records or less, then the largest possible value for THRS would be 139 × 8Ø or 111ZØ, which is a five-digit integer field.

Low-Order Truncation

Low-order truncation occurs when low-order digits, usually to the right of the decimal point, are truncated. This may be as serious a problem as high-order truncation. For example, if the value 123ʌ45 were stored in a four-digit field containing one decimal position, then the following would result:

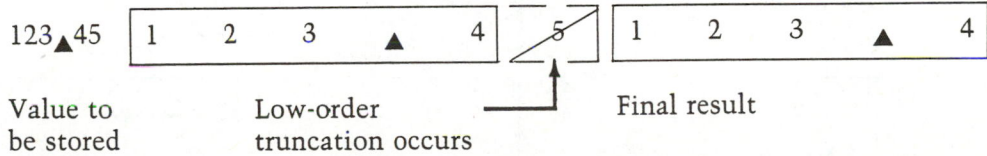

Value to   Low-order   Final result
be stored   truncation occurs

This type of truncation still retains the most significant digits of the original field.

Both these truncation problems can be avoided if the programmer takes the time to determine the maximum size of the field needed for the particular application. Usually the programmer knows in advance the number of decimal positions required for a resultant field. The Printer Spacing Chart is a helpful aid in establishing the size of printed fields, since the location, and thus length, of each field is specified.

b. Field Location in an ADD Operation.   The fields or literals in Factor 1 and Factor 2 may be interchanged for the ADD operation. Transposing the two fields will not affect the result of the operation. In all cases, the Result Field will be the receiving field in an ADD operation. Consider this example:

C		Control Level (L0 – L9, LR, SR, AN/OR)	Indicators				Factor 1	Operation	Factor 2		Result Field				Resulting Indicators				Comments
			And	And										Arithmetic				
										Name	Length	Decimal Positions	Half Adjust (H)	Plus	Minus	Zero		
														Compare				
Line	Form Type		Not	Not	Not									1 > 2	1 < 2	1 = 2		
														Lookup (Factor 2) is				
														High	Low	Equal		
0 1	C			1 0		REG	ADD	OTHRS		HRSWKD	4 2							
0 2	C	*																
0 3	C			1 0		OTHRS	ADD	REG		HRSWKD	4 2							
0 4	C																	

Both statements add the two operands to produce the same results.

2. Adding to a Counter

Counter Concept

A **counter** is used to record how many times an event occurs in a program. Typically, counters are used to count input records, count output lines, and record the number of errors that may occur during the execution of a program. In the sample program in Figure 3.3, the number of employees is counted as each input record is processed. The field called NOEMP (Number Of EMPloyees) will have the value "1" added to it each time indicator 10 is "on." Recall that indicator 10 is turned on each time a record is read. Thus, NOEMP will keep track of the number of employee records processed. Since the counter starts out with an initial value of zero, and one is added each time a record is read and processed, the counter will always reflect the number of employee records processed. In Figure 3.7, the number 1 is a numeric literal or constant (either statement will increment NOEMP by 1).

Counter Summary

Concept: A literal or numeric value is added to a field each time an event occurs.

Figure 3.7
Alternate ways of adding to a counter.

C		Control Level (L0 – L9, LR, SR, AN/OR)	Indicators				Factor 1	Operation	Factor 2		Result Field				Resulting Indicators				Comments
			And	And										Arithmetic				
										Name	Length	Decimal Positions	Half Adjust (H)	Plus	Minus	Zero		
														Compare				
Line	Form Type		Not	Not	Not									1 > 2	1 < 2	1 = 2		
														Lookup (Factor 2) is				
														High	Low	Equal		
0 1	C					NOEMP	ADD	1		NOEMP								FORMAT 1
0 2	C	*																
0 3	C						ADD	1		NOEMP								FORMAT 2
0 4	C																	

Output: Final total counters are usually printed at the end of the run after the last record has been processed , at which time the LR indicator is automatically turned "on."

Remember, counters are used to add a numeric value such as one (1) each time an event occurs. This keeps track of the number of times the event has occurred.

As you can see, the previous addition operations that add to counters can use either Format 1 or Format 2. You can use Format 2 when the Result Field is to be increased by the value of a specific field or literal. With this format, the contents of Factor 2 is added to the Result Field, with no need for a Factor 1. The original value of the receiving field, the Result Field, will be changed. Note, however, that not all compilers accept the second format.

3. Accumulating a Running Total

A **running total** is used to sum or add up the value of a specific field defined in the program. Again, referring to the sample report, note that TOTAL represents the sum or accumulation of all the hours worked (HRSWKD). TOTAL is initialized to zero at the beginning of the program by RPG. This running total is accumulated by adding HRSWKD to total hours (TOTAL) as each employee record is processed. Once HRSWKD is determined by adding REG and OTHRS, it is then added to the total field. The final result reflects the total accumulation of the hours worked.

Consider the instruction in Figure 3.8. This would cause the following calculations to be executed as each record is processed:

Input Record	HRSWKD	+ TOTAL	Giving	TOTAL
Start	0.00	0.00		0.00
1	50.00	0.00		50.00
2	44.50	50.00	$\longrightarrow$	94.50
3	46.30	94.50		140.80
4	52.00	140.80		192.80

The TOTAL field would be printed when the LR indicator is set, that is, after the last record has been processed. The printing of a total line will be discussed in detail at the end of this chapter.

Figure 3.8
Sample ADD operation.

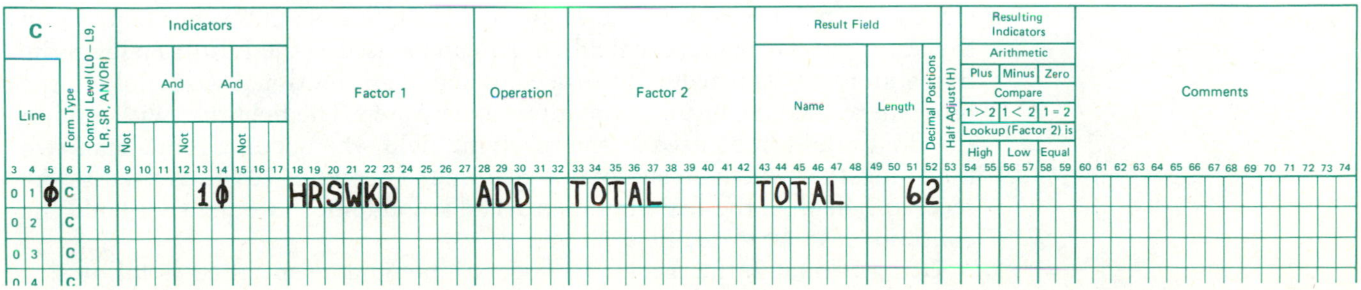

Line	Form Type	Control Level (L0–L9, LR, SR, AN/OR)	Indicators						Factor 1	Operation	Factor 2	Result Field				Resulting Indicators		Comments
			And		And							Name	Length	Decimal Positions	Half Adjust (H)	Arithmetic / Compare / Lookup		
				Not		Not		Not										
0 1	Ø C		1 Ø						HRSWKD	ADD	TOTAL	TOTAL	62					
0 2	C																	
0 3	C																	
0 4	C																	

Summary for Running Total

Concept: A field is added to the total field as each record is processed.

Output: Totals may be printed at the end of the run after the last record has been processed and the LR indicator is "on," or whenever totals are desired.

Other examples of calculations that produce running totals are:

C		Indicators			Factor 1	Operation	Factor 2	Result Field			Resulting Indicators	Comments
Line	Form Type	Control Level (L0–L9, LR, SR, AN/OR)	And Not / And Not / Not		Factor 1	Operation	Factor 2	Name	Length	Decimal Positions / Half Adjust (H)	Arithmetic Plus Minus Zero / Compare 1>2 1<2 1=2 / Lookup (Factor 2) is High Low Equal	Comments
0 1	C				HRSWKD	ADD	THRS	THRS				Add HRSWKD to THRS
0 2	C											
0 3	C				PAY	ADD	TPAY	TPAY				Add PAY to TPAY
0 4	C											
0 5	C				DEDUCT	ADD	TDEDT	TDEDT				Add DEDUCT to TDEDT
0 6	C											
0 7	C											Meaning
0 8	C											

4. Adding More than Two Fields

Note that with both instruction formats, the ADD operation is restricted to two operands. Often, calculations require more than two fields to be added together. Let us consider the following example in which three fields are to be added together in order to produce a total:

```
FLDA + FLDB + FLDC = TOTAL
```

To add FLDA, FLDB, and FLDC in order to produce a total, two steps are required in RPG as illustrated here:

C		Indicators			Factor 1	Operation	Factor 2	Result Field			Resulting Indicators	Comments
Line	Form Type	Control Level (L0–L9, LR, SR, AN/OR)	And Not / And Not / Not		Factor 1	Operation	Factor 2	Name	Length	Decimal Positions / Half Adjust (H)	Arithmetic Plus Minus Zero / Compare 1>2 1<2 1=2 / Lookup (Factor 2) is High Low Equal	Comments
0 1	0 C		10		FLDA	ADD	FLDB	TOTAL	62			
0 2	0 C*				TOTAL	ADD	FLDC	TOTAL				
0 3	0 C		10		TOTAL	ADD	FLDC	TOTAL				
0 4	C											

In this example, the first ADD statement adds together the contents of FLDA and FLDB and places the result in the field TOTAL. This is an intermediate step since FLDC must be added next. A subtotal of FLDA and FLDB is not required in this example. Therefore, the field TOTAL can be used as the Result Field on the first statement. This reduces the need to define an additional work field in the program to hold the result of the intermediate step. The field that will contain the final total can be used as the receiving field when adding more than two fields together where no subtotal is required. Therefore, TOTAL is used as the receiving field on the first statement. The second ADD statement will add the contents of FLDC to the field TOTAL.

Using Format 2, the second ADD operation could be specified as follows:

C			Indicators						Factor 1	Operation	Factor 2	Result Field				Resulting Indicators						Comments
			And		And							Name	Length			Arithmetic						
Line	Form Type	Control Level (L0–L9, LR, SR, AN/OR)		Not		Not		Not						Decimal Positions	Half Adjust (H)	Plus	Minus	Zero				
																Compare						
																1 > 2	1 < 2	1 = 2				
																Lookup (Factor 2) is						
																High	Low	Equal				
3 4 5	6	7 8	9 10 11	12 13 14	15 16 17	18 19 20 21 22 23 24 25 26 27	28 29 30 31 32	33 34 35 36 37 38 39 40 41 42	43 44 45 46 47 48	49 50 51	52	53	54 55	56 57	58 59	60 61 62 63 64 65 66 67 68 69 70 71 72 73 74
0 1	C						ADD	FLDC	TOTAL						
0 2	C														

Self-Test

1. The Calculation Specifications form of a program is used to code all _____.

2. Each operation of a calculation to be performed must be specified on a _____ line.

3. When executing an ADD operation, the Result Field must be a _____ field.

4. A _____ literal is a constant used primarily for arithmetic operations.

5. A constant's _____ never changes in the program.

6. The sum of an ADD operation is always placed in the _____ .

7. _____ truncation occurs when an insufficient number of integer positions are assigned to the left of the decimal point.

8. (T or F) The fields or literals in Factor 1 and Factor 2 may be interchanged in the ADD operation.

9. A _____ is used to record how many times an event occurs in a program.

10. A _____ is used to accumulate the sum for a specific field from several input records.

Use a Calculation Specifications form to code the solutions to Questions 11 through 16:

11. Add a field called HRS into a running total called THRS when indicator 10 is on. Assume HRS is defined on the Input Specifications form and THRS is a seven-position field with two decimal places defined in a Data Structure.

12. Add a field called GROSS into a field called TOTAL when indicator 15 is on. Assume GROSS has been defined on the Input Specifications and TOTAL is a seven-position field with two decimal places defined in a Data Structure on the Input Specifications form.

13. Add a field called GRADE into a running total called AVG when indicator 20 is on. Assume GRADE and AVG have been defined previously.

14. Add one to a three-position counter called CTR when indicator 25 is on. Assume that CTR has not yet been defined.

15. Increment a four-position counter named ODD by two each time indicators 10 and 15 are both on.

16. Add a previously defined field called CREDIT into a total field named TCRED (eight positions, two decimal places) when indicator 35 or 45 is on.

Solutions

1. processing or arithmetic operations
2. separate
3. numeric variable (not a literal)
4. numeric
5. value
6. Result Field
7. High-order
8. T
9. counter
10. running total

11.

Line	Form Type	Indicators	Factor 1	Operation	Factor 2	Result Field Name	Length
01	C	10	HRS	ADD	THRS	THRS	
02	C*			—OR—			
03	C	10	THRS	ADD	HRS	THRS	
04	C*			—OR—			
05	C	10		ADD	HRS	THRS	
06	C						

Note: THRS is defined on the Input Specifications form as a Data Structure.

12.

Line	Form Type	Indicators	Factor 1	Operation	Factor 2	Result Field Name	Length
01	C	15	GROSS	ADD	TOTAL	TOTAL	
02	C*			—OR—			
03	C	15	TOTAL	ADD	GROSS	TOTAL	
04	C*			—OR—			
05	C	15		ADD	GROSS	TOTAL	
06	C						

13.

Line	Form Type	Indicators	Factor 1	Operation	Factor 2	Result Field Name	Length
01	C	20	GRADE	ADD	AVG	AVG	
02	C*			—OR—			
03	C	20	AVG	ADD	GRADE	AVG	
04	C*			—OR—			
05	C	20		ADD	GRADE	AVG	
06	C						

14.

Line	Form Type	Indicators	Factor 1	Operation	Factor 2	Result Field Name	Length
01	C	25	CTR	ADD	1	CTR	30
02	C*			—OR—			
03	C	25	1	ADD	CTR	CTR	30
04	C*			—OR—			
05	C	25		ADD	1	CTR	30
06	C						

15.

Line	Form Type	Control Level	And (Not)	And (Not)	Factor 1	Operation	Factor 2	Result Field Name	Length	Dec Pos	Comments
01	C		10	15	ODD	ADD	2	ODD	40		
02	C	*				——OR——					
03	C		10	15	2	ADD	ODD	ODD	40		
04	C	*				——OR——					
05	C		10	15		ADD	2	ODD	40		

16.

Line	Form Type	Control Level	And (Not)	And (Not)	Factor 1	Operation	Factor 2	Result Field Name	Length	Dec Pos	Comments
01	C		35								
02	C	OR	45		CREDIT	ADD	TCRED	TCRED	82		
03	C	*				——OR——					
04	C		35								
05	C	OR	45		TCRED	ADD	CREDIT	TCRED	82		
06	C	*				——OR——					
07	C		35								
08	C	OR	45			ADD	CREDIT	TCRED	82		
09	C										
10	C										
11	C										

Note: Only the last line of an OR condition contains the calculations.

D. SUBtraction Operation

Operation:	SUB
Meaning:	Subtract one numeric field from another. Decimal alignment will be maintained.
Factors:	Factor 2 is subtracted from Factor 1 to produce a result. The contents of these factors *do not change* (unless either field is used as a result). Factors 1 and 2 can be numeric fields or numeric literals.
Result:	The difference of Factor 1 − Factor 2 is placed in the Result Field.
Limitations:	Make certain the Result Field is large enough to accommodate the answer. The order of the factors is important and affects the results obtained. Result = Factor 1 − Factor 2

The **SUBtraction operation** has the following two instruction formats:

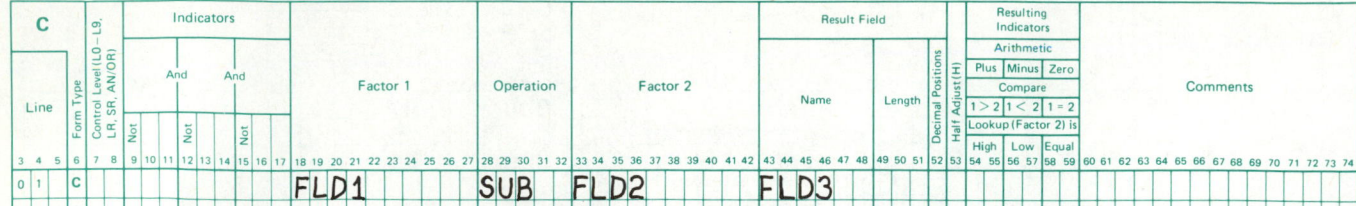

Format 1
(Use Factor 1, Factor 2, and Result Field)

Line	Form Type	Control Level (L0–L9, LR, SR, AN/OR)	Indicators And Not	And Not	Not	Factor 1	Operation	Factor 2	Result Field Name	Length	Decimal Positions	Half Adjust (H)	Resulting Indicators	Comments
0 1	C					FLD1	SUB	FLD2	FLD3					

The contents of the field or literal in Factor 2 is subtracted from the contents of the field or literal in Factor 1. The difference is stored in the Result Field specified in columns 43–48.

Unlike the ADD operation, Factor 1 and Factor 2 *cannot* be interchanged. Reversing the two fields will change the operation, placing the difference of Factor 2 minus Factor 1 in the Result Field.

Format 2
(Use Factor 2 and Result Field)

Line	Form Type	Control Level (L0–L9, LR, SR, AN/OR)	Indicators And Not	And Not	Not	Factor 1	Operation	Factor 2	Result Field Name	Length	Decimal Positions	Half Adjust (H)	Resulting Indicators	Comments
0 1	C						SUB	FLD2	FLD3					
0 2	C													

If Factor 1 is *not* present, Factor 2 is subtracted from the Result Field, and the difference is placed in the Result Field.

In both formats the result of a SUB operation is always placed in the Result Field. The only field that is altered as a result of a subtract operation is the Result Field. Note that Format 2 is not available with all RPG compilers. Check to see if it is available with yours.

Figure 3.9 illustrates the SUBtraction operation using Format 1.

In the example shown in Figure 3.9, indicator 20 must be "on" if the subtraction is to take place. The PRICE field identified as Factor 1 is entered in

Figure 3.9
Sample SUBtraction operation.

Line	Form Type	Control Level (L0–L9, LR, SR, AN/OR)	Indicators And Not	And Not	Not	Factor 1	Operation	Factor 2	Result Field Name	Length	Decimal Positions	Half Adjust (H)	Resulting Indicators	Comments
0 1 0	C		20			PRICE	SUB	DISCT	COST	52				

PRICE	–	DISCT	=	COST
2 3 4 0 0 ▲	–	2 3 4 0 ▲	=	2 1 0 6 0 ▲

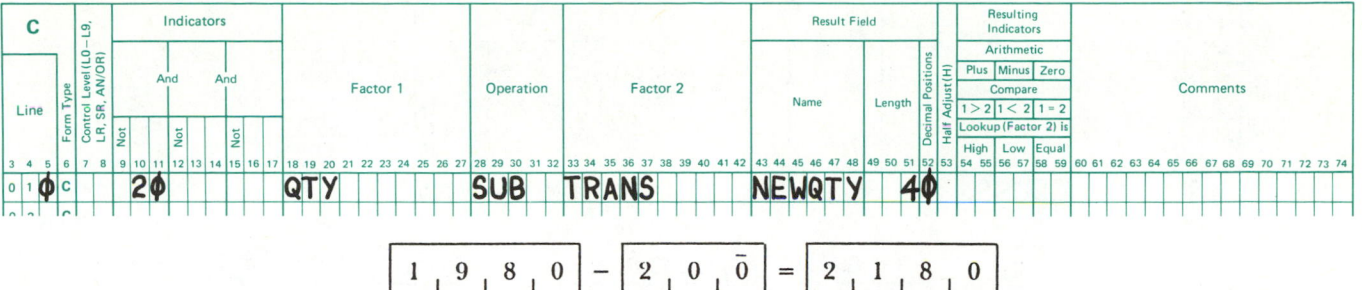

Figure 3.10
Subtraction of a negative quantity from a positive quantity.

columns 18–27 and, as an alphanumeric name, is left-justified. The DISCT field identified as Factor 2 is coded in columns 33–42, also left-justified. Factor 1 minus Factor 2 will produce a difference or answer to the SUBtraction operation in the Result Field. This result or difference is stored in the Result Field named COST. Since COST has not been previously defined, the length and number of decimal positions must be specified in columns 49–51 and column 52, respectively. The operation is entered in columns 28–32 and is again left-justified: names are left-justified, while numeric values are right-justified. We will see at the end of this chapter that it is best to use Data Structures defined on the Input Specifications form to define and describe result fields.

The format for the SUBtraction operation is easy to remember if you think of the calculation as Factor 1 minus Factor 2 giving a Result Field containing the difference.

When subtracting negative numbers, the results may sometimes be confusing unless you are familiar with the rules for subtracting signed numbers. Essentially, there is one basic rule to follow:

SUBTRACTING A NEGATIVE NUMBER

Rule: Change the sign of the number to be subtracted (Factor 2) and proceed as in addition.

Figure 3.10 illustrates the subtraction of a negative quantity from a positive quantity:

$$1980 - (-200) = 1980 + 200 = 2180$$

Numeric literals can be used as either Factor 1 or Factor 2 in a SUBtraction operation. Additional examples of the SUBtraction operation are as follows:

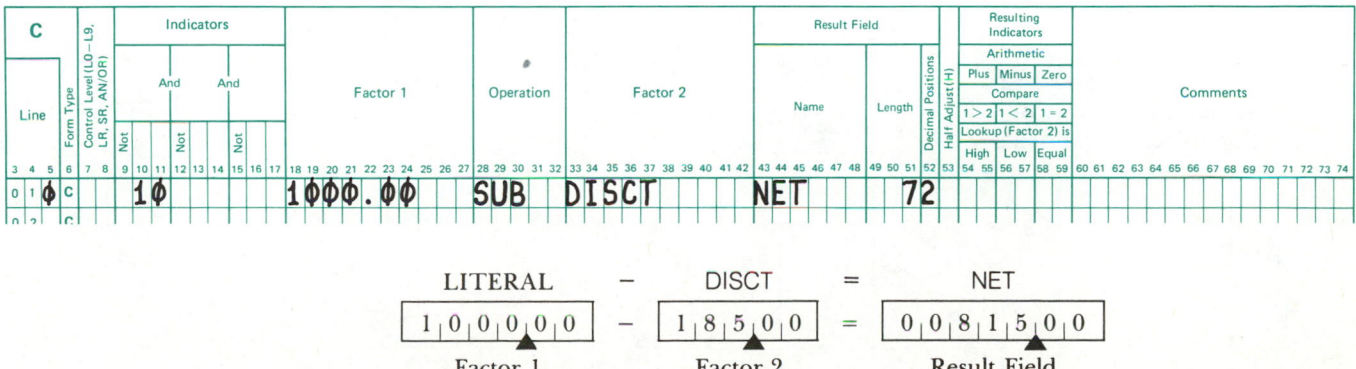

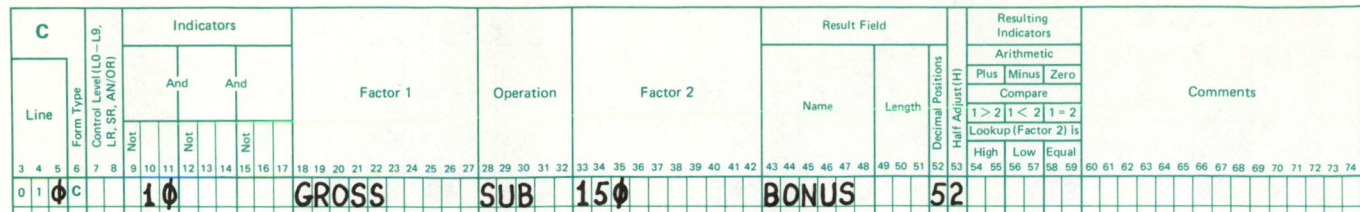

GROSS   —   LITERAL   =   BONUS

| 4 | 8 | 0 | 0 | 0 | — | 1 | 5 | 0 | 0 | 0 | = | 3 | 3 | 0 | 0 | 0 |

Factor 1   Factor 2   Result Field

E. Clearing Fields in Storage

1. Using the SUB Operation

The need to reinitialize a field to zero often arises in a program; frequently, this reinitialization is required when a particular indicator is "on." The example in Figure 3.11 illustrates how the SUB operation could set the DEPHRS field to zero when indicator 15 is "on."

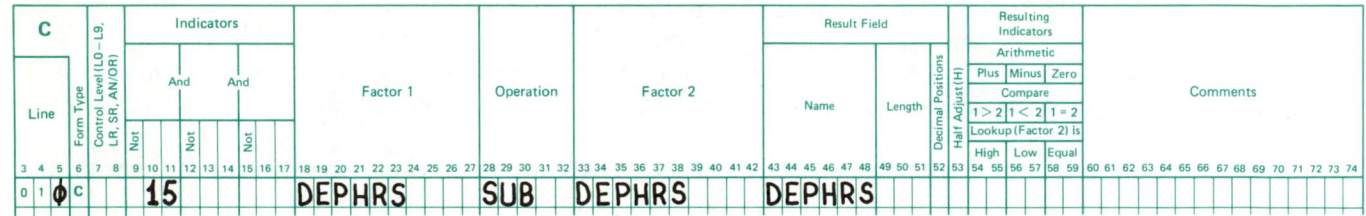

DEPHRS   —   DEPHRS   =   DEPHRS

| 3 | 3 | 5 | — | 3 | 3 | 5 | = | 0 | 0 | 0 |

Figure 3.11
Using the SUB operation to set a field to zero when a designated indicator is on.

Format 2 of the SUB operation can also be used to zero out the contents of a field. See Figure 3.12, which uses Format 2. When using Format 2, the contents of Factor 2 is subtracted from the Result Field. The original value of the Result Field will be changed. Thus, in this example the difference between DEPHRS

Figure 3.12
Use of Format 2 of the SUB operation to zero out a field.

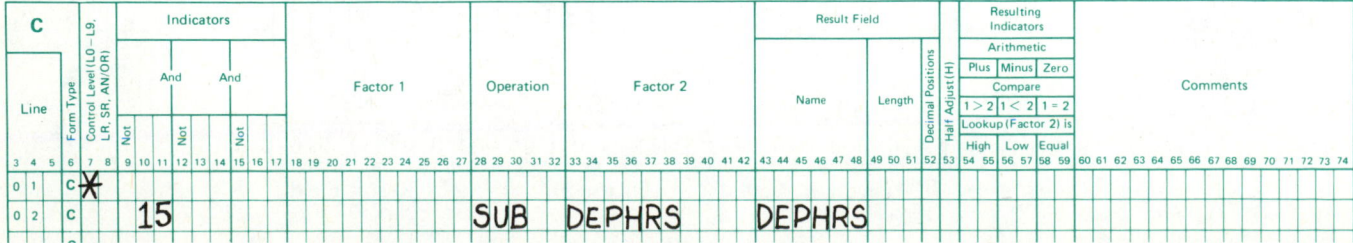

and DEPHRS, which is zero, is placed in DEPHRS. Check if this format is available with your compiler.

2. Using the Z-ADD Operation

Other methods can be used to "clear" or "initialize" a field to zero. The **zero-and-add (Z-ADD) operation** may be used to initialize or set a field to zero or to save the contents of a numeric field that would be lost as a result of the looping procedure used by the RPG cycle. The net effect of this operation is to move or copy data from one storage location to another after clearing the result area. Typically, the Z-ADD operation appears as follows:

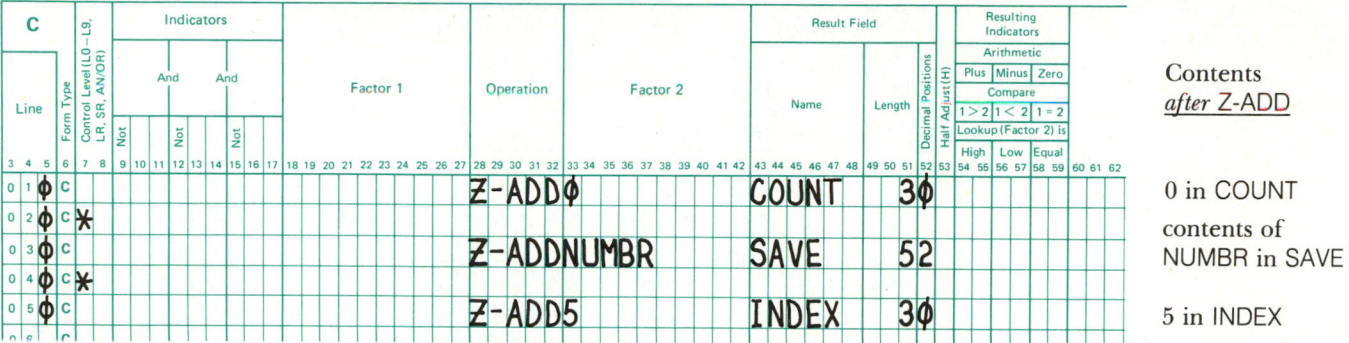

	Contents *after* Z-ADD
Z-ADDØ COUNT 3Ø	0 in COUNT
Z-ADDNUMBR SAVE 52	contents of NUMBR in SAVE
Z-ADD5 INDEX 3Ø	5 in INDEX

Factor 1 is not used in the Z-ADD operation. The Z-ADD operation causes the field specified as the Result Field to be initialized at zero first. The data referenced in Factor 2 is then copied or moved to the Result Field. The first example, in which Ø is Z-ADDed to COUNT, is another method for initializing a field. The following examples illustrate this concept and display the contents of storage before and after each operation shown is executed:

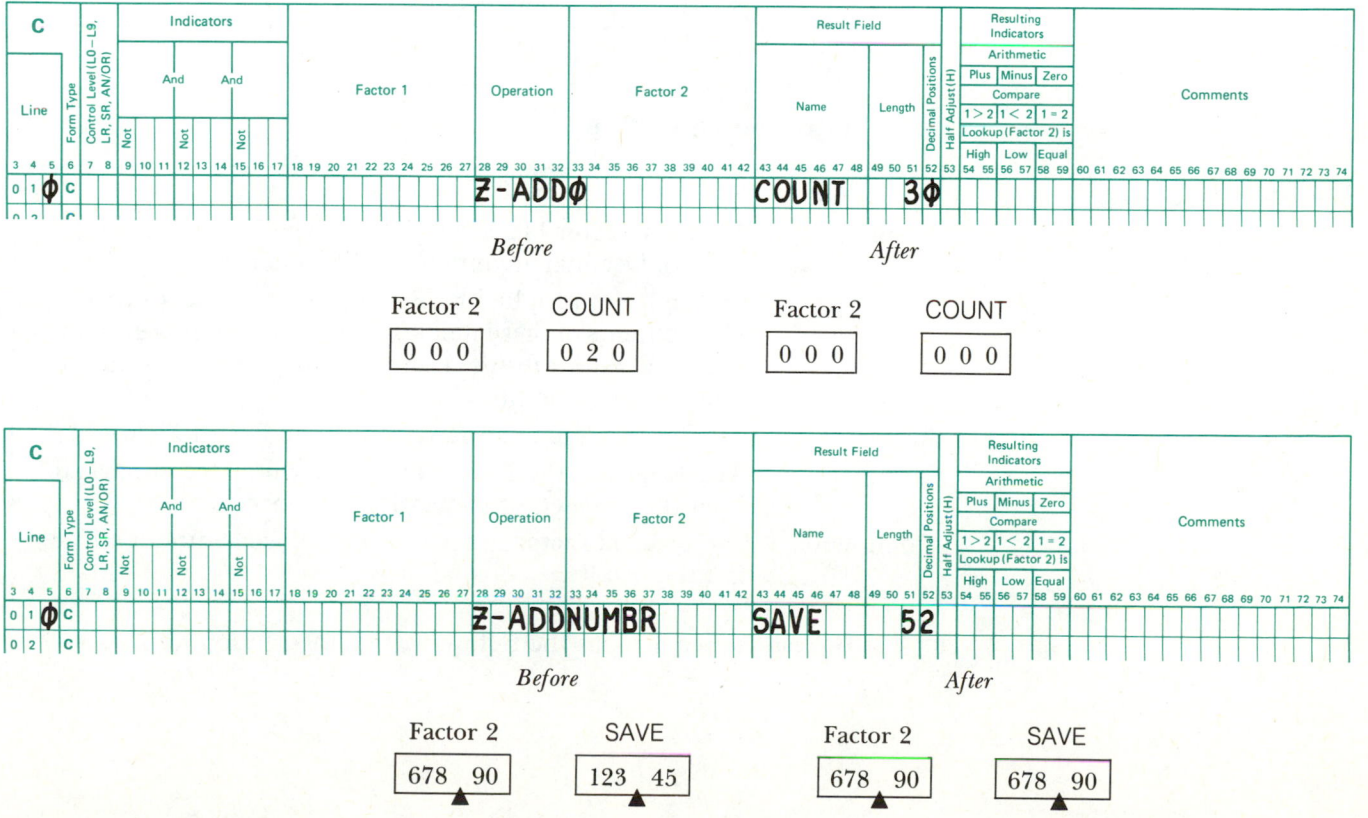

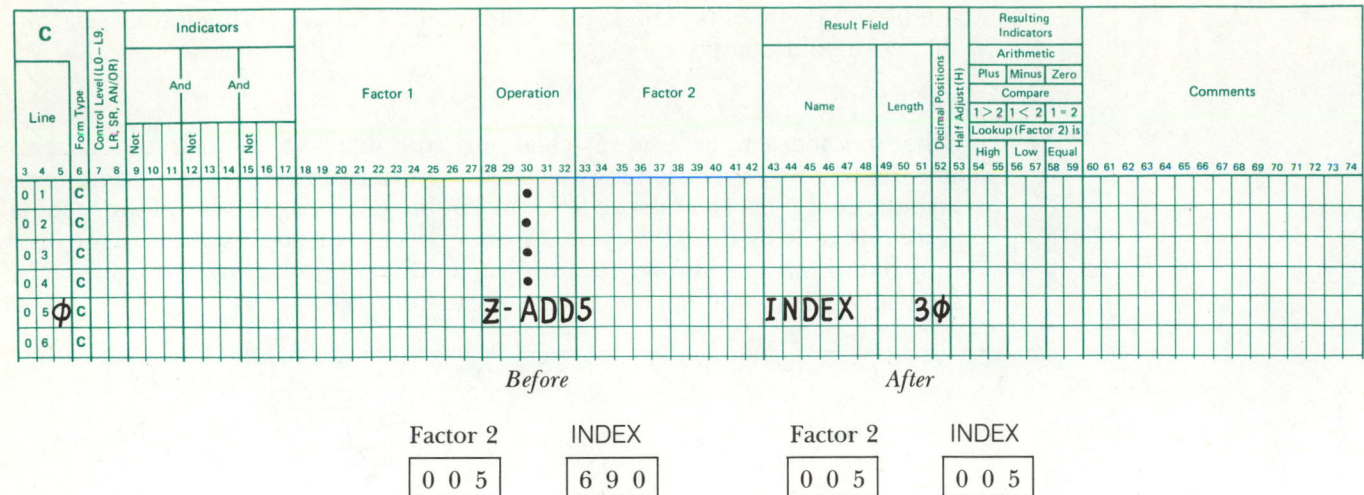

Before   *After*

Factor 2   INDEX   Factor 2   INDEX

| 0 | 0 | 5 | | 6 | 9 | 0 | | 0 | 0 | 5 | | 0 | 0 | 5 |

The `Z-ADD` operation can be summarized as follows:

Operations:	`Z-ADD`
Meaning:	Zero the Result Field, and then move the contents of Factor 2 to the Result Field. Decimal alignment will be maintained.
Factors:	Factor 1 is not used. Factor 2 contains the numeric data to be copied or moved to the Result Field.
Result:	Factor 2 is copied to the Result Field.
Limitations:	The Result Field must be large enough to store the answer. Factor 2 may be a numeric literal.

F. MULTiplication Operation

Operation:	`MULT`
Meaning:	Multiply Factor 1 (the multiplicand) by Factor 2 (the multiplier). Decimal alignment will be maintained.
Factors:	Factor 1 is multiplied by Factor 2 to produce a product. The contents of these fields do not change unless either is specified as the result. Factors 1 and 2 can be numeric fields or numeric literals.
Result:	The resulting product is stored in the Result Field.
Length:	The length of the Result Field must be large enough to hold the product, or truncation may occur.
Comments:	Factor 1 and Factor 2 may be interchanged without affecting the results.

The **MULTiplication operation** has the following two instruction formats:

Format 1
(Use Factor 1, Factor 2, and Result Field)

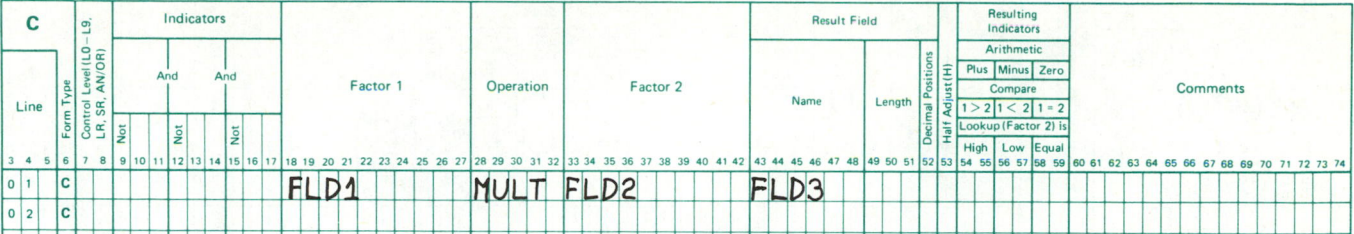

C	Form Type	Control Level (L0 — L9, LR, SR, AN/OR)	Indicators						Factor 1	Operation	Factor 2	Result Field					Resulting Indicators					Comments
Line			And		And							Name	Length	Decimal Positions	Half Adjust (H)	Arithmetic						
			Not		Not		Not									Plus	Minus	Zero				
																Compare						
																1>2	1<2	1=2				
																Lookup (Factor 2) is						
3 4 5	6	7 8	9 10 11	12 13	14 15	16 17	18 19 20 21 22 23 24 25 26 27	28 29 30 31 32	33 34 35 36 37 38 39 40 41 42	43 44 45 46 47 48	49 50 51	52	53	High 54 55	Low 56 57	Equal 58 59	60 61 62 63 64 65 66 67 68 69 70 71 72 73 74
0 1	C						FLD1	MULT	FLD2	FLD3									
0 2	C																		

The contents of the field or literal in Factor 1 is multiplied by the contents of the field or literal in Factor 2. The answer or product is stored in the Result Field.

The MULT operation is similar to the ADD operation in that Factor 1 and Factor 2 can be interchanged. Reversing the two fields contained in Factor 1 and Factor 2 will not affect the result.

Format 2
(Use Factor 2 and Result Field)

C	Form Type	Control Level (L0 — L9, LR, SR, AN/OR)	Indicators						Factor 1	Operation	Factor 2	Result Field					Resulting Indicators				Comments
Line			And		And							Name	Length	Decimal Positions	Half Adjust (H)	Arithmetic				
																Plus	Minus	Zero			
0 1	C ✳																		
0 2	C							MULT	FLD2	FLD3									
0 3	C																		

If Factor 1 is *not* present, the Result Field is multiplied by Factor 2, and the product is placed in the Result Field. (**Note:** Check to see if Format 2 is available with your RPG compiler.)

In both formats, the product of a MULT operation is always placed in the Result Field. The only field that is altered as a result of a multiplication operation is the Result Field.

The input described in Figure 3.13 will be used to demonstrate how multiplication is performed.

Operation to be Performed	Terms	Sample Contents	
PRICE	Multiplicand	999.99	Maximum contents
× QTY	× Multiplier	× 99	
= COST	= Product	= 98,999.01	Maximum result

Determining the Size of the Result Field

Multiplication operations produce Result Fields that usually require more storage than either Factor 1 or Factor 2. The number of digits in the product field of a multiplication can be determined by *adding* together the number of digits contained in the multiplicand and the number of digits contained in the multiplier.

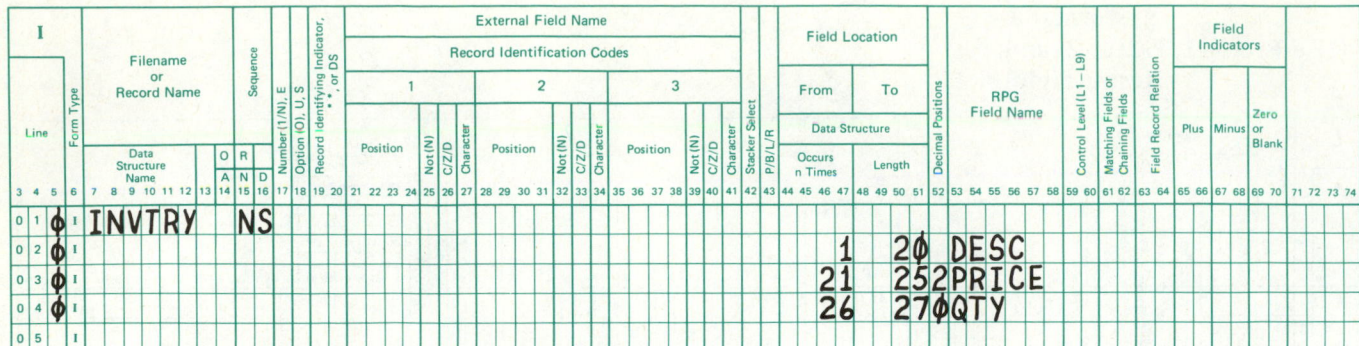

Figure 3.13
Input Specifications to be used
in multiplication example.

		Left of decimal (integers)	Right of decimal	Total no. of digits
Number of digits in multiplicand	=	3	2	5
Number of digits in multiplier	=	2	0	2
Number of digits in product	=	5	2	7

(5 integers, 2 decimal places)

It is essential that the programmer establish a field large enough for the product of a multiplication. If the product field is too small, *truncation* may result. Recall that truncation results in the loss of the most significant digits. In this example, if the programmer had provided a product field six digits in length with two decimal positions, then the Result Field might be too small to store the answer. Hence, the left-most digit could be lost and the results would be incorrect.

If PRICE = 999.99 and QTY = 99 and the product was designated as fewer than five integers, Figure 3.14 would indicate the incorrect results.

Figure 3.14
Example of truncation.

Field containing six digits
including two decimal positions

On most computers,
the left-most digit is lost
due to truncation.

Again, if the multiply operation is to be correctly executed, the programmer must establish the size of the product field very carefully. If you are certain that COST, for example, never exceeds 9,999.99, then a six-digit Result Field would be large enough.

RULES FOR DETERMINING THE FIELD SIZE OF THE PRODUCT

1. Calculate the number of integers (digits to the left of the decimal point) required to hold the product.
2. Decide the number of decimal places (digits to the right of the decimal point) that you would like.
3. Add the two together to determine Result Field length.

To multiply PRICE by QTY and to make certain that the result, called COST, is large enough, code the calculation as shown in Figure 3.15.

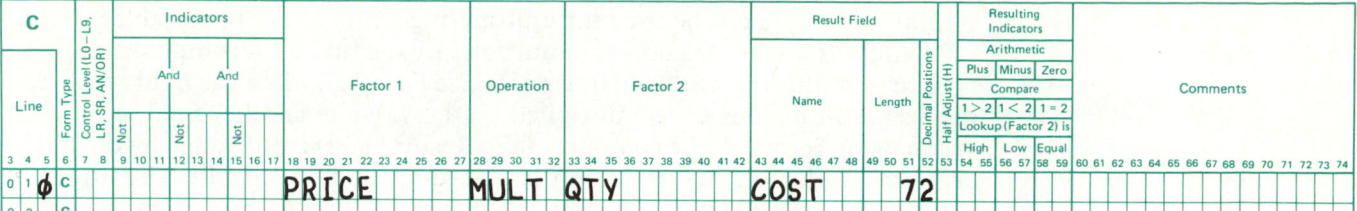

Example

Figure 3.15
Example of MULTiplication.

$$PRICE \qquad QTY \qquad COST$$

$$\boxed{1\,1\,9\,9\,9} \ \times \ \boxed{8\,8} \ = \ \boxed{1\,0\,5\,5\,9\,1\,2}$$

Field Size: 5 (2 decimal places) + 2 = 7 (2 decimal places)

For the multiplication to be performed, the arithmetic operation MULT must be entered in the Operation field in columns 28–32. As with previous illustrations, the variable entries for Factor 1, Factor 2, and the name of the Result Field are left-justified in their respective fields on the Calculation Specifications form.

Example A factor to be used in a MULT operation can be a numeric literal such as:

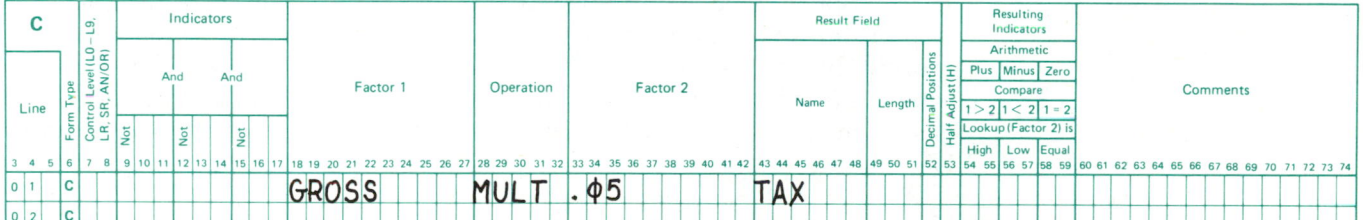

MULTIPLYING 3 NUMBERS TOGETHER

Suppose we want to calculate $D = A \times B \times C$. Note in the following example that the field specifications for D are defined only once, the first time D is used. Note, too, that D can be a factor as in the second operation, as well as a result.

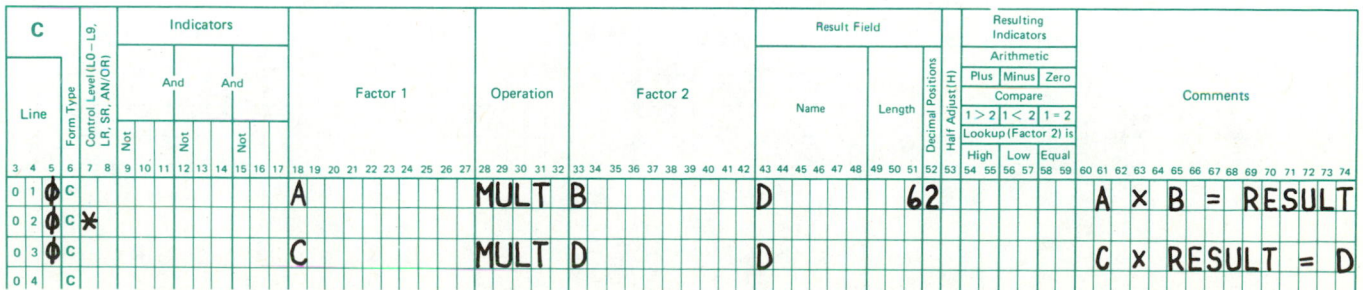

This technique can be used for multiplying any number of variables.

Figure 3.16 illustrates how the multiplication could be accomplished using Format 2 for the second MULT statement. Use Format 2 when the field specified in the Result Field is to be multiplied by the value of another field or literal. When using Format 2, the contents of the Result Field is multiplied by the field or literal in Factor 2 and the result is placed in the Result Field. The original value of the Result Field is replaced. In this example, then, the contents of field D is multiplied by field C and the product is placed in field D.

G. Rounding Concepts

When programming for business applications, results are often expressed as dollars and cents; that is, with two decimal positions. The multiply and divide operations frequently create situations where **rounding** to two decimal places is necessary. For example, the discount (DISC) calculated in the following example will result in a product field containing four decimal digits:

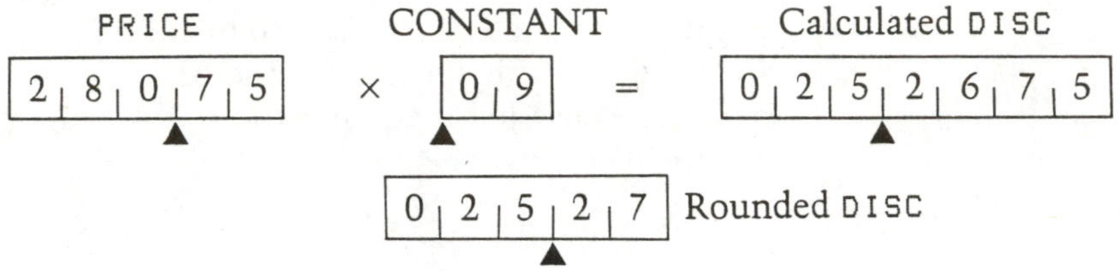

The result of the calculation illustrated is 25.2675. If DISC were specified as four positions in length with two decimal positions, 25.2675 would be truncated and the result would be 25.26. Thus the last two digits would be lost. In business, however, this result would be more properly rounded to 25.27.

Use H in the **Half-adjust** field (column 53) to obtain rounding (see Figure 3.17).

Figure 3.16
Example of MULTiplication using only Factor 2 and the Result Field.

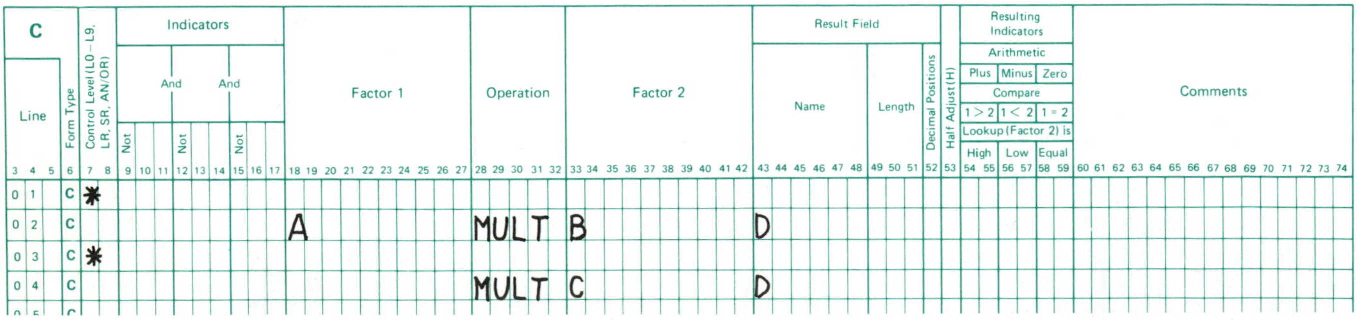

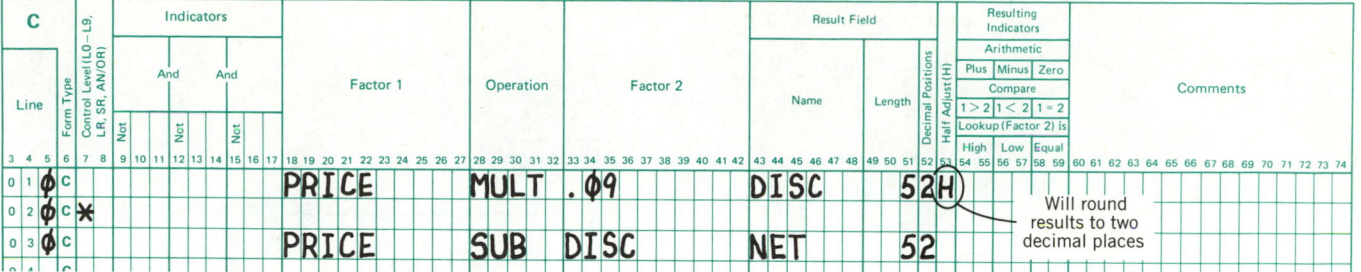

Figure 3.17
Use of the Half-adjust field to
obtain rounding.

To further illustrate the concept of rounding, review the following examples:

Round to the Nearest Cent

Field Contents	Field Rounded
123.4567	123.46
7.9999	8.00
−73.6578	−73.66
9.345	9.35
13.3333	13.33

Round to the Nearest Integer
(Whole Number)

Field Contents	Field Rounded
123.4567	123
7.9999	8
−73.6578	−74
9.345	9
13.3333	13

The rounding calculations are performed as illustrated in Examples 1 and 2 below. Notice that a value of five is added to the digit immediately *to the right of the digit to be rounded.* Once the addition is completed, all digits to the right of the rounded digit are truncated.

Example 1   **Round to the Nearest Cent**

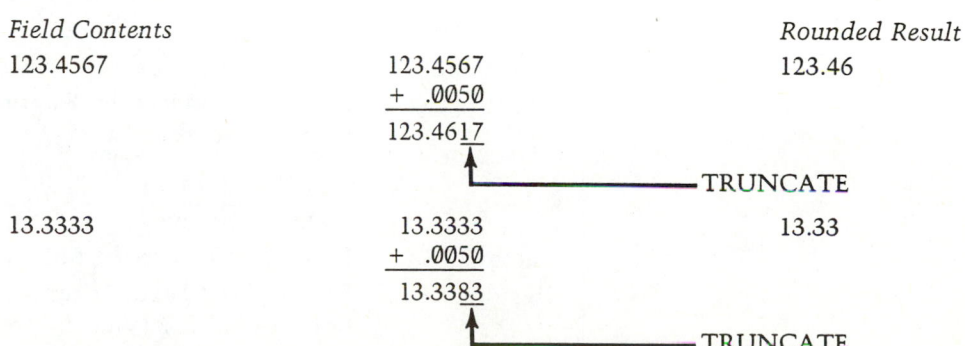

Field Contents		Rounded Result
123.4567	123.4567	123.46
	+ .0050	
	123.4617	
	↑ TRUNCATE	
13.3333	13.3333	13.33
	+ .0050	
	13.3383	
	↑ TRUNCATE	

Example 2   **Round to the Nearest Integer**

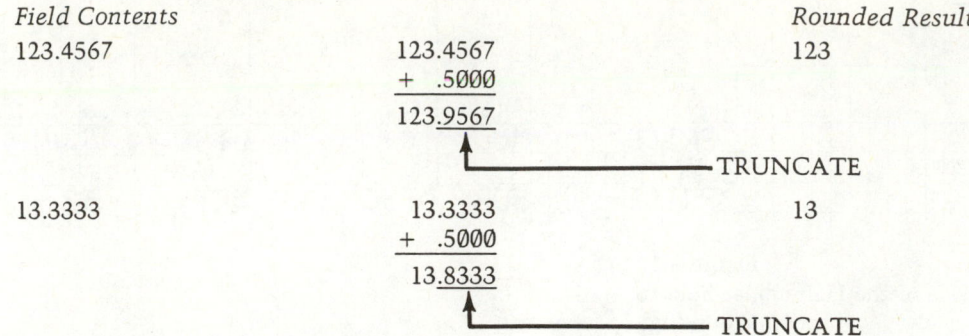

Field Contents   *Rounded Result*
123.4567   123.4567   123
                                    +   .5000
                                    ─────────
                                      123.9567
                                            ↑
                                            └──────────────── TRUNCATE

13.3333   13.3333   13
                                    +   .5000
                                    ─────────
                                       13.8333
                                            ↑
                                            └──────────────── TRUNCATE

A general rule for rounding is that the final result contains the value that is the nearest approximation to the given number. For example, the rounded result in Example 1, 123.46, is closer to 123.4567 than is 123.45. This can be demonstrated as follows:

$$
\begin{array}{r}
123.4567 \\
-123.4500 \\
\hline
.0067
\end{array}
\qquad
\begin{array}{r}
123.4600 \\
-123.4567 \\
\hline
.0033
\end{array}
$$

The error introduced by rounding up and using a value of 123.46 is only .0033, as compared to an error of .0067 that occurs when the result is truncated to 123.45. Therefore, to ensure accuracy and minimize errors resulting from approximation, numbers are rounded by entering an H (Half-adjust) in column 53 of the field to be rounded.

Rounding may also introduce errors when running totals are used in a program. For example, if a bank was to pay 12.4% straight interest on a $1,000 deposit, the investor would expect to receive 124.00 in interest for 1 year (annual interest = .124 × 1,000.00 = $124.00). If the interest were to be paid monthly, the investor would receive the following:

Monthly interest = Annual interest/12 = 124.00/12 = 10.3333

After rounding, the amount of the monthly interest would be 10.33. Twelve payments of 10.33, however, would introduce an error of 4 cents, since 12 times 10.33 = $123.96. Hence, it is critical that the programmer be aware of the errors that may be introduced by rounding and the overall effect on the results produced by the program. In order to compensate for the error just illustrated, an adjustment in the last interest payment would be required.

H. DIVide Operation

Operation:	DIV
Meaning:	Factor 1 is divided by Factor 2. Decimal alignment will be maintained:
	$$\text{Divisor }\overline{\big)\text{Dividend}}\;\;^{\text{Quotient}}$$
Factors:	Factors 1 and 2 can be numeric fields or numeric literals.
Results:	Factor 1 and Factor 2 remain unchanged. The quotient, or result of the DIVide, is referenced by the name entered in the Result Field.

Length: When dividing by a field that is greater than 1, the maximum number of digits in the quotient is equal to the number of digits in the dividend. Additional positions to the right of the decimal may also be specified and rounded.

Limitations: An attempt to divide by zero will cause an error. Factor 2, therefore, cannot have a zero value. It is useful to test Factor 2 for zero before dividing to make certain that errors do not occur.

The **DIVide operation** has the following two instruction formats:

Format 1
(Use Factor 1, Factor 2, and Result Field)

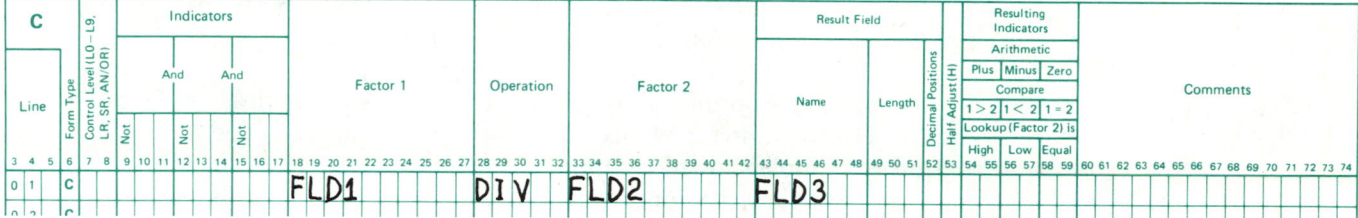

The contents of the field or literal in Factor 1 is divided by the contents of the field or literal in Factor 2. The answer or quotient is stored in the Result Field.

The DIV operation, like the SUB operation, cannot interchange the two fields contained in the operation. Transposing Factor 1 and Factor 2 will produce incorrect results.

Format 2
(Use Factor 2 and Result Field)

If Factor 1 is *not* used, the Result Field is divided by Factor 2 and the result is placed in the Result Field.

In both formats the result of a DIV operation is always placed in the Result Field. The only field that is altered as a result of a division operation is the Result Field.

As in the ADD, SUB, and MULT operations, Format 2 can be used when there is only one operand needed along with the Result Field. The original value of Factor 2 always remains unchanged.

Check to see if Format 2 is available with your RPG compiler.

What if Factor 1 or Factor 2 is Equal to Zero in a DIV Operation?

Zero values for Factor 1 and Factor 2 can cause unexpected results in a DIV operation. If Factor 1 is zero, the result of the DIVide operation will be zero. Factor 2, however, cannot be zero with either Format 1 or Format 2. Moreover, if Factor 2 is zero, an interrupt will occur and the program will halt. An error message will be issued by the system that states that a "divide by zero" error has occurred. Later on, we will see how to test factors to ensure that they are not zero before division is performed.

The Sign of a Quotient

The divide operation requires the entry of DIV in the operation field specified as columns 28–32. The dividend, contained in Factor 1, is divided by the divisor (Factor 2), resulting in the **quotient.** The quotient is stored in the Result Field. The quotient will be algebraically signed depending on the dividend and the divisor. If their signs are the same, that is, both positive or both negative, then the quotient will be positive. If they contain opposite signs, then the quotient will be negative. Remember, to print a result with a sign, you must use the appropriate Edit Code on the Output Specifications form.

Assume, for example, that an input record is defined as in Figure 3.18. Figure 3.19 illustrates how division instructions can be coded.

In the example shown, compute the class average AVG by dividing the total grades (TGRADE) by the number of students (STUDS) in the class. As always, the programmer is responsible for establishing fields of the proper length to store results. In Figure 3.18, the remainder was zero. However, additional positions to the right of the decimal point could have been specified to provide more accurate results if decimal digits were desired. In the example that follows, the results of the division operation could be extended to include two decimal positions:

Figure 3.18
Input Specifications for DIVision example.

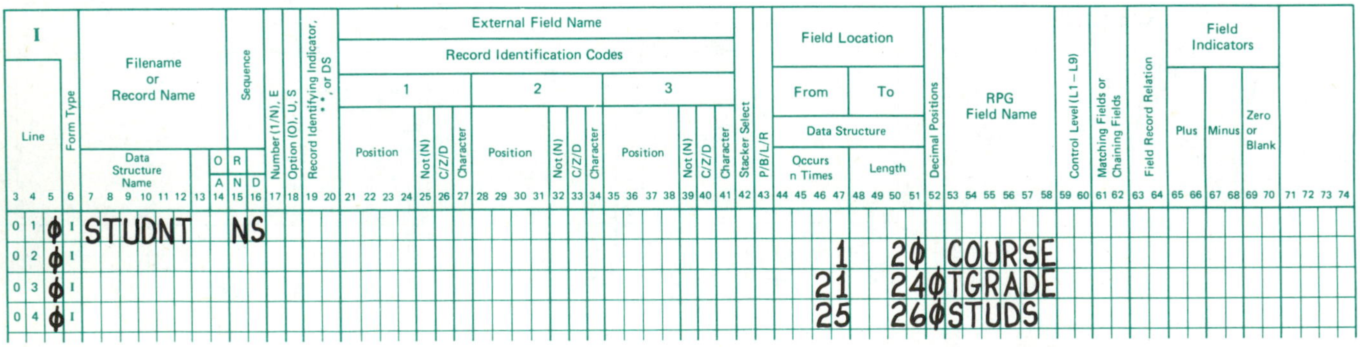

Operation	Terms	Calculation	Formula
AVG ← Quotient		0078	
STUDS)TGRADE ← Dividend		32)2496	$TGRADE/STUDS = AVG$
← Divisor		224	
		256	
		256	
		000	

C			Indicators					Factor 1	Operation	Factor 2	Result Field				Resulting Indicators			Comments
Line	Form Type	Control Level (L0–L9, LR, SR, AN/OR)	And / Not	And / Not	/ Not						Name	Length	Decimal Positions	Half Adjust (H)	Arithmetic: Plus / Minus / Zero; Compare 1>2 / 1<2 / 1=2; Lookup (Factor 2) is High / Low / Equal			
0 1	C							QTY	DIV	12	DOZEN	42						
0 2	C*																	
0 3	C							TGRADE	DIV	STUDS	AVG	52H						
0 4	C																	

$$\text{QTY} \div \text{CONSTANT} = \text{DOZEN}$$

$$\boxed{1\,4\,8} \div \boxed{1\,2} = \boxed{1\,2\,3\,3\,3\,3}$$

Values truncated

$$\text{TGRADE} \div \text{STUDS} = \text{Calculated AVG} \qquad \text{Rounded AVG}$$

$$\boxed{2\,5\,1\,7} \div \boxed{3\,2} = \boxed{0\,7\,8\,6\,5\,6\,2\,5} \qquad \boxed{0\,7\,8\,6\,6}$$

```
        0078.50
    32|2512.00
       224
        272
        256
        160
        160
          0
```

The results of the division may also be rounded in a manner similar to that used in multiplication. Placing an "H" in position 53 (Half-adjust) of the Calculation Specifications form will perform the rounding required for the arithmetic operation. Assume that SALES has a value of 2000ʌ00:

	C			Indicators					Factor 1	Operation	Factor 2	Result Field				Resulting Indicators			Comments
	Line	Form Type	Control Level (L0–L9, LR, SR, AN/OR)	And / Not	And / Not	/ Not						Name	Length	Decimal Positions	Half Adjust (H)	Arithmetic: Plus / Minus / Zero; Compare 1>2 / 1<2 / 1=2; Lookup (Factor 2) is High / Low / Equal			
1.	0 1	C							SALES	DIV	3	AVGS	52H						
	0 2	C*																	
2.	0 3	C							SALES	DIV	3	AVGS	52						
	0 4	C*																	
3.	0 5	C							SALES	DIV	3	AVGS	42H						

The Result Field in Example 1 is of sufficient size and yields correctly rounded results. Example 2 would result in low-order truncation; that is, the right-most position would not be rounded. In many business applications, rounding of the second decimal position is the usual and accepted practice. There are, however, numerous instances where other types of rounding are required.

In Example 3 a more serious error occurs. High-order truncation, as illustrated, is caused when a Result Field is sized too small. The importance of **sizing fields** correctly cannot be overemphasized.

To determine the size of a Result Field used as a quotient, you must know the range of both the dividend and the divisor. Performing the divisions using these ranges yourself will help you determine the size to be allocated for the result. When in doubt, always make the Result Field larger than might be necessary, since it will not adversely affect the processing to do so.

The Remainder

When a DIVide operation is executed and a remainder results, the remainder will be lost. Some applications, however, make use of a remainder. We can save the remainder with the move remainder (**MVR**) **operation** specified as the next instruction immediately following the division.

I. Move Remainder (MVR) Operation

The *move remainder* (MVR) operation moves the remainder of a division operation into the field specified in the Result Field. The MVR operation must immediately follow the division operation as shown in Figure 3.20. If it does not, an error will occur. In this example, JTMINS (job task in minutes) is divided by 60 in order to determine the number of hours to perform a task. If the division operation results in a remainder, that remainder is placed in the #MINS field by the MVR operation following the DIV operation. The field size of the remainder should be the same as the divisor. Since the divisor (60) is established as two integers, the length of the remainder, #MINS, should be specified as two integers.

Both the #HOURS and #MINS fields can be printed to indicate the number of hours and minutes for a job task. We use a # as a prefix to designate work fields within Data Structures defined with length and decimal positions on the Input Specifications form.

If the Result Field in a calculation has no length and decimal specifications, we can assume it is defined on the Input Specifications form as part of the input record or as part of a Data Structure.

MVR must be specified in columns 28–30 of the Operation field. Factors 1 and 2 must be blank. The Half-adjust option (column 53) cannot be specified for this operation or for the division operation preceding it.

If Factors 1 and 2 of the DIV operation have decimal positions, the size of the remainder is determined by using the larger of:

1. The number of decimal positions in Factor 1 of the divide operation, or
2. The sum of the decimal positions in Factor 2 and the Result Field of the divide operation.

Figure 3.20
Use of the move remainder (MVR) operation.

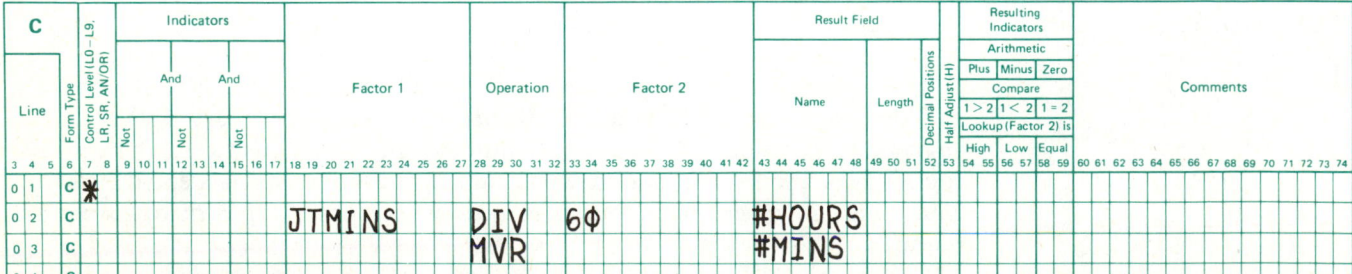

For example, let us consider the calculation of the monthly interest problem stated earlier:

Monthly interest = Annual interest / 12
Annual interest = $124

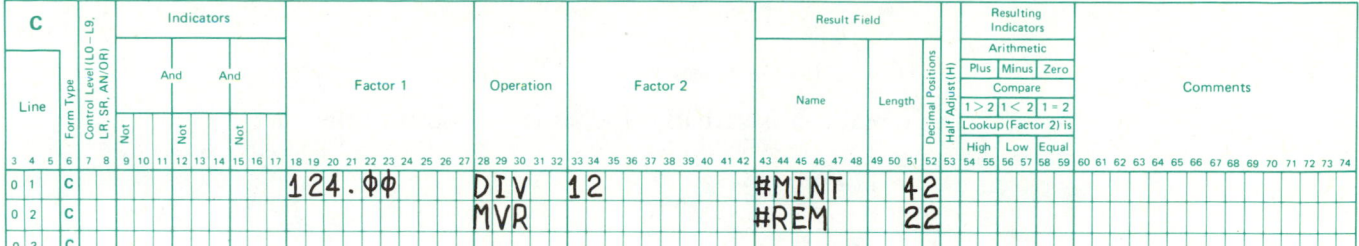

The size of the remainder field #REM would be two decimal positions, which is the number of decimal positions in Factor 1 of the DIV operation.

The actual arithmetic can be shown as follows:

$$
\begin{array}{r}
10.33 \\
12\overline{)124.00} \\
\underline{12} \\
40 \\
\underline{36} \\
40 \\
\underline{36} \\
4 \longleftarrow \text{Remainder}
\end{array}
$$

The remainder is actually .04, as can be shown in the checking of the division:

$$
\begin{array}{r}
10.33 \\
\times \quad 12 \\
\hline
2066 \\
\underline{1033} \\
123.96 \\
+ \quad .04 \text{ Add back the remainder} \\
\hline
124.00
\end{array}
$$

Another example that can be used to illustrate how remainders with decimal positions are determined is:

C		Indicators				Factor 1	Operation	Factor 2	Result Field				Resulting Indicators	Comments
Line	Form Type	Control Level (L0–L9, LR, SR, AN/OR)	And / Not	And / Not	Not				Name	Length	Decimal Positions	Half Adjust (H)	Arithmetic / Compare / Lookup	
0 1	C					124.00	DIV	10.5	#QUOT	62				
0 2	C						MVR		#REM	33				

The size of the remainder field #REM would be calculated by taking the single decimal position in Factor 2 and the two decimal positions in the Result Field, making three, which is larger than the two positions of Factor 1.

The arithmetic is performed as follows:

$$
\begin{array}{r}
11.80 \\
10.5\overline{)124.000} \\
105 \\
\hline
190 \\
105 \\
\hline
850 \\
840 \\
\hline
100 \longleftarrow \text{Remainder}
\end{array}
$$

The remainder is actually .100, as can be seen in the check:

$$
\begin{array}{r}
11.80 \\
\times \quad 10.5 \\
\hline
5900 \\
11800 \\
\hline
123.900 \\
+ \quad .100 \quad \text{Add back the remainder} \\
\hline
124.000
\end{array}
$$

J. Moving or Copying Data During Calculations

When writing RPG programs, it is frequently necessary to move or transfer data from one storage location to another. Sometimes only a single character is moved, but most often fields are transferred.

Numeric and alphanumeric data may be transferred from one field, the *sending field*, to another field, the *receiving field*, by using the following operations:

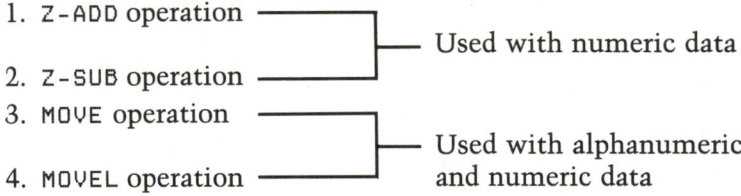

1. Z-ADD operation ⎯⎯⎯⎬⎯ Used with numeric data
2. Z-SUB operation ⎯⎯⎯
3. MOVE operation ⎯⎯⎯⎬⎯ Used with alphanumeric and numeric data
4. MOVEL operation ⎯⎯⎯

The Z-ADD and Z-SUB operations are used to copy numeric fields, whereas the MOVE and MOVEL operations are used with either alphanumeric or numeric data. However, it is strongly recommended that the MOVE and MOVEL operations be limited to *transferring alphanumeric data* only. The reasons for this will be explained in more detail later when we discuss the MOVE and MOVEL operations. It should be noted that the results of these four operations are normally referred to as *moving* data from one location to another, but in fact, the data is *copied* from one location to another. Therefore, the contents of the sending field always remains the same.

1. The Z-ADD Operation

The Z-ADD operation was described earlier in this chapter. To review, the Z-ADD operation:

1. Initializes the contents of the Result Field to zero.
2. Adds Factor 2 to the Result Field.

Consider the following examples:

C			Indicators					Factor 1	Operation	Factor 2	Result Field					Resulting Indicators						Comments	
			And	And							Name	Length				Arithmetic							
																Plus	Minus	Zero					
																Compare							
																1 > 2	1 < 2	1 = 2					
Line			Not	Not		Not										Lookup (Factor 2) is							
																High	Low	Equal					
3 4 5	6	7 8	9 10 11	12 13 14	15 16 17	18 19 20 21 22 23 24 25 26 27	28 29 30 31 32	33 34 35 36 37 38 39 40 41 42	43 44 45 46 47 48	49 50 51	52	53	54 55	56 57	58 59	60 61 62 63 64 65 66 67 68 69 70 71 72 73 74								
0 1	C						Z-ADDØ	COUNT															
0 2	C	*																					
0 3	C	*																					
0 4	C						Z-ADDERATE	#RATE															
0 5	C																						

1. The field COUNT is initialized to zero.
2. The value from the ERATE field (employee rate from input record) is transferred to the Data Structure subfield #RATE.

The value of Factor 2 in the second example does not change as a result of the Z-ADD operation.

Two primary uses for the Z-ADD operation are:

1. To initialize a counter or index before entering a looping routine.
2. To save the contents of a field for later reference in the program.

Let us now examine each of the remaining three data movement operations in detail.

2. The Z-SUB (Zero-and-Subtract) Operation

The Z-SUB operation can be summarized as follows:

Operation:	Z-SUB
Meaning:	Zero the Result Field and then subtract the contents of Factor 2 from the Result Field. Decimal alignment is maintained.
Factor 1:	Factor 1 is not used.
Operation Code:	Contains Z-SUB for a zero and subtract operation.
Factor 2:	Factor 2 contains the numeric data to be subtracted from the Result Field. This subtraction will take place after the Result Field is set to zeros. Thus, Factor 2 will be subtracted from a field containing zeros. Factor 2 may be a numeric field or a numeric literal.

The Z-SUB operation is executed using the following steps:

1. Factor 2 is placed in a temporary area in storage. This prevents the contents of the field from being lost if Factor 2 and the Result Field are the same field.
2. The Result Field is initialized to zeros.
3. Factor 2, which was stored in a temporary storage location, is subtracted from the Result Field (which is zero).
4. The difference, which is actually the negative of Factor 2, is placed in the Result Field (e.g., suppose Factor 2 = −10: ZSUB − (−10) = 10).

The primary use of the Z-SUB operation is to change the sign of a field. That is, if the field is positive it will be changed to negative. If negative, it will be changed to positive. The following examples illustrate this concept and display the contents of storage before and after each Z-SUB operation is executed:

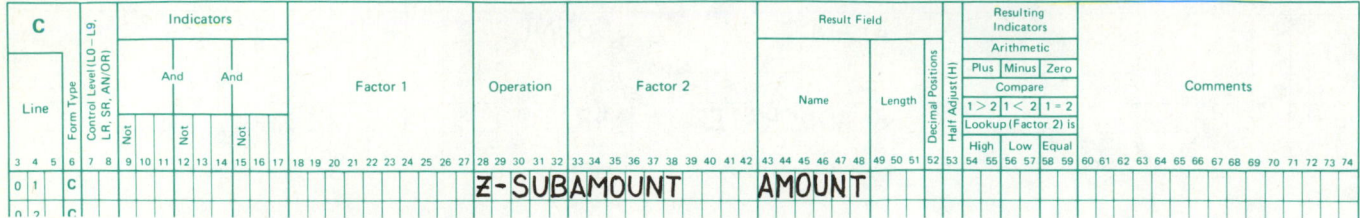

Example 1   If the value of the AMOUNT field was 255.00 before the Z-SUB operation was executed, its contents would be −255.00 after the execution of the Z-SUB operation:

Before   *After*

```
   AMOUNT          AMOUNT
                        ‾
  2,5,5,0,0       2,5,5,0,0        ←— denotes a negative value

  F F F F F       F F F F D      Zone  ⎫
  2 5 5 0 0       2 5 5 0 0      Digit ⎬ Hexadecimal representation
                                       ⎭
                                SIGN  DIGIT
                              → 1101 | 0000   Right-most byte

                              Negative sign
                              in binary
```

Note the letter D in the zone portion of the right-most byte of the AMOUNT field after the Z-SUB operation. The zone portion was changed from an F to a D because the contents changed from a positive 255.00 to −255.00. Subtraction of a positive field is shown here:

$$0 \quad - \quad 2,5,5,0,0 \quad = \quad 2,5,5,0,\overline{0}$$

Thus, the net effect of this operation is to change the sign of the AMOUNT field from positive to negative.

Example 2   This example illustrates the effects on a field that is negative before the execution of the Z-SUB operation.

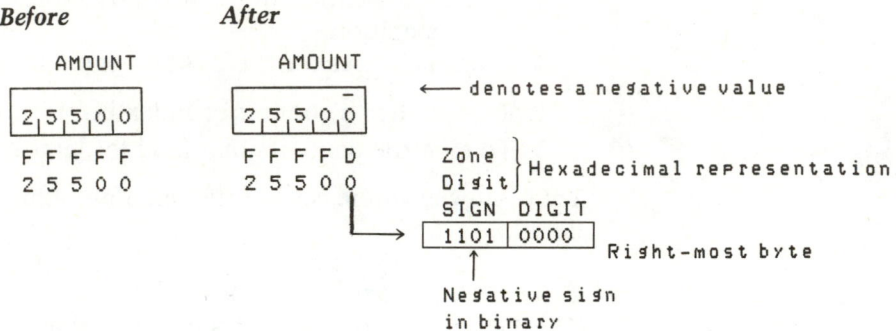

Before   *After*

```
   BALNCE          BALNCE
        ‾
  3,2,5,5,5       3,2,5,5,5

  F F F F D       F F F F F      Zone  ⎫
  3 2 5 5 5       3 2 5 5 5      Digit ⎬ Hexadecimal representation
```

Note the change in the sign when this Z-SUB operation is executed. Before execution, the right-most byte contained a negative sign (D) and after execution the sign changed to a positive F. The zone portion was changed from a D to an F because the contents changed from a negative 325.55 to 325.55. Zero-and-subtraction of a negative field is shown here:

$$\boxed{0} \; - \; \boxed{3\,2\,5\,5\,\overline{5}} \; = \; \boxed{0} \; + \; \boxed{3\,2\,5\,5\,5} \; = \; \boxed{3\,2\,5\,5\,5}$$

3. The MOVE Operation

When moving numeric fields, use the Z-ADD rather than the MOVE operation. The problem with using MOVE instructions to move or copy numeric data fields is that *implied decimal positions are ignored.* Hence, if numeric fields are not the same size and do not contain the same number of decimal positions, the value of the data may be changed as a result of the MOVE. For example, if $1_\wedge00$ is moved into a three-position numeric field with one decimal position, the result is $10_\wedge0$. You should, therefore, avoid using the MOVE operation when numeric data is to be copied to a receiving field. Instead, use the Z-ADD, since alignment of decimal points is automatic with the zero-and-add operation.

When moving integers or whole numbers to numeric fields of the same size, the chances for error with the MOVE are reduced; note, however, that the Z-ADD is still strongly recommended. It is also important for the programmer to recognize that although a field may contain numbers, it is not necessarily always numeric. We define numeric fields as those used in calculations. Data fields such as employee number, Social Security number, and edited dates containing slashes are *not* treated as numeric fields in programming. These can be transmitted to other areas of storage using the MOVE operation. With this in mind, we will now summarize the MOVE operation:

Operation:	MOVE
Meaning:	Move or copy characters from one field to another starting with the *right*-most position.
Factor 1:	Not used.
Factor 2:	Sending field, which remains unchanged.
Result Field:	Receiving field; its contents change.
Limitations:	Half-adjusting and resulting indicators are not used with this operation.
Comment:	Avoid using the MOVE operation when *numeric* data is to be moved. Use the Z-ADD instead for proper decimal alignment of numeric fields.

Example 1

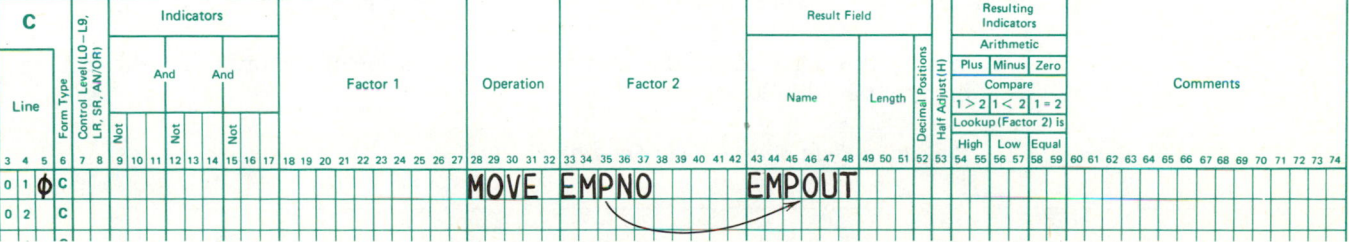

The data in Factor 2 replaces the previous contents of the Result Field. After execution, the Result Field contains an exact copy of Factor 2 if the fields are of the same size. Movement of the characters is from *right to left,* one character at a time. The move operation ends whenever all characters in the sending field are moved or the receiving field is filled. This means that if the Result Field is longer than the sending field, there will be data remaining from the Result Field's previous contents. An example will clarify this point.

Example 2 *Receiving Field Longer than Sending Field*

C	Form Type	Control Level (L0 – L9, LR, SR, AN/OR)	Indicators			Factor 1	Operation	Factor 2	Result Field				Resulting Indicators			Comments
			And	And					Name	Length	Decimal Positions	Half Adjust (H)	Arithmetic: Plus Minus Zero / Compare: 1>2 1<2 1=2 / Lookup (Factor 2) is: High Low Equal			
Line			Not	Not	Not											
0 1	C						MOVE	NAMEIN	NAMEO							
0 2	C															

NAMEIN
Before MOVE | *After* MOVE

| P | O | R | T | → | P | O | R | T |

Contents unchanged

NAMEO
Before MOVE | *After* MOVE

| R | E | M | A | K | E | → | R | E | P | O | R | T |

Contents unchanged ——— Contents change

Note the results in NAMEO after the move. Since NAMEO, the receiving field, contains six characters and only four characters are moved, the *left-most two characters remain unchanged.* There are applications where such a move may prove desirable. In the illustration that follows, for example, we are able to change the year in the date field without disturbing the month and day data.

C	Form Type	Control Level (L0 – L9, LR, SR, AN/OR)	Indicators			Factor 1	Operation	Factor 2	Result Field				Resulting Indicators			Comments
			And	And					Name	Length	Decimal Positions	Half Adjust (H)	Arithmetic: Plus Minus Zero / Compare: 1>2 1<2 1=2 / Lookup (Factor 2) is: High Low Equal			
Line			Not	Not	Not											
0 1	C						MOVE	YRIN	DATEO							

YRIN
Before MOVE | *After* MOVE

| 9 | 2 | → | 9 | 2 |

Contents unchanged

DATEO
Before MOVE | *After* MOVE

| 0 | 4 | 1 | 7 | 4 | 2 | → | 0 | 4 | 1 | 7 | 9 | 2 |

Contents the same ——— Contents change

In the following example, the receiving field (Result Field) is shorter than the sending field contained in Factor 2.

Example 3 *Receiving Field Shorter than Sending Field*

C	Form Type	Control Level (L0 – L9, LR, SR, AN/OR)	Indicators			Factor 1	Operation	Factor 2	Result Field				Resulting Indicators			Comments
			And	And					Name	Length	Decimal Positions	Half Adjust (H)	Arithmetic: Plus Minus Zero / Compare: 1>2 1<2 1=2 / Lookup (Factor 2) is: High Low Equal			
Line			Not	Not	Not											
0 1 0	C						MOVE	LONGFD	SHORT							

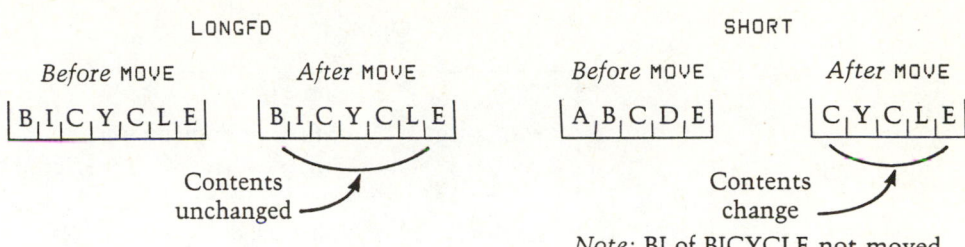

LONGFD

Before MOVE | *After* MOVE

B I C Y C L E | B I C Y C L E

Contents
unchanged

SHORT

Before MOVE | *After* MOVE

A B C D E | C Y C L E

Contents
change

Note: BI of BICYCLE not moved.

Since the receiving or result field, SHORT, is five characters in length and the sending field contains seven characters, two characters will be lost or *truncated* as a result of this operation. Since the MOVE operation begins on the right and progresses one character at a time, there is not any room in the receiving field for the two left-most characters. Consequently, the BI of "BICYCLE" is not transmitted. Also recall that the sending field is not altered; hence "BICYCLE" remains as the contents of LONGFD.

Literals may also be moved with the MOVE operation. Consider the following:

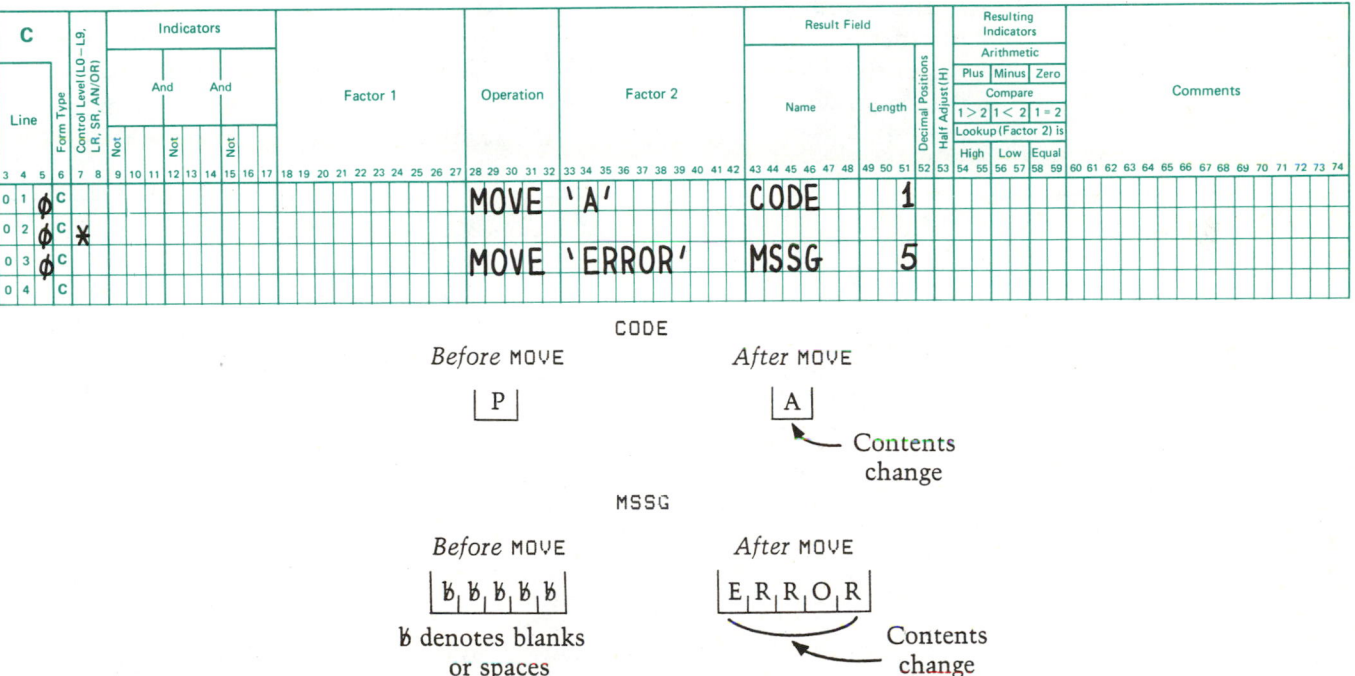

Line	Form Type	Control Level (L0—L9, LR, SR, AN/OR)	Indicators						Factor 1	Operation	Factor 2	Result Field		Decimal Positions	Half Adjust (H)	Resulting Indicators				Comments
			And		And							Name	Length							
0 1	0 C									MOVE	'A'	CODE	1							
0 2	0 C *																			
0 3	0 C									MOVE	'ERROR'	MSSG	5							
0 4	C																			

CODE

Before MOVE | *After* MOVE

P | A

Contents
change

MSSG

Before MOVE | *After* MOVE

ƀ ƀ ƀ ƀ ƀ | E R R O R

ƀ denotes blanks
or spaces

Contents
change

Based on certain indicator conditions, the programmer may want to move a unique code or message into a field. (Note that alphanumeric literals are enclosed in quotes.)

The MOVE operation is subject to several limitations. Recall that Factor 1 is not used in this instruction. No resulting indicators or Half-adjusting are permitted. Numeric fields may be redefined as alphameric fields by simply moving the data to a field defined as alphameric.

To change an alphameric field to a numeric field, move the data to a numeric Result Field, that is, one that is defined by using an integer in the Decimal Positions field. The *format* of the Result Field establishes the format of the contents. Most other programming languages *do not* allow this unique capability of changing the format of a field from alphameric to numeric and vice versa. The potential problems arising from manipulating data in this manner are, however, significant, particularly with respect to decimal alignment of numeric fields. Therefore, it is strongly recommended that this practice *be avoided*.

4. The MOVEL Operation

Operation:	MOVEL
Meaning:	Move or copy characters from one field to another, starting with the *left-most* character and moving from left to right.
Factor 1:	Not used.
Factor 2:	Sending field, which remains unchanged.
Result Field:	Receiving field; its contents change.
Limitations:	Half-adjust and resulting indicators are not used. If the receiving field is shorter than the sending field, right-most positions are truncated. If the receiving field is longer than the sending field, the extra right-most positions in the receiving field remain unchanged.

The MOVEL operation is similar to the MOVE instruction, but the movement of the data begins from the *left* instead of from the right. As with the MOVE instruction, if the sending field contained in Factor 2 is longer than the receiving or Result Field, the extra positions are truncated. However, the positions truncated would be the excess right-most positions in this case. For example, the following operation produces the results indicated:

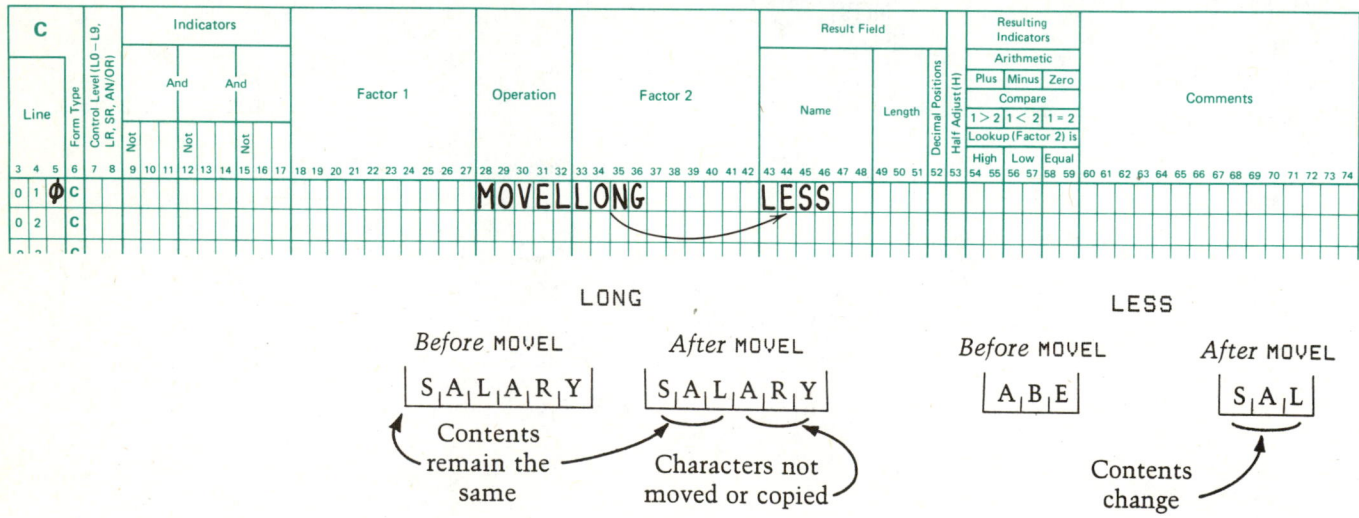

This operation would result in copying only three of the six characters contained in the sending field. Since the MOVEL operation begins the movement of data from the left, only the left-most three characters contained in LONG would be moved or copied into the receiving field called LESS.

If, however, the sending field is smaller than the receiving field, the extra *right-most* positions of the receiving field remain unchanged. Consider the following:

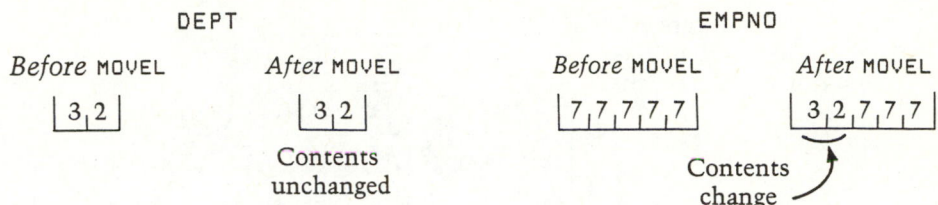

DEPT

Before MOVEL	*After* MOVEL
3 2	3 2
	Contents unchanged

EMPNO

Before MOVEL	*After* MOVEL
7 7 7 7 7	3 2 7 7 7
	Contents change

Again, the MOVEL operation, in effect, copies the left-most positions of the sending field to the receiving field. If the receiving field is the shorter field, the excess positions to the right are truncated or lost. If, however, the receiving field is the longer field, the receiving field's extra right-most positions remain unchanged. To ensure correct results, it is best to use fields of the same length in a MOVEL operation.

Literals may be used in either MOVE or MOVEL operations. They are enclosed in quotes and entered in Factor 2. However, the data moved will be left-justified in the Result Field in a MOVEL operation. Consider the following:

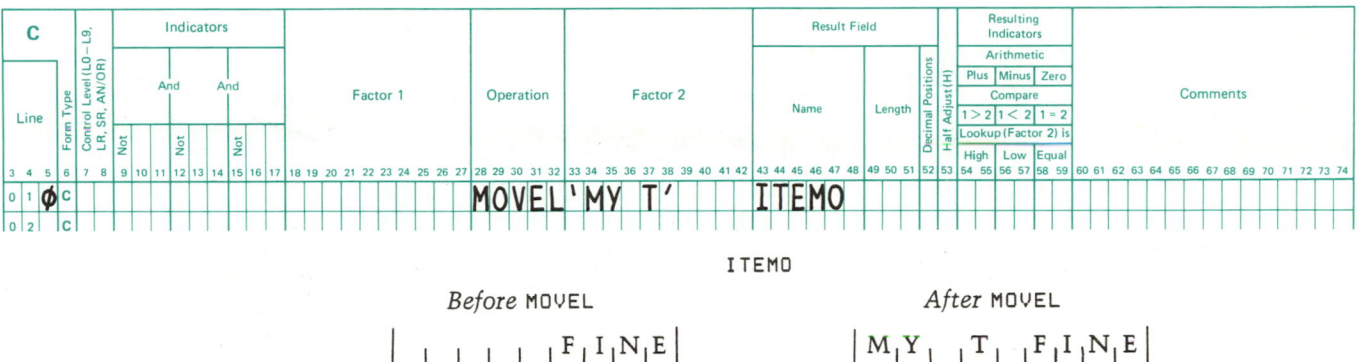

ITEMO

Before MOVEL	*After* MOVEL
F I N E	M Y T F I N E

Recall that the maximum length of an alphanumeric literal is eight characters.

K. Summary of Arithmetic Operations

Factor 1	Operation	Factor 2	Result	Value After Execution		
				A	B	C
A	ADD	B	C	A	B	$A + B$
	ADD	A	B	A	$A + B$	
	Z-ADD	B	C		B	B
A	SUB	A	A	*Zero*		
A	SUB	B	C	A	B	$A - B$
	SUB	B	A	$A - B$	B	
	Z-SUB	B	C		B	$-B$
A	MULT	B	C	A	B	$A \times B$
	MULT	A	B	A	$A \times B$	
A	DIV	B	C	A	B	A/B

Rule. The Result field is *always* assigned new values as shown in italics in each example of the summary chart.

L. Structured Concepts

The following sample program (Figure 3.21), introduced at the beginning of this chapter, has been modified to illustrate new programming techniques and

Figure 3.21
Sample program that illustrates structured concepts.

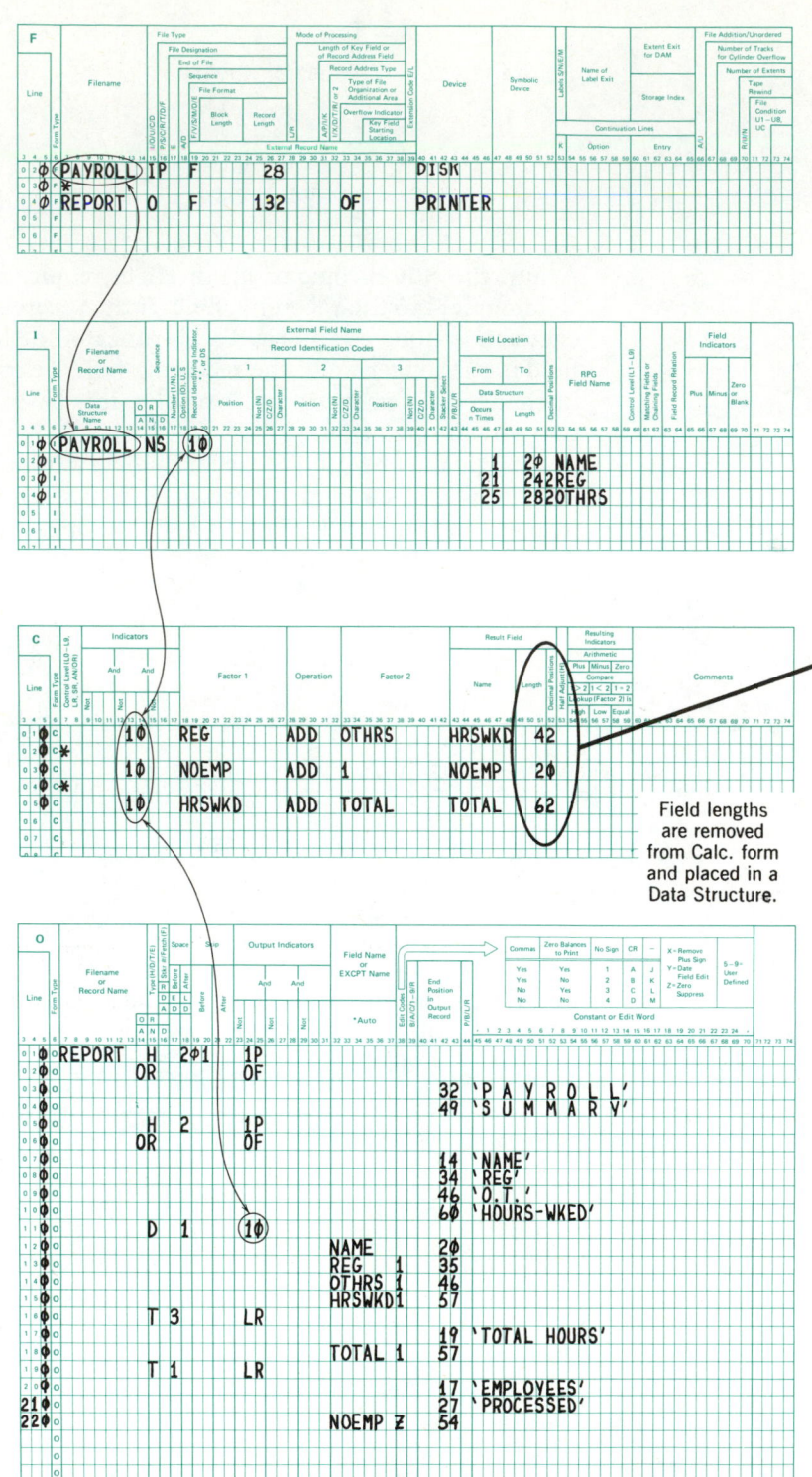

Field lengths
are removed
from Calc. form
and placed in a
Data Structure.

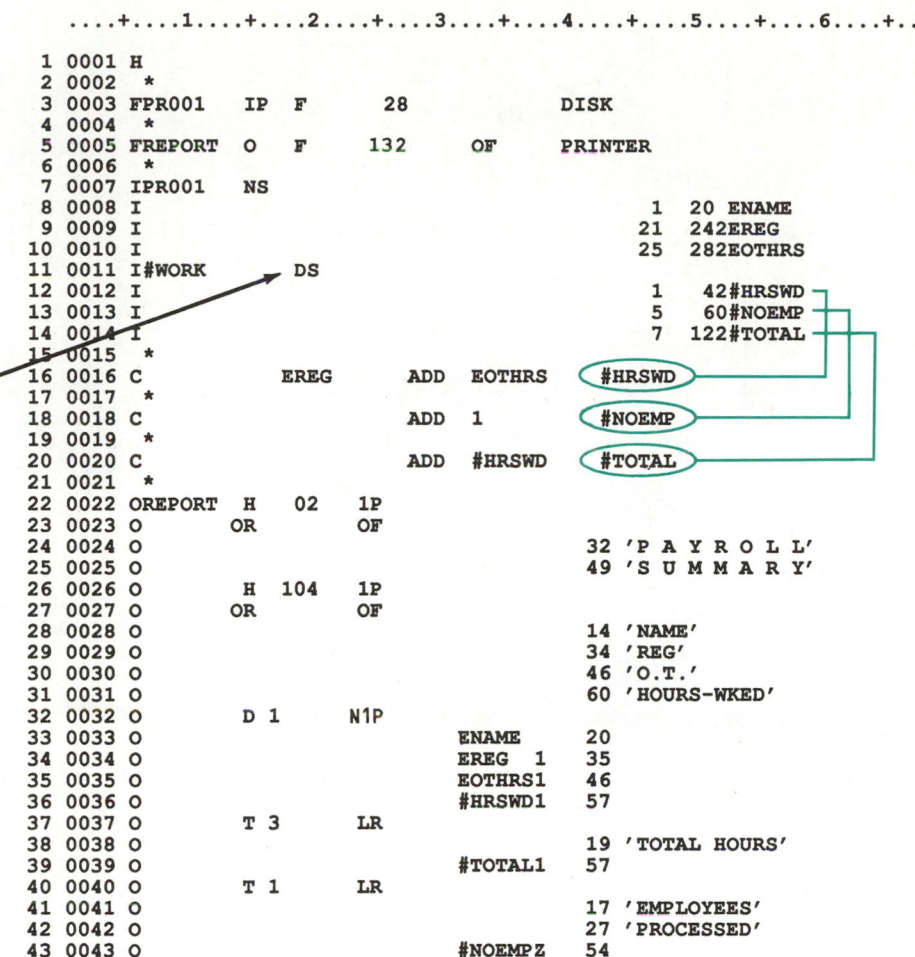

```
        ....+....1....+....2....+....3....+....4....+....5....+....6....+....
 1 0001 H
 2 0002 *
 3 0003 FPR001    IP F     28            DISK
 4 0004 *
 5 0005 FREPORT   O  F    132      OF    PRINTER
 6 0006 *
 7 0007 IPR001    NS
 8 0008 I                                   1   20 ENAME
 9 0009 I                                  21  242EREG
10 0010 I                                  25  282EOTHRS
11 0011 I#WORK        DS
12 0012 I                                   1   42#HRSWD
13 0013 I                                   5   60#NOEMP
14 0014 I                                   7  122#TOTAL
15 0015 *
16 0016 C            EREG      ADD  EOTHRS  #HRSWD
17 0017 *
18 0018 C                      ADD  1       #NOEMP
19 0019 *
20 0020 C                      ADD  #HRSWD  #TOTAL
21 0021 *
22 0022 OREPORT   H  02   1P
23 0023 O            OR        OF
24 0024 O                              32 'P A Y R O L L'
25 0025 O                              49 'S U M M A R Y'
26 0026 O         H  104  1P
27 0027 O            OR        OF
28 0028 O                              14 'NAME'
29 0029 O                              34 'REG'
30 0030 O                              46 'O.T.'
31 0031 O                              60 'HOURS-WKED'
32 0032 O         D  1    N1P
33 0033 O                      ENAME   20
34 0034 O                      EREG  1 35
35 0035 O                      EOTHRS1 46
36 0036 O                      #HRSWD1 57
37 0037 O         T  3    LR
38 0038 O                              19 'TOTAL HOURS'
39 0039 O                      #TOTAL1 57
40 0040 O         T  1    LR
41 0041 O                              17 'EMPLOYEES'
42 0042 O                              27 'PROCESSED'
43 0043 O                      #NOEMPZ 54
```

structured concepts. Study the two programs and note the differences before continuing.

Note that we preface all work fields with a pound sign (#) and all employee input fields with an E. This makes it easier to follow the logic of the program.

Let us now consider the three arithmetic operations in the two programs. In the modified version, the second and third ADD operations do not contain a field in Factor 1. Since Factor 1 would be the same field as the Result Field, the Format 2 version of the ADD operation can be used to eliminate Factor 1 from these statements. Hence, the program will ADD 1 to #NOEMP, and ADD #HRSWD to #TOTAL. Alternatively, we could have specified these instructions as "1 ADD #NOEMP #NOEMP" and "#HRSWD ADD #TOTAL #TOTAL," but this latter method is more cumbersome and requires more coding.

We will now focus on using Data Structures for defining temporary work fields.

1. Defining Work Fields with a Data Structure

As illustrated in Chapter 1, RPG allows the programmer to define an area in storage, called a **Data Structure,** and then subdivide that area into fields, called subfields. As noted earlier, Data Structures are defined on the Input Specifications form and must follow all record definitions for input files (see Figure

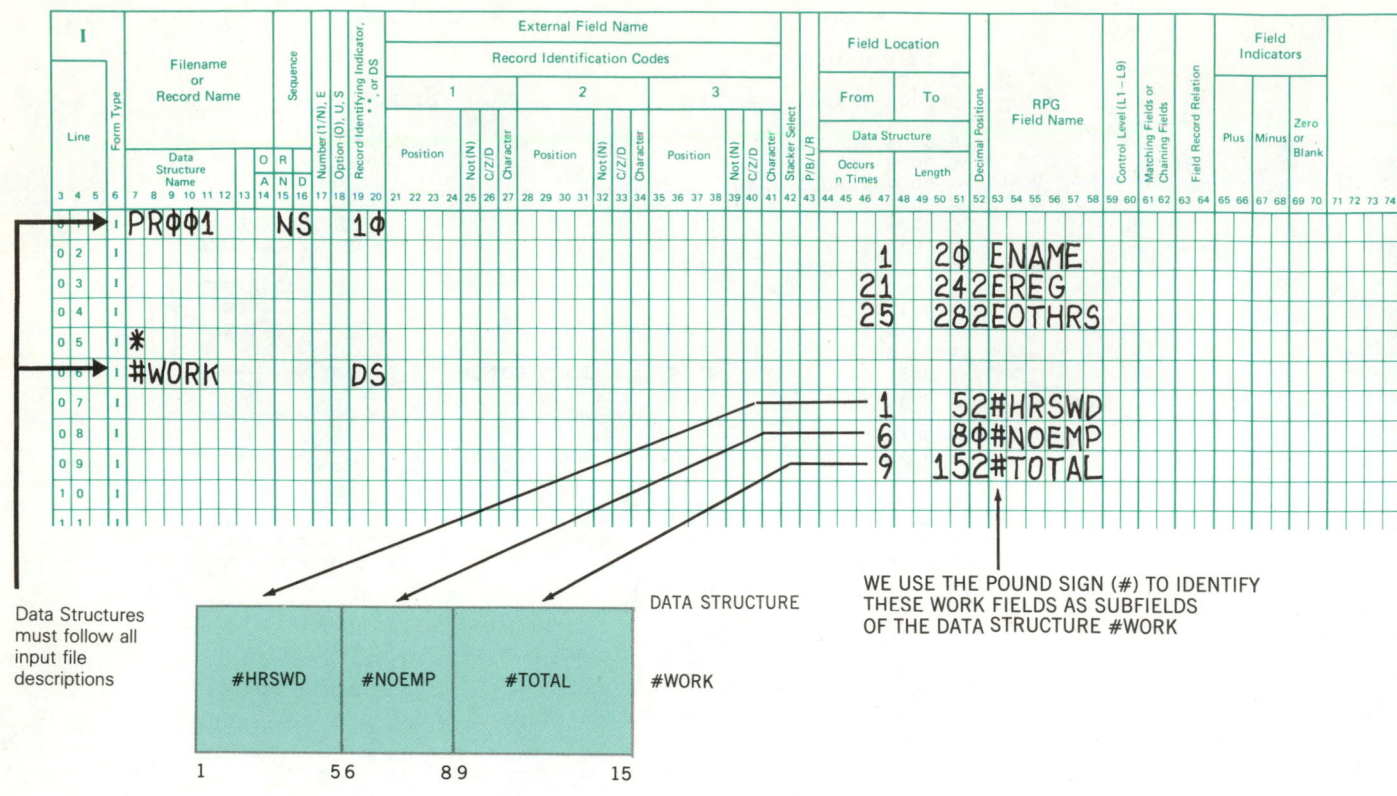

Figure 3.22
Data Structures must follow
all input file descriptions.

3.22). DS is specified in positions 19–20 of the first line of the #WORK to designate it as a Data Structure.

Temporary Fields, necessary for processing but not part of an input record, are defined in a Data Structure. Such fields may include:

1. Total fields necessary for processing.
2. Counters used to accumulate a count of a specific condition.

By using this enhancement of Data Structures, the Input Specifications form contains all storage areas necessary for the processing of data. This provides for better program documentation and makes it easier to determine the attributes of both input and work fields. As noted, we use the pound sign (#) as a prefix for all fields defined within Data Structures so that they are easily identifiable.

Let us examine in more detail the Input Specifications necessary for identifying and establishing temporary work fields in a Data Structure.

The Data Structure (#WORK) is stored in memory as a contiguous string of subfields. Each subfield occupies its own area relative to the beginning of the Data Structure. #WORK is defined and described on the Input Specifications form, thereby eliminating the need to define the length and decimal positions for each new field on the Calculation Specifications form. In this way, all fields used in the modified sample program are identified on the Input Specifications form, leaving the Calculation Specifications form for processing only.

In the modified sample program a Data Structure was established to store the temporary work fields and is identified by the Data Structure name #WORK.

The pound sign prefix "#" will be used in this text to identify subfields within Data Structures.

2. Storing Result Fields

Consider the following excerpt from the sample program. EREG and EOTHRS are input fields defined in the payroll file. E is used as a prefix for fields within the employee record. #HRSWD is a Result Field necessary for calculating the total number of hours worked. It is not part of any input record. As a temporary Result Field, it is given the pound sign prefix (#) and stored as a subfield in the Data Structure #WORK:

Line	Form Type	Control Level	Indicators	Factor 1	Operation	Factor 2	Result Field Name	Length	Decimal Positions	Resulting Indicators	Comments
0 1	C										*
0 2	C			EREG	ADD	EOTHRS	#HRSWD				

3. Storing Counters

We wanted to count the number of input records contained within the file and store that number in a counter field. In our modified program, the following specification was used. #NOEMP, a temporary storage field, was defined within the Data Structure #WORK thus eliminating the need to specify the field length and decimal positions on the Calculation Specifications form. #NOEMP is incremented by one each time a record is read; therefore, it will contain a total count of all employee records read:

Line	Form Type	Control Level	Indicators	Factor 1	Operation	Factor 2	Result Field Name	Length	Decimal Positions	Resulting Indicators	Comments
0 1	C										*
0 2	C				ADD	1	#NOEMP				

Data Structures are a powerful enhancement to RPG. They provide a method of defining temporary work fields on the Input Specifications form, which eliminates the need for extra Calculation Specifications to define these work fields. The fields on the Calculation Specifications labeled *Length* and *Decimal Positions*, both within the *Result Field* heading, are no longer used. Moreover, the Data Structure defines these temporary work fields in one central location making them easier to identify and maintain, and making the program easier to read and debug.

Self-Test
1. Factor 1 and Factor 2 of a SUB operation (*can/cannot*) be interchanged.
2. (T or F) Numeric literals can be used as either Factor 1 or Factor 2 in a SUB operation.
3. What are the two operations of the Z-ADD?

4. To obtain rounding during divide and multiply operations the _____ is used.

5. The _____ operation stores the remainder of a DIVide operation in the field specified in the Result Field.

6. (T or F) For the MVR operation to work properly, it must immediately follow the DIV operation.

7. By using _____, all variable fields in a program can be defined on the Input Specifications form.

8. Determine the contents of the Result Field used in the following MOVE operations. The contents of each field before the MOVE is as follows:

$$FLDA = \text{'AB56'}$$
$$LONG = \text{'XXXZZZ'}$$
$$SHORT = \text{'YY'}$$

```
a. MOVE     FLDA     LONG
b. MOVEL    FLDA     SHORT
c. MOVEL    FLDA     LONG
d. MOVE     FLDA     SHORT
e. MOVEL    SHORT    LONG
f. MOVE     LONG     SHORT
g. MOVEL    LONG     SHORT
h. MOVE     SHORT    LONG
i. MOVEL    'M'      SHORT
j. MOVEL    'L'      LONG
k. MOVEL    '12'     FLDA
l. MOVE     'HI'     FLDA
```

9. (T or F) The MOVEL operation is used to right-justify data transmitted to the receiving field.

10. (T or F) The most efficient way to move numeric data is with the MOVE operation.

Solutions

1. cannot

2. T

3. (a) The field specified as the Result Field is initialized to zero. (b) The value of the field specified in Factor 2 is added to the Result Field.

4. Half-adjust column (column 53)

5. Move remainder (MVR)

6. T

7. Data Structures

8. a. XXAB56   g. XX
   b. AB   h. XXXZYY
   c. AB56ZZ   i. MY
   d. 56   j. LXXZZZ
   e. YYXZZZ   k. 1256
   f. ZZ   l. ABHI

9. F—The MOVE is used for this purpose.

10. F—Always use the Z-ADD.

III. Additional Considerations

A. Expanding the RPG Logic Cycle

Thus far, we have focused on addition operations that accumulate running totals and add to counters. The RPG programming necessary for producing the output was explained in the previous chapter. Recall that the Last Record indicator is turned on or set after all the input records have been processed. When the **LR indicator** is turned on, total calculations and total output operations are to be performed. Figure 3.23 provides an illustration of the RPG Logic Cycle as it relates to detail and LR processing.

Note that the last record indicator is "on" only after all the input records have been processed. Turning on the last record indicator causes:

1. Total Calculations to be performed
2. Total Output to print.

Figure 3.23
Illustration of the RPG Logic Cycle as it relates to detail and LR processing.

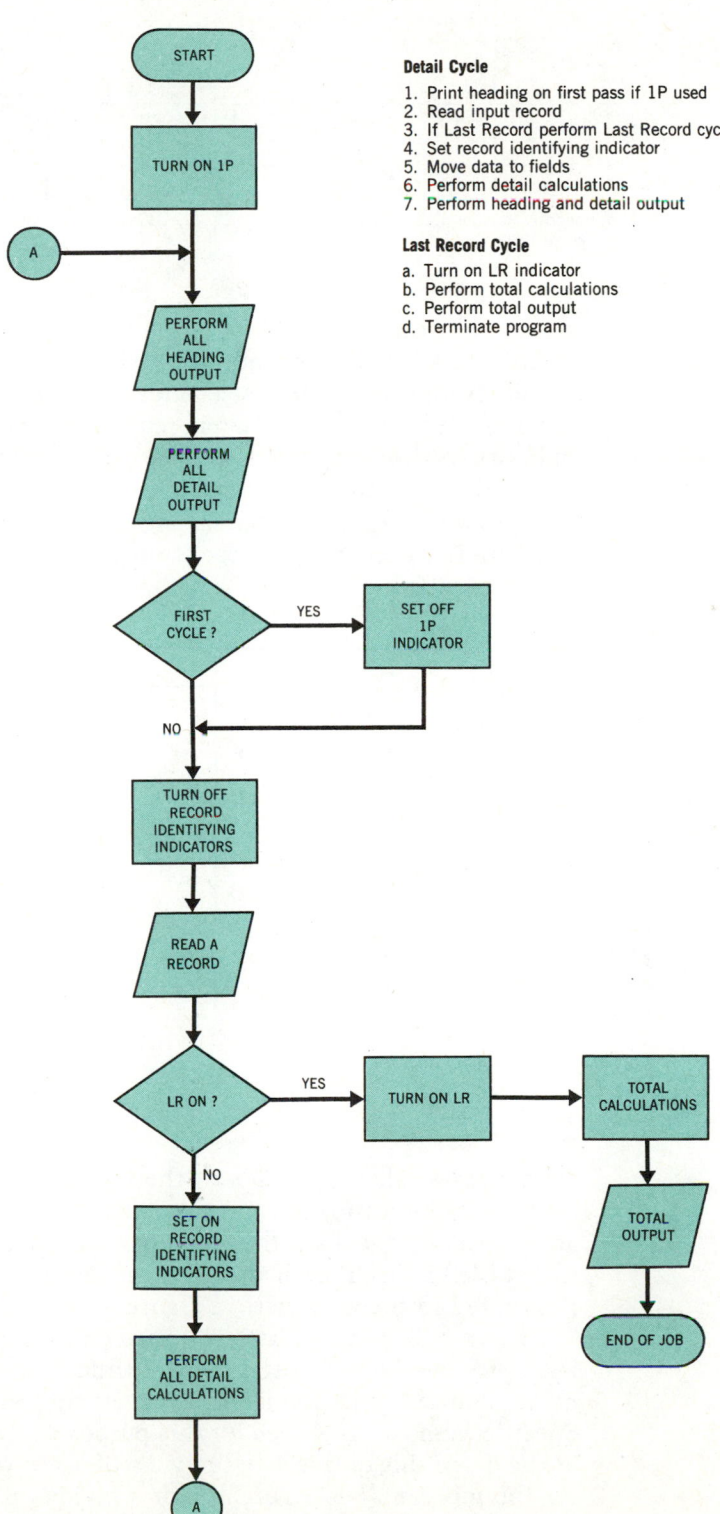

Detail Cycle

1. Print heading on first pass if 1P used
2. Read input record
3. If Last Record perform Last Record cycle
4. Set record identifying indicator
5. Move data to fields
6. Perform detail calculations
7. Perform heading and detail output

Last Record Cycle

a. Turn on LR indicator
b. Perform total calculations
c. Perform total output
d. Terminate program

B. Total Calculations

When it is necessary to perform *calculations* after the last input record has been processed, the characters LR are coded in columns 7–8 of the Calculation Specifications form as follows:

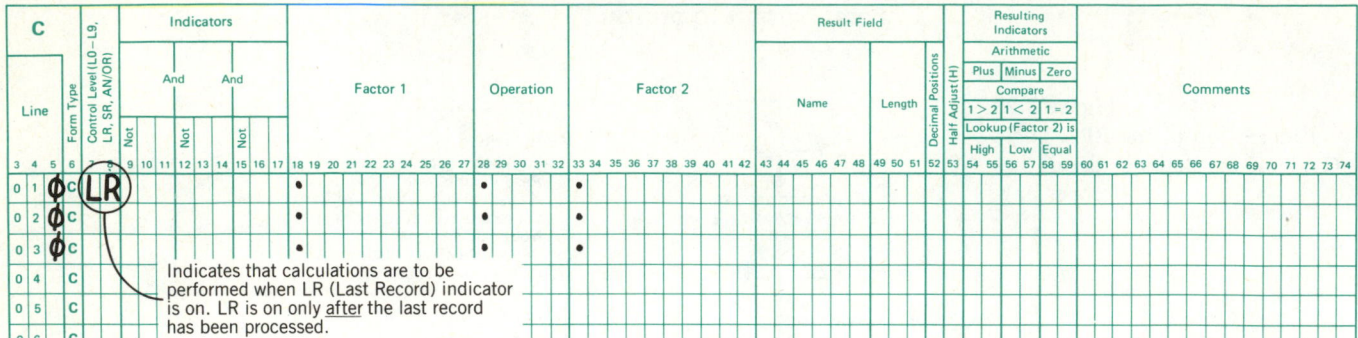

Indicates that calculations are to be performed when LR (Last Record) indicator is on. LR is on only *after* the last record has been processed.

Since LR calculations are the last to be performed by the program, they would similarly be the last entries coded on the Calculation Specifications form. If the sample program had required you to calculate the average number of hours worked per person (AVGHRS), you could have divided the TOTAL (hours worked) by the number of employees (NOEMP) once all the data had been read and processed by the program. Again, this calculation would be performed when the last record indicator is turned "on." The coding to accomplish this calculation is as follows:

C	Form Type	Control Level (L0–L9, LR, SR, AN/OR)	Indicators And And	Factor 1	Operation	Factor 2	Result Field Name Length	Decimal Positions	Half Adjust (H)	Resulting Indicators	Comments
0 1	C										
0 2	C										
0 3	C			Other calculation entries							
0 4	C										
0 5	C	LR		TOTAL	DIV	NOEMP	AVGHRS 52				
0 6	C										

Last entry on the Calculation Form.

C. Total Output

In summary, all the records in the input file are processed using the record identifying indicators to control calculations and output. The RPG Logic Cycle automatically checks if the last record has been processed. Recall that, if the end of file has been reached, the LR indicator is turned on. This process is again illustrated in the flowchart in Figure 3.24.

The Last Record indicator is turned on immediately after the last record has been processed during detail output time. This indicator may then be used to print counters and totals required at the end of the report. The Output Specifications form is used for this purpose. Recalling the example introduced at the beginning of this chapter, we will again review the output requirements for the program. See Figure 3.2 for a review of the Printer Spacing Chart. As

Figure 3.24
Use of the LR indicator.

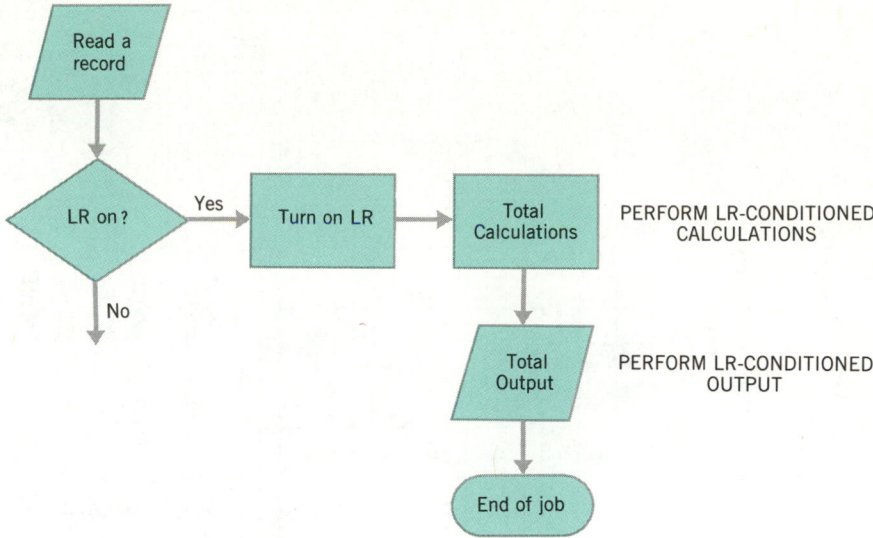

previously noted, detail lines (D) are printed for each input record by coding the letter D in column 15 of the Output Specifications form and using the record indicator specified on the Input Specifications form. In order to print a total line at the end of the report when the last record has been read, the letter T must be entered in column 15 of the Output Specifications form. Total lines follow the detail output specifications and use the last record (LR) indicator to control this last record or end-of-file processing. Figure 3.25 illustrates the Output Specifications form for the sample problem.

Total lines are not printed for each record but are accumulated and printed at a specified "total" time. In the example just presented the last record indicator is being used to control the printing of these totals. The field specifications for total lines follow the same basic format as that used on detail lines. The total lines specifications contain the following:

First Line	T in column 15 denoting Total line.
	1 in column 17 controlling the spacing of the continuous form.
	LR indicator in columns 24–31 specifying when output is to be printed.
Subsequent Lines	End position of fields and/or constants to be printed, including editing.

D. Resulting Indicators/SETON/SETOF

1. Resulting Indicators

Resulting indicators are used on the Calculation Specifications form to test the following:

1. The results of arithmetic calculations to determine whether the resulting field is plus (positive), minus (negative), or zero.
2. The results of compare operations, which are discussed in detail later in this text.

Columns 54–59 on the Calculation Specifications form may be used to test and record the value of a Result Field after an arithmetic operation has been completed. The test determines whether the results are positive, negative, or zero by turning on specific indicators. These indicators are then used to control

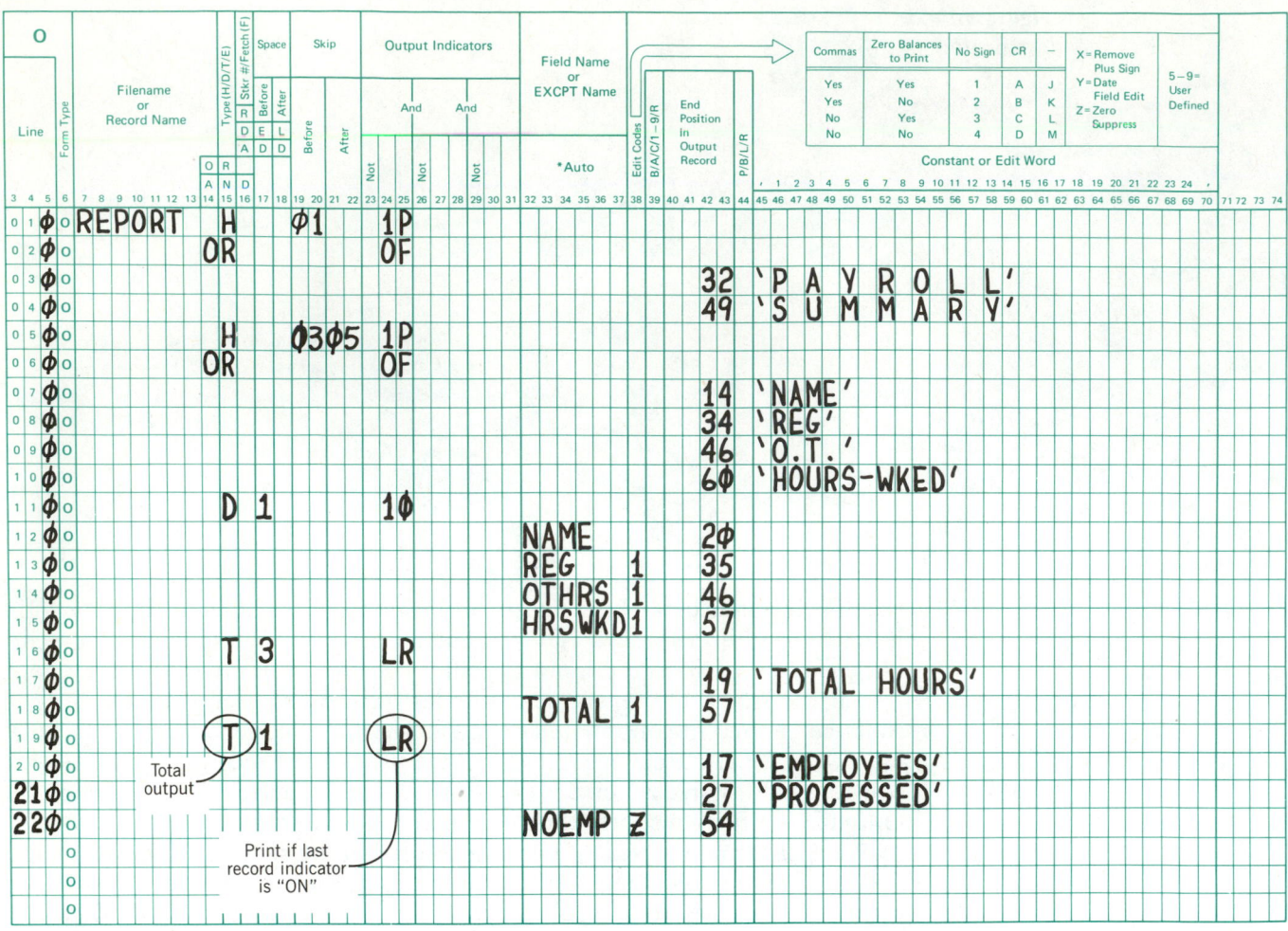

Figure 3.25
Output Specifications form for
the sample problem.

subsequent calculations or output operations. Figure 3.26 provides an illustration of the use of resulting indicators.

An arithmetic operation can also be used to turn on indicators that will specify whether the result is a positive, negative, or zero balance.

In Figure 3.26, note that the resulting field NBAL will always turn "on" one of the resulting indicators, namely 2Ø, 3Ø, or 4Ø. If an account is overdrawn (OBAL − DEBIT = a negative amount), a negative balance will result and indicator 3Ø will be turned on. Thus, indicator 3Ø may be used to print a message that designates the account as overdrawn. Similarly, indicator 4Ø may be used on the Output Specifications form to produce a message denoting a zero balance (OBAL − DEBIT = 0). A positive balance (OBAL − DEBIT = a positive amount) will turn on indicator 2Ø. Since a positive balance is acceptable, no warning messages would be printed. Indicator 2Ø was included in this example for completeness and may be eliminated without changing the logic of the program. Since indicator 2Ø is not used for other calculations or for printing output, it is not necessary in the program. Some RPG compilers will print a warning level error if an indicator is specified in the program but not used.

Keep in mind that these indicators will remain on until reset. It should be noted that the resulting indicators 20, 30, and 40 are set on or off by executing

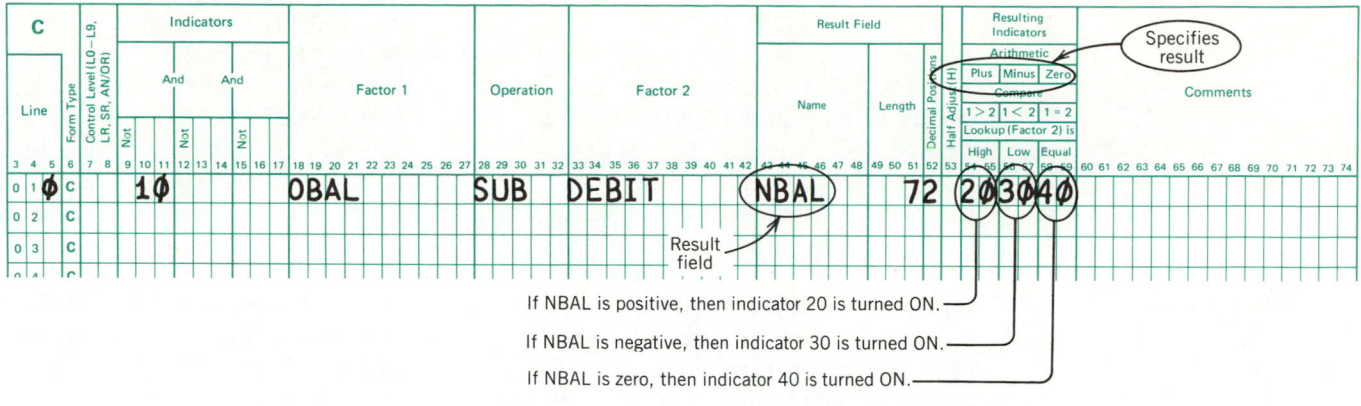

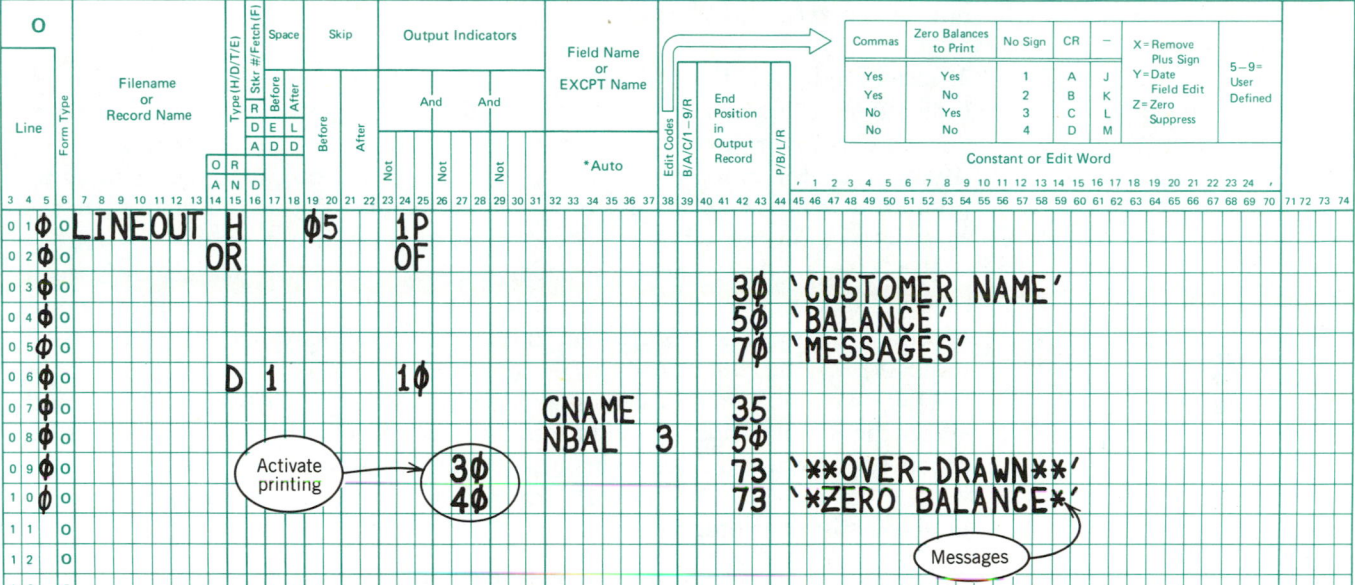

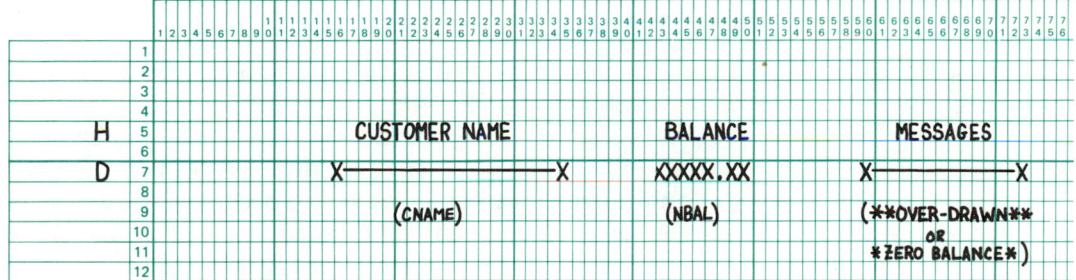

Figure 3.26
Using Resulting Indicators on an Output Specifications form.

the SUB operation. It should also be noted that the indicators are only set off if the SUB operation is executed. The SUB operation is executed if the condition—indicator 10 on—is met. Thus, if indicator 10 is off, the SUB operation is not executed at all and indicators 20, 30, and 40 remain as they were before indicator 10 was tested.

In the next section, we will discuss the use of the SETON and SETOF commands, which can directly affect the logic of a program by turning indicators on and off.

In the example, the resulting indicators are used on the Output Specifications form to produce messages that describe the status of the customer's account. When indicator 30 is on, the message "**OVER-DRAWN**" will print; similarly, indicator 40 will be used to print the message "*ZERO BALANCE*". The Printer Spacing Chart reflects the desired output needed to produce an exception report. Again, note that no output will be produced when a positive balance sets indicator 20 on, since indicator 20 is not used on the Output Specifications form.

Also recall that field indicators can be used on the Input Specifications form. In the previous chapter, you learned that field indicators can be set if the contents of numeric input fields are positive, negative, or zero; similarly, alphanumeric fields may be tested for spaces or blanks. As with resulting indicators, if the specified condition is met, the field indicator is turned "on"; if not, it is turned "off."

2. Setting Indicators On and Off

Indicators are normally controlled throughout a program based on certain conditions being met, for example, reading a record and setting on a record identifying indicator. However, there are certain times during the processing of the program when it is necessary to change the condition of an indicator, that is, turn on an indicator when it is off or turn off an indicator when it is on.

RPG contains two operation codes, **SETON** and **SETOF**, which are used to turn indicators on and off. When either the SETON or SETOF operation code is specified in positions 28–32 of the Calculation Specifications form, we may set indicators on (SETON) or off (SETOF) directly.

One, two, or three indicators may be controlled on one calculation line with either the SETON or SETOF operation. The indicators to be SETON or SETOF are specified in columns 54–59 as shown in Figure 3.27, which we will describe shortly. Use the SETON or SETOF operations when you want to control the indicators in your program to:

1. Keep track of conditions affecting the logic of the program
2. Replace several indicators with one indicator
3. Set off indicators for each RPG cycle or record

Indicators may be used to condition SETON or SETOF operations in a variety of ways. ANd, OR, and Not conditions may be logically combined to set indicators on or off as shown in Examples 2 and 4 of Figure 3.27. Note that on both the OR and ANd specifications, the SETON instruction is on the *last line* that conditions indicators. If you fail to observe this rule, a syntax error will occur.

A key point to remember with the SETON and SETOF operations is that when using numerous indicators it is a good idea to set them all off at one single point in the cycle. Typically this is done at the beginning or end of the calculations, which are specified on the Calculation Specifications form. If the indicators are not set off with each cycle, then several indicators could still be on at the same time, which could result in logic errors that may be difficult to detect. Therefore, it is good practice to set off *all* indicators at the beginning or end of each cycle to prevent logic errors resulting from indicators being left on from a previous cycle.

A brief description of each of the examples in Figure 3.27 will further your understanding of the SETON and SETOF operations.

Example 1   The SETON can be used to keep track of a condition that occurred in your program during the present RPG cycle. In this example, when the overflow (OF) indicator is set on by RPG, we use the SETON operation to set on indicator 55. Indicator 55 will remain on until you set it off.

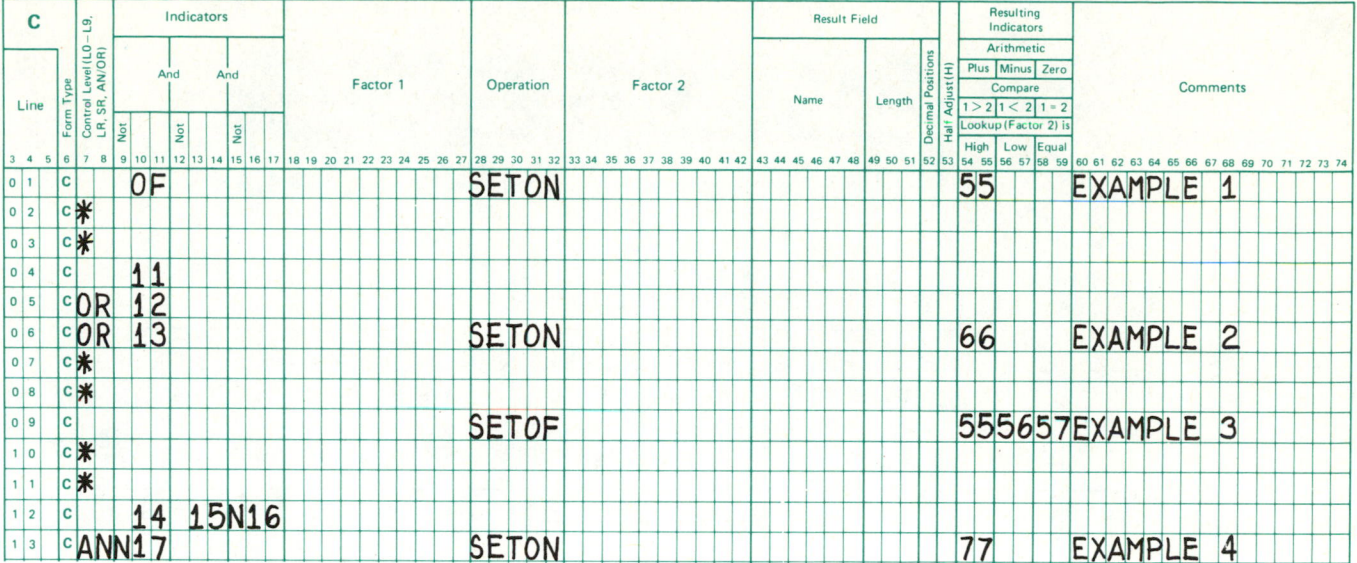

Figure 3.27
Use of resulting indicators.

Example 2 If indicators 11, 12, and 13 represent different error conditions, then 66 can be SETON to signal that an error exists. If indicator 11, 12, or 13 is on, then indicator 66 will be turned on by the SETON operation illustrated.

Example 3 The SETOF operation can set off up to three different indicators. This example will set off indicators 55, 56, and 57 with only one operation.

Example 4 This example illustrates the concept of combining indicators. If several indicators are to be combined for later reference, then the ANd is appropriate. In this example, four conditions must all exist to set on indicator 77. Namely, indicators 14 and 15 must be on, while indicators 16 and 17 must be off. Remember, to satisfy the ANd operator, all conditions must be met or satisfied.

E. Sample Program 2

Consider the problem definition in Figure 3.28. The program is illustrated in Figure 3.29.

Figure 3.28
Problem definition for Sample Program 2.

Systems Flowchart

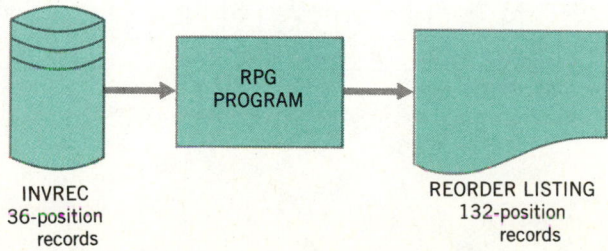

INVREC
36-position
records

RPG PROGRAM

REORDER LISTING
132-position
records

Figure 3.28
(continued)

INVREC Record Layout

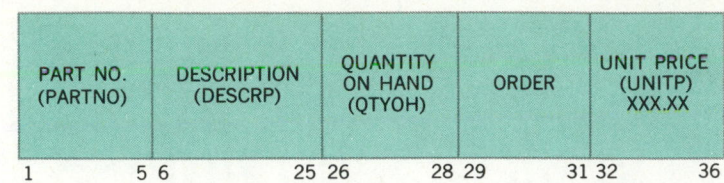

REORDER LISTING Printer Spacing Chart

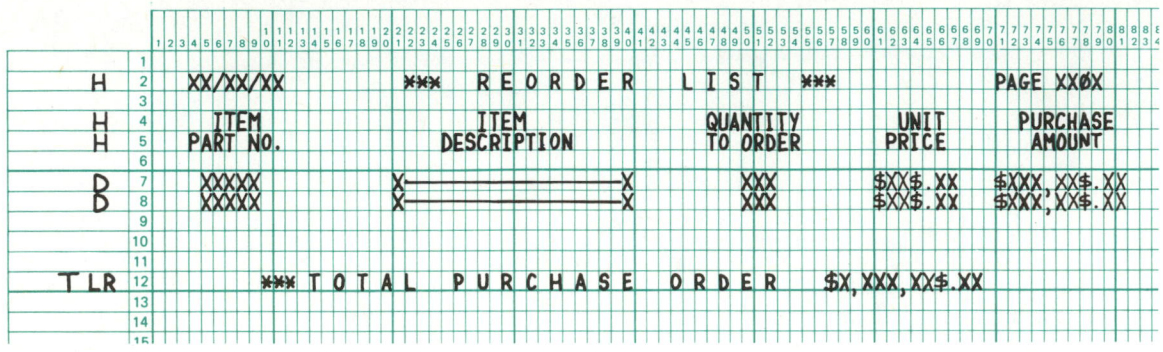

Figure 3.29
Coding sheets for Sample
Program 2.

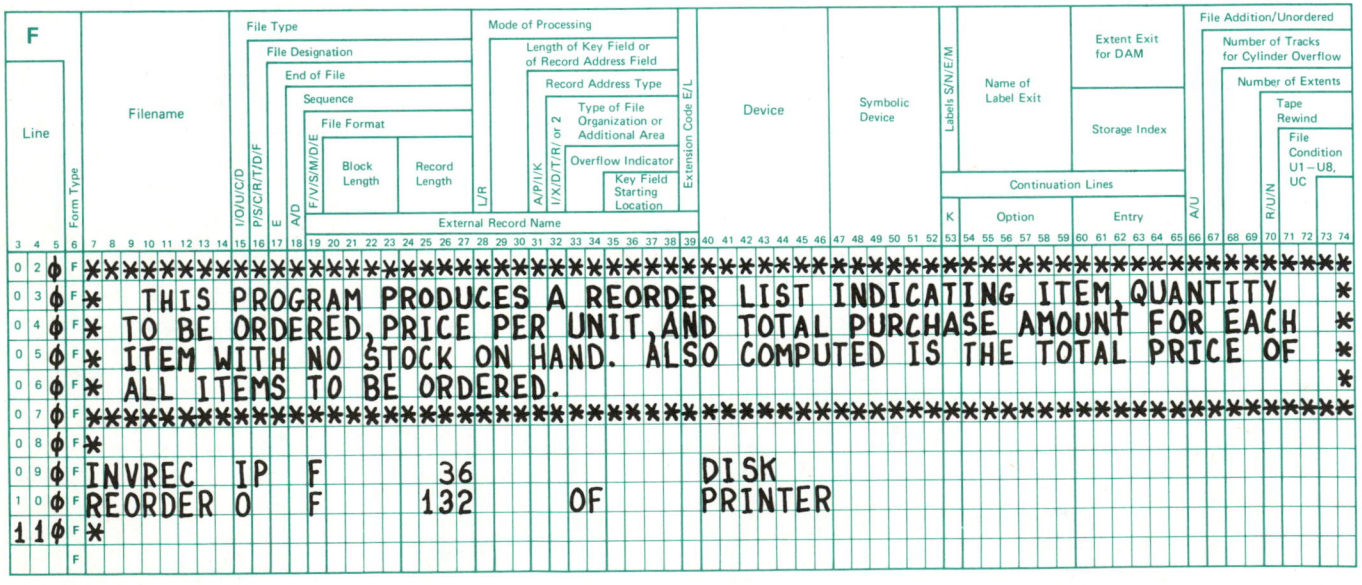

I — Input Specifications

Line	Form Type	Filename or Record Name / Data Structure Name	Field Location From	To	RPG Field Name	Field Indicators
01	I	********************************** INPUT RECORD **********************************				
02	I	*				
03	I	INVREC NS				
04	I		1	5	PARTNO	
05	I		6	25	DESCRP	
06	I		26	28Ø	QTYOH	Ø5
07	I		29	31Ø	ORDER	
08	I		32	362	UNITP	
09	I	*				
10	I	#WORK				
11	I		1	92	#AMT	
12	I		1Ø	182	#TOT	
13	I					

C — Calculation Specifications

Line	Form Type	Indicators	Factor 1	Operation	Factor 2	Result Field Name	Length	Decimal Positions	Half Adjust (H)	Resulting Indicators Comments
01	C	************************** CALCULATIONS ************************************								
02	C	*								
03	C	***								
04	C	***** IF QTYOH FIELD CONTAINS ZEROS								
05	C	***** INDICATOR Ø5 IS TURNED ON AND								
06	C	***** CALCULATIONS ARE PERFORMED								
07	C	***								
08	C	Ø5	ORDER	MULT	UNITP	#AMT			H	
09	C	Ø5	#AMT	ADD	#TOT	#TOT				
10	C	*								

Figure 3.29

(continued)

(continued on next page)

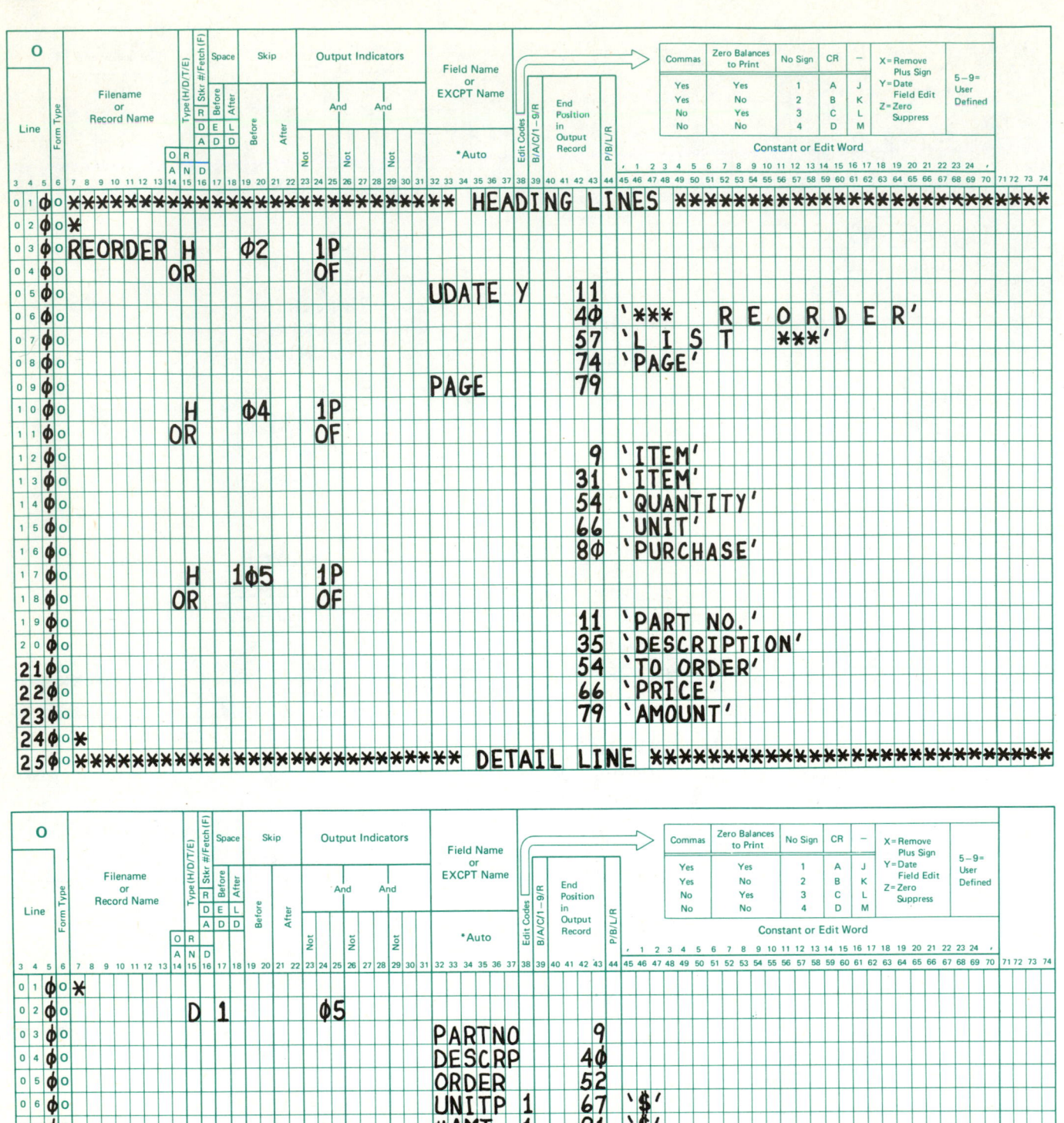

Figure 3.29
(continued)

CHAPTER SELF-TEST

1. Arrange the following steps in the order in which they occur during the RPG cycle.
   a. PERFORM DETAIL CALCULATIONS
   b. READ A RECORD
   c. PERFORM DETAIL OUTPUT
   d. MOVE DATA TO FIELDS
   e. PRINT HEADINGS

2. If you added 1 to a field each time an event occurred, this would be an example of using a _____ .

3. When a field is added to a total field as each record is processed, this would be an example of using a (counter/running total).

4. (T or F) Numeric fields can be defined only by placing an entry in the Decimal Positions field of the Calculation Specifications form.

5. Numeric literals or constants may be up to _____ positions in length.

6. (T or F) Numeric literals or constants may contain commas and dollar signs.

7. (T or F) Numeric fields used for counters and running totals are initially set to zero by the RPG compiler.

8. (T or F) After performing subtraction, the contents of Factor 1 will always be reduced by the quantity stored in Factor 2.

9. (T or F) A numeric field may be set to zero by subtracting the field from itself.

10. If a five-digit field containing two decimal positions (XXX.XX) were to be multiplied by a three-digit field (no decimals), for precise results the product should be stored in a(n) _____(no.)_____-digit field containing _____(no.)_____ decimal positions.

11. Rounding the number 3.141592 to three decimal places would result in a value of _____ .

12. Truncating the number 3.141592 to three decimal places would result in a value of _____ .

13. After all the input records have been processed, the _____ indicator is used to print out the totals accumulated by the program.

14. The _____ and _____ operations are used to set indicators on and off, respectively.

15. Up to _____(no.)_____ indicators can be set on or off with the SETON or SETOF operations.

In Questions 16 through 19, determine the contents of the various fields after the instruction shown has been executed.

16.

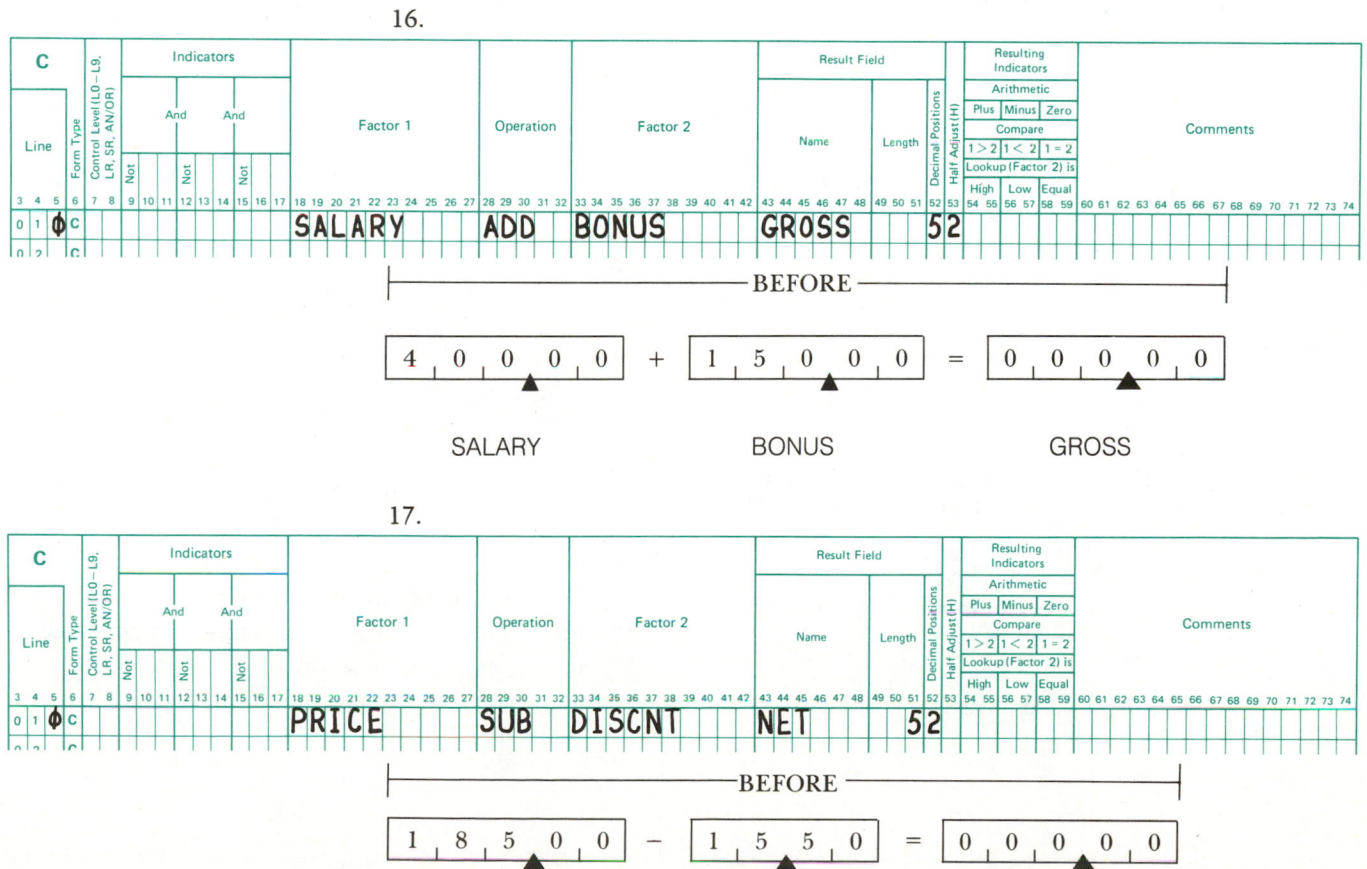

17.

18.

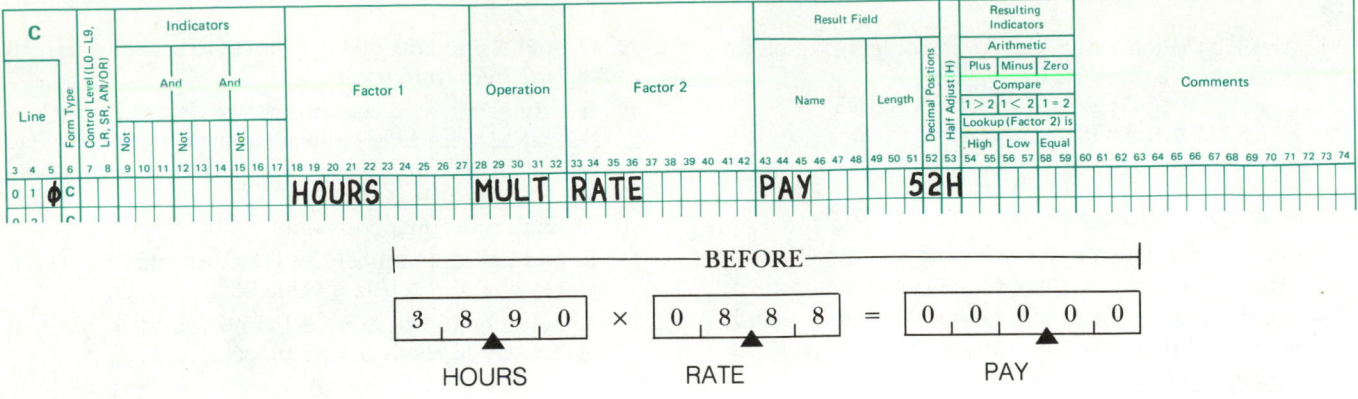

19.

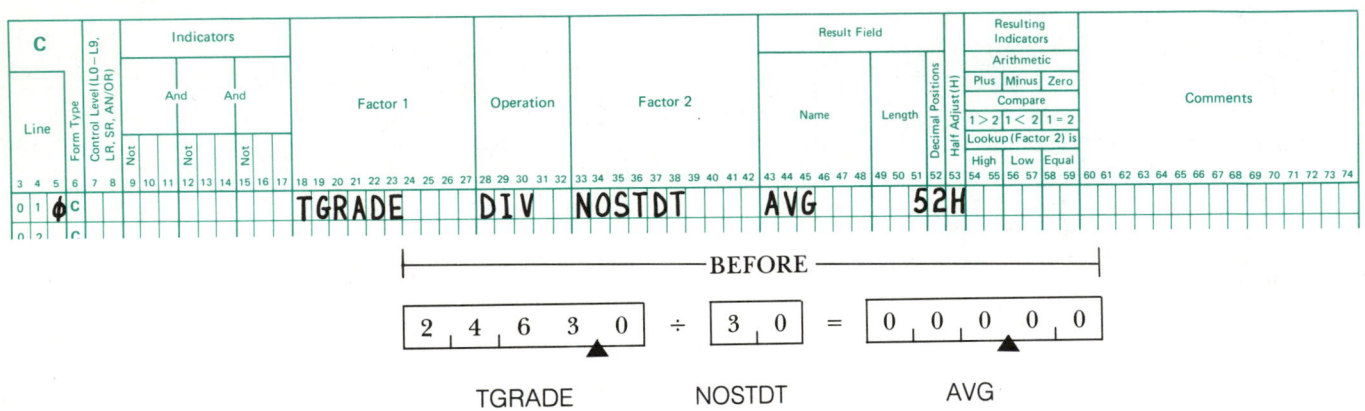

SOLUTIONS

1. e; b; d; a; c
2. counter
3. running total
4. F—Numeric fields may also be defined on the Input Specifications form as part of input or as part of a Data Structure.
5. 1Ø
6. F—Only decimal points and minus signs are permitted.
7. T
8. F—Only the Result Field changes.
9. T
10. eight; two
11. 3.142
12. 3.141
13. LR (denoting last record)
14. SETON and SETOF
15. three
16. GROSS = 550∧00 (SALARY and BONUS are unchanged)
17. NET = 169∧50 (PRICE and DISCNT are unchanged)
18. PAY = 345∧43 (HOURS and RATE are unchanged)
19. AVG = 082∧10 (TGRADE and NOSTDT are unchanged)

KEY TERMS

ADDition operation	Half-adjust	Quotient	Sizing fields
Alphanumeric literal	High-order truncation	Record indicator	SUBtraction operation
Constant	Literal	Result Field	Truncation
Counter	Low-order truncation	Resulting indicator	Variable data
Data Structure	LR indicator	Rounding	Z-ADD operation
DIVide operation	MOVE	RPG Logic Cycle	Z-SUB operation
Factor 1	MOVEL	Running total	
Factor 2	MULTiplication operation	SETOF	
	MVR operation	SETON	
	Numeric literal		

REVIEW QUESTIONS

In each case, code the Calculation Specifications form only.

1. Student registration records contain each student's name, number of credits the student is taking (CRED) for the semester, and the rate per credit (RATE). Each student's tuition is to be calculated using the following formula:

   TUITN = CRED × RATE

   CRED is two positions long (no decimals). RATE is five positions long, including two decimal positions. Approximately 200 students are enrolled in all courses. You are required to count the number of students processed and accumulate a sum of all the students' tuition (SUM). Indicator 10 is to be turned on for all input records and is used for these calculations.

2. An input record contains a customer name, old balance (OBAL), deposits (DEP), and withdrawals (WITH). Write the entries necessary to calculate a new balance (NBAL) using the formula:

   NBAL = OBAL + DEP − WITH

   when indicator 19 is on. Also, count the input records (COUNT) and develop running totals of the deposits (TDEP) and withdrawals (TWITH). All fields should be seven positions long including two decimal positions.

3. S & S Department Store bills customers using an accounts receivable billing system. A service charge of 1.5% of the old balance (OBAL) is assessed each month. The amount due (AMT) each month is calculated as follows:

   Credits = Payments + Returns
   New Balance = Old Balance + Purchases
     + Service Charge − Credits

   All balance fields are six positions in length including two decimal positions. Code the RPG entries for these calculations using indicator 20.

4. Compute Fahrenheit (F) temperatures using inputted Celsius (C) temperatures. The formula for the conversion is: $F = (9/5) \times C + 32$. Round F to two decimal positions.

5. Calculate net sales = total sales less a (rounded) discount of 2%. Allow for a Result Field of six positions, containing 2 decimal places.

6. Convert N (number of feet) to I (number of inches). N will never exceed 99.99 feet.

7. Convert quarts to liters. Recall that 1 quart = 0.946 liters. The maximum entry for quarts is 9.9 for this problem. Do not truncate any digits.

8. Calculate quantity on hand (QOH) = QTYIN − QTYOUT. If QOH is zero or negative, do not perform the succeeding step, which is

   AVG = TCOST/QOH

   Note: All quantity fields are four-position integers, whereas TCOST has an XXXX.XX specification.

9. Assume FLDA = 100.00, FLDB = − 75, and FLDC = 0. Using the instructions depicted here, determine (1) the indicator set on by the instruction, and (2) the contents of the Result Fields ANS1 through ANS6.

C			Indicators							Result Field				Resulting Indicators			(A)	(B)
			And		And									Arithmetic				
	Form Type	Control Level (L0—L9, LR, SR, AN/OR)					Factor 1	Operation	Factor 2	Name	Length	Decimal Positions	Half Adjust (H)	Plus	Minus	Zero	Indicator ON	Contents of Result Field
Line			Not		Not		Not							Compare				
														1 > 2	1 < 2	1 = 2		
														Lookup (Factor 2) is				
														High	Low	Equal		
3 4 5	6	7 8	9	10 11	12 13	14	15 16 17	18 19 20 21 22 23 24 25 26 27	28 29 30 31 32	33 34 35 36 37 38 39 40 41 42	43 44 45 46 47 48	49 50 51	52	53	54 55	56 57	58 59	60 6	
0 1 0	C							FLDA	SUB	FLDB	ANS1	3 0			0 1	0 2	0 3	(a)	
0 2 0	C	*																
0 3 0	C								Z-ADD	FLDC	ANS2	3 0			0 4	0 5	0 6	(b)	
0 4 0	C	*																
0 5 0	C							FLDA	MULT	FLDB	ANS3	4 0			0 7	0 8	0 9	(c)	
0 6 0	C	*																
0 7 0	C								Z-ADD	FLDB	ANS4	2 0			1 0	1 1	1 2	(d)	
0 8 0	C	*																
0 9 0	C							FLDB	ADD	FLDB	ANS5	2 0			1 3	1 4	1 5	(e)	
1 0 0	C	*																
1 1 0	C							FLDB	SUB	FLDB	ANS6	2 0			1 6	1 7	1 8	(f)	
1 2	C																	

DEBUGGING EXERCISES

DEBUGGING EXERCISE 1

Misgiven Reality: A Walkthrough Exercise

The following is an exercise requiring you to predict the results of calculations. Programmers often use a walkthrough technique to verify that the program will accomplish its desired goals. That is, the program is checked manually, and the results obtained are compared to those produced by the actual program.

The objective of this program is to compute the monthly payment (MNPYMT) for each parcel of real estate. The monthly payment is the sum of the monthly tax (MNTAX) and the monthly payment of the mortgage (MNMORG). These calculations (MNTAX and MNMORG) are based on the selling price (SELLPR), the amount of down payment (DNPAY), the annual cost of the mortgage (YRMORG), and the annual tax charges (YRTAX).

Figure 3.30 is the problem definition for this exercise. Figure 3.31 shows the coding sheets used for the program. The program listing and output are shown in Figure 3.32.

For this example, assume a selling price (SELLPR) of $50,000 with a down payment (DNPAY) of $14,500. Perform each operation on the Calculation Specifications form, one at a time, and note your results. Compare your results with the program output. Also answer the questions that follow the program.

Questions

1. Identify the fields in the input record that are numeric.
2. What does the **H** signify on the Calculation form?
3. How is the monthly mortgage calculated?
4. How are new values assigned for each customer in calculating the monthly mortgage?
5. How is the monthly tax calculated?
6. How many dollars are paid for the $35,500 mortgage over a 25-year period?
7. How many total dollars in taxes will be spent over a 25-year period?
8. Indicate the operation that causes the current date to be printed on the output.
9. Are any of the output fields zero-suppressed?
10. Refer to the Calculation Specifications form. Does the selling price (SELLPR) change because the down payment (DNPAY) is subtracted?

Figure 3.30
Problem definition for Debugging Exercise 1.

Systems Flowchart

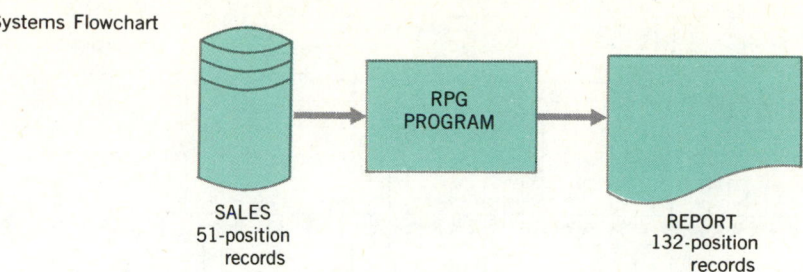

SALES Record Layout

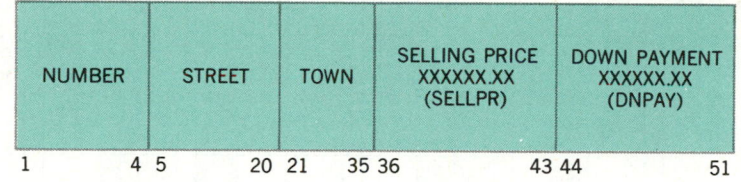

REPORT Printer Spacing Chart

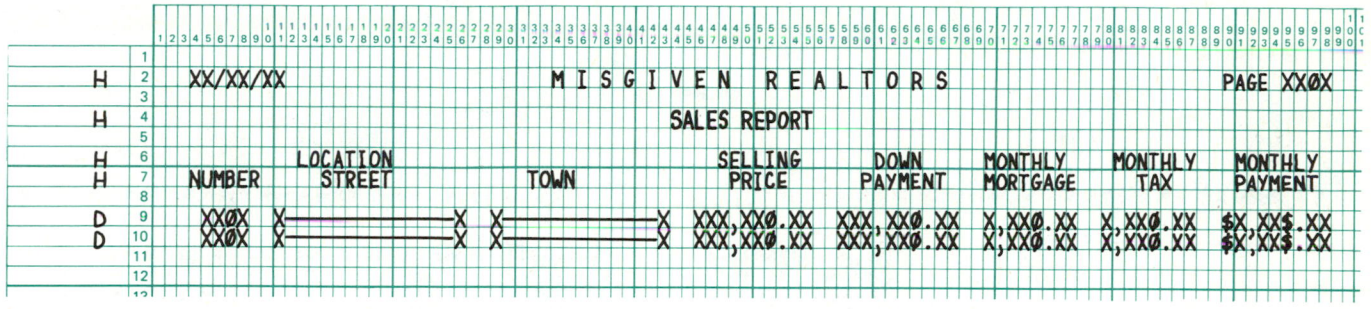

Figure 3.31
Coding sheets for Debugging Exercise 1.
(continued on next page)

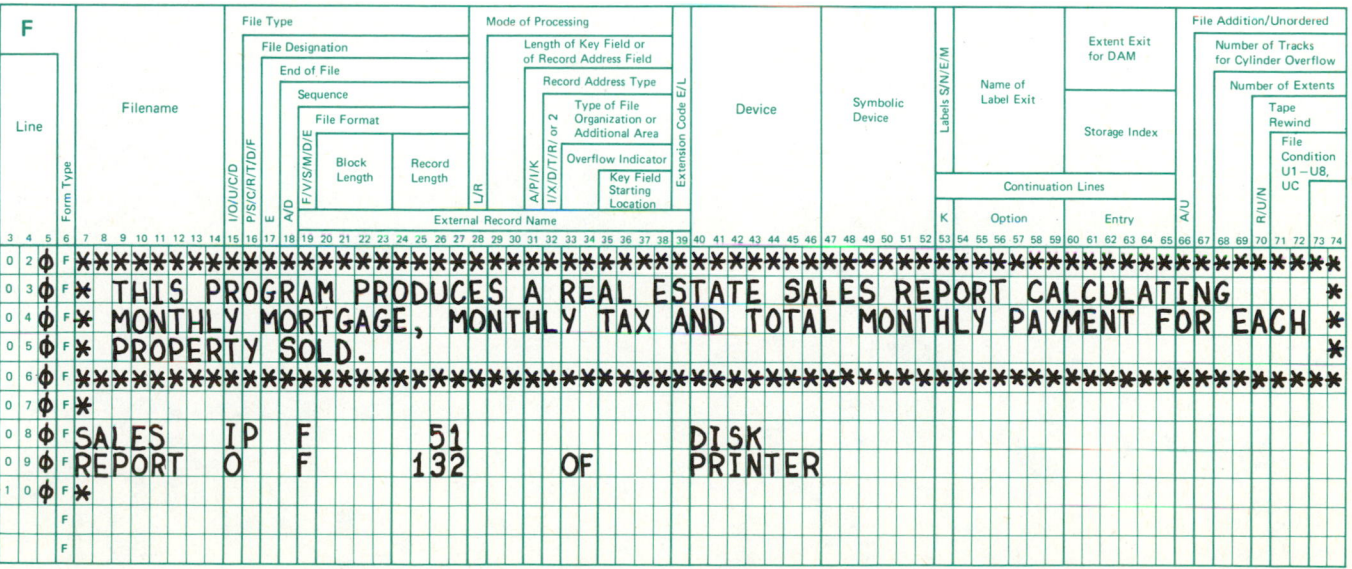

I — Input Specifications

Line	Form Type	Filename or Record Name / Data Structure Name	O/R And	Number (1/N), E Option (O), U, S	Record Identifying Indicator or DS	Record Identification Codes 1 Position / Not(N) / C/Z/D / Character	2 Position / Not(N) / C/Z/D / Character	3 Position / Not(N) / C/Z/D / Character	Stacker Select P/B/L/R	Field Location From (Occurs n Times)	To (Length)	Decimal Positions	RPG Field Name	Control Level (L1–L9)	Matching Fields or Chaining Fields	Field Record Relation	Field Indicators Plus / Minus / Zero or Blank
0 1	Ø I	**********************								INPUT RECORD	******************************						
0 2	Ø I	*															
0 3	Ø I	SALES			NS												
0 4	Ø I									1	4Ø		NUMBER				
0 5	Ø I									5	2Ø		STREET				
0 6	Ø I									21	35		TOWN				
0 7	Ø I									36	43	2	SELLPR				
0 8	Ø I									44	51	2	DNPAY				
0 9	Ø I	*															
1 0																	
1 1																	

C — Calculation Specifications

Line	Form Type	Control Level (L0–L9, LR, SR, AN/OR)	Indicators And Not / And Not / And Not	Factor 1	Operation	Factor 2	Result Field Name	Length	Decimal Positions	Half Adjust (H)	Resulting Indicators Arithmetic Plus 1>2 High / Minus 1<2 Low / Zero 1=2 Equal	Comments
0 1	Ø C	*************************					CALCULATIONS				***************************	
0 2	Ø C	*										
0 3	Ø C			SELLPR	SUB	DNPAY	MRGAMT	82				MONTHLY
0 4	Ø C			MRGAMT	MULT	.137	YRMORG	72H				MORTGAGE
0 5	Ø C			YRMORG	DIV	12	MNMORG	62H				
0 6	Ø C	*										
0 7	Ø C			SELLPR	MULT	.Ø45	YRTAX	72H				MONTHLY
0 8	Ø C			YRTAX	DIV	12	MNTAX	62H				TAX
0 9	Ø C	*										
1 0	Ø C			MNMORG	ADD	MNTAX	MNPYMT	72				MONTHLY PAYMENT
1 1	Ø C	*										

Figure 3.31
(continued)

Figure 3.31
(continued)

Figure 3.32
Program listing and output for
Debugging Exercise 1.

```
          01-020   F*****************************************************************SSS03C
          01-030   F* THIS PROGRAM PRODUCES A REAL ESTATE SALES REPORT CALCULATING   *SSS03C
          01-040   F* MONTHLY MORTGAGE, MONTHLY TAX AND TOTAL MONTHLY PAYMENT FOR EACH*SSS03C
          01-050   F* PROPERTY SOLD.                                                 *SSS03C
          01-060   F*****************************************************************SSS03C
          01-070   F*                                                                SSS03C
0001      01-080   FSALES    IP  F     51              DISK                           SSS03C
0002      01-090   FREPORT   O   F    132        OF    PRINTER                        SSS03C
          01-100   F*                                                                SSS03C
          02-010   I********************** INPUT RECORD **************************SSS03C
          02-020   I*                                                                SSS03C
0003      02-030   ISALES    NS                                                       SSS03C
0004      02-040   I                                       1   40NUMBER               SSS03C
0005      02-050   I                                       5   20 STREET              SSS03C
0006      02-060   I                                      21   35 TOWN                SSS03C
0007      02-070   I                                      36  432SELLPR               SSS03C
0008      02-080   I                                      44  512DNPAY                SSS03C
          02-090   I*                                                                SSS03C
          03-010   C********************** CALCULATIONS **************************SSS03C
          03-020   C*                                                                SSS03C
0009      03-030   C           SELLPR    SUB  DNPAY     MRGAMT  82         MONTHLY     SSS03C
0010      03-040   C           MRGAMT    MULT .137      YRMORG  72H        MORTGAGE    SSS03C
0011      03-050   C           YRMORG    DIV  12        MNMORG  62H                    SSS03C
          03-060   C*                                                                SSS03C
0012      03-070   C           SELLPR    MULT .045      YRTAX   72H        MONTHLY     SSS03C
0013      03-080   C           YRTAX     DIV  12        MNTAX   62H        TAX         SSS03C
          03-090   C*                                                                SSS03C
0014      03-100   C           MNMORG    ADD  MNTAX     MNPYMT  72         MONTHLY PAYMENTSSS03C
          03-110   C*                                                                SSS03C
          04-010   O********************** HEADING LINES **************************SSS03C
          04-020   C*                                                                SSS03C
0015      04-030   OREPORT   H  201        1P                                         SSS03C
0016      04-040   O                  OR          OF                                  SSS03C
0017      04-050   O                             UDATE Y   11                         SSS03C
0018      04-060   O                                      48 'M I S G I V E N'        SSS03C
0019      04-070   O                                      66 'R E A L T O R S'        SSS03C
0020      04-080   O                                      93 'PAGE'                   SSS03C
0021      04-090   O                             PAGE     98                          SSS03C
0022      04-100   O         H  2          1P                                         SSS03C
0023      04-110   O                  OR          OF                                  SSS03C
0024      04-120   O                                      55 'SALES REPORT'           SSS03C
0025      04-130   O         H  1          1P                                         SSS03C
0026      04-140   O                  OR          OF                                  SSS03C
0027      04-150   O                                      20 'LOCATION'               SSS03C
0028      04-160   O                                      64 'SELLING       DOWN'     SSS03C
0029      04-170   O                                      87 'MONTHLY    MONTHLY'     SSS03C
0030      04-180   O                                      97 'MONTHLY'                SSS03C
0031      04-190   O         H  2          1P                                         SSS03C
0032      04-200   O                  OR          OF                                  SSS03C
0033      04-210   O                                      19 'NUMBER    STREET'       SSS03C
0034      04-220   O                                      53 'TOWN          PRICE'    SSS03C
0035      04-230   O                                      77 'PAYMENT   MORTGAGE'     SSS03C
0036      04-240   O                                      97 'TAX       PAYMENT'      SSS03C
          04-250   C*                                                                SSS03C
          05-010   C********************** DETAIL LINE **************************SSS03C
          05-020   C*                                                                SSS03C
0037      05-030   O         D  1         N1P                                         SSS03C
0038      05-040   O                             NUMBERZ    8                         SSS03C
0039      05-050   O                             STREET    26                         SSS03C
0040      05-060   O                             TOWN      43                         SSS03C
0041      05-070   O                             SELLPR1   55                         SSS03C
0042      05-080   O                             DNPAY 1   67                         SSS03C
0043      05-090   O                             MNMORG1   77                         SSS03C
0044      05-100   O                             MNTAX 1   87                         SSS03C
0045      05-110   O                             MNPYMT1   98 '$'                     SSS03C
          05-120   C*                                                                SSS03C
          05-130   C********************** *****************************************SSS03C
```

```
        END  OF  SOURCE

12/17/91                    M I S G I V E N   R E A L T O R S

                                 SALES REPORT

        LOCATION                        SELLING    DOWN     MONTHLY    MONTHLY   MONTHLY
NUMBER  STREET           TOWN           PRICE      PAYMENT  MORTGAGE   TAX       PAYMENT

 1932   HAMILTON DRIVE   OCEANSIDE      50,000.00  14,500.00  405.29   187.50    $592.79
  362   WASHINGTON AVE   LEVITTOWN      61,900.00  18,500.00  495.48   232.13    $727.61
  721   LAFAYETTE ST     UNIONDALE      45,000.00  11,250.00  385.31   168.75    $554.06
 1045   LANCASTER RD     NORTHPORT     105,900.00  37,065.00  785.87   397.13  $1,183.00
   57   DOGWOOD RD       GARDEN CITY    95,900.00  30,560.00  741.40   358.13  $1,099.53
  566   PUMPKIN LANE     HICKSVILLE     59,950.00  15,000.00  513.18   224.81    $737.99
    7   SEAVIEW COURT    OYSTER BAY     87,500.00  21,900.00  748.93   328.13  $1,077.06
```

11. Identify the instruction that numbers each page of the output.
12. Name the primary file used by the program.
13. Do any output fields contain dollar signs?
14. Identify the edited fields in the detail printing of the report.
15. With the editing specified, how will fields containing zeros be printed?

DEBUGGING EXERCISE 2

The problem definition for this exercise is shown in Figure 3.33. The coding sheets in Figure 3.34 contain three syntax errors. Identify them and illustrate the corrections you would make to the program.

The listing in Figure 3.35 includes the error diagnostics produced by running the program as coded. The syntax corrections are circled on the computer listing shown in Figure 3.36. There are, however, logic errors in the program. Your assignment is to desk check the program carefully, find the logic errors, and make the necessary corrections.

Figure 3.33
Problem definition for Debugging Exercise 2.

Systems Flowchart

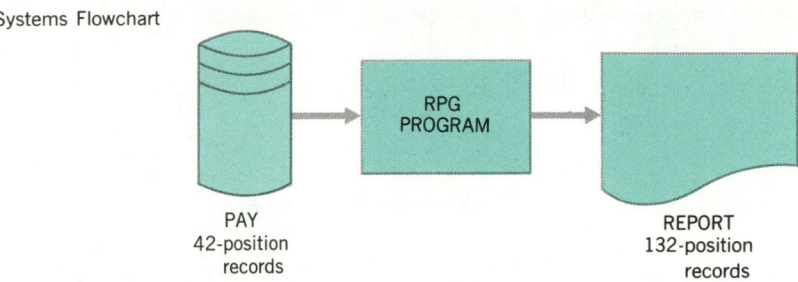

PAY Record Layout

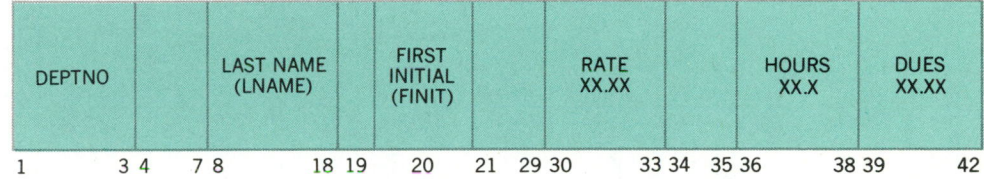

REPORT Printer Spacing Chart

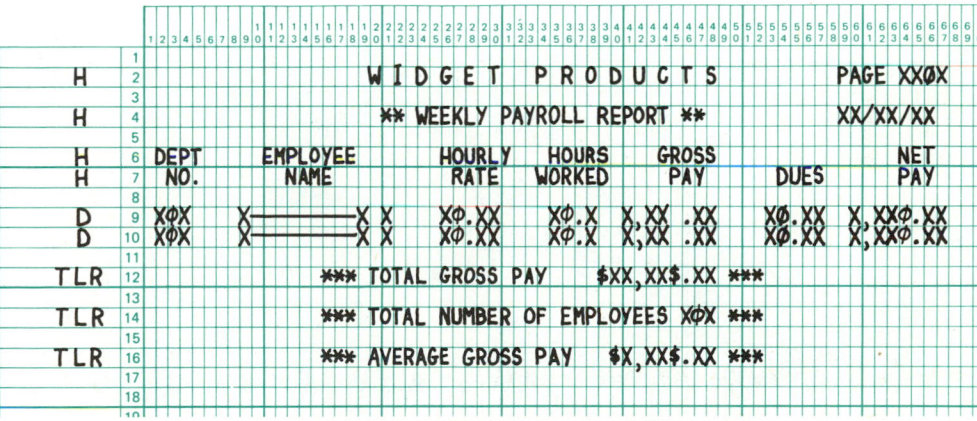

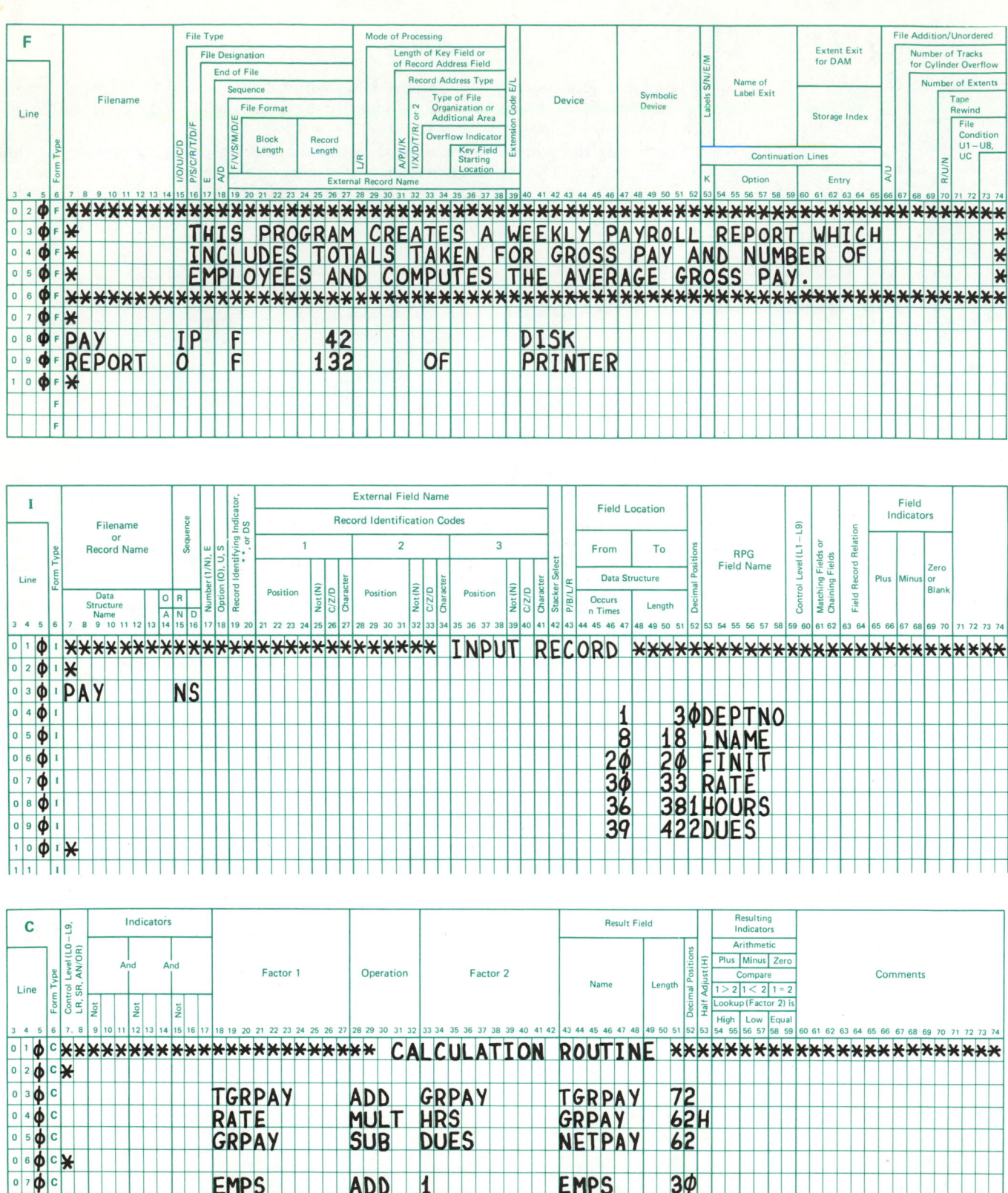

Figure 3.34
Coding sheets for Debugging
Exercise 2.

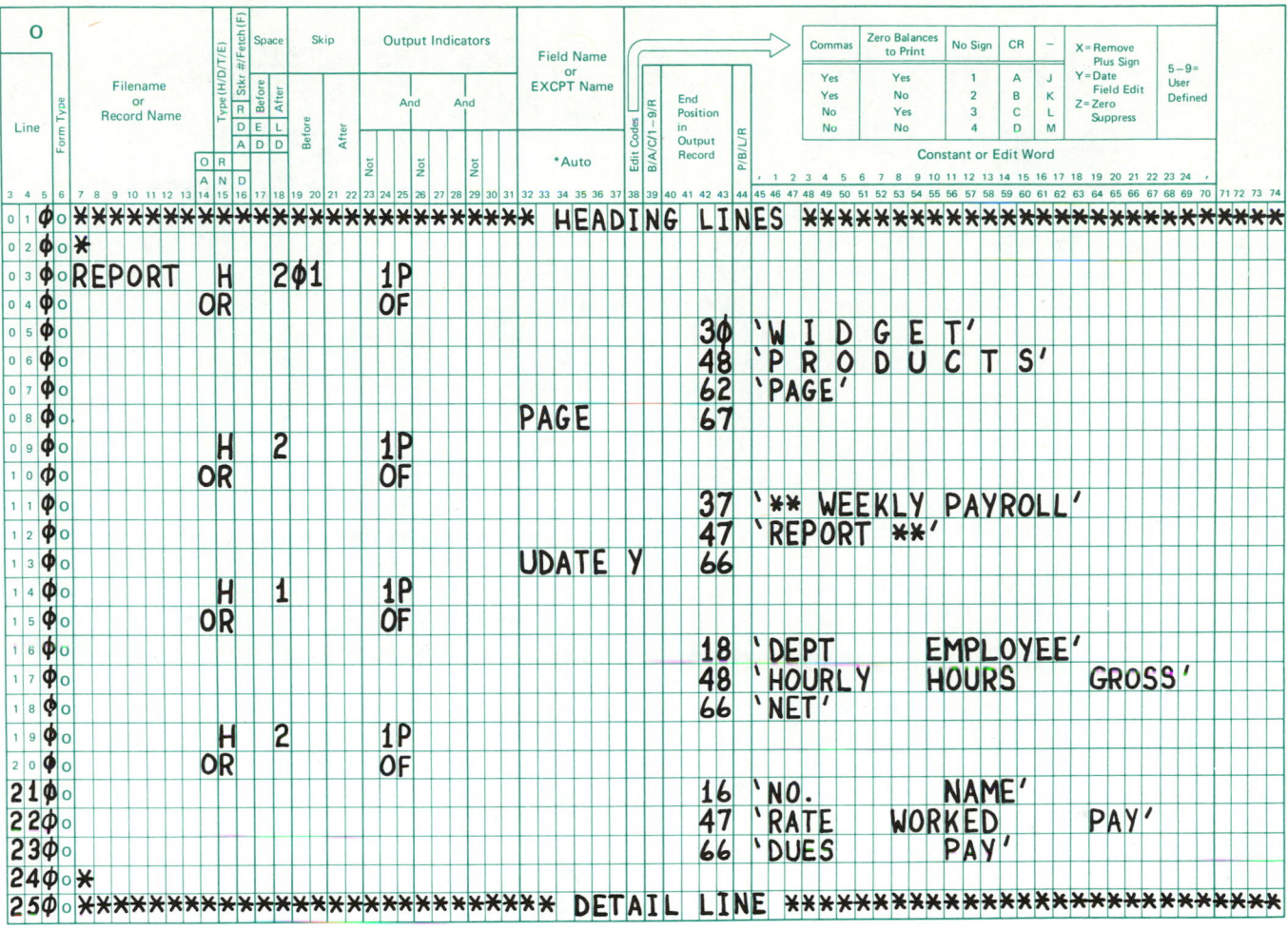

O	Line	Form Type	Filename or Record Name	Type (H/D/T/E)	Stkr #/Fetch (F)	Space Before After	Skip Before	After	Output Indicators And Not	And Not	Not	Field Name or EXCPT Name *Auto	Edit Codes B/A/C/1–9/R	End Position in Output Record	P/B/L/R	Constant or Edit Word
01	0	O	✻✻✻✻✻✻✻✻✻✻✻✻✻✻✻✻✻✻✻ HEADING LINES ✻✻✻✻✻✻✻✻✻✻✻✻✻✻✻✻✻✻✻													
02	0	O	✻													
03	0	O	REPORT	H		201		1P								
04	0	O		OR				OF								
05	0	O												30		'WIDGET'
06	0	O												48		'PRODUCTS'
07	0	O												62		'PAGE'
08	0	O											PAGE	67		
09	0	O		H		2		1P								
10	0	O		OR				OF								
11	0	O												37		'✻✻ WEEKLY PAYROLL'
12	0	O												47		'REPORT ✻✻'
13	0	O											UDATE Y	66		
14	0	O		H		1		1P								
15	0	O		OR				OF								
16	0	O												18		'DEPT EMPLOYEE'
17	0	O												48		'HOURLY HOURS GROSS'
18	0	O												66		'NET'
19	0	O		H		2		1P								
20	0	O		OR				OF								
21	0	O												16		'NO. NAME'
22	0	O												47		'RATE WORKED PAY'
23	0	O												66		'DUES PAY'
24	0	O	✻													
25	0	O	✻✻✻✻✻✻✻✻✻✻✻✻✻✻✻✻✻✻✻✻✻ DETAIL LINE ✻✻✻✻✻✻✻✻✻✻✻✻✻✻✻✻✻✻✻✻✻													

Figure 3.34
(continued)

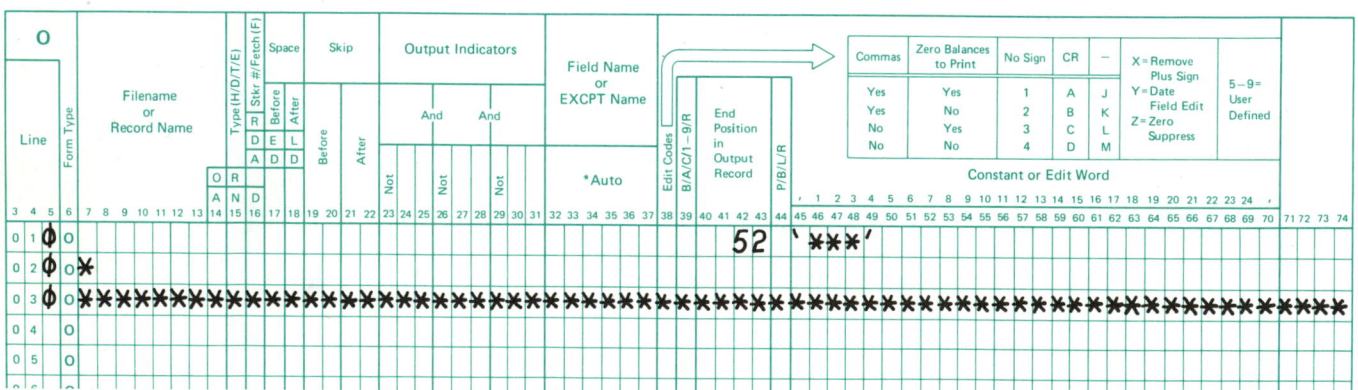

RPG Output Specifications:

```
Line  Form  ...
 01   O  *
 02   O        D  1        N1P
 03   O                        DEPTNOZ       4
 04   O                        LNAME        19
 05   O                        FINIT        21
 06   O                        RATE   1     30
 07   O                        HOURS  1     38
 08   O                        GRPAY  1     48
 09   O                        DUES   1     57
 10   O                        NETPAY1      67
 11   O  *
 12   O  *********************** TOTAL LINES *******************************
 13   O  *
 14   O        T 11       LR
 15   O                                     34  '*** TOTAL GROSS PAY'
 16   O                        TGRPAY1      48  '$'
 17   O                                     52  '***'
 18   O        T 11       LR
 19   O                                     31  '*** TOTAL NUMBER'
 20   O                                     44  'OF EMPLOYEES'
 21   O                        EMPS    Z    48
 22   O                                     52  '***'
 23   O        T 1        LR
 24   O                                     36  '*** AVERAGE GROSS PAY'
 25   O                        AVGPAY       48  '$'
```

(continued)

```
Line  Form  ...
 01   O                                     52  '***'
 02   O  *
 03   O  *****************************************************************************
 04   O
 05   O
```

Figure 3.34
(continued)

Figure 3.35
Program listing with error
diagnostics for Debugging
Exercise 2.

```
        01-020  F*********************************************************SSS03
        01-030  F*        THIS PROGRAM CREATES A WEEKLY PAYROLL REPORT WHICH      *SSS03
        01-040  F*        INCLUDES TOTALS TAKEN FOR GROSS PAY AND NUMBER OF       *SSS03
        01-050  F*        EMPLOYEES AND COMPUTES THE AVERAGE GROSS PAY.           *SSS03
        01-060  F*********************************************************SSS03
        01-070  F*                                                                SSS03
0001    01-080  FPAY      IP  F    42              DISK                            SSS03
0002    01-090  FREPORT   C   F   132        CF    PRINTER                         SSS03
        01-100  F*                                                                SSS03
        02-010  I********************* INPUT RECORD *********************SSS03
        02-020  I*                                                                SSS03
0003    02-030  IPAY      NS                                                       SSS03
0004    02-040  I                               1    30DEPTNO                      SSS03
0005    02-050  I                               8    18 LNAME                      SSS03
0006    02-060  I                              20    20 FINIT                      SSS03
0007    02-070  I                              30    33 RATE                       SSS03
0008    02-080  I                              36    381HOURS                      SSS03
0009    02-090  I                              39    422DUES                       SSS03
        02-100  I*                                                                SSS03
        03-010  C******************** CALCULATION ROUTINE ********************SSS03
        03-020  C*                                                                SSS03
0010    03-030  C           TGRPAY    ADD  GRPAY     TGRPAY  72                     SSS03
0011    03-040  C           RATE      MULT HRS       GRPAY   62H                    SSS03
0012    03-050  C           GRPAY     SUB  DUES      NETPAY  62                     SSS03
        03-060  C*                                                                SSS03
0013    03-070  C           EMPS      ADD  1         EMPS    30                     SSS03
0014    03-080  C           TGRPAY    DIV  EMPS      AVGPAY  62H                    SSS03
        03-090  C*                                                                SSS03
        04-010  O******************** HEADING LINES ********************SSS03
        04-020  C*                                                                SSS03
0015    04-030  OREPORT  H  201       1P                                           SSS03
0016    04-040  O             OR               CF                                  SSS03
0017    04-050  O                                      30 'W I D G E T'            SSS03
0018    04-060  O                                      48 'P R O D U C T S'        SSS03
0019    04-070  O                                      62 'PAGE'                   SSS03
0020    04-080  O                              PAGE    67                          SSS03
0021    04-090  O        H  2          1P                                          SSS03
0022    04-100  O             OR               CF                                  SSS03
0023    04-110  O                                      37 '** WEEKLY PAYROLL'      SSS03
0024    04-120  O                                      47 'REPORT **'              SSS03
0025    04-130  O                              UDATE Y 66                          SSS03
0026    04-140  O        H  1          1P                                          SSS03
0027    04-150  O             OR               OF                                  SSS03
0028    04-160  O                                      18 'DEPT     EMPLOYEE'      SSS03
0029    04-170  O                                      48 'HOURLY    HOURS    GROSS' SSS03
0030    04-180  O                                      66 'NET'                    SSS03
0031    04-190  O        H  2          1P                                          SSS03
0032    04-200  O             OR               CF                                  SSS03
0033    04-210  O                                      16 'NO.      NAME'          SSS03
0034    04-220  O                                      47 'RATE    WORKED     PAY' SSS03
0035    04-230  O                                      66 'DUES       PAY'         SSS03
        04-240  C*                                                                SSS03
        04-250  O********************* DETAIL LINE *********************SSS03
        05-010  C*                                                                SSS03
0036    05-020  O        D  1          N1P                                         SSS03
0037    05-030  O                              DEPTNOZ  4                          SSS03
0038    05-040  O                              LNAME   19                          SSS03
0039    05-050  O                              FINIT   21                          SSS03
0040    05-060  O                              RATE  1 30                          SSS03
0041    05-070  O                              HOURS 1 38                          SSS03
0042    05-080  O                              GRPAY 1 48                          SSS03
0043    05-090  O                              DUES  1 57                          SSS03
0044    05-100  O                              NETPAY1 67                          SSS03
        05-110  C*                                                                SSS03
        05-120  O********************* TOTAL LINES *********************SSS03
        05-130  C*                                                                SSS03
0045    05-140  O        T  11         LR                                          SSS03
0046    05-150  O                                      34 '*** TOTAL GROSS PAY'    SSS03
0047    05-160  O                              TGRPAY1 48 '$'                      SSS03
0048    05-170  O                                      52 '***'                    SSS03
0049    05-180  O        T  11         LR                                          SSS03
0050    05-190  O                                      31 '*** TOTAL NUMBER'       SSS03
0051    05-200  O                                      44 'OF EMPLOYEES'           SSS03
0052    05-210  O                              EMPS  Z 48                          SSS03
0053    05-220  O                                      52 '***'                    SSS03
0054    05-230  O        T  1          LR                                          SSS03
0055    05-240  O                                      36 '*** AVERAGE GROSS PAY'  SSS03
0056    05-250  O                              AVGPAY  48 '$'                      SSS03
0057    06-010  O                                      52 '***'                    SSS03
        06-020  C*                                                                SSS03
        06-030  O*********************************************************SSS03
```

```
        E N D   O F   S O U R C E

        C O M P I L E R   D I A G N O S T I C S   S U M M A R Y


ILN234   INVALID NUMBER OF DIGIT POSITIONS IN EDIT WORD. DROP EDITING.

         00056    05-250    AVGPAY

ILN398   FIELD NAME UNDEFINED. SPEC IS DROPPED.

       D 00011    03-040    HRS

ILN413   EDIT SPECIFIED WITH ALPHAMERIC FIELD. DROP EDITING.

         00040    05-060
```

Figure 3.36
Program listing that contains
logic errors for Debugging
Exercise 2.

```
      01-020  F****************************************************************SSS03
      01-030  F*        THIS PROGRAM CREATES A WEEKLY PAYROLL REPORT WHICH     *SSS03
      01-040  F*        INCLUDES TOTALS TAKEN FOR GROSS PAY AND NUMBER OF      *SSS03
      01-050  F*        EMPLOYEES AND COMPUTES THE AVERAGE GROSS PAY.          *SSS03
      01-060  F****************************************************************SSS03
      01-070  F*                                                               SSS03
0001  01-080  FPAY       IP  F      42                 DISK                    SSS03
0002  01-090  FREPORT    O   F     132        CF       PRINTER                 SSS03
      01-100  F*                                                               SSS03
      02-010  I************************ INPUT RECORD ************************SSS03
      02-020  I*                                                               SSS03
0003  02-030  IPAY       NS                                                    SSS03
0004  02-040  I                                         1   30DEPTNO           SSS03
0005  02-050  I                                         8   18 LNAME           SSS03
0006  02-060  I                                        20   20 FINIT           SSS03
0007  02-070  I                                        30   332RATE            SSS03
0008  02-080  I                                        36   38THOURS           SSS03
0009  02-090  I                                        39   422DUES            SSS03
      02-100  I*                                                               SSS03
      03-010  C********************** CALCULATION ROUTINE ******************SSS03
      03-020  C*                                                               SSS03
0010  03-030  C            TGRPAY    ADD  GRPAY       TGRPAY  72                SSS03
0011  03-040  C            RATE      MULT HOURS       GRPAY   62H               SSS03
0012  03-050  C            GRPAY     SUB  DUES        NETPAY  62                SSS03
      03-060  C*                                                               SSS03
0013  03-070  C            EMPS      ADD  1           EMPS    30                SSS03
0014  03-080  C            TGRPAY    DIV  EMPS        AVGPAY  62H               SSS03
      03-090  C*                                                               SSS03
      04-010  O********************** HEADING LINES ***********************SSS03
      04-020  C*                                                               SSS03
0015  04-030  OREPORT   H  201       1P                                        SSS03
0016  04-040  O              OR          CF                                    SSS03
0017  04-050  O                                        30 'W I D G E T'        SSS03
0018  04-060  O                                        48 'P R O D U C T S'    SSS03
0019  04-070  O                                        62 'PAGE'               SSS03
0020  04-080  O                                 PAGE   67                      SSS03
0021  04-090  O          H  2        1P                                        SSS03
0022  04-100  O              OR          CF                                    SSS03
0023  04-110  O                                        37 '** WEEKLY PAYROLL'  SSS03
0024  04-120  O                                        47 'REPORT **'          SSS03
0025  04-130  O                                 UDATE Y 66                     SSS03
0026  04-140  O          H  1        1P                                        SSS03
0027  04-150  O              OR          CF                                    SSS03
0028  04-160  O                                        18 'DEPT    EMPLOYEE'   SSS03
0029  04-170  O                                        48 'HOURLY   HOURS   GROSS' SSS03
0030  04-180  O                                        66 'NET'                SSS03
0031  04-190  O          H  2        1P                                        SSS03
0032  04-200  O              OR          CF                                    SSS03
0033  04-210  O                                        16 'NO.     NAME'       SSS03
0034  04-220  O                                        47 'RATE    WORKED    PAY' SSS03
0035  04-230  O                                        66 'DUES    PAY'        SSS03
      04-240  C*                                                               SSS03
      04-250  O********************** DETAIL LINE ***********************SSS03
      05-010  C*                                                               SSS03
0036  05-020  O          D  1        N1P                                       SSS03
0037  05-030  O                                 DEPTNOZ 4                      SSS03
0038  05-040  O                                 LNAME   19                     SSS03
0039  05-050  O                                 FINIT   21                     SSS03
0040  05-060  O                                 RATE  1 30                     SSS03
0041  05-070  O                                 HOURS 1 38                     SSS03
0042  05-080  O                                 GRPAY 1 48                     SSS03
0043  05-090  O                                 DUES  1 57                     SSS03
0044  05-100  O                                 NETPAY1 67                     SSS03
      05-110  C*                                                               SSS03
      05-120  O********************** TOTAL LINES ***********************SSS03
      05-130  C*                                                               SSS03
0045  05-140  O          T 11        LR                                        SSS03
0046  05-150  O                                        34 '*** TOTAL GROSS PAY' SSS03
0047  05-160  O                                 TGRPAY1 48 '$'                 SSS03
0048  05-170  O                                        52 '***'                SSS03
0049  05-180  O          T 11        LR                                        SSS03
0050  05-190  O                                        31 '*** TOTAL NUMBER'   SSS03
0051  05-200  O                                        44 'OF EMPLOYEES'       SSS03
0052  05-210  O                                 EMPS  Z 48                     SSS03
0053  05-220  O                                        52 '***'                SSS03
0054  05-230  O          T 1         LR                                        SSS03
0055  05-240  O                                        36 '*** AVERAGE GROSS PAY' SSS03
0056  05-250  O                                 AVGPAY1 48 '$'                 SSS03
0057  06-010  O                                        52 '***'                SSS03
      06-020  C*                                                               SSS03
      06-030  O****************************************************************SSS03


           E N D   O F   S O U R C E
```

(annotations) Numeric field; Corrected field HRS to HOURS; Edit code required

Figure 3.36
(continued)

```
               W I D G E T   P R O D U C T S          PAGE    1

               ** WEEKLY PAYROLL REPORT **            7/29/91

   DEPT    EMPLOYEE        HOURLY  HOURS    GROSS                NET
   NO.      NAME            RATE   WORKED    PAY       DUES      PAY

   10    ADAMS     M        5.00   40.0    200.00      6.75    193.25
   10    BROWN     B        7.00   30.5    213.50      3.50    210.00
   10    DAVIS     C        6.50   39.5    256.75      4.65    252.10
   10    WOLFGANG  N        9.10   40.0    364.00      3.00    361.00
   20    BOSCO     V        8.20   36.0    295.20      5.00    290.20
   20    CARTER    B        4.40   25.5    112.20      4.85    107.35
   20    DONOVAN   D        6.75   33.0    222.75      4.50    218.25
   20    JOHNKE    N        7.10   39.2    278.32      9.50    268.82
   30    EDWARDS   E        3.90   40.0    156.00       .00    156.00
   30    SAGER     A        7.80   36.0    280.80     10.00    270.80
   30    STERN     B        8.00   34.0    272.00      8.00    264.00
   30    WHITE     F        9.90   40.0    396.00     15.00    381.00

        *** TOTAL GROSS PAY       $2,651.52 ***  ← Incorrect total—should be 3,047.52

        *** TOTAL NUMBER OF EMPLOYEES   12 ***

        *** AVERAGE GROSS PAY      $220.96 ***  ← Incorrect total—should be 253.96
```

PROGRAMMING ASSIGNMENTS

Use Data Structures for work fields. Use prefixes for input, output, and work fields. Use SETON and SETOF where appropriate.

1. Consider the following problem definition: Write a program to produce the sales report from the disk records. The profit for each item is determined by subtracting the cost of the item from its sales amount. Final totals are to be printed for the sales amount, cost amount, and profit fields.

Systems Flowchart

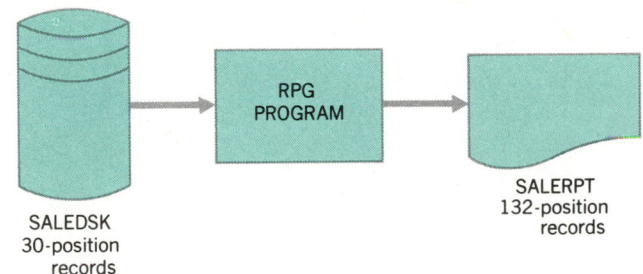

SALEDSK Record Layout

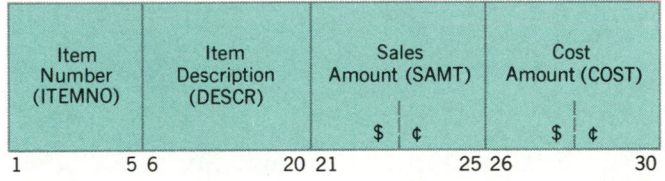

SALERPT Printer Spacing Chart

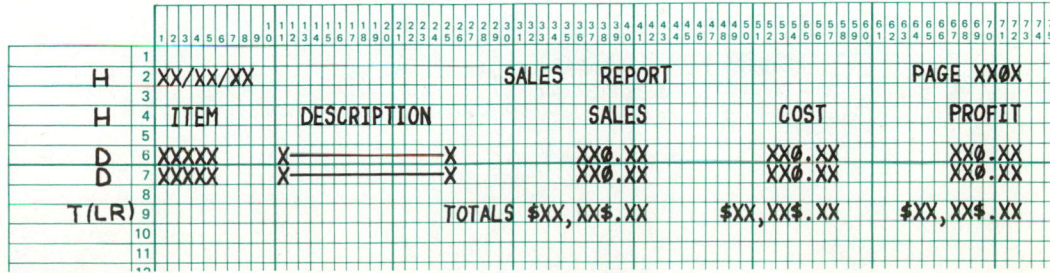

2. Write an RPG program to produce a payroll register. The problem definition is shown in Figure 3.37. The following formulas are to be used.

FICA = 7.65% of gross pay (assume all employees earn less than the maximum amount subject to FICA tax, which is the Social Security tax).

Voluntary deductions = Union dues + credit union + health insurance
Statutory deductions = FICA + federal tax + state tax
Total deductions = Voluntary deductions + statutory deductions
Net Pay = Gross pay − total deductions

Note: Use an edit word for the Social Security number.

Figure 3.37 Problem definition for Programming Assignment 2.

Systems Flowchart

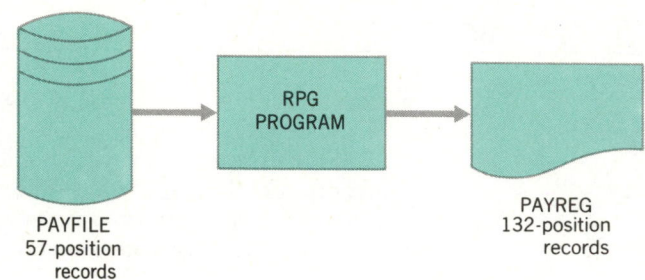

PAYFILE Record Layout

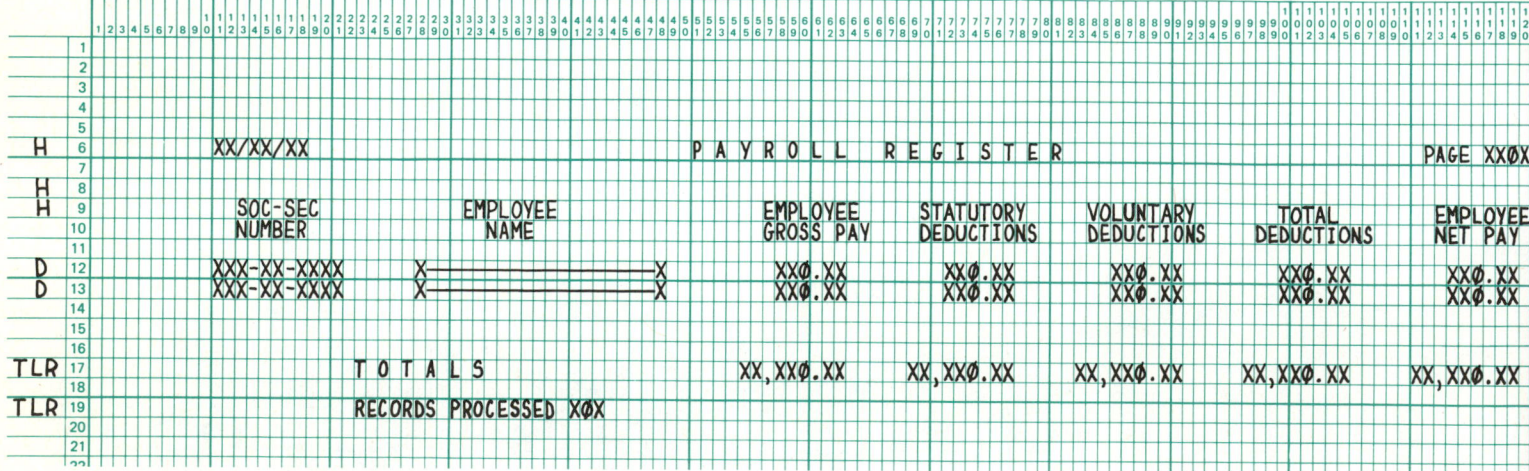

PAYREG Printer Spacing Chart

Figure 3.38
Problem definition for Programming Assignment 3.

Systems Flowchart

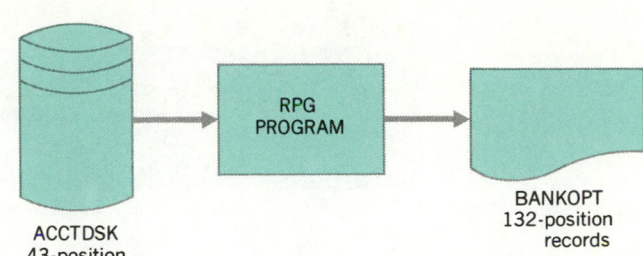

ACCTDSK
43-position
records

BANKOPT
132-position
records

ACCTDSK Record Layout

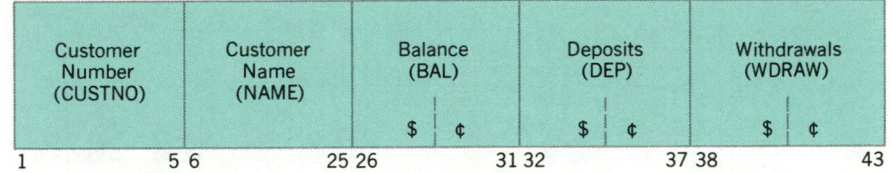

BANKOPT Printer Spacing Chart

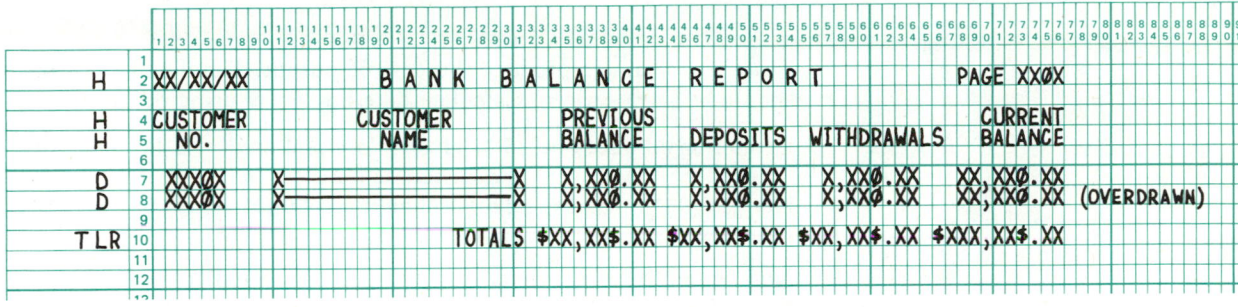

3. Write **an** RPG program that will produce a bank balance report. The problem definition is shown in Figure 3.38.

   If the current balance is negative, indicate this by including the word "OVER-DRAWN" on the detail line. The formula for calculating current balance is as follows:

   Current balance = BAL + DEP − WDRAW

4. Consider the following problem definition:

Systems Flowchart

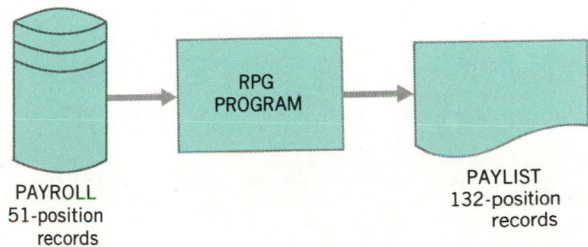

PAYROLL
51-position
records

PAYLIST
132-position
records

PAYROLL Record Layout

EMP NO (EMPNO)	EMP NAME (NAME)	ANNUAL SALARY (SALARY) $ ¢	SSNO	NO OF DEPTS (DEPTS)	DUES $ ¢	INSUR $ ¢
1 5	6 20	21 28	29 37	38 39	40 45	46 51

PAYLIST Printer Spacing Chart

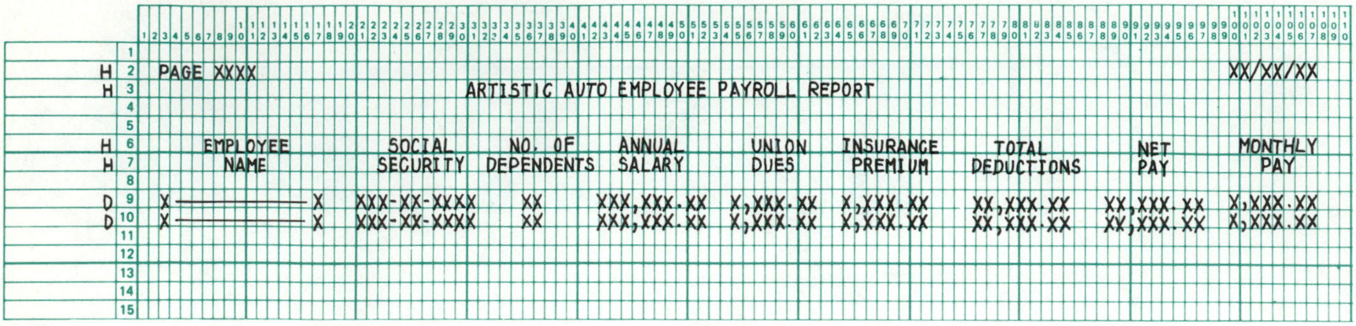

```
      1  PAGE XXXX                                                                              XX/XX/XX
   H  2
   H  3              ARTISTIC AUTO EMPLOYEE PAYROLL REPORT
      4
      5
   H  6      EMPLOYEE      SOCIAL     NO. OF    ANNUAL     UNION    INSURANCE     TOTAL       NET      MONTHLY
   H  7        NAME       SECURITY  DEPENDENTS  SALARY     DUES      PREMIUM   DEDUCTIONS     PAY        PAY
      8
   D  9  X----------X  XXX-XX-XXXX     XX    XXX,XXX.XX  X,XXX.XX  X,XXX.XX  XX,XXX.XX  XX,XXX.XX  X,XXX.XX
   D 10  X----------X  XXX-XX-XXXX     XX    XXX,XXX.XX  X,XXX.XX  X,XXX.XX  XX,XXX.XX  XX,XXX.XX  X,XXX.XX
     11
     12
     13
     14
     15
```

Write a program to produce the desired output. The detail lines on the report should be single-spaced. Calculate take-home pay using the following formulas:

Deduction (DEDUCT) = .25 × gross salary (SALARY) − 2000 × number of dependents (DEPTS)
Net pay (NET) = Gross salary (SALARY) − DEDUCT − INSUR − DUES
Monthly pay = NET / 12

Note: If DEDUCT is negative, set it to zero. Use an indicator to condition the Z-ADD instruction.

Selection: Comparing Fields

OBJECTIVES

To familiarize you with

1. The ways in which RPG can be used for comparing fields.
2. The logical control procedures used in RPG.
3. Comparison operations commonly used in business applications.

I. Introduction

A. An Overview of Program Logic and Comparisons

In prior chapters, we indicated that instructions on the Calculation Specifications form were executed in sequence, one step at a time in the order written. In the business world, however, many problems cannot be solved by this direct sequential approach. Programming problems usually impose a variety of conditions requiring the program to make decisions so that alternative actions can be taken. Frequently it is necessary to alter the normal flow and execute a different set of instructions in order to accomplish the objectives of the program.

For example, if an individual works more than 40 hours in a week, gross pay must be calculated using a premium rate of time and a half applied against the overtime hours. That is, for all hours worked in excess of 40, the employee will be paid at a rate of 1.5 times the regular rate.

To process input data correctly, the RPG program must have the ability to compare the actual hours worked to the number forty (40) and then decide whether overtime calculations should be included or not. When different sets of instructions are used depending on specific conditions, these sets are referred to as **routines.** In this example there are two routines: a regular pay routine used for employees who worked 40 hours or less and an overtime routine used for employees who worked more than 40 hours. For any given input data, the routine that will be used depends on the number of hours worked.

B. The Compare (COMP) Operation

The **compare (COMP) operation** is used in RPG for decision-making purposes. It is used to compare the contents of a field to the contents of a second field or to a **literal.** The data to be compared may be numeric or alphanumeric, but both factors used in the comparison must have the same format. That is, the fields or literals being compared must both be numeric or both be alphanumeric. As noted previously, another term for an **alphanumeric field** is an **alphameric field.** Simply stated, numeric data should not be compared with alphameric data.

Compare operations are coded on the Calculation Specifications form as noted in Figure 4.1. Only Factor 1 and Factor 2 are used; the Result Field is not used with a COMP instruction.

The COMP operation automatically triggers an internal **condition code** that is used to set the **resulting indicators.** A COMPare operation always produces one of three results: HIGH, LOW, or EQUAL. Referring to the instruction in Figure 4.1, consider the following:

Compare			
Factor 1 (HRS)	**Factor 2 (40)**	**Condition Code**	**Indicator On**
20	40	LOW	40
30	40	LOW	40
40	40	EQUAL	40
50	40	HIGH	41
60	40	HIGH	41

COMPare operations can be used to set on indicators if the result of the comparison is a "high," "equal," or "low" condition; subsequent instructions

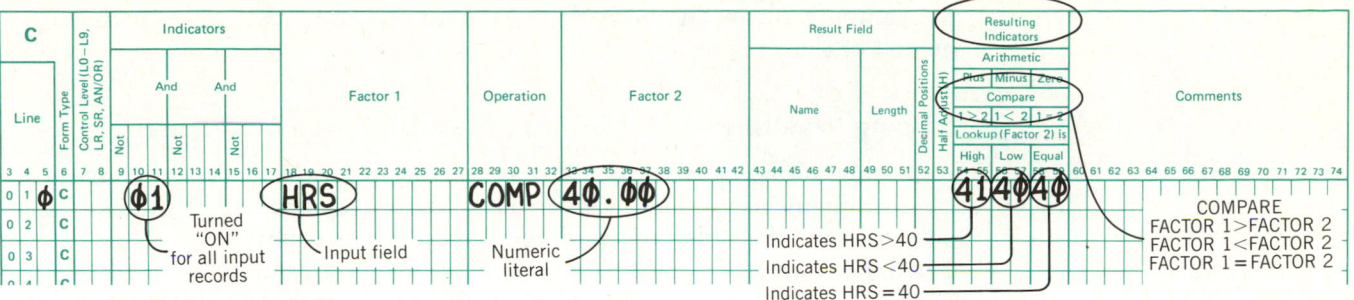

Figure 4.1
Coding COMPare instructions
on the Calculation
Specifications form.

can then be executed depending on whether the indicator coded was "turned on" during the comparison operation.

Factor 1 contains the contents of the hours-worked field. This field is being compared to the numeric literal 40 in Factor 2. Note that when Factor 1 (hours worked) is equal to 40, indicator 40 is "turned on." If the hours worked were less than 40, then Factor 1 would be less than Factor 2 and a "low" condition would result. The low condition will also "turn on" indicator 40. Thus indicator 40 is turned on when HRS is less than or equal to ($\leq$) 40. However, when the hours exceed 40, then indicator 41 is set "on" because we have a "high" condition. That is, Factor 1 is greater than Factor 2.

Thus, when indicator 40 is "on," the employee did not work more than 40 hours; in this case you would calculate the gross as simply the product of rate times the hours worked. This is accomplished at step 020 of Figure 4.2, which represents the regular pay routine.

However, when the hours exceed 40, then indicator 41 would be turned "on" and lines 030–070, the overtime routine, would be executed. Hence, the entries in columns 54–59 of line 010 are used to turn on resulting indicators in order that specific instructions may be executed. In effect, the indicators are used to record the relationship of Factor 1 to Factor 2.

Resulting indicators are *not* turned off automatically by RPG, but *rather remain on until the next record is processed* and the compare instruction is again executed.

Figure 4.2
Payroll program excerpt that
illustrates the COMP operation.

C		Indicators						Factor 1		Operation		Factor 2		Result Field				Resulting Indicators			Comments
Line	Form Type	Control Level (L0–L9, LR, SR, AN/OR)	And Not	And Not	Not									Name	Length	Decimal Positions	Half Adjust (H)	1>2 High	1<2 Low	1=2 Equal	
0 1	0 C							HRS		COMP		40						41	40	40	
0 2	0 C	40						HRS		MULT		RATE		GROSS		52H					
0 3	0 C	41						HRS		SUB		40		OTHRS		31					
0 4	0 C	41						RATE		MULT		1.5		OTRATE		42H					
0 5	0 C	41						OTHRS		MULT		OTRATE		OTPAY		52H					
0 6	0 C	41						RATE		MULT		40.0		REG		52H					
0 7	0 C	41						REG		ADD		OTPAY		GROSS							
0 8	C																				

A sample program that uses these calculations and indicators is included at the end of this chapter.

C. Using Resulting Indicators with the COMPare Operation

Sometimes students using the COMPare operation for the first time misunderstand its application. The problem is in the interpretation of the resulting indicators and the order of events following its execution.

In our example, the hours worked field (HRS) is compared to 40 to determine if the regular pay routine or the overtime pay routine should be executed. Indicator 40 is identified with the regular pay routine while indicator 41 is associated with the operations to be performed for the overtime pay routine.

It may seem like the following flowchart depicts the logic flow for a COMP but it does not:

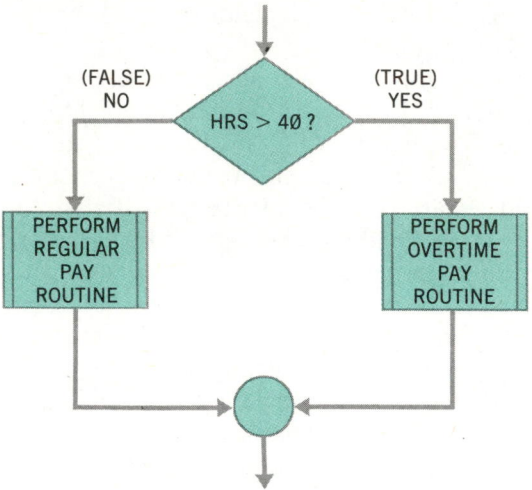

A correct flowchart for an IF/ELSE/END structure, but an incorrect representation of the COMPare operation.

The flowchart illustrates that if the hours worked field is greater than 40, then the program should execute the routine that uses overtime hours to calculate the gross pay. If hours worked is less than or equal to 40, the program should calculate the gross pay in the usual manner by simply multiplying RATE times HRS in the regular pay routine. Thus, according to the flowchart, one of two routines will be executed as a result of the COMPare operation. Based on the flowchart it would seem that one of two paths will be executed by the RPG program and therefore only those operations that meet the condition(s) being tested will be executed. However, this is *not* the procedure used by RPG when executing a COMPare operation. Since the COMPare operation does not itself result in the execution of alternative sets of instructions, it should not be represented in the flowchart form illustrated above. The illustrated flowchart represents the IF/ELSE/END structure, which, as we will see in Chapter 5, is executed in RPG with an IF, not a COMP instruction. We will not use flowcharts to illustrate the logic of a COMP. This may seem like a subtle point, but it is an important one.

The COMPare operation does not make a selection and then execute one particular routine as does an IF/ELSE/END. Very simply, RPG executes every statement *in sequence*.

As RPG encounters each statement, it tests the indicators specified in columns 7–8 or 9–17. If the indicators are on, the corresponding statement is executed. If they are not on, the program continues with the next statement.

Because instructions are executed in sequence, RPG can use resulting indicators to control which operations belong to which routines after a COMPare operation. These indicators control the sequence in which instructions are executed following a COMPare operation.

Every routine that may be performed as a result of a COMPare operation is assigned a particular resulting indicator. In our example, indicator 40 is assigned to the regular pay routine and indicator 41 is assigned to the overtime pay routine. Prior to the execution of the COMPare operation, all resulting indicators are set off. As a result of the COMPare operation, the indicator identifying the outcome of the comparison test is set on. The subsequent operations following the COMPare operation are grouped together into routines and conditioned by the assigned indicator in columns 7–8 or 9–17. In the overtime pay routine, for example, all operations are grouped together and controlled by indicator 41 in columns 10 and 11. Thus, as each statement is encountered, the indicators in columns 7–8 or 9–17 are tested to determine if that statement is to be executed. By using assigned indicators, you can control which operations are executed together and which operations are bypassed. The following is a summary of the COMPare operation and the results of its execution:

SUMMARY OF THE **COMPARE OPERATION**

1. Controlling indicators (Columns 7–8 or 9–17) are tested. If the indicator conditions are satisfied, or "met," the COMPare operation is executed. If the indicator conditions are not satisfied, the COMP operation is *not* executed and the program continues with the *next* statement following the compare operation.

   It should be noted that if the COMPare operation is not executed, any "on" indicators will not be set off. They will remain as they were prior to the COMPare statement. That is, resulting indicators are *not* set off automatically by RPG, but *rather remain on until the next record is processed* and the COMPare operation is again executed. Recall, however, that the SETOF and SETON operations can be used to control indicator settings.

2. When the COMPare operation is executed, the resulting indicators are *set off* with the SETOF prior to the comparison test of the COMP.

3. The comparison (COMP) is made between the contents of Factor 1 and the contents of Factor 2. When compared, the outcome is one of the following relationships:

	Compare	Condition Code
Factor 1 is greater than Factor 2	1 > 2	HIGH
Factor 1 is less than Factor 2	1 < 2	LOW
Factor 1 is equal to Factor 2	1 = 2	EQUAL

4. One, two, or three resulting indicators may be specified in columns 54–59 to identify the outcome of the comparison in step 3. After the comparison is made between Factor 1 and Factor 2, one and only one resulting indicator will be conditioned in the following manner:

   If Factor 1 is greater than Factor 2, the resulting indicator in columns 54–55 (HIGH) is set on.

If Factor 1 is less than Factor 2, the resulting indicator in columns 56–57 (LOW) is set on.

If Factor 1 is equal to Factor 2, the resulting indicator in columns 58–59 (EQUAL) is set on.

It should be pointed out that if no resulting indicator is specified for the resulting condition, then no indicator will be set on as a result of the COMPare operation. That is, if you code FLD1 COMP FLD2 22, with 22 coded in 54–55 (1 > 2) and both fields are equal, no indicator will be set.

5. Once the resulting indicator is set as a result of the comparison, the COMPare operation is completed. The program continues with the next statement following the COMPare operation regardless of the outcome of the COMPare operation. Thus, the COMPare operation has no direct relevance to the subsequent statements other than to have set on the resulting indicator. If an indicator is set as a result of a compare, the subsequent statements will each be evaluated to see which ones are to be executed.

6. Routines that are to be executed as a result of the COMPare operation should be grouped together and conditioned by the appropriate resulting indicator. As control of the program passes from statement to statement, the indicators in columns 7–8 or 9–17 are tested first and, if satisfied, the statement(s) are executed in sequence. In this way, the COMPare operation can control which routines will actually be performed.

As previously noted, COMPare operations are either numeric or alphanumeric (nonnumeric); the two types cannot be mixed. Numeric COMPare operations will be considered first.

A structured programming alternative to the COMP statement, using IF/ELSE/END, will be discussed in detail in the next chapter.

II. Comparing Numeric Fields

A. Summary

COMPARING NUMERIC DATA FIELDS

Operation:	COMP
Meaning:	Compare two data fields algebraically.
Operation:	Condition code is set to high, low, or equal as follows: HIGH: Factor 1 is greater than Factor 2. LOW: Factor 1 is less than Factor 2. EQUAL: Factor 1 is equal to Factor 2.
Resulting Indicators:	When results are "high," the indicator specified in columns 54–55 is turned "on." When results are "low," the indicator specified in columns 56–57 is turned "on." When results are equal, the indicator in columns 58–59 is turned "on."
Limitation:	(1) For numeric compares, both fields being compared must be numeric. Either Factor 1 or Factor 2 may be a numeric literal, but not both.

(2) Numeric fields can store a maximum of 15 digits.

Special note: All indicators are initially set off prior to the COMP operation. Indicators that are set on as a result of a COMP remain on until the COMP instruction is executed again.

B. Specifying Numeric Fields: A Review

First, numeric fields being compared must be specified as numeric in the program. Recall that a **numeric field** requires the coding of an integer in column 52 (Decimal Positions) of the form on which it is defined. This would be either the Input or the Calculation Specifications form. Numeric fields *must* have a numeric entry in the Decimal Positions field of one of these forms as illustrated in Figure 4.3. If a numeric field consists entirely of integers and has no decimal positions, then enter Ø in column 52 of the Input Specifications form, if the field is defined there, or on the Calculation Specifications form if the field is defined during a calculation.

In the example in Figure 4.3, RATE and HRS on the Input Specifications form contain entries in column 52 (Decimal Positions), thereby defining these fields as numeric. Similarly, GROSS is established on the Calculation Specifications form, also with an entry in column 52 (Decimal Positions). Therefore, GROSS is also a numeric field. Only when the fields are properly defined as numeric will numeric comparisons take place. Should the programmer attempt to compare a numeric field with a nonnumeric field (alphameric or alphabetic), an error

Figure 4.3
Specifying numeric fields.

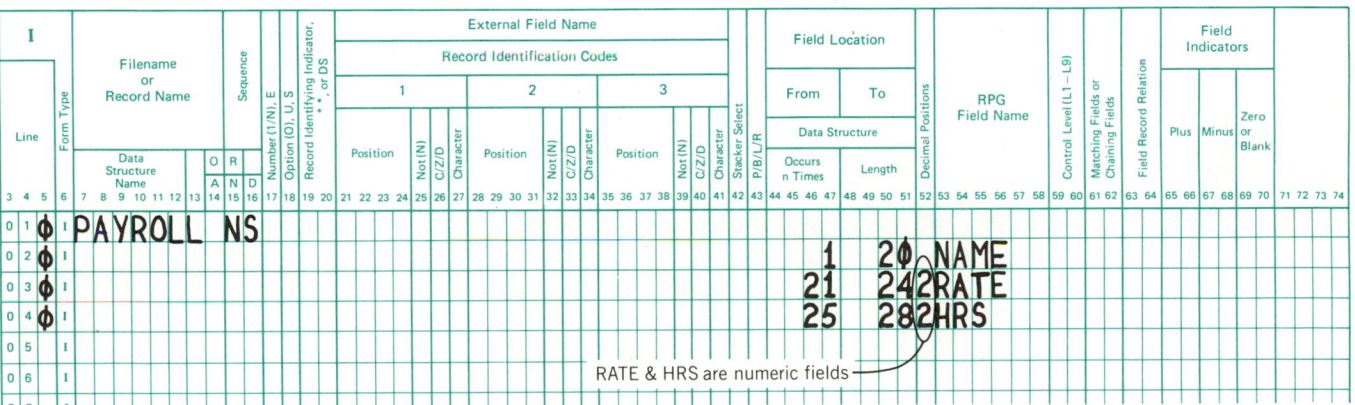

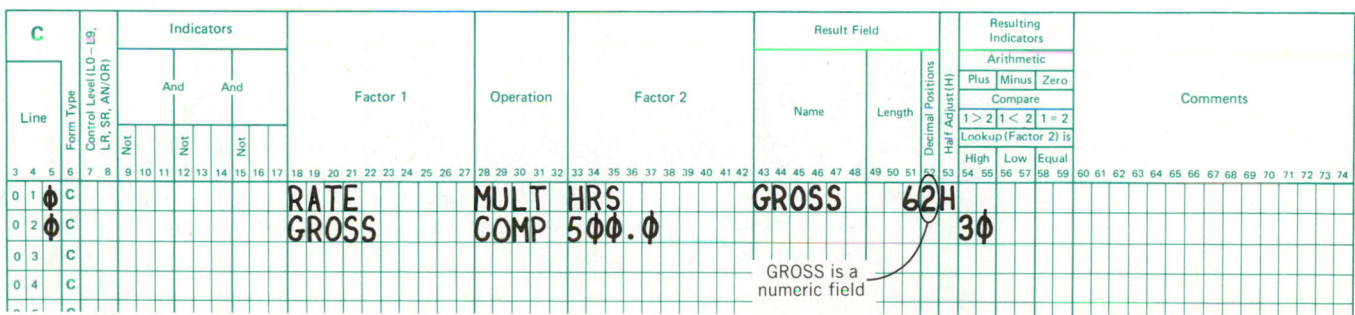

message may result stating *"Factor 1 and Factor 2 of compare or look up must either be numeric or alphanumeric. Specification is dropped."* The precise wording of this diagnostic message may vary from one system to another, but the overall intent will be the same. Do not compare numeric fields with fields that are not numeric since the computer stores the information for each type of field differently. In particular, arithmetic operations must be performed on numeric data only. When error messages occur as a result of a COMP operation, check the fields that are intended to be numeric to be sure that they were defined with an entry in the Decimal Positions column.

C. Comparing Numeric Fields of Equal Length

Numeric comparisons are **algebraic comparisons,** meaning that the sign is included in the test. Negative quantities will always compare LOW when compared to positive quantities.

A condition code is set (HIGH, LOW, EQUAL) depending on the relative value of Factor 1 as compared to Factor 2. Remember that the results will be high, low, or equal, depending on how Factor 1 compares to Factor 2. Both factors must contain the same type of data (in this case, numeric data).

The examples in Figure 4.4 illustrate the concepts of comparing two numeric fields. The examples in the illustration use all three resulting indicators on the Calculation Specifications form. We need only code, however, for the conditions we are trying to check. It may require the use of one indicator, two indicators, or all three. That is, if we want to execute a series of instructions only if Factor 1 is equal to Factor 2, we need only set on an indicator in positions 58–59, when using the COMP instruction.

Figure 4.4
Examples of comparisons.

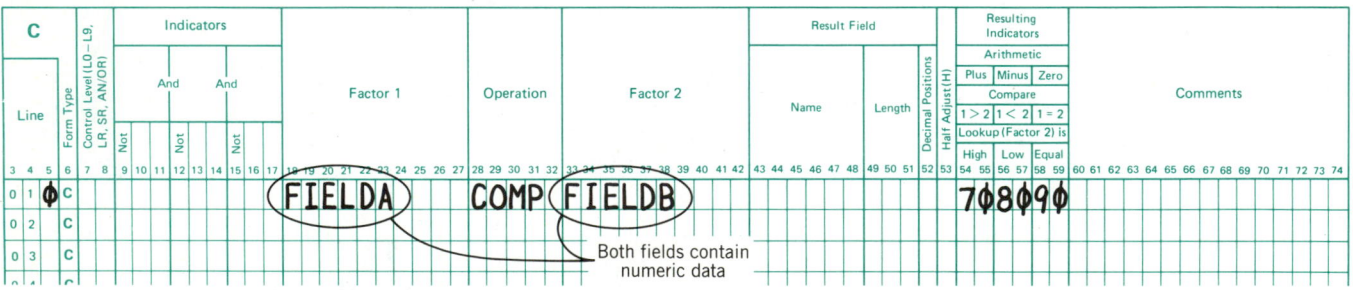

Both fields contain numeric data

FIELDA is compared to FIELDB

| | FIELDA | FIELDB | | | |
Example Number	Factor 1	Factor 2	Condition Result	Indicators "on"	"off"
1	150▲00	100▲00	High	70	80 90
2	−050▲00	−100▲00	High	70	80 90
3	000▲00	−100▲00	High	70	80 90
4	100▲00	100▲00	Equal	90	70 80
5	050▲00	100▲00	Low	80	70 90
6	−050▲00	100▲00	Low	80	70 90

In the illustrations in Figure 4.4, observe that indicators 70, 80, and 90 are set on according to the results of the comparison (high, low, equal). In Example 1, as would be expected, Factor 1 is greater than Factor 2, resulting in a high condition. Thus, indicator 70 is set "on" and indicators 80 and 90 are set off.

Example 2 illustrates and reinforces the fact that −50 is greater than −100. Remember that the comparison is *algebraic.* Consider the illustration in Figure 4.5.

Referring to the scale of values shown, −50 is higher on this scale or greater than −100. Also note in Example 3 of Figure 4.4 that zero has a greater value than −100. When Factor 1 is greater than Factor 2, the result is high and indicator 70 is "turned on." Example 4 compares two fields that are equal. As a consequence, indicator 90 is set "on" and indicators 70 and 80 are set off. Examples 5 and 6 both contain numeric data in Factor 1 that is less than the numeric contents of Factor 2. The condition or result of each comparison is low, setting "on" indicator 80 referenced in columns 56–57 of the Calculation Specifications form and setting off indicators 70 and 90 (Figure 4.4).

D. Comparing Numeric Fields of Unequal Length

Recall that numeric fields are compared algebraically. Before any compare operations can take place, however, RPG decimally aligns the fields. Any missing digits are filled in with zeros. (The maximum length for numeric fields that are to be compared is 15 digits.) For example, suppose the following fields are to be compared:

```
Field 1    1 2 3∧4 5
Field 2         6∧7 8 9
```

RPG would first extend the decimal positions of Field 1 to match the number of decimal positions in Field 2. This is done by adding a zero to the low-order position of Field 1.

```
Field 1    1 2 3∧4 5 0
Field 2         6∧7 8 9
```

Then the high-order or left-most positions of Field 2 would be zero-filled, thereby equalizing the number of positions both to the right and to the left of

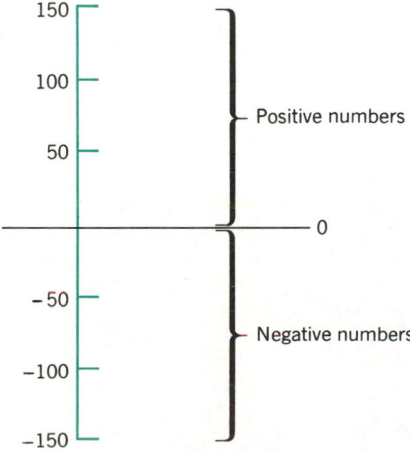

Figure 4.5
Scale of values for algebraic comparisons.

the decimal. Thus the effect would be the same as comparing the following two fields:

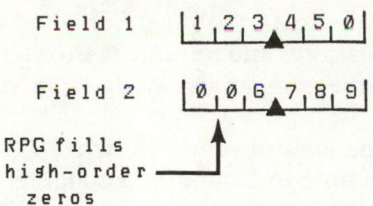

Once the fields are decimally aligned and have the same number of digits, they can be compared. If the number of decimal digits to the right of the decimal points are unequal, the shorter field is padded (on the right) with zeros. If the number of digits to the left of the decimal points are *unequal*, then high-order zeros are added to the shorter field. Let us apply these concepts of field alignment to a few practical examples.

Referring to Figure 4.6, note that SALES contains two decimal digits whereas QUOTA contains none. The first step in aligning these fields is to extend QUOTA by padding *low-order* or right-most zeros. The shorter decimal field is always extended by padding zeros in the right-most positions. Next, we find that QUOTA has fewer digits to the left of the decimal point and is the shorter field in this regard. Again, the shorter field is zero-filled. Following alignment, both fields are six digits in length, containing two decimal positions. The result of the comparison is high since the contents of Factor 1 (9000) is greater than the contents of Factor 2 (900). Indicator 60, coded in columns 54–55 of the Calculation Specifications form, is set "on."

In Figure 4.7, we again find fields of different lengths. In this example, both

Figure 4.6
Example 1. Illustrating alignment of fields for a comparison.

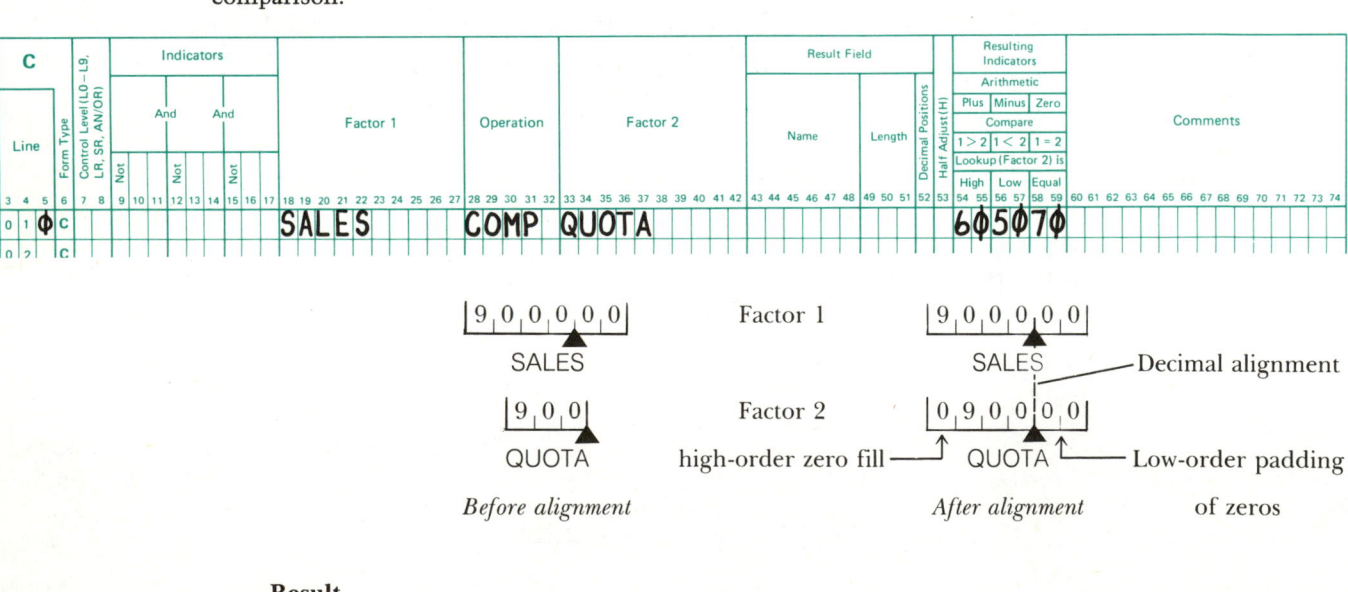

Result
Condition _____ HIGH
Reason _____ 9000 > 900
Indicator set on _____ 60

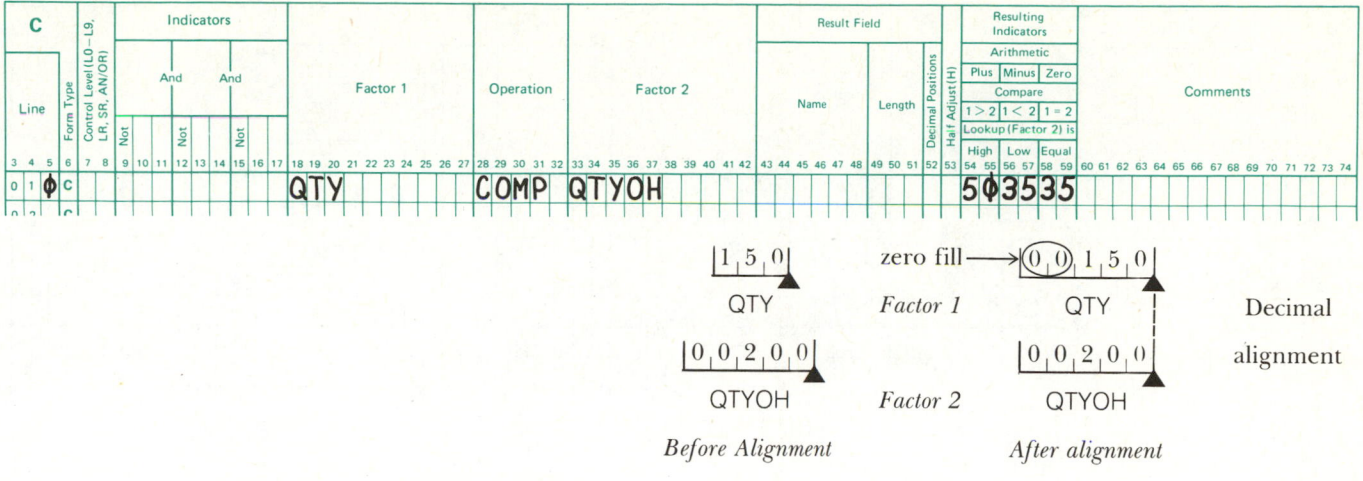

C		Control Level(L0 – L9, LR, SR, AN/OR)		Indicators								Factor 1	Operation	Factor 2		Result Field				Resulting Indicators				Comments
Line	Form Type			And		And										Name	Length	Decimal Positions	Half Adjust (H)	Arithmetic				
					Not		Not		Not											Plus	Minus	Zero		
																				Compare				
																				1 > 2	1 < 2	1 = 2		
																				Lookup (Factor 2) is				
																				High	Low	Equal		
0 1	0	C									QTY	COMP	QTYOH								35	35		

Before Alignment | After alignment

Result

Condition _____ LOW
Reason _____ 150 < 200
Indicator set on _____ 35

Figure 4.7
Alignment of fields for a comparison, Example 2.

fields do not contain any decimal positions. A decimal point is, however, *implied* for each field. Once the fields are aligned around the implied decimal points, we find that Factor 1 has fewer positions to the left of the decimal point. The left-most positions of Factor 1 are zero-filled and the algebraic comparison is performed. In this instance, a low condition occurs and indicator 35, specified in columns 56–57 of the Calculation Specifications form, is turned on.

Note, then, that in RPG, comparisons are performed *logically*. The fact that one field contains fewer characters than another will not adversely affect the logic of the comparison. This is not always the case in other languages.

E. Specifying Numeric Literals: A Review

Thus far, numeric comparisons have focused on comparing one numeric field with another. Compare instructions may also use literals that have numeric values. The comparison is again algebraic, and either Factor 1 or Factor 2 may contain a literal. Let us review the following rules for defining numeric literals:

NUMERIC LITERAL RULE SUMMARY

1. A numeric literal may contain only the digits 0–9, a decimal point, and a + or − sign to the left of the literal.
2. The maximum length of a numeric literal is 10 characters, including a sign and a decimal point.
3. Unsigned literals are assumed positive.
4. Numeric literals must never contain dollar signs, commas, blanks, or any other alphameric character.
5. Numeric literals are left-justified when entered in Factor 1 or Factor 2 of the Calculation form.

Typical examples of numeric literals are illustrated in Figure 4.8. Again, the same rules apply when using numeric literals as when using numeric fields. Alignment is achieved in the same manner.

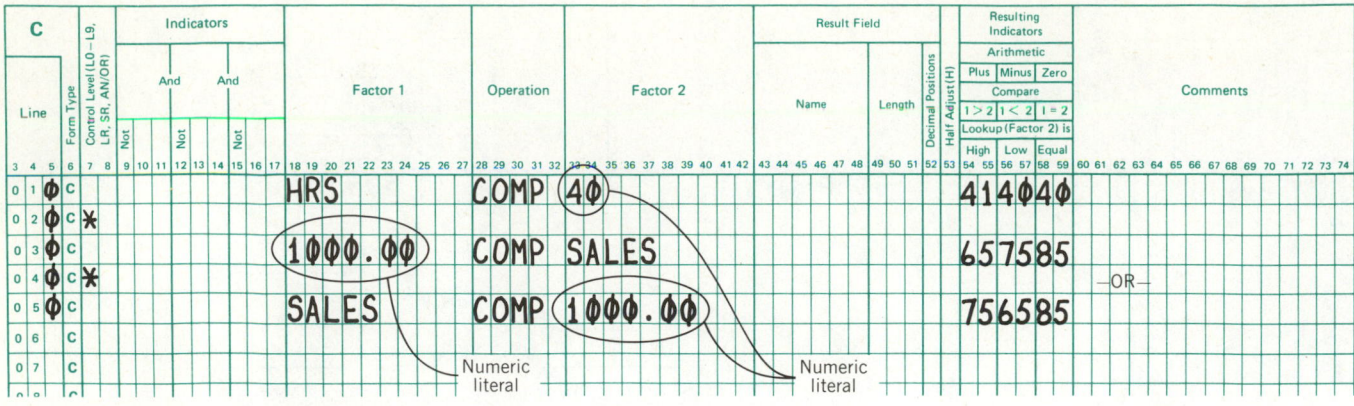

Figure 4.8
Using numeric literals with COMPare instructions.

F. Negating Compares (NOT Entry)

By entering an N in column 9, 12, or 15 of the Calculation Specifications form, a test may be made to determine if an indicator is "off" rather than "on." Referring to Figure 4.9, the need for indicator 40 (defined in Figure 4.2) has been eliminated by using the NOT entry. The overtime routine will be executed when indicator 41 is on. However, when indicator 41 is "off," then the regular pay instruction would be used to calculate the gross. The NOT operation therefore extends the use of indicators to include NOT HIGH, NOT LOW, and NOT EQUAL conditions. In many instances, the programmer may find these additional relational tests more direct and useful in refining a program by eliminating unnecessary indicators.

If Factor 1 compared NOT HIGH to Factor 2, this would mean that Factor 1 was less than or equal to Factor 2. Similarly, if Factor 1 compared NOT LOW to Factor 2, this would mean that Factor 1 was greater than or equal to Factor 2.

G. Comparing Date Fields

In business, it is often necessary to determine if payments are late in order to bill the customer for late charges. This requires the comparison of date fields,

Figure 4.9
Using the NOT entry in a
COMPare.

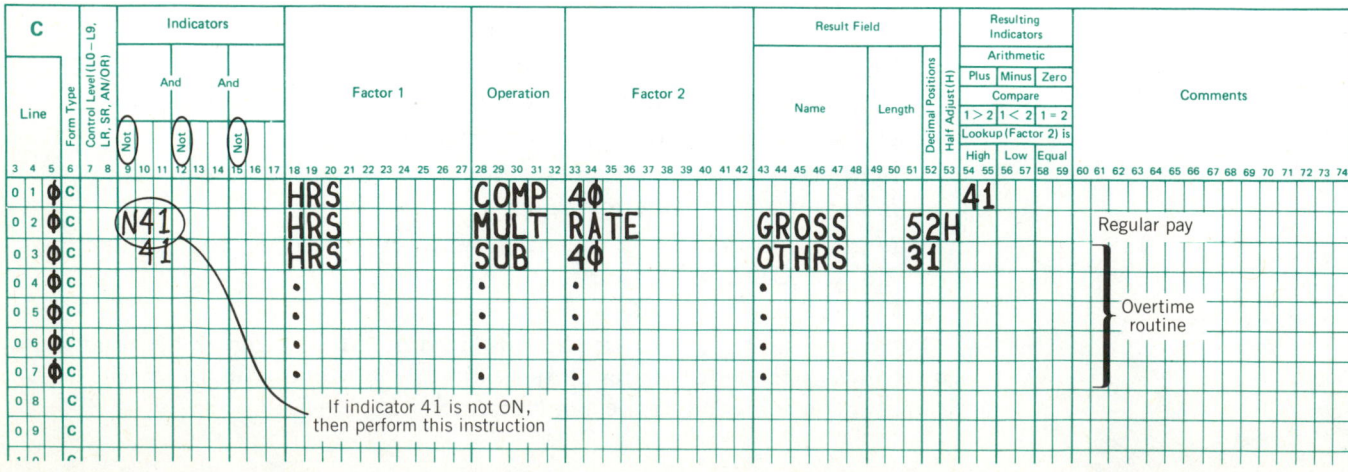

which usually are stored in the typical month, day, year format. Let us examine an accounts receivable problem in which we need to determine whether late charges should be imposed on charge-account customers. The Input and Calculation Specifications forms are illustrated in Figure 4.10.

The DATEDU (for date due) field description contains the subordinate fields, DMONTH, DUDAY, and DUYR. The advantage of using this group specification is that the programmer may reference a field either as a group or individually by the subordinate field names assigned.

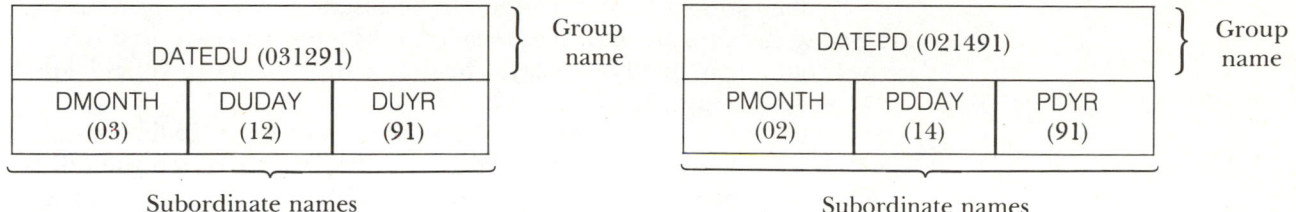

Figure 4.10
Comparing date fields.

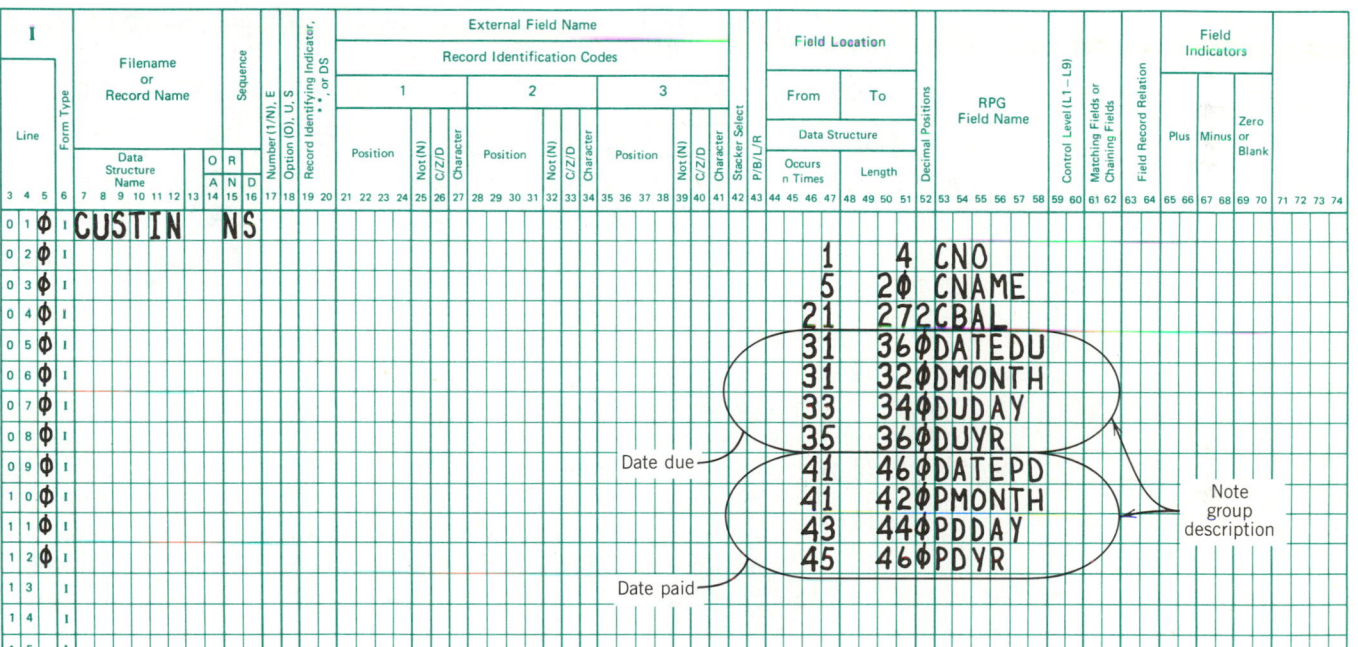

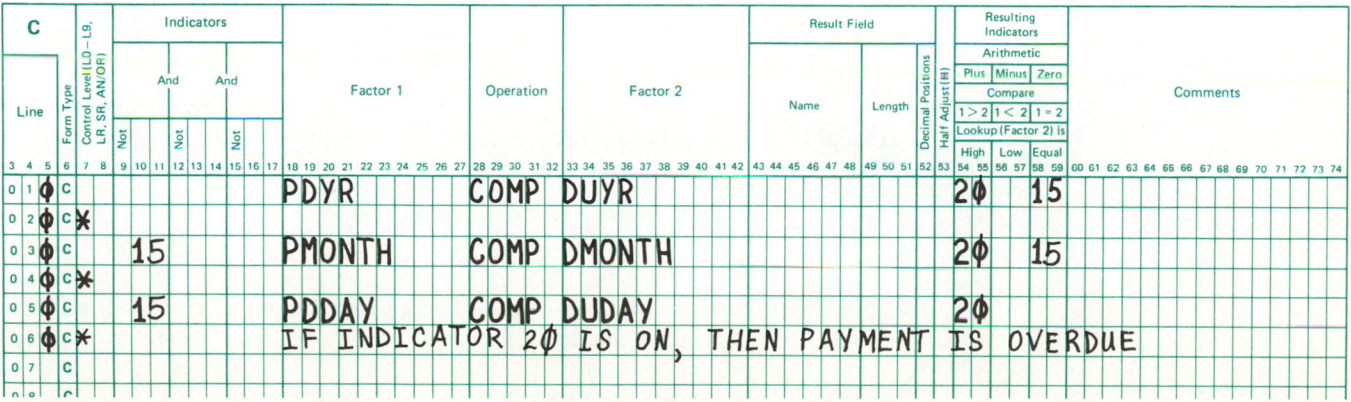

DATEDU is a six-character numeric field. Ø31291 in DATEDU refers to a date of March 12, 1991. The DATEDU field could be edited in the usual manner by coding the letter 'Y' in column 38 of the Output Specifications form. Moreover, the subordinate fields, DMONTH (Ø3), DUDAY (12), and DUYR (91), may also be referenced *individually*. Again, the primary reason for referencing data either as a group or by individual field names is that the programmer has the option of using the field definition that best suits his or her needs. For comparing date fields, it will be necessary to reference the individual fields—DMONTH, DUDAY, and DUYR.

To determine if late charges are to be assessed, the date paid must be compared to the date due in three steps in the sequence shown: first the year, then the month, and, finally, the day. The year is the most critical field, followed by the month, and then the day.

In Figure 4.1Ø, a payment will be designated as late if indicator 2Ø is set on. Again, the year field is compared first. If the year in which the bill was paid (PDYR) is greater than the year due, a high condition occurs turning "on" indicator 2Ø. That is, if payment was made in a year greater than the year it was due, then a late charge should be incurred. When, however, the year in which the bill was paid is equal to the year due, you must next check the month.

If the payment was early, that is, if the PDYR is less than the DUYR, a low condition results; in this case no indicator would be turned "on." No further checking is required; clearly, there would not be any late charges incurred. Steps Ø3Ø and Ø5Ø would not be executed because indicator 15 has not been conditioned or "turned on."

If the PDYR was equal to DUYR, check the month of payment (PMONTH) against the month due (DMONTH) and, as before, a HIGH condition would only be caused by a late payment; in this instance, indicator 2Ø would again be turned "on."

If the month paid and the month due are equal, it will be necessary to check the least-significant field, the day. When indicator 15 is "on," then both steps Ø1Ø and Ø3Ø resulted in equal comparisons, thereby requiring the day fields to be checked. When the year and month are equal, the last comparison to be made will compare the PDDAY and the DUDAY. If the PDDAY is greater than the DUDAY, the payment is late and, as before, indicator 2Ø is set "on." Again, indicator 2Ø denotes a late payment. This last comparison will not be made, however, if the month paid is less than the month due; if PMONTH < DMONTH, this would mean that the customer's payment was early, and indicator 15 would be "off" as a result. This general approach to comparing dates is useful to the programmer; there are, however, advanced techniques that are more efficient that we will discuss later.

At this point, you should again review the logic used by the program excerpt in Figure 4.1Ø. It is a good idea to substitute values for the dates and walk through the problem validating that the logic is indeed correct. For example, use the following data and determine if indicator 2Ø will be set "on" by the program:

Date Paid	Date Due
Ø1/15/92	12/Ø1/91
11/29/91	12/Ø1/91
12/Ø2/91	12/Ø1/91

By substituting values and performing each step, one at a time, the logic can be verified. This **program walkthrough** procedure is used for determining if the logic of a program is correct. It is used to test the logic of RPG programs as well as programs written in other languages. Desk checking a program with walkthroughs will minimize the number of syntax and logic errors. We recommend that you use the SETOF instruction at the beginning of the calculations to set off any indicators that may have been set on in the previous cycle. This not only simplifies the coding, but prevents potential logic errors. When we compared dates, we used only two indicators, namely indicators 15 and 20. In that example, both indicators were set off immediately before the first compare instruction. The logic, then, was correct. When numerous indicators are required throughout a program, however, the SETOF should be used to ensure that when calculations begin for each record, the indicators are set off.

The programmer may also find instances when dates are to be compared to the current date. The reserved word UDATE may be divided into its three component parts (month, day, year) if you need to access a part of the date. Each part has its own reserved name: UMONTH, UDAY, and UYEAR. UDATE is stored by the computer and need not be read in as input.

```
┌─────────────────────────────────┐ ⎫ Group name
│             UDATE               │ ⎬ Current date
├─────────────┬────────┬──────────┤ ⎭
│   MONTH     │  DAY   │   YEAR   │
│   UMONTH    │  UDAY  │  UYEAR   │
└─────────────┴────────┴──────────┘
```

Subordinate names
Current date

UDATE can be coded as follows:

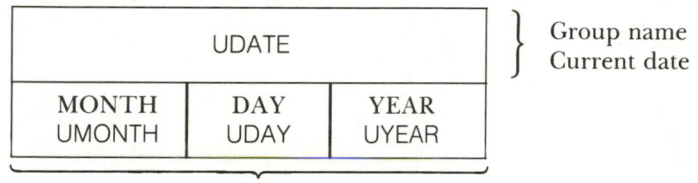

The entire UDATE field is subdivided into component fields. Referencing an area by a group name, or a subdivision of the group, is an important feature in RPG. The date due and date paid fields are subdivided in the same manner as the UDATE field. Remember, by subdividing a field you can access the data in two ways—on a group basis and also on an individual subordinate basis. Later in the text other advantages in using these procedures will be covered.

H. Using Data Structures to Group Fields

In the previous example, two date fields (DATEDU and DATEPD) are compared to determine if the payment is late. Since the date fields are in the month/day/

year format, each subfield has to be compared independently to determine if the payment date is greater than the due date. Here, we will illustrate how the Data Structure technique can be used to simplify this comparison of two date fields.

When Data Structures are used to group fields, nonadjacent fields from the input record can be grouped together to occupy adjacent locations internally. The internal area defined by the Data Structure can then be referenced by a group name, thus allowing fields arranged in a different sequence to be used in comparisons or other operations.

Figure 4.11 illustrates the Input and Calculation Specifications forms that define two new Data Structures and perform the necessary comparison operation on the date fields. Since both dates are in yymmdd format, a full one-pass comparison is sufficient (e.g., 910307 < 910326 which means that 03/07/91 < 03/26/91).

As shown in the Input Specifications form in Figure 4.11, Data Structures can be used to rearrange fields for easier reference.

Figure 4.11   Let us consider the due date in more detail to illustrate how Data Structures

Line	Form Type	Filename or Record Name / Data Structure Name	Sequence	Number (1/N), E	Option (O), U, S	Record Identifying Indicator, ** or DS	Position (1)	Not(N)	C/Z/D	Character	Position (2)	Not(N)	C/Z/D	Character	Position (3)	Not(N)	C/Z/D	Character	Stacker Select / P/B/L/R	From	To	Decimal Positions	RPG Field Name	Control Level (L1–L9)	Matching Fields or Chaining Fields	Field Record Relation	Plus	Minus	Zero or Blank
01	I	CUSTIN	NS			01																								
02	I																			1	4		CNO						
03	I																			5	20		CNAME						
04	I																			21	27	2	CBAL						
05	I																			31	36	0	DATEDU						
06	I																			31	32	0	DMONTH						
07	I																			33	34	0	DUDAY						
08	I																			35	36	0	DUYR						
09	I																			41	46	0	DATEPD						
10	I																			41	42	0	PMONTH						
11	I																			43	44	0	PDDAY						
12	I																			45	46	0	PDYR						
13	I			DS																										
14	I																			1	6	0	#DDATE						
15	I																			1	2	0	DUYR						
16	I																			3	4	0	DMONTH						
17	I																			5	6	0	DUDAY						
18	I			DS																										
19	I																			1	6	0	#PDATE						
20	I																			1	2	0	PDYR						
	I																			3	4	0	PMONTH						
	I																			5	6	0	PDDAY						

Line	Form Type	Control Level (L0–L9, LR, SR, AN/OR)	Not	And	Not	And	Not	Factor 1	Operation	Factor 2	Result Field Name	Length	Decimal Positions	Half Adjust (H)	Plus 1>2	Minus 1<2	Zero 1=2	Comments
01	C							#PDATE	COMP	#DDATE					20			
02	C																	

can be used to rearrange subfields into a different order. Examine the following comparison between DATEDU defined in the CUSTIN input record and #DDATE defined as a Data Structure:

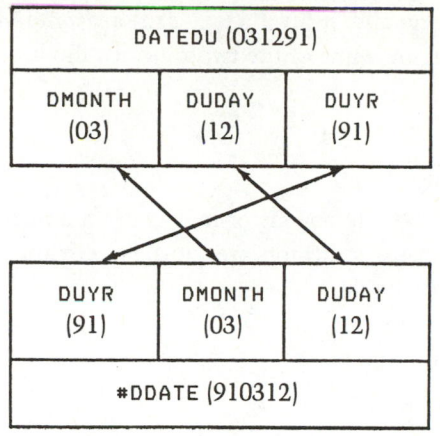

DATEDU as defined in the CUSTIN input record

The date due (#DDATE) defined as a Data Structure

The Data Structure #DDATE (due date) is a group field containing the subfields DUYR, DMONTH, and DUDAY. These subfields are the same fields defined on the Input Specifications form for the CUSTIN record. However, in the Data Structure #DDATE they have been grouped into a different order. This will allow the program to reference the due date in the year/month/day format.

It should be noted that when a Data Structure is used to group fields together, the fields are still stored in only one internal location. Thus, the Data Structure is allowing access to the fields in a different order and not creating new fields.

Similarly, the payment date has been specified on the Input Specifications form as a Data Structure in which the subfields are arranged in the same year/month/day format.

An advantage of using Data Structures to group fields into a different order is shown on the Calculation Specifications form. Because the two date fields have been rearranged into the order necessary for comparison, the group fields can now be compared in one operation, thereby eliminating indicator 15 and two compare operations.

Self-Test

1. The contents of both Factor 1 and Factor 2 must be _____ if an algebraic comparison is to take place.

2. Resulting indicators are set according to the relative value of Factor _____ compared to Factor _____.

3. When the contents of Factor 1 is greater than the contents of Factor 2, the resulting condition is _____.

4. If Factor 1 contains a numeric literal, then Factor 2 (may/may not) contain a numeric literal.

5. (T or F) Resulting indicators are automatically turned off by RPG at the end of the cycle.

6. The three conditions of the resulting indicators in the order found on the coding form are from left to right, _____, _____, and _____.

7. Since numeric compares are algebraic, negative quantities are (greater than, less than) positive quantities.

8. When numeric fields are of different lengths, the shorter field is extended by adding _____ once the _____ is aligned.

9. Assume a comparison is made and an equal condition results in turning on indicator 3Ø. How can we execute an instruction to be performed if an unequal condition occurs?

10. Review the illustration in Figure 4.12 and indicate whether the instructions are valid or invalid. If invalid, state the reason. (Assume that all fields are numeric.)

11. State the meaning of the two routines illustrated in Figure 4.13.

Solutions
1. numeric
2. 1, 2
3. high
4. may not—Only one factor may contain a numeric literal.
5. F—Resulting indicators are set the next time the COMP instruction is executed.
6. high, low, equal
7. less than
8. zeros, decimal point

Figure 4.12
Illustration for Question 10.

	Line	Form Type	Control Level	And Not	And Not	Not	Factor 1	Operation	Factor 2	Result Field Name	Length	Decimal Positions	Half Adjust	Plus / 1>2 High	Minus / 1<2 Low	Zero / 1=2 Equal	Comments
(a)	0 1	Ø C					CTAX	COMP	LIMIT								
	0 2	Ø C ✱															
(b)	0 3	Ø C					YTDGRS	COMP	6785.ØØ					4Ø	5Ø	6Ø	
	0 4	Ø C ✱															
(c)	0 5	Ø C					WAGES	COMP	1Ø,ØØØ.ØØ					7Ø	8Ø	9Ø	
	0 6	Ø C ✱															
(d)	0 7	Ø C					45Ø	COMP	MIN					75	85	95	
	0 8	Ø C ✱															
(e)	0 9	Ø C					SLRY	COMP	$5ØØ.ØØ					45	55	65	
	1 0	Ø C ✱															
(f)	1 1	Ø C					SALES	COMP	SLS8Ø					3Ø	3Ø	3Ø	
	1 2	Ø C ✱															
(g)	1 3	Ø C					YTDFCA	COMP	MAX					1Ø	2Ø	3Ø	

Figure 4.13
Illustration for Question 11.

Line	Form Type	Control Level	And Not	And Not	Not	Factor 1	Operation	Factor 2	Result Field Name	Length	Decimal Positions	Half Adjust	Plus / 1>2 High	Minus / 1<2 Low	Zero / 1=2 Equal	Comments
0 1	Ø C		1Ø			AGE	COMP	3Ø							66	
0 2	Ø C		1Ø 66			OVER3Ø	ADD	1	OVER3Ø	3Ø						
0 3	Ø C ✱															
0 4	Ø C ✱															
0 5	Ø C		2Ø			HRS	COMP	4Ø.ØØ						3Ø	3Ø	
0 6	Ø C		2Ø N3Ø			OVER4Ø	ADD	1	OVER4Ø	3Ø						
0 7	Ø C		2Ø N3Ø			HRS	SUB	4Ø.ØØ	OTHRS	52						
0 8	Ø C		2Ø N3Ø			OTHRS	ADD	TOTAL	TOTAL	72						

9. By coding N3Ø in columns 9–17 of the Calculation form.
10. a. Invalid—no resulting indicators.
    b. Invalid—Factor 2 must be left-justified.
    c. Invalid—numeric literal may not contain a comma.
    d. Valid.
    e. Invalid—dollar sign not permitted in a numeric literal.
    f. Invalid—will always turn on indicator 3Ø.
    g. Valid
11. The first routine counts all records when the field AGE is greater than 3Ø. The counter, OVER3Ø, is updated each time a record is found where the age is greater than 3Ø. The second routine counts the number of records where HRS exceeds 4Ø. In addition, the TOTAL overtime hours, that is, the hours in excess of 4Ø, are accumulated in a running total.

III. Comparing Alphanumeric Fields

A. Collating Sequence

For comparison purposes, the computer treats alphabetic fields in exactly the same manner as alphanumeric fields. Let us consider the comparison of two alphabetic fields called NAME1 and NAME2 contained in main storage areas. In the illustration that follows, once the values in the two areas are compared, the result would indicate that NAME1 is less than NAME2:

R O B E R T S	<	S A M U E L S
NAME1	Less than	NAME2

S A M U E L S	<	T H O M A S
NAME1	Less than	NAME2

When comparing alphabetic data, A < B, B < C, and so on. Thus, in the example just presented, the sequence is ROBERTS < SAMUELS < THOMAS since the letter "R" is less than the letter "S," and similarly the letter "S" is less than the letter "T." The comparison begins with the left-most letter of each name. The entire contents of the field referenced as NAME1 is considered less than the contents of NAME2 in the two examples shown.

The computer, then, will compare alphabetic characters logically. If the first character of the two factors were equal, the computer would then compare the subsequent characters. Consider the following example:

Z O R R O	>	X E R O X
NAME1	Greater than	NAME2

X E R O X	>	E X X O N
NAME1	Greater than	NAME2

Again, the *first* letter of each name is compared; NAME1 is greater than NAME2 because the letter "Z" is greater than the letter "X"; in the second example, NAME1 is also greater than NAME2 because the letter "X" is greater than the letter "E." As a consequence, the entire contents of NAME1 is considered greater than NAME2. That is, ZORRO > XEROX > EXXON.

Alphameric comparisons may not, however, be as simple as those illustrated. Sometimes, the comparison of alphameric data includes fields containing letters, blanks, numbers, and special characters as typically found in street addresses such as "112-Ø5 FIFTY-FIRST AVENUE." In order for programmers to understand alphameric comparisons, they must first be aware of the **collating sequence** used by the computer.

Every computer system has a collating sequence, which is the order by which it sorts characters. The collating sequence is instrumental in determining the results of alphameric comparisons. Figure 4.14 illustrates the two most common collating sequences used for representing data:

1. EBCDIC, which is widely used on IBM and IBM-compatible computers, and

2. ASCII, which is used on most micros and other types of mainframes.

EBCDIC (pronounced eb-se-dik) is an acronym for Extended Binary Coded Decimal Interchange Code. ASCII (pronounced as-key) is an acronym for American Standard Code for Information Interchange.

With both collating sequences, the blank or space has the lowest value in the collating sequence. Thus a blank field will always be considered "low" when compared to any nonblank field. For EBCDIC computers, special characters are followed by the 26 uppercase letters of the alphabet (A–Z), which in turn are followed by digits (Ø–9). As a consequence, the letter "B" has a higher value than the letter "A." Uppercase letters are considered less than lowercase letters. Zero has a higher value than the letter "Z" and, as we would expect, numbers increase in ascending sequence.

Figure 4.14
Collating sequences for EBCDIC and ASCII computers.

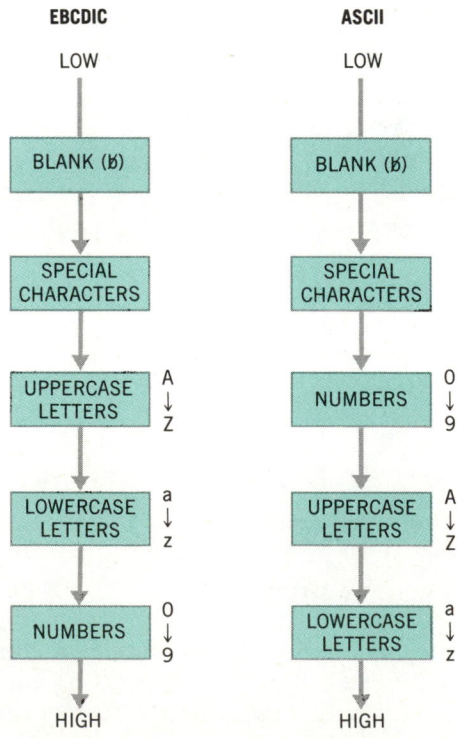

Note that with ASCII computers, numbers are considered less than letters and uppercase letters are less than lowercase letters. Most computers that have RPG compilers, however, use the EBCDIC collating sequence.

B. Rules for Alphanumeric Comparisons

1. The data in Factor 1 and Factor 2 must both be alphameric.
2. Factor 1 is compared to Factor 2.
3. Fields are aligned on the left; if one field is shorter, blanks are added to the low-order position(s) of the shorter field. Thus, a field containing ABC is equal to a field containing ABCƀƀ.
4. The comparison begins in the left-most position and proceeds from left to right, one character at a time, until an inequality occurs or until the fields have been fully compared and all the characters are found equal.
5. Alphameric literals can have a maximum length of eight characters and are enclosed in single quotes or apostrophes.
6. Fields up to 256 characters may be compared using an alphameric compare.

C. Comparing Alphanumeric Fields of Equal Length

When fields are defined on the Input and/or Calculation Specifications form, and the Decimal Position (column 52) is left blank, the fields are considered alphanumeric. RPG compares alphameric fields quite differently from numeric fields; that is, a different set of rules applies.

As with numeric fields, Factor 1 is compared to Factor 2 and resulting indicators are used to record the result of the comparison. Consider the following as a review:

Factor 1 is greater than Factor 2	HIGH
Factor 1 is less than Factor 2	LOW
Factor 1 is equal to Factor 2	EQUAL

Alphameric fields are compared by aligning their left-most characters. If one field is shorter than the other, the shorter field is extended by padding blanks or spaces on the right in the **low-order positions.** The comparison begins in the **high-order position** (left-most) and thereafter proceeds from left to right, one character at a time. As soon as an unequal condition occurs, the comparison is terminated. When an inequality is found, one of the following results:

1. If the character in Factor 1 is greater than the character in Factor 2, a HIGH result occurs.
2. If the character in Factor 1 is less than the character in Factor 2, a LOW result occurs.

However, if each position is compared and the end of both factors is reached without an unequal condition occurring, then the result of the comparison is equal. Now that the basis for alphameric comparisons has been established, an example will serve to illustrate the points made (see Figure 4.15).

The example in Figure 4.15 illustrates in detail precisely how the COMPare instruction operates. Beginning on the left, the high-order positions of both fields are compared. Since both contain the letter "B" they are equal; therefore the next position is compared. Again, we find the characters (R) equal. This process continues until an unequal condition occurs or the right-most charac-

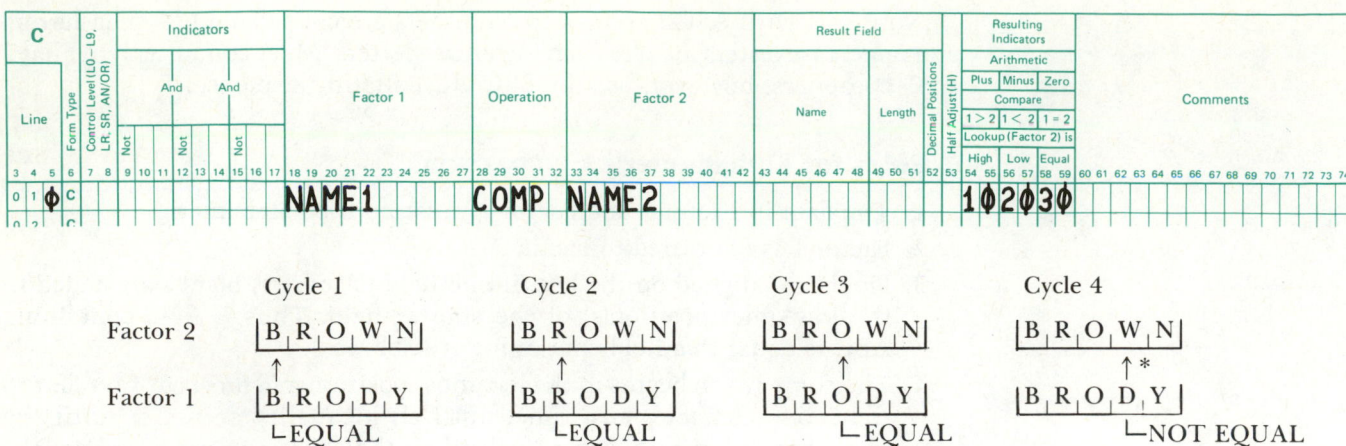

Figure 4.15
Alphameric comparison.

ters of the factors are reached. In the example, the computer compared four characters before an unequal condition was found. Note that each character is compared, one at a time, from left to right. The collating sequence will determine the relative weight of each character being compared.

D. Comparing Alphanumeric Fields of Unequal Length

Again referring to the instruction in Figure 4.15, note that the conditions HIGH, LOW, and EQUAL will set on indicators 1Ø, 2Ø, and 3Ø, respectively.

Figure 4.16
Alphameric comparisons.

Example 1

Factor 1	Factor 2	
J O H N S O N	J O H N	Before alignment
J O H N S O N	J O H N ʬ ʬ ʬ	After alignment

Result

Number of characters compared	5
Condition	HIGH
Reason	S > ʬ
Indicator set on	10

Example 2

Factor 1	Factor 2	
P E T E R S	P E T E R S O N	Before alignment
P E T E R S ʬ ʬ	P E T E R S O N	After alignment

Result

Number of characters compared	7
Condition	LOW
Reason	ʬ < O
Indicator set on	20

Let us evaluate a variety of conditions using NAME1 as Factor 1 and NAME2 as Factor 2 in Figure 4.16.

In Example 1 of Figure 4.16, Factor 2 contains fewer characters than Factor 1. Hence, Factor 2 is extended by padding blanks in the right-most positions. After alignment, both factors contain seven characters. We find the result of this comparison to be high since the weighted value of the "S" in Factor 1 is greater than the blank in Factor 2. Thus we see that Factor 1 compared to Factor 2 is high and results in turning on indicator 1Ø.

In Example 2, Factor 1 contains fewer characters than Factor 2. Therefore, during alignment, blanks are padded in the right-most positions of Factor 1. After alignment, both fields are eight characters in length. A low condition results from this comparison since the blank in Factor 1 has a lower weight than the letter "O" in Factor 2. Recall that the low condition turns on indicator 2Ø.

Example 1 of Figure 4.17 illustrates an equal comparison of Factors 1 and 2. Again, alignment causes Factor 1 to be extended by padding blanks in the low-order position(s). However, each character is compared and found equal. Since all nine of the characters compare equal, including the last character of both factors, the compare instruction terminates with the resulting condition code set to equal.

The collating sequence must again be known in order to determine the results of the comparison illustrated in Example 2. Remember, letters have a lesser value in the collating sequence than do numbers for most computers; hence the letter "F" has a lower value than the number 4. This results in the low condition indicated in the example.

Figure 4.17
Alphameric comparisons.

Example 1

Factor 1	Factor 2	
J O N E S R	J O N E S R	Before alignment
J O N E S R ƀ ƀ	J O N E S R	After alignment

Result

Number of characters compared	9
Condition	EQUAL
Reason	All characters equal
Indicator set on	30

Example 2

Factor 1	Factor 2
F O U R T H S T R E E T	4 T H S T R E E T

No alignment necessary. Both factors contain 13 characters.

Result

Number of characters compared	1
Condition	LOW
Reason	F < 4
Indicator set on	20

E. Specifying Alphanumeric Literals

When comparing alphanumeric fields, a literal may be used instead of a field name in either Factor 1 or Factor 2. The mechanics of the compare operation are essentially the same as when comparing two alphanumeric fields; however, the literal must be properly defined. The following rules will serve as a review of alphanumeric literals:

RULES FOR FORMING ALPHANUMERIC LITERALS

1. Any combination of characters may be used.
2. Alphanumeric literals must be enclosed in single quotes or apostrophes.
3. The apostrophes are not part of the literal, but rather serve to indicate its beginning and end points.
4. The maximum length is eight characters, excluding the enclosing apostrophes.
5. When an apostrophe is to be included as part of the literal, as for example in O'CONNOR, then the literal would be written 'O''CONNOR'. Note the two apostrophes preceding the C would ensure that an actual apostrophe is part of the literal.

Figure 4.18 contains an alphabetic literal in Factor 2. Alphabetic literals represent actual information and must be enclosed in quotes to distinguish them from field names. Note that alphabetic literals are treated by the computer in exactly the same manner as alphanumeric literals. In Figure 4.18, if the quotes had been omitted, RPG would interpret ALABAMA to be a field name, thereby causing an error in the program. The quotes, however, are not included in the comparison. Also observe that Factor 2 is longer than Factor 1 in Figure 4.18. You will recall that the shorter field is extended by padding blanks in the low-order position. Once aligned, the comparison again proceeds from left to right, one character at a time until an unequal condition is found. According to the collating sequence, the S in ALASKA has a higher value than the B in ALABAMA. Therefore, the result is high, setting indicator 1Ø on.

Figure 4.18
Using an alphanumeric literal,
Example 1.

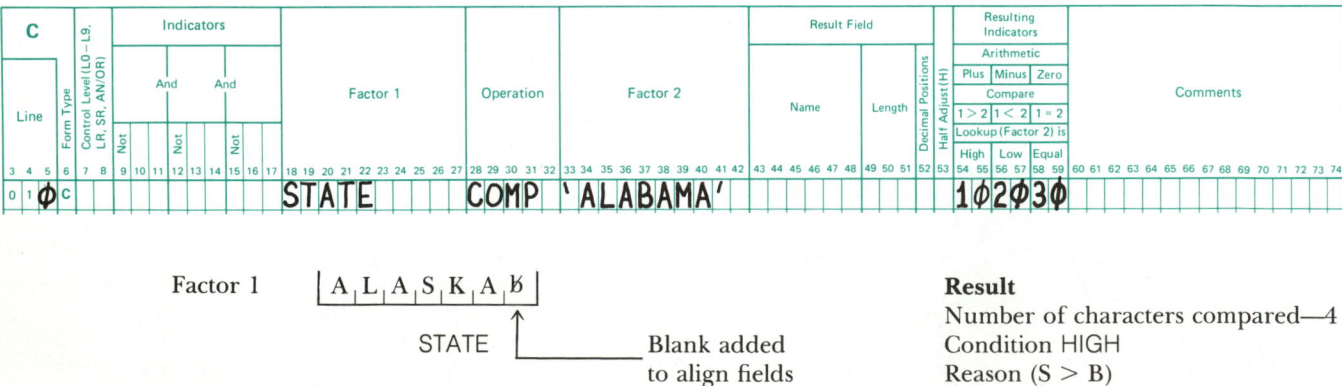

Factor 1 | A L A S K A ♭ |
              STATE ↑
                     Blank added
                     to align fields

Factor 2 | A L A B A M A |
              Literal
                     Compare ends here

Result
Number of characters compared—4
Condition HIGH
Reason (S > B)
Indicator set on: 10

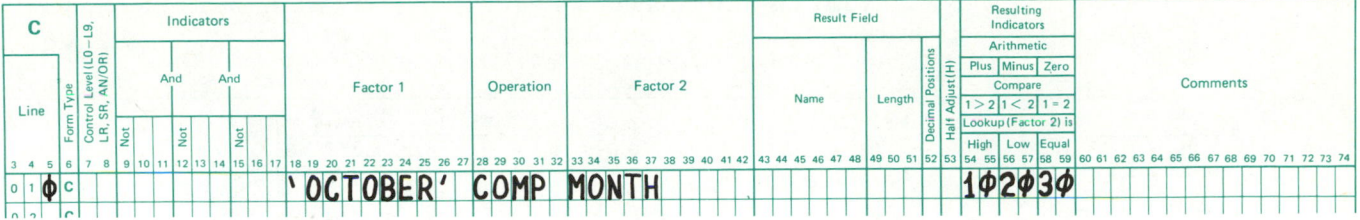

Factor 1 | O C T O B E R ♭ ♭ |
          Literal

Result
Number of characters compared—1
Condition   LOW
Reason   (O < S)
Indicator set on: 20

Factor 2 | S E P T E M B E R |
          MONTH

Figure 4.19
Using an alphanumeric literal,
Example 2.

Figure 4.19 illustrates the use of an alphabetic literal as Factor 1. Since the letter "O" is less than "S" in the collating sequence, a low condition will result. Indicator 20 will therefore be set on.

IV. Applications of the COMPare Operation

Example 1
Code the instructions necessary to count the number of records containing an AMT field that is between 50 and 100, inclusive of the endpoints.

First, the AMT field is compared to the numeric value 50, and if AMT is equal to or greater than 50, indicator 10 is set "on." Only when indicator 10 is "on" will the next test be performed. If indicator 10 is "off," the AMT field will not be compared to 100. When the second COMP instruction is executed, the AMT field is compared to the number, 100. If the AMT field is less than or equal to 100, then indicator 10 is set "on."

Indicator 10, in effect, signals the program that the AMT field is between 50 and 100. Indicator 10 is thus used to condition the instruction: ADD 1 to COUNT. The coding necessary for this problem is shown here:

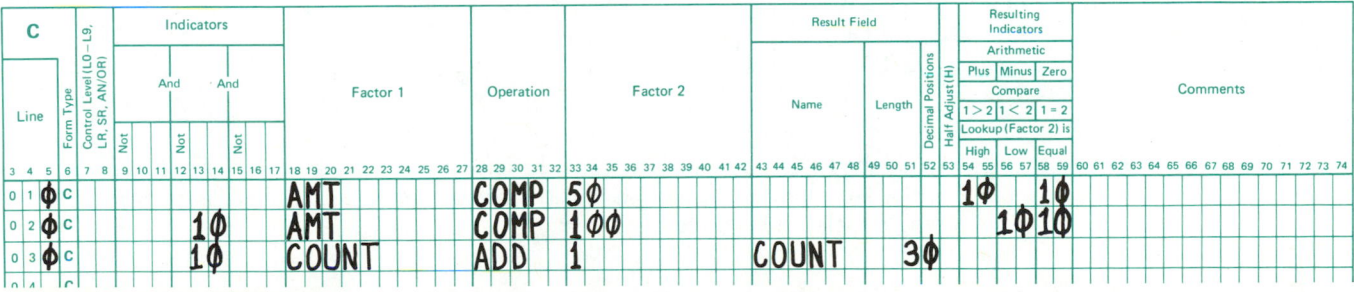

Example 2
The pay rate for employees varies depending on the shift worked. Code the steps necessary to provide an adjustment in the pay rate depending on the SHIFT. Then calculate the GROSS as RATE × HRS. The RATE adjustment is as follows:

Shift	Adjustment
1	0 (simply use the RATE)
2	10% premium or 1.10 × RATE
3	15% premium or 1.15 × RATE

See Figure 4.20 for coding of this problem. Note that the RATE is changed if SHIFT = 2 or 3. The last instruction multiplies RATE by HRS for each input record regardless of whether RATE has been changed.

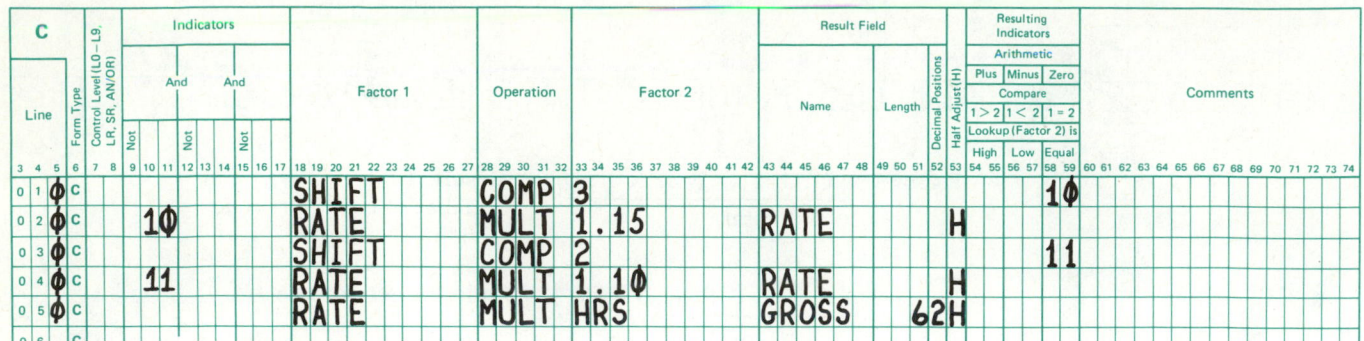

Figure 4.20
Coding for Example 2.

Note in the coding that we did not test for a SHIFT = 1. The reason for this is that the rate is not supposed to change when the SHIFT is equal to 1. Hence, if the condition was found to be true, that is, if the SHIFT was equal to 1, we would not modify the value of RATE. We would be wasting time with an instruction that is unnecessary. An alternative to the solution in Figure 4.20 is as follows:

C	Form Type	Control Level (L0–L9, LR, SR, AN/OR)	And Not	And Not	Not	Factor 1	Operation	Factor 2	Result Field Name	Length	Decimal Positions	Half Adjust (H)	Arithmetic Plus High 54 55	Minus Low 56 57	Zero Equal 58 59	Comments
0 1 0	C					SHIFT	COMP	2					10		11	
0 2 0	C		10			RATE	MULT	1.15	RATE			H				
0 3 0	C		11			RATE	MULT	1.10	RATE			H				
0 4 0	C					RATE	MULT	HRS	GROSS	62		H				
0 5	C															
0 6	C															
0 7	C															

Example 3   Provide the RPG coding to determine the largest of three numbers, identified as N1, N2, and N3. No duplicate values within the set of the three numbers is permitted. The coding to solve this problem follows:

Summary	
Largest Value	Indicator "ON"
N1	21
N2	22
N3	23

Line	Form Type	Control Level (L0–L9, LR, SR, AN/OR)	Indicators And Not	And Not	And Not	Factor 1	Operation	Factor 2	Result Field Name	Length	Decimal Positions	Half Adjust (H)	Resulting Indicators Arithmetic Plus 1>2 / High	Minus 1<2 / Low	Zero 1=2 / Equal	Comments
0 1	C					N1	COMP	N2					21	22		
0 2	C		21			N1	COMP	N3					21	23		
0 3	C		22			N2	COMP	N3					22	23		
0 4	C															

Example 4 Develop a program excerpt to calculate FICA, where SALARY is read from an input record. FICA is calculated as 7.65% of the first $51,300 earned. FICA is the Social Security tax paid by employees.

Line	Form Type	Control Level	Indicators And Not	And Not	And Not	Factor 1	Operation	Factor 2	Result Field Name	Length	Decimal Positions	Half Adjust (H)	Resulting Indicators Plus High	Minus Low	Zero Equal	Comments
0 1 0	C					SALARY	COMP	51300					10	11	10	
0 2 0	C		10				Z-ADD	3924.45	FICA	92						
0 3 0	C		11			SALARY	MULT	.0765	FICA			H				
0 4	C															

The need for indicator 11 could be eliminated by conditioning line 030 with an N10 entry, meaning that indicator 10 is in the "off" state. The effect of line 030 would be to multiply SALARY by .0765. Recall that *none* of these statements change the contents of the SALARY field in any way because SALARY is *not* a Result Field. A field must be used as a Result Field in order for its contents to change. The exception to this rule is the reading of data from an input medium. Once data has been read in and *moved* to the respective fields, new values would be assigned to these fields and the previous input values would no longer be available for processing unless they had been stored elsewhere. Sometimes students have difficulty in differentiating between the use of a field as a factor and using the field to store a result. Remember, Result Fields are *always* assigned new values each time an arithmetic instruction is executed. Result Fields are not used, however, with COMP instructions.

Example 5 Code the RPG Calculation Specifications to calculate SALES discounts for customers based on the amount of the sale. Use the following table and set on the indicators as noted:

Sales Amount	Discount	Set "ON"
0–99.99	0%	
100–199.99	2%	22
200–299.99	3%	23
300 and over	6%	26

Subtract the discount (DISCT) from the SALES, giving the NET sales. When SALES are less than 100, no discount is offered.

The Calculation Specifications to solve this problem are as follows:

C	Line	Form Type	Control Level (L0–L9, LR, SR, AN/OR)	Indicators And Not	And Not	Not	Factor 1	Operation	Factor 2	Result Field Name	Length	Decimal Positions	Half Adjust (H)	Resulting Indicators Arithmetic / Compare / Lookup High	Low	Equal
C	01							Z-ADD	0	DISCT						
C	02						SALES	COMP	200.00					26	22	23
C	03			26			SALES	COMP	300.00					26	23	26
C	04			22			SALES	COMP	100.00					22		22
C	05			22			SALES	MULT	.02	DISCT			H			
C	06			23			SALES	MULT	.03	DISCT			H			
C	07			26			SALES	MULT	.06	DISCT			H			
C	08						SALES	SUB	DISCT	NET						
C	09															
C	10															

Must be specified for rounding each calculation →

Note that we begin by resetting the DISCT (discount) field to zero. Thus, if SALES are less than 100.00, DISCT will be automatically set to zero.

Next, we compare SALES to 200.00. If SALES are equal to or greater than 200.00, there is no need to test the first two conditions (SALES between 0 and 99.99, and SALES between 100 and 199.99). This practice of beginning our test with the *middle* condition is a common programming technique. It is designed specifically to save computer time. When a field compares "greater than or equal to" the middle entry, there is no need to compare it to the first half of the table. In general, then, this technique reduces the number of comparisons that will be required to determine the appropriate course of action.

When SALES is compared to 200.00, two things happen. First, all three indicators (26, 22, 23) are set off initially. Second, one of the three indicators is set on as a result of the comparison:

Line 02: SALES COMP 200.00

If SALES is less than 200.00, indicator 22 is set on.

If SALES is equal to 200.00, indicator 23 is set on.

If SALES is greater than 200.00, indicator 26 is set on.

Once the program has completed the COMP operation on line 02 it continues with the next sequential statement in the program (line 03). It should be noted that the program continues with this next statement regardless of which indicator is set on during line 02. On line 03, the program tests the condition of indicator 26. If it is on, line 03 is executed. If it is off, the program continues with the next statement (line 04). Again, it is worth noting that indicator 26 is tested first to determine if line 03 is to be executed. If it is on, indicators 23 and 26 are set off prior to the COMP operation. In this way, only the correct indicator will be on as a result of the COMP operation.

Recall that the SETOF indicator could be used to simplify the program logic and prevent logic errors that could result from multiple indicators having been set in a previous cycle that should be off for subsequent cycles. Indicators 22, 23, and 26 could be set off with a single SETOF instruction.

On line 03, SALES is compared to 300.00 and the outcome is as follows:

Line 03: SALES COMP 300.00

If SALES is less than 300.00, indicator 23 is set on.

If SALES is equal to or greater than 300.00, indicator 26 is set on.

If 23 is on, SALES must be greater than 200.00 and less than 300.00, since the previous operation (line 02) determined that SALES was greater than 200.00.

If indicator 26 is on, then SALES must be equal to or greater than 300.00.

Line 04 is executed only if indicator 22 was set on during line 02, that is, SALES < 200.00. The outcome of line 04 is as follows:

> Line 04: SALES COMP 100.00
>
> If SALES is equal to or greater than 100.00, indicator 22 is set on.
>
> If no indicator is set on, SALES must be less than 100.00.

Once the comparison operations are completed, the DISCT is calculated using the appropriate discount value (numeric literal). However, if SALES < 100.00, a value for DISCT is not calculated since this field was set to zero at the beginning of this routine.

Self-Test

1. The character with the lowest value in the collating sequence is the _____.
2. The letter "A" is (greater than, less than) the letter "B."
3. The digit zero is (higher in, lower in) value relative to the letter "Z."
4. (T or F) When alphanumeric fields of different length are compared, the comparison ends when the last character of the shorter field is tested.
5. If we compared the name "JOHNS" with "JOHNSON," we would find (number) characters were compared, with the name _____ having the higher value.
6. When alphanumeric literals are entered in Factor 1 or Factor 2, they are enclosed in _____.
7. Suppose a month field in Factor 1 can take on values JAN, FEB, . . . DEC. If we compare Factor 1 to the literal 'APR' in Factor 2, we would have (number) of equal comparisons, (number) of high comparisons, and (number) of low conditions after comparing the 12 months of the year.
8. Could we use 'SEPTEMBER' as an alphabetic literal?
9. If in an alphanumeric compare, we compared a field containing 'NEWARK' with 'NEW YORK', how many characters would be compared and which field would have the higher value?
10. A field named SOCSEC contains an entry in column 52 of the Input form. We are required to perform an alphanumeric compare using SOCSEC. Is this acceptable in RPG?

Solutions

1. blank or space
2. less than
3. higher in
4. F—Blanks or spaces are padded on the right of the shorter field.
5. 6; JOHNSON
6. apostrophes or single quote marks
7. 1; 11; 0
8. No. It has more than 10 characters, including the apostrophes, and therefore will not fit in either Factor 1 or Factor 2.
9. four; NEWARK (NEW YORK has a blank in the fourth position)
10. No. The data in both fields must be numeric.

V. RPG Indicator Summary Form

The RPG Indicator Summary form is used to assist the programmer in keeping track of all indicators established in a program. Unlike the other RPG Speci-

F*							Circle Indicators Used:											Note: All indicators are not valid with all systems.

(RPG Indicator Summary form)

Line	Form Type	Record Identifying	Input Field	Calculation Result and Command Key	Halt and User	Control Level and Overflow	FUNCTION OF INDICATORS
0 1	⌀F*	I	D	F	C	H	L	FUNCTION OF INDICATORS
0 2	⌀F*						
0 3	⌀F*	⌀1						MASTER ACCOUNTS RECEIVABLE RECORD
0 4	⌀F*	⌀2						CREDIT TRANSACTION RECORD
0 5	⌀F*	⌀3						DEBIT TRANSACTION RECORD
0 6	F*						

Figure 4.21
RPG Indicator Summary form.

fications forms considered thus far, the Indicator Summary form has no effect on the translation or execution of the program; it is used primarily for documentation and commentary purposes. Note that all entries on this form have an asterisk (*) in column 7 designating each entry as a comment.

When a programmer sets on numerous indicators in a program, it is quite possible that he or she may inadvertently use the same indicator number for two different purposes. Unless the programmer finds this error before execution, debugging could be a timely and difficult task. The Indicator Summary form is useful in helping the programmer avoid such errors. See Figure 4.21 for an illustration of an RPG Indicator Summary form.

CHAPTER SELF-TEST

1. A compare instruction always produces one of three results: _____, _____, or _____ .

2. (T or F) It is permissible in RPG to compare a numeric field to an alphanumeric field.

3. The COMP instruction automatically triggers an internal _____ that is used to set the resulting indicators.

4. (T or F) The COMP instruction can be used to turn on up to three indicators.

5. (T or F) Resulting indicators are turned off automatically in an RPG program unless they are used immediately.

6. (T or F) In a numeric compare, both Factor 1 and Factor 2 may be numeric literals.

7. To accomplish a numeric comparison of two fields, each field must have a numeric entry in the _____ Positions column of the form on which it is defined.

8. Numeric comparisons are algebraic comparisons, which means that the _____ is included in the test.

9. Before numeric fields of unequal length are compared, they are automatically aligned according to their _____ and missing digits are _____ .

10. (T or F) An example of a valid numeric literal is $1,000.

11. A _____ is a technique used to manually follow the logic of a program before actually running the program.

12. (T or F) When comparing alphanumeric fields, the comparison begins with the low-order or right-most positions.

13. When comparing alphameric fields of different lengths, the shorter field is padded with _____ in the _____ -order positions.

14. (T or F) 'REGISTRATION' is an example of a valid alphanumeric literal.

SOLUTIONS
1. high; low; equal
2. F

3. condition code

4. T—Any one or all the high, low, and equal indicators can be used.

5. F—They remain on until the next record is processed and the compare instruction is again executed.

6. F—Either Factor 1 or Factor 2 may be a numeric literal, but not both.

7. Decimal

8. sign

9. decimal points; filled with zeros

10. F—Numeric literals cannot contain dollar signs, commas, blanks, or any other alphanumeric character except a sign and a decimal point.

11. structured program walkthrough

12. F—It begins with the left-most position.

13. blanks; low

14. F—The maximum length is eight characters, excluding the apostrophes.

KEY TERMS

Algebraic comparison
Alphameric field
Alphanumeric field
Collating sequence

Compare (COMP) operation
Condition code
High-order position

Literal
Low-order position
Numeric field
Program walkthrough

Resulting indicator
Routine

REVIEW QUESTIONS

1. Indicate the results of the following comparisons assuming the EBCDIC collating sequence:

Factor 1	Factor 2
Ø12	12
12+	12
AEF	AED
12A	B2A
12-	12
AEFG	AEF
4Ø.ØØ	4Ø

2. If Factor 1 is less than Factor 2, a COMP instruction will turn on the _____ indicator.

3. (T or F) Resulting indicators that are turned on as a result of a COMP operation remain on until the next record is processed.

4. Indicate how an RPG programmer defines a field as numeric.

5. (T or F) Alphanumeric fields may be used in arithmetic operations.

6. (T or F) All fields must be the same length if they are to be compared.

7. (T or F) A numeric literal may contain a dollar sign.

8. (T or F) Numeric literals are right-justified when entered in Factor 1 or Factor 2 of the Calculation form.

9. (T or F) By entering an N in column 9, 12, or 15, a test may be made to determine if an indicator is off rather than on.

10. A field that is further subdivided into subordinate fields is referred to as a(n) _____ item.

11. A(n) _____ is a desk-checking procedure that enables the programmer to manually step through the set of procedures used in the program to ensure that the logic is correct.

12. The reserved word _____ contains the current month, day, and year.

13. Alphameric literals are enclosed in _____ to distinguish them from numeric literals.

14. (T or F) An alphanumeric field should only be compared to an alphanumeric literal.

15. (T or F) A blank or space has the lowest value in the collating sequence.

DEBUGGING EXERCISES

Debugging Exercise 1
The purpose of this program is to produce a weekly payroll register (PAYREG) from employee input records contained in the PAYMAST file. Employees working more than 4Ø hours in a week are paid time and a half for the overtime hours. Note that if the hours field is blank, the record will not be processed. The problem definition is shown in Figure 4.22.

Figure 4.22
Problem definition for Debugging Exercise 1.

Systems Flowchart

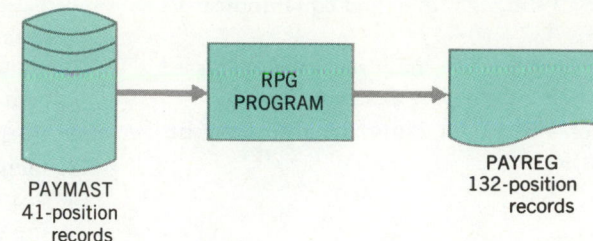

PAYMAST
41-position
records

RPG
PROGRAM

PAYREG
132-position
records

PAYMAST Record Layout

EMPNO	LNAME	FNAME	HRS (2 DECIMALS)	RATE

1   3 4   23 24   33 34   37 38   41

PAYREG Printer Spacing Chart

```
        1111111111222222222233333333334444444444555555555566666666667777777777888888888899999999990
1234567890123456789012345678901234567890123456789012345678901234567890123456789012345678901234567890

 H   2  XX/XX/XX                         P A Y R O L L   R E G I S T E R                      PAGE XXØX
 H   4  EMPLOYEE                                   REG      O/T     PAY     REGULAR    OVERTIME      TOTAL
 H   5  NUMBER          EMPLOYEE NAME              HRS      HRS    RATE    EARNINGS    EARNINGS   GROSS PAY
 D   7    XXX   X=====================X X======X  XØ.XX    XØ.XX   XØ.XX    XXØ.XX     XXØ.XX      XXØ.XX
 D   8    XXX   X=====================X X======X  XØ.XX    XØ.XX   XØ.XX    XXØ.XX     XXØ.XX      XXØ.XX
TLR 10                    *** FINAL TOTALS XXØ.XX  XXØ.XX          $X,XX$.XX $X,XX$.XX  $X,XX$.XX
```

The program coding sheets in Figure 4.23 contain syntax errors. Identify the errors and indicate the corrections you would make to the program.

The program listing in Figure 4.24 includes the error messages produced by running the program. The syntax corrections are circled on the computer listing shown in Figure 4.25. There are, however, logic errors. (Remember, indicators remain "on" unless set off by the programmer.) Your assignment is to carefully desk check the program, find the logic errors, and make the necessary corrections.

Debugging Exercise 2

The problem definition for this exercise is shown in Figure 4.26. The program coding sheets in Figure 4.27 contain syntax errors. Identify them and indicate the corrections you would make to the program.

The listing in Figure 4.28 includes the error diagnostics produced by running the program as shown. The syntax corrections are circled on the computer listing shown in Figure 4.29. There are, however, logic errors. Your assignment is to desk check this program carefully, find the logic errors, and make the necessary corrections.

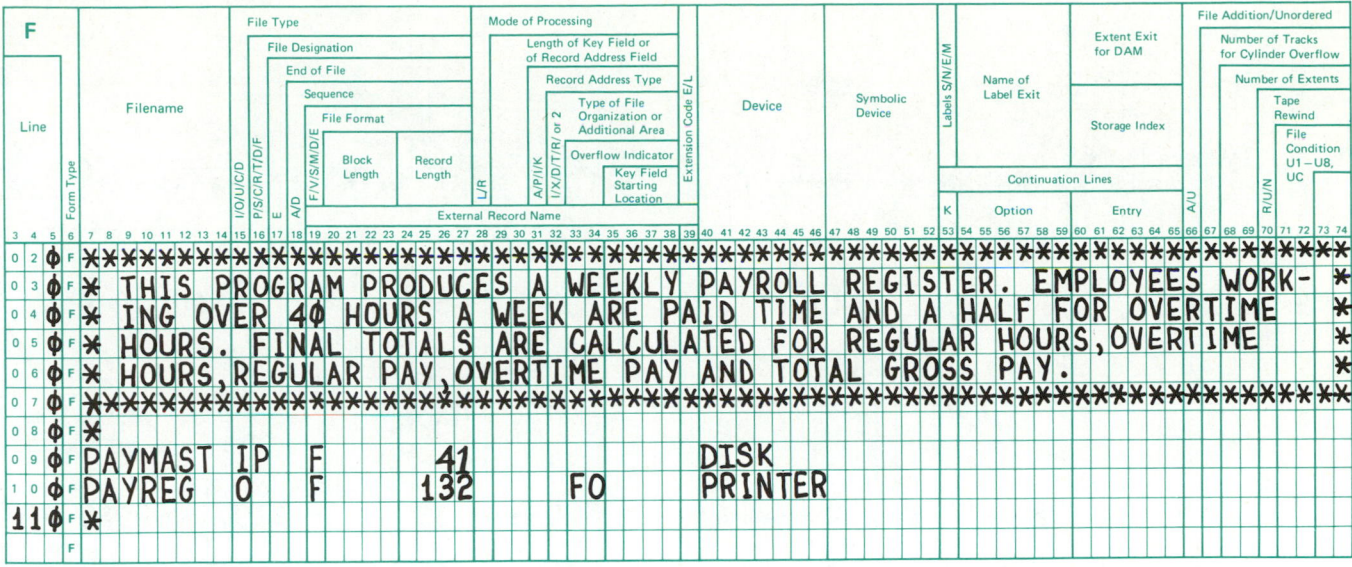

Figure 4.23
Coding sheets for Debugging
Exercise 1.
(continued on next page)

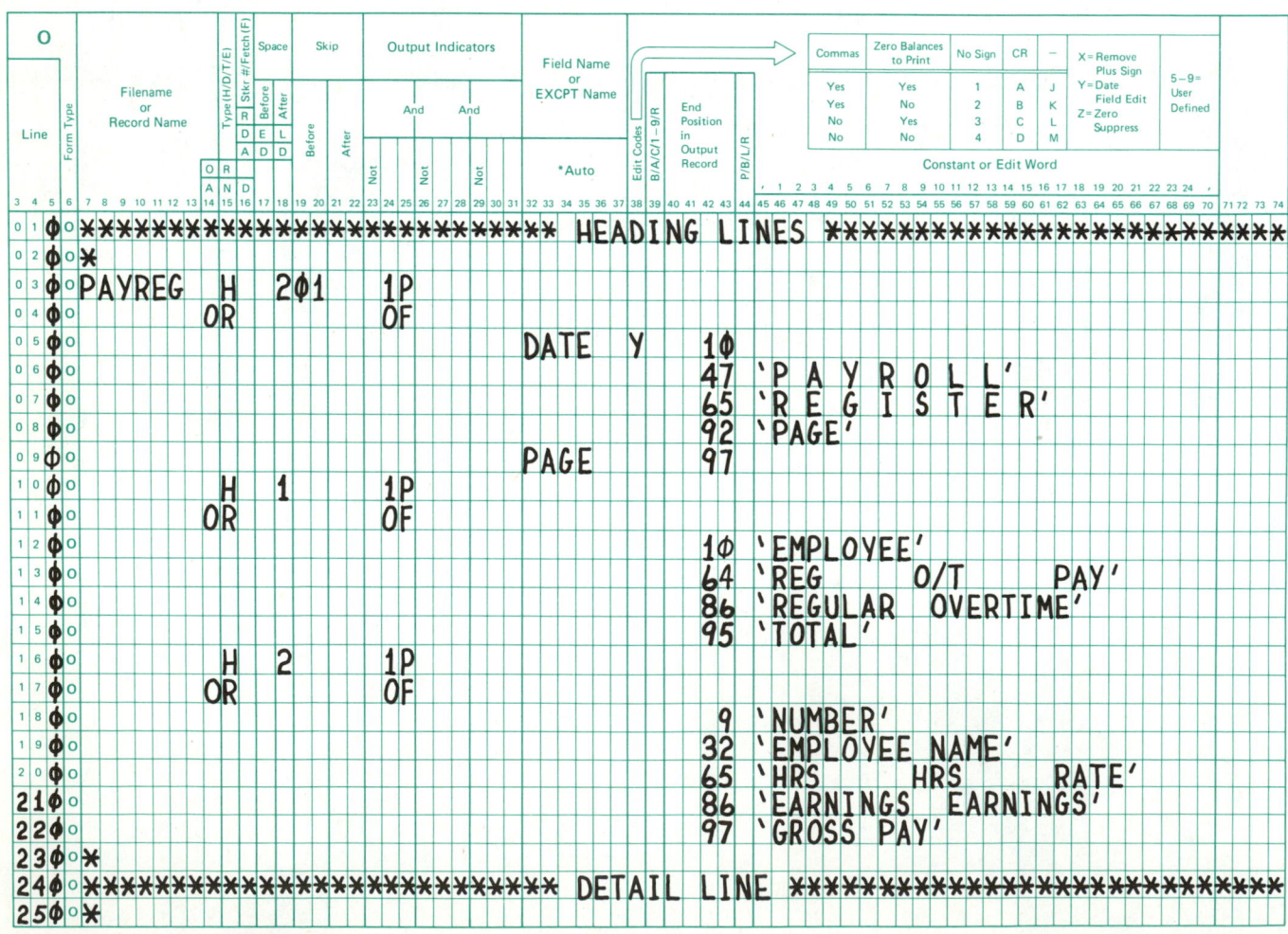

RPG Calculation Specifications (C)

Line	Form	Indicators	Factor 1	Operation	Factor 2	Result Field Name	Length	Dec/H	Resulting Indicators	Comments
01	C		*****************************		CALCULATIONS	**********************************				
02	C		*							
03	C	01	HRS	COMP	40				10 11 11	
04	C		*							
05	C	10	HRS	MULT	RATE	REG	52	H		REGULAR PAY
06	C		*							
07	C	11	HRS	SUB	40.00	OTHRS	42			O T
08	C	11	RATE	MULT	1.5	OTRATE	42	H		V I P
09	C	11	OTHRS	MULT	OTRATE	OTPAY	52	H		E M A
10	C	11	RATE	MULT	40.00	REG		H		R E Y
11	C		*							
12	C		REG	ADD	OTPAY	GROSS	52			TOTAL GROSS PAY
13	C		*							
14	C		THRS	ADD	HRS	THRS	52			F I T
15	C	11	TOTHRS	ADD	OTHRS	TOTHRS	52			I O T
16	C		TREG	ADD	REG	TREG	62			N T A
17	C	11	TOTPAY	ADD	OTPAY	TOTPAY	62			A A L
18	C		TGROSS	ADD	GROSS	TGROSS	62			L L
19	C		*							S

RPG Output Specifications (O)

Line	Form	Filename/Record	Type	Space/Skip	Output Indicators	Field/EXCPT Name	Edit	End Pos	Constant or Edit Word
01	O	**********************************				HEADING LINES			******************************
02	O	*							
03	O	PAYREG	H	201	1P				
04	O		OR		OF				
05	O					DATE	Y	10	
06	O							47	'PAYROLL'
07	O							65	'REGISTER'
08	O							92	'PAGE'
09	O					PAGE		97	
10	O		H	1	1P				
11	O		OR		OF				
12	O							10	'EMPLOYEE'
13	O							64	'REG O/T PAY'
14	O							86	'REGULAR OVERTIME'
15	O							95	'TOTAL'
16	O		H	2	1P				
17	O		OR		OF				
18	O							9	'NUMBER'
19	O							32	'EMPLOYEE NAME'
20	O							65	'HRS HRS RATE'
21	O							86	'EARNINGS EARNINGS'
22	O							97	'GROSS PAY'
23	O	*							
24	O	**********************************				DETAIL LINE			******************************
25	O	*							

Figure 4.23
(continued)

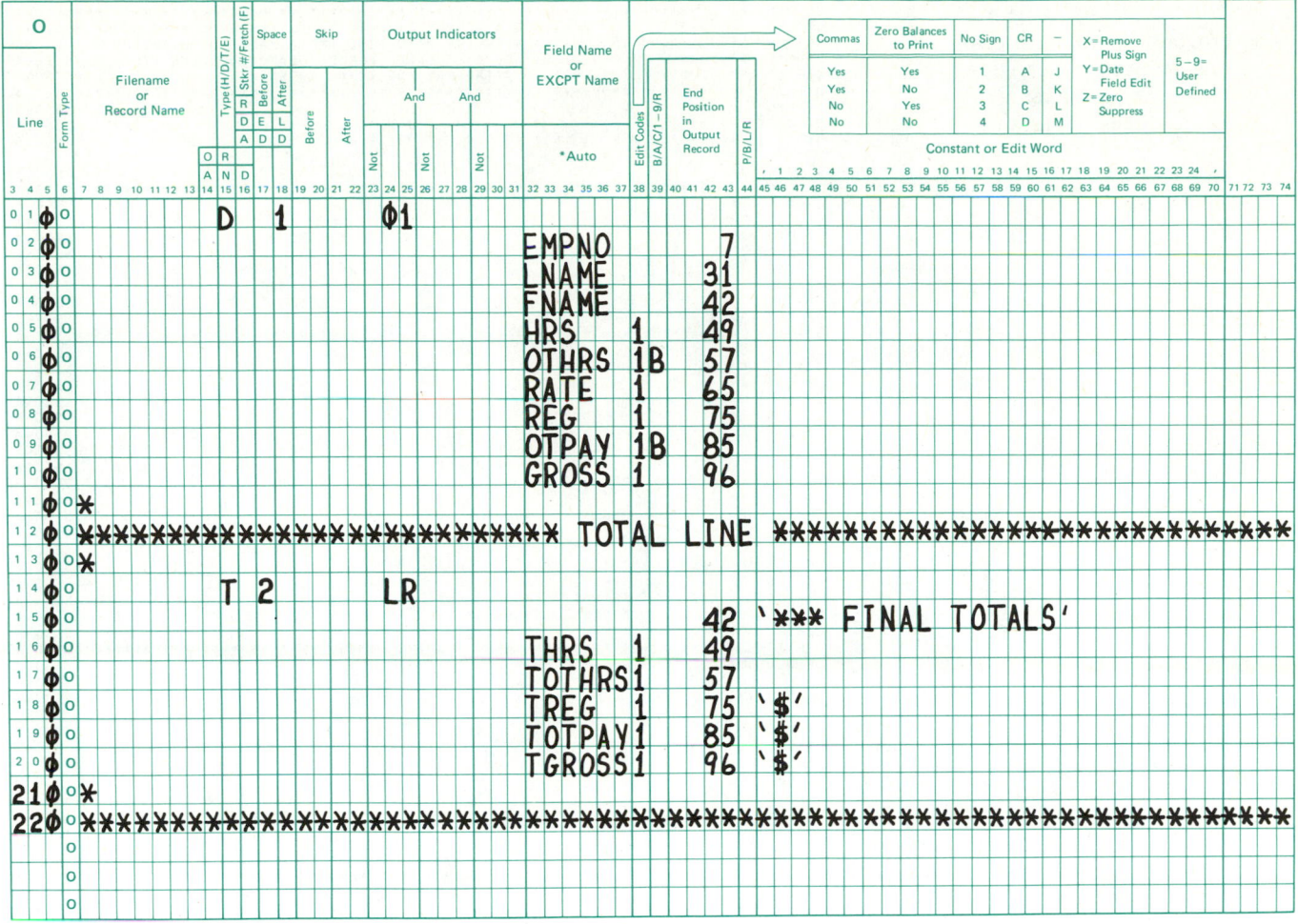

Figure 4.23
(continued)

Figure 4.24
Program listing with error
diagnostics for Debugging
Exercise 1.
(continued on next page)

```
                       01-020  F********************************************************SSS04A
                       01-030  F* THIS PROGRAM PRODUCES A WEEKLY PAYROLL REGISTER. EMPLOYEES WORK- *SSS04A
                       01-040  F* ING OVER 40 HOURS A WEEK ARE PAID TIME AND A HALF FOR OVERTIME   *SSS04A
                       01-050  F* HOURS. FINAL TOTALS ARE CALCULATED FOR REGULAR HOURS,OVERTIME   *SSS04A
                       01-060  F* HOURS,REGULAR PAY,OVERTIME PAY AND TOTAL GROSS PAY.             *SSS04A
                       01-070  F********************************************************SSS04A
                       01-080  F*                                                                 SSS04A
          0001         01-090  FPAYMAST IP  F    41            DISK               SSS04A
          0002         01-100  FPAYREG  C   F   132        FC  PRINTER            SSS04A
                                                            $
                       01-110  F*                                                 SSS04A
                       02-010  I******************** INPUT RECORD ****************************SSS04A
                       02-020  I*                                                 SSS04A
          0003         02-030  IPAYMAST NS  10                                    SSS04A
          0004         02-040  I                              1   30EMPNO         SSS04A
          0005         02-050  I                              4   23 LNAME        SSS04A
          0006         02-060  I                             24   33 FNAME        SSS04A
          0007         02-070  I                             34   372HRS          SSS04A
          0008         02-080  I                             38   412RATE         SSS04A
                       02-090  I*                                                 SSS04A
                       03-010  C******************** CALCULATIONS ****************************SSS04A
                       03-020  C*                                                 SSS04A
          0009         03-030  C   01      HRS       COMP 40                101111 SSS05A
                       03-040  C*                                                 SSS05A
          0010         03-050  C   10      HRS       MULT RATE     REG   52H       REGULAR PAY SSS04A
                       03-060  C*                                                 SSS04A
          0011         03-070  C   11      HRS       SUB  40.00    OTHRS  42       O T SSS04A
          0012         03-080  C   11      RATE      MULT 1.5      OTRATE 42H      V I P SSS04A
          0013         03-090  C   11      OTRATE    MULT OTRATE   OTPAY  52H      E M A SSS04A
          0014         03-100  C   11      RATE      MULT 40.00    REG    H        R E Y SSS04A
                       03-110  C*                                                 SSS04A
          0015         03-120  C           REG       ADD  OTPAY    GROSS  52       TOTAL GROSS PAYSSS04A
                       03-130  C*                                                 SSS04A
          0016         03-140  C           THRS      ADD  HRS      THRS   52       F T SSS04A
          0017         03-150  C   11      TOTHRS    ADD  OTHRS    TOTHRS 52       I O SSS04A
          0018         03-160  C           TREG      ADD  REG      TREG   62       N T SSS04A
          0019         03-170  C   11      TOTPAY    ADD  OTPAY    TOTPAY 62       A A SSS04A
          0020         03-180  C           TGROSS    ADD  GROSS    TGROSS 62       L L SSS04A
                       03-190  C*                                              S   SSS04A
                       04-010  O******************** HEADING LINES ****************************SSS04A
                       04-020  C*                                                 SSS04A
          0021         04-030  OPAYREG  H  201    1P                              SSS04A
          0022         04-040  O           OR           OF                        SSS04A
                                                          $
          0023         04-050  O                    DATE Y  10                    SSS04A
          0024         04-060  O                            47 'P A Y R O L L'    SSS04A
          0025         04-070  O                            65 'R E G I S T E R'  SSS04A
          0026         04-080  O                            92 'PAGE'             SSS04A
          0027         04-090  O                    PAGE    97                    SSS04A
          0028         04-100  O           H   1    1P                            SSS04A
          0029         04-110  O           OR           OF                        SSS04A
                                                          $
          0030         04-120  O                            10 'EMPLOYEE'         SSS04A
          0031         04-130  O                            64 'REG    O/T    PAY' SSS04A
          0032         04-140  O                            86 'REGULAR  OVERTIME' SSS04A
          0033         04-150  O                            95 'TOTAL'            SSS04A
          0034         04-160  O           H   2    1P                            SSS04A
          0035         04-170  O           OR           OF                        SSS04A
                                                          $
          0036         04-180  O                             9 'NUMBER'           SSS04A
          0037         04-190  O                            32 'EMPLOYEE NAME'     SSS04A
          0038         04-200  O                            65 'HRS    HRS    RATE' SSS04A
          0039         04-210  O                            86 'EARNINGS  EARNINGS' SSS04A
          0040         04-220  O                            97 'GROSS PAY'        SSS04A
                       04-230  O*                                                 SSS04A
                       04-240  O******************** DETAIL LINE ****************************SSS04A
                       04-250  O*                                                 SSS04A
          0041         05-010  O           D   1    01                            SSS04A
                                                          $
          0042         05-020  O                    EMPNO      7                  SSS04A
          0043         05-030  O                    LNAME     31                  SSS04A
          0044         05-040  O                    FNAME     42                  SSS04A
          0045         05-050  O                    HRS    1  49                  SSS04A
          0046         05-060  O                    OTHRS 1B  57                  SSS04A
          0047         05-070  O                    RATE   1  65                  SSS04A
          0048         05-080  O                    REG    1  75                  SSS04A
          0049         05-090  O                    OTPAY 1B  85                  SSS04A
          0050         05-100  O                    GROSS  1  96                  SSS04A
                       05-110  O*                                                 SSS04A
                       05-120  O******************** TOTAL LINE ****************************SSS04A
                       05-130  O*                                                 SSS04A
          0051         05-140  O           T   2    LR                            SSS04A
          0052         05-150  O                            42 '*** FINAL TOTALS' SSS04A
          0053         05-160  O                    THRS   1  49                  SSS04A
          0054         05-170  O                    TOTHRS1   57                  SSS04A
          0055         05-180  O                    TREG   1  75 '$'              SSS04A
          0056         05-190  O                    TOTPAY1   85 '$'              SSS04A
          0057         05-200  O                    TGROSS1   96 '$'              SSS04A
                       05-210  O*                                                 SSS04A
                       05-220  O********************************************************SSS04A
```

Figure 4.24
(continued)

```
                    C O M P I L E R   D I A G N O S T I C S   S U M M A R Y


ILN019   OVERFLOW INDICATOR (POSITIONS 33-34) IS INVALID. ASSUME BLANK.

         0002   01-100    PAYREG

ILN202   INDICATOR IS INVALID OR UNDEFINED. DROP ENTRY.

         0022   04-040
         0029   04-110
         0035   04-170
         0041   05-010

ILN387   INDICATOR REFERENCED BUT NOT DEFINED. DROP INDICATOR.

         0009   03-030    01

ILN398   FIELD NAME UNDEFINED. SPEC IS DROPPED.

      D  0023   04-050    DATE
```

Figure 4.25
Program listing that contains logic errors for Debugging Exercise 1.

(continued on next page)

```
        01-020   F*******************************************************************SSS04A
        01-030   F* THIS PROGRAM PRODUCES A WEEKLY PAYROLL REGISTER. EMPLOYEES WORK- *SSS04A
        01-040   F* ING OVER 40 HOURS A WEEK ARE PAID TIME AND A HALF FOR OVERTIME   *SSS04A
        01-050   F* HOURS. FINAL TOTALS ARE CALCULATED FOR REGULAR HOURS,OVERTIME    *SSS04A
        01-060   F* HOURS,REGULAR PAY,OVERTIME PAY AND TOTAL GROSS PAY.              *SSS04A
        01-070   F******************************************************************* SSS04A
        01-080   F*                                       Correction 1               SSS04A
0001    01-090   FPAYMAST IP  F     41               CF        DISK                  SSS04A
0002    01-100   FPAYREG  O   F    132               CF        PRINTER               SSS04A
        01-110   F*                                                                  SSS04A
        02-010   I********************** INPUT RECORD ****************************SSS04A
        02-020   I*                                                                  SSS04A
0003    02-030   IPAYMAST NS  01        Correction 2                                 SSS04A
0004    02-040   I                                          1   30EMPNO              SSS04A
0005    02-050   I                                          4   23 LNAME             SSS04A
0006    02-060   I                                         24   33 FNAME             SSS04A
0007    02-070   I                                         34   372HRS               SSS04A
0008    02-080   I                                         38   412RATE              SSS04A
        02-090   I*                                                                  SSS04A
        03-010   C********************** CALCULATIONS ****************************SSS04A
        03-020   C*                                                                  SSS04A
0009    03-030   C   01    HRS     COMP 40                        101111             SSS05A
        03-040   C*                                                                  SSS05A
0010    03-050   C   10    HRS     MULT RATE      REG    52H        REGULAR PAY      SSS04A
        03-060   C*                                                                  SSS04A
0011    03-070   C   11    HRS     SUB  40.00     OTHRS  42         O  T             SSS04A
0012    03-080   C   11    RATE    MULT 1.5       OTRATE 42H        V  I  P          SSS04A
0013    03-090   C   11    OTHRS   MULT OTRATE    OTPAY  52H        E  M  A          SSS04A
0014    03-100   C   11    RATE    MULT 40.00     REG    H          R  E  Y          SSS04A
        03-110   C*                                                                  SSS04A
0015    03-120   C         REG     ADD  OTPAY     GROSS  52         TOTAL GROSS PAYSSS04A
        03-130   C*                                                                  SSS04A
0016    03-140   C         THRS    ADD  HRS       THRS   52         F  T             SSS04A
0017    03-150   C   11    TOTHRS  ADD  OTHRS     TOTHRS 52         I  O             SSS04A
0018    03-160   C         TREG    ADD  REG       TREG   62         N  T             SSS04A
0019    03-170   C   11    TOTPAY  ADD  OTPAY     TOTPAY 62         A  A             SSS04A
0020    03-180   C         TGROSS  ADD  GROSS     TGROSS 62         L  L             SSS04A
        03-190   C*                                                  S               SSS04A
        04-010   O********************** HEADING LINES ****************************SSS04A
        04-020   C*                                                                  SSS04A
0021    04-030   OPAYREG  H  201    1P                                               SSS04A
0022    04-040   O          OR      OF                    Correction 3               SSS04A
0023    04-050   O                        UDATE Y  10                                SSS04A
0024    04-060   O                                  47 'P A Y R O L L'               SSS04A
0025    04-070   O                                  65 'R E G I S T E R'             SSS04A
0026    04-080   O                                  92 'PAGE'                        SSS04A
0027    04-090   O                        PAGE       57                             SSS04A
0028    04-100   O       H  1    1P                                                  SSS04A
0029    04-110   O          OR      OF                                               SSS04A
0030    04-120   O                                  10 'EMPLOYEE'                    SSS04A
0031    04-130   O                                  64 'REG    O/T    PAY'           SSS04A
0032    04-140   O                                  86 'REGULAR  OVERTIME'           SSS04A
0033    04-150   O                                  95 'TOTAL'                       SSS04A
0034    04-160   O       H  2    1P                                                  SSS04A
0035    04-170   O          OR      OF                                               SSS04A
0036    04-180   O                                   9 'NUMBER'                      SSS04A
0037    04-190   O                                  32 'EMPLOYEE NAME'               SSS04A
0038    04-200   O                                  65 'HRS     HRS     RATE'        SSS04A
0039    04-210   O                                  86 'EARNINGS  EARNINGS'          SSS04A
0040    04-220   O                                  97 'GROSS PAY'                   SSS04A
        04-230   O*                                                                  SSS04A
        04-240   O********************** DETAIL LINE ****************************SSS04A
        04-250   O*                                                                  SSS04A
0041    05-010   O       D  1    01                                                  SSS04A
0042    05-020   O                        EMPNO      7                               SSS04A
0043    05-030   O                        LNAME      31                              SSS04A
0044    05-040   O                        FNAME      42                              SSS04A
0045    05-050   O                        HRS   1    49                              SSS04A
0046    05-060   O                        OTHRS 1B   57                              SSS04A
0047    05-070   O                        RATE  1    65                              SSS04A
```

Figure 4.25
(continued)

```
CC48    C5-C80   0                              PEG    1  75                                            SSS04A
CC49    C5-C90   0                              CTPAY 1B  85                                            SSS04A
CC5C    C5-100   0                              GRCSS  1  96                                            SSS04A
        C5-110   C*                                                                                     SSS04A
        C5-120   C**************************** TOTAL LINE ****************************SSS04A
        C5-130   C*                                                                                     SSS04A
CC51    C5-140   C              T  2      LR                                                            SSS04A
CC52    C5-150   0                                      42 '*** FINAL TOTALS'                           SSS04A
CC53    C5-16C   0                              THRS   1  49                                            SSS04A
0054    C5-170   C                              TCTHRS1   57                                            SSS04A
0055    C5-18C   0                              TREG   1  75 '$'                                         SSS04A
0056    C5-190   0                              TCTPAY1   85 '$'                                         SSS04A
0057    C5-200   C                              TGROSS1   96 '$'                                         SSS04A
        C5-210   0*                                                                                     SSS04A
        C5-22C   C**************************************************************SSS04A
```

E N D   C F   S C U R C E

```
12/27/91                    P A Y R C L L   R E G I S T E R                    PAGE    1

EMPLCYEE                                  REG      C/T     PAY     REGULAR   OVERTIME    TOTAL
NUMBER          EMPLCYEE NAME             HRS      HRS     RATE    EARNINGS  EARNINGS  GRCSS PAY
                                                           .20                                   Straight
010    BEASELY      CARCLE       60.00     .00    10.00    600.00      .00    600.00     time
485    ALBERTSCN    JAMES        37.00    3.00     5.75    230.00    25.89    204.11
172    DCBERMAN     HANS         42.25     .00     6.25    264.06      .00    264.06
5C1    KAVANAGH     EILEEN       15.00   25.00     5.00    200.00   187.50     12.50
224    LCMBARDO     ANTHONY      45.00     .00     9.50    427.50      .00    427.50
654    LYNCH        ALICE        43.50     .00     8.75    380.63      .00    380.63
345    MACFARLAND   SUSAN        40.00     .00     9.25    370.00      .00    370.00
293    PHILLIPS     DAVID        35.50    4.50    10.00    400.00    67.50    332.50
481    RCSENKRANZ   SAUL         46.25     .00     8.25    381.56      .00    381.56
799    SCHAEFFER    MARICN       21.75   18.25     5.75    230.00   157.50     72.50
888    SMITH        RCBERT       4C.CC     .00     6.25    250.00      .00    250.00
910    TAYLOR       ECWARD       21.75   18.25     5.50    220.00   150.56     69.44
577    ZIMMERMAN    KAREN        45.C0     .00     7.50    337.50      .00    337.50


              *** FINAL TCTALS 493.00    69.00           $4,291.25  $588.95 $3,702.30
```

Figure 4.26
Problem definition for Debugging Exercise 2.

Systems Flowchart

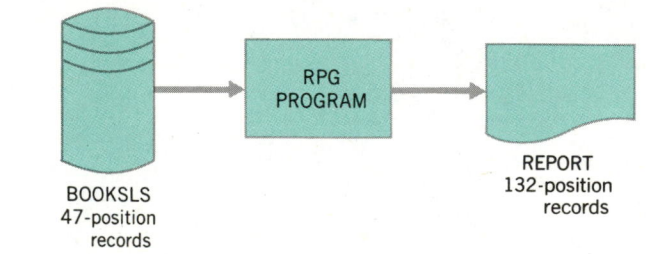

BOOKSLS
47-position
records

RPG
PROGRAM

REPORT
132-position
records

BOOKSLS Record Layout

AUTHOR	TITLE	NET (2 DECIMALS)	QTY
1 12	13 37	38 41	42 47

REPORT Printer Spacing Chart

```
       1234567890123456789012345678901234567890123456789012345678901234567890123456789012345678901234567890

H  1   XX/XX/XX                            ABC PUBLISHING COMPANY                               PAGE XXØX
   2
H  3                                        ROYALTY REPORT
   4
H  5   AUTHOR              TITLE                  NET     QUANTITY        NET      ROYALTY     ROYALTY
H  6                                              COST     SOLD          SALES     RATE        PAID
   7
D  8   X-------------X X----------------X  XØ.XX  XXX,XØX  XXX,XXØ.XX    ØX%    $XXX,XX$.XX
D  9   X-------------X X----------------X  XØ.XX  XXX,XØX  XXX,XXØ.XX    ØX%    $XXX,XX$.XX
  10
  11
TLR 2  *** TOTAL ROYALTIES PAID      $X,XXX,XX$.XX
  13
```

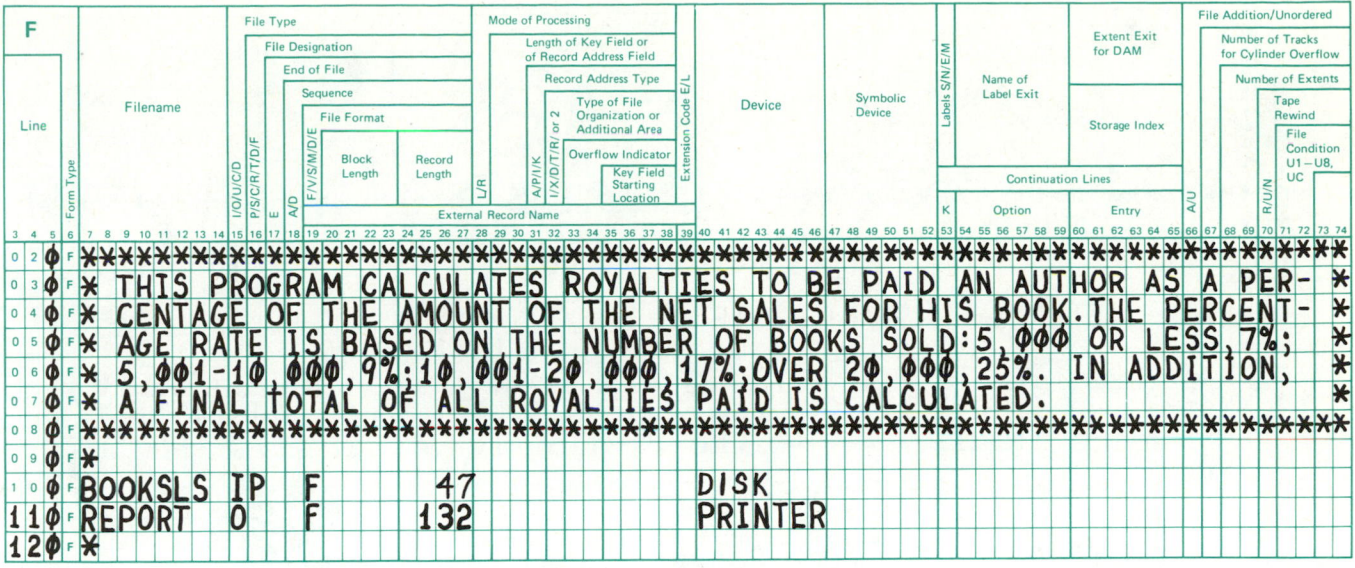

Figure 4.27
Coding sheets for Debugging
Exercise 2.
(continued on next page)

Line	Form Type	Control Level (L0 – L9, LR, SR, AN/OR)	Indicators And Not	And Not	Not	Factor 1	Operation	Factor 2	Result Field Name	Length	Decimal Positions	Half Adjust (H)	Resulting Indicators Arithmetic Plus High 1>2	Minus Low 1<2	Zero Equal 1=2	Comments
0 1	ФC	******************************					CALCULATIONS ********************************									
0 2	ФC	*														
0 3	ФC		Ф1			QTY	MULT	NET	NETSLS	82	H					NET SALES
0 4	ФC	***														
0 5	ФC	****** DETERMINE ROYALTY RATE BY QUANTITY SOLD:														
0 6	ФC	******				IF QTY < OR = 5ФФФ TURN ON INDICATOR Ф7										
0 7	ФC	******				IF QTY > 5ФФФ AND < OR = 1ФФФФ TURN ON INDICATOR Ф9										
0 8	ФC	******				IF QTY > 1ФФФФ AND < OR = 2ФФФФ TURN ON INDICATOR 17										
0 9	ФC	******				IF QTY > 2ФФФФ TURN ON INDICATOR 25										
1 0	ФC	***														
1 1	ФC					QTY	COMP	5ФФФ					Ф7	Ф7		
1 2	ФC		NФ7			QTY	COMP	1ФФФФ					Ф9	Ф9		
1 3	ФC		NФ7	NФ9		QTY	COMP	2ФФФФ					25	1717		
1 4	ФC	***														
1 5	ФC	****** COMPUTE ROYALTY														
1 6	ФC	***														
1 7	ФC		Ф7			NETSLS	MULT	.07	ROYLTY	82	H					
1 8	ФC		Ф9			NETSLS	MULT	.Ф9	ROYLTY		H					
1 9	ФC		17			NETSLS	MULT	.17	ROYLTY		H					
2 0	ФC		25			NETSLS	MULT	.25	ROYLTY		H					
2 1	ФC	*														
2 2	ФC					ROYTLY	ADD	TOTROY	TOTROY	92						TOTAL ROYALTIES
2 3	ФC	*														

Figure 4.27
(continued)

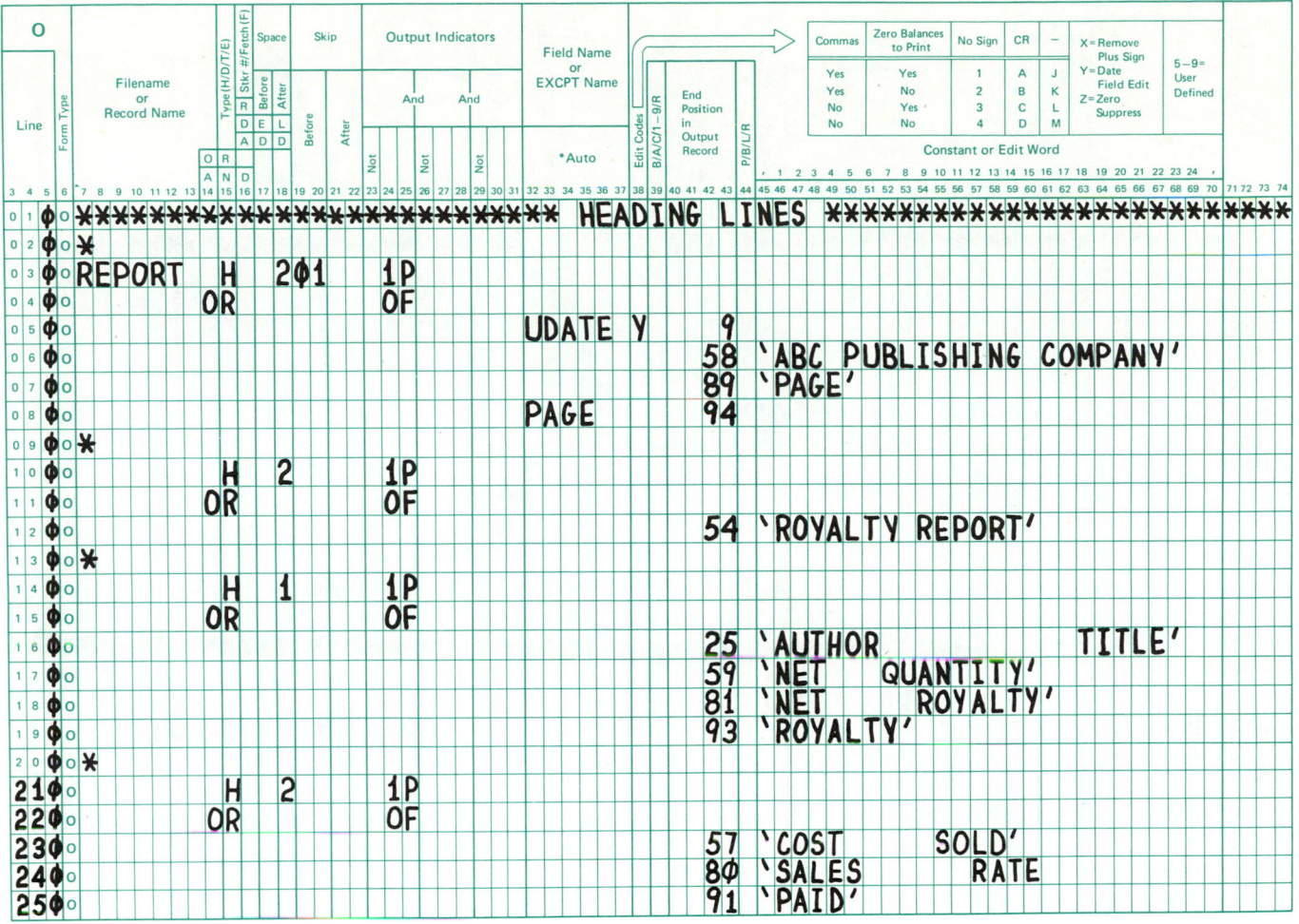

Figure 4.27
(continued)

```
01 0 O*
02 0 O************************** DETAIL LINE ****************************
03 0 O*
04 0 O      D 1    N1P
05 0 O                          AUTHOR      13
06 0 O                          TITLE       40
07 0 O                          NET     1   48
08 0 O                          QTY     1   58
09 0 O                          NETSLS1     73
10 0 O                  07                  79 '7%'
11 0 O                  09                  79 '9%'
12 0 O                  17                  79 '17%'
13 0 O                  25                  79 '25%'
14 0 O                          ROYLTY1        '$'
15 0 O*
16 0 O************************** TOTAL LINE *****************************
17 0 O*
18 0 O      T 2     LR
19 0 O                                      25 '*** TOTAL ROYALTIES PAID'
20 0 O                          TOTROY1     45 '$'
21 0 O*
22 0 O*****************************************************************
```

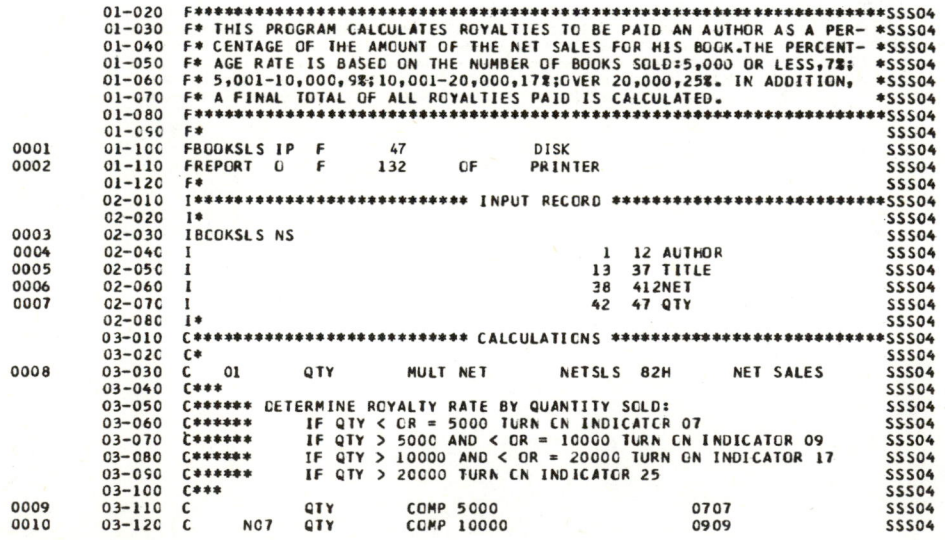

Figure 4.27
(continued)

```
          01-020  F********************************************************************SSS04
          01-030  F* THIS PROGRAM CALCULATES ROYALTIES TO BE PAID AN AUTHOR AS A PER- *SSS04
          01-040  F* CENTAGE OF THE AMOUNT OF THE NET SALES FOR HIS BOOK.THE PERCENT- *SSS04
          01-050  F* AGE RATE IS BASED ON THE NUMBER OF BOOKS SOLD:5,000 OR LESS,7%;  *SSS04
          01-060  F* 5,001-10,000,9%;10,001-20,000,17%;OVER 20,000,25%. IN ADDITION,  *SSS04
          01-070  F* A FINAL TOTAL OF ALL ROYALTIES PAID IS CALCULATED.               *SSS04
          01-080  F********************************************************************SSS04
          01-090  F*                                                                   SSS04
0001      01-100  FBOOKSLS IP  F      47            DISK                               SSS04
0002      01-110  FREPORT  O   F     132      OF    PRINTER                            SSS04
          01-120  F*                                                                   SSS04
          02-010  I*************************** INPUT RECORD ****************************SSS04
          02-020  I*                                                                   SSS04
0003      02-030  IBCOKSLS NS                                                          SSS04
0004      02-040  I                                            1  12 AUTHOR            SSS04
0005      02-050  I                                           13  37 TITLE             SSS04
0006      02-060  I                                           38  412NET               SSS04
0007      02-070  I                                           42  47 QTY               SSS04
          02-080  I*                                                                   SSS04
          03-010  C*************************** CALCULATICNS ****************************SSS04
          03-020  C*                                                                   SSS04
0008      03-030  C   01       QTY        MULT NET       NETSLS  82H      NET SALES    SSS04
          03-040  C***                                                                 SSS04
          03-050  C****** CETERMINE ROYALTY RATE BY QUANTITY SOLD:                     SSS04
          03-060  C******      IF QTY < OR = 5000 TURN CN INDICATCR 07                 SSS04
          03-070  C******      IF QTY > 5000 AND < OR = 10000 TURN CN INDICATOR 09     SSS04
          03-080  C******      IF QTY > 10000 AND < OR = 20000 TURN ON INDICATOR 17    SSS04
          03-090  C******      IF QTY > 20000 TURN CN INDICATOR 25                     SSS04
          03-100  C***                                                                 SSS04
0009      03-110  C            QTY        COMP 5000                 0707               SSS04
0010      03-120  C      N07   QTY        COMP 10000                0909               SSS04
```

Figure 4.28
Program listing with error diagnostics for Debugging Exercise 2.
(continued on next page)

```
0011      03-130   C     NO7NO9QTY       COMP 20000                   251717            SSSO4
          03-140   C***                                                                 SSSO4
          03-150   C****** COMPUTE ROYALTY                                              SSSO4
          03-160   C***                                                                 SSSO4
0012      03-170   C     07   NETSLS      MULT .07       RCYLTY 82H                      SSSO4
                                                    $
0013      03-180   C     09   NETSLS      MULT .09       RCYLTY     H                    SSSO4
0014      03-190   C     17   NETSLS      MULT .17       ROYLTY     H                    SSSO4
0015      03-200   C     25   NETSLS      MULT .25       RCYLTY     H                    SSSO4
          03-210   C*                                                                   SSSO4
0016      03-210   C          RCYLTY      ADD  TCTROY    TCTROY 92     TOTAL ROYALTIESSSSO4
          03-230   C*                                                                   SSSO4
          04-010   O*********************** HEADING LINES ***********************SSSO4
          04-020   O*                                                                   SSSO4
0017      04-030   CREPCRT  H  201     1P                                               SSSO4
0018      04-040   C       OR          CF                                               SSSO4
0019      04-050   O                            UDATE Y    9                             SSSO4
0020      04-060   C                                     58 'ABC PUBLISHING COMPANY'    SSSO4
0021      04-070   C                                     89 'PAGE'                      SSSO4
0022      04-080   C                            PAGE     94                             SSSO4
          04-090   O*                                                                   SSSO4
0023      04-100   O       H   2        1P                                              SSSO4
0024      04-110   O       CR           CF                                              SSSO4
0025      04-120   C                                     54 'ROYALTY REPORT'            SSSO4
          04-130   C*                                                                   SSSO4
0026      04-140   C       H   1        1P                                              SSSO4
0027      04-150   O       CR           CF                                              SSSO4
0028      04-160   O                                     25 'AUTHCR          TITLE'     SSSO4
0029      04-170   O                                     59 'NET    QUANTITY'           SSSO4
0030      04-180   C                                     81 'NET    ROYALTY'            SSSO4
0031      04-190   O                                     93 'RCYALTY'                   SSSO4
          04-200   C*                                                                   SSSO4
0032      04-210   C       H   2        1P                                              SSSO4
0033      04-220   C       OR           CF                                              SSSO4
0034      04-230   C                                     57 'CCST      SCLD'            SSSO4
0035      04-240   C                                     80 'SALES      RATE            SSSO4
                                                                $
0036      04-250   C                                     91 'PAID'                      SSSO4
          05-010   C*                                                                   SSSO4
          05-020   O********************** DETAIL LINE ************************SSSO4
          05-030   C*                                                                   SSSO4
0037      05-040   C       D   1        N1P                                             SSSO4
0038      05-050   O                            AUTHCR    13                            SSSO4
0039      05-060   C                            TITLE     40                            SSSO4
0040      05-070   O                            NET   1   48                            SSSO4
0041      05-080   C                            QTY   1   58                            SSSO4
0042      05-090   O                            NETSLS1   73                            SSSO4
0043      05-100   C                      07             79 '7%'                        SSSO4
0044      05-110   C                      09             79 '9%'                        SSSO4
0045      05-120   C                      17             79 '17%'                       SSSO4
0046      05-130   C                      25             79 '25%'                       SSSO4
0047      05-140   C                            ROYLTY1   94 '$'                        SSSO4
          05-150   C*                                                                   SSSO4
          05-160   C********************** TCTAL LINE ***********************SSSO4
          05-170   C*                                                                   SSSO4
0048      05-180   C       T   2        LR                                              SSSO4
0049      05-190   O                                     25 '*** TOTAL ROYALTIES PAID'  SSSO4
0050      05-200   O                            TCTROY1   45 '$'                         SSSO4
          05-210   C*                                                                   SSSO4
          05-220   C********************************************************SSSO4
```

```
E N D   O F   S C U R C E
```

```
C O M P I L E R   D I A G N C S T I C S   S U M M A R Y
```

ILN178   FACTOR 2 IS INVALID. SPEC IS DROPPED IF AN ENTRY IS REQUIRED.

    D 00C12   C3-170   MULT

ILN214   LEADING/CLOSING APOSTROPHE IS MISSING CN CLNSTANT. SPEC IS DROPPED.

    D 00035   04-240

ILN413   EDIT SPECIFIED WITH ALPHAMERIC FIELD. DRCP EDITING.

    00041   05-08C

ILN442   OPERAND MUST BE NUMERIC. SPEC IS DROPPED.

    D 00008   C3-030   FACTCR 1 ENTRY

ILN485   FACTOR 1 AND FACTOR 2 CF CCMP CR LCKUP MUST BCTH BE EITHER NUMERIC OR ALPHAMERIC. SPEC IS DROPPED.

    D 00009   C3-110
    D 00010   C3-120
    D 00011   C3-130

Figure 4.28
(continued)

Figure 4.29
Program listing that contains
logic errors for Debugging
Exercise 2.
(continued on next page)

```
     01-020  F***************************************************************SSS04
     01-030  F* THIS PROGRAM CALCULATES ROYALTIES TO BE PAID AN AUTHOR AS A PER- *SSS04
     01-040  F* CENTAGE OF THE AMOUNT OF THE NET SALES FCR HIS BOCK.THE PERCENT- *SSS04
     01-050  F* AGE RATE IS BASED ON THE NUMBER OF BOCKS SOLD:5,000 OR LESS,7%;  *SSS04
     01-060  F* 5,001-10,000,9%;10,001-20,000,17%;OVER 20,000,25%. IN ADDITION, *SSS04
     01-070  F* A FINAL TOTAL CF ALL ROYALTIES PAID IS CALCULATED.              *SSS04
     01-080  F***************************************************************SSS04
     01-090  F*                                                                  SSS04
0001 01-100  FBOOKSLS IP  F      47              DISK                            SSS04
0002 01-110  FREPORT   C  F     132       CF     PRINTER                         SSS04
     01-120  F*                                                                  SSS04
     02-010  I***************************** INPUT RECCRD ******************************SSS04
     02-020  I*                                                                  SSS04
0003 02-030  IBOOKSLS NS                                                         SSS04
0004 02-040  I                                            1  12 AUTHOR           SSS04
0005 02-050  I                                           13  37 TITLE            SSS04
0006 02-060  I                                           38  412NET             SSS04
0007 02-070  I                                           42  470QTY             SSS04
     02-080  I*                                                                  SSS04
     03-010  C***************** CALCULATIONS ***************************SSS04
     03-020  C*                                                                  SSS04
0008 03-030  C    01       QTY       MULT NET       NETSLS 82H      NET SALES    SSS04
     03-040  C***                                                                SSS04
     03-050  C****** DETERMINE ROYALTY RATE BY QUANTITY SOLD:                    SSS04
     03-060  C******      IF QTY < OR = 5000 TURN CN INDICATOR 07                SSS04
     03-070  C******      IF QTY > 5000 AND < OR = 10000 TURN CN INDICATOR 09    SSS04
     03-080  C******      IF QTY > 10000 AND < OR = 20000 TURN CN INDICATOR 17   SSS04
     03-090  C******      IF QTY > 20000 TURN CN INDICATOR 25                    SSS04
     03-100  C***                                                                SSS04
0009 03-110  C            QTY       CCMP 5000                    0707            SSS04
0010 03-120  C    NO7     QTY       CCMP 10000                   0909            SSS04
0011 03-130  C    NO7N09QTY         CCMP 20000                   251717          SSS04
     03-140  C***                                                                SSS04
     03-150  C****** COMPUTE ROYALTY                                             SSS04
     03-160  C***                                                                SSS04
0012 03-170  C    07      NETSLS    MULT .O7       ROYLTY 82H                    SSS04
0013 03-180  C    09      NETSLS    MULT .09       RCYLTY    H                   SSS04
0014 03-190  C    17      NETSLS    MULT .17       ROYLTY    H                   SSS04
0015 03-200  C    25      NETSLS    MULT .25       RCYLTY    H                   SSS04
     03-210  C*                                                                  SSS04
0016 03-220  C            ROYLTY    ADD  TCTRCY    TCTRCY 92      TOTAL ROYALTIESSSS04
     03-230  C*                                                                  SSS04
     04-010  O***************** HEADING LINES ***************************SSS04
     04-020  C*                                                                  SSS04
0017 04-030  OREPORT   H  201       1P                                          SSS04
0018 04-040  O            OR        CF                                          SSS04
0019 04-050  O                           UDATE Y   9                            SSS04
0020 04-060  O                                     58 'ABC PUBLISHING COMPANY'  SSS04
0021 04-070  O                                     89 'PAGE'                    SSS04
0022 04-080  O                           PAGE      94                           SSS04
     04-090  O*                                                                  SSS04
0023 04-100  O         H  2         1P                                          SSS04
0024 04-110  O            OR        CF                                          SSS04
0025 04-120  O                                     54 'ROYALTY REPORT'          SSS04
     04-130  O*                                                                  SSS04
0026 04-140  O         H  1         1P                                          SSS04
0027 04-150  O            OR        CF                                          SSS04
0028 04-160  O                                     25 'AUTHOR         TITLE'    SSS04
0029 04-170  O                                     59 'NET     QUANTITY'        SSS04
0030 04-180  O                                     81 'NET      ROYALTY'        SSS04
0031 04-190  O                                     93 'ROYALTY'                SSS04
     04-200  C*                                                                  SSS04
0032 04-210  O         H  2         1P                                          SSS04
0033 04-220  O            OR        CF                                          SSS04
0034 04-230  O                                     57 'COST    SOLD'            SSS04
0035 04-240  O                                     80 'SALES      RATE'         SSS04
0036 04-250  O                                     91 'PAID'                    SSS04
     05-010  C*                                                                  SSS04
     05-020  O***************** DETAIL LINE ***************************SSS04
     05-030  C*                                                                  SSS04
0037 05-040  O         D  1         N1P                                         SSS04
0038 05-050  O                           AUTHOR    13                           SSS04
0039 05-060  O                           TITLE     40                           SSS04
0040 05-070  O                           NET  1    48                           SSS04
0041 05-080  O                           QTY  1    58                           SSS04
0042 05-090  O                           NETSLS1   73                           SSS04
0043 05-100  O                        07           79 '7%'                      SSS04
0044 05-110  O                        09           79 '9%'                      SSS04
0045 05-120  O                        17           79 '17%'                     SSS04
0046 05-130  O                        25           79 '25%'                     SSS04
0047 05-140  O                           RCYLTY1   94 '$'                       SSS04
     05-150  O*                                                                  SSS04
     05-160  O***************** TOTAL LINE ***************************SSS04
     05-170  O*                                                                  SSS04
0048 05-180  O         T  2         LR                                          SSS04
0049 05-190  O                                     25 '*** TOTAL ROYALTIES PAID' SSS04
0050 05-200  O                           TCTRCY1   45 '$'                       SSS04
     05-210  O*                                                                  SSS04
     05-220  O***************************************************************SSS04


                    E N D   O F   S C U R C E
```

Numeric field (annotation pointing to line 0007 02-070)

Zero—not a letter (annotation pointing to line 0012 03-170 .O7)

Missing quote (annotation pointing to line 0035 04-240)

```
12/17/91                    ABC PUBLISHING COMPANY                 PAGE    1

                               ROYALTY REPORT

    AUTHOR         TITLE              NET    QUANTITY      NET    ROYALTY   ROYALTY
                                      COST     SOLD       SALES    RATE      PAID

   GREEN,A.C.    NEVER SAY NEVER      7.95    7,890     62,725.50   9%      $5,645.30
   JONES,S.S.    GUIDE TO DOWNTOWN HOBOKEN  11.95  5,000   55,750.00  9%7%  $5,377.50  ← Incorrect royalty
   SMITH,H.A.    RPG II FOR FUN AND PROFIT  14.95  25,050  374,497.50  25%  $93,624.38
   BROWN,J.B.    THE SENSUOUS COMPUTER  9.95  15,100  150,245.00  17%   $25,541.65
   TAYLOR,P.J.   PLUMBING MADE EASY    4.95   10,000   49,500.00  17%9%   $8,415.00  ← Incorrect royalty
   WHITE,R.D.    DIARY OF A MAC PROGRAMMER  9.95  4,999  45,740.05  17%7%  $8,455.81  ← Incorrect royalty
   JENSEN,N.E.   WILL FRIDAY EVER COME  10.95  19,999  218,989.05  17%   $37,228.14


   *** TOTAL ROYALTIES PAID        $184,287.78 ── Incorrect
                                                    total
```

royalty % rate — Incorrect logic to determine royalty % rate (annotation pointing at ROYALTY RATE column)

Figure 4.29
(continued)

PROGRAMMING ASSIGNMENTS

Notes

a. Use SETOF and SETON where appropriate.

b. Use Data Structures for work fields. Use prefixes for input, output, and work fields.

1. A real estate salesperson is paid a commission based on the amount of the sale. If the sale is over $50,000.00, then the salesperson receives a 6% commission. For sales of $50,000 or less, the salesperson receives only a 4.5% commission. Sales over $100,000.00 result in a bonus of $1,500.00 added to the 6% commission. The total commission is the sales commission plus the bonus. Using the following problem definition, write an RPG program to produce the required results.

Systems Flowchart

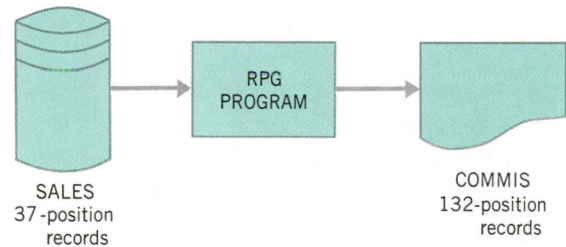

SALES
37-position
records

RPG
PROGRAM

COMMIS
132-position
records

SALES Record Layout

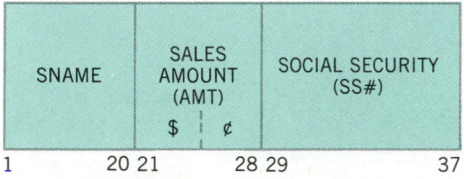

SNAME	SALES AMOUNT (AMT) $ ¢	SOCIAL SECURITY (SS#)
1	20 21 28	29 37

COMMIS Printer Spacing Chart

```
     ┌──────────────────────────────────────────────────────────────────────────────
  H  3  PAGE XXXX      BREWSTER & BREWSTER REALTORS COMMISSION REPORT      XX/XX/XX
  H  6  SOCIAL        SALESPERSON        AMOUNT OF        AGENT        AGENT        AGENT
  H  7  SECURITY        NAME               SALES        COMMISSION     BONUS        TOTAL
  D  9  XXX-XX-XXXX    X──────────X      XX,XXX.XX      XX,XXX.XX    X,XXX.XX     XX,XXX.XX
  D 10  XXX-XX-XXXX    X──────────X      XX,XXX.XX      XX,XXX.XX    X,XXX.XX     XX,XXX.XX
  D 11  XXX-XX-XXXX    X──────────X      XX,XXX.XX      XX,XXX.XX    X,XXX.XX     XX,XXX.XX
  D 12   (ss#)          (sname)           (amt)          (comm)
 TLR 14                   TOTALS       XXX,XXX.XX     XXX,XXX.XX    XX,XXX.XX    XXX,XXX.XX
```

2. Using the following problem definition, code an RPG program to produce the required results. Counters must be used to count the number of employees, the number paying union dues, the number earning less than $2,500.00, etc.

Systems Flowchart

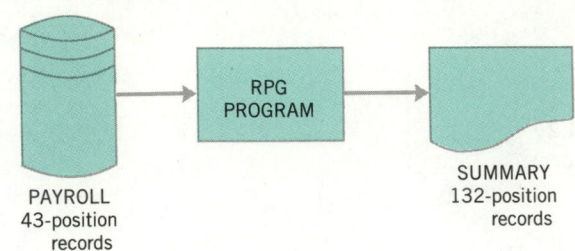

PAYROLL
43-position
records

RPG
PROGRAM

SUMMARY
132-position
records

PAYROLL Record Layout

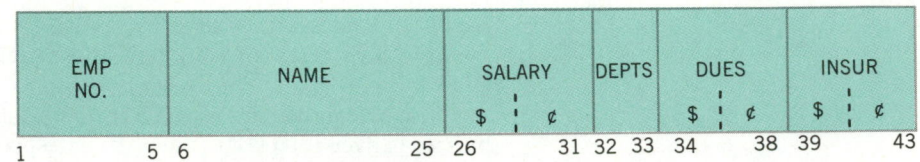

SUMMARY Printer Spacing Chart

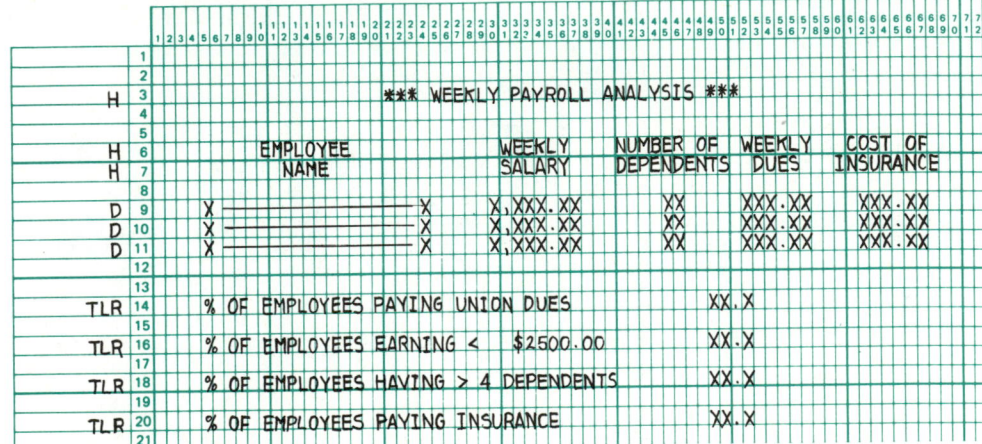

3. Code an RPG program to calculate the royalty to be paid to an author by a publishing house. The input record contains fields describing the quantity of books sold (QTY) and the (NET) cost of each. The royalty rate is a sliding scale based on the quantity of books sold.

No. of Books Sold	Royalty Rate %
5000 or less	7
5001–10,000	9
10,001–20,000	17
over 20,000	25

The royalty paid is computed by multiplying the royalty rate by the net sales. In order to determine the net sales, multiply the quantity sold by the net cost. The problem definition is shown here:

Systems Flowchart

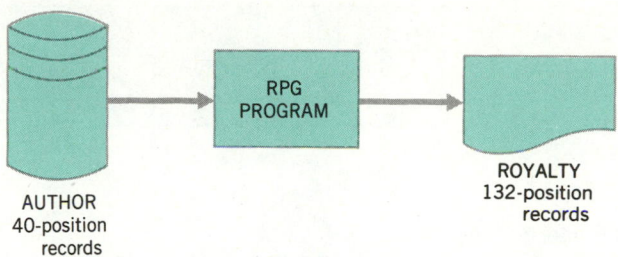

AUTHOR
40-position
records

RPG
PROGRAM

ROYALTY
132-position
records

AUTHOR Record Layout

AUTHOR	NO. OF BOOKS SOLD (QTY)	COST OF BOOK $ ¢ (NET)	TITLE
1 15	16 20	21 25	26 40

ROYALTY Printer Spacing Chart

```
                                      ROYALTY REPORT FOR PERIOD ENDING XX/XX/XX
H  3
H  6        AUTHOR'S          TITLE OF        CURRENT   CURRENT   RATE    TOTAL         AUTHOR'S
H  7          NAME            TEXTBOOK         SALES     PRICE     %      SALES         ROYALTY
D  9   X----------X   X----------X    XX,XØX    XXØ.XX    XX    X,XXX,XØX.XX    XXX,XØX.XX
D 10   X----------X   X----------X    XX,XØX    XXØ.XX    XX    X,XXX,XØX.XX    XXX,XØX.XX
D 11   X----------X   X----------X    XX,XØX    XXØ.XX    XX    X,XXX,XØX.XX    XXX,XØX.XX
D 12   X----------X   X----------X    XX,XØX    XXØ.XX    XX    X,XXX,XØX.XX    XXX,XØX.XX
TLR 16               TOTAL ROYALTIES DISTRIBUTED    XXX,XXX,XØX.XX
```

4. Code an RPG program to identify items in an inventory file that are below or equal to the reorder point (sometimes referred to as the minimum), or greater than the maximum number that should be on hand. The quantity on hand (QOH) is calculated as follows:

QOH = old balance + receipts − usage

For each item, calculate the quantity on hand and compare to the minimum and the maximum. If QOH > Maximum, print the message "OVERSTOCKED". However, if QOH < or = Minimum, then print the message "REORDER". Note that the report is an exception report and only "REORDER" and "OVERSTOCKED" items are to be listed.

Systems Flowchart

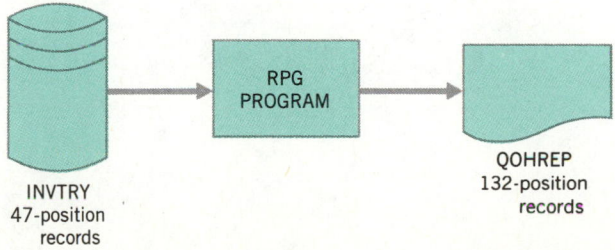

INVTRY
47-position
records

RPG
PROGRAM

QOHREP
132-position
records

INVTRY Record Layout

PART NO.	DESCRIPT.	OLD BALANCE	RECPTS	USAGE	MIN.	MAX.
1 5	6 20	21 26	27 31	32 36	37 41	42 47

QOHREP Printer Spacing Chart

```
      1         1111111111222222222233333333334444444444555555555566666666667777777777888888888899999999990000000
 1234567890123456789012345678901234567890123456789012345678901234567890123456789012345678901234567890123456
1
2
3 H  xx/xx/xx                         EXCEPTION INVENTORY REPORT                              PAGE XXXX
4
5
6 H  PART         PART        OPENING   (PLUS)     (MINUS)   QUANTITY   MINIMUM   MAXIMUM   EXCEPTION
7 H  NO.          DESCRIPTION BALANCE   RECEIPTS   USAGE     ON HAND    LEVEL     LEVEL     MESSAGE
8
9  D  X---X   X---------X     XXX,XXX   XX,XXX     XX,XXX    XXX,XXX    XXX,XXX   XXX,XXX   OVERSTOCKED
10 D  X---X   X---------X     XXX,XXX   XX,XXX     XX,XXX    XXX,XXX    XXX,XXX   XXX,XXX   REORDER
11 D  X---X   X---------X     XXX,XXX   XX,XXX     XX,XXX    XXX,XXX    XXX,XXX   XXX,XXX   REORDER
```

UNIT 2

DESIGNING STRUCTURED PROGRAMS

5

Structured Programming Design: Concepts and Tools

OBJECTIVES

To familiarize you with

1. The way structured programs should be designed.
2. Flowcharts and pseudocode as planning tools used to map out the logic in a structured program.
3. Hierarchy or structure charts as planning tools used to illustrate the relationships among modules in a top-down program.
4. The logical control structures of sequence, selection, case, and iteration.
5. Techniques used to make programs easier to code, debug, maintain, and modify.
6. The use of subroutines in RPG.

I. Writing Well-Designed Programs

In the early days of programming, people learning to program believed that mastering the rules of a programming language was all that was needed to write well-designed programs. Often, instruction formats and coding rules necessary for writing programs were taught without ever fully explaining the way programs are actually designed. It is, of course, true that you must learn programming rules, or *syntax*, before instructions can be coded. Unfortunately, however, knowledge of a programming language's rules will not guarantee that programs will be designed properly. That is, it is possible for elements of a program to be coded correctly and yet the entire set of procedures might not work properly or efficiently. In addition to learning syntax, then, programmers must learn how to *design a program* so that it functions effectively *as an integrated whole*. We define the term *program design* to mean the development of a program so that its elements fit together logically and effectively in an integrated way. Thus, programmers must be familiar with the techniques used to structure programs as well as with the programming or syntax rules.

Learning syntax, then, is only one step in the process of developing programs. The syntax you learn is language-specific, meaning that each programming language has *its own particular rules.* But the *techniques* for developing well-designed programs are *applicable to all languages.* That is, the logical control structures for designing an RPG program are very similar to those in all the other languages. Once you know how to design programs efficiently and effectively, you need only learn the syntax rules of a specific language to implement these design elements. It is also important to point out that learning the techniques and the environment in which RPG is used is as important as learning the rules of RPG programming.

Note that the concepts that will be explained in this chapter include structured techniques that are available in most programming languages. We will begin by showing you general concepts used to construct or design a program so that you can create structures that are easy to understand, debug, maintain, and modify. Then, we will apply some of these structured programming techniques to RPG. Additional structured concepts will be illustrated in subsequent chapters.

A. Programs Should Use a Top-Down Modular Approach

Each well-defined unit or program segment should be written as an independent module and coded in a *hierarchical order.* The main module of a top-down program is coded first, with the secondary modules initially sketched out and the details filled in later, after the structure has been clearly described.

The coding of modules in a hierarchical manner is called **top-down programming.** Only after the organization of the program has been determined will the programmer code the specific instructions in each module.

In RPG, modules or program segments are called *subroutines* and are executed in their entirety from specific places in a program. This feature allows control to pass temporarily from one module or subroutine to another and then return to the original one from which it was executed.

An unconditional branch to different routines, called a GOTO in RPG and other languages, is *avoided entirely* in a top-down structured program. Thus, GOTO instructions should *not* be used in well-designed programs.

B. Programs Should Be Structured

Well-designed programs are those that have a logical structure, where the order in which instructions are executed is *standardized.* Structured programming is a technique that provides this logical construct. With well-designed structured programs, each set of instructions that performs a specific function is represented by a logical control structure.

Logical control structures refer to the different ways in which instructions may be executed. Sometimes instructions are executed in order, that is, in the sequence in which they appear in the program. Other times, different sequences of instructions are executed depending on the outcome of a test between two fields. Or, a series of instructions might be executed repeatedly from different points in a program. The way in which a set of instructions is executed is called a *logical control structure.*

C. Program Design Tools

Well-designed programs are systematically planned before they are coded. The planning process minimizes logic errors by helping the programmer determine how all instructions will interrelate when the program is actually coded. Planning tools that help programmers map out program logic consist of the following:

1. Hierarchy charts.
2. Flowcharts.
3. Pseudocode.

Flowcharts and **pseudocode** are planning tools used to depict the instructions and logical control structures that will be used when a program is actually written. They help plan a program so that the coded instructions will be implemented properly and efficiently in a standardized manner. Typically, a programmer uses either a flowchart or pseudocode to map out program logic. The overall relationship among major and minor components of a well-designed program is accomplished using **hierarchy charts.** This tool, however, is not intended to map out specific logical control structures, but to illustrate the top-down relationships among the modules in a program.

Thus, before writing a program you will need to plan the logic in two ways:

1. With a *hierarchy chart* to illustrate how the modules should relate to one another in a top-down fashion.
2. With a *flowchart* or *pseudocode* to illustrate the logical structure, that is, how instructions are actually executed.

Let us first consider the use of hierarchy charts in the modular approach to program design.

II. Hierarchy Charts for Top-Down Programming

The planning tool best used for illustrating a *top-down approach* to a program is a *hierarchy* or **structure chart.** A hierarchy or structure chart provides a graphic method for dividing a problem into components called **modules.** You will find that the hierarchy chart clearly illustrates the breakdown of a complex problem into small segments; this permits you to program smaller, simpler program excerpts, as opposed to one large complex program. Its main purpose is to provide a visual or graphic overview of the relationships among modules in a program. That is, hierarchy charts are a top-down method used to divide the problem into subtasks and illustrate them in the order in which they will be executed.

In RPG, the concept of top-down or hierarchical programming is accomplished by coding main modules first, with minor ones detailed later. These modules, then, are said to be coded hierarchically.

A main module is subdivided into its components, which are considered subordinate modules. Think of a top-down design as an outline of a term paper. Begin by penciling in the main subject areas and components and focus on the minor details after the main organization has been defined.

Note the following about hierarchy charts:

HIERARCHY CHARTS

1. A hierarchy chart is a structure chart that represents program modules as rectangular boxes and illustrates the interrelationships among these modules with the use of connecting lines.
2. A module is a well-defined program segment that performs a specific function. A module may be a heading routine, an error-checking routine, a specific calculation routine, and so forth.

Figure 5.1 illustrates a hierarchy chart showing the relationship between the modules. In practice, we would use meaningful names for modules. The letters A through H are used here as module names for the sake of brevity and to highlight the concepts being illustrated. In actual programs, we use more meaningful module names.

Figure 5.1
Example of a hierarchy chart.

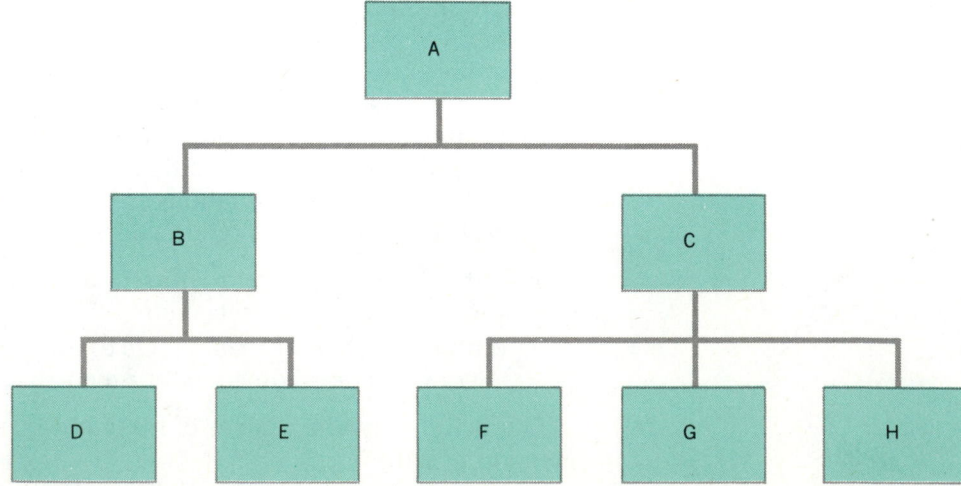

Each module is represented by a rectangle:

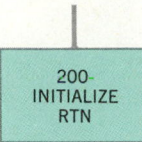

Note that letters A through H represent module names that are executed or performed from different points in the program. Figure 5.1 has modules executed as follows:

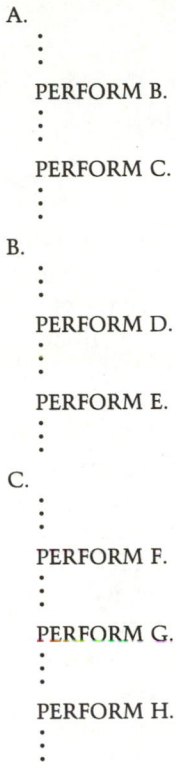

A.

    PERFORM B.

    PERFORM C.

B.

    PERFORM D.

    PERFORM E.

C.

    PERFORM F.

    PERFORM G.

    PERFORM H.

The hierarchy chart, then, only illustrates modules executed from other modules. Unlike a flowchart or pseudocode, actual instructions are not depicted in a hierarchy chart. Each block or box in a hierarchy chart represents a module. If a module calls for another module, this is depicted in a separate box. Consider the following section of the hierarchy chart in Figure 5.1:

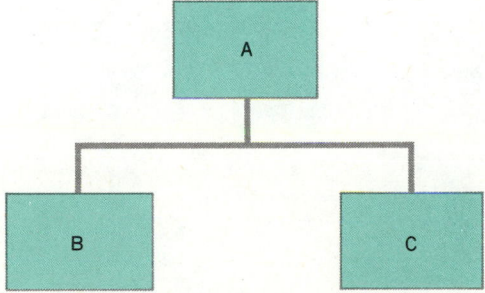

From this excerpt, we see that modules B and C are executed from module A.

Note that a module executed from another module can itself execute yet another module. Referring to Figure 5.1, Module D is performed in Module B, which itself is executed from the main module, Module A.

Consider the following excerpt, which is different from the preceding:

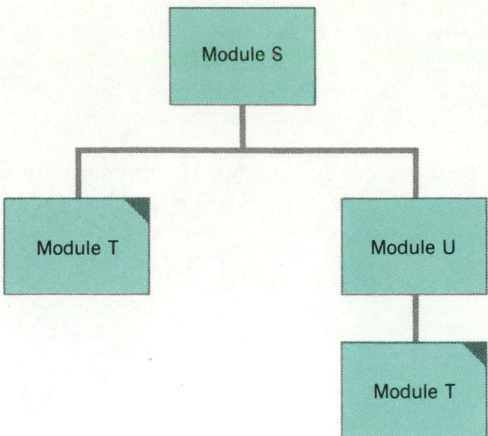

This excerpt indicates that Module T is executed from both Module S and Module U. To highlight the fact that Module T is executed from more than one point in the program, we use a corner-cut in both boxes labeled Module T.

In summary, the hierarchy chart illustrates how modules relate to one another, which modules are subordinate to others, and whether or not a module is executed from more than one point in the program. Moreover, if a module must be modified at some later date, the hierarchy chart will tell you how the change might affect the entire program. It does not consider the actual instructions within each module, just the relationships among them. The actual sequence of instructions is depicted in a flowchart or pseudocode, either of which would accompany a hierarchy chart as a program planning tool.

A hierarchy chart is sometimes called a **Visual Table of Contents (VTOC)** because it provides a graphic overview of a program. Consider the hierarchy chart or VTOC in Figure 5.2 for a payroll program that calculates wages for each employee, where overtime is calculated as time-and-a-half. You will note that the hierarchy chart provides a visual overview of the relationships among modules. Module names should be as descriptive as possible. Modules marked

Figure 5.2
Hierarchy chart for a payroll program.

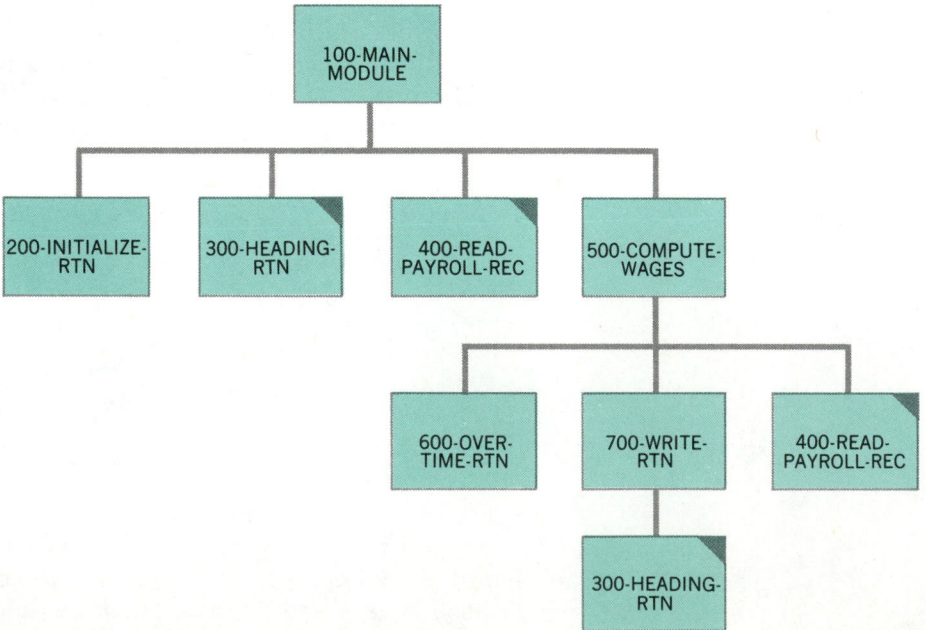

with a corner-cut are performed from more than one point in the program.

Note that when a subordinate module such as 600-OVERTIME-RTN is executed in its entirety, control then returns to the next highest module, 500-COMPUTE-WAGES in this instance. When 500-COMPUTE-WAGES has been executed in its entirety, control returns to MAIN-MODULE. Because logical control is depicted in this hierarchical fashion in a hierarchy or structure chart, it is referred to as a *top-down* tool.

For now, we will use descriptive module names. Later in this chapter, when we discuss RPG rules for coding procedures and subroutines, we will focus on valid RPG names.

In summary, then, a hierarchy chart has the following advantages:

ADVANTAGES OF A HIERARCHY OR STRUCTURE CHART

1. It helps programmers, systems analysts, and users see how modules interrelate.
2. It helps programmers debug and modify programs.
3. It helps users understand the logical flow in a program.
4. It helps programming managers assess the efficiency of programs.

Thus, the hierarchy chart is both a design and documentation tool.

You can see that a hierarchy chart is not designed to highlight individual instructions; flowcharts or pseudocode serve that purpose. Rather, a hierarchy chart provides an overview of the interrelationships, hierarchy, and structure of modules. It also serves as a kind of table of contents, helping users and programmers locate modules in a program. This is why the term "visual table of contents" (VTOC) is sometimes used.

III. Modularizing Programs

We have seen that top-down programs are written with main units or modules planned and coded first, followed by more detailed ones. Structure or hierarchy charts illustrate the relationships among these modules. All statements that represent a unit or a set of instructions that together achieve a given task should be coded as a module or subroutine. Consider the following:

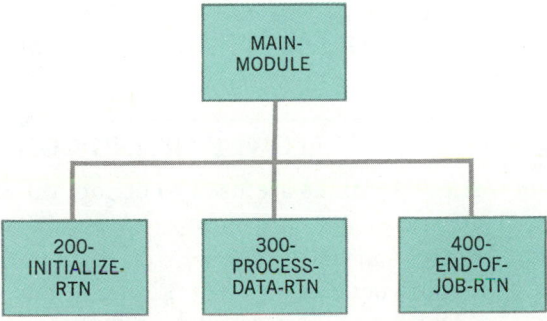

200-INITIALIZE-RTN would perform any operations required prior to the processing of data. These instructions could have been coded directly in MAIN-MODULE, but because they are really a related set of operations we treat them as a separate unit. We encourage this type of modularity especially for complex programs or when standard initializing procedures are required by an organization.

Similarly, `400-END-OF-JOB-RTN` would include procedures such as the printing of final totals. Here, again, such statements represent a unit and should be modularized.

Most programmers use initializing and end-of-job procedures as modules rather than including the individual instructions in the main module. In this way, the main module provides a "bird's-eye view" of the entire structure in the program. This modularization eliminates the need to get involved in detailed coding until after the structure has been fully developed.

Later on, our RPG programs will consist of modules written and executed in a top-down manner. For these programs, we will use hierarchy charts to depict the relationships among these modules.

IV. Designing Program Logic

Two useful tools for planning the logic to be used in a program are *flowcharts* and *pseudocode*. Both of these planning tools are language-independent. That is, they help plan the logic to be used in *any program* regardless of the language in which the program will be coded. Thus, they afford us the benefit of illustrating the control structures in a general or theoretical way, without being dependent on any specific language rules.

A *flowchart* is a diagram or pictorial representation of the instructions and logical control structures that will be used in a program. Similarly, *pseudocode* is a set of written statements that specifies the instructions and logical control structures that will be used in a program.

Flowcharts and pseudocode are planning tools that should be prepared *before* the program specifications are written. They map out and then verify the logic to be incorporated in the program. Usually a program is planned with *either* a flowchart or pseudocode.

For now, we will focus on flowcharts and pseudocode and how they illustrate the ways in which a program can be logically structured. Once you understand how to plan the logical control structure of a program using pseudocode and flowcharts, the specific RPG rules to implement that logic will be introduced.

A. Flowcharts

The symbols in Figure 5.3 are the ones most frequently used in program flowcharts.

FLOWCHARTING CONVENTIONS

1. Various symbols are used to denote different operations or functions.
2. An explanatory note is written inside each symbol to indicate the specific operations to be performed. Since a symbol signifies a major category of operations such as input/output or processing, a note is required within the symbol to describe the *specific* operations to be performed such as "read a record" or "subtract total deductions from gross pay giving net pay."
3. The symbols are connected by flowlines.

---

4. Flowcharts are drawn and read from top to bottom unless a specific condition is met that alters the path.
5. A sequence of operations is performed until a terminal symbol designates the end of the sequence or the end of the program.
6. Sometimes several RPG steps or statements are combined in a single processing symbol for ease of reading.

Figure 5.3
Commonly used program flowchart symbols.

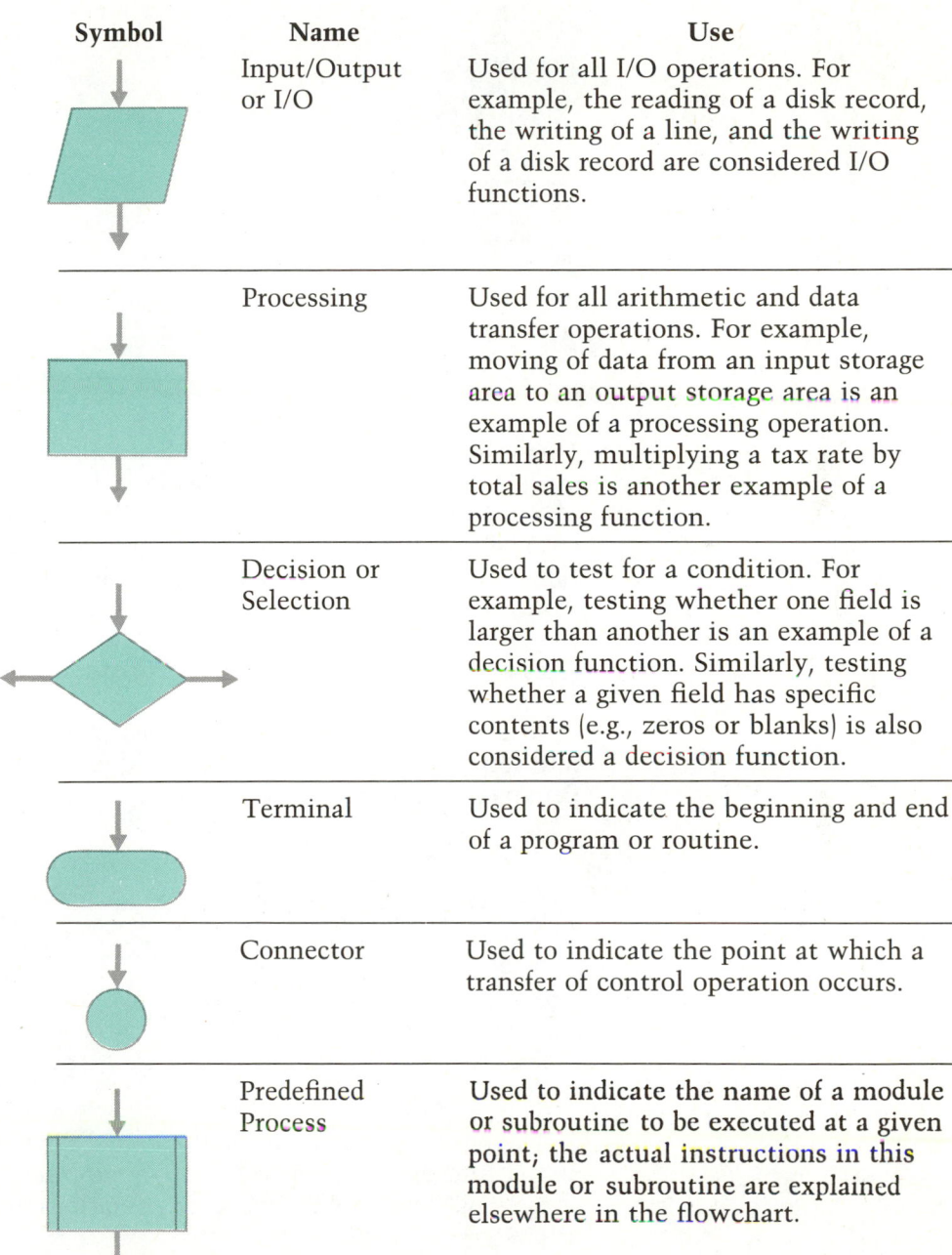

Symbol	Name	Use
	Input/Output or I/O	Used for all I/O operations. For example, the reading of a disk record, the writing of a line, and the writing of a disk record are considered I/O functions.
	Processing	Used for all arithmetic and data transfer operations. For example, moving of data from an input storage area to an output storage area is an example of a processing operation. Similarly, multiplying a tax rate by total sales is another example of a processing function.
	Decision or Selection	Used to test for a condition. For example, testing whether one field is larger than another is an example of a decision function. Similarly, testing whether a given field has specific contents (e.g., zeros or blanks) is also considered a decision function.
	Terminal	Used to indicate the beginning and end of a program or routine.
	Connector	Used to indicate the point at which a transfer of control operation occurs.
	Predefined Process	Used to indicate the name of a module or subroutine to be executed at a given point; the actual instructions in this module or subroutine are explained elsewhere in the flowchart.

Consider the following simple flowchart:

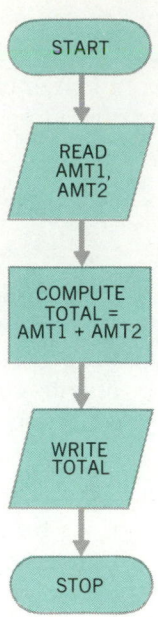

This sequence of instructions is called a *module.* The beginning and end of the module or sequence are designated with terminal symbols that are labeled START and STOP, respectively. The first instruction or statement is READ AMT1, AMT2, meaning "read into storage a value for a field called AMT1 and a value for a field called AMT2." This is an input operation and is coded in an input/ouput or I/O symbol. Because a flowchart is a planning tool that is language-independent, you need not follow any language's specific syntax rules when drawing the flowchart. For example, INPUT AMT1, AMT2 would also be acceptable.

When coded and executed, the first instruction in the sequence will read into storage a value for AMT1 and a value for AMT2, where AMT1 and AMT2 are field names or symbolic addresses:

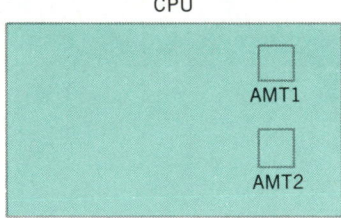

The next instruction in the illustrated flowchart module computes TOTAL as the sum of AMT1 and AMT2; it is a processing operation and is coded in a processing symbol. All arithmetic operations are considered processing operations.

In the program, this computation will add AMT1 and AMT2 and put the result in a field or symbolic storage address called TOTAL. Suppose 10 is entered as input for AMT1 and 15 is entered as input for AMT2. Then the CPU would have the following contents in the fields or symbolic storage addresses defined in this program:

CPU

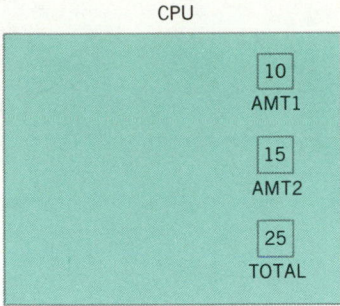

The next instruction in the illustrated flowchart module, WRITE TOTAL, is an output operation that will print the contents of the field called TOTAL. It is also coded in an I/O symbol.

The flowchart is read from top to bottom. Since there is no need to repeat instructions or to test for any conditions, this simple flowchart indicates that two numbers will be read, added together, and the sum printed.

Specific instructions or statements are coded in each of the following flow-chart symbols: input/output, processing, and decision. Terminal symbols indicate the beginning and end points of each module. A predefined process is drawn as a single step within the sequence; it indicates that another module is to be executed at that point. The steps within the named module are specified in detail in a different module or sequence.

Suppose we wish to print not only TOTAL but a series of headings and other data. We can include each of these processing steps in our module or sequence, or we can indicate a "PRINT-MODULE" as a separate series of steps to be performed. The following illustrates how we would draw a flowchart symbol to indicate that a predefined process called PRINT-MODULE is to be executed at a specific point:

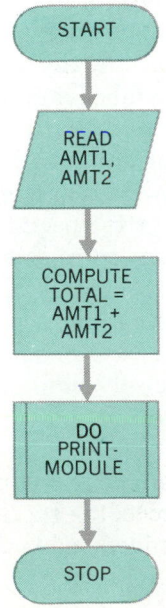

PRINT-MODULE, then, would be defined in detail in a separate sequence:

PRINT-MODULE

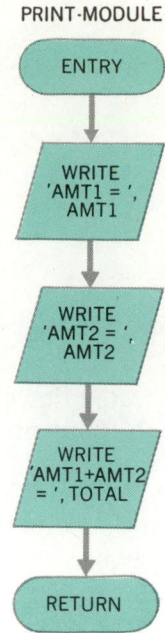

B. Pseudocode

Flowcharts have been used as planning tools for four decades. Structured programming, on the other hand, is a technique that has been developed only in the last two or three decades. When structured programming became an established method for designing programs, flowchart symbols had to be modified to accurately depict a structured design. Many programmers and managers have found that these modifications make flowcharts difficult to use as a planning tool. As a result, although flowcharts are still widely used in some organizations, other tools have been developed for more clearly depicting the logic in a *structured program.* Pseudocode is one such tool.

Pseudocode has been designed specifically as a method for representing the logic in a structured program. No symbols are used as in a flowchart; rather, a series of logical control terms defines the structure. Each processing or input/output step is denoted by a line or group of lines in a pseudocode. As with flowcharts, you need not follow any language rules when using pseudocode; it is a language-independent tool. Thus, the pseudocode need not indicate *all* the processing details; abbreviations are permissible. The actual words used in pseudocode need not follow any specific rules. We can say "Housekeeping Operations" to mean any initializing steps, or we can say "Initialize Variables." The degree of detail used in pseudocode can vary, although the logical control structures need to be precisely defined as we will see later in this section. We will see that logical control structures are easily specified using pseudocode.

Like a flowchart, pseudocode is read in sequence unless a logical control structure is encountered. In the preceding section we focused on a flowchart for a program that reads in two numbers, adds them, and prints the total. The pseudocode for this sequence is as follows:

```
START
   Read Amt1, Amt2
   Compute Total = Amt1 + Amt2
   Write Total
STOP
```

As with flowcharts, the START and STOP delineate the beginning and ending points of the program module. The words such as "Read Amt1, Amt2" are used to convey a message and need not be written precisely as shown. Thus, "Input Amt1, Amt2" would be acceptable. Similarly, "Add Amt1 to Amt2 Giving Total" could be used rather than "Compute Total = Amt1 + Amt2" for the second instruction.

To illustrate the performing of a `PRINT-MODULE` as we did with a flowchart, we would have the following in pseudocode:

DO
   Write "AMT1 = ", Amt1
   Write "AMT2 = ", Amt2
   Write "THE SUM OF AMT1 and AMT2 = ", Total
ENDDO

PSEUDOCODE RULES

1. Pseudocode is written and read from top to bottom. Instructions are to be executed in sequence unless a logical control construct is used that alters the sequence of how instructions are executed.

2. The logical control structure of pseudocode is defined with the use of key terms such as DO . . . ENDDO and IF-ELSE-ENDIF.

3. The operations to be executed with a DO group or `IF-ELSE-ENDIF` are coded in sequence.

  a. DO
      .
      . Instructions to be executed go here
      .
    ENDDO
  b. IF condition
      .
      .
      .
    ELSE
      .
      .
      .
    ENDIF

4. Similarly, the case structure, which will be discussed later, is defined with a CASE . . . ENDCASE format.

When you design your own programs, particularly long and complex ones, we recommend that you begin by drawing a hierarchy chart and flowchart or pseudocode. You will find that these tools are extremely helpful in mapping out the logic to be used in your program. Although our early programs have relatively simple logical control constructs, the habitual use of program planning tools will be extremely helpful later on when you write more complex programs. When a flowchart or pseudocode is written correctly, it is a relatively easy matter to convert it to a program, assuming you know the syntax or rules of the programming language. You may also find that these planning tools will help you detect potential logic errors that, if coded in a program, will produce erroneous results.

Experienced programmers use either flowcharts or pseudocode as a planning tool. Writing both is really "overkill." Some computing organizations specify whether you should use pseudocode or flowcharting; others allow the programmer to choose the tool to be used.

C. The Four Logical Control Structures

Structured programs use logical control structures to specify the order in which instructions are executed. These structures are the same for all languages and when integrated form the logical design in a program. They are used to make programs easier to write, debug, maintain, and modify. They avoid the use of unconditional branches (GOTOs), which make program logic difficult to follow.

The following are the four logical control structures:

LOGICAL CONTROL STRUCTURES

1. Sequence.
2. Selection.
3. Case Structure.
4. Iteration.

---

1. Sequence

When instructions are to be executed in the order in which they appear, we call this a **sequence.** The first flowchart and pseudocode in the preceding section illustrated a module executed as a sequence, one instruction after the other. Thus if all data is to be processed step-by-step in some fixed way, we use a sequence to depict the logic. That is, when instructions are executed in order *regardless of any existing condition,* we code them as a sequence. As another example, the instructions in Figure 5.4 would represent a sequence. The ellipses (dots) within each symbol just mean that each statement has other components.

The preceding sequence of instructions would always be executed in the order in which it appears. These instructions, when they are coded in a program, will be executed as they appear in the flowchart, from top to bottom.

Figure 5.4
Example of a sequence.

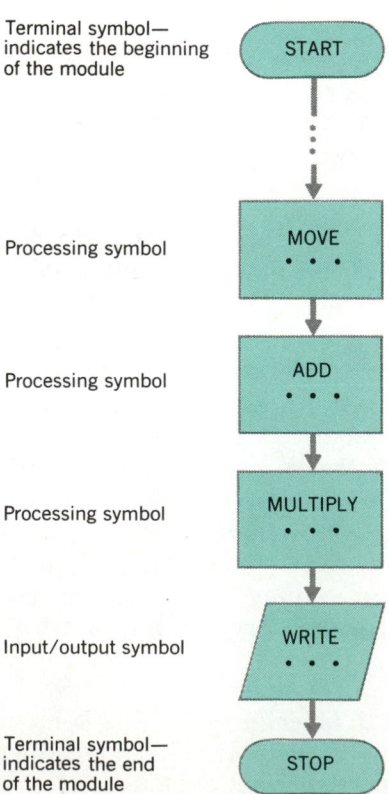

Terminal symbol—
indicates the beginning
of the module

START

Processing symbol — MOVE · · ·

Processing symbol — ADD · · ·

Processing symbol — MULTIPLY · · ·

Input/output symbol — WRITE · · ·

Terminal symbol—
indicates the end
of the module

STOP

Beginning and Ending Modules

All modules or sequences in a program flowchart and a pseudocode should be clearly delineated. To denote the beginning and ending of a module or sequence in a flowchart, we use a terminal symbol. Similarly, the pseudocode could use START and STOP as code words to delineate a sequence or module, particularly the main module.

START

———————
———————
———————

STOP

Each instruction in a structured program is executed in sequence unless one of the other logical control structures is specified. We now consider these other structures.

2. Selection

Selection is a logical control construct that executes instructions *depending on the existence of a condition*. In RPG it is sometimes called an IF-ELSE-END logical control structure. Using pseudocode, we can code an IF-ELSE-ENDIF structure as follows:

IF   (condition)

———————
———————   Indicates what is to be done
———————   if the condition exists

ELSE

———————
———————   Indicates what is to be done
———————   if the condition does not exist

ENDIF

   Consider this problem to illustrate the IF-ELSE-END logical control structure. Suppose that a field called AMT is in error if its value is less than zero and we would want to ADD 1 to an error counter. If the AMT field were zero or greater than zero, we would want to write a record.

   The general flowchart representation for an IF-ELSE-END logical control structure along with the specific flowchart excerpt for the preceding example are as follows:

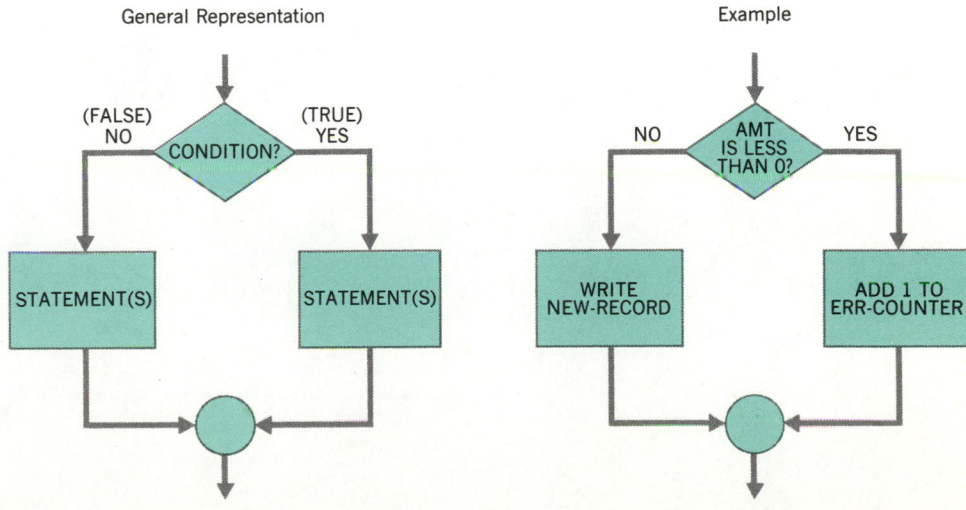

If the condition is true (or exists), we execute the statement or statements on the right. If the condition does not exist, we execute the statement or statements on the left. In either case, the flow returns to the circle or connector, where the next instruction, in sequence, is executed.

The general pseudocode format for the IF-ELSE-ENDIF logical control structure along with the specific pseudocode for the preceding example are as follows:

Pseudocode Format for a Selection	**Example**
IF *condition*	IF Amt1 is Less Than Zero
_____	Add 1 to Error Counter
_____	ELSE
_____	Write a New Record
ELSE	ENDIF
_____	
_____	
_____	
ENDIF	

In pseudocode, the word IF is followed by the condition to be tested. Following the IF condition clause are the statements to be executed if the condition exists. The word ELSE is followed by the statements to be executed if the condition does not exist, and the word ENDIF ends the selection process. We capitalize only the logical control terms IF, ELSE, and ENDIF, which also helps to highlight the structure.

Here we presented the general form for the IF-ELSE-END control structure and focused on the flowchart and pseudocode techniques that illustrate this logical control structure. The precise details for coding RPG programs using IF-ELSE-END are discussed later in this chapter.

3. Case Structure

The **case structure** is a special form of the IF logical control structure used when there are numerous paths to be followed depending on the contents of a given field. For example, if a code field is equal to 1, we want to perform a print routine; if it is equal to 2, we want to perform a total routine, and so on. With the case structure, then, we wish to perform one of several possible procedures or subroutines depending on some condition.

Consider a payroll program that reads in an update code and executes one of several subroutines depending on the value of the code. This can best be described with a flowchart as shown in Figure 5.5.

Figure 5.5
Case structure for a payroll program.

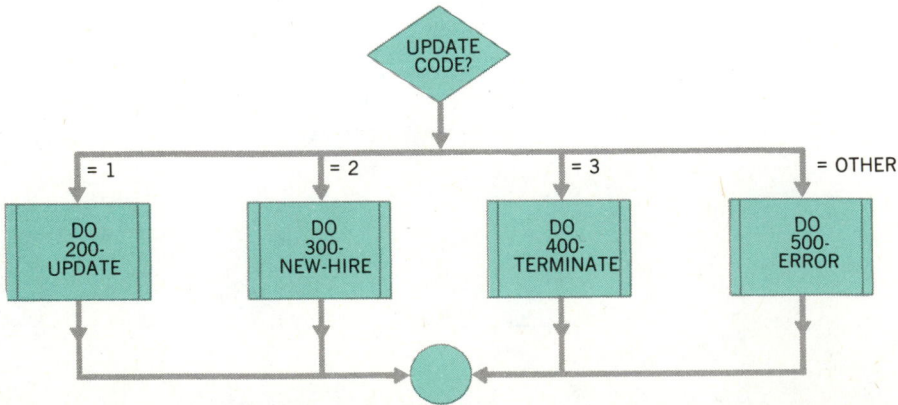

Although this could be coded with a series of simple conditions, such coding can be complex because once a valid entry such as 1, 2, or 3 has been determined, we want to skip over the other tests. If additional valid values need to be added, it is a simple task to add the appropriate operations.

With the use of the CASE, you can execute different routines depending on the contents of a field. You can also determine if a field has valid contents with the use of the OTHERWISE CASE statement. In the preceding, we executed the appropriate subroutine depending on the contents of the update code entered; if the code is invalid with a value other than 1, 2, or 3, an error message would be printed.

The pseudocode for a case structure is as follows:

```
CASE Update-Code
    When 1          Salary Update Procedure
    When 2          New Hire Procedure
    When 3          Terminate Procedure
    When Other      Error Procedure
ENDCASE
```

4. Iteration

Here we will illustrate the logical control structure referred to as *iteration* or DO Groups. These operations enable us to execute a series of steps repeatedly until a specific condition exists. When writing computer programs, the ability to perform or execute a series of operations repeatedly is an essential feature. For example, if we wanted to print five mailing labels for each customer, we would not run a program five times. The program would be run once with it repeating the operations required to produce the five labels for each customer. **Iteration** is a term used in programming for indicating the repeated execution or **looping** of a series of steps. Iteration consists of two main formats: the DO WHILE (DOW) structure and the DO UNTIL (DOU) structure. Another format, the DO structure, is also available in RPG and will be illustrated in Chapter 6. For now we will consider the DO WHILE and DO UNTIL structures.

Consider the preceding example where five mailing labels are to be printed for each customer. Figure 5.6 illustrates the DO WHILE iteration for this problem.

In the example, the module we have called 300-WRITE-RTN is executed *repeatedly* as long as the field #COUNT *is less than* 5. The flowchart symbol used to indicate a DO group operation (DO 300-WRITE-RTN) is referred to as a *predefined process.*

Once the structure is entered the condition is tested (is #COUNT less than 5?) first before any operations are performed. If #COUNT is less than 5 (the condition is *true*) we execute the named module using the predefined process symbol. This means that the operations in the module named within the predefined process symbol will be defined or described in detail in a separate module. The flowchart indicates that we continue to execute that named module *while* the specified condition is met. In the example, the paragraph named 300-WRITE-RTN will be executed *while* the field called #COUNT contains a value less than 5. #COUNT must be incremented within the loop (300-WRITE-RTN) to ensure that the loop will eventually stop when #COUNT equals 5. Thus, when the condition is no longer met (false), we continue with the next step in sequence after the decision test.

We use the terms "looping" and "iteration" interchangeably here.

The module defined in the predefined process symbol would be flowcharted

Figure 5.6
Format and example of the DO
WHILE iteration.

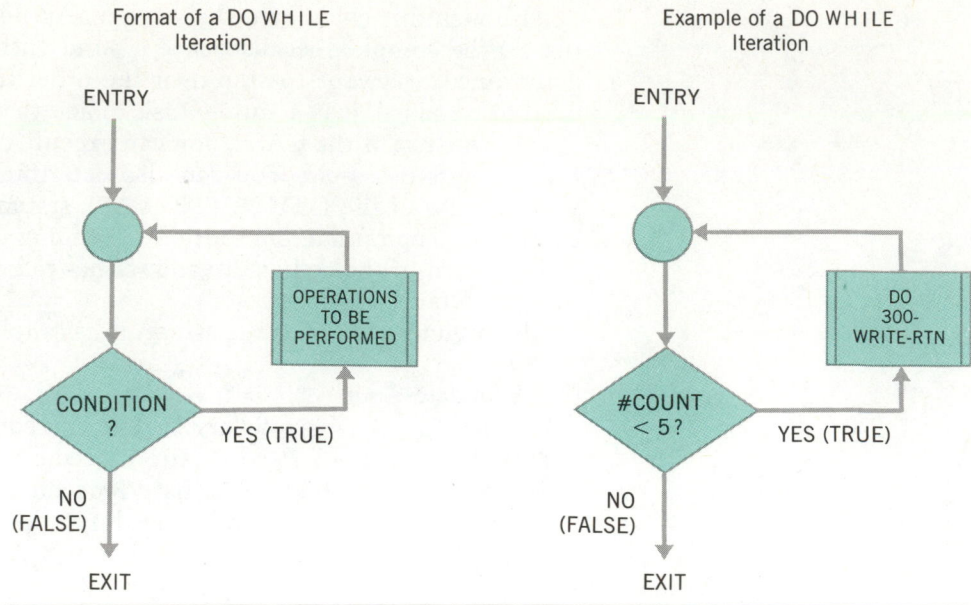

as a separate sequence. The following is an example of the relationship between the two modules:

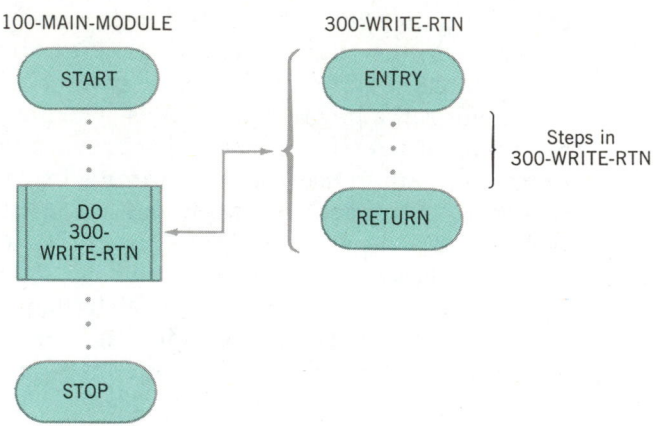

The pseudocode for a DO . . . WHILE type of iteration is as follows:

Do WHILE Format	**Example**

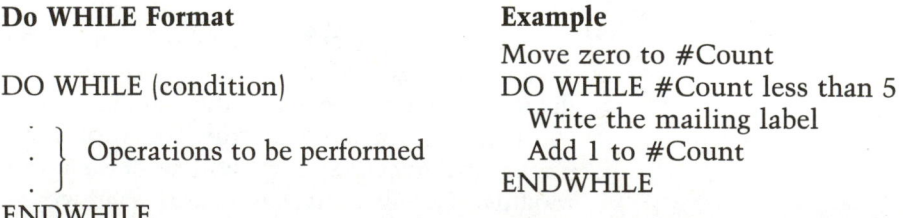

The module or series of steps to be performed would be coded on the lines between the words DO and ENDWHILE. These instructions are indented to highlight the fact that they are part of a separate logical control structure.

Let us use the same mailing label problem to illustrate the DO UNTIL iteration. (See Figure 5.7.)

The major difference between the DO WHILE structure and the DO UNTIL structure is the execution of the first loop through the structure. With the DO

Figure 5.7
Illustration of the DO UNTIL iteration for the mailing label problem.

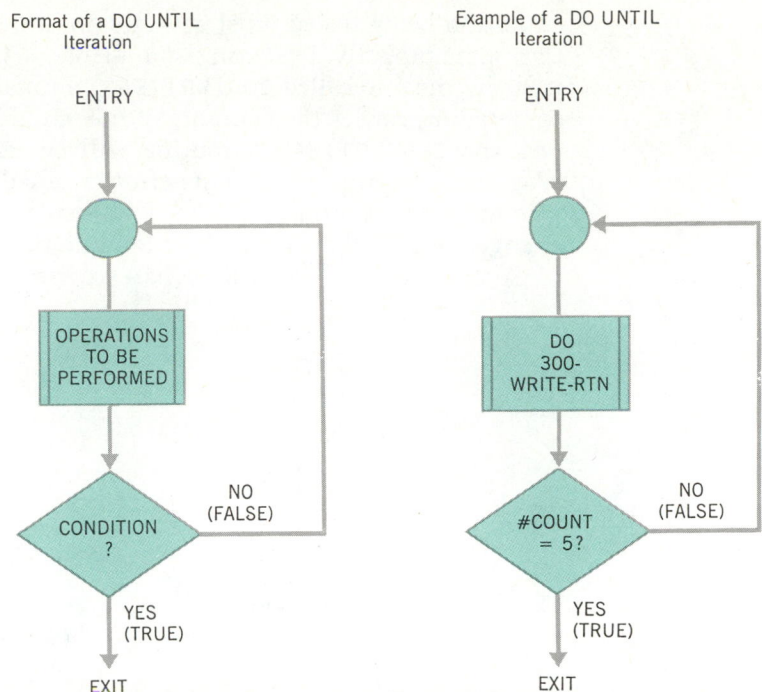

UNTIL structure (Figure 5.7), the predefined process is executed before the condition is tested, whereas, with the DO WHILE structure, the condition is tested before the predefined process is executed. Therefore, with the DO UNTIL structure, the predefined process is executed at least once. This means that the module we have called 300-WRITE-RTN is executed at least one time and then executed *repeatedly* until the field labeled #COUNT is *equal to* 5.

If the condition tested in the decision symbol is not met (false), we execute the module indicated in the predefined process symbol. When the condition is finally met (true), we continue with the next step in sequence after the decision test.

The pseudocode for a DO . . . UNTIL type of iteration is as follows:

Do UNTIL Format	**Example**
	Move zero to #Count
DO UNTIL (condition)	DO UNTIL #Count equals 5
.	Write the mailing label
. Operations to be performed	Add 1 to #Count
.	ENDUNTIL
ENDUNTIL	

Similar to the DO WHILE structure, the series of steps to be performed would be coded on the lines between the words DO UNTIL and ENDUNTIL and are indented to highlight the fact that they are part of a separate logical control structure. Again, with the DO UNTIL structure the Write operation and the Add operation would be performed at least one time.

The Infinite Loop: An Error to Be Avoided

Let us again consider the DO . . . UNTIL in which a predefined process is executed as part of an iteration. Keep in mind that the operations executed within the loop are under the control of the DO UNTIL structure. The module will be executed repeatedly until a specified condition exists or is true. The condition being tested must at some point be true for the DO . . . UNTIL to terminate properly. Executing 300-WRITE-RTN Until #COUNT equals 5 means that the module called 300-WRITE-RTN must contain an instruction that, at some point, causes the contents of the variable #COUNT to be changed to 5. If not, the 300-WRITE-RTN routine will be executed repeatedly without any programmed termination. This error is called an **infinite loop.** We avoid infinite loops by ensuring that the field tested in the UNTIL clause of a DO is changed within the paragraph or module that is being executed.

Consider the following flowchart excerpt:

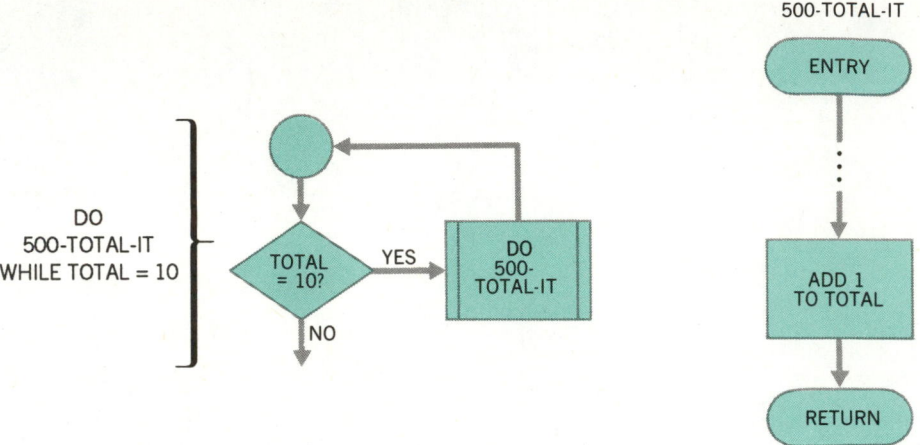

If the instruction ADD 1 TO TOTAL were omitted from the 500-TOTAL-IT module, then the sequence of instructions at 500-TOTAL-IT would result in an infinite loop.

The next section of this chapter will focus on subroutines and the first three structures (sequence, selection, and case) using RPG. RPG iteration structures will be discussed in the next chapter.

Self-Test

True-False Questions   T   F

___ ___   1. In general, programs that are first planned with a flowchart or pseudocode take less time to code and debug.

___ ___   2. Programmers should draw a flowchart and write a pseudocode before coding a program.

___ ___   3. To ensure that flowcharts are correct, it is best to draw them after you have coded the program.

___ ___   4. Well-designed programs should be structured.

___ ___   5. The terms "top-down" and "structured" have the same meaning in this chapter.

___ ___   6. The terms "module" and "subroutine" may be used interchangeably in RPG.

___ ___   7. A flowchart for an RPG program should generally be the same as for a COBOL program.

___ ___   8. The syntax for RPG and COBOL are, in general, the same.

___ ___   9. A hierarchy chart can illustrate how the logical control structure of selection is used in a program.

___ ___ 10. The four logical control structures used in well-designed programs are sequence, selection, case structure, and iteration.

Fill in the Blanks

1. The program planning tool specifically designed for depicting the logic in a structured program is _____ .

2. The program planning tool specifically designed for depicting the top-down approach used in a structured program is the _____ .

3. If instructions are executed step-by-step without any change in control, we call this a _____ .

4. Another name for selection, when used in pseudocode or in an RPG program, is called _____ .

5. Iteration, or the repeated execution of a module is accomplished using one of the _____ operations.

6. When executing an iteration structure, the field tested in the condition must be changed in order for the program to _____ properly from the structure.

7. The flowchart symbol used for performing a module is called _____ .

8. The pseudocode structure for a selection begins with the word _____ and ends with the word _____ .

9. Another name for a hierarchy chart is _____ .

10. All flowchart symbols have notes within them indicating the specific _____ to be performed.

General Questions

Indicate in each case whether the flowchart and pseudocode accomplish the same thing:

(a)

Flowchart

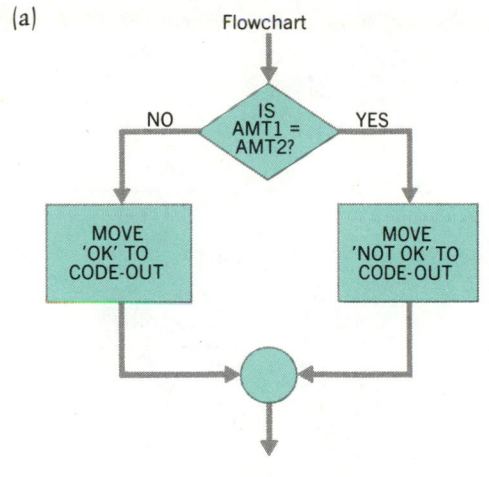

Pseudocode

```
IF      Amt1 = Amt2
             Move 'OK' to Code-Out
ELSE
             Move 'Not OK' to Code-Out
ENDIF
```

(b)

Flowchart

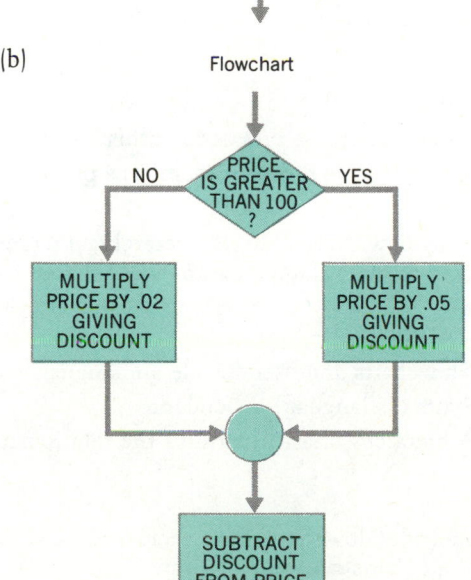

Pseudocode

```
IF    Price is Greater Than 100
          Multiply Price by .05
                    Giving Discount
ELSE
          Multiply Price by .02
                    Giving Discount
ENDIF
Subtract Discount from Price
```

(c)

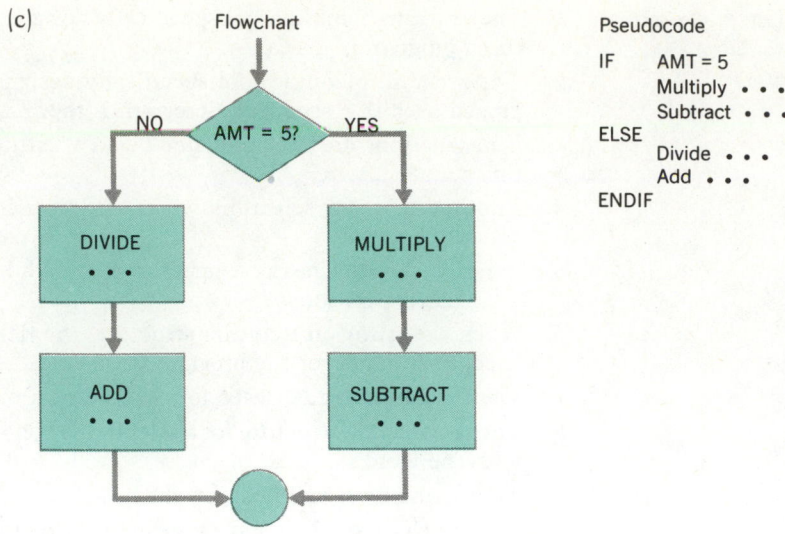

Flowchart

Pseudocode

```
IF      AMT = 5
        Multiply  • • •
        Subtract  • • •
ELSE
        Divide  • • •
        Add  • • •
ENDIF
```

(d)

CASE Structure
Flowchart

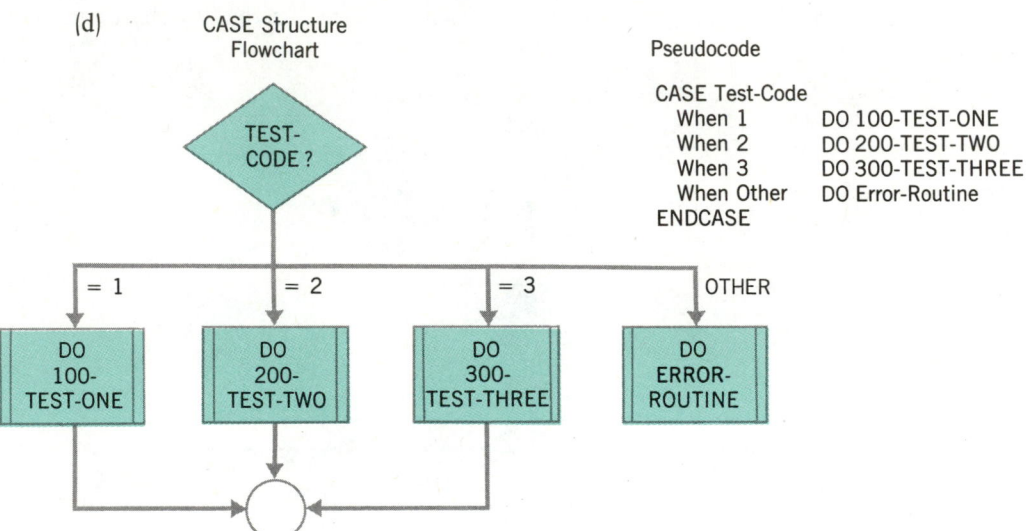

Pseudocode

```
CASE Test-Code
     When 1        DO 100-TEST-ONE
     When 2        DO 200-TEST-TWO
     When 3        DO 300-TEST-THREE
     When Other    DO Error-Routine
ENDCASE
```

Solutions: True-False

1. T
2. F—Usually they use one or the other.
3. F—A flowchart is not very useful as a planning tool if it is drawn after a program.
4. T
5. F—"Top-down" refers to the hierarchical representation of modules; "structured" refers to the fact that a program uses the four basic logical control structures in its design.
6. T
7. T—Flowcharts and pseudocode are language-independent.
8. F—Syntax is language-dependent.
9. F—A hierarchy chart illustrates the relationships among modules.
10. T

Solutions: Fill in the Blanks

1. pseudocode (Flowcharts have been used for several decades and were not originally developed for structured programs.)
2. hierarchy or structure chart

3. sequence
4. IF/ELSE/END or IF-ELSE-ENDIF
5. DO group
6. exit
7. a predefined process
8. IF; ENDIF
9. structure chart or visual table of contents (VTOC)
10. operations

Solutions: General Questions
(a) No
(b) Yes
(c) Yes
(d) Yes

V. The Application of Structured Concepts

A. Subroutines

One way to code structured programs in RPG is with the use of subroutines. A *subroutine* is a self-contained module that includes a series of operations that can be executed from anywhere in a program. Each of the predefined process modules referenced previously could become statements within a subroutine to be executed at the appropriate time within the Calculation Specifications. There are two main reasons for coding subroutines in a program:

1. Using a top-down, structured approach, a main module can call and execute subroutines as needed. Each subroutine is an entity in itself designed to perform a single function, such as calculating totals, printing a series of lines, or executing an end-of-job routine. Consequently, these shorter, precise modules are easier to modify and debug. They also help to make the logic of a program much easier to follow.
2. If the same series of operations is to be executed from more than one point in a program, it can be specified as a subroutine and executed as needed. Specifying a series of operations once as a subroutine will reduce coding and make more efficient use of primary storage.

A subroutine may be either an internal subroutine or an exteral subroutine:

1. An **internal subroutine** is part of the actual RPG program, and therefore, part of the compiled program.
2. An **external subroutine** is independent of the program and called into the program from a library when needed. External subroutines are available for use in many programs. A sequence check routine, error procedure, and control total routine are examples of external subroutines that may be called into different programs as needed. External subroutines are rarely used in today's RPG environment and will not be discussed in this text.

1. Internal Subroutines

Internal subroutines are specified on the Calculation Specifications form *after* all other processing operations. Even so, they may be executed at any point in the calculations.

Figure 5.8 illustrates the specifications required to execute a subroutine and how subroutines must be defined in the program. In this example the subroutine name is SR400. "EXSR SR400" is the instruction that executes or performs the subroutine.

The actual subroutine can be specified with SR in columns 7–8 to distinguish it from other parts of the program. The SR specification is optional on IBM mid-range computers but is recommended to help distinguish subroutine modules from mainline specifications. It should be noted that for some compilers the SR in columns 7–8 is required.

In this example, SR400 is executed at two different points in the program, on line 010 and line 040. After each execution, control returns to the operation directly following EXSR. The second EXSR operation is controlled with indicator 77 and therefore will be executed only when indicator 77 is on. It is important to understand that subroutines can be executed at any point on the Calculation Specifications form and can be executed more than once.

The actual subroutine or module itself specified as SR400 will be located at the end of the Calculation Specifications form. The beginning of the subroutine will be identified with a BEGSR statement, and an ENDSR statement will be used to terminate or end the subroutine. Let us consider these different parts of a subroutine.

2. BEGSR (Begin Subroutine)

The **BEGSR** operation code (designating "beginning of subroutine") must be the first statement of the subroutine, thus serving as its *entry point*. To identify the beginning of a subroutine, BEGSR is specified as the operation code (columns 29–32). It is specified on the same line as the subroutine name, specified in Factor 1. The subroutine name can be 1–6 characters in length and must begin with an alphabetic character. The remaining characters can be any combination or alphabetic or numeric characters. Subroutine names cannot contain blanks. These names must be unique. Essentially, subroutine names follow the same rules as field names.

Figure 5.8
Defining and executing a subroutine.

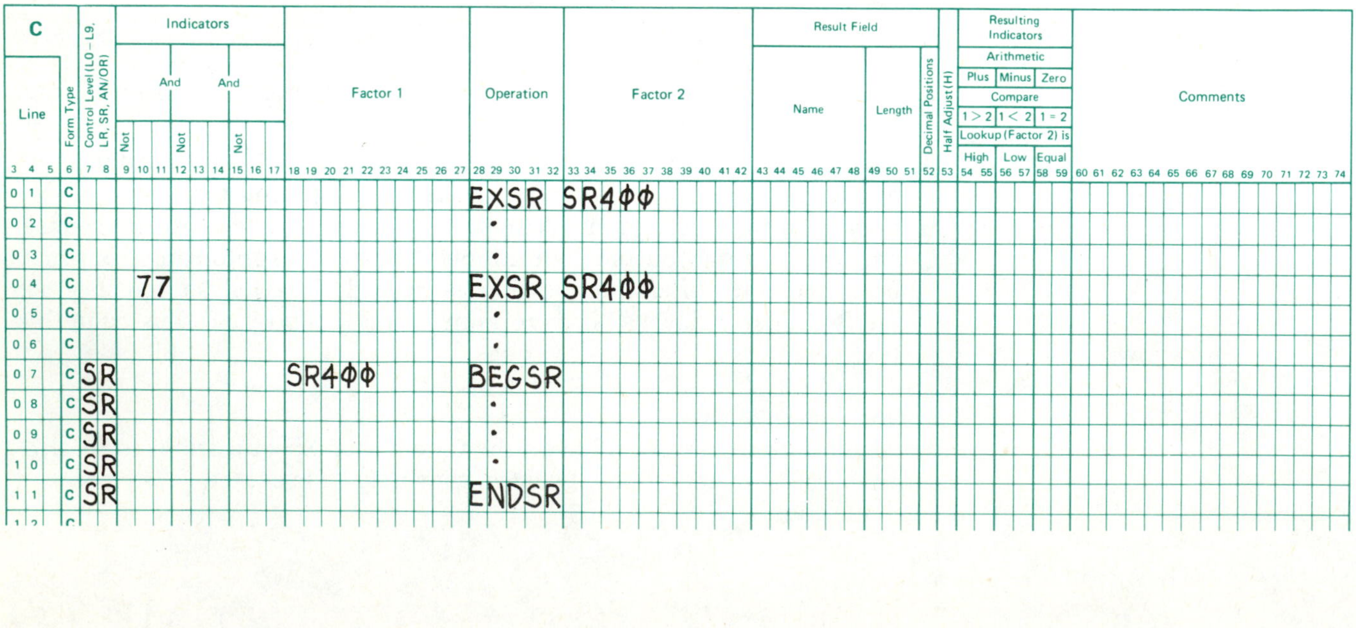

3. ENDSR (End Subroutine)

The **ENDSR** operation code (designating "end of subroutine") must be the last statement of a subroutine, thus serving to terminate the subroutine. When the ENDSR statement is executed, program control is transferred back to the first operation following the specific EXSR operation that executed the subroutine.

4. EXSR (Execute Subroutine)

To execute an internal subroutine from anywhere in a program, the **EXSR** (Execute Subroutine) operation code is used. The operations between the BEGSR and ENDSR statements are executed and then control returns to the operation directly following the specific EXSR operation that executed the module or subroutine. The subroutine name in Factor 2 of an EXSR operation must be the same as the name in Factor 1 of the BEGSR statement to be executed. Moreover, the *same* subroutine may be executed from several points in a program. A program may have more than one subroutine. If more than one subroutine is specified, a subroutine may not be contained within another subroutine as shown here:

Incorrect Coding

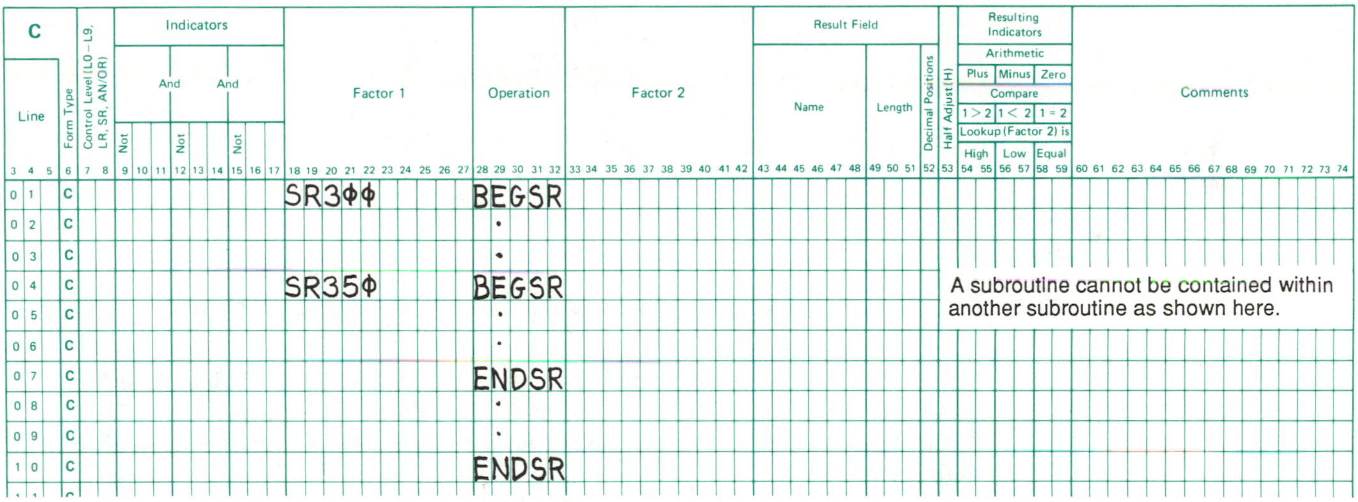

Line	Factor 1	Operation	Factor 2	Comments
0 1	SR3ØØ	BEGSR		
0 2		•		
0 3		•		
0 4	SR35Ø	BEGSR		A subroutine cannot be contained within another subroutine as shown here.
0 5		•		
0 6				
0 7		ENDSR		
0 8		•		
0 9				
1 0		ENDSR		

In addition, a subroutine *cannot* execute itself:

Incorrect Coding

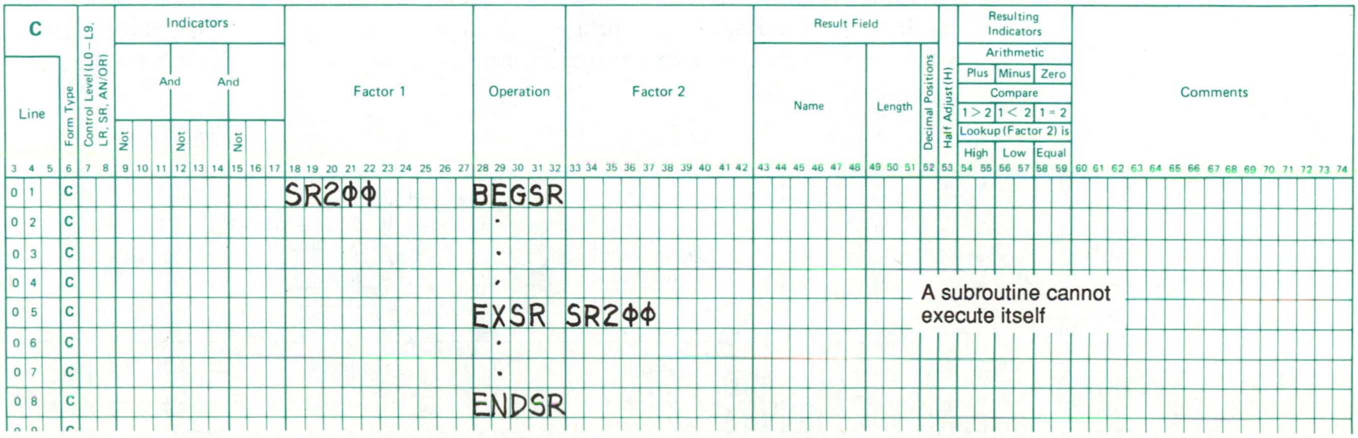

Line	Factor 1	Operation	Factor 2	Comments
0 1	SR2ØØ	BEGSR		
0 2		•		
0 3		•		
0 4		•		
0 5		EXSR	SR2ØØ	A subroutine cannot execute itself
0 6		•		
0 7				
0 8		ENDSR		

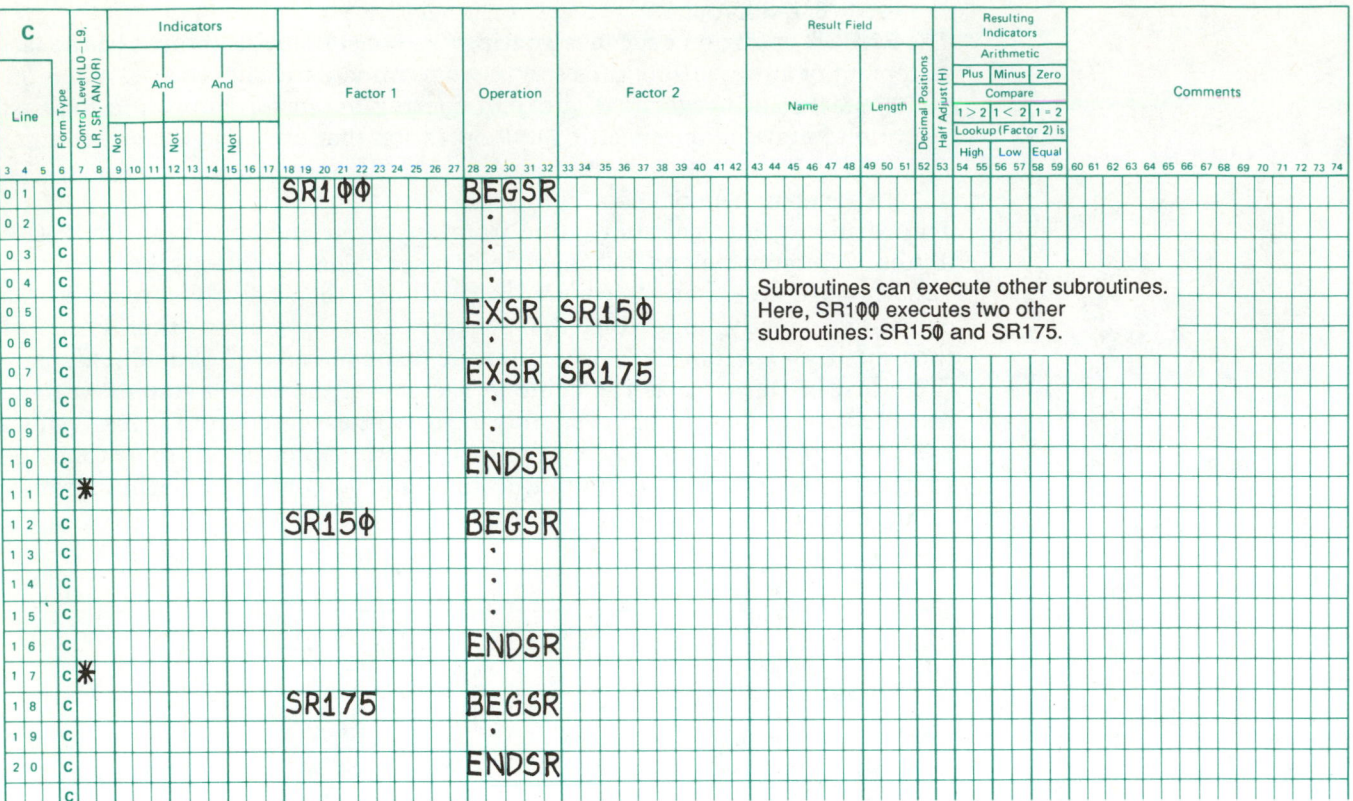

Figure 5.9
A subroutine can execute
other subroutines.

However, subroutines can execute other subroutines, as shown in Figure 5.9.

EXSR may be conditioned by indicators in columns 7–8 or 9–17 on the Calculation Specifications form to control when a subroutine is to be executed. If no indicators are specified for the EXSR operation, the subroutine identified in Factor 2 is always executed.

Each subroutine should be viewed as an independent entity. Thus, if branching (coded with GOTO or CABxx in RPG) cannot be avoided in a subroutine, it should cause a branch to another point *within* the subroutine or to the ENDSR statement and not cause a branch external to the subroutine. To branch to a point outside the subroutine can cause logic errors.

With the use of internal subroutines, the modular approach to programming can be realized. That is, if a program is to perform edit functions, tally control totals, and check for errors, the calculations can be coded in the main or calling module as follows:

The RPG program is executed using the preceding three modules. At SETUP, indicator 02 will be turned on, which means that SETUP will be executed only *once* at the beginning. After indicator 02 is on, the PROCES module performs all calculations:

Line	Form Type	Control Level (L0–L9, LR, SR, AN/OR)	Indicators And Not	And Not	Not	Factor 1	Operation	Factor 2	Result Field Name	Length	Decimal Positions	Half Adjust (H)	Resulting Indicators Arithmetic Plus/1>2	Minus/1<2	Zero/1=2 Lookup(Factor 2) is High Low Equal	Comments
0 1	0 C	*				PERFORM ALL INITIALIZING										
0 2	0 C	*														
0 3	0 C	SR				SETUP	BEGSR									
0 4	0 C	SR					•									
0 5	0 C	SR					•									
0 6	0 C	SR					•									
0 7	0 C	SR					SETON							02		
0 8	0 C	SR					ENDSR									

WRAPUP performs all end-of-job functions:

Line	Form Type	Control Level (L0–L9, LR, SR, AN/OR)	Indicators And Not	And Not	Not	Factor 1	Operation	Factor 2	Result Field Name	Length	Decimal Positions	Half Adjust (H)	Resulting Indicators Arithmetic Plus/1>2	Minus/1<2	Zero/1=2 Lookup(Factor 2) is High Low Equal	Comments
0 1	0 C	SR				WRAPUP	BEGSR									
0 2	0 C	SR					•									
0 3	0 C	SR					•									
0 4	0 C	SR					•									
0 5	0 C	SR					ENDSR									

PROCES is executed from the main module for all records with indicator 01 on; 02 will remain on for the entire run. Thus, PROCES is executed for each record read. At PROCES, indicator 99 is turned on when the last record has been processed:

Line	Form Type	Control Level (L0–L9, LR, SR, AN/OR)	Indicators And Not	And Not	Not	Factor 1	Operation	Factor 2	Result Field Name	Length	Decimal Positions	Half Adjust (H)	Resulting Indicators Arithmetic Plus/1>2	Minus/1<2	Zero/1=2 Lookup(Factor 2) is High Low Equal	Comments
0 1	0 C	SR				PROCES	BEGSR									
0 2	0 C	SR					•									
0 3	0 C	SR					•									
0 4	0 C	SR					•									
0 5	0 C	SR				ACCTNO	COMP	99999							99	
0 6	0 C	SR					ENDSR									

At the end-of-job, when 99 has been turned on, WRAPUP is executed.

To code this entire procedure under the control of a main module, we would have the following:

C	Form Type	Control Level (L0–L9, LR, SR, AN/OR)	Indicators							Factor 1	Operation	Factor 2	Result Field				Resulting Indicators				Comments
Line			And Not	Not	And Not								Name	Length	Decimal Positions	Half Adjust (H)	Plus 1>2 High	Minus 1<2 Low	Zero 1=2 Equal		
0 1	0 C		0 1								EXSR	MAIN									
0 2	0 C	*																			
0 3	0 C	SR								MAIN	BEGSR										
0 4	0 C	SRN0 2									EXSR	SETUP									
0 5	0 C	SR	0 2 N9 9								EXSR	PROCESS									
0 6	0 C	SR	9 9								EXSR	WRAPUP									
0 7	0 C	SR									ENDSR										

Thus the main sequence of steps will themselves be under the control of a module called MAIN.

More than one programmer can be called on to code and debug each of these subroutines independently. Moreover, if a modification is required to one subroutine, it will not affect the logic of other modules. In this way, subroutines can be *tested* independently.

The modular approach to programming, using internal subroutines, helps to standardize the programming activity and makes it easier to code, debug, and modify programs. It also makes it easier for managers to assess individual programs and to evaluate the programming proficiency of their staff.

Figure 5.10 illustrates the use of internal subroutines in a program that produces a weekly payroll register. After studying this program, you will see that it contains three subroutines that are executed from the mainline processing. Subroutine SR100 is executed if indicator 10 is on, that is, if the employee hours (EHRS) is equal to or less than 40. If EHRS is greater than 40, indicator 11 is turned on. This means that the employee has worked overtime and subroutine SR200 is to be executed to perform the overtime calculations. Finally, subroutine SR300 is executed to accumulate the final totals. Thus, the main module or series of calculations from lines 31–34 is greatly simplified. It is easier to code and read. In a top-down manner, you indicate that one of two methods for calculating pay will be executed depending on the outcome of the comparison. Then a subroutine will be executed to accumulate final totals. The details for each module are then specified in a top-down manner.

Figure 5.10
Use of internal subroutines in
a payroll program.

```
    ....+....1....+....2....+....3....+....4....+....5....+....6....+...
 1 0001   ******************************************************************
 2 0002   * THIS PROGRAM PRODUCES A WEEKLY PAYROLL REGISTER. EMPLOYEES
 3 0003   * WORKING OVER 40 HOURS ARE PAID TIME AND A HALF FOR OVERTIME
 4 0004   * HOURS. FINAL TOTALS ARE CALCULATED FOR REGULAR HOURS, OVER-
 5 0005   * TIME HOURS, REGULAR PAY, OVERTIME PAY AND TOTAL GROSS PAY.
 6 0006   ******************************************************************
 7 0007   *
 8 0008   FPR100    IP  F    150            DISK
 9 0009   FREPORT   O   F    132      OF    PRINTER
10 0010   *
11 0011   IPR100    NS
12 0012   I                                      1   30EEMPNO
13 0013   I                                      4   23 ELNAME
14 0014   I                                     24   33 EFNAME
15 0015   I                                     34   372EHRS
16 0016   I                                     38   412ERATE
17 0017   I#WORK        DS
18 0018   I                                      1   52#REG
19 0019   I                                      6   92#OTHRS
20 0020   I                                     10  132#OTRTE
```

Figure 5.10
(continued)

```
    ....+....1....+....2....+....3....+....4....+....5....+....6....+...
21 0021 I                                                14   182#OTPAY
22 0022 I                                                19   232#GROSS
23 0023 I                                                24   282#THRS
24 0024 I                                                29   342#TREG
25 0025 I                                                35   402#TOTPY
26 0026 I                                                41   462#TGROS
27 0027 I                                                47   512#TOTHR
28 0028 *
29 0029 *                                      MAIN-LINE-RTN
30 0030 *
31 0031 C            EHRS      COMP 40                              111010
32 0032 C    10                EXSR SR100
33 0033 C    11                EXSR SR200
34 0034 C                      EXSR SR300
35 0035 *    SUBROUTINES
36 0036 *                                      100-NO-OVERTIME-PAY-RTN
37 0037 CSR          SR100     BEGSR
38 0038 CSR          EHRS      MULT ERATE      #REG        H
39 0039 CSR                    Z-ADD0          #OTHRS
40 0040 CSR                    Z-ADD0          #OTPAY
41 0041 CSR                    ENDSR
42 0042 *
43 0043 *                                      200-PAY-WITH-OVERTIME-RTN
44 0044 CSR          SR200     BEGSR
45 0045 CSR          EHRS      SUB  40.00      #OTHRS
46 0046 CSR          ERATE     MULT 1.5        #OTRTE      H
47 0047 CSR          #OTHRS    MULT #OTRTE     #OTPAY      H
48 0048 CSR          ERATE     MULT 40.00      #REG        H
49 0049 CSR                    ADD  #OTHRS     #TOTHR
50 0050 CSR                    ADD  #OTPAY     #TOTPY
51 0051 CSR                    ENDSR
52 0052 *
53 0053 *                                      300-FINAL-TOTALS-RTN
54 0054 CSR          SR300     BEGSR
55 0055 CSR          #REG      ADD  #OTPAY     #GROSS
56 0056 CSR                    ADD  EHRS       #THRS
57 0057 CSR                    ADD  #REG       #TREG
58 0058 CSR                    ADD  #GROSS     #TGROS
59 0059 CSR                    ENDSR
60 0060 *
61 0061 OREPORT   H   01   1P
62 0062 O      OR          OF
63 0063 O                                      10 'PR5010XR'
64 0064 O                            UDATE Y   30
65 0065 O                                      47 'P A Y R O L L'
66 0066 O                                      65 'R E G I S T E R'
67 0067 O                                      92 'PAGE'
68 0068 O                            PAGE      97
69 0069 O         H   03   1P
70 0070 O      OR          OF
71 0071 O                                      10 'EMPLOYEE'
72 0072 O                                      64 'REG      O/T     PAY'
73 0073 O                                      86 'REGULAR   OVERTIME'
74 0074 O                                      95 'TOTAL'
75 0075 O         H   104  1P
76 0076 O      OR          OF
77 0077 O                                       9 'NUMBER'
78 0078 O                                      32 'EMPLOYEE NAME'
80 0080 O                                      65 'HRS      HRS       RATE'
81 0081 O                                      86 'EARNINGS   EARNINGS'
82 0082 O                                      97 'GROSS PAY'
83 0083 *
84 0084 O         D   1    N1P
85 0085 O                            EEMPNO     7
86 0086 O                            ELNAME    31
87 0087 O                            EFNAME    42
88 0088 O                            EHRS   1  49
89 0099 O                            #OTHRS1   57
90 0090 O                            ERATE  1  65
91 0091 O                            #REG   1  75
92 0092 O                            #OTPAY1   85
93 0093 O                            #GROSS1   96
94 0094 *
95 0095 O         T   2    LR
96 0096 O                                      42 '*** FINAL TOTALS'
97 0097 O                            #THRS  1  49
98 0098 O                            #TOTHR1   57
99 0099 O                            #TREG  1  75 '$'
100 0100 O                           #TOTPY1   85 '$'
101 0101 O                           #TGROS1   96 '$'
```

5. Naming Modules or Subroutines

In summary, a module or set of related instructions is defined as a subroutine. Subroutines must be identified in a program using a unique name. That name can be a combination of letters and digits up to six characters. We will, however, establish a standard method for naming subroutines in all programs. First, it is difficult to choose a meaningful name, one that describes the subroutine. Names such as MNMDLE for MAIN-MODULE, PRODAT for PROCESS-DATA, and ERRRTE for ERROR-ROUTINE are *not* descriptive in that they are meaningful only to the person who wrote the program; others would have no idea of the type of instructions within the module. Hence, a different naming convention is required.

If you refer back to hierarchy charts discussed earlier in this chapter, you will see that full descriptive names were used to identify routines or modules. In addition, a numbering system was often used as a prefix for each module. To establish subroutine names in our examples, we will use SR to identify the module as a subroutine followed by the prefix number associated with the module in the hierarchy chart. The numbering system 100, 200, and so on will distinguish these modules from one another and make the module *stand out* from field names. Hence, subroutine names will be determined by appending the three-digit numbers from the hierarchy chart to the prefix SR. In doing so, the hierarchy chart acts as documentation along with the program. Subroutine names are given the number designation to provide information on their location. That is, subroutine SR100 precedes subroutine SR200, which precedes subroutine SR300, and so forth. You will find that in very large programs that require several pages for listing, this type of numbering makes it much easier to locate a module during debugging or program modification. In addition, the full descriptive name used in the hierarchy chart for each module should be placed in the subroutine as a comment line (asterisk in column 7).

This numbering system usually uses intervals of 100 for ease of reading and to allow for possible insertions later on. Prior to each subroutine, you could use a series of comment lines to define the purpose of the module.

B. The Sequence Structure in RPG

We already know how to use sequence as a logical control structure in our programs. We simply specify each line in the order we want it executed. *Subroutines* help enhance the sequence structure by allowing us to divide long sequences of instructions into separate independent modules consisting of a series of related instructions.

C. The IFxx/ELSE/END Operation in RPG

Here, we will focus on selection or the IFxx/ELSE/END operation structure, which permits us to execute an operation or series of operations depending on the result of a comparison of two fields or literals. It is a more structured way of comparing fields than using the COMP instruction.

The IFxx operation can be specified using the IFxx/ELSE/END instruction format or the IFxx/END instruction format with no ELSE. The following specifications illustrate the use of both of these formats:

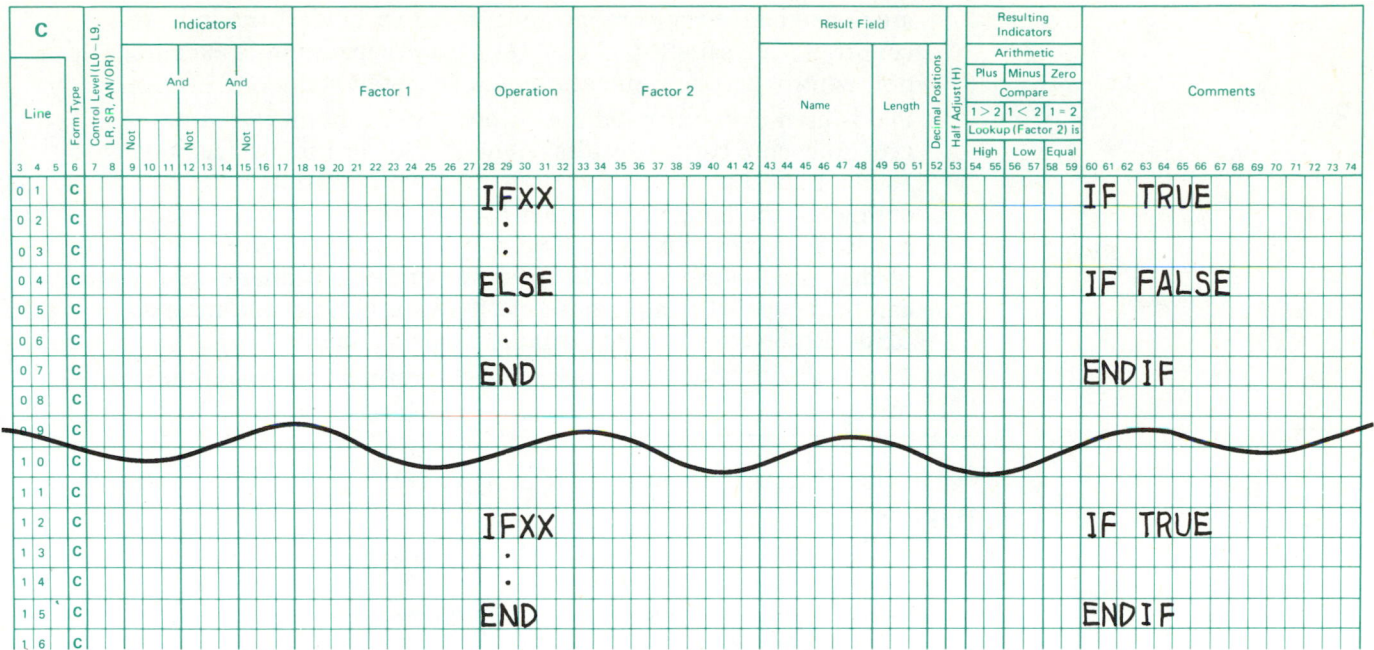

The `IFxx/ELSE/END` operation compares the contents of Factor 1 to the contents of Factor 2.

The `xx` portion of the operation identifies the comparison operation that is to take place between Factor 1 and Factor 2. It is the controlling factor for the outcome of the comparison and determines which of two possible paths the program will take.

The relational operator, specified as `xx`, indicates the comparison test to be performed between Factor 1 and Factor 2. The following relational operators can be used to replace `xx`:

Relational Operator	Comparison Test
GT	Factor 1 greater than Factor 2.
LT	Factor 1 less than Factor 2.
EQ	Factor 1 equal to Factor 2.
NE	Factor 1 not equal to Factor 2.
GE	Factor 1 greater than or equal to Factor 2.
LE	Factor 1 less than or equal to Factor 2.

That is, you would code `IFGT`, `IFLT`, and so on, *not* `IFxx`. We will see later that the CASE operation (`CASxx`), the Compare and Branch operation (`CABxx`), the DO WHILE operation (`DOWxx`), and the DO UNTIL operation (`DOUxx`) all support the use of a relational operator to test for the existence of a condition that relates Factor 1 to Factor 2.

Following is a summary of the rules used in the execution of the `IF/ELSE/END` operation.

SUMMARY OF IF/ELSE/END EXECUTION RULES

1. The indicators in columns 7–8 and 9–17 are specified to control execution of the operation. They are called Conditional Indicators and

are tested before the comparison test is executed. If the indicator conditions are satisfied, the IF/ELSE/END operation is executed; if not, control passes to the associated END statement.

2. Fields used in comparison operations must contain the same data type to ensure correct results. Hence, fields or literals specified in Factor 1 and Factor 2 of the IF/ELSE/END operation must be defined in the program as either *both* numeric or *both* alphanumeric. They may contain a field name, a literal, an array element (to be discussed later), or a data structure subfield. Alphanumeric fields can be compared to alphanumeric fields or literals, and numeric fields can be compared to numeric fields or literals.

3. The IFxx/ELSE/END operation must terminate with an END statement.

The flowchart that corresponds to an IFxx/ELSE/END selection structure is as follows:

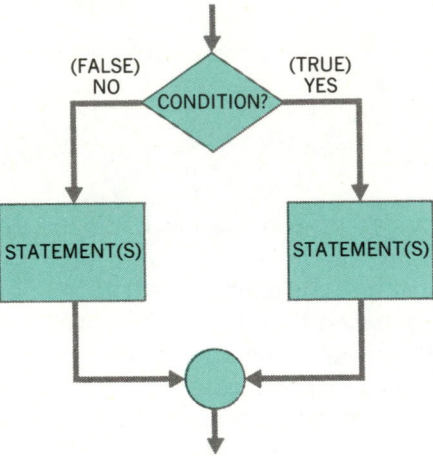

The pseudocode is as follows:

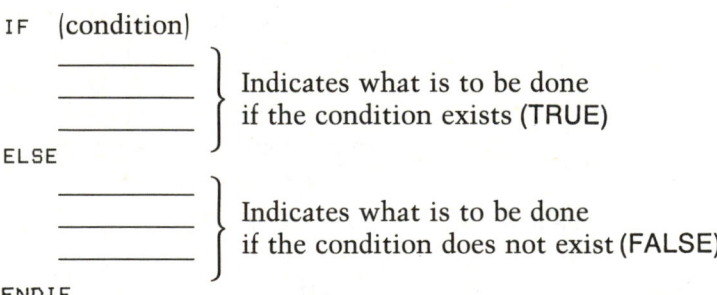

ELSE Option

The ELSE is optional when using the RPG IFxx structure. If an operation is to be executed only if a condition exists (is true) and nothing is to be done if the condition does not exist, the entire ELSE option may be omitted. The structure, then, would be as follows:

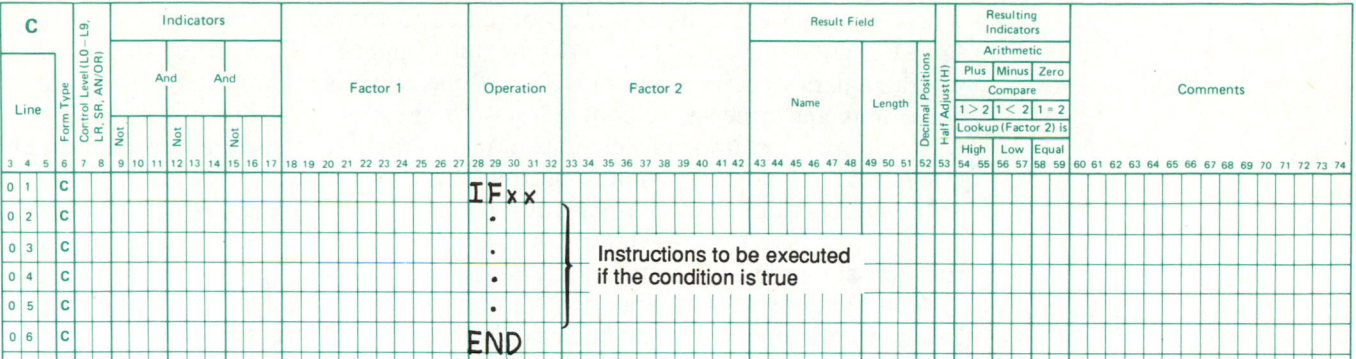

If conditional indicators (column 9–17) are specified to control execution of an IFxx operation, they are tested before the IFxx condition is tested. If the indicator conditions are satisfied, the IFxx operation is executed; if not, control passes to the associated END statement, even if an ELSE option is specified.

Basic Conditional Statements

We define **conditional statements** as those that are executed only when the condition specified by the relational operator has been satisfied. As stated earlier, the **IFxx/ELSE/END** operation permits execution of conditional statements depending on the result of a comparison of two fields or literals. Such conditions consist of the following:

1. A single action conditional test.
2. The Not condition.
3. A double action conditional test with an ELSE branch option.
4. Testing for a range of values.
5. Testing multiple conditions.
6. Compound conditions with nesting.

We will now discuss each in detail.

Applications of the IFxx/ELSE/END Operation

Let us consider the IFxx operation by illustrating each of the conditional tests mentioned above.

1. A Single Action Conditional Test

An IFxx/END operation may test for a simple specific relation. That is, instructions are executed only if the condition tested is true. A *simple condition* may be a single test of the following form:

C		Control Level (L0–L9, LR, SR, AN/OR)	Indicators						Factor 1	Operation	Factor 2	Result Field				Resulting Indicators			Comments
				And		And						Name	Length	Decimal Positions	Half Adjust (H)	Arithmetic			
	Form Type		Not		Not		Not									Plus	Minus	Zero	
																Compare			
																1>2	1<2	1=2	
Line																Lookup (Factor 2) is			
																High	Low	Equal	
3 4 5	6	7 8	9 10 11	12 13	14	15 16	17	18 19 20 21 22 23 24 25 26 27	28 29 30 31 32	33 34 35 36 37 38 39 40 41 42	43 44 45 46 47 48	49 50 51	52	53	54 55	56 57	58 59	60 61 62 63 64 65 66 67 68 69 70 71 72 73 74
0 1	C							SALES	IFGT	QUOTA								
0 2	C							SALES	MULT	.Ø3	#COMM							
0 3	C								END									
0 4	C																	

The SALES field in Factor 1 is compared to the QUOTA field in Factor 2. If SALES *is greater than* (GT) QUOTA, the MULT operation is executed to calculate #COMM, a data structure subfield. The IF operation is terminated with the END statement and processing continues with the first statement following the END statement. #COMM, as a data structure subfield, has its length and number of decimal positions designated on the Input Specifications form.

If SALES *is not* greater than QUOTA, the MULT operation is *not executed.* Control passes to the associated END statement and processing continues with the first statement following the END statement.

Note that both SALES and QUOTA must be numeric fields. (SALES is used in an arithmetic operation and both fields must be of the same type.)

Recall that the ELSE option is optional in an IF statement.

2. The Not Condition

There are times when you might want to execute a series of operations only if a certain condition *does not* exist. This is equivalent to testing for the negative. For example, if we wanted to count all employees, *excluding* those in the Sales department, the following coding could be used:

Example of a Not operator

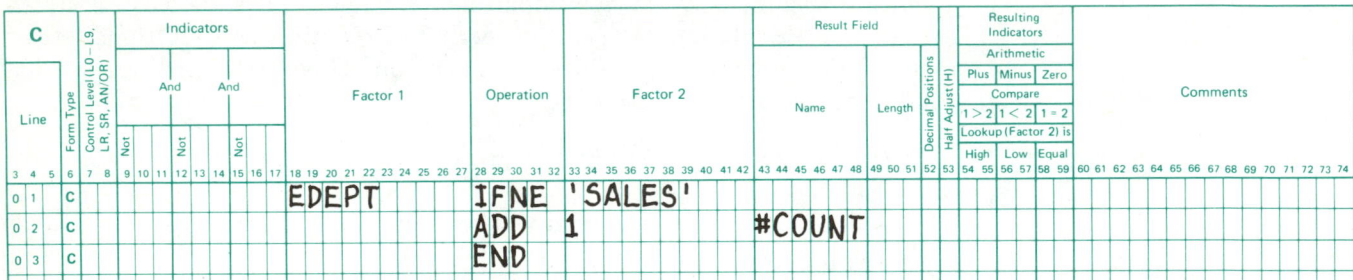

Here, 1 is added to the counter field #COUNT when EDEPT is *not equal* (NE) to the alphanumeric literal 'SALES'. Note that EDEPT should be defined as an alphanumeric field to make this comparison correct since EDEPT is compared to an alphanumeric literal.

3. A Conditional Test with an ELSE Branch Option

We learned from the first two examples that we test for a condition, then execute operations if the result of that test is true. However, there are times when a test is required and operations are to be executed for both the true and false conditions. By using the ELSE option, we can execute operations if the initial condition is *not met* or is "false."

A simple conditional operation can be expanded using the ELSE option to allow for execution of two different sets of operations depending on the outcome of the initial test. The example in Figure 5.11 illustrates an IFxx conditional test with an ELSE branch option.

If the field containing the employee's shift worked (ESHIFT) is *equal to* 2, the ADD operation is performed to add .25 cents to the employee's rate field (ERATE). The result is stored in the data structure subfield #RATE. The second part of the operation, beginning with the ELSE option, is ignored and the program continues executing with the first operation following the END statement.

If the two fields are not equal, the ADD operation is *not executed.* Control

C	Line	Form Type	Control Level (L0—L9, LR, SR, AN/OR)	Indicators							Factor 1	Operation	Factor 2	Result Field					Resulting Indicators							Comments
				And		And								Name	Length	Decimal Positions	Half Adjust (H)		Arithmetic							
					Not		Not		Not										Plus	Minus	Zero					
																			Compare							
																			1 > 2	1 < 2	1 = 2					
																			Lookup (Factor 2) is							
																			High	Low	Equal					
0 1		C									ESHIFT	IFEQ	2													
0 2		C									ERATE	ADD	.25	#RATE												
0 3		C										ELSE														
0 4		C									ERATE	MULT	1.1Ø	#RATE												
0 5		C										END														
0 6		C									#RATE	MULT	EHRS	#GROSS												

Figure 5.11
Illustration of an IFxx conditional test with an ELSE branch option.

passes to the ELSE statement and ERATE is multiplied by 110 percent (1.10) with the product stored in #RATE.

In either case, the program continues executing with the first operation following the END statement, the calculation of the gross pay.

Executing More than One Operation

The IFxx/ELSE/END operation format also indicates that more than one operation may be executed for each condition. Thus, the following example will perform two Z-ADD operations if RATE1 is equal to RATE2, or two MULT operations if RATE1 and RATE2 are not equal:

C	Line	Form Type	Control Level (L0—L9, LR, SR, AN/OR)	Indicators							Factor 1	Operation	Factor 2	Result Field					Resulting Indicators							Comments
				And		And								Name	Length	Decimal Positions	Half Adjust (H)		Arithmetic							
					Not		Not		Not										Plus	Minus	Zero					
																			Compare							
																			1 > 2	1 < 2	1 = 2					
																			Lookup (Factor 2) is							
																			High	Low	Equal					
0 1		C									RATE1	IFEQ	RATE2													
0 2		C										Z-ADD	RATE1	PRICE												
0 3		C										Z-ADD	Ø.1Ø	DISCT												
0 4		C										ELSE														
0 5		C									RATE2	MULT	1.Ø5	PRICE												
0 6		C										MULT	1.12	DISCT												
0 7		C										END														

If *numerous* operations are required if a condition is met or not met, it is best to code the operations in a separate module:

```
SALES  IFGE QUOTA
       EXSR SR100
       END
```

This results in a more structured, top-down program.

Ending Conditional Statements with an END Terminator

As indicated, several statements may appear within one conditional operation. Therefore, it is imperative to identify the termination point of the operation.

The END statement is used to specify the boundary limit or closing of an IF operation. The statement contains the word "END" in positions 28–30 of the Operation Field; all other columns are left blank. Let us consider the importance of the END statement using Figure 5.11 again as an illustration.

The placement of the END statement can affect the logic in an IF operation. If the END statement were to be inadvertently placed after the second MULT operation, then #RATE   MULT EHRS   #GROSS would be considered part of the ELSE branch and would not be executed if ESHIFT was equal to 2. You can see, then, that the placement of the END terminator can significantly affect the logic.

Nested Conditional

A **nested conditional** is a conditional in which an IF operation itself can contain additional IF operations. Conditional tests can be nested by using multiple IFxx operations. Multiple IFxx operations are executed beginning with the first or outer level IFxx statement; if the result of the comparison is *true*, the next level IFxx statement is executed. Let us continue with our examination of IFxx operations by considering three programs using nested IFxx operations.

4. Testing for a Range of Values (Multiple Conditions)

A test for a *range of values* can be accomplished by using nested IFxx operations as shown below. In this example, we wish to add 1 to the counter field, #COUNT, if an employee has between 5 and 10 years of service (EYRSER). Nesting IFxx operations in this manner results in an AND condition between the IFxx operations. That is, to follow EYRSER IFGE 5 with EYRSER IFLE 10 is the same as saying "IF EYRSER is greater than or equal to 5 and less than or equal to 10." When IFxx operations are nested, or follow one another, we have an AND condition. Consequently, the conditioned operations are executed only if the first condition AND the second condition are true. The result is that two conditions must be met before the conditioned operation(s), in this example, the ADD operation, is executed:

Line	Form Type		Indicators						Factor 1	Operation	Factor 2	Result Field Name	Length					Comments
0 1	C								EYRSER	IFGE	5							
0 2	C								EYRSER	IFLE	10							
0 3	C									ADD	1	#COUNT						
0 4	C									END								
0 5	C									END								
0 6	C																	

In this example, 1 is added to the counter #COUNT when the years of service field (EYRSER) is between 5 and 10. First, EYRSER is tested to see if it contains a value *equal to* or *greater than* 5. If the test is *true*, EYRSER is tested to see if the value is *less than* or *equal to* 10. If the second test is *true*, the ADD operation is executed, adding 1 to the #COUNT field.

During the two tests, if EYRSER is *less than* 5 or *greater than* 10, control of the program is transferred to the associated END statement and the ADD operation is not executed. Processing would then continue with the first operation following the second END statement.

5. Testing Multiple Conditions

Consider the nested IFxx operation below. Here we join (AND) the IFxx operations again, not to select a range of values but rather to perform a comparison test based on multiple conditions. In order for the MOVE and ADD operations to be executed, EDEPT (department title) must be *equal to* 'SALES' and EYRSER (years service) must be *greater than* 3 and EMSTAT (marital status) must be *equal to* 'S' (single):

Line	Form Type	Factor 1	Operation	Factor 2	Result Field Name
0 1	C	EDEPT	IFEQ	'SALES'	
0 2	C	EYRSER	IFGT	3	
0 3	C	EMSTAT	IFEQ	'S'	
0 4	C		MOVE	EEMPNO	#EMPNO
0 5	C		ADD	1	#COUNT
0 6	C		END		
0 7	C		END		
0 8	C		END		

Remember, an END statement must terminate each IFxx operation; therefore, three END statements are used to close the multiple conditions.

6. Compound Conditions with Nesting

To illustrate how we might solve a problem with compound IF conditions, let us consider the employees in the Sales department.

The employees in the Sales department (EDEPT = 'SALES') have just finished their yearly review. It was decided that junior sales people, those with a code 'J' in the ELEVEL field, will receive a flat $100.00 increase before calculating the yearly raise. If a person's yearly sales exceeded their quota, they will be given a 7% increase; otherwise they will receive a 5.5% increase in their salary.

Besides the salary increase, the number of vacation days will be increased according to the years of service. For each year of service, employees in the Sales Department will receive an additional half day of vacation rounded up to the nearest full day. Before writing the program, the flowchart or pseudocode in Figure 5.12 should be developed to show the conditions for this problem. Figure 5.13 illustrates the specifications required to accomplish this task.

Self-Test

True-False Questions

T   F

___ ___ 1. A subroutine can be executed from any point on the Calculations Specifications form.

___ ___ 2. RPG cannot use internal subroutines.

___ ___ 3. Internal subroutines are placed first on the Calculation Specifications.

Flowchart

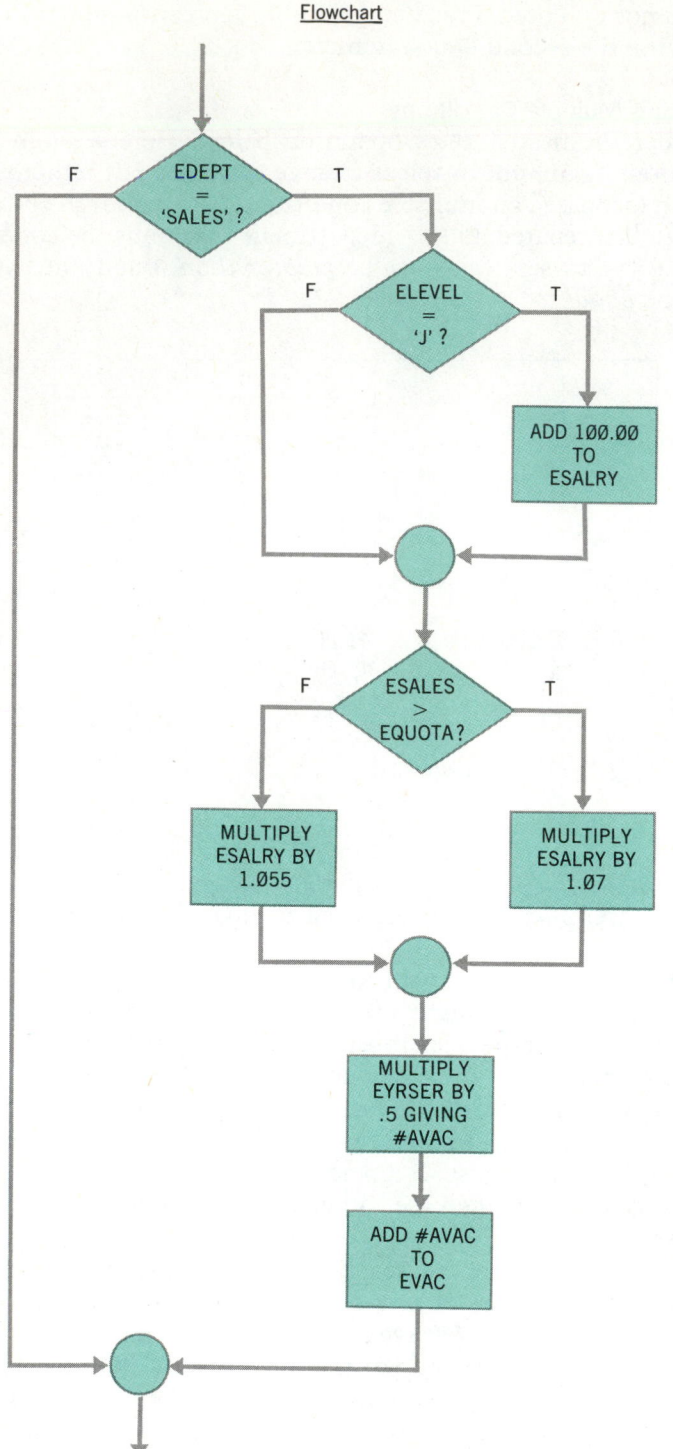

Pseudocode

```
If EDEPT = "SALES"
Then
      If ELEVEL = "J"
      Then
            Add 100 to ESALRY
      End
      If ESALES > EQUOTA
      Then
            Multiply ESALRY by 1.07
      Else
            Multiply ESALRY by 1.055
      End
      Multiply EYRSER by .5 Giving #AVAC
      Add # AVAC to EVAC
Endif
```

Figure 5.12
Flowchart and pseudocode for
the sample problem.

C	Form Type	Control Level (L0—L9, LR, SR, AN/OR)	Indicators						Factor 1	Operation	Factor 2	Result Field		Decimal Positions	Half Adjust (H)	Resulting Indicators			Comments
			And		And							Name	Length			Arithmetic			
Line			Not		Not		Not									Plus	Minus	Zero	
																Compare			
																1>2	1<2	1=2	
																Lookup (Factor 2) is			
																High	Low	Equal	
0 1	C								EDEPT	IFEQ	'SALES'								
0 2	C								ELEVEL	IFEQ	'J'								
0 3	C									ADD	100.00	ESALRY							
0 4	C									END									
0 5	C								ESALES	IFGT	EQUOTA								
0 6	C									MULT	1.07	ESALRY							
0 7	C									ELSE									
0 8	C									MULT	1.055	ESALRY							
0 9	C									END									
1 0	C								EYRSER	MULT	.5	#AVAC			H				
1 1	C									ADD	#AVAC	EVAC							
1 2	C									END									

Figure 5.13
Calculation Specifications
form for the sample problem.

T F

___ ___ 4. The IFxx/ELSE/END operation can be used to perform the same function as the COMP operation.

___ ___ 5. Unlike the COMP operation, the IFxx operation can compare numeric fields to alphanumeric fields.

___ ___ 6. A nested conditional can be an IFxx operation that contains another IFxx operation.

___ ___ 7. An IFxx operation is limited to testing for only one condition.

___ ___ 8. Every IFxx operation must have an ELSE statement.

Fill in the Blanks

1. A _____ is a self-contained module that includes a series of operations to be performed.

2. An _____ subroutine is one that is part of the program, whereas an _____ subroutine is independent of the program.

3. If a hierarchy chart showed a module as *200-List-Inventory-Items*, an RPG subroutine for this module could be called _____ .

4. To execute a subroutine, the _____ operation must be specified.

5. A test for a range of values can be accomplished by using a _____ IFxx operation.

6. The xx portion of an operation specifies the _____ between Factor 1 and Factor 2.

7. All logical control structures must terminate with an _____ statement.

Solutions: True-False

1. T
2. F
3. F—They are placed at the end of the Calculation Specifications form.
4. T
5. F—Both fields or literals must be of the same data type.
6. T
7. F
8. F

1. subroutine
2. internal; external
3. SR200 (the first line of the subroutine should be a comment line such as : * 200-
   List-Inventory-Items)
4. EXSR
5. nested
6. relationship
7. END

D. The CASE (CASxx) Operation In RPG

The *case structure* is a logical control structure used to *compare* the contents of two fields or literals and *select or execute* one of several subroutines as a result of that comparison. For example, if a code is equal to 'S', the salary payroll routine is to be executed; if it is an 'H', the hourly payroll routine is to be executed, and so on.

As with IFxx, the xx portion of the **CASE (CASxx) operation** specifies the relationship between Factor 1 and Factor 2. This relationship must be satisfied before a subroutine named in the Result Field is selected for execution. In addition to the xx options previously discussed, a blank is also valid with the CASxx operation. A blank is considered a nonconditional operation because no comparison test is performed. If the nonconditional (CASE) operation is executed, the subroutine located in the Result Field will be executed in all instances.

With the case structure, then, we perform one of several possible subroutines, depending on the condition tested.

CASxx offers some advantages over the IFxx/ELSE/END structure. CASxx is easier to read, especially when the IFxx structure contains a high level of nesting or when each condition contains many lines of RPG specifications. Also, the CASxx structure can be used to separate the program into sections or modules in order to implement the top-down approach.

In the following problem, each record contains a job classification level code to designate which level an employee is currently working at. The codes 'J' (Junior), 'I' (Intermediate), 'S' (Senior), and 'E' (Executive) are used to determine which subroutine from a group is to be executed. Moreover, if the inputted code is not one of the codes specified, an error routine is to be executed. The CASE structure flowchart and pseudocode in Figure 5.14 illustrate the use of the CASxx operation to solve this problem. The RPG CASxx specifications for the problem are shown in Figure 5.15.

The first CASEQ operation (on line 04) compares the employee's job classification level (ELEVEL) field to 'J'. If ELEVEL is equal to 'J', subroutine SR100 specified in the Result Field is executed. The program transfers control to the END statement and processing continues with the operation specified on line 10.

If ELEVEL is *not equal* to 'J', the program executes the next CASEQ operation on line 05.

The program continues in this manner, that is, passing control down the CASxx operations until one of the following three conditions is met:

1. The tested condition is satisfied and the corresponding subroutine is executed; then the case structure is terminated.
2. If no case operation is executed in the first four lines of the case structure, then the CAS operation containing the blank operation (CAS) is encountered. Since no comparison test is performed here, the program ex-

Figure 5.14
Example of a CASE structure
flowchart and pseudocode.

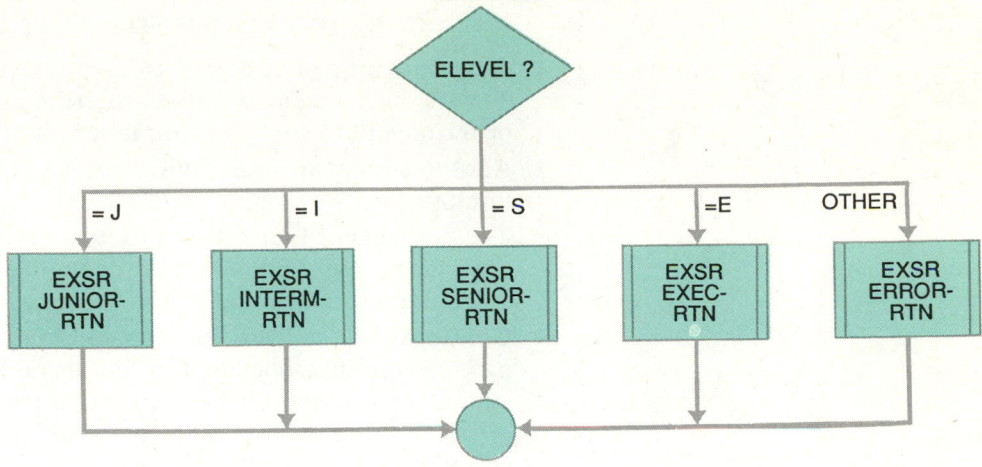

Pseudocode

```
CASE ELEVEL
   When J        DO JUNIOR-RTN
   When I        DO INTERM-RTN
   When S        DO SENIOR-RTN
   When E        DO EXEC-RTN
   When Other    DO ERROR-RTN
ENDCASE
```

ecutes the "catchall" subroutine found in the Result Field. Note that this CAS is executed only if none of the previous conditions were met.

3. If the group of CASxx operations did not contain a blank operator (xx), the END statement would terminate the CASxx group even if a match was not found.

In conclusion, study the following list for considerations when using the CASxx operation:

Figure 5.15
CASxx specifications for the
sample problem.

C	Form Type	Control Level (L0–L9, LR, SR, AN/OR)	Indicators						Factor 1	Operation	Factor 2	Result Field		Decimal Positions	Half Adjust (H)	Resulting Indicators			Comments
			And		And							Name	Length			Plus / Minus / Zero; Compare 1>2 / 1<2 / 1=2; Lookup (Factor 2) is High / Low / Equal			
Line			Not		Not		Not												
0 1	C	※																	JOB
0 2	C	※																	CLASSIFICATION
0 3	C	※																	
0 4	C								ELEVEL	CASEQ'J'		SR1ΦΦ							JUNIOR
0 5	C								ELEVEL	CASEQ'I'		SR2ΦΦ							INTERMEDIATE
0 6	C								ELEVEL	CASEQ'S'		SR3ΦΦ							SENIOR
0 7	C								ELEVEL	CASEQ'E'		SR4ΦΦ							EXECUTIVE
0 8	C								ELEVEL	CAS		SR5ΦΦ							ERROR
0 9	C									END									
1 0	C									.									
1 1	C									.									

CONSIDERATIONS FOR THE CASxx OPERATION

1. A nested group of CAS operations must contain only CAS operations. That is, once you start a CAS structure all operations must be CAS operations until the structure is terminated with an END statement.

2. An END statement must follow the last CAS operation to terminate or close the CAS group.

3. The contents of Factor 1 and Factor 2 must be of the same data type. They may contain a field name, a character or numeric literal, a data structure subfield name, or be blank.

4. Control is passed from one CAS operation to the next until the comparison condition specified in the operator xx is satisfied or an END statement is encountered. If the condition specified in the xx operator exists between Factor 1 and Factor 2, the subroutine specified in the Result Field is selected and executed.

5. A *blank* or *nonconditional* CAS (CASⱼⱼ) operation, if used, is placed after all other CASxx operations in the CAS group. Used in this manner, the nonconditional CAS operation is considered a catchall CAS operation. That is, the subroutine specified in the Result Field will be executed if all other previous CAS conditions compare false.

6. When the subroutine selected for execution finishes, control returns to the next operation following the END statement of the CAS structure.

E. Compare and Branch Operation (CABxx)

The **CABxx (Compare And Branch) operation,** illustrated in Figure 5.16, is used to permanently transfer control to another point in the program as a result of a comparison. This is a form of branch or GOTO. We recommend that, where possible, you avoid it in order to keep programs structured. We include it here because it has the same xx conditional tests as the logical control structures.

The CABxx operation *compares* the contents of the fields or literals in Factor 1 and Factor 2. If the comparison agrees with the specified operator (xx), the result of the test is a *transfer* of control to a specified label (TAG) within the program. The TAG statement will be discussed in the next section. As with the other control structures, data contained in Factor 1 and Factor 2 must be defined as the same type, that is, both numeric or both alphanumeric.

The CABxx operation, similar to the IF and CAS, contains an xx relational operator to indicate the test condition between Factor 1 and Factor 2. When the relationship between Factor 1 and Factor 2 satisfies the xx operator, control transfers to the label found in Factor 1 of a TAG or ENDSR statement.

1. TAG Operation

The *TAG* operation identifies a target label to which the program can transfer control. The label is specified in Factor 1, and the operation code, TAG, is specified in columns 28–32 of the Calculation Specifications form. This is a nonexecutable statement; that is, it is used only as the target of a branch operation.

2. Two Examples of the CABxx Operation

Figure 5.16 illustrates two examples of the CABxx operation. Example 1 illustrates how control of the program transfers to the TAG statement labeled BRANCH if FIELDA is greater than FIELDB. Example 2 demonstrates how the CABxx operation can be used to exit from a subroutine. Here FIELDA is com-

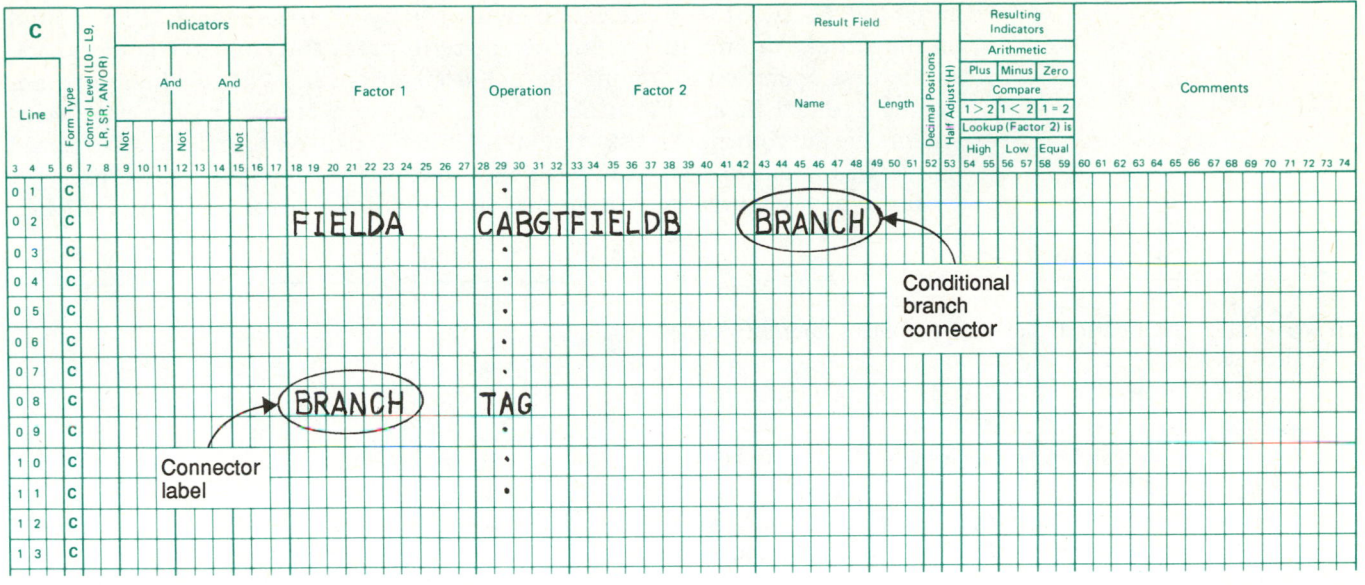

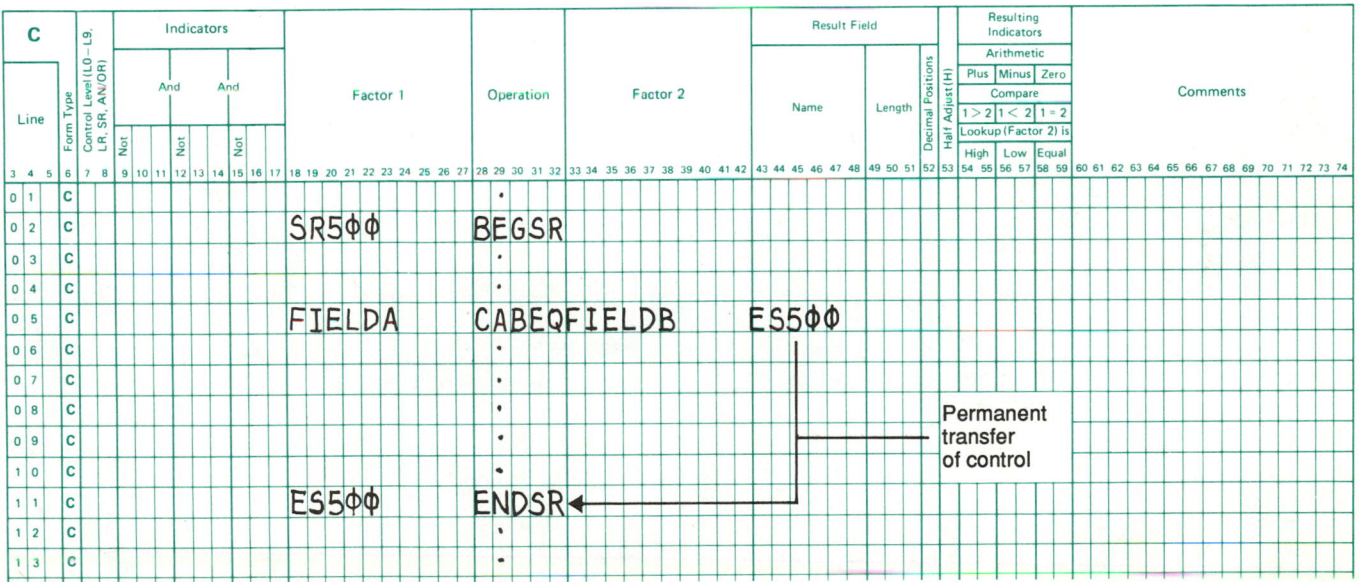

Figure 5.16

Examples of the CABxx (Compare And Branch) operation.

pared to.FIELDB; if they are equal, control transfers to the label ES500 found on the ENDSR statement. The subroutine terminates and control transfers back to the first operation following the EXSR operation. If a CABxx operation cannot be avoided in a subroutine, it should cause a branch to the exit point *within* the subroutine (ENDSR statement) and not cause a branch to an external point. To branch to a point outside the subroutine can cause logic errors.

In the next chapter we will discuss the iteration control structure for RPG.

CHAPTER SELF-TEST

1. Write the specification that will execute a subroutine called SR725.
2. After a DO operation is executed, control returns to _____ .
3. Write the specifications to execute SR455 if A is between 5 and 18.
4. Write the specifications to execute SR125 if ESEX = 'M', SR130 if ESEX = 'F', or SR150 if ESEX is not equal to 'M' or 'F'.
5. To prevent erroneous results, numeric fields must be compared to _____ fields.

SOLUTIONS

1. EXSR SR725
2. the operation following the terminating END statement of the DO operation.
3.
```
A     IFGE 5
A     IFLE 18
      EXSR  SR455
      END
      END
```
4.
```
ESEX   CASEQ 'M'    SR125
ESEX   CASEQ 'F'    SR130
       CAS          SR150
       END
```
5. numeric

KEY TERMS

BEGSR	EXSR	Iteration	Sequence
CABxx (Compare And Branch) operation	External subroutine	Logical control structure	Structure chart
CASE (CASxx) operation	Flowchart	Looping	Top-down programming
Case structure	Hierarchy chart	Module	Visual Table of Contents (VTOC)
Conditional statements	IFxx/ELSE/END	Nested conditional	
ENDSR	Infinite loop	Pseudocode	
	Internal subroutine	Selection	

REVIEW QUESTIONS

Code the following flowchart exercises using nested IFxx operations:

1.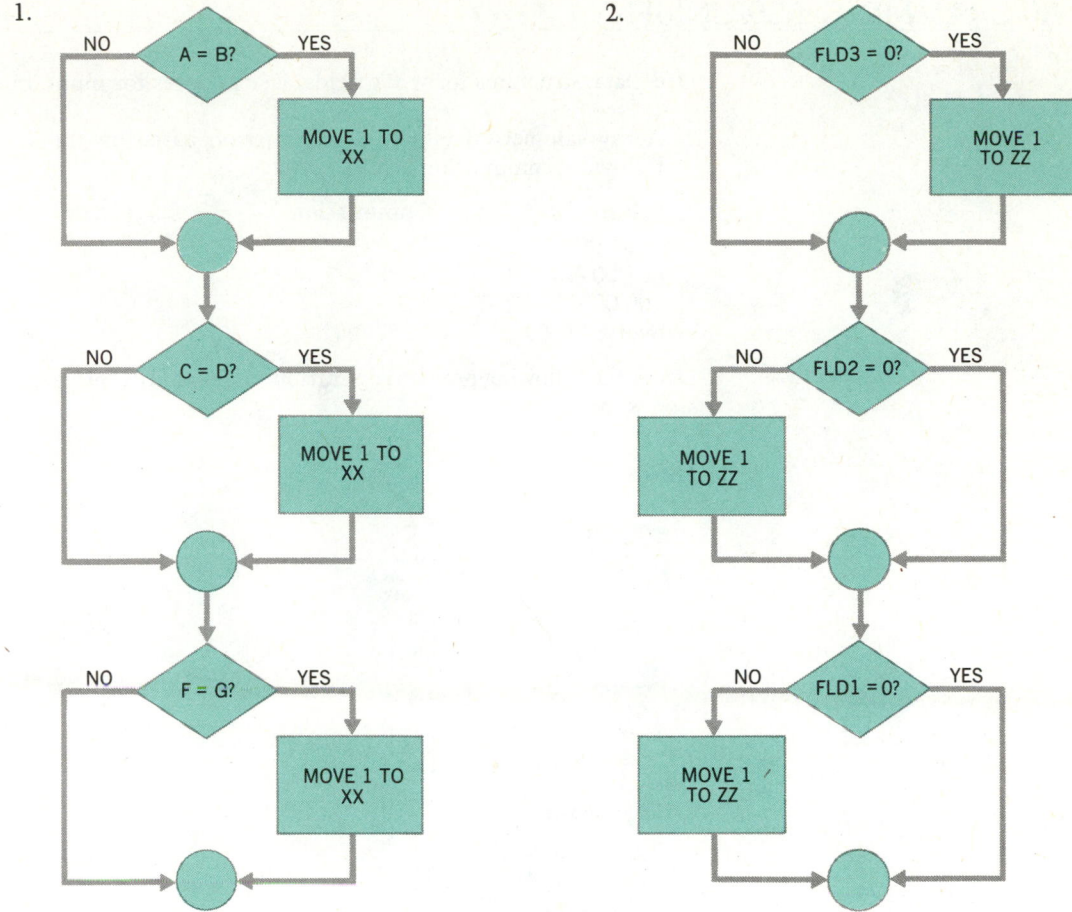

2.

3. Code the following CASE structure (flowchart).

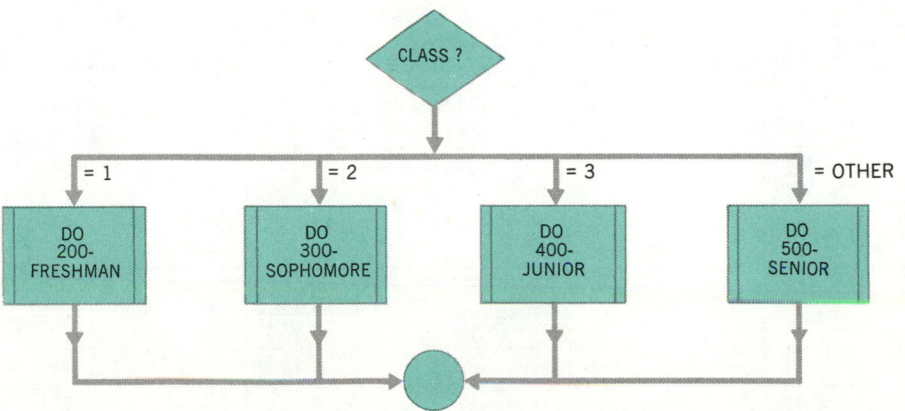

PROGRAMMING ASSIGNMENTS

Use Data Structures for work fields. Use prefixes for input, output, and work fields.

1. A toy salesperson is paid a commission based on the amount of each sale. The following commission scale is used:

Sales	Commission
0–59,999	3%
60,000–99,999	4.5%
100,000–200,000	6%
over 200,000	7.5%

Using the following problem definition, write an RPG program to produce the Commission Report:

Systems Flowchart

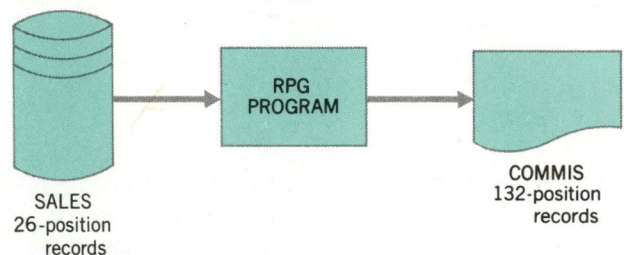

SALES
26-position
records

RPG PROGRAM

COMMIS
132-position
records

SALES Record Layout

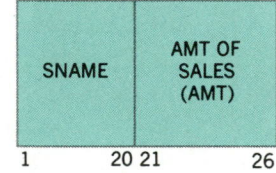

COMMIS Printer Spacing Chart

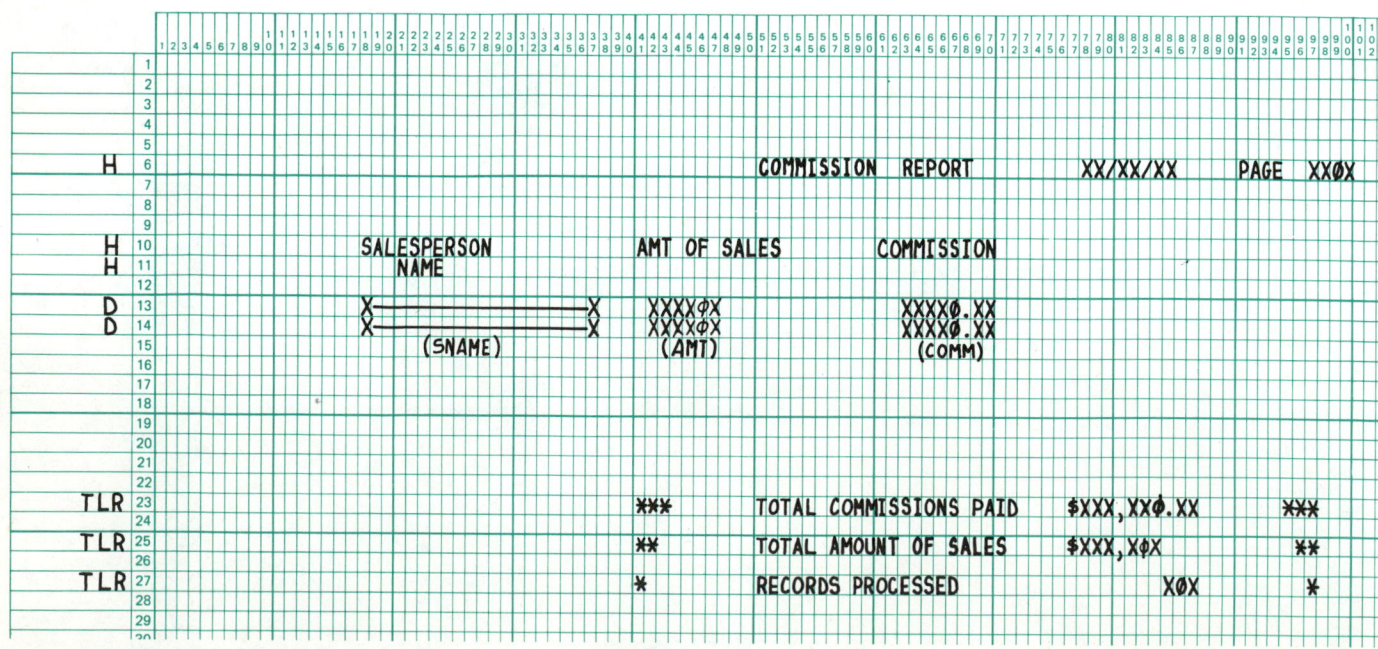

2. Using the following problem definition, code an RPG program to produce the required results:

Systems Flowchart

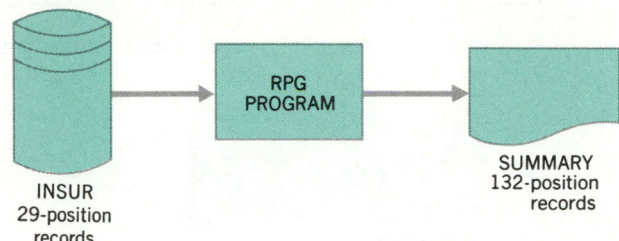

INSUR Record Layout

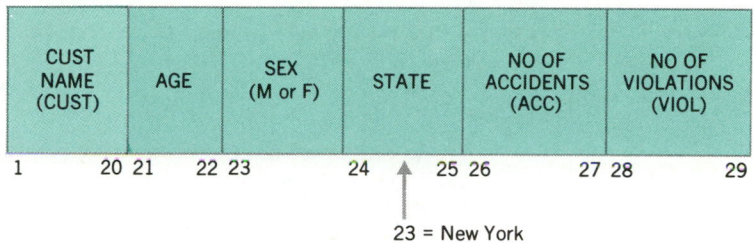

SUMMARY Printer Spacing Chart

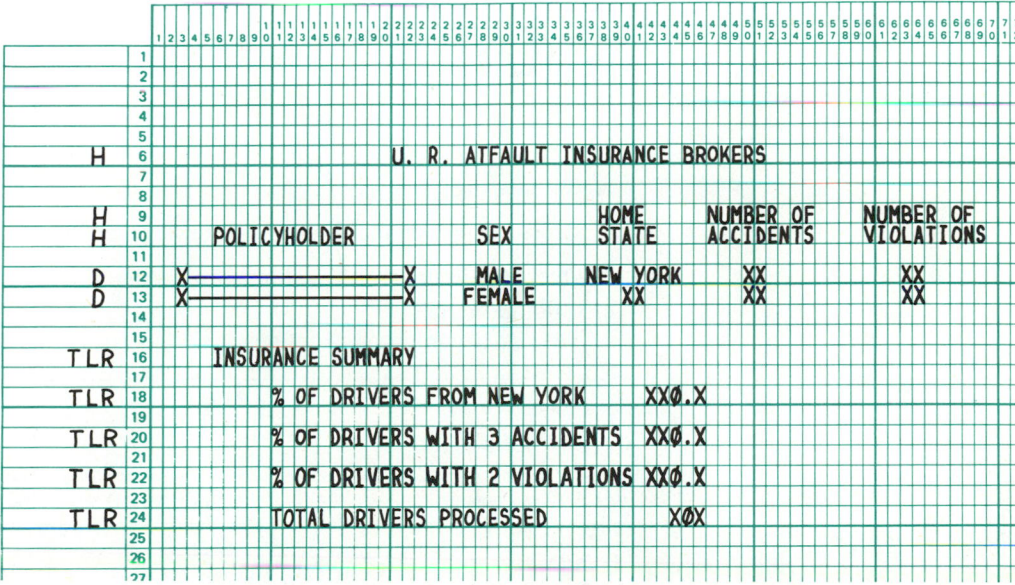

3. The terms of a revolving credit account are as follows:

Current Balance	Interest Rate Per Month
$0–$500	1.5%
$500.01–$1000	1.25%
Over $1000	1%

New Balance	Minimum Payment
(Current balance and interest for first month)	
$0–$10	New balance (all)
$10.01–$250	$10
Over $250	10% of new balance

Read in customer records with the following format:

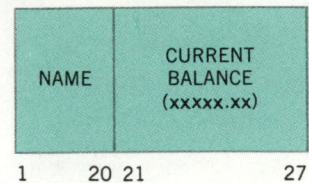

```
              CURRENT
              BALANCE
 NAME         (xxxxx.xx)

1        20 21          27
```

Print the new balance for each customer and the minimum payment he or she must make. Design the Printer Spacing Chart for this problem including headings, run date, and page numbers. Assume that all balances are positive numbers.

4. Write a program to create a sequential disk file from the following input records:
Input:
   1–5   Employee number
   6–25 Employee name
  26–27 Hours worked
  28–31 Rate xx.xx

Output: Sequential disk file
   1–5   Employee number
   6–25 Employee name
  26–31 Gross pay xxxx.xx
  32–37 Tax xxxx.xx

Notes

a. Calculating gross pay

   Gross pay = Regular hours × Rate + Overtime hours × 1.5 × Rate

   Overtime hours are those hours exceeding 40.

b. Calculating tax
   The tax is computed as follows:

Gross Pay	Tax
Less than 150.00	0
Between 150.00 and 500.00	5% of Gross pay greater than 150.00
Over 500.00	$25.00 + 10% of the Gross pay over 500.00

c. Validate the results by printing the contents of the sequential disk file.

d. Design the Printer Spacing Chart needed for this problem.

Iteration and Looping

OBJECTIVES

To familiarize you with

1. The concepts used in looping.
2. Exception reporting in RPG programs.
3. How structured iteration is accomplished in RPG.
4. Which iterative technique to use in different situations.

I. Introduction to Looping Concepts

In programming business applications, there are many instances where a series of instructions is to be executed a fixed number of times. This repetition of a group of instructions, called a **loop,** is an important programming concept. Loops are used for a wide variety of programming applications and represent a logic control construct called **iteration.** We begin by discussing standard loops using GOTOs and then focus on structured loops using DO statements without GOTOs.

Looping requires that a comparison be made. Figure 6.1a provides one illustration. In RPG, if the condition specified is true, then a resulting indicator is set "on." The resulting indicator may then be used to condition a GOTO instruction that will cause the computer to leave one point in the calculations of a program and begin executing instructions at some other point. If, however, the condition tested is not satisfied, the resulting indicator would not be set and the next instruction in the top-down sequence would then be executed. That is, if the condition tested is not met, the GOTO instruction, which transfers control to some other point in the program, is not executed and the next sequential instruction is performed. The structured version of a loop, which is illustrated in Figure 6.1b, executes a routine repeatedly until CTR is no longer

Figure 6.1
(a) Nonstructured loop.
(b) Structured loop. (c) RPG program excerpt for nonstructured loop.

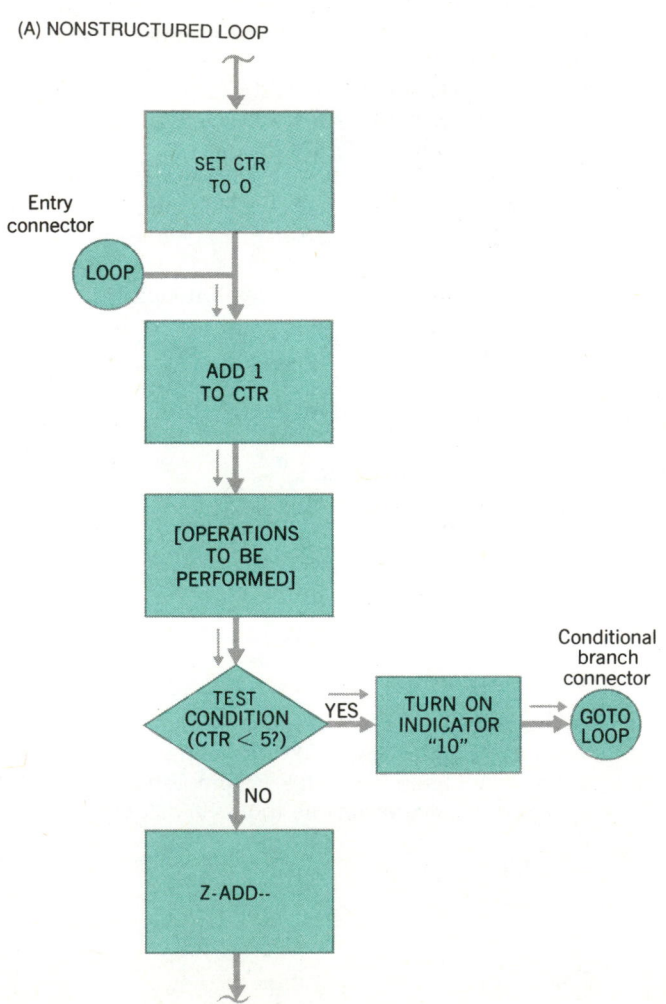

Figure 6.1   (B) STRUCTURED LOOP
(continued)

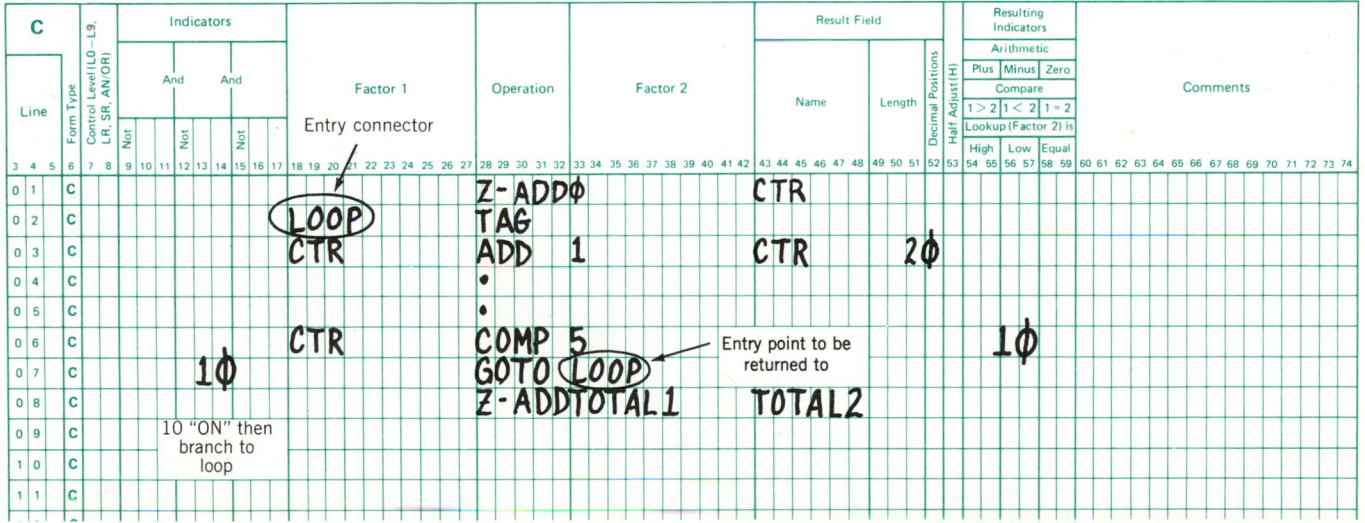

(C) PROGRAM EXCERPT FOR THE NONSTRUCTURED LOOP

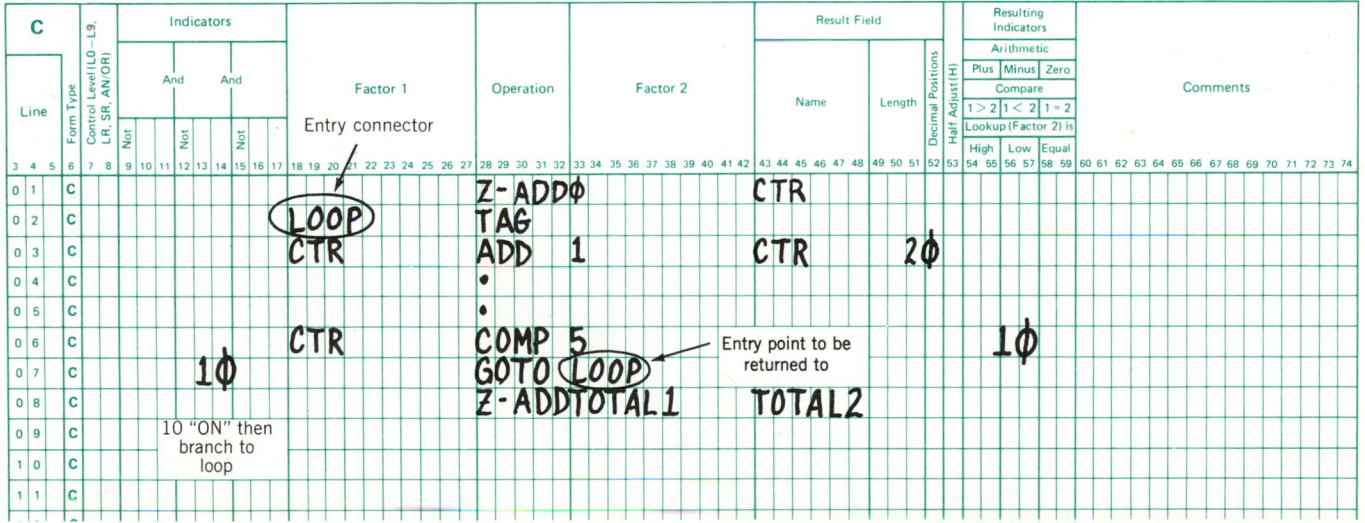

less than 5; the routine that is executed increments CTR so that at some point it is no longer less than 5 and the loop is terminated.

In the illustrations in Figure 6.1, the second Z-ADD (zero-and-add) instruction would be executed *only* when CTR is no longer less than 5. Thus, the sequence of instructions denoted with the arrows will be continually executed as long as a specific condition (CTR is less than 5) was met. The sequence of instructions denoted by the arrow is called a *loop*. Once the condition is no longer met, then the computer will terminate the loop and proceed with the Z-ADD. Thus, when CTR is greater than or equal to 5, the loop is terminated.

We will focus on nonstructured or standard looping in this section but later on in section III we will show you how to code a structured DO loop without using GOTOs.

Let us consider the RPG program excerpt that performs a nonstructured loop, which is illustrated in Figure 6.1c. CTR is initialized at Ø. A **TAG** operation then provides a name to which the program can branch. The name is specified in Factor 1, and the operation code, TAG, is specified in columns 28–32 of the Calculation Specifications form. It represents an **entry point** of a **routine** to be branched to. Initially, 1 is added to CTR and the required operations are performed. Then, CTR is compared to the numeric literal 5. Resulting indicator 1Ø is turned "on" when the *compare* yields a low result, that is, as long as CTR is less than 5. If indicator 1Ø is "on," the program branches to line Ø2Ø, the TAG specification bearing the name LOOP. If CTR is greater than or equal to 5, then the next statement, the Z-ADD, is performed.

Let us consider Figure 6.1a again. The decision symbol specifies a branch or transfer point using a conditional branch connector. This branch connector, coded as GOTO LOOP, must correspond to an entry connector (TAG) indicating where the LOOP begins. Thus, every branch connector must be matched to an entry connector as illustrated in Figure 6.2. Note that the name specified in Factor 1 of the TAG instruction is the name referenced in Factor 2 of the GOTO on line Ø8Ø. Each TAG statement in the program must be assigned a unique name in Factor 1. Once this name is assigned to the TAG statement, it *cannot* be used with another TAG. It can only be used again in a **GOTO instruction** to indicate where to transfer control. Hence, TAG statements are used to identify entry points in the program. These entry points are the targets for the GOTO operations.

Once again, referring to Figure 6.1a, when a low condition results from the *compare* operation, the GOTO instruction will be executed and the program

Figure 6.2
Every branch connector must
be matched to an entry
connector.

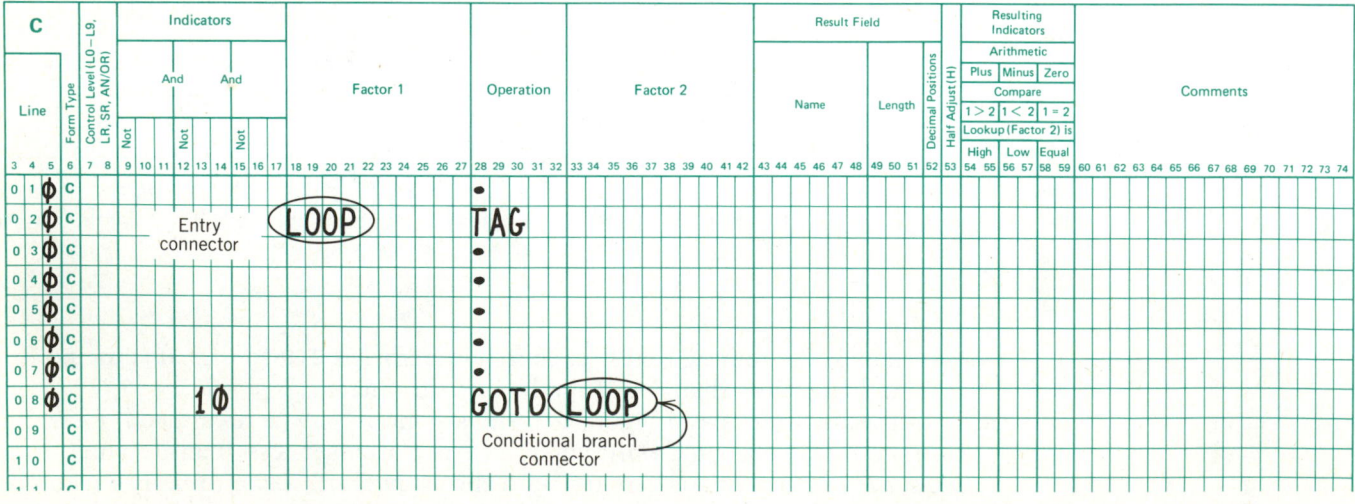

will branch to the entry point called LOOP. However, when an equal or high condition occurs, indicator 10 will be turned "off," the GOTO will *not* be conditioned, and the next instruction in the sequence after the conditional branch will be carried out.

Recalling the counter concepts previously discussed in Chapter 4, note that with each pass through the loop, 1 is added to the counter. As a result, the loop coded in Figure 6.1*a* would be repeated *five* times. If, instead, you were required to perform the loop 12 times, the numeric literal in the *compare* operation would simply be changed from 5 to 12 as illustrated here:

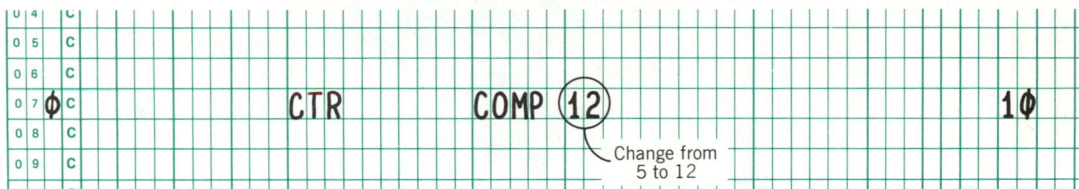

During the twelfth pass through the loop, CTR would contain the value 12; an equal condition would result, and indicator 10 would be set "off." With indicator 10 in the "off" state, the looping process would terminate. That is, the GOTO conditioned by indicator 10 would *not* be executed and the program would continue with the next sequential step. Be sure to initialize CTR before the loop is executed.

A. Programmed Loops

Several fundamental steps are involved in developing a loop. One way to control the number of times the loop or set of desired instructions is to be executed is to use a counter. The counter is initialized before the loop is executed. With each pass through the loop, the counter is increased or incremented by one. The value of the counter is tested in order to determine if the loop should be repeated or not. Thus, if the counter is less than a fixed number (for example, 12), the loop will be repeated. Once the counter is equal to or exceeds that number, the program continues with the next instruction rather than branching. In this way, the loop procedure would be executed 12 times, assuming that the counter was set to zero prior to entering the loop. The process is summarized in Figure 6.3.

Figure 6.3
Steps involved with a loop.

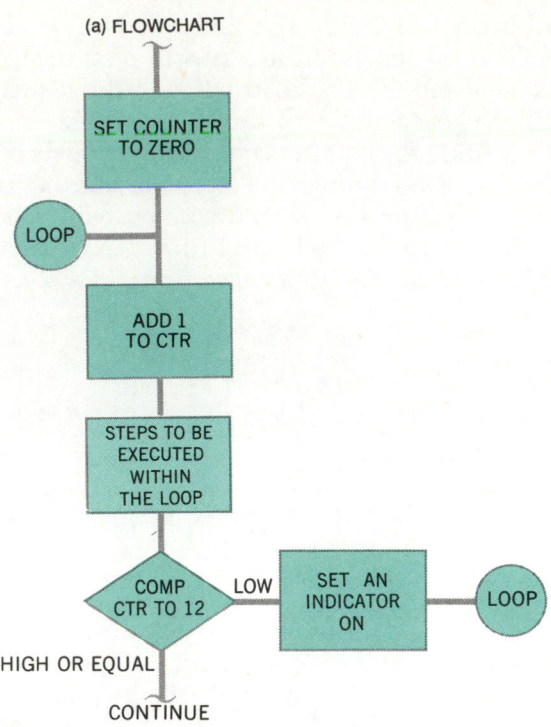

(a) FLOWCHART

(B) CODING

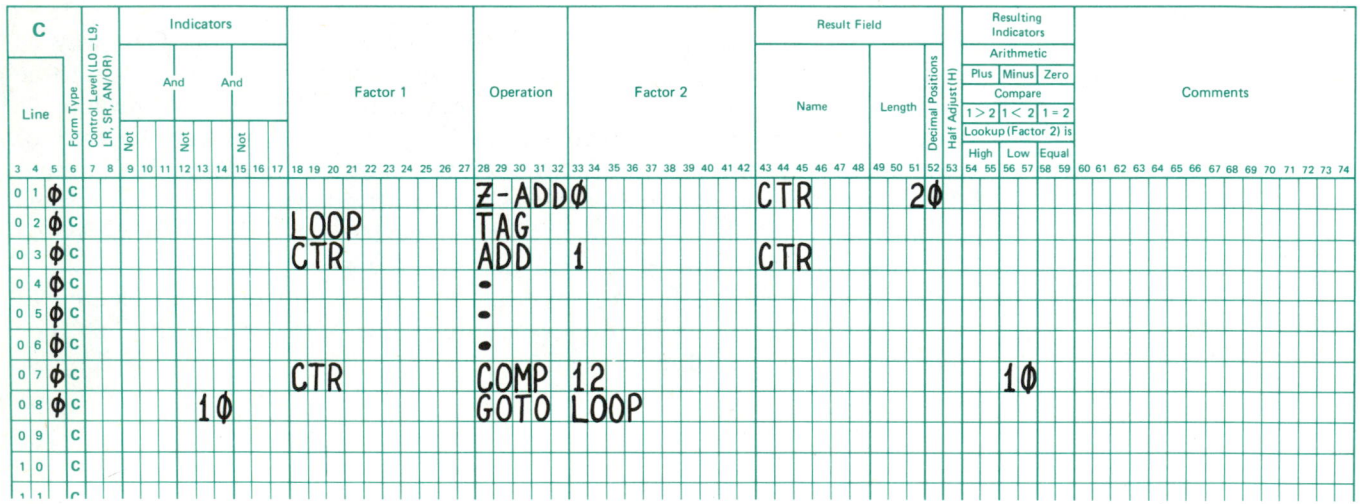

C		Indicators			Factor 1	Operation	Factor 2	Result Field			Resulting Indicators	Comments
0 1 Ø C						Z-ADDØ		CTR	2Ø			
0 2 Ø C					LOOP	TAG						
0 3 Ø C					CTR	ADD 1		CTR				
0 4 Ø C						•						
0 5 Ø C						•						
0 6 Ø C						•						
0 7 Ø C					CTR	COMP 12					1Ø	
0 8 Ø C		1Ø				GOTO LOOP						
0 9 C												
1 0 C												
1 1 C												

B. Applications of Looping Procedures

Application 1

Problem Definition. Sum all the even numbers between Ø and 1ØØ and accumulate the result in a field named TOTAL using the nonstructured approach that we have been focusing on.

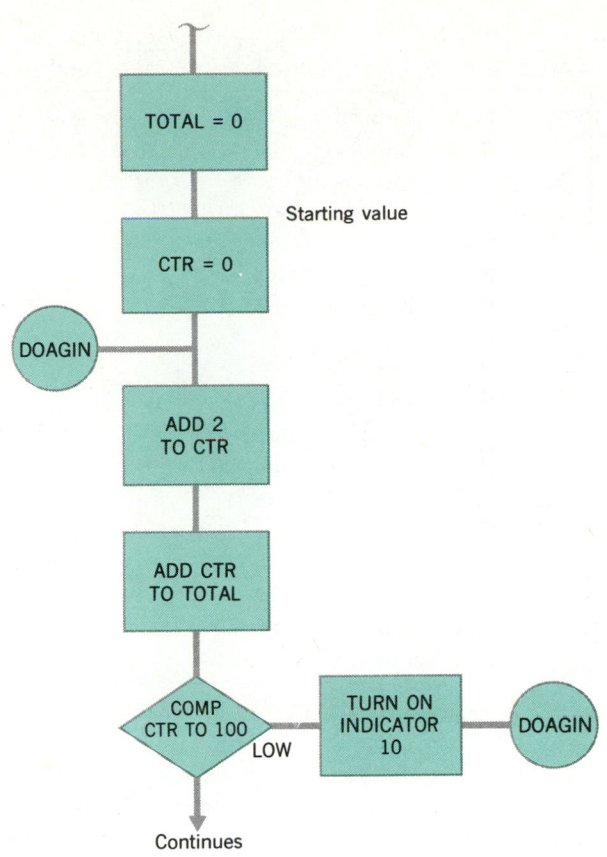

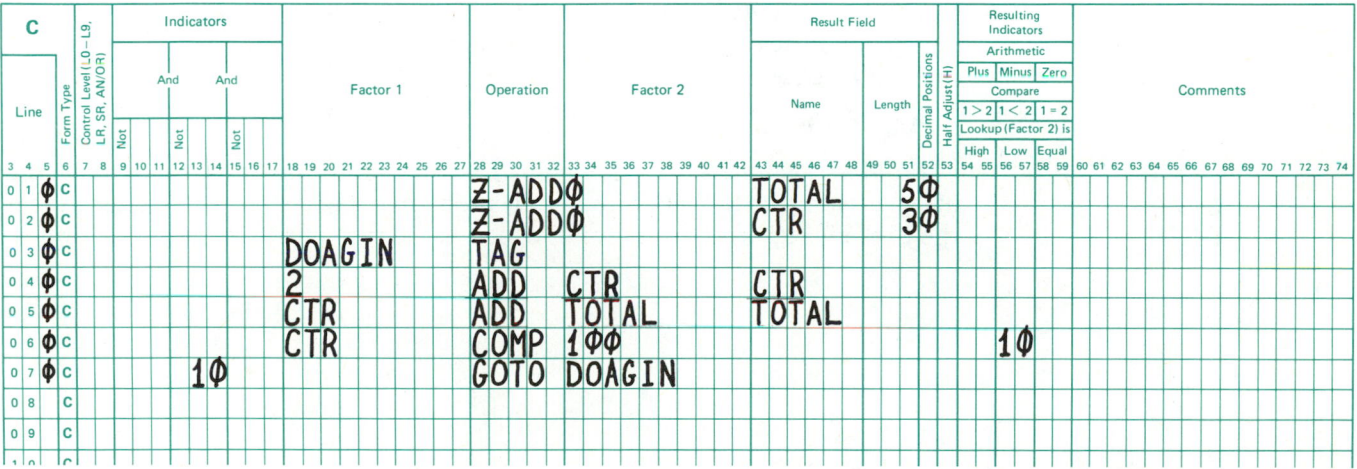

Study the Calculation Specifications form to reinforce your understanding of looping. Walk through the problem, substituting values to see if the program will operate as intended. Try this for even numbers from Ø to 6. It is not necessary to manually test the program until CTR reaches 1ØØ; that is, if the logic performs correctly from Ø–6, then presumably it will work from Ø–1ØØ. The only difference is that we think of Factor 2 of the *compare* instruction having a value of 6 rather than of 1ØØ. The table that follows illustrates the summing of the even numbers from Ø to 6:

TAG	Line	Instruction	Value in Total	Value in CTR	Result of Compare	GOTO
	Ø1Ø	Zero TOTAL	Ø			
	Ø2Ø	Zero CTR	Ø	Ø		
X	Ø3Ø	Entry point				
	Ø4Ø	Add 2 to CTR		2		
	Ø5Ø	Add CTR to TOTAL	2			
	Ø6Ø	Compare CTR:6			LOW	
	Ø7Ø	Indicator 10 on; GOTO				DOAGIN
X	Ø3Ø	Entry point				
	Ø4Ø	Add 2 to CTR		4		
	Ø5Ø	Add CTR to TOTAL	6			
	Ø6Ø	Compare CTR:6			LOW	
	Ø7Ø	Indicator 10 on; GOTO				DOAGIN
X	Ø3Ø	Entry point				
	Ø4Ø	Add 2 to CTR		6		
	Ø5Ø	Add CTR to TOTAL	12			
	Ø6Ø	Compare CTR:6			EQUAL	
	Ø7Ø	Indicator 10 is off				
		___ Loop terminates ___				

Note that the program does function correctly since TOTAL contains the value 12 when the loop terminates. That is, the sum of the even numbers 2, 4, 6 is equal to 12. Since the walkthrough produced the correct result, we can assume that the program that sums even numbers through 1ØØ is correct.

It may seem an unnecessary task to walk through each step in a program, but this form of *desk checking* is a very useful part of programming. It will help detect any logic errors in the RPG program. Apply this technique to the following applications.

Application 2

Problem Definition. A value named N is read into the program. Sum all the integers from 1 to N. Walk through the problem using an N of 3 and determine if the SUM ends up with a value of 6, which is the sum of the integers 1, 2, and 3.

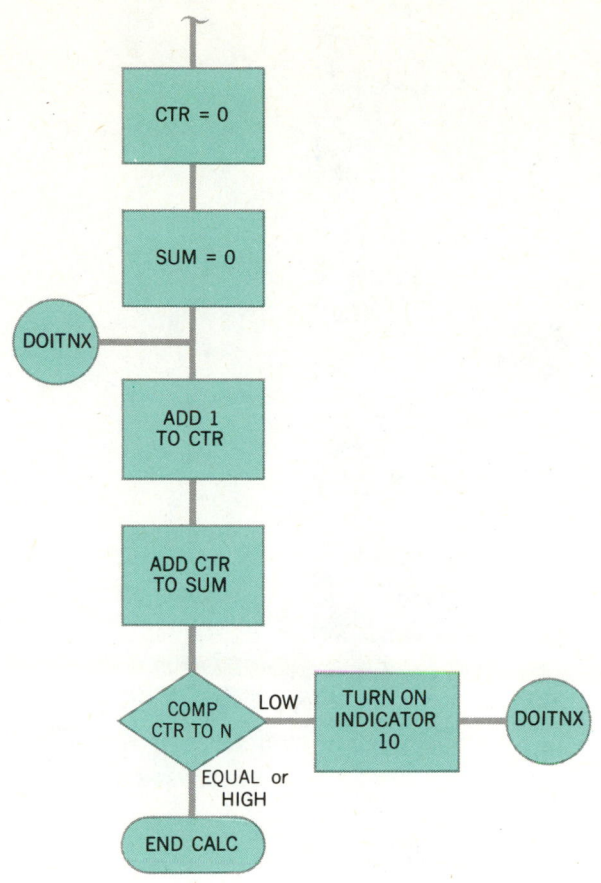

C			Indicators																				Result Field				Resulting Indicators						
				And		And			Factor 1		Operation		Factor 2			Name		Length			Arithmetic						
																					Plus	Minus	Zero			
																					Compare					
																					1>2	1<2	1=2		Comments	
					Not		Not		Not												Lookup(Factor 2) is					
Line	Form Type	Control Level(L0–L9, LR, SR, AN/OR)																	Decimal Positions	Half Adjust(H)	High	Low	Equal			
3 4 5	6	7 8	9	10 11	12	13 14	15	16 17	18 19 20 21 22 23 24 25 26 27		28 29 30 31 32		33 34 35 36 37 38 39 40 41 42			43 44 45 46 47 48		49 50 51	52	53	54 55	56 57	58 59	60 61 62 63 64 65 66 67 68 69 70 71 72 73 74		
0 1 Ø	C										Z-ADDØ					CTR		4Ø								
0 2 Ø	C										Z-ADDØ					SUM		7Ø								
0 3 Ø	C								DOITNX		TAG															
0 4 Ø	C								CTR		ADD		1			CTR										
0 5 Ø	C								CTR		ADD		SUM			SUM										
0 6 Ø	C								CTR		COMP		N										1Ø			
0 7 Ø	C			1Ø							GOTO		DOITNX													
0 8	C																									
0 9	C																									
1 0	C																									

Application 3

Problem Definition. A value, M, is read into the program. Calculate M factorial, which is M times (M − 1) times (M − 2) . . . times (1) = FACT. M factorial is usually specified as M!.

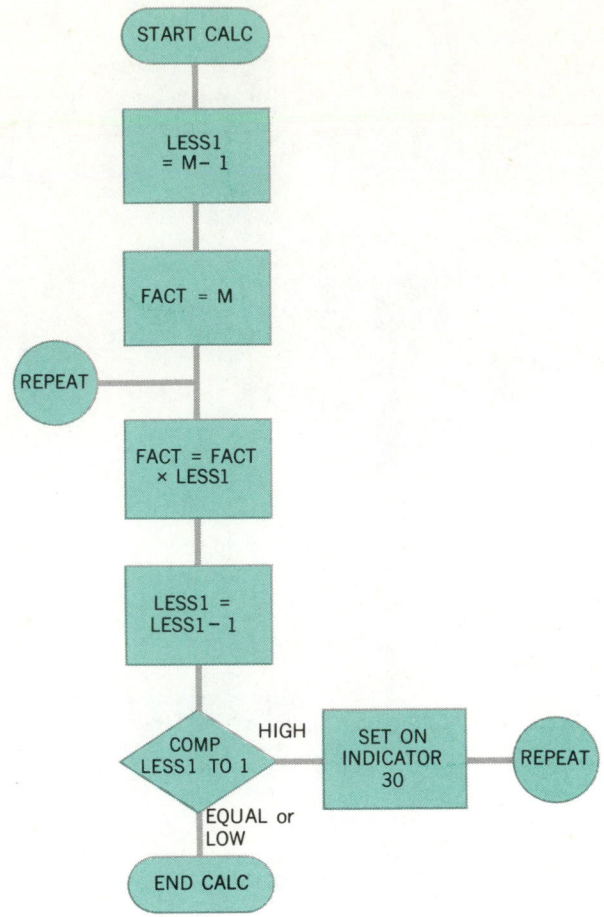

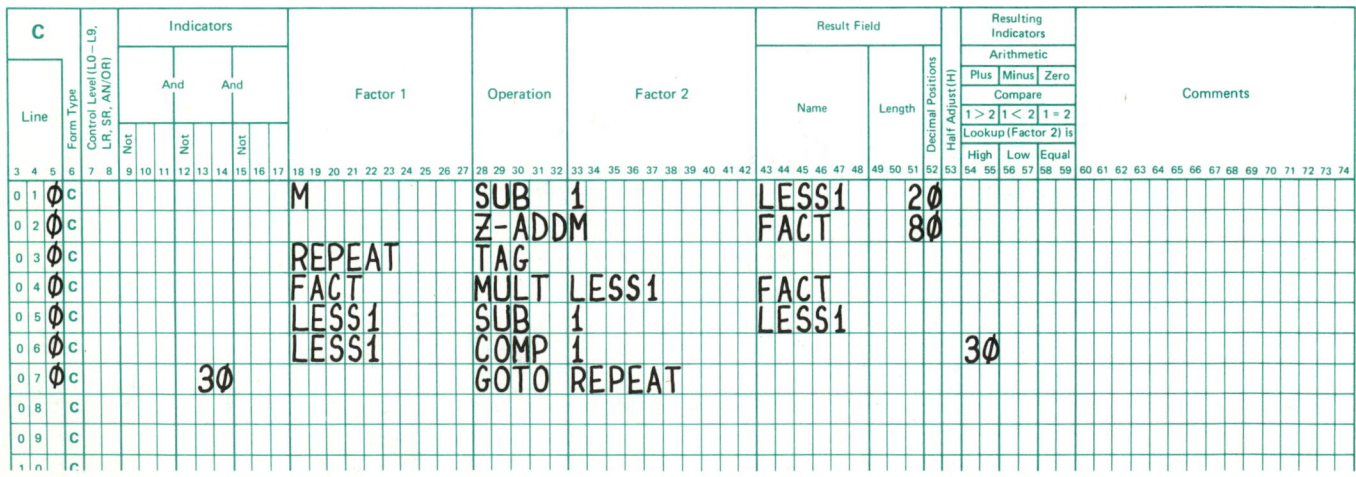

If M was equal to 4, for example, M factorial ($FACT$) would be $4 \times 3 \times 2 \times 1$ or 24. The result of your walkthrough should produce the value of 24 in the field called $FACT$. If the result of a walkthrough does not produce the correct answer, check your own calculations first. If the walkthrough was performed properly and the answer is still wrong, then the program logic must be revised.

C. Summary of Looping and Branching

> **Looping**
> 1. Initialize the counter to zero *before* entering the loop. The Z-ADD can be used for this purpose.
> 2. Recall that the variable name for a counter must always appear as either Factor 1 or Factor 2.
> 3. A literal is added to the counter within the loop. The counter is usually incremented by 1 in a loop, but could be incremented by any value, depending on the application.
> 4. The counter is tested for loop control purposes with a compare instruction. Indicators are set according to the desired objectives of the looping procedure.

> **GOTO/TAG Operation Codes**
> 1. The GOTO operation can be used to branch around certain calculations or to loop back and repeat certain operations.
> 2. When looping procedures are used, be sure there is a provision within the loop to exit to outside the loop when the procedure has been executed the required number of times.
> 3. For each GOTO statement indicating the name of a branch point, there must be a corresponding TAG or entry point with the same name in Factor 1.
> 4. Many GOTOs can branch to the same TAG instruction, but the entry point named in the TAG, as specified in Factor 1, must be unique.
> 5. A conditional branch is simply a GOTO that is executed if specific indicators are on.

If a programmer had to perform a loop five times, the following instructions could be used to control the looping process:

Nonstructured Loop with GOTO

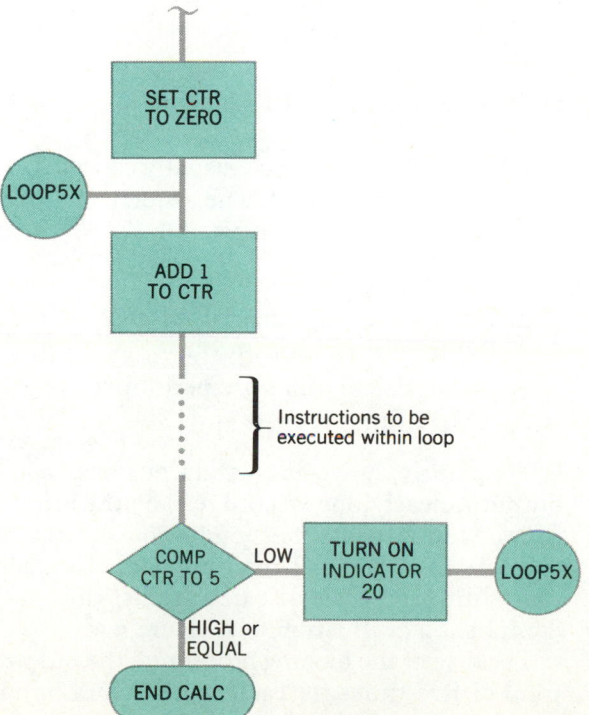

The instructions used are part of the fundamental operations of all looping procedures:

> **Looping Procedures**
> 1. Initialize a counter (CTR) to zero before entering the loop.
> 2. Increment or add 1 to the counter with each pass through the loop.
> 3. Execute instructions within the loop.
> 4. Test the counter to determine if the loop should be continued.

Therefore, any instructions inserted in the looping procedure just shown would be executed five times.

Self-Test
1. The GOTO and TAG operations are coded on the _____ form.
2. (T or F) Several GOTO instructions may branch to the same TAG.
3. When the GOTO operation is conditioned with an indicator, it is considered a(n) _____ branch.
4. (T or F) TAG names may be repeated if the logic of the program requires it.
5. (T or F) For each GOTO operation, an entry point or tag must exist in order for the program to branch properly.
6. (T or F) With a looping procedure, it is best to initialize the counter to zero inside the loop.
7. We usually add (number) to a counter with each pass through the loop.
8. (T or F) The GOTO and TAG commands are entered in the operation field of the Calculation Specifications form and are left-justified.

Solutions
1. Calculation Specifications
2. T
3. conditional branch—The instruction is executed only when the indicator is "on."
4. F—TAGs that have the same name in Factor 1 are not permitted.
5. T
6. F—Always initialize the counter *before* entering the loop.
7. 1
8. T

II. Program Control of Output

The basic RPG Logic Cycle usually causes *each* input record to print *one* detail line on an output report. The sequence of operations in the RPG Logic Cycle includes the following steps:

1. A record is read.
2. Input data may then be referenced by the field names specified on the Input Specifications form.
3. Detail calculations are performed.
4. A detail line is written.

Frequently, however, certain business applications require several lines of output for each input record read by the program. For example, an input record may contain a customer's name and address, and the program may be required to print five identical mailing labels for each customer. By using a looping procedure in the detail calculations, this multiple-line printing could be accomplished as illustrated in Figure 6.4.

Because of the looping procedure, the output operations would be executed a total of five times for each input record, producing five copies of the printed

Figure 6.4
Logic for nonstructured looping procedure for multiple-line printing.

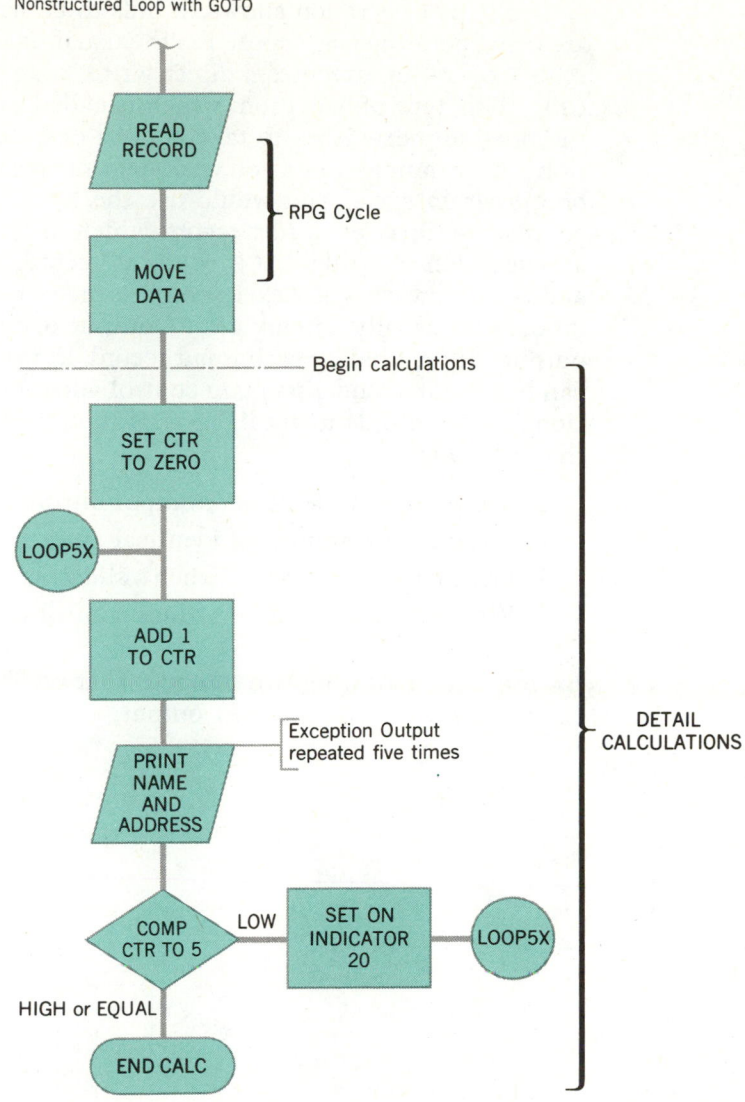

Nonstructured Loop with GOTO

RPG Cycle

Begin calculations

Exception Output repeated five times

DETAIL CALCULATIONS

output. The printing of a group of detail lines for each input record would be repeated, thereby producing five labels for each customer. The output operations, however, which are to be executed five times, must be performed from the Calculation Specifications form and *not* from the Output Specifications form as is usual with the fixed logic of RPG. This is because output indicated on the Output Specifications form is under the control of the RPG Logic Cycle and is printed once for each input record read and processed. In order for the program to output records during calculations, a new operation is required— the **EXCPT operation.** We will now consider the use of the EXCPT operation in conjunction with looping applications.

A. The EXCPT Operation

At times, it is necessary to *write* a record to a file or print lines to a report during the processing or calculations portion of the program. That is, sometimes we need to allow records to be written during calculation time instead of during the normal output time of the RPG Logic Cycle. The RPG operation that alters this sequence is the EXCPT operation. The EXCPT operation is RPG's method of performing "write" operations at specified times that are independent of the logic cycle. Examples of structured RPG programs using EXCPT output will be illustrated throughout the remainder of this text.

The `EXCPT` operation allows records to be written at the time calculations are being performed as opposed to the usual fixed logic output time. Thus, the `EXCPT` operation executes a direct write to an output file during calculation time. This type of operation, which is called **exception output,** is used when the programmer wishes to take control of output operations during calculations. For example, when you wish to print five identical mailing labels *during one program cycle*, You would use the `EXCPT`. EXCPT output is not to be confused with an *exception report*, which prints detail output that represents an exception to a rule. `EXCPT` outputs records under direct program control, and thus represents an "exception" to the normal RPG Logic Cycle. Looping procedures usually employ `EXCPT` output operations when multiple lines of output are required for each input record. In this way, these output operations can be executed under program control when printing is required, before additional input records are read. Practical applications of exception output include the following:

1. Printing multiple lines of output during the same cycle.
2. Printing any number of identical mailing labels.
3. Printing error messages when validating input records.
4. Writing records under program control in a structured program.

Examine the following two methods that can be used to write records during calculation time, using `EXCPT` output:

Example 1
Exception output controlled by indicators

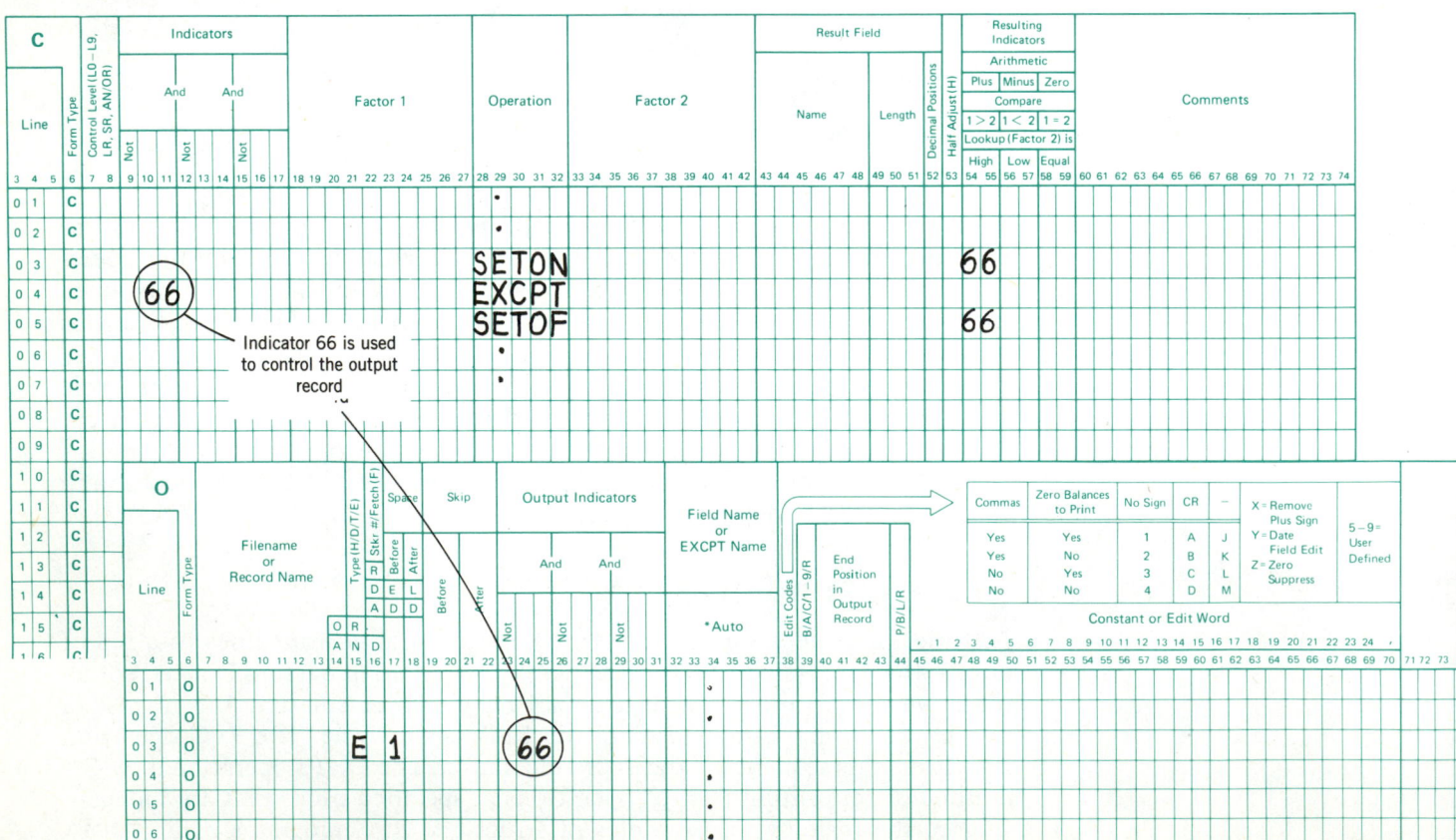

Indicator 66 is used to control the output record

Example 2
Using EXCPT labels to control output

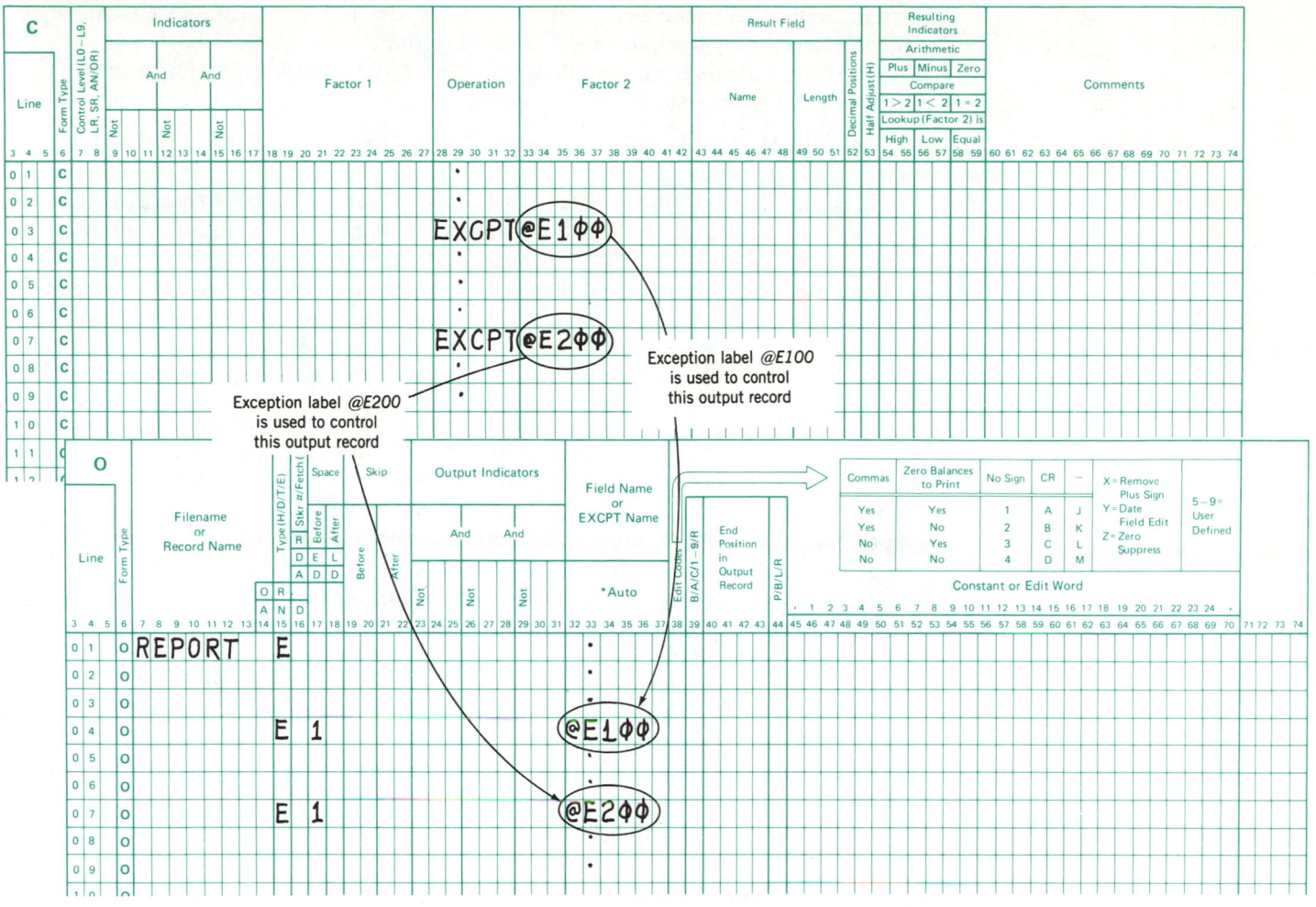

Exception label @E100 is used to control this output record

Exception label @E200 is used to control this output record

To execute the EXCPT operation on the Calculation Specifications form, use either the indicator method with:

Columns 7–17 (Indicators) containing indicators to condition the execution of the operation.
Columns 28–32 (Operation) containing EXCPT to identify this line as an exception operation during calculation time.

or the EXCPT labels method to control output with:

Columns 28–32 (Operation) containing EXCPT to identify this line as an exception operation during calculation time.
Columns 33–42 (Factor 2) containing an identifying label or EXCPT name. This name can identify an output record or a group of output records to be written. Using an EXCPT name reduces the need for indicators to condition which records are to be written.

Multiple EXCPT operations can appear on the Calculation Specifications form with the same EXCPT name. EXCPT names must follow the rules used for field names. In addition, EXCPT names must be unique; they cannot be the same as a field name, Data Structure name, or array name used in the program.

It should be noted here that the use of a label in Factor 2 of an EXCPT operation is not available with older RPG compilers. Check with your computer center or instructor to verify the availability of this option. The use of labels for EXCPT output using RPG III and structured RPG II is, however, available and is the normal way of writing records from a structured RPG program. Even if your compiler does not permit you to use EXCPT labels, we recommend that you learn it since you are apt to use structured programming techniques if you work as an RPG programmer.

To write records from the program using EXCPT output, the Output Specifications form consists of the following:

Column 15 (Type) must contain the letter E to identify that this record is to be written using EXCPT output.

Columns 23–31 (Output Indicators) can contain indicators to control which records are to be written (see Example 1). Or, as in Example 2, we use:

Columns 32–37 (EXCPT Name) can contain an EXCPT label or name to identify a particular record or group of records to be written during calculation time. This label must be the same label specified in Factor 2 on the Calculation Specifications line that contains the EXCPT operation. The same EXCPT name can appear on multiple EXCPT output records.

In our first example, indicator 66 is used to identify and control the exception routine. In addition, it is used to identify the record to be written during EXCPT output and thus is the link between the Calculation and Output Specifications. Indicator 66 is SETON prior to the execution of the EXCPT operation. The EXCPT operation is then controlled by indicator 66, thus controlling which output record is written. Once the EXCPT operation is complete the next operation is used to SETOF indicator 66. This results in complete program control of an output operation.

Our second example is an illustration of EXCPT output using EXCPT names or labels to identify each output record to be written. Here, @E100 is used to identify one output record while @E200 is used to identify a different output record. Thus, when either of the EXCPT operations is executed, the corresponding output record will be written to the file. In this example, when the EXCPT operation on line 03 is executed, control is transferred from the Calculation Specifications form to line 04 of the Output Specifications form where the first EXCPT output operation is executed. Then, after all related output for @E100 is produced, control returns to line 04 of the Calculation Specifications form. Similarly, when line 07 of the Calculation Specifications form is executed, control transfers to line 07 of the Output Specifications form. Output relating to @E200 is produced and control returns to line 08 of the Calculation Specifications.

RULES FOR **EXCPT** OUTPUT

1. All columns on the Calculation and Output Specifications forms, except those described above, must be blank.

2. When using indicators with EXCPT operations (as in Example 1), use a *unique* indicator to control exception output for each record to be written. This can be accomplished with the SETON and SETOF operations. The controlling indicator can be SETON prior to the execution of the EXCPT operation and SETOF can be executed after the record has been written. In this way, you take direct control of all output operations in the program.

3. We suggest that EXCPT output *not* be mixed with RPG Logic Cycle output (H, D, and T) on the Output Specifications form. Combining program-controlled output, which can be controlled by the EXCPT, and fixed logic output operations controlled by the RPG Logic Cycle, can make the overall logic of a program more difficult to follow

and maintenance of that program more complicated. There is less confusion in the program if only one method of output operations is used. Thus, use either traditional H, D, and T output operations or perform all output using the EXCPT (more on this later).

4. On the Output Specifications, only Type E (column 15) records, not heading (H), detail (D), or total (T) records, can contain an EXCPT name in columns 32–37.

5. When the EXCPT operation containing an EXCPT name in Factor 2 on the Calculation Specifications is executed (as in Example 2), only those EXCPT output records (E in column 15) with the same EXCPT name in columns 32–37 on the Output Specifications are written.

6. EXCPT output, which contains the letter E in column 15 of the Output Specifications, *cannot* be conditioned with overflow indicators.

In the next section, we will consider examples of looping and EXCPT output. We will introduce structured looping operations for RPG and illustrate examples of these using EXCPT output with EXCPT names.

B. Looping and the EXCPT Operation

We would like to write an RPG program to print five mailing labels for each customer in the master file. The customer records are read from the master file CUST. The information is to be printed on mailing labels that are 1″ in length by 3½″ wide. The systems flowchart and Record Layout are shown below.

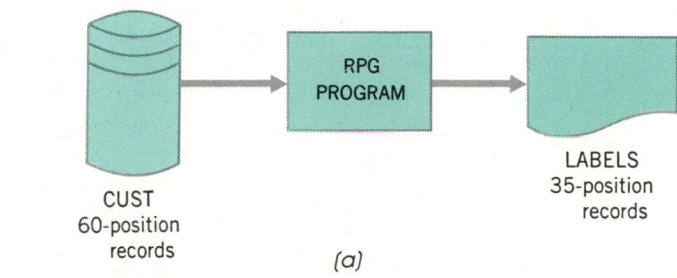

(a)

CUST Record Layout

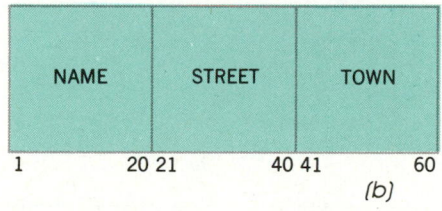

(b)

Figure 6.5 illustrates the flowchart to perform the looping routine necessary to print five mailing labels per customer. Figure 6.6 contains the required RPG specifications.

The objective of this program is to produce five mailing labels for each customer. In order to accomplish this task a loop is required within the program (see Figure 6.5) and a counter is established to control the loop process. Before entering the loop, the counter (#CTR) is initialized to zero. With each pass through the loop, the counter (#CTR) will be incremented by 1 in order to control the processing of the loop. Within the loop, an EXCPT operation is required to write the customer's mailing label to the print file called LABELS.

Figure 6.5
Flowchart for program that is
to print five mailing labels per
customer.

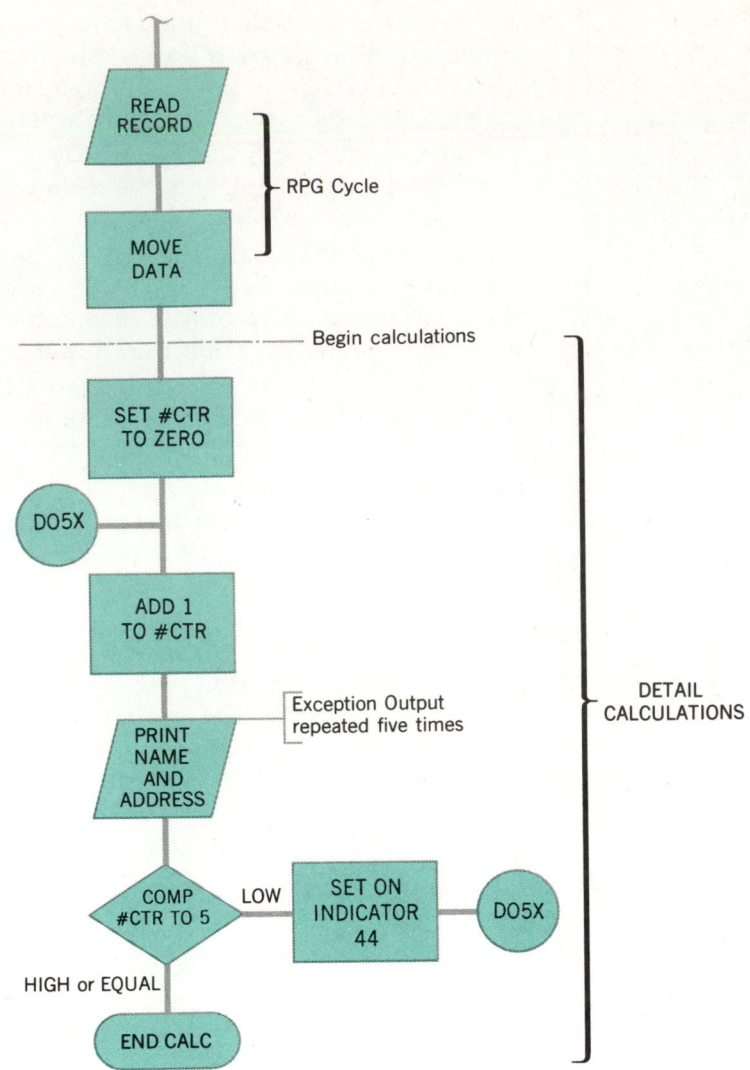

Figure 6.6
RPG specifications for printing
five mailing labels per
customer.

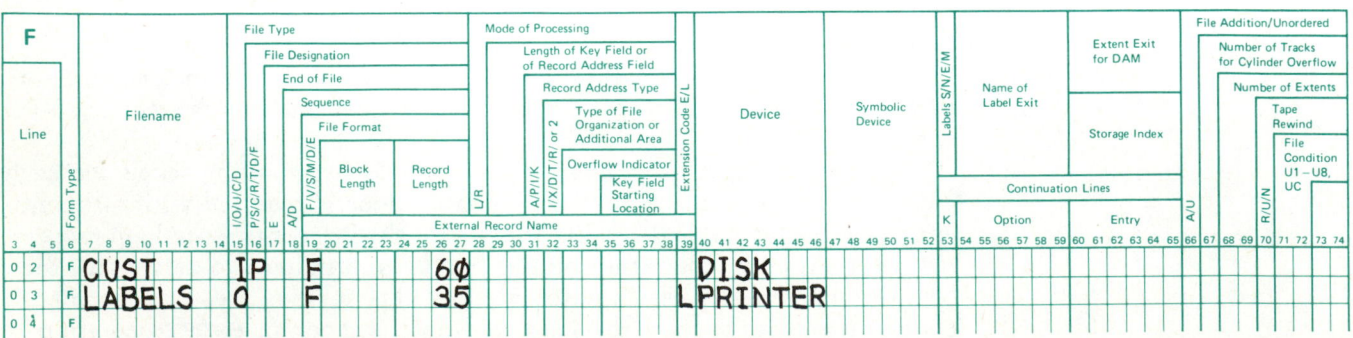

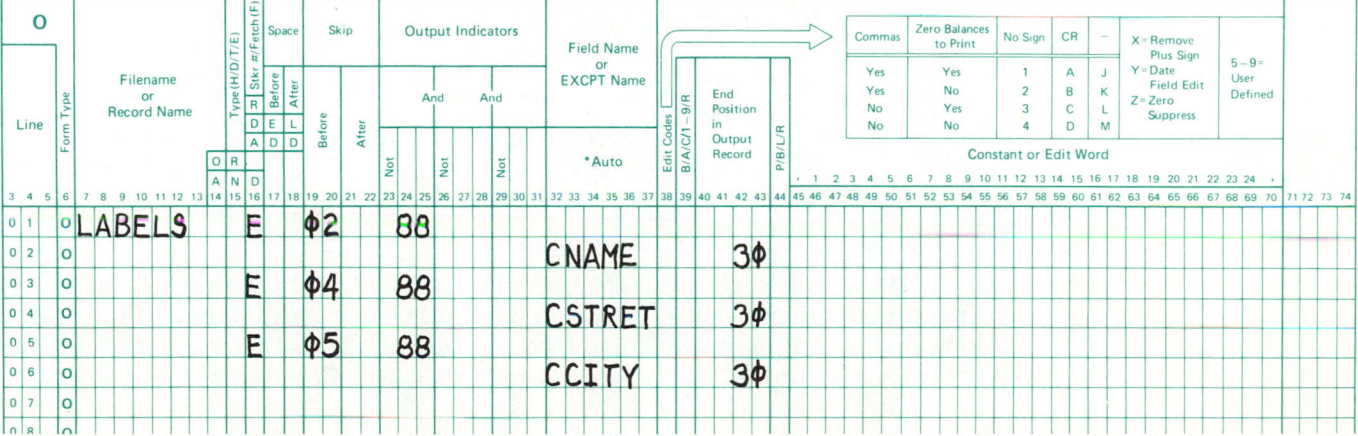

Figure 6.6
(continued)

The indicator method for EXCPT output has been used in this sample program. Indicator 88 is SETON to identify the output line to be written. The EXCPT operation is executed next, forcing an output mailing label to be printed. Then indicator 88 is SETOF to finish the EXCPT print routine. At the top of the loop the counter field (#CTR) is increased by 1 and at the bottom of the loop it is compared to five (5 mailing labels). If the counter field (#CTR) is less than five, that is, we have not printed all five labels yet, indicator 44 is SETON and control of the program is transferred back to the DO5X tag label using the GOTO operation. However, if the counter field (#CTR) is equal to five, meaning we have printed five labels, indicator 44 is *not* set on, and control of the program continues with line Ø9Ø. That is, the loop is terminated and processing for that particular customer is complete. The counter field (#CTR) is reinitialized to zero and the looping process begins again.

Below is the RPG source listing to print five mailing labels for each customer.

```
....+....1....+....2....+....3....+....4....+....5....+....6....+....7
0001   ********************************************************************
0002   *
0003   *   PROGRAM DESCRIPTION:
0004   *
0005   *       THIS PROGRAM PRODUCES FIVE MAILING LABELS FOR
0006   *       EACH CUSTOMER IN THE "CUST" FILE.
0007   *
0008   *
0009   *   FUNCTION OF INDICATORS:
0010   *
0011   *       44     #CTR LESS THAN 5 - CONTINUE DO5X LOOP
0012   *       88     CONTROL PRINTING OF LABEL
0013   *
0014   ********************************************************************
0015   *
0016   H
0017   FCUST     IP  F      60              DISK
0018   FLABELS   O   F      35              LPRINTER
0019   *
0020   LLABELS      6FL   6OL
0021   *
0022   ICUST     NS
0023   I                                        1   20 CNAME
0024   I                                       21   40 CSTRET
0025   I                                       41   60 CCITY
0026   *
0027   C                    Z-ADD0        #CTR    20
0028   C           DO5X     TAG
0029   C           #CTR     ADD  1        #CTR
0030   C                    SETON                     88
0031   C     88             EXCPT
0032   C                    SETOF                     88
0033   C           #CTR     COMP 5                        44
0034   C     44             GOTO DO5X
0035   *
0036   OLABELS  E   02   88
0037   O                            CNAME    30
0038   O        E   04   88
0039   O                            CSTRET   30
0040   O        E   05   88
0041   O                            CCITY    30
```

Mailing labels typically require nonstandard continuous forms and thus require additional specifications to define the new form length to the computer. To print on nonstandard forms we use the Line Counter Specification that was introduced in Chapter 2. Recall that Line Counter Specifications are used to:

1. Modify the default setting for the number of lines per page.
2. Modify the default setting for the overflow line number.

You may wish to review Line Counter Specifications in Chapter 2 at this time.

The mailing labels being used in the program in this section are 1″ in length or six lines long. Thus, a Line Counter Specification form is required to indicate to the computer the new form length of six (6) lines. The Line Counter Specifications form establishes the form length as six lines. Although overflow is not used in this situation, we must include an overflow line on the form. Typically, we specify the last line to be printed on as the overflow line even though it is not used in the program.

Let us now consider a looping problem that requires headings to be printed along with the exception output.

Example Code the RPG program to list a 12-month payment book for each customer. The customer records are contained in the input file named CUST. The Record Layout and the Printer Spacing Chart depicting the output requirements are illustrated here.

Systems Flowchart

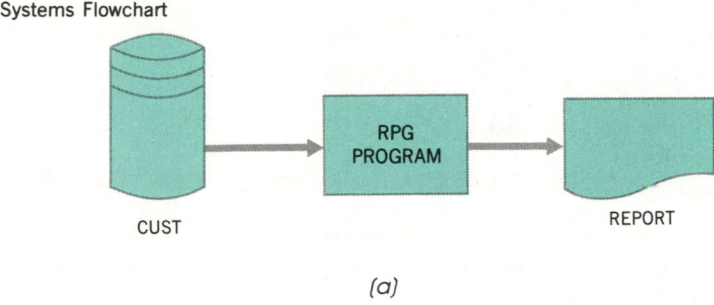

(a)

CUST Record Layout

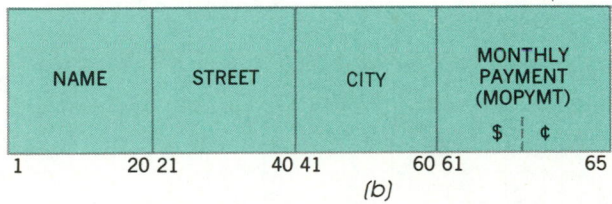

(b)

REPORT Printer Spacing Chart

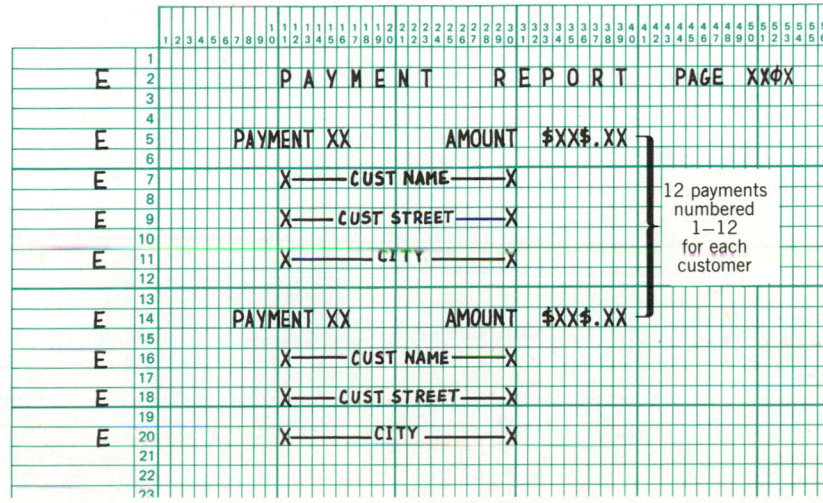

(c)

The RPG program appears in Figure 6.7. The objective of the sample program is to print 12 copies of each customer record and to number each payment, starting with one and continuing until the twelfth payment is printed.

Control of page overflow and printing of the heading have purposely been left out of the specifications in Figure 6.7. We will see in the next section how headings can be printed using exception output when page overflow occurs.

Figure 6.7
Program to print a 12-month payment book for each customer.

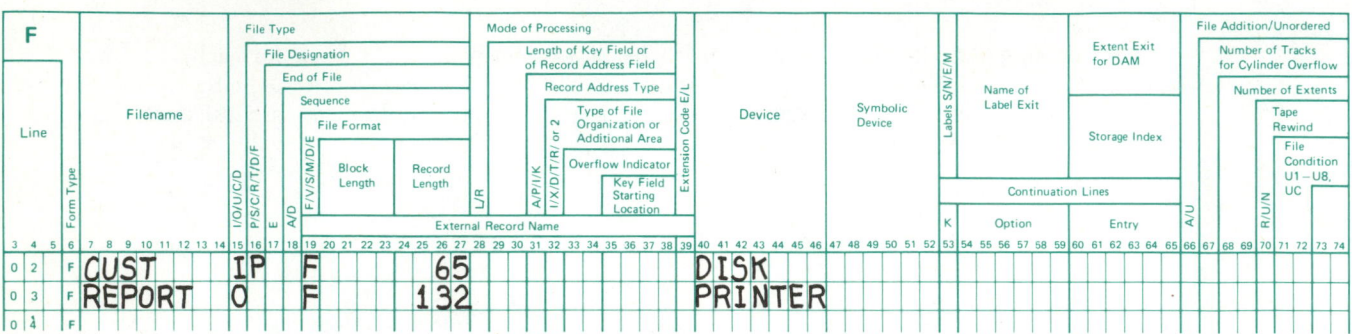

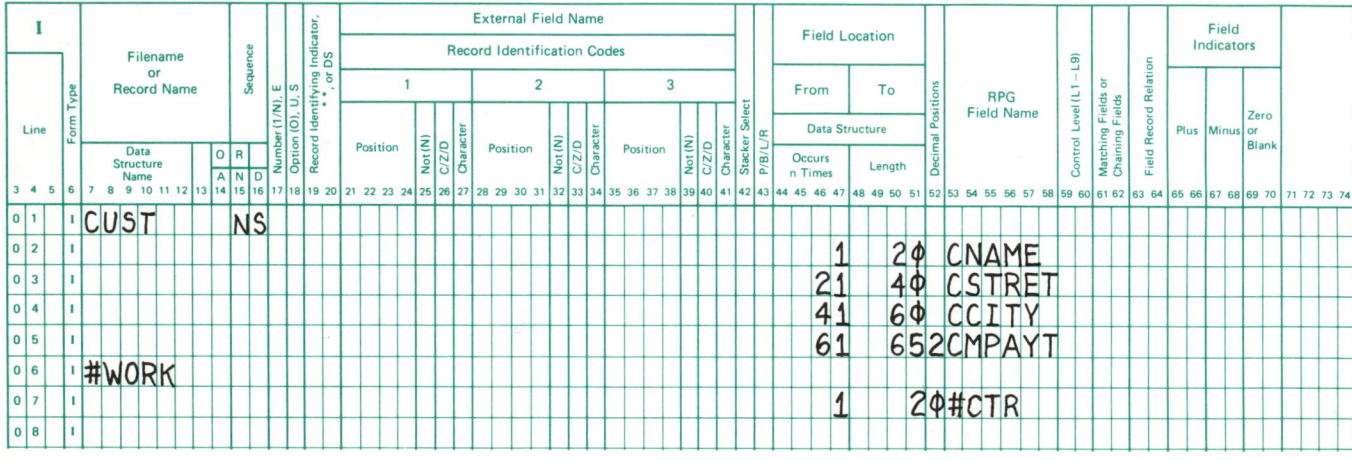

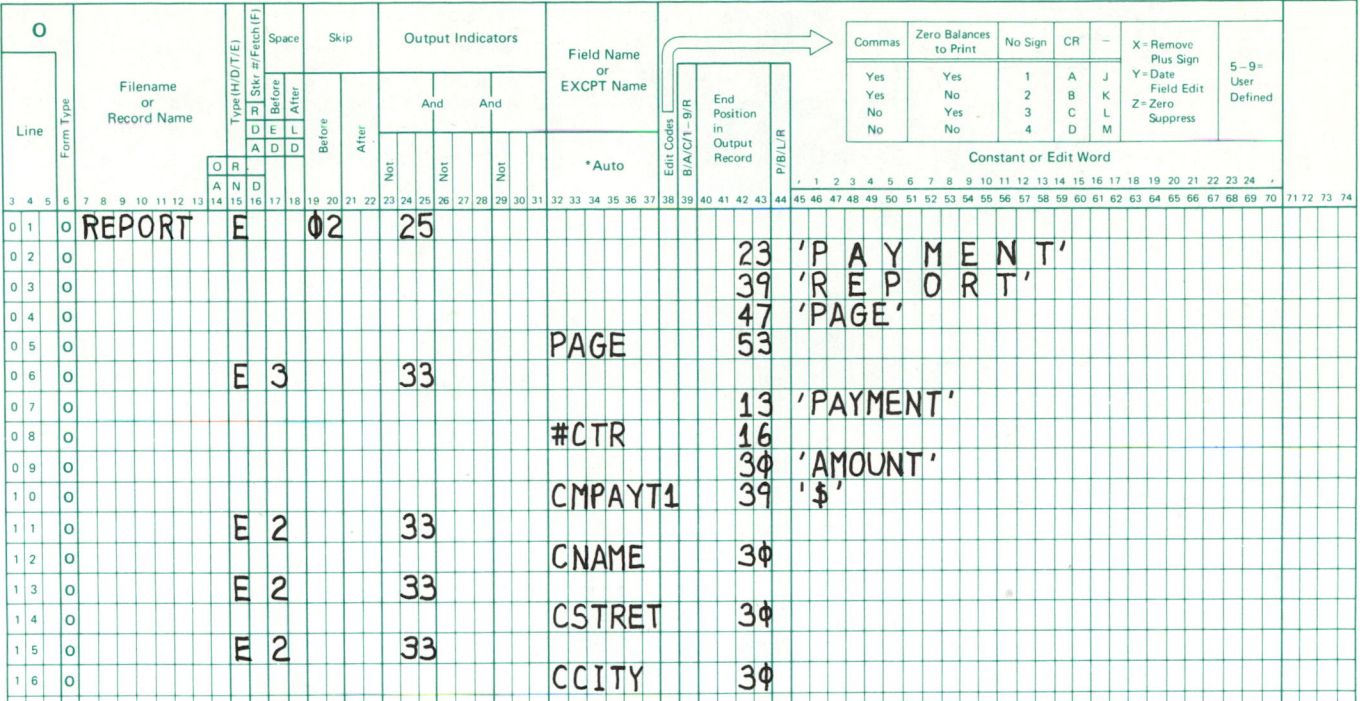

Figure 6.7
(continued)

We will first begin by illustrating the loop required to print the 12 payments from the input record. Then, we will expand our exception output to include the heading.

In order to create 12 copies of each input record, a loop will be necessary. With each pass through the loop, a counter (#CTR) will be used in the looping process. This #CTR field can also be used to indicate the number of the payment. The first time through, #CTR is 1, the second time it is 2, and so on.

The flowchart depicted in Figure 6.8 illustrates the logic used on the Calculation form of the program. Note that the EXCPT operation is depicted as a write operation in the flowchart. Its effect is precisely the same as an output instruction; however, it is executed during calculation time when the EXCPT operation is encountered. That is, the EXCPT interrupts the normal RPG Logic Cycle to print output. After all EXCPT output has been printed, control returns to the next calculation. As with any output operation, EXCPT output may be written on the printer or disk. In this instance, we are using the printer.

Referring to line Ø1Ø of the Calculation Specifications form, we find the counter (#CTR) is initialized to zero using the Z-ADD operation. Each time a new record is to be processed, the counter is reset to zero before the looping procedure is executed. Had this initialization step been omitted, the looping procedure would have executed properly for the first input record only. All subsequent records would only pass through the loop once since the counter would continue to have a value of 12 or more. Be sure to initialize counters prior to entering a loop. Failure to do so may mean that the second attempt to execute the loop will produce erroneous results since the counter would not contain the proper initial value.

The next instruction on the Calculation Specifications form, line Ø2Ø, is the TAG statement, which specifies an entry point that is referenced by the GOTO operation. In the sample program, the TAG serves as the first instruction of the loop. The counter is incremented at line Ø3Ø as previously discussed. On the first pass through the loop, note that the counter will have a value of one. Recall from the Printer Spacing Chart that the counter is used to number each payment as well as count the number of passes through the loop. Hence, the first payment will be listed as Ø1, the second as Ø2, and so on until the last payment, 12, is finally printed. The exception output using the EXCPT operation

Figure 6.8
Logic used on the Calculation
form for the program in
Figure 6.7.

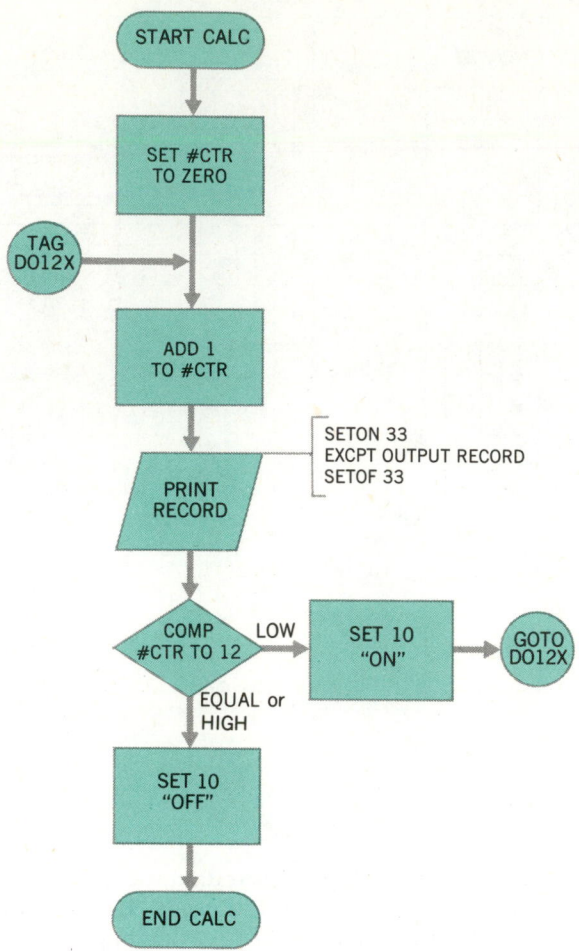

serves to print the desired output. Output is described on the Output Specifications form and may be summarized as follows:

Output Specifications Form Summary	
Column 15	**Type of Record**
H	Heading record
D	Detail record
T	Total record
E	Exception record

All four types of output may be used in any one program and should be specified on the Output Specifications form in the order shown above. However, it is not recommended to mix fixed logic cycle output methods with the program-controlled EXCPT operation. It is much easier to understand and maintain a program when consistent methods of output operation are used. For this reason, the following rules are recommended:

1. When the RPG Fixed Logic Cycle is used to control output operations, use only Heading, Detail, and Total output, not Exception output.
2. When using the EXCPT operation to write output from the calculations, control *all* output in the program with the EXCPT operation. For clarity, it is recommended that exception output *not* be combined with RPG's fixed logic output.

Again, it is important to be consistent. Programs using only EXCPT output will be easier to understand and maintain if not used with H, D, and T output.

In addition to writing records directly from the Calculation Specifications form, records can also be read directly into a program during calculations. We will see in Chapter 8 how records can be read into a program under direct control of the program, overriding the RPG Logic Cycle.

Referring to the sample program, note how the EXCPT operation on the Calculation Specifications form references the output specified with an "E" in column 15 of the Output Specifications form. Hence, each time the EXCPT is executed, and indicator 33 is conditioned "on," the customer payment, name, address, and so on will be listed on the output device.

Referring to Figure 6.7, we find that EXCPT operations may be conditioned with indicators in a way similar to that used on detail lines. After printing, indicator 33 is set off and the counter (#CTR) is compared to the value 12 with each pass through the loop. A low condition will turn on indicator 10. The GOTO is executed each time indicator 10 is "on"; the program then branches to the TAG entry called DO12X and the loop is repeated. After the printing of the twelfth copy of the output, the *compare* operation will yield an equal condition, setting indicator 10 "off." The GOTO is no longer conditioned and therefore is not executed. This will terminate the processing in the calculation section.

As each input record is read, 12 copies of the input data will be printed and numbered as required by the output specifications contained in the Printer Spacing Chart.

C. Page Overflow Considerations Using EXCPT

The normal RPG Logic Cycle will *not* automatically control page overflow when the EXCPT operation is used. The reason for this will be made clear when we again review precisely how RPG handles overflow. In the illustration in Figure 6.9, note that the RPG Logic Cycle tests for overflow *after* the data has been outputted using H, D, or T lines. The EXCPT operation may be used *during* detail calculation time before the RPG Logic Cycle outputs H, D, or T lines, as illustrated in the flowchart in Figure 6.9.

In the sample program presented earlier, overflow would not be detected while the loop is printing the 12 copies of the payment records because these are printed with the EXCPT, not as part of the standard RPG Logic Cycle. Therefore, if the end of page was reached, printing would continue from the end of the page to the beginning of the next, over the perforation *without* execution of the necessary overflow procedure. The overflow indicator may be set "on" when an exception line is printed. RPG does not, however, automatically test for overflow during *detail calculation time*, only during output time.

Study the flowchart in Figure 6.9 before continuing and note that the overflow will not be checked by the RPG Logic Cycle until the next record is read.

As noted, it is not recommended to mix heading (H) and exception (E) output in the Output Specifications. Heading output is controlled by the RPG Fixed Logic Cycle, whereas exception output is a program-controlled operation executed during calculation time. Thus, if EXCPT output is going to be used in a program, we suggest using EXCPT output to control *all* output operations. Therefore, the output heading line in our sample program will be specified as an exception output line.

By specifying our heading line as an output exception line (letter E in column 15) we will need to print that line from the Calculation Specifications form, *not* the Output Specifications form, as has thus far been the case. Remember, the only way to write exception output is with an EXCPT operation in the Calculation Specifications form. Thus, we need to develop a routine to print headings and control page overflow from the Calculation Specifications form. This can be accomplished as shown in the flowchart in Figure 6.10.

Figure 6.9
Use of the EXCPT operation
during detail calculation time.

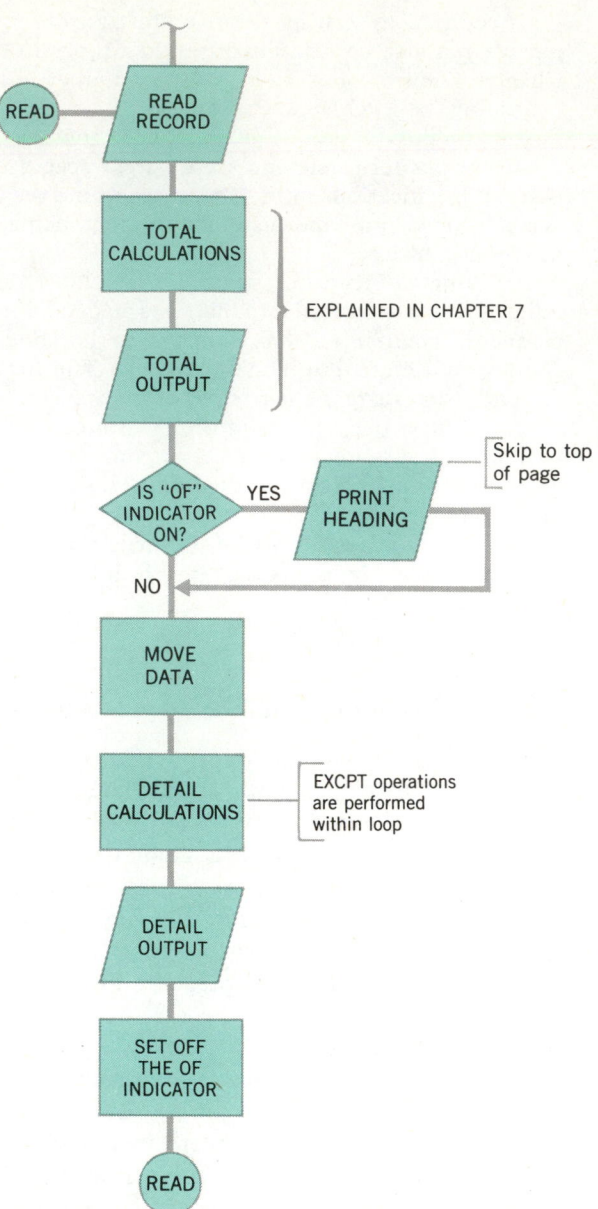

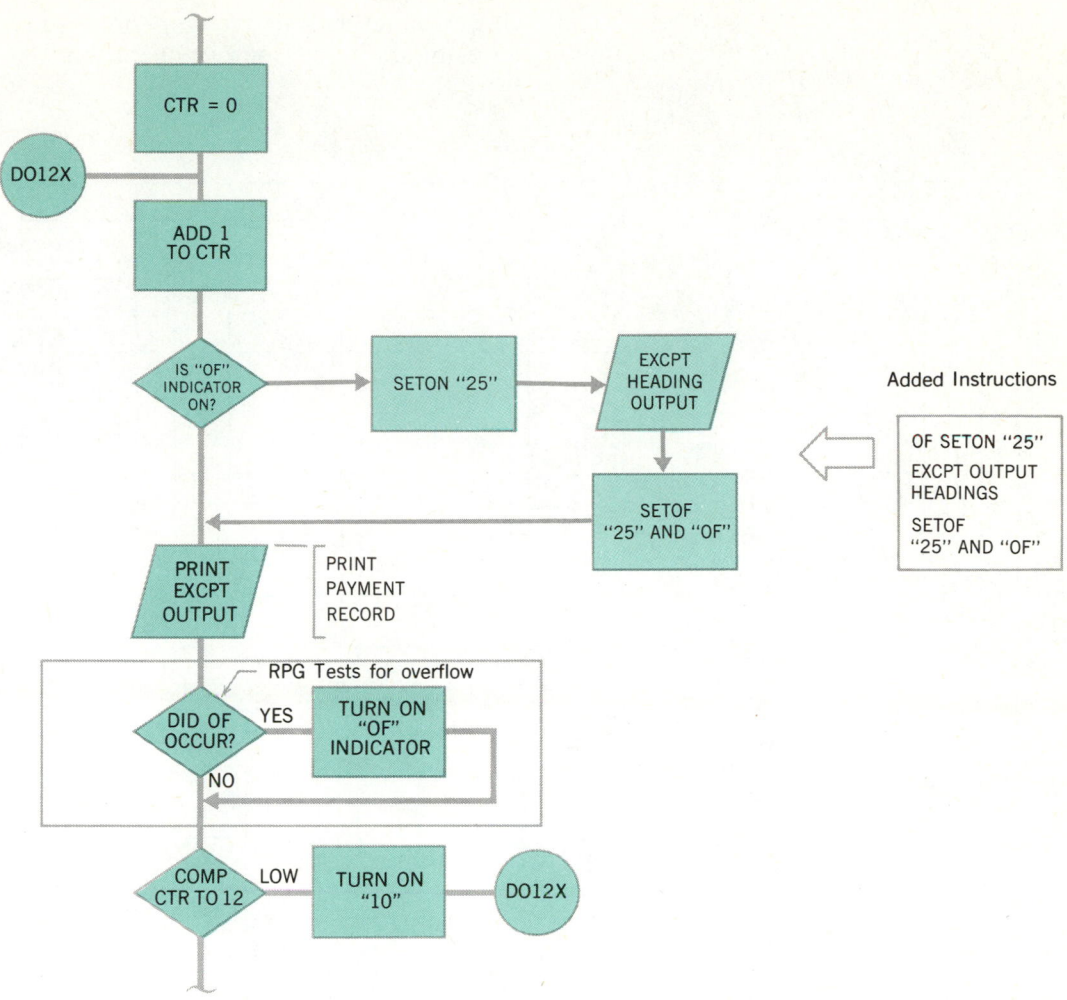

Figure 6.10
Illustration of printing headings with EXCPT output.

The following two methods are recommended when you need to force page overflow when using the EXCPT output operation:

Method 1

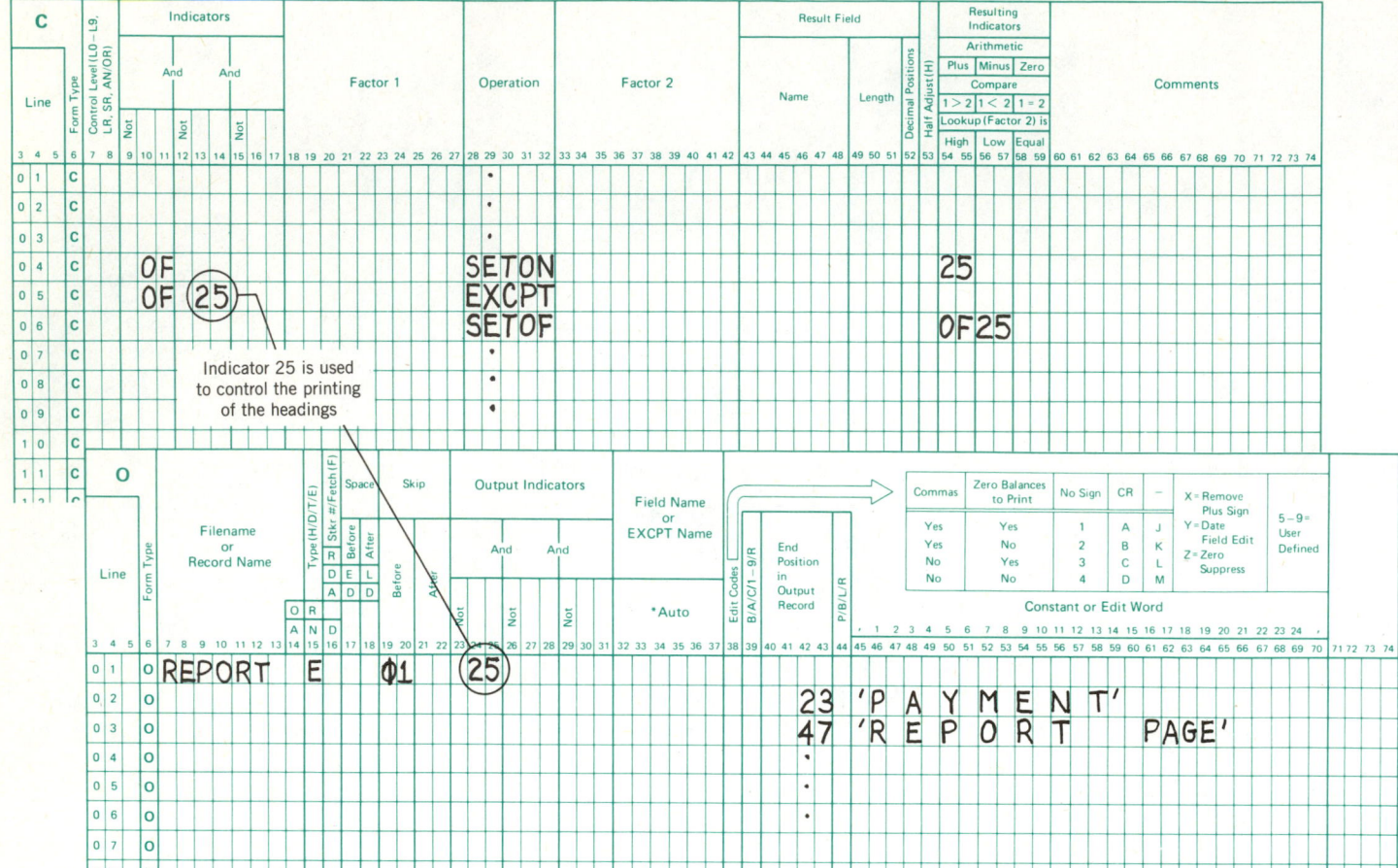

When an EXCPT output operation prints on or beyond the overflow line it will set on the overflow indicator (OF). This overflow indicator can be used *during calculations* to force headings on a new page. The above example using indicator 25 requires two operations to perform this heading routine on the Calculation Specifications form. First, a test is made to see if the OF indicator is on, and if so, another indicator is set on to identify the heading lines to be printed. Remember that the overflow indicator cannot be used on an EXCPT output line. Thus, a different indicator, indicator 25 in our example, is set on and used to control the printing of the heading lines using an EXCPT operation. The EXCPT operation controlled by indicator 25 is then executed and will print all EXCPT output conditioned by indicator 25. After printing the headings on a new page, indicators 25 and OF must be set off with the SETOF operation on the Calculation Specifications form. Normal EXCPT output operations can now be performed until another overflow condition occurs.

Method 2

The following method illustrates the same operation but uses an EXCPT label instead of an indicator to identify the heading lines to be printed.

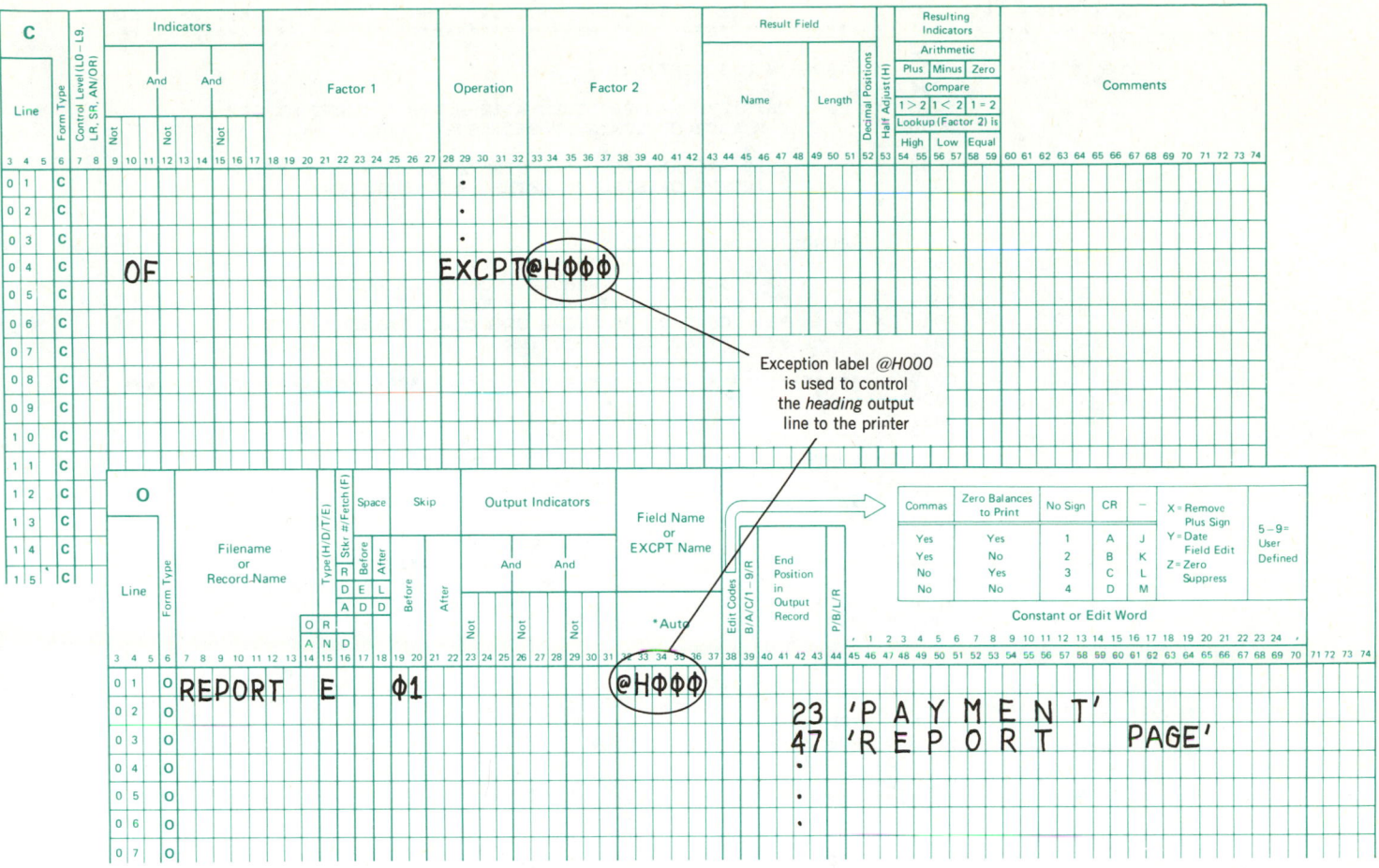

Exception label *@H000* is used to control the *heading* output line to the printer

By using either Method 1 or Method 2, the programmer can force the skipping to a new page and the printing of headings when a page overflow occurs. However, once an overflow routine is executed under the control of an EXCPT, the programmer must *set off* the overflow indicator to ensure that it does not affect subsequent printing.

Figure 6.11 illustrates our complete sample program with a test for page overflow.

We have seen how headings can be printed on page overflow when using exception output. But how do we print the headings on the first page of the report? Simple. We add a new operation at the beginning of the program that turns on the overflow indicator during the first cycle and then never executes that operation again. Indicator 99 is used in our sample program to perform this function. Indicator 99 is off when the program begins. During the first cycle, when indicator 99 is off, a SETON operation is executed that sets on the overflow (OF) indicator and indicator 99. Thus, the overflow indicator (OF) will be on when the first EXCPT operation is executed, forcing the report to skip to a new page initially. Since indicator 99 is also set on during this first SETON operation, this operation will be executed only on the first cycle. Hence, this operation is normally called the *first cycle routine* or *initialization routine*.

Figure 6.11
Sample program with a test for
page overflow.

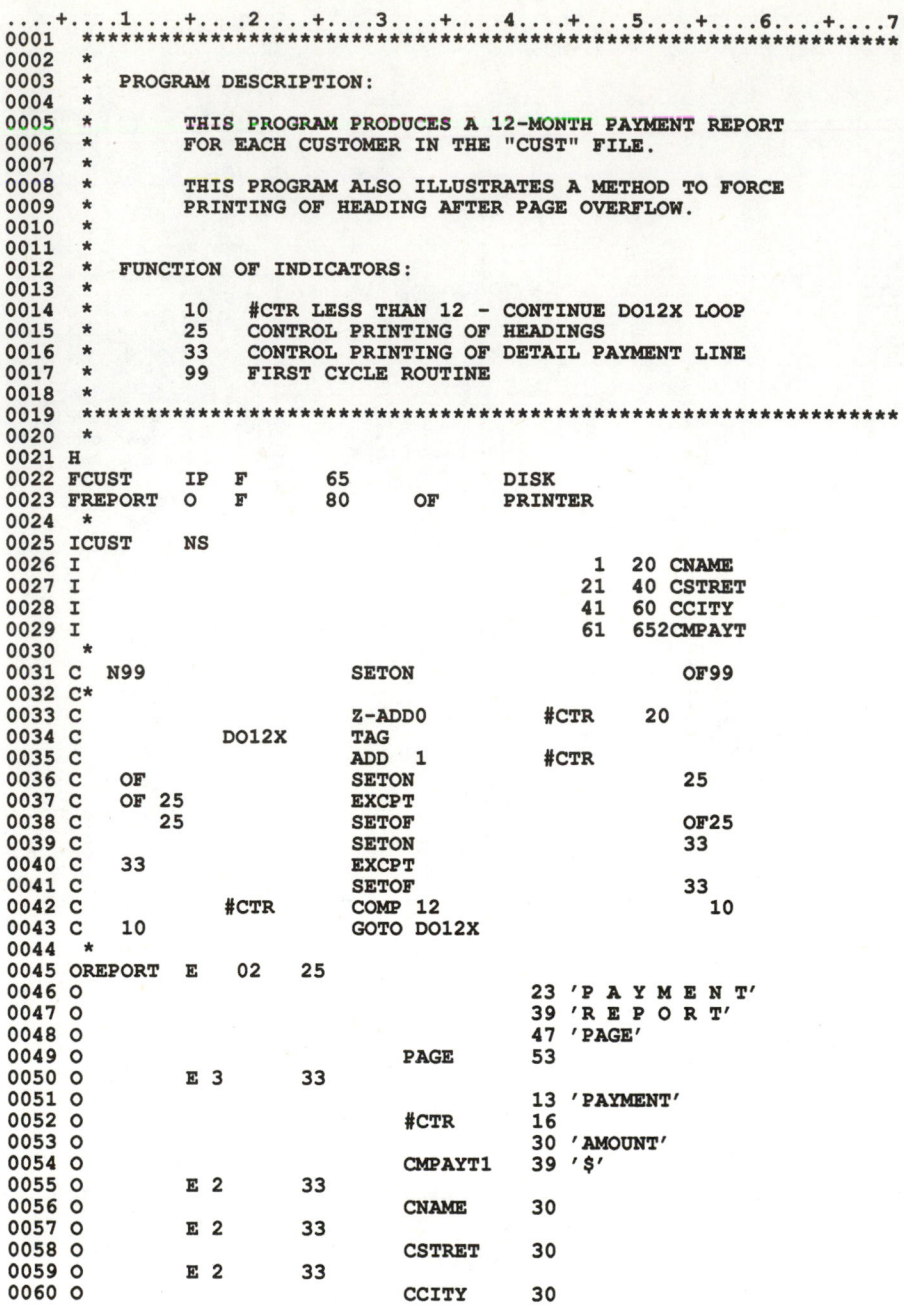

```
....+....1....+....2....+....3....+....4....+....5....+....6....+....7
0001 ********************************************************************
0002 *
0003 *   PROGRAM DESCRIPTION:
0004 *
0005 *       THIS PROGRAM PRODUCES A 12-MONTH PAYMENT REPORT
0006 *       FOR EACH CUSTOMER IN THE "CUST" FILE.
0007 *
0008 *       THIS PROGRAM ALSO ILLUSTRATES A METHOD TO FORCE
0009 *       PRINTING OF HEADING AFTER PAGE OVERFLOW.
0010 *
0011 *
0012 *   FUNCTION OF INDICATORS:
0013 *
0014 *       10    #CTR LESS THAN 12 - CONTINUE DO12X LOOP
0015 *       25    CONTROL PRINTING OF HEADINGS
0016 *       33    CONTROL PRINTING OF DETAIL PAYMENT LINE
0017 *       99    FIRST CYCLE ROUTINE
0018 *
0019 ********************************************************************
0020 *
0021 H
0022 FCUST     IP  F      65              DISK
0023 FREPORT   O   F      80      OF      PRINTER
0024 *
0025 ICUST     NS
0026 I                                  1   20 CNAME
0027 I                                 21   40 CSTRET
0028 I                                 41   60 CCITY
0029 I                                 61   652CMPAYT
0030 *
0031 C    N99              SETON                        OF99
0032 C*
0033 C                     Z-ADD0      #CTR      20
0034 C          DO12X      TAG
0035 C                     ADD 1       #CTR
0036 C    OF               SETON                        25
0037 C    OF 25            EXCPT
0038 C       25            SETOF                        OF25
0039 C                     SETON                        33
0040 C    33               EXCPT
0041 C                     SETOF                        33
0042 C          #CTR       COMP 12                           10
0043 C    10               GOTO DO12X
0044 *
0045 OREPORT   E   02  25
0046 O                                      23 'P A Y M E N T'
0047 O                                      39 'R E P O R T'
0048 O                                      47 'PAGE'
0049 O                            PAGE      53
0050 O         E 3     33
0051 O                                      13 'PAYMENT'
0052 O                            #CTR      16
0053 O                                      30 'AMOUNT'
0054 O                            CMPAYT1   39 '$'
0055 O         E 2     33
0056 O                            CNAME     30
0057 O         E 2     33
0058 O                            CSTRET    30
0059 O         E 2     33
0060 O                            CCITY     30
```

D. Summary of the EXCPT Operation

EXCPT Operation	
Instruction:	EXCPT
Meaning:	Exception output is produced during calculation time. That is, the EXCPT instruction may be included in detail calculations and/or total calculations on the Calculation Specifications form.
Calculation Specifications form:	EXCPT is entered in columns 28–32. Conditioning indicators may be specified in columns 7–17. An EXCPT label may be specified in columns 33–42 to

> identify an output record. All other columns must be blank.
>
> `EXCPT` may be incorporated within a looping procedure in order to produce multiple copies of similar records.
>
> Output form: `E` is entered in column 15.

Self-Test

1. When output is required during calculation time, the _____ operation is used.
2. Looping operations are entered on the _____ Specifications form.
3. When multiple copies of labels are needed, the `EXCPT` operation is contained within a(n) _____.
4. (T or F) When `EXCPT` output is used, overflow is handled automatically by RPG.
5. List the following steps in the sequence in which they occur in the RPG Logic Cycle. Begin with the Read instruction.
   a. Test for overflow
   b. Total calculations
   c. Read record
   d. Detail calculations
   e. Detail output
   f. Move data to fields
   g. Total output
6. A conditional branch requires that _____ be used in conjunction with the `GOTO` instruction.
7. Entry points in the program are identified by _____ statements.
8. When exception output is used, the Type field (column 15) on the Output Specifications form is coded with a(n) _____.
9. (T or F) The overflow indicator may be used on the Calculation Specifications form to `SETON` and `SETOF` indicators.
10. (T or F) The overflow indicator may be coded on the Output Specifications form to condition exception printing.

Solutions

1. `EXCPT`
2. Calculation
3. loop
4. F—`EXCPT` output occurs during calculation time, and the RPG Logic Cycle is not able to check or test for overflow until the calculation section is completed.
5. c b g a f d e
6. indicators
7. `TAG`
8. `E`
9. T
10. F—The overflow indicator (`OF`) cannot be used on the Output Specifications form with an `EXCPT` operation.

III. Structured RPG Iteration

A. Review of Structured Iteration

Chapter 5 introduced the four logical control structures used in structured RPG programming. The fourth and final control structure we need to consider in detail is the structure known as `DO` groups or *iteration*. Iteration refers to the logic required for looping or executing a series of steps until a given condition is met. Many business applications require routines that must be executed repeatedly until a particular condition has been met. For example, looping can provide the logic for printing five mailing labels for each customer in a customer master file. Also, looping could be used for calculating and printing payment information for a twenty-year mortgage.

There are three types of iteration or looping structures in RPG, each providing a different method to perform repetitive operations:

> The first type of iteration executes a group of operations *while* a condition is true and stops execution when the condition tested is no longer met (DOW or DO While).
>
> The second type of iteration is a looping operation that executes a routine *until* a certain condition is met or is true (DOU or DO Until).
>
> The third type of iteration is the *counter* loop, in which a variable is set equal to a starting value and increased in equal increments until it is greater than a specified ending value (DO).

1. DO Groups: An Overview

In this section, we will focus on DO group structures, which initiate the repetitive execution of a group of operations. A DO group operation, used for repetitive processing, begins with a **DOWxx** (DO While), **DOUxx** (DO Until), or **DO** operation and ends with an **END** operation. The following specifications illustrate the general format of DO group operations:

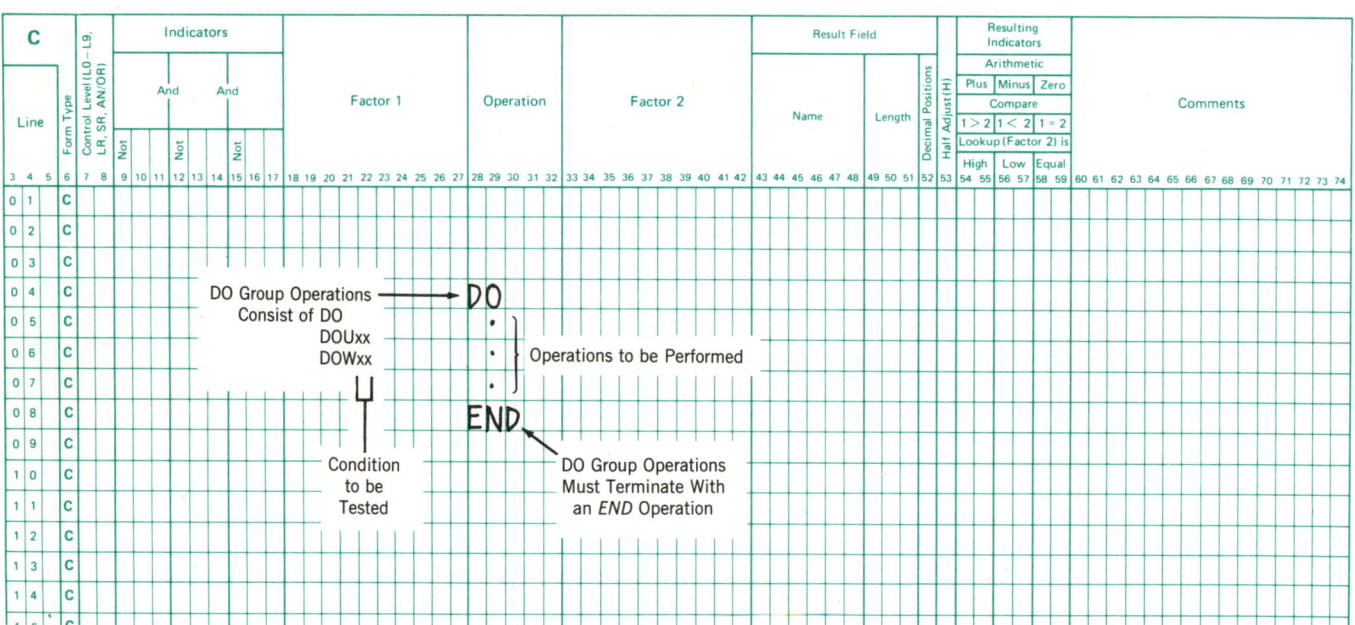

All DO group operations include the following:

1. Testing for a specific condition.
2. Executing an operation or group of operations based on the result of the condition tested.
3. Altering the field or factor being tested for the specific condition.
4. Checking the condition again to determine whether the repetitive routine or looping operation should continue.

Performing iteration in RPG requires the execution of an operation referred to as DO groups and consists of the following three types:

DO While (DOWxx/END) operation
DO Until (DOUxx/END) operation
DO/END operation

These DO/END groups can be used in place of loops using unconditional branching (GOTOs), thus providing for GOTO-less programming, a structured programming standard.

Before considering the three types of DO/END groups in detail, let us discuss some rules when specifying DO/END group operations.

2. Rules for Using **DO** Group Operations

1. Indicators (columns 7–8 and 9–17) can be specified to control execution of a DO/END group operation. If indicators are specified, they are tested *before* execution of the DO/END operation begins. If the indicator conditions are satisfied, the DO/END operation is executed. If not, control passes to the first operation following the corresponding END statement. If no indicators are specified in columns 7–8 or 9–17, the DO/END operation will be executed every time the program encounters the DO/END operation.

2. Each DO group must begin with a DO, DOUxx, or DOWxx operation and end with a corresponding END operation.

3. DO group operations can be executed during detail time, total time, or within a subroutine on the Calculation Specifications form.

4. Fields used in comparison operations, such as DOUxx and DOWxx operations, must contain the same data types to ensure correct results. That is, fields or literals specified in Factor 1 and Factor 2 must be defined as *both numeric* or *both alphanumeric*. They may contain a field name, character or numeric literals, a literal containing blanks, a Data Structure subfield, or an array element (see Chapter 10).

Next, we will illustrate each of the iteration or looping types used for structured RPG programming.

B. The DOWxx/END (DO While) Operation

The first and most common type of iteration, the DOWxx/END operation or DO While operation is illustrated below:

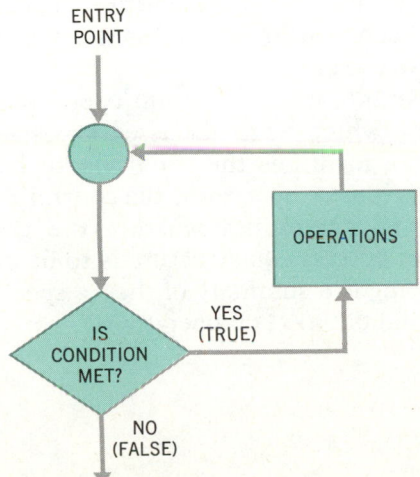

The DOWxx/END operation initiates the execution of a group of operations as long as the condition specified in the relational operator (xx) is *true*. That is, a DOWxx/END operation will continue to execute *while* a condition is met or is true.

The DOWxx/END operation has the following format:

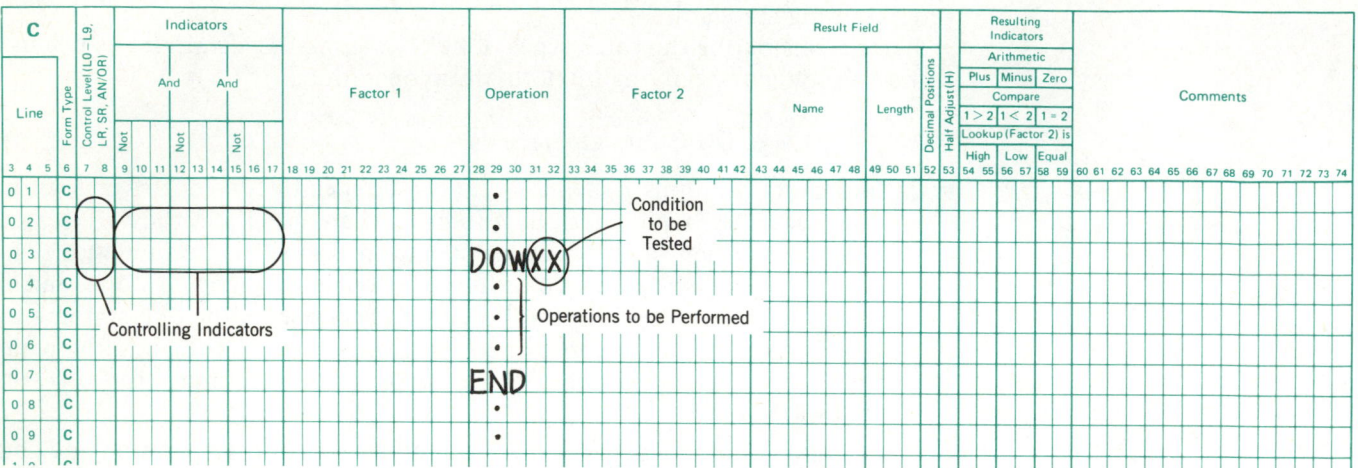

Repetitive execution of the DOWxx/END operation is determined by the comparison of the contents of Factor 1 to the contents of Factor 2. This comparison is made at the *top* of the loop (at the DOWxx statement). Therefore, if the DOWxx operation is to be executed *even once*, the condition tested must be satisfied (or true) at least initially. If the condition tested is not satisfied, the DOWxx/END iteration will not be executed and control of the program will transfer to the first statement following the associated END statement. Hence, it is possible that the group of operations within a DOWxx/END structure will not be executed at all if the condition being tested is not met.

When the DOWxx operation is executing and the END statement is reached, control transfers to the top of the loop where Factor 1 is compared to Factor 2. If the relationship between Factor 1 and Factor 2 is met, program control is passed to the first operation in the DOWxx structure and the operations within the DOWxx are executed again. If, however, the relationship between Factor 1 and Factor 2 specified by the xx operator is not true, the DOWxx/END operation is terminated and program control is transferred to the first operation following the END statement.

The DOWxx/END and DOUxx/END operations support the use of relational operators (xx), which were discussed in Chapter 5. The relational operator specified as xx identifies the condition to be tested between Factor 1 and Factor 2. Thus, the xx operator is the controlling factor for the outcome of the comparison and determines whether the group of operations within the DOWxx/END or DOUxx/END structure is to be executed.

The following is a summary of the xx specifications available for both the DOWxx/END and DOUxx/END operations:

xx Specifications for **DOWxx/END** and **DOUxx/END**	
Relational Operator (xx)	**Comparison Test**
GT	Factor 1 is greater than Factor 2
LT	Factor 1 is less than Factor 2
EQ	Factor 1 is equal to Factor 2
NE	Factor 1 is not equal to Factor 2
GE	Factor 1 is greater than or equal to Factor 2
LE	Factor 1 is less than or equal to Factor 2

Let us consider two examples in which the DOWxx/END operation can be used for iteration within a program.

Example 1 Suppose as a member of a family business you can take a one-time loan at zero percent interest. All you have to do is guarantee to repay the loan.

We wish to write the RPG program to print a payment schedule. In doing so, we wish to determine the number of payments (months) it would take to repay the loan given a loan amount and a payment amount. The record layout and printed output for a loan amount of $10,000 with payments of $425.00 are illustrated here.

LNFILE Record Layout

Loan Amount (LAMT) XXXXX	Payment (LPMT) XXXXX.XX

```
1            5 6          12
```

```
                    PAYMENT SCHEDULE

PAYMENT -      425.00        LOAN AMOUNT - 10,000

    MONTH    PAYMENT                         BALANCE
      1       425.00                          9,575
      2       425.00                          9,150
      3       425.00                          8,725
      4       425.00                          8,300
      5       425.00                          7,875
      6       425.00                          7,450
      7       425.00                          7,025
      8       425.00                          6,600
      9       425.00                          6,175
     10       425.00                          5,750
     11       425.00                          5,325
     12       425.00                          4,900
     13       425.00                          4,475
     14       425.00                          4,050
     15       425.00                          3,625
     16       425.00                          3,200
     17       425.00                          2,775
     18       425.00                          2,350
     19       425.00                          1,925
     20       425.00                          1,500
     21       425.00                          1,075
     22       425.00                            650
     23       425.00                            225
     24       225.00                              0
```

The DOWxx/END operation specifications required to print the payment schedule are as follows:

```
C  | Indicators      | Factor 1 | Operation | Factor 2 | Result Field      | Resulting Indicators | Comments
Line|And  And  Not    |          |           |          | Name   Length Dec | Plus Minus Zero ...
01 C                                          .
02 C                           Z-ADDLAMT             #BAL
03 C                           Z-ADD0               #MTHS
04 C              #BAL         DOWGTLPMT
05 C                           ADD  1               #MTHS
06 C                           SUB  LPMT            #BAL
07 C    OF                     EXCPT@H000
08 C                           SETOF                              OF
09 C                           EXCPT@PMT
10 C                           END
11 C                                          .
12 C                                          .
```

This `DOWxx/END` operation would be executed in the following manner:

1. The loan amount (`LAMT`) is transferred to a Data Structure subfield (`#BAL`) in order to keep track of the decreasing balance of the loan during the `DOWxx/END` operation.

2. The payment number (`#MTHS`) is set to zero before each payment schedule is printed. This assures us that the payment number or number of payments will be correct throughout the routine.

3. As in all other operations, a test is made to determine if conditioning indicators in columns 9–17 have been set. If any were present they would be tested first to determine if the `DOWxx/END` operation was to be executed. Since none are specified, the `DOWxx/END` operation is executed each time.

4. The `DOWxx` operation compares the contents of `#BAL` (Factor 1) with the contents of the loan payment (`LPMT`) in Factor 2 to determine if the relationship specified by the `xx` (`GT`) operator exists. If `#BAL` is greater than `LPMT`, the condition specified in the `xx` (`GT`) operator is satisfied and the operations within the DO While loop are executed. These operations include the following:

   a. `#MTHS` is increased by 1 in order to maintain a running total of the number of payments. `#MTHS` is also used to print the payment number on the report.

   b. A new loan balance (`#BAL`) is calculated by subtracting the loan payment (`LPMT`) from `#BAL`.

   c. The `OF` indicator is checked to determine whether a page overflow occurred on the previous loop. If so, the paper is advanced to a new page, headings are printed, and the `OF` indicator is `SETOF`.

   d. The payment line (`@PMT`) is then printed.

5. When the `END` statement is encountered at the end of a loop, control transfers back to the top of the loop (`DOWGT` statement), where the test between `#BAL` and `LPMT` is performed again to determine if the loop is to continue.

6. If the relationship specified by the `xx` (`GT`) operator is not met, that is `#BAL` is *not greater than* `LPMT`, control is transferred to the first statement following the associated `END` statement.

7. The `DOWGT` operation continues until the relationship (`#BAL` is greater than `LPMT`) is no longer true. At this time, control transfers to the statement following the `END` statement and processing continues.

Once the DOWxx/END operation is completed (#BAL is not greater than LPMT), one final step is required, the calculation and printing of the final payment. The DOWxx/END operation is terminated when the balance of the loan is no longer greater than the payment. However, when this occurs there still is a balance owing that is equal to or less than the LPMT. This is shown in the Payment Schedule Report.

Figure 6.12 illustrates the payment program in its entirety, including the calculation and printing of the final payment. Review the DOWxx/END operation and the final payment calculations carefully.

If the Condition Tested in the DOWxx Loop Is Not Met Initially, the Loop Is Not Executed at All

Note that the test for the specific condition (#BAL is greater than LPMT) is made *before* the series of steps within the loop is executed even once. A DOWxx/END loop was used in

Figure 6.12
Program for Example 1.

```
....+....1....+....2....+....3....+....4....+....5....+....6....+....7
0001 **********************************************************************
0002 *
0003 *    PROGRAM DESCRIPTION:
0004 *
0005 *        THIS PROGRAM PRODUCES A LOAN PAYMENT SCHEDULE.
0006 *
0007 *
0008 *    FUNCTION OF INDICATORS:
0009 *
0010 *        NONE
0011 *
0012 **********************************************************************
0013 *
0014 H
0015 FLNFILE IP  F      12              DISK
0016 FREPORT O   F      80       OF     PRINTER
0017 *
0018 ILNFILE  NS
0019 I                                  1    50LAMT
0020 I                                  6   122LPMT
0021 I#WORK      DS
0022 I                                  1    30#MTHS
0023 I                                  4    80#BAL
0024 *
0025 C                   EXCPT@H000                      NEW PAGE
0026 C                   Z-ADDLAMT    #BAL
0027 C                   Z-ADD0       #MTHS
0028 C           #BAL    DOWGTLPMT
0029 C                   ADD  1       #MTHS
0030 C                   SUB  LPMT    #BAL
0031 C     OF            EXCPT@H000
0032 C                   SETOF                    OF
0033 C                   EXCPT@PMT
0034 C                   END
0035 C                   ADD  1       #MTHS        CALCULATE
0036 C                   Z-ADD#BAL    LPMT         AND
0037 C                   Z-ADD0       #BAL         PRINT
0038 C     OF            EXCPT@H000                FINAL
0039 C                   SETOF                    OF    PAYMENT
0040 C                   EXCPT@PMT                      HERE
0041 *
0042 OREPORT E   02      @H000
0043 O                                 40 'PAYMENT SCHEDULE'
0044 O       E   04      @H000
0045 O                                 10 'PAYMENT -'
0046 O                   LPMT   1      20
0047 O                                 43 'LOAN AMOUNT -'
0048 O                   LAMT   1      50
0049 O       E   0607    @H000
0050 O                                 10 'MONTH'
0051 O                                 20 'PAYMENT'
0052 O                                 50 'BALANCE'
0053 O       E 1         @PMT
0054 O                   #MTHS  Z       9
0055 O                   LPMT   1      20
0056 O                   #BAL   1      50
```

this example because the possibility exists that you may wish to make a one-time payment in which your payment is equal to the loan balance, as shown here:

```
                        PAYMENT SCHEDULE

     PAYMENT - 10,000.00              LOAN AMOUNT - 10,000

        MONTH    PAYMENT                        BALANCE

           1   10,000.00                           0
```

In this case, the statements within the DOWxx/END loop are not executed at all because the loan balance would not be greater than the payment amount. Thus, control transfers to the line following the associated END statement where the final payment (in this case, the only payment) is calculated and printed (see Figure 6.12 again). This would be the correct procedure, because the payment is equal to the loan amount and thus only the final payment calculation is required. Therefore, we would want to bypass the loop entirely.

If the possibility exists that the contents of Factor 1 and Factor 2 *may not* be equal at the beginning, a DOWxx/END operation should be used. If it was determined beforehand that the loan would never be paid in one payment, then a DOUxx/END loop would be more appropriate. We will use this same example when we discuss the DOUxx/END operation to illustrate why.

Note that the DOWxx/END operation tests the relationship between Factor 1 and Factor 2 at the beginning of the loop. Therefore, the contents of the two factors must be *initialized* or contain valid data before execution of the DOWxx/END operation so that the result of the test will be true the first time. If the condition specified with the DOWxx is *not* met initially, the operations within the DOWxx/END operation will not be performed at all.

Example 2 Write the RPG program to produce a customer loan report. The input file CL301 contains a customer loan number (CLNUMB) and current balance (CLCBAL). The systems flowchart, record layout, and printed output are as follows:

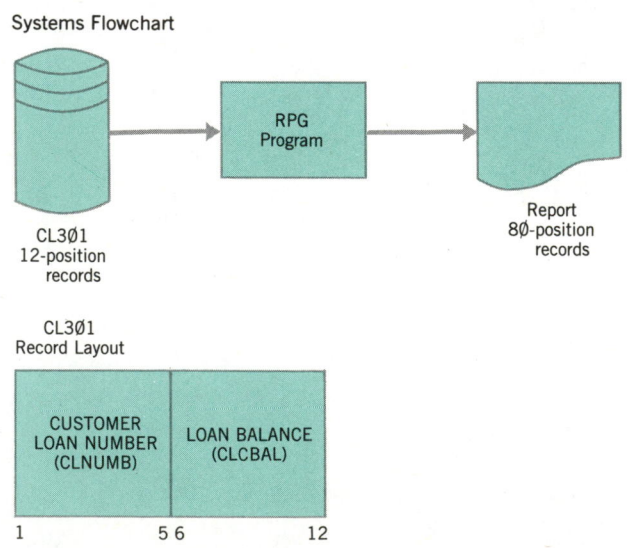

Systems Flowchart

CL301
12-position
records

RPG
Program

Report
80-position
records

CL301
Record Layout

CUSTOMER
LOAN NUMBER
(CLNUMB)

LOAN BALANCE
(CLCBAL)

1   5 6   12

```
                      CUSTOMER LOAN REPORT

                        LOAN # 6365
              CURRENT BALANCE    $485.00
              PAYMENT                                    NEW
               NUMBER     INTEREST        PAYMENT      BALANCE

                  01        7.28           59.07        433.21
                  02        6.50           52.77        386.94
                  03        5.80           47.13        345.61
                  04        5.18           42.09        308.70
                  05        4.63           37.60        275.73
                  06        4.14           33.58        246.29
                  07        3.69           30.00        219.98
                  08        3.30           26.79        196.49
                  09        2.95           23.93        175.51
                  10        2.63           21.38        156.76
                  11        2.35           19.09        140.02
                  12        2.10           17.05        125.07
                  13        1.88           15.23        111.72
                  14        1.68           13.61         99.79
                  15        1.50           12.15         89.14
                  16        1.34           10.86         79.62
                  17        1.19            9.70         71.11
                  18        1.07            8.66         63.52
                  19         .95            7.74         56.73
                  20         .85            6.91         50.67
                  21         .76            6.17         45.26
```

The purpose of this report program is to determine how many payments are required to reduce the loan balance to a value less than or equal to $50.00. When calculating the new monthly balance, an interest charge of 1.5% is added to the previous month's balance before calculating the payment. The payment is calculated by multiplying the loan balance amount by 12%. Thus, the following calculations are required:

Monthly Interest = Previous Month's Balance $*$ .015 (1.5%)

New Balance = Previous Month's Balance + Monthly Interest

Payment = New Balance $*$ .12 (12%)

New Monthly Balance = New Balance − Payment

The Calculation Specifications form to perform these calculations is shown in Figure 6.13.

Figure 6.13
Calculation Specifications for Example 2.

A DOWxx/END operation was used in this program because the current balance from the input record could be a value below $50.00, in which case we do not want the DOWxx/END operation to be executed. Remember, we want to determine how many payments are required to bring the balance *equal to or less than $50.00*. Therefore, if the current balance is already equal to or below $50.00, the DOWxx/END operation should not be executed at all. Figure 6.14 illustrates the complete RPG specifications for the customer loan report program.

Figure 6.14
Program for Example 2.

```
....+....1....+....2....+....3....+....4....+....5....+....6....+....7
0001  ******************************************************************
0002  *
0003  *   PROGRAM DESCRIPTION:
0004  *
0005  *       THIS PROGRAM PRODUCES A CUSTOMER LOAN REPORT.
0006  *       THE PROGRAM READS THE CUSTOMER'S LOAN BALANCE,
0007  *       ADDS A MONTHLY INTEREST CHARGE, CALCULATES AND PRINTS
0008  *       THE MONTHLY PAYMENTS AND DETERMINES HOW MANY PAYMENTS
0009  *       ARE REQUIRED TO REDUCE THE LOAN BALANCE TO A VALUE
0010  *       LESS THAN OR EQUAL TO $50.00.
0011  *
0012  *
0013  *   FUNCTION OF INDICATORS:
0014  *
0015  *       NONE
0016  *
0017  ******************************************************************
0018  *
0019  H
0020  FCL301    IP  F       12              DISK
0021  FREPORT   O   F       80      OF      PRINTER
0022  *
0023  ICL301    NS
0024  I                                     1    5 CLNUMB
0025  I                                     6  122CLCBAL
0026  I#WORK        DS
0027  I                                     1   72#NBAL
0028  I                                     8  122#INT
0029  I                                    13  192#PAYMT
0030  I                                    20  210#MONTH
0031  *
0032  *                               MAIN-LINE-RTN
0033  C                   EXSR SR100
0034  *
0035  *                               SR100-CALCULATE-CUSTOMER-LOAN-RTN
0036  CSR        SR100    BEGSR
0037  CSR                 EXCPT@H000
0038  CSR                 Z-ADD0          #MONTH
0039  CSR                 Z-ADDCLCBAL     #NBAL
0040  CSR        #NBAL    DOWGE50.00
0041  CSR        #NBAL    MULT .015       #INT        H
0042  CSR                 ADD  #INT       #NBAL
0043  CSR        #NBAL    MULT .12        #PAYMT      H
0044  CSR                 SUB  #PAYMT     #NBAL
0045  CSR                 ADD  1          #MONTH
0046  CSR OF              EXCPT@H000
0047  CSR                 SETOF                       OF
0048  CSR                 EXCPT@E100
0049  CSR                 END
0050  CSR                 ENDSR
0051  *
0052  OREPORT   E    02           @H000
0053  O                                    30 'CUSTOMER LOAN REPORT'
0054  O         E    04           @H000
0055  O                                    20 'LOAN #'
0056  O                           CLNUMB   26
0057  O         E    05           @H000
0058  O                                    20 'CURRENT BALANCE'
0059  O                           CLCBAL1  30 '$'
0060  O         E    06           @H000
0061  O                                    15 'PAYMENT'
0062  O                                    50 'NEW'
0063  O         E    107          @H000
0064  O                                    15 'NUMBER'
0065  O                                    25 'INTEREST'
0066  O                                    40 'PAYMENT'
0067  O                                    50 'BALANCE'
0068  O         E  1              @E100
0069  O                           #MONTH   15
0070  O                           #INT   1 25
0071  O                           #PAYMT1  40
0072  O                           #NBAL  1 50
```

Figure 6.15
DO Until xx/END control structure.

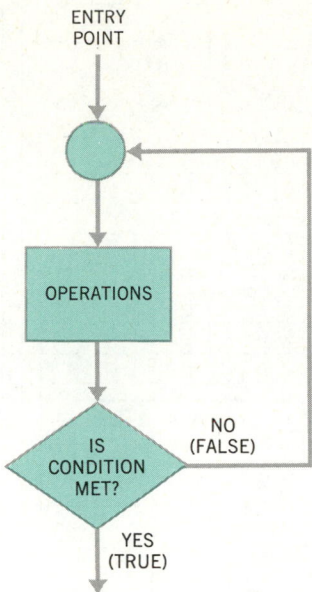

C. The DOUxx/END (DO Until) Operation

The second form of iteration is the DOUxx/END operation illustrated in the flowchart in Figure 6.15.

The DOUxx/END operation, known as the DO Until operation, executes a group of instructions *until* a specified condition is met. That is, the DOWxx/END loop achieves iteration for as long as a given condition is true, whereas the DOUxx/END loop achieves iteration *until* a given condition is true. The specifications below illustrate the use of the DOUxx/END operation format.

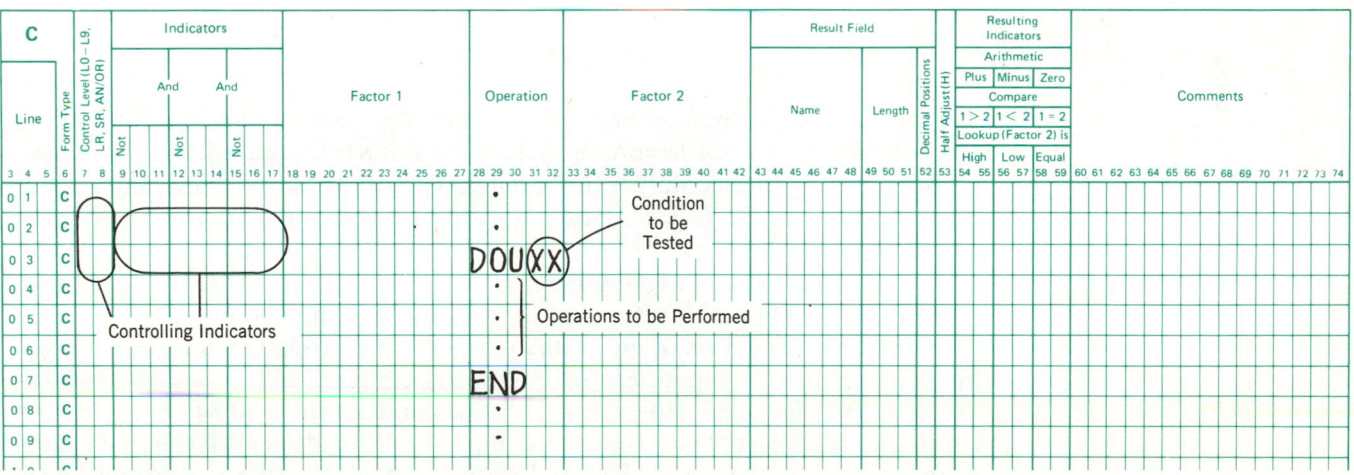

The DOUxx/END operation follows the same general rules as the DOWxx/END operation. The following two structures are equivalent:

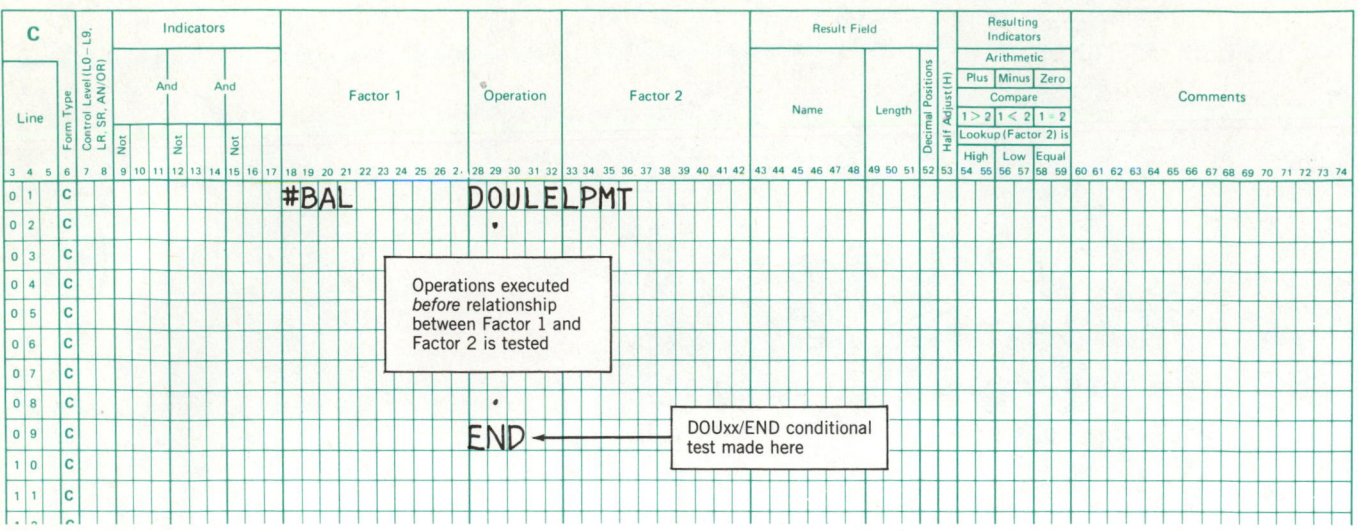

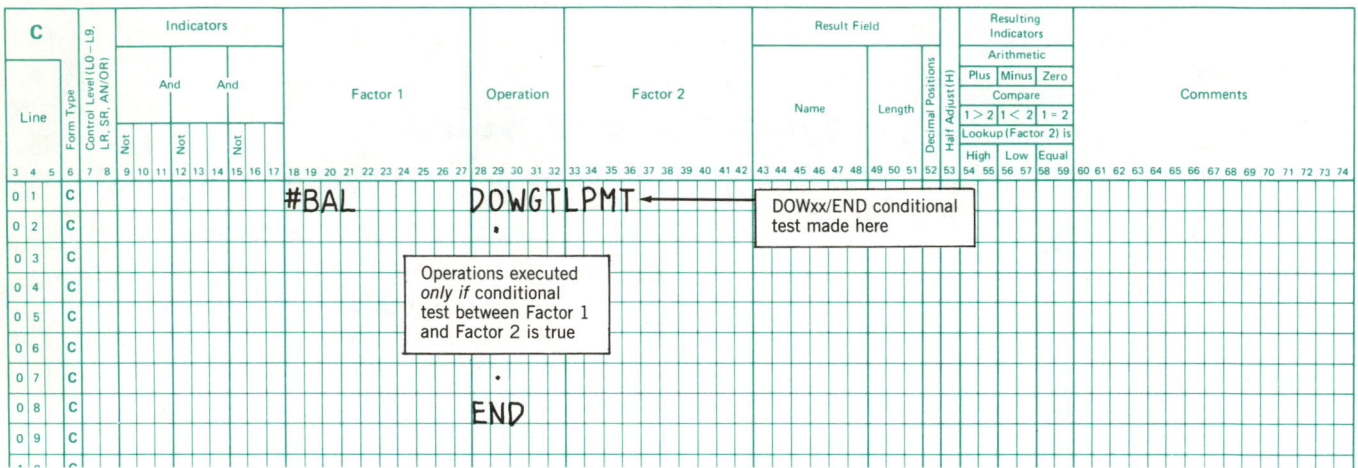

To execute a loop *until* #BAL *is less than or equal to* LPMT is the same as executing the loop *while* #BAL is greater than LPMT. These are essentially two different ways to accomplish the same task. Note that the same instructions used in Figure 6.12 to calculate and print the last payment would again be needed.

There is, however, a major difference in the execution of the two structures: that difference is in the setup and in the way they may be used.

Repetitive execution of the DOUxx/END operation is determined by the comparison of the contents of Factor 1 with the contents of Factor 2. Unlike the DOWxx/END, however, this comparison is made *at the end of the loop* (END statement). Thus, the first time the comparison is made is *after* the first execution of the DOUxx loop. Fields used in the comparison, then, need not be set before the looping operation is executed. They can be altered during the DOUxx/END loop because the comparison is not performed until the end of the loop.

Once the END statement has been reached in a DOUxx/END loop, Factor 1 is compared with Factor 2. If the relationship between Factor 1 and Factor 2 specified by the xx operator is true, the DOUxx/END is terminated and program control is transferred to the first operation following the END operation. However, if the relationship between Factor 1 and Factor 2 is not true, program control is passed to the first operation in the DOUxx structure and the operations within the loop are executed again. The operators specified within the DOUxx/END operation, then, are executed *at least once*, regardless of the condition specified in the xx operator or the values specified in Factor 1 and Factor 2.

Thus, when deciding whether to use a DOUxx/END operation or a DOWxx/END operation, consider the following:

1. Will the data fields in Factor 1 and Factor 2 be initialized before the execution of the looping operation? If they will, a DOWxx/END loop can be used. If, however, the values for Factor 1 or Factor 2 will be initialized during the loop, a DOUxx/END operation is necessary.
2. Do you want a loop executed at least once? Then use the DOUxx/END, because a DOWxx/END may not be executed at all if the conditions being tested are met initially.

Consider the payment schedule program discussed earlier. The following DOUxx/END operation could have been used to accomplish the same task:

Line	Form Type	Control Level (L0–L9, LR, SR, AN/OR)	Indicators (And/Not/And/Not/And/Not)	Factor 1	Operation	Factor 2	Result Field Name	Length	Decimal Positions	Half Adjust (H)	Resulting Indicators Plus / Minus / Zero — Compare 1>2 / 1<2 / 1=2 — High / Low / Equal	Comments
0 1	C				.							
0 2	C				Z-ADD LAMT	#BAL						
0 3	C				Z-ADD 0	#MTHS						
0 4	C			#BAL	DOULE LPMT							
0 5	C				ADD 1	#MTHS						
0 6	C				SUB LPMT	#BAL						
0 7	C		OF		EXCPT @H00							
0 8	C				SETOF						OF	
0 9	C				EXCPT @PMT							
1 0	C				END							
1 1	C				.							
1 2	C				.							
1 3	C				.							

To execute this DOUxx/END loop until #BAL is less than or equal to LPMT is the same as executing the DOWxx/END operation while #BAL is greater than LPMT. However, there is a major difference in the execution of the two structures.

The DOUxx/END operation tests the relationship between #BAL and LPMT at the bottom of the loop, that is, during the END operation. Thus, the operations within the DOUxx/END loop are executed at least once before the comparison test is made.

The DOWxx/END operation, however, tests the relationship between #BAL and LPMT at the beginning of the loop. If the condition specified with the DOWxx is *not* met initially, the operations within the DOWxx/END operation will not be performed at all.

Let us consider a more detailed example of the DOUxx/END operation.

Example   Write the RPG program to read an employee's salary, add a cost-of-living allowance and salary increase to the employee's salary, and determine how many years it would take to double the salary.

The employee records are contained in the input file called EM222. The systems flowchart, record layout, and printed report describing the output requirements are illustrated here.

Systems Flowchart

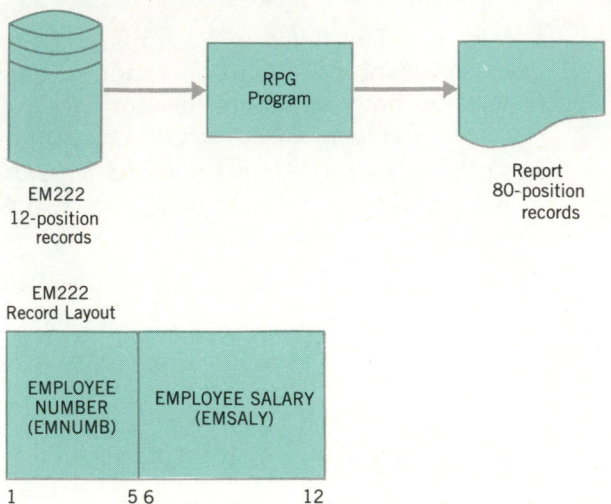

EM222
12-position
records

RPG
Program

Report
80-position
records

EM222
Record Layout

EMPLOYEE NUMBER (EMNUMB)	EMPLOYEE SALARY (EMSALY)

1   5 6   12

```
        SALARY PROJECTION REPORT

        EMPLOYEE # 6365
          CURRENT SALARY   $485.00

              COST OF   SALARY      NEW
       YEAR   LIVING    INCREASE    SALARY

        01    15.52     29.10       529.62
        02    16.95     31.78       578.35
        03    18.51     34.70       631.56
        04    20.21     37.89       689.66
        05    22.07     41.38       753.11
        06    24.10     45.19       822.40
        07    26.32     49.34       898.06
        08    28.74     53.88       980.68
```

Each input record contains an employee number (EMNUMB) and the employee's current salary (EMSALY). Using a cost-of-living allowance of 3.2% and a salary increase of 6.0% each year, we use a DOUxx/END operation to calculate the actual cost of living allowance in dollars and cents, the salary increase, and the new salary for each year. Figure 6.16 illustrates the Calculation Specifications required for this program.

Examine the full RPG source listing for this program illustrated in Figure 6.17. The mainline for this program consists of just one operation, EXSR SR105, which executes a subroutine that calculates the cost of living allowance, salary increase, and new salary for each year, and prints the required output report.

Prior to the DOUxx/END operation, the original salary is multiplied by two and placed in the field #DSALY. During the DOUxx/END operation, the new salary field #NSALY will be compared to #DSALY to determine when execution of the DOUxx/END operation is to terminate.

The eight instructions between the DOUGT and END statements are executed at least once because the comparison is not made in a DOUxx operation until the end of the loop. Once the END statement is encountered the new salary (#NSALY) is compared to #DSALY. If the condition is met, that is, #NSALY is greater than or equal to #DSALY, the

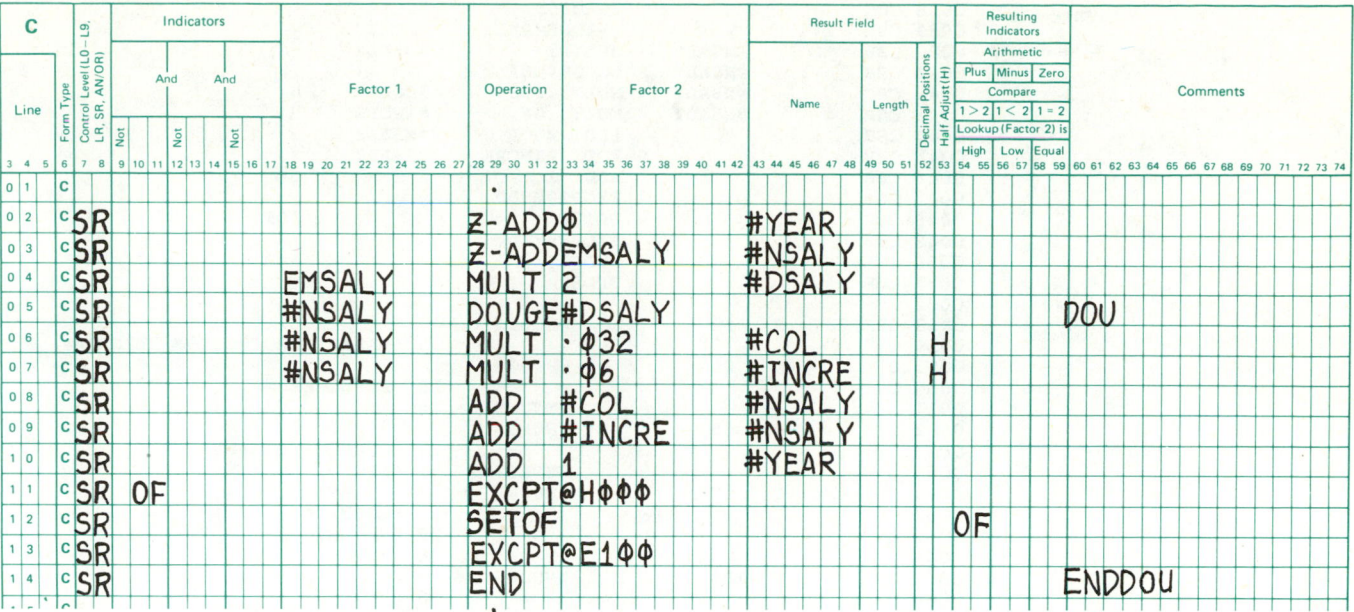

Figure 6.16
Calculation Specifications for
sample program.

Figure 6.17
RPG specifications for sample
program.

```
....+....1....+....2....+....3....+....4....+....5....+....6....+....7
0001  ***************************************************************
0002  *
0003  *   PROGRAM DESCRIPTION:
0004  *
0005  *       THIS PROGRAM PRINTS A SALARY PROJECTION REPORT.
0006  *       THE PROGRAM READS AN EMPLOYEE'S SALARY AND DETERMINES
0007  *       HOW MANY YEARS IT WOULD TAKE TO DOUBLE THE SALARY
0008  *       WHEN A COST OF LIVING AND SALARY INCREASE
0009  *       ARE ADDED EACH YEAR TO THE SALARY.
0010  *
0011  *
0012  *   FUNCTION OF INDICATORS:
0013  *
0014  *       NONE
0015  *
0016  ***************************************************************
0017  *
0018  H
0019  FEM222    IP  F      12              DISK
0020  FREPORT   O   F      80        OF    PRINTER
0021  *
0022  IEM222    NS
0023  I                               1    5 EMNUMB
0024  I                               6  122EMSALY
0025  I#WORK       DS
0026  I                               1   52#COL
0027  I                               6  102#INCRE
0028  I                              11  172#NSALY
0029  I                              18  242#DSALY
0030  I                              25  260#YEAR
0031  *
0032  *                                    MAIN-LINE-RTN
0033  C                           EXSR SR105
0034  *
0035  *                                    SR105-CALCULATE-SALARY-RTN
0036  CSR          SR105      BEGSR
0037  CSR                     EXCPT@H000
```

Figure 6.17
(continued)

```
0038 CSR                       Z-ADD0         #YEAR
0039 CSR                       Z-ADDEMSALY    #NSALY
0040 CSR          EMSALY       MULT 2         #DSALY
0041 CSR          #NSALY       DOUGE#DSALY
0042 CSR          #NSALY       MULT .032      #COL      H
0043 CSR          #NSALY       MULT .06       #INCRE    H
0044 CSR                       ADD  #COL      #NSALY
0045 CSR                       ADD  #INCRE    #NSALY
0046 CSR                       ADD  1         #YEAR
0047 CSR OF                    EXCPT@H000
0048 CSR                       SETOF                    OF
0049 CSR                       EXCPT@E100
0050 CSR                       END
0051 CSR                       ENDSR
0052  *
0053 OREPORT  E    02          @H000
0054 O                                        35 'SALARY PROJECTION REPORT'
0055 O         E    04          @H000
0056 O                                        10 'EMPLOYEE #'
0057 O                         EMNUMB         16
0058 O         E    05          @H000
0059 O                                        15 'CURRENT SALARY'
0060 O                         EMSALY1        25 '$'
0061 O         E    07          @H000
0062 O                                        21 'COST OF'
0063 O                                        29 'SALARY'
0064 O                                        38 'NEW'
0065 O         E    108         @H000
0066 O                                        10 'YEAR'
0067 O                                        20 'LIVING'
0068 O                                        30 'INCREASE'
0069 O                                        40 'SALARY'
0070 O         E  1             @E100
0071 O                         #YEAR          10
0072 O                         #COL  1        20
0073 O                         #INCRE1        30
0074 O                         #NSALY1        40
```

DOUGT operation is terminated and execution of the program continues with the operation following the END statement. The ENDSR statement would then be executed, terminating the subroutine and passing control of the program back to the main body of the program.

However, if #NSALY is not greater than or equal to #DSALY (the salary doubled), then control of the program transfers to the beginning of the DOUxx operation and the operations within the DOU operation are repeated.

D. The DO/END Operation

Repeating or iterating a series of steps as long as a certain condition exists is called *looping*. We saw earlier how these types of looping routines can be executed using the DOWxx and DOUxx operations.

1. Using a Counter (Index Value) for Looping a Predetermined Number of Times

Sometimes, however, we know in advance the *number of times* we want to execute a loop. In such cases we can use a *counter* along with a looping operation to control the number of times a routine is repeated or iterated. Instead of testing for a condition to be met to terminate the loop, we test the counter to see if the loop has been executed the required number of times.

In this section, we consider the DO/END looping operation in which a counter controls the looping procedure.

2. A Simple DO/END Operation

Here, we will examine the simplest DO/END operation, which is used for executing a group of operations a *fixed number of times*. With this DO/END format, we perform a series of operations using a counter or index value that begins at 1 and is incremented by 1 until it reaches a maximum or limit value. For example, an input record containing a customer's name and address is read into the program. If we wanted to print five mailing labels for each customer record in the file, we would begin our counter or index value at 1 and loop until the counter or index field is greater than 5, thus producing five mailing labels. Printing five mailing labels for each customer can be performed using unconditional branching as described previously, or it can be performed using a structured simple DO/END operation as shown below:

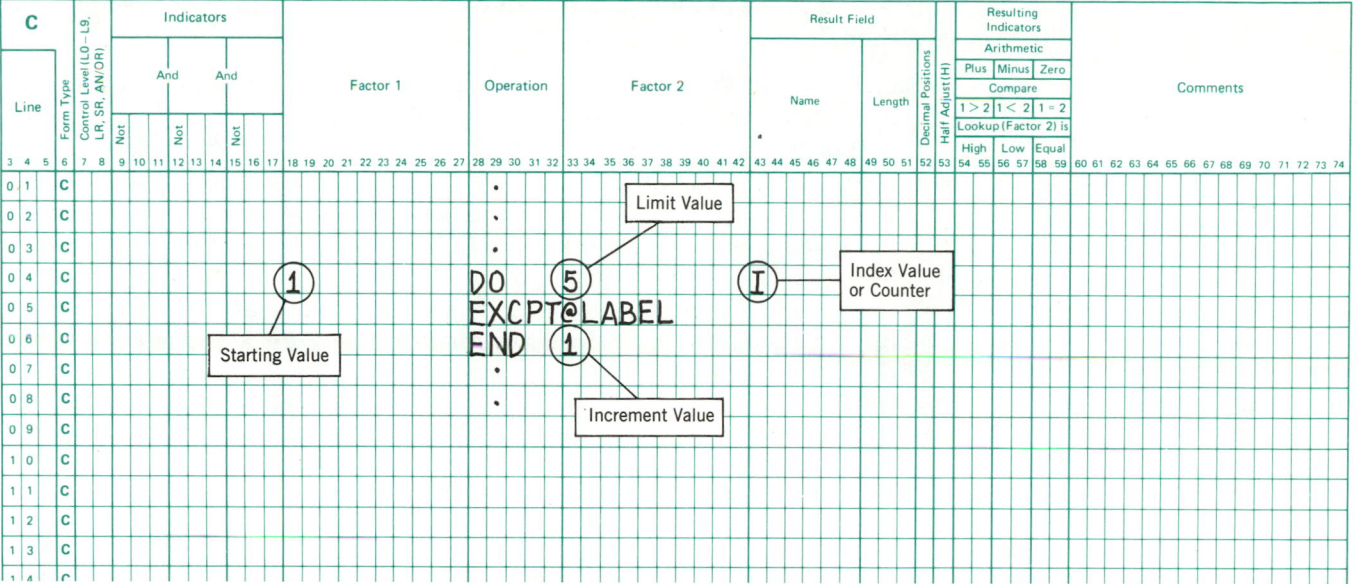

In this program excerpt a *counter* or *index value* (I) is used to keep track of the number of times the DO/END iteration is performed. Before execution, the index (Result Field) is set equal to the starting value of 1 specified in Factor 1. That is, the index value will typically begin as 1 during the first execution of the iteration, then be set to 2, etc., until it reaches 5.

When the END statement is reached at the end of each loop, the index value is increased by the increment value 1 found in Factor 2 of the END statement. Control is then returned to the top of the loop where the index value is compared to the limit value. If the index value *is greater than* the limit value, the loop is terminated and control is transferred to the first operation following the END statement. However, if the index value *is not greater than* the limit value, the loop is executed again. Processing of the loop continues repeatedly until the index value is greater than the limit value, at which time the DO/END operation is terminated.

In our example, this structure will execute the EXCPT operation within the DO/END loop five times. The EXCPT operation is the only one required within the DO loop and is used to output a label to a printer each time a pass is made through the DO loop.

The DO/END operation is typically used when we wish to perform a loop a *predefined number of times* in which a counter or index value needs to be incremented, as in this case.

To determine the number of times the loop will be executed, the DO/END operation:

Establishes a counter or index value (Result Field) that keeps track of the number of times the loop is executed.

Increases or decreases the index value each time through the loop using an increment value (Factor 2 of the END statement).

Specifies the range in which the index value is to vary. This range includes a starting value (Factor 1) and a limit or maximum value (Factor 2).

A DOWxx/END or DOUxx/END could be used in place of a DO/END to achieve the same result, but to do so would require more programming effort to initialize an index and increment it each time through the loop. We recommend using a DO/END for executing a loop a fixed number of times.

Let us examine in more detail each component or parameter of the DO/END operation.

Factor 1 (columns 18–27) contains a *starting value* from which the DO/END operation is to begin. Upon execution of the DO/END operation this value is transferred to the index value or counter. This initializes the counter before looping begins.

The starting value in Factor 1 can contain a numeric literal, a numeric field name, a Data Structure subfield name, or an array element (see Chapter 10).

Factor 1 is optional and if not specified will default to 1. Thus, in the DO/END operation to produce five mailing labels, the starting value is not required if we wish to begin the counter at the value 1 (which we do).

Factor 2 (columns 33–42) contains the *limit value* or the maximum value of the index. At the beginning of each loop, the index value is compared to the limit value to determine if looping is to continue.

Like the starting value, the limit value can contain a numeric literal, a numeric field name, a Data Structure subfield name, or an array element.

The limit value in Factor 2 is also optional and if not specified will default to 1. To print five mailing labels for each record we must specify 5 for the limit value in order to have the loop terminate after looping five times.

Operation code for the DO statement (columns 28–32) must contain the letters DO in columns 28 and 29. Unlike the DOUxx and DOWxx operation, the DO/END operation does not contain an xx relational operator. Thus, a conditional test is not explicitly performed with the DO operation. Rather, the loop will be executed until the index value exceeds the specified limit value.

Result Field (columns 43–48) contains the current *index value* or counter variable, which is adjusted during each execution of the DO/END operation. The index value is compared to the limit value at the beginning of each loop to determine when to exit the DO operation. When the index value becomes greater than the limit value, the DO operation is terminated and control transfers to the first operation following the END statement.

The index value contains the count of the number of times through the loop and can be used within the loop procedure as a variable field. For example, the index value might be used to specify the number of customer payments or the number of months. This concept will be illustrated later in this chapter.

The Result Field or index value *cannot contain a numeric literal* but must be a numeric data field, a Data Structure subfield, or array element (see Chapter 10). If the Result Field is not specified, RPG will create a numeric index field with no decimals to serve as the DO operation counter.

Since we do not want to make reference to the index value or counter during the looping procedure there is no need to identify a variable field in our mailing label example.

Operation code for the END statement (columns 28–32) must contain the letters END in columns 28–30. Every DO/END operation must terminate with an END statement.

Factor 2 of the END statement specifies the *increment value*. The increment value is added to the index value each time the END statement is encountered. If the increment value is not specified, the increment value will default to 1.

Again, in our example, we use an increment of 1. That is, each time through the loop, the index value is increased by 1.

Each of these delimiters has a default value of 1. Thus, they need not be specified with all DO/END operations, although we recommend that you use them. As we examine different variations of the DO/END operation we will explain in more detail how each delimiter is used.

Our mailing label problem, then, could be specified as follows:

C	Form Type	Control Level (L0–L9, LR, SR, AN/OR)	Indicators			Factor 1	Operation	Factor 2	Result Field				Resulting Indicators				Comments
Line			And Not	And Not	Not				Name	Length	Decimal Positions	Half Adjust (H)	Plus 1>2 High	Minus 1<2 Low	Zero 1=2 Equal		
0 1	C						•										
0 2	C						•										
0 3	C						•										
0 4	C						DO 5										
0 5	C						EXCPT@LABEL										
0 6	C						END										
0 7	C						•										
0 8	C						•										

With this type of a DO operation, it is *not* necessary to establish a counter or index value that must be incremented each time through the loop. When the counter or *index value* field (Result Field) is not used, an internal variable field with a default value of 1 is established by RPG to maintain the count or index value.

In addition, if the loop is to begin at 1, it is not necessary to specify the starting value in Factor 1. When the starting value is not specified, RPG establishes a default value of 1 and transfers that value to the index variable in the Result Field. The DO 5 line is sufficient to indicate that we want to execute the EXCPT five times.

As noted, we could also have used a DOWxx/END or a DOUxx/END to achieve the same type of looping. However, the DO/END type of iteration better accommodates a looping procedure when a counter is required.

Let us consider additional examples of the DO/END operation in order to illustrate how and when to use the different delimiters.

Variable Starting and Limit Values

In the mailing label example, numeric literals were used for the *starting* and *limit* values. The starting and limit values or delimiters of the DO/END operation could also be numeric *variables*. Moreover, the starting value or delimiter need not be 1. See the following examples:

Line	Factor 1	Operation	Factor 2	Result Field (Name)	Comments
01	1	DO	L	I	If L = 8,
02		.			I will vary from 1 to 8
03		.			(Loop will execute 8 times)
04		.			
05		END			
06					
07					
08	S	DO	25	I	If S = 1,
09		.			I will vary from 1 to 25
10		.			(Loop will execute 25 times)
11		.			
12		END			
13					
14					
15	S	DO	L	I	If S = 4 and L = 60,
16		.			I will vary from 4 to 60
17		.			(Loop will execute 57 times)
18		.			
19		END			
20	C				

Examples   **If the Starting Value Is Greater Than the Limit Value in a DO/END, the Loop Is Not Executed at All**

Suppose we wish to print the mailing labels, but we want to enable the user to determine the number of mailing labels desired. We could add a new field, number of labels (LNUMB), to the input record. This field would contain the number of labels required for each customer. Thus, the following would be required to print a variable number of labels for each customer:

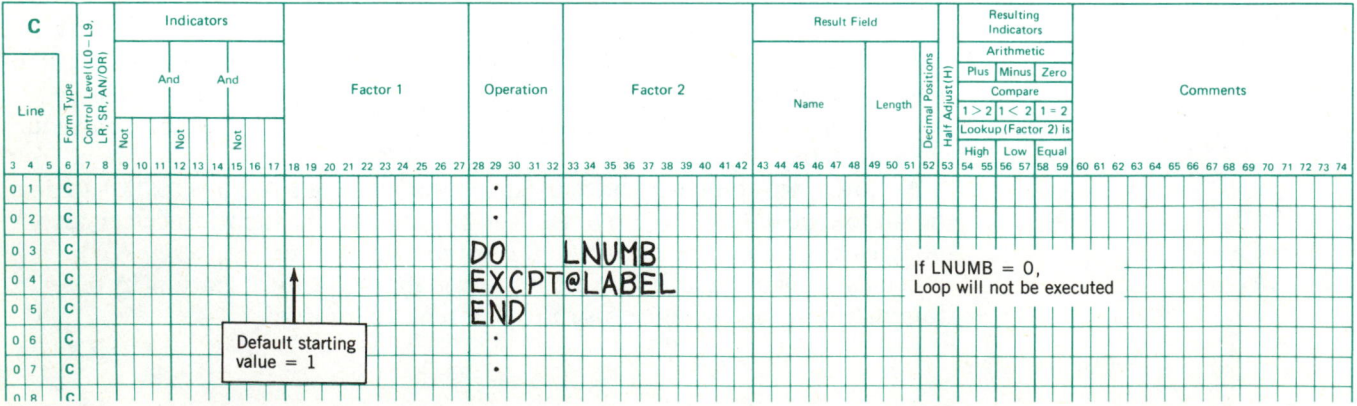

The operations within the DO/END loop will be *skipped entirely* if the starting value is greater than the limit value. That is, if the user has entered a 0 into the LNUMB field, the operation DO LNUMB would result in *zero* or *no executions* of the loop. Note that LNUMB is incremented by 1, by default.

Incrementing the Index Value in a DO/END by a Value Other Than One

Consider the following:

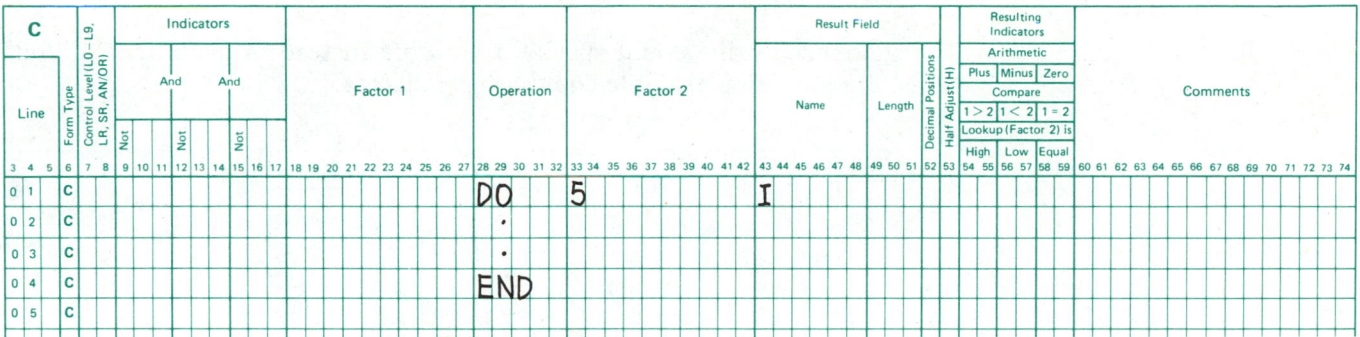

The computer executes the loop five times. The first time, I has a value of 1, then 2, until it reaches 5. When I is 5, the loop is executed a fifth time; then the operation following the END statement is executed.

Thus, I is incremented by one each time the loop is performed. Using the increment value (Factor 2 of the END statement), however, we can increment I by any value we wish.

Suppose we want to sum the odd numbers from 1 to 101, inclusive of the end points, using a DO/END loop, and place the result in #SUM. We could specify the following:

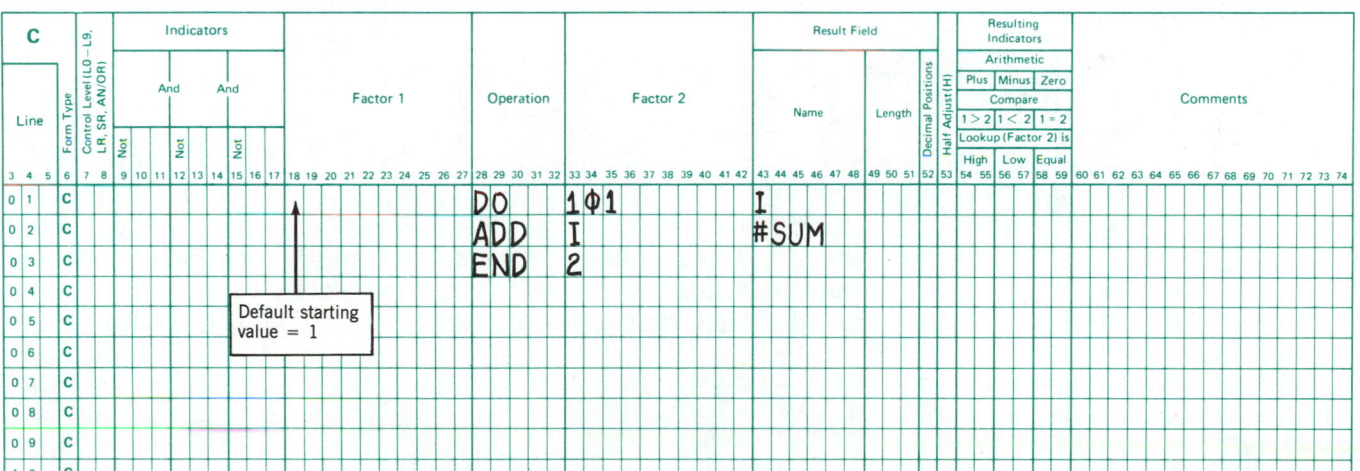

In this DO/END operation, I is set equal to 1. Each time through the loop, the value of I is added to #SUM and then I is incremented by 2. Note that this is an example of how the index value may be used during calculations within the looping procedure. Here, the index value I is added to #SUM. The following indicates how the operations are performed:

	Value in I After	
No. of Times Through Loop	Loop is Performed	Value in #SUM
0	1	0
1	3	1
2	5	1 + 3
:	:	:
50	103	1 + 3 + 5 + . . . 101

The increment value could specify a *variable* instead of a numeric literal. Thus, the preceding example could be specified as:

Line	Form Type	Factor 1	Operation	Factor 2	Result Field Name	Comments
0 1	C		DO	1Ø1	I	If V = 2,
0 2	C		ADD	I	#SUM	I will be incremented
0 3	C		END	V		by 2 each time through the loop
0 4	C					
0 5	C					

Moreover, we can use the increment value to *decrease* the index value. The following is also correct:

Line	Form Type	Factor 1	Operation	Factor 2	Result Field Name
0 1	C	1Ø1	DO	1	I
0 2	C		ADD	I	#SUM
0 3	C		END	-2	
0 4	C				

If the increment value is omitted, the *default* increment value is 1. This means that the computer assumes we wish to increment the index value by one each time. Thus, the following two instructions produce identical results:

Line	Form Type	Factor 1	Operation	Factor 2	Result Field Name
0 1	C		DO	5	I
0 2	C		.		
0 3	C		.		
0 4	C		.		
0 5	C		END		
0 6	C				

Line	Form Type	Control Level (L0–L9, LR, SR, AN/OR)	Indicators And / And	Factor 1	Operation	Factor 2	Result Field Name	Length	Decimal Positions	Half Adjust (H)	Resulting Indicators	Comments
01	C				DO	5	I					
02	C				.							
03	C				.							
04	C				.							
05	C				END	1						
06	C											
07	C											

To start I at 5 and decrease to 1, however, we must use:

Line	Form Type	Control Level (L0–L9, LR, SR, AN/OR)	Indicators And / And	Factor 1	Operation	Factor 2	Result Field Name	Length	Decimal Positions	Half Adjust (H)	Resulting Indicators	Comments
01	C			5	DO	1	I					
02	C				.							
03	C				.							
04	C				.							
05	C				END	-1						
06	C											
07	C											

In summary, the DO/END operation results in the execution of a group of operations a specified or fixed number of times. The number of times the loop is to be executed is identified in the DO/END operation by supplying a starting value, a limit value, an increment value, and an index value. Each of these has default values that can be changed by the programmer if desired.

Example Suppose we wish to sum all the even numbers between 2 and 100. To perform this operation we can initialize the index value at 2 and increment the index by 2 during each cycle through the loop. The specifications to perform this DO/END operation are shown in Figure 6.18.

The following steps describe the execution of this DO/END operation:

Step 1. The first line of the DO operation is examined for the presence of indicators (columns 7–17). If indicators are specified, they are checked to determine if the DO/END operation is to be executed. In our example here, no indicators are specified; therefore, the DO/END operation will be performed each time the instruction is encountered.

Step 2. When the DO operation is executed, the *starting value* of 2 in Factor 1 is transferred to the *index value field* (#NUMB) specified in the Result Field.

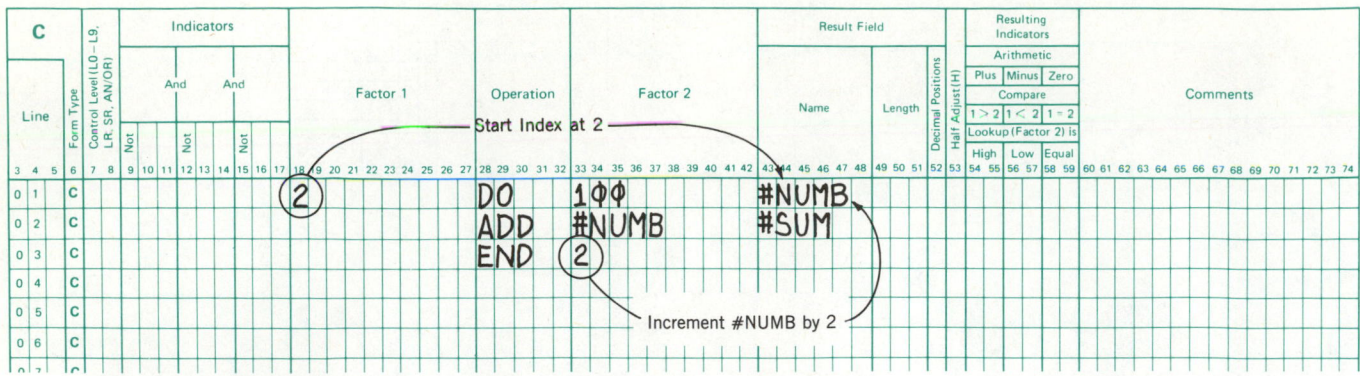

Figure 6.18
Specifications to perform
sample DO/END operation.

Step 3. The index value contained in #NUMB is compared with the limit value (100) specified in Factor 2. If the *index value* is less than or equal to the *limit value* (100), control transfers to the first operation within the DO/END loop.

When the *index value* becomes greater than the *limit value*, the DO/END loop is complete and control transfers to the first operation following the associated END statement (*step 5*).

Step 4. When the END operation is reached, the increment value of 2 in Factor 2 is added to the *index value field* #NUMB. Control is transferred to the beginning of the DO operation (*step 3*) to determine if the DO/END loop is to continue.

Step 5. The DO/END loop is terminated when the index value is greater than the limit value and control continues with the first operation following the END statement.

In Figure 6.18, the DO/END loop is executed 50 times because #NUMB begins at 2 (starting value) and is incremented by 2 until it exceeds 100:

```
 2  ⎫
 4  ⎪
 6  ⎪
 8  ⎬  50 times
10  ⎪
 •  ⎪
 •  ⎪
 •  ⎪
100 ⎭
```

E. Which Iterative Technique To Use

1. DOUxx and DOWxx operations are used when a repetitive routine is required based on the result of a comparison of two factors.

2. The DOWxx/END operation tests for a condition first. If the condition is true, the routine between DOWxx and the END statements is executed. The condition is again tested and the looping continues as long as the condition tested is met.

3. With the DOUxx operation, the operations between the DOUxx and END statements are executed at least once and continue to execute *until* a certain condition is met. That is, the program terminates looping when the condition is true.

4. The DO operation is preferred when the number of times a process is to be executed is predefined. The DO/END operation is implemented when a counter is used to control the number of times the loop is to be executed.

Remember that DO loops are preferable to using GOTOs because they result in structured programs with logical control constructs that make programs easier to read, debug, maintain, and modify.

F. Summary of DO Group Operations

The DO Group

I. A Review of the DO Group Iteration Construct
   A. A series of steps is executed repeatedly, based on whether or not a given condition or conditions are met.
   B. DO Groups consist of DOWxx/END, DOUxx/END, and DO/END.
   C. DO Group operations can be nested. That is, DO groups can be contained within DO groups. **Note:** Each DO is matched to the closest END.

II. The DOWxx Operation
   A. The loop is repeated as long as a certain condition exists. Execution is terminated when the condition being tested is no longer met.
   B. If the condition is not met initially, the loop will never be executed, because the test is performed before the first execution of the loop.

III. The DOUxx Operation
   A. The loop is executed and then repeated until a specified condition is met.
   B. The loop is executed at least one time because the condition test is performed at the bottom of the loop.

IV. The DO/END Operation
   A. The DO operation is used when we wish to perform a loop a predefined number of times. In this case, a variable or counter needs to be incremented (or decremented) by the same amount each time the loop is repeated.
   B. The DO operation accomplishes the following:
      1. Establishes a variable (index value).
      2. Increments (or decrements) the variable using a specified value.
      3. Specifies the range (starting value and limit value) in which the variable is to vary.
   C. Refinements of the DO operation.
      1. The starting value, limit value, and increment (or decrement) value may be numeric literals or numeric variables.
      2. The index value, if specified, must be a numeric variable.
      3. Any values not specified are assigned the default value 1.

V. Which Iterative Technique to Use
   A. The DOWxx operation is utilized when you first test for a condition and then execute a series of steps as long as that condition is true.
   B. The DOUxx operation is employed when a series of steps is executed at least once and then continues until a certain condition is met.
   C. The DO operation is preferred when the number of times that a process is to be executed is a predetermined number.

Self-Test

1. Structured iteration can be performed using the _____ operation, _____ operation, or the _____ operation.

2. Every DO group operation must terminate with an _____ operation.

3. After a DO group operation is executed, control transfers to _____.

4. (T or F) All DO group operations test for a specific condition.

5. When a routine is to be executed a pre-defined number of times, we use the (DO While/DO/DO Until).

6. The DOUxx operation executes a routine _____ the condition specified is satisfied.

7. The DOWxx operation executes a routine _____ a specified condition is _____.

8. The DOUxx operation tests the relationship between Factor 1 and Factor 2 at the _____ of the operation.

9. The DOWxx operation tests the relationship between Factor 1 and Factor 2 at the _____ of the operation.

10. Using the flowcharts below, identify the DOUxx operation and the DOWxx operation:

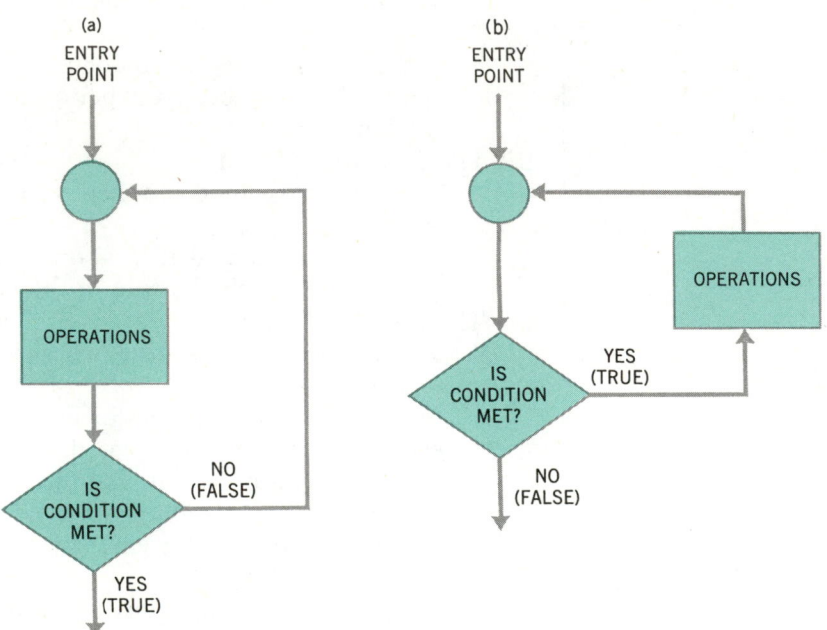

11. (T or F) The increment value in a DO operation may be negative.

Solutions

1. DO, DOUxx, DOWxx

2. END

3. the first operation following the END operation

4. T—Even the DO operation itself must test for the specified number of times in order to terminate the loop.

5. DO

6. until

7. while; true or is met

8. end

9. beginning

10. a. DO Until control structure (DOUxx)
    b. DO While control structure (DOWxx)
11. T

KEY TERMS

DO	END	EXCPT operation	Loop
DOUxx/END	Entry point	GOTO instruction	Routine
DOWxx/END	Exception output	Iteration	TAG

REVIEW QUESTIONS

1. Using the Calculation form, code the RPG instruction to test if CTR > 17. If CTR > 17, then branch to NOGO routine; otherwise, branch to OK.
2. Using the flowchart excerpt shown below at left, code the program segment.
3. Using the Calculation Specifications form, code the excerpt illustrated below on the right.

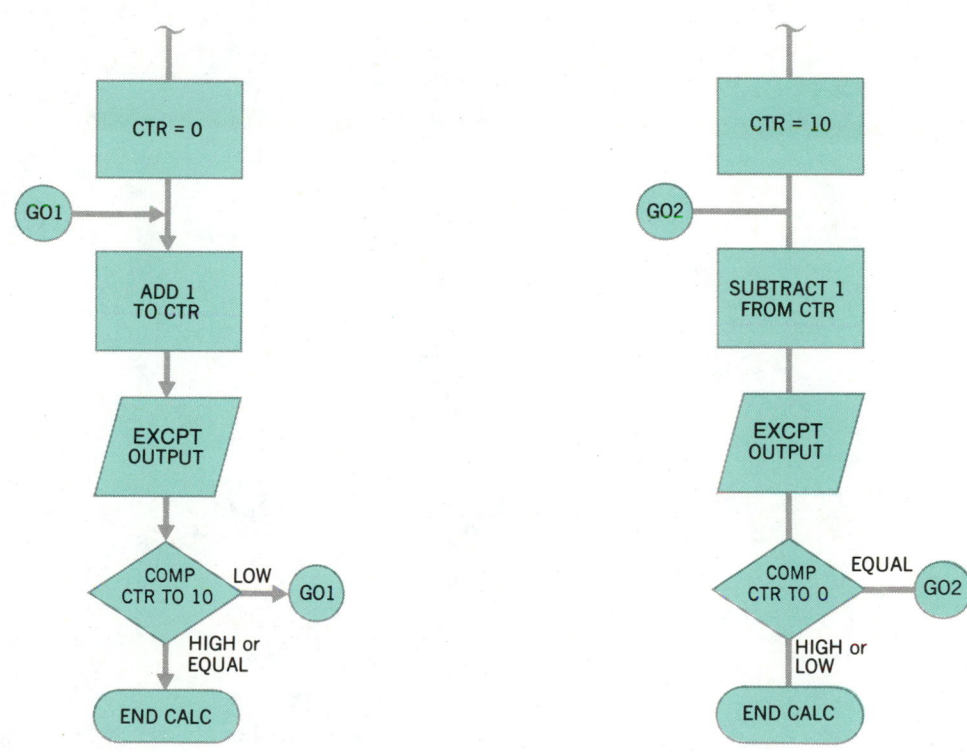

4. Referring to the flowchart below, code the Calculation Specifications form to accomplish the sequence of steps shown.

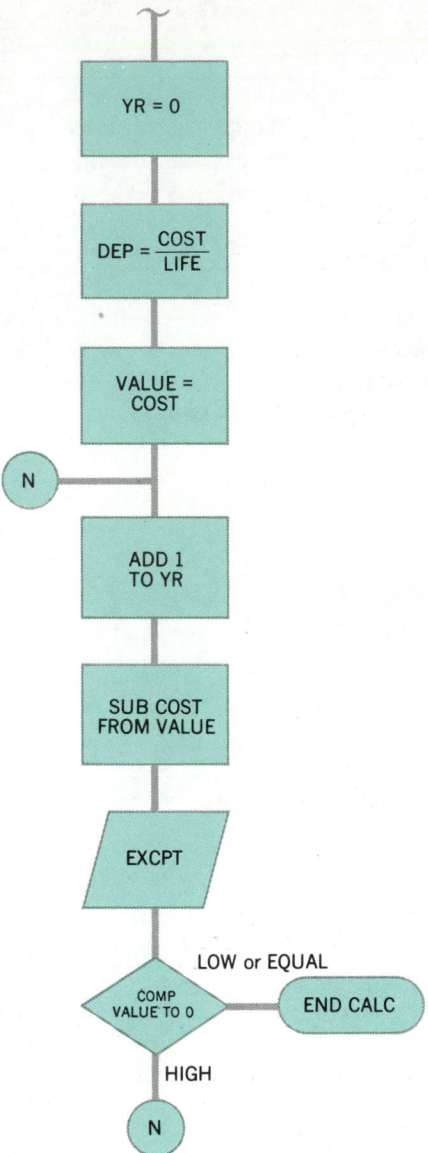

5. Suppose a programmer wishes to use EXCPT output when overflow occurs in a program using exception output. Identify what is required within the following loop.

C	Form Type	Control Level (L0 – L9, LR, SR, AN/OR)	Indicators						Factor 1	Operation	Factor 2	Result Field		Decimal Positions	Half Adjust (H)	Resulting Indicators			Comments
			And		And							Name	Length			Arithmetic			
																Plus	Minus	Zero	
																Compare			
																1>2	1<2	1=2	
																Lookup (Factor 2) is			
Line			Not		Not		Not									High	Low	Equal	
3 4 5	6	7 8	9 10 11	12 13 14	15 16	17	18 19 20 21 22 23 24 25 26 27	28 29 30 31 32	33 34 35 36 37 38 39 40 41 42	43 44 45 46 47 48	49 50 51	52	53	54 55	56 57	58 59	60 61 62 63 64 65 66 67 68 69 70 71 72 73 74
0 1	Φ	C						BEGIN	TAG										
0 2	Φ	C							ADD 1		#CTR								
0 3	Φ	C							EXCPT										
0 4	Φ	C						#CTR	COMP 1Φ								2Φ		
0 5	Φ	C		2Φ					GOTO BEGIN										
0 6		C																	
0 7		C																	

6. Code the following flowchart excerpt.

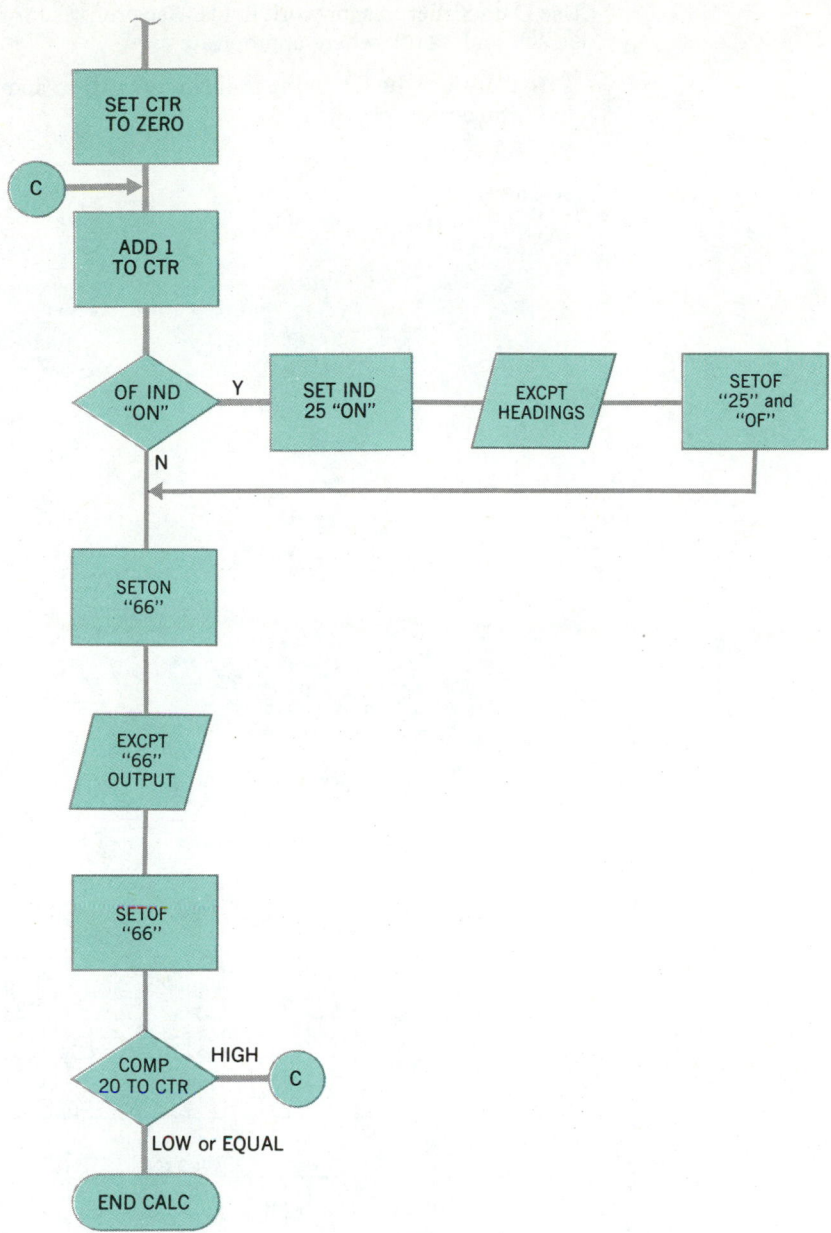

PROGRAMMING ASSIGNMENTS

Use Data Structures for work fields. Use prefixes for input, output, and work fields. Use SETON and SETOF where appropriate.

1. Consider the following problem definition and code the RPG program to produce the desired results.

Systems Flowchart

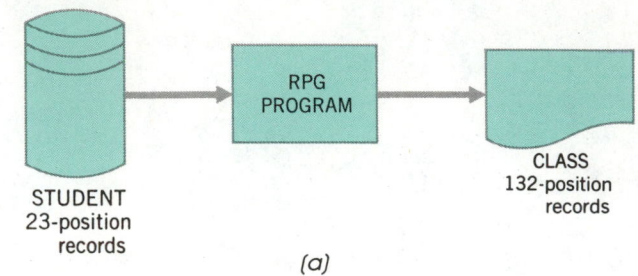

STUDENT
23-position
records

RPG
PROGRAM

CLASS
132-position
records

(a)

STUDENT Record Layout

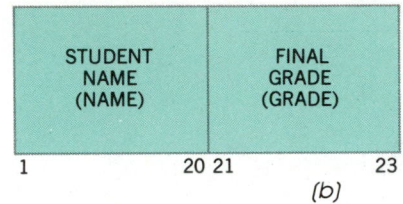

(b)

CLASS Printer Spacing Chart

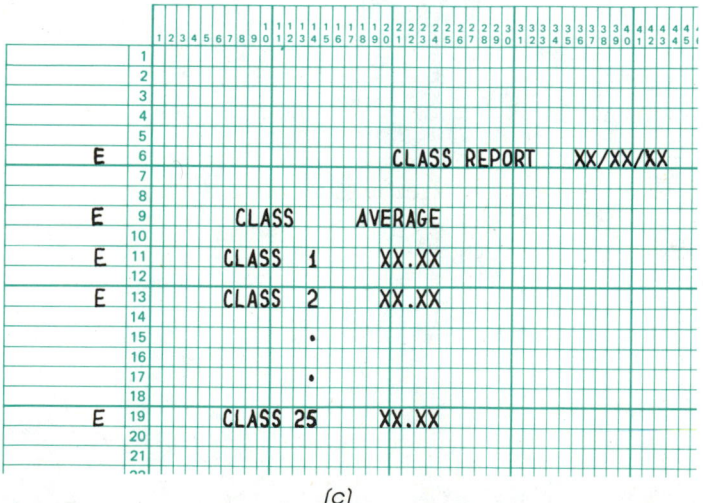

(c)

Notes:

a. Each class has a variable number of students. However, the trailer record for each class contains a grade of 999.

b. The grade for each student is in each record and ranges from 000 to 100. We do not need the student name for this problem.

    c. Thus, the first set of records is for the students in class 1 and ends with a 999 trailer. The second set of records is for students in class 2, and so on. There are exactly 25 classes.

    d. Print a report with the class average for each class.

2. Consider the following problem definition and code the RPG program to produce the desired results. The monthly payment is calculated using these formulas:

Number of payments $(N) = 12 \times$ number of loan years

Monthly payment $= ($Loan amount $\times 1.005^N)/N$

Systems Flowchart

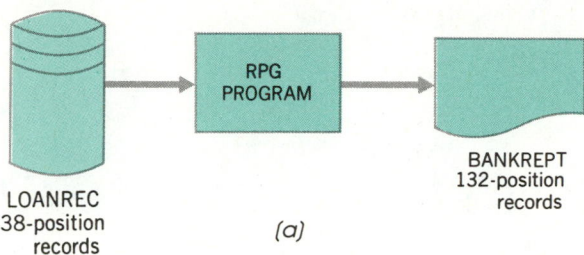

(a)

LOANREC Record Layout

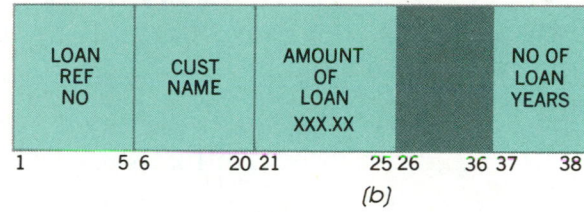

(b)

BANKREPT Printer Spacing Chart

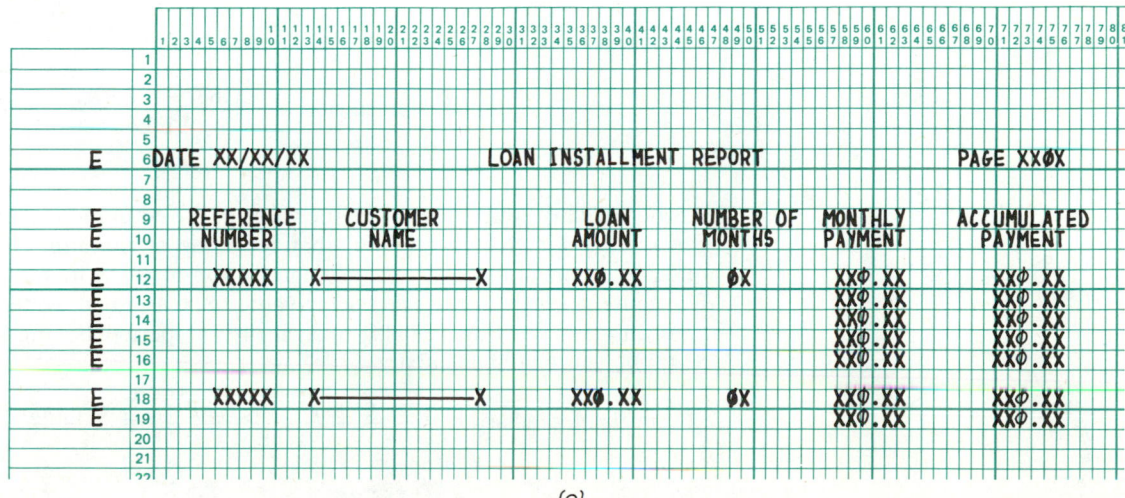

(c)

3. Consider the following problem definition and code an RPG program to provide the desired results. Use the formula shown to calculate annual depreciation of capital equipment for this programming assignment.

Systems Flowchart

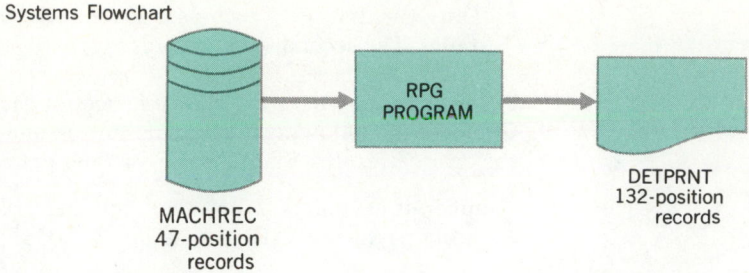

MACHREC Record Layout

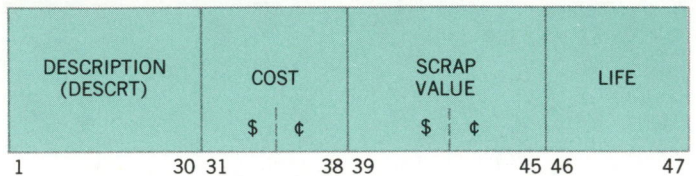

DETPRNT Printer Spacing Chart

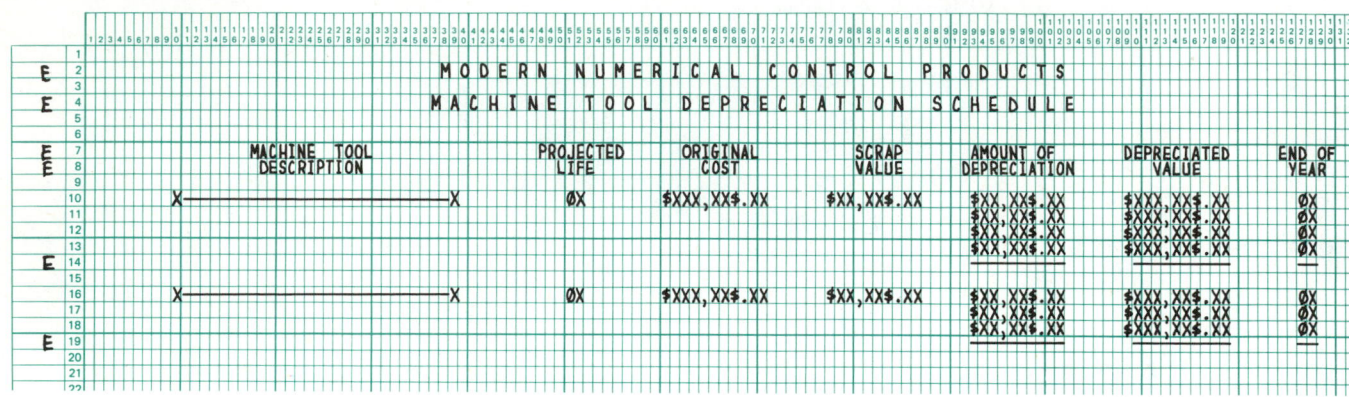

$$\text{Annual depreciation} = \frac{\text{COST} - \text{SCRAP}}{\text{LIFE}}$$

At the end of the anticipated life, the value of the equipment should depreciate to the scrap value. Note, however, that rounding of the annual depreciation frequently occurs and the last year's depreciation must be increased or decreased a few cents in order for the exact scrap value to be attained. For example, to depreciate an item costing \$78,000 over a 14-year period having a scrap value of \$14,000, you would calculate

$$\text{Annual depreciation} = \frac{\text{COST} - \text{SCRAP}}{\text{LIFE}} = \frac{\$78,000 - \$14,000}{14}$$

$$= \frac{\$64,000}{14} = \$4,571.43 \text{ per year}$$

If you used this figure for a 14-year period, however, you would depreciate the equipment by \$64,000.02 and not the \$64,000.00 we had intended. Thus you have an error of 2 cents. The program, however, should recalculate the annual depreciation during the last pass through the loop, thus avoiding this problem.

7

Control Break Processing

OBJECTIVES

To familiarize you with

1. What a control break is and how it is used in printing.
2. Programming requirements for single, double, and triple level control break printing.
3. How data can be printed as a group-indicated field.
4. How to handle the test for a page overflow condition.

I. An Introduction to Control Break Processing

A. A Review of Detail and Group Printing

Thus far, we have focused on the printing of an individual line for each input record read. This is called **detail printing.** Sometimes, however, we wish to print total or summary lines for a group of records. This is called **group printing.** Group printing can be performed either in place of, or in addition to, detail printing. Thus far, we have considered group printing only for purposes of printing a final total. You will recall that we may accumulate a total field by adding to it each time a record is read. We print the T or total line that will contain the final total when the LR (last record) indicator is turned on. For a comparison of detail printing and group printing, see Figure 7.1.

This chapter considers group printing in far more depth, focusing on a specific type of group printing that uses **control fields** to indicate when totals are to print.

B. An Example of Single Level Control Break Processing

Consider the problem definition in Figure 7.2. The output requires the processing of three input fields: DEPT, SLSNAM, and AMT. Each input record consists of

Figure 7.1
Comparison of detail printing
and group printing.

(a)

Detail
Report

```
                    SALES REPORT
                    BY ITEM NUMBER                          08/04/91

                                                            PAGE    1


    ITEM                        ITEM                        SALES
    NO.                         DESCRIPTION                 AMOUNT

    587                         WIDGETS                     142.38
    587                         WIDGETS                     382.27
    763                         WAXED PAPER                 872.53
    763                         WAXED PAPER                 821.33
    763                         WAXED PAPER                 168.38
    923                         BALLOONS                    858.21
    923                         BALLOONS                    923.73
    923                         BALLOONS                    15.82
    923                         BALLOONS                    77.93
```

(b)

Group
Report

```
                SUMMARY SALES REPORT
                    BY ITEM NUMBER
                                                            08/04/91

                                                            PAGE    1

    ITEM                        ITEM                        SALES
    NO.                         DESCRIPTION                 AMOUNT

    587                         WIDGETS                     524.65*
    763                         WAXED PAPER                 1862.24*
    923                         BALLOONS                    1875.69*
```

Figure 7.2
Problem definition for a single-level control break program.

Systems Flowchart

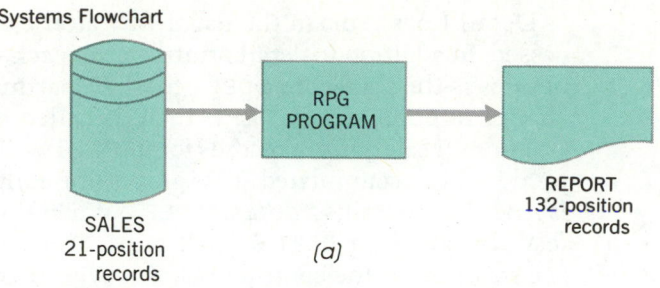

SALES
21-position
records

(a)

RPG
PROGRAM

REPORT
132-position
records

SALES Record Layout

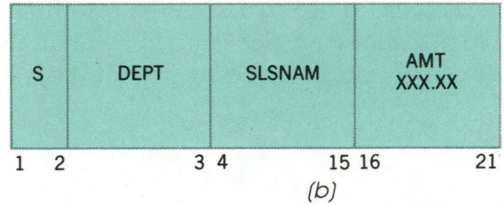

(b)

REPORT Printer Spacing Chart

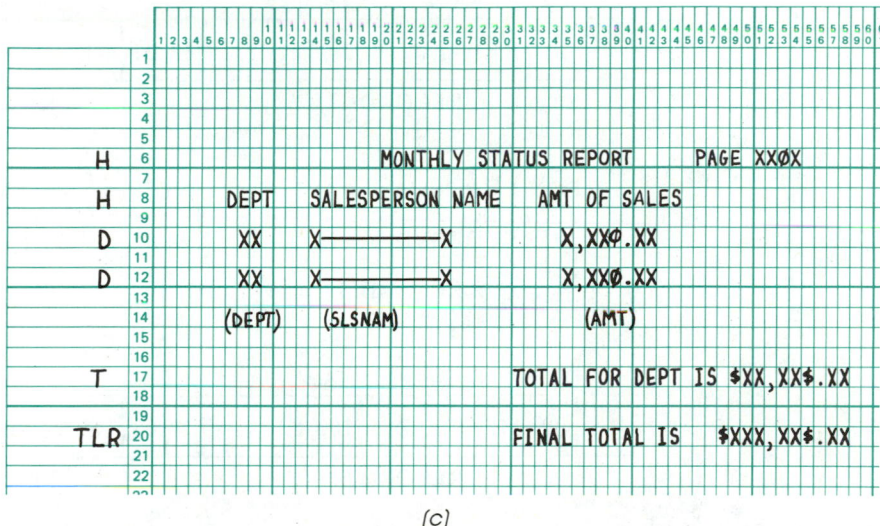

(c)

the salesperson's department number, the salesperson's name, and the amount of sales that he or she accrued for the week. There may be numerous salesperson records for DEPT Ø1, Ø2, and so on. Thus each department will contain records for several different salespersons.

For this problem, detail printing is required; that is, each input record is to be printed, as in previous examples. In addition to this detail printing, summary lines indicating department totals must also print. Thus group printing is required where a group or total line is written for each department.

In summary, after all records for DEPT Ø1 have been read and printed, a total for DEPT Ø1 will print. Similarly, after all records for DEPT Ø2 have been read and printed, a total for DEPT Ø2 will print. This type of processing requires all DEPT Ø1 records to be entered first followed by the next DEPT's records, and so on. That is, the file of input records must be in sequence by department number.

Detail lines print in the usual way after each input record is read and processed. In addition to detail printing after each input record is read, the amount of sales is then added to a DEPT total. Department totals will print whenever a change in DEPT occurs. DEPT, then, is called the control field.

Thus all salesperson records for DEPT 01 will be read and printed, and a DEPT total will be accumulated. This processing continues until a salesperson record is read that contains a *different* DEPT. When this record with a different DEPT is read, the total for DEPT 01 will print. Since a total is printed after a change occurs in DEPT, the control field, this type of group processing is called **control break** processing.

In order for the department totals to print correctly, one for each department, the input records must be sorted into DEPT sequence. That is, all salesperson records for DEPT 01 must be read first, followed by salesperson records for DEPT 02, and so on. See Figure 7.3 for an illustration of the output that this type of control break processing produces.

Figure 7.3
Example of input and output for a control break procedure.

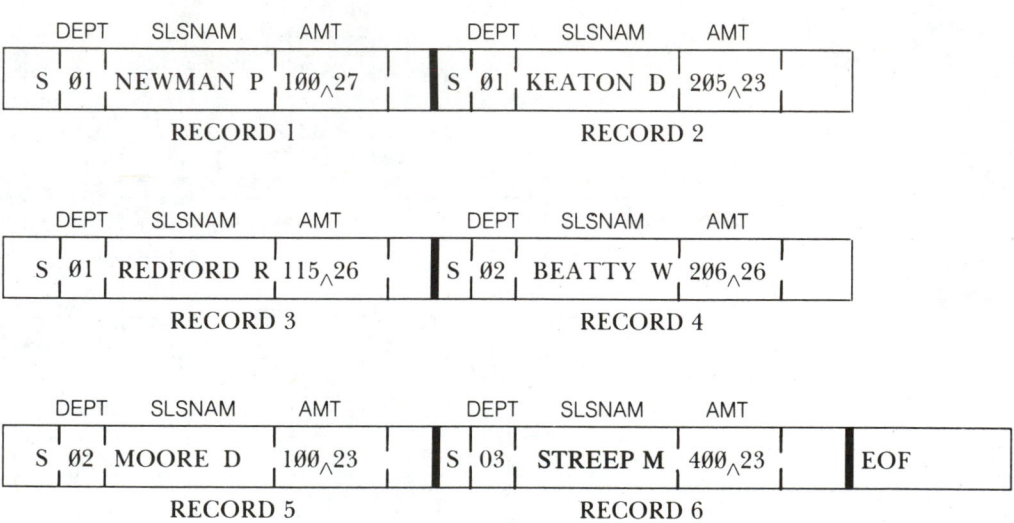

CONTROL FIELD: DEPT

RECORD 1: S | 01 | NEWMAN P | 100∧27
RECORD 2: S | 01 | KEATON D | 205∧23
RECORD 3: S | 01 | REDFORD R | 115∧26
RECORD 4: S | 02 | BEATTY W | 206∧26
RECORD 5: S | 02 | MOORE D | 100∧23
RECORD 6: S | 03 | **STREEP M** | 400∧23 | EOF

MONTHLY STATUS REPORT		PAGE 1
DEPT	SALESPERSON NAME	AMT OF SALES
01	NEWMAN P	100.27
01	KEATON D	205.23
01	REDFORD R	115.26
		TOTAL FOR DEPT IS $420.76
02	BEATTY W	206.26
02	MOORE D	100.23
		TOTAL FOR DEPT IS $306.49
03	**STREEP M**	400.23
		TOTAL FOR DEPT IS $400.23
		FINAL TOTAL IS $1,127.48

II. Program Requirements for Control Break Processing

A. Single Level Control Breaks

For each input record read, a detail line will be printed. In addition, to accumulate a department summary total, the AMT field will be added to a department total, which we will call DTOTAL.

All DEPT Ø1 records, then, will be read, and the DTOTAL will be accumulated. The total line, "TOTAL FOR DEPT IS $XX,XXX.XX", will print only *after* a record with the next DEPT is read. However, the total line for DEPT Ø1 must be printed before processing the first detail record for DEPT Ø2. That is, the total for the previous group (DEPT Ø1) must be printed before processing the first detail record of the new group, DEPT Ø2. If it is not, the AMT field from the first DEPT Ø2 record would be added to the wrong DTOTAL accumulator field, thereby producing incorrect department totals. For this reason, total time calculations are executed to produce the group totals for the previous group before the first record of the current group is processed at detail time.

The File Description Specifications are similar to those in previous programs.

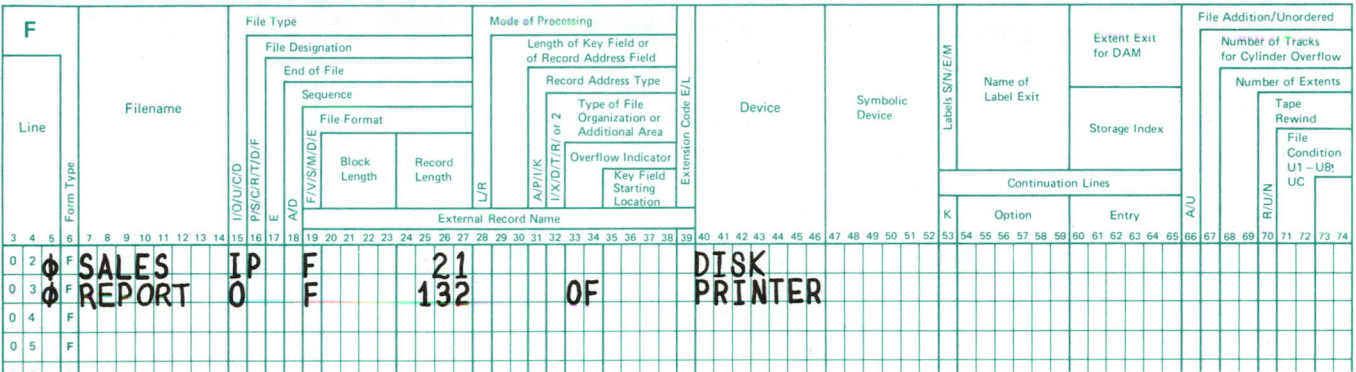

The specific input field to be used for the control field is assigned the **level indicator** L1 (level one control field). Thus, to indicate that control break processing will occur, we specify the control field on the Input Specifications form by coding L1 in the Control Level Positions (columns 59–60) of the appropriate input field, in this case, DEPT. Note that one and only one field may be designated as the L1 field.

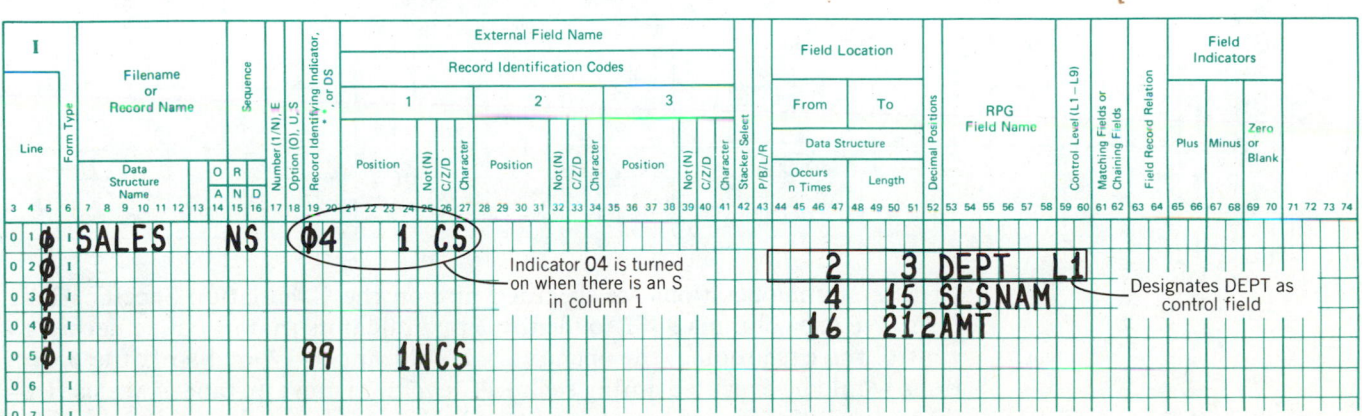

L1 designates DEPT as a "level one" control field. Level one is used when there is a **single level control break** field to be processed. Multiple level control breaks designated by L1, L2, L3, and so on will be considered later in this chapter.

B. Identifying Control Break Calculations

In order to write RPG programs containing control breaks or summary totals, it is important to understand the difference in specification requirements between calculations performed during detail processing and those executed during control break processing.

When calculations are performed during each RPG cycle for records read, this is called **detail time** processing. On the other hand, calculations performed as the result of a control break are total or summary calculations and are executed during **total time** processing.

Columns 7 and 8 and columns 9–17 of the Calculation Specifications form distinguish detail time processing from total time processing. In addition, where we place these calculations within the program will also determine the type of processing. Consider the following:

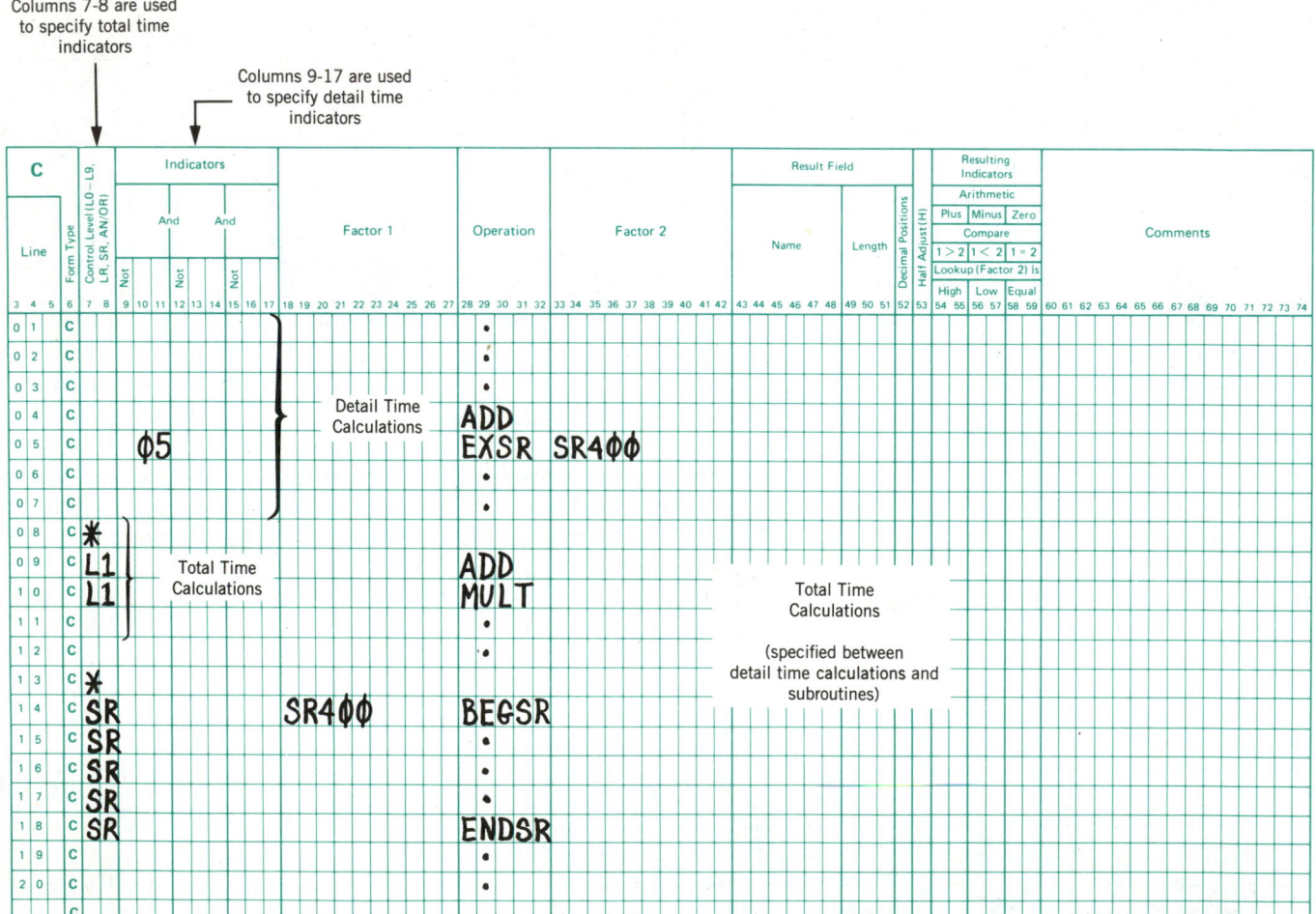

Detail time operations are specified first on the Calculation Specifications form. We use columns 9–17 to identify any indicators that might be needed to control the execution of the operations. If columns 9–17 are blank, the operations would be executed during each RPG cycle. In most instances, we use 01– 99 as detail time indicators, but we may also include total time indicators in columns 9–17, as we will see later in this chapter. Columns 7 and 8 must be blank during detail time processing as these two columns are reserved for total time processing. We can use positions 10–11, 13–14, or 16–17 to designate a single indicator.

Control or *total time* operations are identified with the use of L1–L9 and LR (last record) indicators in columns 7 and 8.

Total time calculations must be specified on the Calculation Specifications form after detail calculations but before subroutines. In other words, Calculation Specifications consist of detail calculations, followed by total time calculations, which are followed by subroutines. It is important to point out that although total time calculations follow detail time calculations, the only way they can be executed is when a control break occurs.

Indicator Summary

	Columns 7 and 8	Columns 9–17
Detail Time	must be blank, or AN/OR	01–99, L1–L9, OF, or blank
Total Time	L1–L9 or LR	must be 01–99, OF, or blank
Subroutines	SR	01–99, L1–L9, LR, or blank

In the problem previously described in Figure 7.2, there are two main calculations to be performed, one that is performed at *detail time*, after each detail record is read, and one that is performed at "control break" or *total time*, when there is a change in the DEPT field (L1).

When a record with an "S" in the first position is read, indicator 04 is set on. Indicator 04 is specified on the detail calculation line where AMT is to be added to a department total (DTOTAL). The detail time operation is placed first on the Calculation Specifications form and controlled with indicator 04 in columns 10 and 11.

Control break or total time occurs when there is a change in the control field DEPT. Therefore, when a record is read containing a department different from the previous record a control break occurs, and DTOTAL is to be added to a final total, FTOTAL. This operation is controlled by the L1 indicator in columns 7–8, which specifies total time processing.

The following illustrates the calculations performed at detail time and at total time:

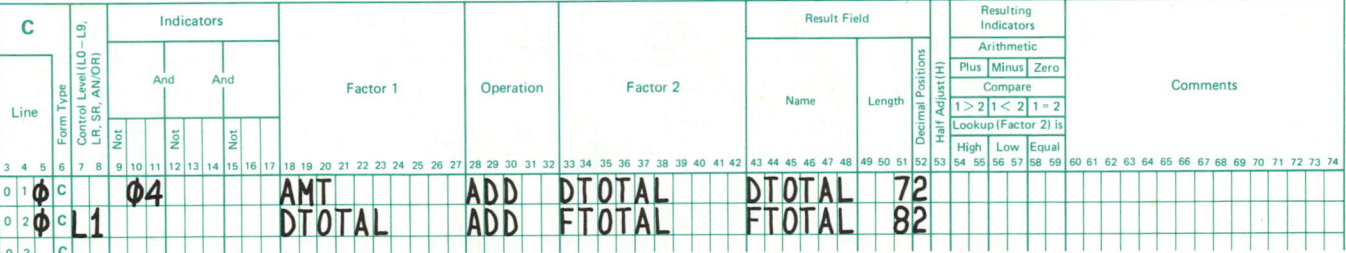

Once again, it is important to be familiar with the RPG Logic Cycle, which specifies the sequence of operations performed by the computer. After a record is read, the computer tests for end of file. If there are still records to process, the next operation the computer performs is a test for a change in the control field. For the first record read, all control break indicators are set on. However, RPG knows that it is executing the first cycle and therefore does not perform total time calculations. On the other hand, since the control break indicators are on during the first cycle they may be used in columns 9–17 for the first detail cycle. For each subsequent read, if there is no change in the control field, then detail time processing is performed and the next record is read. Once the program recognizes a control break, that is, a change in the value of the control field, processing transfers to the total time section of the program. Total time calculations are executed for those operations conditioned by the appropriate control level indicators (L1–L9) in columns 7–8. Once total time calculations are completed, processing transfers to total time output where output identified with L1 specifications is printed. Processing then continues with detail time operations for the current record that forced the control break.

Both the L1 total time calculations and total time printing are performed *prior* to processing the new detail record. In this way, a record with a change in DEPT will first cause the previous DEPT total (DTOTAL) to print, prior to any detail calculations or printing for the next DEPT.

It is important to remember that, after being set on during input, a control break indicator stays on throughout total time, detail time, and until the next record is read from the file. In other words, a control break indicator stays on for one complete RPG program cycle.

The Output Specifications form for a control break problem would include coding for the following:

H records for printing Headings.
D records for printing Detail lines.
T records for printing Control Totals.

The T or Total line will print when the L1 indicator is on. We also wish to print a final total when the LR or Last Record indicator is on. But after the last record has been processed it is necessary to first print the last control total before printing this final total. This is handled automatically by RPG. When the LR indicator is turned on, all control level indicators are automatically turned on as well. Thus, when the LR indicator is turned on, the L1 indicator will be turned on too. The computer will print the last DEPT total (DTOTAL) and then the final total (FTOTAL).

The Output Specifications for our control break procedure would be as follows:

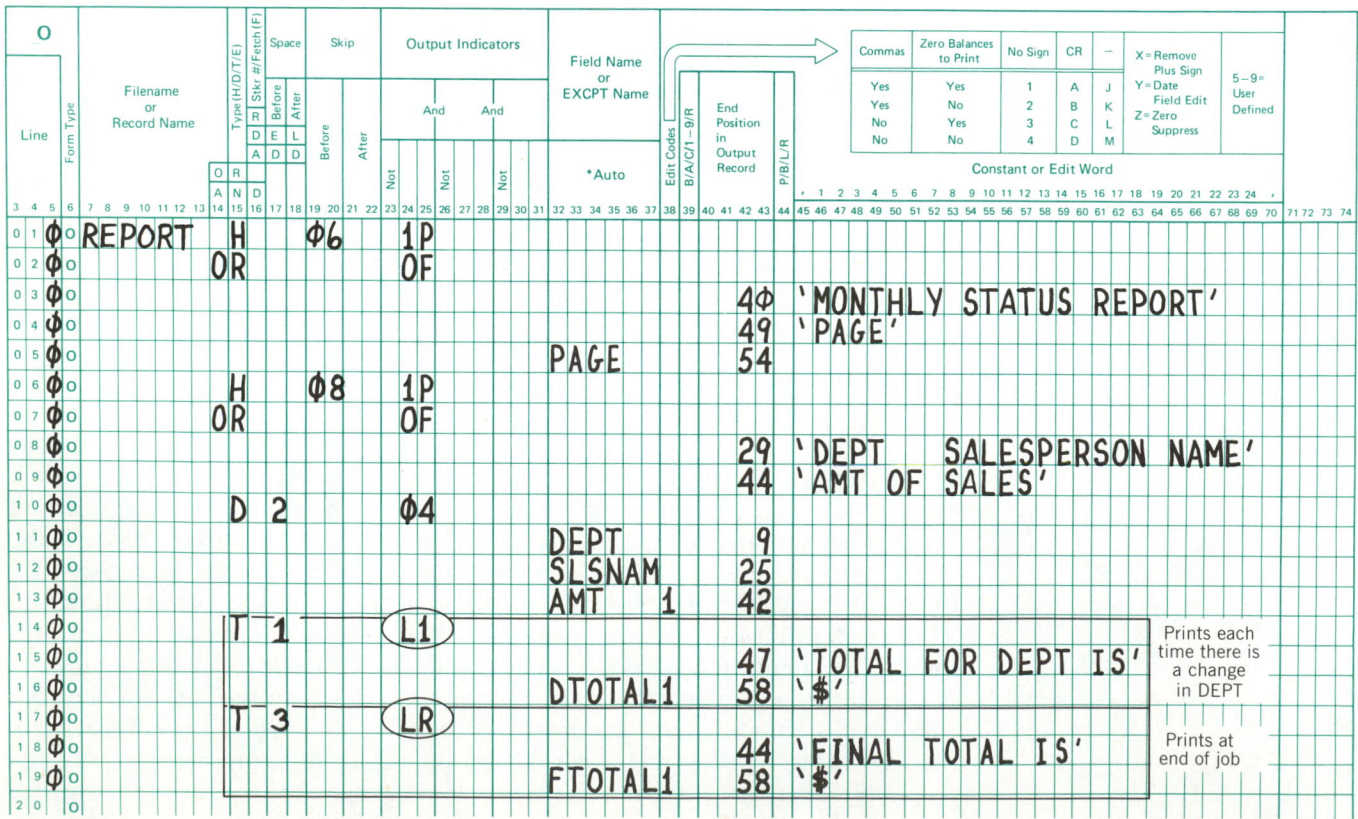

Generally, we have the following:

H lines print on 1P or OF indicators.
D lines print on record or resulting indicators.
T lines print on L indicators.

C. Clearing Total Fields after Printing

There is, however, a major element missing from this sample program. Remember that when the L1 control break occurs (first record for DEPT 02) two steps are performed. First, DTOTAL is added to FTOTAL, and second, DTOTAL is printed for the previous group (DEPT 01).

After printing DTOTAL for DEPT 01, processing continues with detail time processing of the first record for DEPT 02. At this point AMT is added to DTOTAL. Here is where the problem exists. DTOTAL still contains the accumulated total for DEPT 01 (the previous group) because it was not reset to zero after printing or before accumulation was to begin for DEPT 02.

This department total, DTOTAL, must be reset or cleared to *zero* before processing the first record of a new group. This can be accomplished by one of three methods:

1. The Blank After Method

The *Blank After* method is a technique used on the Output Specifications form to reset fields to zero after the field has printed. In addition to reinitializing numeric fields to zero, the Blank After method can also be used to reset alphanumeric fields to blanks after printing.

The illustration below shows how the Blank After method can be utilized to reset DTOTAL to zero before processing the current record that triggered a control break. To do this, we code the letter B in the Blank After field for DTOTAL on the Output Specifications form:

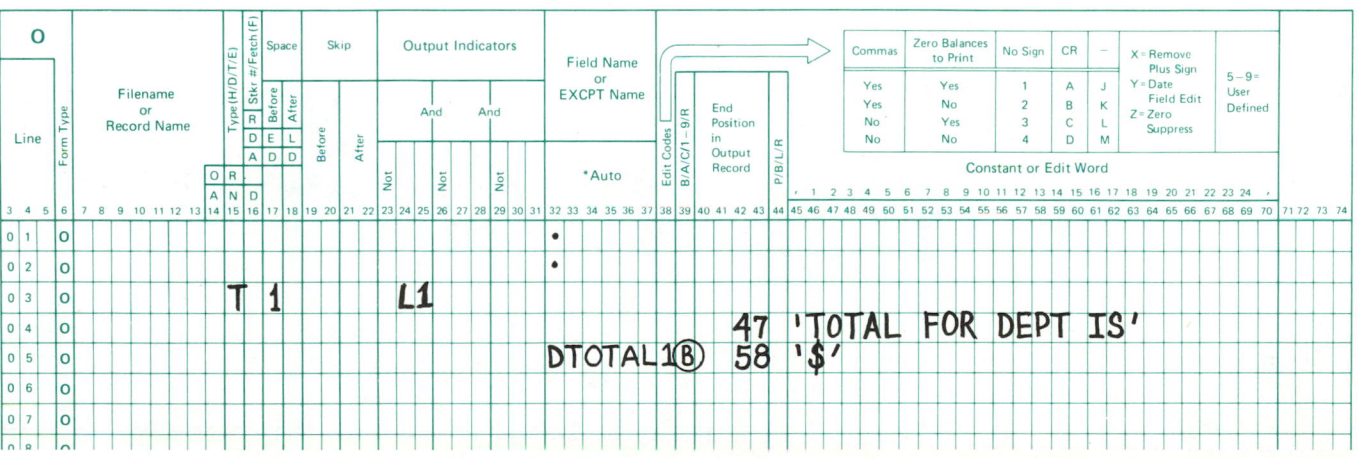

Using Blank After to reset DTOTAL to zero after printing.

The letter B in column 39 of the DTOTAL line means that the contents of DTOTAL will be reset to zero after printing. DTOTAL will thus be reinitialized before the AMTs are accumulated for the next DEPT.

When we need to zero-out total fields in a program, an arithmetic operation is required to perform the task. Output Specifications, however, are used to output or write records from the program and should not, in general, be used to perform functions requiring arithmetic operation such as clearing fields. That function is better performed during the Calculation Specifications of the program. This is especially true when designing structured RPG programs. The Blank After method, therefore, will not be emphasized in our programs. However, you should be aware that many RPG programs exist that use the Blank After method.

We will now discuss and illustrate the preferred method of resetting fields to zero on the Calculation Specifications form after printing subtotal fields.

2. Initializing Fields during Calculations

Once the program recognizes a control break, that is, a change in the value for the control field, processing transfers to the *total time* section of the program. Once total time calculations and output are completed, processing continues with detail time calculations for the current record. Even though the program has started the detail processing, control break indicators are still on because the program is still in the *same* RPG cycle. The control level indicators can be used at detail time to condition the operations required to reset the accumulator fields to zero before processing begins on the current detail record. Examine Figure 7.4. One more operation has been added to the previous calculations. The Z-ADD operation line is used to reset DTOTAL to zero after the department total has printed. DTOTAL will thus be reinitialized before the AMTs are accumulated for the next DEPT. L1 is specified in columns 10 and 11 (that is, during detail time) to control execution of the operation. This calculation is an example of an L1 indicator being used during detail time. To ensure that this calculation is executed at detail time and not total time, L1 is specified in columns 10 and 11, not in 7 and 8.

The placement of the Z-ADD operation in the program is critical. If DTOTAL was reset to zero during total time, that is, if L1 was specified in columns 7 and 8 and not columns 10 and 11, the department total DTOTAL would always print as zero since total time calculations are performed prior to total time output. That is, DTOTAL would be set to zero during total time processing and then printed as zero during total time printing. Consequently, total fields that need to be reset to zero after totals are printed must be initialized as the first step of detail time processing for the first record of the new control group.

3. Using Figurative Constants

When writing programs, there are times when it is necessary to have Factor 1 or Factor 2 contain a field or literal with a value of numeric zeros or alphanumeric spaces (blanks).

Besides using the numeric zero (∅) or literal spaces (' '), there is an alternative method to specifying these values. That alternative is called a **figurative constant.**

Figure 7.4
Using an L1 indicator during detail time.

Figurative constants consist of *BLANK, *BLANKS, *ZERO, and *ZEROS. *BLANK or *BLANKS mean all spaces and *ZERO or *ZEROS mean all 0s. The following four examples illustrate how you might compare a numeric field to zeros, compare an alphanumeric field to blanks, set a numeric field to zeros, or move blanks to an alphanumeric field.

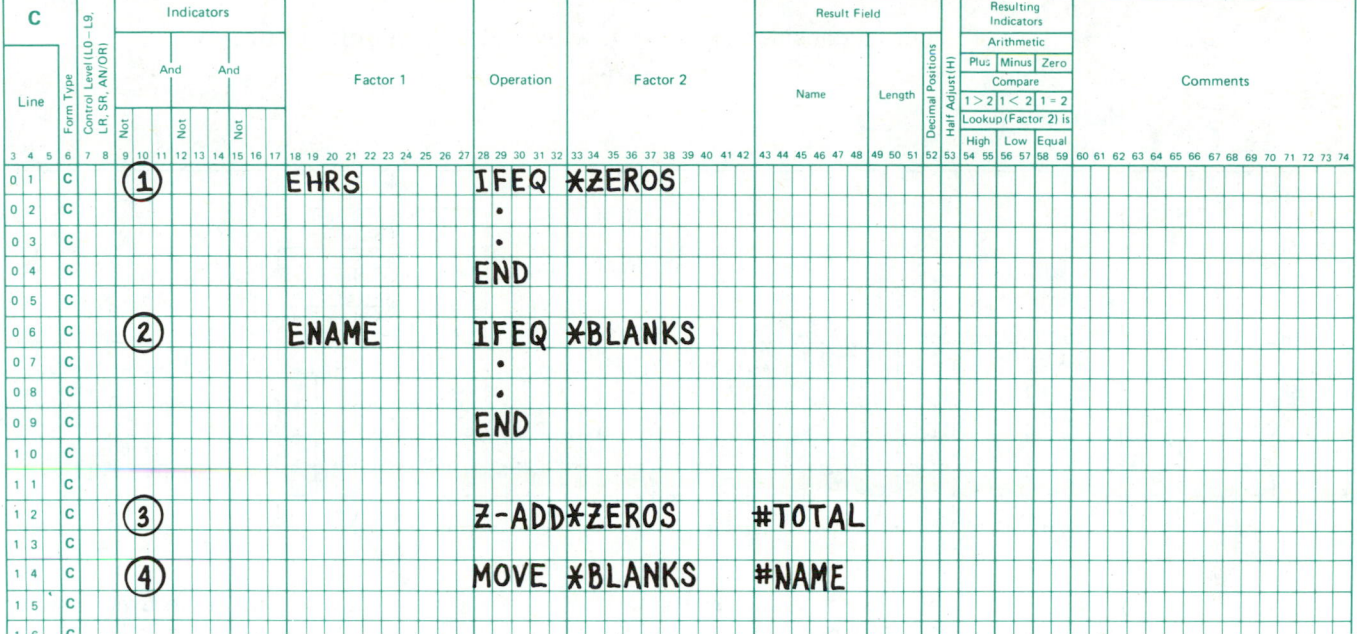

Figure 7.5 illustrates how the figurative constant of *ZEROS can be used in the Z-ADD operation described previously.

The following is a list of rules for using figurative constants:

RULES FOR FIGURATIVE CONSTANTS

1. *BLANK and *BLANKS can be used *only* with alphanumeric fields.
2. *ZERO and *ZEROS can be used with *either* numeric or alphanumeric fields.

Figure 7.5
Using the figurative constant *ZEROS.

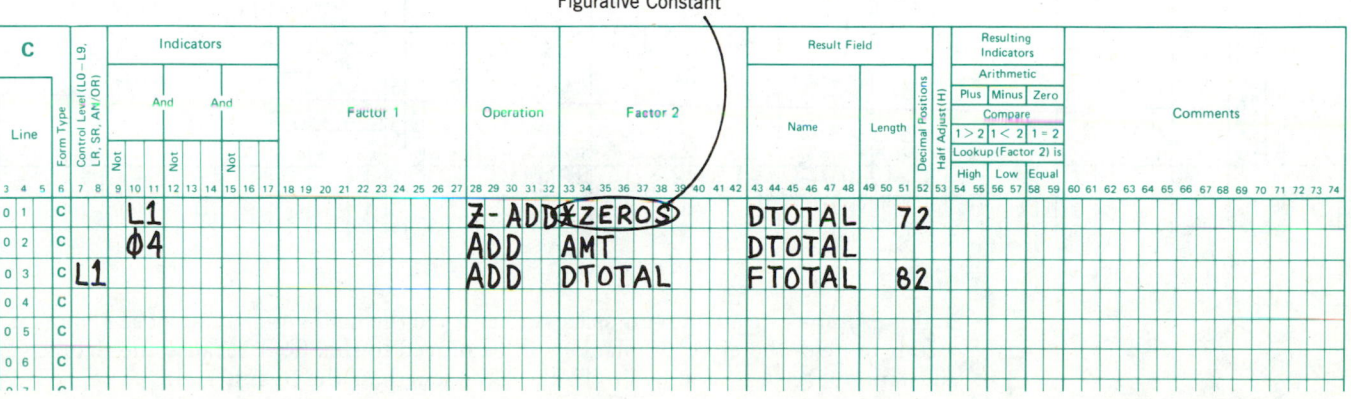

3. The length of a figurative constant is derived from either the other factor in the operation or from the Result Field. If both factor fields are present, where one is a figurative constant, then the length of the constant is assumed to be that of the other factor. However, if the only factor field in the operation is a figurative constant, then the length is assumed to be that of the Result Field.

Let us consider Example 1, which illustrates rule number 3.

Example 1

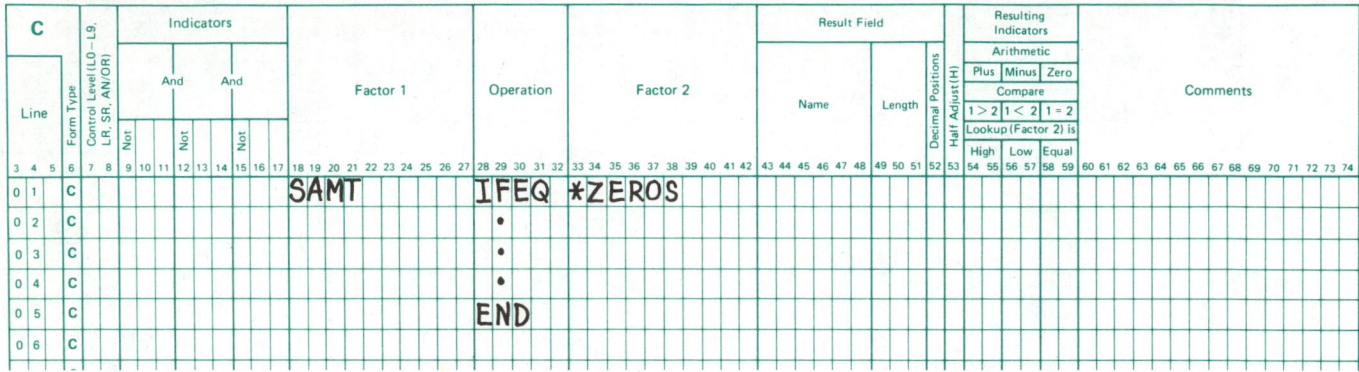

In this example, the sales amount (SAMT) field is compared to the figurative constant *ZEROS using an IF/END operation. The length of the *ZEROS constant in Factor 2 is considered to be the same length as the field SAMT in Factor 1.

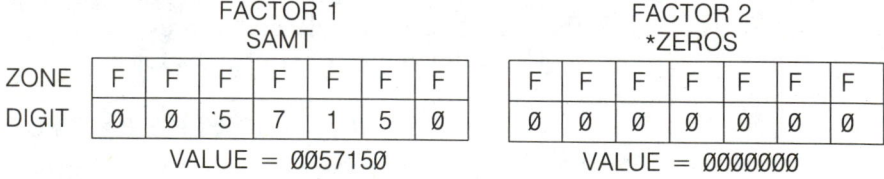

Since SAMT is a seven-byte field, the constant in Factor 2 is assumed to be the same length, that is, seven bytes.

Example 2

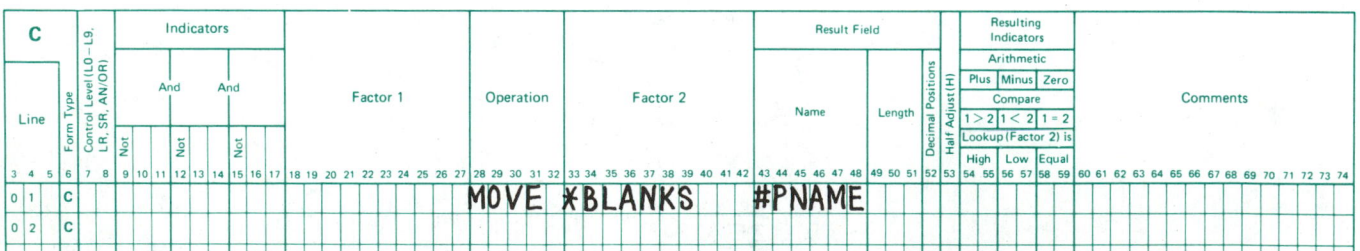

In this example, we are moving spaces or blanks to the field #PNAME. Suppose #PNAME is a 20-byte field; therefore, 20 blanks will be moved to this field because the figurative constant *BLANKS is assumed to be the same length as the Result Field.

D. Interpreting Control Break Procedures

Suppose the following data is read in:

	CODE	DEPT	SLSNAM	AMT
1.	S	01	BROWN S	1158∧22
2.	S	01	ADAMS T	1873∧22
3.	S	02	SMITH J	0922∧11
4.	S	02	JONES R	0123∧47
5.	S	02	FIELD F	3217∧23

1. The computer reads the first record. L1 is set on at this time but RPG does not perform total time calculations or total time output. (Note that total calculations and total output are *not* performed in the first cycle.) The AMT is accumulated using DTOTAL, and a detail line is printed.

2. The second record is read. Since it is not an end-of-file record, the computer checks to see if the DEPT is the same as the previous DEPT. Since it is the same, the AMT is accumulated and a detail record is printed.

3. The third record is not an end-of-file record, but it has 02 in DEPT, which means there is a change in DEPT. L1 signals a change in the control field. L1 calculations, if any, would then be processed, and total time printing, which uses L1 coding, occurs. In this instance, the L1 Calculation Specifications add the department total, DTOTAL, to a final total, called FTOTAL. Then the total line that contains the sum for DEPT 01, the previous group, will print.

4. After the total line is printed, the program continues with detail time processing. Since the current record to be processed is the first record of a new control group, the field DTOTAL must be reset to zero before processing begins. The L1 indicator, still on from the change in the control field, is used during detail time to control the operation necessary to reset the field DTOTAL to zero. This Z-ADD operation must be performed prior to operations executed on the current record that triggered the control break. Then the new AMT for DEPT 02 can be accumulated and the first detail line for DEPT 02 can be printed.

At the end of the file, it is important to print the total that has been accumulated for the last DEPT. Recall that the last record or LR indicator in RPG is turned on at the end of the file; this indicator automatically turns on all level indicators as well. This means that the control level calculations and the total line will print for the last department group without the need for additional coding. All other programming languages require the programmer to "force" the last control break at the end of the job in order to have the computer print the last group of totals. This additional coding is not necessary in RPG, because it is a language uniquely designed to handle these specific types of applications.

Figure 7.6 provides a program flowchart excerpt that depicts the sequence of operations in the RPG cycle that have just been described. Study the flowchart carefully so that you understand the sequence in which operations are performed.

Figure 7.6
RPG Logic Cycle depicting
single-level control break
processing.

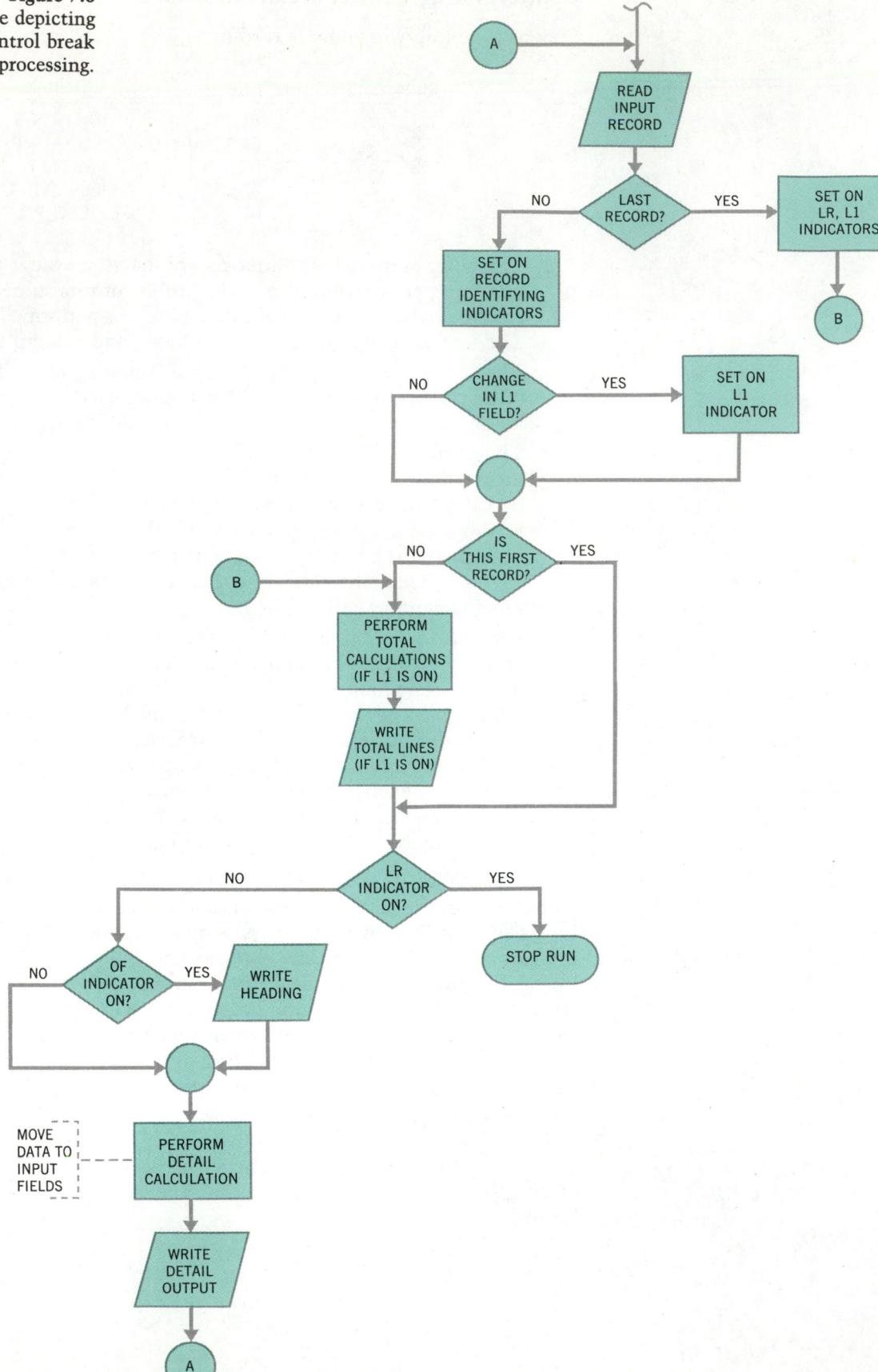

E. Group Indicate Procedure

If DEPT 01 had numerous salespeople, the output would print as follows:

DEPT	SALESPERSON NAME		AMT OF SALES
01	JONES	J	4,826.33
01	DAVIS	T	3,872.17
01	STERN	N	1,173.23
01	ROBERTS	S	6,322.43
.	.		.
.	.		.
.	.		.
	TOTAL FOR DEPT IS $44,326.22		

It is unnecessary to print 01 for DEPT *each* time a detail line is printed, since it will always be the same until a break occurs. We may instruct the computer to print the department number only *once* at the beginning of each control break. In this way, DEPT 01 is assumed for all subsequent records in that group and redundant information is suppressed. The next group is highlighted by having its DEPT print only once at the beginning of the group.

DEPT	SALESPERSON NAME		AMT OF SALES
01	JONES	J	4,826.33
	DAVIS	T	3,872.17
	STERN	N	1,173.23
	ROBERTS	S	6,322.43
	.		.
	.		.

The output DEPT field, then, would be referred to as a **group indicate** field. Only one change would be required in the detail printing to accomplish group indicate printing:

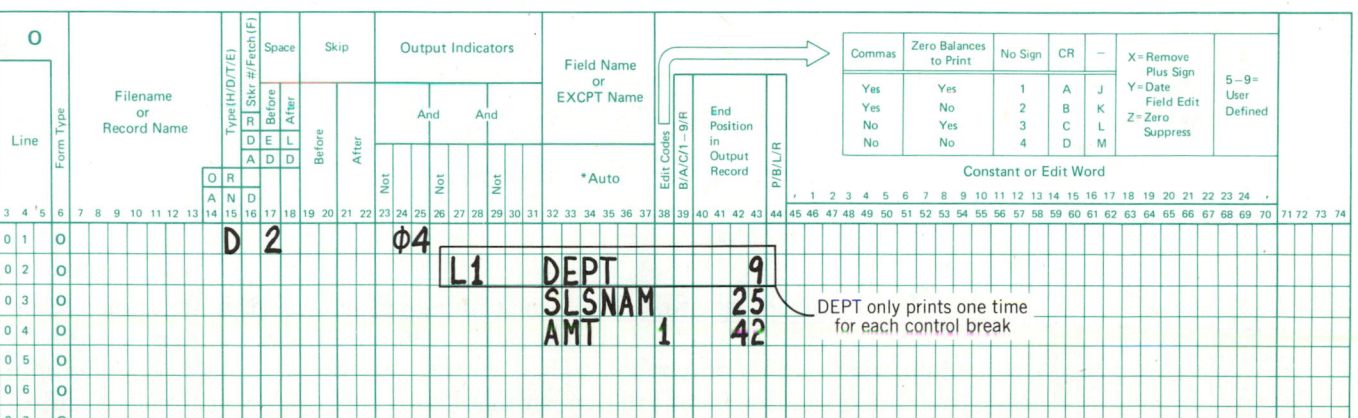

If a change in the L1 field has not yet occurred, the DEPT will not print.

The L1 indicator can be used for detail printing as well as total printing to control which fields will print. That is, because control level indicators remain on until after detail printing has been completed, an L1 indicator can be used for D or Detail lines as well as for T or Total lines, as in the preceding. A change in DEPT will first cause the T line to print, which would write the previous DEPT's total. L1 is coded on the same line as the DEPT field; this means we print the department number only when the L1 indicator is on. For Detail level processing, L1 would only be on for the first record of each group; hence the DEPT prints only once for each group.

When using the group indication procedure, a problem may occur if a detail record belonging to the same group forces page overflow. For example, suppose the detail records for DEPT 03 are printing toward the bottom of the page. A DEPT 03 record then causes page overflow. The program jumps to the next page and prints the headings and the next detail record, which is also for DEPT 03. However, in this case the DEPT number does not print.

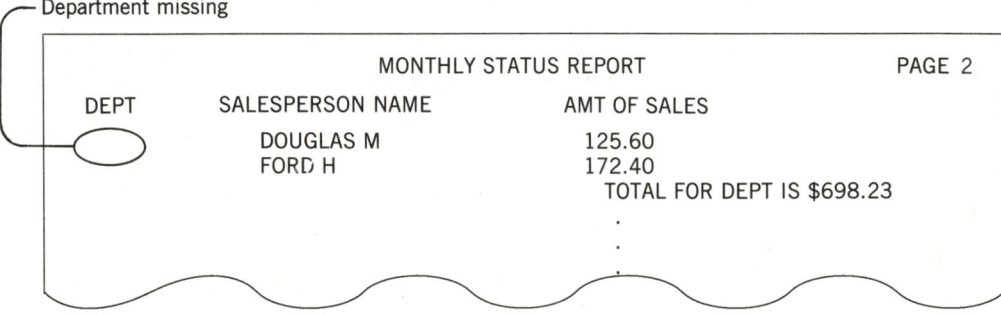

The result of page overflow with group indication

If this happens, the first detail line printed on the new page will not contain the DEPT field because it is printed only when L1 is on. Remember, the L1 indicator is set on only when a change occurs in the DEPT field. Therefore, in order to make the report more meaningful, we need to add additional specifications that will allow us to print the DEPT when L1 is on and also when overflow (OF) occurs. This can be accomplished as shown here:

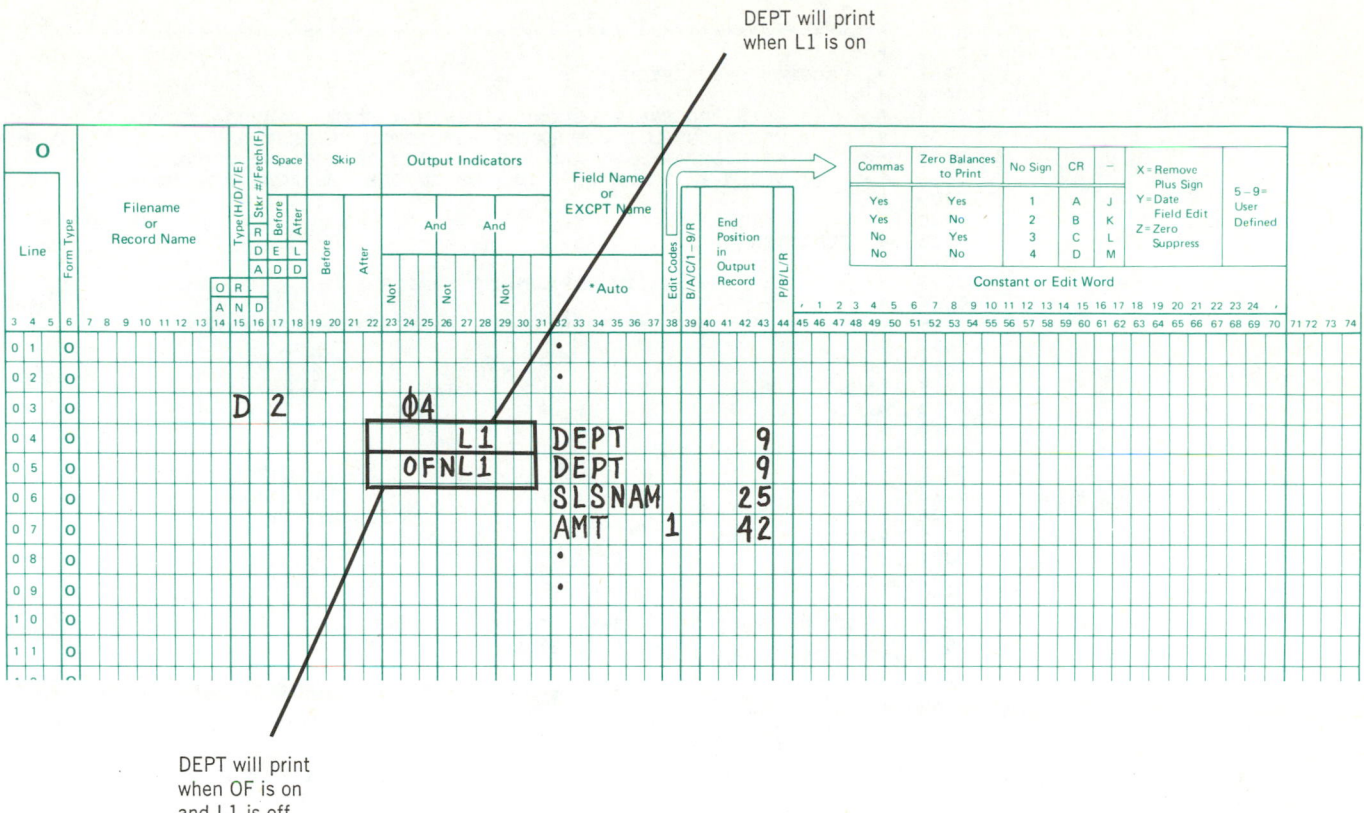

DEPT will print
when L1 is on

DEPT will print
when OF is on
and L1 is off

We specify the DEPT to print when one of two conditions occurs. On the first line, we specify the DEPT field to print if L1 is on, that is, the program is printing the first detail record for a new DEPT group. On the second line, we specify DEPT to print if the overflow (OF) indicator is on. In addition, we specify that L1 has to be off when overflow (OF) is on. The reason for this is that if the overflow (OF) indicator and the L1 indicator were on at the same time, the DEPT field would be moved to the print area twice, on the first line when the L1 indicator is on, and again on the second line when the OF indicator is on. Specifying NL1 with OF will make this operation more efficient because DEPT would only be moved once to the print area.

Figure 7.7 illustrates the complete RPG program to produce the group-printed monthly sales report illustrated throughout this section. In addition to illustrating all the concepts presented so far in this chapter, the program uses some newer concepts of structured RPG programming.

See Figure 7.8 for a summary of control level indicators as they are used in RPG.

Self-Test

1. When a line of output is generated for each input record, this is called _____ printing.

2. When a total or summary line is printed for a group of input records, this is called _____ printing.

3. Suppose a file is entered in ACCTNO (account number) sequence where all records for a given ACCTNO appear together, followed by records for another ACCTNO, and so on. If output is to include totals for each ACCTNO, a _____ procedure is required.

Figure 7.7
RPG program to produce the group-printed monthly sales report.

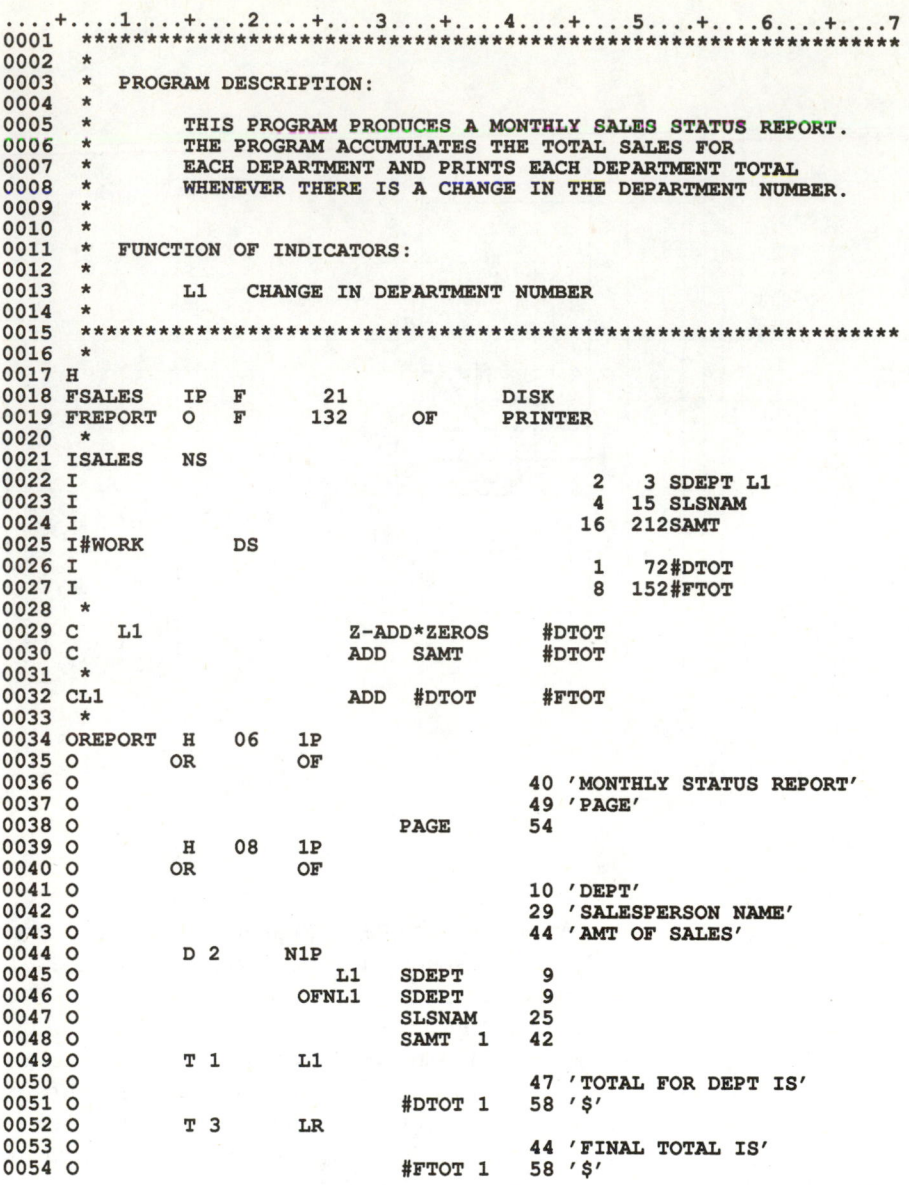

```
....+....1....+....2....+....3....+....4....+....5....+....6....+....7
0001  ****************************************************************
0002  *
0003  *    PROGRAM DESCRIPTION:
0004  *
0005  *        THIS PROGRAM PRODUCES A MONTHLY SALES STATUS REPORT.
0006  *        THE PROGRAM ACCUMULATES THE TOTAL SALES FOR
0007  *        EACH DEPARTMENT AND PRINTS EACH DEPARTMENT TOTAL
0008  *        WHENEVER THERE IS A CHANGE IN THE DEPARTMENT NUMBER.
0009  *
0010  *
0011  *    FUNCTION OF INDICATORS:
0012  *
0013  *        L1    CHANGE IN DEPARTMENT NUMBER
0014  *
0015  ****************************************************************
0016  *
0017  H
0018  FSALES    IP  F      21            DISK
0019  FREPORT   O   F     132      OF    PRINTER
0020  *
0021  ISALES    NS
0022  I                                      2    3 SDEPT L1
0023  I                                      4   15 SLSNAM
0024  I                                     16  212SAMT
0025  I#WORK        DS
0026  I                                      1   72#DTOT
0027  I                                      8  152#FTOT
0028  *
0029  C    L1              Z-ADD*ZEROS    #DTOT
0030  C                    ADD    SAMT    #DTOT
0031  *
0032  CL1                  ADD    #DTOT   #FTOT
0033  *
0034  OREPORT   H   06    1P
0035  O         OR        OF
0036  O                                           40 'MONTHLY STATUS REPORT'
0037  O                                           49 'PAGE'
0038  O                               PAGE        54
0039  O         H   08    1P
0040  O         OR        OF
0041  O                                           10 'DEPT'
0042  O                                           29 'SALESPERSON NAME'
0043  O                                           44 'AMT OF SALES'
0044  O         D   2     N1P
0045  O                   L1    SDEPT             9
0046  O                   OFNL1 SDEPT             9
0047  O                         SLSNAM           25
0048  O                         SAMT  1          42
0049  O         T   1     L1
0050  O                                           47 'TOTAL FOR DEPT IS'
0051  O                         #DTOT 1          58 '$'
0052  O         T   3     LR
0053  O                                           44 'FINAL TOTAL IS'
0054  O                         #FTOT 1          58 '$'
```

Figure 7.8
Summary of control break indicators.

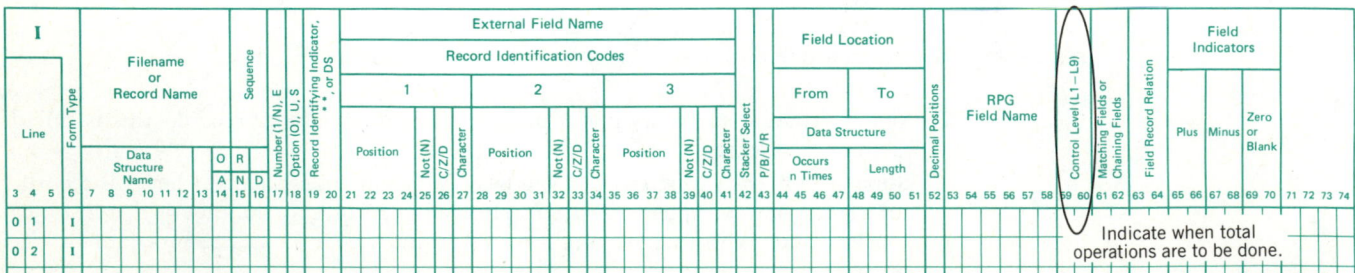

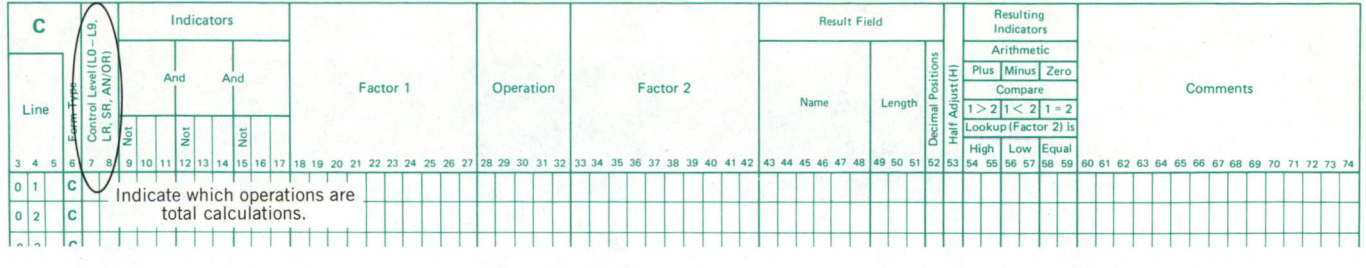

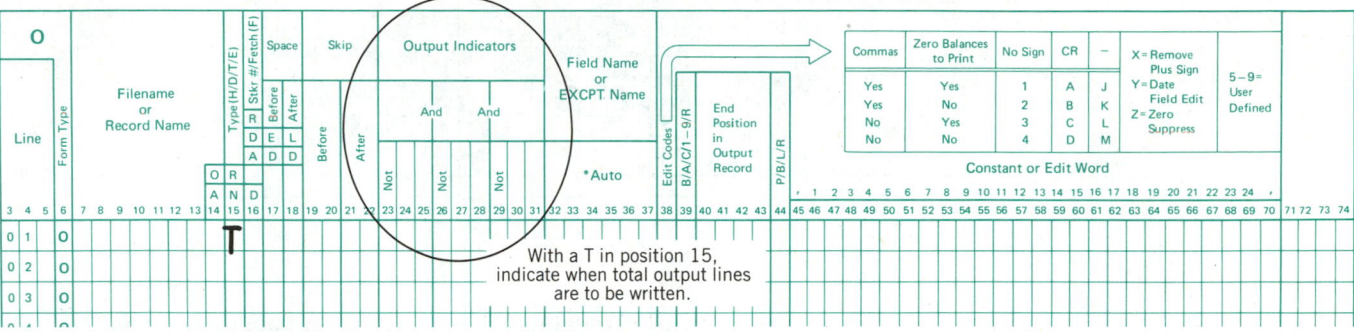

Figure 7.8
(continued)

4. In Question 3, ACCTNO would be called a(n) _____ field and would be defined on the Input Specifications form along with an entry in the _____ columns of the form.

5. (T or F) Control break problems require input to be sorted into the correct sequence by control field.

6. Using L1 to control a calculation would mean that the calculation would only be performed when a change in the _____ occurred.

7. After a control break is detected by the computer, _____ are performed, followed by _____ .

8. (T or F) When an end-of-file condition occurs, the LR indicator along with all control level indicators are turned on.

9. Suppose the last group in a control break problem has ACCTNO 999. Once the end-of-file indicator is turned on, the computer will perform two operations. Name them.

10. (T or F) The computer does not perform total calculations or total output when the first record is read.

11. Code an RPG program using the specifications in Figure 7.9.

Figure 7.9
Problem definition for
Question 11.

Systems Flowchart

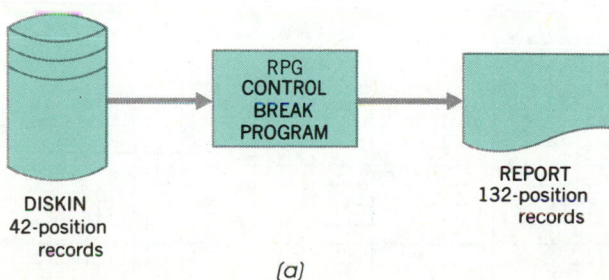

DISKIN
42-position
records

RPG
CONTROL
BREAK
PROGRAM

REPORT
132-position
records

(a)

(continued on next page)

Figure 7.9
(continued)

DISKIN Record Layout

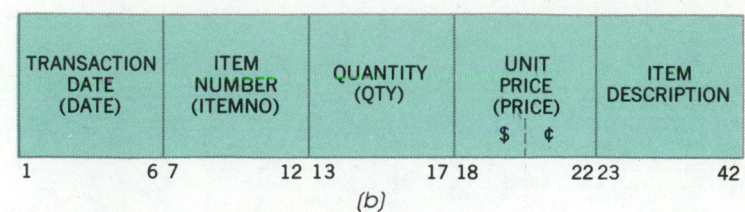

(b)

REPORT Printer Spacing Chart

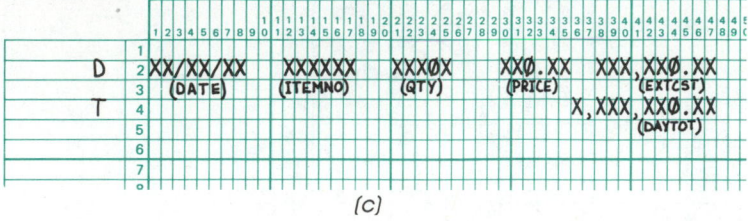

(c)

Note:

Extended cost (EXTCST) is equal to QTY × PRICE. Compute daily totals. Records are in sequence by DATE, which is the control field.

12. Code an RPG program to produce the output specified in the problem definition in Figure 7.10.

Figure 7.10
Problem definition for
Question 12.

Systems Flowchart

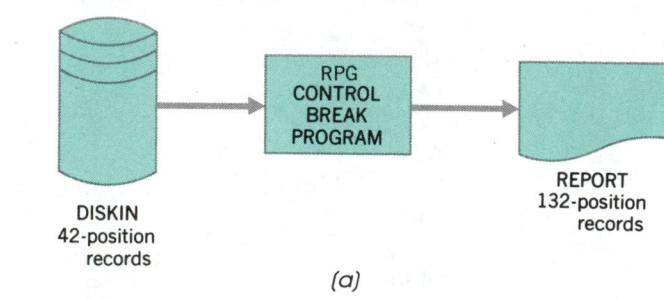

(a)

DISKIN Record Layout

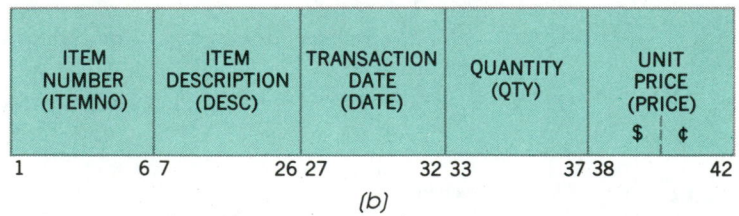

(b)

REPORT Printer Spacing Chart

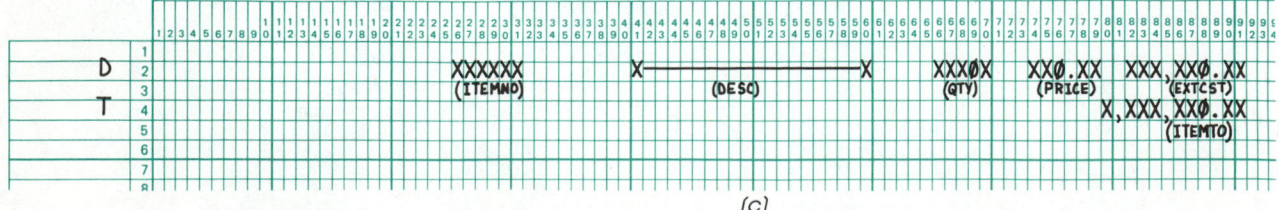

(c)

Notes:

a. The input records are in sequence by item number (ITEMNO), which is the control field. There will be several records for each ITEMNO.

b. ITEMNO and DESC are group indicated.

c. ITEMTO is the total to be computed for each item. It is the total of all the extended costs for each item.

d. Each extended cost is equal to QTY times PRICE.

Solutions
1. detail
2. group or summary
3. control break
4. control; control level (59–60)
5. T
6. control field
7. L1 calculations; total time printing
8. T
9. control level and LR total calculations; control level and LR total output
10. T, but the control break indicator is set on and can be used during detail time.
11. See Figure 7.11.
12. See Figure 7.12.

Figure 7.11
Solution for Question 11.

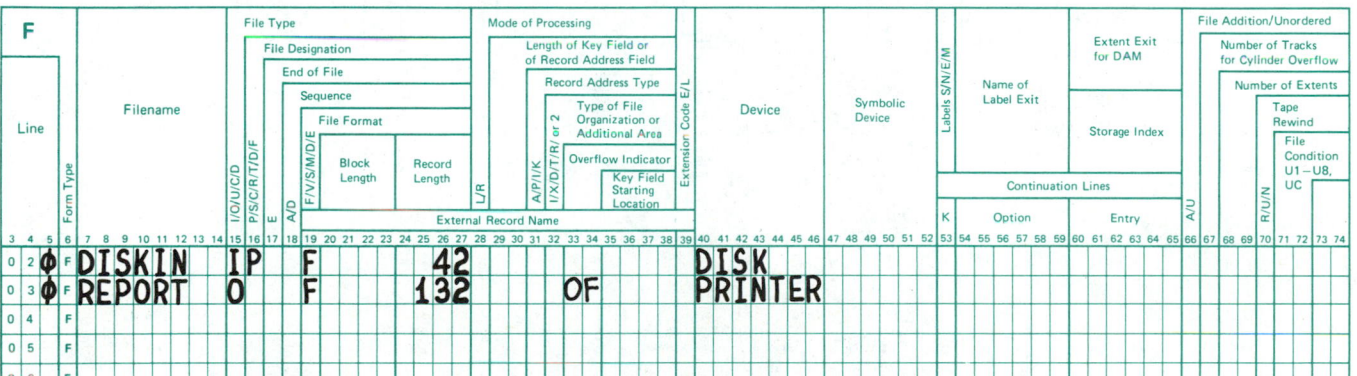

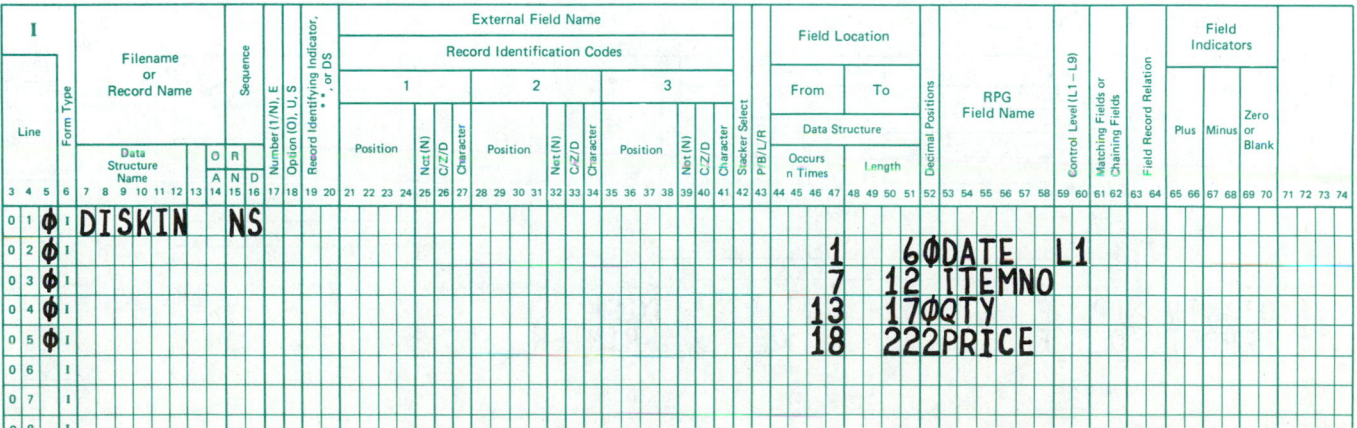

(continued on next page)

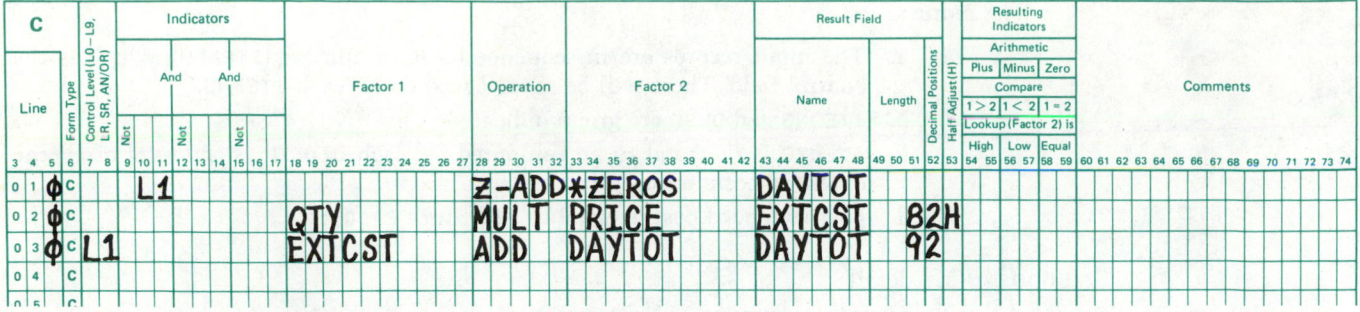

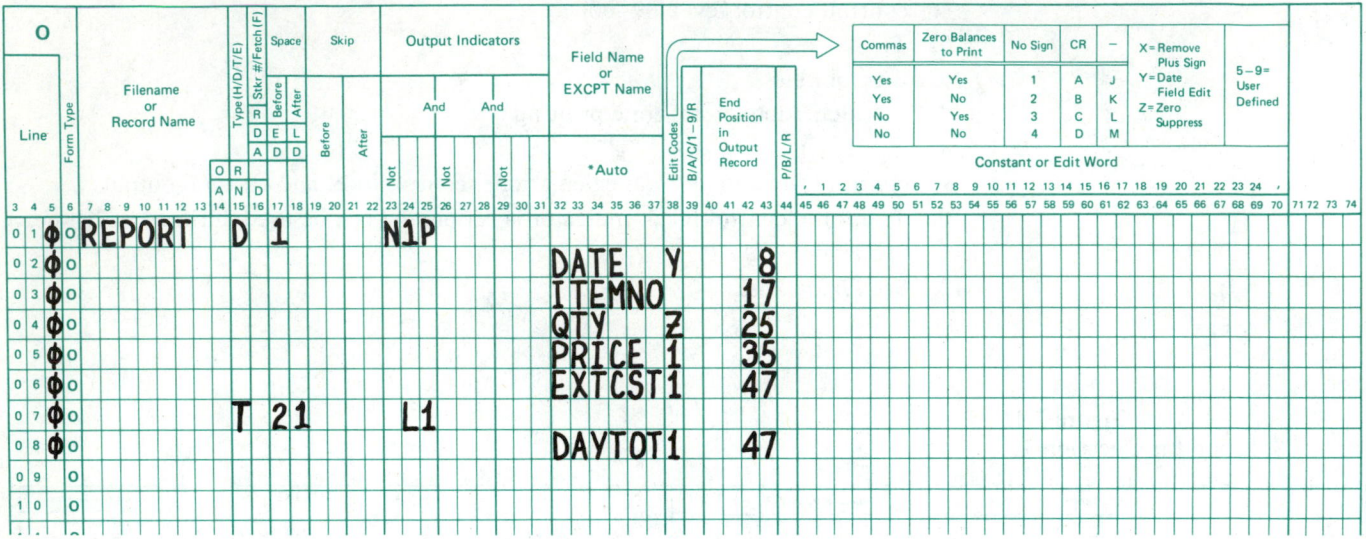

Figure 7.11
(continued)

Figure 7.12
Solution for Question 12.

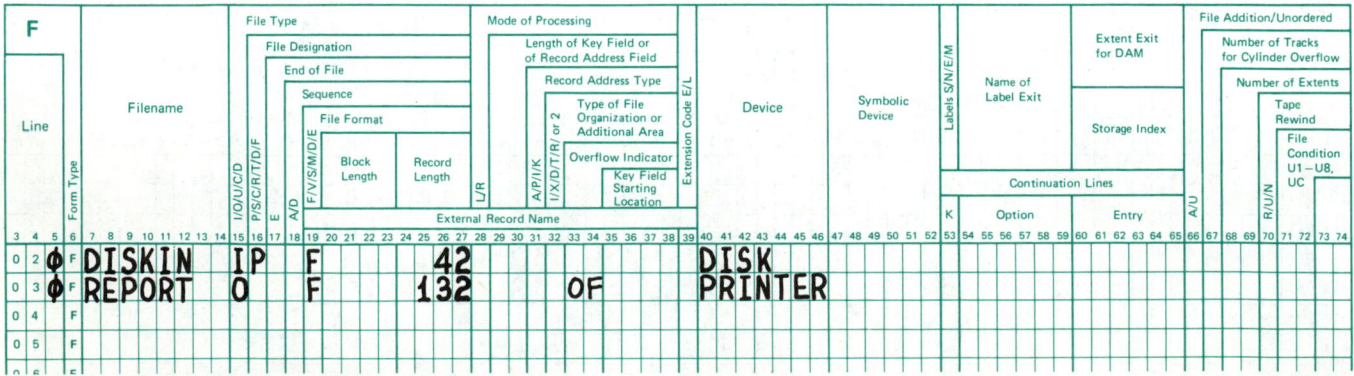

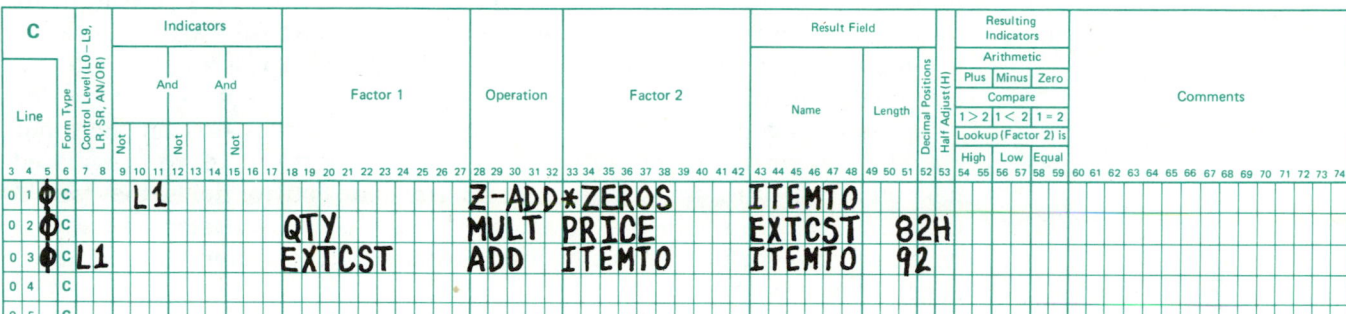

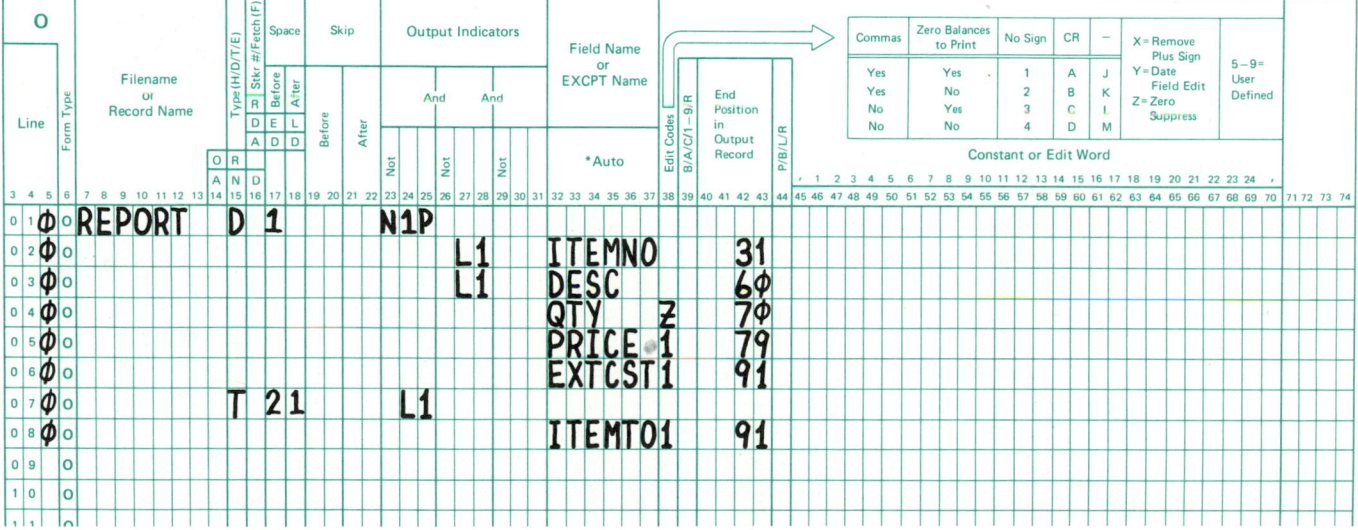

Figure 7.12
(continued)

III. Multiple Level Control Breaks

A. Defining the Problem

It is often useful to have different levels of control fields determine when printing is to occur. The RPG specifications permit **multiple level control**

breaks. Up to *nine* levels of control may be used with the use of level indicators L1–L9. We will consider double level controls in this section and end with an illustration of a triple level control break procedure.

Examine the report in Figure 7.13. It uses control break procedures that produce summary data on lines 13, 19, 21, 25, 29, 31, and 33. It also prints detail data from each input record as indicated on lines 9, 11, 15, 17, 23, and 27.

Every time a customer charges a purchase, an input record is created that consists of the customer name, amount of purchase, territory in which purchase was made, and department in which purchase was made. Control fields are usually placed in the left-most positions of an input record because they are used for control and sorting purposes. Since territory and department are control fields in this instance, they would typically be coded first on the Input Specifications form.

Detail printing is required as well as group printing of department totals and territory totals. Since departments exist within each territory, department is a *minor control field* and territory is a *major control field*. Major control fields have higher control level numbers than do minor control fields. Hence we could code department as an L1 control field and territory as an L2 (or L3, L4, etc.) control field.

Territory is considered the major control field, so it is first on the input record. Department, within territory, is a minor control field, so it is placed next on the input record. If there were intermediate control fields, they would typically be placed between TERR and DEPT. In general, data is stored in records with major key fields followed by intermediate and then minor ones, but this is not always the case.

Each input record is printed, and a department total is accumulated. When there is a control break or a change in department, the following occur:

1. Calculations: The department total is added to the territory total.
2. Printing: The total for the previous department is printed.

Figure 7.13
Printer Spacing Chart illustrating multiple-level control breaks.

Printer Spacing Chart (Figure 7.13):

Line	Type	TERRITORY	DEPARTMENT	CUSTOMER NAME	AMT OF PURCHASE		
6	H			CUSTOMER REPORT		PAGE 1	
7	H	TERRITORY	DEPARTMENT	CUSTOMER NAME	AMT OF PURCHASE		
9	D	01	01	PAUL NEWMAN	$100.50		
11	D	01	01	EDDIE MURPHY	$250.00		
13	TL1				TOTAL DEPT 01	$350.50*	
15	D	01	02	ROBERT REDFORD	$5,250.40		
17	D	01	02	BARBRA STREISAND	$525.10		
19	TL1				TOTAL DEPT 02	$5,775.50*	
21	TL2					TOTAL TERR 01	$6,126.00**
23	D	02	01	WOODY ALLEN	$200.50		
25	TL1				TOTAL DEPT 01	$200.50*	
27	D	02	02	JACK NICHOLSON	$425.30		
29	TL1				TOTAL DEPT 02	$425.30*	
31	TL2					TOTAL TERR 02	$625.80**
33	TLR					FINAL TOTAL	$6,751.80***

The territory total keeps accumulating for each department within the specific territory. This processing continues until there is a major break in territory. A major control break performs the following:

1. Accumulates a final total.
2. Forces the previous department total to print.
3. Prints the territory total.

The final total is printed at the end of the job, when the LR indicator is on. This LR indicator first turns on indicators L1–L9, causing minor and major control breaks before printing final totals.

A change in department, the minor level control break, causes a department total to print and that total to be added to the territory total. Minor level controls are the lowest level indicated. We use L1 to denote a department break and we print an asterisk (*) on the report to designate the department total as a control total.

As noted, a change in the major level control field, territory, results in the *printing* of the following as well as the accumulating of a final total:

1. The last department total in the previous territory.
2. The previous territory total.

Major level control fields must have a level number higher than minor level ones. We use L2 to denote the major control field, territory, and we print two asterisks (**) on the report to designate the territory total as a major control total. Keep in mind, however, that we could have used any level L2–L9 for denoting the territory as a major control field, although L2 is usually used.

When a control level indicator is turned on because there is a change in the control field, all lower level indicators are automatically set on as well. Hence, if an L2 territory break occurs, this will automatically turn on the L1 indicator, which will cause the last department total for the territory to print.

If five control levels, L1–L5, were used, a break in the L5 control field would automatically turn on indicators L1–L4 (and L5) forcing lower level breaks. Printing and calculations occur from low to high (L1→L5). This is a logical sequence because we would always want to print the last department total for a specific territory before we printed the territory total.

Records must be entered in sequence by department within territory. If records are in a different sequence, they would need to be sorted before being inputted. Thus all DEPT 01 records for TERR 01 would be entered first, followed by DEPT 02 records (if any) for TERR 01, and so on, until all DEPTs in TERR 01 were read and processed; then records for the first DEPT in TERR 02 would be read, and so on. Suppose a group of records were processed as shown in Figure 7.14.

Each time there is a change in DEPT a department total prints. When there is a change in TERR, the total for the previous department prints followed by the TERR total.

In this example, there is one instance where a change in territory occurs but the DEPT number remains the same. We would still want to print DEPT 03 and TERR 01 totals before processing the new TERR. In this instance, it might appear as if the L2 indicator is turned on but not the L1 indicator. The processing proceeds properly, however, because the L2 indicator automatically turns on the L1 indicator. Thus the DEPT 03 break is "forced" when there is a change in TERR even if it happens that the first DEPT in the next TERR is also 03. This guarantees that the processing will be correct.

At the end of the job, three totals print:

Figure 7.14
Sample output illustration for
multiple-level control breaks.

TERRITORY	DEPT	CUSTOMER NAME	AMT OF PURCHASE
Ø1	Ø1	X_____X	X_____X
Ø1	Ø1	X_____X	X_____X
		TOTAL DEPT Ø1 $_____	
Ø1	Ø3	X_____X	X_____X
Ø1	Ø3	X_____X	X_____X
		TOTAL DEPT Ø3 $_____	
		TOTAL TERR Ø1 $_____	

Ø2   Ø3 ◄——— (Note that this DEPT Ø3 relates to a different TERRITORY.)

1. Department total (*).
2. Territory total (**).
3. Final total (***).

The asterisks (*) are frequently used to designate the level of the total field printing.

The LR indicator automatically turns on all level indicators L1–L9, which will cause all accumulated totals to print.

At total time, the computer prints L1 totals first, followed by L2 totals, and so on. The last total line to print is the LR total line. *You should code L1 totals first, followed by L2 totals, and so on, and end with LR totals.*

B. RPG Coding for Multiple Control Breaks

Recall that Figure 7.13 provides the sample output for a double-level control break problem in which DEPT is the minor control field and TERR is the major control field. Figure 7.15 illustrates the RPG coding.

It is important to understand the sequence in which the computer performs control processing. Suppose we are using level indicators L1, L2, L3.

1. A record is read.
2. Level testing is performed in the following sequence.
   a. LR test: If an end-of-file condition exists, L1–L3 indicators are turned on (whichever levels are used by program), as well as LR.

Figure 7.15
Coding for a double-level
control break problem.

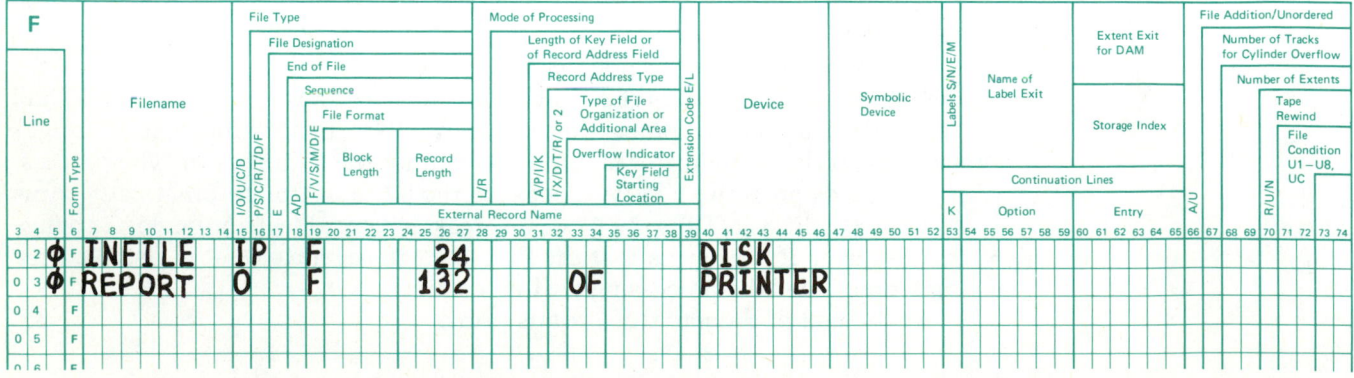

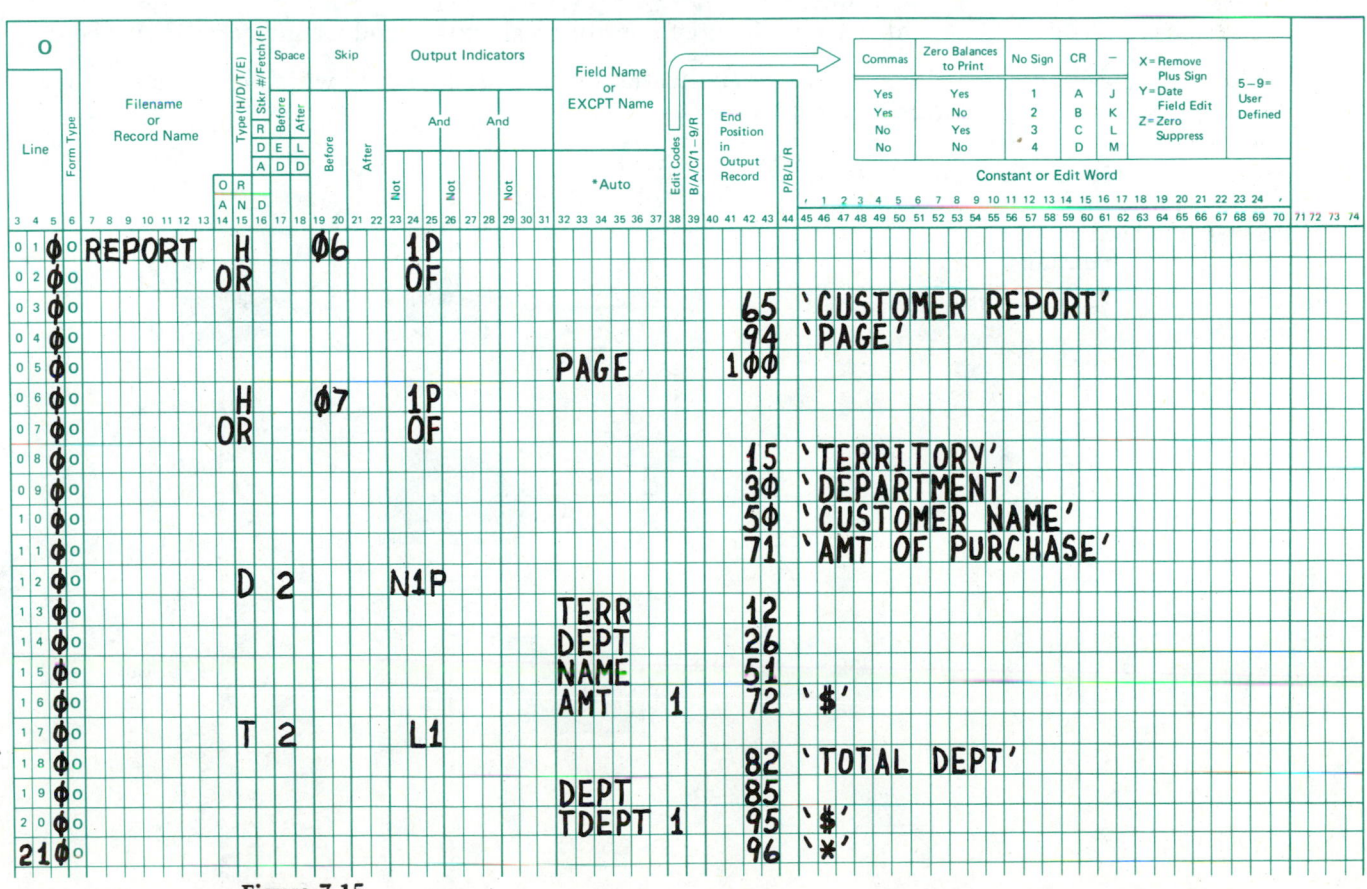

Figure 7.15
(continued)

(continued on next page)

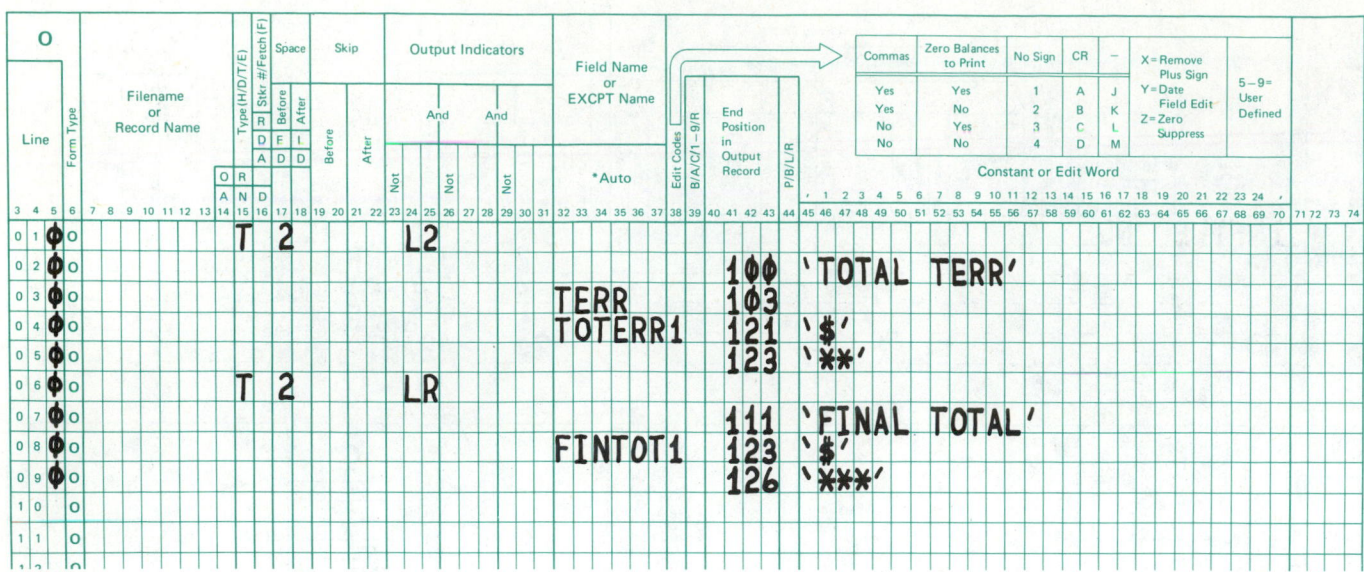

Figure 7.15
(continued)

b. L3 test: If an L3 control break exists, the L3, L2, and L1 indicators are turned on.

c. L2 test: If an L2 control break exists, the L2 and L1 indicators are turned on.

d. L1 test: If an L1 control break exists, and L1 indicator is turned on.

See Figure 7.16 for an illustration of the sequence in which RPG tests the level control indicators.

Figure 7.16
The sequence in which RPG tests the level control indicators.

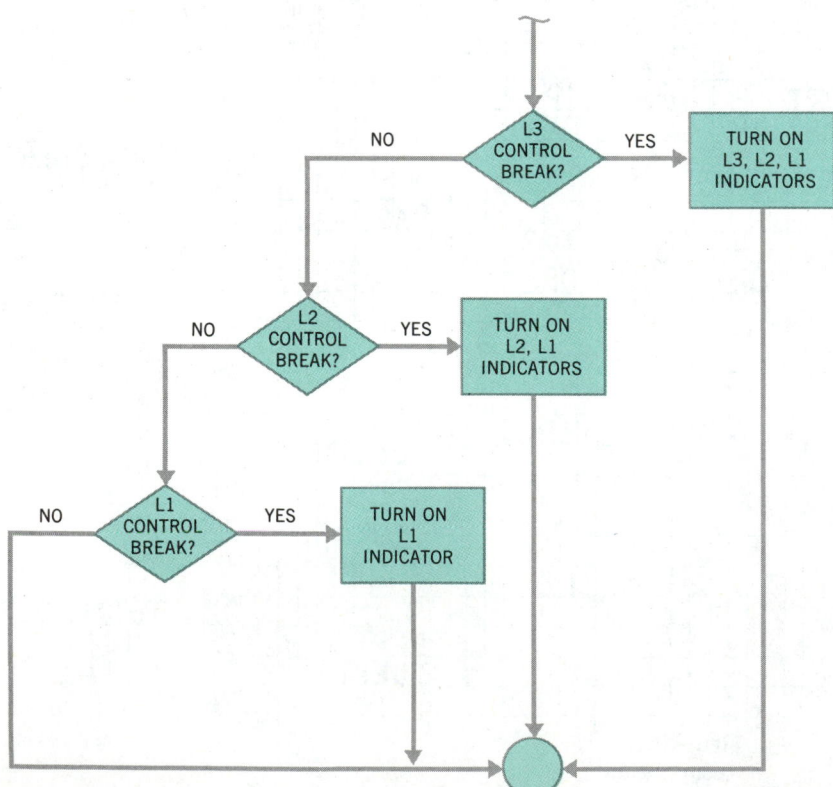

3. Control level calculations are performed in sequence: L1, L2, L3, . . . LR. The calculations must be coded in that sequence as well.

4. Control level totals are printed in sequence: L1, L2, L3, . . . LR. The output specifications should be coded in that sequence as well.

5. If LR is off, detail calculations and printing are performed.

6. If LR is off, all level indicators are turned off and another record is read.

The following is a summary of the steps involved:

Indicator On	Calculation Performed	Field That Is Printed
None	ADD AMT to TDEPT	AMT
L1	ADD TDEPT to TOTERR	TDEPT
L2	ADD TOTERR to FINTOT	TOTERR
LR	None	FINTOT

The flowchart for this facet of the RPG Logic Cycle appears in Figure 7.17.

Figure 7.17
RPG Logic Cycle depicting triple-level control break processing.

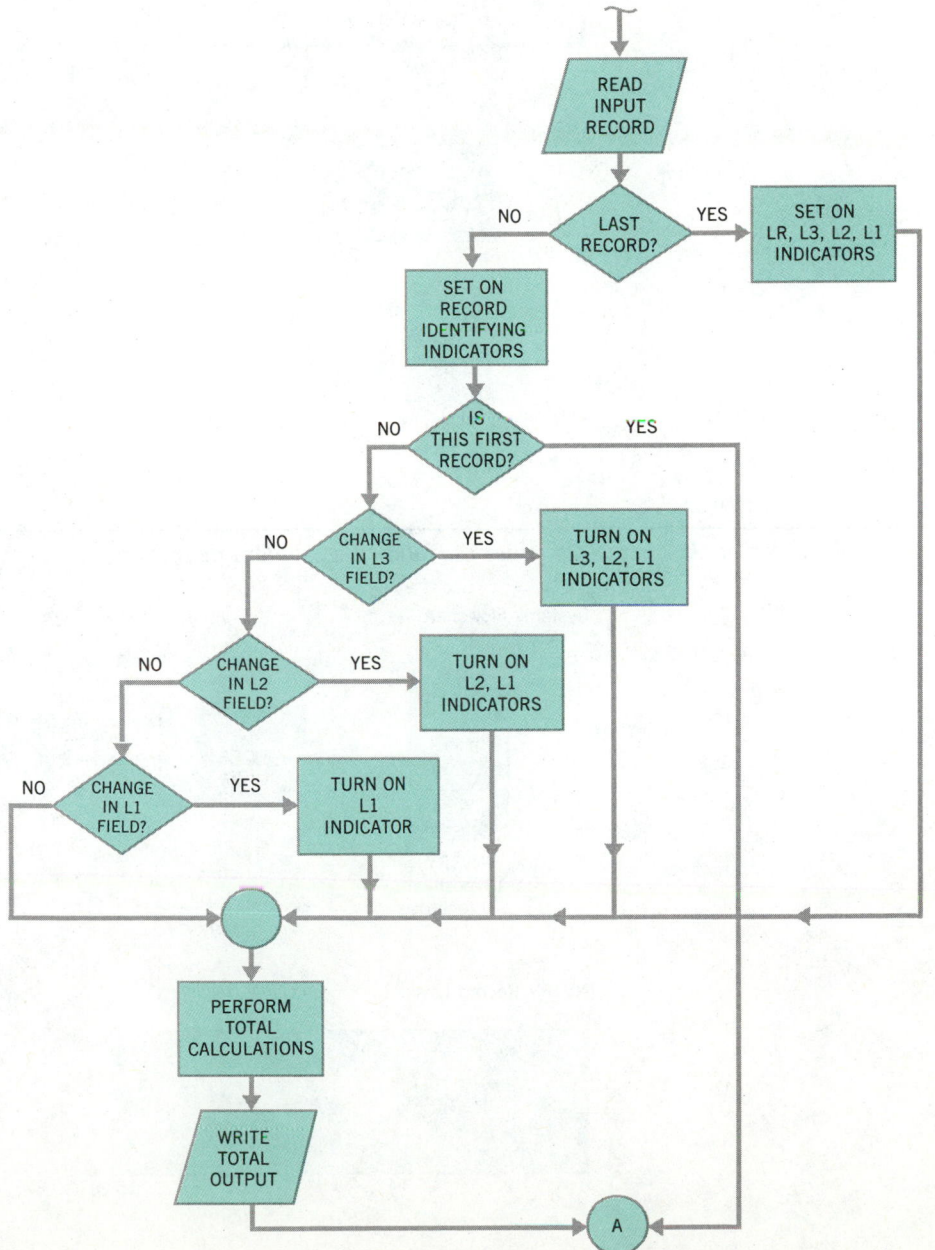

(continued on next page)

Figure 7.17
(continued)

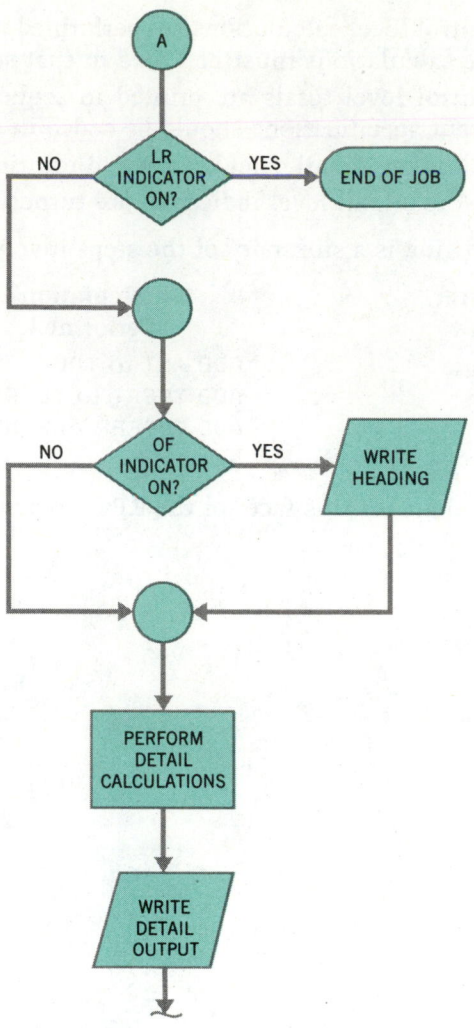

Self-Test   *Consider the following problem definition:*

Systems Flowchart

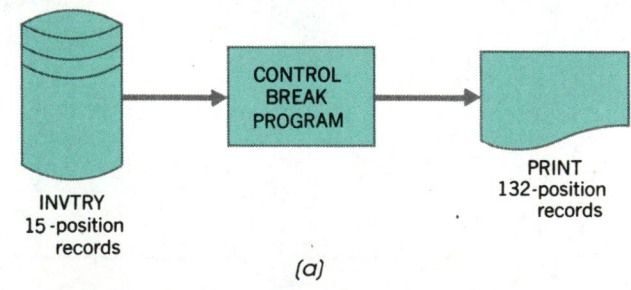

(a)

INVTRY Record Layout

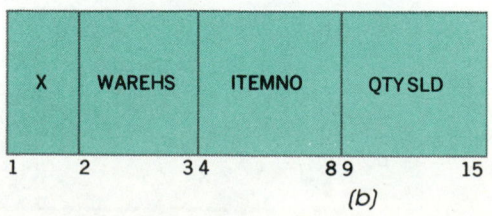

(b)

PRINT Printer Spacing Chart

H				INVENTORY STATUS REPORT		
H		WAREHOUSE ITEM NO		QTY		
D		XX	XXXXX	XXXXXX		
D				XXXXXX		
D				XXXXXX		
T L1				TOTAL FOR ITEM XXXXXXXX		
D		XX	XXXXX	XXXXXX		
D				XXXXXX		
T L1				TOTAL FOR ITEM XXXXXXXX		
				TOTAL FOR WH XXXXXXXXX		
T L2						
T LR				FINAL COUNT OF ALL ITEMS XXXXXXXXX		

(c)

Part 1
1. This would be considered a(n) _____ control break problem.
2. The major control field would be _____ , and the minor control field would be
   _____ .
3. The L1 level would be associated with _____ .
4. The L2 level would be associated with _____ .
5. When an L2 break occurs, _____(no.)_____ totals print in the following sequence:
   _____ and _____ .
6. An end-of-job condition would turn on which indicators?
7. (T or F) For double-level control problems, the input need not be in any particular sequence.
8. In this problem definition, L1 calculations would include _____ .
9. In this problem definition, L2 calculations would include _____ .
10. In this problem definition, the LR indicator would cause the printing of
    _____ .

Part 2
Code the program required to produce the output specified in Part 1.

Solutions *Part 1*
1. double-level
2. WAREHS
   ITEMNO
3. ITEMNO
4. WAREHS
5. two; ITEMNO total; WAREHS total
6. LR; L2; L1
7. F—It must be in ITEMNO sequence within WAREHS.
8. adding ITEMTO to WHTOT
9. adding WHTOT to FINTOT
10. the final total

Part 2

F — File Description Specifications

Line	Form Type	Filename	I/O/U/C/D	P/S/C/R/T/D/F	E	F/V/S/M/D/E	Block Length	Record Length	L/R	A/P/I/K	1/X/D/T/R or 2	External Record Name	Extension Code E/L	Device	Symbolic Device
0 2 0	F	INVTRY	I P		F			15						DISK	
0 3 0	F	REPORT	O		F			132				OF		PRINTER	
0 4	F														
0 5	F														
0 6	F														

I — Input Specifications

Line	Form Type	Filename or Record Name	Sequence	Number (1/N), E	Option (O), U, S	Record Identifying Indicator, * * *, or DS	From	To	Decimal Positions	RPG Field Name	Control Level (L1–L9)	Matching Fields or Chaining Fields	Field Record Relation	Plus	Minus	Zero or Blank
0 1 0	I	INVTRY	NS													
0 2 0	I						2	3		WAREHS	L2					
0 3 0	I						4	8		ITEMNO	L1					
0 4 0	I						9	150		QTYSLD						
0 5	I															
0 6	I															

C — Calculation Specifications

Line	Form Type	Control Level (L0–L9, LR, SR, AN/OR)	Indicators And	And	Factor 1	Operation	Factor 2	Result Field Name	Length	Decimal Positions	Plus 1>2	Minus 1<2	Zero 1=2	Comments
0 1 0	C	L1				Z-ADD	*ZEROS	ITEMTO						
0 2 0	C	L2				Z-ADD	*ZEROS	WHTOT						
0 3 0	C				QTYSLD	ADD	ITEMTO	ITEMTO	80					
0 4 0	C	L1			ITEMTO	ADD	WHTOT	WHTOT	90					
0 5 0	C	L2			WHTOT	ADD	FINTOT	FINTOT	100					

```
O  | Filename   |Type| Space | Skip | Output Indicators | Field Name | End   | Constant or Edit Word
   | or Record  |    |       |      |                   | or EXCPT   | Pos.  |
   | Name       |    |Before | Before| And   And         | Name       |       |
Line|           |    | After | After | Not  Not  Not      | *Auto      |       |
01 0 REPORT   H      06          1P OF
02 0          OR                 OF
03 0                                              37 'INVENTORY STATUS'
04 0                                              44 'REPORT'
05 0          H      08          1P OF
06 0          OR                 OF
07 0                                              11 'WAREHOUSE'
08 0                                              20 'ITEM NO'
09 0                                              29 'QTY'
10 0          D  2           N1P
11 0                              L2  WAREHS       6
12 0                              L1  ITEMNO      19
13 0                                  QTYSLD      31
14 0          T  2               L1
15 0                                              44 'TOTAL FOR ITEM'
16 0                                  ITEMTO      53
17 0          T  2               L2
18 0                                              46 'TOTAL FOR WH'
19 0                                  WHTOT       56
20 0          T  3               LR
21 0                                              30 'FINAL COUNT'
22 0                                              43 'OF ALL ITEMS'
23 0                                  FINTOT      55
```

C. Control Break Printing with No Detail Output (Group-Printed Reports)

Sometimes the user does not need detail output at all, but requires a summary report consisting of totals by specific categories. In this instance, control break processing can be performed without the need for any D or detail output. Figure 7.18 provides the problem definition for such a program, and Figure 7.19 illustrates the RPG program.

D. Handling Page Overflow Conditions for Group Printing

1. Review of Overflow (OF) Indicator

Detail reports typically contain one output line for each input record read. If no overflow or OF indicator is used, then output will continue to print from one sheet on a continuous form to another, with no attention being given to top and bottom page margins or to perforations separating each sheet. See Figure 7.20 for an illustration of a poorly designed report that might be printed when no attention is given to page overflow.

Usually, we want the computer to print a heading on each page of a report.

Figure 7.18
Problem definition for control break procedure with no detail print.

Systems Flowchart

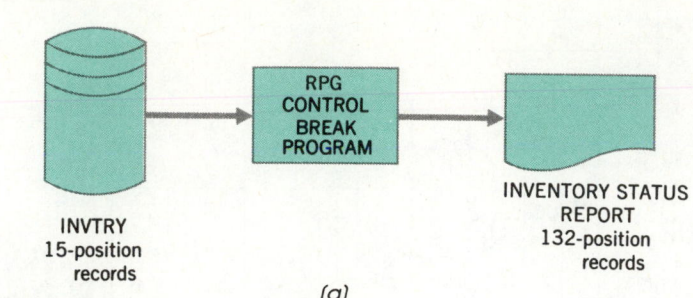

INVTRY
15-position
records

RPG
CONTROL
BREAK
PROGRAM

INVENTORY STATUS
REPORT
132-position
records

(a)

INVTRY Record Layout

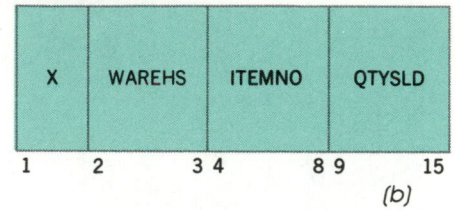

INVENTORY STATUS REPORT Printer Spacing Chart

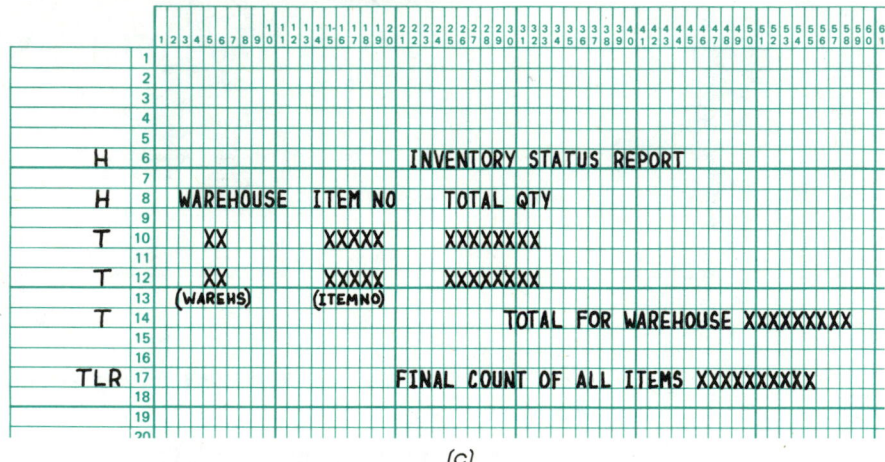

(c)

Figure 7.19
Coding for control break procedure with no detail print.

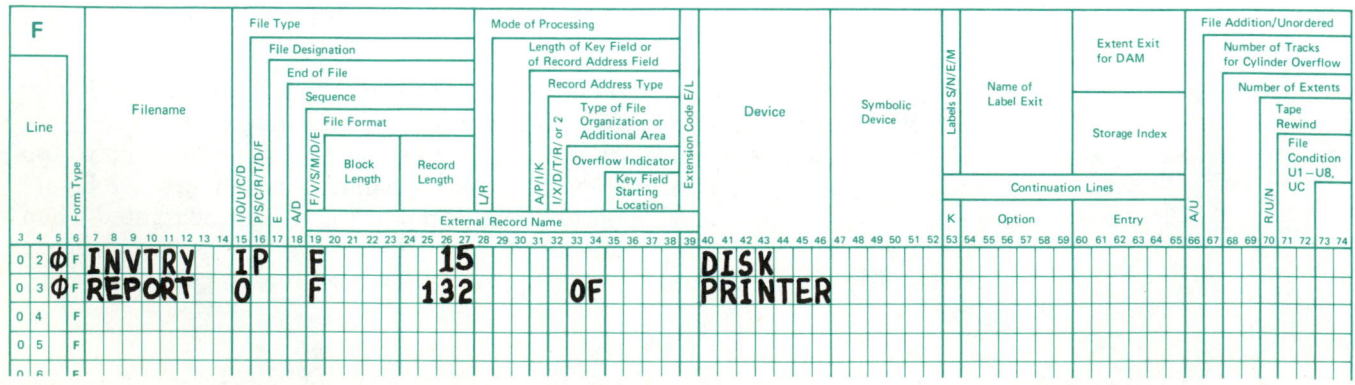

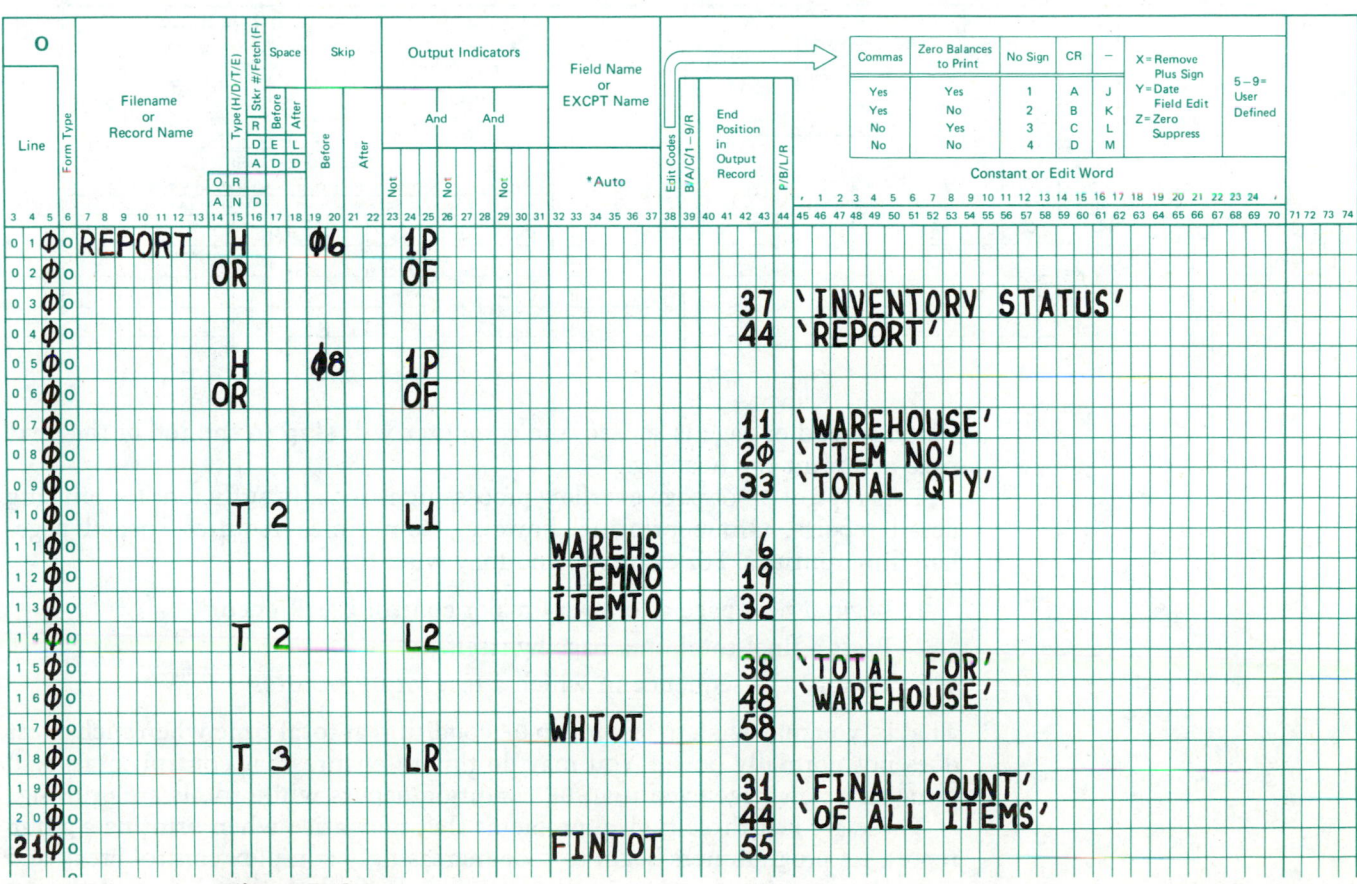

Figure 7.19
(continued)

Figure 7.20
Example of a poorly designed
output report.

MONTHLY SALES REPORT

Poor Design of Output

1. Printing occurs over perforation.
2. Heading appears only on the first page.
3. Page numbers are not used.

The following Output Specifications will result in the printing of headings when the first page (1P) or overflow (OF) indicator is on.

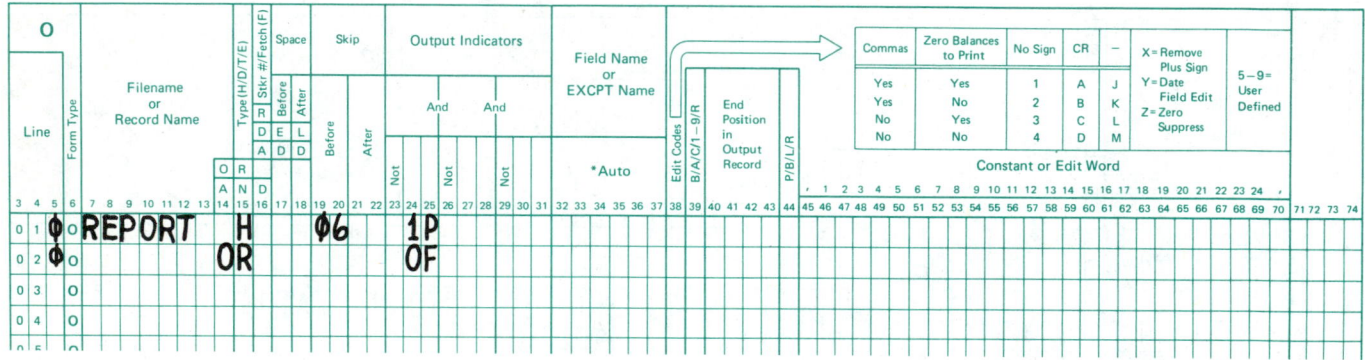

When an end of page is sensed, the computer will skip to the top of the next page and print the heading.

This type of OF or **page overflow** processing is usually sufficient for printing detail reports. Group printing, however, sometimes requires special page-handling routines. For example, you may wish to:

1. Begin a new page after every major control break occurs.
2. Print a final total on a page by itself.
3. Change the sequence in which a test for OF occurs.

That is, you may wish to test for an OF condition at total time when such a test does not normally occur. You may do this to ensure that control totals will print on a new page even if an OF condition occurs while totals are printing.

These are just three typical problems that may arise when printing a group report. As programmers begin to code increasingly complex control break and other group print procedures, they frequently find the need to use the OF indicator in ways that have not yet been explained.

2. Forcing an End-of-Page Condition after Control Totals Have Printed

As noted, you may wish to force an end-of-page condition so that after control totals print, a new page is started that specifies a heading followed by new detail lines. To "force" an end-of-page condition, you must code an operation that turns on the OF indicator. This instruction would be executed when a control level break has occurred. Since this is to be done after all control level calculations have been performed, code a SETON operation on the Calculation form as the last control level operation. If you use only one control level, L1, the Calculation Specifications form might appear as follows:

C	Form Type	Control Level (L0—L9, LR, SR, AN/OR)	Indicators						Factor 1	Operation	Factor 2	Result Field		Decimal Positions	Half Adjust (H)	Resulting Indicators			Comments
			And		And		Not					Name	Length			Arithmetic Plus / Minus / Zero; Compare 1>2 / 1<2 / 1=2; Lookup (Factor 2) is High / Low / Equal			
Line			Not		Not														
0 1 0	C								DTOTAL	ADD	AMT	DTOTAL	72						
0 2 0	C	L1							FTOTAL	ADD	DTOTAL	FTOTAL	82						
0 3 0	C	L1								SETON						OF			
0 4	C																		
0 5	C																		

For each input record, add AMT to DTOTAL. For each L1 break, add this DTOTAL to a final total called FTOTAL. The FTOTAL will print at the end of the run.

In addition, you may wish to set on the OF indicator when an L1 occurs:

C	Form Type	Control Level (L0—L9, LR, SR, AN/OR)	Indicators						Factor 1	Operation	Factor 2	Result Field		Decimal Positions	Half Adjust (H)	Resulting Indicators			Comments
			And		And		Not					Name	Length			Arithmetic Plus / Minus / Zero; Compare 1>2 / 1<2 / 1=2; Lookup (Factor 2) is High / Low / Equal			
Line			Not		Not														
0 1 0	C	L1								SETON						OF			
0 2	C																		
0 3	C																		

The SETON command is used for turning on one, two, or three indicators using columns 54–55, 56–57, 58–59, respectively, to specify the indicators. As noted in Chapter 3, resulting indicators set on by the programmer remain on until the program turns them off. The OF indicator remains, however, under the control of the RPG cycle and will "turn off" after there is a skip to a new page.

The operation to SETON the overflow indicator is executed after a change in DEPT, the L1 field, occurs. This SETON operation will be executed after the DTOTAL is added to the FTOTAL because it is coded after the ADD. Recall that if there are numerous calculations that are performed when a specific indicator is on, they are executed in the sequence in which they are coded.

After all the L1 calculations are peformed, the total lines that specify the L1 indicator will print. It is important to note that the computer does *not* automatically check for an overflow condition at total time. This means that these totals will print on the same page as the previous detail data. After the total lines print, and before new detail data is written, the computer will test for an overflow condition.

Figure 7.21
Using the RPG Logic Cycle to
cause headings to print after
each control break.

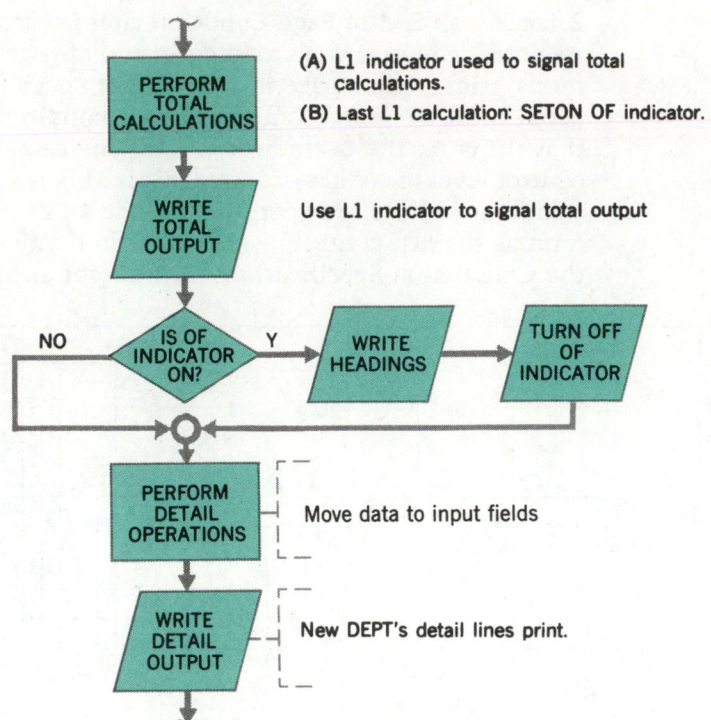

(A) L1 indicator used to signal total
    calculations.
(B) Last L1 calculation: SETON OF indicator.

Use L1 indicator to signal total output

Move data to input fields

New DEPT's detail lines print.

Note that the OF indicator will always be on at T or total time because the programmer sets it on, using the Calculation Specifications form. Thus, prior to printing a detail line that will contain a new control field, the computer will check for page overflow; since the page overflow indicator will be on, the headings will print on a new page followed by this first detail line for the new control group.

Figure 7.21 provides an illustration of how this RPG cycle can be used to cause headings to print after each control break.

3. An Alternative Method for Beginning Control Totals on a New Page
Thus far, we have begun a new page for each control group by setting on the overflow indicator whenever a major control break occurs. In our example, a major break is denoted by the L2 indicator.

Consider Example 1, which, on first glance, may seem to perform the same function more easily: the printing of a heading each time there is a control break. There is, however, a major flaw in Example 1.

Example 1

Line	Form Type	Filename or Record Name	Type (H/D/T/E)	Stk #/Fetch (F)	Space Before/After	Skip Before/After	Output Indicators And / And	Field Name or EXCPT Name *Auto	End Position in Output Record	Constant or Edit Word
0 1	O	TOTSLS	H		2 0 6		1P			
0 2	O		OR				OF			
0 3	O		OR				L2			
0 4	O							5 0	'SALES REPORT'	
0 5	O		•							
0 6	O		•							
0 7	O		•							
0 8	O									

Note that the heading will print if either the 1P, OF, or L2 indicator is on. There is an initial problem, however. You may recall that the RPG Logic Cycle *turns on* all level indicators when the first input record of a control group is read. This means that after the first input record is read, 1P *and* L2 are on. Since each indicator is tested separately, the heading would print *twice* on two separate pages before the first detail record is printed.

Thus, the logic in Example 1 is fine *except* for the initial heading, which prints twice. Since all level indicators are automatically turned on prior to any processing of the first record, you may use the L2 indicator to force a heading to print *in place of* the 1P indicator. See Example 2. This would certainly seem to alleviate this problem. Thus a heading prints if there is an overflow condition *or* an L2 break. This works fine for all normal processing and for the first record as well, which forces an L2 break.

Example 2

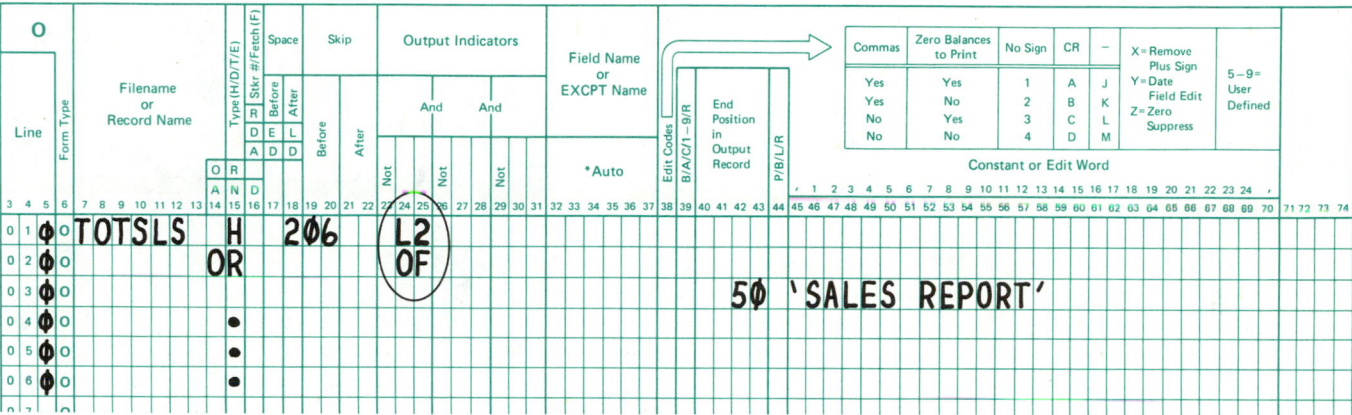

There is *still* a potential error, however. If an overflow condition occurs when there is an L2 break, then once again *two* headings will print on two separate pages. To alleviate this problem, print a heading if:

1. The L2 indicator is on; or
2. The OF indicator is on *and* the L2 indicator is off.

See Example 3, which can be used to force a page overflow whenever there is a major control break. This eliminates the need for setting on the OF indicator. This represents the best solution to the problem.

Example 3

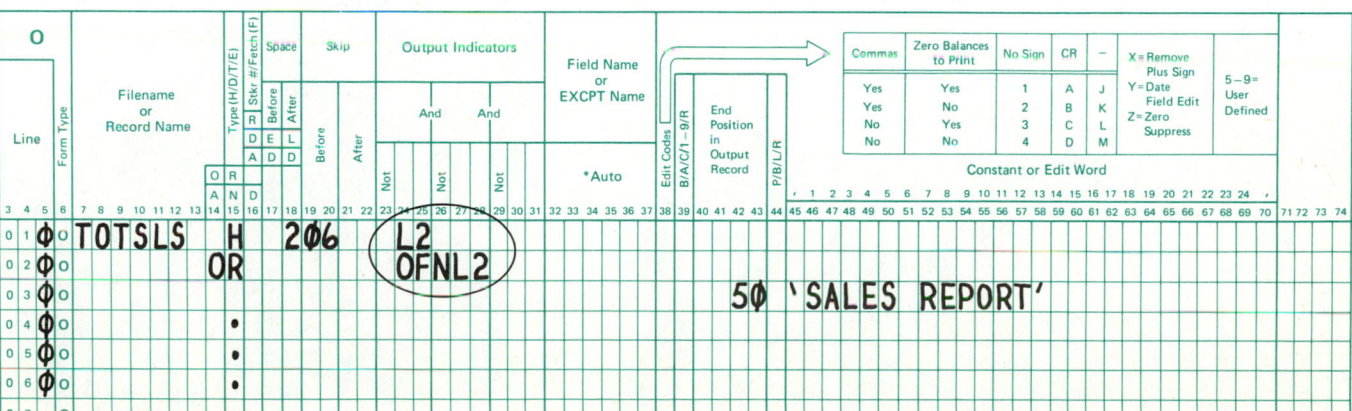

4. Using Fetch Overflow to Check for an Overflow Condition

In the normal RPG cycle, the test for overflow occurs after total time and before detail time. If several total or control lines are to print and we are at the bottom of a page, it is very likely that we would print over page perforations. Even though the overflow indicator has been set on, the RPG cycle will not test for overflow until all of the total lines have printed. For example, suppose there are five levels of controls to print, each requiring two lines of output. The overflow indicator may turn on after the first line prints. But since OF is not tested again until detail time, the subsequent nine control lines will continue printing on the same page, over the perforation and onto the next page:

```
                    .
                    .
        CONTROL LEVEL 1
            TOTALS $1234.56 *
        CONTROL LEVEL 2
            TOTALS $3345.89 **
------------CONTROL LEVEL 3--------------------
            TOTALS $2135.79 ***
        CONTROL LEVEL 4
            TOTALS $2156.76 ****
        CONTROL LEVEL 5
            TOTALS $4533.12 *****
```
Page perforation

Because OF is not tested at total time, you run the risk of having totals print over perforations producing a decidedly unprofessional-looking report. To avoid this, you can *force* an overflow test at total time by using the **Fetch Overflow** option on the Output Specifications form.

Column 16 on the Output Specifications form is called the *Fetch Overflow* position and is used to execute the Fetch Overflow option. If you wish to test for overflow as several total lines are printed, simply place an 'F' in column 16 for each total output line. Prior to each line printing, a test will be made to see if the overflow indicator is on. If on, all headings controlled by the overflow indicator are *fetched* and written out. Usually, the first heading line will force a skip to a new page. Then, the total output line that executed the Fetch Overflow option will be printed. Note that the Fetch Overflow does not force an overflow condition; it merely tests to see if the OF indicator is on during total time.

Thus, the following control total Output Specifications will avoid the possibility of missing an overflow condition and printing over the perforations of a continuous form:

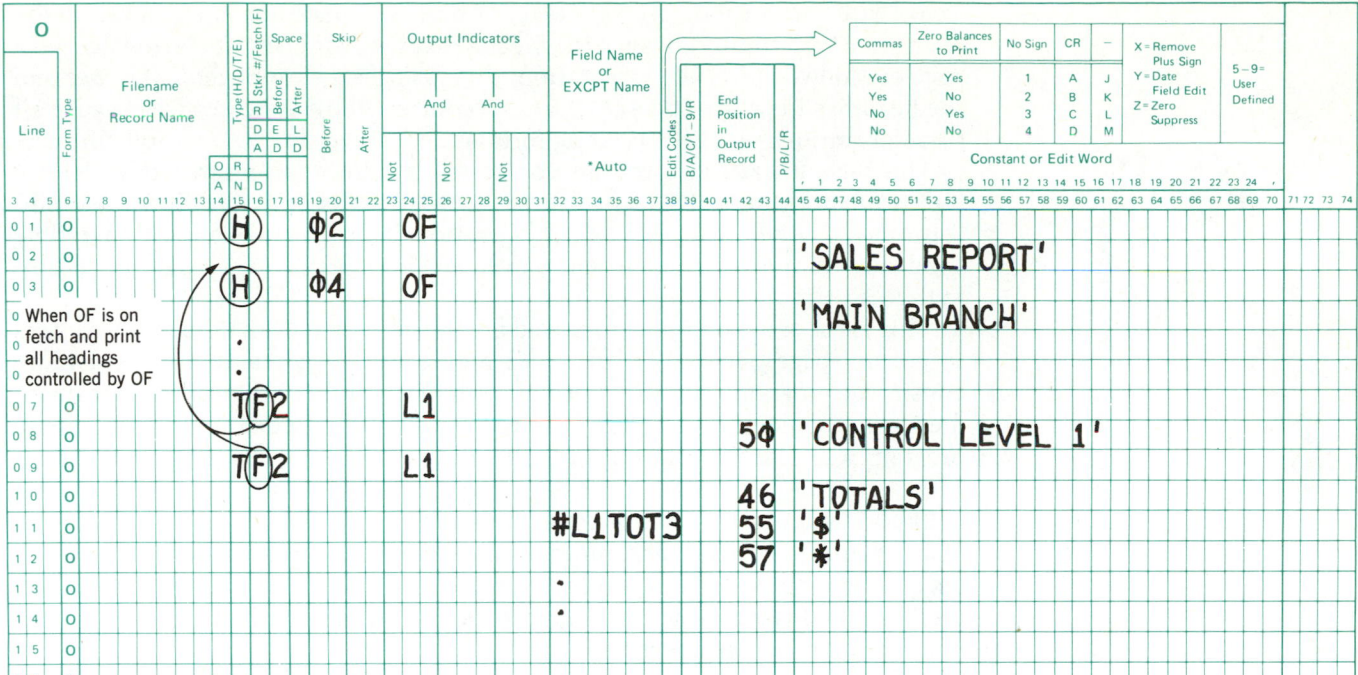

Note that the F in the Fetch Overflow field causes an overflow test to be performed before the specific total output line prints.

5. An Alternative to Fetch Overflow: EXCPT Output

We saw that when page overflow occurs during the printing of total lines the overflow indicator (OF) is set on. This caused a problem since the overflow (OF) indicator is not tested until detail time. The previous section illustrated Fetch Overflow, which can be used to *alter* the normal fixed logic cycle for printing and *force* the heading lines to print at total time.

EXCPT output is an alternative method to force the printing of headings on a new page if a page overflow condition occurs. Since the Fetch Overflow method alters the basic processing cycle of an RPG program, EXCPT output can be employed as a consistent method of printing output using the Calculation Specifications form, so that all output is printed under control of the program.

The following is a simple alternative for handling page overflow:

Two EXCPT operations are necessary. The first operation is executed if the overflow indicator (OF) is on. This means that the last print operation caused a page overflow. This EXCPT operation, then, causes a skip to the next page and the headings to print. The EXCPT is also controlled by indicator L1 because all three operations on the preceding form are executed during L1 total time.

The second EXCPT operation controlled by the appropriate control level indicator (L1) prints the control level totals. Finally, the overflow (OF) indicator has to be set off with a SETOF operation. This prevents another overflow condition from executing since the overflow indicator is not set off until normal detail time.

This is the same method employed previously when EXCPT output was used to control page overflow with detail processing. The result here is a more consistent program structure with all print lines including heading lines handled in the same manner, namely with the use of the EXCPT. Our next sample program will illustrate the use of EXCPT output with control break processing.

6. EXCPT Output with Control Break Processing

The Inventory Status Report program illustrated earlier in this chapter will be used here to illustrate control break processing using the EXCPT. Figure 7.22 presents the Inventory Status Report program written with the EXCPT, which results in a more structured approach.

The EXCPT operation is used in this program to perform *all* output operations. As we saw in Chapter 5, output operations using the EXCPT are handled under program control and are executed at the exact time output is required. This makes for a much more uniform program since all output is written in the

Figure 7.22
Structured RPG program for producing an Inventory Status Report.

```
....+....1....+....2....+....3....+....4....+....5....+....6....+....7
0001  ****************************************************************
0002  *
0003  *   PROGRAM DESCRIPTION:
0004  *
0005  *       THIS PROGRAM PRODUCES AN INVENTORY STATUS REPORT.
0006  *       THE PROGRAM ACCUMULATES AND PRINTS TOTALS
0007  *       FOR EACH ITEM NUMBER (L1) AND EACH WAREHOUSE (L2).
0008  *
0009  *
0010  *   FUNCTION OF INDICATORS:
0011  *
0012  *       L1      CHANGE IN ITEM NUMBER (ITEM)
0013  *       L2      CHANGE IN WAREHOUSE (IWHSE)
0014  *
0015  ****************************************************************
0016  *
0017  H
0018  FINVTRY   IP  F     15              DISK
0019  FREPORT   O   F     132     OF      PRINTER
0020  *
0021  IINVTRY   NS
0022  I                                    2   3 IWHSE L2
0023  I                                    4   8 IITEM L1
0024  I                                    9 150IQTYSD
0025  I#WORK        DS
0026  I                                    1   80#ITOT
0027  I                                    9  170#WTOT
0028  I                                   18  270#FTOT
0029  *
0030  C   L1              Z-ADD*ZEROS    #ITOT            RESET #ITOT TO ZERO
0031  C   L1              EXCPT@H000                      PRINT HEADINGS FOR
0032  *                                                   NEW ITEM GROUP
```

```
0033 C    L2                        Z-ADD*ZEROS      #WTOT            RESET #WTOT TO ZERO
0034 *
0035 C                              ADD  IQTYSD      #ITOT
0036 *
0037 C    OFNL1                     EXCPT@H000                        IF OF, PRINT HEADINGS
0038 C                              SETOF                       OF    AND SET OF OFF
0039 C                              EXCPT@D100                        PRINT DETAIL RECORD
0040 *
0041 CL1                           ADD  #ITOT       #WTOT
0042 CL1                           EXCPT@T200                        PRINT ITEM TOTAL
0043 CL2                           ADD  #WTOT       #FTOT
0044 CL2                           EXCPT@T300                        PRINT WAREHOUSE TOTAL
0045 CLR                           EXCPT@T400                        PRINT FINAL TOTAL
0046 *
0047 OREPORT    E    02            @H000
0048 O                                            44 'INVENTORY STATUS REPORT'
0049 O              E    08            @H000
0050 O                                            11 'WAREHOUSE'
0051 O                                            20 'ITEM NO'
0052 O                                            32 'QUANTITY'
0053 O              E  2            @D100
0054 O                       L2     IWHSE          6
0055 O                       OFNL2  IWHSE          6
0056 O                       L1     IITEM         19
0057 O                       OFNL1  IITEM         19
0058 O                              IQTYSD        32
0059 O              E  2            @T200
0060 O                                            29 'TOTAL FOR ITEM'
0061 O                              #ITOT 1       40
0062 O              E  2            @T300
0063 O                                            28 'TOTAL FOR WAREHOUSE'
0064 O                              #WTOT 1       40
0065 O              E  3            @T400
0066 O                                            26 'FINAL COUNT OF ALL ITEMS'
0067 O                              #FTOT 1       40
```

Figure 7.22
(continued)

same consistent manner. Let us examine the program in Figure 7.22 in more detail:

1. Lines 30 and 33 reinitialize the two subtotal fields #ITOT and #WTOT to zero after the appropriate control breaks occur. These Z-ADD operations are performed at the beginning of detail calculations in order to reset these subtotal fields before accumulation is to begin for the next group. Thus, for example, #ITOT is reset to zero prior to IQTYSD being added to #ITOT on line 35.

2. As illustrated earlier, we saw how to begin a new page for each new control group processed in the program. To do so, the overflow indicator (OF) had to be set on at total time when a control level break had occurred. During detail output the overflow indicator (OF) then forced the computer to skip to a new page prior to printing the detail records for a new control group.

   Line 31 of our sample program performs the same function. Here, we wish to skip to a new page whenever the L1 indicator is on, that is, when we have a change in the department field. As noted earlier, if L1 is on during detail time, the program must be processing the first record of a new department control group. Since we wish to start each new control group (department) on a new page, an EXCPT operation, controlled by the L1 indicator at detail time, is executed to print out the headings.

   Moreover, it is line 31 that provides for the headings to print on the first page. Recall that L1 is set on when the first record is read into the program and thus used during detail processing. L1 is set on for the first record because it is the first record of a new control group. Therefore, line

31 is executed during the first detail cycle, which forces the computer to skip to the first page and print headings.

3. Line 39 of the program contains the operation to print the detail information on the report. That is, each time a record is read from the INVTRY file line 39 is executed at detail time, which prints the necessary detail line (@D100).

However, before printing this detail line it is necessary to determine if page overflow has occurred during the last detail cycle. Thus, prior to printing @D100, line 37 is executed to determine if page overflow has occurred. If so, the program skips to a new page and the headings are printed. Line 37 is controlled by two indicators: OF and NL1. This means that the headings will only print if OF is on and the L1 indicator is off. Since we print new headings on line 31 if L1 is on, we want to guarantee that L1 is off when we print the headings on line 37. Otherwise, we could print the headings twice in the same cycle.

After the headings are printed, line 38 is used to set off the overflow indicator (OF). This is necessary because the overflow indicator is set off only during normal detail output time. Thus, to prevent the overflow (OF) indicator from staying on and printing headings during the next cycle, the overflow indicator is set off at this time.

4. Lines 42, 44, and 45 are executed to print the appropriate control level totals #ITOT, #WTOT, and #FTOT. For example, if L1 is on during total calculation time, lines 41 and 42 are executed. First, line 41 adds the accumulated item total #ITOT to #WTOT. Then, line 42 prints the item total, #ITOT.

The following is a summary of the control break procedure:

SUMMARY

1. There are nine control level indicators: L1–L9, with L1 being the lowest and L9 being the highest.

2. A control level indicator is assigned on the Input Specifications form. It is used to identify an input field as a control field. Fields may be located within the record in any sequence, but, if feasible, it is good practice to specify control fields on the Input Specifications form beginning with the major field and continuing in descending sequence to the minor field (L1).

3. When an input record is read, the computer determines if there is a change in the control field; if there is:

   Total calculations using the specified level indicator (L1–L9) are performed in the sequence indicated on the Calculation Specifications form.

   Total output corresponding to the same level indicator is printed.

4. After a control field is tested and total processing is performed when a change in the control field occurs, then:

   Detail calculations are performed in the sequence in which they appear on the Calculation Specifications form.

   Detail output is produced.

Note: The record that caused a control break is not printed until the previous totals have been computed and printed.

5. Control level arithmetic operations are entered on the Calculation Specifications form and follow the detail calculations. These entries are also in L1, L2, L3, etc. sequence. Remember, these instructions are executed during total calculation time only if the level indicators are coded in columns 7–8 of the Calculation Specifications form.

6. When a control level indicator is coded in columns 9–17, and columns 7–8 contain blanks, the indicator is turned on only for the *first* record of each group. The programmer could use this to advantage by setting a counter to zero when the first record of a new group is processed. The number of detail records within each group could then be counted by the program. It should again be emphasized that control level indicators entered in columns 9–17 are processed during detail calculation time.

7. Control level entries on the Output Specifications form require a T in column 15 as well as control level indicator entries in columns 23–31. Again, these entries follow the detail output specifications in ascending level (L1, L2, L3, etc.) sequence. These instructions are executed during total output time and print the *previous group's* totals.

8. Control level indicators L1–L9 are automatically turned off at the end of the RPG Logic Cycle.

9. Despite the fact that control break totals are calculated and printed before detail data, output should be coded in the following sequence: H, D, T. Moreover, total output should be coded with the lowest level (L1) followed by subsequent levels if used.

10. Calculations should be specified with detail calculations coded before total calculations. Total calculations should also be in sequence, with L1 calculations preceding L2, L3, etc. The LR or last record indicator forces all other total calculations from L1 to L9.

11. Level indicators are normally used to condition total lines but may condition fields on detail lines as well, specifically for group indicate purposes.

12. Any fields used for accumulating group totals must be reset to zero once they have been printed. We use a Z-ADD to accomplish this.

Figure 7.23 provides the problem definition for a triple level control break problem. The RPG coding required to produce the output indicated is in Figure 7.24.

Figure 7.23 Problem definition for a triple-level control break program.

Systems Flowchart

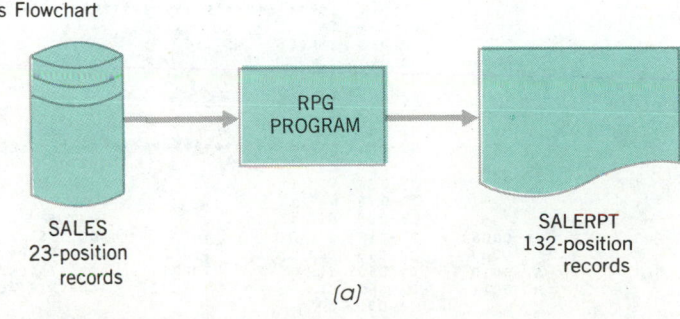

SALES
23-position
records

RPG
PROGRAM

SALERPT
132-position
records

(a)

(continued on next page)

Figure 7.23
(continued)

SALES Record Layout

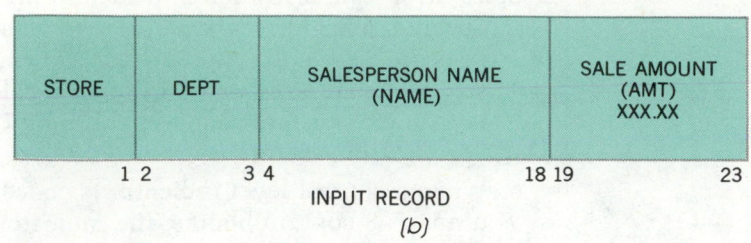

INPUT RECORD

(b)

SALERPT Printer Spacing Chart

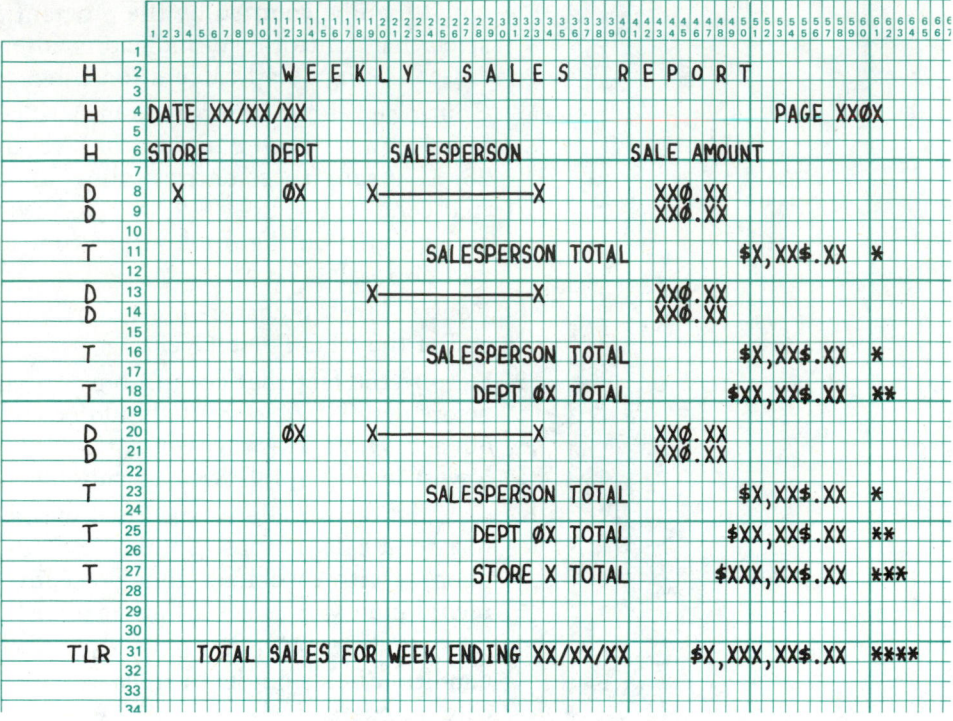

(c)

Figure 7.24
Triple-level control break
program with output.

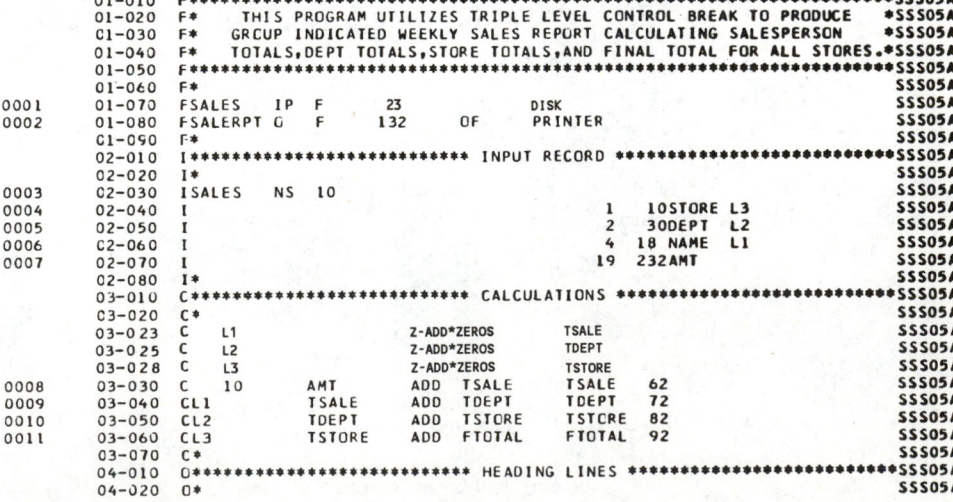

Figure 7.24
(continued)

```
0012   04-030   OSALERPT H   201     1P                                                     SSSO5A
0013   04-040   O          OR       OF                                                      SSSO5A
0014   04-050   O                                          35 'W E E K L Y    S A L E S'     SSSO5A
0015   04-060   O                                          50 'R E P O R T'                  SSSO5A
0016   C4-070   C          H   2    1P                                                       SSSO5A
0017   04-080   O          OR       OF                                                       SSSO5A
0018   04-090   O                                           4 'DATE'                          SSSO5A
0019   C4-100   O                              UDATE Y     13                                 SSSO5A
0020   C4-110   O                                          56 'PAGE'                          SSSO5A
0021   04-120   O                              PAGE        61                                 SSSO5A
0022   04-130   O          H   2    1P                                                        SSSO5A
0023   04-140   O          OR       CF                                                        SSSO5A
0024   04-150   C                                           5 'STORE'                          SSSO5A
0025   04-160   O                                          14 'DEPT'                           SSSO5A
0026   04-170   C                                          31 'SALESPERSON'                     SSSO5A
0027   04-180   O                                          51 'SALE AMOUNT'                      SSSO5A
       C4-190   O*                                                                             SSSO5A
       04-200   O****************** DETAIL LINE ***************************SSSO5A
       04-210   C*                                                                             SSSO5A
0028   04-220   O          D   1    10                                                         SSSO5A
0029   04-230   C                              L3 STORE     3                                  SSSO5A
0030   04-240   O                              L2 DEPT  Z  13                                  SSSO5A
0031   04-250   O                              L1 NAME     33                                  SSSO5A
0032   04-260   G                                 AMT  1   48                                  SSSO5A
       04-270   O*                                                                             SSSO5A
       05-010   O****************** TOTAL LINES ***************************SSSO5A
       C5-020   O*                                                                             SSSO5A
0033   05-030   C          T  12    L1                                                        SSSO5A
0034   C5-040   O                                          40 'SALESPERSON TOTAL'               SSSO5A
0035   05-050   C                              TSALE 1     58 '$'                               SSSO5A
0036   05-060   O                                          61 '*'                               SSSO5A
0037   C5-070   O          T   2    L2                                                         SSSO5A
0038   05-080   G                                          31 'DEPT'                            SSSO5A
0039   05-090   O                              DEPT  Z     34                                  SSSO5A
0040   05-100   G                                          40 'TOTAL'                           SSSO5A
0041   05-110   G                              TDEPT 1     58 '$'                               SSSO5A
0042   05-120   O                                          62 '**'                              SSSO5A
0043   05-130   C          T   3    L3                                                         SSSO5A
0044   05-140   O                                          32 'STORE'                           SSSO5A
0045   05-150   O                              STORE       34                                  SSSO5A
0046   05-160   O                                          40 'TOTAL'                           SSSO5A
0047   05-170   O                              TSTORE1      58 '$'                              SSSO5A
0048   05-180   O                                          63 '***'                             SSSO5A
0049   05-190   O          T   1    LR                                                          SSSO5A
0050   05-200   O                                          15 'TOTAL SALES'                      SSSO5A
0051   05-210   C                                          31 'FOR WEEK ENDING'                  SSSO5A
0052   05-220   O                              UDATE Y     40                                   SSSO5A
0053   05-230   C                              FTOTAL1     58 '$'                               SSSO5A
0054   05-240   O                                          64 '****'                            SSSO5A
       05-250   O*                                                                              SSSO5A
       05-260   O***************************************************************SSSO5A
```

```
           W E E K L Y    S A L E S    R E P O R T

DATE 11/29/91                                        PAGE    1

STORE    DEPT     SALESPERSON          SALE AMOUNT

  1        2      CHARLIE SMITH            29.95
                                          37.63

                    SALESPERSON TOTAL          $67.58   *

                  SHIRLEY GREENE          101.01

                    SALESPERSON TOTAL         $101.01   *

                        DEPT  2 TOTAL         $168.59   **

           5      JOE THOMPSON             68.57

                    SALESPERSON TOTAL          $68.57   *

                        DEPT  5 TOTAL          $68.57   **

          10      DANIEL MURPHY            87.65
                                           9.97

                    SALESPERSON TOTAL          $97.62   *

                        DEPT 10 TOTAL          $97.62   **

                        STORE 1 TOTAL         $334.78   ***


  2        1      ALLAN DARRONE            52.34

                    SALESPERSON TOTAL          $52.34   *

                  MIKE WILLIAMS           298.50

                    SALESPERSON TOTAL         $298.50   *

                        DEPT  1 TOTAL         $350.84   **
```

(continued on next page)

Figure 7.24
(continued)

```
          5      JOANNA LITTLE              49.98

                      SALESPERSON TOTAL          $49.98  *

                         DEPT  5 TOTAL           $49.98  **

                         STORE 2 TOTAL          $400.82  ***


    3     5      BOB ALBERTSON              99.99

                      SALESPERSON TOTAL          $99.99  *

                         DEPT  5 TOTAL   .        $99.99  **



              W E E K L Y   S A L E S   R E P O R T

        DATE 11/29/91                        PAGE   2

        STORE    DEPT    SALESPERSON     SALE AMOUNT

                  7     ELAINE RICHARDS        62.73
                                               4.89

                      SALESPERSON TOTAL          $67.62  *

                        JOHN JOHNSON           112.34
                                               24.98

                      SALESPERSON TOTAL         $137.32  *

                        HARRY HIGGINS           79.98

                      SALESPERSON TOTAL          $79.98  *

                         DEPT  7 TOTAL          $284.92  **

                 12     FRANK JONES             9.95

                      SALESPERSON TOTAL           $9.95  *

                        MARY CUMMINGS           34.48
                                                47.89
                                                27.45

                      SALESPERSON TOTAL         $109.82  *

                        JIM ANDERSON          100.00

                      SALESPERSON TOTAL         $100.00  *

                         DEPT 12 TOTAL         $219.77  **

                         STORE 3 TOTAL         $604.68  ***


        TOTAL SALES FOR WEEK ENDING 11/29/91   $1,340.28  ****
```

CHAPTER SELF-TEST

1. When summary totals for each DEPT are required and the input is in sequence by department number, then the type of processing to be performed is called _____ .

2. In Question 1, DEPT is referred to as the _____ field.

3. Suppose that detail printing was required in Question 1 as well. If the DEPT field is printed only on the *first* detail line of each group, then it is referred to as a(n) _____ field.

4. (T or F) Using control break processing, detail records must be printed.

5. (T or F) Using control break processing, control totals must be accumulated if a final total is required.

6. (T or F) If a final total is required in a control break procedure, then it can be accumulated at detail time or at L1 time.

7. If three control breaks are needed and L1–L3 are used to define them, then the _____ level is considered the major level.

8. Suppose you are using L1–L3. A change in the input field associated with the L2 level will automatically force *(no.)* breaks.

9. (T or F) When the last record has been processed, L1–L9 indicators, when used, are turned on along with the LR indicator.

10. (T or F) In a control break procedure, the last record at the end of the job will not be accumulated properly unless the programmer makes specific changes to the normal flow of logic.

11. When an L1 control break occurs, (calculation, detail output, total output) operations that use L1 indicators are executed, followed by (calculation, detail

output, total output) operations that use L1 indicators.

12. When an L1 control break occurs, L1 operations (precede, follow) detail operations. Explain your answer.

13. When performing a multiple-level control break operation, the computer checks for a change in the (highest, lowest) level of control first.

14. Using the following input, how would you tell the computer that branch offices are arranged within regions and that control totals will be necessary for branch offices within regions and for regions as well?

Line	Form Type	Filename or Record Name	Sequence	Number (1/N), E	Option (O), U, S	Record Identifying Indicator	Position 1	Not(N)	C/Z/D	Character	From	To	Decimal Positions	RPG Field Name	Control Level (L1-L9)
01	I	SALES	NS	01		1	1		C	S					
02	I										2	5		SLSNO	
03	I										6	10	2	AMT	
04	I										11	12	0	BRANCH	
05	I										13	14	0	REGION	

15. Using the input specifications for Question 14, code the calculations for producing double level control breaks for the AMT field, with branch totals and region totals printing.

16. Could the following coding be used to produce correct branch and region totals? Explain your answer.

Line	Form Type	Control Level	Indicators And Not	Factor 1	Operation	Factor 2	Result Field Name	Length
01	C		01	BRTOT	ADD	REGTOT	REGTOT	
02	C	L1		REGTOT	ADD	FINTOT	FINTOT	

17. Code the Output Specifications form for Question 16, printing detail lines as well as branch totals and region totals when control breaks occur.

18. (T or F) After each control break, clearing the region total field after printing is entirely optional.

19. (T or F) The programmer must turn off all level indicators prior to processing each record.

20. (T or F) If data is not in sequence by the control field, then control break processing cannot be used.

SOLUTIONS

1. control break processing

2. control

3. group indicate

4. F—It is feasible to produce just summary data from detail input using control break processing.

5. T

6. T—It is, however, more efficient to accumulate a final total when there is a control break. Suppose, for example, that there are 10,000 input records but only five control fields, such as DEPT Ø1—DEPT Ø5. If final totals were accumulated at detail time, there would be 10,000 additions necessary; if final totals were accumulated whenever there was a change in DEPT, there would only be five additions necessary.

7. L3

8. two (L2 and L1)

9. T

10. F—The LR indicator as well as all level indicators are turned on at the end of the job. This forces appropriate control breaks when there is no more data.

11. calculation; total output

12. precede (This enables a control total that has been accumulated to print *prior to* the new control field.)

13. highest

14.

I	Filename or Record Name	Sequence	Number (1/N), E	Option (O), U, S	Record Identifying Indicator, ** or DS	Position	Not(N)	C/Z/D	Character	Position	Not(N)	C/Z/D	Character	Position	Not(N)	C/Z/D	Character	Stacker Select	P/B/L/R	From	To	Decimal Positions	RPG Field Name	Control Level (L1–L9)	Matching Fields or Chaining Fields	Field Record Relation	Plus	Minus	Zero or Blank
01 Ø I	SALES	NS	Ø1		1 CS																								
02 Ø I																				2	5		SLSNO						
03 Ø I																				6	10	2	AMT						
04 Ø I																				11	12	Ø	BRANCH	L1					
05 Ø I																				13	14	Ø	REGION	L2					
06 I																													
07 I																													

15.

C	Line	Control Level (L0–L9, LR, SR, AN/OR)	Not	And Not	And Not	Factor 1	Operation	Factor 2	Result Field Name	Length	Decimal Positions	Half Adjust (H)	High	Low	Equal	Comments
01 Ø C		Ø1				AMT	ADD	BRTOT	BRTOT	72						
02 Ø C		L1				BRTOT	ADD	REGTOT	REGTOT	82						
03 Ø C		L2				REGTOT	ADD	FINTOT	FINTOT	92						
04 C																
05 C																

Note: This line is coded only if final total is required

16. No. AMT should be added to BRTOT when the 01 indicator is on; BRTOT should be added to REGTOT when the L1 indicator is on; REGTOT should be added to FINTOT when the L2 indicator is on.

17.

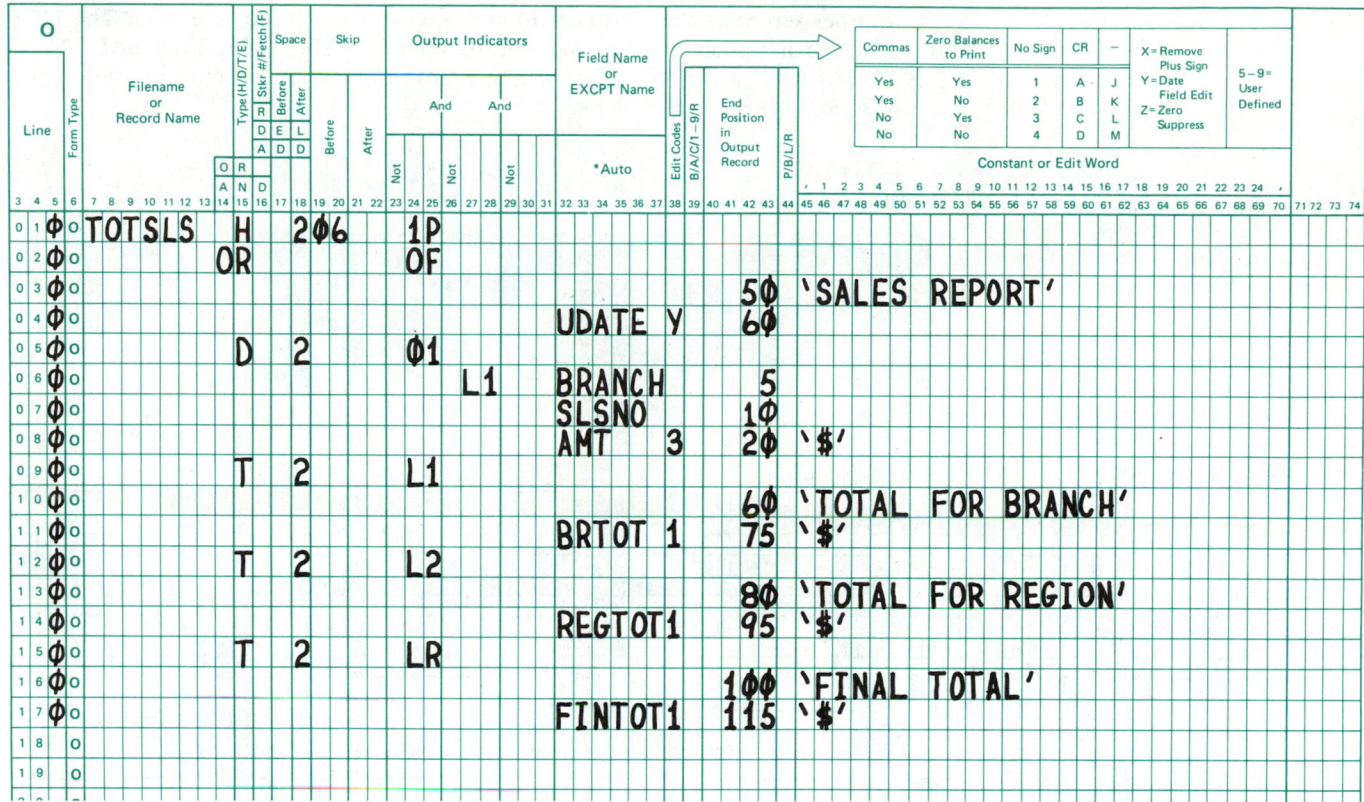

18. F—Failing to clear it will result in incorrect processing of region totals.

19. F—These are automatically turned off.

20. T

KEY TERMS

Control break	Fetch Overflow	Level indicator	Page overflow
Control field	Figurative constant	Multiple level control	Single level control break
Detail printing	Group indicate	break	Total time
Detail time	Group printing		

REVIEW QUESTIONS

Define the meaning of the following (1–3).

1. Control break
2. Group indicate field
3. Fetch overflow

4. Indicate how a triple level control break is performed. Specify the RPG Logic Cycle for this procedure.

5. Provide a sample listing for a program that has double level control breaks, a group indicate field, and detail printing.

PROGRAMMING ASSIGNMENTS

Use Data Structures for work fields. Use prefixes for input, output, and work fields. Use SETON and SETOF where appropriate.

1. Using the problem definition shown below, code an RPG program to produce the required results. This is a single level control break problem. The department number serves as the control field and is also a group indicate field. The NET SALARY is calculated using the formula NET SALARY = WEEKLY SALARY – TOTAL DEDUCTIONS. Note the three running totals to be accumulated and printed with each level break.

PAYROLL Record Layout

DEPT	EMPNO	EMPLOYEE NAME	WEEKLY SALARY	TOTAL DEDUCTIONS
1 2	3 7	8 27	28 33	34 38

CLIST Printer Spacing Chart

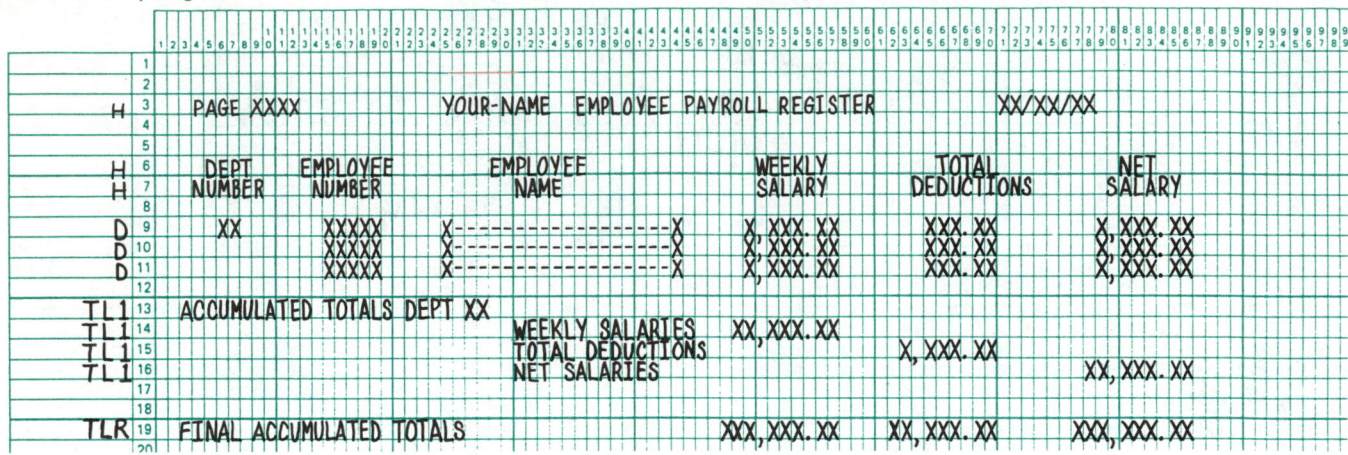

2. Using the problem definition shown below, code an RPG program to produce the required results. This is a two level control break problem wherein a change in the Purchase Order number controls Level 1 calculations while a change in the date controls Level 2 calculations. Note the date is the only group indicate field. **We calculate the** TOTAL PRICE using the formula:

PURCHASE Record Layout

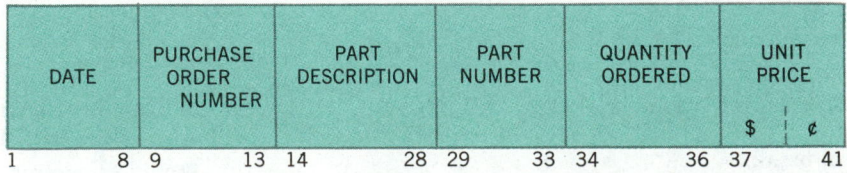

DATE	PURCHASE ORDER NUMBER	PART DESCRIPTION	PART NUMBER	QUANTITY ORDERED	UNIT PRICE
1 8	9 13	14 28	29 33	34 36	37 41

PURLIST Printer Spacing Chart

```
       |1234567890123456789012345678901234567890123456789012345678901234567890123456789012345678901234567890|
 H   3 | PAGE XXXX              MONTHLY PURCHASE ORDER ANALYSIS              XX/XX/XX                         |
 H   6 | DATE      PURCHASE     PART         PART            QUANTITY        UNIT              TOTAL          |
 H   7 | OF P.O.   ORDER #      NUMBER       DESCRIPTION     ORDERED         PRICE             PRICE          |
 D   9 | XX/XX/XX       XXXXX       XXXXX    X-----------X       XXX          XXX.XX          X,XXX.XX        |
 D  10 |               XXXXX       XXXXX     X-----------X       XXX          XXX.XX          X,XXX.XX        |
 D  11 |               XXXXX       XXXXX     X-----------X       XXX          XXX.XX          X,XXX.XX        |
TL1 13 |           TOTAL COST OF P.O. # XXXXX IS                                           $XX,XX$.XX        |
TL2 15 |           TOTAL PURCHASES FOR XX/XX/XX IS                                        $XXX,XX$.XX        |
TLR 17 |           TOTAL MONTHLY PURCHASES                                              $X,XXX,XX$.XX        |
```

3. Using the problem definition shown below, code an RPG program to produce the required results. This is a three level control break problem. There will be one input record for each sale. A change in salesperson name controls Level 1 calculations, while a change in district conditions Level 2 calculations. Level 3 calculations use the state to control the major control break. Assume the input records have been correctly sorted for this problem.

PURCHASE Record Layout

STATE	DISTRICT	SALESPERSON NAME	VEHICLE DESCRIPTION	SALES PRICE $ ¢
1 2	3 5	6 25	26 45	46 54

PURLIST Printer Spacing Chart

```
       |1234567890123456789012345678901234567890123456789012345678901234567890123456789012345678901234567890|
 H   1 | PAGE XXXX              MOTORSPORT EXOTIC AUTO ENTERPRISE              XX/XX/XX                       |
 H   4 | TITLE     DISTRICT          NAME OF              VEHICLE                       SALES                |
 H   5 | STATE     NO.               SALESPERSON          DESCRIPTION                   PRICE                |
 D   7 |   XX        XXX        X----------------X    X-----------------X           X,XXX,XXX.XX             |
 D   8 |   XX        XXX        X----------------X    X-----------------X           X,XXX,XXX.XX             |
TL1 11 |           * TOTAL SALES BY X--------------X   $X,XXX,XX$.XX *                                       |
TL2 13 |          ** TOTAL DISTRICT XXX SALES        $XX,XXX,XX$.XX **                                       |
TL3 15 |         *** TOTAL SALES BY STATE XX        $XX,XXX,XX$ XX ***                                       |
```

4. Using the following problem definition, code an RPG program to produce the required results.

Notes:

a. There is one input record for each employee. Records are in sequence by level within department within branch office.

b. Add 1 to the total fields for each input record to accumulate proper sums. Individual records do not print.

Systems Flowchart

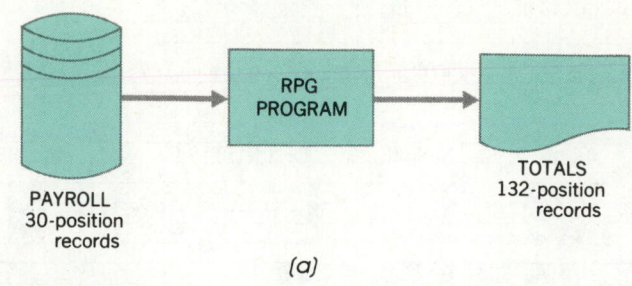

PAYROLL
30-position
records

RPG
PROGRAM

TOTALS
132-position
records

(a)

PAYROLL Record Layout

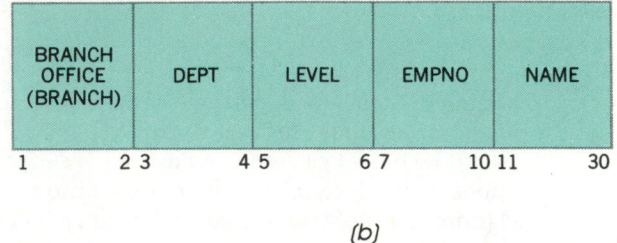

BRANCH OFFICE (BRANCH)	DEPT	LEVEL	EMPNO	NAME
1 2	3 4	5 6	7 10	11 30

(b)

TOTALS Printer Spacing Chart

```
        H   6                                          EMPLOYEE  DISTRIBUTION  SUMMARY     XX/XX/XX      PAGE  XXØX

        H   9        BRANCH     DEPT      LEVEL     TOTAL NO. OF
        H  10        OFFICE                         EMPLOYEES

        T  12          XX        XX         XX        X,XØX
        T  13          XX        XX         XX        X,XØX

        T  15                                        TOTAL EMPLOYEES IN DEPT XX    XX,XØX

        T  17                                        TOTAL EMPLOYEES IN BRANCH XX  XX,XØX

       TLR 19                                        TOTAL EMPLOYEES IN COMPANY    XXX,XØX
```

(c)

FILE PROCESSING, ARRAYS, AND TABLES

File Concepts and Sequential File Processing

I. TYPES OF DISK FILE ORGANIZATION
   A. Review of File Processing Concepts
   B. Sequential File Organization
   C. Random Access Files
      1. Indexed File Organization
      2. Direct File Organization
II. TYPICAL SEQUENTIAL FILE PROCEDURES: AN OVERVIEW
   A. Creating a Sequential Master File
   B. Creating a Transaction File
   C. Updating a Master File
   Self-Test
III. TRANSACTION FILE CREATION AND VALIDATION PROCEDURES
   A. Data Validation Procedures
      1. The Class Test
      2. Missing Data Test
      3. Testing for Reasonableness
      4. Coded Field Test
      5. Sequence Test
   B. When to Validate Data and What to Do If Errors Occur
   C. Creating the Transaction File of Changes
   D. Programmed Control of Input Operations
      1. Demand Files
      2. Full Procedural Files
      3. The READ Operation
      4. Program Control of Input and Output Operations
   Self-Test
IV. SEQUENTIAL FILE MAINTENANCE PROCEDURE
   A. Files Required for a Sequential File Maintenance
      1. Input Master File
      2. Input Transaction File
      3. Output Master File
   B. Sequential File Update: An Illustration
      1. The Main Module
      2. How Input Transaction and Master Records Are Processed
      3. Illustrating the Update Procedure with Examples
   C. End-of-File Conditions
   D. Updating Sequential Master Records in Place
   E. Adding Records to a Sequential File
   Self-Test
V. SORT UTILITY PROCEDURES
   A. The Sort Utility Program
   B. Files Used in a Sort Procedure
   C. Ascending or Descending Key
      1. Collating Sequence
      2. Sorting on More Than One Control Field

OBJECTIVES

To familiarize you with

1. The different types of disk file organization.
2. Master file processing concepts.
3. How transaction files are created and validated.
4. Sequential file update procedures.
5. Sort Utility procedures.

I. Types of Disk File Organization

A. Review of File Processing Concepts

You will recall that a file is a collection of data records for a given application. In the business world, we have accounts receivable files, payroll files, and so on. The major collection of records for each of these applications is called a **master file**. There are many types of procedures that must be performed on files in order to satisfy the need for information. To perform these procedures requires that data files be accessed and processed by different methods depending on the needs of the organization. The following are file processing procedures frequently used in many RPG applications:

File Processing Procedures

1. Edit a file—check for accuracy.
2. Update a file—incorporate changes to make the file current by
   a. Posting transactions or changes.
   b. Adding records.
   c. Deleting records.
3. Print a report.
4. Answer inquiries.

Two methods can be used to process a file.

File Processing Methods

1. Sequential access.
2. Random access.

Thus far, in all of our programs using disk files as input and output, we have used files in a **sequential access** mode; that is, we have always processed files in sequence. This chapter, along with Chapter 9 and Chapter 11, will be used to expand on file processing concepts. In addition, examples and illustrations will be presented to demonstrate all of the file processing procedures listed above. Let us first discuss the different types of file organizations that are most often used in RPG programs.

B. Sequential File Organization

The simplest type of disk file organization is *sequential*. Sequential access means that the file is processed in sequence, starting with the record that is physically located at the beginning of the file and processing sequentially through the file until the last record is processed or until the program is terminated.

The order in which records are accessed in **sequential files** is determined by the order in which the records are written to the file. Thus, to sequentially access the 24,000th record in a file, for example, the computer reads past the first 23,999 records in sequence.

Sequential File Organization

1st record	2nd	3rd	4th	5th	6th

Records are stored in the file in the same sequence in which they are written to the file. No index is kept and no spaces are left between records.

Typically, the records to be stored in a sequential file are first *sorted* into sequence by a control or key field such as customer number, part number, or employee number. It is then relatively easy to locate a given record. The record with employee number 00766, for example, would be physically located between records with employee numbers 00765 and 00767 if employee numbers are consecutive. To access that record, the computer must read past the first 765 records.

In addition, suppose an accounts receivable file is arranged in customer number sequence. If you wish to print the file alphabetically in customer name sequence, you would first sort the file into alphabetical sequence by name, and then print it sequentially. We will see later in this chapter how *sort procedures* can be used to put a file into the required sequence.

In summary, files organized for sequential access must be either read as input in the sequence in which they were originally created, or resorted into another sequence and then accessed sequentially.

If a file is organized for sequential access, then, there is no convenient method for moving directly to the middle of the file or to some point near the end of the file. There are, however, two methods of *random access* file organization, called *indexed* and *direct*, that enable a disk file to be accessed randomly as well as sequentially. **Random access** *permits the user to directly access records in any order.*

C. Random Access Files

Indexed and direct disk files can be accessed randomly as well as sequentially. That is, with indexed file organization or direct file organization, records can be accessed in any sequence. With such files, changes to records can be entered randomly; the corresponding master records can be updated and then rewritten in place. As noted, when files need to be accessed in some manner other than sequentially, the methods of file organization that can be used are called *indexed* and *direct*. We discuss each in detail.

1. Indexed File Organization

When an **indexed file** is created, each record is placed on the disk in ascending sequence by a unique field designated as the key or index field. At the same time, the computer establishes an index or key file on the disk that keeps track of where each record is physically located. The data file and the index file work together in order for a program to access records either sequentially or randomly from the file:

Indexed File Organization

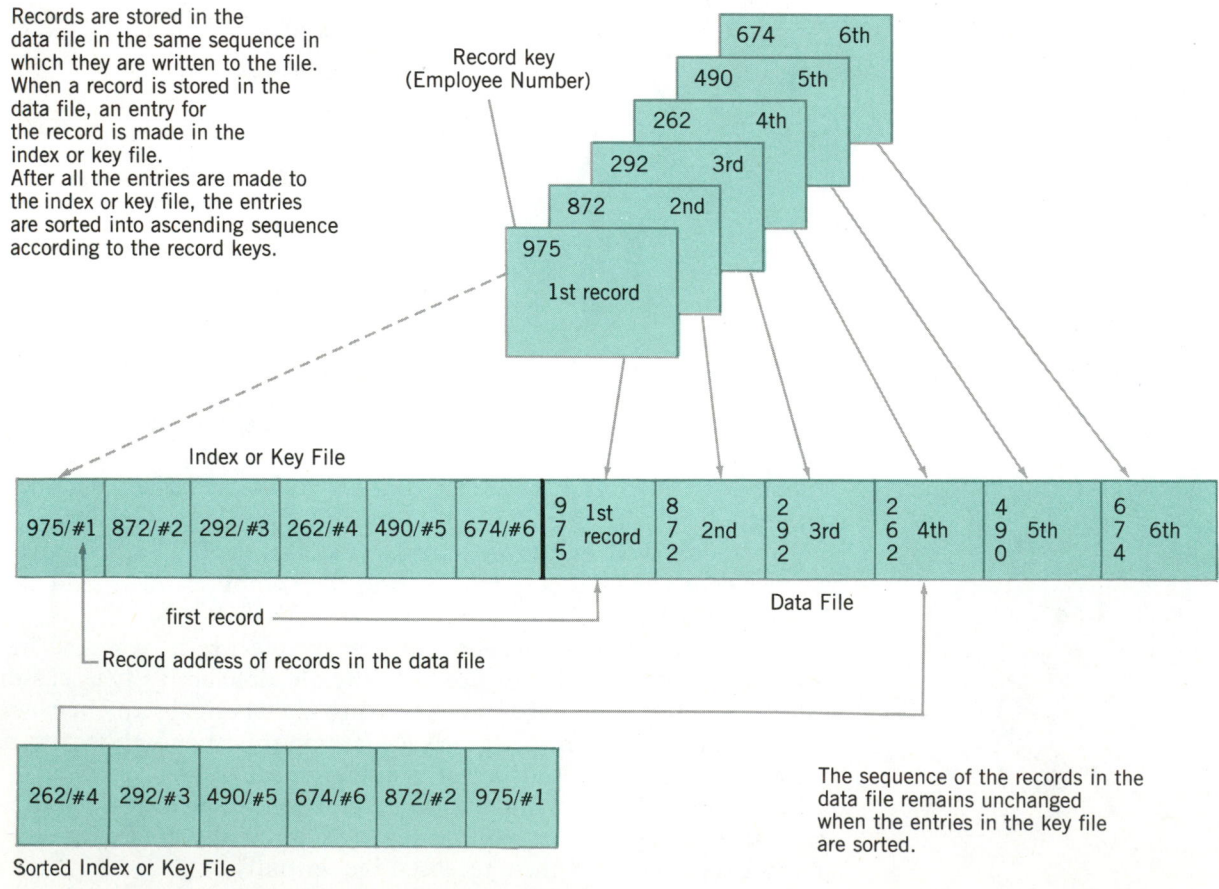

Records are stored in the data file in the same sequence in which they are written to the file. When a record is stored in the data file, an entry for the record is made in the index or key file.

After all the entries are made to the index or key file, the entries are sorted into ascending sequence according to the record keys.

Record key (Employee Number)

Index or Key File

| 975/#1 | 872/#2 | 292/#3 | 262/#4 | 490/#5 | 674/#6 |

first record

Record address of records in the data file

Data File

Sorted Index or Key File

| 262/#4 | 292/#3 | 490/#5 | 674/#6 | 872/#2 | 975/#1 |

The sequence of the records in the data file remains unchanged when the entries in the key file are sorted.

As noted, a **key field** in the record uniquely identifies the record to the computer. For a payroll file, the key field may be Social Security number or employee number; for an inventory file, the key field may be part number. The computer then stores in the index file the key field and the disk address of that corresponding physical record. This index file enables the user to access a disk file randomly. If, at some later time, you wish to access any record, the computer uses the value given for the key field to "look up" the record's actual address in the index file; the disk's access mechanism goes directly to that location to find the record. The index file, then, operates exactly like a book index. To locate data, "look up" the address in the index.

When only a few records are to be changed, or data is entered as it is transacted, we process the data randomly because it is far more efficient to look up the address of each corresponding disk record than to search the entire file sequentially.

Random access is a very useful technique for **interactive processing,** where a user communicates directly with the computer using a terminal and the key field values entered are not necessarily in sequence.

Chapter 9 discusses indexed files in more detail and illustrates how to process them. Chapter 11 will demonstrate interactive processing of indexed files.

2. Direct File Organization

Direct files or relative files, as they are sometimes called, are disk files in which each record is assigned a specific location depending on the value of its key field. A record with a key field value of 3 is placed in the third record location, a record with a key field of 22 is placed in the 22nd location, and so on.

Direct File Organization

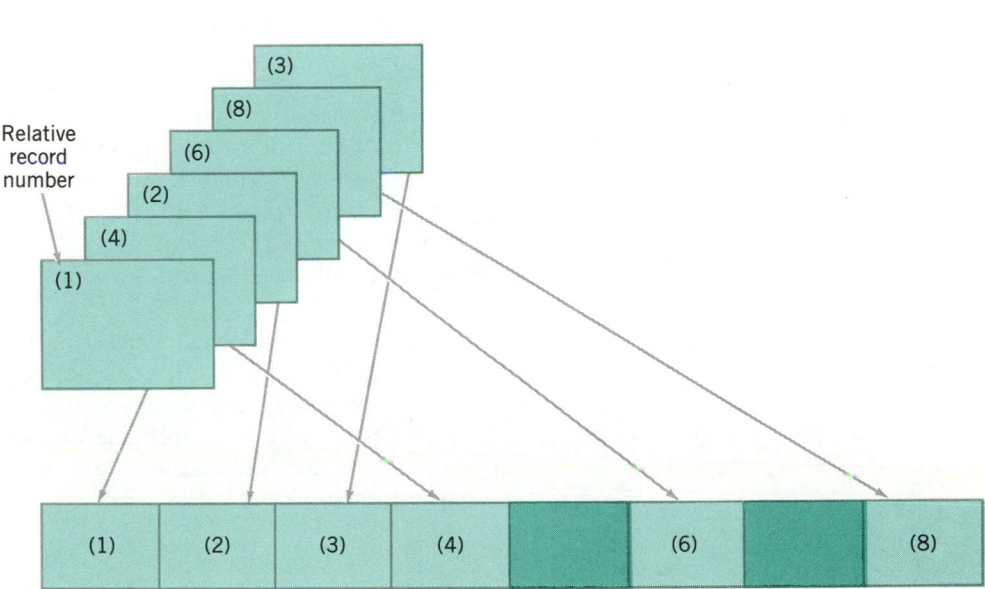

Records are stored in the file in the order indicated by the relative record numbers. Spaces are left in the file for missing records (in this case, records 5 and 7).

If customer numbers vary from 1 to 999, for example, they can be used as relative record numbers. If there is no key field that can be used as a relative record number, the computer can assign a relative record number as the records are created on disk. For example, consider a file containing 4500 records that has no usable key field to serve as a relative record number. Each record in the file is given a relative record number based on its location from the beginning of the file. That is, the first record is given the number 1, the second 2, the third 3, and so on. Thus, the numbers 1, 2, 3, etc., indicate a given record's position relative to the beginning of the file regardless of the order in which they are placed in the file. This method of numbering records from the beginning of the file is called the **relative record number** technique. Each record position in a direct file is assigned a relative record number when the file is created, that is, before any records are actually placed into the file. When records are loaded into a direct file they occupy the specific record location assigned by the relative record number. Thus, a record with a relative record number of 5 would occupy the 5th record location within the file. A record with a relative record number of 1500 would occupy the 1500th record location. A record can be retrieved from a direct file or placed into a direct file by specifying its record position within the file.

As noted previously, direct files may also contain a key field within the records for directly determining the location of each record. The key field may serve as a relative record number if it is consecutive and begins at 1 (e.g., Customer Numbers 1–999). Or, key fields can be converted to relative record numbers using some mathematical formula (e.g., SSNO can be converted to a relative record number).

In this way, unlike an indexed file, a key file is not needed, and a "look-up" of the index is not required to access a record. Since no look-up is required, accessing relative files randomly can be faster than accessing indexed files randomly.

Employee numbers and part numbers, for example, could be used as key fields for direct files. In this way, these fields would be used as the relative record numbers when placing the records into the file. However, when a key field is used in this manner, the value of the field can sometimes exceed the size of the direct file. If, for example, there are 4500 records but employee numbers are nonconsecutive and vary from 1 to 8300, we could either exceed the size allotted for the file or end up with a file that has many blank areas. When this is the case, a conversion process called a **hashing technique** is used. A hashing technique employs a formula that converts the key field into a relative record number in the direct file.

Since most randomly accessed files are indexed files, we will not dwell on direct files in this text.

This chapter will focus on file processing procedures to maintain and process sequential files. We will first discuss typical sequential file procedures and then illustrate these procedures using structured RPG concepts. Finally, we will discuss sort procedure concepts used to arrange records into a different order for processing. The next chapter will explore random access features on disk files using indexed keys.

II. Typical Sequential File Procedures: An Overview

When a business system is computerized, it must be determined whether the master file is to be organized for sequential processing, random processing, or both. As noted, random processing provides the advantage of accessing files in any sequence required and thus is the most popular type of file organization in use today. However, there is still a need for sequential files in applications having a high volume of activity where batch processing of files is required. For example, consider a company's main office that receives daily transactions from its different branches where most master records have some transactions occurring each day. These transactions would be grouped together, sorted, and transmitted to the main office once a day for sequential processing along with the master file. That is, it would be far more efficient to process these transactions sequentially as a batch than to use random access techniques in an interactive environment. The following procedures are required with sequential file processing:

A. Creating a Sequential Master File

When a new system is implemented, or used for the first time, a master file must be initially *created*. Creating a master file is a one-time procedure. That is, once the master file is created, changes to it are made by a different procedure.

Creating a sequential file is simply a matter of writing records to a file designated as output on the File Description Specifications form except that data validation procedures are often incorporated to minimize the risk of errors. We have already created sequential output files in an earlier chapter. Therefore, this chapter will not explore how master files are created but assume that they already exist.

As an additional note, sequential files may be created using a Control Language (CL) procedure. With this method of file creation, no programming is needed and thus time is saved when new files are required. See Appendix A for a discussion of the IBM System/36 Control Language procedure BLDFILE (for build file) used to create files.

B. Creating a Transaction File

After a master file is created, a procedure must be developed to make changes to it. Change records are stored in a separate file referred to as a **transaction file**. Changes to an accounts receivable master file, for example, may consist of sales records and credit records. Changes to a payroll master may consist of name changes, salary changes, and so on. Such change records would be stored in a transaction file. The transaction file should be validated to ensure data integrity in order to minimize the risk of errors. Any errors found should be listed in a validation report or control listing so that necessary corrections can be made.

C. Updating a Master File

The process of making a master file current is referred to as *updating*. The master file is updated or made current by incorporating the changes from the transaction records. Sequential updates process transaction records that are stored *in sequence in a file*, rather than interactively. We call this **batch processing.** Chapter 9 illustrates techniques used for performing *random access updates* where the transaction records need not be in sequence. Chapter 11 adds to this discussion by considering the interactive processing of random files. Such processing is required where master files must always be current and where waiting for transactions to be processed in batches is not efficient.

Self-Test

1. A collection of data records for a given application is called a _____.
2. The main file or major collection of records for a payroll application would be considered the payroll's _____.
3. _____ and _____ are two methods that can be used to process a file.
4. When a file is always accessed in some sequence, we call it a _____ file.
5. If you want to access the 1200th record in a sequential file, the program must first read the first _____ records.
6. Records in a sequential file are normally _____ into sequence by the _____ field.
7. When records are placed into a sequential file, no _____ are left between records.
8. _____ and _____ files can be accessed randomly as well as sequentially.
9. When an indexed file is created, a _____ field uniquely identifies each record to the computer.
10. When indexed files are created, two corresponding files are built; they are the _____ file and the _____ file.
11. After all entries are made to the index or key file, it is _____ into _____ sequence according to the record _____.
12. The sequence of the records in the data file remains _____ after the index or key file is sorted.
13. Direct files, sometimes called _____, are assigned _____.
14. With direct files, _____ are left in the file for missing records.
15. Changes to a master file are sometimes stored in a _____ file.
16. _____ is the process of making a master file current.

Solutions

1. file
2. master file
3. Sequential access; random access
4. sequential
5. 1199
6. sorted; control or key
7. spaces
8. indexed; direct
9. key
10. data; index or key
11. sorted; ascending; key
12. unchanged
13. relative files; relative record numbers
14. spaces
15. transaction
16. Updating

III. Transaction File Creation and Validation Procedures

The master file is created only once when a system is implemented. After the initial creation, it is kept current using an **update procedure**.

A file of change records, called a *transaction file*, is created on a regular basis and is used to update the master file. For a payroll application, this transaction file may consist of payroll changes, new hires, separations from the company, name changes, and so on. The transaction file is created and *edited* or checked for reasonableness and then used to update the master file. A **control listing** or **audit trail** is produced as part of an update for users to check. This listing typically indicates totals of records processed, error conditions encountered, erroneous data, and so forth.

Note that indexed files are also created and updated using the same edit procedures that we will discuss here.

Let us consider the basic data validation or **edit procedures** that should be performed on unedited transaction records before updating a master file.

A. Data Validation Procedures

1. The Class Test

If an input field is to contain numeric data only, the program processing the data should make certain that the field is, in fact, numeric before actually processing the data. The numeric **class test** uses the **TESTN operation** as follows:

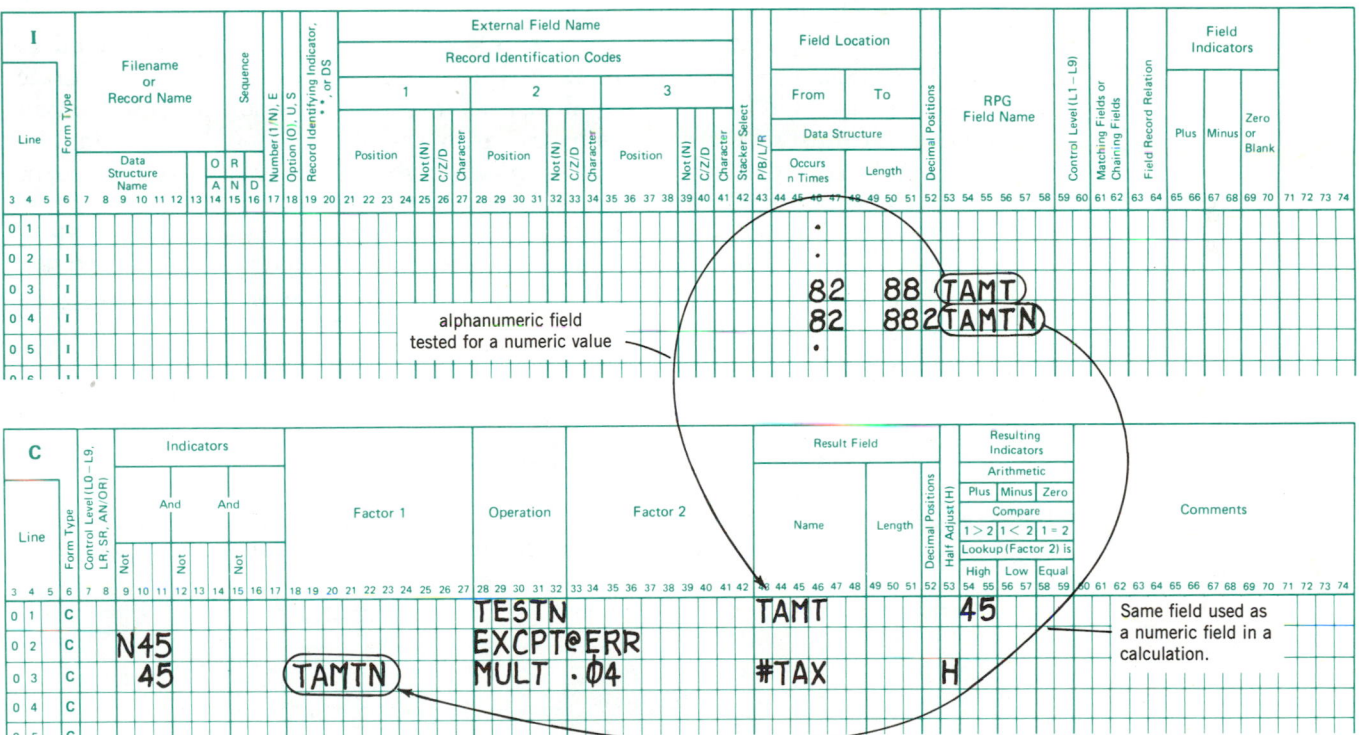

The TESTN operation is used to validate that the contents of an *alphanumeric field* is, in fact, numeric data. In our example, TAMT, defined as an alphanumeric field, is validated for numeric data. If TAMT contains a numeric value, indicator 45 is set on.

If the field tested is to be used in an arithmetic operation, it must be redefined as a numeric field. In our example, TAMT is redefined in the Input Specifications as TAMTN. Thus, if TAMT contains a numeric value and indicator 45 is set on, TAMTN can be used in the MULT operation to calculate the #TAX field. If, however, TAMT is not numeric and indicator 45 is *not* set on, an error has occurred and the appropriate message is written to the error report.

Note that TESTN will not work on all systems.

2. Missing Data Test

Sometimes it is necessary to verify the presence of data in a field. If the test indicates that data was not found in the field when in fact data should be present, an error condition exists. This validation procedure can be accomplished with the **missing data test:**

C	Form Type	Control Level (L0–L9, LR, SR, AN/OR)	Indicators And	And	Factor 1	Operation	Factor 2	Result Field Name	Length	Decimal Positions	Half Adjust (H)	Resulting Indicators	Comments
0 1	C												
0 2	C				ENAME	IFEQ	*BLANKS						
0 3	C					EXCPT@ERR3							
0 4	C					END							

If ENAME = Blanks, write an error message.

3. Testing for Reasonableness

If a data entry operator enters a weekly salary field for a payroll record as 326550 ($3,265.50) instead of 126550 ($1,265.50), the result will be inaccurate output. It would be extremely difficult for a program itself to find such an error. We must rely on the employees within the payroll department to double-check the control listing for such errors when records are created or updated, or when checks are produced.

Programs, however, can prevent many errors from being processed by at least making certain that the input is *reasonable.* A weekly salary of $50,000 or $25, for example, is likely to fail a test for reasonableness. The following are two tests for reasonableness:

a. Range Tests. One way to check for reasonableness is to make certain that the field passes a **range test;** that is, the value contained in a particular field should fall within preestablished guidelines.

Example   Assume that the value of a salary field ESALRY may be between 500 and 7000. A programmed range test could be accomplished using one of the following two methods:

C	Form Type	Control Level (L0–L9, LR, SR, AN/OR)	Indicators And	And	Factor 1	Operation	Factor 2	Result Field Name	Length	Decimal Positions	Half Adjust (H)	Resulting Indicators High 54 55	Low 56 57	Equal 58 59	Comments
0 1	C	*													
0 2	C				ESALRY	IFLT	500								
0 3	C					EXCPT@ERR4									
0 4	C					ELSE									
0 5	C				ESALRY	IFGT	7000								
0 6	C					EXCPT@ERR4									
0 7	C					END									
0 8	C					END									
0 9	C	*													
1 0	C	*													
1 1	C				ESALRY	COMP	500							57	
1 2	C		N57		ESALRY	COMP	7000						57		
1 3	C		57			EXCPT@ERR4									

Example of a range test.

b. Limit Test.   Another test for reasonableness is the **limit test**. We use this test to ensure that the value in a field does not exceed an established limit.

Example   The value of a commission field `ECOMM` is tested to ensure that it does not exceed an upper limit of 3500. That is, if $3,500 is the highest commission that can be paid, no commission should be greater than $3,500:

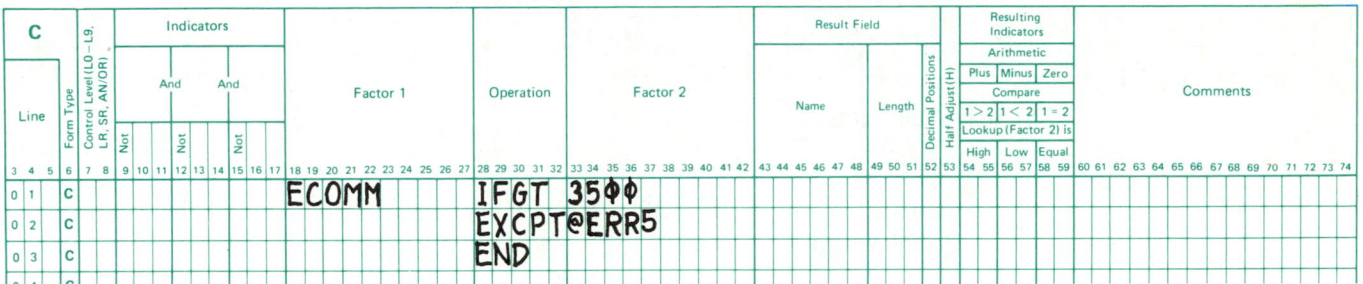

IF ECOMM is greater than 3500, write an error message.

4. Coded Field Test

Coded fields are frequently used in input records to minimize keystrokes for data entry operators and to keep the input record format shorter and more manageable. A marital status field, for example, is likely to be a coded field. Programs should make certain that the contents of these coded fields are valid. Two methods can be used depending on the action you wish to take after the **coded field test:**

1. Suppose a job classification code (`EJOBC`) may contain the values H for Hourly, S for Salary, and P for Piece Work. If you wish to validate the job classification field `EJOBC` to ensure that the field contains a correct value, the following could be used:

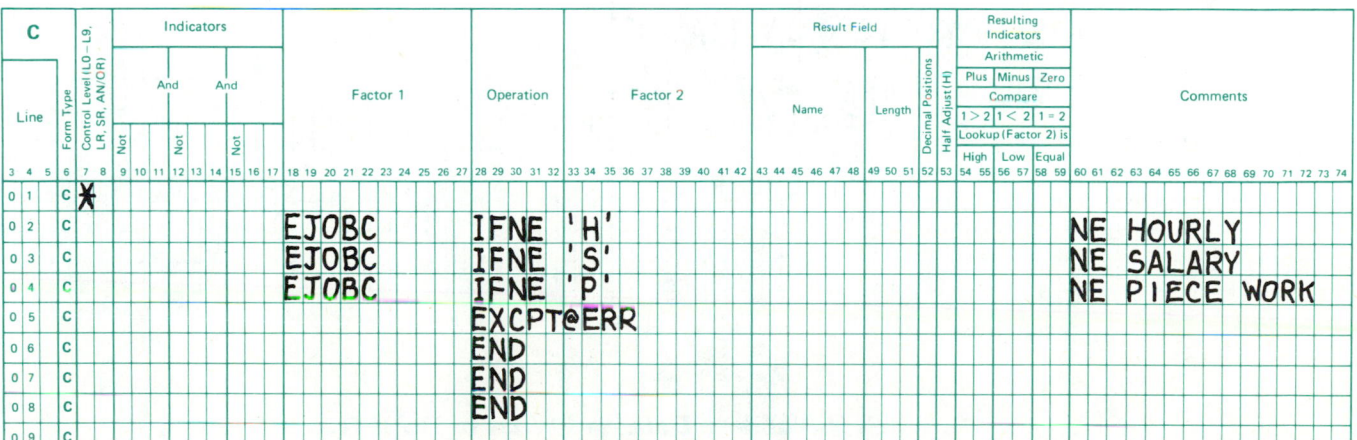

Coded field test using IFxx/END.

2. If you wish to check the job classification field `EJOBC` for particular values and then execute a subroutine based on the value of the field, the following could be used:

C			Indicators				Factor 1	Operation	Factor 2	Result Field				Resulting Indicators			Comments
Line	Form Type	Control Level (L0—L9, LR, SR, AN/OR)	And Not	And Not	Not					Name	Length	Decimal Positions	Half Adjust (H)	Arithmetic: Plus Minus Zero / Compare 1>2 1<2 1=2 / Lookup (Factor 2) is High Low Equal			
0 1	C	✳															
0 2	C						EJOBC	CASEQ	'H'	SRH100							
0 3	C						EJOBC	CASEQ	'S'	SRS200							
0 4	C						EJOBC	CASEQ	'P'	SRP300							
0 5	C							CAS		SRERR							
0 6	C							END									

Coded field test using CASxx.

In this example, if `EJOBC` did not contain a correct value the subroutine `SRERR` would be executed.

5. Sequence Test

Frequently, input records are entered in sequence by a key or control field. If a sorting procedure or a Sort Utility is not used to sort the records into the proper sequence, the program may need to determine whether input records are in proper sequence, either ascending or descending, based on the control or key field. For example, if you are reading records from an inventory transaction file and you wish to check that the records are in ascending sequence by part number (`IPART`), use a **sequence test** as follows:

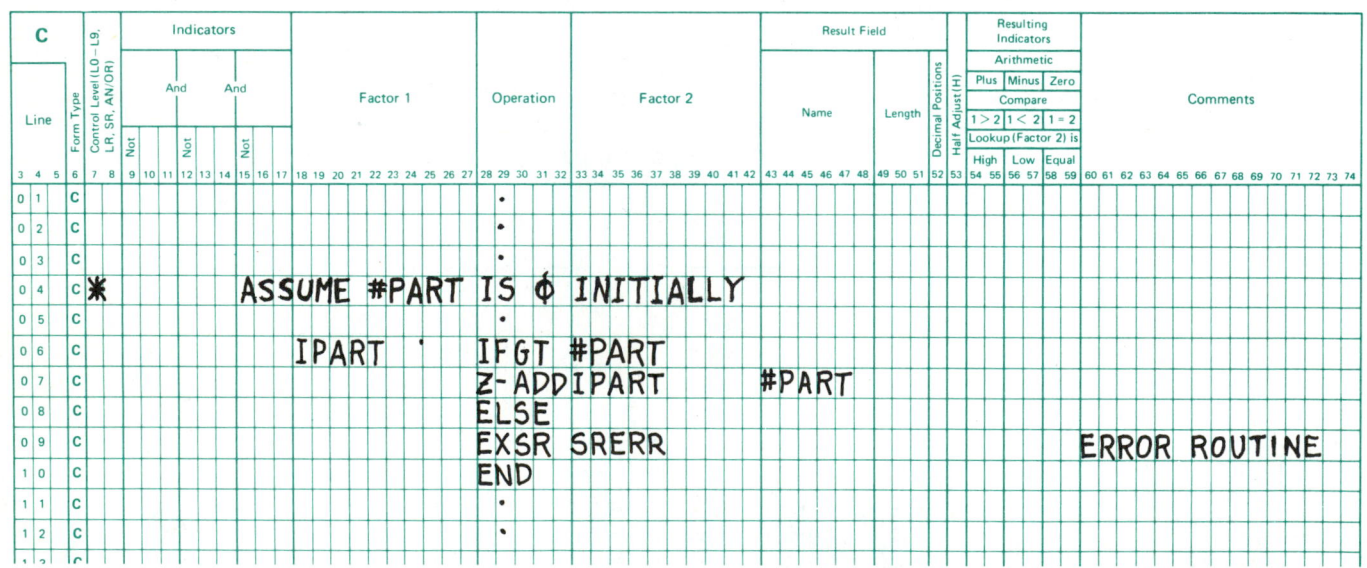

C			Indicators				Factor 1	Operation	Factor 2	Result Field				Resulting Indicators			Comments
Line	Form Type	Control Level (L0—L9, LR, SR, AN/OR)	And Not	And Not	Not					Name	Length	Decimal Positions	Half Adjust (H)	Arithmetic: Plus Minus Zero / Compare 1>2 1<2 1=2 / Lookup (Factor 2) is High Low Equal			
0 1	C							•									
0 2	C							•									
0 3	C							•									
0 4	C	✳					ASSUME #PART IS 0 INITIALLY										
0 5	C							•									
0 6	C						IPART	IFGT	#PART								
0 7	C							Z-ADD	IPART	#PART							
0 8	C							ELSE									
0 9	C							EXSR	SRERR								ERROR ROUTINE
1 0	C							END									
1 1	C							•									
1 2	C							•									

Sequence test

B. When to Validate Data and What to Do If Errors Occur

When should data be validated? Whenever data is entered into a system from an outside source the data should be validated and checked for every possible error.

All programs to be run on a regularly scheduled basis that *change* or *update* *master files* should include **data validation** techniques to minimize errors.

Once data is validated and entered into master files, data validation is not required when you wish to retrieve and manipulate the data from a file. Thus, data should be validated only once—when it enters the system.

If a major error occurs, it may be best simply to stop the run. Usually, this procedure is followed when data integrity is the primary consideration and errors must be kept to an absolute minimum.

Normally, however, when errors occur during the validation process, the program continues to execute. One method for minimizing the risk of any errors going undetected is to print a control listing or audit trail that includes (1) the key fields of each invalid record, (2) the contents of the erroneous fields, (3) error messages describing the errors encountered, and (4) totals of the types of errors encountered. Someone in the user department should be responsible for checking the control listing to make certain that the processing was performed correctly and that errors are corrected.

C. Creating the Transaction File of Changes

Let us consider an example that illustrates the procedures required to validate an unedited file and then create a transaction file of changes. Figure 8.1 illustrates the problem definition for this edit program. For **sequential processing** the input for this procedure would be records from an unedited disk file. Input from a terminal would typically be used for random updates.

Figure 8.1
Problem definition for edit program.

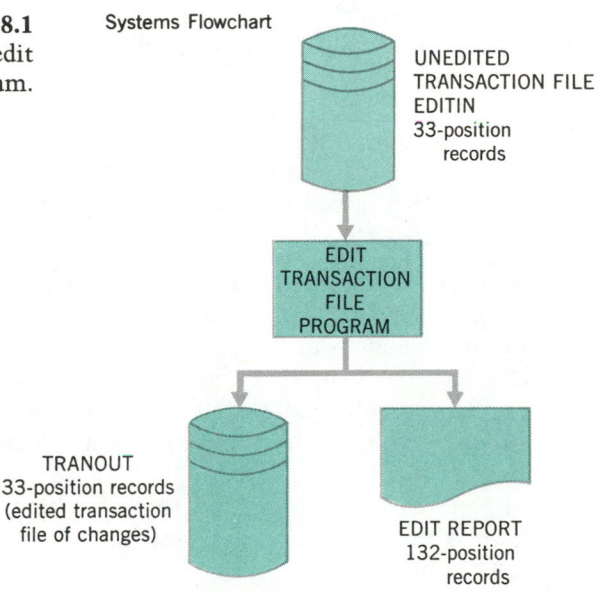

Systems Flowchart

UNEDITED
TRANSACTION FILE
EDITIN
33-position
records

EDIT
TRANSACTION
FILE
PROGRAM

TRANOUT
33-position records
(edited transaction
file of changes)

EDIT REPORT
132-position
records

EDITIN Record Layout

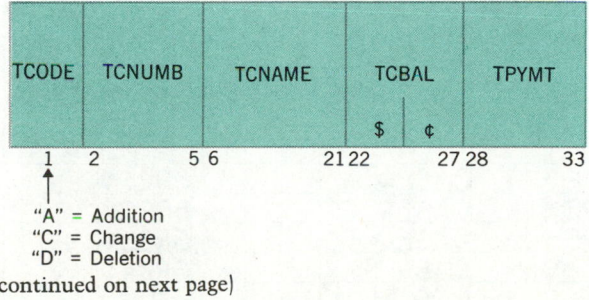

TCODE	TCNUMB	TCNAME	TCBAL	TPYMT
			$ ¢	

1 2   5 6   21 22   27 28   33

"A" = Addition
"C" = Change
"D" = Deletion
(continued on next page)

REPORT Printer Spacing Chart

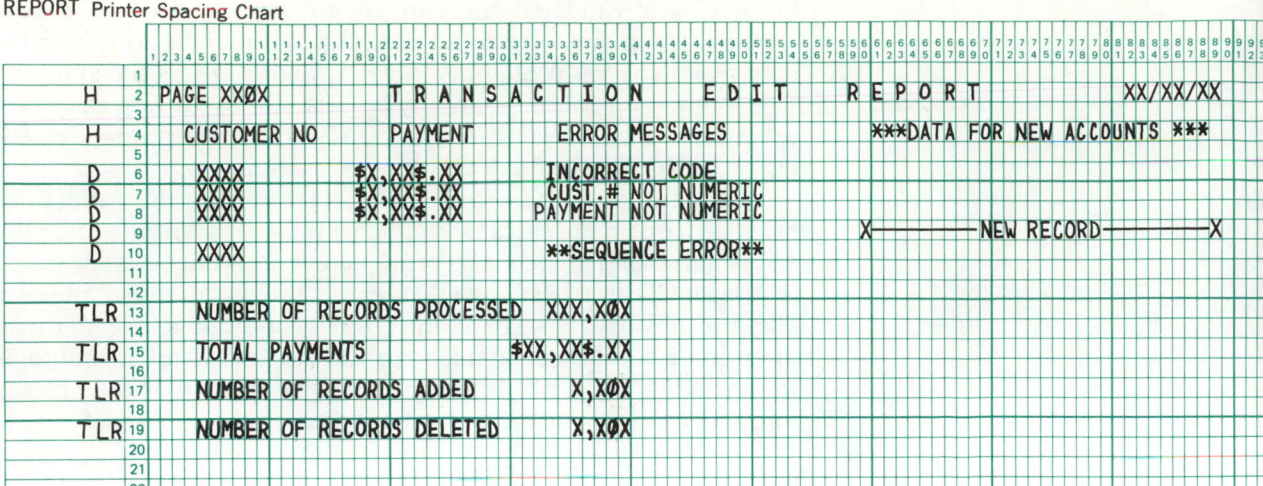

Figure 8.1
(continued)

Since the transaction file will be used to update the *sequential* master file, it must be *in the same sequence* as the master file. In this instance, the transaction file is in customer number sequence, the same as the master file. If the transaction file was not created in the same sequence as the master file, it must be sorted before a sequential update could be performed. We will see later in this chapter how a sort procedure can be used to arrange the transaction records in the proper sequence.

The program in this illustration must perform the following validation procedures:

1. The transaction code (TCODE) field should contain one of the following:

A—Denotes a record to be added to the master file.
C—Denotes a record to be changed on the master file.
D—Denotes a record to be deleted from the master file.

The transaction code is checked for an "A" (addition of a record), "C" (change or update of a record), or "D" (deletion of a record). Any other transaction code is unacceptable and will be flagged by the program as an error. The following Calculation Specifications illustrate the case structure operation (CASxx), which we use for the appropriate transaction code validation. In addition to determining which subroutine to execute depending on the value of TCODE, the case operation contains an "otherwise" or "catchall" operation that will be executed if TCODE is invalid. SR240 is the subroutine that will print the appropriate error message if TCODE is incorrect.

Line	Form Type	Control Level	Ind And Not	And Not	And Not	Factor 1	Operation	Factor 2	Result Field Name	Length	Decimal Positions	Half Adjust	Compare High	Low	Equal	Comments
0 1	C						•									
0 2	C						•									
0 3	C	SR				TCODE	CASEQ	'A'	SR21Ø							
0 4	C	SR				TCODE	CASEQ	'C'	SR22Ø							
0 5	C	SR				TCODE	CASEQ	'D'	SR23Ø							
0 6	C	SR					CAS		SR24Ø							CODE ERROR
0 7	C	SR					END									
0 8	C						•									
0 9	C						•									

2. TCNUMB, the customer number field, and TPYMT, the payment field, are tested to ensure that they contain numeric data only. Recall that the TESTN operation tests a field defined as *alphanumeric* for the presence of numeric data. This means that the field must be defined with a blank in the Decimal Positions column. As a result of the TESTN, the resulting indicator specified in columns 54–55 will be set on if the field has numeric contents. The field must be redefined in the Input Specifications as a numeric field if arithmetic operations are to be performed. In this example, indicator 08 is set on if the TPYMT field is numeric. The TPYMT field is redefined in the Input Specifications as TPYMTN, a numeric field, for subsequent addition to #TOTAL.

Line	Form Type	Control Level (L0–L9, LR, SR, AN/OR)	Not	Indicators And Not	And Not	Factor 1	Operation	Factor 2	Result Field Name	Length	Decimal Positions	Half Adjust (H)	Resulting Indicators Arithmetic Plus/High 54 55	Minus/Low 56 57	Zero/Equal 58 59	Comments
0 1	C						TESTN	TCNUMB					Ø9			
0 2	C		NØ9				EXCPT@ENUMB									
0 3	C		NØ9				MOVE 'E'		#EFLAG							
0 4	C						.									
0 5	C						.									
0 6	C						.									
0 7	C						TESTN	TPYMT					Ø8			
0 8	C		ØM8				ADD TPYMTN		#TOTAL							
0 9	C		NØ8				MOVE 'E'		#EFLAG							
1 0	C						.									

Use Switches to Identify an Error Condition

Suppose we perform multiple validity tests on each record, as in our example here, and we wish to process valid records only, that is, records without any errors. We may use a **switch** or **flag** for this purpose in place of indicators.

A switch is a field (usually defined in a Data Structure) that is established in the program; it is used to identify a particular condition within the program, such as an error condition. The term "flag" is used to denote a field that signals or flags an error condition.

Before processing any records, the error flag is initialized with a blank. In each error routine, if any error occurs, we move 'E' to the error flag (#EFLAG in our example). Thus, once the record is validated, if #EFLAG contains the letter E, we know an error has occurred and we proceed accordingly. If #EFLAG is equal to blank, however, no error has occurred and we write the valid record to the file. Before processing each new record, be sure to reinitialize #EFLAG with a blank.

As an alternative, a specific indicator in the program can be used as a switch. With this technique, the indicator is initialized as "off" and set on only when an error occurs.

In our example, if either field (TCNUMB or TPYMT) is not numeric, 'E' is moved to the error flag, #EFLAG. This is a signal that an error has occurred in the current record and the record is not to be written to the new transaction file TRANOUT.

We will see in Chapter 11 that the TESTN operation is not necessary with interactive programming. Testing for numeric data in interactive applications is performed at the data entry screen, which automatically prevents an operator from entering nonnumeric data into numeric fields.

3. The customer number field is checked to verify that the records are in ascending sequence by customer number. This edit routine verifies that the transaction records are in the same sequence as the master file, which is also in ascending sequence by customer number. The procedure is shown here.

C	Form Type	Control Level (L0–L9, LR, SR, AN/OR)	Indicators						Factor 1	Operation	Factor 2	Result Field				Resulting Indicators						Comments
Line			And Not	Not	And Not							Name	Length	Decimal Positions	Half Adjust (H)	Plus 1>2 54 55	Minus 1<2 56 57	Zero 1=2 58 59				
3 4 5	6	7 8	9 10 11	12 13	14 15	16 17			18 19 20 21 22 23 24 25 26 27	28 29 30 31 32	33 34 35 36 37 38 39 40 41 42	43 44 45 46 47 48	49 50 51	52	53				60 61 62 63 64 65 66 67 68 69 70 71 72 73 74			
0 1	C									•												
0 2	C									•												
0 3	C		Ø9						TCNUMB	IFGT	#PCNUM											
0 4	C									MOVE	TCNUMB	#PCNUM										
0 5	C									ELSE												
0 6	C									EXCPT@ESEQ												
0 7	C									MOVE	'E'	#EFLAG										
0 8	C									END												
0 9	C																					

It should be pointed out that this sequence test is executed only if indicator 09 is on, that is, TCNUMB is numeric and therefore a valid numeric field. Note that if computer sorts were performed on the files prior to processing it would *not* be necessary to do a sequence check.

As long as each customer number is greater than the previous customer number, we know the file is in sequence. If TCNUMB is less than or equal to the previous record's customer number (#PCNUM), however, 'E' is moved to #EFLAG. #EFLAG, as discussed earlier, is a field established as an error flag that indicates an error has occurred and the appropriate error message is to be written out.

4. A running total of all payments (#TOTAL) is accumulated as shown in Figure 8.1. For verification purposes, this total would typically be compared by a user to a manually computed total of all monies received.

5. The number of new accounts (#ADDS), records deleted (#DELS), and the number of records processed (#RECS) are listed at the end of the "Transaction Edit Report," which is the control listing. See the Printer Spacing Chart in Figure 8.1. Again, a user would verify these totals against manually prepared totals.

The complete program for creating the new edited transaction file is shown in Figure 8.2. Again, the validation of transaction data is of paramount importance in developing an effective program. Data validation is important to ensure *system integrity;* this means that errors must be minimized by validating the transaction data prior to updating the master file. Although these edit procedures require additional programming, the result will be a transaction file that is relatively free of errors. In this way, the risk of updating a master file with inaccurate data can be minimized.

When errors in the transaction record are detected by the program, the transaction data should *not* be used to update the master file. Only when the transaction file is free from errors and all totals prove correct can the updating procedure begin.

Figure 8.2
Program for creating an edited
transaction file.

```
....+....1....+....2....+....3....+....4....+....5....+....6....+....7
001 ******************************************************************
002 *
003 *   PROGRAM DESCRIPTION:
004 *
005 *       THIS PROGRAM WILL PRODUCE THE REQUIRED OUTPUT FOR
006 *       FIGURE 8.1.
007 *       THIS PROGRAM EDITS TRANSACTION RECORDS (EDITIN) AND
008 *       CREATES A FILE (TRANOUT) OF CORRECTLY EDITED DATA.
009 *       A REPORT IS PRINTED OF THOSE RECORDS
010 *       CONTAINING ERRORS.
011 *
012 *
013 *   FUNCTION OF INDICATORS:
014 *
015 *       08    PAYMENT (TPYMTN) NUMERIC
016 *       09    CUSTOMER NUMBER (TCNUMB) NUMERIC
017 *       99    CONTROL FIRST CYCLE ROUTINE
018 *
019 ******************************************************************
020 H
021 FEDITIN  IP  F      33            DISK
022 FTRANOUT O   F      33            DISK
023 FREPORT  O   F      132    OF     PRINTER
024 *
025 IEDITIN   NS
026 I                                    1   1 TCODE
027 I                                    2   5 TCNUMB
028 I                                    6  21 TCNAME
029 I                                   22  272TCBAL
030 I                                   28  33 TPYMT
031 I                                   28  332TPYMTN
032 I                                    1  33 EREC
033 *
034 I#WORK       DS
035 I                                    1   62#NUMFD
036 I                                    7  132#TOTAL
037 I                                   14  160#ADDS
038 I                                   17  190#DELS
039 I                                   20  220#RECS
040 I                                   23  26 #PCNUM
041 *
042 I#FLAGS      DS
043 I                                    1   1 #EFLAG
044 *
045 *                          MAIN-MODULE-RTN
046 C  N99              EXSR SR100             FOR 1ST PAGE HEADINGS
047 C                   EXSR SR200             EDIT INPUT RECORD
048 C                   EXSR SR300             WRITE RECORD, IF GOOD
049 *
050 CLR                EXSR SR400             EOJ TOTALS
051 *
052 *                          SR100-INITIALIZATION-RTN
053 CSR        SR100   BEGSR
054 CSR                SETON                  OF99
055 CSR                ENDSR
056 *                          SR200-EDIT-TRANSACTION-RECORDS-RTN
057 CSR        SR200   BEGSR
058 CSR        TCODE   CASEQ'A'     SR210     VALUATE CODE
059 CSR        TCODE   CASEQ'C'     SR220        AND EXECUTE
060 CSR        TCODE   CASEQ'D'     SR230        ADD, CHANGE,
061 CSR                CAS          SR240        DEL, OR ERROR
062 CSR                END
063 CSR                TESTN        TCNUMB      09  IS NUMBER NUMERIC?
064 CSR    N09         EXCPT@ENUMB
065 CSR    N09         MOVE 'E'     #EFLAG
066 CSR    09  TCNUMB  IFGT #PCNUM              IF SO, CHECK SEQUENCE
067 CSR                MOVE TCNUMB  #PCNUM
068 CSR                ELSE
069 CSR                EXCPT@ESEQ
070 CSR                MOVE 'E'     #EFLAG
071 CSR                END
072 CSR                ADD  1       #RECS       ACCUM TOTAL # OF REC
073 CSR                ENDSR
074 *                          SR210-ADD-RTN
075 CSR        SR210   BEGSR
076 CSR                ADD  1       #ADDS
077 CSR    OF          EXCPT@H000
078 CSR                SETOF                    OF
079 CSR                EXCPT@ADD
080 CSR                ENDSR
081 *                          SR220-CHANGE-RTN
082 CSR        SR220   BEGSR
083 CSR                TESTN        TPYMT       08  IS PAYMENT NUMERIC?
084 CSR    08          ADD  TPYMTN  #TOTAL
085 CSR    N08         MOVE 'E'     #EFLAG
086 CSR    OF          EXCPT@H000
```

Figure 8.2
(continued)

```
....+....1....+....2....+....3....+....4....+....5....+....6....+....7
087 CSR                     SETOF                        OF
088 CSR                     EXCPT@CHG
089 CSR                     ENDSR
090 *                                       SR230-DELETE-RTN
091 CSR          SR230      BEGSR
092 CSR                     ADD  1           #DELS
093 CSR      OF             EXCPT@H000
094 CSR                     SETOF                        OF
095 CSR                     EXCPT@DEL
096 CSR                     ENDSR
097 *                                       SR240-INVALID-CODE-RTN
098 CSR          SR240      BEGSR
099 CSR                     EXCPT@ECODE
100 CSR                     MOVE 'E'         #EFLAG
101 CSR                     ENDSR
102 *                                       SR300-WRITE-TRANSACTION-RECORD-RTN
103 CSR          SR300      BEGSR
104 CSR      #EFLAG         IFEQ 'E'
105 CSR                     MOVE *BLANK      #EFLAG
106 CSR                     ELSE
107 CSR                     EXCPT@REC
108 CSR                     END
109 CSR                     ENDSR
110 *                                       SR400-EOJ-OF-JOB-RTN
111 CSR          SR400      BEGSR
112 CSR                     EXCPT@EOJ
113 CSR                     ENDSR
114 *
115 OREPORT   E    02               @H000
116 O                                    5 'PAGE'
117 O                               PAGE 10
118 O                                   41 'T R A N S A C T I O N'
119 O                                   69 'E D I T    R E P O R T'
120 O                               UDATE Y 89
121 O         E    104              @H000
122 O                                   14 'CUSTOMER NO'
123 O                                   27 'PAYMENT'
124 O                                   48 'ERROR MESSAGES'
125 O                                   84 '***DATA FOR NEW ACCOUNTS'
126 O                                   88 '***'
127 O         E 1                  @ADD
128 O                               TCNUMB 8
129 O                                   26 '******'
130 O                                   47 'NEW ACCOUNT'
131 O                                   68 'NAME:'
132 O                               TCNAME 90
133 O         E 1                  @ADD
134 O                                   85 'OPENING BALANCE'
135 O                               TCBAL 1 95
136 O         E 1                  @CHG
137 O                               TCNUMB 8
138 O                      N08      TPYMT 26
139 O                      08       TPYMTN1 26 '$'
140 O                      N08         51 'PAYMENT NOT NUMERIC'
141 O         E 1                  @DEL
142 O                               TCNUMB 8
143 O                                   26 '******'
144 O                                   51 'RECORD TO BE DELETED'
145 O         E 1                  @ECODE
146 O                               TCNUMB 8
147 O                                   45 'INCORRECT CODE-'
148 O                                   53 'CONTAINS'
149 O                               TCODE 55
150 O         E 1                  @ENUMB
151 O                                   51 'CUST. # NOT NUMERIC'
152 O         E 1                  @ESEQ
153 O                                   51 '***SEQUENCE ERROR***'
154 O         E 2                  @EOJ
155 O                                   21 'NUMBER OF RECORDS'
156 O                                   31 'PROCESSED'
157 O                               #RECS 1 40
158 O         E 2                  @EOJ
159 O                                   18 'TOTAL PAYMENTS'
160 O                               #TOTAL1 40 '$'
161 O         E 2                  @EOJ
162 O                                   21 'NUMBER OF RECORDS'
163 O                                   27 'ADDED'
164 O                               #ADDS 1 40
165 O         E 2                  @EOJ
166 O                                   21 'NUMBER OF RECORDS'
167 O                                   29 'DELETED'
168 O                               #DELS 1 40
169 O*
170 OTRANOUT E                     @REC
171 O                               EREC   33
```

D. Programmed Control of Input Operations

We have seen in earlier chapters how the programmer could take control of the sequence of output operations by using the EXCPT operation, so that the program is not directly under the control of the RPG Fixed Logic Cycle. We would do this in order to write a record to an output file in some sequence other than the one provided by the logic cycle (e.g., during calculation time). Similarly, input operations can be performed under the programmer's control if the input file is specified as a *Demand file* or a *Full Procedural file*.

1. Demand Files

A **Demand file** is a disk file that must be processed *sequentially* regardless of the file's disk organization (sequential, indexed, or direct). Thus, any type of file may be defined as a Demand file. To define a file as a Demand file the letter D is placed in column 16 of the File Description Specifications. See Figure 8.3.

Demand files are normally processed as *input* files where sequential access is required. However, a Demand file can also be defined as an *update* file where records can be accessed sequentially, updated, and rewritten back to the same location on the disk.

To define a Demand file as input requires the letter I in column 15 (File Type) of the File Description Specifications. An update file is defined by specifying the letter U for File Type in column 15.

A Demand file can also be defined as a combined file that refers to a WORKSTN or workstation file used for interactive processing. We will discuss Demand files as WORKSTN files in Chapter 11.

Records are accessed from Demand files during calculations; that is, they are not processed according to the normal fixed logic cycle. Hence, files defined as Demand files access records on *demand* at the time they are required in the Calculation Specifications.

Both Demand files and Full Procedural files must use the READ operation to access or read records sequentially. We will discuss Full Procedural files next and then consider the READ operation later on.

2. Full Procedural Files

In addition to Demand files, **Full Procedural files** can also be used to control the processing of disk files from the Calculation Specifications. A Full Pro-

Figure 8.3
Defining a Demand file on the File Description Specifications form.

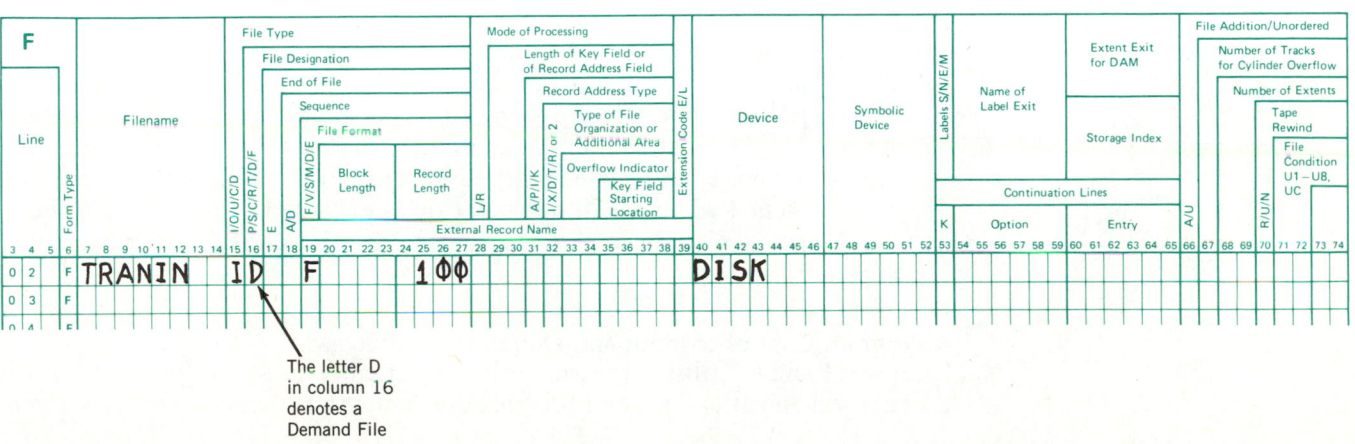

The letter D
in column 16
denotes a
Demand File

cedural file is a much more powerful version of the Demand file feature. While Demand files can be accessed only sequentially, Full Procedural files may be accessed both sequentially and randomly. To sequentially access records from a file defined as a Full Procedural file, the READ operation is also used during the Calculation Specifications.

In addition, the file can be accessed randomly using the chaining operation (CHAIN), which we will discuss in Chapter 9. The Full Procedural feature, then, provides all the features of the Demand files in addition to offering additional features for randomly accessing records.

To define a file as a Full Procedural file, the letter F is specified for the File Type in column 16 of the File Description Specifications. Recall that a Demand file uses the letter D in this column.

As noted, for a program to sequentially access records from either a Demand or Full Procedural file a READ operation must be specified in the Calculation Specifications. We will now examine the READ operation in detail.

3. The READ Operation

The **READ operation** reads the next record from a demand file or a full procedural file. This operation is executed within the Calculation Specifications and calls for immediate input of a record from the file specified in the READ operation. Thus, a record is read directly into the program under the programmer's control, rather than waiting for the fixed logic cycle to perform the read. The format of the READ operation is as follows:

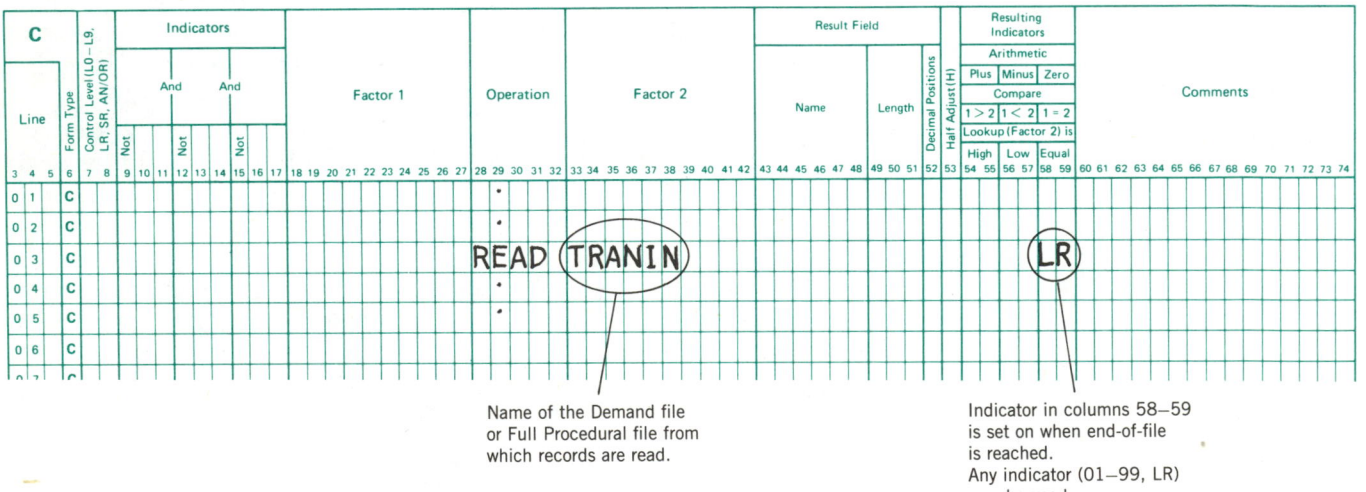

Name of the Demand file or Full Procedural file from which records are read.

Indicator in columns 58–59 is set on when end-of-file is reached. Any indicator (01–99, LR) may be used.

The **Operation Code** (columns 28–32) must contain READ.

Factor 2 (columns 33–42) must contain the name of the Demand file or Full Procedural file from which records are to be read.

Columns 58–59 must contain an end-of-file indicator to identify when the end-of-file has been reached on the file. This indicator is set on if end-of-file is reached when the READ operation is executed. That is, when there are no more records to process in the file, the end-of-file indicator is automatically set on.

4. Program Control of Input and Output Operations

Figures 8.4 and 8.5 illustrate two methods that can be used to loop within the Calculation Specifications and control both input and output operations. Input

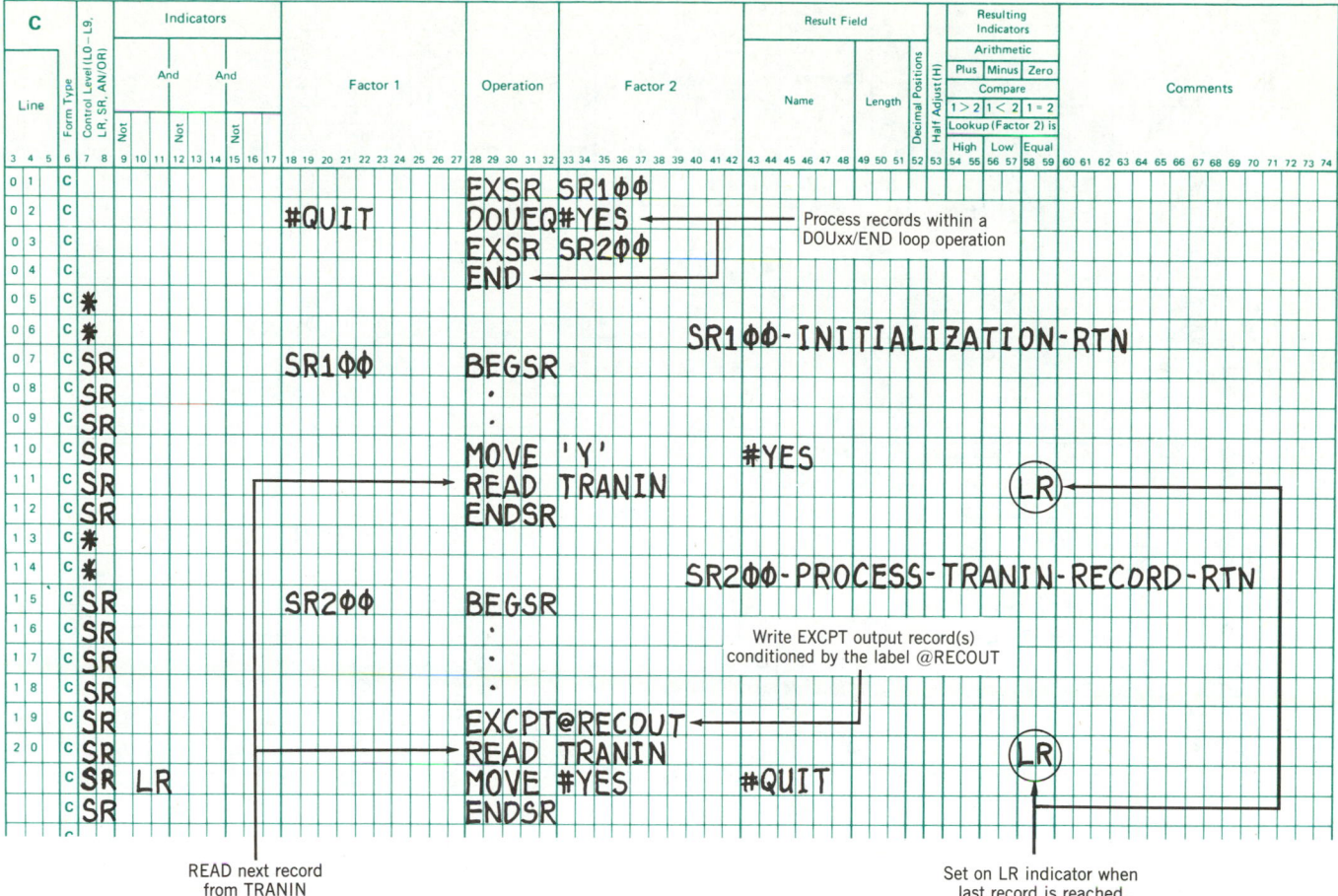

Figure 8.4
Program control of input and
output operations—Method 1.

operations are performed by the READ operation, while the EXCPT operation is used to control output operations. In this way, the program is executed under the programmer's complete control. This method of programming is primarily used when structured programming is desired. Note that the traditional RPG Logic Cycle is superseded by using this processing technique.

In both examples, the initialization routine, SR100, is executed as the first operation in order to perform any necessary initialization operations.

Figure 8.4 is the more structured method of the two. In addition to reading the first record from the file TRANIN, the subroutine SR100 initializes the Data Structure subfield, #YES, to 'Y'. #QUIT is used to control the execution of the DOUxx operation. As long as #QUIT is not equal to #YES the looping process continues. #YES and #QUIT are meaningful field names established in the program to replace the use of indicators or constants and thus make the program more readable and self-documenting.

Prior to looping back to the beginning of the DOU/END operation, a record is read from the TRANIN file. If end-of-file is encountered, indicator LR is set on and #YES is moved to #QUIT. When processing returns to the DOUxx loop, the loop is terminated because #QUIT is now equal to #YES. We will demonstrate this procedure later in this chapter.

Output in Figure 8.4 is controlled by an EXCPT operation. When this EXCPT

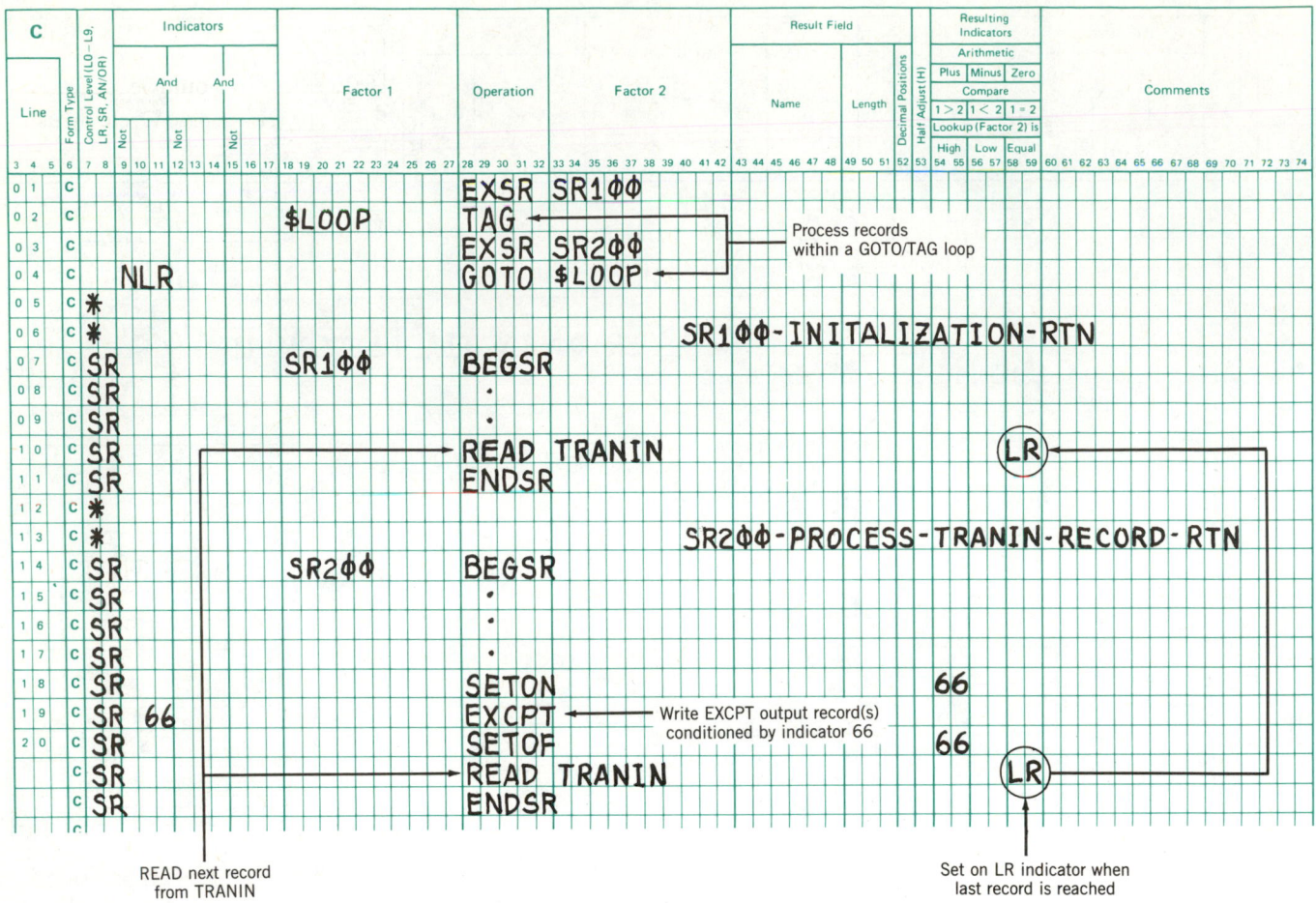

Figure 8.5
Program control of input and
output operations—Method 2.

operation is encountered, all output records controlled by the label @RECOUT are written out.

Figure 8.5 uses the older, traditional GOTO/TAG method of looping. In this example, the SR200 subroutine continues to execute until the LR indicator is set on during a READ operation of the TRANIN file.

Output in Figure 8.5 is also controlled by the use of the EXCPT operation. However, in this example, indicator 66 is used to control the output operation. Here, indicator 66 is set on, the record is written using the EXCPT operation, and then indicator 66 is set off.

Self-Test
1. After initial creation, a master file is kept up-to-date using an _____.
2. A(n) _____, also called a(n) _____, is produced as the result of a transaction file being edited.
3. The TESTN operation is a test to ensure a field contains _____ data only.
4. The TESTN operation must test fields that are defined as _____ in the program.
5. Two tests for reasonableness are a _____ test and a _____ test.
6. One method to minimize keystrokes for data entry operators is to use _____ fields.

7. A sequence test is not required if data records are _____ prior to running an update procedure.

8. When data is being entered into a system for the first time it should be _____ .

9. The programmer can take control away from the RPG Fixed Logic Cycle by using the _____ and _____ operations.

10. When using the READ operation, the file must be defined as either a _____ file or a _____ file.

Solutions

1. update procedure
2. control listing; audit trail
3. numeric
4. alphanumeric
5. range; limit
6. coded
7. sorted
8. validated
9. READ; EXCPT
10. Demand; Full Procedural

IV. Sequential File Maintenance Procedure

Sequential master files can be updated by reading in the master file and a transaction file and creating a new master file. This means that the update procedure uses *three* files. Most often, a fourth print file that is used as a *control listing* or *audit trail* (for printing all changes made, any errors found, and totals) is created as well.

Later in this chapter we will see that sequential master files can be updated using another method where the records to be updated on the master file are *rewritten in place.* This means that only two files would be needed: an input transaction file and a master file that is read and rewritten. Prior to updating a master file in place, it is good practice to create a backup or copy of the master file. If, for any reason, errors occur and the newly created master file is unusable, the backup or copy can still be used. For now, we focus on the traditional method of updating sequential files where there are two input files and one output file.

A. Files Required for a Sequential File Maintenance

The systems flowchart in Figure 8.6 summarizes the files used in a typical sequential master file update procedure.

1. Input Master File

The input master file is the master file that is current through the previous update period. That is, if updates are performed weekly, the input master file is the file that was created as the new output master during the previous week. This file is in sequence by a key or control field. For the current update procedure we generally refer to this file as the OLD-MASTER file because it does not contain current changes.

2. Input Transaction File

The transaction file is the one that contains data to be used for updating the OLD-MASTER file. The input transaction file contains all additions, changes, and deletions that have occurred since the previous updating cycle. This file is

Figure 8.6
Systems flowchart of a sequential update procedure.

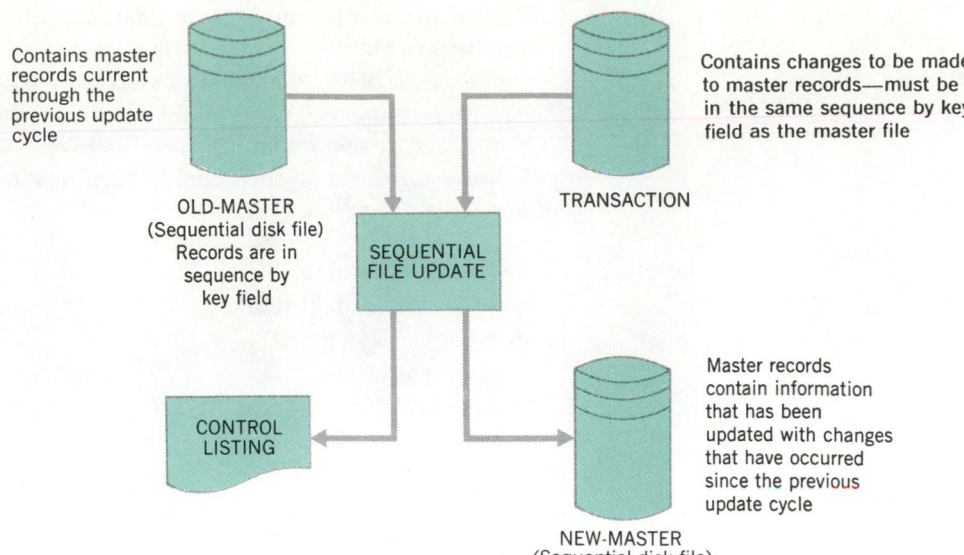

in sequence by the same key or control field as used in the master file. This file is referred to as the TRANSACTION file.

3. Output Master File

The output master file is the file that becomes the new master file as a result of the updating procedure. The output master file will integrate data from the OLD-MASTER and the TRANSACTION file. This file is called the NEW-MASTER file and will become the OLD-MASTER file for the next week's update run.

In summary, the OLD-MASTER file contains master data that was complete and current through the previous updating cycle. The TRANSACTION file contains transactions or changes that have occurred since the previous updating cycle. These transactions or changes must be incorporated into the master file to make it current. The NEW-MASTER file will include all the OLD-MASTER data in addition to the changes stored on the TRANSACTION file that have occurred since the last update. The NEW-MASTER file will in turn become the OLD-MASTER file for the next update cycle.

As noted, a print file or *control listing* is usually created during a sequential file update. This print file would list (1) changes made to the master file, (2) errors encountered during processing, and (3) totals to be used for control and checking purposes. Since you are already familiar with the techniques for creating print files, we will omit them from our sequential update illustrations for the sake of simplicity.

In a sequential update, all records in the master file are in sequence by a *key field*, such as account number, Social Security number, or part number, depending on the type of master file. This key field uniquely identifies each master record. To update records in a sequential master file, the transaction file containing the change records must also be *in sequence by the same key field*. Thus, a transaction record will similarly be identified with this key field.

B. Sequential File Update: An Illustration

Let us consider the updating of a sequential master accounts receivable file. The key field used to identify records in the old master file is account number, called MACCTN, for master account number. All records in the OLD-MASTER file are in sequence by MACCTN.

The TRANSACTION file contains all transactions (additions, changes, and deletions) to be posted to the master file that have occurred since the previous update. The TRANSACTION file also has an account number as a key field, called TACCTN, for transaction account number. Records in the TRANSACTION file are in sequence by TACCTN.

The formats for the two input files are:

OLD-MASTER Record **MASTOLD**		**TRANSACTION** Record **TRANIN**	
1–5	MACCTN (Account Number)	1–5	TACCTN (Account Number)
6–9	MADUE (Amount Due)	6–9	TAMT (Purchased Amount)
10–100	Not Used	10–100	Not Used

Note: MADUE and TAMT are both packed fields.

Each transaction record contains the *total* amount of purchases during the current period for a specific master record. Hence, there will be *at most one transaction record* for each master record to be updated.

The NEW-MASTER file becomes the current master accounts receivable file after the update procedure. It must have the same format as the MASTOLD file. The NEW-MASTER file has the following format:

NEW-MASTER File
MASTNEW

1–5	Account Number
6–9	Amount Due (Amount due is a packed field)
10–100	Not used

The files contain additional data (positions 10–100) used in other programs that are not related to this update; thus, these fields will not be described in detail in this program.

Keep in mind that records within the MASTOLD file are in sequence by MACCTN and that records within the TRANIN file are in sequence by TACCTN. The NEW-MASTER file MASTNEW, then, will also be created in account number sequence.

Figure 8.7 is a flowchart of the procedures to be coded in this update program. We will consider each procedure in detail. Figure 8.8 shows the pseudocode for this program; Figure 8.9 is the hierarchy chart. Examine these charts carefully before looking at the program in Figure 8.10.

1. The Main Module

The initialization routine, SR800, executes two subroutines, SR600 and SR700, that read a record from the MASTOLD and TRANIN files. Subroutine SR200, which compares account numbers, is then executed until all records are processed. At that point, an end-of-file condition has been reached on both files and the program terminates.

2. How Input Transaction and Master Records Are Processed

Subroutine SR200 compares the transaction account number, TACCTN of the TRANIN file, to MACCTN of the MASTOLD file. Since both files are in sequence by their respective account numbers, a comparison of TACCTN to MACCTN will determine the next subroutine to be executed. One of three possible conditions may result when comparing TACCTN to MACCTN:

Figure 8.7
Flowchart of procedures to be used in sample accounts receivable update program.

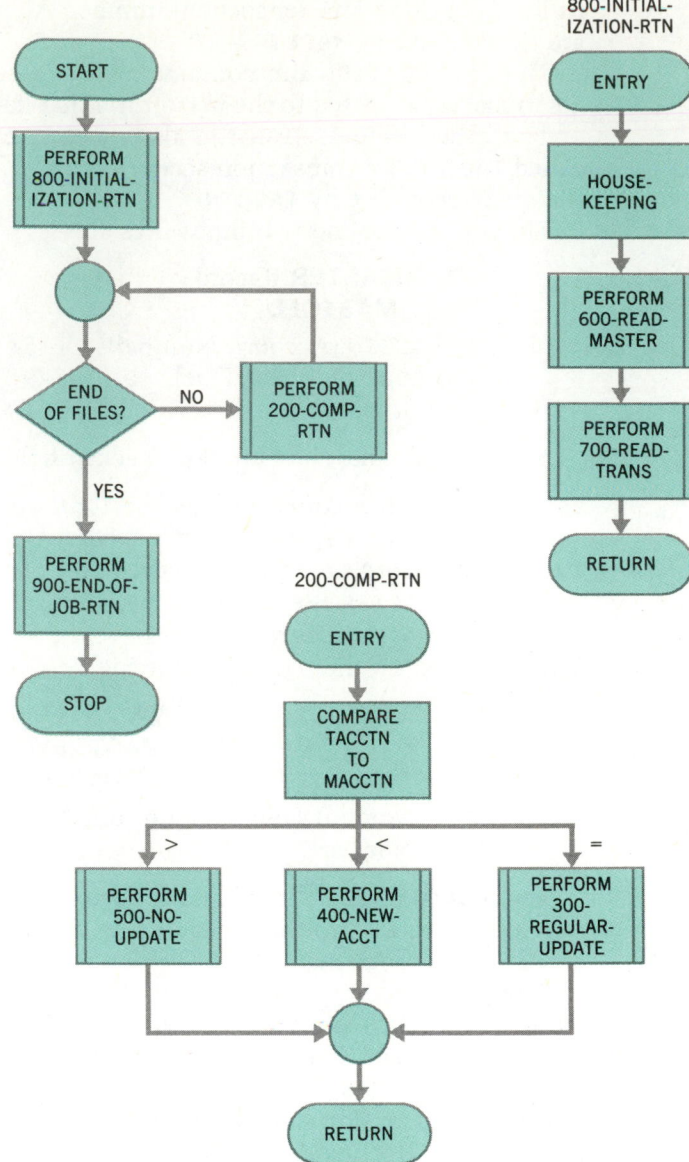

Figure 8.8
Pseudocode for sample accounts receivable update program.

```
PERFORM
    Read Master Record
ENDPERFORM
PERFORM
    Read Transaction Record
ENDPERFORM
PERFORM UNTIL no more input (#QUIT = #YES)
    IF   T-Acct-No = M-Acct-No
    THEN
        PERFORM
            Update the Master Record
            Read a Master Record
            Read a Transaction Record
        ENDPERFORM
    ELSE
        IF   T-Acct-No < M-Acct-No
        THEN
            PERFORM
                Write a New Master Record from Transaction Record
                Read a Transaction Record
            ENDPERFORM
        ELSE
            PERFORM
                Write a New Master from Old Master
                Read a Master Record
            ENDPERFORM
        ENDIF
    ENDIF
ENDPERFORM
PERFORM
    End-of-Job Operations
ENDPERFORM
```

Figure 8.9
Hierarchy chart for sample accounts receivable update program.

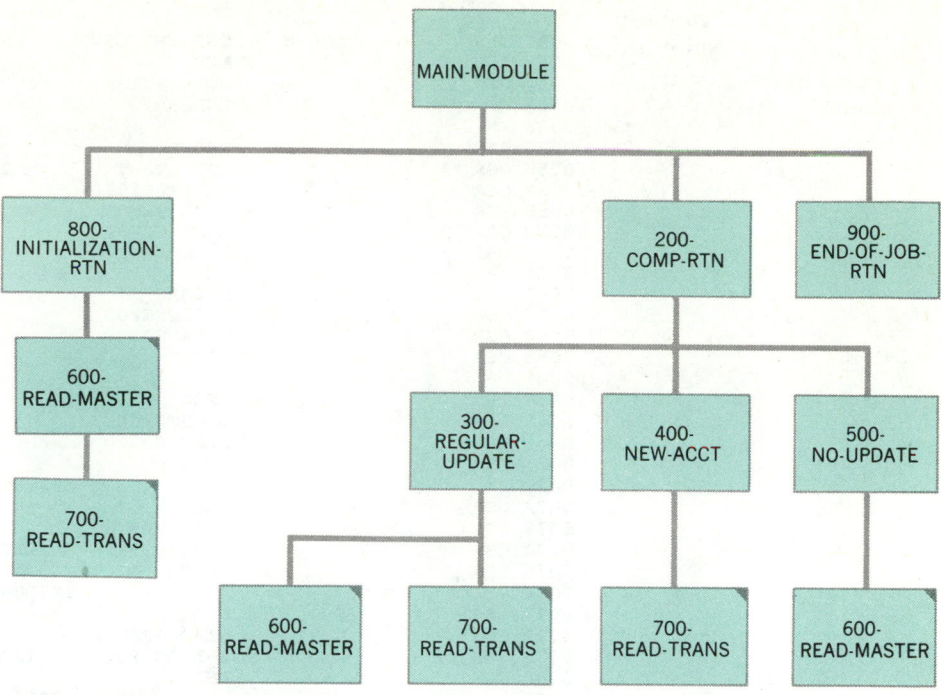

Figure 8.10
Sample accounts receivable update program.

```
0001    ****************************************************************
0002    *
0003    *   PROGRAM DESCRIPTION:
0004    *
0005    *       THIS PROGRAM PERFORMS AN ACCOUNTS RECEIVABLE
0006    *       SEQUENTIAL UPDATE.
0007    *       THE PROGRAM READS TWO FILES (MASTOLD AND TRANIN),
0008    *       COMPARES THE ACCOUNT NUMBERS, AND PERFORMS
0009    *       THE NECESSARY UPDATE PROCEDURE CREATING A
0010    *       NEW FILE (MASTNEW).
0011    *
0012    *
0013    *   FUNCTION OF INDICATORS:
0014    *
0015    *       61    END-OF-FILE FOR "MASTOLD"
0016    *       62    END-OF-FILE FOR "TRANIN"
0017    *
0018    ****************************************************************
0019    *
0020    H
0021    FMASTOLD ID  F      100              DISK
0022    FTRANIN  ID  F      100              DISK
0023    FMASTNEW O   F      100              DISK
0024    *
0025    IMASTOLD NS
0026    I                                      1 100 MREC
0027    I                                      1   50MACCTN
0028    I                                   P  6    92MADUE
0029    ITRANIN  NS
0030    I                                      1 100 TREC
0031    I                                      1   50TACCTN
0032    I                                   P  6    92TAMT
0033    I#FLAGS      DS
0034    I                                      1   1 #YES
0035    I                                      2   2 #QUIT
0036    *
0037    *                              MAIN-MODULE-RTN
0038    C                     EXSR SR800                 INITIAL READS
0039    *
0040    C           #QUIT     DOUEQ#YES                  TEST FOR STOP
0041    C                     EXSR SR200                 COMPARE RTN
0042    C                     END
0043    *
0044    C                     EXSR SR900                 END OF JOB RTN
0045    *
0046    *                              SR200-COMPARE-ACCT-NUMBERS-RTN
0047    CSR         SR200     BEGSR
0048    CSR         TACCTN    CASEQMACCTN      SR300     TACCTN = MACCTN
0049    CSR         TACCTN    CASLTMACCTN      SR400     TACCTN < MACCTN
```

Figure 8.10
(continued)

```
0050 CSR          TACCTN      CASGTMACCTN    SR500          TACCTN > MACCTN
0051 CSR                      END
0052 CSR 61 62                MOVE #YES      #QUIT          END OF BOTH FILES
0053 CSR                      ENDSR
0054  *                                     SR300-REGULAR-UPDATE-RTN
0055 CSR          SR300       BEGSR
0056 CSR                      ADD   TAMT     MADUE
0057 CSR                      EXCPT@E100
0058 CSR                      EXSR SR600                    READ NEXT MASTTER
0059 CSR                      EXSR SR700                    READ NEXT TRAN
0060 CSR                      ENDSR
0061  *                                     SR400-NEW-ACCOUNT-RTN
0062 CSR          SR400       BEGSR
0063 CSR                      EXCPT@E200
0064 CSR                      EXSR SR700
0065 CSR                      ENDSR
0066  *                                     SR500-NO-UPDATE-RTN
0067 CSR          SR500       BEGSR
0068 CSR                      EXCPT@E100
0069 CSR                      EXSR SR600
0070 CSR                      ENDSR
0071  *                                     SR600-READ-OLD-MASTER-FILE-RTN
0072 CSR          SR600       BEGSR
0073 CSR                      READ MASTOLD                  61
0074 CSR 61                   Z-ADD99999     MACCTN
0075 CSR                      ENDSR
0076  *                                     SR700-READ-TRANSACTION-FILE-RTN
0077 CSR          SR700       BEGSR
0078 CSR                      READ TRANIN                   62
0079 CSR 62                   Z-ADD99999     TACCTN
0080 CSR                      ENDSR
0081  *                                     SR800-INITIALIZATION-RTN
0082 CSR          SR800       BEGSR
0083 CSR                      MOVE '1'       #YES
0084 CSR                      EXSR SR600
0085 CSR                      EXSR SR700
0086 CSR 61 62                MOVE #YES      #QUIT          END OF BOTH FILES
0087 CSR                      ENDSR
0088  *                                     SR900-END-OF-JOB-RTN
0089 CSR          SR900       BEGSR
0090 CSR                      SETON                         LR
0091 CSR                      ENDSR
0092  *
0093 OMASTNEW E               @E100
0094 O                        MREC      100
0095 O                        MADUE     9P
0096 O        E               @E200
0097 O                        TREC      100
0098 O                        TAMT      9P
```

a. TACCTN Is Equal to (EQ) MACCTN. This means that a transaction record exists with the same account number that is on the master file. If this condition is met, we execute a subroutine called SR300, Regular Update, where the record from the Old-Master (MASTOLD) file is updated. That is, the transaction data is posted to the Old-Master record (MASTOLD), which means that the new New-Master record will contain the previous Amount Due (MADUE) plus the Purchase Amount (TAMT) of the transaction record. After a New-Master record is written using an EXCPT operation, another record from both the MASTOLD and TRANIN files must be read. Here again, we are assuming that each master record can be updated by only *one* transaction record so that the next TRANIN record will pertain to a different master record.

b. TACCTN Is Greater Than (GT) MACCTN. If TACCTN is greater than MACCTN, then there is a master record with an account number *less than* the account number on the transaction file. This condition occurs in our program if the last case operation is executed in SR200. If TACCTN is not equal to MACCTN, or TACCTN is not less than MACCTN, then TACCTN *must be* greater than MACCTN.

Since both files are in sequence by account number, this condition means that a master record exists for which there is *no corresponding transaction record*. That is, the master record has had no activity or changes occurring during the current update cycle and should be written onto the MASTNEW file *as is*. Thus, this subroutine is a *no-update* routine and is called SR500. At SR500, we write the new master record for MASTNEW from the MASTOLD record and read another record from the Old-Master file MASTOLD. Since we have not yet processed the last transaction record that caused TACCTN to compare greater than MACCTN of the MASTOLD file, we should not read another transaction record at the SR500 subroutine. Consider the following example that illustrates the processing to be performed if MACCTN is less than TACCTN, which is the same as TACCTN is greater than MACCTN:

MACCTN	TACCTN	Action
00001	00001	Update master record
00002	00003	00002 is rewritten to the New-Master file MAST-NEW as is; the next master record is read; TACCTN 00003 has not yet been processed

c. TACCTN **Is Less Than** (LT) MACCTN. Since both files are in sequence by account number, this condition would mean that a transaction record exists for which there is no corresponding master record. Depending on the type of update procedure being performed, this could mean either (1) a new account is to be processed from the transaction file TRANIN or (2) an error has occurred; that is, the TACCTN is incorrect. In our illustration, we will assume that when a TACCTN is less than MACCTN, this is a *new account*; but first let us consider the full range of procedures that could be executed if TACCTN is less than MACCTN:

(1) **Create a New Account** if TACCTN **Is Less Than** MACCTN. As noted, for some applications a transaction record with no corresponding master record means a new account. This procedure is called the NEW-ACCOUNT routine and is identified as SR400 in our program. In this instance, a new master record is created entirely from the transaction record. Then the next transaction record is read. We do *not* read another record from the Old-Master file MASTOLD at this time, since we have not yet processed the master record that compared greater than TACCTN. The other possibility is to do the following:

(2) **Specify an Error Condition** if TACCTN **Is Less Than** MACCTN. For some applications, all account numbers on the transaction file *must* have corresponding master records with the same account numbers. For these applications, new accounts are handled by a different program and are *not* part of the update procedure.

Thus, if TACCTN is less than MACCTN, an error routine should be executed. The error routine would usually print out the transaction record that has a nonmatching account number and then read the next transaction record.

In many instances when TACCTN is less than MACCTN and we assume this to be a new account, we add a code to the transaction record that explicitly defines the record as a new account.

3. Illustrating the Update Procedure with Examples

In our program, a master and a transaction record are read in subroutine SR800—the initialization routine. Then SR200 (the compare subroutine) using the CASxx structure is executed, where the account numbers are compared. Based on the comparison, SR300, SR500, or SR400 will be executed. SR200 is then repeated until the last record has been processed from both the TRANIN and MASTOLD files.

The following examples illustrate the subroutines to be executed depending on the comparison of the account numbers:

TACCTN	MACCTN	Condition	Action
00001	00001	TACCTN = MACCTN	SR300 (Regular Update)
00004	00002	TACCTN > MACCTN	SR500 (No Update-Write MASTOLD)
00004	00003	TACCTN > MACCTN	SR500 (No Update-Write MASTOLD)
00004	00005	TACCTN < MACCTN	SR400 (New Account)
00005	00005	TACCTN = MACCTN	SR300 (Regular Update)

Remember that this update procedure assumes there is no more than a *single transaction record for each master record.*

One element in the program requires further clarification. Since two files are being processed simultaneously, one file will more than likely reach an end-of-file condition before the other file. Consideration must be given to the end-of-file procedures in order to properly terminate the program.

C. End-of-File Conditions

Because we have two input files, two possible end-of-file conditions may occur. First, an end-of-file condition for the transaction file may occur *before* we have reached the end of the Old-Master file MASTOLD. Or, we may run out of records in the MASTOLD file before we reach the end of the transaction file TRANIN. We must account for both possibilities in our program.

To accomplish a proper end-of-file condition we use a combination of two indicators (61 and 62) and a Data Structure subfield called #QUIT. We do not use the LR indicator here because we want to perform different operations depending on which file ends first.

Indicator 61 is set on when an end-of-file condition occurs on the MASTOLD file. An end-of-file condition on the TRANIN file will set on indicator 62. Indicator 61 is used in the SR600 subroutine (Read MASTOLD File) and indicator 62 is used in the SR700 subroutine (Read TRANIN File). Consider first the subroutine SR600 to read records from the Old-Master file MASTOLD. When the MASTOLD file has reached the end, there may be additional transaction records to process. Hence, we would not want to automatically terminate all processing at a MASTOLD end-of-file condition; instead, we want to continue processing transaction records as new accounts. To accomplish this, we place the highest possible values (99999) in MACCTN of the MASTOLD record when an end-of-file condition occurs for that file.

All 9's in MACCTN ensures that subsequent attempts to compare the TACCTN of new transaction records to this MACCTN will always result in a "less than" condition. Thus, subroutine SR400 (Add New Account) would be executed until there are no more transaction records, because MACCTN has the highest possible value and will always compare "high" to TACCTN. The use of 9's in the key fields TACCTN and MACCTN is possible only, however, if the account number fields could not, in reality, have a valid value of 9's. That is, if an account number of 99999 is a feasible entry, moving 99999 to an account number when an end-of-file condition is reached could produce erroneous results. For our program here, we will assume that the account number field could not contain 99999.

Now consider the SR700 subroutine (Read Transaction Record). We may reach the end-of-file for the TRANIN file while there are still records to process in the Old-Master file MASTOLD. In this case, we would continue processing MASTOLD records at SR500 (No Update) until we have read the file in its entirety. Hence, at SR700 (Read Transaction File) we set on indicator 62 and move all 9's to TACCTN on an end-of-file condition. All 9's is a kind of "dummy" TACCTN that will always compare high, or greater than, MACCTN. In this way, SR500 (No Update) will continue to be executed. Any remaining records in MASTOLD will be read and processed using this SR500 subroutine (No Update). This procedure will be repeated until an end-of-file condition for MASTOLD is reached.

Thus, we continue to process records at SR200 (Compare Account Numbers) even if one of the two input files has reached an end-of-file condition. Only when *both* files reach an end-of-file condition and indicators 61 and 62 are both on will #YES be moved to the subfield #QUIT. At this point, control would return to the main module where the program is terminated.

Later on, we will consider other methods of updating.

D. Updating Sequential Master Records in Place

As we have noted, disk files can be organized sequentially and updated using a sequential update procedure as described in the previous section of this chapter. Updating a master file in this manner means recreating the master with a new file that incorporates Old-Master data along with the transaction data. This procedure results in an automatic backup, with MASTOLD serving as the backup in case something happens to the new master.

Disk files, however, can serve as *both input and output during the same run*. Thus, it is possible to read a disk record, make changes *directly to the same record*, and rewrite it or update it back into its original location. With this capability of updating sequential disk files, we need use only two files:

File	Defined as
Master File	Update (will serve as both input and output)
Transaction File	Input

The following example illustrates how a disk file can be defined as an input/output or update file, which means records from the file will be read, changed, and rewritten. Note that if we update disk records in place we should always copy the master onto a new disk for backup purposes before processing.

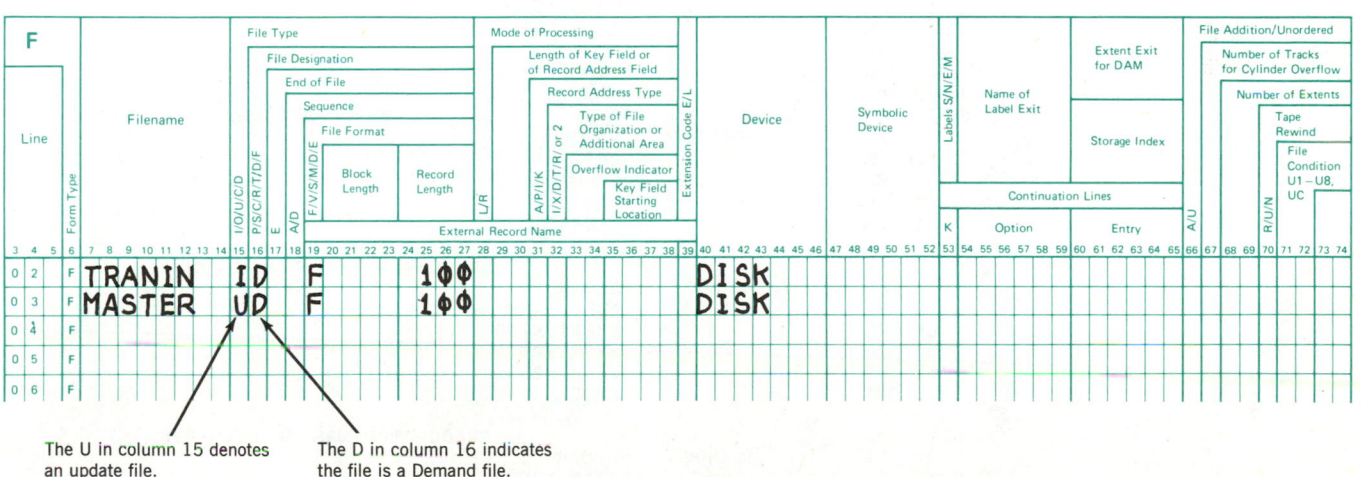

The U in column 15 denotes an update file.

The D in column 16 indicates the file is a Demand file.

In RPG, we define an update file by placing the letter U in column 15 (File Type) of the File Description Specifications. This will designate the file as an input/output file to be *updated*. As an update file, it must be described on both the Input Specifications form and the Output Specifications form. The Input Specifications for this file are defined as they would be for any input file. The

Output Specifications also include the master file descriptions so that updating can take place.

We read each disk record in sequence; when a record is to be updated, we make the changes directly to the record in the master file and *rewrite* it.

The program in Figure 8.11 provides an alternative method for updating a

Figure 8.11
Updating a master file directly
in place.

```
....+....1....+....2....+....3....+....4....+....5....+....6....+....7
0001  ******************************************************************
0002  *
0003  *   PROGRAM DESCRIPTION:
0004  *
0005  *        THIS PROGRAM PERFORMS A SEQUENTIAL UPDATE IN PLACE
0006  *        BY READING TWO FILES, TRANIN AND MASTER,
0007  *        AND UPDATING THE MASTER IN PLACE.
0008  *
0009  *
0010  *   FUNCTION OF INDICATORS:
0011  *
0012  *        61   END-OF-FILE FOR "MASTER"
0013  *
0014  ******************************************************************
0015  *
0016  H
0017  FTRANIN   ID  F     100           DISK
0018  FMASTER   UD  F     100           DISK
0019  *
0020  IMASTER   NS
0021  I                                        1 100 MREC
0022  I                                        1   50MACCTN
0023  I                                     P  6   92MADUE
0024  ITRANIN   NS
0025  I                                        1 100 TREC
0026  I                                        1   50TACCTN
0027  I                                     P  6   92TAMT
0028  I#FLAGS       DS
0029  I                                        1   1 #YES
0030  I                                        2   2 #QUIT
0031  *
0032  *                             MAIN-MODULE-RTN
0033  C                  EXSR SR100
0034  *
0035  C         #QUIT    DOUEQ#YES
0036  C                  EXSR SR200
0037  C                  END
0038  *
0039  *                             SR100-INITIALIZATION-RTN
0040  CSR       SR100    BEGSR
0041  CSR                MOVE '1'       #YES
0042  CSR                EXSR SR600
0043  CSR                EXSR SR700
0044  CSR                ENDSR
0045  *
0046  *                             SR200-COMPARE-ACCOUNT-NUMBERS-RTN
0047  CSR       SR200    BEGSR
0048  CSR       TACCTN   CASEQMACCTN    SR300         TACCTN = MACCTN
0049  CSR       TACCTN   CASGTMACCTN    SR600         TACCTN > MACCTN
0050  CSR                END
0051  CSR                ENDSR
0052  *
0053  *                             SR300-REGULAR-UPDATE-RTN
0054  CSR       SR300    BEGSR
0055  CSR                ADD  TAMT      MADUE
0056  CSR                EXCPT@E100
0057  CSR                EXSR SR600
0058  CSR                EXSR SR700
0059  CSR                ENDSR
0060  *
0061  *                             SR600-READ-MASTER-FILE-RTN
0062  CSR       SR600    BEGSR
0063  CSR                READ MASTER                  61
0064  CSR                ENDSR
0065  *
0066  *                             SR700-READ-TRANSACTION-FILE-RTN
0067  CSR       SR700    BEGSR
0068  CSR                READ TRANIN                  LR
0069  CSR LR             MOVE #YES      #QUIT
0070  CSR                ENDSR
0071  *
0072  OMASTER   E                   @E100
0073  O                             MREC       100
0074  O                             MADUE        9 P
```

sequential master file. This alternative uses the master file both as input and output and *updates* it directly in place. *This program assumes that transaction records will always have a corresponding master record.* Also, it assumes that there is no more than a single transaction record for each master record.

The previous sample sequential file update program in Figure 8.10 has been modified in order that the file can be updated in place. In Figure 8.11 the master file is called MASTER since it is both the input file and output file. Note that when the EXCPT operation is executed it replaces the disk record on the MASTER file that was accessed by the preceding READ operation to the file.

Since we are updating in place it is not possible to make additions to the MASTER file using this procedure. For this procedure, we can only read records in sequence, modify the fields, and write the records back to disk in their original locations. Later, we will see how additions can be made when master records are updated in place.

Creating a Backup File When Updating Sequential Files in Place

Accessing a disk as an update file and rewriting records in place saves us the need for creating an entirely new file, but some caution must be exercised when using this procedure. As noted, since the master file is itself updated, there is no Old-Master available for backup purposes after an update. This means that if the master file gets damaged, there is no way of conveniently recreating it.

When performing a sequential update procedure using an Old-Master input file that is separate from a New-Master output file, we always have the Old-Master as backup in case we cannot use the new master. However, since there is no comparable backup when we update a master file in place, we must make provisions to create a duplicate copy of the master file after the update procedure is performed. This duplicate is called a *backup copy* and is typically stored on tape or diskette. Backup copies should always be kept in a safe place in case something happens to the original.

Normally, the computer operator schedules backup procedures to be run on a regularly scheduled basis. These backup procedures would be run daily, weekly, or monthly depending on the importance of the files being backed up.

A Control Language command procedure is usually used to back up files. These commands, which are hardware dependent, allow a *group of files* to be backed up at one time. This method of backing up files is faster than having a procedure that backs up each file after it has been updated. For example, the inventory files might be backed up every Monday, Wednesday, and Friday, whereas the accounts receivable files might be backed up Tuesday and Thursday. The backup schedule for any file or group of files depends on how important the files are and how much activity each file might have on a daily basis.

E. Adding Records to a Sequential File

Figure 8.11 illustrates how the update procedure is performed on a file specified as an *update file*. In this program, records were rewritten back to the master file in their original place.

We have not considered in our update-in-place program the technique used to add records to a master file. In Figure 8.10, where an input master and an input transaction file were used to create a separate output master, if a transaction record existed for which there was no corresponding master, we were able to add it to the New-Master *in its proper sequence*. This is not, however, possible when rewriting onto a file specified as update on the File Description Specifications form.

Suppose the first two master records have account numbers of 00101 and 00103. If a transaction record with a TACCTN of 00102 is read and is a new account, there is *no physical space* to insert it in its proper place on the master update (input/output) file. That is, it is not feasible to add records in sequence to a sequential file. You cannot "squeeze" them between existing records. Thus, when a file is specified as an update file we can rewrite records to it but *we cannot physically add or insert records* in their correct place in the file.

It is, however, possible to write a separate program to add records to the *end of a sequential file*. If the records to be added contain account numbers greater than the last one currently in the file, then the master file will still be in sequence. If the records to be added have key fields not in sequence at the end of the file, then the master file will need to be sorted before it is processed again.

The program required to specifically add records to an *existing* sequential master file is illustrated in Figure 8.12. In this example, records are read from the NEWDATA file and added to the output file MASTER. The File Description Specifications for the MASTER file contains the letter A in column 66, which

Figure 8.12
Specifications to ADD a new record to an existing sequential file.

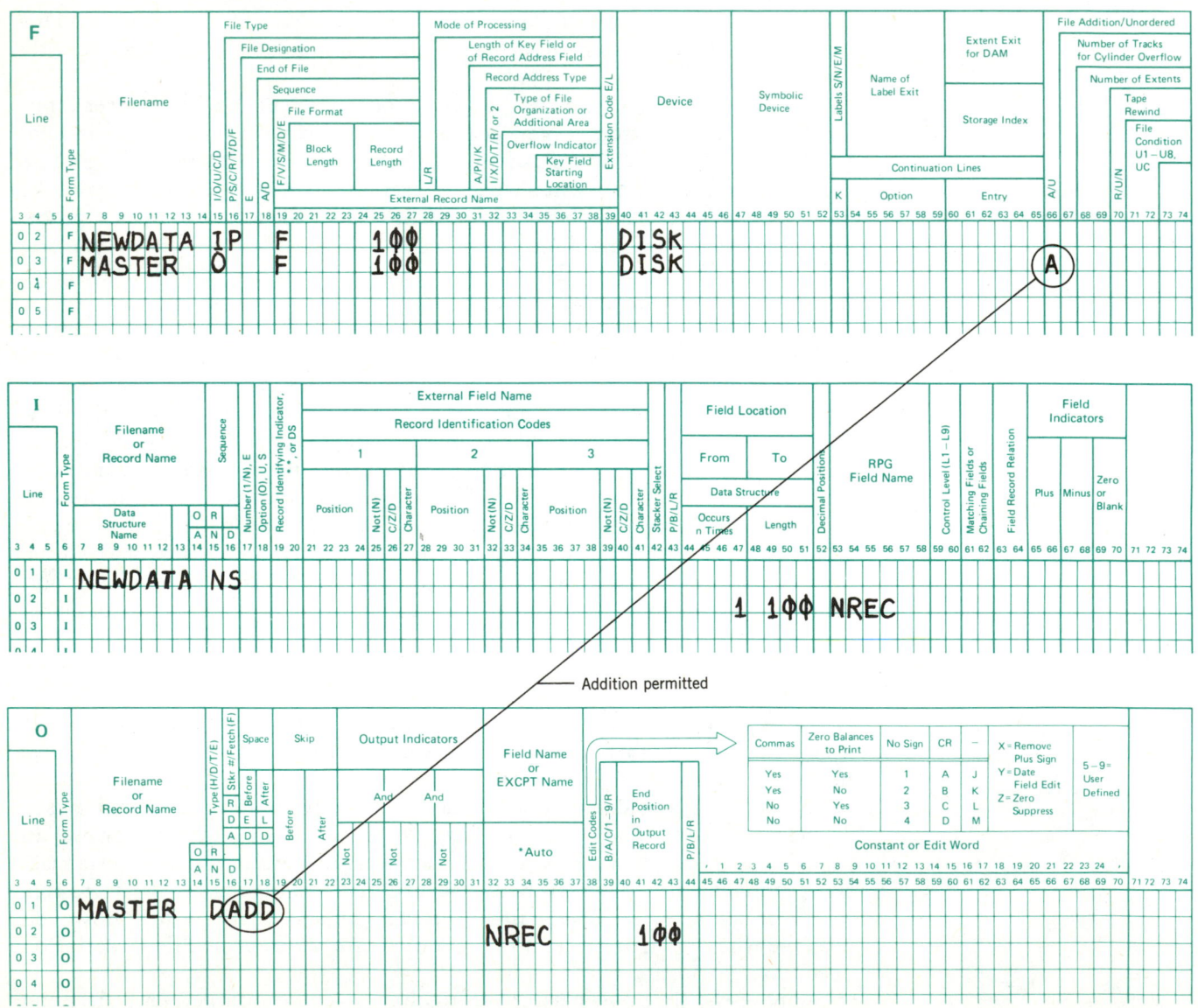

indicates that the file will have records *added* to it by the program. To do so, program control first positions the record pointer at the *end* of the file, immediately after the last record. When records are written to the file, then, they are added to the *end of the file* after all existing records. As noted, if the records that are added are not in sequence (e.g., they do not contain key fields greater than those currently on the master file), the file must be sorted before it is processed again. Thus, if the 00102 TACCTN record is added to the end of the file, the file will need to be sorted so that it is in proper sequence by TACCTN.

The importance of the A in column 66 should be emphasized here. If specified, output records will be *added* at the end of the existing sequential file. If column 66 is blank, however, an entirely new output file will be created.

In the Output Specifications, ADD is specified in columns 16–18 to indicate that each NREC is to be added to the file.

SUMMARY: UPDATING A MASTER FILE IN PLACE

To Update in Place:
1. Define the file as update; specify File Type as U in column 15 of File Description Specifications.
2. Read the master record to be updated and rewrite the record with changes.

To Add Records to a Sequential File:
1. Specify the file as Output (O in column 15 of File Description Specifications).
2. Specify the letter A in column 66 of the File Description Specifications.
3. Specify ADD in columns 16–18 of the Output Specifications of the records to be added.
4. Read the transaction record to be added to the master file.
5. Write the record to the existing master output file.

Self-Test

1. (number) files are used for a sequential file update procedure where a new master is separate from an old master.
2. (number) files are used when a master file is updated in place.
3. When updating a master file in place, the master file must be defined on the File Description Specifications form as a(n) _____ file.
4. When a master file is being updated in place, records (can/cannot) be added to the file.
5. The File Description Specifications form must contain the letter _____ in column _____ when records will be added to the file.
6. The Output Specifications form for a record being added to a file must contain _____ in columns _____.

Solutions

1. Three
2. Two
3. update (U)
4. cannot
5. A, 66
6. ADD, 16–18

V. Sort Utility Procedures

When processing disk files, we frequently wish to access records in a particular sequence. The **Sort Utility** feature of your computer system can be used to accomplish this function.

A. The Sort Utility Program

Utility programs are typically supplied with the operating system to perform specific tasks. The Sort Utility program is an integral part of any computer system's utility programs. The task of the Sort Utility is to sort records into a particular sequence before reading them into a program. To use a Sort Utility, the programmer provides specifications about the data files and how the sort is to be performed. A Sort Utility requires the programmer to indicate the name of the unsorted and sorted files, the characteristics of each file's records, the position and number of key fields, and whether ascending or descending sorting is required. The Sort Utility can provide three basic functions:

1. It can rearrange records into a different sequence.
2. It can include or omit specific records from a file.
3. It can reformat records into a different structure with fields in a different order.

In this section, we will discuss sort procedure concepts in general. We will then illustrate in detail a sort procedure that will select specific records from a file and arrange them into a particular sequence for the printing of a report.

B. Files Used in a Sort Procedure

1. *Input file:* File of unsorted input records.
2. *Work or Sort file:* The file used by the Sort Utility to store records temporarily during the sorting process. The work file prevents loss of records from the original input file if the Sort procedure is not completed properly.
3. *Output file:* File of sorted records.

Work or Sort file (temporary storage)

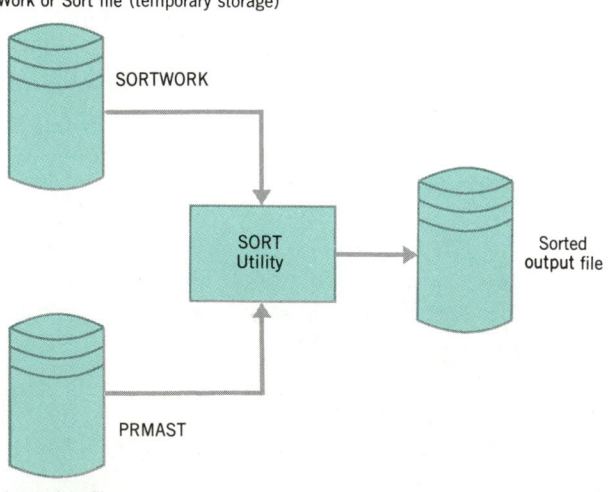

C. Ascending or Descending Key

The programmer must specify the control fields that will be used by the sort program. These are fields in the input file's records that are used to determine the sequence of the output file. Each control field can be identified as an *ascending control field* or a *descending control field*, depending on which sequence is required:

Ascending: From lowest to highest.
Descending: From highest to lowest.

If all control fields are to be sorted in either ascending or descending sequence, one default sequence may be specified in the sort program. That is, the sort sequence specification (either ascending or descending) need only be specified once.

Records may be sorted using either numeric or nonnumeric control fields. Ascending sequence used with an alphabetic field will cause sorting into standard alphabetic order.

Sorting can be performed on more than one control field. We can, for example, sort records into ascending alphabetic name sequence within ascending department sequence:

```
DEPT    NAME
01      Allan
        Brown
        Carter
02      Andrews
        Drake
        Fisher
```

1. Collating Sequence

The two major codes used for representing data in a computer are **EBCDIC,** an abbreviation for Extended Binary Coded Decimal Interchange Code, and **ASCII,** an abbreviation for American Standard Code for Information Interchange.

Most IBM computers that use RPG as a primary language use the EBCDIC code for the internal representation of data.

The sequence of characters from lowest to highest, which is referred to as the **collating sequence,** is slightly different in EBCDIC from the way it appears in ASCII:

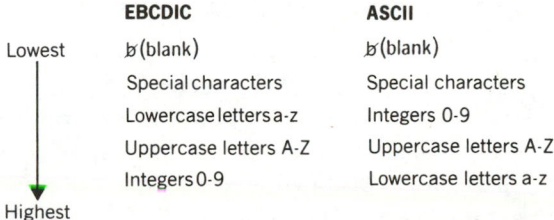

	EBCDIC	ASCII
Lowest	ƀ (blank)	ƀ (blank)
	Special characters	Special characters
	Lowercase letters a-z	Integers 0-9
	Uppercase letters A-Z	Uppercase letters A-Z
Highest	Integers 0-9	Lowercase letters a-z

We have not included the collating sequence for the individual special characters here because we rarely sort on special characters.

Basic numeric sorting and basic alphabetic sorting are performed the same way in both EBCDIC and ASCII. The results of a sort, however, may be somewhat different when alphanumeric fields containing both letters and numbers or special characters are sorted on an ASCII as opposed to an EBCDIC computer. That is, an ASCII computer could produce different sorting from that of an EBCDIC computer if an alphanumeric field is being sorted or if a combination of upper- and lowercase letters is used. "PO Box 891" will appear *before* "891 PO Box" in an address field on EBCDIC computers, for example, but will appear *after* it on ASCII computers. Similarly, "abc" is less than "ABC" on EBCDIC computers, but "abc" is greater than "ABC" on ASCII computers. Thus, when performing alphanumeric sorts or sorts on fields that could contain both upper- and lowercase characters or both letters and digits, you should know what collating sequence is being used.

2. Sorting on More Than One Control Field

As noted, the Sort Utility may be used to sequence records *using more than one control field*. Suppose we wish to sort a payroll file so that it is in ascending alphanumeric sequence by employee number, within each department, for each territory. That is:

Territory is the *major* sort field.
Department is the *intermediate* sort field.
Employee number is the *minor* sort field.

We may use a *single* sort program to perform this sequence. The first control field indicates the *major* field to be sorted; the next control field represents the *intermediate* sort field, followed by the *minor* sort field.

When specifying the sort specifications, a default sequence, either ascending or descending, may be specified for all sort fields. Alternatively, because all control fields are independent, one control field can be sorted in *ascending* sequence while others can be sorted in *descending* sequence.

Two types of output sort files can be produced from the Sort Utility program: Tagalong Sort files and Address Out Sort files. We will explain both types of output sort files next and then provide a sample problem to illustrate the Address Out Sort procedure.

D. Types of Sorts

1. Tagalong Sort

The **Tagalong Sort** procedure produces a new sequential output file after selecting and sorting records from an input file. The output records can contain all of the fields from the input records or just selected fields from the input records being sorted.

When executing a Tagalong Sort you must specify two types of fields:

1. *Control fields.* These are data fields from the input records used by the Sort Utility to sort the records into the required sequence. These fields will determine the sequence or order of the new output file. In addition, these fields will be included in the new sorted records and thus become part of the output file.
2. *Data Fields.* These are fields extracted from the original input records and *included* as part of the new sorted output file. These fields are considered "tagalong" fields because they have no effect on the sort procedure. They are extracted from the original file and are included or tagalong with the new sorted records.

Figure 8.13 illustrates the results of a Tagalong Sort procedure on an Employee master file (PRMAST). In this example, all data fields in the input file are to be included in the new sorted output tagalong file.

When the Tagalong Sort is executed, records from the input file PRMAST are

Figure 8.13
Sample Tagalong Sort
procedure.

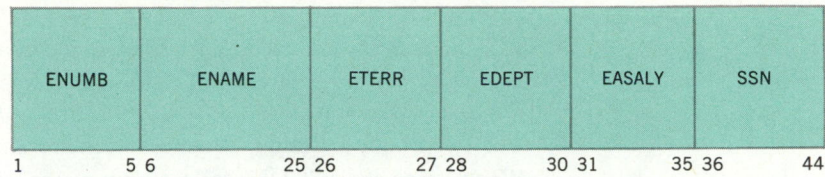

PRMAST Record Layout

ENUMB	ENAME	ETERR	EDEPT	EASALY	SSN

1   5 6   25 26   27 28   30 31   35 36   44

SORTWORK (work file) and TAGSORT (output) Record Layouts

ETERR	EDEPT	ENUMB	ENAME	EASALY	SSN

1   2 3   5 6   10 11   30 31   35 36   44

Control fields are sorted ENUMB within EDEPT within ETERR

Input File (unsorted) — PRMAST	Output File (sorted) — TAGSORT
10245 CONNORS, SANDRA 01 CIS 35000 537954013	01 CIS 00750 WILLIAMS, ROBERT 26000 883562836
00748 PITFIELD, JOHN 01 MKT 29500 774956237	01 CIS 10245 CONNORS, SANDRA 35000 537954013
10567 FARR, KEN 02 CIS 31000 753001384	01 CIS 10586 KERR, HARRY 80000 797253745
00397 PETERS, TED 02 PUR 32000 884673847	01 MKT 00748 PITFIELD, JOHN 29500 774956237
00750 WILLIAMS, ROBERT 01 CIS 26000 883562836	02 CIS 00876 MILLS, BARRY 27000 201738064
00876 MILLS, BARRY 02 CIS 27000 201738064	02 CIS 10567 FARR, KEN 31000 753001384
10022 ROBINSON, JUDY 02 MKT 32500 891423836	02 PUR 00397 PETERS, TED 32000 884673847
10586 KERR, HARRY 01 CIS 80000 797253745	02 MKT 10022 ROBINSON, JUDY 32500 891423836

Note: spaces have been provided between fields for clarity. These spaces do not exist in the record
layout shown above.

read by the Sort Utility. New records are built from the input records using the
control fields (ETERR, EDEPT, and ENUMB) and the data fields specified. The
newly created records are moved to the work area and then sorted into the
sequence ENUMB within EDEPT within ETERR. Therefore, the major control
field is ETERR, the intermediate control field is EDEPT, and the minor control field is ENUMB.

A sequential output file containing records with the control fields and data
fields, in the order specified, is written to disk. This new file can now be used
as a sequential input file to another program.

It should be noted that the record lengths for all three files used in our
sample Tagalong Sort are the same, that is, 44 bytes. The reason for this is that
all data fields from the PRMAST records are going to "tagalong" into the new
sorted file. Since all data fields are required in the new sorted file, the Sort
Utility must include them as part of the procedure. Therefore, in this example,
the Tagalong Sort will produce a new file containing exactly the same data as
the original PRMAST file. However, the fields in the new file will be arranged in
a different order and the records will be sorted into a different sequence within
the file.

Note that outputted records in a Tagalong Sort file need not be the same
length as input records. That is, sometimes fields from the input record are
omitted from the sorted output file.

Self-Test   1. The utility used to arrange records into a particular sequence is the _____
Utility.
2. (T or F) When a file is being sorted, records from the input file can be omitted or
not selected for sorting.

3. The SORT Utility uses a separate _____ file to sort the records into the correct sequence.

4. _____ fields are used to arrange the records into the proper sequence.

5. The sequence of each control field can be specified in _____ or _____ order.

6. The two major collating sequences used are _____ and _____.

7. When using the EBCDIC collating sequence, the value "Box 1059" will be <u>less than/greater than</u> the value "8306 Main Street."

8. When using the EBCDIC collating sequence, the value "marketing dept." will be <u>less than/greater than</u> the value "CIS dept."

9. The _____ Sort produces a new sequential output file that can be processed by an RPG program.

10. Tagalong Sort files contain two types of fields: _____ and _____.

Solutions

1. Sort
2. T
3. work or sort
4. Control
5. ascending; descending
6. EBCDIC; ASCII
7. less than ("B" < "8")—letters are less than numbers
8. less than ("m" < "C")—lowercase letters are less than uppercase letters
9. Tagalong
10. control fields; data fields

2. Address Out Sort

Unlike a Tagalong Sort, an **Address Out Sort** produces a special type of file, called an **ADDROUT file.** An ADDROUT (address Out) file is a *record address file* organized sequentially and used to process records from another file. The contents of the ADDROUT sort file is a series of relative record numbers of all or part of the records contained in the file to be sorted. For the System/36, each record in the ADDROUT file is a three-byte binary field containing the relative record number of the records in the associated file; for the AS/400 it is a four-byte binary field. These relative record numbers indicate the sequence in which the records are to be read from the corresponding disk file in order to obtain a sequential read. There is no actual data included in the ADDROUT file. Rather, it contains the relative location in sequence of every control field selected from the original file.

An ADDROUT file may be used in an RPG program to process a corresponding input or update file that is designated as a primary or secondary file on the File Description Specifications form. During processing of an RPG program, records are read sequentially from the ADDROUT file. The binary relative record number from each record is converted to a disk address that is then used to access the corresponding record from the original input file.

The following is a list of rules for using ADDROUT sort files:

RULES FOR ADDROUT (ADDRESS OUT) SORTS

1. An ADDROUT file is described on the File Description and the Extension Specifications forms.

2. Input Specifications are never used with an ADDROUT file since this file contains only the relative record locations of the records in the actual input file.

3. The corresponding file to be processed by an ADDROUT file must also be specified on the Extension Specifications form.

Tagalong versus **ADDROUT** Sort Files

The major advantage of using an Address Out Sort over a Tagalong Sort is the savings in disk space. The ADDROUT sort produces a file containing only relative record numbers used to access the records from a corresponding file. The record length for an ADDROUT file is either three or four bytes, depending on the computer. The Tagalong Sort, on the other hand, creates a new file containing all or part of the original file. If all data fields are included in the Tagalong Sort, this will double the space required to store both files.

The output file from an Address Out Sort is used in conjunction with an associated file in order to access the required records. This procedure requires the RPG program to read the ADDROUT sort file sequentially and then randomly access the record from the associated input file. Even though this procedure is transparent to the programmer it takes longer for the RPG program to process a file using this method. Tagalong Sorts, however, create a new file that is read directly by the RPG program. But this new file requires more disk space since the Tagalong Sort file is a full or partial copy of the main input file.

E. Processing with an ADDROUT File

To illustrate the use of Address Out (ADDROUT) Sort files, let us consider a sample problem in which we want to produce a Salary Report. Figure 8.14 illustrates the problem definition for our sample problem. For this report, we wish to extract only those employees who work in the Computer Information Services (CIS) department, sort them into the proper sequence, and produce the CIS Salary Report. Before printing the report, the records are to be sorted by

Figure 8.14
Problem definition for an Address Out Sort procedure.

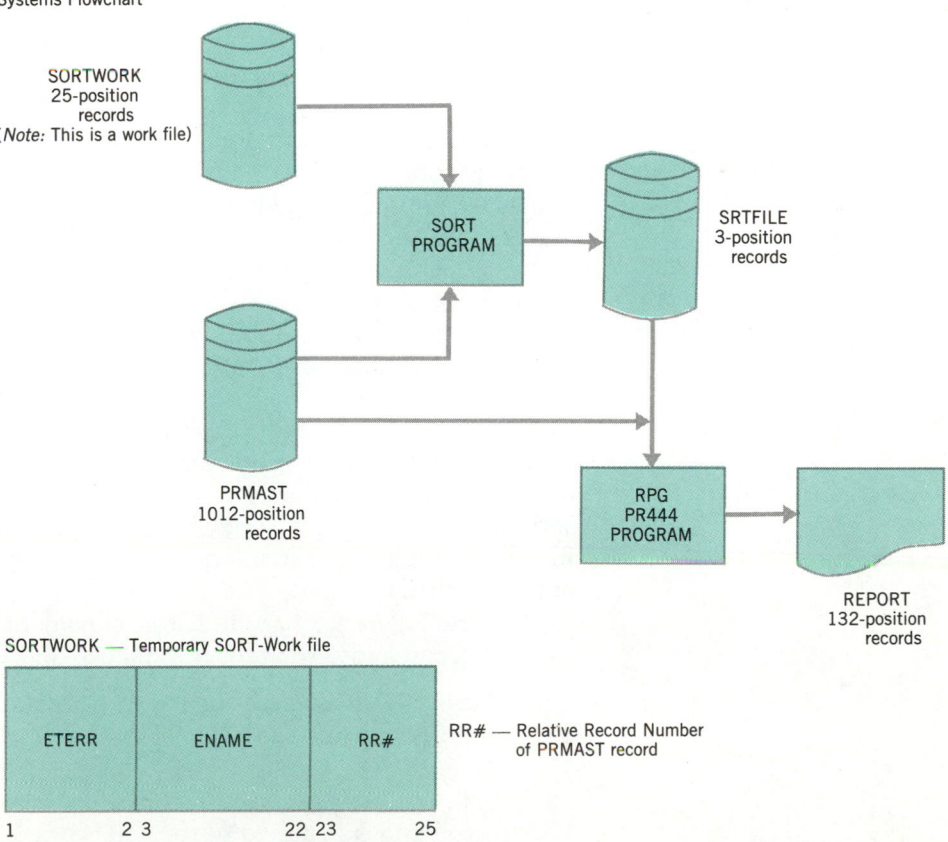

Systems Flowchart

SORTWORK
25-position
records
(*Note:* This is a work file)

SORT PROGRAM

SRTFILE
3-position
records

PRMAST
1012-position
records

RPG
PR444
PROGRAM

REPORT
132-position
records

SORTWORK — Temporary SORT-Work file

ETERR	ENAME	RR#

RR# — Relative Record Number of PRMAST record

1　　2 3　　　22 23　　25

(continued on next page)

Figure 8.14
(continued)

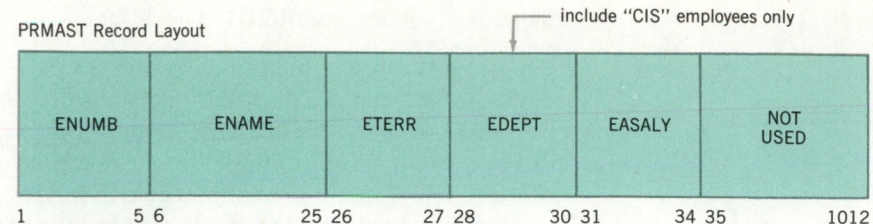

PRMAST Record Layout

include "CIS" employees only

| ENUMB | ENAME | ETERR | EDEPT | EASALY | NOT USED |

1   5 6   25 26   27 28   30 31   34 35   1012

Note: Annual Salary (EASALY) is a packed field containing 7 digits, no decimals

SRTFILE — Address Out Sort file

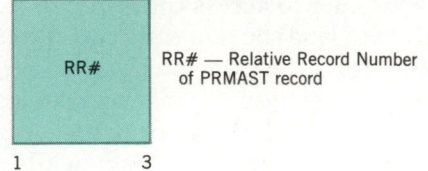

RR#   RR# — Relative Record Number
                of PRMAST record

1   3

CIS Salary Report

PR444	CIS SALARY REPORT	91/01/15	PAGE 1
TERR	NAME		SALARY
01	CONNORS, SANDRA		$35,000
01	KERR, HARRY		$80,000
01	WILLIAMS, ROBERT		$26,000
02	FARR, KEN		$31,000
02	MILLS, BARRY		$27,000

(Records are sequenced by ENAME within ETERR)

ENAME within ETERR (employee name within territory). Thus, ETERR and EDEPT are *control fields* used to determine the output of the sort operation.

CIS people can be identified as having the code "CIS" in the EDEPT field. Therefore, the sort program will include the necessary specifications to select only those records that contain "CIS" in the field EDEPT and sort them by ENAME within ETERR.

When running an Address Out Sort, you specify only the control fields required by the Sort Utility to sort the records into the required sequence. Again, as with the Tagalong Sort, these fields will determine the sequence or order of the control fields in the new ADDROUT file. Remember, data fields are *not* included as part of an ADDROUT sort file. An Address Out Sort file, therefore, uses much less disk space than a Tagalong Sort.

When an Address Out Sort is executed, records are read by the Sort Utility from the input file specified in the sort program. New records are built using only the control fields from the input record and the input record's relative record number. The newly created records are placed into the work area and sorted into the sequence specified by the control fields. The output ADDROUT file, containing only the relative record numbers of the associated input records, is written to disk.

Examine Figure 8.14 again. Let us consider the steps required to select and sort the records into the proper sequence and then print the Salary Report.

1. The Sort Utility reads the PRMAST file and selects or includes only those employees working in the CIS group (EDEPT is equal to "CIS").
2. For each record selected, the control fields (ETERR and ENAME) and the PRMAST record's relative record number are placed into a new temporary record and transferred to the sort work file (SORTWORK).

3. After the Sort Utility has read through the PRMAST file and selected the required records, step one of the sort procedure is complete.

4. The records in the temporary SORTWORK file are sorted into ENAME sequence within ETERR. This completes step 2 of the sort operation.

5. When the sort is finished, the address out file SRTFILE is written to disk. It contains the relative record locations in sequence of all employees in the CIS department by name within territory. Note that it does not contain the records themselves. This completes all phases of the sort procedure.

6. RPG program PR444 is then executed to print the CIS Salary Report in the proper sequence.

7. When program PR444 is executed, the SRTFILE file is read sequentially by ENAME within ETERR. The relative record number from each record is translated into a disk address, which in turn is used to access the associated record from the PRMAST file. Thus, only those "CIS" records necessary from the PRMAST file are read.

8. Once the end-of-file has been reached on the SRTFILE file, the report is complete and the program is terminated.

This sample problem requires two programs. First, a sort program (Sort Specifications) must be coded to select the required records, sort them, and create the necessary record address file (steps 1–5 above).

Next, an RPG program must be written that will read the ADDROUT sort file and the associated PRMAST file and print the CIS Salary Report (steps 6–8 above).

Let us first examine the program specifications required for the sample RPG program that will sequentially process the record address file SRTFILE in order to access the PRMAST file. The program assumes that SRTFILE has already been created and is in the correct sequence. Then, we will briefly consider the sort specifications necessary to create the ADDROUT file for this program.

The File Description Specifications and the Extension Specifications required for our sample program are as follows:

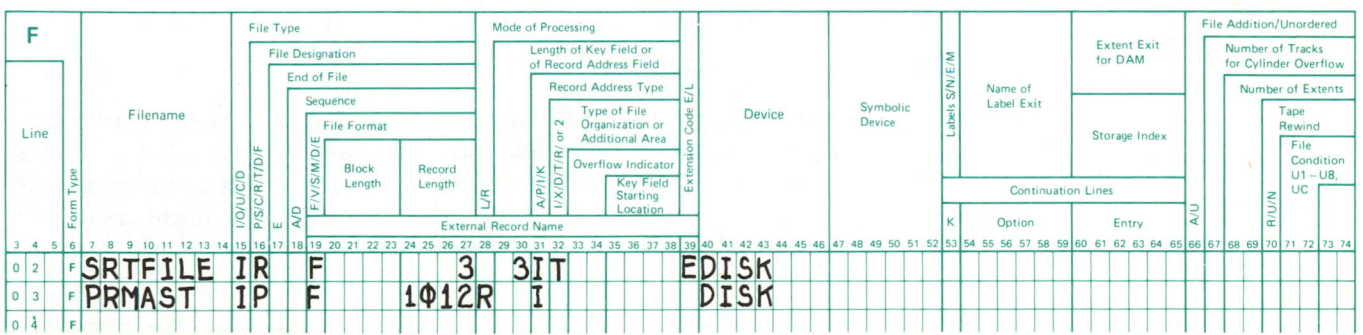

Let us consider the new entries that are required when processing a file with an ADDROUT sort file.

File Description Entries

File Designation (Column 16)

The File Designation field must contain the letter R to designate a file as a *record address file*. An ADDROUT (*Address Out*) sort file is one type of record address file that is organized sequentially and used to process records from an associated file.

Record Length (Columns 24–27)

The Record Length for ADDROUT sort files on the IBM System/36 is 3 bytes, but on the AS/400 the Record Length is 4 bytes. Each record in the SRTFILE file contains the binary relative record number of the corresponding location of the record on the input disk file, PRMAST.

Mode of Processing (Column 28)

The Mode of Processing indicates the method by which records are to be read from the file. In our example, PRMAST is to be read randomly using the address out file SRTFILE. That is, the sequence of PRMAST is not the same sequence used to actually read the file. The letter R is specified when the file is to be read randomly by an ADDROUT file.

Record Address Field (Columns 29–30)

This field contains the length of the relative record numbers in the ADDROUT sort file. For the System/36 this field is always 3; for the AS/400 the length is 4.

Record Address Type (Column 31)

Specify the letter I in this field when the file is an address out file consisting of relative record numbers, or the main input file is to be processed using relative record numbers from an address out file. Both input files in our example, then, require the letter I in column 31.

File Organization (Column 32)

The letter T is specified in column 32 to identify a file as an ADDROUT file.

Extension Code (Column 39)

The letter E in column 39 means that there is an Extension Specification that further describes the file. For an ADDROUT sort file, specifying an E in this column directs RPG to the Extension Specifications where it can identify the corresponding file that will be read using the relative record numbers of this ADDROUT file.

Extension Specifications

From Filename (Columns 11–18)

Columns 11–18 specify the ADDROUT sort file identified on the File Description Specifications. This file contains the relative record numbers that will be used to read records from the file specified in columns 19–26.

To Filename (Columns 19–26)

Columns 19–26 are used to identify the input file to be processed by the relative record address file named in columns 11–18.

Figure 8.15
Sample Sort program.

```
....+....1....+....2....+....3....+....4....+....5....+....6....+....7
0001 *****************************************************************
0002 *
0003 *   PROGRAM DESCRIPTION:
0004 *
0005 *       THIS PROGRAM PRODUCES A SALARY REPORT FOR THE
0006 *       CIS DEPARTMENT.
0007 *       THE PROGRAM READS THE PAYROLL FILE (PRMAST)
0008 *       USING AN ADDRESS OUT SORT FILE (SRTFILE).
0009 *
0010 *
0011 *   FUNCTION OF INDICATORS:
0012 *
0013 *       NONE
0014 *
0015 *****************************************************************
0016 *
0017 H
0018 FSRTFILE IR  F        3  3IT        EDISK
0019 FPRMAST  IP  F     1012R  I         DISK
0020 FREPORT  O   F      132     OF      PRINTER
0021 *
0022 E       SRTFILE PRMAST
0023 *
0024 IPRMAST  NS
0025 I                                          1    5 ENUMB
0026 I                                          6   25 ENAME
0027 I                                         26   27 ETERR
0028 I                                         28   30 EDEPT
0029 I                                    P    31  340EASALY
0030 *
0031 OREPORT  H    02    1P
0032 O        OR         OF
0033 O                                      10 'PR444'
0034 O                                      40 'CIS SALARY REPORT'
0035 O                             UDATE Y   60
0036 O                             PAGE  Z   70
0037 O                                      67 'PAGE'
0038 O        H   104    1P
0039 O        OR         OF
0040 O                                      11 'TERR'
0041 O                                      35 'NAME'
0042 O                                      70 'SALARY'
0043 O        D    1     N1P
0044 O                             ETERR    10
0045 O                             ENAME    50
0046 O                             EASALY1  70 '$'
```

Figure 8.15 illustrates the complete RPG program that will print the CIS Salary Report.

In our sample program, we wanted to select only CIS employees and sort those records in ascending alphanumeric sequence by employee name (ENAME) within territory (ETERR).

We will now briefly consider the System/36 sort specifications required for our sample sort.

F. Sort Utility Requirements

Here, we will consider the sort specifications necessary to create the ADDROUT sort file SRTFILE used in our sample problem. Again, the purpose for the address out file SRTFILE is to include or select only those employees working in the CIS department and to sort them by ENAME within ETERR. Thus, we are using an Address Out sort procedure to access records from the file PRMAST in a sequence different from the one in which PRMAST is stored.

Each type of sort procedure, whether a Tagalong or ADDROUT sort, requires sort specifications relevant to the type of sort specified. As mentioned earlier, these statements would include the specifications about the data files, the control fields to be used for sorting, whether records are to be included or omitted in the sort, and whether the sort is to be performed in ascending or

Figure 8.16
Output from Sort Utility when sample ADDROUT sort procedure was executed.

```
         1    1    2    2    3    3    4    4
     5....0....5....0....5....0....5....0....5

         HSORTA    22A                     $1012
         I C   28  30EQCCIS
         FNC   26  27
         FNC    6  25
SORT-7451 I 1012 bytes- input record length
SORT-7452 I 25 bytes- work file record length
SORT-7453 I 3 bytes- output record length
SORT-7462 I 4 sequence specification statements
SORT-7402 I No errors found
SORT-7401 I Job completed generation phase
SORT-7600 I Initial phase started
SORT-7602 I 782 input records were read in
SORT-7603 I 63 records were selected to be sorted
SORT-7690 I Sort starting final pass
SORT-7691 I Final pass successfully completed
SORT-7692 I 63 sorted records placed on output file
SORT-7901 I Normal end of job
```

descending sequence. Figure 8.16 illustrates the Address Out sort specifications required for our sample problem. In addition, the sequence specifications, diagnostic messages, and program status messages that are produced as a result of running this sort are included. This illustration is not meant to be a detailed explanation of the sort procedure, but rather an introduction to the sort specifications. Refer to your Sort Utility manual for a complete detailed explanation of the sort procedure used on your computer.

The Sort Utility used on IBM mid-range computers consists of three specifications:

1. The Header Specification.
2. The Record Specification.
3. The Field Specification.

You should refer to your Sort Utility manual for a detailed explanation of the various entries on the Header, Record, and Field specifications. Here, we will offer a brief summary of each of the specifications.

1. The Header Specification

Each sort procedure must contain a header specification to identify the type of sort procedure being executed. Moreover, only one header specification is required for each sort job. In addition, not all fields designated on this specification are required for both the Tagalong and Address Out sorts. Thus, the information contained in the header specification will vary with each type of sort. The header specification supplies the following:

1. The type of sort.
2. The total length of all control fields.
3. Whether the sort is to be in ascending or descending order.
4. The length of output records for Tagalong Sorts.
5. The input record length.

The following are coded on the first line in our sample sort in Figure 8.16:

Columns	Entry
6	H identifies this as a header line.
7–12	SORTA identifies this as an ADDROUT sort.

Columns	Entry
13–17	The control fields used to sort the records are ETERR and ENAME. The total length of these fields is 22.
18	The A specifies ascending order. The output records are to be sorted by ENAME within ETERR in ascending order.

2. The Record Specification

The record specification identifies which records from the input file are to be selected for the sort. The record specification indicates records to be *included* in the sort or records to be *omitted* from the sort. In our sample problem, for example, we wish to include and sort only employees working in the CIS department (EDEPT equal to "CIS"). Another example might be to omit all records that can be identified by the inactive code of I.

The following are coded on the second line in our sample sort in Figure 8.16:

Columns	Entry
6	I identifies this as an "include" record specification.
8	The C indicates that a character compare (both zone and digit portion) will be performed on the field EDEPT.
9–12	Identifies the starting position of the EDEPT field within the input record. EDEPT begins in position 28 of the record.
13–16	Identifies the ending position of the EDEPT field within the input record. EDEPT ends in position 30 of the record.
17–18	Defines the "EQ" comparison between the EDEPT field and the constant CIS.
19	C indicates that the field EDEPT is being compared to a constant.
20–27	Identifies the constant CIS

3. The Field Specification

The field specification is used to specify the format of the records in the output file. A field specification is specified for each field and supplies the following information:

1. The control fields that will be used by the sort utility to determine the order of the output records.

   For Tagalong Sorts only, the individual data fields that are to be included as part of the new sorted output records.
   When specifying the control and data fields on the field specifications, the beginning and ending locations of the fields within the input records.

2. The sort sequence, that is, ascending or descending, can be specified for each field.

The following are coded on lines 3 and 4 in our sample sort in Figure 8.16:

Columns	Entry
6	F identifies this as a field specification line.
7	The N defines this field as a normal control field.
8	C indicates that the zone and digit portions of all characters in all fields are used as they appear in the input records.
9–16	Specifies the location of the fields in the input record.

CHAPTER SELF-TEST

1. Two methods of random access file organization, called _____ and _____, enable a disk file to be accessed randomly as well as sequentially.

2. (T or F) Updating a sequential master file is typically done using interactive processing.

3. (T or F) The TESTN operation is used to validate that the contents of an alphanumeric field does, in fact, contain numeric data.

4. A (Demand file/Full Procedural file) is a disk file that must be processed sequentially regardless of the file's disk organization.

5. The READ operation, when used with Demand or Full Procedural files, must contain an indicator in columns _____ to indicate _____.

6. (T or F) Sequential master files can be updated using a method where the records to be updated on the master file are written in place.

7. The files used in a sort procedure are: _____, _____, and _____.

8. (T or F) Basic numeric sorting and basic alphabetic sorting are performed the same way in both EBCDIC and ASCII.

9. A (Tagalong Sort/Address Out Sort) produces a new sequential output file after selecting and sorting records from an input file.

10. (T or F) If records are to be added to a sequential file, specify ADD in the File Description Specifications.

SOLUTIONS

1. indexed; direct
2. F—Batch processing is used.
3. T
4. Demand file
5. 58–59; end-of-file
6. T
7. the input file; the work or sort file; the output file
8. T—Note, however, that (1) lowercase letters are less than uppercase letters in EBCDIC, while uppercase letters are less than lowercase letters in ASCII, and (2) letters are less than numbers in EBCDIC whereas the reverse is true in ASCII.
9. Tagalong Sort
10. F—Specify ADD in columns 16–18 of the Output Specifications of the records to be added.

KEY TERMS

ADDROUT file	Demand file	Key field	Sequential access
Address Out Sort	Direct file	Limit test	Sequential file
ASCII	EBCDIC	Master file	Sequential processing
Audit trail	Edit procedure	Missing data test	Sort Utility
Batch processing	Flag	Random access	Switch
Class test	Full Procedural file	Range test	Tagalong Sort
Coded field test	Hashing technique	READ operation	TESTN operation
Collating sequence	Indexed file	Relative record number	Transaction file
Control listing	Interactive processing	Sequence test	Update procedure
Data validation			

REVIEW QUESTIONS

1. What are the major types of file organization?
2. Explain what occurs when an indexed file is created.
3. What files are involved when a sequential file is updated?
4. Explain how the TESTN operation can be used to validate data.
5. When should data be validated and what should be done if errors occur?
6. What are the differences between Demand files and Full Procedural files?
7. What is meant by the collating sequence of a computer?
8. What are the differences between a Tagalong Sort and an Address Out Sort?

PROGRAMMING ASSIGNMENTS

Use Data Structures for work fields. Use prefixes for input, output, and work fields. Use SETON and SETOF where appropriate.

1. Using the problem definition shown below, code an RPG program to produce the required results. The RPG program should match the professor and course files in order to produce the output depicted on the Printer Spacing Chart:

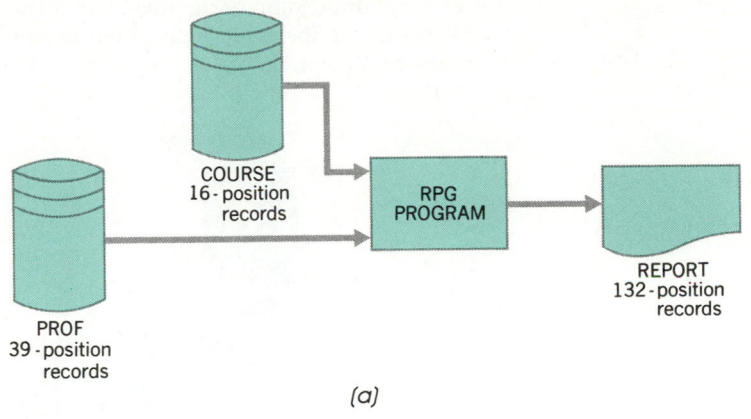

(a)

PROF Record Layout

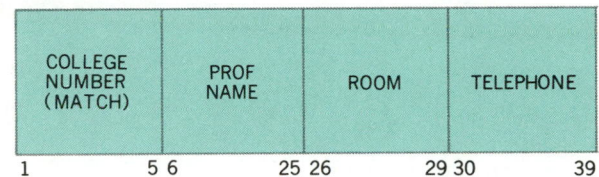

COURSE Record Layout

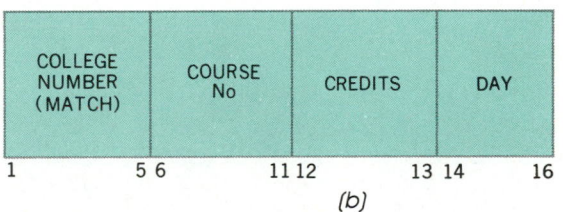

(b)

REPORT Printer Spacing Chart

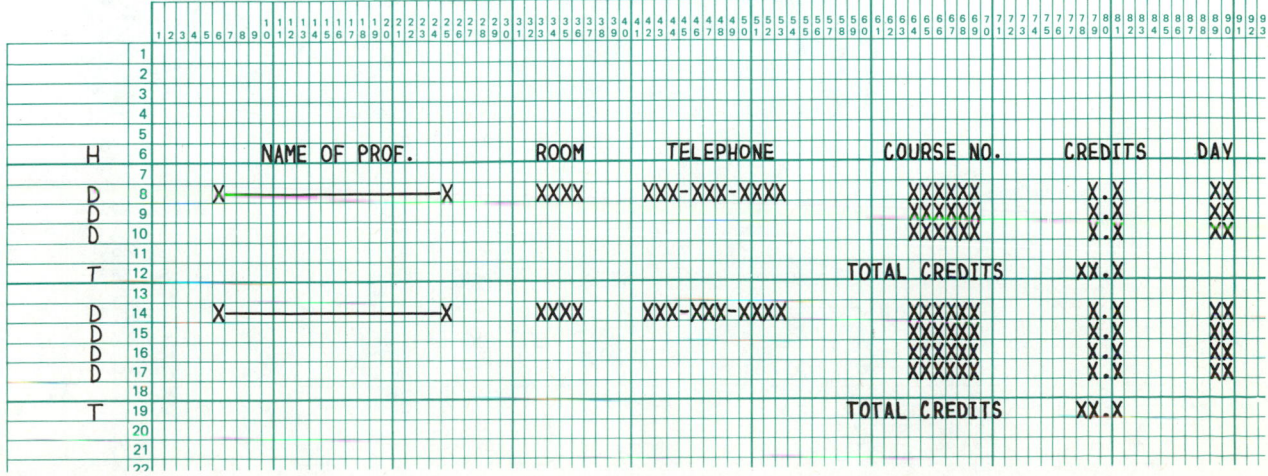

(c)

2. Using the problem definition shown below, code an RPG program to produce the required results. This program requires the Master file to be updated by the HOURS records and CLIST to be printed. All USED fields in the Master file are initialized to zero. The fields containing the hours LEFT in the master are all initialized to 40. The vacation, sick, and personal hours appearing in the HOURS file are used to update the corresponding hours in the master. For example, if the sick hours field of the HOURS file contained the value eight, then we would add this value to the SICK HOURS USED of the MASTER. In addition, the eight sick hours would be subtracted from the SICK HOURS LEFT of the MASTER:

Systems Flowchart

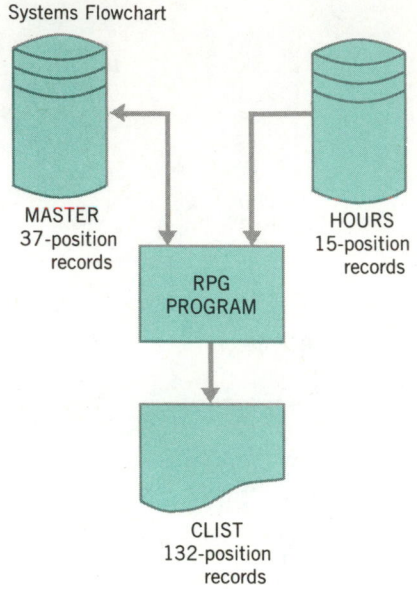

HOURS Record Layout

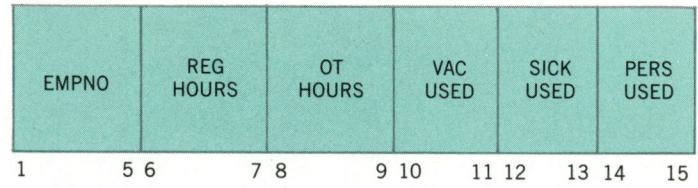

EMPNO	REG HOURS	OT HOURS	VAC USED	SICK USED	PERS USED
1 5	6 7	8 9	10 11	12 13	14 15

MASTER Record Layout

EMPNO	NAME	VAC USED	VAC LEFT	SICK USED	SICK LEFT	PERS USED	PERS LEFT
1 5	6 25	26 27	28 29	30 31	32 33	34 35	36 37

CLIST Printer Spacing Chart

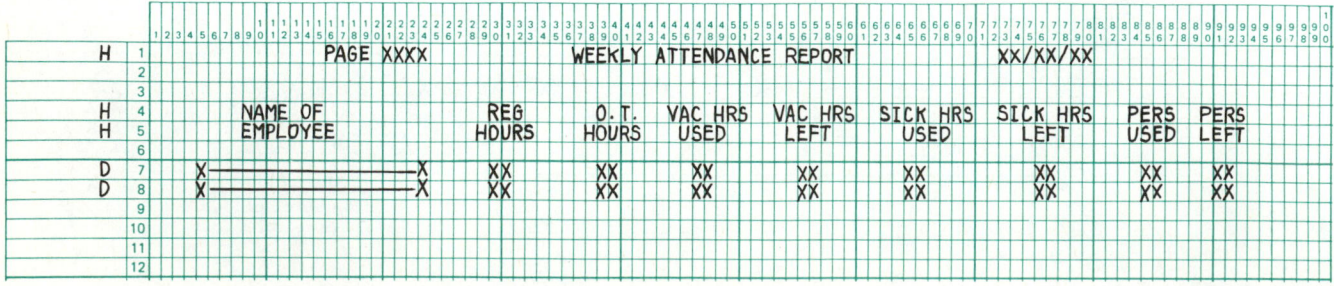

3. Using the problem definition shown below, code an RPG program to produce the required results. This program requires the Master file to be updated by the CHANGE records and CLIST to be printed. A change code of 1 denotes a change in annual salary, while a 2 indicates a change in address. When both a change of address and annual salary are required, a code of 3 is used. Once the Master has been updated, display the contents of the file and validate that all changes have been correctly made.

Systems Flowchart

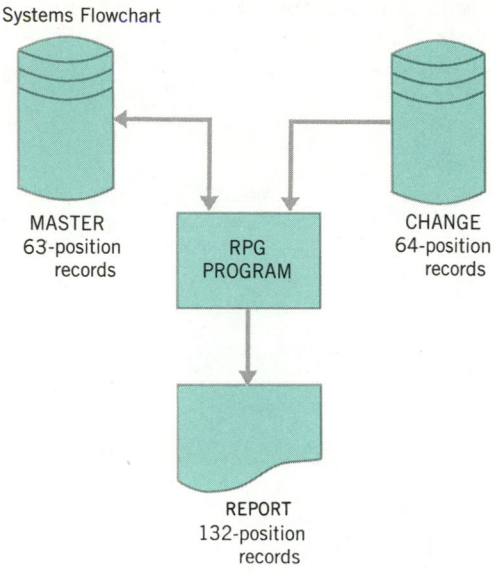

MASTER
63-position
records

RPG
PROGRAM

CHANGE
64-position
records

REPORT
132-position
records

CHANGE Record Layout

EMPNO	NAME	(code=1) NEW ANNUAL SALARY $:¢	(code=2) NO & STREET ADDRESS	(code=2) TOWN OR CITY	CHANGE CODE
1 5	6 25	26 33	34 48	49 63	↑ 64

1—change salary
2—change street/city
3—change both

MASTER Record Layout

EMPNO	NAME	NO & STREET ADDRESS	TOWN OR CITY	ANNUAL SALARY
1 5	6 25	26 40	41 55	56 63

REPORT Printer Spacing Chart

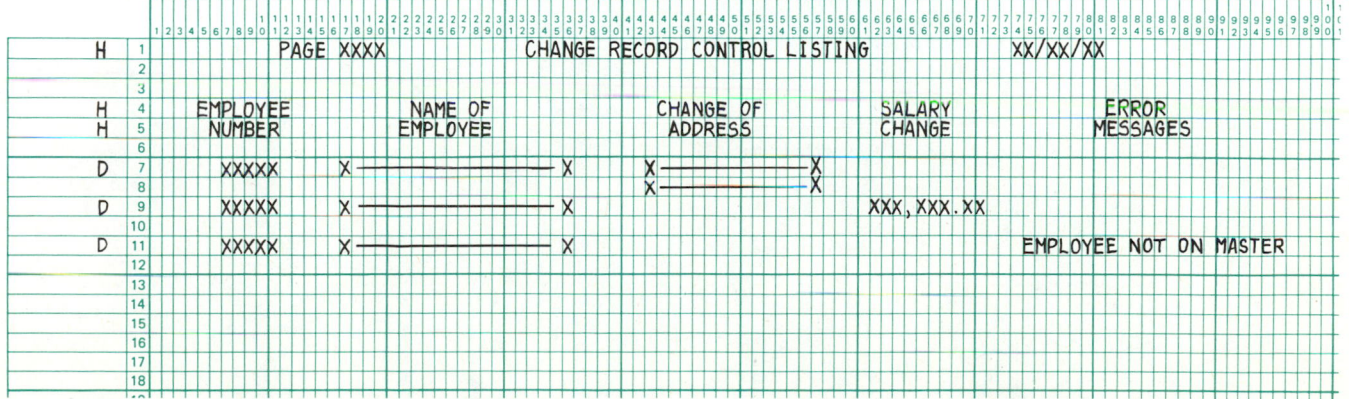

4. Using the problem definition shown below, code an RPG program to produce the required results. This program creates an updated master file called NEWMSTR using the transaction file TRANSIN, and the master file MASTER, as input. When the change code in the TRANSIN record contains the letter "A", the transaction record is to be added to the MASTER file. Similarly, a "D" is used for deleting records from the file and "C" denotes a change or update to the MASTER file. For changes, the PAYMENT is subtracted from the OLD BALANCE to produce the NEW BALANCE. The output listing, PRNTOUT, is depicted in the Printer Spacing Chart. Once the MASTER has been updated, display the contents of the file and validate that all changes have been correctly made.

Systems Flowchart

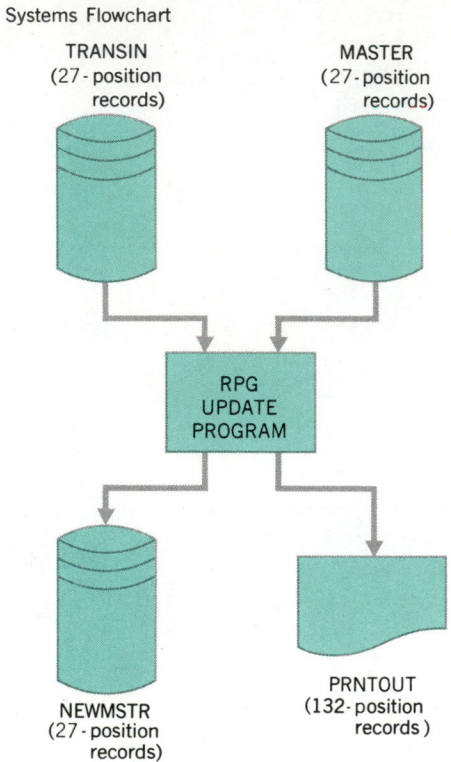

TRANSIN Record Layout (Additions)

CODE	CUSTNO	CNAME	NEW BALANCE $ ¢

| 1 | 2   5 | 6   21 | 22   27 |

CODE = A: add record to MASTER
       D: delete record from MASTER
       C: update balance

TRANSIN Record Layout (Changes and Deletions)

CODE	CUST#	PAYMENT $ ¢	NOT USED
1	2 5	6 11	12 27

MASTER Record Layout

"M"	MCUST#	MNAME	MBALNCE $ ¢
1	2 5	6 21	22 27

M in first position denotes MASTER file.

PRNTOUT Printer Spacing Chart

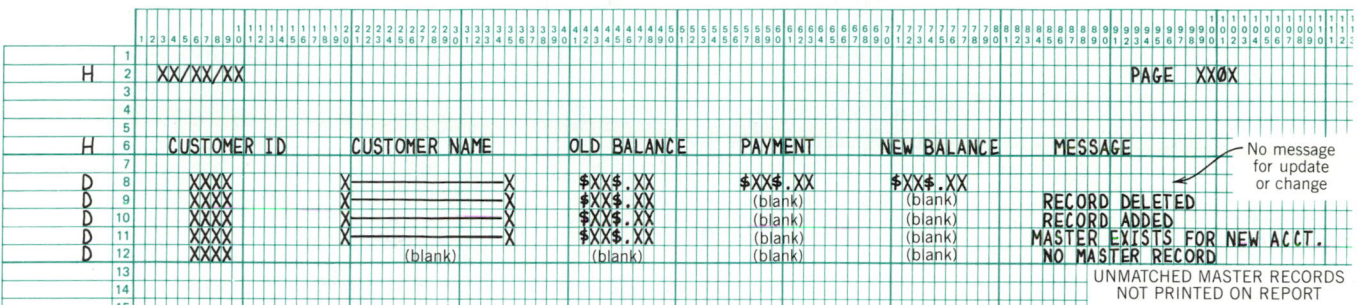

9

Indexed File Processing

OBJECTIVES

To familiarize you with

1. Methods used to create and update indexed files.
2. Different ways of accessing indexed files.
3. How dynamic processing of an indexed file can be accomplished in RPG.

I. An Introduction to Indexed File Processing

Thus far, our programs have used sequential disk files that serve as input to or output from a computer program. In this chapter, we focus on indexed files that are organized so that an index may be used for directly accessing records.

A. An Overview of Indexed File Processing

In a *sequential file*, the physical sequence of records is the same as that in which the records were written to the file and read from the file. Normally, this is in ascending or descending sequence by a particular field within the records. This field, sometimes called the key field, is used to sort the sequential records into the proper sequence before placing them into the file. A given record can be accessed *only* by first accessing all records that physically precede it. That is, to read the 887th record in a sequential file, you must read past the first 886 records.

With **indexed files,** records are also stored in physical sequence according to a particular field also called the **key field.** The key field is used to establish an indexed file, which contains each key field and the disk address of the record with that key field.

Unlike a sequential file, the key field of an indexed file is used to directly retrieve records from the file. As shown below, a key field is a field within the record that is used to identify that record in the indexed file. In this illustration of a Product master file, the product code (PMCODE) field is labeled as the key field that will be used to identify each record. The key field for an indexed file must always be in the same location within each record of the file.

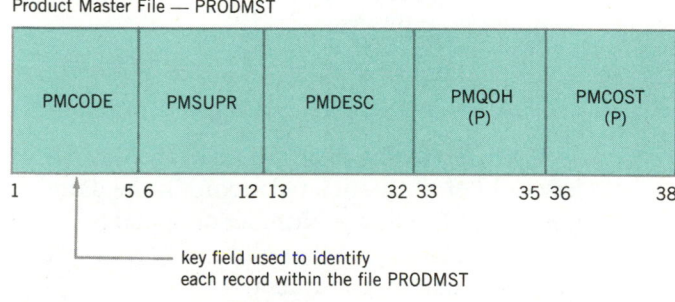

Record Layout for
Product Master File — PRODMST

| PMCODE | PMSUPR | PMDESC | PMQOH (P) | PMCOST (P) |

1   5 6   12 13   32 33   35 36   38

key field used to identify
each record within the file PRODMST

Note: (P) denotes a packed field

Unlike a sequential file, an indexed file when created actually establishes two files on disk: the data file and a separate key file or index that contains the key field and the physical disk address of the record with that key field. (See Figure 9.1.)

When an indexed file is created, the data file is established on disk and contains the physical data records stored in the sequence in which they were written to the file.

When creating an indexed file, the programmer must designate one field that *uniquely* identifies each record. This key field, called the **primary key,** becomes part of the index and can be used to randomly access individual records without accessing other records. In Figure 9.1, PMCODE would be specified as the primary key for the file since it can be used to uniquely identify each record.

Figure 9.1

A data file and a separate key file are established when an indexed file is created.

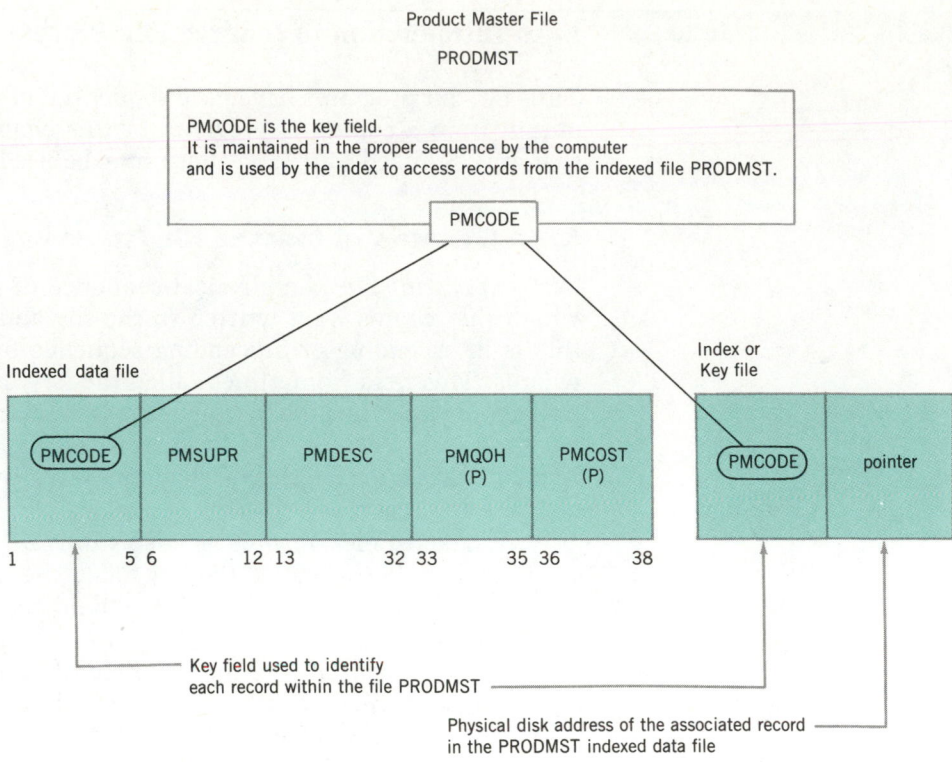

Product Master File

PRODMST

PMCODE is the key field.
It is maintained in the proper sequence by the computer
and is used by the index to access records from the indexed file PRODMST.

PMCODE

Indexed data file

| PMCODE | PMSUPR | PMDESC | PMQOH (P) | PMCOST (P) |

1   5 6   12 13   32 33   35 36   38

Index or Key file

| PMCODE | pointer |

Key field used to identify
each record within the file PRODMST

Physical disk address of the associated record
in the PRODMST indexed data file

Note: (P) denotes a packed field

As noted, when an indexed file is created, a **key file** or **index** is created separate from the data file. As shown in Figure 9.1, each record in the key file or index contains two fields:

1. The key field.
2. A pointer to the associated data record in the indexed data file.

The first field in each record of the key file or index contains the value of the key field of the associated record in the data file. For a payroll file, the key field may be an Employee Number or Social Security Number; for an inventory file, the key field may be Part Number; for an accounts receivable file, the key field may be Customer Number.

The second field, the **pointer,** is a field containing the location (actual physical disk address) of the record in the data file that is identified by the key field.

When records are added to an indexed file, they are added to the end of the data file. At the same time, the key file or index is updated with a record containing the key field and the record address of that record in the data file. With some computer systems, after the record is added to the key file or index, the key file is sorted into its correct sequence using the key field. With other systems, sorting of the key file is not necessary since the key field is placed in its correct location when a record is added to the indexed file. In either case, the key file is always maintained in the proper order by key field regardless of the physical location of the disk records in the data file.

Thus the computer establishes a key file or index on the disk in the sequence of the key field that keeps track of where each record in the data file is physically located. The computer stores in the key file or index the key field and the actual disk address where the corresponding record is located. This allows indexed files to be accessed at random without accessing other records by looking up the address of a record from the index and going directly to that address or disk location for the desired record. In addition, the indexed file may also be accessed sequentially in the sequence of the key file or index.

As noted, the records in the key file are stored and maintained in sequence according to the key field. During processing, record retrieval from the indexed file is performed by the computer system using the key file in a procedure that is *completely transparent* to the program. The data file and the key file or index may be thought of as one file.

If, at some time, you wish to access any record randomly, the computer locates the address of the data record from the key file and goes directly to that location to find the record. The index, then, operates exactly like a book index. To locate data, you "look up" the address in the index rather than sequentially reading each "page" looking for the required topic.

The key field may be located anywhere within the record and may vary in length from one byte to a maximum of 255 bytes. In addition, the key field may be either numeric or alphanumeric.

As stated earlier, every indexed file must be identified by one unique key field called the *primary key*. This primary key is never permitted to have duplicate values. Two Product records on the file with a product code of 10725, for example, would not be allowed.

Indexed files, however, can be created with multiple key fields, used to create alternate indexes. Thus, an indexed file can have more than one key field for randomly accessing records:

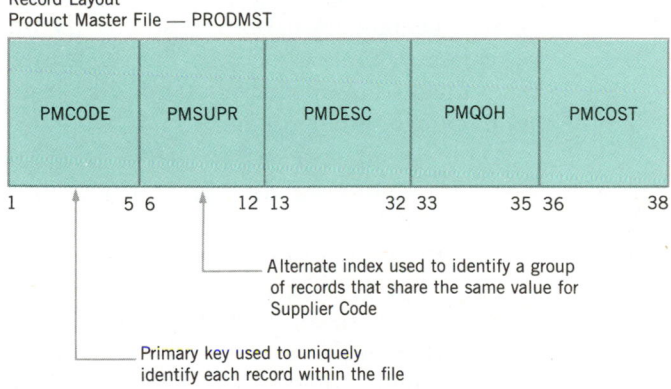

Record Layout
Product Master File — PRODMST

An **alternate key** is a field within the record that could uniquely identify the record (e.g., product name). Normally, however, an alternate key does not uniquely identify a record but identifies a number of records in a group that share the same value (e.g., supplier, dept no, etc.).

When alternate keys are established, a separate key file or index is created on disk for each alternate key specified. Each alternate key file is organized like the original primary key file, but reflects a different key field within the record and thus a different sequence. Records can be randomly accessed either by the primary key or an alternate key.

Alternate indexes allow duplication of the same value within the same alternate key field and thus provide the ability to access the indexed file in different ways. For example, PMCODE can be a primary key to uniquely identify each record, whereas the supplier code field PMSUPR can be an alternate index used to identify a group of records belonging to the same supplier:

Alternate Key   **Physical Disk Address**

Supplier 1
⎧ _____
⎨ _____
⎩ _____

Supplier 2
⎧ _____
⎩ _____

With such an alternate index, you can easily select all records related to Supplier 1, then all records related to Supplier 2, and so on.

This provides a major advantage when processing indexed files in that you do not need multiple copies of the same data organized in different sequences. Thus, if an indexed file has been created with two keys, Product Code (PMCODE) as the primary key and Supplier Code (PMSUPR) as the alternate key, it is possible to access a record directly from the file if the user knows either the Product Code or the Supplier Code. Moreover, all records for a given supplier can be accessed directly and quickly without the need for a Sort or sequential read.

A field that may not be unique, such as Supplier Code, can be used as an alternate key field but not as a primary key field because primary keys must be unique.

Indexed files, then, are created sequentially with each record placed on the file as it is read in. When the indexed file is created, the key file or index is also created associating actual disk addresses to each record's index. After the indexed file has been created, it may be accessed or updated randomly or sequentially, as the need arises. Indexed files can be summarized as follows:

1. Indexed files can be processed *either sequentially or randomly*; they can also be processed *both* sequentially and randomly at the same time (called *dynamic processing*) in the same program. That is, you may want to update an indexed file randomly and then print a report sequentially, all in the same program.

2. New records can be inserted into an indexed file and processed either randomly or sequentially. This is accomplished by the computer adding the necessary data to the key file or index and then sorting the key file into the proper sequence using the key field of the indexed file. Again, the processing of the indexed file either randomly or sequentially is transparent to the program. When reading data, you need only supply the key field and the computer will locate the corresponding record.

    Sequential files, on the other hand, do not allow additions between existing records unless a complete sequential update procedure is performed or records are added to the end of the file and the file is then sorted.

3. For interactive applications, indexed files offer faster access for record retrieval.

4. Indexed files can be created with alternate indexes in addition to the primary index. These alternate indexes allow duplicate values and provide the ability to access the file in different ways. With alternate indexes, then, any field can serve as a key field or index. For example, it is possible to access all records directly with PMSUPR equal to 0067702, where PMSUPR or Supplier Code is an alternate index. In this case, PMSUPR need not be a unique field since several records could have the same supplier. Only primary key fields need to be unique.

After a discussion of general procedures required for indexed file processing, this chapter will present applications of indexed processing in detail.

B. Methods Used to Create Indexed Files

Once a programmer or systems analyst decides what data is required in an indexed file, the method used to build or create the file must be determined. The following two methods can be used to create an indexed file:

1. Using a Control Language Command
2. Using an RPG Program

The operating system is the interface between application programs and the hardware or computer systems on which the programs are to be run. Programmers communicate directly with the operating system by issuing **control language commands,** which the operating system executes. One such command enables programmers to build or create a data file. Using a control language command is the most common method for creating a disk file. However, before control languages were available for this purpose, programmers had to build data files using computer programs.

Using a computer program rather than a control language command to create a file requires much more time and effort. Also, since the program would be operational only once, during file creation, this process wastes programming effort.

Control language, on the other hand, is much faster and can produce the same results in a matter of minutes. Depending on the particular computer system, the command is issued to the operating system along with the necessary file information. The operating system responds by creating an empty indexed file. In other words, disk space is initially reserved or allocated for the file by the control language command and records are added later using an RPG program. See Appendix A for a description of how the System/36 procedure BLDFILE can be used to create files.

The difference between the two methods, then, is *when* records are placed in the file. When building a file from an RPG program, the file is created on disk and the initial records are usually loaded into the file at the time it is created. With a control language command, however, the file format is established on disk without any records being placed in the file. The records will be added later using an RPG program.

Regardless of how an indexed file is created initially, it can be updated or kept current using a file maintenance program that will add, change, and delete records in the file.

Even though the control language method is the more widely used for creating indexed files, it is hardware dependent. That is, the command that you would issue to build an indexed file would depend on the computer system you are working on. For this reason, we will not illustrate the different commands that could be used to create an indexed file on disk. Instead, you should obtain the necessary information to perform this function from your computer center.

For our purposes, we will illustrate the programming required to create an indexed file as output using an RPG program. This procedure is not hardware dependent.

C. Creating an Indexed File Using an RPG Program

Consider the situation in which you have a sequential transaction file that you wish to use to create a new Product indexed file so that you can access records randomly. Consider the following illustration of the record layouts and systems flowchart indicating the processing required for creating the new indexed Product file (PRODMST) from the existing sequential transaction file (PTTRAN).

Systems Flowchart

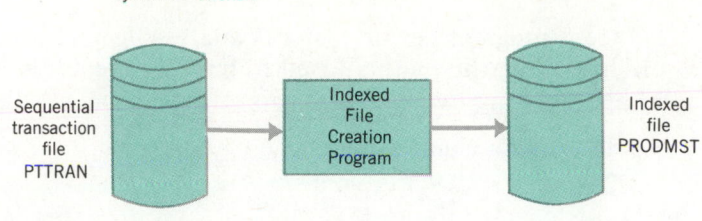

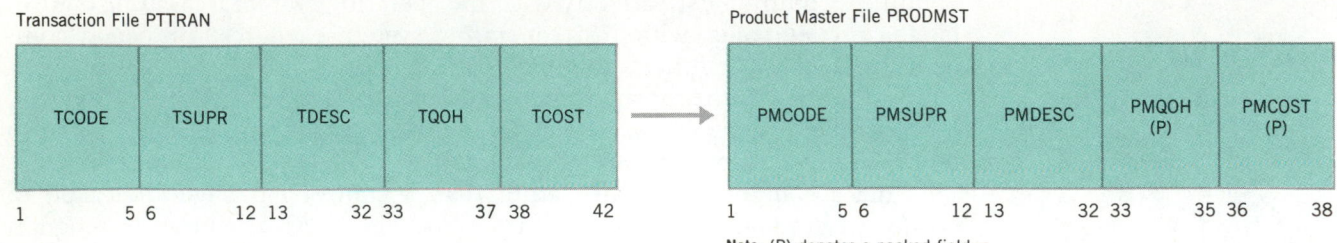

Transaction File PTTRAN				
TCODE	TSUPR	TDESC	TQOH	TCOST

1   5 6   12 13   32 33   37 38   42

Product Master File PRODMST				
PMCODE	PMSUPR	PMDESC	PMQOH (P)	PMCOST (P)

1   5 6   12 13   32 33   35 36   38

Note: (P) denotes a packed field

Indexed files are typically created *in sequence* by key field; that is, the indexed file is created by reading each record from the transaction file (PTTRAN) in sequence by a field designated as the key field, TCODE in our example. The output indexed records are written to PRODMST *in the same sequence*. Thus, creating an indexed file is performed in the same manner as creating a sequential file, with some minor differences. We will explore those differences as well as illustrate some of the techniques that may be used to process indexed files. Note that when an indexed file is created, the corresponding key file or index must also be created for future random access of the file.

Depending on the programming application, it might be necessary to edit or validate the data from the sequential file before writing the records to the new indexed file. We have already seen in Chapter 8 several techniques used to validate data. In our program illustrations in this chapter we will concentrate entirely on indexed file processing and assume that data has already been validated. (This will be done in order to clearly demonstrate indexed file concepts without confusing them with other programming procedures.) Thus, the *validated* input used to create the indexed file PRODMST will come directly from the sequential file PTTRAN, where we assume that PTTRAN has already been validated.

In our example, then, the master indexed file PRODMST will consist of all records from the transaction file PTTRAN, since PTTRAN consists of only valid records. The computer would also establish a *key file* or index using the PMCODE field on the indexed file as the primary key field. Recall that the primary key is a unique field on the record that identifies the record to the system. Once the RPG program designates the key field and indicates that the output file is an indexed file, the program will *automatically* create the indexed file and its corresponding index.

The File Description Specifications for creating an indexed file are similar to creating a sequential file except that the computer system requires some additional information pertaining to the field designated as the key field. The information necessary to identify the file as an indexed file includes the key field's attributes, such as length, location in the record, and field type. The name of the key field itself is specified on the Input Specifications form.

Let us examine the File Description Specifications necessary to create the PRODMST indexed file as output from a program.

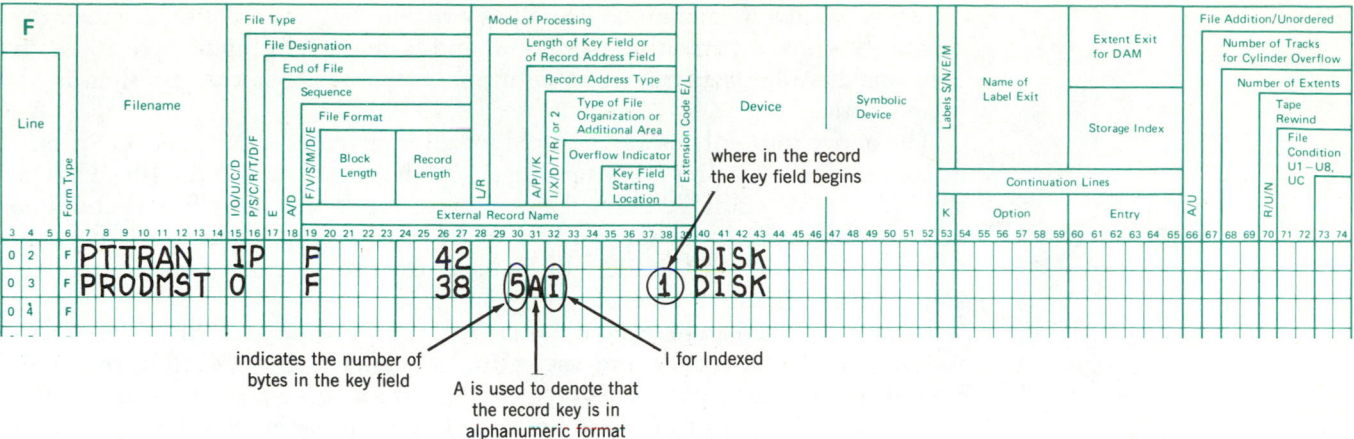

Figure 9.2
The four components required
for defining an indexed file.

D. The File Description Specifications Form for Creating Indexed Files

Examine Figure 9.2. The File Description Specifications for the sequential file PTTRAN are identical to previous program examples. The File Description Specifications for the new indexed file PRODMST, however, contains additional information not previously discussed. To define the file as an indexed file, the key field must be specified in order for the computer to establish an index. The following are the four primary entries needed to define an indexed file:

Columns 29–30 (Length of Key Field)

This specifies the length or number of bytes of the field designated as the key field. The length must be right-justified in this field and leading zeros can be omitted.

Column 31 (Record Address Type)

Column 31 applies to indexed files or ADDROUT sort files (see Chapter 8). For indexed files, column 31 contains one of the following:

A indicates that the key to the file is alphanumeric. This is the normal entry.
P indicates that the key is packed. Packing index keys is not recommended.

Thus, key fields are usually alphanumeric. We will, therefore, illustrate alphanumeric indexes in our program examples.

Column 32 (Type of File Organization)

For indexed files, column 32 contains an I to identify the file as indexed.

Columns 35–38 (Key Field Starting Location)

The starting location of the key field within the record is specified in columns 35–38. It must be right-justified on the form and leading zeros can be omitted. When indexed files are designed, the key field is normally the first field of the record, although this is not required. Therefore, the entry in columns 35–38 is usually 1, as shown in Figure 9.2. This means that the starting location of the key field, which is PMCODE, begins in position 1 of the record. The key field can, however, appear anywhere in the record.

In our example, then, the file is indexed as stated by the letter I in column

32 (Type of File Organization). The file's key field begins in the first byte of the record (there is a 1 in columns 35–38) and is five bytes long (there is a 5 in columns 29–30). The letter A in column 31 denotes that the key field is alphanumeric.

The above four entries are required for all indexed File Description Specifications regardless of the type of processing to be performed on the file. That is, the indexed file could be defined as either an input or output file; it could be accessed sequentially or randomly or both in a given program. Regardless of the method in which the file will be used, the four primary components described above must be present.

Normally, when an indexed file is created from a sequential file, the sequential file would be sorted into ascending sequence using the field that will become the key field on the new indexed file. If for some reason the sequential file is not in sequence by the key field, the letter U must be specified in column 66 of the File Description Specifications form for the indexed file to tell the computer that the keys used to build the index will be *unordered*. This is rarely the case, however, since most, if not all, files are sorted into key field sequence. The operating system's Sort Utility is typically used for this purpose. In our examples, therefore, we will assume that transaction files are sorted into proper key field sequence before creating an indexed file.

Let us continue with our indexed file creation example by considering the Input and Output Specifications.

In a simple application where the records in an indexed file are to be exactly the same length and contain the same data types as the sequential records, the entire sequential record can be defined as one long field on the Input Specifications and similarly written to the indexed file as one field.

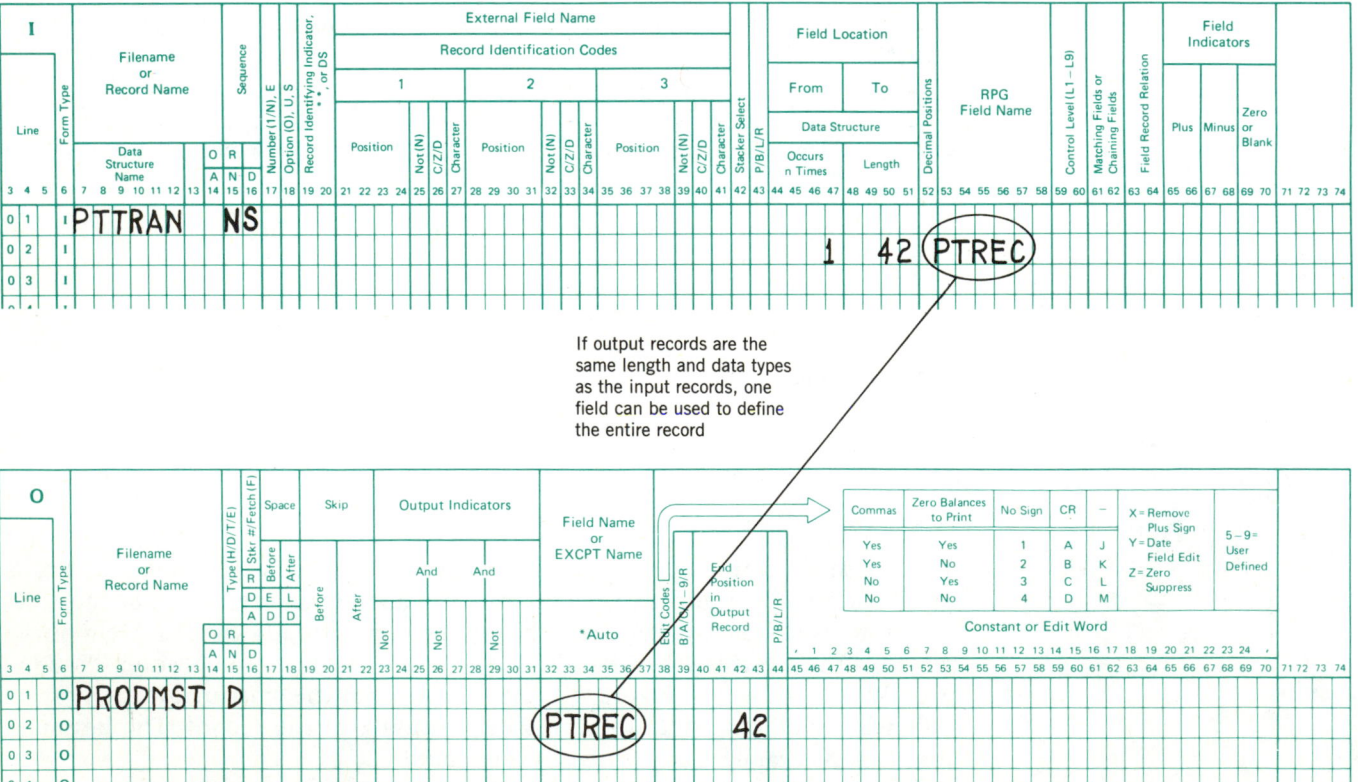

If output records are the same length and data types as the input records, one field can be used to define the entire record

As records are read from the PTTRAN file and written to the PRODMST file there may not be a need to alter or change the contents of the individual fields. Therefore, the individual fields need not be defined in this program; only one field is required that defines the entire data record.

In actuality, this is rarely the case. Typically, input fields are modified or rearranged, new fields are added, or some fields are deleted. If this is the case, then individual fields would need to be described on the Input and Output Specifications forms.

The purpose of our sample program is to transfer the sequential records from file PTTRAN to the new indexed file PRODMST. The format for the PTTRAN sequential records is as follows:

Record Description for PTTRAN

Field Description	Field Type (C,N,P)	Width	Dec. Pos.	RPG Field Name
Product Code	C	5		TCODE
Supplier Code	N	7	0	TSUPR
Product Description	C	20		TDESC
Quantity on Hand	N	5	0	TQOH
Product Cost	N	5	2	TCOST

Note: C = character; N = numeric; P = packed

The Input Specifications are described below.

Consider the following Output Specifications for the indexed file PRODMST to be created:

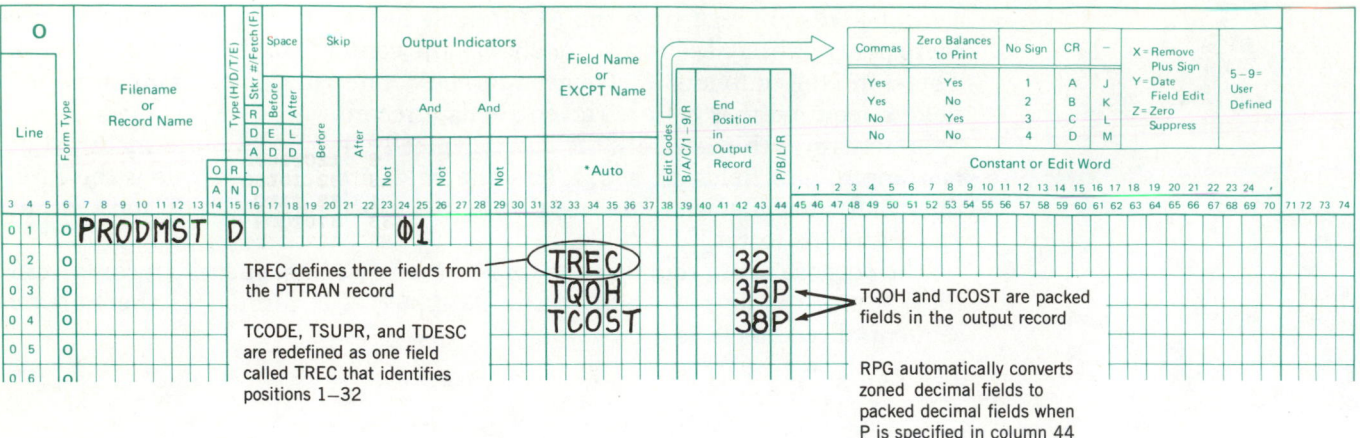

In comparing the Output Specifications of the indexed file PRODMST with the Input Specifications of the sequential transaction file PTTRAN, you will note some similarities as well as some differences. First, the fields Part Code, Supplier Code, and Part Description have been grouped into one field called TREC that identifies position 1–32 of the input record. These fields can be defined as one collective field called TREC since they are to be written out to the indexed file in the same order and data format as in the sequential input file. If the entire record would not have changed, as discussed earlier, then TREC could have been specified for the entire record. Again, remember that this technique of grouping fields can be used only if the outgoing fields have the same length and data format as the incoming fields.

Next, the Quantity on Hand (TQOH) and Product Cost (TCOST) fields, specified as zoned decimal numeric fields on the Input Specifications form, have been specified as packed fields on the Output Specifications. This, of course, reduces the size of the two fields within the record of the indexed file. The letter 'P' is placed in column 44 of the Output Specifications to identify these fields as *packed* fields in the outputted indexed file. Remember, all numeric fields, *with the exception of key fields*, should be defined as packed fields to save space and to improve program efficiency. Therefore, as the record is written to the indexed file, PRODMST, TQOH and TCOST are written out in the packed format. The RPG program automatically converts zoned decimal fields to packed format on output when P is placed in column 44 of the Output Specifications form. No additional programming is required.

The RPG program to create the indexed file PRODMST using the records from the transaction file PTTRAN is illustrated in Figure 9.3.

Special mention should be made of indicator 01 in this program. Indicator 01 is used to prevent the program from writing a "garbage" record to the file during the first cycle. Recall, if *detail* output records are not controlled by either an indicator or an EXCPT label, a record will be written to the output file *before* the program reads the first record from the input transaction file.

Self-Test   1. An indexed file has one field called the _____ field used for establishing the index and for randomly accessing records.

2. The primary key field in an indexed file must contain a value that is _____ .

3. (T or F) Indexed files can be processed either sequentially and/or randomly.

4. The four primary components that are specified on the File Description Specifications form for an indexed file are (a) _____ , (b) _____ , (c) _____ , and (d) _____ .

Figure 9.3
Sample program to create an
indexed file.

```
....+....1....+....2....+....3....+....4....+....5....+....6....+....7
0001 H
0002 FPTTRAN  IP  F     42              DISK
0003 FPRODMST  O  F     38  5AI     1 DISK
0004 *
0005 IPTTRAN   NS  01
0006 I                                      1   5 TCODE
0007 I                                      6 120TSUPR
0008 I                                     13  32 TDESC
0009 I                                      1  32 TREC
0010 I                                     33 370TQOH
0011 I                                     38 422TCOST
0012 *
0013 OPRODMST D      01
0014 O                            TREC     32
0015 O                            TQOH     35P
0016 O                            TCOST    38P
```

5. Indexed files that are processed both sequentially and randomly in the same program are said to be _____ .

6. (T or F) Alternate index fields need not be unique.

7. (T or F) Indexed files can be accessed randomly using either a primary or alternate key field.

8. (T or F) Indexed files can be created by using a command language procedure that interfaces with the operating system or by writing a program to create the files.

9. (T or F) Indexed files often minimize the need for creating other versions of the same file in different sequences.

10. (T or F) Sequential files are more efficiently processed than indexed files for interactive applications.

Solutions

1. primary key

2. unique (different for each record in the file)

3. T

4. (a) Length of Key Field (columns 29–30)
   (b) Record Address Type (column 31); usually the letter A is used to denote the key field as alphanumeric
   (c) Type of File Organization (column 32); contains the letter I to identify the file as an indexed file
   (d) Key Field Starting Location (columns 35–38)

5. dynamic

6. T—For example, Department Number can be used as an alternate key.

7. T

8. T

9. T

10. F

II. Processing Indexed Files

A. Accessing an Indexed File Sequentially

The main reason for creating indexed files is so that they can be accessed randomly. Indexed files are most often accessed randomly when updates are to be performed in no particular sequence or when on-line inquiries about specific records are requested. There are times, however, when it is best to access or retrieve records from an indexed file sequentially, that is, to read the entire

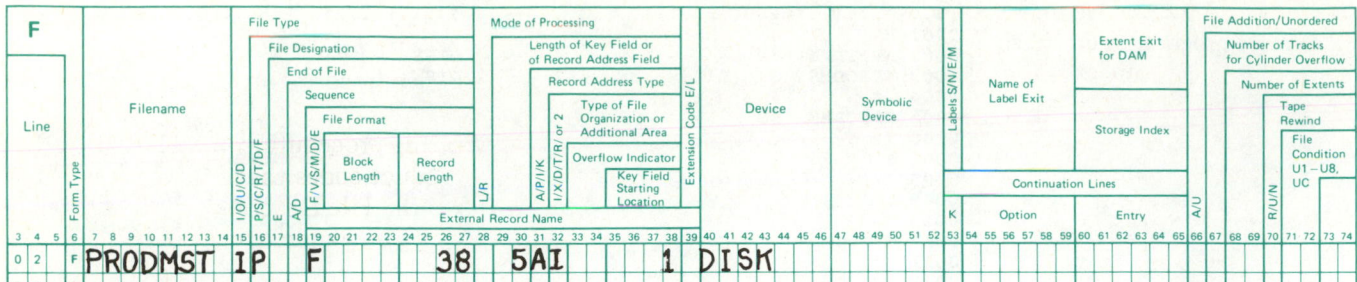

Figure 9.4
Accessing an indexed file sequentially as an input file.

file from beginning to end in sequence. Such a case might be the printing of a product master listing containing all products for the company or printing payroll checks in Social Security number sequence. Figure 9.4 illustrates the File Description Specifications form required to sequentially access the indexed Product file called PRODMST. When compared with the File Description Specifications in Figure 9.2, which created the indexed file, we see that it is identical except that the file is specified as an input file (File Type contains an I in column 15 rather than an O for output file). Also note in Figure 9.4 that the File Designation (column 16) has been specified as P for Primary file. This means that the file is to be accessed sequentially using the built-in RPG Fixed Logic Cycle.

Column 16, however, could have also been specified as D for Demand file or F for Full Procedural file. In these cases, the file would be accessed sequentially using the READ operation on the Calculation Specifications form.

When defining an indexed file as a sequential input file it is necessary to include the four primary components discussed in the preceding section. Even though the computer will read the indexed file sequentially it must still access the records through the key file or index established during the create procedure. Remember, the PRODMST's data file is in the sequence in which records are entered into the file, not necessarily in product code sequence maintained in the key file or index. Thus, the computer requires the key field information in order to process the indexed file.

Once an indexed file has been created, the file can be accessed sequentially in the same way sequential files were processed earlier.

B. Accessing an Indexed File Randomly

As noted, indexed files may be accessed randomly to respond to special requests or inquiries, or accessed randomly to verify the existence of a master record and to update that record. Let us consider an example of random inquiries about an indexed file for the purpose of printing a Product Request report.

Suppose salespeople submit daily requests for product information required for the next business day. All requests submitted are grouped together and entered into one batch sequential transaction file called PTREQT (Product Request file). Since these requests are not made in any specific sequence we will need to access the indexed file randomly in order to print a reply to each request. This file, which we will call a *query file*, would then be an input file in a program that would randomly access the indexed Product file PRODMST. With this type of processing, only those product records requested are selected from the PRODMST file and printed on the Product Request report. Note that records in the PTREQT query file are read in sequence (record 1, record 2, etc.) but the key fields of each record are in no particular order.

In our example we will illustrate how this procedure can be accomplished by processing the query file containing product codes that we wish to extract from the indexed file. Figure 9.5 illustrates the File Description Specifications form necessary to access the indexed file randomly. It includes the specifications for the query or product request file (PTREQT) that contains the product code field used to access the indexed file. Thus, the product request file will consist of records containing a field (TCODE) that will be used as a pointer to randomly access the indexed file called PRODMST.

The indexed file PRODMST in Figure 9.5 is being used as input only. Therefore, the letter I is specified for its File Type in column 15. The file is being accessed randomly, so the letter R is specified in column 28. The letter R stands for *random* access and must be specified any time an indexed file is being accessed randomly. The letter C in column 16, which stands for *CHAIN*, must also be specified. Chaining is a calculation operation that will be used to randomly access the records from the file. Thus, for reading an indexed file randomly, two new specifications are required on the File Description Specifications form:

> **File Type (column 16)** must contain the letter C for the CHAIN operation.
> The CHAIN operation will be discussed in the next section.
> **Mode of Processing (column 28)** must contain the letter R for random access.

1. The CHAIN Operation

As we have seen, indexed files can be processed in several different ways. However, any time an indexed file is to be accessed or read randomly, the **CHAIN operation** must be used. Figure 9.6 illustrates the Calculation Specifications form to access an indexed file randomly using the CHAIN operation. *Chaining*, which occurs during the Calculation cycle, is an operation that is executed under control of the program and results in a random access of the indexed file. The CHAIN operation uses a key field value from a second file to access the record with the corresponding key from the indexed file. This key field value, used for chaining, should *not* be defined as part of the indexed file but as part of the query file. In our example, the field used to access the PRODMST file, TCODE, is a field in the PTREQT or query file.

Figure 9.5
Accessing an indexed file randomly.

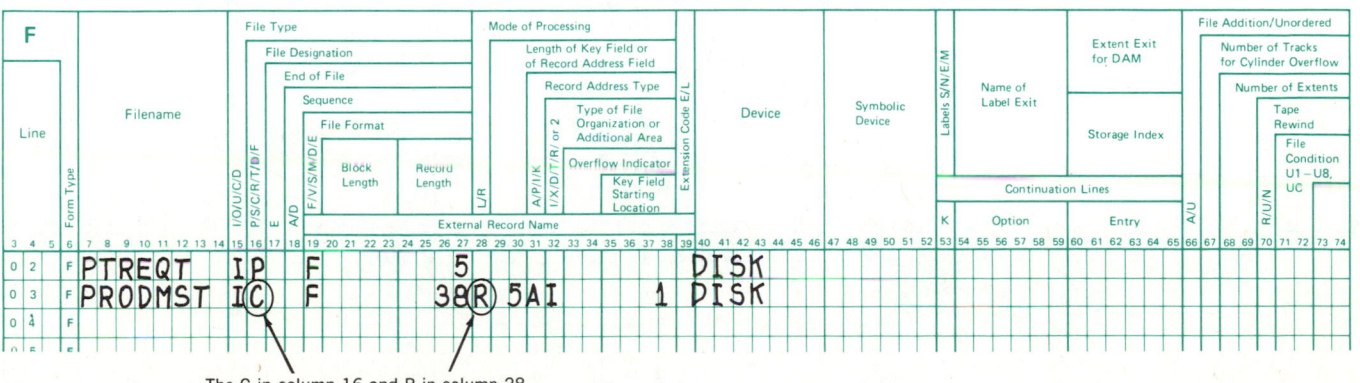

The C in column 16 and R in column 28 must both be specified if indexed records are to be read randomly using the CHAIN operation

When reading an indexed file randomly, we do not test for an *end-of-file condition* because we are not reading the file in sequence; instead, we include a *record-not-found* or *invalid-key indicator* test. If there is no record in the indexed file with a record key equal to the value of the field in Factor 1, the record-not-found indicator specified in column 54–55 is set on. This is sometimes called an *invalid-key test* because the key value in Factor 1 could be invalid rather than not being found. However, in our illustrations we will refer to it as a record-not-found test, meaning the key value from the query file, specified in Factor 1, was not found in the indexed file. Thus, the computer sets on the record-not-found indicator only if TCODE of the PTREQT file does not match any of the keys found in the index of the PRODMST indexed file.

If a match for TCODE is found in the index of the indexed file, then the corresponding record is read and that record's values are immediately placed in the variables declared in the indexed file's Input Specifications.

Chaining, then, is the process of *randomly accessing* an indexed file using a value stored in a field from another file or using a field established within the program. The value stored in the field serves as a "pointer" to the corresponding indexed record (see Figure 9.6).

Note that PRODMST was previously created as an indexed file with product code (positions 1–5 in the record) as the primary key.

In our sample problem, the product code field (TCODE) of the PTREQT query file contains the index or key value used to access the corresponding record in the indexed file. Figure 9.6 illustrates the CHAIN operation to access the indexed file randomly. In summary, this CHAIN operation specifies the following:

1. The field or literal in Factor 1 contains the *index key value* of the record you wish to access from the indexed file. It is a field that is part of another file (PTREQT in our example) or one that is established in the program; it is *not* a field in the indexed file. The record in the indexed file with a key field equal to the index key value in Factor 1 will be accessed by the CHAIN operation.

2. The operation code CHAIN is specified in columns 28–32.

3. The indexed file to be accessed or chained is specified in Factor 2.

4. Columns 54 and 55 contain an indicator that will be set on if the CHAIN operation is unsuccessful. That is, the indicator is set on if the record in

Figure 9.6
Accessing an indexed file randomly using the CHAIN operation.

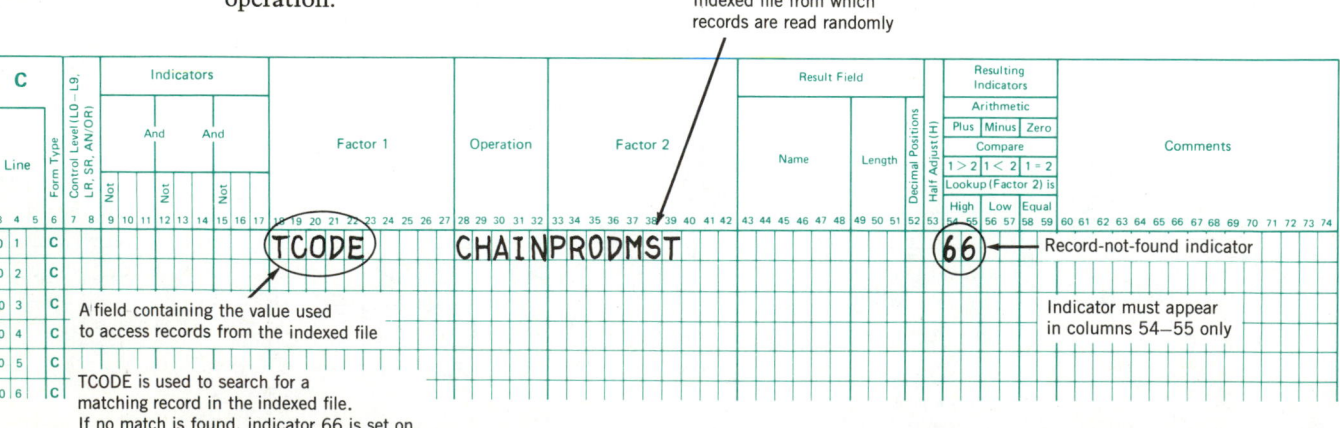

the indexed file is not found. This indicator, which must be specified in columns 54 and 55, is a record-not-found indicator for this operation.

The CHAIN operation causes a search through the PRODMST indexed file specified in Factor 2 and attempts to retrieve a record *equal to* the TCODE field specified in Factor 1. If the record is not found indicator 66 is set on.

2. Verifying an Update Record by Comparing It Against the Master File

Let us consider a payroll application in which a transaction file contains employee data that will eventually be used to update an Employee Master File. Again, we will assume all fields in the transaction file contain valid data. Our example here will demonstrate a procedure to check that each transaction record is actually associated with an active Employee Master record. That is, each transaction record would be checked to see that it corresponds to an existing, active master record. To do this, we must use the CHAIN operation.

The transaction file in our example consists of records that are to be used later to update an existing master file. This program reads a transaction record and determines if the record corresponds to an active master record. To perform this procedure, a key field in the transaction record is used to *access* the record in the indexed file with the corresponding key field value. If employee number is the key field of an indexed file, then the employee number key field in each input transaction record is used to find the corresponding indexed record. Thus, we need two input files for verifying that a transaction record corresponds to an active master record:

1. *Transaction file.* This is the *primary* file for our application because it controls which indexed master records are to be accessed. A 'P' in column 16 of the File Description Specifications form for the transaction file designates the transaction file as a primary file.

2. *Indexed file.* This file is accessed using the transaction file to determine which record is required. The CHAIN operation is used to perform this procedure. A 'C' in column 16 and an 'R' in column 28 of the File Description Specifications form for the indexed file indicate that the indexed file will be *randomly chained to,* in order to access records.

With this program example, the transaction record serves as a "pointer" to the corresponding indexed record using the key field as the source (see Figure 9.7).

Figure 9.7
Example of chaining.

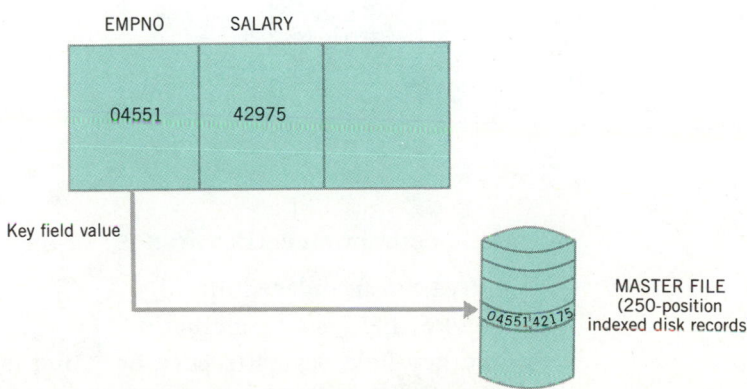

The key field on the transaction file is specified on the Calculation Specifications form along with the CHAIN operation. The precise location, length, and specification of the index key field that was used to create the indexed file must be defined on the File Description Specifications form.

The following File Description Specifications form may be used for a program in which a transaction file will be compared against the master file. An audit trail or control listing is produced. If a transaction record is not associated with a corresponding active master record, an error message will print.

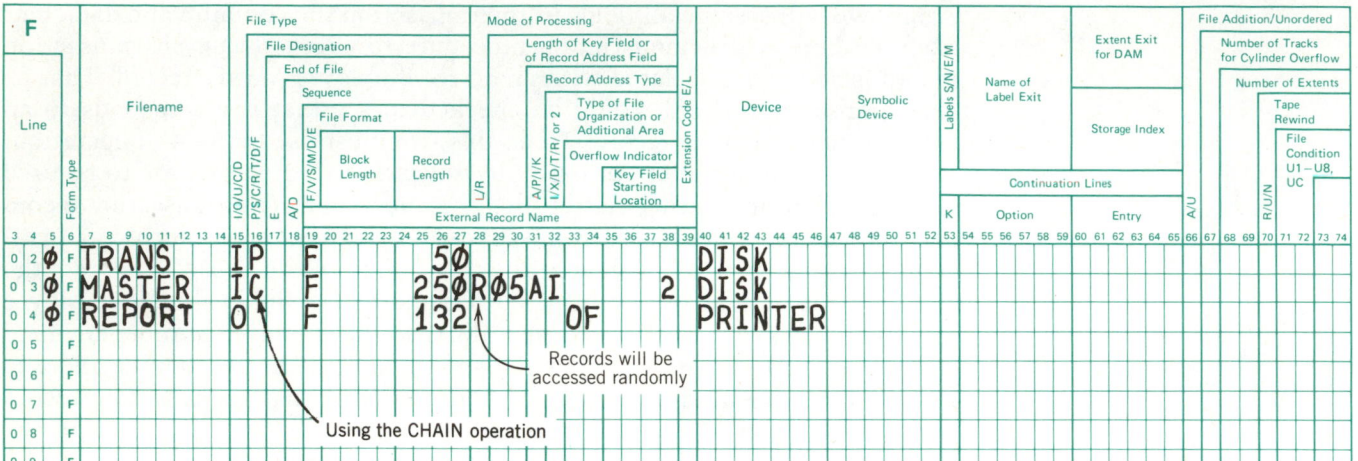

The file description entries for the TRANS and REPORT files are self-explanatory and are similar to other programs that have been illustrated. The file description entries for the MASTER file, however, may require some explanation. Let us consider them separately.

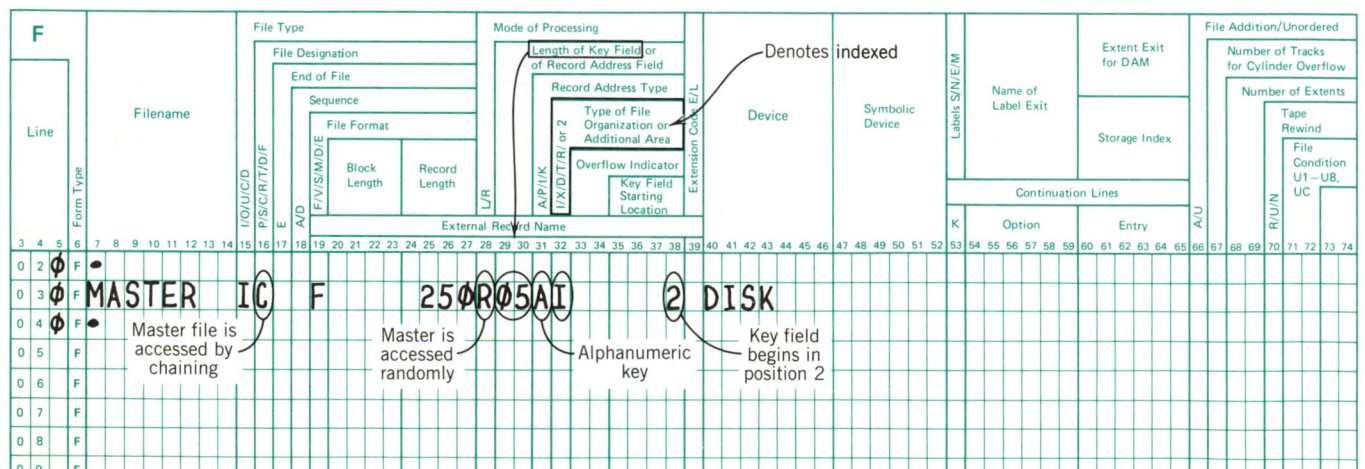

The file description entries for MASTER indicate the following:

1. MASTER is an indexed file.
2. The key field is alphanumeric.
3. The key field begins in position 2 and is five positions long; that is, it appears in positions 2–6 of each indexed record.

4. The indexed file is accessed randomly by chaining, using a field from the transaction file.

If the program is simply used to determine that a record exists in the indexed file for each corresponding transaction record, then only those fields necessary for the comparison are specified on the Input Specifications form. Note that the key field of the indexed file does not need to be indicated on the Input Specifications form since we already included its specification (Key Field Starting Location, Length of Key Field, and Type) on the File Description Specifications form.

Often, each master record includes a coded field that indicates if it is an active record or if it has been deactivated. For a master payroll file, deactivated records may pertain to employees who have left the company. They are retained on the master file for some reporting purposes, but they should not be updated by transaction data. That is, a transaction record corresponding to an inactive master file should be printed as an error.

Let us assume that the first character in the master record will designate STATUS: 'A' for active and 'I' for inactive. Our Input Specifications form may be as follows:

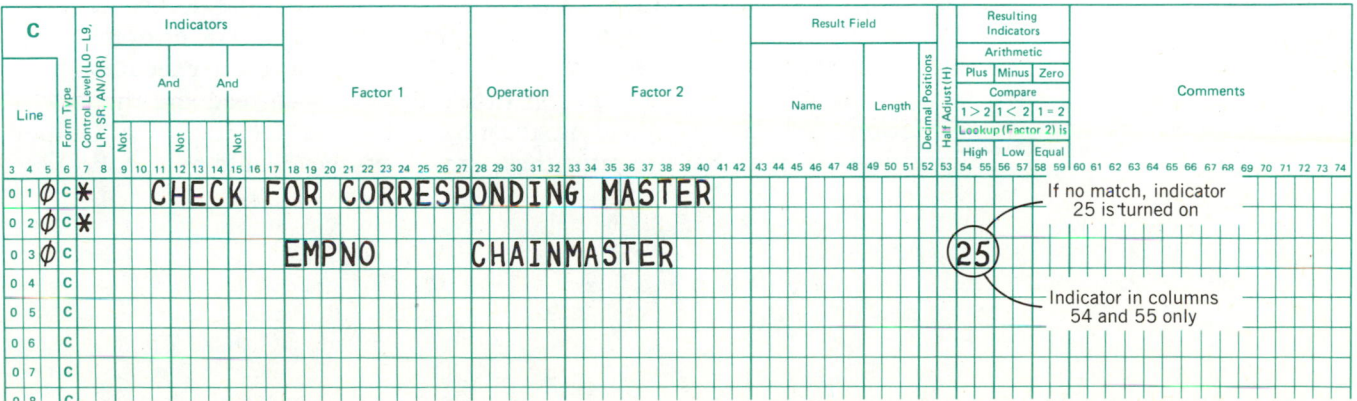

On the Calculation Specifications form, we determine if a master record exists for a given transaction record by using a CHAIN operation:

This operation specifies the following:

1. The field in the transaction file (EMPNO) that serves as the index key value for look-up purposes.
2. The file to chain against (MASTER).
3. The indicator to be turned on if the record on the master with that key does not exist. This must be coded in columns 54 and 55 only, and serves as an invalid key or record-not-found indicator.

EMPNO is a TRANS field that serves as the index key value. The CHAIN operation is performed for each transaction record. This chain operation compares the EMPNO from the transaction file against the five-byte key field in positions 2–6 of each master record. If no match is found, then indicator 25 is turned on. When indicator 25 is off, then a match has occurred; that is, there is a corresponding master record for the transaction record.

If there is a match, we must determine if the status in the master record is 'A' for active; if it is not, then the transaction record corresponds to an inactive master. This would be an error because transaction data should not be used to update inactive records.

The following coding will be used to print *two* types of errors:

1. When indicator 25 is on, we print the error message 'NO CORRESPONDING MASTER RECORD'.
2. When indicator 25 is off and the STATUS field = I, we print the error message 'CORRESPONDING MASTER RECORD IS INACTIVE'.

Line	Form Type	Control Level (L0–L9, LR, SR, AN/OR)	Not	And	Not	And	Not	Factor 1	Operation	Factor 2	Result Field Name	Length	Decimal Positions	Half Adjust (H)	High 54 55	Low 56 57	Equal 58 59	Comments
0 1	C							EMPNO	CHAIN	MASTER					25			
0 2	C			25					EXCPT	@E100								NOT FOUND
0 3	C			N25				STATUS	IFEQ	'I'								FOUND/INACTIVE
0 4	C								EXCPT	@E200								
0 5	C								END									
0 6	C																	

The IF/END operation is performed to make certain that when a match occurs, the master record is active. Thus, if STATUS is equal (EQ) to 'I', the EXCPT output line labeled @E200 is used to print the appropriate error message. Note that the indicator used to cause the IF/END operation to execute is N25. N25 occurs when a record from the TRANS file has been read and the CHAIN operation finds a corresponding record in the MASTER file. The Output Specifications form used to print these error messages would be as follows:

O	Line	Form Type	Filename or Record Name	O A N / R	Type (H/D/T/E) R D E D / L D	Stkr #/Fetch (F)	Space Before	After	Skip Before	After	Output Indicators / And	Not	And	Not	Not	Field Name or EXCPT Name / *Auto	Edit Codes / B/A/C/1-9/R	End Position in Output Record / P/B/L/R	Constant or Edit Word
0 1	O						•												
0 2	O						•												
0 3	O				E	2										@E10Φ			
0 4	O																	75	'NO CORRESPONDING'
0 5	O																	89	'MASTER RECORD'
0 6	O	✱																	
0 7	O				E	2										@E20Φ			
0 8	O																	72	'CORRESPONDING'
0 9	O																	86	'MASTER RECORD'
1 0	O																	98	'IS INACTIVE'
1 1	O																		
1 2	O																		

An Alternate Method

The following coding uses a COMP operation to print the *two* types of errors:

1. When indicator 25 is on, we print the error message 'NO CORRE-SPONDING MASTER RECORD'.
2. When indicator 35 is on, we print the error message 'CORRESPONDING MASTER RECORD IS INACTIVE'.

C	Line	Form Type	Control Level (L0-L9, LR, SR, AN/OR)	Indicators And	Not	And	Not	Not	Factor 1	Operation	Factor 2	Result Field Name	Length	Decimal Positions	Half Adjust (H)	Resulting Indicators Arithmetic / Plus / Minus / Zero / Compare 1>2 / 1<2 / 1=2 / Lookup High / Low / Equal	Comments
0 1	C								EMPNO	CHAIN	MASTER					25	
0 2	C			25						EXCPT							
0 3	C			N25					STATUS	COMP	'I'					35	
0 4	C			35						EXCPT							
0 5	C									SETOF		25 35					
0 6	C																
0 7	C																

The COMP operation is performed to make certain that when a match occurs, the master record is active. If it is not, indicator 35 is turned on and the above message prints. Note that the indicator used to cause the COMP instruction to execute is N25. This occurs when a record from the TRANS file has been read that chains properly to MASTER. The Output Specifications form used to print these messages with this method would be as follows:

Line	Form Type	Filename or Record Name		Type (H/D/T/E)	Stkr #/Fetch (F)	Space Before	Space After	Skip Before	Skip After	Output Indicators And	And	Field Name or EXCPT Name *Auto	Edit Codes	B/A/C1–9/R	End Position in Output Record	P/B/L/R	Constant or Edit Word
0 1	O																
0 2	O																
0 3	O			E	1			25									
0 4	O														75		'NO CORRESPONDING'
0 5	O														89		'MASTER RECORD'
0 6	O			E	1			35									
0 7	O														72		'CORRESPONDING'
0 8	O														86		'MASTER RECORD'
0 9	O														98		'IS INACTIVE'
1 0	O																

Checking for New Employees

Suppose the transaction file contains a record that does not correspond to an existing master record. That is, when the CHAIN operation is executed, the record-not-found indicator specified in columns 54 to 55 of the CHAIN operation is set on. Depending on the application, this could mean one of two things:

TRANSACTION RECORD FOR WHICH THERE IS NO CORRESPONDING MASTER RECORD

1. The transaction record has an erroneously entered key field.
2. The transaction record represents a record to be added to the master file.

(For a payroll file, this may be a new employee; for an accounts receivable file, this may be a new account, and so on.)

If transaction data has not been set up to also enter new records, then transaction records that do not correspond to master records would be designated as errors just as they have been in the preceding illustrations.

If transaction data can, however, denote a new employee we can use the new record code field called NEWCDE, which appears in column 1 of the transaction record as follows:

Line	Form Type	Filename or Record Name / Data Structure Name		Sequence	Number (1/N), E	Option (O), U, S	Record Identifying Indicator, ** , or DS	Position 1	Not (N)	C/Z/D	Character	Position 2	Not (N)	C/Z/D	Character	Position 3	Not (N)	C/Z/D	Character	Stacker Select	P/B/L/R	From / Occurs n Times	To / Length	Decimal Positions	RPG Field Name	Control Level (L1–L9)	Matching Fields or Chaining Fields	Field Record Relation	Plus	Minus	Zero or Blank
0 1	I	TRANS		NS																											
0 2	I																					1	1		NEWCDE						
0 3	I																														
0 4	I																														
0 5	I																														
0 6	I																														
0 7	I																														

As noted, on the Calculation Specifications form shown below, a *record-not-found* condition on the CHAIN operation could mean a new employee on the transaction file. Thus, the CHAIN operation would then be followed by a test to see if there was an 'N' in NEWCDE for transaction records with no corresponding master. An 'N' in NEWCDE would mean that the transaction record represents a new employee. Thus, if the record-not-found indicator is set on and there is an 'N' in NEWCDE, the transaction record is meant to be a new employee.

Line	Form Type	Control Level (L0–L9, LR, SR, AN/OR)	Indicators						Factor 1	Operation	Factor 2	Result Field				Resulting Indicators				Comments
			And		And							Name	Length	Decimal Positions	Half Adjust (H)	Arithmetic / Compare / Lookup				
			Not		Not		Not									Plus / High	Minus / Low	Zero / Equal		
0 1	C								EMPNO	CHAINMASTER						25				
0 2	C	25							NEWCDE	IFEQ	'N'									
0 3	C									EXCPT@ADD										NEW EMPLOYEE
0 4	C									ELSE										
0 5	C									EXCPT@E100										NOT FOUND & NOT
0 6	C									END										NEW EMPLOYEE
0 7	C	N25							NEWCDE	IFEQ	'N'									
0 8	C									EXCPT@E200										FOUND &
0 9	C									END										NEW EMPLOYEE
1 0	C	N25							STATUS	IFEQ	'I'									
1 1	C									EXCPT@E300										FOUND &
1 2	C									END										INACTIVE
1 3	C																			
1 4	C																			

Valid conditions to add employee:
— NEWCDE = 'N'
— Record not found on master (Indicator 25 ON)

However, a different type of error condition can occur if the transaction record designates a new employee that is to be added to the indexed file and the record is already on the file. In this instance, if the record-not-found indicator is not set on with the CHAIN operation but NEWCDE = 'N' in the transaction record, this, too, is an error. In this case, the transaction record NEWCDE denotes a new employee but that employee's record was found on the indexed file.

Note that master records, like transaction records, sometimes include codes. NEWCDE in the transaction file denotes whether the record refers to a new employee. On master indexed files, we often have an activity STATUS code to denote whether the record is active or inactive (e.g., A in STATUS is for active and I in STATUS is for inactive). Sometimes we retain inactive records on a master file, but only want to process active ones. Thus, we would consider it an error if a transaction record referred to an inactive master record.

The Calculation Specifications that test for the error conditions discussed above are as follows:

1. The transaction record did not match any master file record (indicator 25 on) and the employee is not a new employee (NEWCDE not equal to 'N'); thus, an error has occurred. "NO CORRESPONDING MASTER RECORD" should print.

2. The transaction record did match the master file record (indicator 25 off), but the STATUS field equals 'I'; thus, an error has occurred. "MASTER RECORD IS INACTIVE" should print.

3. The transaction record did match the master file record (indicator 25 on) and the employee transaction record is a new employee (NEWCDE equal to 'N'); thus, an error has occurred. "MASTER RECORD ALREADY EXISTS" should print.

The new valid condition can be stated as follows:

4. If the transaction record's index key value did not match a key field on the master indexed file (that is, indicator 25 is on), but the employee is a new employee, then a valid condition would exist. That is, the transaction record contains a new employee (NEWCDE equal to 'N'), which was not found on the master file (indicator 25 on). The new employee could then be added to the indexed master file.

The following illustrates an alternative method to the previous IF/ELSE/END operation using a COMP operation:

C	Control Level (L0 – L9, LR, SR, AN/OR)	Indicators					Factor 1	Operation	Factor 2	Result Field				Resulting Indicators			Comments
		And		And						Name	Length			Arithmetic			
														Plus / Minus / Zero			
														Compare			
			Not		Not									1>2 / 1<2 / 1=2			
														Lookup (Factor 2) is			
Line	Form Type						Factor 1	Operation	Factor 2	Name	Length	Decimal Positions	Half Adjust (H)	High / Low / Equal			Comments
0 1	C						EMPNO	CHAIN	MASTER					25			
0 2	C						NEWCDE	COMP	'N'					4848		50	
0 3	C		25	48				EXCPT	@E100								NOT FOUND & NOT
0 4	C*																NEW EMPLOYEE
0 5	C		25	50				EXCPT	@ADD								NEW EMPLOYEE
0 6	C	N25	50					EXCPT	@E200								FOUND & NEW EMP
0 7	C	N25					STATUS	COMP	'I'							35	FOUND &
0 8	C	N25	35					EXCPT	@E300								INACTIVE
0 9	C																
1 0	C																

With the above specifications, the following will be known if indicators 25 and 50 are set on:

1. The transaction record did not match any master record.
2. The transaction record has an 'N' in column 1, designating it as a new account.

All other conditions denote errors as previously discussed.

Self-Test

1. A _____ is a major collection of data for a particular application.
2. The process of keeping a master file current is called _____ .
3. The file of change records used to update the master file is called the _____ file.
4. The first program to be executed when a system is implemented is usually one that _____ the master file.
5. Before a master file is updated with transaction data, the transaction file should be _____ to minimize the risk of errors.
6. If a program checks to see that each transaction record corresponds to an active master record, then a(n) _____ operation is required.
7. In a chaining operation, the specifications for the key field on the master file are denoted on the _____ Specifications form.
8. In a chaining operation, the transaction field used for looking up the corresponding master record is specified on the _____ Specifications form along with the _____ .

Solutions

1. master file
2. updating

3. transaction
4. creates
5. edited
6. chaining
7. File Description. These include (a) the starting position of the key field, (b) the length of the key field, and (c) the format of the key field.
8. Calculation; name of the file to be "looked up," that is, the master file

III. File Maintenance Procedures for Indexed Files

We will discuss indexed file updating in general and then consider a specific illustration.

A. The Files That Are Used

In this section, we will assume the existence of an indexed master disk file and an edited transaction file. The procedure used to make the master file current by incorporating transaction change data is called the **update** or **file maintenance procedure** (see Figure 9.8). The edited transaction file will contain all changes that have occurred during an update cycle.

Changes to an indexed file are made directly to the file itself. Thus the master file serves as both input and output. This is in contrast to sequential update procedures that use the input master file and a transaction file to create an entirely new master file as output.

B. Updating or Changing Existing Records in an Indexed File

A field in the edited transaction file is used to chain to the master file. If the transaction record is a change record, one that is to revise a master record, then the chaining procedure should cause the corresponding master record to be read into storage. If the transaction record does not have a corresponding master record, then an error has occurred and a message should be printed on the error control listing.

Transaction records that denote changes are the most common types of update records. For an accounts receivable master file, transaction change records would include sales, or purchases, and credits. If an update procedure is performed daily, the transaction file would include all sales and credits that

Figure 9.8
Update procedure.

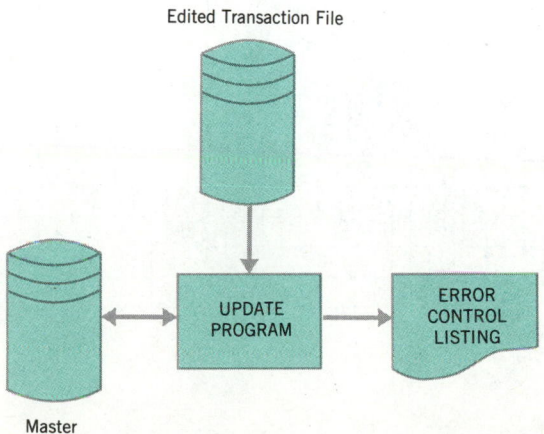

occurred during the preceding day. In Chapter 11, we will see that updates can be made interactively as the change occurs. That is, when a transaction is made, the data is used to instantly update the corresponding master record. This is referred to as interactive processing. With such applications, the master file is always current.

Transaction records used to update a payroll master file might include changes to salary, level, job description, name, address, number of dependents, and job location.

The transaction record would include a code to indicate the type of change. For example, a payroll transaction record may include the following:

SSNO	NAME	ADDRESS	ANNUAL SALARY	LEVEL	JOB DESCRIPTION	JOB LOCATION	NUMBER OF DEPENDENTS	CODE
1 9	10 30	31 50	51 55	56 57	70	71	72	73

CODE
1 = salary change
2 = level change
3 = job description change
4 = name change
5 = address change
6 = number of dependents change
7 = job location change

For an accounts receivable transaction file, we might have:

```
1-5  ACCTNO
6-10 AMT
 15  CODE        (1 = Purchase; 2 = Credit)
```

The RPG programmer would turn on an indicator depending on the code in the transaction record. Then the corresponding changes would be made to update the master record. The programming excerpt for the accounts receivable procedure is as follows:

Line	Form Type	Control Level	And	And	And	Factor 1	Operation	Factor 2	Result Field Name	Length	Dec Pos	Half Adjust	Plus	Minus	Zero	High	Low	Equal	Comments
01	C					ACCTNO	CHAIN	MSTR								25			
02	C	N25				CODE	COMP	'1'										01	
03	C	N25	N01			CODE	COMP	'2'										02	
04	C	N25	01			AMT	ADD	BAL	BAL										
05	C	N25	02			BAL	SUB	AMT	BAL										
06	C																		
07	C																		
08	C																		

O		Filename or Record Name		Type(H/D/T/E)	Stkr #/Fetch (F)	Space		Skip		Output Indicators				Field Name or EXCPT Name		Edit Codes	B/A/C/1 – 9/R	End Position in Output Record	P/B/L/R	Commas	Zero Balances to Print	No Sign	CR	–	X = Remove Plus Sign / Y = Date Field Edit / Z = Zero Suppress	5 – 9 = User Defined
						Before	After	Before	After	And	And			*Auto						Yes / Yes / No / No	Yes / No / Yes / No	1 / 2 / 3 / 4	A / B / C / D	J / K / L / M		
Line	Form Type		OR AND		R D E L A D D					Not	Not	Not										Constant or Edit Word				
0 1	O										•															
0 2	O										•															
0 3	O										•															
0 4	O									01				'AMT OF PURCHASE'												
0 5	O									02				'AMT OF CREDIT'												
0 6	O																									
0 7	O																									

C. Changing the Status of Master Records

Recall that an indexed master disk file includes active records, which are those that are currently part of the file, as well as inactive records, which are those that are retained for legal, control, or historical purposes but are no longer used for normal updating or reporting. An inactive master payroll record, for example, might pertain to an employee who has retired, resigned, or been fired. An inactive master accounts receivable record might pertain to a customer who no longer has an active charge account.

Transaction records are sometimes created to change the status of master records from active to inactive. That is, a transaction record might specify a master record to be deactivated. Consider the following transaction accounts receivable record:

```
1–5  ACCTNO
6–10 AMT
25   CODE      (1 = Purchase; 2 = Credit; 3 = Deactivate the account)
```

In this instance, as in the previous cases, a CHAIN operation is used to read the corresponding master record with the same ACCTNO. If no corresponding master record exists, this would be an error and an error message should be printed.

Assuming that a valid master record exists with the same ACCTNO as the transaction record, then the CODE is checked. If CODE is equal to 3, the constant 'I' (for inactive) is put in the STATUS field of the master record and the record is rewritten:

C		Control Level (L0–L9, LR, SR, AN/OR)	Indicators						Factor 1	Operation	Factor 2	Result Field				Resulting Indicators			Comments
			And		And							Name	Length	Decimal Positions	Half Adjust (H)	Arithmetic			
																Plus 1>2	Minus 1<2	Zero 1=2	
Line	Form Type		Not		Not		Not									High Low Equal Lookup (Factor 2) is			
0 1	C								ACCTNO	CHAIN	MSTR						25		
0 2	C		N25						CODE	COMP	'3'						03		CHANGE TO INACT

O	Line	Form Type	Filename or Record Name	Type (H/D/T/E)	Stkr #/Fetch (F)	Space Before/After	Skip	Output Indicators And And	Field Name or EXCPT Name *Auto	Edit Codes B/A/C/1 - 9/R	End Position in Output Record	P/B/L/R	Commas / Zero Balances to Print / No Sign / CR / - / X=Remove Plus Sign Y=Date Field Edit Z=Zero Suppress / 5-9= User Defined	Constant or Edit Word
	0 1	0	0						•					
	0 2	0	0						•					
	0 3	0	0						•					
	0 4	0	0					Ø3			1			'I'
	0 5	0	0					NØ3			1			'A'
	0 6	0												

D. Adding New Records to a Master Indexed File

As noted, transaction records are sometimes used to designate a new record that must be *added to* the master file. In this instance, a CHAIN operation should be executed to ensure that a corresponding master record does *not* already exist. That is, if ACCTNO 12345 is designated as a new account on the transaction file, the programmer must make certain that ACCTNO 12345 does not already exist on the master. If a match occurs, then this would be an error condition and an error message should print.

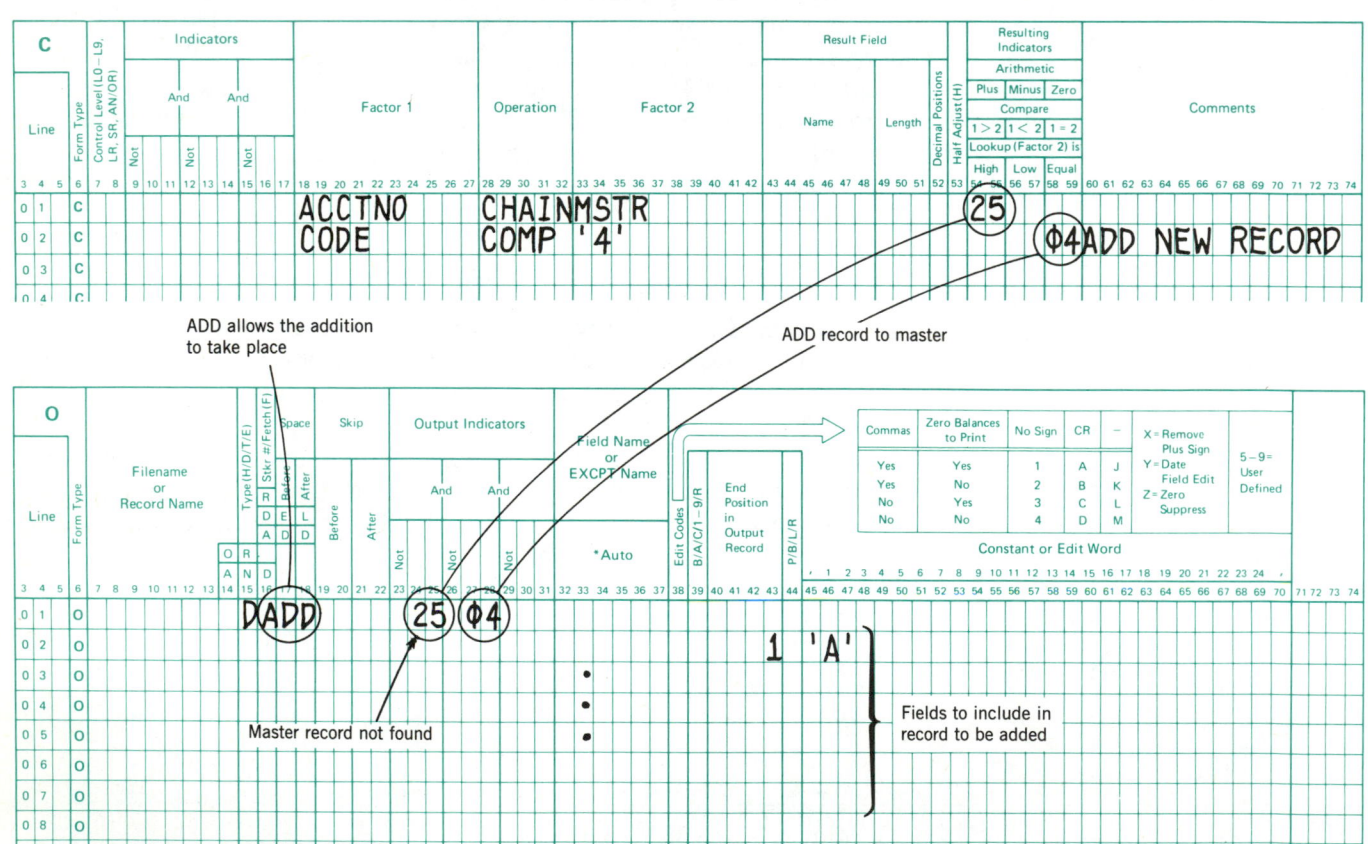

Calculation form:

C	Line	Indicators And And	Factor 1	Operation	Factor 2	Result Field Name	Length	Resulting Indicators	Comments
	0 1		ACCTNO	CHAIN	MSTR			25	
	0 2		CODE	COMP	'4'			Ø4	ADD NEW RECORD
	0 3								
	0 4								

ADD allows the addition to take place

ADD record to master

Output form:

O	Line				Output Indicators	Field Name / EXCPT Name				Constant or Edit Word
	0 1	O	D ADD		25 Ø4					
	0 2	O							1	'A'
	0 3	O				•				
	0 4	O				•				
	0 5	O				•				
	0 6	O								
	0 7	O								
	0 8	O								

Master record not found

Fields to include in record to be added

Thus, if the CHAIN operation sets on the record-not-found indicator, then check to see if the transaction record specifies a new account. If it does, add the new record to the master file. Later in this chapter, we will see in detail the procedure that is used to add records to an indexed file. Basically, we use the appropriate output indicators to write an output record and code "ADD" in columns 16–18 of the Output Specifications form.

If, however, the transaction record denotes an update, then the CHAIN operation resulted in an error since a corresponding master record should have been found. If this type of error condition occurs, an appropriate error message should print indicating that a record was not found.

E. Deleting Records from a Master Indexed File

In addition to changing fields within an existing record, adding new records, or changing an existing record's status, it is sometimes necessary to *delete* records from an indexed file so that they are no longer part of the file.

Deleting records from an indexed file should not be confused with changing the status of a record. Changing a record's status is a method used to suspend processing or to flag a record as inactive for future reference. Take for example, an accounts receivable file for a retail store. Here, active accounts may be deactivated or changed to inactive accounts by changing a status code in order to identify accounts that have not been used for a certain period of time. This is accomplished by establishing a *status field* in the record into which the letter I for inactive (or the letter D for deactivated) is placed. The value A in the status field would mean that the record status is active as discussed in previous examples. If a customer has not used the account for a certain period of time or if the account is in arrears the store may deactivate the account by changing the status field from A to I. The account record still remains on the file, however, but it is now inactive and the customer can no longer make transactions.

Deleting records, on the other hand, refers to the physical *removal* of the record from the file. Once a record is deleted, the data is gone and the only way to restore the record's contents is to reenter the data into the file.

This is sometimes referred to as a *system delete* because once the RPG program issues the "delete" operation, the operating system takes over. The operating system issues a system delete by destroying the record's contents and flagging the deleted record so that it cannot be referenced again. Technically speaking, records are not physically removed from a file when they are deleted. Instead, the computer system destroys all data in the record by replacing it with hexadecimal F's and then flags the record as being deleted. This becomes a signal to the system that the record has been deleted and is no longer part of the file. When the file is processed, those deleted records are then bypassed by the computer. So, as far as the program is concerned, deleted records do not exist. Records deleted in this manner cannot be restored. For a deleted record to become active again the entire record would have to be reentered as an addition. (For inactive records to become active, we simply change the status code.)

Deleted records can be physically removed from a file by using an operating system command that is system dependent. If you wish to learn more about these commands contact your computer center. Alternatively, you could read an indexed file sequentially and write all records to a new file; records identified by the computer as being system-deleted would not be recognized by the system and thus would not be copied to the new file.

To delete a record from an indexed file, the key field must first be read into the program from another file or interactively from the keyboard, and then the CHAIN operation would be executed.

Deleting records in an indexed file

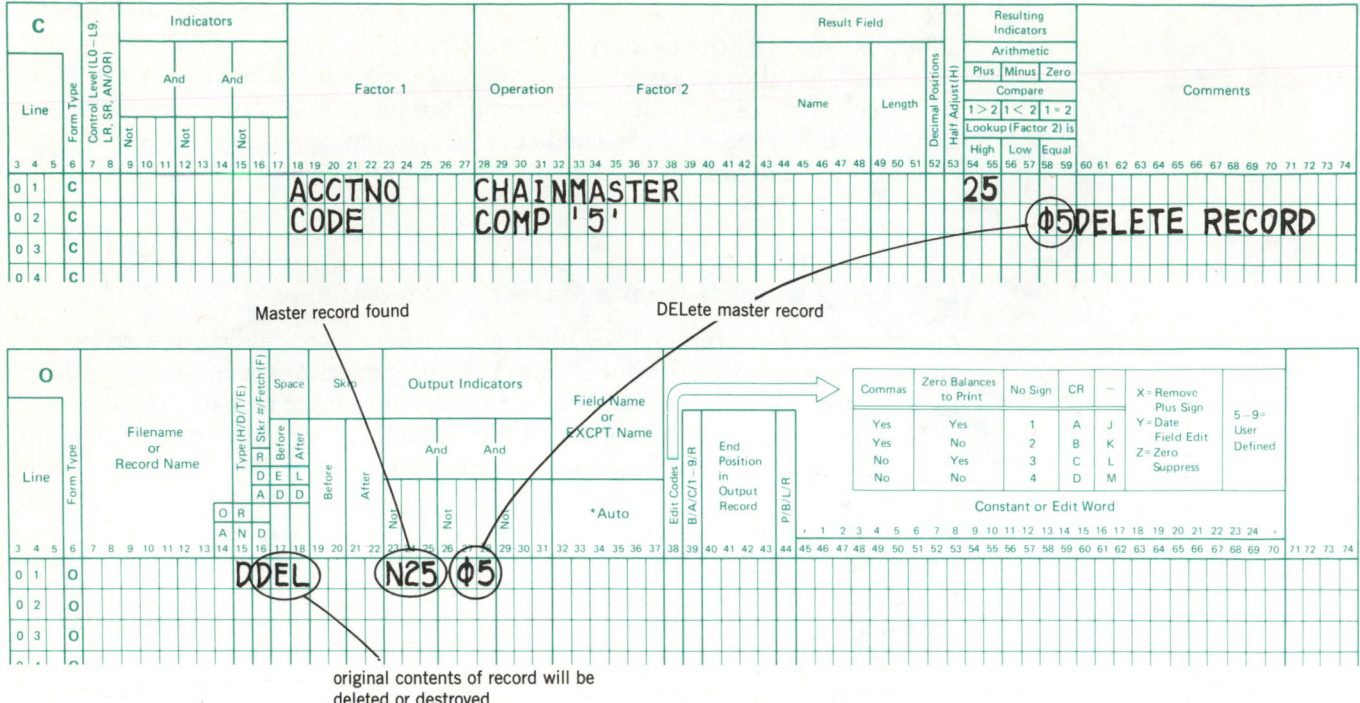

Master record found

DELete master record

original contents of record will be deleted or destroyed

If the CHAIN operation does not turn on the *record-not-found* indicator then the record sought was found and moved into storage. A check must then be made to see if the transaction record specifies a delete record code. If it does, the corresponding record in the indexed file can be deleted. To delete a record from an indexed file, the letters DEL must be specified in columns 16—18 of the output record line. This will instruct the computer to destroy the contents of the record and flag the record as being deleted.

Remember, before a record can be deleted from an indexed file it must be read into the program first, using the CHAIN operation. Trying to delete a record before reading it will cause a system error and the program will terminate abnormally, called an **abend**.

Again, as with all other file maintenance routines, the program should check for errors. For example, if the transaction record code specified a delete code and the CHAIN operation revealed that the record did not exist (record-not-found indicator on) an error condition would occur. When an error condition occurs, the program should print out an appropriate error message.

When records are deleted from an indexed file, that file must be defined on the File Specifications form as an update file (U in column 15). Specifying the file as an update file will allow the program to read a record from the file and write back or rewrite to the file.

All updating procedures should produce control listings indicating the following:

1. All changes made.
2. The number of records processed, added, and deleted.
3. The number of occurrences of each type of error and a listing of each error record.

In many instances, there might be more than one transaction record for a specific master record. For a transaction accounts receivable file, for example, a given ACCTNO may have several purchases or transactions that need to be chained to the master. Similarly, a transaction payroll file may include two change records for the same employee. Suppose a female employee marries; typically, a name change record and an address change record might be required.

If, in fact, there is more than one transaction for a given master record, each is chained as per our illustration and each is processed individually. The fact that there may be numerous changes for a given master record just means that the indexed master record will be retrieved and rewritten more than once.

Before considering a specific illustration of an indexed update procedure, the following will serve as a general review of concepts:

All Transactions

Always check the transaction record's action code for validity—it should be add, change, or delete. If valid, make the appropriate change.

SUMMARY OF UPDATE PROCEDURES

Changes
1. For each transaction record, CHAIN to the master indexed file to make certain that an active master record exists.
2. If an active master record exists, be sure that the transaction record is a "change" record or a "delete," but not an "add" record.
3. Rewrite the master record by indicating on the Output Specifications form all the fields to be changed.
4. For control purposes, add 1 to the count of records updated.
5. As an extra edit check, you may want to determine if the field to be changed is, in fact, different from the field currently in the master record.

Deletions
1. CHAIN to the master file to bring the master record corresponding to the transaction record into storage.
2. For control purposes, add 1 to the count of records deleted.
3. Delete the record from the file.

Additions
1. CHAIN to the master file to make sure that a record with the same key field does not already exist in the master file.
2. Add the new record to the master file.
3. Add 1 to the count of new records.

Self-Test

1. The main advantage of using indexed files is for _____ .
2. The _____ operation is used to read indexed files randomly.
3. When an indexed file is read randomly, we *do not* test for _____ .
4. When a CHAIN operation is executed, a test is made for _____ .
5. When an indexed file is to be accessed randomly, the File Description Specifications form includes the letter _____ in column 16 and the letter _____ in position 28.
6. In a chaining operation, the field used for looking up the corresponding record in the indexed file is specified on the _____ Specifications form along with the _____ . The field used for look-up purposes is defined _____ . This field must equal the _____ of an indexed record in order for the CHAIN to be executed properly.

7. Write the Calculation Specifications line to randomly read the indexed file IN-VENT using the key field PARTNO.

8. The procedure for keeping an indexed file current is called the _____ .

9. To add records to an indexed file, _____ is specified on the Output Specifications form. To delete a record, _____ is specified.

10. The three major types of file maintenance procedures result in _____ , _____ , and _____ .

Solutions

1. random retrieval

2. CHAIN

3. end-of-file

4. no record found

5. C, R

6. Calculation; name of the file to be "looked up," that is, the indexed file; as either an input field or as the result of a calculation; key field

7. PARTNO   CHAIN   INVENT   88

8. update procedures or file maintenance

9. ADD; DEL

10. changes to a file; deletions from a file; additions to a file

IV. Illustrating an Update Procedure in Its Entirety Using a Master Indexed File

The following is the format for a master sales file called SMSTR:

SMSTR 31-position records

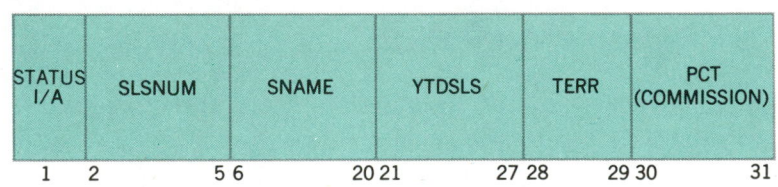

STATUS I/A	SLSNUM	SNAME	YTDSLS	TERR	PCT (COMMISSION)
1 2	5 6	20 21	27 28	29 30	31

SMSTR is an indexed master file with SLSNUM (salesperson number) as the key field. It will be accessed randomly, so that only those master records to be updated with corresponding transaction records need to be read into storage. SNAME is the salesperson's name, YTDSLS is the year-to-date sales credited to the salesperson, TERR is the person's territory, PCT is the commission percent, STATUS is 'A' for active records and 'I' for inactive records.

SMSTR is an indexed input/output file. We read from it to access master records that correspond to the transaction file, and we write to it with changes, additions, and deletions. It is accessed randomly. Its File Type is 'U' for 'UPDATE'.

The transaction file called MAINT contains the changes that will update SMSTR. Position 1 of each transaction record will always contain the CODE, which must be included to indicate the type of transaction. TSLSNO must always be coded to indicate the key field. The format for MAINT is as follows:

MAINT 24-position records

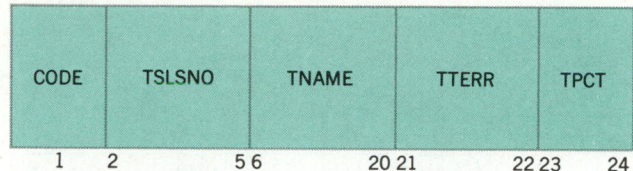

CODES
1 = new salesperson
   (all fields are coded)
2 = delete master record
   (only TSLSNO is coded)
3 = change of name
   (only TSLSNO and TNAME
   are coded in the record)
4 = change of territory
   (only TSLSNO and TTERR
   are coded in the record)
5 = change of commission rate
   (only TSLSNO and TPCT are coded)
6 = deactivate record by changing status to I
   (only TSLSNO is coded)

Note that in using these codes, only *one* record format is required for MAINT. All records—updates, additions, and deletions—use this same format.

In this sample problem, we will incorporate the following file maintenance procedures discussed in the previous sections:

1. *Adding a record to the file.* We will use this procedure to add new salespeople to the indexed file, that is, when CODE is equal to 1.

2. *Updating fields within a record.* This procedure will illustrate how a particular field can be updated or changed within a record. Updates to an existing record will occur when CODE is equal to 3, 4, or 5.

3. *Status change procedure.* This procedure is no different from the procedure to update fields within a record.

   A status field that is established as part of the record in the master indexed file can be used to identify particular conditions. Such conditions might consist of A for an active record or I for an inactive record. In this way, the record continues to be part of the file and can be identified by its special status code during future processing.

   A record's status will be changed to I when CODE is equal to 6.

4. *Deleting a record from the file.* This procedure will be illustrated to demonstrate how records can be eliminated from the file. Caution, however, must be exercised when implementing this procedure. Deleting a record from the file will destroy all data contained in the record and thus should only be performed when the record is not required for future reference (or it has been saved in an archive file).

   If a record is not required for normal processing, but the data is still required for future reference, then the record *should not* be deleted in this manner. Rather, the status change procedure discussed above should be used. In this way, the record will be flagged as a special record that will not normally be processed but can still be referenced at a later date.

   Record deletion will occur when CODE is equal to 2.

The control listing, called REPORT, has the following format:

REPORT Printer Spacing Chart

```
              1
              2
              3
    H    4              MAINTENANCE REPORT
              5
    H    6      EMP NO.   SALES PERSON    TERR.   COMM.   YTD SALES   MESSAGES
              7
    D    8      XXXX    X─────────X  XX    .XX   XX,XXØ.XX ⎧ADDITION
              9                                             DELETE
    D   10      XXXX    X─────────X  XX    .XX   XX,XXØ.XX ⎨CHANGE
             11                                             ERROR-INACTIVE
    D   12      XXXX    X─────────X  XX    .XX   XX,XXØ.XX ⎩ERROR-NO MASTER
             13     (EMPNO)      (SNAME)   (TERR) (PCT)   (YTDSLS)  ⎩ERROR-EXISTING MASTER
             14
             15                    ─────NEW PAGE─────
             16
   TLR   17     XXØX RECORDS ADDED   XXØX RECORDS CHANGED   XXØX RECORDS DELETED   XXØX TOTAL ERRORS
             18    (ACTR)               (CHCTR)               (DCTR)                (ECTR)
             19
             20
             21
```

The File Description Specifications form for this update procedure is as follows:

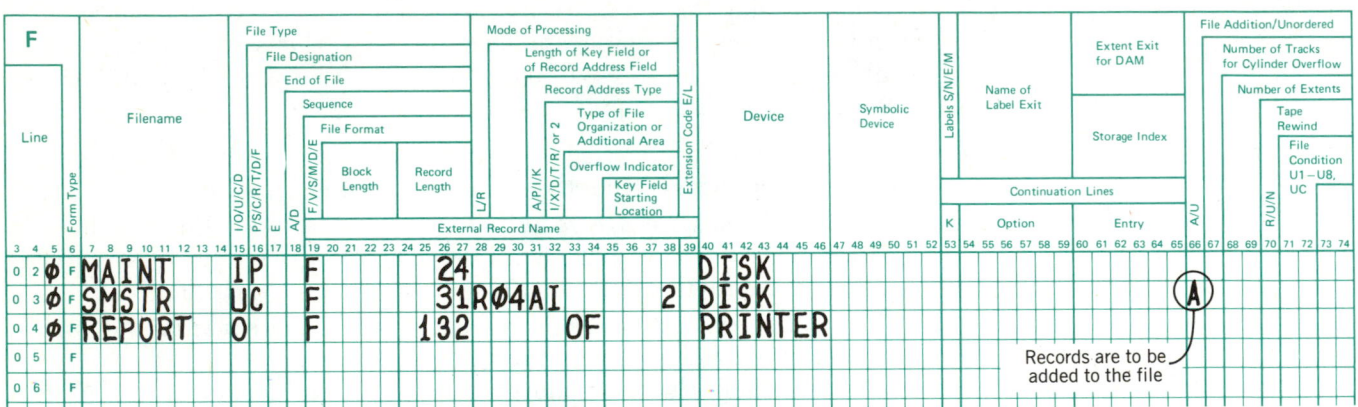

The transaction file called MAINT is considered to be the primary input file. That is, each record from MAINT is read first and the key field is used to find, by chaining, the corresponding master record, if one exists.

SMSTR is an *Update*, *Chained* file that is to be processed randomly. Thus, the Mode of Processing must be specified as 'R'. A file designated with a File Type of 'U' is treated as both an input and output file. For indexed file processing, the following entries are required:

1. Key field length: Ø4 in this illustration.
2. Starting location of the key field: 2 in this illustration. (The key field, SLSNUM, starts in column 2.)
3. Record Address Type or Data Format for Key: A for alphanumeric in this illustration.
4. File organization: I for indexed in this illustration.

Since we will also be adding records to the indexed file, we code A for "Additions" in column 66 of the File Description Specifications form. The index is always in sequence so that, even if a record is added, it can be accessed correctly later on. That is, the index is resequenced after each update procedure if records have been added to the master file.

The Input Specifications form for SMSTR is as follows:

Line	Form Type	Filename or Record Name	From	To	Decimal Positions	RPG Field Name
01	I	SMSTR NS				
02	I		1	1		STATUS
03	I		2	5		SLSNUM
04	I		6	20		SNAME
05	I		21	27	2	YTDSLS
06	I		28	29		TERR
07	I		30	31	2	PCT
08	I					

All input fields on SMSTR that are necessary for processing are included on the Input Specifications form. STATUS is the field that will include 'A' for active records and 'I' for inactive records. Numeric fields must include the number of decimal positions in the field by coding a digit in column 52.

The Input Specifications for MAINT are as follows:

Line	Form Type	Filename or Record Name	From	To	Decimal Positions	RPG Field Name
01	I	MAINT NS				
02	I		1	1		CODE
03	I		2	5		TSLSNO
04	I		6	20		TNAME
05	I		21	22		TTERR
06	I		23	24	2	TPCT
07	I					

TSLSNO of MAINT will be used for chaining to the indexed master file SMSTR.

A. Calculation Specifications for Updating Existing Master Records

The transaction field TSLSNO is used to CHAIN to the SMSTR indexed file. That is, TSLSNO is compared to SLSNUM on the SMSTR indexed file to find the matching record. The CHAIN operation compares the field specified in Factor 1 to the designated key field SLSNUM identified on the File Description Specifications form.

If the corresponding master record is found, then the programmer should make certain that the transaction code field does not equal 1, which would indicate a new salesperson. For update transaction records, the CHAIN operation *should* result in a corresponding master being read in. For new salespeople, however, the CHAIN operation should result in the record-not-found indicator being set on.

If the CHAIN operation results in the record-not-found indicator being set on and the transaction record is *not* a new salesperson, this would be an error. It would mean that the transaction file contains a record to be used to update the SMSTR master file, but that no corresponding record on the indexed file exists. The program should print an error message in this instance.

If the CHAIN operation results in a match, meaning a corresponding master record was found, make certain that the STATUS of the master record is 'A' for active. If it is not 'A', this, too, would be an error.

The Calculation Specifications form for this series of steps is as follows:

C	Form Type	Control Level (L0–L9, LR, SR, AN/OR)	Indicators						Factor 1	Operation	Factor 2	Result Field				Resulting Indicators			Comments
Line			Not	And	Not	And	Not					Name	Length	Decimal Positions	Half Adjust (H)	Plus 1>2 High	Minus 1<2 Low	Zero 1=2 Equal	
0 1	C	***							CHAIN TO MASTER AND MAKE CERTAIN THAT PROPER										
0 2	C	***							CORRESPONDENCE EXISTS										
0 3	C	*																	
0 4	C								TSLSNO	CHAIN	SMSTR						22		
0 5	C								CODE	COMP	'2'					44	10	80	
0 6	C			N22					STATUS	COMP	'A'							33	
0 7	C	*																	
0 8	C			N22	33		44			EXSR	SRCHGE								
0 9	C			22	10					EXSR	SRADD								
1 0	C			N22	80					EXSR	SRDEL								
1 1	C	*																	
1 2	C			22N10															
1 3	C	OR	N22N33																
1 4	C	OR	N22	10															
1 5	C	OR	22	80					ECTR	ADD	1	ECTR	40						
1 6	C																		
1 7	C																		
1 8	C																		

The following indicators, then, denote a valid change or update condition:

Indicators	Meaning
N22	A master record with the same salesperson number as the transaction record was found.
33	The status of the master record is 'A' for active.
44	The type of transaction indicated with the CODE field is an update transaction because CODE is between 3 and 6 (CODE is greater than 2).

If N22, 33, and 44 are on, then the specific type of change record must be determined by again testing the CODE field. This is performed in the subroutine named SRCHGE, illustrated below. Recall that a code of 3 is a NAME change, 4 is TERR change, 5 is PCT change, and 6 indicates that the STATUS field of the master is to change to I. The RPG coding necessary for designating the appropriate change is as follows:

C			Indicators						Factor 1	Operation	Factor 2	Result Field				Resulting Indicators			Comments
			And		And											Arithmetic			
												Name	Length			Plus	Minus	Zero	
																Compare			
																1>2	1<2	1=2	
Line	Form Type	Control Level	Not		Not		Not							Decimal Positions	Half Adjust (H)	Lookup (Factor 2) is			
																High	Low	Equal	
3 4 5	6	7 8	9 10 11	12 13	14 15	16	17	18 19 20 21 22 23 24 25 26 27	28 29 30 31 32	33 34 35 36 37 38 39 40 41 42	43 44 45 46 47 48	49 50 51	52	53	54 55	56 57	58 59	60 61 62 63 64 65 66 67 68 69 70 71 72 73 74
0 1	C	***						CHANGE THE MASTER RECORD											
0 2	C	*																	
0 3	C	SR						SRCHGE	BEGSR										
0 4	C	SR						CODE	COMP	'3'							4Φ		TNAME
0 5	C	SR	4Φ						MOVE	TNAME	SNAME								
0 6	C	SR						CODE	COMP	'4'							5Φ		TTERR
0 7	C	SR	5Φ						MOVE	TTERR	TERR								
0 8	C	SR						CODE	COMP	'5'							6Φ		TPCT
0 9	C	SR	6Φ						Z-ADD	TPCT	PCT								
1 0	C	SR						CODE	COMP	'6'							7Φ		INACTIVE
1 1	C	*																	
1 2	C	SR						CHCTR	ADD	1	CHCTR	4Φ							
1 3	C	SR							ENDSR										
1 4	C																		

For transaction records that designate new accounts, we would have the following indicators set on:

Indicators	Meaning
22	No master record exists for the transaction record.
10	The CODE on the transaction record is equal to 1, denoting a new account.

For new salespeople, all transaction fields would be written to the master record and the STATUS would be set to 'A' for active.

The following calculations are used to move the fields from the transaction record to the fields defined in the SMSTR record for subsequent addition of the record to the indexed file during output time:

C			Indicators						Factor 1	Operation	Factor 2	Result Field				Resulting Indicators			Comments
			And		And											Arithmetic			
												Name	Length			Plus	Minus	Zero	
																Compare			
																1>2	1<2	1=2	
Line	Form Type	Control Level	Not		Not		Not							Decimal Positions	Half Adjust (H)	Lookup (Factor 2) is			
																High	Low	Equal	
3 4 5	6	7 8	9 10 11	12 13	14 15	16	17	18 19 20 21 22 23 24 25 26 27	28 29 30 31 32	33 34 35 36 37 38 39 40 41 42	43 44 45 46 47 48	49 50 51	52	53	54 55	56 57	58 59	60 61 62 63 64 65 66 67 68 69 70 71 72 73 74
0 1	C	***						ADD NEW MASTER RECORD TO FILE											
0 2	C	*																	
0 3	C	SR						SRADD	BEGSR										
0 4	C	SR							MOVE	TSLSNO	SLSNUM								
0 5	C	SR							MOVE	TNAME	SNAME								
0 6	C	SR							MOVE	TTERR	TERR								
0 7	C	SR							Z-ADD	Φ	YTDSLS								
0 8	C	SR							Z-ADD	TPCT	PCT								
0 9	C	SR						ACTR	ADD	1	ACTR	4Φ							
1 0	C	SR							ENDSR										
1 1	C																		
1 2	C																		

If indicators 22 and 10 are on, the new record will be added to the indexed master file during output time.

Transaction records that designate a deletion of a record from the master file are identified by the following indicators:

Indicators	Meaning
N22	A master record with the same salesperson number as the transaction record was found.
80	The CODE on the transaction record is equal to 2, denoting that the record is to be deleted from the master file.

If the two indicators N22 and 80 are set on, the record chained from the SMSTR indexed file will be deleted. That is, the data contained in the record is destroyed and is no longer available for future use.

The following calculations add 1 to a counter used to count the number of deletions. The count is printed out at the end for control purposes. The actual deletion of the record takes place on the Output Specifications form discussed in the next section.

	C		Indicators						Factor 1	Operation	Factor 2	Result Field				Resulting Indicators					Comments
Line	Form Type	Control Level	And Not	And Not	Not							Name	Length	Decimal Positions	Half Adjust (H)	Plus	Minus	Zero	High	Low	Equal	
0 1	C	SR							SRDEL	BEGSR												
0 2	C	*																				
0 3	C	***							ADD 1 TO DELETE COUNTER													
0 4	C	*																				
0 5	C	***							RECORD WILL BE DELETED DURING												
0 6	C	***							DETAIL OUTPUT TIME WITH												
0 7	C	***							INDICATORS N22 AND 80												
0 8	C	*																				
0 9	C	SR							DCTR	ADD	1	DCTR	40									
1 0	C	SR								ENDSR												

There are two types of output in this program: disk output, which will be the updated indexed file, and printed output, indicating errors and control totals.

Disk Output

In most of our previous problems that used disk output, each output field was defined on the Output Specifications form. This is required if each output record is created anew from an input record.

In the update procedure defined in this chapter, an SMSTR record already exists—in the input area—for transaction records in which a successful CHAIN operation was performed. Thus, for records to be changed, only the fields that require changing need be defined on the Output Specifications form. You will recall that the following indicators denote a successful CHAIN, where an active master record exists:

N22 A chain to the master file results in a corresponding record.

33 The master record is active.

In this instance, the changes to the master file are defined by the following indicators, which would be turned on during calculations:

Indicators	Meaning
40	SNAME change
50	STERR change
60	PCT change
70	STATUS change (record is to be deactivated)

The following Output Specifications would result in the appropriate changes to the indexed file SMSTR:

Updating the indexed file SMSTR with changes

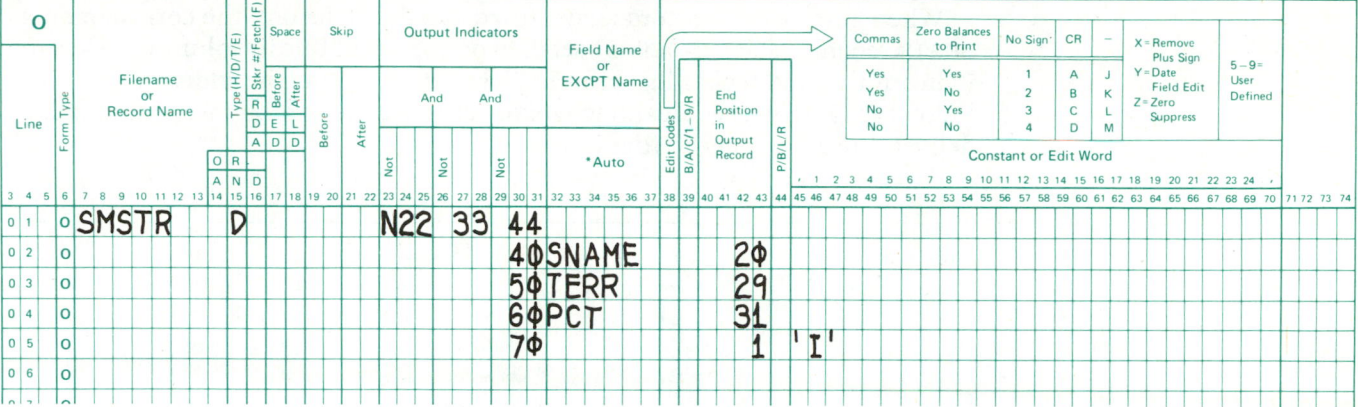

For transaction records that denote new salespeople, all MAINT fields must be moved to the SMSTR record and then specified in the output area since a new record is to be created. You will recall that the following indicators are used to designate a new salesperson:

Indicators	Meaning
22	A corresponding record does not exist.
10	The CODE field in the MAINT record indicates a new salesperson (CODE is equal to 1).

For these transaction records, a new SMSTR record must be created. ADD is specified on the detail line in columns 16–18 to indicate that an entirely new record is to be added to the indexed file. The fields to serve as output must also be specified:

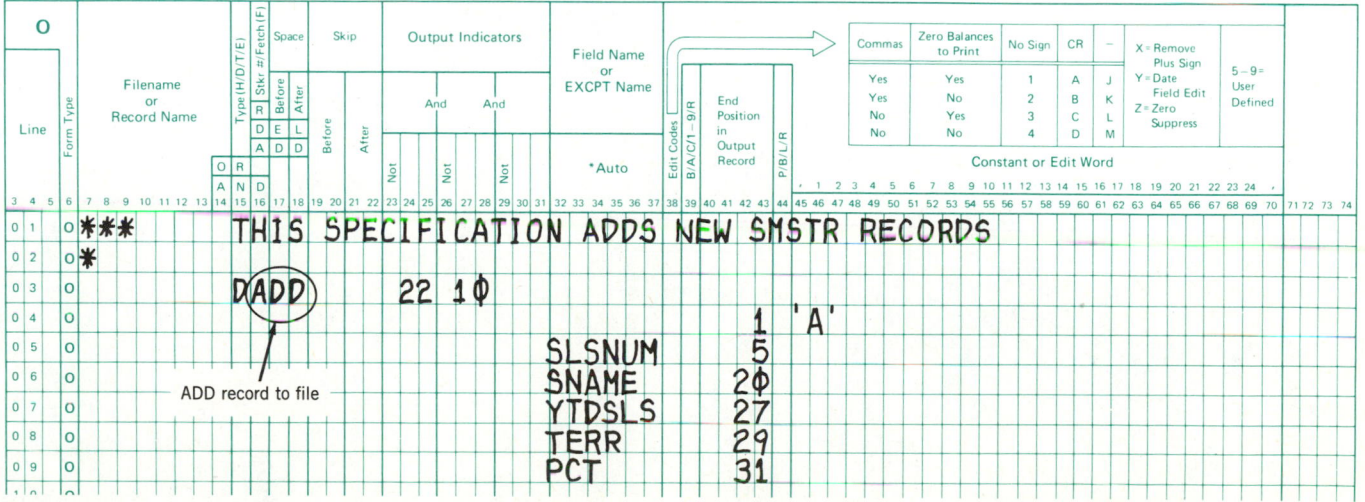

For transaction records containing the value 2 in the CODE field, the corresponding record from the indexed file is to be read using the CHAIN operation and then *deleted*. The following indicators are used to designate a record that is to be deleted:

Indicators	Meaning
N22	A CHAIN to the indexed file resulted in a corresponding record; that is, a match was found.
80	The CODE field in the MAINT record indicates a record is to be deleted from the indexed file.

When a transaction record is identified as a delete record, the corresponding SMSTR record is deleted. DEL is specified on the detail line in columns 16–18 to indicate that the record just read is to be deleted from the indexed file. The following Output Specifications would result in the appropriate record being deleted from the indexed file:

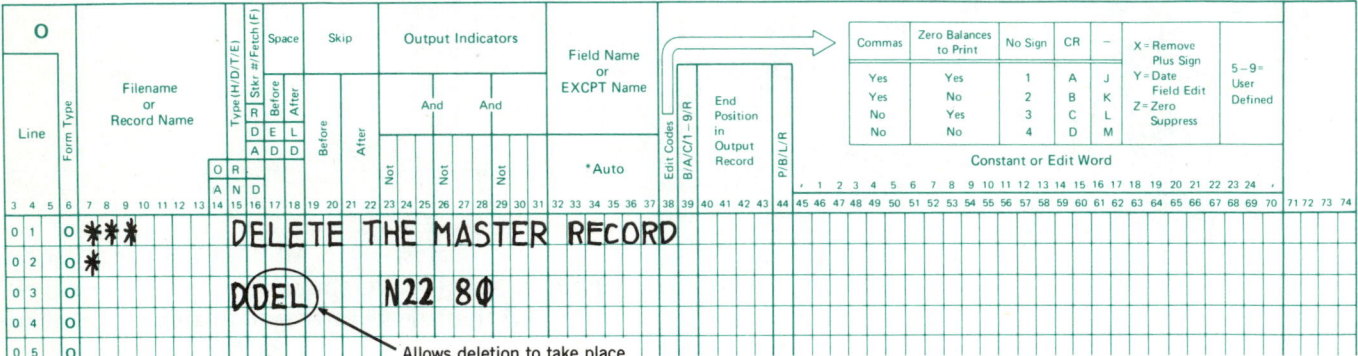

Printed Output

The following Output Specifications will produce the printed results specified on the Printer Spacing Chart:

RPG Output Specifications

```
Line  Form  Filename/    Type  Stk  Space  Skip   Output Indicators   Field Name   End    Constant or Edit Word
      Type  Record Name               B/A   B/A                       or EXCPT     Pos
                                                   And    And    And   Name
01    O   REPORT    H        04              1P
02    O             OR                       OF
03    O                                                                             39    'MAINTENANCE REPORT'
04    O             H        06              1P
05    O             OR                       OF
06    O                                                                             15    'EMP NO.'
07    O                                                                             31    'SALES PERSON'
08    O                                                                             48    'TERR.     COMM.'
09    O                                                                             69    'YTD SALES   MESSAGES'
10    O             D   2                    N1P
11    O                                                                  SLSNUM     13
12    O                                                                  SNAME      33
13    O                                                                  TERR       39
14    O                                                                  PCT    3   46
15    O                                                                  YTDSLS1    59
16    O                                       N22 33 44                            67    'CHANGE'
17    O                                       N22 80                               67    'DELETE'
18    O                                        22 10                               69    'ADDITION'
19    O                                       N22N33                               75    'ERROR-INACTIVE'
20    O                                        22N10                               76    'ERROR-NO MASTER'
21    O                                       N22 10                               82    'ERROR-EXISTING MASTER'
22    O                                       N22 80                               84    'ERROR-NO MASTER FOR DEL'
23    O*
24    O             T   4                    LR
25    O                                                                  ACTR   Z   10
26    O                                                                             24    'RECORDS ADDED'
27    O                                                                  CHCTR  Z   30
28    O                                                                             46    'RECORDS CHANGED'
29    O                                                                  DCTR   Z   52
30    O                                                                             68    'RECORDS DELETED'
31    O                                                                  ECTR   Z   74
32    O                                                                             87    'TOTAL ERRORS'
```

Note that this printed output is used for correcting errors and for providing control totals. In general, the more information provided on an error control report, the better.

B. File Maintenance Procedures Using Structured Programming

The update program presented in the previous illustration performs the update task effectively, but does not incorporate the full structured concepts used in more modern RPG programming. In this section, we write the required RPG specifications for the previous problem using structured programming concepts. Figure 9.9 presents an illustration of the program using structured

Figure 9.9
Example of program that uses
structured programming
concepts.

```
....+....1....+....2....+....3....+....4....+....5....+....6....+....7
0001  ******************************************************************
0002  *
0003  *   PROGRAM DESCRIPTION:
0004  *
0005  *       THIS PROGRAM IS A FILE MAINTENANCE PROGRAM USED TO
0006  *       UPDATE THE FILE "SMSTR". TRANSACTION RECORDS
0007  *       ARE READ FROM THE FILE "MAINT" WHICH ARE USED TO
0008  *       ADD, CHANGE, AND DELETE RECORDS IN THE "SMSTR" FILE.
0009  *       A REPORT IS ALSO PRODUCED IDENTIFYING THE TRANSACTIONS
0010  *       MADE TO THE SMSTR FILE.
0011  *
0012  *
0013  *   FUNCTION OF INDICATORS:
0014  *
0015  *       22    UPDATE RECORD NOT FOUND IN SMSTR FILE
0016  *
0017  ******************************************************************
0018  *
0019 H
0020 FMAINT    ID F    64           DISK
0021 FSMSTR    UC F    128R04AI  2 DISK                                 A
0022 FREPORT   O  F    132    OF   PRINTER
0023  *
0024 ISMSTR    NS
0025 I                                          2    5 SMSNUM
0026 I                                          6   20 SMNAME
0027 I                                         21  272SMYTDS
0028 I                                         28   29 SMTERR
0029 I                                         30  312SMPCT
0030 I                                        128  128 SMSTAT
0031  *
0032 IMAINT    NS
0033 I                                          2    5 TSLSNO
0034 I                                          6   20 TNAME
0035 I                                         21   22 TTERR
0036 I                                         23  242TPCT
0037 I                                         64   64 TCODE
0038  *
0039 I#WORK       DS
0040 I                                          1   40#ECTR
0041 I                                          5   80#DCTR
0042 I                                          9  120#CCTR
0043 I                                         13  160#ACTR
0044 I                                         17   19 #FOUND
0045 I                                         20   34 #MESAG
0046  *
0047 IFLAGS       DS
0048 I                                          1    1 #FRST
0049 I                                          2    4 #LR
0050  *
0051  *                              MAIN-MODULE-RTN
0052 C                    EXSR SRFRST
0053  *
0054 C         #LR        DOWEQ' OFF'
0055 C         TSLSNO     CHAINSMSTR                    22
0056 C    N22             MOVE 'YES'     #FOUND
0057 C     22             MOVE 'NO '     #FOUND
0058 C                    MOVE *BLANKS   #MESAG
0059 C    OF              EXCPT@H100
0060 C                    SETOF                    OF
0061 C         TCODE      CASEQ'1'       SRADD
0062 C         TCODE      CASEQ'2'       SRDEL
0063 C         TCODE      CASGE'3'       SRCHG
0064 C                    END
0065 C                    EXCPT@D200
0066 C                    READ MAINT                    LR
0067 C    LR              MOVE 'ON '     #LR
0068 C                    END
0069  *
0070 C                    EXCPT@T300
0071  *
0072  *                              SRADD-ADD-RECORD-RTN
0073 CSR       SRADD      BEGSR
0074 CSR       #FOUND     IFEQ 'NO '                   IF-01
0075 CSR                  ADD  1         #ACTR
0076 CSR                  MOVE 'ADDITION'#MESAG
0077 CSR                  MOVE TSLSNO    SMSNUM
0078 CSR                  MOVE TNAME     SMNAME
0079 CSR                  Z-ADD*ZEROS    SMYTDS
0080 CSR                  MOVE TTERR     SMTERR
0081 CSR                  MOVE TPCT      SMPCT
0082 CSR                  EXCPT@ADD
```

Figure 9.9   ....+....1....+....2....+....3....+....4....+....5....+....6....+....7
(continued)

```
0083 CSR                      ELSE                                  ELSE
0084 CSR                      ADD   1        #ECTR
0085 CSR                      MOVEL'ER-EXIST'#MESAG
0086 CSR                      MOVE 'ING MAST'#MESAG
0087 CSR                      END                                   ENDIF-01
0088 CSR                      ENDSR
0089  *
0090  *                                      SRDEL-DETETE-RECORD-RTN
0091 CSR          SRDEL       BEGSR
0092 CSR          #FOUND      IFEQ 'YES'                            IF-01
0093 CSR                      ADD   1        #DCTR
0094 CSR                      MOVE 'DELETE'  #MESAG
0095 CSR                      EXCPT@DEL
0096 CSR                      ELSE                                  ELSE
0097 CSR                      ADD   1        #ECTR
0098 CSR                      MOVEL'ERROR-NO'#MESAG
0099 CSR                      MOVE ' MASTER' #MESAG
0100 CSR                      END                                   ENDIF-01
0101 CSR                      ENDSR
0102  *
0103  *                                      SRCHG-UPDATE-RECORD-RTN
0104 CSR          SRCHG       BEGSR
0105 CSR          #FOUND      IFEQ 'YES'                            IF-01
0106 CSR          SMSTAT      IFEQ 'A'                              IF-02
0107 CSR          TCODE       IFEQ '3'                              IF-03
0108 CSR                      MOVE TNAME     SMNAME
0109 CSR                      EXCPT@CHGE3
0110 CSR                      ELSE
0111 CSR          TCODE       IFEQ '4'                              IF-04
0112 CSR                      MOVE TTERR     SMTERR
0113 CSR                      EXCPT@CHGE4
0114 CSR                      ELSE
0115 CSR          TCODE       IFEQ '5'                              IF-05
0116 CSR                      MOVE TPCT      SMPCT
0117 CSR                      EXCPT@CHGE5
0118 CSR                      ELSE
0119 CSR          TCODE       IFEQ '6'                              IF-06
0120 CSR                      EXCPT@CHGE6
0121 CSR                      END                                ENDIF-06
0122 CSR                      END                                ENDIF-05
0123 CSR                      END                                ENDIF-04
0124 CSR                      END                                ENDIF-03
0125 CSR                      ADD   1        #CCTR
0126 CSR                      MOVE 'CHANGE'  #MESAG
0127 CSR                      ELSE
0128 CSR                      ADD   1        #ECTR
0129 CSR                      MOVEL'ERROR-IN'#MESAG
0130 CSR                      MOVE 'ACTIVE'  #MESAG
0131 CSR                      END                                   ENDIF-02
0132 CSR                      ELSE
0133 CSR                      ADD   1        #ECTR
0134 CSR                      MOVEL'ERROR-NO'#MESAG
0135 CSR                      MOVE ' MASTER' #MESAG
0136 CSR                      END                                   ENDIF-01
0137 CSR                      ENDSR
0138  *
0139 CSR          SRFRST      BEGSR
0140 CSR                      MOVE 'OFF'     #LR
0141 CSR                      SETON                         OF
0142 CSR                      READ MAINT                       LR
0143 CSR LR                   MOVE 'ON '     #LR
0144 CSR                      ENDSR
0145  *
0146 OSMSTR    E             @CHGE3
0147 O                       SMNAME     20
0148 O         E             @CHGE4
0149 O                       SMTERR     29
0150 O         E             @CHGE5
0151 O                       SMPCT      31
0152 O         E             @CHGE6
0153 O                       128 'I'
0154  *
0155 O         EADD          @ADD
0156 O                         1 'M'
0157 O                       SMSNUM      5
0158 O                       SMNAME     20
0159 O                       SMYTDS     27
0160 O                       SMTERR     29
0161 O                       SMPCT      31
0162 O                       128 'A'
0163 O         EDEL          @DEL
```

Figure 9.9
(continued)

```
          ....+....1....+....2....+....3....+....4....+....5....+....6....+....7
0164   *
0165 OREPORT   E    04            @H100
0166 O                                             39 'MAINTENANCE      REPORT'
0167 O         E    06            @H100
0168 O                                             15 'EMP NO '
0169 O                                             31 'SALES PERSON'
0170 O                                             48 'TERR.    COMM.'
0171 O                                             69 'YTD SALES  MESSAGES'
0172   *
0173 O         E 2                @D200
0174 O                            SMSNUM   13
0175 O                            SMNAME   33
0176 O                            SMTERR   39
0177 O                            SMPCT 3  46
0178 O                            SMYTDS1  59
0179 O                            #MESAG   82
0180   *
0181 O         E 4                @T300
0182 O                            #ACTR Z  10
0183 O                                             24 'RECORDS ADDED'
0184 O                            #CCTR Z  30
0185 O                                             46 'RECORDS CHANGED'
0186 O                            #DCTR Z  52
0187 O                                             68 'RECORDS DELETED'
0188 O                            #ECTR Z  74
0189 O                                             87 'TOTAL ERRORS'
```

concepts. Examine and compare this program with the previous illustration. Let us point out some of the features used in this structured example:

1. This program has complete control of input. That is, the sequential file MAINT is defined as a Demand file and processed on the Calculations Specifications form using the READ operation.

2. The program also has complete control of output operations. All output in this program is written using the EXCPT (write) operation at the time it is required. Again, like input operations, output operations are executed during calculation-time.

3. Variable names or switches that have been established in the Data Structure FLAGS are used to replace indicators used as conditional switches. These variable names give more meaning to the conditions tested within the program and make the program more structured. In addition, structures such as IF/ELSE/END operations are used in place of indicators to achieve better structuring of the program. In these situations, a test is performed and operations are executed based on the outcome of various tests. There is no need to establish indicators or flags for these conditions.

By comparison, the structured program that is illustrated is much longer than the previous figure, which uses traditional specifications. But, after examining the structure of this program, you will see that it is much easier to understand and follow. In general, structured techniques make programs easier to debug, maintain, and modify when the need arises.

Summary of Indexed File Updating

You may have noticed that it is possible to update both sequential and indexed sequential disks in similar ways. By using the file type of U (column 15) on the File Description Specifications form, you may designate an existing disk as a file to be updated. If we want to add records to that file as well as change existing records, we code 'A' in column 66 on the File Description Specifications form.

For indexed files we code the following:

INDEXED FILE DESCRIPTION ENTRIES

File Type (column 15)	Use U.
File Designation (column 16)	For records to be processed randomly, the letter C is placed in column 16 to denote the CHAIN operation.
Mode of Processing (column 28)	For records to be processed randomly (use R).
Type of File Organization (column 32)	Use I for indexed.
Length of Key Field (columns 29–30)	This is a numeric entry, right-justified.
Record Address Type (column 31)	Use A for alphanumeric.
Key Field Starting Position (columns 33–38)	This is a numeric entry, right-justified.
File Additions (column 66)	Use A for adding records.

To add records to a file designated as an update file, code ADD in columns 16–18 of the Output Specifications line. This will add records to the end of the indexed file and the index itself will be updated. Likewise, to delete records from a file designated as an update file, code DEL in columns 16–18 of the Output Specifications line. This will delete the record previously read using the CHAIN operation.

For indexed files, it is not necessary to sort the file after additions are made, since the index itself is automatically sorted into the correct key field sequence after each update. That is, the physical location of the records is not as important since the index can direct us to the appropriate record on a random access basis. Note, however, that an indexed file that is physically in sequence by record key could be accessed more efficiently than one that is out of order. Hence, it is a good idea to periodically sort the indexed file, not because it is necessary, but because it will, overall, reduce access time.

Making Inquiries Into an Indexed File

Thus far, we have seen one benefit of indexed files—you can CHAIN to the master with transaction records in no specific sequence and update the file as necessary. A second major advantage of indexed files is that you can randomly retrieve and display any record and check its status or contents. This is referred to as an inquiry.

UPDATING AN INDEXED DISK FILE

1. The file to be updated is treated as both an input and output file.
2. The update file is described on the following forms:
   File Description Specifications form
   Input Specifications form
   Output Specifications form
3. Only the fields to be changed need be described on the Input Specifications form.

4. Records to be changed or deleted must already exist on the master file.
5. Records to be added should not have the same key field as one already on the master file.

V. Dynamic Processing of an Indexed File

A. Processing within Limits

As stated earlier, the most important feature of indexed files is the ability to access them randomly. That is, it is possible to process only those indexed records we wish to, without the need to access every record in the file in sequence. We have also seen how indexed files can be accessed sequentially for reporting purposes where every record is read in sequence. In addition to a full sequential procedure or a random procedure, sometimes we wish to access a *select group* of *related records* from an indexed file. For example, we may wish to print the quantity on hand for products stored in a particular warehouse or print billing statements for those customers whose last names begin with a particular character.

To perform this function requires **dynamic processing** or **processing within limits.**

Processing within limits means that we access an indexed file randomly first, to locate the initial record we want, and then sequentially from that point on. Dynamic processing, then, combines both random and sequential access in the same program in order to process only a select group of records from the file. This is accomplished by randomly "jumping" to a record location within the file and then processing the file in a sequential manner from that point on, thus allowing access to only those records required.

Example 1   To illustrate the different steps involved in dynamic processing or processing within limits we will consider a problem to print billing statements for a retail store. The record layout for the customer master file CUSTMST is shown in Figure 9.10. The primary key for this file, CACCT, consists of two parts: the first letter of the customer's last name in the first position and a five-digit *unique* customer number in positions 2–6. By using the first character of the account code, redefined as CLNCDE, we will be able to identify and process records for customers whose last names begin with a specific letter.

The retail store sends billing statements to customers once a month. Since the accounts receivable department is small, the manager has decided to process the customer account file daily and produce smaller groups of billing statements using the first

Figure 9.10
Record layout for the customer master file CUSTMST.

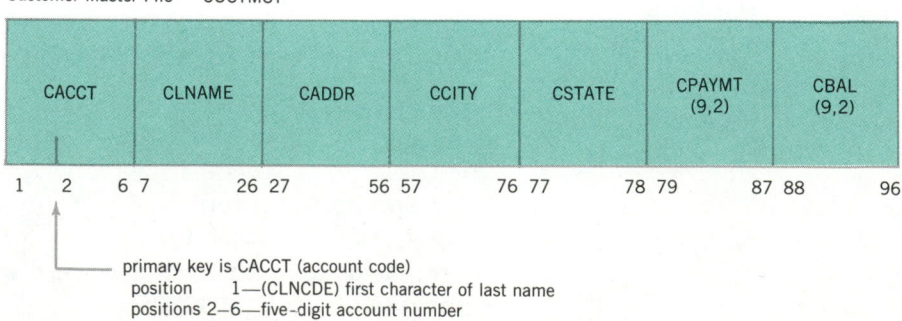

Record Layout for
Customer Master File — CUSTMST

CACCT	CLNAME	CADDR	CCITY	CSTATE	CPAYMT (9,2)	CBAL (9,2)

1   2   6 7   26 27   56 57   76 77   78 79   87 88   96

primary key is CACCT (account code)
position   1—(CLNCDE) first character of last name
positions 2–6—five-digit account number

Figure 9.11
Sample customer master file where only records with an account code that begins with 'H' are to be processed.

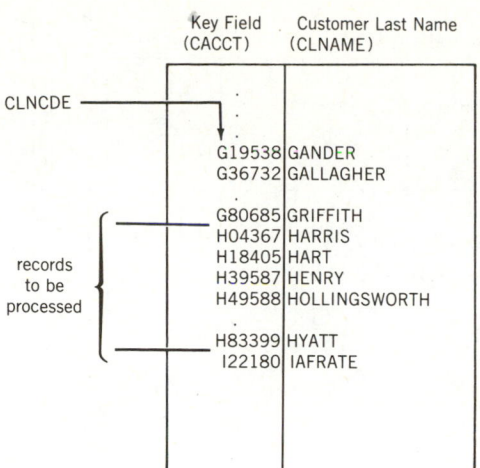

letter of the customer's last name (CLNCDE) to determine which bills are to be prepared each day.

To simplify our example, we will consider the specifications required to process only the customer account records in which the account code begins with the character H, as shown in Figure 9.11. The first position of the primary key field CACCT has been redefined as CLNCDE to identify the first character of the customer's last name.

The File Description entries necessary for processing the CUSTMST file between limits to produce billing statements are shown in Figure 9.12. In this example, only customers whose last names begin with 'H' will be processed.

To process an indexed file within limits requires one new File Description Specification. The Mode of Processing (column 28) must contain the letter L for the indexed file to be processed within limits.

In addition, processing an indexed file within limits requires that the file be accessed under control of the program, *not* under control of the RPG Logic Cycle. For this reason, the File Designation (column 16) must be an F (Full Procedural file) or D (Demand file). In our example, we will use a Demand file to sequentially access the records from the CUSTMST indexed file beginning with those records whose CLNCDE, which is part of CACCT, is equal to 'H'.

The four primary components of indexed files must also be specified.

Before the indexed file can be accessed sequentially, program control must position the record pointer at the first record to be read (CLNCDE of CACCT is equal to 'H'). This is accomplished by using the SETLL operation.

Figure 9.12
File Description entries necessary for a file to be processed between limits.

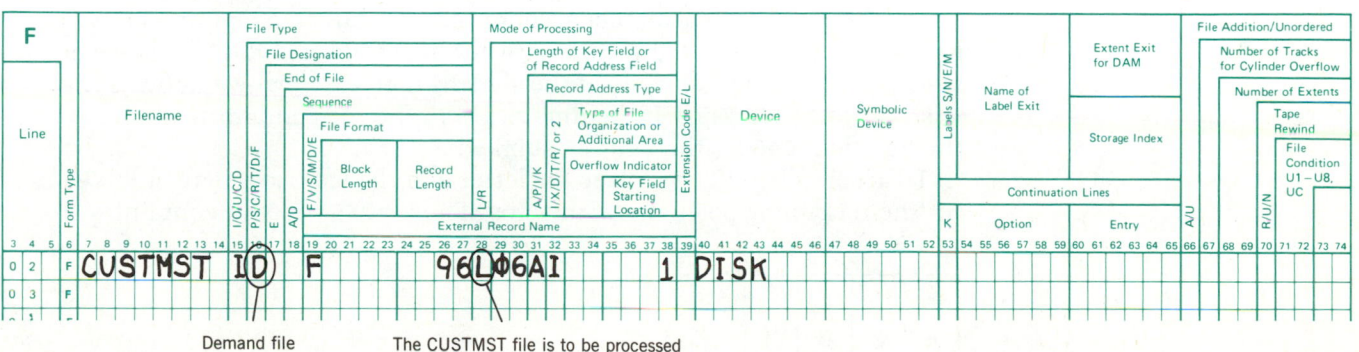

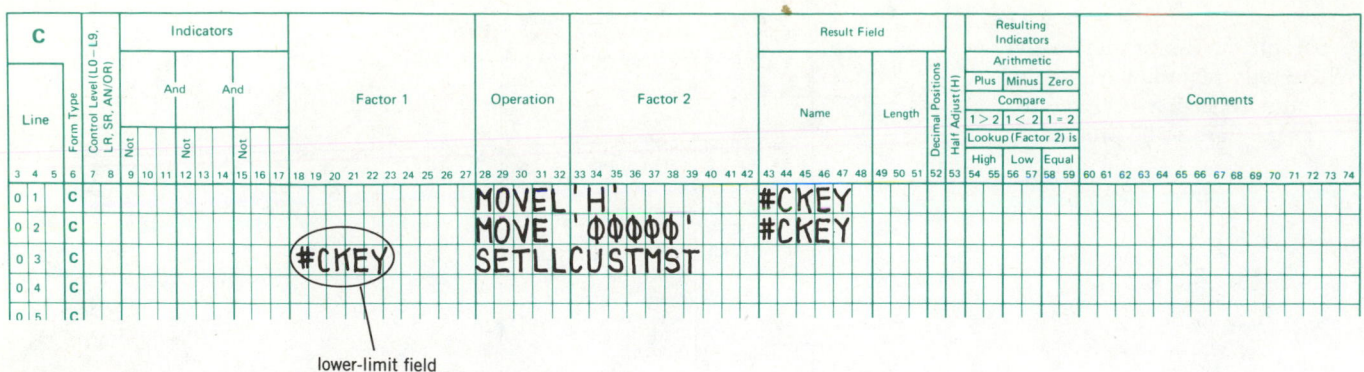

	C			Indicators							Factor 1		Operation	Factor 2		Result Field					Resulting Indicators			Comments
0 1	C												MOVEL	'H'		#CKEY								
0 2	C												MOVE	'ØØØØØ'		#CKEY								
0 3	C										#CKEY		SETLL	CUSTMST										
0 4	C																							
0 5	C																							

lower-limit field

Figure 9.13
Use of the SETLL operation in
a billing program.

B. The SETLL (Set Lower Limit) Operation

The **SETLL operation** enables a program to begin processing an indexed file sequentially at a record location other than the first or next record in the file. Since we want to start processing at the first customer record that begins with the letter 'H', the SETLL operation is required to position the record pointer. Figure 9.13 illustrates the SETLL operation for our billing problem.

When the SETLL operation is executed, the record pointer randomly "jumps" to the first record in the file in which CACCT is equal to or greater than #CKEY.

Factor 1 (columns 18–27) of the SETLL operation contains a field or literal specifying the starting value where sequential processing is to begin. This field is called the *lower limit field* because it contains the lowest value where processing is to begin.

Operation Code (columns 28–32) contains the operation SETLL.

Factor 2 (columns 33–42) contains the name of the indexed file to be accessed within limits.

C. Establishing the Lower Limit Field

To process an indexed file within limits, a field or literal must be placed in Factor 1 that will contain a value representing the lowest value or starting point where sequential processing is to begin. This field should be the same length and data type as the key field in the indexed file. Using this field, the SETLL operation will locate the first record in the file with a key value equal to or greater than the lower limit field. This is our starting point.

For our example of customer account records shown in Figure 9.11, we need to start processing at the record with the key field 'H04367'. However, we would normally not know what the starting digits are. All we know is that we wish to start processing at the first record in the file containing the letter H in the key field CACCT (the CLNCDE subfield).

To accomplish this, we place the letter H in the left-most byte of #CKEY and fill the remaining positions with zeros. Thus, #CKEY would contain:

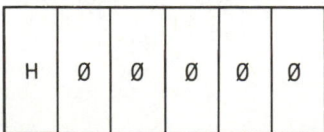

#CKEY is initialized this way so that when the SETLL operation is executed it will locate the first record in the file that contains a key field equal to or greater than #CKEY. That record is 'H04367', the first record beginning with the letter H.

The field #CKEY is initialized to its starting value (lower limit) in Figure 9.13 using the MOVEL and MOVE operations preceding the SETLL operation. The MOVEL operation moves the letter H to the left-most position of #CKEY and the MOVE operation initializes the remaining bytes with zeros.

When the SETLL operation is executed, the record pointer is positioned at the first record in the indexed file in which the key field is *equal to* or *greater than* the value stored in #CKEY. This will position the record pointer at the first record to be read sequentially from the file. The SETLL operation does *not* read a record from the indexed file but only moves the record pointer to the first sequential record to be read.

After execution of the SETLL in our sample problem, the record pointer should be positioned as follows:

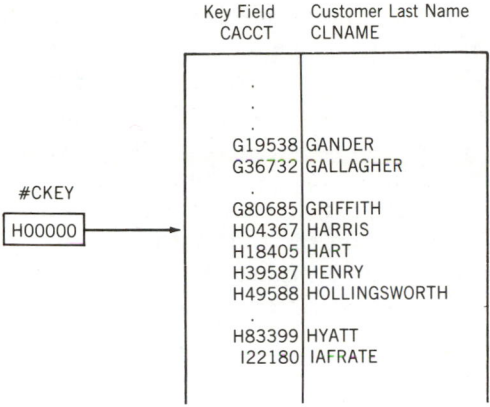

The SETLL operation will position the record pointer to the first record in the file in which CACCT is greater than or equal to #CKEY.

Remember, when the SETLL operation is executed, the record pointer will be positioned at the first record equal *to* or *greater than* the value in Factor 1. Thus, by placing the letter H and zeros in #CKEY the record pointer will be moved to the first record in the file in which CACCT is greater than #CKEY, that is, the first account record beginning with the letter H.

D. Sequentially Reading the Indexed File

To indicate that we wish to read records in sequence from a file processed within limits, we must use the following READ operation after the SETLL:

Line	Form Type	Control Level (L0–L9, LR, SR, AN/OR)	Indicators And Not	And Not	Not	Factor 1	Operation	Factor 2	Result Field Name	Length	Decimal Positions	Half Adjust (H)	Plus	Minus	Zero	1>2 High 54 55	1<2 Low 56 57	1=2 Equal 58 59	Comments
0 1	C						•												
0 2	C						•												
0 3	C							READ	CUSTMST										LR
0 4	C	NLR				CLNCDE	COMP	'H'									LR		
0 5	C						•												
0 6	C																		

Upon execution of the READ operation, the next sequential record is read from the indexed file CUSTMST. Columns 58–59 must contain an end-of-file indicator to identify if the end-of-file has been reached on the file.

Since the SETLL operation positioned the record pointer at record 'H04367', that record will be read into the program when the READ operation is executed the first time.

Once a record is read from the indexed file, it must be determined if the record is to be processed. That is, it must be determined if the record just read belongs to the group of records we wish to process in this program. In our example, we want to process only those records in which the CLNCDE field is equal to 'H'.

E. Checking for the Upper Limit

When processing an indexed file within limits a procedure must be executed in order to determine when processing is to terminate. Normally, when processing within limits we continue to sequentially access records from the file until we read a record that exceeds an upper limit value established in the program. In our example, we stop processing when the field CLNCDE begins with a letter greater than H as shown in the READ operation above. Thus, our upper limit in this example is a record with a CLNCDE greater than 'H'.

The first character of each customer account code, defined as CLNCDE, is compared to the letter 'H' to determine if the upper limit has been reached (CLNCDE is greater than 'H'). When CLNCDE is greater than 'H' or an end-of-file has occurred on the indexed file, the program is terminated because the program has read beyond the required upper limit of processing.

Figure 9.14 shows the complete RPG program for our accounts receivable billing problem.

Figure 9.14
RPG program for accounts receivable billing problem.

```
....+....1....+....2....+....3....+....4....+....5....+....6....+....7
0001 **************************************************************
0002 *
0003 *   PROGRAM DESCRIPTION:
0004 *
0005 *       THIS PROGRAM PRINTS BILLING STATEMENTS FOR A
0006 *       PARTICULAR GROUP OF RECORDS (CUSTOMER ACCOUNT RECORDS
0007 *       IN WHICH THE ACCOUNT CODE BEGINS WITH "H").
0008 *
0009 *
0010 *   FUNCTION OF INDICATORS:
0011 *
0012 *       NONE
0013 *
0014 **************************************************************
0015 *
0016 H
0017 FCUSTMST ID  F     96L 6AI      1 DISK
0018 FREPORT   O  F     80             PRINTER
0019 *
0020 ICUSTMST NS
0021 I                              1   6 CACCT
0022 I                              1   1 CLNCDE
0023 I                              7  26 CLNAME
0024 I                             27  56 CADDR
0025 I                             57  76 CCITY
0026 I                             77  78 CSTATE
0027 I                             79  872CPAYMT
0028 I                             88  962CBAL
0029 I          DS
0030 I                              1   6 #CKEY
0031 *
0032 *                                MAIN-LINE-RTN
0033 C                    EXSR SR100
0034 C        $LOOP       TAG
0035 C                    EXSR SR200
```

Figure 9.14
(continued)

```
0036 C   NLR                 GOTO $LOOP
0037 *
0038 *                                  SR100-INITIALIZATION-RTN
0039 CSR         SR100       BEGSR
0040 CSR                     MOVEL'H'        #CKEY
0041 CSR                     MOVE '00000'    #CKEY
0042 CSR         #CKEY       SETLLCUSTMST
0043 CSR                     READ CUSTMST                      LR
0044 CSR    NLR  CLNCDE      COMP 'H'                     LR
0045 CSR                     ENDSR
0046 *
0047 *                                  SR200-PRINT-STATEMENT
0048 CSR         SR200       BEGSR
0049 CSR                     EXCPT@BILL
0050 CSR                     READ CUSTMST                      LR
0051 CSR    NLR  CLNCDE      COMP 'H'                     LR
0052 CSR                     ENDSR
0053 *
0054 OREPORT   E    05           @BILL
0055 O                           CACCT     15
0056 O                           CLNAME    45
0057 O         E    08           @BILL
0058 O                           CADDR     45
0059 O         E    09           @BILL
0060 O                           CCITY     45
0061 O                                     46 ','
0062 O                           CSTATE    49
0063 O         E    14           @BILL
0064 O                           CBAL   1  60 '$'
0065 O                           CPAYMT1   60 '$'
```

Example 2   Let us consider another problem to illustrate the specifications required to process an indexed file within limits.

In this problem we will use the product master indexed file called PRODMST used earlier in this chapter. To demonstrate processing within limits we will add a new field called PMWHSE to the record. This warehouse field has been added to the PRODMST record layout as shown in Figure 9.15 so that an inventory of products can be maintained at more than one warehouse.

Let us consider the specifications required to produce an inventory report by warehouse.

In this example, unlike the earlier one that used the PRODMST file, products can be stored at more than one warehouse. In this situation, PMCODE is no longer a unique primary key. For example, if two records existed, one for warehouse 01 and another for warehouse 05, and both contained the product 10055, the two records would begin with the following data:

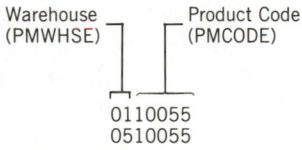

```
Warehouse         Product Code
(PMWHSE)          (PMCODE)


        0110055
        0510055
```

Figure 9.15
Sample record layout for the master file used in Example 2.

Record Layout for
Product Master File — PRODMST

PMWHSE	PMCODE	PMSUPR	PMDESC	PMQOH (P)	PMCOST (P)
1	2 3	7 8	14 15	34 35 37	38 40

Index consists of PMWHSE and PMCODE joined together

These two records both contain 10055 in the PMCODE field. This is because the product is located at two different warehouses. To ensure that the key field is unique, the warehouse and product code fields are joined or concatenated to form one unique primary key.

Thus, a record with warehouse 01 and product code 10055 would have a unique primary key of 0110055; and warehouse 05, product 10055, would have a unique key of 0510055. *Concatenation* is the term used for combining fields in this way. The following illustrates the File Description Specifications form required to define the file PRODMST to be processed within limits:

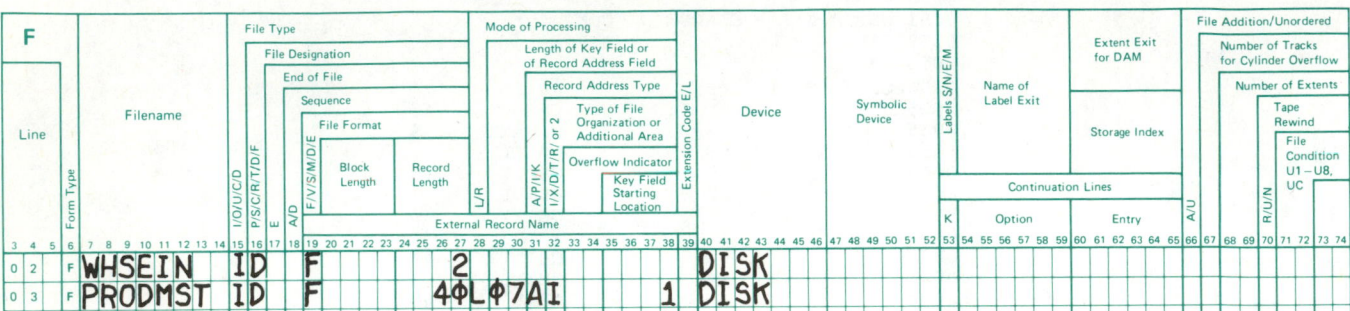

The purpose of this program is to produce a listing of the inventory at any particular warehouse. The file, WHSEIN in this program, is a Demand file that specifies the warehouse whose inventory is to be printed.

The key field of the PRODMST file consists of the concatenated subfields, Warehouse and Product Code, and is seven bytes long.

In our example, PRODMST is defined as a Demand file (D in column 16) and will be accessed sequentially using the READ operation. That is, PRODMST is processed sequentially beginning with a warehouse code that is inputted from the WHSEIN file. The Mode of Processing (column 28) for PRODMST must contain the letter L in order to process the file within limits. The four primary components of indexed files must also be specified.

Recall that we wish to print a report of all products found in a *particular* warehouse. This will require the program to locate the first record in the PRODMST file for the selected warehouse and then read each of the records for that warehouse in sequence. Remember, the first two bytes of the key field PMWHSE contains the warehouse code.

To accomplish this task the program will first input the warehouse code (TWHSE) from the WHSEIN file. We will then print the product codes from PRODMST for that warehouse. The product codes are not required in the WHSEIN file, however, since we wish to print *all* products for the selected warehouse. To print from PRODMST only those products for the warehouse contained in the field TWHSE requires processing within limits. That is, we need to randomly "jump" to the first record for the required warehouse (our lower limit) regardless of the product code and then process the file sequentially until we reach the last record for the selected warehouse (our upper limit) or until the program reaches an end-of-file.

The following illustration shows the Calculation Specifications form required to process the PRODMST file within limits and produce the required warehouse listing:

C		Indicators				Factor 1	Operation	Factor 2	Result Field				Resulting Indicators								
		And	And						Name	Length			Arithmetic						Comments		
													Plus	Minus	Zero						
Line	Form Type	Control Level (L0–L9, LR, SR, AN/OR)	Not	Not	Not						Decimal Positions	Half Adjust (H)	Compare								
													1 > 2	1 < 2	1 = 2						
													Lookup (Factor 2) is								
													High	Low	Equal						
3 4 5	6	7 8	9 10 11	12 13 14	15 16 17	18 19 20 21 22 23 24 25 26 27	28 29 30 31 32	33 34 35 36 37 38 39 40 41 42	43 44 45 46 47 48	49 50 51	52	53	54 55	56 57	58 59	60 61 62 63 64 65 66 67 68 69 70 71 72 73 74					
0 1	C						·														
0 2	C						·														
0 3	C						MOVEL	TWHSE	#WPKEY	7											
0 4	C						MOVE	'ΦΦΦΦ'	#WPKEY												
0 5	C					#WPKEY	SETLL	PRODMST													
0 6	C						READ	PRODMST							LR						
0 7	C		NLR			PMWHSE	COMP	TWHSE							LR						

First, the lower limits for processing must be set using the SETLL operation. This will cause the record pointer to be positioned at the first record where sequential processing is to begin.

In the above, the field #WPKEY is initialized to its starting key value with the MOVEL and MOVE operations prior to the execution of the SETLL operation. The MOVEL operation moves the required warehouse value to the left-most positions of #WPKEY and the MOVE operation initializes the product code portion of #WPKEY to zeros. Zeros are required for the product code because we wish to select *all* product codes for the particular warehouse and we do not know the first product code for this particular warehouse. Remember, when the SETLL operation is executed, the record pointer will point to the first record equal to or greater than the value of Factor 1. Thus, with the product code equal to zeros the record pointer will move to the first record for the specified warehouse. Recall that the SETLL operation does *not* read a record from the indexed file but only moves the record pointer to the first sequential record to be read.

The next step when processing within limits is reading the records from the indexed file *sequentially*. This operation requires the READ operation to process the PRODMST file sequentially, as shown above.

Upon execution of the READ operation the next sequential record is read from the indexed file PRODMST. The warehouse code from the indexed record is then compared to the input warehouse code (TWHSE) to determine if the upper limit has been reached. Once PWHSE in the PRODMST file is greater than TWHSE in the WHSEIN file or an end-of-file has occurred for the indexed PRODMST file, the program is terminated because it has read beyond the required upper limit of processing.

Figure 9.16 illustrates the complete RPG program to process the PRODMST file within limits as discussed throughout this section.

An Alternate Structured Approach

Figure 9.17 offers an alternate approach to our warehouse listing program. This program illustrates how structured programming concepts can be employed in this problem. Examine both Figure 9.16 and Figure 9.17 carefully and note the differences in the more structured approach.

Figure 9.16
Program for Example 2.

```
....+....1....+....2....+....3....+....4....+....5....+....6....+....7
0001   ****************************************************************
0002   *
0003   *   PROGRAM DESCRIPTION:
0004   *
0005   *        THIS PROGRAM PRODUCES AN INVENTORY REPORT BY WAREHOUSE.
0006   *        THE PROGRAM WILL ACCESS THE FILE "PRODMST' WITHIN LIMITS
0007   *        TO SELECT RECORDS FOR A PARTICULAR WAREHOUSE.
0008   *
0009   *
0010   *   FUNCTION OF INDICATORS:
0011   *
0012   *        NONE
0013   *
0014   ****************************************************************
0015   *
0016 H
0017 FWHSEIN  ID  F       2            DISK
0018 FPRODMST ID  F       40L07AI   1 DISK
0019 FREPORT  O   F       80     OF    PRINTER
0020 IWHSEIN  NS
0021 I                                       1    2 TWHSE
0022 IPRODMST NS
0023 I                                       1    2 PMWHSE
0024 I                                       3    7 PMCODE
0025 I                                       8  140PMSUPR
0026 I                                      15   34 PMDESC
0027 I                                   P  35  370PMQOH
0028 I                                   P  38  402PMCOST
0029 C*
0030  *                                  MAIN-MODULE-RTN
0031 C                       EXSR SR100
0032 C*
0033 C          $LOOP        TAG
0034 C                       EXSR SR200
0035 C  NLR                  GOTO $LOOP
0036 C*
0037 C                       EXSR SR300
0038 C*
0039  *                                  SR100-INITIALIZATION-RTN
0040 CSR        SR100        BEGSR
0041 CSR                     SETON                       OF
0042 CSR                     READ WHSEIN                 LR
0043 CSR                     MOVELTWHSE     #KEY
0044 CSR                     MOVE '    '    #KEY      7
0045 CSR        #KEY         SETLLPRODMST
0046 CSR                     READ PRODMST                LR
0047 CSR                     ENDSR
0048 C*
0049  *                                  SR200-PROCESS-PRODMST-RECORD-RTN
0050 CSR        SR200        BEGSR
0051 CSR        PMQOH        MULT PMCOST    #TCOST  72
0052 CSR    OF               EXCPT@H000
0053 CSR                     SETOF                       OF
0054 CSR                     EXCPT@D100
0055 CSR        #GCOST       ADD  #TCOST    #GCOST  72
0056 CSR                     READ PRODMST                LR
0057 CSR    NLR PMWHSE       COMP TWHSE              LR
0058 CSR                     ENDSR
0059 C*
0060  *                                  SR300-END-OF-JOB-RTN
0061 CSR        SR300        BEGSR
0062 CSR                     EXCPT@T300
0063 CSR                     SETON                  LR
0064 CSR                     ENDSR
0065 C*
0066 OREPORT  E   05         @H000
0067 O                                50 ' WAREHOUSE LISTING'
0068 O        E   07         @H000
0069 O                                19 'PRODUCT'
0070 O                                27 ' QTY'
0071 O        E   108        @H000
0072 O                                18 'CODE'
0073 O                                29 'ON HAND'
0074 O                                49 'COST'
0075 O                                65 'EXTENDED COST'
0076 O        E  1           @D100
0077 O                       PMCODE   18
0078 O                       PMQOH Z  27
0079 O                       PMCOST1  49
0080 O                       #TCOST1  65
0081 O        E  2           @T300
0082 O                                55 ' GRAND TOTAL'
0083 O                       #GCOST1  65
```

Figure 9.17
Alternate approach to the program in Figure 9.16.

```
....+....1....+....2....+....3....+....4....+....5....+....6....+....7
0001 *******************************************************************
0002 *
0003 *  PROGRAM DESCRIPTION:
0004 *
0005 *       THIS PROGRAM IS AN ALTERNATIVE STRUCTURED APPROACH
0006 *       TO THE WAREHOUSE INVENTORY LISTING PRESENTED EARLIER.
0007 *
0008 *
0009 *  FUNCTION OF INDICATORS:
0010 *
0011 *       NONE
0012 *
0013 *******************************************************************
0014 *
0015 H
0016 FWHSEIN   ID  F     2           DISK
0017 FPRODMST  ID  F     40L07AI   1 DISK
0018 FREPORT   O   F     80    OF    PRINTER
0019 *
0020 IWHSEIN   NS
0021 I                                        1   2 TWHSE
0022 IPRODMST  NS
0023 I                                        1   2 PMWHSE
0024 I                                        3   7 PMCODE
0025 I                                        8 140PMSUPR
0026 I                                       15  34 PMDESC
0027 I                                     P 35 370PMQOH
0028 I                                     P 38 402PMCOST
0029 I          DS
0030 I                                        1   7 #KEY
0031 I                                        1   2 TWHSE
0032 I                                        3   7 #PCODE
0033 I#WORK     DS
0034 I                                        1  72#TCOST
0035 I                                        8 142#GCOST
0036 I#FLAGS    DS
0037 I                                        1   1 #YES
0038 I                                        2   2 #NO
0039 I                                        3   3 #QUIT
0040 C*
0041  *                              MAIN-MODULE-RTN
0042 C                   EXSR SR100
0043 C*
0044 C          #QUIT    DOWEQ#NO
0045 C                   EXSR SR200
0046 C                   END
0047 C*
0048 C                   EXSR SR300
0049 C*
0050  *                              SR100-INITIALIZATION-RTN
0051 CSR        SR100    BEGSR
0052 CSR                 SETON                        OF
0053 CSR                 MOVE 'Y'      #YES
0054 CSR                 MOVE 'N'      #NO
0055 CSR                 MOVE #NO      #QUIT
0056 CSR                 MOVE *BLANKS  #PCODE
0057 CSR                 READ WHSEIN            LR
0058 CSR        #KEY     SETLLPRODMST
0059 CSR                 READ PRODMST           LR
0060 CSR    LR           MOVE #YES     #QUIT
0061 CSR                 ENDSR

0062  *
0063  *                              SR200-PROCESS-PRODMST-RECORD-RTN
0064 CSR        SR200    BEGSR
0065 CSR        PMQOH    MULT PMCOST   #TCOST
0066 CSR    OF           EXCPT@H000
0067 CSR                 SETOF                        OF
0068 CSR                 EXCPT@D100
0069 CSR                 ADD  #TCOST   #GCOST
0070 CSR                 READ PRODMST           LR
0071 CSR    NLR PMWHSE   COMP TWHSE            LR
0072 CSR    LR           MOVE #YES     #QUIT
0073 CSR                 ENDSR
0074 C*
0075  *                              SR300-END-OF-JOB-RTN
0076 CSR        SR300    BEGSR
0077 CSR                 EXCPT@T300
0078 CSR                 SETON                 LR
0079 CSR                 ENDSR
0080 C*
0081 OREPORT  E   05          @H000
0082 O                             50 ' WAREHOUSE LISTING'
0083 O        E   07          @H000
```

Figure 9.17 `....+....1....+....2....+....3....+....4....+....5....+....6....+....7`
(continued)

```
0084 O                                      19 'PRODUCT'
0085 O                                      27 ' QTY'
0086 O        E   108        @H000
0087 O                                      18 'CODE'
0088 O                                      29 'ON HAND'
0089 O                                      49 'COST'
0090 O                                      65 'EXTENDED COST'
0091 O        E   1          @D100
0092 O                       PMCODE         18
0093 O                       PMQOH  Z       27
0094 O                       PMCOST1        49
0095 O                       #TCOST1        65
0096 O        E   2          @T300
0097 O                                      55 ' GRAND TOTAL'
0098 O                       #GCOST1        65
```

CHAPTER SELF-TEST

1. When created, an index file establishes two files on disk: the _____ and a separate _____ .

2. (T or F) The primary key uniquely identifies each record in an indexed file.

3. A key file or index contains two fields: _____ and _____ .

4. (T or F) The most common method for creating an indexed file is with the use of a program specifically written by a programmer for that purpose.

5. The _____ operation must be used any time an indexed file is to be accessed or read randomly.

6. When records are deleted from an indexed file, that file must be defined on the Input Specifications form as a(n) _____ file.

7. _____ processing combines both random and sequential access to allow processing of only a select group of records in an indexed file.

8. (T or F) The SETLL operation enables a program to begin processing an indexed file sequentially at a record location other than that of the first record.

9. When the SETLL operation is executed, the record pointer will be positioned at the first record (equal to/greater than/equal to or greater than) the value in Factor 1.

10. Concatenation is a term used to denote the _____ .

SOLUTIONS

1. data file; key file or index

2. T

3. the key field; a pointer specifying the disk address for the record with that key field

4. F—Use of a control language command is the most common method.

5. CHAIN

6. update (U in column 15)

7. Dynamic (or processing within limits)

8. T

9. equal to or greater than

10. combining of fields

KEY TERMS

Abend

Alternate key

CHAIN operation

Control language commands

Dynamic processing

File maintenance procedure

Index

Indexed file

Key field

Key file

Pointer

Primary key

Processing within limits

SETLL operation

Update procedure

REVIEW QUESTIONS

1. Distinguish between alternate indexes and a primary index, indicating how each is used.

2. Indicate the major advantages of using a control language command to create an indexed file.

3. Explain what is meant by chaining.

4. Describe how dynamic processing can be used with an indexed file.

5. What is the purpose of the SETLL operation?

PROGRAMMING ASSIGNMENTS

Use Data Structures for work fields. Use prefixes for input, output, and work fields. Use SETON and SETOF where appropriate.

1. Using the problem definition shown in Figure 9.18, write an RPG program to update a master payroll file with salary changes. Print the error control listing as specified. (Continued on the next page.)

Figure 9.18
Problem definition for Programming Assignment 1.

Systems Flowchart

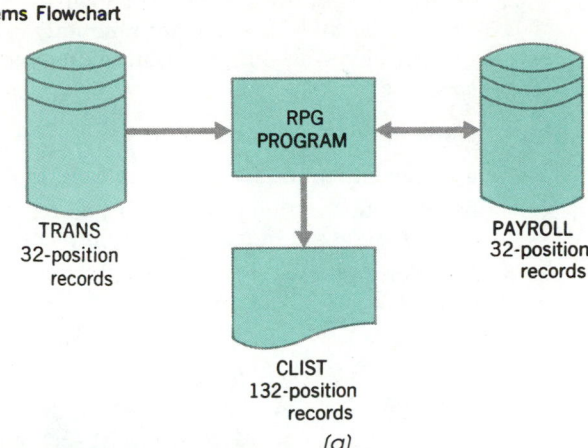

(a)

TRANS Record Layout

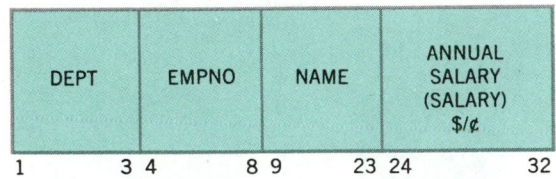

PAYROLL Record Layout

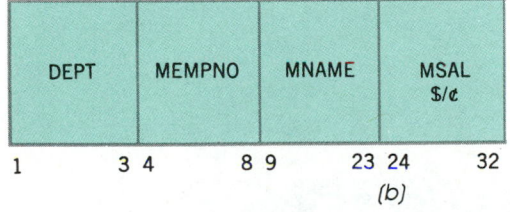

(b)

CLIST Printer Spacing Chart

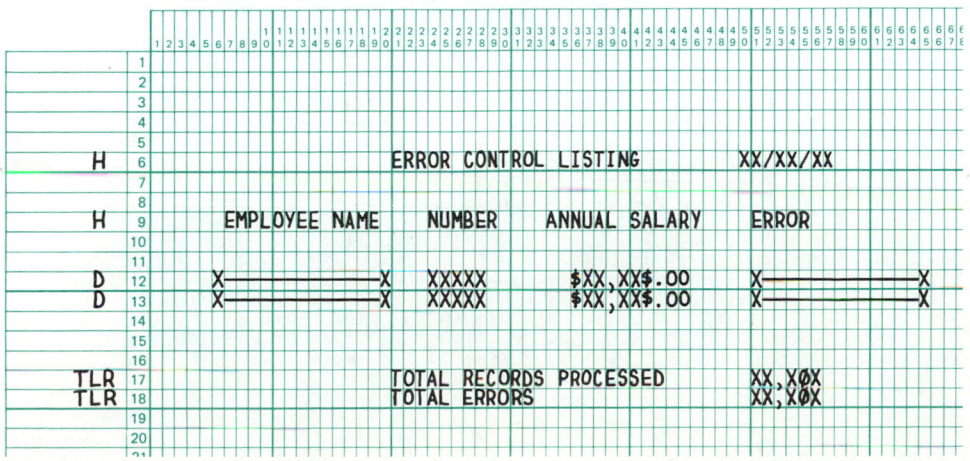

(c)

Notes:

a. All records in the transaction file should be in the master file. If any transaction record does not have a corresponding master record, list the record and the error.

b. Employee number is the key field.

c. `Z-ADD SALARY to MSAL`.

d. Display the Payroll file to validate the correctness of the update procedure.

2. Using the problem definition shown in Figure 9.19, write an RPG program to update, add, and delete records randomly from an indexed master file, depending on the activity code in each transaction record. Print the error control listing as specified.

Notes:

a. Customer number is the key field in `MSTR`.

b. For a transaction record with a corresponding master record, add the amount of sales (`SALES`) in the transaction record to `MSALES` in the master record.

(Continued on the next page.)

Figure 9.19
Problem definition for Programming Assignment 2.

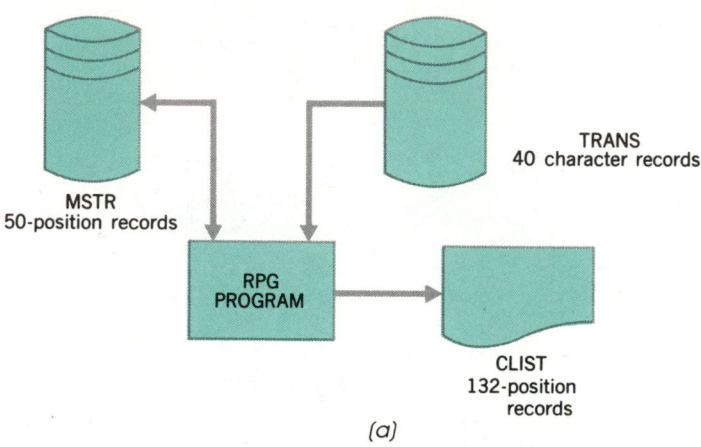

(a)

TRANS Record Layout

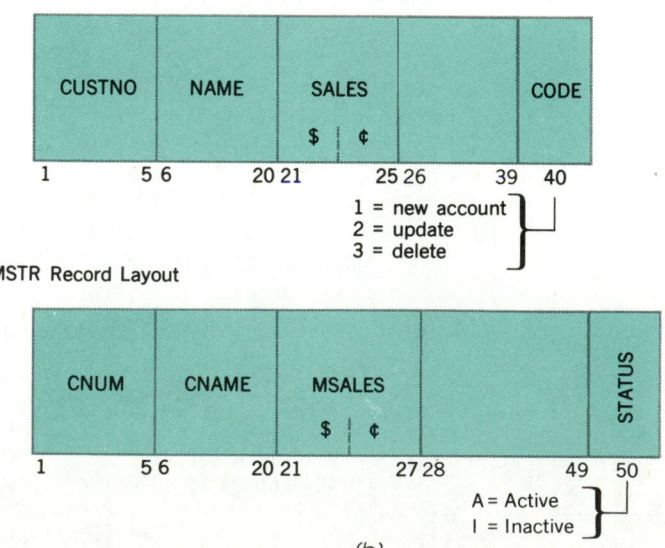

(b)

Figure 9.19
(continued)   CLIST Printer Spacing Chart

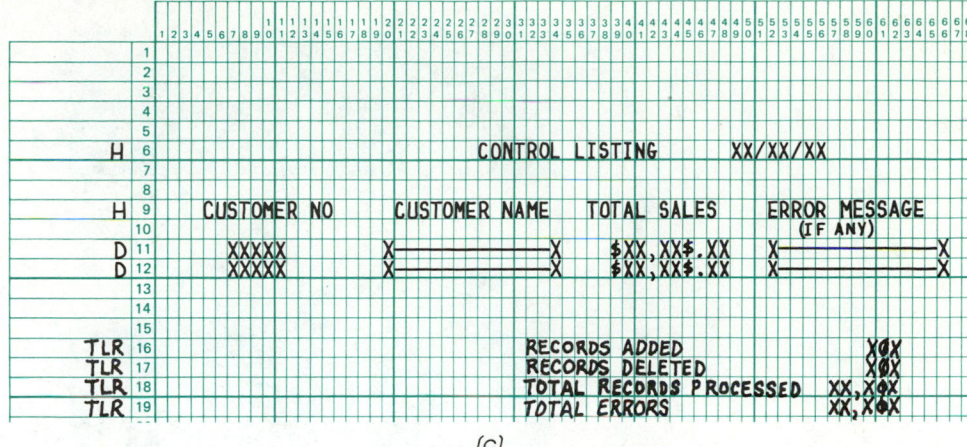

```
                                          CONTROL  LISTING        XX/XX/XX


        CUSTOMER NO      CUSTOMER NAME      TOTAL SALES       ERROR MESSAGE
                                                                (IF ANY)
           XXXXX        X--------------X    $XX,XX$.XX       X--------------X
           XXXXX        X--------------X    $XX,XX$.XX       X--------------X



                                          RECORDS ADDED                    XØX
                                          RECORDS DELETED                  XØX
                                          TOTAL RECORDS PROCESSED   XX,XØX
                                          TOTAL ERRORS              XX,XØX
```

(c)

    c. For a new account transaction record, add the record to the master file.

    d. For a delete record, deactivate the corresponding master record.

    e. Display the master to validate the results.

3. Using the problem definition shown in Figure 9.20, write an RPG program to update an indexed disk file. Print the error control listing as specified.

    Notes:

    a. Customer number is the key field in MSTR.

    b. Create a disk record for any transaction record that does not have a corresponding master record.

    c. For a transaction record with a corresponding master record, (1) add the amount of purchase from the transaction record to the amount owed in the master record, and (2) update the date of last purchase.

    d. There does not need to be a transaction record for each master record.

    e. The transaction records are not in sequence.

    f. Display MSTR to validate the correctness of this procedure.

Figure 9.20
Problem definition for Programming Assignment 3.   Systems Flowchart

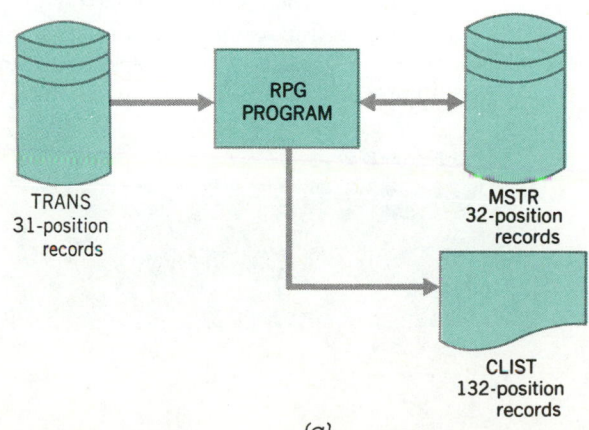

(a)

TRANS Record Layout

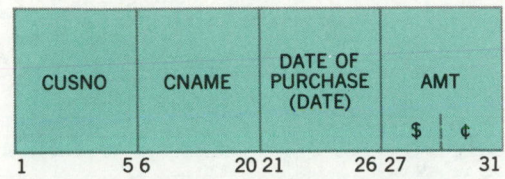

MSTR Record Layout

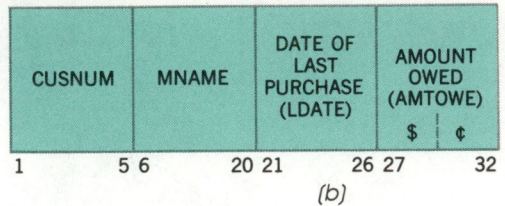

(b)

CLIST Printer Spacing Chart

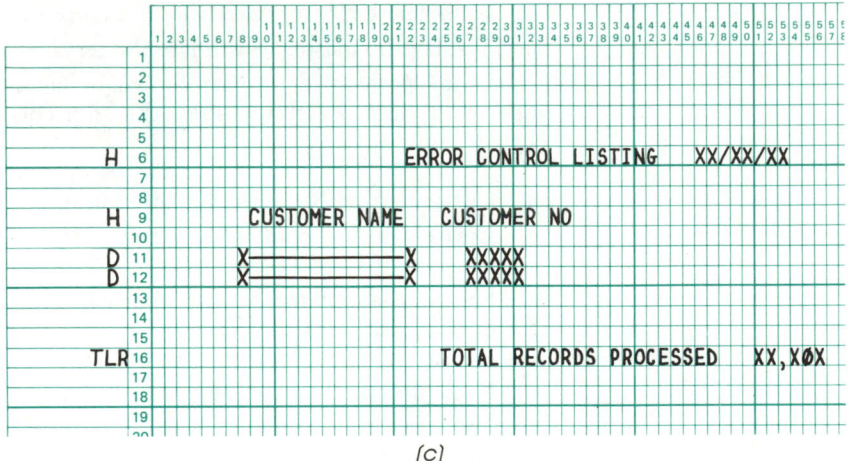

(c)

4. Using the PAYROLL record layout illustrated below, code an RPG program to produce the output contained in the Printer Spacing Chart. List all personnel with an annual salary greater than $42,000.00 per year and having a department code of 02, denoting Executive Officers. The SETLL operation should be used to process the records sequentially, once department 02 is accessed. The key field is DEPT/ MEMPNO concatenated to form one field.

PAYROLL Record Layout

DEPT	MEMPNO	MNAME	MSAL
			$ ¢
1 3	4 8	9 23	24 32

CLIST   Printer Spacing Chart

```
                1         1 1 1 1 1 1 1 1 1 2 2 2 2 2 2 2 2 2 2 3 3 3 3 3 3 3 3 3 3 4 4 4 4 4 4 4 4 4 4 5 5 5 5 5 5 5 5 5 5 6 6
      1 2 3 4 5 6 7 8 9 0 1 2 3 4 5 6 7 8 9 0 1 2 3 4 5 6 7 8 9 0 1 2 3 4 5 6 7 8 9 0 1 2 3 4 5 6 7 8 9 0 1 2 3 4 5 6 7 8 9 0 1 2 3 4 5 6 7 8 9 0 1

H  1   XX/XX/XX DEPARTMENT 02 EXECUTIVE PAYROLL CONTROL LISTING
   2
   3
H  4      EMPLOYEE           NAME OF          CURRENT ANNUAL
H  5       NUMBER           EMPLOYEE             SALARY
   6          X                                    X
E  7        XXXXX        X————————X          XX,XXX,XX.XX
E  8        XXXXX        X————————X          XX,XXX,XX.XX
E  9        XXXX         X————————X          X,XXX,XX.XX
  10
TLR 11     NUMBER OF RECORDS LISTED ABOVE XX
  12
```

10

Array Processing and Table Handling

OBJECTIVES

To familiarize you with

1. Array and table processing.
2. Why, when, and how arrays and tables should be used in an RPG program.
3. The advantages and disadvantages of compile time arrays and tables and pre-execution time arrays and tables.
4. How arrays and tables are established and used in a LOKUP procedure.
5. Processing single-entry and related tables in RPG.

I. Introduction to Arrays

An **array** is a list of related data items stored in consecutive locations in main storage. Arrays consist of individual elements or fields that may be accessed or addressed individually and, in addition, can be referenced as a whole entity. Each element or individual field in an array must have the same attributes. That is, all of the elements of a given array must be the same length and must also be of the same type, either numeric or nonnumeric (alphanumeric). For numeric arrays, each element must not only have the same length, but the same number of decimal positions.

Once an array has been established, each element may be referenced directly by specifying its relative position within the array. An **index**, also called a **subscript,** is used to indicate which element in an array is to be accessed. The index thus serves as a pointer to identify the particular element of the array that is to be processed. Since the array name is the same for each element, the index is used to identify the specific element to be accessed for calculation or output operations.

Suppose you have an array called TEMP (for weekly temperatures), which contains seven temperature figures, one for each day of the week. To access the temperature of the third day of the week you would use TEMP,3. This reference uses the array name, TEMP, and the index, 3, separated by a comma (see Figure 10.1).

Accessing an array called EXAM that has five elements is performed in exactly the same way. EXAM,3 refers to the third element or third exam in the array (see Figure 10.2).

Consider the array in Figure 10.3, called MOT, which stores monthly sales totals. To add an inputted sales amount to a specific monthly total, specify the array name and the index that indicates the element to be changed or updated. To add to the monthly total for February, for example, add to MOT,2. Again, the array name is separated from the index by a comma. Suppose an input record includes a sales amount called AMT and a field called MO, which contains a number from 1 to 12 representing the month of the transaction. We can add

Figure 10.1
Accessing an array.

TEMP

Ø88.9
Ø75.7
Ø93.6
Ø99.5
Ø88.8
Ø85.6
Ø77.7

Index points → (to third element)

TEMP, 3
— Third element
— Array name

Figure 10.2
Accessing an array called
EXAM.

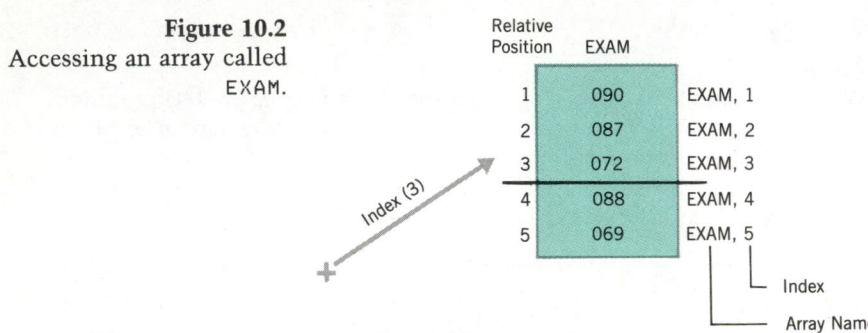

Relative
Position   EXAM

1	090	EXAM, 1
2	087	EXAM, 2
3	072	EXAM, 3
4	088	EXAM, 4
5	069	EXAM, 5

Index (3)

— Index
— Array Name

the AMT field to the correct element of the MOT array by using the inputted MO field as the index. Depending on the contents of the month field, the AMT would be added to the correct element of the monthly sales total array, MOT. Thus, each element of the MOT array serves as a running total and accumulates the sales month by month, as shown in Figure 10.4.

To print the contents of an array after all the calculations have been performed on the elements, use a loop with the EXCPT command. One main advantage to looping is that the index changes with each pass through the loop. Typically the index begins with a value of 0 and is incremented each time you step through the routine that accesses the array. You continue with this procedure until the entire array has been processed and you then exit from the loop. In this instance, the index begins at 0 and varies, within the loop, from 1 to 12 to print all 12 monthly totals (see Figure 10.5).

We will now examine the limitations imposed by the RPG coding forms in naming an array and using the index.

Figure 10.3
Example of an array that stores
monthly totals.

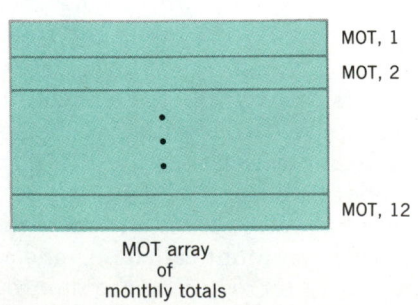

MOT, 1
MOT, 2

·
·
·

MOT, 12

MOT array
of
monthly totals

Figure 10.4
Adding an input amount to
the proper element of an array.

Input

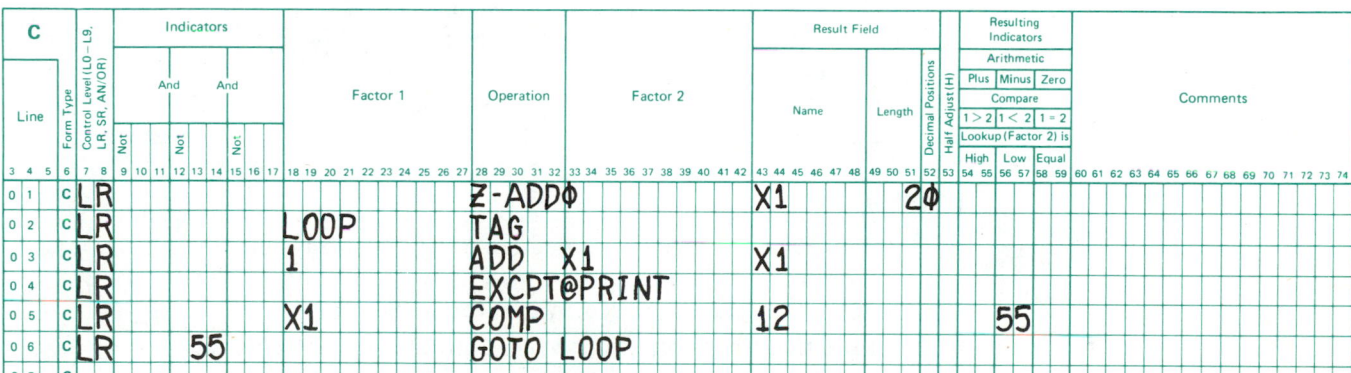

C		Indicators				Factor 1	Operation	Factor 2	Result Field				Resulting Indicators			Comments
			And	And					Name	Length			Arithmetic Plus Minus Zero			
Line	Form Type	Control Level (L0–L9, LR, SR, AN/OR)	Not	Not	Not						Decimal Positions	Half Adjust (H)	Compare 1>2 1<2 1=2 Lookup (Factor 2) is			
3 4 5	6	7 8	9 10 11	12 13 14	15 16 17	18 ... 27	28 ... 32	33 ... 42	43 ... 48	49 50 51	52	53	High Low Equal 54 55 56 57 58 59		60 ... 74	
0 1	C					AMT	ADD	MOT,MO	MOT,MO						
0 2	C														

FROM INPUT   ARRAY   INDEX   LIMITED TO
RECORD   NAME   SIX POSITIONS

C		Indicators				Factor 1	Operation	Factor 2	Result Field				Resulting Indicators			Comments
			And	And					Name	Length			Arithmetic Plus Minus Zero			
Line	Form Type	Control Level (L0–L9, LR, SR, AN/OR)	Not	Not	Not						Decimal Positions	Half Adjust (H)	Compare 1>2 1<2 1=2 Lookup (Factor 2) is			
3 4 5	6	7 8	9 10 11	12 13 14	15 16 17	18 ... 27	28 ... 32	33 ... 42	43 ... 48	49 50 51	52	53	High Low Equal 54 55 56 57 58 59		60 ... 74	
0 1	C	LR					Z-ADD0		X1	20						
0 2	C	LR				LOOP	TAG									
0 3	C	LR				1	ADD	X1	X1							
0 4	C	LR					EXCPT@PRINT									
0 5	C	LR				X1	COMP	12						55		
0 6	C	LR	55				GOTO LOOP									

Figure 10.5
Printing monthly totals at LR
time.

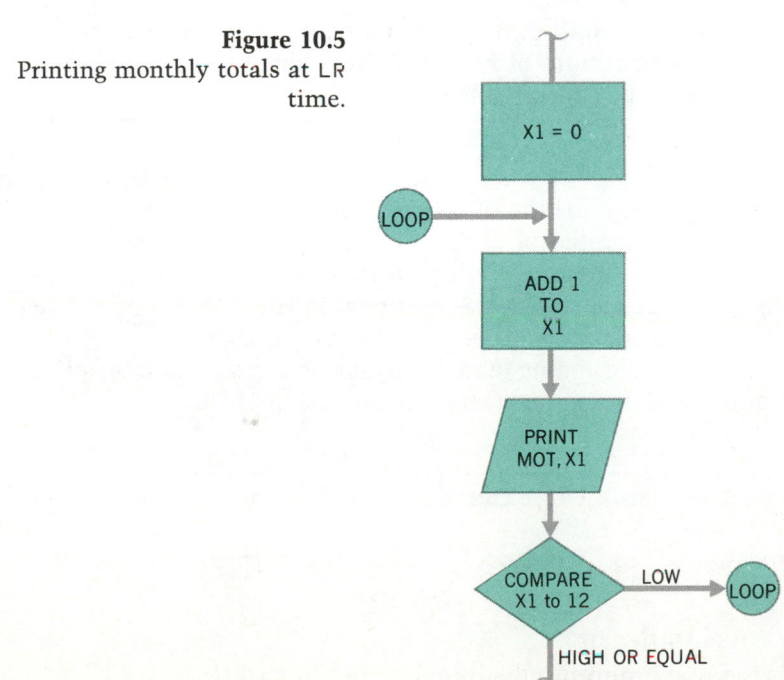

II. Naming an Array and Using an Index

Every array used in a program must be assigned a name consisting of from one to six characters. Array names must begin with a letter, but cannot begin with the letters TAB since this unique three-character string is reserved for TABles, to be discussed later. However, several problems may arise, particularly in the Calculation and Output Specifications, if you do not limit array names to four characters or less. In order to reference an element of an array, we use the array name followed by a comma plus an index. As noted, an index can be an integer constant (a number such as 1, 2, etc.) referring to a specific array element or a field name whose value (1, 2, etc.) refers to a specific array element. The field name, if used, must be defined as a numeric field with zero decimal positions. Since the comma and index occupy at least two positions, the name of the array must be restricted to four positions on the Calculation Specifications form if used as a Result Field. Refer to Figure 10.4 and recall that we add AMT to the Monthly Sales Total array name MOT. The Result Field, which can only contain six characters, is specified as MOT,MO and is completely filled. It is best, therefore, to use short array and index names since the combination must not exceed six characters when included in the Result Field. In the illustration below, the invalid array references contain too many characters if used as Result Fields:

Valid Array References	Invalid Array References
EXAM,1	GRADE,1
SLS,X1	EXAM,10
PAY,99	PAY,100
TL,INX	SLS,SUB

GENERAL RULES FOR NAMING AN ARRAY

1. When an index is used to reference an element of an array, such as (MOT,MO), limit the combined length of the array name, comma, and index name to a maximum of six characters. This is the maximum length that can be placed in the Result Field.
2. Limit the array name to a maximum of four characters.
3. Limit the index name to a maximum of two characters.
4. Limit the combined length of the array name and the index name (or constant) to a maximum of five characters since the array name and the index must be separated by a comma.

The index for the array must be a numeric field or literal that points to an existing element of the array. In other words, the index must never be less than one or greater than the number of elements in the array. If either of these conditions occurs, the halt indicator will be turned on and the program interrupted. Therefore, be sure the index does not exceed the number of elements specified for the array. You can use a validity check for this.

We will now examine the coding required to set up arrays in storage. Defining an array requires use of the Extension Specifications form.

III. Defining Arrays Using the Extension Specifications Form

With array processing, the Extension Specifications form is used to do the following:

1. Assign a name to the array.
2. Establish the maximum number of elements in the array.

3. Define the length of the elements. Each element in an array must be the same length.
4. Specify the array type as numeric or nonnumeric by using the Decimal Positions entry. As always, if the Decimal Positions entry is left blank, the array is assumed to contain nonnumeric entries. If it contains a number, the array is assumed to contain numeric entries.

The programmer is often required to define an array that is read from an input record. In Figure 10.6, the EXAM array is defined as numeric with zero decimal positions (column 44) on the Extension Specifications form. The array to be inputted consists of five elements (columns 36–39), each containing three digits (columns 40–42). Since the array is being read in, it must also be coded on the Input Specifications form. Care must be exercised to ensure that the EXAM array be correctly sized on both Specifications forms. Since the array extends from columns 31 to 45, we find it contains 15 positions. (Remember to subtract the lower number from the higher number and add 1 to determine the size of a field or array.)

The Extension Specifications form specifies five fields, each containing three digits. Thus, the array is consistently defined as occupying 15 positions on both the Input and Extension Specification forms.

Note in Figure 10.6 that the Decimal Positions field of the Input Specifica-

Figure 10.6
Defining an array on the Extension and the Input Specifications.

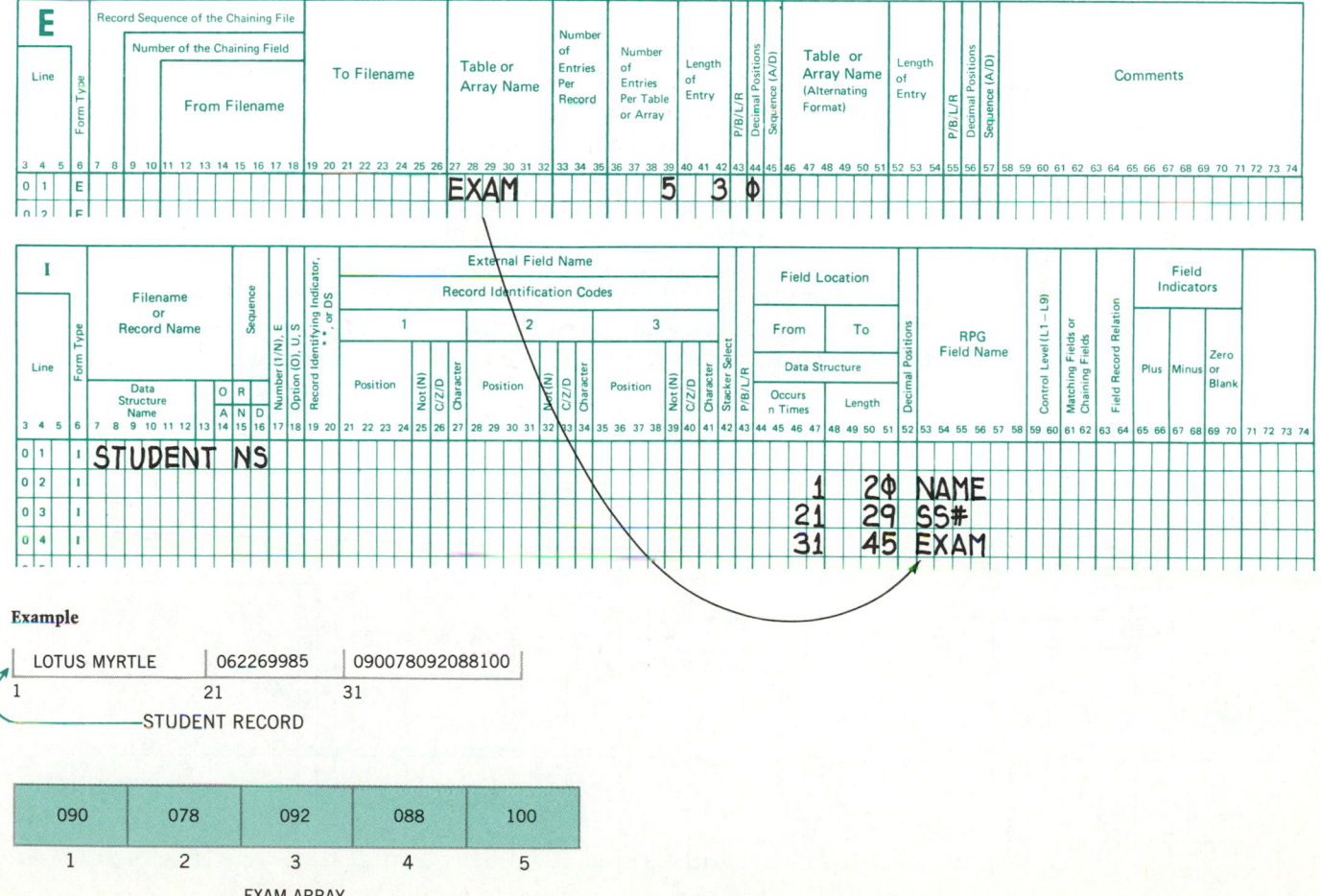

tion contains a blank for the array and not a zero. The zero is specified on the Extension Specifications form.

Thus, an array should always be defined as alphanumeric on the Input Specifications form and numeric on the Extension Specifications form. Remember, we omit the number in the Decimal Positions column of the Input Specifications form only when an array is loaded from an input record. The Decimal Positions for an array is specified instead on the Extension Specifications form. Note, too, that the length of the field defined on the Input Specifications form must be the same as the length specified for the array on the Extension Specifications form.

The Extension Specifications form in Figure 10.6 includes the following entries:

1. **Table or Array Name (Columns 27–32)**
   The name of the table must begin in columns 27–32 of the Extension Specifications form. We chose the name EXAM to denote student exams or grades.
2. **Number of Entries per Table or Array (Columns 36–39)**
   The EXAM array consists of five elements. Thus 5 is coded in column 39.
3. **Length of Entry (Columns 40–42)**
   Each exam or grade is three characters in length. We therefore code a 3 in column 42. Since the highest possible grade is 100, a three-position field is required.
4. **Decimal Positions (Column 44)**
   The Decimal Positions entry is left blank when the array elements are not numeric. Here, the Decimal Positions entry, column 44, is coded with a zero indicating that the EXAM array is numeric and has no decimal positions.

In addition to the EXAM array, which is defined as part of the input record, other arrays could be created in main storage during calculation time. In Figure 10.7 we define two additional arrays and call them AVG and TOT, respectively. Note that each line of the Extension Specifications form is used to describe an array.

The AVG array could be used to save each student's average. Assuming class size is limited to 30 persons, a 30-element array would be necessary to save the 30 student average grades. Also note that we have defined the average as containing one decimal position. The array named TOT could be used to accumulate running totals of each of the five exams. This would prove useful if a class average of each exam were needed. The TOT array would therefore contain five elements. At the end of the input file, we would divide each TOT by the number of records processed to get an average for each of the five exams. Since 30 records will be accumulated or summed, and the largest valid entry in

Figure 10.7
Definining arrays on the Extension Specifications form.

Line (3–5)	Form Type (6)	Record Sequence of the Chaining File (7–8)	Number of the Chaining Field (9–10)	From Filename (11–18)	To Filename (19–26)	Table or Array Name (27–32)	Number of Entries Per Record (33–35)	Number of Entries Per Table or Array (36–39)	Length of Entry (40–42)	P/B/L/R (43)	Decimal Positions (44)	Sequence (A/D) (45)	Table or Array Name (Alternating Format) (46–51)	Length of Entry (52–54)	P/B/L/R (55)	Decimal Positions (56)	Sequence (A/D) (57)	Comments (58–74)
01	E					EXAM		5	3		0							
02	E					AVG		30	4		1							
03	E					TOT		5	5		0							
04	E																	

a three-position exam field is 100, then the largest valid result would be 100 ×
30 or 3000. Thus, we allow for a five-position TOTal field. At the end, each
running total in the TOT array would be divided by the total number of students processed to obtain each EXAM's average.

Note that during data entry an error could be made by entering a grade
greater than one hundred. However, full programs usually include a validation
procedure to ensure that each entry is within accepted limits. In this instance,
the validation procedure would include tests to ensure that grade entries do
not exceed 100. Validation procedures are used in a program to prevent errors
of this type from occurring.

IV. Array Concepts

A. Dynamic and Static Arrays

A major advantage of arrays is that they may be created during calculation
time as a program is executing. Arrays created in this manner are frequently
referred to as *dynamic*. Consider a program that reads student records, each
containing five test scores. The five exams will be averaged to produce a final
grade for each student. Assume that we need to save each student's final grade
for later processing. A dynamic array called AVG could be used to save the final
grade of each student. Hence, if there were 30 students in the class, an AVG
array of 30 elements or averages would be needed. As each student's final
average is calculated, it could be moved or saved in the next available element
of the AVG array. When all 30 final averages have been calculated, the array AVG
will be full. We could then process the AVG array using any statistical methods
we wish because all of the final grades will have been saved and will be available to us. In Figure 10.8, the final grade, FGRADE, for the first student is being
loaded into the AVG array.

The AVG array could then be summed and divided by the number of students
to produce a class average, sorted into any desired sequence, or processed in

Figure 10.8
Loading the final grade for the
first student into the AVG
array.

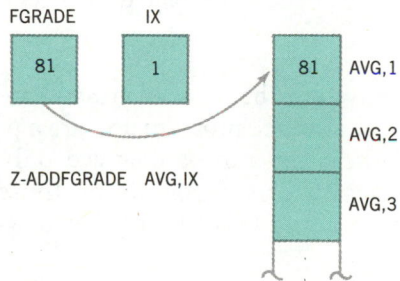

C			Indicators								Result Field				Resulting Indicators				
				And		And			Factor 1	Operation	Factor 2		Name	Length		Arithmetic			
																Plus	Minus	Zero	
																Compare			
																1>2	1<2	1=2	
																Lookup (Factor 2) is			
Line					Not		Not									High	Low	Equal	Comments
3 4 5	6	7 8	9 10 11	12 13	14 15	16 17	18 19 20 21 22 23 24 25 26 27			28 29 30 31 32	33 34 35 36 37 38 39 40 41 42	43 44 45 46 47 48	49 50 51	52	53	54 55	56 57	58 59	60 61 62 63 64 65 66 67 68 69 70 71 72 73 74
0 1	C							Z-ADDFGRADE			AVG,IX								
0 2	C																		
0 3	C																		

Note: FGRADE is calculated elsewhere in the program.

any other way we wish. The important point to remember is that the five student exams are used to create the AVG array *during the execution of the program*. Furthermore, the five exams for each student could be stored in an array such as the EXAM array presented earlier. In this case, each time a student record is read, the EXAM array would receive new data. That is, the EXAM array would hold a single student's five exams. When that student's average has been calculated, the next student's five exams are read from the next record and loaded into the input area reserved for the EXAM array. Note that the contents of input arrays may be replaced over and over again as with the EXAM array, or created during calculation time and *saved* for future processing as with the dynamic AVG array. An array can be referenced as a whole, meaning that a single instruction causes operations to be performed on all of the elements of the array. For example, arrays may be added to other arrays to produce totals in a single operation. Typically, running totals can be created using this technique. That is, each student's EXAM array could be added to a total array that would maintain a running total of each exam. Since there are five exams for each student, five elements would be needed in the total array. When the input file has been completely processed, this running total for each exam would be divided by the number of students to obtain a separate class average for each exam. Note in Figure 10.9 that the total array is called TOT.

That is, after all records have been read and processed, TOT,1 would contain the running total of all of the EXAM,1 scores. Similarly, TOT,2 contains a total of all of the EXAM,2 scores and so on. The ability to manipulate and process an entire group or set of data, often with a single instruction, provides RPG with vast and extended computational capabilities.

B. Types of Static Arrays

Keep in mind that **dynamic arrays** are those created during execution time; **static arrays** are those defined and described at compile time or pre-execution time. We could, for example, establish a MOnth array with 12 fields containing the literals JAN, FEB, . . . , DEC. Since the contents of the array are defined prior to execution, we call the array a static array. Compile time arrays and pre-execution time arrays will be discussed next. These two types of static arrays differ only in the way they are loaded or receive their assigned values.

1. Compile Time Arrays

Compile time arrays are "hard coded arrays," meaning that they are to contain data loaded with the source program and are a permanent part of that program. The content of the array can be changed only when the source program is recompiled. Typically, arrays containing the days of the week (the literals MON–SUN), months of the year (the literals JAN–DEC), or a standardized set of

Figure 10.9
Accumulating running totals
in an array.

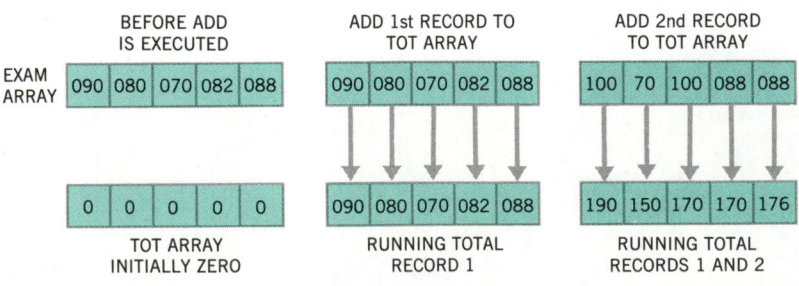

Processing Entire Array As a Whole

error messages are likely candidates for compile time arrays. The data records holding the values to be loaded follow the Output Specifications form of the source program. The source statements and the array data are separated by a record containing two asterisks in the first two positions, followed by a blank in the third. The sequence of the source program and array data for a compile time array is shown in Figure 10.10. Note that following the data records for the array is a line containing slash asterisk (/*), which designates the end of the array to the compiler.

The advantage of compile time arrays is that the array is always an integral part of the program itself. The disadvantage is that when the values stored within the array require change, the entire RPG program must be recompiled.

Again, compile time arrays are best suited for applications where the data is seldom subject to change, such as the names of the days of the week. Using this as an example, we will consider the programming requirements necessary to establish an array of DAYs of the week.

The DAY array would consist of seven elements, each representing a different day of the week. Note that WEDNESDAY is the longest entry and requires nine positions. Because the length of all elements within a given array must be the same, blanks are padded to the right of the other DAY names to make each of them nine characters or positions in length. An array representing the DAYS of the week may be conceptualized as shown below.

```
DAY ARRAY
  element 1    M O N D A Y b b b
  element 2    T U E S D A Y b b
      .        W E D N E S D A Y
      .        T H U R S D A Y b
      .        F R I D A Y b b b
      .        S A T U R D A Y b
  element 7    S U N D A Y b b b
```

Array consists of seven elements, each nine positions in length. Note that all entries or elements are of the same length. Elements that are shorter than the nine positions are padded with blanks.

In Figure 10.11, we have seven entries consisting of nine characters, each representing a day of the week. The DAY entries could be entered by seven records, as shown, where each record is nine positions long. Or, the DAY entries could be entered by two records, with each record containing 36 positions, four day entries in record 1 and three in record 2 and shown in Figure 10.12. Note that record 2 contains the data for the three remaining elements that are

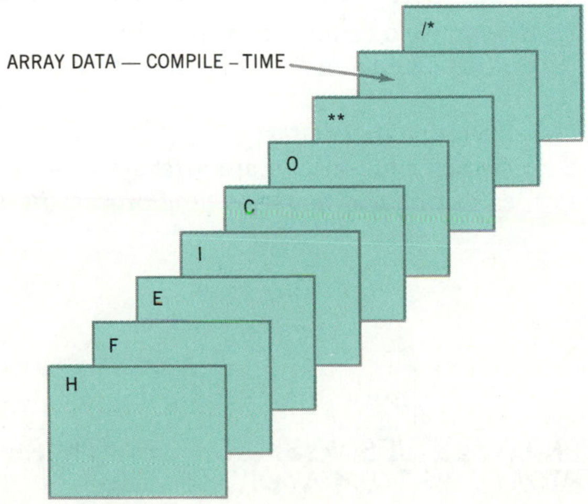

Figure 10.10 The sequence of the source program and array data for a compile time array.

Figure 10.11
Input records for loading the DAY array using a separate record for each element.

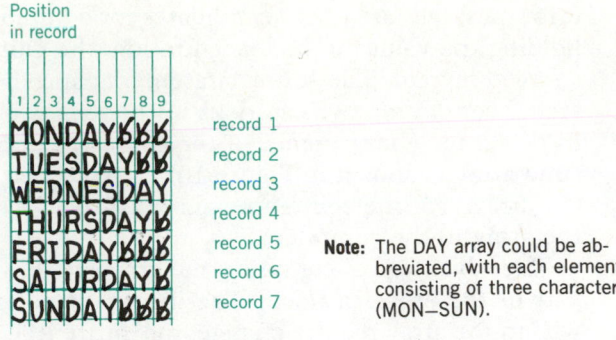

Note: The DAY array could be abbreviated, with each element consisting of three characters (MON—SUN).

necessary to complete the array. Note also that array entries always begin in position 1 of the record.

The Extension Specifications required in allocating storage for the DAY array using seven data records, and the alternative, consisting of two data records, is shown in Figure 10.13. The only difference in the two examples is the Number of Entries Per Record field specification.

An alternate method for establishing a DAY array would be to have seven elements, each three characters long, consisting of MONTUEWEDTHUFRISATSUN.

The following rules apply when entering compile time array data with your program:

Loading Compile Time Array Data
1. A record containing two asterisks in positions 1 and 2, followed by a blank in position 3, signals the compiler that compile time array data is to be loaded.
2. Always begin the array entries in position 1 of the record.
3. One or more entries may be recorded on each input record; however, individual entries may not be split or continued from one record to another.
4. The number of Entries Per Record field of the Extension Specifications form must contain the actual number of entries found on each input record. Note that the last record may have fewer entries than the number specified, as in Figure 10.12.
5. As a general rule, it is best to specify one array element per record (columns 33–35). This makes it easier to read and modify the data.
6. When more than one array is required, each begins with a ' ** ' record.
7. The array to be loaded must be in the same physical sequence as specified on the Extension Specifications form.

2. Pre-execution Time Arrays
Pre-execution time arrays are arrays whose values are loaded from external data files during the housekeeping processing in the RPG Fixed Logic Cycle,

Figure 10.12
Alternative method of loading the DAY array.

Position in record

| 1 2 3 4 5 6 7 8 9 0 | 1 1 1 1 1 1 1 1 1 2 0 1 2 3 4 5 6 7 8 9 0 | 2 2 2 2 2 2 2 2 2 3 1 2 3 4 5 6 7 8 9 0 | 3 3 3 3 3 3 1 2 3 4 5 6 | |

MONDAYɃɃɃTUESDAYɃɃWEDNESDAYTHURSDAYɃ   record 1
FRIDAYɃɃɃSATURDAYɃSUNDAYɃɃɃ   record 2

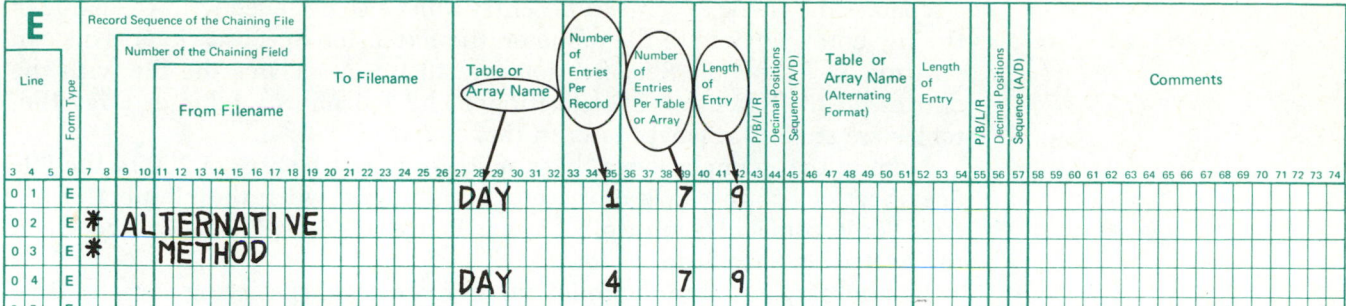

Figure 10.13
The Extension Specifications
for defining the DAY array.

prior to the execution of the first instruction of the program. The data values for the arrays are stored in independent files, and not in the program as with compile time arrays. An obvious advantage of pre-execution time arrays is that changes to the array do not necessitate a recompilation of the program. Pre-execution time arrays are used when entries change with some frequency.

Values such as inventory items and their associated prices are candidates for pre-execution time arrays since price changes are relatively frequent and the price arrays may be used by several programs. When necessary, the prices in the data file can be changed so that the next time the program is to be executed, the newly changed values are loaded without having to change the program. In addition, any and all programs using this price array data will have access to the latest prices.

The major difference in the definition of compile time arrays and pre-execution time arrays is the presence of a From Filename entry on the Extension Specifications form. (See Figure 10.14.) Since the array values are stored in

Figure 10.14
Defining a pre-execution time
array on the Extension and the
File Specifications.

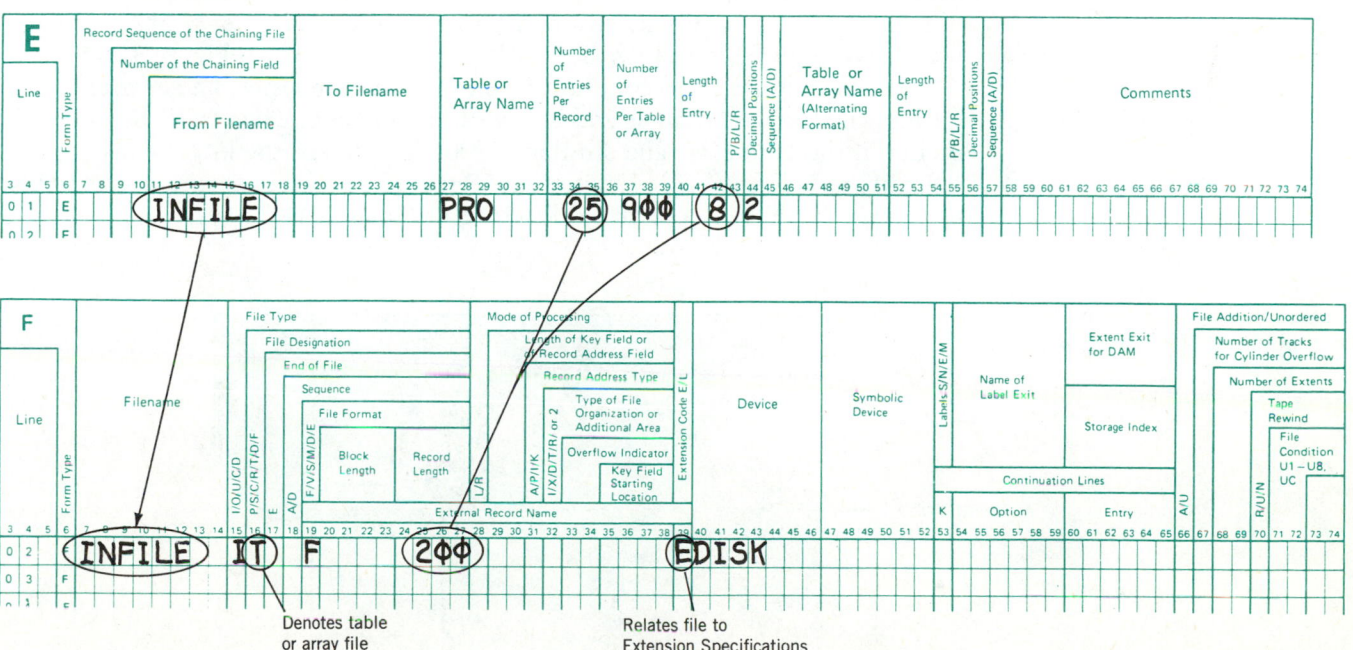

a separate file, a File Specifications entry must also be coded with the name of the file corresponding to the name on the Extension Specifications. The T in position 16 of the File Specification for INFILE associates the file with the entries on the Extension Specifications. The T denotes a table or array file; tables are studied at length later in this chapter.

Note in the example above that the Record Length entry of 200 in the File Specifications corresponds to the product obtained when the Number of Entries Per Record (25) is multiplied by the Length of (each) Entry (8) as coded on the Extension Specifications form.

In summary, we note the following differences in specifying compile time arrays and pre-execution time arrays:

	Pre-compile Time Array	Pre-execution Time Array
Extension Specifications		
From Filename (11–18)	Blank	Provides name of input array file identified on File Specifications form
File Specifications		
Filename (7–14)	Not used	Same name as referenced in From Filename entry on Extension Specifications form
File Designation (6)		T entry denotes table or array file
Extension Code (39)		E entry relates file to Extension Specifications form

3. Alternating-parallel Arrays

Alternating arrays consist of two parallel arrays usually having the same number of elements. An example of an alternating array could include an array of Employee Numbers and the corresponding hourly Pay Rate for each employee. We will call the Employee Number array ENO, while the corresponding or parallel Pay Rate array is called RATE. The arrays would be stored in a disk file in an alternating format, meaning that the input records first contain an Employee Number, followed by the Pay Rate, as illustrated in Figure 10.15.

Each input record is to contain two entries for each array. The entries begin with an Employee Number and end with a Pay Rate. There will be 100 elements in the ENO array, and similarly, 100 elements in the RATE array. Again referring to Figure 10.15, we note that 50 records, each containing two entries per array, would be necessary to load the ENO and RATE arrays.

Figure 10.15
Example of alternating arrays.

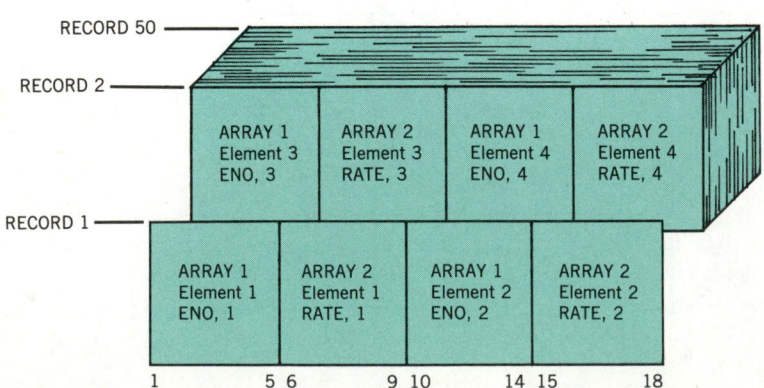

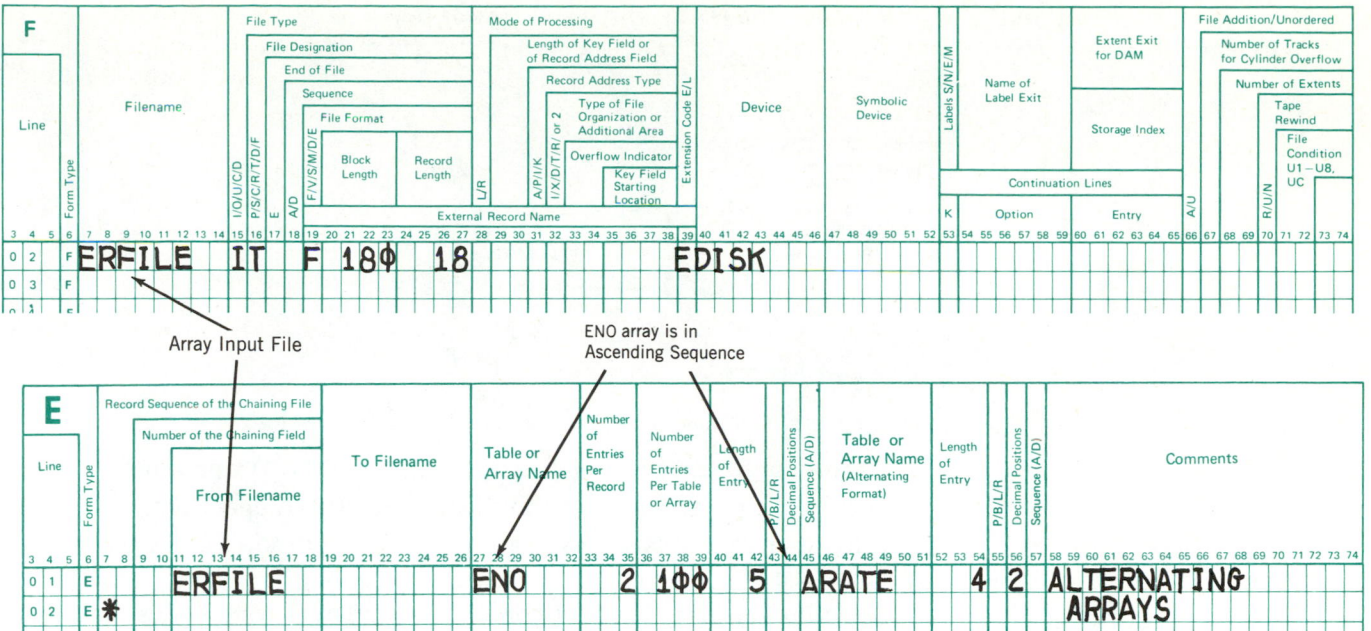

Array Input File

ENO array is in
Ascending Sequence

Figure 10.16
File and Extension
Specifications for defining
alternating arrays.

The Employee Number array, ENO, will contain 100 alphanumeric elements, each five characters in length. The ENO array will be in ascending sequence as indicated by the A entry in position 45 of the Extension Specifications form in Figure 10.16. The Pay Rate array, RATE, will contain 100 numeric elements, each four digits in length with two decimal positions. Therefore, the maximum Pay Rate is limited to $99.99 per hour.

The File and Extension Specifications forms in Figure 10.16 should be familiar to you, since the arrays will be loaded at pre-execution time. The only additional coding is found on the Extension Specifications form. Note the entry of the name of the alternating RATE array (46–56) including length and decimal positions, and the A entry in position 45 denoting that the ENO array is in ascending sequence. That is all that is required to define the parallel, alternating arrays called ENO and RATE respectively.

Once the arrays have been defined and loaded at pre-execution time, they can then be used for look-up purposes. This means that when an Employee Number is entered into the program, the appropriate Pay Rate for that employee could be "looked up" and retrieved from the RATE array. Remember, in order to reference an array element, the array name must be followed by a comma and an index. Again, the index must be defined as a numeric field with zero decimal positions.

The index would typically begin with a value of one, and would then be incremented in the loop to search for the matching Employee Number in the (ENO) array. Once found, the index is used to retrieve the corresponding Pay Rate from the RATE array.

Referring to Figure 10.17 we find that, given an employee number of 00007, the search through the ENO array would find a match at element 3. The index would therefore contain the value of 3. If the field name for the index is X, by referring to RATE,X the corresponding Pay Rate of 08.25 per hour would be retrieved from element 3 of the RATE array.

The details of coding an array look-up are presented later in this chapter.

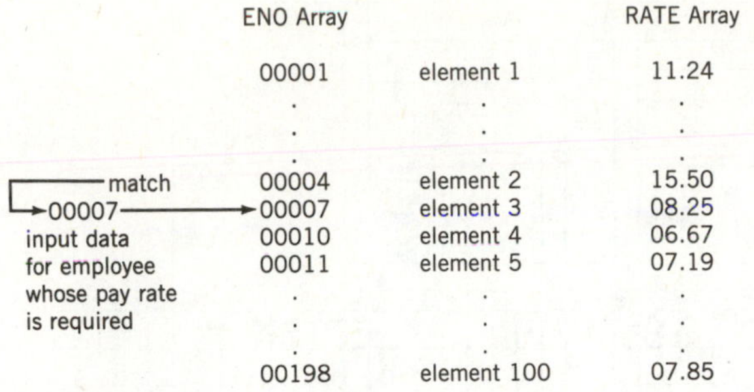

Figure 10.17
Example of parallel arrays.

	ENO Array		RATE Array
	00001	element 1	11.24
	.	.	.
	.	.	.
	.	.	.
match	00004	element 2	15.50
00007 →	00007 →	element 3	08.25
input data	00010	element 4	06.67
for employee	00011	element 5	07.19
whose pay rate	.	.	.
is required	.	.	.
	00198	element 100	07.85

C. Uses of Arrays

Array processing may include any or all of the following:

1. Summing the elements of an array using the **XFOOT operation.**
2. Sorting the elements of an array using the **SORTA operation.**
3. Moving character data into an array for search purposes using the **MOVEA operation.**
4. Selecting the array element containing the largest or smallest values.
5. Averaging the elements of an array.
6. Updating specific elements of an array.
7. Adding elements of one array to another.

We have seen that the elements of an array can be referenced individually using an index, or the array may be referenced as a whole. The array name *alone* implies a reference to the entire array.

We will now examine different methods for processing arrays.

V. Processing Array Elements

A. Adding Elements in an Array: The XFOOT Operation

Suppose you have five exam grades for each student, which you wish to average. If the five exam grades were entered as individual fields, five ADD instructions would be necessary to obtain a sum that you would then divide by five to obtain an average. If a student took 20 or 30 exams, then obtaining an average would require even more ADD instructions and prove exceedingly cumbersome. The use of an array minimizes the coding of a procedure to operate on 10, 20, or 50 similar items.

Consider an array that contains five exam scores for a student. To obtain the average of these five scores, you could use the coding shown in Figure 10.18. This figure illustrates both the nonstructured coding as well as the structured approach that does not use GOTOs.

Array processing can be simplified even further. An operation called "cross-foot" and coded as XFOOT can be used to sum all the elements in an array. Thus, the elementary loop summing the five elements of the array just presented could be simplified even further as shown in Figure 10.19.

To obtain an average, then, simply code the two operations shown in Figure 10.20.

Regardless of the number of entries of the array, XFOOT can be used to sum all the elements. The array to be summed is entered in Factor 2, and the field to serve as the sum is entered in the Result Field. When required, the programmer may use Half-adjust for rounding.

Figure 10.18
Averaging five exam grades.

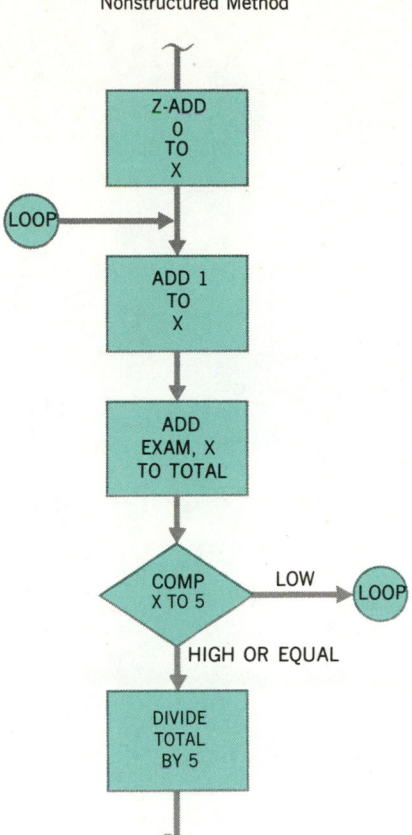

Nonstructured Method

Nonstructured

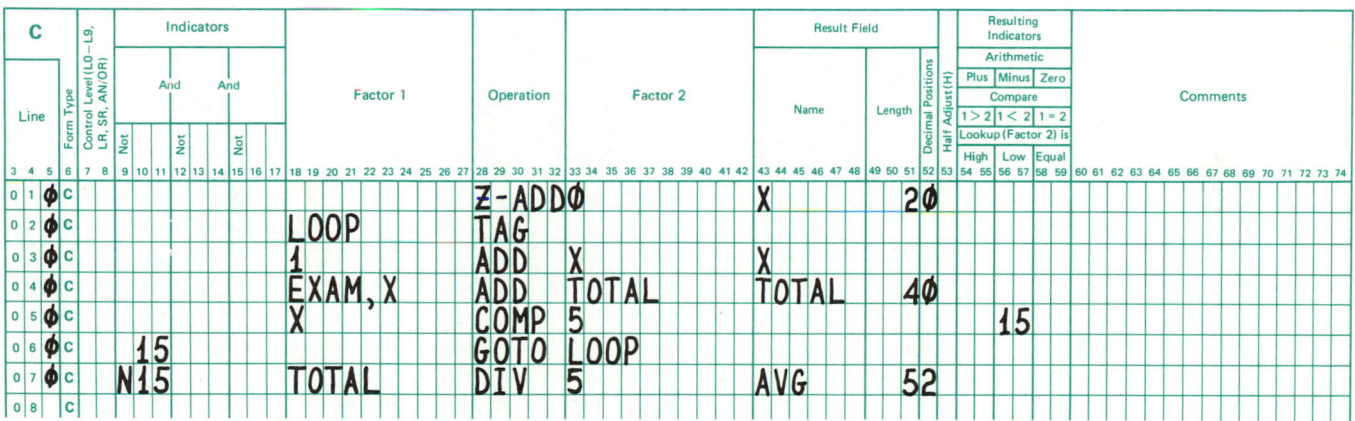

C			Indicators				Factor 1	Operation	Factor 2	Result Field				Resulting Indicators				Comments
Line	Form Type	Control Level (L0—L9, LR, SR, AN/OR)	And Not	And Not	Not		Factor 1	Operation	Factor 2	Name	Length	Decimal Positions	Half Adjust (H)	Plus / 1>2 / High	Minus / 1<2 / Low	Zero / 1=2 / Equal		Comments
0 1	Ø C							Z-ADD Ø		X	2Ø							
0 2	Ø C						LOOP	TAG										
0 3	Ø C						1	ADD	X	X								
0 4	Ø C						EXAM,X	ADD	TOTAL	TOTAL	4Ø							
0 5	Ø C						X	COMP	5						15			
0 6	Ø C		15					GOTO	LOOP									
0 7	Ø C	N15					TOTAL	DIV	5	AVG	52							
0 8	C																	

(continued on next page)

Figure 10.18   Structured Method
(continued)

Structured

C			Indicators										Factor 1	Operation	Factor 2		Result Field				Resulting Indicators					Comments
		Control Level (L0 — L9, LR, SR, AN/OR)	And		And												Name	Length	Decimal Positions	Half Adjust (H)	Arithmetic				
Line	Form Type		Not		Not		Not														Plus	Minus	Zero		
																					Compare				
																					1 > 2	1 < 2	1 = 2		
																					Lookup (Factor 2) is				
																					High	Low	Equal		
3 4 5	6	7 8	9 10 11	12 13 14	15 16 17	18	19 20 21 22 23 24 25 26 27		28 29 30 31 32	33 34 35 36 37 38 39 40 41 42	43 44 45 46 47 48	49 50 51	52	53							54 55	56 57	58 59	60 61 62 63 64 65 66 67 68 69 70 71 72 73 74	
0 1	C								Z-ADDø		X	2ø													
0 2	C					X			DOWLT5																
0 3	C					1			ADD	X	X														
0 4	C					EXAM,X			ADD	TOTAL	TOTAL	4ø													
0 5	C								END																
0 6	C					TOTAL			DIV	5	AVG	52													
0 7	C																								

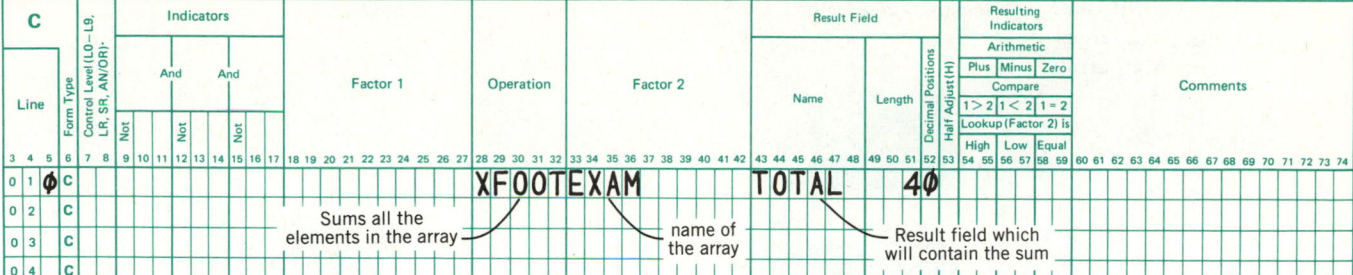

Figure 10.19
The XFOOT instruction.

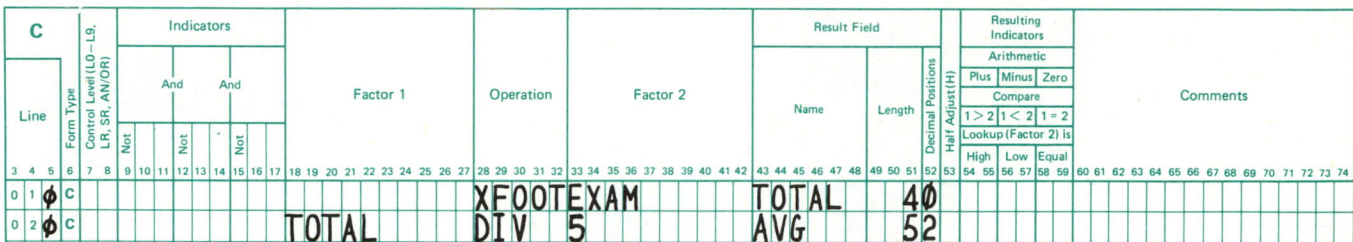

Figure 10.20
A simplified way of finding
an average.

B. Determining the Largest Element In an Array

A common programming requirement is to examine the contents of an array to determine the largest element. This is best accomplished with the use of a program loop. Refer to Figure 10.21, which illustrates both the nonstructured and structured flowcharts.

Suppose you have five exams and you wish to select the highest grade (see Figure 10.22). Establish an index and call it X. X varies from 1 to n, where n is the number of elements in the array. In this instance, there are five exams, so X varies from 1 to 5.

For each value of X from 1 to 5, compare the element in the array called EXAM to a field we will call BIGEX. If the element referenced by EXAM,X is smaller than or equal to BIGEX, do not process that element but simply increment the index, X, and test the next element. If the element referenced by EXAM,X is larger than BIGEX, move it into BIGEX with the use of a Z-ADD instruction. In this way, five passes through the loop will produce, in the field called BIGEX, the largest value in the array. Figure 10.22 illustrates both the nonstructured and structured coding techniques.

Hence, each element is compared during the looping procedure and the largest exam is selected by the program and stored in BIGEX. The variable BIGEX may therefore be referenced on the Output Specifications form and printed as necessary.

C. Counting Elements Greater Than the Average

Now consider an array of final grades called GRD. Suppose we wish to determine the number of individual GRD scores that exceed the average of these five GRD scores.

Figure 10.21
Logic for finding the largest
element in an array.

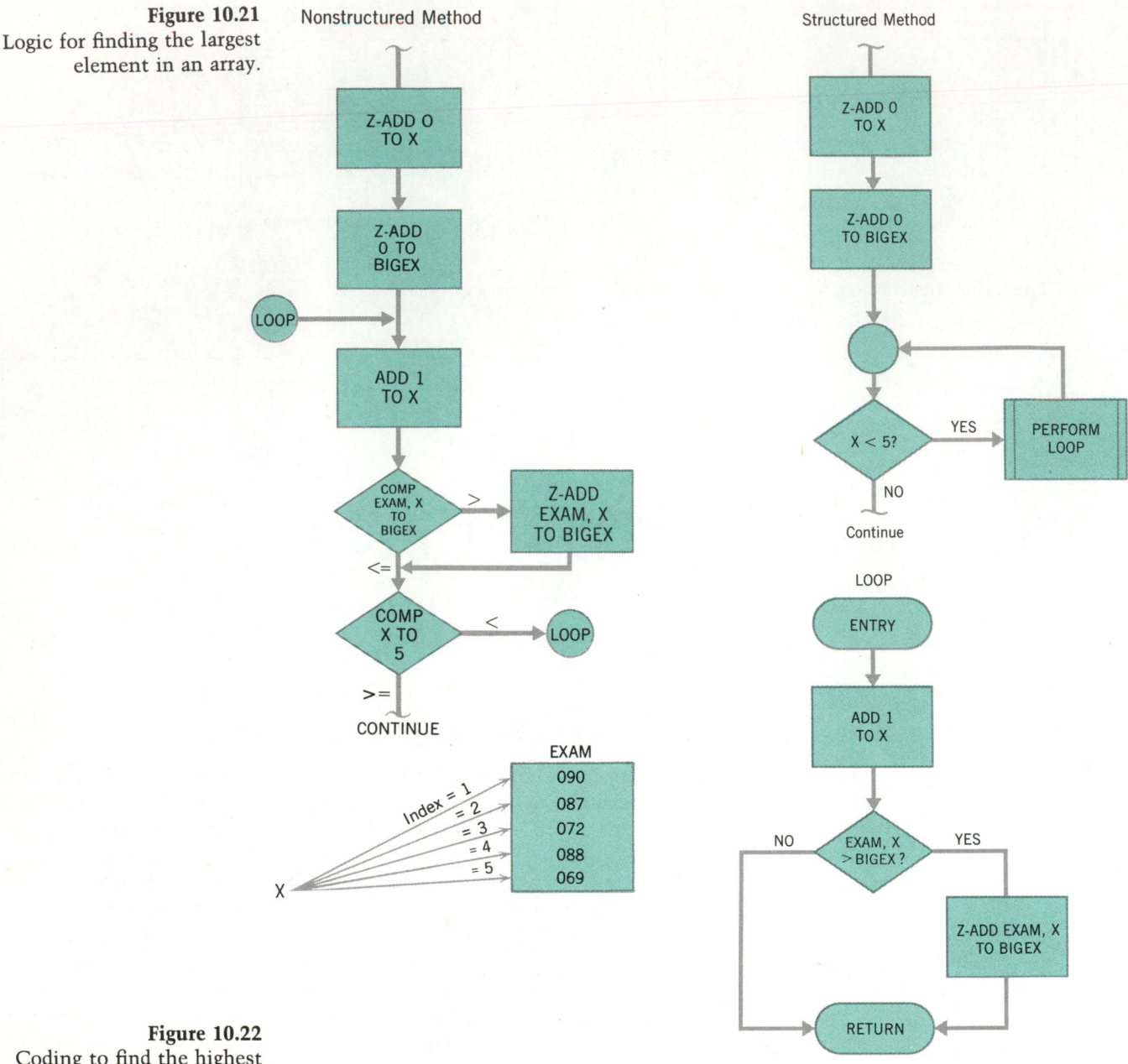

Figure 10.22
Coding to find the highest
value in an array. Nonstructured

C		Indicators					Factor 1	Operation	Factor 2	Result Field				Resulting Indicators			Comments
Line	Form Type	Control Level (L0—L9, LR, SR, AN/OR)	And		And		Factor 1	Operation	Factor 2	Name	Length	Decimal Positions	Half Adjust (H)	Arithmetic / Compare			Comments
			Not		Not	Not								High	Low	Equal	
0 1	Ø C							Z-ADD Ø		X	20						
0 2	Ø C							Z-ADD Ø		BIGEX	30						
0 3	Ø C						LOOP	TAG									
0 4	Ø C						X	ADD 1		X							
0 5	Ø C						EXAM, X	COMP	BIGEX					15			
0 6	Ø C		15					Z-ADD EXAM, X		BIGEX							
0 7	Ø C						X	COMP	5							25	
0 8	Ø C		25					GOTO	LOOP								

Structured

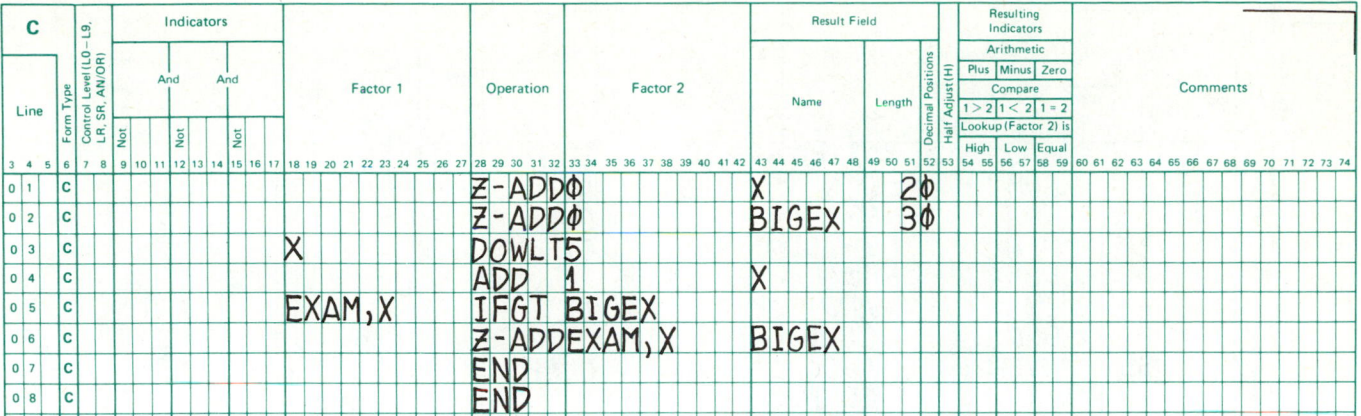

Figure 10.22
(continued)

Element	GRD
1	090
2	087
3	072
4	087
5	069

We use a short name such as GRD as the name of the grade array. Remember, a comma and index will also be needed to reference the array on the Output Specifications form, where we are restricted to a total of six characters.

The average of 81 is calculated by using the XFOOT operation to sum the elements of the GRD array, which is then divided by the number of grades (five). In other words we obtain the sum of the numbers 90, 87, 72, 87, and 69. The sum, 405, is then divided by 5 to produce an average of 81. A loop is needed to compare each element of the GRD array to the calculated average. If the value contained in an element of the GRD array is greater than the calculated average, an indicator is set on. One is added to a count field when that indicator is on. We will turn indicator 35 on if a GRD score exceeds the calculated average.

By adding 1 to a counter each time a value larger than the average is found, a count of the grades greater than the average is obtained. See Figure 10.23 for an illustration of this procedure in both nonstructured and structured form.

D. Sample Program

Each input record contains student identifying data along with five test grades. The five grades in each input record are treated as an array to reduce the coding necessary to solve the problem. The array of five grades is named EXAM on the Extension Specifications form. The EXAM array is to be summed with the XFOOT operation and averaged to produce the student's final grade. In addition, each student's highest exam score will be found and printed along with the student's final grade and identifying data. The systems flowchart and input record layout for the program are shown in Figure 10.24.

The program with sample output is shown in Figure 10.25. The Extension Specifications form should be familiar to you since the coding is the same as illustrated earlier. The XFOOT is used to sum the EXAM array, which is the first step in calculating the student's final average. A loop is used to extract the

Line	Form Type	Control Level	And	And	Factor 1	Operation	Factor 2	Result Field Name	Length	Dec. Pos.	Half Adjust	High 1>2	Low 1<2	Equal 1=2	Comments
01	C					XFOOTGRD		SUM	41						
02	C				SUM	DIV	5	AVG	41						
03	C					Z-ADD0		OVER	20						
04	C					Z-ADD0		IX	20						
05	C				DO5X	TAG									
06	C				IX	ADD	1	IX							
07	C				GRD,IX	COMP	AVG					35			
08	C			35	OVER	ADD	1	OVER							
09	C				IX	COMP	5							40	
10	C			40		GOTO	DO5X								
11	C														
12	C	****							*						
13	C	*		STRUCTURED VERSION IS:											
14	C	*							*						
15	C					XFOOTGRD		SUM	41						
16	C				SUM	DIV	5	AVG	41						
17	C					Z-ADD0		OVER	20						
18	C					Z-ADD0		IX	20						
19	C				IX	DOUGT5									
20	C					ADD	1	IX							
	C				GRD,IX	COMP	AVG					35			
	C			35	OVER	ADD	1	OVER							
	C					END									
	C														
	C														

Figure 10.23
Example of counting elements greater than the average.

Figure 10.24
Problem definition for sample array problem.

Systems Flowchart

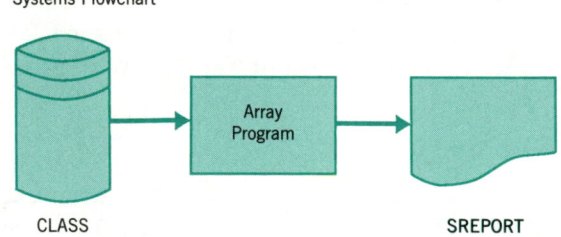

CLASS   SREPORT

Input Record Layout

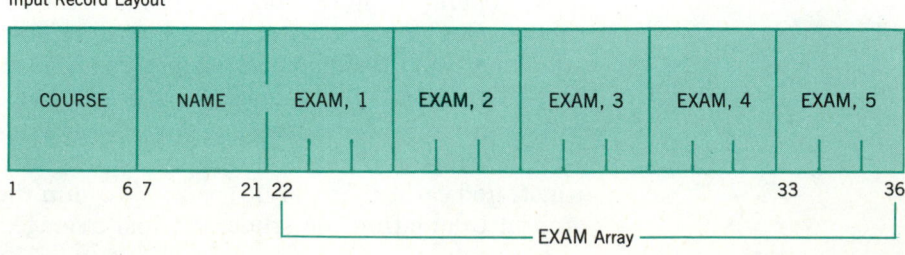

| COURSE | NAME | EXAM, 1 | EXAM, 2 | EXAM, 3 | EXAM, 4 | EXAM, 5 |

1   6 7   21 22   33   36

—— EXAM Array ——

Figure 10.25
Program for sample array
problem.

```
                    H
                    F*****************************************************************
                    F*    PROGRAM READS AN ARRAY AND PRODUCES A FINAL GRADE,        *
                    F*    CLASS AVERAGE AND AN AVERAGE FOR EACH OF THE 5 EXAMS       *
                    F*****************************************************************
0001                FCLASS   IP F      36              DISK
0002                FSREPORT O  F     132       OF     PRINTER
                    E*
0003                E                   EXAM      5  3 0
0004                E                   TOT       5  5 1
                    I*
0005                ICLASS   NS 01
0006                I                                       1   6 COURSE
0007                I                                       7  21 NAME
0008                I                                      22  360EXAM
                    C*****************************************************************
0009                C          P        ADD  1         P        20
0010                C                   XFOOTEXAM       TOTAL    30
0011                C          TOTAL    DIV  5          FGRADE   41H
0012                C          FGRADE   ADD  TGRADE     TGRADE   61
0013                C                   Z-ADD0          BIG      30
0014                C                   Z-ADD0          N        20
                    C*
0015                C          LOOP     TAG
0016                C          N        ADD  1          N
0017                C          EXAM,N   COMP BIG                         15
0018                C       15          Z-ADDEXAM,N     BIG
0019                C          N        COMP 5                              20
0020                C       20          GOTO LOOP
                    C*
0021                C          EXAM     ADD  TOT        TOT
                    C*
0022                CLR        TOT      DIV  P          TOT      H
0023                CLR        TGRADE   DIV  P          CLAVG    51H
                    O*****************************************************************
0024                OSREPORT H  201       1P
0025                O        OR           OF
0026                O                                   33 'S T U D E N T'
0027                O                                   60 'G R A D E   R E P O R T'
0028                O        H  11        1P
0029                O        OR           OF
0030                O                                    7 'COURSE'
0031                O                                   24 'STUDENT'
0032                O                                   52 'EXAM    EXAM    EXAM'
0033                O                                   69 'EXAM    EXAM '
0034                O                                   78 'FINAL'
0035                O                                   89 'HIGHEST'
0036                O        H  1         1P
0037                O        OR           OF
0038                O                                    5 'NO.'
0039                O                                   22 'NAME'
0040                O                                   51 '#1      #2      #3'
0041                O                                   67 '#4      #5'
0042                O                                   88 '  AVERAGE    GRADE'
0043                O        D  21        01
0044                O                          COURSE    7
0045                O                          NAME     28
0046                O                          EXAM,13  35
0047                O                          EXAM,23  43
0048                O                          EXAM,33  51
0049                O                          EXAM,43  59
0050                O                          EXAM,53  67
0051                O                          FGRADE3  78
0052                O                          BIG   1  87
0053                O        T  1         LR
0054                O                                   25 '** EXAM AVERAGES **'
0055                O                          TOT,1 1  35
0056                O                          TOT,2 1  43
0057                O                          TOT,3 1  51
0058                O                          TOT,4 1  59
0059                O                          TOT,5 1  67
0060                O                          CLAVG 1  78

          E N D  O F  S O U R C E
```

Figure 10.25
(continued)

S T U D E N T   G R A D E   R E P O R T

COURSE NO.	STUDENT NAME	EXAM #1	EXAM #2	EXAM #3	EXAM #4	EXAM #5	FINAL AVERAGE	HIGHEST GRADE
CMP1Ø1	PORSCHE FERDY	88	75	88	9Ø	7Ø	82.2	9Ø
CMP1Ø1	BENZ DAIMLER	92	87	91	7Ø	88	85.6	92
CMP1Ø1	DELOREAN JOHN Z	8Ø	9Ø	95	7Ø	6Ø	79.Ø	95
CMP1Ø1	DUSENBERG HARRY	6Ø	7Ø	88	99	77	78.8	99
CMP1Ø1	FERRARI ENZO	91	92	93	95	96	93.4	96
CMP1Ø1	DODGE HORACE	8Ø	76	56	98	93	8Ø.6	98
CMP1Ø1	TUCKER PRESTON	86	83	91	78	92	86.Ø	92
CMP1Ø1	CORD WILHELM	67	86	91	76	78	79.6	91
CMP1Ø1	LOWE RAYMOND	56	87	91	84	9Ø	81.6	91
** EXAM AVERAGES **		77.8	82.9	87.1	84.4	82.7	83.Ø	

highest exam score and save it under the name BIGEX. Later, you will find the SORTA instruction could also be used for this purpose. All of the other instructions in this example should already be familiar to you.

VI. Referencing an Entire Array

To reference an entire array, use the array name *without* an index. The following array operations may be used with an array name: Z-ADD, ADD, SUB, MOVEA, and SORTA.

A. Z-ADD Operation

The **Z-ADD operation** may be used to move data from one array to another. If it is necessary to move data to an array that is to be used in a subroutine, for example, it can be accomplished with a single instruction. However, the more common problem of swapping or interchanging arrays requires that a third temporary array be used. If the data in ARR1 and ARR2 are to be interchanged, the coding in Figure 10.26 would be used.

Similarly, an entire array may be initialized with a single instruction. For example, if it was necessary in a program to reinitialize an entire array to zero, the instruction in Figure 10.27 would accomplish this objective.

B. ADDing Arrays

A programmer may frequently find the need to add arrays together. For example, a business may require a total of the sales for each of ten departments for January, February, and March in order to create a first quarter total. In other words, the corresponding ten elements of the arrays SJAN, SFEB, and SMAR are to be accumulated in a first quarter TOTAL array.

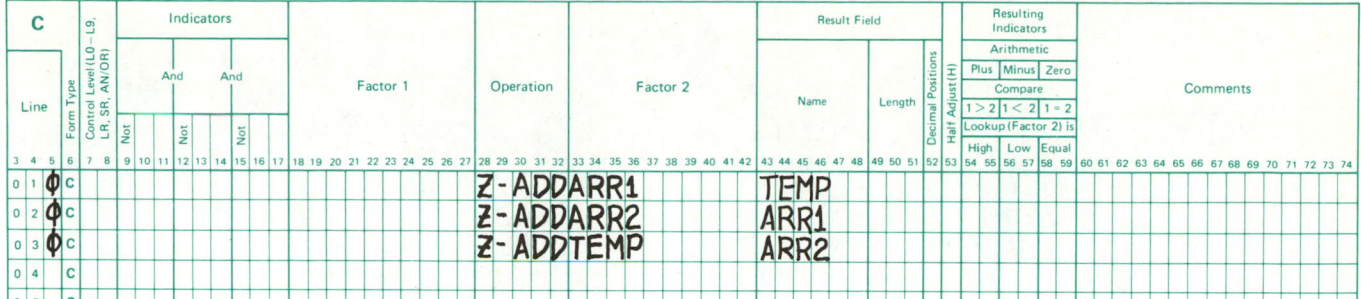

Figure 10.26

Use of the Z-ADD to move data from one array to another.

Dept.	SJAN Jan Sales		SFEB Feb Sales		SMAR March Sales		TOTAL 1st Quarter
01	2,500.00	+	6,106.00	+	7,800.00	→	16,400.00
02	800.00		790.00		839.00		2,429.00
.	.		.		.		.
.	.		.		.		.
10	1,300.00		2,500.00		1,800.00	→	5,600.00

Each element of TOTAL is calculated by adding SJAN + SFEB + SMARCH

In Figure 10.28, the elements are added individually to the total. Since Factor 1, Factor 2, and the Result Field are all arrays with the same number of elements, the operation is performed using the first element from each array, then the second, and so on until all the elements in the arrays are processed. However, if the arrays do not have the same number of elements, the operation terminates when the last element of the shortest array is processed. The coding in Figure 10.28 provides for the addition of the SJAN, SFEB, and SMAR arrays.

This ability to process all elements in an array with just one instruction is a relatively unique feature for a programming language. It provides RPG with a capability that surpasses that of most third-generation languages like COBOL and BASIC.

C. MOVEArray Operation

The MOVEArray **operation** is frequently used in applications that require the programmer to *search* an array. A search refers to a procedure that steps

Figure 10.27

Initializing an array to zero.

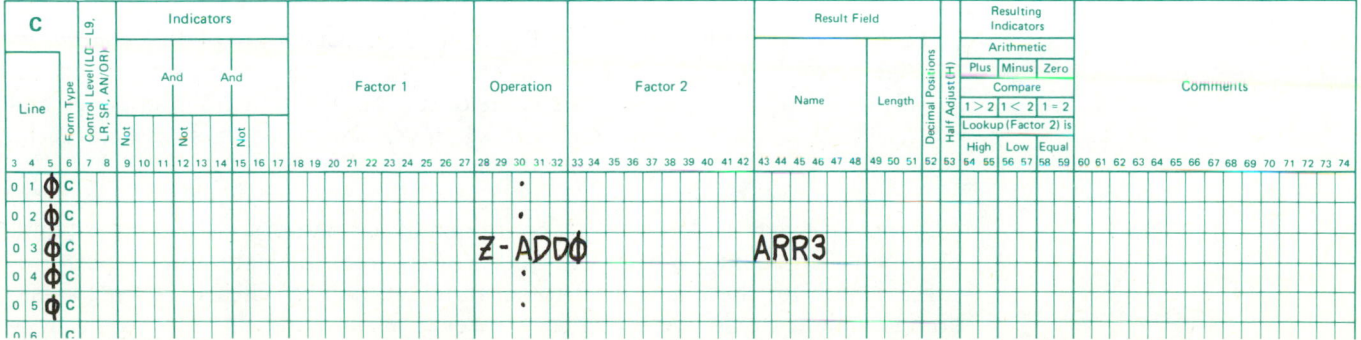

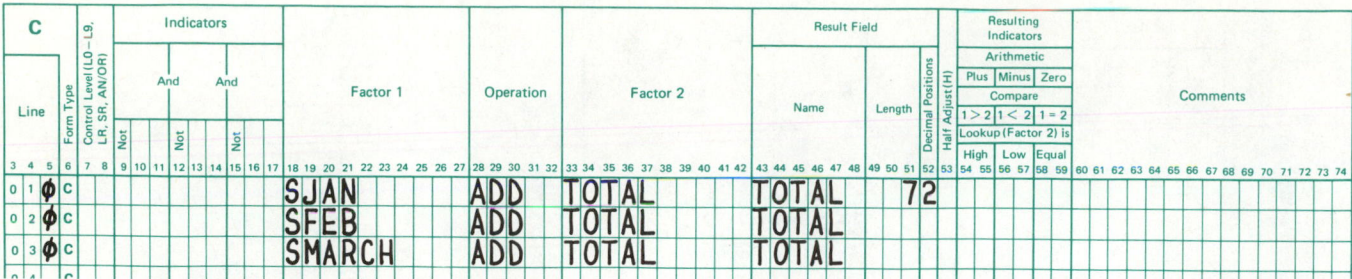

Figure 10.28
ADDing arrays.

through each element in an array and tests for a specific condition. For example, a grade of 999 could be used to indicate the end of a group of grades in a numeric array. The trailer grade of 999 is not to be used in any calculations but rather serves as a sentinel value that indicates that all of the grades have been processed. In this instance, we would search the array by stepping through each element and testing for a value of 999 until we find the element containing the trailer value. Once the trailer or sentinel value is found, the search is terminated.

An array element referenced with the MOVEA instruction must be nonnumeric, meaning that this instruction is designed to move alphanumeric data. The MOVEA operation makes it possible to do the following:

1. *Move a single alphanumeric field to an array.* In this way each character in the field becomes an array element that can be accessed by indexing. Searches for certain characters can be performed using this technique.

2. *Move several array elements to a single field.* The results of a search may be placed in an array and later moved to an output field for printing.

Either Factor 2 or the Result Field must be an array in a MOVEA operation. For example, in order to move a 25-character field, NAMEIN, to an array called NME, consisting of 25 elements, the MOVEA instruction in Figure 10.29 would be coded. Recall that NME must be defined on the Extension Specifications form.

One reason for moving the NAMEIN field to the array is to perform a search (e.g., how many nonblank characters are there in NAMEIN). In such a case, the Result Field, the NME array, and the field coded in Factor 2, NAMEIN, would be the same length. If, however, they were not the same length, then the following rules would apply:

Condition	Result Field
Factor 2 contains more characters than the Result Field	The Result Field does not receive all of the characters from Factor 2. Truncation of the rightmost characters occurs.
Factor 2 contains fewer characters than the Result Field	The Result Field receives all of the characters from Factor 2. In addition, the extra or excess characters of the Result Field are unchanged and contain whatever data that existed before the MOVEA was executed.

Suppose a field called NAMEIN contained a last name, followed by a blank and then a first name. We wish to isolate or separate the last name by performing a search for the blank used to separate the names. Clearly, NAMEIN as a standard field cannot be searched. However, by moving NAMEIN to an array (NME), a search for the blank as a name separator could be performed since each character in NME can be accessed separately.

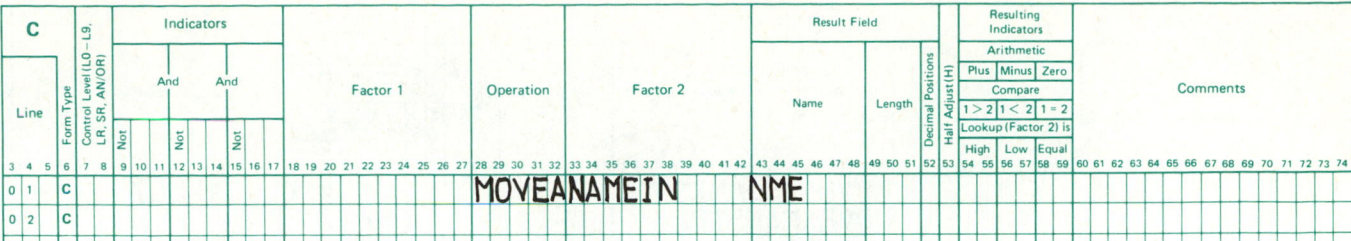

C			Indicators											Result Field				Resulting Indicators					
			And	And														Arithmetic					
Line	Form Type	Control Level (L0–L9, LR, SR, AN/OR)	Not	Not	Not	Factor 1	Operation	Factor 2	Name	Length	Decimal Positions	Half Adjust (H)						Plus	Minus	Zero		Comments	
																		Compare					
																		1 > 2	1 < 2	1 = 2			
																		Lookup (Factor 2) is					
3 4 5	6	7 8	9 10 11	12 13	14 15	16 17 18 19 20 21 22 23 24 25 26 27	28 29 30 31 32	33 34 35 36 37 38 39 40 41 42	43 44 45 46 47 48	49 50 51	52 53		High 54 55	Low 56 57	Equal 58 59	60 61 62 63 64 65 66 67 68 69 70 71 72 73 74								
0 1	C					MOVEANAMEIN		NME															
0 2	C																						

Figure 10.29
Example of the MOVEA instruction.

We would simply move 1 character at a time from the NME array to another array (LST) until we found the blank. We use a loop to perform the series of moves with the NME index being incremented by 1 each time through the loop. When we find a blank we terminate the loop and move the array containing the last name, called LST, to an output field for printing. The coding of the Calculation Specifications form for this excerpt appears in Figure 10.30. When a blank is encountered, we want to terminate the loop, so we Z-ADD 26 to X. This results in the termination of the DO loop since X would then be greater than 25.

D. SORTArray Operation

The SORTA operation is used to sort the elements of an array into either ascending or descending order. When column 45 of the Extension Specifications form contains an A, then the array is sorted into ascending order. If column 45 contains the letter D, then the array is sorted in descending sequence. How-

Figure 10.30
Performing a search for a blank used in a name field to separate first and last names.

E			Record Sequence of the Chaining File		To Filename	Table or Array Name	Number of Entries Per Record	Number of Entries Per Table or Array	Length of Entry	P/B/L/R	Decimal Positions	Sequence (A/D)	Table or Array Name (Alternating Format)	Length of Entry	P/B/L/R	Decimal Positions	Sequence (A/D)	Comments	
			Number of the Chaining Field																
Line	Form Type		From Filename																
3 4 5	6	7 8	9 10 11 12 13 14 15 16 17 18	19 20 21 22 23 24 25 26	27 28 29 30 31 32	33 34 35	36 37 38 39	40 41 42	43	44 45	46 47 48 49 50 51	52 53 54	55	56 57	58 59 60 61 62 63 64 65 66 67 68 69 70 71 72 73 74				
0 1	E				NME		25	1											
0 2	E				LST		25	1											

I						External Field Name			Field Location					Field Indicators		
					Record Identification Codes											
Line	Form Type	Filename or Record Name	Sequence	Number (1/N)	Option (O), U, S	Record Identifying Indicator, * or DS	1	2	3	From	To	Decimal Positions	RPG Field Name	Control Level (L1–L9)	Matching Fields or Chaining Fields	Field Record Relation	Plus	Minus	Zero or Blank
		Data Structure Name	O R	A N D			Position	Not (N)	C/Z/D	Character	Position	Not (N)	C/Z/D	Character	Position	Not (N)	C/Z/D	Character	Stacker Select	P/B/L/R	Occurs n Times	Length
3 4 5	6	7 8 9 10 11 12 13	14	15 16	17	18 19 20	21 22 23 24	25	26	27	28 29 30 31	32	33	34	35 36 37 38	39	40	41	42	43	44 45 46 47	48 49 50 51	52 53	54 55 56 57 58	59 60	61 62	63 64	65 66 67 68	69 70	71 72 73 74
0 1	I									1	25		NAMEIN						
0 2	I																		

(continued on next page)

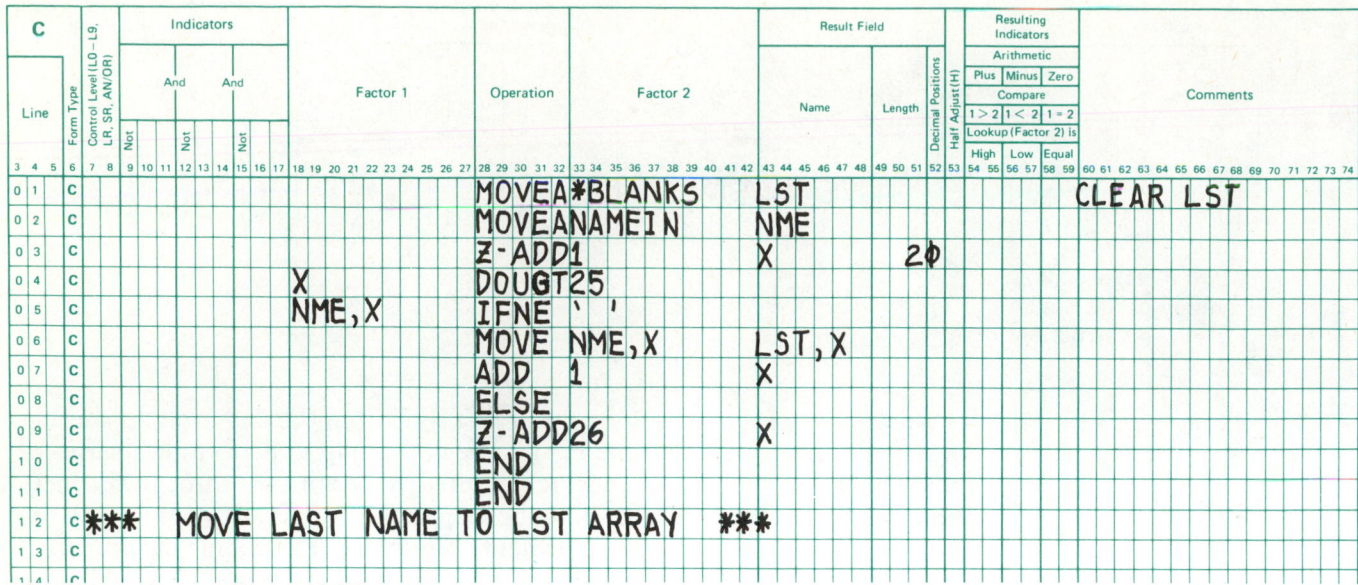

C			Indicators				Factor 1	Operation	Factor 2	Result Field				Resulting Indicators				Comments

Line							Factor 1	Operation	Factor 2	Name	Length							Comments
0 1	C							MOVEA*BLANKS		LST								CLEAR LST
0 2	C							MOVEANAMEIN		NME								
0 3	C							Z-ADD1		X	20							
0 4	C			X				DOUGT25										
0 5	C			NME,X				IFNE ' '										
0 6	C							MOVE NME,X		LST,X								
0 7	C							ADD 1		X								
0 8	C							ELSE										
0 9	C							Z-ADD26		X								
1 0	C							END										
1 1	C							END										
1 2	C	***	MOVE LAST NAME TO LST ARRAY						***									
1 3	C																	
1 4	C																	

Figure 10.30
(continued)

ever, if column 45 of the Extension Specifications form is blank, then the default is to ascending order, as shown in Figure 10.31.

Another useful application of the SORTA operation would be the sorting of dates. To make the sorting of dates meaningful, they must be set up as year-month-day. If the dates were in month-day-year sequence the resulting order would be incorrect. (For example, 12-01-90 would be considered greater than months 01 through 11 regardless of the year.) To correctly sort the array, the data must be in year-month-day sequence since year has greater value than month, which has greater value than day.

Before SORTA	After SORTA
YYMMDD	YYMMDD
910417	900519
910718	900801
900519	910417
920323	910718
900801	920323

Remember, the default with the SORTA operation is ascending sequence.

VII. Other Types of Array Processing

A. Two-dimensional Arrays

Unlike some other programming languages, only one-dimensional arrays are available in RPG. However, the programmer, by carefully manipulating the index, can reference an array by the row and column format normally associated with two-dimensional arrays. An array consisting of four columns and three rows contains 12 cells or storage positions as shown below. The number in each cell illustrates the relative position of each element in the array.

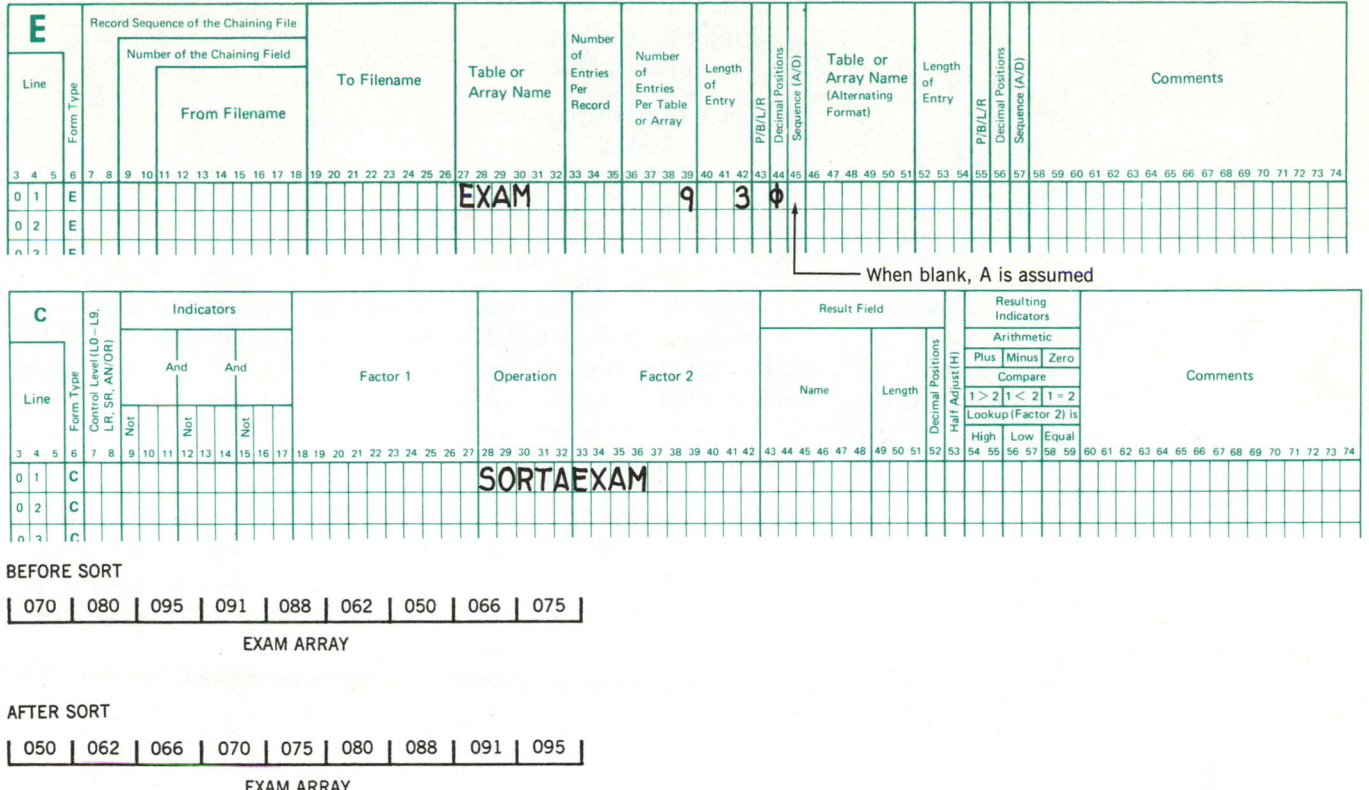

NOTE: EXAM, 9 contains highest test grade after sorting.

Figure 10.31
Example of the SORTArray
instruction.

```
          COLUMNS
         1   2   3   4
row 1    1   2   3   4
row 2    5   6   7   8
row 3    9  10  11  12
```

If it were necessary to access row 3, column 2, we can see that this is the 10th element of the array. The general equation for locating any cell in a row-column or two-dimensional array is:

index = column + ((row − 1) × number of columns)

To find the index for the element in row 3, column 2 where the number of columns = 4, we compute:

index = 2 + ((3 − 1) × 4) = 10

It is important to note that each cell is one storage location and can therefore only store one item of data. We can access this data by calculating an index for a particular row and column combination.

Let us consider an example of a two-dimensional array.

The Hit Parade Music Stores is a small chain of four retail stores sharing a central computer. As sales occur, they are transmitted to the mainframe and posted; hence the sales records are in random order. Each store sells 3 types of musical media. Type 1 denotes cassettes, Type 2 is used for LP records, and Type 3 is reserved for compact disks. The array SLS needed for this problem may be visualized as shown below.

Two-dimensional Array—SLS

```
                        STORE #
                      1  2  3  4
CASSETTES             X  X  X  Ⓧ ◄── row 1, column 4
LP RECORDS            X  X  X  X
COMPACT DISKS         X  X  X  Ⓧ ◄── row 3, column 4
```

The objective is to develop running totals for sales by type, for each store. If store 2 sold four compact disks for $68.00, then the sales amount would be added to the cell located at column 2, row 3. Recall, this is the tenth element in the array. The input record for this transaction is illustrated below:

```
┌──────┬──────┬──────────┬───────┐
│ 0 2  │ 0 3  │ 0 0 6 8 0 0 │ 0 0 4 │
└──────┴──────┴──────────┴───────┘
  store   type     amount     qty
```

All that is needed is to add the amount field to the proper cell in the array. Instead of using rows and columns in the general equation, we substitute STORE for column and TYPE for row. The index, IX, is calculated from the store number and type. The proper element of the SLS array is then updated with the ADD instruction as shown in Figure 10.32.

Some applications require us to process the array using columns as the major index while others may have the rows as the major index. In the example presented, the total sales for any store can be obtained by adding the column data. Totals for each type of media are calculated by summing a row. For our example:

to index	first cell location	increment by
column	column number	4, the number of columns
row	(row number − 1) × 4 + 1	1

In a similar fashion, another two-dimensional array could be used to store the quantities of each type of media sold. Hence, one array would contain the total dollar amount of sales, and a corresponding array would keep track of the quantities of each of the media by type and by store.

Figure 10.32
Updating elements in a two-dimensional array.

		Indicators				Factor 1	Operation	Factor 2	Result Field			Resulting Indicators	Comments
Line	Form Type	And / And							Name	Length	Decimal Positions / Half Adjust (H)	Arithmetic / Compare / Lookup	
0 1	C					TYPE	SUB	1	IX	20			
0 2	C					IX	MULT	4	IX				
0 3	C					IX	ADD	STORE	IX				
0 4	C	*											
0 5	C					SLS,IX	ADD	AMOUNT	SLS,IX				
0 6	C												

B. Printing an Entire Array

It is sometimes convenient to print an entire array on one line of output with a single instruction. For example, during the debugging phase of program development, the printing of an array every time a record is processed would assist the programmer in tracking down logic errors. Again, each array would be printed on a single line. Therefore, when specifying the End Position on the Output Specifications form, sufficient space must be allowed to output all of the elements of the array. It is recommended that edit codes be used for punctuation and to improve readability. Be aware of the additional space needed for punctuation, namely decimal points, commas, and so forth. When an edit code is specified, every element of the array is edited accordingly. Furthermore, two spaces will be embedded between each element. The embedded blanks are automatically inserted by the program. The last element of the array ends in the End Position specified on the Output Specifications form. If space is limited, the programmer may elect to print the array without editing (see Figure 10.33).

Using a loop and `EXCPT` instruction, we could also print each individual array element on a separate line, thereby illustrating the flexibility available to the RPG programmer when printing arrays.

C. Array LOKUP Operation

The array **LOKUP operation** performs a sequential search of an array until the search condition is satisfied or the end of the array has been reached. When an index is specified, the number of the array element that first satisfies the search condition is saved in the index. If the search is unsuccessful, the resulting indicator is turned off and the index is set to 1. When the search is successful, the resulting indicator is turned on and the index or subscript points to the element of the array that satisfies the search condition.

Figure 10.33
Printing an array.

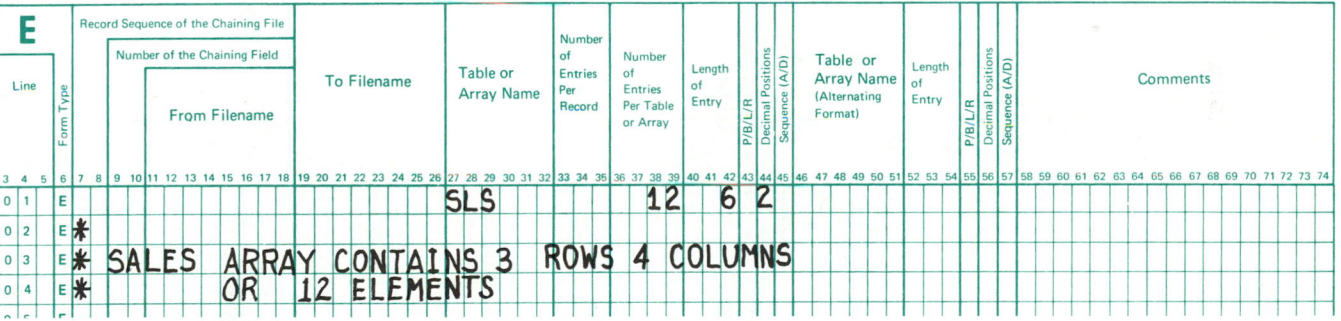

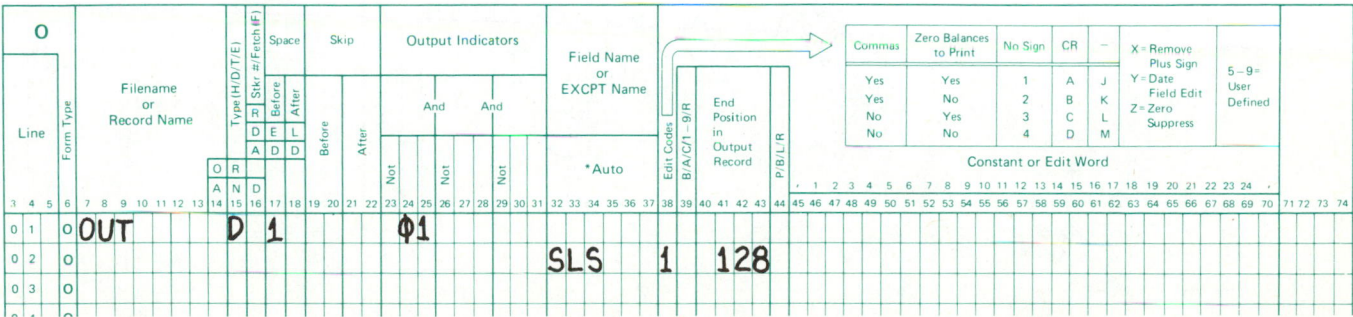

After a successful search, the index may be used to access another array or to further facilitate the processing of the array that has been searched. For example, recall the search process used to extract the last name from an array containing both first and last names. The NME array was searched until the blank used to separate the first and last names was found. If we were required to select the first name, rather than the last, the coding would be entirely different. In order to select the first name only, we would need to move the characters after the blank was found. If the index was called IX, then we would begin moving the characters from IX + 1:

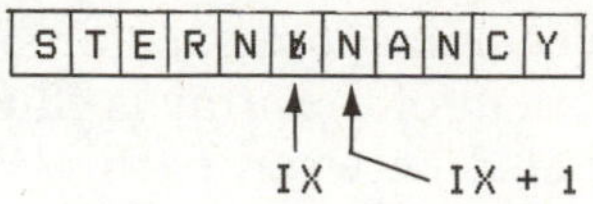

The coding of the Calculation Specifications form for this program excerpt is shown in Figure 10.34. You will note later in this chapter that the LOKUP operation is ideally suited for tables and table processing.

D. Developing Totals for Control Breaks

A frequent problem in the coding of RPG control break programs is the difficulty in determining when to accumulate the various control fields. Arrays may be used to eliminate this confusion. Examine the coding in Figure 10.35 and note that sales totals are being accumulated as follows:

Sales are added to a salesperson total.
Salesperson totals are accumulated by department.
Department totals are summed into store totals.
Store totals are added to a final total.

Figure 10.36 can perform the same operation with a single instruction.

TARRAY consists of four elements, where TARRAY,1 represents the salesperson (SPER) total, TARRAY,2 denotes the department total (DEPTOT), TARRAY,3 corresponds to the store total (STRTOT), and TARRAY,4 is the final total.

Figure 10.34
Program excerpt that uses the LOKUP operation.

```
01 C                            MOVEANAMEIN    NME
02 C                            Z-ADD0         Y       20
03 C                            Z-ADD1         X       20
04 C                   ' '      LOKUPNME,X                   10
05 C     10            X        DOWLT25
06 C                            ADD  1         X
07 C                            ADD  1         Y
08 C                            MOVE NME,X     FST,Y
09 C                            END
10 C*
11 C*** MOVE FIRST NAME TO FST ARRAY ***
12 C*
13 C
```

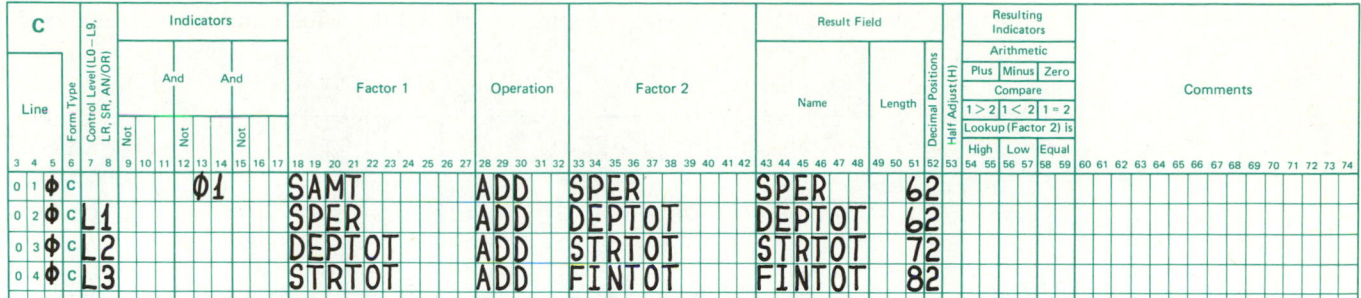

Figure 10.35
Use of arrays in a control
break program.

The ADD instruction adds the sales amount (SAMT) to all four elements of the total array (TARRAY).

All that is necessary is to reset the totals to zero once they are printed using the Z-ADD operation. Therefore, when an L1 break occurs, the accrued sales-person total *must* be reset to zero once the total output has been completed. Similarly, the department total is reset to zero for an L2 control break. The store total (STRTOT) is reset to zero after printing as a result of the L3 level indicator.

Self-Test

1. Suppose you name an array EMP. The fourth element is called _____ . In addition to using the array name, you would use a(n) _____ .

2. Consider the following fields on a CUSTFILE Input Specifications Form:

    ```
     1  20 CNAME
    21  25 CAMT1 0
    26  30 CAMT2 0
    31  35 CAMT3 0
    36  40 CAMT4 0
    41  45 CAMT5 0
    ```

    The amount fields could instead be established as a(n) _____ because all amount fields are _____ .

3. Suppose CAMT1 had two decimal positions and CAMT3 was six positions long. Could the amount fields be established as an array?

4. Recode the above as an array.

5. Code a routine to determine the total of all five amounts, defined as an array.

Solutions

1. EMP, 4; index or subscript
2. array; the same size and have the same number of decimal positions

Figure 10.36
Using only one array in a
control break program.

| C | | | Indicators | | | | | | | Factor 1 | Operation | Factor 2 | | Result Field | | | | Resulting Indicators | | | Comments |

3. No—All fields must have the same length and the same number of decimal positions.

4.

E			Record Sequence of the Chaining File				Table or Array Name	Number of Entries Per Record	Number of Entries Per Table or Array	Length of Entry	P/B/L/R	Decimal Positions	Sequence (A/D)	Table or Array Name (Alternating Format)	Length of Entry	P/B/L/R	Decimal Positions	Sequence (A/D)	Comments
			Number of the Chaining Field																
	Line	Form Type	From Filename		To Filename														
01	E						CAMT		5	5	2								
02	E																		

I			Filename or Record Name	Sequence	Number (1/N), E	Option (O), U, S	Record Identifying Indicator, * , or DS	External Field Name										Field Location			RPG Field Name	Control Level (L1—L9)	Matching Fields or Chaining Fields	Field Record Relation	Field Indicators		
								Record Identification Codes										From	To							Plus	Minus	Zero or Blank
								1				2				3												
	Line	Form Type	Data Structure Name	O R / A N D				Position	Not (N)	C/Z/D	Character	Position	Not (N)	C/Z/D	Character	Position	Not (N)	C/Z/D	Character	Stacker Select	P/B/L/R	Occurs n Times / Data Structure	Length	Decimal Positions			
01	I	CUSTFILENS		01																								
02	I																			1	20	CNAME					
03	I																			21	45	CAMT					
04	I																										

5.

C		Control Level (L0–L9, LR, SR, AN/OR)	Indicators							Factor 1	Operation	Factor 2	Result Field				Resulting Indicators							Comments
				And		And											Arithmetic								
																	Plus	Minus	Zero					
													Name	Length	Decimal Positions	Half Adjust (H)	Compare							
																	1>2	1<2	1=2					
	Line	Form Type		Not		Not		Not									Lookup (Factor 2) is							
																	High	Low	Equal					
01	C										XFOOT	CAMT	TOTAL	62										
02	C																							

VIII. How Tables Are Used

A **table** is a group of related data items contained in main or auxiliary storage that may be accessed or referenced by an RPG program. The table consists of a group of entries of the same type and size, not part of the actual program, which are stored in consecutive locations within storage as illustrated in Figure 10.37. Since tables are used by the program and occupy storage, the computer system must be made aware of the following:

1. The name to be assigned to the table.
2. The maximum number of entries in the table.
3. The length of the table entries.

This information is necessary in order to allocate storage for the tables in the RPG program and is handled by the coding of the Extension Specifications form.

Tables are typically used when processing or calculations are based on data that varies from one run to another. Examples of tables include:

1. A discount table that includes discount rates based on the quantity of items ordered.
2. A table of accounts that are no longer valid.

Figure 10.37
Examples of tables.

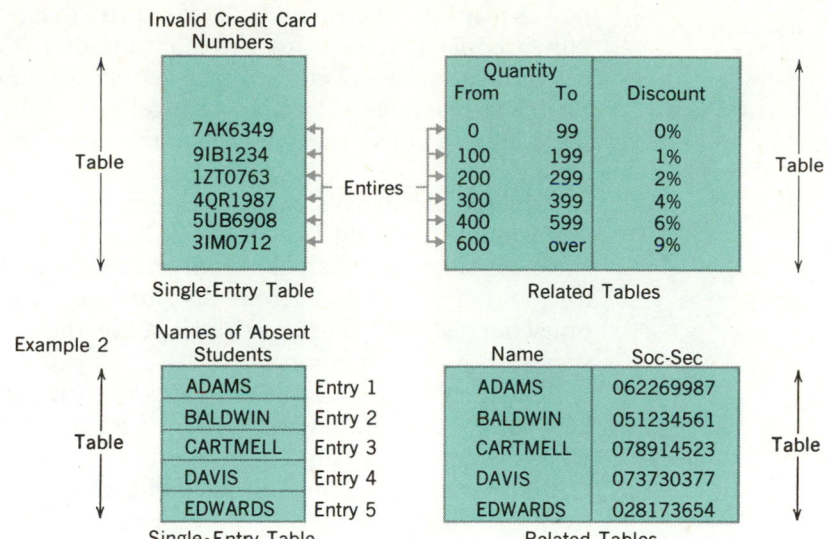

3. A tax table indicating federal tax based on each employee's gross pay.
4. A table of shipping charges based on the weight of items mailed.

Why Tables Are Stored Externally

Tables are entered as variable data and are not defined as constants within a program. Suppose you had a table of discount rates for each item sold by a company. You would *not* define the table containing discount rates for each product as a *constant*. The reason that tables are not usually defined as constants is that table *entries* change from time to time. If the table were actually coded as part of the program, then each change would require a modification of the program coding, and the program would have to be recompiled. One rule of programming is that you code procedures so that changes or subsequent modifications are minimized. Since each program change increases the risk of error, we do not include as constant data any item that is apt to change. Note that compile-time tables are not considered constants within the program, but are handled as separate input records.

Thus table data that changes frequently is always entered as *variable* input along with the specific input to be processed. In this way, if a table entry is to be changed, you simply alter the entry and do not need to modify the program. Thus table programs are processed as follows:

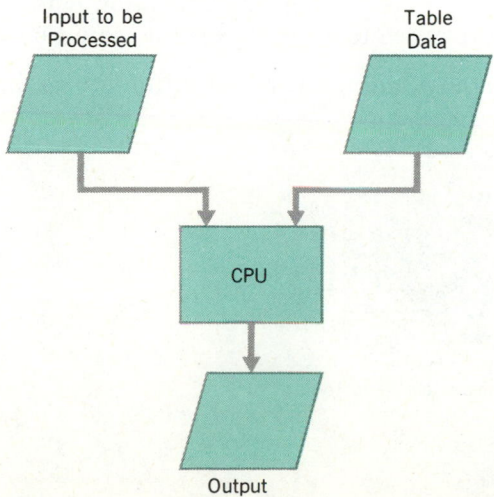

Without a table, the discounts shown in Figure 10.37 that are given for ranges of quantities ordered would require the programmer to code a number of COMPare instructions using the input quantity field to determine the discount percentage. We avoid entering the actual discounts on the Calculation Specifications form since they may change over time. Changes are easily made to table entries but changes to constants established in a program can result in errors.

Another alternative to maintaining an external table that is loaded into main memory would be to build a disk file and access the data directly from the disk. However, there is usually not enough data to justify the use of a disk for looking up values such as discount percentages, tax percentages, or shipping charges, and the access time is somewhat slower for disk searches than for searches in main memory.

The function of the table is to organize the data systematically so that it can be readily referenced within the program. The table serves as a small file, which, when loaded into storage, provides the programmer with access to any of the entries. Based on an input field, you can look up a corresponding value from the table.

The two general categories of tables are single-entry tables and related or parallel tables. A **single-entry table** simply consists of a series of entries. Examples of single-entry tables include a table of out-of-stock part numbers and a table of account numbers that are in arrears. **Related** or **parallel tables** are two or more tables that have related entries, such as discount percentages corresponding to each quantity ordered, or credit ratings corresponding to each customer number. This chapter will present sample programs illustrating the use of both single-entry and related tables.

IX. Single-entry Tables

A. Applications

A single-entry table is simply a group of single entries or items such as a table of overdrawn checking account numbers (see Figure 10.38).

Single-entry tables are frequently used for checking purposes. Before processing a personal check, a bank teller should enter the account number via a computer terminal or other device, checking to determine if the account is overdrawn. If the account number is listed in the table that contains all overdrawn accounts, a message would be issued instructing the teller not to cash the check. This is a typical application using a single-table lookup. The processing required to accomplish this would be as follows:

1. A teller enters the account number as input.

Figure 10.38
Example of a single-entry table.

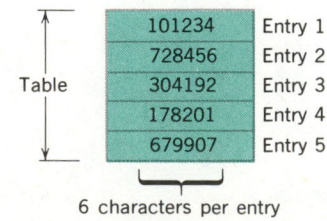

Table		Entry
	101234	Entry 1
	728456	Entry 2
	304192	Entry 3
	178201	Entry 4
	679907	Entry 5

6 characters per entry

2. A lookup or search is performed to determine if the account entered is equal to any of the table entries.
3. If an equal condition is found, an indicator will be set on.
4. The indicator would then be used to condition printing a message to reject the transaction.
5. If the account number is not in the table, the indicator would not be set on, the account number would be considered valid, and the transaction would be processed in the normal way.

B. Size Considerations

Single-entry tables, like arrays, may consist of either numeric or alphanumeric entries that are arranged in ascending order, descending order, or in no specific sequence at all. Similarly, all entries in a table or array must be exactly the same length. The table in Figure 10.39, for example, lists the months of the year. The month of September, with nine letters, is the longest entry in the table. Because the length of all entries must be the same, blanks are padded to the right of the other month names to make each of them nine characters in length. Note the similarity when defining arrays.

In other words, one table entry cannot be three positions long (MAY) and another nine positions long (SEPTEMBER). All the entries must be nine positions, which is the length of the *longest* table entry. The shorter month names contain right-justified spaces so that all are the same length.

When numeric table entries are employed, again the same rule applies and the largest entry is used for determining the size requirement. Since numeric fields are right-justified, high-order zeros are placed in the unfilled left-most positions of entries with fewer digits than the longest entry. Decimal points are not included in tables but are, however, specified on the Extension Specifications form using the Decimal Positions field. Thus the decimal point is implied.

A single-entry table is used when it is necessary to determine if a certain name or account number in a table matches an input or a Result Field used in the program. If, however, the program requires data to be retrieved from the table when a match occurs, then *related tables* should be used for those applications. That is, if a match between an input NAME and a table NAME is used to print the corresponding Social Security number from the table specified previously in Figure 10.37, then the table is called a related table. If, however, the input name is used simply to determine if a match exists in the table, a single-entry table is sufficient.

Figure 10.39
Table of months.

```
J A N U A R Y ƀ ƀ
F E B R U A R Y ƀ
M A R C H ƀ ƀ ƀ ƀ
A P R I L ƀ ƀ ƀ ƀ
M A Y ƀ ƀ ƀ ƀ ƀ ƀ
J U N E ƀ ƀ ƀ ƀ ƀ
J U L Y ƀ ƀ ƀ ƀ ƀ
A U G U S T ƀ ƀ ƀ
S E P T E M B E R
O C T O B E R ƀ ƀ
N O V E M B E R ƀ
D E C E M B E R ƀ
```

All entries must have the same length. Those items that are not as long as the longest item must be padded with blanks (ƀ).

TABMO

X. Processing Single-entry Tables

A. Creating Table Input Records

The table data is typically stored on disk. Regardless of the device used, the following rules will always apply:

RULE SUMMARY

1. Begin the table entries in position 1 of the record.
2. One or more entries may be recorded on each input record; however, entries may not be split or continued from one record to another. Suppose for example that each table entry is 10 characters long. Each disk record could contain a single table entry or a group of table entries.
3. Whatever number of entries you choose per record must be the same for all records except the last, which may contain a complete number of entries or only the remaining entries necessary to complete the table.
4. The maximum number of table names permitted in a program is 60.

In Figure 10.38, we have five table entries each consisting of a six-character checking account number. The checking account entries in Figure 10.38 could be entered by five records as in Figure 10.40, where each record is six positions long. Or, the checking accounts in Figure 10.38 could be entered on two records, with each record containing 18 positions (three checking-account entries in record 1 and two in record 2 as in Figure 10.41). Note that record 2 in Figure 10.41 contains only the two remaining entries that are necessary to complete the table.

B. Compile Time and Pre-execution Time Tables

The two most popular types of tables are:

1. **Compile time table.** The table records are read in along with the program during compilation.
2. **Pre-execution time table.** The table records are read in just before the program is executed.

C. Loading Compile Time Tables

Compile time tables are entered along with the RPG program using the sequence specified in Figure 10.42. The Extension Specifications form directly

Figure 10.40
Input records for loading the table in Figure 10.38.

1 0 1 2 3 4	Record 1
7 2 8 4 5 6	Record 2
3 0 4 1 9 2	Record 3
1 7 8 2 0 1	Record 4
6 7 9 9 0 7	Record 5

Figure 10.41
Alternative layout for input records.

| 1 0 1 2 3 4 | 7 2 8 4 5 6 | 3 0 4 1 9 2 | Record 1

| 1 7 8 2 0 1 | 6 7 9 9 0 7 | (unused) | Record 2

Figure 10.42
Placing compile-time tables with a source program.

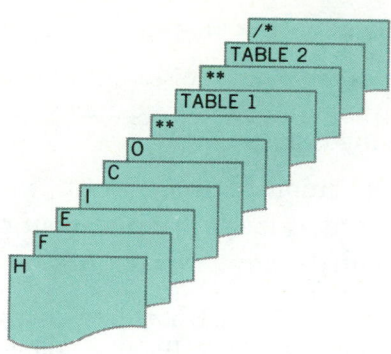

follows the File Description Specifications form. The record following the Output Specifications form contains a double asterisk (**) to indicate that table data follows. Table data, then, is part of the program and is not treated as ordinary input.

The advantage of compile time tables is that the table is always an integral part of the program itself. The disadvantage is that when the table changes, the entire RPG program must be recompiled. If a table does not change or changes infrequently, the compile time table is usually used. The student will find the compile time table to be the most popular and the most frequently used type, especially with IBM System 36, 38, or AS/400 users.

Pre-execution time tables are *not* compiled with the program, but rather, the table records are typically stored on disk. They are entered just prior to standard input. Thus, after the program is loaded and immediately before the RPG cycle begins, the pre-execution table(s) are read into the program as shown in Figure 10.43.

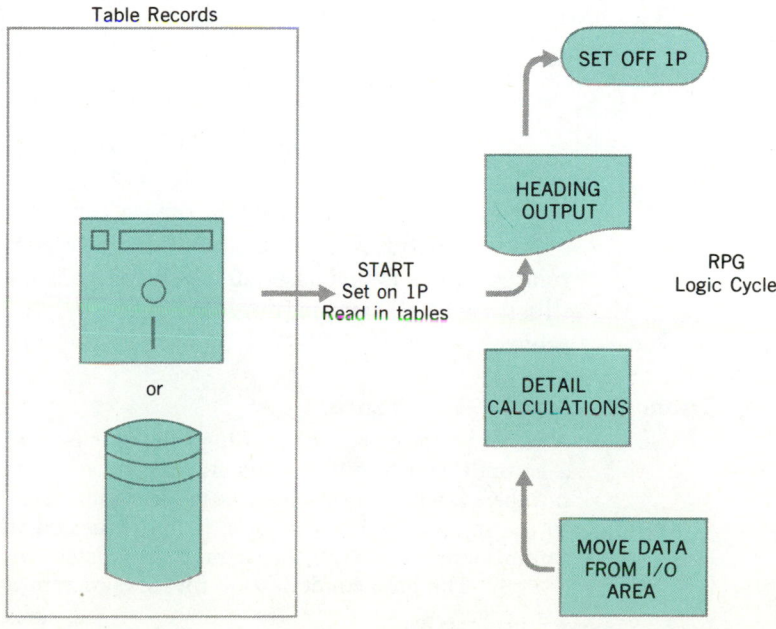

Figure 10.43
Reading in pre-execution tables.

Pre-execution time tables are used when entries change with some frequency. With a pre-execution time table, changes do not necessitate a recompilation since the table is stored on an external device. Thus, once the table data is read in, it is exactly the same as if it had been originally included as part of the program.

D. LOKUP Instruction for Single-entry Tables

As noted earlier, a table may be searched for a high, low, and/or equal condition. That is, an input or Result Field may be compared against table entries until the following is true:

1. An equal condition exists.
2. The table entry is lower than the input or Result Field.
3. The table entry is greater than the input or Result Field.

When simple tables are used, however, always specify the equal condition in a look-up procedure. The LOKUP operation causes a comparison to be made between Factor 1, referred to as the **search argument,** and each entry of the table, called a **table argument,** which is coded as Factor 2. If an equal condition is found, that is, the search argument equals one of the table arguments, then the indicator is set on and is used to condition further processing or output. With the LOKUP operation, Factor 2 always contains the name of the table. In the example that follows, an account number (ACCTNO) has been entered as input and the table containing invalid account numbers (TABACC) is to be searched. If the input account number is found in the table, indicator 10 will be set on. That is, if the input ACCTNO field matches a table entry, indicator 10 is set. The coding for this search is as follows:

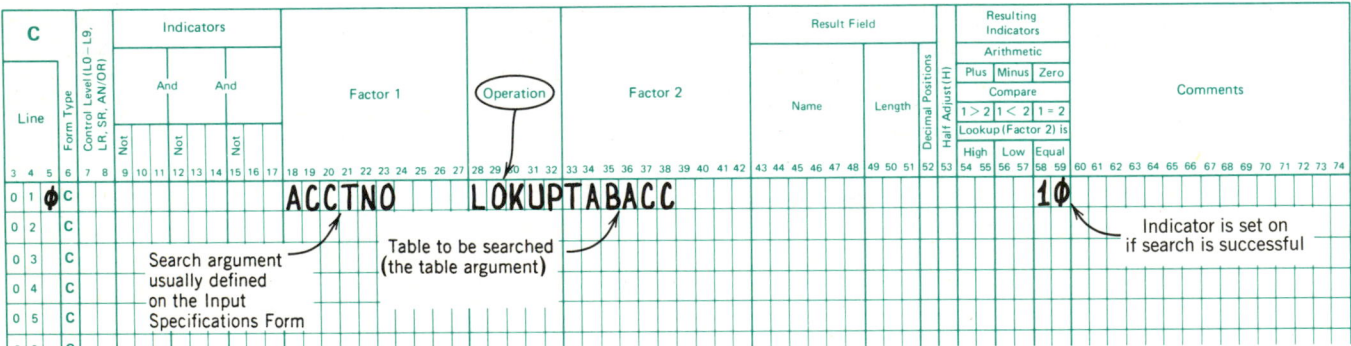

This illustrates a LOKUP with a *single table*. The use of the LOKUP with related tables is discussed and summarized later in this chapter. We will now illustrate a full sample program using the LOKUP instruction with single-entry tables.

Example   **Sample Table Program 1**

A table is to be created containing a list of out-of-stock part numbers. We will establish a compile time table for this illustration on the assumption that out-of-stock part numbers rarely change. When parts are requested, they are checked against the table file to see if they are out of stock. If the requested item is found in the table, the part number and requesting department are listed on a report entitled "OUT OF STOCK ITEMS." The problem definition for this program is shown in Figure 10.44.

Figure 10.44
Problem definition for Sample
Table Program 1.

Systems Flowchart

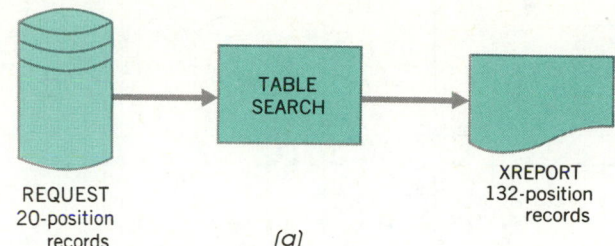

REQUEST
20-position
records

TABLE
SEARCH

XREPORT
132-position
records

(a)

REQUEST Record Layout

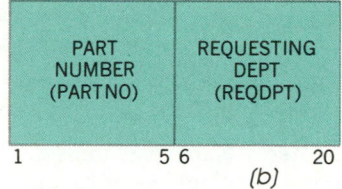

PART NUMBER (PARTNO)	REQUESTING DEPT (REQDPT)

1   5 6   20

(b)

XREPORT Printer Spacing Chart

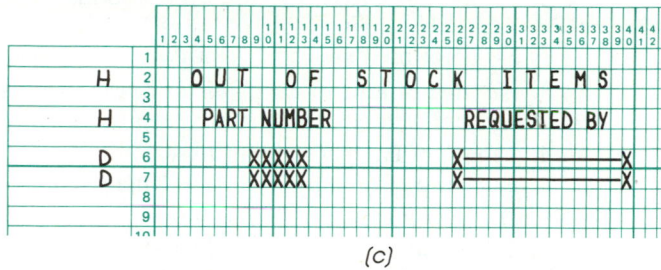

(c)

The File Specifications for the program are familiar and no different from any of our previous programs. However, since we will be using a compile time table, we will use the Extension Specifications form that we used when processing arrays. This form directly follows the File Specifications form.

The Extension Specifications are used to:

1. Identify the name of the table.
2. Allocate storage for the table in the program.

In this example, each part number consists of five characters, and the table is to contain 32 part-number entries. Hence the table will be 160 positions long (see Figure 10.45).

The table will be created from 80-position input disk records. Each input record is to contain 16 five-position part number fields. Since the table is to contain 32 entries, only

Figure 10.45
Table for Sample Program 1.

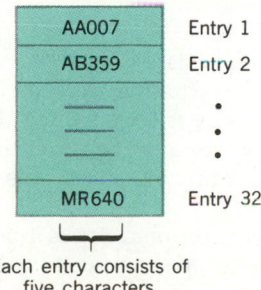

AA007 — Entry 1

AB359 — Entry 2

⋮

MR640 — Entry 32

Each entry consists of
five characters

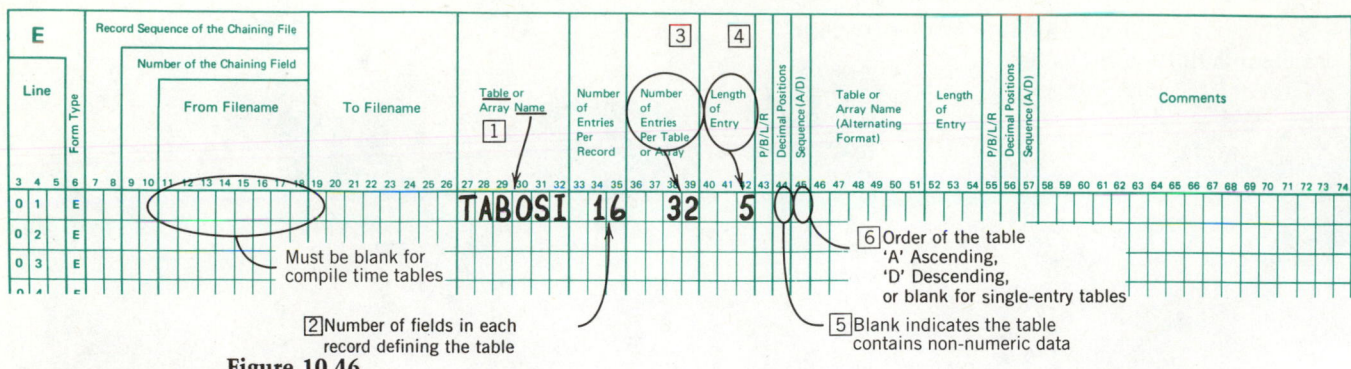

Figure 10.46
Extension Specifications for
Sample Table Program 1.

two 80-character records will be necessary to fill the table. The Extension Specifications are indicated in Figure 10.46. The numbered entries have the following meanings:

1. *Table or Array Name (Columns 27–32)*
   The name of the table must begin with TAB in columns 27–29 of the Extension Specifications form. We chose the name TABOSI to denote out-of-stock items. However, any name is acceptable, providing it begins with TAB.

2. *Number of Entries per Record (Columns 33–35)*
   Each table input record contains 16 table entries. Thus 16 is coded in columns 34–35 of the Extension Specifications form.

3. *Number of Entries per Table or Array (Columns 36–39)*
   The entire table is to contain 32 entries. Thus 32 is coded in columns 38–39.

4. *Length of Entry (Columns 40–42)*
   Each entry is five characters in length. Thus 5 is coded in column 42.

5. *Decimal Positions (Column 44)*
   The Decimal Positions field (column 44) is blank when the table fields are *not* numeric. Decimal Positions must contain a digit for numeric table entries.

6. *Sequence (Column 45)*
   With single-entry tables, no order need be specified. However, with related tables, the table data may be organized in ascending (A) or descending (D) sequence by specifying A or D in column 45.

The rest of the Extension Specifications form is left blank for compile time tables.

Thus the entries just listed represent all the coding necessary to describe the TABOSI table to the program. The programmer should prepare the 160-character table data on two 80-character disk records (16 entries of five positions each per record). The source program should be organized as previously noted in Figure 10.42. Remember that the compile time table data always follows the double asterisk (**) line in the source program.

Also note that the table entries will be listed on the Table MAPs, as illustrated in Figure 10.47. During debugging, the MAP listing should be carefully reviewed by the programmer to validate the accuracy of the table. Inaccuracies in the table could cause extensive debugging effort. Always validate the contents of tables before checking the logic of the program.

The program is shown in Figure 10.48. Figure 10.49 shows sample output produced by the program. Note that there is a LOKUP operation, which is used to search the TABOSI table. Using the LOKUP operation, the search argument, PARTNO, is compared to the table arguments; indicator 50 is set on when the input PARTNO is equal to a table argument. Indicator 50 is then used to condition the printing of the detail lines in the exception report. All the other instructions in this program should already be familiar to you.

Remember, any time an application requires a check to determine if a specific name, number, or item is present, a single-entry table may be used. An input or Result Field is

TABLES AND MAPS

RESULTING INDICATOR TABLE

OFFSET	RI	OFFSET	RI	OFFSET	RI	OFFSET	RI	OFFSET	RI	OFFSET	RI	OFFSET	RI
0503	0A	0525	LR	0526	HO	0531	1P	0534	01	0535	50		

OFFSETS OF VARIABLE NAMES AND CONSTANT NAMES

OFFSET	NAME	OFFSET	NAME	OFFSET	NAME	OFFSET	NAME	OFFSET	NAME
0638	ILF TABOSI	03C9	*ERROR	064D	PARTNO	0652	REQDPT		

TABLE/ARRAY ⟨TABOSI⟩   000698

```
AA007AB359AB913AR375AS009AT332AX198BB142BC963BE111BG653BT301BZ193CA165CB338CC654
CD328CT123DD001DR610DT387DX921GE199GS333GU610JR017JX910LE370LG989LX328MM321MR640
```

Table data. Every 5 characters represent a new entry.

Figure 10.47
Listing of the table entries.

Figure 10.48
Sample Table Program 1.

```
           01-010   F*                                                                     SSS10A
           01-020   F*********************** FILE DESCRIPTION ***************************    SSS10A
           01-030   F*                                                                     SSS10A
0001       01-040   FREQUEST IP  F      20              DISK                                SSS10A
0002       01-050   FXREPORT  O  F     132              PRINTER                             SSS10A
           02-010   E*                                                                     SSS10A
           02-020   E***************** EXTENSION SPECIFICATIONS***********************       SSS10A
           02-030   E*                                                                     SSS10A
0003       02-040   E                      TABOSI 16 32  5                                   SSS10A
           03-010   I*                                                                     SSS10A
           03-020   I*********************** INPUT RECORD **************************          SSS10A
           03-030   I*                                                                     SSS10A
0004       03-040   IREQUEST NS  01                                                         SSS10A
0005       03-050   I                                         1   5 PARTNO                  SSS10A
0006       03-060   I                                         6  20 REQDPT                  SSS10A
           04-010   C*                                                                     SSS10A
           04-020   C***************** PERFORM TABLE SEARCH ************************          SSS10A
           04-030   C*                                                                     SSS10A
0007       04-040   C      01     PARTNO    LOKUPTABOSI                    50               SSS10A
           05-010   O*                                                                     SSS10A
           05-020   O***************** HEADING LINES *****************************           SSS10A
           05-030   O*                                                                     SSS10A
           05-040   O*                                                                     SSS10A
0008       05-050   OXREPORT H  201    1P                                                   SSS10A
0009       05-060   O                                26 'OUT OF STOCK'                      SSS10A
0010       05-070   O                                38 'ITEMS'                             SSS10A
0011       05-080   O         H  1     1P                                                   SSS10A
0012       05-090   O                                15 'PART NUMBER'                       SSS10A
0013       05-100   O                                38 'REQUESTED BY'                      SSS10A
           05-110   O*                                                                     SSS10A
           05-120   O***************** DETAIL LINES***************************              SSS10A
           05-130   O*                                                                     SSS10A
0014       05-140   O         D  1    50 01                                                 SSS10A
0015       05-150   O                     PARTNO     13                                     SSS10A
0016       05-160   O                     REQDPT     40                                     SSS10A
           05-170   O***************** END OF SOURCE ***************************            SSS10A
```

END OF SOURCE

Notes: 1. Assume one page of output.
2. Tables and Maps are not illustrated.

Figure 10.49
Sample output produced by
Table Program 1.

```
OUT OF STOCK ITEMS

PART NUMBER          REQUESTED BY
   MR640             MACHINE PARTS
   JX910             SPINNING DEPT
   AA007             WELDING DEPT
   LG989             WELDING DEPT
   BE111             DIE CASTING
   AS009             TOOL & DIE SHOP
   JR017             CARPENTER SHOP
   CB338             ELECTRICAL ASSY
```

simply compared to the table and an indicator is set if the LOKUP produces a match or equal condition. If, however, additional data stored in the table is to be *retrieved* when a match occurs, then *related* or *multiple tables* are necessary. That is, if a match exists between an input field and a table entry in a related table, then a corresponding table entry is accessed.

XI. Related or Parallel Tables

A. Applications

Related or *parallel tables* are two or more tables that are related to one another. For every entry in one table, there is a corresponding entry in another table. See Figure 10.50 for an illustration.

A typical application using the table illustrated would be to calculate the cost of shipping items of different weights. When a match in a weight category is found, a second table is accessed to determine the corresponding shipping cost for that category. The processing of the related tables would include the following steps:

1. Load the tables into storage—one contains weights and one contains corresponding shipping charges.
2. Input a transaction record that contains the weight of the item to be shipped.
3. Search the weight table to find a match with the transaction record's weight specification; if no match is found, find the entry that is closest to the input item weight, but greater than it. For example, if the weight of the transaction input item was 38 pounds, the charge would be $24.95 because the item is more than 25 pounds but not greater than 50 pounds.
4. Once the correct argument has been found, use the corresponding charge in the function table for that weight category.
5. The charge retrieved from the function table is used in any required program calculations. Again, note that with related tables, we search the argument table in order to find an entry, then return with the corresponding field from the function table.

The *argument* table is used to compare against an input or Result Field. If a match is found, the corresponding entry in the *function* table is used to calculate a total price. Thus the weight of an input item is compared to the weight indicated in the argument table. When the input weight is less than the argument weight, the corresponding freight charge from the function table is added to the total price.

B. Loading Related or Parallel Tables

If you were required to enter the related tables illustrated in Figure 10.50, you would define them separately as shown in Example 1 of Figure 10.51.

The Extension Specifications form for Example 1 is illustrated in Figure 10.52.

In Example 1, the related tables were coded as two individual or parallel tables. However, when the look-up operation is performed in the weight table, the corresponding entry in the charge table can be referenced and used by the program. That is, if a match occurs on entry 2 of the weight table, then the second element in the Function table is the desired one.

Note the following in the Extension Specifications form for Example 1:

1. The table names always begin with TAB.

Figure 10.50
Example of related tables.

	Weight*	Charge
Entry 1	Up to 10	Ø5.95
Entry 2	Up to 25	12.50
Entry 3	Up to 50	24.95
Entry 4	Up to 100	48.ØØ
	Argument table	Function table

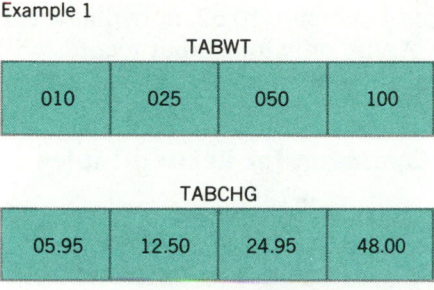

Related tables

Note: No item over 100 lbs. will be shipped.

Figure 10.51
Alternative ways of entering
related tables.

Example 1

TABWT

010	025	050	100

TABCHG

05.95	12.50	24.95	48.00

Two Single-Entry Tables

Example 2

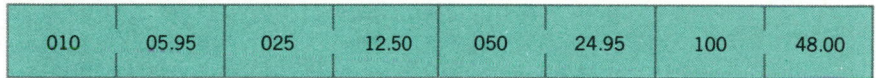

010	05.95	025	12.50	050	24.95	100	48.00

Related Tables with Alternating Format

2. Each table entry is contained on a single record. Because the table contains four entries, the weight table would be defined on four records. Similarly, the charge table would also be defined on four records.

The sequence of the table data must follow the same order as coded on the Extension Specifications form. Again refer to Figure 10.42 on page 559 for the organization of the source program.

Figure 10.52
Extension Specifications for
Figure 10.51.

Line	Form Type		From Filename	To Filename	Table or Array Name	Number of Entries Per Record	Number of Entries Per Table or Array	Length of Entry	P/B/L/R	Decimal Positions	Sequence (A/D)	Table or Array Name (Alternating Format)	Length of Entry	P/B/L/R	Decimal Positions	Sequence (A/B)	Comments
0 1	Ø E	* EXAMPLE ONE															
0 2	Ø E				TABWT	1	4	3		Ø	A						
0 3	Ø E				TABCHG	1	4	4		2							
0 4	Ø E	* EXAMPLE TWO															
0 5	Ø E				TABWT	1	4	3		Ø	A	TABCHG	4		2		
0 6	E																

The Extension Specifications form also specifies that:

1. The length of each weight entry is three and the length of the charge field is four with two decimal places. These definitions are identical to those previously used on the Input or Calculation Specifications form.
2. An "A" is coded in column 45, denoting that the weight table is in ascending sequence. If the search argument is not equal to the weight (in the illustration it could be less than or equal to), the programmer must specify the sequence of the table data in order for the program to select the correct corresponding entry based on the high/low condition.

Example 2 contains the coding for related tables in an alternating format. All the entries in the two examples contain the same specifications. However, the input records are formatted as indicated in Figure 10.53.

In Example 2 of Figure 10.52, note that the input records contain the data for both tables. Again, only four input records will be used to define the tables, as shown in Figure 10.53.

C. LOKUP Operation for Related Tables

With single-entry tables, the LOKUP operation always searches for an equal condition. With related tables, RPG uses the same LOKUP operation to search one table and return with the corresponding entry from a parallel table in order to perform calculations and/or output operations. This concept is illustrated in the example in Figure 10.54, in which we search the weight table (TABWT) to determine the appropriate amount due from the charge table (TABCHG).

The LOKUP operation is used to search TABWT and return with the data from TABCHG. The search argument, WEIGHT, is a field contained in the input record and is coded in Factor 1. The table to be searched, the argument table, is coded in Factor 2. The related function table, TABCHG, is entered in the Result Field. Note that the specifications for the resulting indicators are set for high and equal.

The coding causes the computer to search and find the exact weight on the table equal to the input field; or the search finds the table argument closest to the weight but *higher* than the input field. For example, an item weighing 38 pounds has a shipping charge of $24.95. If the search is successful (Factor 1 = Factor 2, or Factor 1 > Factor 2), indicator 10 is set on and the field TOTAL is calculated using the resulting field called TABCHG (see Figure 10.55).

When the search is successful, the name of the table TABCHG is used to reference the corresponding table entry that is needed for calculations.

The LOKUP instruction may be summarized as follows:

Figure 10.53
Format of input records for Example 2.

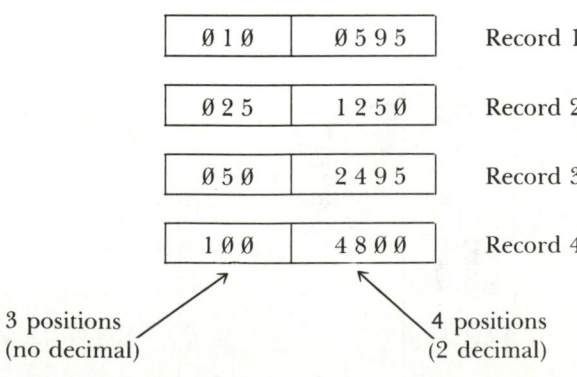

Ø 1 Ø	Ø 5 9 5	Record 1
Ø 2 5	1 2 5 Ø	Record 2
Ø 5 Ø	2 4 9 5	Record 3
1 Ø Ø	4 8 Ø Ø	Record 4

3 positions   4 positions
(no decimal)   (2 decimal)

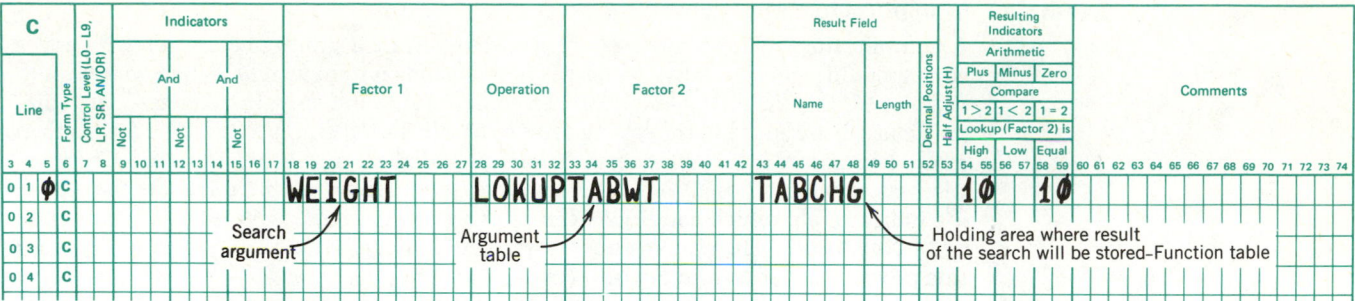

Figure 10.54
LOKUP operation.

Operation:	**LOKUP**
Meaning:	Search a table for the conditions specified by the resulting indicators.
Factor 1:	Specifies the search argument containing the data for the search and is usually defined on the Input Specifications form or the Calculation Specifications form. The length of the search argument must always be the same as the length of the entry in the argument table. If the argument table contains numeric data, then the search argument must also be defined as numeric.
Factor 2:	The name of the table to be searched is coded in Factor 2. The argument table is always defined on the Extension Specifications form.
Result Field:	When related tables are used, the function table name is coded in the Result Field. If the search is successful, the data from the corresponding function table is copied and moved to a special holding area that is referenced by the function table name.
Limitations:	Related tables must be in ascending or descending order if a condition other than equal is specified. Hence, A or D is entered in column 45 of the Extension Specifications form when either a high or low resulting indicator is specified.

Figure 10.55
Example of search.

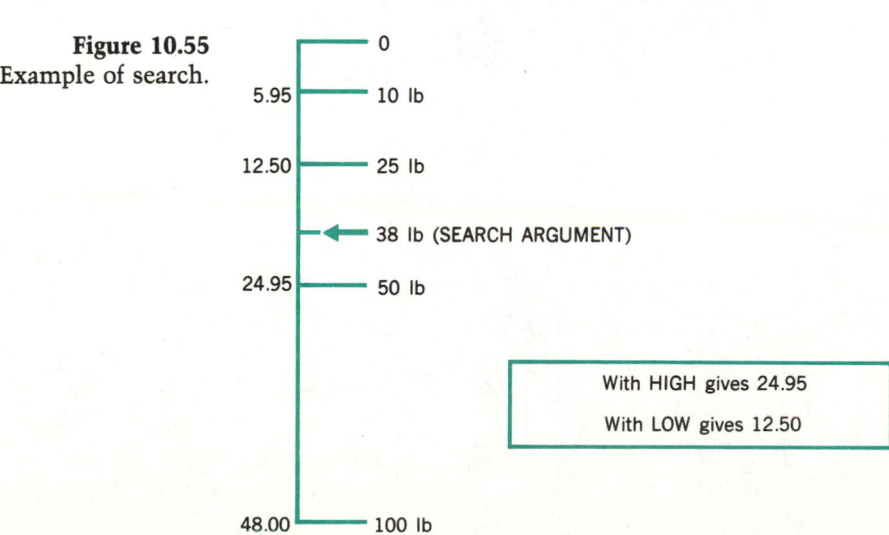

Example   **Sample Table Program 2**

A compile time table is to be established containing a group of item weights and a corresponding group of delivery charges that depend on item weight. When an item is to be shipped, the weight table is searched to determine the shipping charges. The shipping charges are added to the selling price to obtain a total amount due. The data is then printed in accordance with specifications provided in the Printer Spacing Chart. In addition, when the weight of an item exceeds 100 pounds, the program sets the resulting indicator off, which conditions the printing of the message '***WEIGHT EXCEEDS 100 POUNDS***'. The systems flowchart, record layout, and Printer Spacing Chart for this program are shown in Figure 10.56.

Again, the Extension Specifications are used to allocate storage within the program for the tables. The Extension Specifications form in this sample program is coded as previously illustrated in Example 2 of Figure 10.52. The specifications provide the following:

The name of the table.
The number of entries coded on each input record.
The maximum number of entries required for the table.
The length of each entry and the decimal positions required (for numeric fields).
The order of the table (ascending or descending) when a resulting indicator other than equal is specified in the LOKUP instruction.

Review Figures 10.53 and 10.54 to ensure your understanding of this material. The LOKUP operation is used to compare the WEIGHT of the input field with the argument

Figure 10.56
Problem definition for Sample Table Program 2.

Systems Flowchart

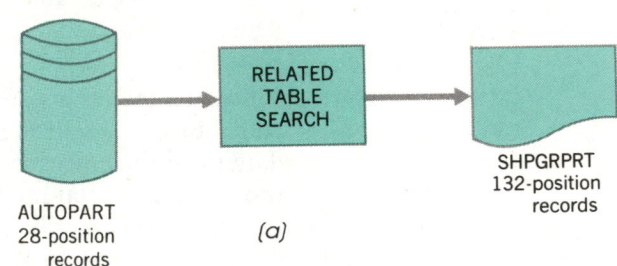

(a)

AUTOPART Record Layout

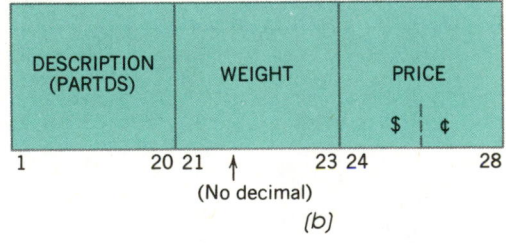

(b)

SHPGRPRT Printer Spacing Chart

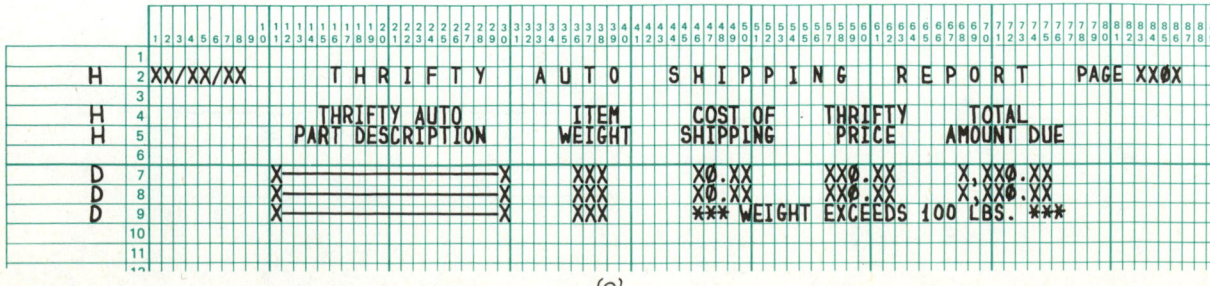

(c)

table (TABWT) in order to determine the shipping charges that are found in the function table TABCHG. If the search is successful, the corresponding charges are placed in a field called TABCHG so that they can be used in calculations. The search will be successful if the search argument is less than or equal to 100. Also note that the field TABCHG is used with the Output Specifications in printing the detail lines. The coding for this program is illustrated in Figure 10.57.

Also recall that the table should be checked for accuracy by referring to the Table Map before attempting to debug the program. See Figure 10.58 for an illustration of the Table Map.

The output generated by this program conforms to the Printer Spacing Chart as established in the problem definition (see Figure 10.59).

XII. Pre-execution Time Tables

Thus far, all the tables used have been compile time tables. Pre-execution tables may also be used in RPG programs. Indeed, they are preferable where table entries are likely to change.

Figure 10.57
Sample Table Program 2.

```
       01-010  F*                                                               SSS10B
       01-020  F********************** FILE DESCRIPTION ********************     SSS10B
       01-030  F*                                                               SSS10B
0001   01-040  FAUTOPARTIP  F    28            DISK                             SSS10B
0002   01-050  FSHPGRPRTO   F   132      OF    PRINTER                          SSS10B
       02-010  E*                                                               SSS10B
       02-020  E**************** EXTENSION SPECIFICATIONS******************     SSS10B
       02-030  E*                                                               SSS10B
0003   02-040  E            TABWT   1    4   3 OATABCHG   4 2                    SSS10B
       03-010  I*                                                               SSS10B
       03-020  I********************** INPUT RECORD *********************       SSS10B
       03-030  I*                                                               SSS10B
0004   03-040  IAUTOPARTNS                                                      SSS10B
0005   03-050  I                                     1   20 PARTDS              SSS10B
0006   03-060  I                                    21  232WEIGHT               SSS10B
0007   03-070  I                                    24  282PRICE                SSS10B
       04-010  C*                                                               SSS10B
       04-020  C********************** CALCULATIONS ********************        SSS10B
       04-030  C*                                                               SSS10B
0008   04-040  C            WEIGHT    LOKUPTABWT     TABCHG      10 10           SSS10B
0009   04-050  C       10   PRICE     ADD  TABCHG    TOTAL    62                SSS10B
       05-010  O*                                                               SSS10B
       05-020  O********************** HEADING LINES ********************       SSS10B
       05-030  O*                                                               SSS10B
0010   05-040  OSHPGRPRTH  2      1P                                            SSS10B
0011   05-050  O           CR      OF                                           SSS10B
0012   05-060  O                            UDATE Y     8                       SSS10B
0013   05-070  O                                  39 'T H R I F T Y    A U T O' SSS10B
0014   05-080  O                                  58 'S H I P P I N G'          SSS10B
0015   05-090  O                                  73 'R E P O R T'              SSS10B
0016   05-100  O                                  81 'PAGE'                     SSS10B
0017   05-110  O                            PAGE  86                            SSS10B
0018   05-120  O           H   1  1P                                            SSS10B
0019   05-130  O           CR      OF                                           SSS10B
0020   05-140  O                                  26 'THRIFTY AUTO'             SSS10B
0021   05-150  O                                  39 'ITEM'                     SSS10B
0022   05-160  O                                  52 'COST OF'                  SSS10B
0023   05-170  O                                  63 'THRIFTY'                  SSS10B
0024   05-180  O                                  73 'TOTAL'                    SSS10B
0025   06-010  O           H   2  1P                                            SSS10B
0026   06-020  O           OR      OF                                           SSS10B
0027   06-030  O                                  28 'PART DESCRIPTION'         SSS10B
0028   06-040  O                                  40 'WEIGHT'                   SSS10B
0029   06-050  O                                  52 'SHIPPING'                 SSS10B
0030   06-060  O                                  62 'PRICE'                    SSS10B
0031   06-070  O                                  76 'AMOUNT DUE'               SSS10B
       06-080  O*                                                               SSS10B
       06-090  O********************** DETAIL LINES********************         SSS10B
       06-100  O*                                                               SSS10B
0032   06-110  O           D   1      10                                        SSS10B
0033   06-120  O                            PARTDS    30                        SSS10B
0034   06-130  O                            WEIGHT    38                        SSS10B
0035   06-140  O                            TABCHG1   50                        SSS10B
0036   06-150  O                            PRICE 1   62                        SSS10B
0037   06-160  O                            TOTAL 1   75                        SSS10B
       07-010  O*                                                               SSS10B
       07-020  O********************** ERROR MESSAGE ********************       SSS10B
       07-030  O*                                                               SSS10B
0038   07-040  O           D   1     N10                                        SSS10B
0039   07-050  O                            PARTDS    30                        SSS10B
0040   07-060  O                            WEIGHT    38                        SSS10B
0041   07-070  O                                  63 '*** WEIGHT EXCEEDS'       SSS10B
0042   07-080  O                                  76 '100 LBS. ***'             SSS10B
       07-090  O********************** END OF SOURCE ********************       SSS10B
```

```
                              T A B L E S   A N D   M A P S

     RESULTING INDICATCR TABLE

     OFFSET  RI      OFFSET  RI      OFFSET  RI      OFFSET  RI      OFFSET  RI      OFFSET  RI      OFFSET  RI

      0508   OF       0525  LR        0526  HO        0531  1P        0534  01        0535  10


     OFFSETS OF VARIABLE NAMES AND CONSTANT NAMES

     OFFSET  NAME      OFFSET  NAME      OFFSET  NAME      OFFSET  NAME      OFFSET  NAME

      0638 TLF TABWT    0648 TLF TABCHG   03C9   *ERROR    0650   PARTDS    0671   WEIGHT
      0673   PRICE      0676   TOTAL      0400   UDATE     067E   PAGE

           ┌─────────────────────────────────────────────────┐
           │  TABLE/ARRAY - TABWT      00073F                 │
           │  TABLE/ARRAY - TABCHG     000747                 │
           │                                                  │
           │              0100595                             │
           │              0251250                             │
           │              0502495                             │
           │              1004800                             │
           └─────────────────────────────────────────────────┘
```

Figure 10.58
Illustration of a table map.

Figure 10.59
Sample output produced by
Table Program 2.

```
1/5/92       T H R I F T Y   A U T O   S H I P P I N G   R E P O R T   PAGE   1

         THRIFTY AUTO        ITEM      COST OF     THRIFTY      TOTAL
         PART DESCRIPTION     WEIGHT    SHIPPING     PRICE     AMOUNT DUE

         CARBURETOR ASSEMBLY    017      12.50      128.50       141.00
         FUEL PUMP #12835       025      12.50       73.20        85.70
         CAMSHAFT  #37085       088      48.00      311.00       359.00
         ELECTRICAL BOX ASSY    003       5.95       17.85        23.80
         TRANSMISSION #12812    245     *** WEIGHT EXCEEDS 100 LBS. ***
         VALVE COVER PLATE      061      48.00       79.95       127.95
         T-ROOF INSERT RIGHT    034      24.95      183.95       208.90
         ELECTRONIC DISTRIB.    003       5.95       89.95        95.90
         POWER BRAKE CYL ASSY   100      48.00      362.85       410.85
         DISK BRAKE CALIPERS    026      24.95       70.90        95.85
```

A. Single-entry Tables

Pre-execution tables are *not* compiled with the program but instead are maintained on a disk, independent of any program using them. After the program is compiled but before the RPG cycle begins, the program will read the table data from disk into the program. Once the table is read and stored in the program, it is used in the same way as if it had been originally defined within the program. In order to read the table from a disk, an additional File Specification entry is required. This is because the table is, in actuality, a separate file. The File Description Specifications form serves to link the device with the table area of the program. Since pre-execution tables are entered as a file, they must be assigned a file name in the same manner as names are given to input and output files. The File Description and Extension Specifications forms for out-of-stock table items stored on disk would be as shown in Figure 10.60.

We are already familiar with most of the entries on the File Description Specifications form. However, the following additional details should be noted:

Columns 15 and 16 of the File Description Specifications form indicates that the file OSITABLE is an input table file.

Since each of the disk records is five characters long, the record length is five.

To link the File Description Specifications form with the area in the program set aside for the table, an E is specified in column 39. RPG will then refer to the Extension Specifications form for more detailed information required to store the table. The entries on the Extension Specifications

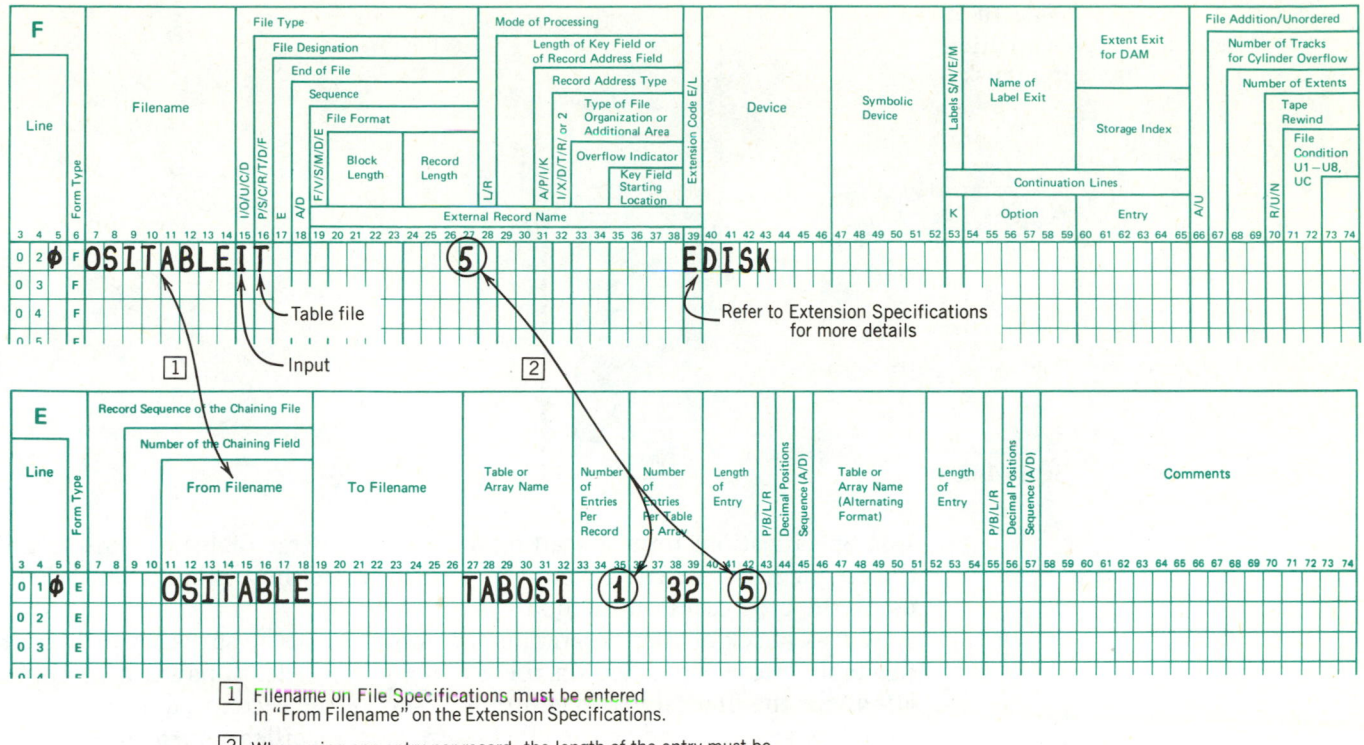

Figure 10.60
Defining a pre-execution,
single-entry table.

form remain the same except for the addition of the filename entry. This entry informs the computer system that the named file is to be read before the program begins (see Figure 10.61).

Again, the File Description Specifications form identifies the device from which the table file is to be read, whereas the Extension Specifications provide the detailed description of the storage area needed for the table.

The following features of pre-execution tables should be kept in mind:

Advantage of Pre-execution Tables

The advantage of this type of table is that a program run on a regular basis does not have to be recompiled whenever the table changes.

Disadvantage of Pre-execution Tables

The disk containing the table must always be available whenever the program is run.

Thus, when table data changes with great frequency, pre-execution tables are usually used; otherwise, the compile time tables are more efficient.

B. Pre-execution Related or Parallel Tables

Pre-execution related or parallel tables are defined in much the same manner as pre-execution single-entry tables. The only difference occurs on the Exten-

Figure 10.61
Reading in a pre-execution
table from disk.

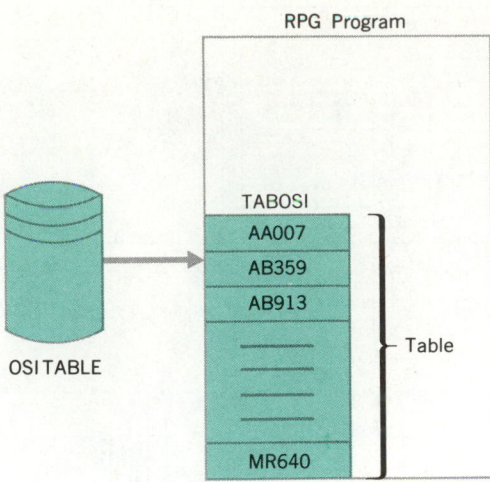

sion Specifications form. Recalling the weight/charge tables presented earlier, the coding in Figure 10.62 would be used to create these tables from a disk file using the pre-execution method.

A desk check of your program is recommended to be sure that the length of the table entries specified on the Extension Specifications form in columns 40–42 for the first table and columns 52–54 of the second table add up to the record length specified on the File Description Specifications form in columns 24–27. Your program will not execute properly if the table lengths are defined incorrectly. In the example given, the length of the table entries (3 plus 4) equals the record length of 7 specified on the File Description Specifications form.

Figure 10.62
Defining pre-execution related
tables.

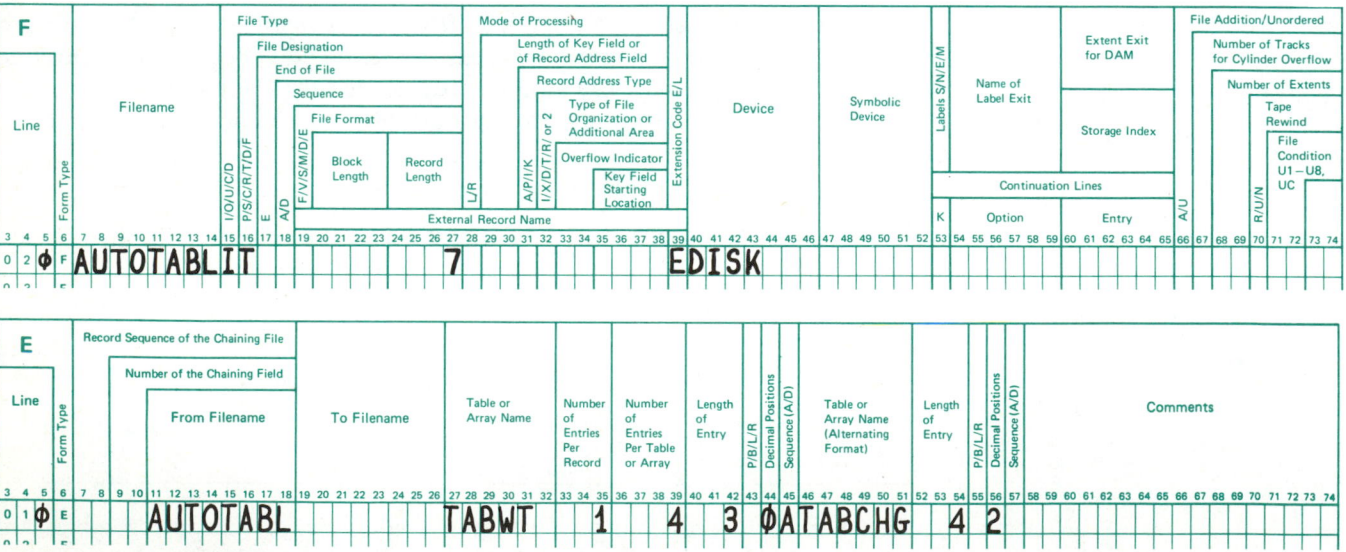

Self-Test   1. (T or F) If a search is not successful, the resulting indicator(s) specified in the LOKUP are set off.

2. When the LOKUP is used with a simple table, the table to be searched is entered in (Factor 1/Factor 2/Result Field) of the Calculation Specifications form.

3. The search argument is usually defined on the (Output Specifications, Input Specifications, Extension Specifications) form.

4. (T or F) When tables do not change or change infrequently, compile time tables are a good choice.

5. When compile time tables change, the programmer must _____ the program before executing it.

6. Code the Extension Specifications form to define the related tables shown here. Each record contains data for both tables; therefore, five input disk records would be used to create the table.

TABNO	TABMSG
01	PARCEL POST
02	S & S TRUCKING
03	AIR MAIL
04	UNITED PARCEL SERVICE
05	MESSENGER SERVICE

7. For the tables defined in Question 6, assume the search argument is a field called CODE. Complete the Calculation Specifications form to search the TABNO table and set on indicator 77.

8. If the search in Question 7 is successful, what field will be referenced in the Output Specifications in order to print the messages 'AIR MAIL', and so forth?

9. Would CODE in Question 7 be defined as a numeric or nonnumeric field?

10. In creating table input records, can more than two entries be placed on each input record?

11. What coding on the File Description Specifications form tells RPG that a pre-execution table is to be read in before the RPG Logic Cycle begins?

12. What entry on the Extension Specifications form informs RPG as to where the table data is coming from?

13. (T or F) When the equal condition is specified for the resulting indicators, then performing a LOKUP requires the table to be in ascending order.

14. When a LOKUP indicator assigned to HIGH is on, what is the relationship between the search argument and the table argument entered as Factor 2?

15. Differentiate between the Number of Entries Per Table and the Number of Entries Per Record on the Extension Specifications form.

16. The RPG form used to allocate or reserve storage in the program for tables is the _____ Specifications form.

Solutions
1. T
2. Factor 2
3. Input Specifications
4. T
5. recompile
6.

E		Record Sequence of the Chaining File												
Line	Form Type	Number of the Chaining Field			Table or Array Name	Number of Entries Per Record	Number of Entries Per Table or Array	Length of Entry	P/B/L/R	Decimal Positions	Sequence (A/D)	Table or Array Name (Alternating Format)	Length of Entry	P/B/L/R	Decimal Positions	Sequence (A/D)	Comments
		From Filename	To Filename												
0 1 0 E					TABNO	1	5	2	0				TABMSG	21			

7.

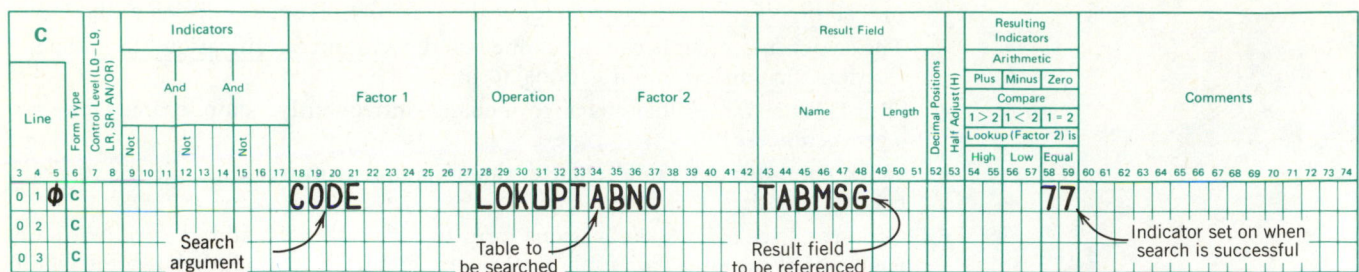

8. `TABMSG`. Remember, when the search is successful the data from the corresponding related table is placed in a special holding area assigned to the name of the array.

9. `CODE` must be numeric if `TABNO` entries are numeric. If `TABNO` entries are not numeric, then `CODE` would not be numeric. This is checked by referring to the Extension Specifications form. If column 44 is blank, `TABNO` is not numeric. However, if a zero was entered, then the field is numeric.

10. Yes. You may use as many table entries on a record as will fit completely. Remember, table entries cannot be split between two records.

11. The filename is entered on the File Specifications form. Column 16 contains the letters "T" denoting that a table file is used, and column 39 contains the letter "E" meaning that additional information is provided on the Extension Specifications form.

12. The From Filename entry in columns 11–18 of the Extension Specifications form.

13. F. When the equal condition is specified, the organization of the table data is of no consequence. However, items having a high activity should be placed near the top of the table to reduce the amount of time used in performing the search. This will improve the efficiency of the table `LOKUP` operation.

14. The table argument selected will be the one greater than the search argument. Therefore, Factor 1, the search argument, is less than Factor 2, the table argument.

15. Number of Entries Per Table denotes the total number of entries or elements for the table. A table of states, for example, would consist of 50 entries. Number of Entries Per Record designates the number of entries contained on each input record used to create the table.

16. Extension.

XIII. Comparing Arrays and Tables

Once the table is entered as input, it is used exclusively for look-up purposes. That is, you compare an input field search argument against the entries in the table to find the condition specified by the indicators. In our table, for example, along with the corresponding product number, we would enter our discount rate. For each customer purchase order, we would compare the product number purchased with the product number in the table to find the corresponding discount rate. When we find a match, the discount associated with the product number, which is in the related table, would be used for computing the customer's bill.

Tables, then, remain constant or unchanged during the execution of a program. They are used exclusively for look-up; if a table entry requires modification, it would be changed by a different program prior to execution of the program that uses it. User programs, then, generally use tables for read-only purposes.

However, in instances in which you would want to establish areas in storage that contain repeated occurrences of a specific entry that you will alter as the program is executed or that will be used for storing totals, then arrays are used.

Each element of an array, like a table, has similar characteristics. The contents of an array, however, usually change during program execution. Array processing greatly extends the ability of RPG programs to calculate results for specific applications. The following provides a comparison of arrays and tables:

COMPARISON OF ARRAYS AND TABLES

1. Similarities
   Elements within an array or table have the same field lengths, the same type of data, the same number of decimal positions (if numeric).
2. Differences
   A table generally contains data that will be used for look-up purposes. An array is generally used for accumulating results or storing totals or amounts.

Example   **Sample Table Program 3**

This sample program creates a discount report listing all customer payments made within a 15-day discount period. The program lists the total amount of sale, amount of discount at two percent, and net payment.

Notice that this program uses a Julian date format to determine if customer payments have been made within a 15-day discount period. Using the Julian date format basically means that we will convert month and day to a day number that will vary from 1 to 365. Assume that the date is not in a leap year. For example, February 10th would have a day number equal to 041 (31 days in January and 10 days in February). The table is shown below for your reference. The table data would consist of a single line of contiguous or consecutive characters; however, we have separated each month to improve readability:

Table Entries   01000   02031   03059   04090   05120   06151
                07181   08212   09243   10273   11304   12334

The problem definition is in Figure 10.63 and the program appears in Figure 10.64.

Figure 10.63
Problem definition for Sample
Table Program 3.

Systems Flowchar

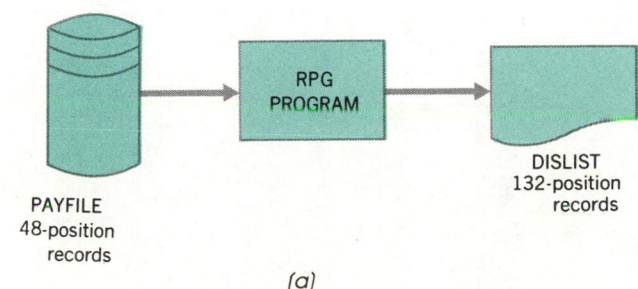

(a)

Figure 10.63   PAYFILE Record Layout
(continued)

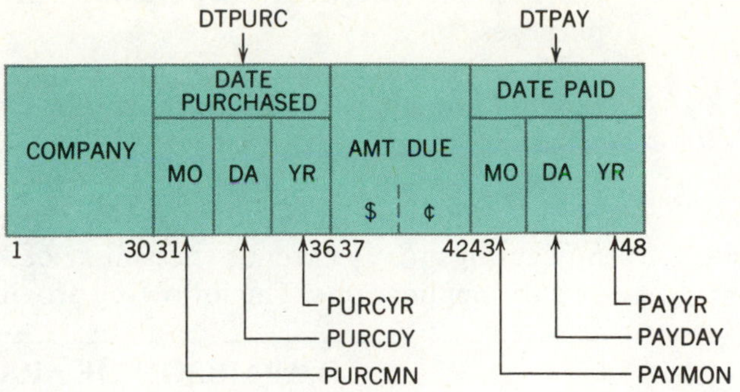

(b)

DISLIST Printer Spacing Chart

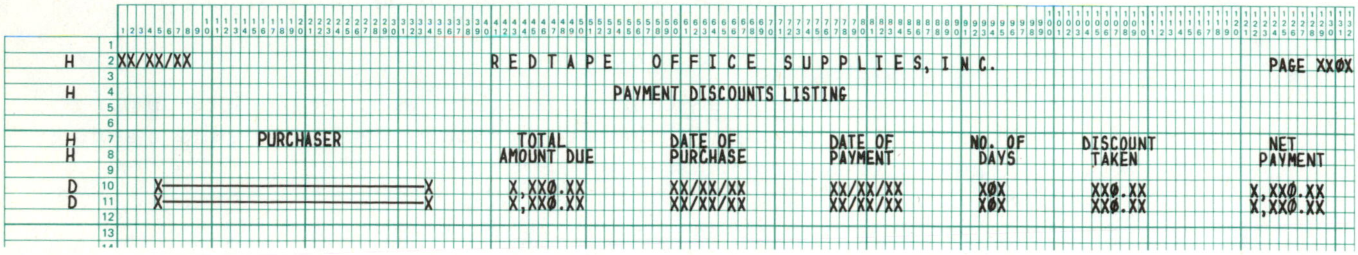

(c)

Figure 10.64
Sample Table Program 3.

```
                    H
0001                FPAYFILE IP  F      48           DISK
0002                FDISLIST O   F     132     OF    PRINTER
0003                E                       TABMON 12  12  2 0ATABDAY  3 0
0004                IPAYFILE NS  01
0005                I                                    1   30 COMPNY
0006                I                                   31  360DTPUR
0007                I                                   31  320PURMN
0008                I                                   33  340PURDY
0009                I                                   35  360PURYR
0010                I                                   37  422AMTDUE
0011                I                                   43  480DTPAY
0012                I                                   43  440PAYMN
0013                I                                   45  460PAYDY
0014                I                                   47  480PAYYR
                    C*
                    C**    CONVERT DATE OF PURCHASE TO JULIAN
                    C*
0015                C     01       PURMN     LOKUPTABMON     TABDAY        10
0016                C     01 10    PURDY     ADD  TABDAY     PURDT   30
                    C*
                    C**    CONVERT DATE PAID TO JULIAN
                    C*
0017                C     01       PAYMN     LOKUPTABMON     TABDAY        11
0018                C     01 11    PAYDY     ADD  TABDAY     PAYDT   30
                    C*
                    C**    IF YEAR OF PAYMENT IS GREATER THAN YEAR OF PURCHASE,
                    C**       NODAYS = (365 - PURDT) + PAYDT
                    C*
0019                C     01       PAYYR     COMP PURYR                    12
0020                C     01 12    365       SUB  PURDT      XDAYS   30
0021                C     01 12    XDAYS     ADD  PAYDT      NODAYS  30
0022                C     01N12    PAYDT     SUB  PURDT      NODAYS
0023                C     01       NODAYS    COMP 15                     1515
0024                C     01 15    AMTDUE    MULT .02        DISCNT  52H
0025                C     01 15    AMTDUE    SUB  DISCNT     NETAMT  62
0026                C     01 15    AMTDUE    ADD  TOTAMT     TOTAMT  72
0027                C     01 15    DISCNT    ADD  TOTDIS     TOTDIS  62
0028                C     01 15    NETAMT    ADD  TOTNET     TOTNET  72
                    O*
0029                ODISLIST H  201     1P
0030                O         OR        OF
0031                O                           UDATE Y  12
0032                O                                 54 'REDTAPE'
0033                O                                 68 'OFFICE'
0034                O                                 95 'SUPPLIES, INC.'
```

Figure 10.64
(continued)

```
0035  O                                        124 'PAGE'
0036  O                               PAGE      129
0037  O        H  3      1P
0038  O   OR             OF
0039  O                                         70 'PAYMENT DISCOUNTS'
0040  O                                         78 'LISTING'
0041  O        H  1      1P
0042  O   OR             OF
0043  O                                         66 'DATE OF        DATE OF'
0044  O                                         98 'NO. OF           TOTAL'
0045  O                                        129 'DISCOUNT           NET'
0046  O        H  2      1P
0047  O   OR             OF
0048  O                                         17 'CUSTOMER NAME'
0049  O                                         66 'PURCHASE        PAYMENT'
0050  O                                         98 'DAYS            AMOUNT'
0051  O                                        129 'AMOUNT          AMOUNT'
0052  O        D  1     01 15
0053  O                          COMPNY          34
0054  O                          DTPUR Y         51
0055  O                          DTPAY Y         66
0056  O                          NODAYSZ         79
0057  O                          AMTDUE1         98
0058  O                          DISCNT1        114
0059  O                          NETAMT1        129
0060  O        T  2        LR
0061  O                                         79 'TOTALS'
0062  O                          TOTAMT1         98 '$'
0063  O                          TOTDIS1        114 '$'
0064  O                          TOTNET1        129 '$'

              E N D   O F   S O U R C E
```

CHAPTER SELF-TEST

1. A group of related items indicating the percentage of federal tax to be paid based on each employee's gross pay is called a(n) _____ .

2. A group of related items that is used for storing totals and calculations is called a(n) _____ .

3. (T or F) Typically, tables remain unchanged during the execution of a program.

4. The number of storage positions allocated to an array is established on the _____ Specifications form.

For Questions 5 to 8, consider the following array of population figures for a specific state.

	POP
DISTRICT 1	12387
DISTRICT 2	24282
	•
	•
	•
	•
	•
DISTRICT 25	4362

5. To access the population for District 5, you would use _____ .

6. The simplest way to obtain the total state population is to use the _____ operation.

7. Write a routine to find the district with the smallest population assuming that no two districts have the same popuation.

8. Write a routine to find the total number of districts with population figures less than 5000.

9. (T or F) Table names may begin with any letter and may contain up to six characters.

10. In order to reference an entire array, the programmer simply references the _____ .

11. When an index is used to reference specific elements of an array, it is a good idea to limit the array name to _____ positions.

12. (T or F) The Extension Specifications form may be used to initialize the contents of an array with some specific nonzero value.

13. (T or F) When an index is used to reference a specific element of an array, the index must always be defined as numeric.

14. A two-dimensional array consists of 5 rows and 4 columns. In order to reference column 4 of the 3rd row, we would refer to the _____ element of the array.

15. (T or F) Any array referenced with the MOVEA operation must be defined as nonnumeric in the program.

16. The _____ operation is used to sort the contents of an array into either ascending or descending order.

17. An array may be searched sequentially using the _____ operation.

18. (T or F) The number of elements in an array is right justified in positions 36 to 39 (Number of Entries per Array) of the Extension Specifications form.

19. If an attempt is made to access an element that is greater than the maximum specified on the Extension Specifications form, an abnormal ending (may, will, will not) occur.

20. (T or F) In order to print the contents of an array, an index must always be specified in the field name of the Output Specifications form.

SOLUTIONS

1. table
2. array
3. T
4. Extension
5. POP,5
6. XFOOT
7.

Line	Form Type	Control Level	Indicators (And / And, Not)	Factor 1	Operation	Factor 2	Result Field Name	Length	Dec. Pos.	Resulting Indicators
01 0	C				Z-ADD0		X1	20		
02 0	C				Z-ADD9999999		SMALL	70		
03 0	C				Z-ADD0		DSML	20		
04 0	C			LOOP	TAG					
05 0	C			X1	ADD	1	X1			
06 0	C			POP,X1	COMP	SMALL				20
07 0	C		20		Z-ADD	POP,X1	SMALL			
08 0	C		20		Z-ADD	X1	DSML			
09 0	C			X1	COMP	25				25
1 0 0	C		25		GOTO	LOOP				

Alternative Solution

Line	Form Type	Control Level	Indicators (And / And, Not)	Factor 1	Operation	Factor 2	Result Field Name	Length	Dec. Pos.	Resulting Indicators
01	C	✱								
02	C				Z-ADD9999999		SMALL	70		
03	C				Z-ADD0		DSML	20		
04	C				DO	25	X1			
05	C			POP,X1	IFLT	SMALL				
06	C				Z-ADD	POP,X1	SMALL			
07	C				Z-ADD	X1	DSML			
08	C				END					
09	C				END					
1 0	C									

8.

Line	Form Type	Control Level	And (Not)	And (Not)	(Not)	Factor 1	Operation	Factor 2	Result Field Name	Length	Decimal Positions	Half Adjust	Plus/Minus/Zero · Compare 1>2	1<2	1=2 / Lookup High	Low	Equal	Comments
0 1	0 C						Z-ADD 0		X1	20								
0 2	0 C						Z-ADD 0		COUNT	20								
0 3	0 C					LOOP	TAG											
0 4	0 C					X1	ADD	1	X1									
0 5	0 C					POP,X1	COMP	5000					50					
0 6	0 C		50			COUNT	ADD	1	COUNT									
0 7	0 C					X1	COMP	25					25					
0 8	0 C		25				GOTO	LOOP										
0 9	C																	

Alternative Solution

Line	Form Type	Control Level	And (Not)	And (Not)	(Not)	Factor 1	Operation	Factor 2	Result Field Name	Length	Decimal Positions	Half Adjust	Plus/Minus/Zero · Compare 1>2	1<2	1=2 / Lookup High	Low	Equal	Comments
0 1	c X																	
0 2	C						Z-ADD 0		COUNT	20								
0 3	C						DO	25	X1									
0 4	C					POP,X1	IFLT	5000										
0 5	C						ADD	1	COUNT									
0 6	C						END											
0 7	C						END											
0 8	C																	
0 9	C																	

9. F—Must begin with the letters TAB

10. array name

11. four. This allows you to specify the array name, followed by a comma, and a one-position index. Again, recall that only six positions are available in the Result Field of the Calculation Specifications form and the Field Name of the Output Specifications form.

12. F—The contents of an array may be initialized with the Z-ADD operation on the Calculation Specifications form.

13. T

14. 12th

15. T

16. SORTA

17. LOKUP

18. T

19. will. It is a good idea to include tests in the program to avoid this problem.

20. F—Specifying an array name without any index will cause the entire array to be printed.

KEY TERMS

Alternating arrays	LOKUP operation	Search argument	Table
Array	MOVEA operation	Single-entry table	Table argument
Compile time table	Parallel table	SORTA operation	XFOOT operation
Dynamic array	Pre-execution time table	Static array	Z-ADD operation
Index (for an array)	Related table	Subscript	

REVIEW QUESTIONS

1. Indicate how the XFOOT operation is used in RPG and provide an example.
2. Describe the use of dynamic arrays and give an example.
3. Give examples of procedures that might require the use of the ADD operation to add arrays.
4. Describe how an array could be used to simplify the calculations in a three-level control break.
5. Describe the output produced when an array is printed using an EXCPT operation instead of a detail line.
6. What is a two-dimensional array and how is the data organized?
7. Describe how to search character strings for blanks or any special character.
8. What occurs if an array name is referenced on the Output Specifications form, but no index is specified?
9. What is a table look-up? How is it used in programming?
10. State the differences between an array and a table.
11. Discuss the differences between a single-entry table and a related table.
12. Compare the differences found on the Extension Specifications form when using tables versus arrays.
13. When performing a table look-up, describe the different results obtained when specifying high or low indicators.
14. What advantages, if any, are derived by converting to Julian date with a table rather than using the conventional Gregorian date (Month/Day/Year)?
15. An alternate method to using a table (look-up) would be to use a series of compares or a nested IF. Discuss the differences in coding techniques when using a two-character abbreviation to obtain the name of each of the fifty states of the United States of America.
16. Both state and federal tax percentages could be stored as a function in a single table. By using the MOVE and MOVEL operations, these entries may be separated since the MOVE is right-justified and the MOVEL is left-justified. Discuss this technique of moving table entries to separate fields for futher processing.
17. How does the RPG compiler determine that all of the table records have been read and the data input records are to begin? (*Hint:* Review Extension Specifications entries.)

PROGRAMMING ASSIGNMENTS

1. Write an RPG program to compute each student's final average from five inputted exams per student, and save the final average for each student in an array called FAVG. Since class size is restricted to 30 students, allocate 30 entries for the FAVG array. Once all of the records have been processed, determine the class average by dividing the sum of the FAVG array by the number of students. Also process the FAVG array to determine the highest average.

   In addition, include an error routine to ensure that the user does not attempt to process more than 30 student records. The problem definition is shown on the next page.

Systems Flowchart

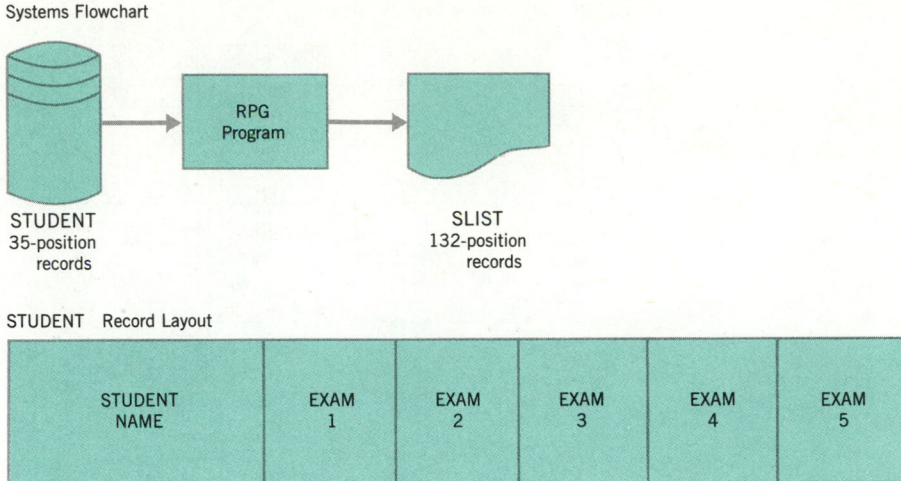

STUDENT
35-position
records

SLIST
132-position
records

STUDENT   Record Layout

STUDENT NAME	EXAM 1	EXAM 2	EXAM 3	EXAM 4	EXAM 5
1 20	21 23	24 26	27 29	30 32	33 35

SLIST Printer Spacing Chart

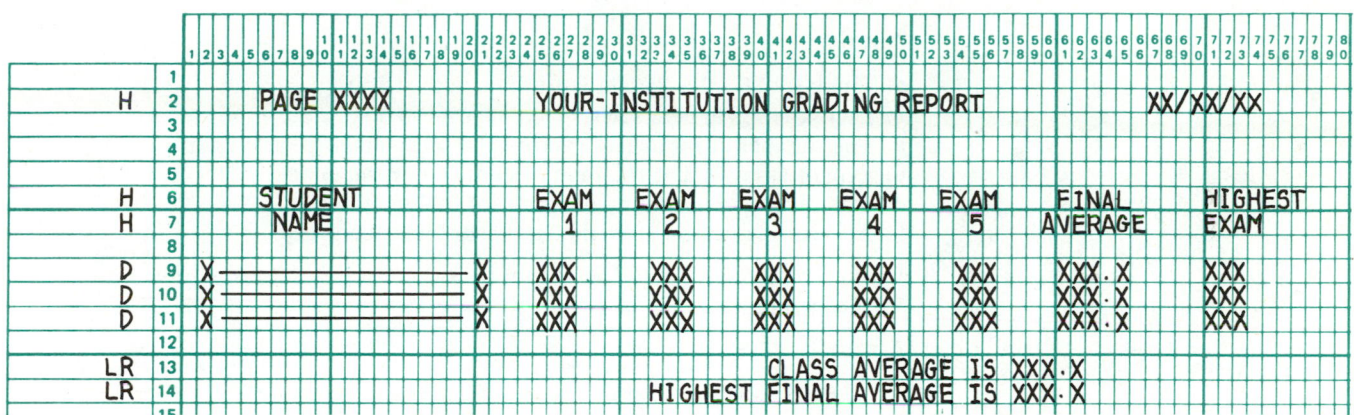

H	2	PAGE XXXX YOUR-INSTITUTION GRADING REPORT XX/XX/XX
H	6	STUDENT EXAM EXAM EXAM EXAM EXAM FINAL HIGHEST
H	7	NAME 1 2 3 4 5 AVERAGE EXAM
D	9	X—————X XXX XXX XXX XXX XXX XXX.X XXX
D	10	X—————X XXX XXX XXX XXX XXX XXX.X XXX
D	11	X—————X XXX XXX XXX XXX XXX XXX.X XXX
LR	13	CLASS AVERAGE IS XXX.X
LR	14	HIGHEST FINAL AVERAGE IS XXX.X

2. Using the following problem definition, write an RPG program to print the total amount of sales for each salesperson.

Systems Flowchart

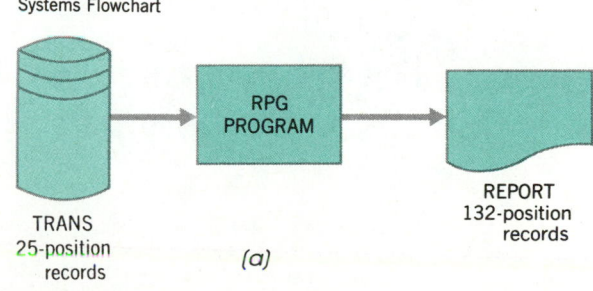

TRANS
25-position
records

(a)

RPG PROGRAM

REPORT
132-position
records

TRANS Record Layout

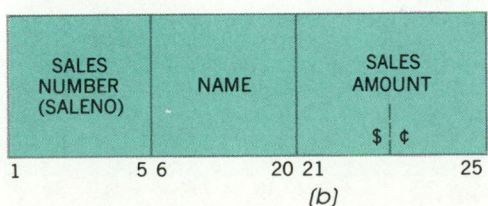

SALES NUMBER (SALENO)	NAME	SALES AMOUNT
		$ ¢
1 5	6 20	21 25

(b)

REPORT Printer Spacing Chart

H	6	TOTAL AMOUNT OF SALES BY SALESPERSON XX/XX/XX
H	8	SALESPERSON TOTAL AMOUNT
TLR	10	1 XX,XX.XX
TLR	12	2 XX,XX.XX
	14-18	. .
TLR	20	20 XX,XX.XX

(c)

Notes:

a. There are 20 salespeople, with sales numbers ranging from 1 to 20.
b. Each sale made by a salesperson appears in a separate input record.
c. The number of input records for each salesperson is unknown.
d. Do not assume that the input records are in sequence.
e. Use an array containing 20 totals for this problem.
f. All printing occurs after the last record has been read.

3. Using the problem definition shown below, code an RPG array program to print the desired report.

Notes:

a. An unknown number of records will serve as input for each salesperson.
b. The input records are in SALENO (salesperson number) sequence only. Totals must be accumulated for each salesperson for each day of the week. In addition, accumulate a weekly sales total for each salesperson and a daily total of all sales in the company.
c. Use an L1 level indicator on the Salesperson Number.

Systems Flowchart

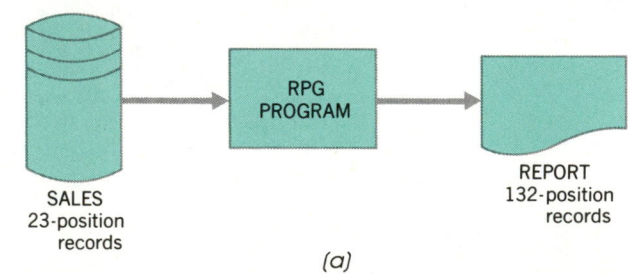

(a)

SALES Record Layout

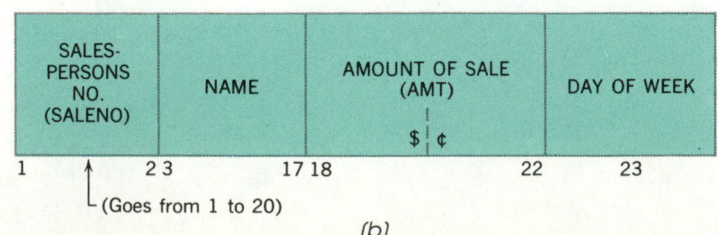

(b)

REPORT Printer Spacing Chart

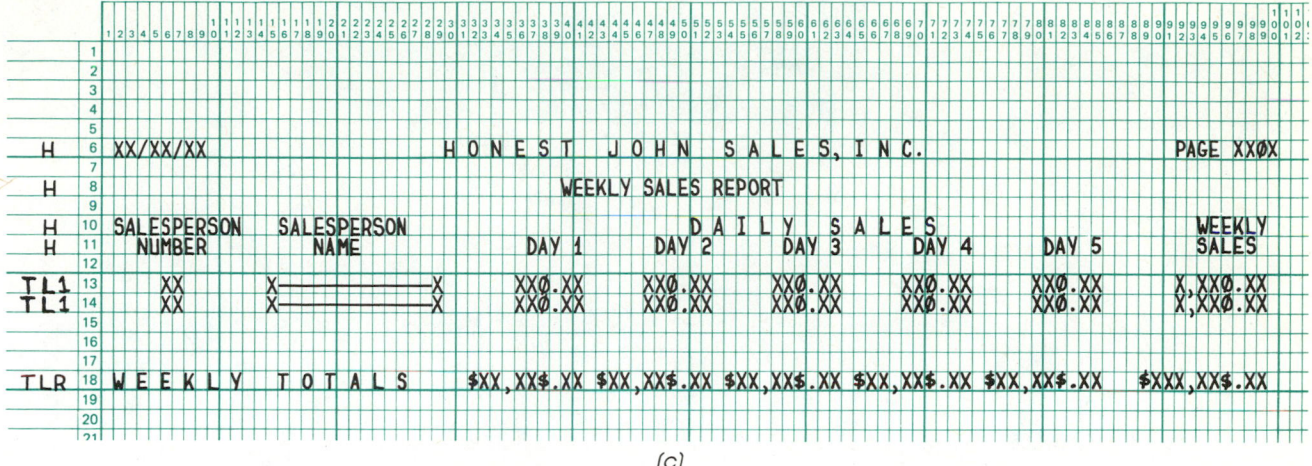

(c)

4. Using the problem definition shown below, code an RPG table look-up program to print the desired report. Use the product number for the search argument. The total price is equal to the unit price × quantity ordered.

Systems Flowchart

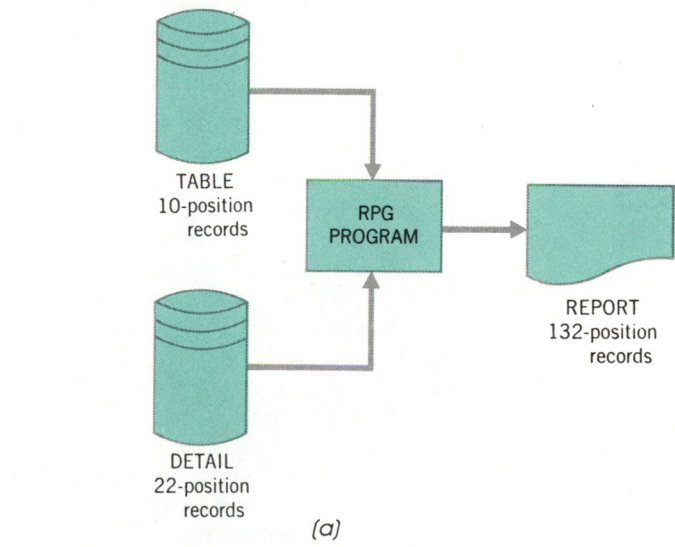

(a)

TABLE Record Layout

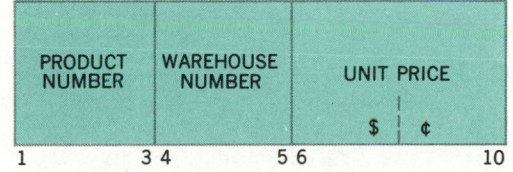

DETAIL Record Layout

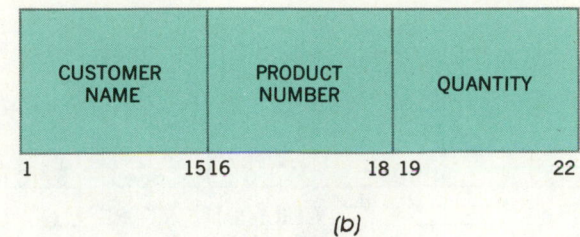

(b)

REPORT Printer Spacing Chart

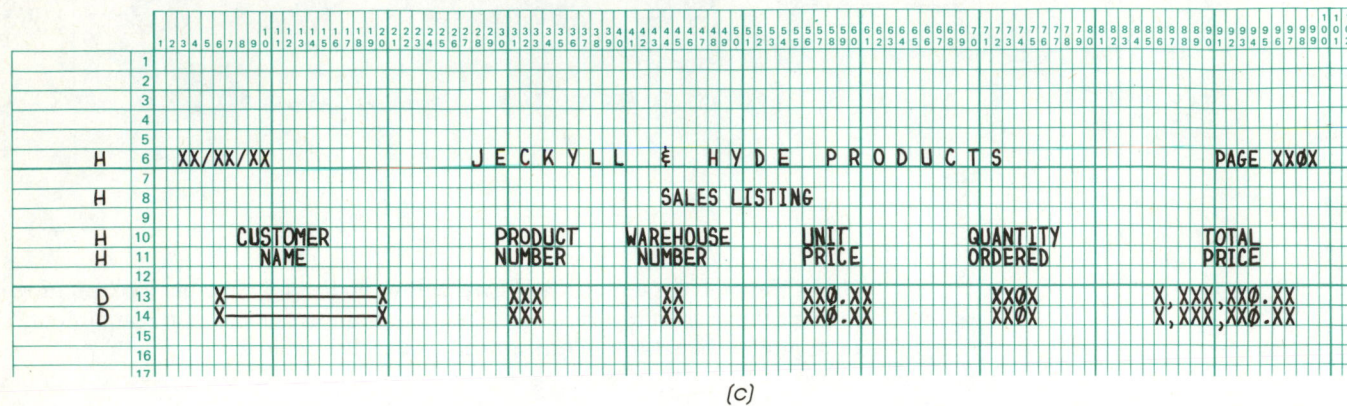

(c)

5. Using the problem definition shown below, code an RPG table look-up program to print the desired report.

   Notes:

   a. There are 20 input table records.

   b. The High Bound Salary field in each input table record indicates the maximum salary for the corresponding state and federal tax percentage figures. An implied decimal point is used in the percentages, therefore a figure of 105 in positions 9 to 11, for example, is to be interpreted as 0.105 or 10.5%.

   c. Monthly take-home pay is computed as follows:

   (1) Standard deduction = 10% of the first $10,000 of annual salary.

   (2) Dependent deduction = $2000 times the number of dependents.

   (3) FICA (Social Security tax) = 7.65% of the first $51,300 of annual salary.

   (4) Taxable income = annual salary − standard deduction − dependent deduction.

   (5) The tax on taxable income is found in the tax table.

   (6) Annual take-home pay = annual salary − (state tax % × taxable income) − (federal tax % × taxable income) − FICA.

   (7) Monthly take-home pay = annual take-home pay ÷ 12.

Systems Flowchart

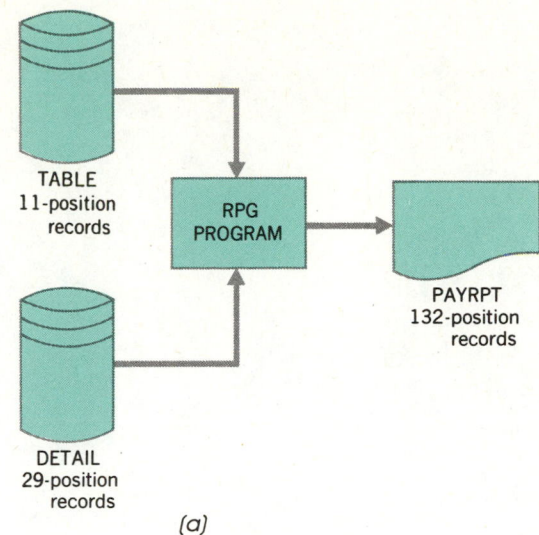

(a)

TABLE Record Layout

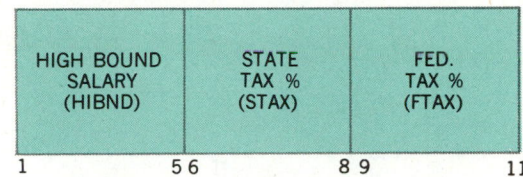

Note: Salary figures are in dollars (no cents).

DETAIL Record Layout

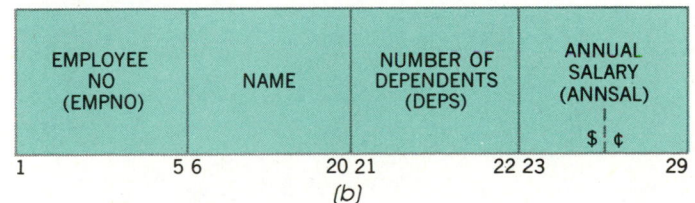

(b)

PAYRPT Printer Spacing Chart

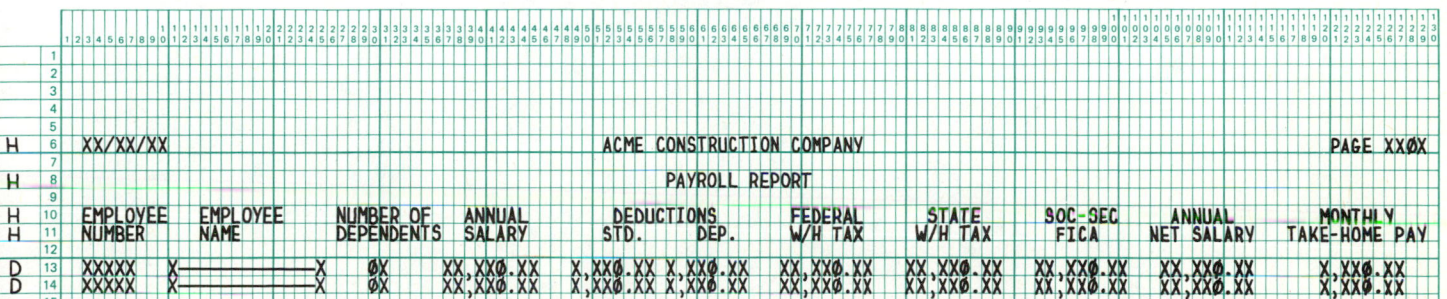

(c)

UNIT 4

ADVANCED TOPICS

11

Interactive Processing

OBJECTIVES

To familiarize you with

1. The differences between batch processing and interactive processing.
2. The different types of display screen formats.
3. How to design display screen format layouts.
4. How to write an interactive program in RPG.

I. Interactive Processing: An Introduction

A. Batch Processing

In previous chapters, our sample problems used batch processing concepts. Batch processing is a data processing technique where transactions are first gathered together, then all transactions are processed as a group during one complete job. For example, businesses typically collect payroll data over a period of time and produce payroll checks for each pay period at one time. This is an example of **batch processing**, that is, collecting and holding all data until output is requested or needed, and then processing the batch all at once.

Several methods can be used for collecting data in a batch environment. In one such method, data is entered on a computer that is not even connected to the main CPU. This type of data entry for future batch processing is called an **off-line operation.** For example, payroll data might be entered at several different corporate sites and then transmitted via disk or telephone lines to the computer at corporate headquarters once a week so that paychecks can be produced in a batch-processing operation.

With batch processing, the user must wait for the results to be returned. The time from submission of batch jobs until the user has the output in his or her hands may vary from a few minutes to a few days, depending on the computer load. Because batch processing does not process data immediately as it is transacted, users may not be getting the output from the computer at the time they need it.

Thus, batch processing is useful only if there is no need to process records as soon as the data is transacted or entered. It may be that payroll files need to be current only at the end of a payroll period when it is time to produce checks; in such a case, batch processing is feasible, less costly, and more efficient.

B. Interactive Processing

In an *on-line* or *interactive environment*, processing occurs somewhat differently. First, files are always kept current. This means that when data is transacted, the associated files are updated immediately. Any request for information can be answered by the computer immediately and will be up-to-date.

Stock exchange systems, for example, must be updated instantly so that stock brokers know at all times exactly what offers and bids have been issued and what the current prices of stocks are. Stock brokers require immediate information so that they can match bids to purchase with offers to sell in order that trades can be conducted. A stock exchange system, therefore, is an example of a system that uses *on-line* or *interactive processing*. **On-line or interactive processing,** then, refers to a system that provides immediate access to files, processes data immediately when it is entered, and always keeps files up-to-date.

Suppose, as another example, that you wish to take a trip to Bermuda and you call your local travel agent to make the plans. Your travel agent would immediately access the airline reservations system to obtain the required information for you to make your decision. Because the travel agent is on-line with the central computer, he or she can tell you immediately which flights are available, with which airlines, the departure and arrival times, and most importantly, the cost of the flight.

In airline reservations systems, there are terminals at many sites, including travel agencies and airport airline desks. Although the terminals are off-site or at remote locations, they communicate directly and instantly with the central computer via communications lines. These systems immediately update ticket information on all flights. Updating data in this manner is called an *on-line operation*, and the person at the terminal is said to be "on-line" with the main computer. The updated information that is produced as a result of an on-line operation is available almost instantly.

One form of interactive processing is called **transaction processing.** Transaction processing allows a user to input data and complete a transaction immediately. The associated files are updated immediately, reflecting the results of the transaction just entered. With this type of processing a user would enter an input transaction and complete that transaction before entering the next transaction.

Files that are to be updated immediately must be randomly accessible; that is, they must be indexed or relative files. Since transaction data is typically entered in a nonsequential manner and, similarly, inquiries are not entered in any specific sequence, the file must be randomly accessible for processing to be timely.

In this chapter, we will consider the different characteristics and procedures of interactive processing. We will then examine how interactive processing takes place using an illustrative RPG program example.

II. Designing Display Screen Format Layouts

A. Systems Considerations

Consider an application in which a user wants to inquire about a record on an indexed file. The keyboard may be used for entering the key field or value that will be used to randomly retrieve the indexed record. This input is keyed on a keyboard and also displayed on the screen, which is sometimes referred to as a monitor, video display, or CRT (Cathode Ray Tube). The program then reads the key value as input. Next, the computer looks up the address of the record with that key value and randomly accesses the corresponding record from the indexed file. The information relating to that record is then displayed on the screen.

This type of processing is used to find or display records for informational purposes. It is also used for enabling a user to change or update a displayed record. The user could make changes to the information on the screen, the program could accept those changes, and then rewrite the updated record back to the file.

Interactive processing of this nature is normally performed on a computer terminal sometimes referred to as a workstation. The keyboard and display screen together make up the components of a workstation. RPG programs written for interactive applications refer to the display screen component as a workstation (WORKSTN) device and in turn refer to this type of processing as **WORKSTN file processing.**

If a program includes interactive dialogue between user and computer, the programmer or systems analyst must carefully design the elements of that exchange. Since users may not be familiar with computers, the exchange must be clear, concise, and as user-friendly as possible.

The following are systems concepts that should be considered when designing display screen formats:

1. The screen layout should be informative but not cluttered. Most screens can display 24 lines with 80 characters per line:

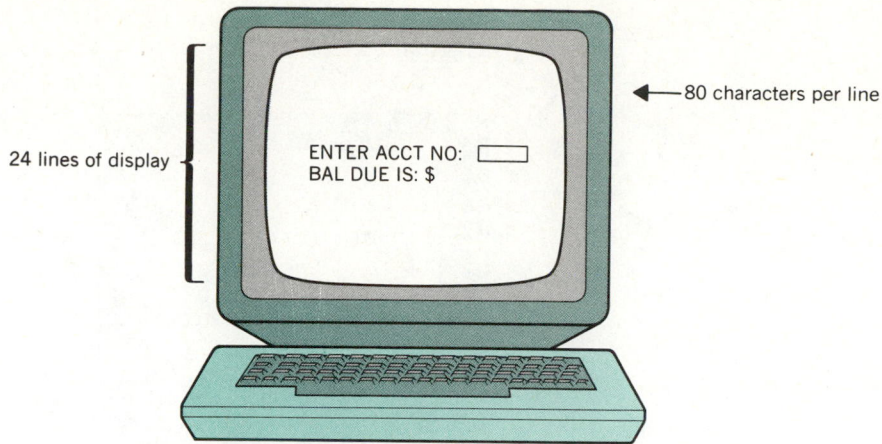

Include blank lines and wide margins to achieve an uncluttered look:

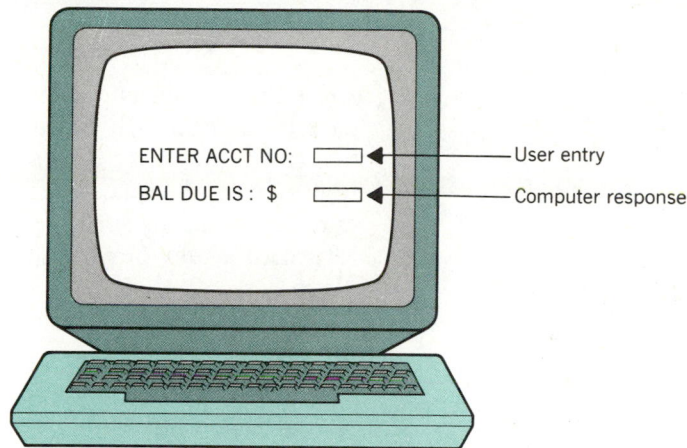

2. Directions to the user, called **prompts,** should be clear and concise. To say `"ENTER ACCT NO:"` is a relatively clear and concise prompt. If you use the word `"ENTER"` in this exchange, be sure to use the same word in other prompts within the same program. That is, it could be confusing to change to a different type of prompt such as `"KEY IN:"` or `"TYPE IN:"`. If terminology is standardized, there will be fewer misunderstandings. Depending on the experience of the user, you may want to add prompts such as `"THEN PRESS ENTER"` or `"WHEN YOU PRESS THE ENTER KEY THE RECORD WILL BE RETRIEVED"`. Such a prompt or message may be obvious to an experienced user but not to a novice.

You may also want to add prompts such as `"PRESS Q TO END PROGRAM"` if entering a `Q` signals an end of job.

Note that command keys, rather than prompts, are used more often with mid-range computers.

3. Vertically align data for ease of reading, and position the cursor at appropriate places. With printed output, as opposed to displayed output, one line at a time in sequence is written. You cannot skip back to previous lines, for example, to print additional data. With a screen display, however, it is possible to display a full screen of data and then direct the user to key in entries on previous lines.

Consider the following:

a. Display 1.

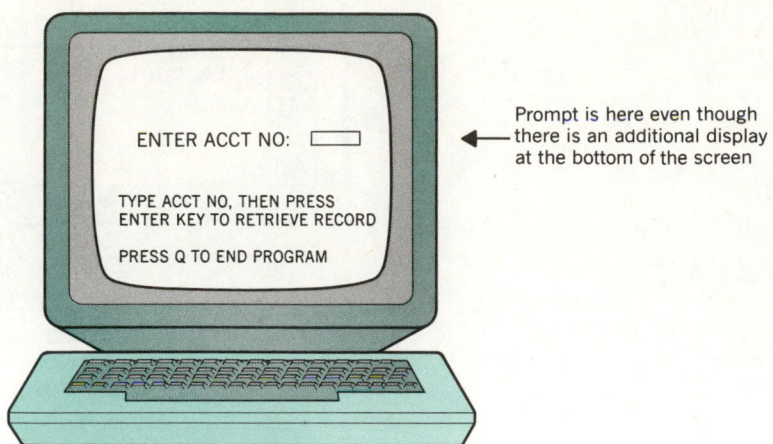

Prompt is here even though there is an additional display at the bottom of the screen

After this screen is displayed, an area for the account number that the user is to enter will be displayed adjacent to the prompt "ENTER ACCT NO:". There will be a **cursor,** which is a blinking square or underscore, highlighting the space after "ENTER ACCT NO:" to remind the user that an entry is required. For the preceding, the cursor must be programmed to return to a previous line (ENTER ACCT NO:) after the full screen is displayed.

When the user responds, a new display can appear such as the following:

b. Display 2.

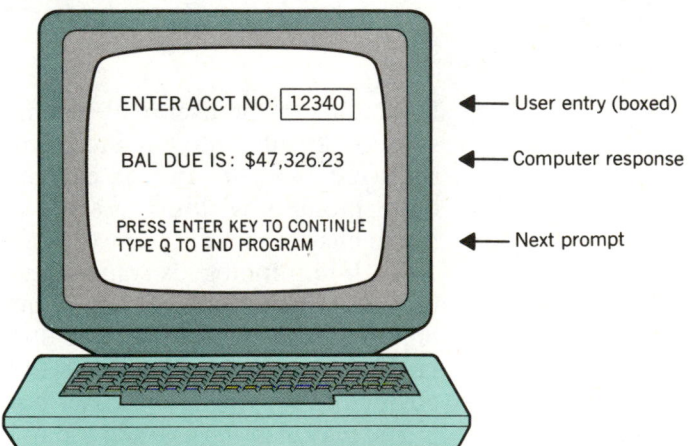

User entry (boxed)

Computer response

Next prompt

Screen displays such as this must be designed by the programmer or analyst to ensure a clear and concise exchange between user and computer. We use a Printer Spacing Chart for planning the format of a printed report; similarly, we use a **Display Screen Layout Sheet** (see Figure 11.1) for planning display formats and exchanges between the user and an interactive computer program. The Display Screen Layout Sheet, which is 80 positions across and 24 lines down, represents the actual display screen. More recent terminals with advanced graphics capabilities can display 132 positions on a line.

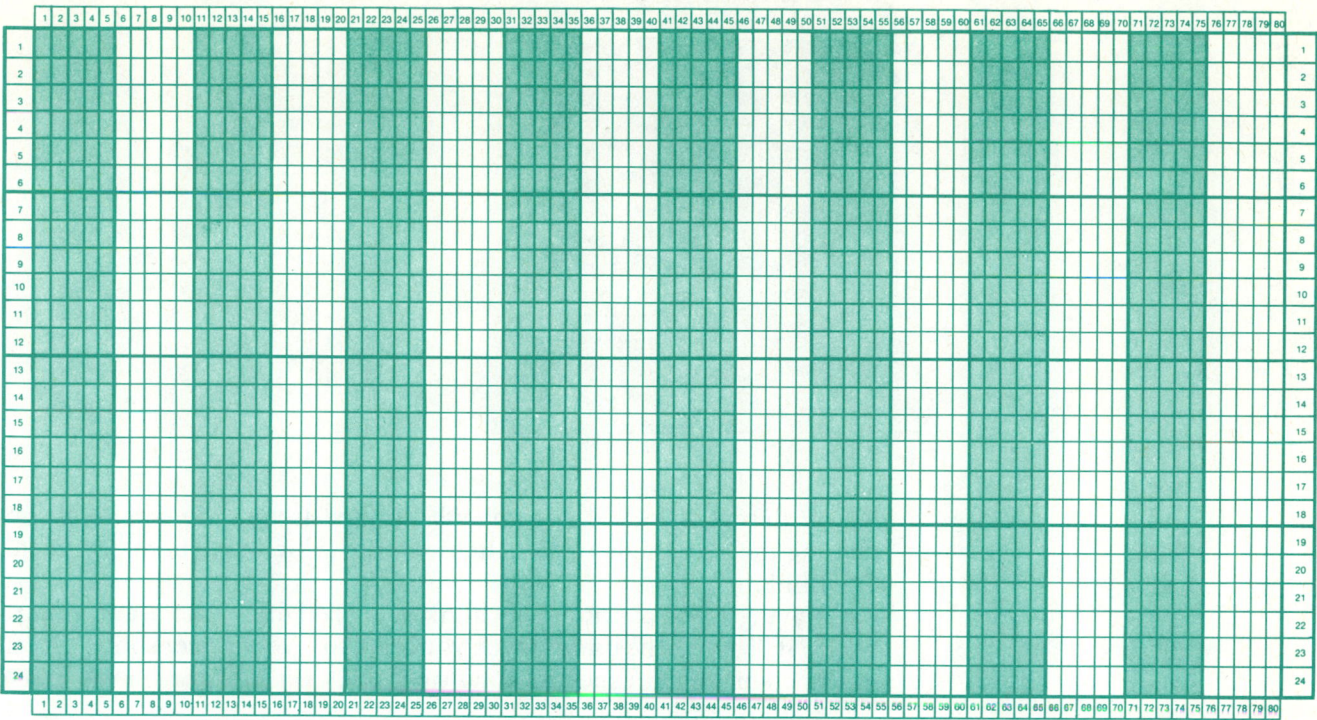

Figure 11.1
Display Screen Layout Sheet.

4. When feasible, provide a **menu** of options available to the user from which he or she can select the desired operations to be performed:

```
PRESS 1 TO MODIFY A RECORD
PRESS 2 TO ADD A RECORD
PRESS 3 TO DELETE A RECORD
PRESS 4 TO INQUIRE ABOUT A RECORD
PRESS 5 WHEN DONE
```

The display of options that would be shown at the bottom of the screen represents a menu. The user selects a course of action by pressing the keys corresponding to the choice required. The program would then evaluate the action taken by the user and proceed to the appropriate routine.

5. Use screen features for highlighting.
   There are numerous ways in which screen displays can be highlighted. We discuss a few here.
   a. Color.
      Where color terminals are available, screens can display certain data in color to highlight it. The user-friendliness of a system can be greatly improved by incorporating color into the display screen. For example, the readability of the screen may be enhanced by using the color red for error messages or fields in error. Another example might be to distinguish user entries from computer responses by the use of different colors. Or, if headings are required, you may want to display a company's name in color.
   b. Reverse Image.
      Most screens display data in a light color on a dark screen. This display can be programmed to be reversed for specific entries that are to be highlighted, as shown on the next page:

With reverse video, a box may be formed around the data field showing the user the length of the field into which data is to be keyed.
c. Blinking entries.
   Having a field continuously blink on and off draws the user's attention
   to it. This can be useful when you wish to give the user some direction
   or to highlight a specific condition.
d. High intensity or boldface.
   An entry can be highlighted by displaying it in boldface.
e. Underlining.
   Key entries can be underlined.
f. Beeping.
   The computer can be programmed to beep whenever an entry has been
   completed, whenever an error has occurred, and so on.

B. Types of Display Screen Formats

As noted, output appears on a screen display. Screen displays can contain
company logos, other headings, data fields to be entered by the user or produced as output by the computer, and messages to the user. The organization
of the screen display is called a *format*.

There are several types of formats commonly used in business applications
written for the RPG environment. We will discuss three of the more common
types here.

1. Menu Format

A menu is an organized list of items from which a user can select an entry by
keying the applicable code. Figure 11.2 is an illustration of a menu format
showing how the various segments of a Music Company application might be
displayed. From the list of available options, the user makes a selection and
that particular option is executed. Each option listed on the menu is a brief
description of the procedure to be run when that option is selected. Each
option has a corresponding number or letter or function key that is used to
select and run each specific procedure. The numbers in the menu with no
entries are those not available to the current user.

A selection from the menu can represent a procedure to be run, an individual command to be executed, or a branch to another menu. For example,
option 1 in Figure 11.2 will run the music master file maintenance procedure
allowing a user to update the music master file. Option 22, on the other hand,
will allow the user to branch to the payroll menu, and option 24 will execute
the command to sign the user off the system. It should be reiterated, however,
that a selection of an option that is not identified by a description, such as 2 or

Figure 11.2
Example of a menu format.

```
COMMAND                                          MENU: MUSIC

Select one of the following:

  1. Music Master File Maintenance    13. Print All Music Titles
  2.                                  14. Print Music Titles by Type
  3.                                  15. Print Music Titles by Category
  4. View Music Record                16.
  5. View Music Titles by Type        17.
  6. View Music Titles by Category    18.
  7.                                  19.
  8.                                  20.
  9.                                  21. Accounts Receivable Menu
 10.                                  22. Payroll Menu
 11.                                  23.
 12.                                  24. Sign Off


Ready for option number or command
```

3, will not result in any action since no available procedure has been identified with that particular option.

Menus are used primarily to simplify the interaction between the user and the computer. The ability to select a procedure from a menu makes it easier for the user to interact with the computer. The user does not need to know the names of any programs to be run or have the specific knowledge of the operating system or a programming language. The user need only know how and when to select a particular option from the menu. In addition, the number of keystrokes required is greatly reduced by the selection of an entry; this reduces the risk of keying errors.

A menu can be used to group related or similar procedures for an application. For example, all procedures relating to payroll may be selected from one menu and all procedures related to inventory control may be grouped on another menu, thus making selection and execution of jobs much easier.

2. Query or Informational Format

A *query* or *informational format*, as shown below, is designed solely to provide information to the user. It does not allow new data to be entered into a file or existing data to be changed.

```
VIEW                                             PROGRAM MU101R
                                                 SCREEN  2
                    INTERNATIONAL MUSIC COMPANY

              Music code:  00070

             Music Title:  EAGLES' GREATEST
                  Artist:  THE EAGLES
                    Type:  LP
                Category:  PP

        Quantity on Hand:  109

                             Enter __ Select another music code

                             CMD  7 __ End of Job
```

The query format presents the user with a sequence of fields identified by captions or headings. Each field on a query format is protected so that the user cannot accidentally make changes to the existing data. When a query format is displayed, the data fields are either "protected" or specified as "output only" so that they are *viewed* but not changed by the user. Similarly, some fields may be further protected so that they will not be displayed on a screen even if the user asks for them. Sensitive data such as salary information might be protected in this way.

Consider a music store application in which a user wants to inquire about the quantity on hand for a particular music title. The user, using the keyboard, enters the music identification code as the key field. The program reads the music code as input and randomly accesses the corresponding record from the indexed file for the music application. From the record read, the program displays the information about the requested music title on the screen for the user.

In this type of interactive application, the user is requesting information only and entering of new data or updating existing data is not required.

3. Data Entry Format

The data entry format presents the user with a sequence of captioned blank fields that the user fills in with the required data. This type of format is used to enter new data into a file or update existing records that are already in the file. When using a data entry format, the user must understand each caption or field heading and the permissible values allowed for each field.

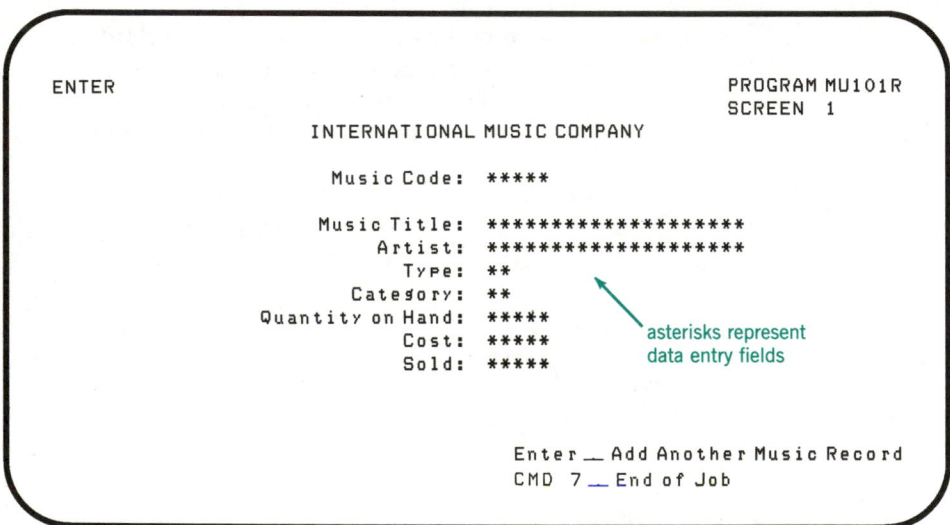

With this type of application, the program displays a data entry format on the screen containing captions for data fields and data entry areas for each field to be entered. The user then completes the display screen by "filling-in" or entering the requested data. Once the user enters the new data, the computer transmits the entered data to the program, which then adds a new record to the file or updates an existing record in the file.

A second and slightly different data entry format is as follows:

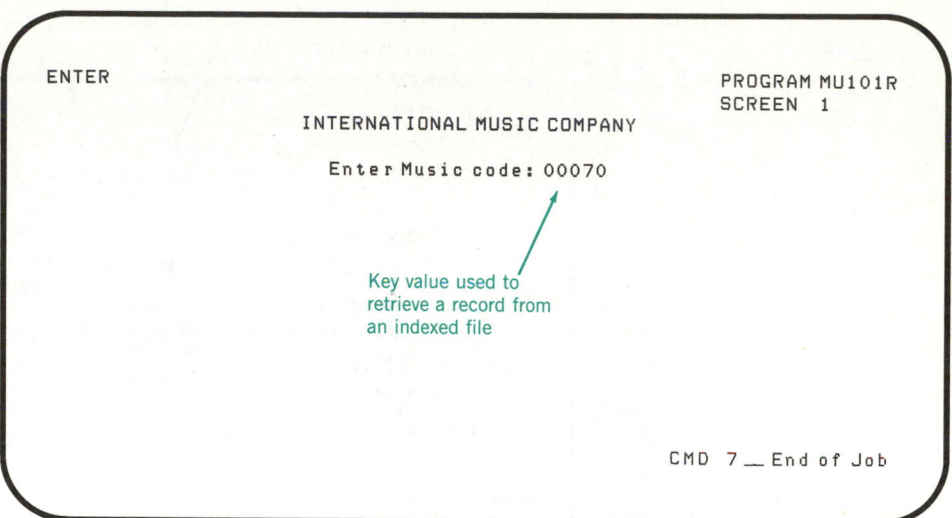

Here, the screen format is prompting the user to enter just one field. When a single field is entered into a screen format as in this example it is normally the key field of an indexed file. The program will use the value entered by the user to retrieve the requested record from the file.

This format is used primarily when a user wishes to select a particular record from a file so that it can be viewed or updated. Thus, this type of data entry screen is used in an application where the user first supplies the requested key value as shown above and then the program displays a second format containing the requested information.

4. Multipurpose Format

Multipurpose formats are a combination of both the query format and the data entry format. This type of format is used primarily to update existing records in a file.

The user would make a request for a record from an indexed file by entering a key value. The program would randomly read the corresponding record from the file and display the information on the screen. Each field on the display would be protected so that the user could not accidentally make changes to the existing data. The user would then have the opportunity to select an option at the bottom of the screen that would remove the protection from the data fields and thus allow him or her to modify the information that is currently in the record. If the user, however, did not want to modify the data, another selection could be made to view a different record or end the program.

III. Elements of a Display Format

Figure 11.3 illustrates a display screen format identified by its elements. Each element is discussed below.

Format Identification

Now and then a user inadvertently causes an interactive application to abend. Although we try to plan for all situations, we sometimes do not succeed.

Imagine a user in a remote office running a critical month-end procedure and the procedure fails or the screen "locks-up." The user calls the computer

Figure 11.3
Elements of a display screen
format.

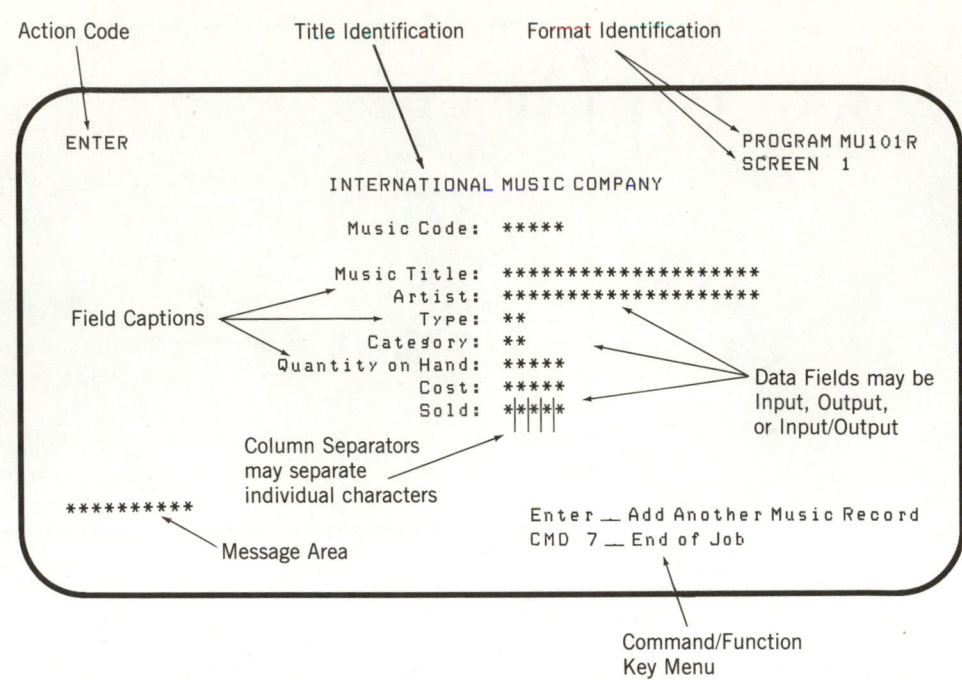

department for help. For the person in the computer department to be able to help, the best information the user can supply is the program identification consisting of the program name and screen number shown in the upper-right corner of the screen.

This immediately makes it clear what program is producing the format and which screen number it is. In that way, no one has to search to identify the program and assistance can be provided immediately to the user.

Action Code

The action code identifies the action required by the user. In the example above, the action code is ENTER, which means that data entry is required in this screen format. If a user had requested a program that allowed only queries into the file in order to view information, that action code could be specified as VIEW or QUERY. Thus, the action code provides immediate direction (ENTER or VIEW) for the user.

Title Identification

Every screen format should have an identification. This identification could be the company name or the application name, such as Payroll, Accounts Payable, and so on.

Field Captions

Field captions are to interactive screen formats as column headings are to printed reports. That is, they provide identification for the different fields that appear on the screen format.

Fields Defined for Input or Entry

When a screen format is displayed that requires the user to enter new data into the fields displayed on the screen, these fields are defined as input or data entry fields. Input fields may be used to create new records or update existing records in a file.

Fields Defined for Output or Query

Unlike input fields, output or query fields can only be displayed to the user. The user is not permitted to enter data into fields specified as output-only fields. Thus, fields defined as output-only fields protect the user from accidentally making changes to data.

Fields Defined for Both Input and Output

Sometimes a user may want to view fields in order to determine if modifications are required. When this is necessary, fields are defined as both output and input or I/O fields.

They are first read as input and then displayed by the program as output fields to allow the user to view the necessary information. If required, the user then enters new data into the fields, which are then returned or rewritten into the fields.

Column Separators

Column separators may be used to separate individual characters when a screen format is displayed. This is especially useful for fields to be inputted, or entry fields, because they help show the size of the field. In this way, the maximum length of each field in which data is to be entered is fully visible to the user.

The type of column separator is often a vertical line, but it may vary depending on the type of workstation being used. Each character position of a field is preceded and followed by the column separator character. However, the column separator character does not take up a position in the field.

Message Area

When entering new data into a data entry format, users sometimes make keying errors. A special area is normally established on the screen format so that error messages can be communicated back to the user. Once the user reads the error message, he or she can take the appropriate action to correct the error. Error messages are normally highlighted in some fashion to draw the user's attention.

Command/Function Key Menu Area

In most interactive applications, programmable keys are used extensively to aid in the selection of the different options available to the user.

Programmable keys consist of two types depending on the type of keyboard being used. These keys are called *Command* keys, identified as CMD keys, and *Function* keys, identified as PF keys. Command keys are found on older keyboards and require the user to press *two* keys—the CMD key and a numeric key—when making a selection. More recent keyboards have 24 function keys that are available to the user.

Normally when a user is running an interactive program several courses of action will exist for a screen format. For example, the user may press the Enter key to add another record to the file, CMD 3 (Command key 3) might be used to permit the user to modify a record, or CMD 7 (Command key 7) might be used to end the job. These options must be placed on the screen in an area where the user can identify them easily. Normally, these options are provided in the form of a menu in the lower-right corner of the screen. From the menu list the user can easily identify the different options available.

Data Attributes

In addition to defining elements, particular highlighting characteristics of the data can be defined. These characteristics are called *attributes* and can be used to highlight or draw the user's attention to a specific data field. We will describe later the different attributes available and how they are defined.

IV. Illustrative Example of Interactive Programming

The International Music Company

The International Music Company has developed an interactive computer system to maintain an inventory of all music titles at each store location. Figure 11.4 contains the description and record layout for the indexed file MUSMST, which uses a five-byte field called MUSCDE (positions 1–5) as its key field.

In our sample problem to follow, we will retrieve records randomly from MUSMST using the key field so that we may make random inquiries into the file.

There are two fields in the MUSMST file, MTYPE and MCATGY, which are coded fields. That is, these fields are used to minimize keystrokes by identifying the actual contents of the fields with abbreviations. The values for MTYPE and MCATGY are as follows:

MTYPE	Type	MCATGY	Category
LP	Long Play Records	CL	Classical
CT	Cassette Tape	CY	Country
CD	Compact Disk	JZ	Jazz
		PP	Pop
		RK	Rock
		VL	Vocal

Figure 11.4
Description and record layout for the sample interactive program.

File Name: MUSMST		Organization: Indexed		
Key Field: MUSCDE				
Record Description	File — MUSMST			
Field Description	Field Type (C,N,P)	Width	Dec. Pos.	RPG Field Name
Music Code	N	5	0	MUSCDE
Music Title	C	20		MTITLE
Artist	C	20		MARTST
Type	C	2		MTYPE
Category	C	2		MCATGY
Quantity on Hand	P	5	0	MQOH
Sold	P	5	0	MSOLD
Cost	P	5	2	MCOST

MUSMST Record Layout

MUSCDE	MTITLE	MARTST	MTYPE	MCATGY	MQOH (P)	MSOLD (P)	MCOST (P)
1 5	6 25	26 45	46 47	48 49	50 52	53 55	56 58

Figure 11.5
Systems flowchart for the sample interactive program.

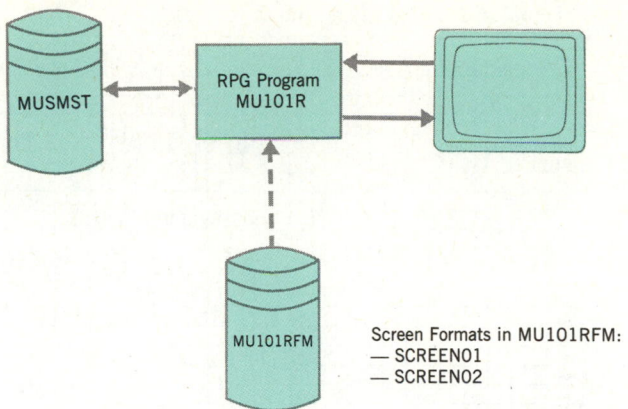

Screen Formats in MU101RFM:
— SCREEN01
— SCREEN02

Interactive Query Program

Our sample interactive program is a query program used to inquire into the indexed file MUSMST. This program will allow the user to retrieve and view the various information about the music records contained in the file MUSMST. Such information as the music title, artist, type, category, and quantity on hand may be displayed on the screen.

This program will demonstrate the concepts of interactive RPG programming using display screen formats. Figure 11.5 shows the systems flowchart for our sample program, which will display music records from the chained file MUSMST. In addition, Figure 11.6 shows the screen layout sheets used to design the two screen formats that will be used in this interactive program.

Program Description

Program MU101R is an interactive *inquiry* program that uses the MUSMST indexed master file. The user is presented with a data entry screen format (SCREEN01) that allows the user to enter a music code. Using the music code entered by the user, the program chains to the MUSMST master file to obtain the requested record. If the music code is found in the MUSMST file, the program displays, using a second screen format called SCREEN02, the music code, music title, artist, type, category, and quantity on hand. If the music code is

Figure 11.6
Screen layout sheets for designing screen formats that will be used in the sample interactive program.

Format SCREEN01 (prompt user for music code)

Figure 11.6   Format SCREEN02 (view music record)
(continued)

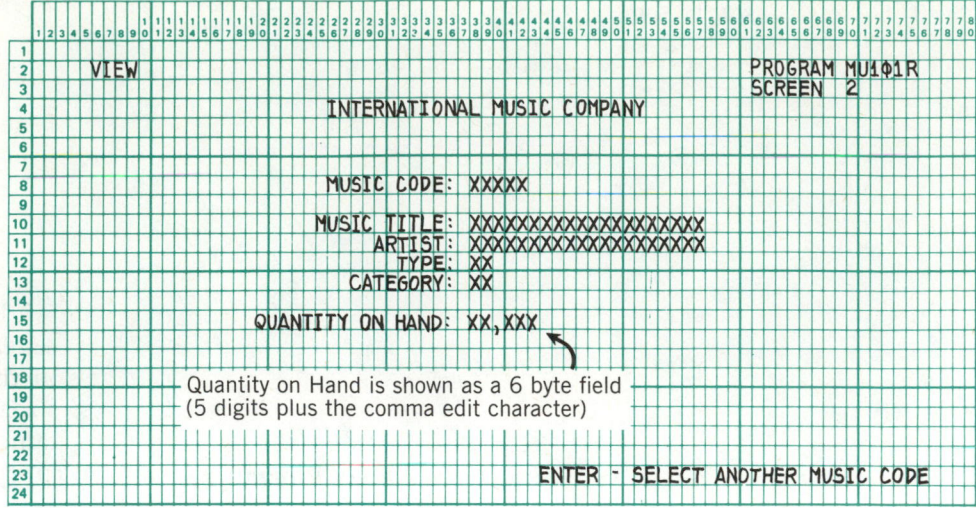

not found, however, the message "MUSIC RECORD NOT FOUND" is displayed on line 24 of the first display screen to notify the user that an incorrect music code was entered.

Program MU101R allows the user to continue to view records from the MUSMST file until the user signals the end of job by pressing CMD 7, at which time the program is terminated.

As we develop our interactive music application you will notice that there are just a few new RPG concepts to learn with respect to interactive programming. Most of the new concepts that you will learn in this chapter pertain to the development of the screen formats used in interactive applications.

Utility Programs Used for Interactive Applications

Many computer systems have utility programs that assist in the design and development of screen formats. These *utility programs* provide a meaningful and user-friendly interaction between the programmer and the computer. A **utility program,** sometimes called just a utility, is a general purpose program or set of programs provided with the operating system to perform specific functions. For example, we discussed the Sort Utility in Chapter 8.

In addition, special utilities are designed to aid the programmer with his or her interactive application programming requirements. IBM, for example, has a utility called Screen Design Aid (SDA). With this screen design utility, it is possible to eliminate the use of the display screen layout forms. In its interactive mode, the screen layout can be designed directly at the workstation. SDA allows the programmer to add, delete, or move display elements until the screen format is completed, at which time SDA will print a copy of the design that is similar to the display layout sheet. In addition, SDA generates the load module that will be used to display the format on the screen when the program is running.

As we develop our interactive music application, we will use several utility programs. We will introduce and discuss each utility when the need arises.

Before we discuss the interactive RPG program requirements for our sample music application we need first to develop the display screen formats (SCREEN01 and SCREEN02) that are to be used.

V. Steps for Creating a Display Screen Format

When developing a display screen format for an interactive program, several steps are involved as shown in Figure 11.7. We will now describe in detail each of the required steps for the development of the screen formats for our sample music problem.

A. Design the Screen Formats for Program MU101R

The first step in writing an interactive program is to design the display screen formats that will be used for communication between the user and the program. The display screen layout sheet shown earlier in Figure 11.1 is used to lay out the formats as they will appear on the display screen. Figure 11.6 illustrates the display screen layout sheets for the two formats that will be required in our sample inquiry music program.

Display screens can display elements in uppercase or lowercase letters. Some companies use all uppercase letters for captions and headings while

Figure 11.7
Steps for creating a display screen format.

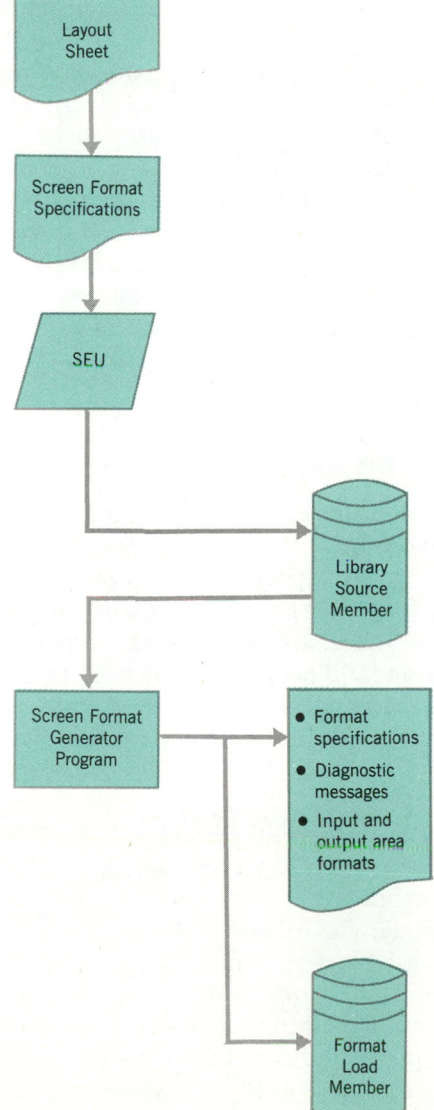

Note: SEU or Source Entry Utility is a line editor used for entering programs, procedures, and screen format specifications.

others use a combination of both uppercase and lowercase letters. What you use will depend on the rules established at your particular computer installation.

The program MU101R uses two screen formats, as described below.

Screen Format **SCREEN01**

Format SCREEN01, shown in Figure 11.6, is an *enter format* that prompts the user to enter a music code so that the corresponding record from the master file can be located. The program will read format SCREEN01 into the program and use the music code field (SMCODE) read from the display screen to randomly access the requested record from the MUSMST indexed file. If, however, the user wishes to terminate the program, CMD 7 is pressed to end the job.

We will use the line and column numbers from this layout sheet in the next step to identify the locations of each element on the display screen.

Screen Format **SCREEN02**

If the music code entered in format SCREEN01 is found in the MUSMST file, format SCREEN02 is displayed on the screen as shown in Figure 11.6. Format SCREEN02 is an informational or query screen used to display the music code, music title, artist, type, category, and quantity on hand for the requested music code.

Once the user is finished viewing the information from the music record the Enter key is pressed to allow another selection to be made. When the Enter key is pressed, format SCREEN01 is again displayed so that the user can select another music code to view.

Every screen format needs to be identified by a screen identifier. This enables the RPG program to identify which screen format has been read into the program. In our example, we use the screen number as the screen format's identifier. In this way, each screen format can be identified by the RPG program. In addition, this number serves as an identification code (program number plus screen number) that can be used if the user requires assistance when a problem arises.

B. Define the Display Screen Format Specifications

The specifications for each display format used in an interactive RPG program are described on the Display Format Specifications form shown in Figure 11.8. The Display Format Specifications form contains two areas that are used to describe the format. The first area, the **Display Control (S) Specification,** is used to define the characteristics of the entire format. The second area, the **Field Definition (D) Specification,** is used to define the characteristics of each element that will appear on the display format.

Let us describe each of the two areas of the Display Format Specifications form.

Display Control (S) Specification

The first entry on the Display Format Specifications form is called the Display Control Specification or S Specification. The S Specification for format SCREEN01 is shown in Figure 11.9. It provides information about the entire display screen format in general terms; that is, it does not specify the fields being defined.

Each format defined in the display screen format member must contain one S Specification. In addition, the S Specification must be the first specification for each format.

Define Format

Display Control Specification

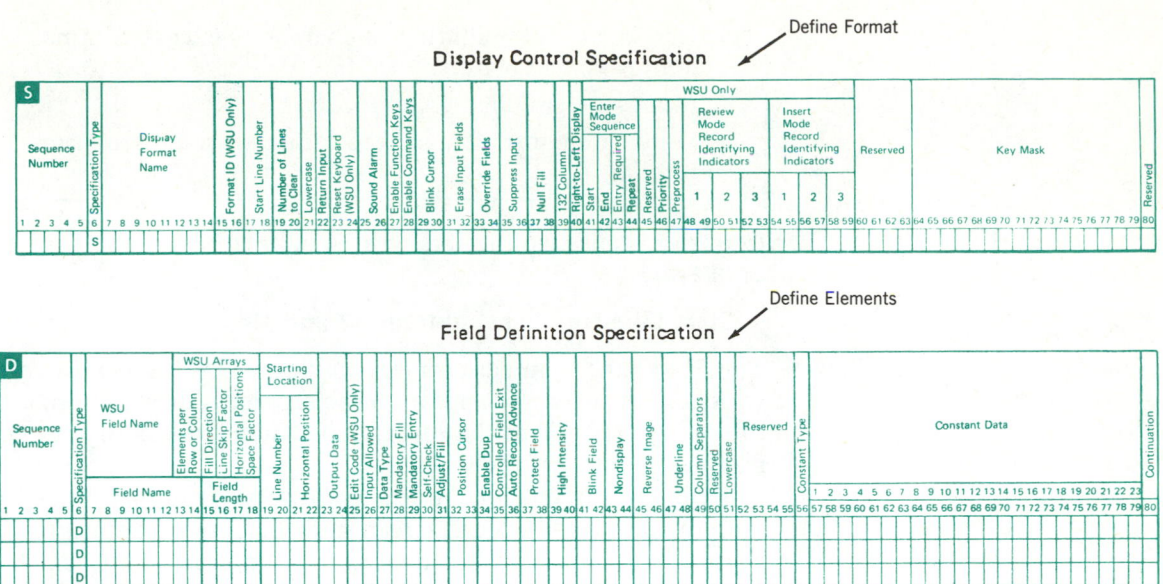

Define Elements

Field Definition Specification

Figure 11.8
System/36 Display Format
Specifications form.

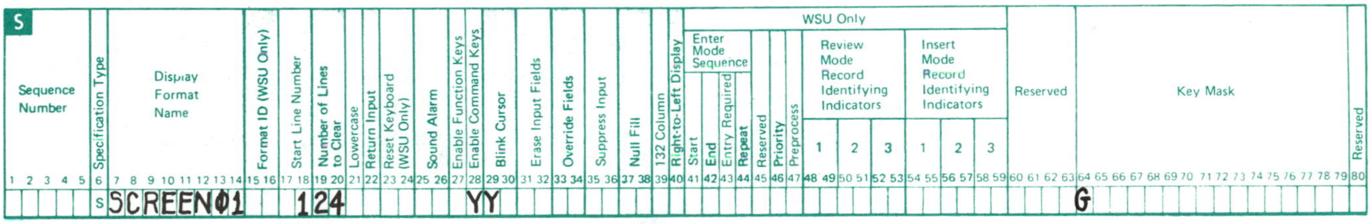

Figure 11.9
S Specification for format
SCREEN01.

Let us examine the entries on the Display Control Specification form shown in Figure 11.9.

Form Type (Column 6)

The letter S identifies this specification as the Screen Display Control Specification or S Specification.

Format Name (Columns 7–14)

This entry assigns a *unique* format name to the format being defined. The rules for defining format names are as follows:

RULES FOR DEFINING FORMAT NAMES

1. Must begin in column 7 (left-justified).
2. Must begin with an alphabetic character.

3. Can be any combination of characters except commas (,), single quotes ('), and blanks.

4. Must be eight characters or less.

5. Duplicate names assigned to formats used by the same program are *invalid*.

In our example two formats will be defined, using the names SCREEN01 and SCREEN02.

Start Line Number (Columns 17 and 18)

The Start Line Number entry in columns 17–18 specifies the starting line at which the display will appear on the screen. A display format can start on any line of the screen but the line number must be less than or equal to the total number of lines on the screen.

Thus, if 12 is specified for the starting line number, lines 1 through 11 will remain unchanged on the screen and the screen format being displayed will begin at line 12. Varying this entry, then, will allow you to display screen formats without disturbing existing information on the screen.

In our example, both formats (SCREEN01 and SCREEN02) are going to use the entire screen, therefore, 1 is specified as the starting line number in column 18.

Number of Lines to Clear (Columns 19 and 20)

This entry specifies the number of lines to be cleared on the screen before the format is displayed. Any number of lines from zero to the maximum number of lines on the screen (usually 24 or 25) may be cleared. If the entire screen is to be cleared before displaying a format, the maximum number of lines on the screen, usually 24 or 25, should be specified. If a value is not specified in columns 19–20 (the entry is left blank), then the entire screen is cleared before the format is displayed.

In our example we specify 24, meaning that the entire screen will be cleared before the format is displayed.

Sound Alarm (Columns 25 and 26)

This entry is sometimes used to sound the audible alarm when the format is displayed on the screen. The alarm feature is normally used when you wish to get the attention of the user, such as when an error has occurred. We did not use the "sound alarm" feature in our sample problem.

Command Keys

Most keyboards have command keys or function keys that can be programmed and used for identifying given tasks. They are one method the user has of selecting a function to be performed. This method, like menu selection, reduces keystrokes and thus errors.

A total of 24 command or function keys are designated on the keyboard. Keyboard keys may vary, depending on the type of keyboard you are using. You should refer to your manual to determine the proper keys to press for each of the command or function keys.

Each command key or function key is assigned an RPG indicator that may be used to condition Calculation and Output operations in your program. The following list shows the command keys and the corresponding alphabetic command key indicators used in an RPG program.

Command Key	RPG Command Key Indicator
1	KA
2	KB
3	KC
4	KD
5	KE
6	KF
7	KG
8	KH
9	KI
10	KJ
11	KK
12	KL
13	KM
14	KN
15	KP
16	KQ
17	KR
18	KS
19	KT
20	KU
21	KV
22	KW
23	KX
24	KY

All command keys can be used in an interactive program. All command keys are set off prior to the program reading a screen format. If a command key is pressed by the user when the screen format is read into the program, RPG will set on the corresponding command key indicator, which can then be used to condition operations within the program.

Enable Command Keys (Column 28)

The entry Y in column 28 signifies that the program using this format will accept only certain command keys. If Y (YES) is specified in column 28, the command keys identified by alphabetic characters in the Key Mask Entry (columns 64–79) are enabled (allowed):

Display Control Specification

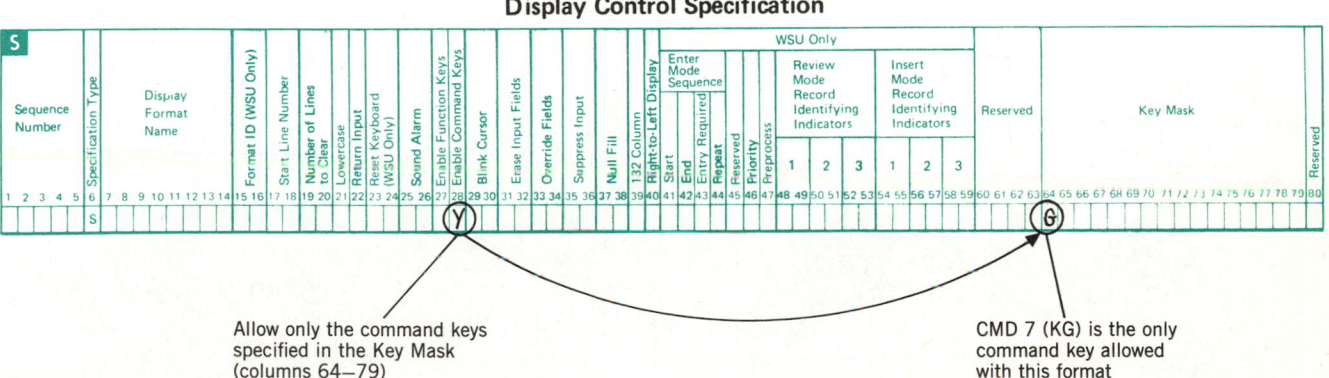

Allow only the command keys specified in the Key Mask (columns 64–79)

CMD 7 (KG) is the only command key allowed with this format

If a Y is specified in column 28 and no command keys are specified in the Key Mask (columns 64–79 blank), all command keys are disabled. That is, command keys will not be allowed with this format.

If the user presses a disabled command key, a warning bell rings and the user must re-key the correct command key.

For the SCREEN01 format, Y is placed in column 28 and the letter G is specified in the Key Mask (column 64). This means that the user can use only command key 7, which will be used to signal "end of job".

Blink Cursor (Columns 29 and 30)

If Y (YES) is specified in column 29, the cursor blinks when the format is displayed. Normally, we have the cursor blinking for data entry formats. For query formats, however, it is not necessary for the cursor to blink since the user is viewing information and not entering data into fields.

C. Define the Field Definition (D) Specifications

Once the characteristics for the entire display have been defined using the S Specification, each element on the format must be defined. The Field Definition Specification or D Specification is used to describe each element of the screen format. Each Field Definition Specification completely describes an element of the screen format. The entries for our Field Definition Specification for SCREEN01 shown in Figure 11.10 are as follows:

Form Type (Column 6)

The Form Type 'D' identifies this record as a Field Definition Specification.

Field Name (Columns 7–14)

Columns 7–14 are used to name elements that are specified as data fields. Format SCREEN01 contains three data fields: SCNID, SMCODE, and SERROR.

Figure 11.10
Field Definition Specification
for SCREEN01.

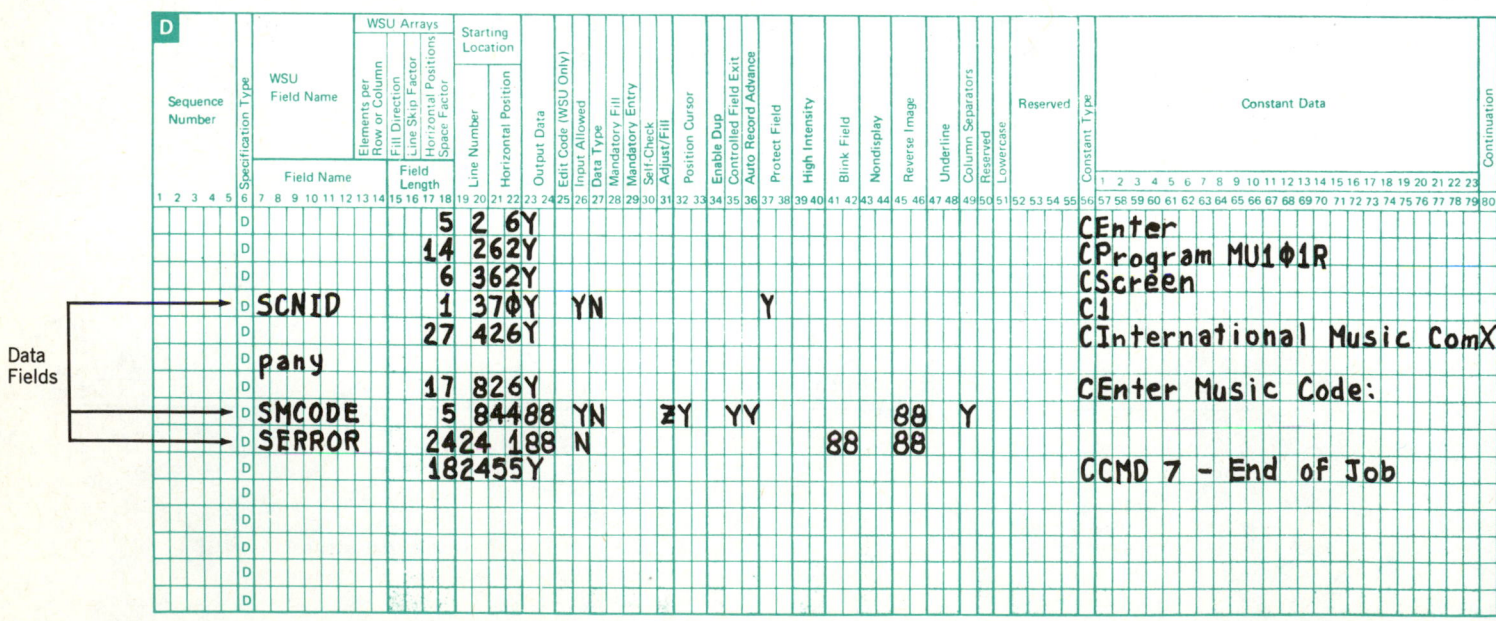

Field Length (Columns 15–18)

This specifies the length of the element. The length of an element can be any number from 1 to 1840. Leading zeros are not required, but the value must be right-justified in this entry.

When a numeric field is specified as an output field, edit codes and edit words may be used to make the data easier to read. If editing is performed on output fields, the length of the field must be adjusted accordingly in order to allow for the additional edit characters.

Note, however, that a problem could occur if a field is edited on output and then read back into the program. When the data is read back into the program it would contain the edit characters that appear on the screen. The programmer must strip the edit characters from the data field before any processing is to take place on the field.

Line Number (Columns 19 and 20)

This specifies the number of the line, relative to the start line, on which the field begins. The start line is specified on the S-Specification. The line number can be any number from 1 to 24. Leading zeros are not required, but the value must be right-justified.

Horizontal Position (Columns 21 and 22)

This specifies the column number of the first position of the element. The column number can be any number from 1 to 80. Leading zeros are not required, but the value must be right-justified in the entry.

Output Data (Columns 23 and 24)

Columns 23 and 24 are used to specify whether an element is an output field. If Y (YES) is specified in column 23, the element is displayed as output. If N (NO) is specified, however, the element will not be displayed as output.

In addition to Y or N, an indicator may be specified. If so, the field will be displayed as output only if the specified indicator is on when the format is displayed by the RPG program.

Input Allowed (Column 26)

If Y (YES) is specified, the element is an input field. If N (NO) or blank is specified, the element is not an input field.

Data Type (Column 27)

Column 27 specifies the type of data that can be placed in the *input* field. Data Type *cannot* be specified for an output field. Data type consists of the following:

- A The field can contain only alphabetic characters, commas, periods, hyphens, or blanks.
- N The field can contain only numeric data.
- B The field can contain any character.
- S The field can contain only signed numeric data.

Adjust Fill (Column 31)

Normally, when data is entered into a field, it should be right-justified. The letter Z is required in column 31 for an input numeric field requiring right justification. Data entered into a field specified as numeric adjust-fill will be right-adjusted with the unused positions to the left filled with zeros.

For an alphanumeric field, a B will right-adjust and fill the unused positions with blanks before the field is transmitted to the program.

In SCREEN01, adjust fill is specified for the input field SMCODE.

Position Cursor (Columns 32–33)

There are times, such as when an error condition occurs, that you may want to position the cursor at the first position in a particular field for the format being displayed on the screen. To accomplish this, the letter Y is placed in column 32 or an indicator is placed in columns 32–33.

The cursor is placed at position 1 of the *first field* on the display that has specified an indicator (01-99 in columns 32–33). The letter Y, if specified, can be designated for only one field and will position the cursor at the beginning of that field.

Controlled Field Exit (Column 35)

When the letter Y is specified in column 35, one of the field exit keys must be pressed before the cursor will leave the field. The most common field exit keys are the Field Advance, Field Exit, Field +, and Field − keys.

Automatic Record Advance (Column 36)

This option is normally used with the last input field of a screen format. If Y (YES) is specified in column 36, the input fields on the screen *automatically* return to the program when the operator enters the last character in the field or presses the field exit key. If N (NO) is specified, the automatic record advance feature does not apply for this field.

Protect Field (Columns 37–38)

Columns 37–38 can be used to protect a field that is displayed on the screen from having new data entered into it.

An entry of Y in column 37 will cause the cursor to bypass this field. An indicator (01-99) specified in columns 37–38 will cause the cursor to bypass this field only if the indicator is on.

High Intensity (Columns 39–40)

Columns 39–40 can be used to display a field with high intensity. An entry of Y in column 39 will display the field with high intensity. An indicator (01-99) specified in columns 39–40 will cause the field to be displayed with high intensity only when the indicator is on.

Blink Field (Columns 41–42)

Columns 41–42 can be used to have a field blink when displayed. An entry of Y in column 41 will cause the field to blink when displayed. An indicator (01-99) specified in columns 41–42 will cause the field to blink only when the indicator is on.

Nondisplay (Columns 43–44)

An entry of Y in column 43 will identify this field as a nondisplay field, meaning it will not be visible on the screen. An indicator in columns 43–44 will cause the field to be a nondisplay field only if the specified indicator is on.

Reverse Image (Columns 45–46)

Columns 45–46 can be used to specify a field as dark characters on a light background (reverse image). An entry of Y in column 45 will display the field in reverse image. An indicator (01-99) in columns 45–46 will cause the field to appear in reverse image only if the specified indicator is on.

Underline (Columns 47–48)

Columns 47–48 can be used to underline a field when displayed on the screen. An entry of Y in column 47 will automatically display a field with underlining. An indicator (01-99) in columns 47–48 will cause the field to be underlined only if the specified indicator is on.

Column Separators (Column 49)

An entry of Y in column 49 will cause each character position within the field to be preceded and followed by a column separator character. Normally, fields defined as input also contain column separators to help identify them to the user.

Constant Type (Column 56)

The entry C in column 56 indicates that the characters in columns 57–79 are displayed in the output field as a constant.

Constant Data (Columns 57–79)

This specifies the data to be placed in an output or input/output field when the format is displayed.

Continuation (Column 80)

The letter X in column 80 indicates that the constant data from this line continues to the next line. A line is continued when the constant data is longer than 23 characters (columns 57–79).

Displaying Constant Data

For the format to display an element as a constant, the letter C must be specified on the D Specification in column 56 (Constant Type). The constant value itself is specified in columns 57–79 (Constant Data).

In format SCREEN01, for example, the format's action code is specified as a constant. The letter C is specified in column 56 and the word ENTER is specified in columns 57–61. The field is also specified as an output field only. Thus, this constant will be displayed on the screen when the format is displayed but will not be read into the program when the format is read.

The screen identifier on the other hand is described as both an input field and an output field. Again, the letter C is specified in column 56. The constant identifier 1 is specified in column 57. This constant is specified as an input (Y in column 26) and output (Y in column 23) field. Therefore, it will be displayed on the screen when the format is displayed and also read into the program along with the format. Even though this constant field is an input field its value cannot change. The letter Y in column 37 (Protect Field) prevents the user from keying data into this field. This enables the program to use this field to identify which format has been read from the screen.

The S and D Specifications for the second format, SCREEN02, are shown in Figure 11.11.

D. Create the Display Screen Format Source Member

After the display screen format specifications have been entered onto the S and D Specifications forms, they must now be entered into a source member and stored in a library. The library we are using for our music application is MUSCLIBR. The SEU utility is used to enter the specifications shown in Figures 11.9, 11.10, and 11.11 into the source member called MU101RFM.

S Specification

Sequence Number	Specification Type	Display Format Name	Format ID (WSU Only)	Start Line Number	Number of Lines to Clear	...	Suppress Input	...
	S	SCREEN02	1	24			Y	

Field Definition Specification

Spec Type	WSU Field Name / Field Name	Field Length	Starting Location (Line Number / Horizontal Position)	Output Data	Input Allowed	Protect Field	Constant Type / Constant Data
D		5	2 6	Y			CView
D		14	26 2	Y			CProgram MU101R
D		6	36 2	Y			CScreen
D	SCNID	1	37 0	Y	YN	Y	C2
D		27	42 6	Y			CInternational Music Com X
D	pany						
D		11	82 6	Y			CMusic Code:
D	MUSCDE	5	83 8	Y			
D		12	102 5	Y			CMusic Title:
D	MTITLE	20	103 8	Y			
D		7	113 0	Y			CArtist:
D	MARTST	20	113 8	Y			
D		5	L23 2	Y			CType:
D	MTYPE	2	123 8	Y			
D		9	132 8	Y			CCategory:
D	MCATGY	2	133 8	Y			
D		17	152 0	Y			CQuantity on Hand:
D	MQOH	6	153 8	Y		Y	
D		33	234 4	Y			CEnter - Select another X
D	music code						

Figure 11.11
S and D Specifications for
SCREEN02.

Source Entry Utility (SEU)

Source Entry Utility (SEU) is a line editor that provides a method for entering source programs, procedures, and display screen format specifications into a library. Once these source members are stored in a library, you can also modify them using SEU.

SEU assists the programmer by displaying "special-purpose" formats (from a format menu list) for each specification into which the S and D specifications can be entered or modified.

SEU also assigns command keys for use by the programmer. These command keys are defined using the top row of keys on the keyboard. They provide the ability to ENTER/UPDATE, DELETE, SCAN, MOVE/COPY, and INCLUDE source specifications in addition to other options. Each of these commands is selected by using a particular command key.

In addition to SEU, another utility called Development Support Utility (DSU) is available. DSU is a full screen editor that allows the programmer to edit an entire screen at one time.

For a complete description on how to use SEU and DSU consult the reference manual in your computer center.

Screen formats are *not* stored with the RPG program that uses them. They are *compiled* separately from the RPG program and are stored in a **format load member.** Normally, but not always, the format load member has the same name as the RPG program that uses it. To make the name unique however, FM is generally added to the end of the name, as in MU101RFM for our sample problem.

E. Create the Format Load Member for MU101RFM

1. Screen Design Aid (SDA)

Screen Design Aid (SDA) is a utility used by the programmer to develop menus and display screen formats. Once display screen formats are developed, SDA can also be used to create the initial RPG program specifications needed to use the formats in an interactive application. In addition, SDA can be used to change and delete display screen formats and menus.

SDA can be accessed by entering the command SDA or selecting the SDA option from the main help menu. Regardless of the method used, the display of the SDA MAIN OPTIONS menu shown in Figure 11.12 appears on the screen.

Option 9 of the SDA MAIN OPTIONS menu can be used to compile the source screen format member. In addition to option 9, there are other methods in which the display screen format member can be compiled. We will not, however, discuss those options at this time. When option 9 is selected, the Screen Format Generator program is executed.

2. Screen Format Generator ($SFGR)

The utility for generating display screen formats for interactive processing on the S/36 is supplied by IBM and is called Screen Format Generator ($SFGR). $SFGR provides an interface between RPG programs and the operating system.

Note, then, that the task of designating and generating format screen displays is not part of the actual program but is handled by a utility serving as an interface between the operating system and the program. This utility or interface is machine dependent and will vary from one computer to another.

Figure 11.12
SDA MAIN OPTIONS menu.

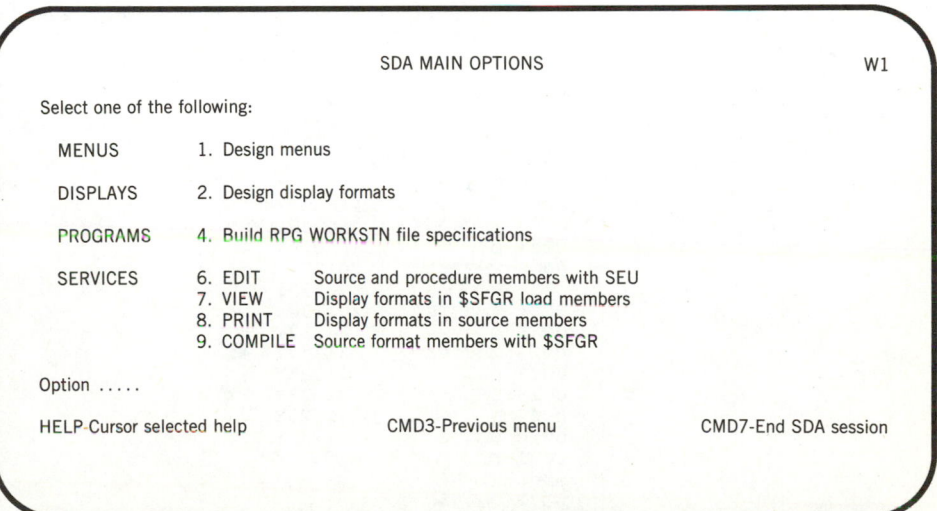

```
                          SDA MAIN OPTIONS                                W1

       Select one of the following:

          MENUS        1.  Design menus

          DISPLAYS     2.  Design display formats

          PROGRAMS     4.  Build RPG WORKSTN file specifications

          SERVICES     6.  EDIT      Source and procedure members with SEU
                        7.  VIEW      Display formats in $SFGR load members
                        8.  PRINT     Display formats in source members
                        9.  COMPILE   Source format members with $SFGR

       Option . . . . .

       HELP-Cursor selected help          CMD3-Previous menu          CMD7-End SDA session
```

Figure 11.13 illustrates the generated output from $SFGR when the source member MU101RFM is compiled.

The $SFGR utility processes Display Screen Format Specifications designed by the programmer and produces Display Screen Formats in a specified file.

In addition to the display screen formats, $SFGR generates the following:

Source Specifications
Diagnostic or Informational Messages
Indicators Used

Figure 11.13
The relationship between the
$SFGR Output Specifications
and the RPG Input
Specifications.

```
....+....1....+....2....+....3....+....4....+....5....+....6....+....7.....
0001 SSCREEN01    124          YY                                        G
0002 D            50205Y  N                Y             CEnter
0003 D            140262Y                                CProgram MU101R
0004 D            60362Y                                 CScreen
0005 DSCNID       10370Y  YN         Y                   C1
0006 D            270426Y                                CInternational Music
ComX
0007 Dpany
0008 D            170826Y                                CEnter Music code:
0009 DSMCODE      5084488 YN    ZY  YY          88  Y
0010 DSERROR      24240188 N                 88  88
0011 D            182455Y                                CCMD 7 - End of Job


EXECUTION TIME OUTPUT BUFFER DESCRIPTION
FIELD NAME     LENGTH      START       END

   SMCODE          5         1          5
   SERROR         24         6         29


INPUT BUFFER DESCRIPTION
FIELD NAME     LENGTH      START       END

   SCNID           1         1          1
   SMCODE          5         2          6


INDICATORS USED

   88



RPG Input Specifications for format SCREEN01


11 0011 IWSFILE  NS
12 0012 I* FORMAT- SCREEN01
13 0013 I                                     1    10SCNID
14 0014 I                                     2    60SMCODE


....+....1....+....2....+....3....+....4....+....5....+....6....+....7.....
0012 SSCREEN02    124          Y
0013 D            50206Y  N                Y             CView
0014 D            140262Y                                CProgram MU101R
0015 D            60362Y                                 CScreen
0016 DSCNID       10370Y  YN         Y                   C2
0017 D            270426Y                                CInternational Music
ComX
0018 Dpany
0019 D            110826Y                                CMusic code:
0020 DMUSCDE      50838Y  NN
0021 D            121025Y                                CMusic Title:
0022 DMTITLE      201038Y NA
0023 D            71130Y                                 CArtist:
0024 DMARTST      201138Y NA
0025 D            51232Y                                 CType:
0026 DMTYPE       21238Y  NA
0027 D            91328Y                                 CCategory:
0028 DMCATGY      21338Y  NA
0029 D            171520Y                                CQuantity on Hand:
0030 DMQOH        61538Y  NN           Y
0031 D            332344Y                                   CEnter - Select
another X
0032 Dmusic code
```

Figure 11.13
(continued)

```
EXECUTION TIME OUTPUT BUFFER DESCRIPTION
FIELD NAME     LENGTH      START        END

    MUSCDE         5           1          5
    MTITLE        20           6         25
    MARTST        20          26         45
    MTYPE          2          46         47
    MCATGY         2          48         49
    MQOH           6          50         55

INPUT BUFFER DESCRIPTION
FIELD NAME     LENGTH      START        END

    SCNID          1           1          1

No Observation Errors
No Warning Errors
No Fatal Errors
```

VI. Generating an RPG **WORKSTN** Program

SDA provides the ability to create a skeleton RPG program generated from the Display Screen Specifications. To execute this procedure, option 4 is selected from the SDA MAIN OPTIONS menu (see Figure 11.12). Figure 11.14 illustrates the skeleton WORKSTN program generated by SDA.

VII. Completing the RPG Program

Figure 11.14 is a listing of the skeleton RPG program created by SDA. This listing is created by SDA from information found in the Format Load Member created earlier. Since this information relates only to the WORKSTN file, only the specifications pertaining to the WORKSTN file were included in the skeleton program. Since SDA creates the skeleton program from information found in the Format Load Member it is imperative that the display screen format member be created first before generating the skeleton program.

After the skeleton program is generated, SEU is used to add those instructions required to make the skeleton program a *complete* WORKSTN file program. Figure 11.15 illustrates the entire WORKSTN program required for this interactive application.

Figure 11.14
Skeleton WORKSTN program
generated by SDA.

```
....+....1....+....2....+....3....+....4....+....5....+....6....+....7
0001 H                                                          MU101R
0002 FWSFILE  CD  F      55              WORKSTN
0003 F                                              KFMTS  MU101RFM
0004 FMUSMST  IC  F      58R 5AI    1 DISK
0005 IWSFILE   NS
0006 I* FORMAT- SCREEN01
0007 I                                      1    10SCNID
0008 I                                      2    60SMCODE
0009 I* FORMAT- SCREEN02
0010 I                                      1    10SCNID
0011 OWSFILE   E
0012 O                                              K8 'SCREEN01'
0013 O                      88      SMCODE   5
0014 O                      88      SERROR  29
0015 OWSFILE   E
0016 O                                              K8 'SCREEN02'
0017 O                              MUSCDE   5
0018 O                              MTITLE  25
0019 O                              MARTST  45
0020 O                              MTYPE   47
0021 O                              MCATGY  49
0022 O                              MQOH    55
```

Figure 11.15
Entire WORKSTN program required for sample interactive application.

```
....+....1....+....2....+....3....+....4....+....5....+....6....+....7
0001  ************************************************************
0002  *
0003  *  PROGRAM DESCRIPTION:
0004  *
0005  *      THIS IS AN INTERACTIVE PROGRAM WHICH WILL ACCESS THE
0006  *      FILE "MUSMST" AND ALLOW THE USER TO VIEW
0007  *      MUSIC RECORDS IN THE FILE.
0008  *
0009  *
0010  *  FUNCTION OF INDICATORS:
0011  *
0012  *      88   MUSIC CODE (SMCODE) NOT FOUND IN MUSMST
0013  *      KG   CMD KEY 7
0014  *
0015  ************************************************************
0016 H                                                       MU101R
0017 FWSFILE   CD  F      55              WORKSTN
0018 F                                           KFMTS  MU101RFM
0019 FMUSMST   IC  F      58R 5AI   1 DISK
0020 IWSFILE   NS
0021 I* FORMAT- SCREEN01
0022 I                                  1    10SCNID
0023 I                                  2    60SMCODE
0024 I         NS
0025 I* FORMAT- SCREEN02
0026 I                                  1    10SCNID
0027 I*
0028 IMUSMST   NS
0029 I                                  1     50MUSCDE
0030 I                                  6    25 MTITLE
0031 I                                 26    45 MARTST
0032 I                                 46    47 MTYPE
0033 I                                 48    49 MCATGY
0034 I                              P  50   520MQOH
0035 I                              P  53   550MSOLD
0036 I                              P  56   582MCOST
0037 I#FLAGS    DS
0038 I                                  1     3 #QUIT
0039 C*
0040  *                              MAIN-LINE-RTN
0041 C              EXSR SR100
0042 C*
0043 C         #QUIT    DOWNE'YES'
0044 C         SCNID    CASEQ1         SR210
0045 C         SCNID    CASEQ2         SR220
0046 C                  END                        END-CAS
0047 C                  READ WSFILE
0048 C     KG           MOVE 'YES'     #QUIT
0049 C                  END                        END-DOW
0050  *
0051 C                  SETON                      LR
0052  *
0053  *                              100-INITIALIZATION-RTN
0054 CSR       SR100    BEGSR
0055 CSR                EXCPT@SCN01
0056 CSR                READ WSFILE
0057 CSR   KG           MOVE 'YES'     #QUIT
0058 CSR                ENDSR
0059  *                              210-PROCESS-SCREEN01-RTN
0060 CSR       SR210    BEGSR
0061 CSR       SMCODE   CHAINMUSMST              88
0062 CSR 88             EXCPT@SCN01              NOT FND - ERROR
0063 CSRN88             EXCPT@SCN02              DISPLAY RECORD
0064 CSR                ENDSR
0065 C*
0066  *                              220-PROCESS-SCREEN02-RTN
0067 CSR       SR220    BEGSR
0068 CSR                EXCPT@SCN01
0069 CSR                ENDSR
0070  *
0071 OWSFILE   E              @SCN01
0072 O                             K8 'SCREEN01'
0073 O                     SMCODE   5
0074 O                             29 ' MUSIC RECORD NOT FOUND '
0075 O         E              @SCN02
0076 O                             K8 'SCREEN02'
0077 O                     MUSCDE   5
0078 O                     MTITLE  25
0079 O                     MARTST  45
0080 O                     MTYPE   47
0081 O                     MCATGY  49
0082 O                     MQOH  2 55
```

If it is necessary to modify the Display Screen Format Specifications (S or D specifications) at a later date, it will be necessary to recompile this source member in order to create a new format load member. Changes to the screen format specifications may also affect the WORKSTN file specifications contained in the RPG program. If so, changes to the RPG program will be necessary. You may make the modifications directly to the RPG program or generate a new skeleton program and then copy the changes into the new program. It should be pointed out, however, that if a new skeleton program is generated the old program should be saved under a different name or the new skeleton program should be generated using a new name. This will prevent the new skeleton program from destroying the old program and all the changes that were made earlier.

Let us consider the modifications that were made to the skeleton program in order to complete the full program.

File Description Specifications Form

Figure 11.16 contains modifications to the File Description Specifications form that were made to the skeleton program.

First, the WORKSTN file is defined as a special type of file called a **Combined file** (C in column 15). This allows the program to read records from or write records to the workstation device.

Note that disk files cannot be defined as combined files. Recall that for a disk file to be both input and output, it is defined as an update file (U in column 15).

The record length for a WORKSTN file used in an interactive program is obtained from the format load member generated by $SFGR.

The second change we made to the skeleton program was to define the WORKSTN file as a *Demand file* (D in column 16). This was done so that we could read records from the WORKSTN file under control of the program, that is, when a READ operation is executed on the Calculation Specifications form.

Figure 11.16
Modifications to the File Description Specifications that were made to the skeleton program.

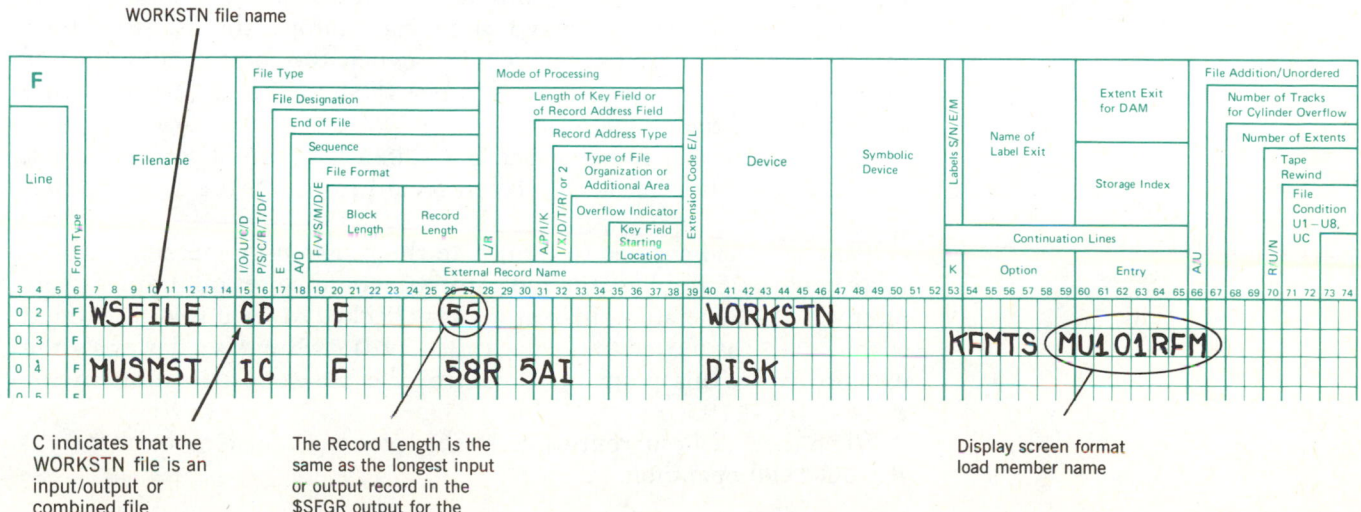

WORKSTN file name

C indicates that the WORKSTN file is an input/output or combined file

The Record Length is the same as the longest input or output record in the $SFGR output for the format load member

Display screen format load member name

Input Specifications Form

The only modification necessary to the Input Specifications form was to add the entry "NS" in columns 15 and 16 for the record definition.

Output Specifications Form

Before we consider the processing of this program, let us discuss the modifications that were made to the Output Specifications form.

On the File Description Specifications form we defined the file as a Demand file so that we could control the reading of the screen formats into the program. Similarly, we changed the output operations to EXCPT output. In this way, both input and output operations to the WORKSTN file will be controlled by the programmer. In addition, we used EXCPT labels to identify the different formats. Format SCREEN01 is displayed under control of the EXCPT label @SCN01, while @SCN02 controls format SCREEN02.

The display screen format names are specified in the RPG program as constants on the Output Specifications form. The end positions for these constants are both specified as K8. These constants are specified as 'Kn', where 'n' is the length of the format name (SCREEN01 = K8).

WORKSTN file input and output records must be described in the RPG program according to the *record format* generated by $SFGR.

Constants, such as the headings and field captions described on the D Specifications form, are maintained with the screen format in the format load member. The RPG program, then, does not have to describe them.

Fields that will be input to or output from the interactive RPG program are the only items required to be described on the Input and Output Specifications forms.

The quantity on hand (MQOH) field illustrates the editing capabilities of an output field. MQOH, which is a five-byte input field, is specified as a six-byte display field for format SCREEN02 on the Output Specifications. Edit code 2 is specified for this field, which allows for a comma to appear in the field when it is displayed on the screen.

Calculation Specifications Form

Let us now consider the Calculation Specifications.

The MAIN-LINE-RTN consists of the following parts:

1. The initialization subroutine, SR100, is executed first. An EXCPT operation writes the first screen format (SCREEN01) to the WORKSTN file WSFILE. SCREEN01 is a display format that prompts the user to enter a music code. The user has two choices when the format SCREEN01 is displayed: (1) enter a music code and press the Enter key or (2) press CMD 7 to terminate the program.

    Once the user has responded to the SCREEN01 prompt screen format, the READ operation reads the screen record from WSFILE into the program.

    If the user had decided to terminate the program by pressing CMD 7 instead of the Enter key, the indicator KG would be set on. Immediately after the READ operation, indicator KG is checked to see if it was set on. If it was, 'YES' is moved to the flag called #QUIT, which is a flag or switch established in this program to control the DOW/END operation in the MAIN-LINE-RTN.

    When the SR100 subroutine is finished, control transfers to the start of the DOW/END operation.

2. The DOW/END operation is executed next. The DOW/END operation continues to execute while #QUIT is not equal to 'YES'. That is, it continues to loop until 'YES' is moved to #QUIT, at which time the loop terminates.

Once inside the loop, the field SCNID from the screen format is evaluated to determine which screen was read into the program.

The screen format record code (SCNID) is either 1 or 2. It is described on the D Specifications form as an Output/Input, Protect, and Constant field. It is used by the RPG program to identify which screen format has been read. SCREEN01 is identified by the code 1, while SCREEN02 is identified by 2.

Because the SCNID is a *constant*, no output field is required on the Output Specifications form. All *constants* are stored as part of the screen format SCREEN01.

Based on the evaluation of the field SCNID, either subroutine SR210 or SR220 is executed.

Subroutine SR210—Screen Format **SCREEN01**

Format SCREEN01 is used to prompt the user to enter a music code. The program reads the format (SCREEN01) into the program and uses the music code field (SMCODE) read from the display screen to randomly access the requested record from the MUSMST indexed file.

If the master record is not found (indicator 88 on), the screen format SCREEN01 is displayed back to the screen. This time, however, indicator 88 is on and thus the error message "MUSIC RECORD NOT FOUND" will appear on line 24. In addition, the error message and the music code field will appear in reverse image. This is because indicator 88 was specified on the D Specifications form under reverse image for both elements.

If the master record is found (N88), the master record is read into the program from the MUSMST file. Then the screen format SCREEN02 is displayed to the WORKSTN file WSFILE.

Subroutine SR220—Screen Format **SCREEN02**

The format SCREEN02 is used to display the music code, music title, artist, type, category, and quantity on hand if the record was found in the MUSMST file. Once the user is finished viewing the information from the music record the Enter key is pressed to allow another selection to be made. When the Enter key is pressed, format SCREEN01 is displayed again so that the user can select another music code to view. If, however, the user is finished and wishes to terminate the program, CMD 7 is pressed to end the job.

Regardless of what condition occurs when the SCNID is evaluated in the CAS/END operation, a screen format record is always displayed to the WORKSTN file WSFILE.

At the end of the DOW/END loop, a READ operation is executed to read the next screen record into the program. If CMD 7 is pressed, 'YES' is moved to #QUIT. If not, processing continues with the DOW/END operation. The DOW/END operation continues to execute as long as #QUIT is not equal to 'YES'.

Terminating a WORKSTN Program

Programs using a WORKSTN file may be terminated in several ways. The easiest way to end a WORKSTN program is to set on the last record indicator (LR) as shown in our example. The user should press a command key (normally CMD

7) to specify end-of-job. The program logic, then, could recognize this command key and terminate the program. Or, release the WORKSTN file when CMD 7 has been pressed. Releasing the WORKSTN causes the file to be treated as though it were at the end-of-file. The WORKSTN may be released by specifying the letter R in column 16 of the output record identification specifications.

CHAPTER SELF-TEST

1. When data is collected and held for later processing, this is a form of _____ processing.

2. When data is entered on a computer not connected to the main CPU and stored for future processing, this is called a(n) _____ operation.

3. With _____ processing, files are accessed and updated immediately thus keeping files up-to-date at all times.

4. Updating files in an interactive environment is called a(n) _____ operation.

5. With _____ processing, every change to the master file is entered and processed as it occurs.

6. When RPG programs are written for interactive applications, the display file is called a _____.

7. _____ are used in interactive processing to signal the user that an entry is required to indicate what is to be done.

8. Screen display formats are normally designed on a _____ first to achieve an effective layout.

9. A _____ on a screen provides a list of options from which a user can select the desired operations to be performed.

10. A program called a _____, such as IBM's _____, can be used by programmers to design and develop display screen formats.

SOLUTIONS

1. batch
2. off-line
3. interactive
4. on-line
5. transaction
6. WORKSTN file
7. Prompts
8. display screen layout sheet
9. menu
10. utility; Screen Design Aid (SDA)

KEY TERMS

Batch processing
Combined file
Cursor
Display Control (S) Specification

Display Screen Layout Sheet
Field Definition (D) Specification
Format load member
Interactive processing

Menu
Off-line operation
On-line processing
Prompt

Source Entry Utility (SEU)
Transaction processing
Utility program
WORKSTN file processing

PRACTICE PROGRAMS

1. Using the problem definition shown in Figure 11.17, write an interactive RPG program to inquire about individual records in the employee master file. The record layout for EMPMST is as follows:

File Name: EMPMST

Key Field: Employee Number

Field Description	Type	Length	Decimal Positions	RPG Name
Employee Number	N	5	0	ENUMB
Employee Name	A	15		ENAME
Employee Salary	N	7	0	ESALRY

Figure 11.17
Problem definition for Practice
Program 1.

Systems Flowchart for Program PR101R
(View employee records)

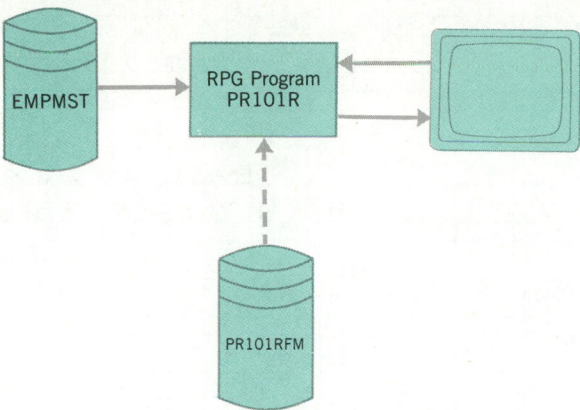

Screen Formats in PR101RFM
—SCREEN01 (prompt user for employee number)
—SCREEN02 (display corresponding employee record)

Screen Formats in SL101RFM

Format SCREEN01 (prompt user for employee number)

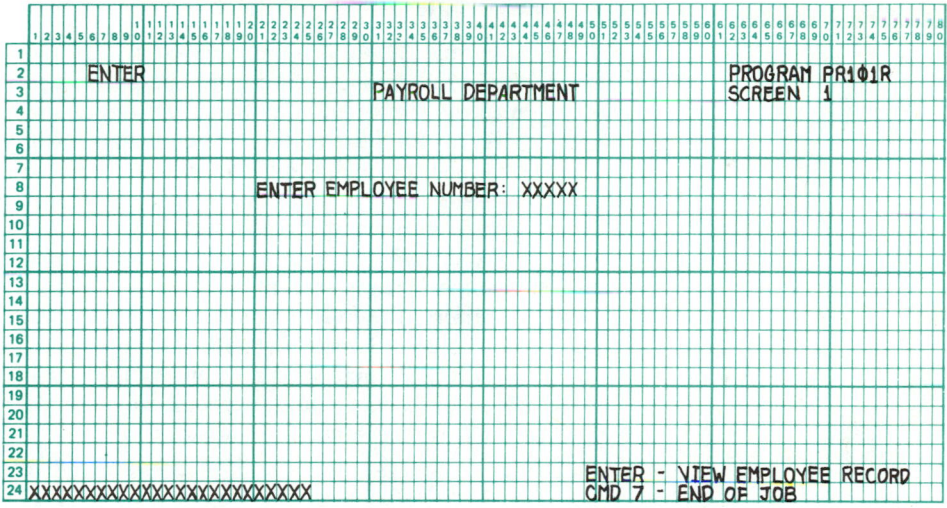

(continued on next page)

Figure 11.17   Format SCREEN02 (view employee record)
(continued)

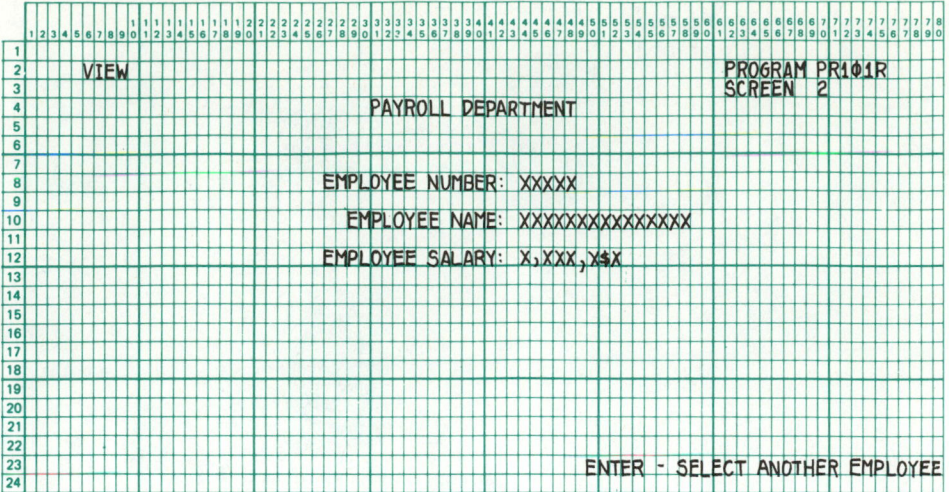

Note: If an employee record is requested that is not found in the employee master
file, display the message "EMPLOYEE RECORD NOT FOUND".

Format SCREEN01 is displayed on the screen to allow the user to enter the
requested employee number. The program reads format SCREEN01 and tries to
read the requested employee record from the EMPMST file.

As noted, if the record is not found, an error message is displayed on the screen
and the user is requested to enter a new employee number. If the requested record
is found in the EMPMST file, format SCREEN02 is displayed showing the information from the employee record.

To terminate the program, the user presses CMD 7 when format SCREEN01 is
displayed on the screen.

Perform the following steps for this assignment:

a. Using the Screen Layout Sheets provided in Figure 11.17, complete the Display
   Screen Format Specifications by transferring the information from the layout
   sheets to the S and D Specifications forms.
b. Create the screen format source member.
c. Compile the screen format source member to generate a screen format load
   member.
d. Generate a skeleton RPG program.
e. Make the necessary changes to the skeleton program that will be required for
   this interactive application.
   Include the necessary error messages that might be required.

2. Using the problem definition shown in Figure 11.18, write an interactive RPG
   program to add new employees to the master employee file. See Practice Program
   1 for the record layout for EMPMST.

Figure 11.18
Problem definition for Practice
Program 2.

Systems Flowchart for Program PR1O2R
(Add employee records)

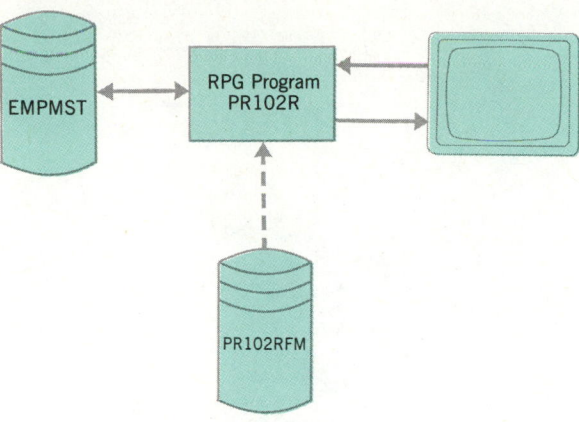

Screen Format in PR1O2RFM
—SCREENO1 (enter new employee record)

Format SCREENO1 (enter new employee record)

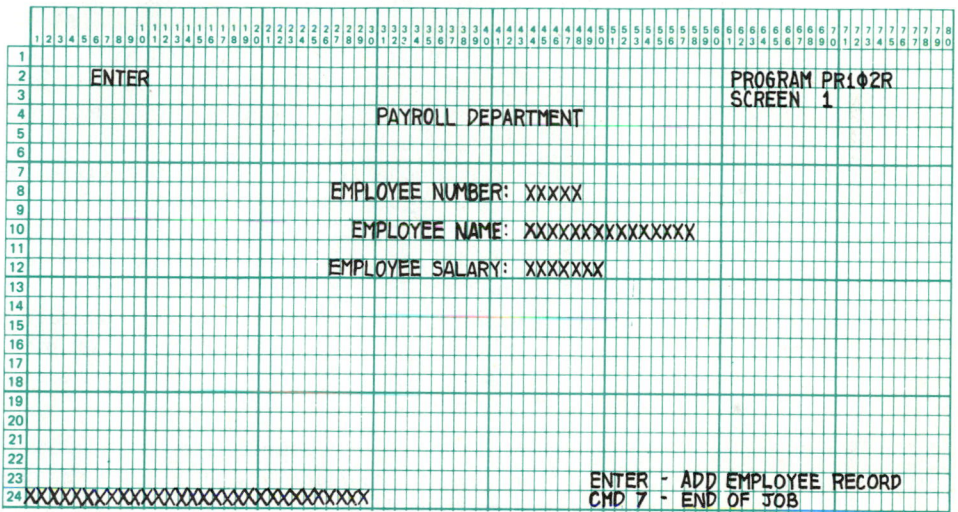

Note: If the user tries to add an employee number that is already on the file,
display the message "EMPLOYEE RECORD ALREADY EXISTS".

Only one format is used in this interactive application. Format SCREEN01 is
used to prompt the user for the data needed to add a new employee to the master
file.

Upon processing format SCREEN01, the program will verify that the employee
number does not already exist in the master file. If the new record is found in the
master file, an error message will be displayed to inform the user that a new
employee is about to be added that already exists on the file.

If the employee number is not found in the employee master file, the new
record is then added. Format SCREEN01 is again displayed in order that another
employee may be added.

The user terminates the program by pressing CMD 7.

3. Using the problem definition shown in Figure 11.19, write an interactive RPG
program to update an employee master file with salary changes. See Practice
Program 1 for the record layout for EMPMST.

Figure 11.19
Problem definition for Practice
Program 3.

Systems Flowchart for Program PR103R
(Update employee records with salary)

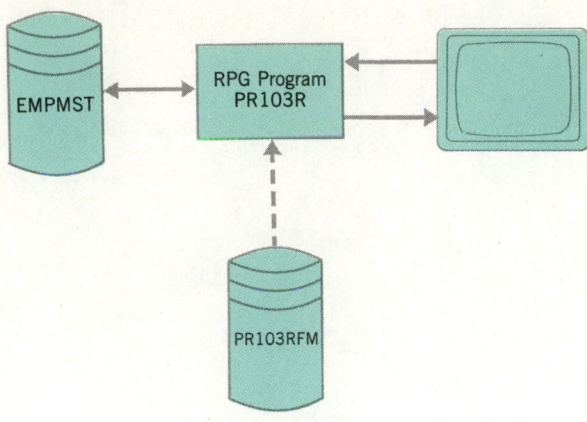

Screen Format in PR103RFM
—SCREEN01 (prompt user for employee record)
—SCREEN02 (enter new salary)

Note: If an employee record is requested that is not found in the employee master file, display the message "EMPLOYEE RECORD NOT FOUND".

Design the two screen formats necessary for this interactive application.

Format SCREEN01 is displayed on the screen to allow the user to enter the requested employee number. The program tries to retrieve the requested employee record from the file.

If the record is not found, an error message is displayed on the screen and the user enters a new employee number. If the employee number is found in the file, format SCREEN02 is displayed showing the information from the employee record. The user would then enter the new salary for the employee and press the Enter key. The program would read format SCREEN02 and update the employee record with the new salary. Once the transaction is completed, format SCREEN01 is displayed so that another employee record can be updated.

To terminate the program, the user presses CMD 7 when format SCREEN01 is displayed on the screen.

4. Using the problem definition shown in Figure 11.20, write an interactive program to perform file maintenance (additions, changes, and deletions) on a master Customer file. The record layout for CSTMST is as follows:

File Name: CSTMST				
Key Field: Customer Number				
Field Description	**Type**	**Length**	**Decimal Positions**	**RPG Name**
Customer Number	N	5	0	CCNUMB
Customer Name	A	15	0	CCNAME
Credit Rating	N	1	0	CCREDIT
Date of Last Purchase	N	6	0	CLPDTE
Year-to-Date Sales	N	11	2	CYTDSL
Outstanding Balance	N	9	2	CBAL

For this assignment, complete all phases for the creation of the display screen formats.

Figure 11.20
Problem definition for Practice
Program 4.

Systems Flowchart for Program SL104R
(File Maintenance for Customer master)

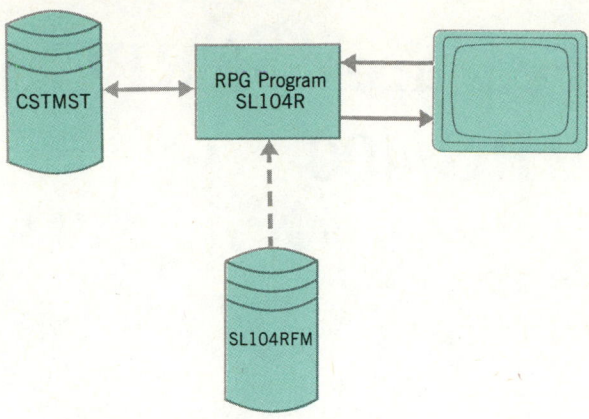

Screen Format in SL104RFM
—SCREEN01 (prompt user for customer number and action code)
—SCREEN02 (view customer record)
—SCREEN03 (enter new customer record)

12

Features of RPG III and RPG/400

OBJECTIVES

To familiarize you with

1. The concept of Full Procedural files, which do not rely on the RPG Fixed Logic Cycle for records to be accessed.
2. How externally described files can be used in RPG III and RPG/400 programs.
3. New operations that are unique to RPG III and RPG/400.
4. How to communicate with a computer in an interactive mode using workstation devices.

I. Full Procedural Files

In early versions of RPG, file processing was always performed under direct control of the RPG Fixed Logic Cycle. In more recent years however, another approach, using **Full Procedural files,** is being used. When a file is specified as a Full Procedural file, it is accessed in the Calculation Specifications by programmer-specified operations such as the READ and CHAIN operations. The RPG Fixed Logic Cycle, then, is not responsible for accessing files defined as Full Procedural files. Both RPG III and RPG/400 support Full Procedural files. (RPG/400 is RPG for the IBM AS/400 computer.)

Full procedural files do not rely on the RPG Fixed Logic Cycle for records to be accessed. Instead, operations are specified in the Calculation Specifications, which are executed under the direction of the programmer, who controls when records are read from and written to the file.

Full Procedural file processing is now optional with RPG II compilers on the System/36 and can be used in place of Chained and Demand files. For RPG III and RPG/400 however, column 16 entries of C (chained) or D (demand) on the File Description Specifications are not permitted. For these types of processing, Full Procedural files must be specified. All operations discussed in earlier chapters that used Chained and Demand files can, however, also be used with Full Procedural files.

When using Full Procedural files, control break indicators (L1–L9) cannot be used because file processing is executed in the Calculation Specifications under the programmer's control, whereas control break indicators are maintained with primary files under control of the RPG Fixed Logic Cycle.

The illustration below shows how an indexed customer master file called CUSTMST could be specified as a Full Procedural file. The letter F in column 16 of the File Description Specifications denotes the file as a Full Procedural file. The letter U (update) in column 15 indicates that the file will be both an input and output file. In order for this file to be processed, programmer-specified operations such as CHAIN and EXCPT would have to be used in the Calculation Specifications.

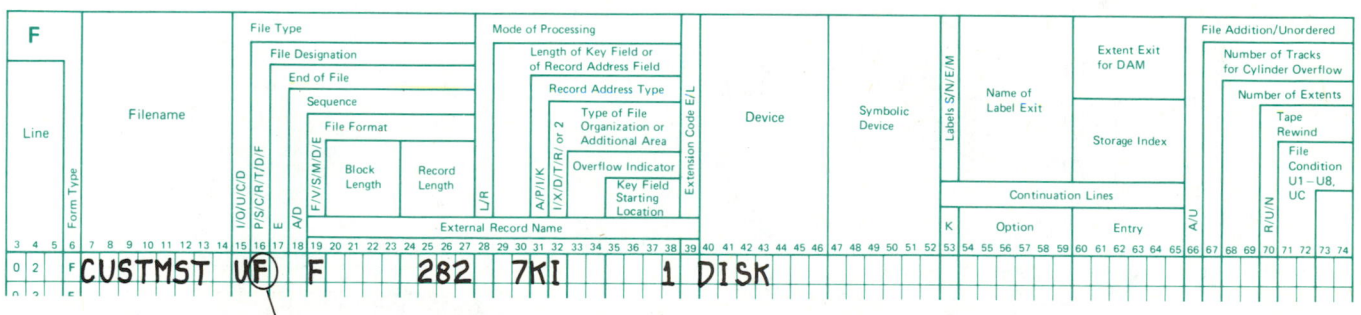

Designates the file as a Full Procedural file

Specifies that all I/O is controlled by operations in Calculation Specifications

II. Externally Described Files

One major innovation in information processing in recent years is the design of a single, integrated, centralized **database** for all data stored, manipulated, or used by an organization. Traditionally, each unit or department within an organization had its own unique files. Several files would normally be accessed in order to provide the necessary data required by a program. An integrated database, however, requires a *single* storage medium containing data accessible by *all* subsystems. In this way, data does not need to be redefined or duplicated by each system or program that requires it. It can be stored as a single database and accessed as needed.

Files defined within an RPG program are referred to as *program-described files.* This means that both the File Description and Input Specifications are described internally within the program. Both RPG III and RPG/400, however, enable the programmer to use record descriptions for a file or database that is external to the RPG program. A file described in this manner is referred to as **an externally described file.** In this way, a file used by many programs within a system is described only once; it need not be described by each user program that accesses it.

Using externally described files makes it easier for a programmer to code programs. It helps standardize the system by defining a file with a *single* set of data descriptions that are used by all programmers. It also makes it easier to modify a file or database; the changes required need to be made *only once.* Thus, if the format of the file changes, the description of the externally described file is changed and the RPG code need not be modified at all.

A. Data Description Specifications (DDS)

To define an externally described file, we use a specification form called Data Description Specifications or DDS as shown in Figure 12.1.

The description of the records in an externally described file is called a record format. In the following discussion, the numbers in brackets ([]) refer to

Figure 12.1
The Data Description
Specifications form.

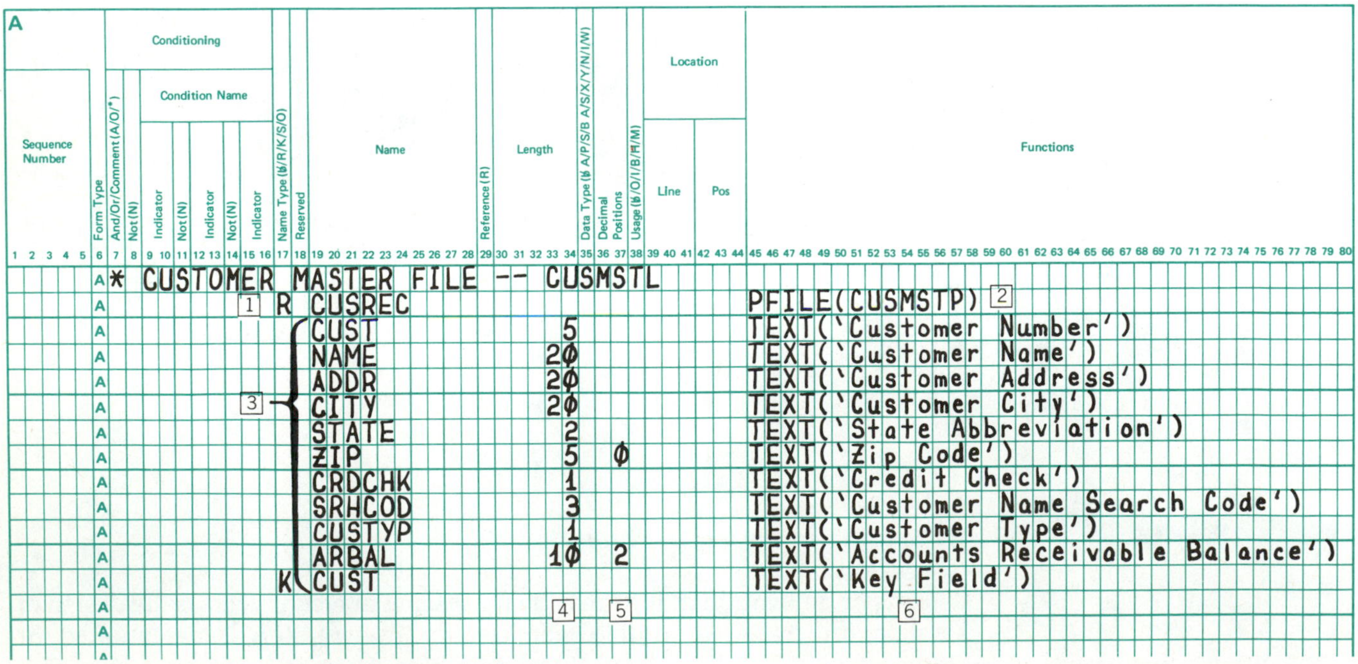

specific elements in Figure 12.1. The record format is identified by a unique name and by an R in column 17 [1]. The PFILE keyword identifies the physical file CUSMST that contains the data to be used by this file [2]. The record format contains the field names [3], the field lengths [4], and other field attributes (such as decimal positions, which indicates whether the field is alphanumeric or numeric). An entry in the decimal positions columns [5] indicates a numeric field. As in RPG II, if these columns are blank, the field is assumed to be alphanumeric. The TEXT keyword and the description in columns 45–80 [6] identify the contents of the field.

B. Using Externally Described Files

Figure 12.2 is a schematic of how processing is performed using externally described files. The programmer enters the source DDS into the system and uses control language commands to compile the DDS in order to create a file object, usually referred to as a file. After the file is created, data is entered into the system and stored in the file; that data can then be accessed by the program that uses the file. Thus, the file and its description are stored in the system's database, external to any application program and can be used by application programs (see Figure 12.2b). The RPG program references the externally described file by the name that is assigned to the Data Description Specifications or by a record format name assigned on the DDS. When the RPG program is compiled, the external description of the file is retrieved from the system and

Figure 12.2
Schematic of how externally
described files can be
(a) created and (b) referenced.

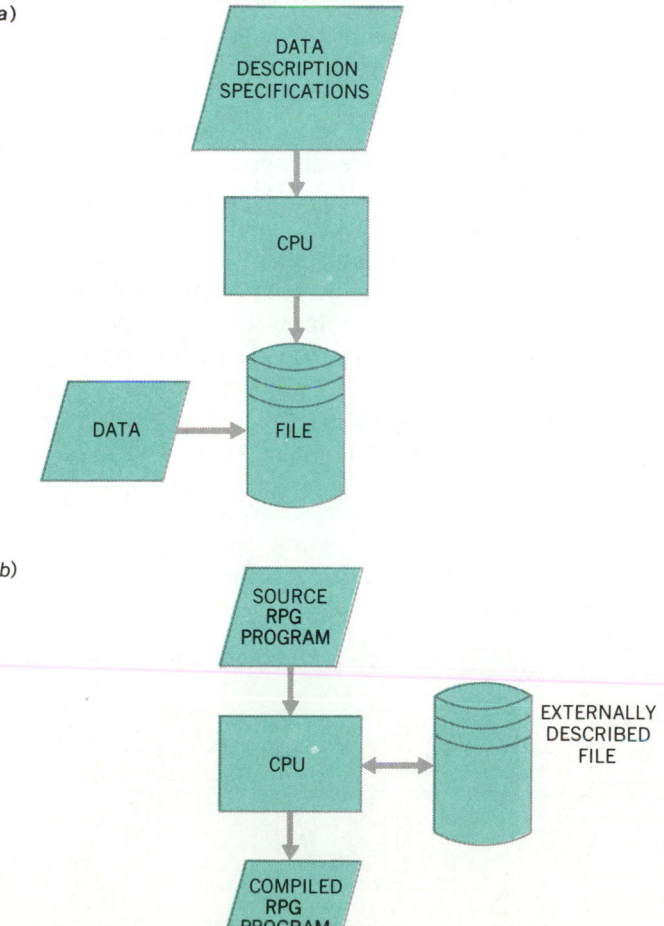

included in the compiled RPG program. Because the fields are defined in the Data Description Specifications, Input Specifications are not required in the RPG program to further define the file. Input Specifications can be used in the RPG program to modify the external DDS.

C. Sample Program

The purpose of this program is to print a list of the records read from an externally described file called DETORDL (detail orders). The output file, which is a program-described print file, is named REPORT. No calculations are performed on the data in the input records. Only the fields QTYORD, ITEM, DESCRP, and EXTENS are to be printed in the detail output record.

To write the specifications for this program, you will need to do the following:

1. Refer to the description of the externally described file DETORDL so you can use the correct field names and field lengths in describing the output REPORT file.
2. Refer to the format of the printed report specified by a Printer Spacing Chart (see Figure 12.3).
3. Code the File Description Specifications.

1. Externally Described Files

The description of the externally described file (DETORDL), which was created by Data Description Specifications (DDS), is stored in the system independently of any program.

The Data Description Specifications that were used to define the DETORDL file are shown in Figure 12.4. The external description of the DETORDL file includes [1] the record format name (which is identified by the R in column 17), [2] the name of each field in the record, [3] the length of each field, and [4] the number of decimal positions in numeric fields. If no entry is made for decimal positions, the field is assumed to be alphanumeric. The TEXT descriptions in columns 45–80 further describe the fields. The PFILE keyword identifies the physical file DETORDP that contains the data to be used by this file. When the RPG program is compiled, the compiler retrieves this description of the DETORDL file and includes it in the program.

2. File Description Specifications

In this sample program, there is one input file (DETORDL) and one output file (REPORT). The File Description Specifications are shown in Figure 12.5.

Figure 12.3
Printer Spacing Chart for the
Sample Program.

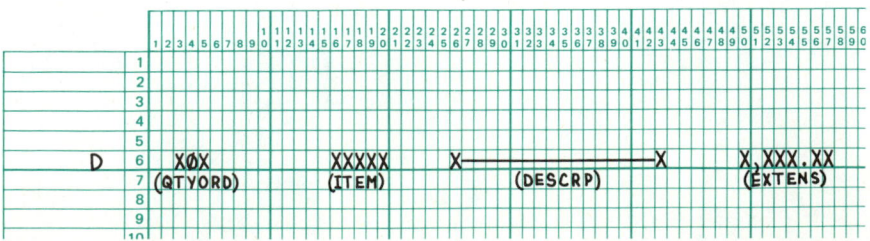

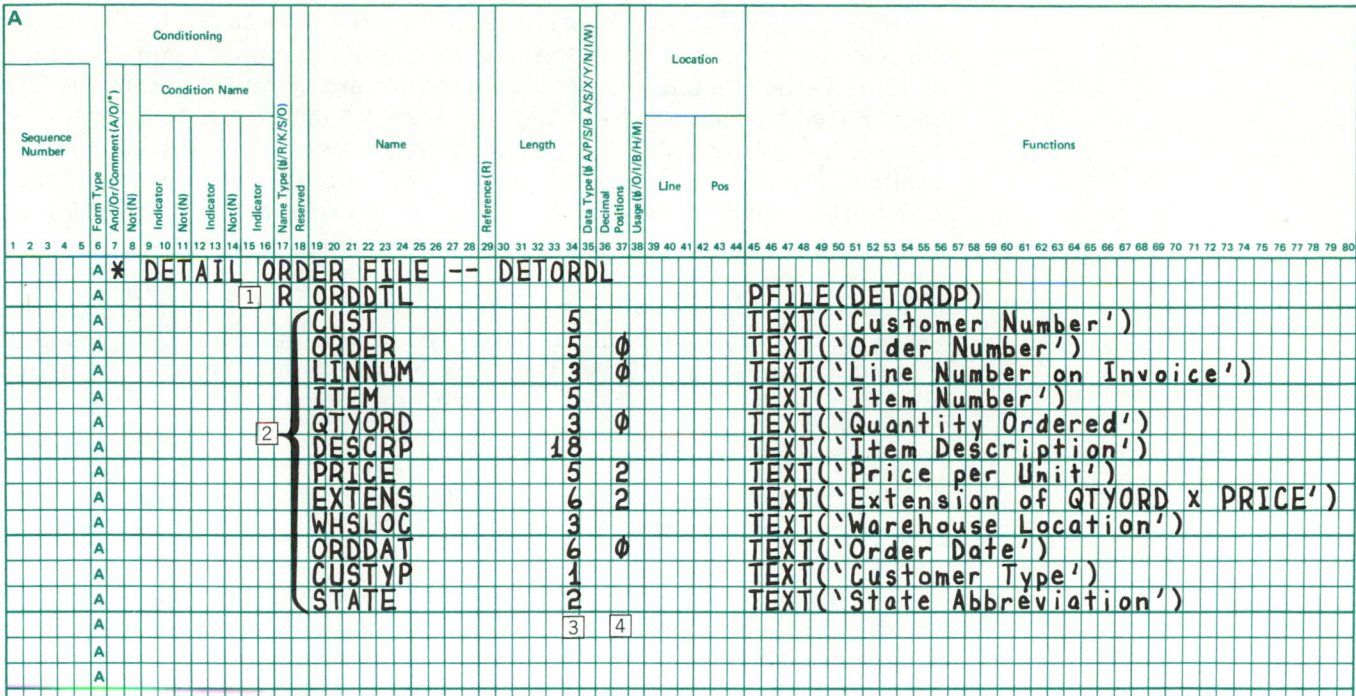

Figure 12.4
Data Description Specifications for the Sample Program.

The specifications on line 02 describe the input file DETORDL. Columns 7–14 contain the name of the file. The I in column 15 identifies the file as an input file and the F in column 16 identifies it as a Full Procedural file. The device associated with the file is DISK (columns 40–46). Because the file is an externally described file, column 19 contains the letter E, which tells the compiler to retrieve the description of the file from the system.

The specifications on line 03 describe the output file REPORT. Columns 7–14 contain the name of the file. The letter O in column 15 identifies the file as

Figure 12.5
File Description Specifications for the Sample Program.

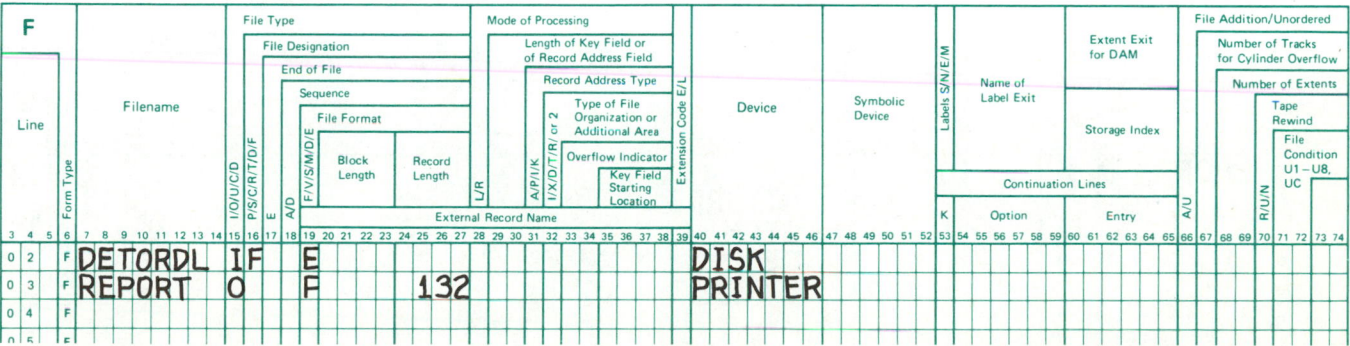

an output file. The device associated with the file is PRINTER (columns 40–46). Because the file is a *program-described file*, column 19 contains an F, which tells the compiler that the file's records are described within the program. For a program-described file, the record length must be specified in columns 24–27, and the entry must be right-justified. The record length specified for a printer file can be the actual length of the output record (which is 57 in this program), or it can be the length of the print line (which is 132). The length of the print line is used in this example.

3. Output Specifications

Just as data files are defined on the System/38 and AS/400 using DDS, report or printer files can also be defined using DDS. In our example, however, we define our output report specifications as a traditional program-described file.

The Output Specifications for this program are shown in Figure 12.6. Line 01 (called a record specification line) contains the name of the output file (REPORT) in columns 7–14, and it identifies the line to be printed as a detail line, which is indicated by a D in column 15. The fields are defined on lines 02 through 05.

Note that the 1 in column 17 causes the printer to space one line before printing. The N1P entry in columns 23–25 conditions the line so it is not printed on the first program cycle, and the Z and 2 entries in column 38 edit the QTYORD and EXTENS fields, respectively.

III. RPG III and RPG/400 Operations

With the introduction of RPG III and RPG/400 has come a number of new operation codes that can be specified on the Calculation Specifications. These new operations are unique to RPG III on the System/38 and RPG/400 on the AS/400. In the following section we introduce each new operation code, include an illustrative example for each operation, and summarize how each operation is used.

A. CALL (Call a Program) Operation

Recall that structured programs should consist of a series of independent modules that are executed from the main module.

Figure 12.6
Output Specifications for the Sample Program.

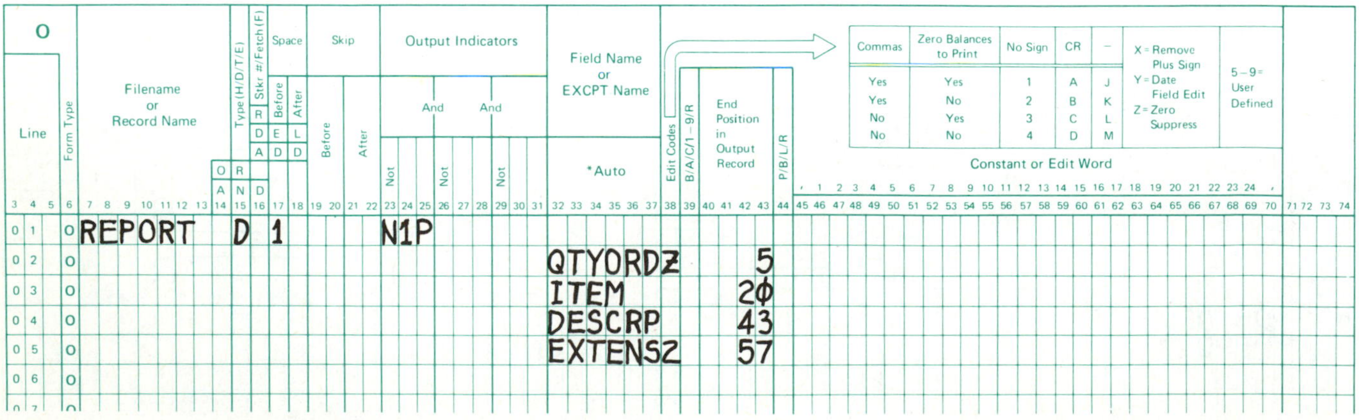

When programs are properly structured each module may be written, compiled, and perhaps even tested independently. Also, the modules may be written in different stages, in a top-down manner. They may even be coded by different programmers. Then, if a specfic module needs to be modified, the entire logical flow should still function properly without the need for extensive revision to other parts of the program.

In our study of modular programming in Chapter 5, we pointed out that modules within a program can be viewed as subroutines that are called or executed from the main module using the EXSR (Execute Subroutine) operation. But a program may also CALL or reference independent **subprograms** or **external subroutines** stored in a library that are *entirely separate* from the main program itself. The main program that references or calls a subprogram is referred to as the **calling program.** The subprogram that is linked and executed within the main program is referred to as the **called program.**

The called program would need to be compiled, debugged, and catalogued (stored) in a library so that it may be accessed when needed. Typical subgroups that may be used by numerous calling programs include edit routines, error control checks, and standard calculations.

The technique of enabling a main program to call a subprogram has some advantages. For example, subprograms avoid duplication of effort. When specific modules need to be included in more than one program, it is best to write them separately and call them into each program. A second advantage of subprograms is that they improve programmer productivity. When common routines are written and stored as subprograms, programmers need not recode them again for each program that requires them. And finally, subprograms provide greater flexibility. Changes to called programs can be made without the need to modify the calling programs.

Since a subprogram is really an independent module that is external to the main program, it may be called in just as one would use an EXSR operation to execute an internal module.

The following is the format for the CALL operation:

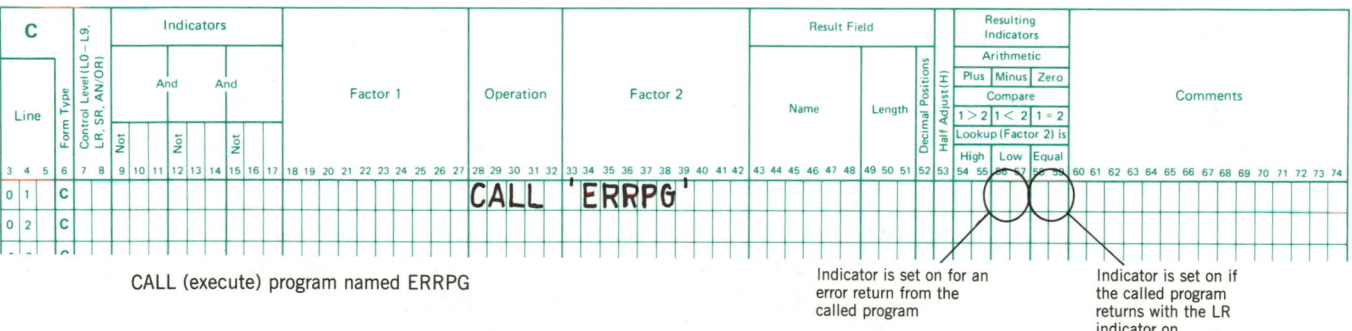

CALL (execute) program named ERRPG

Indicator is set on for an error return from the called program

Indicator is set on if the called program returns with the LR indicator on

The **CALL operation** transfers control from the program currently being executed to the program specified in Factor 2 (ERRPG in the preceding). When the called program is completed, control returns to the calling program, which commences with the operation following the CALL.

CALL OPERATION

1. Factor 2 contains the name of the program to be called. The called program may be specified as a data field, a literal, or an array element in Factor 2. When used, a data field or array element cannot

exceed 21 characters. A literal, which must be enclosed in quotation marks, cannot exceed 8 characters.

2. Factor 2 must contain a character entry.

3. An indicator may be specified in columns 56–57. The indicator is set on when an error occurs in the called program.

4. An indicator may be specified in columns 58–59 if the called program is an RPG program. This indicator will be set on if the called program returns with the LR indicator on.

5. A parameter list (PLIST) may be used to transmit values between the calling program and the called program. Parameter lists will not be covered in this text.

Factor 2 may also contain the library name in which the called program is located. The method for specifying the program and library names differs slightly between the S/38 and the AS/400 as shown below:

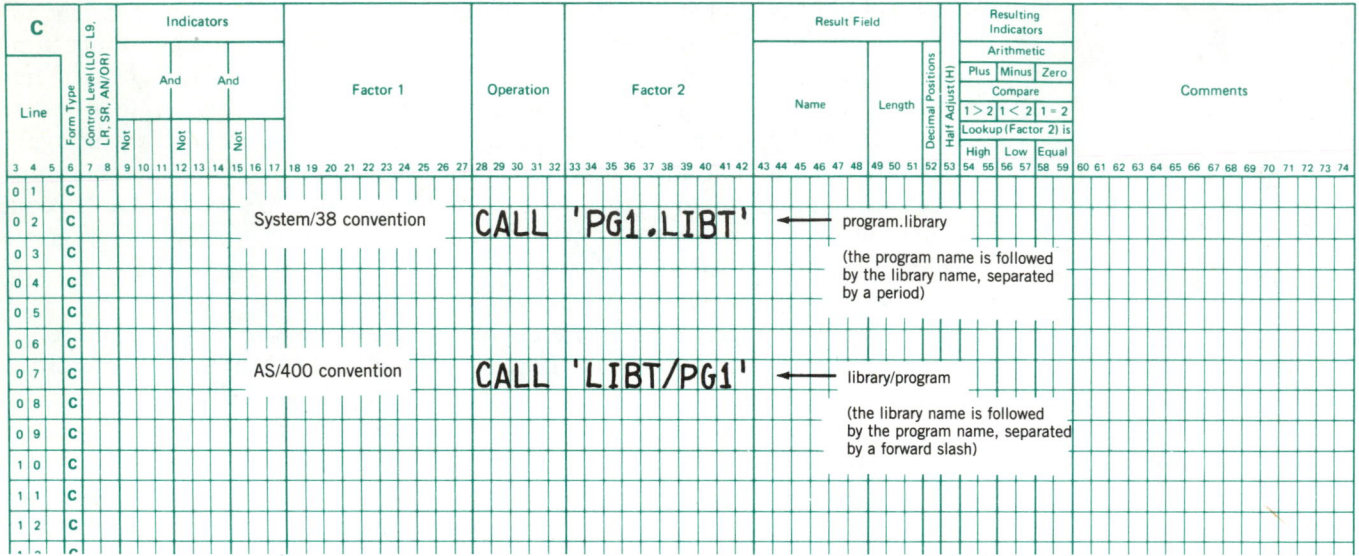

Note that the CALL may be used with some versions of RPG II as well.

B. CLOSE (Close a File) Operation

For some programs, all specified files may not need to be open at the same time. When this situation occurs, files can be released from the program by issuing the **CLOSE operation** as shown below:

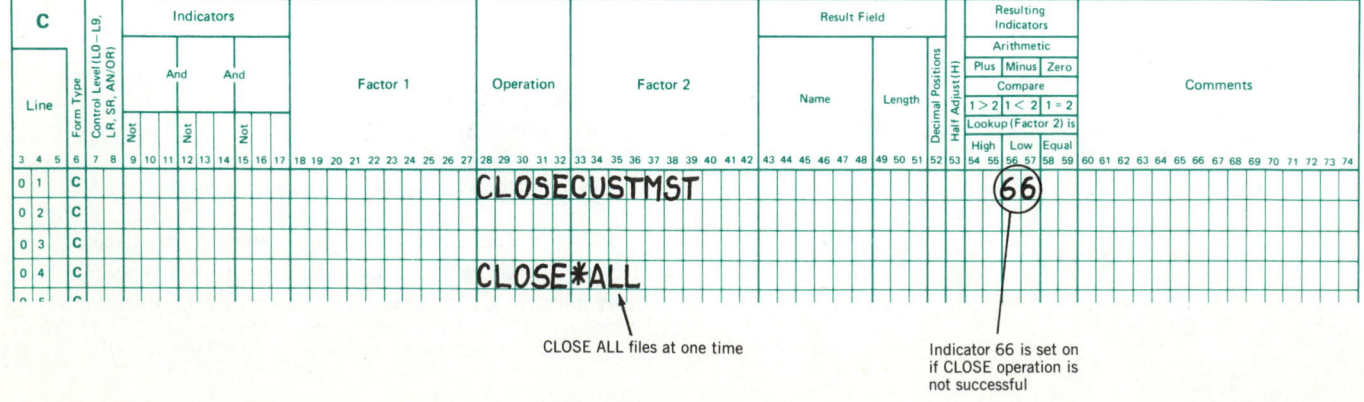

CLOSE OPERATION

1. The CLOSE operation closes and releases a file from the program and deactivates the devices assigned to the file.
2. Factor 2 must contain the name of the file to be closed.
3. The keyword *ALL can be specified in Factor 2 to close all files in the program at once.
4. A program may contain more than one CLOSE operation for a file.
5. If a CLOSE operation is executed for a file that is already closed, the operation is ignored.
6. An indicator may be specified in columns 56–57. This indicator is set on if the CLOSE operation is not successful.

C. DELET (Delete a Record) Operation

The **DELET operation,** shown below, deletes a record from a file. This operation can be used only with a file specified as an update file (letter U in column 15 of the File Description Specifications).

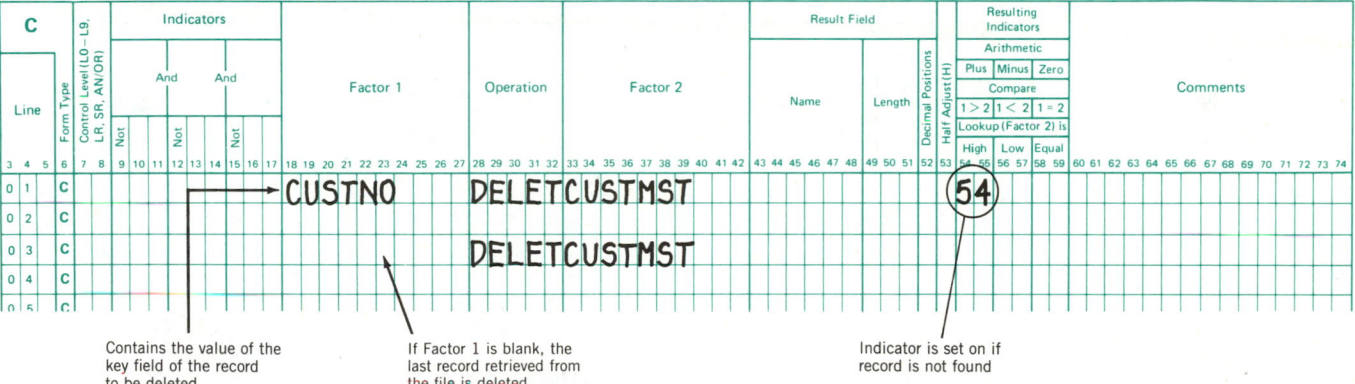

Contains the value of the key field of the record to be deleted

If Factor 1 is blank, the last record retrieved from the file is deleted

Indicator is set on if record is not found

The DELET operation is similar to the DEL operation discussed in Chapter 9 (Indexed Files). With both operations the record is not physically removed from the file. Instead, the system replaces each byte of the record with Hex F's (all bits on) and makes the record no longer accessible to any program. Therefore, once a record has been deleted with the DELET operation it can never be retrieved.

DELET OPERATION

1. The DELET operation deletes a record from a file specified as an update file. The system replaces each byte of the record with Hex F's making the record no longer accessible.
2. The DELET operation deletes a record by specifying the key value or relative record number. In addition, the DELET operation can be used to delete the last record read from an update file.
3. Factor 1 contains the value of the key field or relative record number of the record to be deleted. If Factor 1 is blank, the DELET operation deletes the last record retrieved from the file.
4. Factor 2 can contain one of two entries. For files defined within the program (program described files) Factor 2 must contain the name of the update file containing the record to be deleted. For externally

defined files, Factor 2 can be either the name of the file or the name of the file's record format whose record will be deleted.

5. An indicator may be specified in columns 54–55. This indicator is set on if the record specified in Factor 1 is not found.

6. An indicator may be specified in columns 56–57. This indicator is set on if the DELET operation fails.

D. EXFMT (Execute Format) Operation

The **EXFMT operation** used with WORKSTN files performs a combined WRITE followed by a READ operation to a workstation file. This operation combines two other operations that were discussed earlier in the text; the EXCPT and READ operations. Whereas the EXCPT can be used to perform an output operation followed by a READ operation, the EXFMT can be used to combine both. The EXFMT causes a screen format to be displayed on the screen, waits for the Enter key or a valid command key to be pressed, and then reads the format from the screen. Thus, the processing of the program pauses during the EXFMT operation while the program waits for the user to respond to the format displayed on the screen:

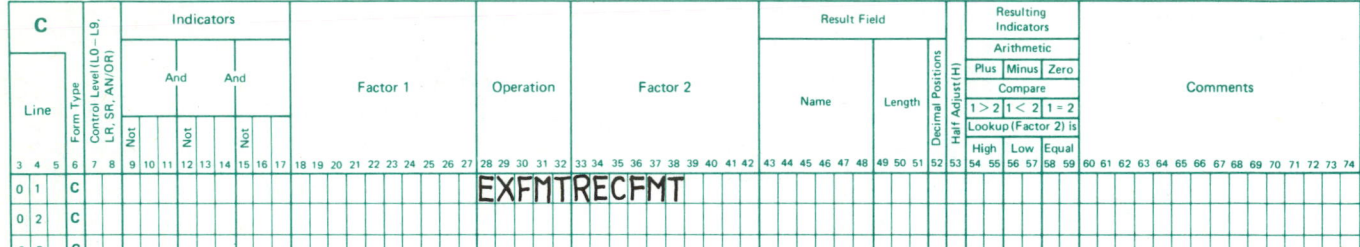

EXFMT OPERATION

1. The EXFMT performs a WRITE followed by a READ to a WORKSTN file.

2. Factor 2 must contain the name of the record format that is written to and read from the WORKSTN file.

3. The EXFMT operation can be used only with a WORKSTN file defined as a combined (C in column 15 of the File Description Specifications) Full Procedural file (F in column 16 of the File Description Specifications) that is described as an externally described file (E in column 19 of the File Description Specifications).

4. An optional indicator may be specified in columns 56–57. When specified, this indicator will be set on if the EXFMT operation is unsuccessful.

E. OPEN (Open a File) Operation

The **OPEN operation,** which is initiated by the programmer, opens a file for processing. The file is not under control of the RPG Fixed Logic Cycle. The file must be specified as a Full Procedural file (F in column 15 of the File Description Specifications):

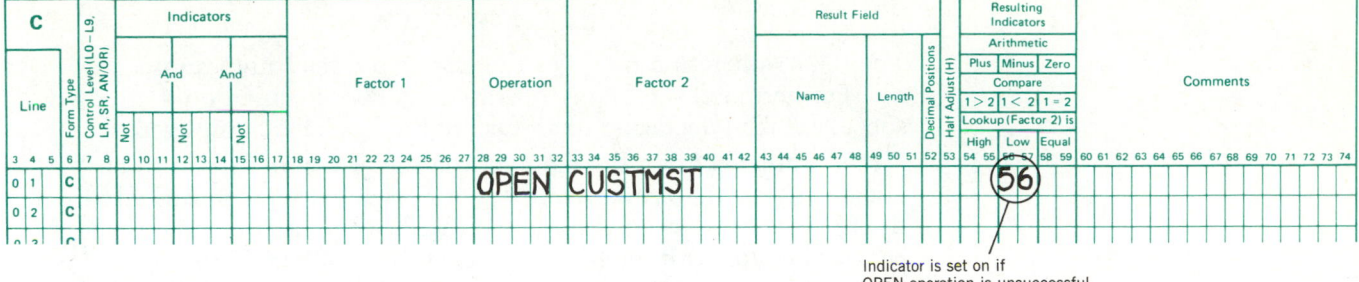

Indicator is set on if
OPEN operation is unsuccessful

OPEN OPERATION

1. The OPEN operation opens the file specified in Factor 2 and makes it available for processing.
2. The file must be defined as a Full Procedural file by specifying the letter F in column 15 of the File Description Specifications.
3. Factor 2 contains the name of the file being opened.
4. An indicator may be specified in columns 56–57. The indicator will be set on if the OPEN operation is unsuccessful.
5. If an OPEN operation is executed for a file opened previously, an error will occur.

File Description Specification entries in columns 71–72 affect the execution of the OPEN operation. The following rules apply:

1. The letters UC (User Control) in columns 71–72 of the File Description Specifications for the file determine how the file will be opened. If the file is to be opened for the first time by the programmer specifying an OPEN operation, the File Description Specifications for the file must contain the letters UC in columns 71–72.
2. If columns 71–72 are blank, the file will be opened during the initialization stage of the RPG Fixed Logic Cycle.

F. UPDAT (Modify Existing Record) Operation

The **UPDAT operation** modifies or changes the last record read from an update file (U in column 15 of the File Description Specifications):

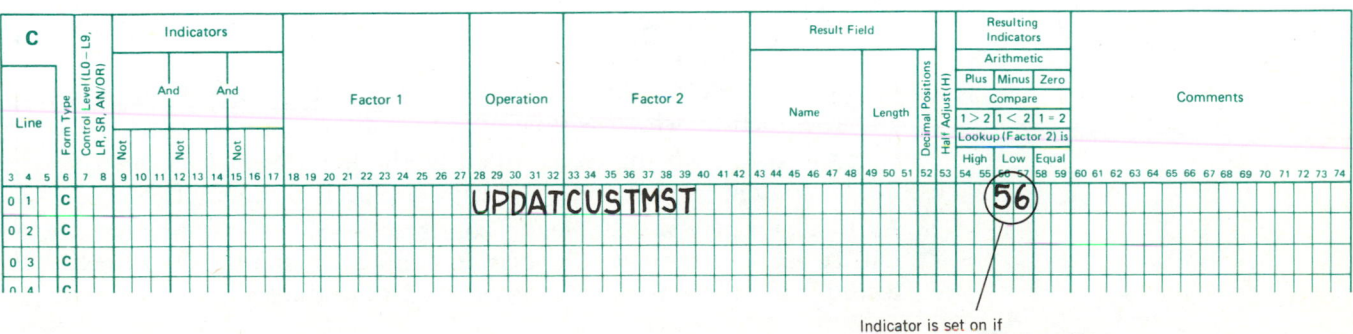

Indicator is set on if
UPDAT operation is unsuccessful

UPDAT OPERATION

1. The UPDAT operation modifies the last record read from an update file. Furthermore, the UPDAT operation can be executed only after a successful read operation of an update file has been completed.

2. Factor 2 must contain the name of the file or record format to be updated. A record format name may be specified in Factor 2 only if the file is defined as an externally described file. A file name may be specified for both program-described files and externally described files.

3. The Result Field must contain a Data Structure name if a file name is specified in Factor 2. The program will update the file directly from the Data Structure specified in the Result Field. If Factor 2 contains a record format name, the Result Field must be blank.

4. An indicator may be specified in columns 56–57. This indicator will be set on if the UPDAT operation cannot be completed successfully.

G. WRITE (Create New Record) Operation

The WRITE operation writes a new record to a file:

C		Indicators			Factor 1	Operation	Factor 2	Result Field			Resulting Indicators	Comments

(RPG coding form showing on line 01, columns 28–42: `WRITECUSTREC`)

WRITE OPERATION

1. The WRITE operation writes a new record to a file.

2. Factor 2 is required and must contain:
   a. a *filename* if the WRITE operation is writing to a program-defined file.
   b. a *record format name* if the WRITE operation is writing to an externally defined file.

3. For program-defined files, the Result Field must contain the name of a Data Structure, which will be used to add the record to the file.

4. When records are being *added* to a file, the letter A must be specified in column 66 of the File Description Specifications for the file.

5. An indicator may be specified in columns 56–57. This indicator will be set on if the WRITE operation is not successful (e.g., if the record being added to the file already exists in the file).

H. The *IN Array for Referencing Indicators as Data Fields

The RPG general-purpose indicators 01 through 99 can be referenced and manipulated in the same manner as data fields. This is an alternative method provided with RPG III and RPG/400 to verify the condition of an indicator. When indicators must be referenced, the reserved words *IN and *INxx may be used.

1. The *IN Array

*IN is a predefined array of one-byte elements. This array consists of 99 one-byte elements representing the RPG general-purpose indicators 01 through 99. Each element, which represents the appropriate indicator, can contain only the character values 0 (zero) or 1 (one). A value of zero in an element (indicator) indicates that the associated indicator is *off*. A value of one indicates that the associated indicator is *on*. Elements in the predefined array *IN can be referenced using the data fields *IN,01 through *IN,99.

2. The *INxx Data Field

*INxx represents a one-byte character data field, where xx represents one of the RPG general-purpose indicators 01 through 99.

The field *INxx can be specified and used in the same manner as any character field except that *INxx cannot be specified as a subfield in a Data Structure or in a SORTA operation.

The following examples illustrate the use of the *INxx data field:

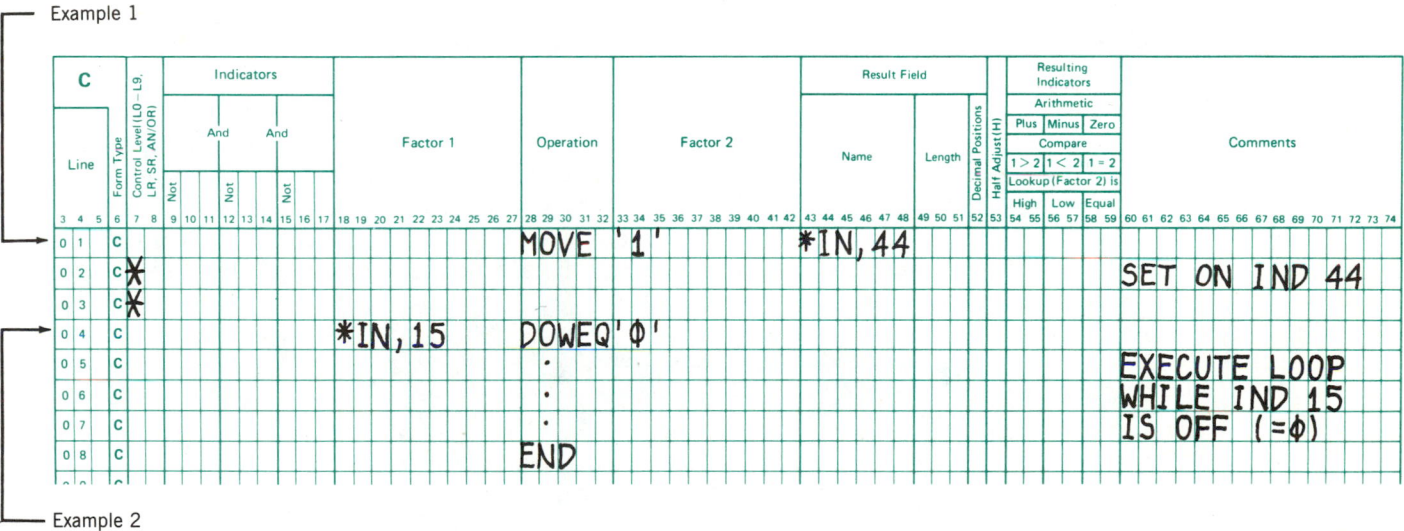

Example 1

Example 2

In Example 1, the MOVE operation moves the value '1' to element 44 of the *IN array. The result is that indicator 44 has been set on (value = 1).

In Example two, element 15 (indicator 15) of the *IN array is used to control the execution of the DOWhile/END operation. The DOW/END operation will continue to execute as long as indicator 15 is off (value = 0). For the DOW/END operation to terminate, indicator 15 must be set on (value = 1) *inside* the DOW/END loop.

I. The *ALL'x' Figurative Constant

RPG III and AS/400 support the use of the *ALL'x' figurative constant. *ALL'x' produces a repetitive string consisting of a pattern of characters or numbers. The data specified within the apostrophes ('x') represents the pattern or string of data that will be repeated in the receiving field specified as the Result Field.

When the receiving field is a numeric field, the data string within the apostrophes must be numeric.

The following example illustrates the use of the *ALL'x' operation:

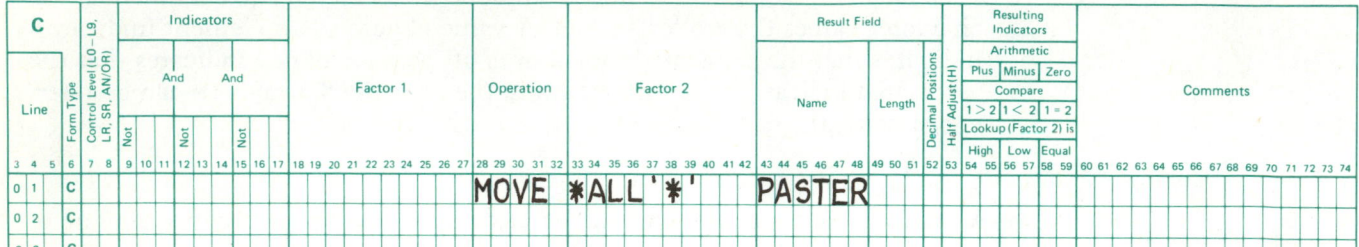

In this example a repetitive string of asterisks is moved to the field PASTER. The result is that the field PASTER will contain an asterisk in every byte.

IV. Processing Inquiries or Data from an Interactive Workstation

With workstation devices, the user communicates with the computer in an interactive mode. The program displays a prompt, which is a message requesting the user to enter some data. The user must then respond to the prompt. Subsequent processing by the program depends on the user's response. The following display shows a prompt for a customer number and also the command key list as a prompt to tell the user which command keys may be used:

The program prompts the user for a customer number. If the user enters a customer number, the program proceeds. If, instead, the user responds to the prompts by pressing command key 3 (CF3), the program will terminate.

Command keys may be specified in the DDS using the CFxx (Command Function) or CAxx (Command Attention) keywords. We will discuss command keys later.

With RPG III and RPG/400, Data Description Specifications are used to create the external descriptions to a workstation file (defined as WORKSTN). To retrieve the description of the WORKSTN file that has already been defined, the specifications shown here are used:

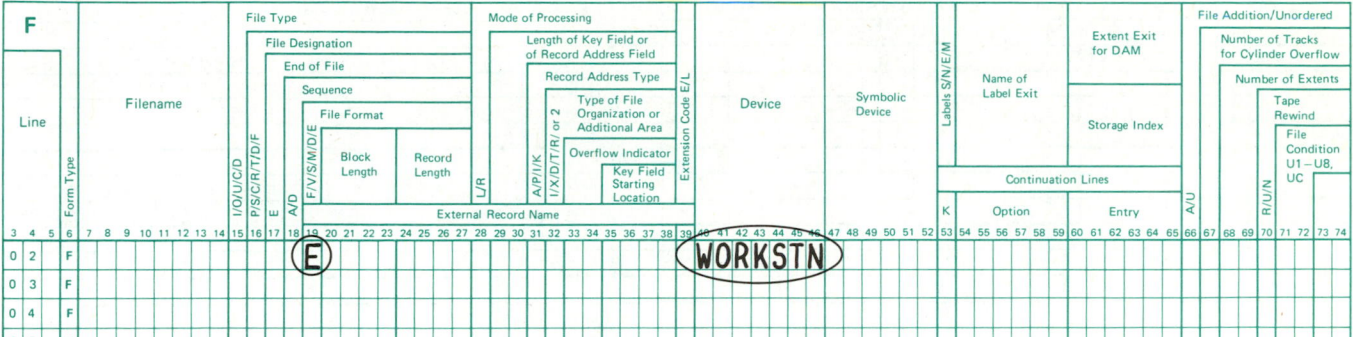

WORKSTN entries, then, may be used to:

1. Inquire about the status of records in a file.
2. Update records on a file.

The format for the WORKSTN entries can be defined on the Data Description Specifications external to the program. See Figure 12.7 for entries that would be used in an update procedure.

The Data Description Specifications for this display file, which is named CUSUPD (customer update), includes the following information:

[1] The name of each record format in the file. In Figure 12.7, there are two record formats: CUSRQST and CUSMAIN.

[2] Association of command key 3 (CF3) with indicator 15. When the user presses CF3, indicator 15 is set on in the RPG program.

 As with RPG II, the command keys 1 to 24 are associated with the RPG indicators KA through KY. Thus, if CF03 is specified in the DDS, it is associated with indicator KC in the RPG program.

 With RPG III and RPG/400, however, another method for assigning indicators is available. If, for example, command key 3 is specified as CF03(15) in the DDS, indicators KC and 15 are both set on when CF03 is pressed. Thus, indicator 15 is associated with the Command Function key 03 and can be used by itself or as *IN,15 to control operations in the program.

[3] For each record format, constants are defined that are to appear on the screen as prompts for the user and as informational messages. The constant 'CUSTOMER MASTER UPDATE' identifies the purpose of this display. The constant 'CUSTOMER NUMBER' is the prompt for the user to enter a customer number. The constant 'USE CF3 TO END THIS PROGRAM' tells the user how to end the program.

[4] CUST is the name of the input field into which the user enters a customer number in response to the prompt 'CUSTOMER NUMBER'. The input field is five characters long and is identified as an input field by the letter I in column 38. If a field is identified as an input field, the user can enter information into that field.

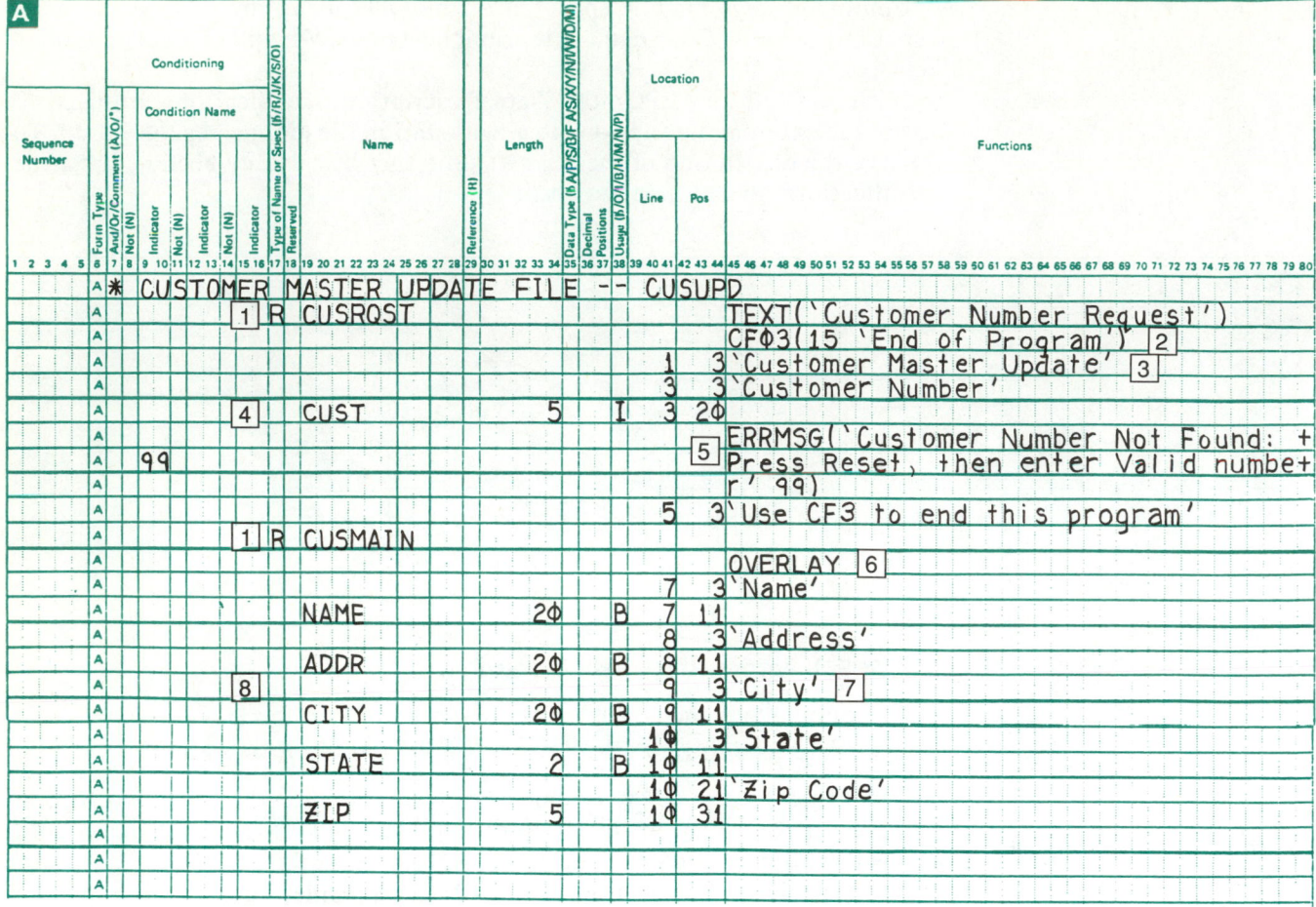

Figure 12.7
WORKSTN entries for an update procedure.

[5] The ERRMSG keyword identifies an error message. This message appears on the display only if indicator 99 is set on in the RPG program.

[6] The OVERLAY keyword indicates that the CUSMAIN record overlays the CUSRQST record. Because of the OVERLAY keyword, both records appear on the display at the same time. If OVERLAY is not specified, the CUSRQST record is erased when the CUSMAIN record is written to the display.

[7] These constants identify the fields that are written to the display when the CUSRQST and CUSMAIN records are displayed. The user cannot change these constants when the program is executing.

[8] Data fields, which include CUST, NAME, ADDR, CITY, STATE, and ZIP are written to the display from the program. The lengths of the fields are specified in columns 30–34. The B in column 38 identifies each field as both an input field and an output field (an input/output field). Data is written to the display from the program, and the user can change this data before the fields are read back into the program.

The CUSRQST record format defines the following display, which is the first record written to the display by the program. This record prompts the user to enter a customer number. The message 'CUSTOMER NUMBER NOT FOUND' is written to the display only if indicator 99 is set on by the program.

```
CUSTOMER MASTER UPDATE
CUSTOMER NUMBER _____
USE CF3 TO END THIS PROGRAM




CUSTOMER NUMBER NOT FOUND: PRESS RESET, THEN ENTER VALID NUMBER
```

The CUSMAIN record format defines the following display. Because the OVERLAY keyword is specified for the CUSMAIN record, the CUSRQST record remains on the display. The NAME, ADDR, CITY, and STATE fields are defined as output/input fields, which means that data is written to these fields from the program and that data can be changed by the user before it is read back into the program.

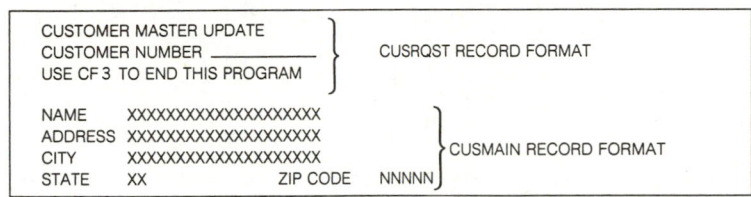

```
CUSTOMER MASTER UPDATE
CUSTOMER NUMBER _____ }  CUSRQST RECORD FORMAT
USE CF3 TO END THIS PROGRAM

NAME     XXXXXXXXXXXXXXXXXX
ADDRESS  XXXXXXXXXXXXXXXXXX  }
CITY     XXXXXXXXXXXXXXXXXX     CUSMAIN RECORD FORMAT
STATE    XX           ZIP CODE   NNNNN
```

The operation code used to write records to and read records from a WORKSTN file is EXFMT (Execute Format). The EXFMT operation performs two functions.

1. It writes a screen format to the screen.
2. When the user responds to the format displayed on the screen the EXFMT returns the screen format record to the program.

One screen format record in our illustration is defined as CUSRQST. To execute it, the following specifications are used:

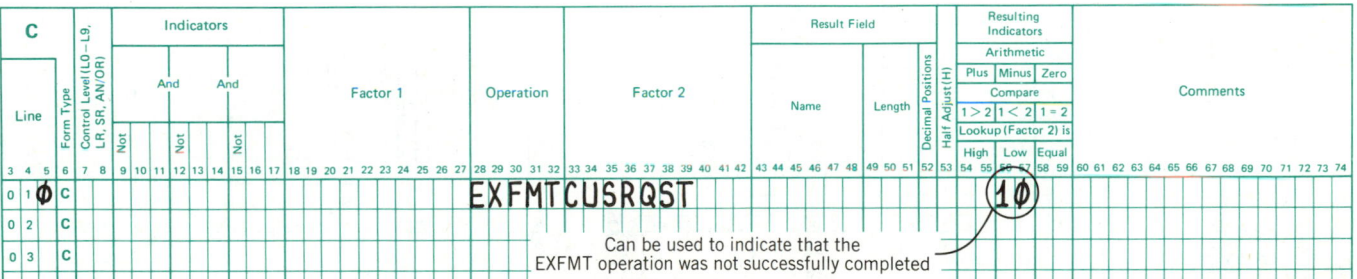

Figure 12.8 shows the Calculation Specifications form for processing our sample interactive workstation program.

To modify existing records in the file, we use the UPDAT operation. After the EXFMT operation has been executed successfully, a CUST number will be read. We CHAIN to the CUSMSTL file to obtain the CUSTREC record. We then display the existing record using the format specified under CUSMAIN. CUSMAIN enables the user to make any changes necessary to CUSTREC. After the user presses enter, the UPDAT operation is executed, which automatically changes all entries indicated by the user. To execute these operations repeatedly, we use a Do While (DOWxx/END) operation. To terminate the job, we will SETON

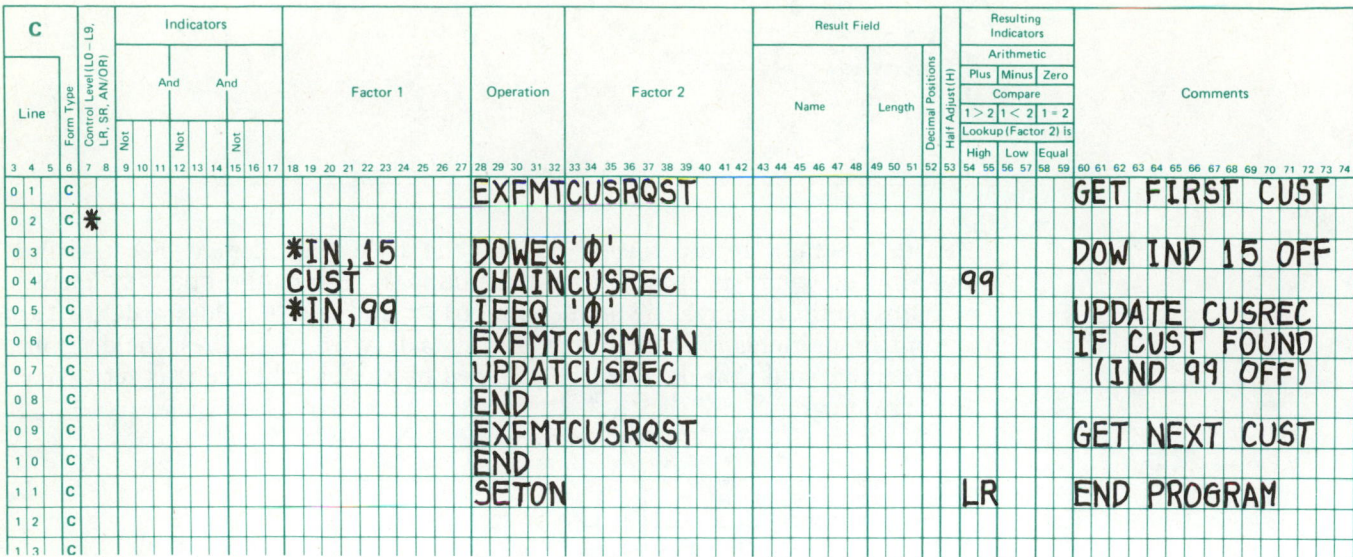

Figure 12.8
Calculation Specifications for processing the sample interactive workstation program.

the LR indicator when indicator 15 is on. Recall that indicator 15 is turned on when the user depresses command key 3 (CF3) to indicate the end of the job.

Note that no Input Specifications are required for this program since the Data Description Specifications includes all entries needed. No Output Specifications are needed since the UPDAT operation will write to the disk. The File Description Specifications are shown in Figure 12.9.

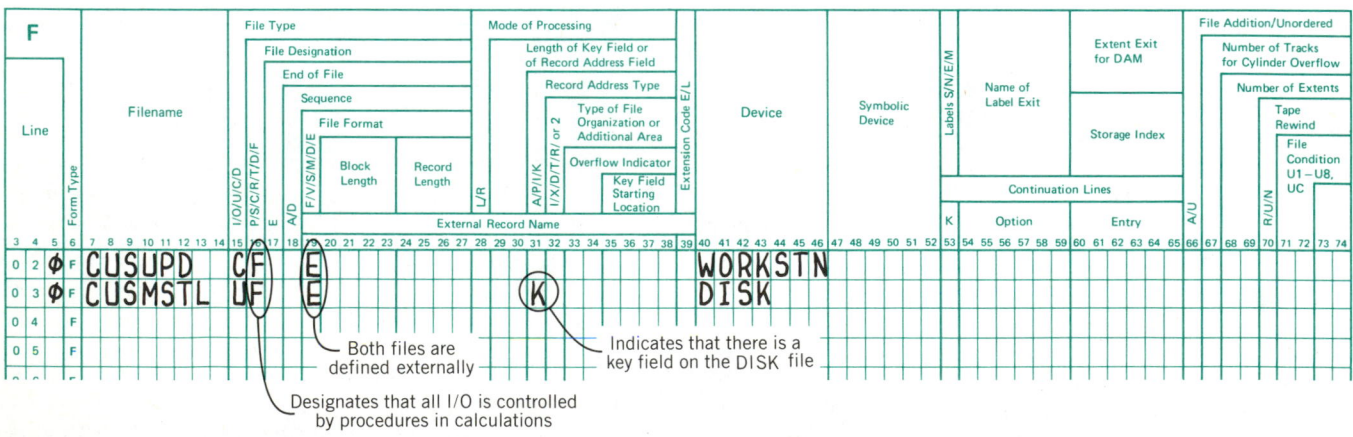

Figure 12.9
File Description Specifications for the Sample Program.

CHAPTER SELF-TEST

1. (T or F) There are operations available in RPG III that make it ideally suited for structured programming.

2. Using an integrated _____, a single-storage medium can contain all the data used by the organization as a whole.

3. Using _____, RPG III and RPG/400 enable the record descriptions to be standardized for the organization as a whole.

4. (T or F) With externally described files, each time a record changes, the RPG programmer must alter the Input Specifications form.

5. A program that executes a subprogram is referred to as the _____ program.

6. The program that is executed from another program is referred to as the _____ program.

7. (T or F) The keyword *ALL used with the CLOSE operation will close all files in the program.

8. (T or F) The DELET operation deletes records only from files defined as output files (O in column 15 of the File Description Specifications).

9. (T or F) Only Full Procedural files (F in column 15 of the File Description Specifications) can be made available for processing using the OPEN operation.

10. The operation code used to write records to and read records from a workstation file is _____.

11. A workstation file is typically defined in RPG as _____.

12. Before an UPDAT operation can be executed to modify a record, a _____ operation must be executed to retrieve the record to be updated.

13. When using the WRITE operation to add a record to an externally described file, Factor 2 must contain a _____.

14. The *IN array consists of 99 _____ elements representing the RPG general-purpose indicators _____ through _____.

15. The *ALL'x' figurative constant produces a _____.

SOLUTIONS

1. T
2. database
3. externally described files
4. F
5. calling
6. called
7. T
8. F—The file must be defined as an update file (U in column 15 of the File Description Specifications).
9. T
10. EXFMT
11. WORKSTN
12. READ
13. record format name
14. one-byte; 01; 99
15. repetitive string of data

KEY TERMS

CALL operation	Database	Externally described file	OPEN operation
Called program	DELET operation	External subroutine	Subprogram
Calling program	EXFMT operation	Full Procedural file	UPDAT operation
CLOSE operation			

REVIEW QUESTIONS

1. Indicate in your own words the major advantages of RPG III and RPG/400 as compared to RPG II.

2. When would externally described files be advantageous in a system? Give specific examples.

3. When would inquiries from an interactive terminal be used in a system? Give specific examples.

4. How is a "prompt" used in a system? Give specific examples.

5. Indicate the meaning of the following terms:
   a. called program
   b. calling program
   c. database
   d. Full Procedural file
   e. WORKSTN

APPENDIXES

Appendix A

Communicating with Operating Systems

What Is an Operating System?

All programs, whether written for a mainframe, mid-range, or microcomputer, run under the control of an **operating system.** An operating system is a complex group of programs that provides an interface between hardware, the user, and application software.

Two functions performed by the operating system are: managing or supervising the computer's resources efficiently and providing an interface for the execution of procedures by users.

Managing the computer's resources includes controlling the CPU, primary storage, and peripheral devices. The operating system must be *loaded* into storage each day before any processing takes place. If the computer operates on a 24-hour basis however, the operating system permanently resides in storage. This loading procedure (called the IPL procedure) is the *Initial Program Load* function, which loads the operating system from the disk to the processor unit. Since the operating system manages or controls all the computer's activity, this IPL process must be the first function performed each day.

The **user interface** is the part of the operating system that permits users to communicate with the hardware. For example, if a user instructs the computer to execute a particular program that prints the company's paychecks, the user interface must ensure that the printer is ready.

A programmer who writes a program in RPG must, for example, instruct the operating system to do the following:

1. Call in the RPG compiler program from the operating system.
2. Release control to the compiler for compilation of the source program.
3. Load the program (load module) into primary storage for execution.
4. Link the files stored on disk with the programs accessing them.
5. Release control to the load program for execution.
6. At the end of the job, pass control to a new job.

Operating systems, provided by the manufacturer, differ from computer to computer and thus are tailored to include features unique to each particular computer system. The type of operating system employed with a computer depends on its size and processing requirements. Many operating systems are available for mainframes, mid-range, and microcomputers. The two most common types of operating systems for IBM mid-range computers are the following:

TYPES OF IBM MID-RANGE OPERATING SYSTEMS:

SSP   System Support Program Product (System/36)
OS/400   (Full) Operating System (AS/400)

These operating systems reside on direct-access devices such as disk.

Control language is the method of communicating with the operating system. It differs somewhat depending on which operating system is used.

Control Language

As noted, control language is a programming language that allows the programmer to communicate with the operating system. Control language is used to identify programs and their processing requirements to the operating system. The precise rules for communicating with an operating system are computer-dependent. You will need to check with your computer center for instructions for your particular operating system.

The set of operating commands used with a VAX or other DEC computer is called DCL (DEC Command Language). IBM calls their set of operating system commands JCL (Job Control Language), OCL (Operation Control Language), or CL (Control Language) depending on the type of computer.

Control language used on the System/36 is called Operation Control Language or OCL, whereas on the AS/400 it is called Control Language or CL.

Purpose of Control Language

1. To communicate the programmer's needs to the supervisor.
2. To access features of the operating system required by the programmer.

Every programmer must become familiar with control language specifications. We would like to supply them in their entirety as part of this text. Unfortunately, there are too many options and entries to be coded that are dependent on the requirements of each computer installation. Hence, the control language used at one information processing center will differ, if only slightly, from that used at another center. Therefore, we will discuss only those control language specifications required for basic program execution on the IBM System/36.

It should be noted that coding rules for control language must be followed *precisely*. If a command requires // LOAD in positions 1–7, for example, with a blank in position 3, then *no* variations are permitted.

Program Execution

To get a program to run on an IBM computer, you have to describe the program very specifically to the operating system. You have to supply the name of the program, the names of any disk files, and any special requirements. Figure A.1 illustrates control language specifications for an RPG program run on an IBM System/36.

Control language is the means of describing a program to the operating system. If control language is correctly specified, the operating system will ensure that your program is executed.

Every program executed on the computer requires control language to describe it. These control language statements may be entered at the keyboard

Figure A.1
Operation Control Language
(OCL) to run program EM401R
on an IBM System/36.

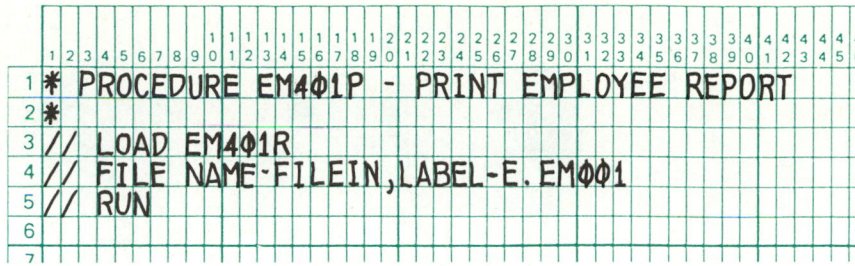

```
1 * PROCEDURE EM401P - PRINT EMPLOYEE REPORT
2 *
3 // LOAD EM401R
4 // FILE NAME-FILEIN,LABEL-E.EM001
5 // RUN
6
7
```

one statement at a time and executed directly by the operating system. A set of precoded statements may also be stored as a **procedure** in a library and executed by the operating system when required.

Procedures

Procedure coding gives you considerable power in the implementation of program execution. A procedure is a source member stored in a library that contains the necessary control language statements to run a particular program or programs. A user can then simply enter the name of the procedure when the program is to be executed.

Multiple programs can also be stored under one procedure name, called a nested procedure. In this way, several programs or utilities may be executed in sequence.

The following is the sequence of events necessary when using procedures to execute programs:

1. Code the control language statements (shown in Figure A.1) to describe the program to be run.
2. Using a utility program, such as SEU, enter the control language statements into a procedure and store the procedure in a library.
3. When required, submit the procedure to the computer for execution.
4. The operating system interprets each of the statements and performs the required action.
5. The program executes using the files described.
6. When the program ends, the operating system waits for the next job.

The next section focuses on the OCL statements required to describe and run programs on the IBM System/36.

Control Language for System/36

Let us consider the following example to illustrate System/36 OCL.

Figure A.2 presents the problem definition for our sample problem. The purpose of this program is to print from the employee master file E.EM001 an employee listing report. The report will consist of the employee's name, department, and rate.

Figure A.3 contains the RPG specifications for program EM401R, which will produce the required report.

In addition, Figure A.3 includes the OCL procedure EM401P required to execute the program. The procedure is shown below the program listing.

Figure A.2
Problem definition for the
sample problem.

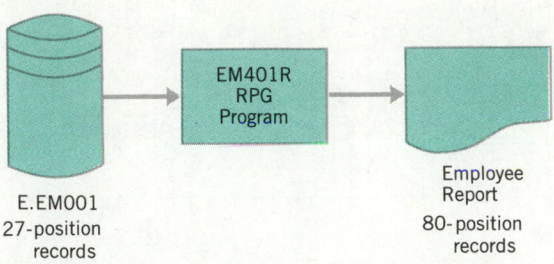

Systems Flowchart

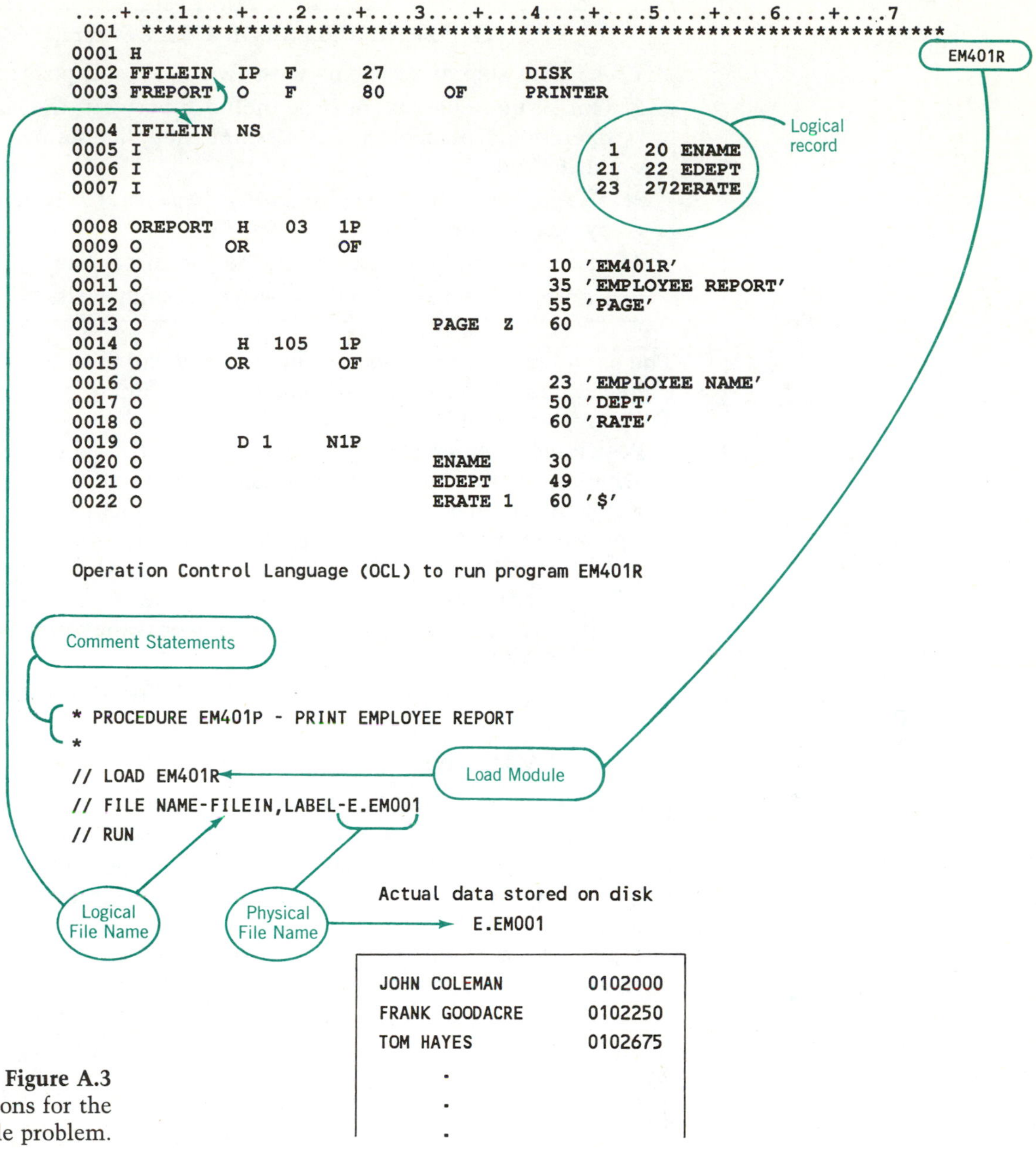

....+....1....+....2....+....3....+....4....+....5....+....6....+....7
001 **
EM401R
0001 H
0002 FFILEIN IP F 27 DISK
0003 FREPORT O F 80 OF PRINTER
0004 IFILEIN NS
0005 I 1 20 ENAME
0006 I 21 22 EDEPT
0007 I 23 272ERATE
Logical record
0008 OREPORT H 03 1P
0009 O OR OF
0010 O 10 'EM401R'
0011 O 35 'EMPLOYEE REPORT'
0012 O 55 'PAGE'
0013 O PAGE Z 60
0014 O H 105 1P
0015 O OR OF
0016 O 23 'EMPLOYEE NAME'
0017 O 50 'DEPT'
0018 O 60 'RATE'
0019 O D 1 N1P
0020 O ENAME 30
0021 O EDEPT 49
0022 O ERATE 1 60 '$'
Operation Control Language (OCL) to run program EM401R
Comment Statements
* PROCEDURE EM401P - PRINT EMPLOYEE REPORT
*
// LOAD EM401R
Load Module
// FILE NAME-FILEIN,LABEL-E.EM001
// RUN
Logical File Name
Physical File Name
Actual data stored on disk
E.EM001
JOHN COLEMAN 0102000
FRANK GOODACRE 0102250
TOM HAYES 0102675
.
.
.

Figure A.3
RPG specifications for the sample problem.

General Format for an OCL Statement

// operation parameter-list
Optional parameters
One or more blanks
OCL operation
One or more blanks
Two slashes in positions 1 and 2

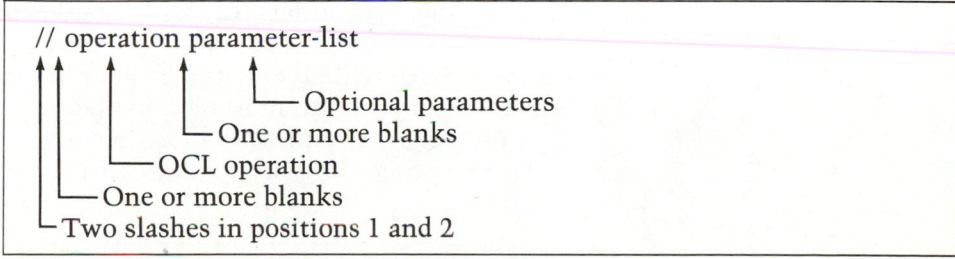

GENERAL RULES FOR OCL STATEMENTS

1. An OCL statement begins with two slashes in positions 1 and 2.
2. One or more blanks must be included between the slashes and the operation. The operation is a system-supplied name, such as, LOAD, FILE, RUN, etc.
3. The first parameter specified must be separated from the operation by one or more blanks.
4. Blanks are not allowed within the parameter list.
5. Commas serve as separators between parameters.

The parameter list provides information and variables to the procedure during execution. Parameters are either positional parameters or keyword parameters. They are separated by commas.

Positional parameters are parameters that must appear in the same position relative to other positional parameters in the same OCL statement.

Keyword parameters are parameters that are identified by a keyword within the parameter itself, for example, NAME-EM001, where NAME is the keyword used to identify the parameter and EM001 is the value assigned to the parameter. A dash separates the keyword and the value of a keyword parameter. Since keyword parameters are identified by keywords they may be placed anywhere within the parameter list.

Let us consider the System/36 OCL statements used in our sample problem.

Comment Statement

Comments are used for documentation purposes. They are displayed in the source program but are considered nonexecutable statements when the program or a procedure is running. That is, when a comment statement is encountered during execution of a program or procedure, the comment statement is ignored.

One method to designate a comment statement is to begin the statement with an asterisk (*) in position 1, for example:

```
┌─position 1
│
▼
* PROCEDURE EM401P - PRINT EMPLOYEE REPORT
```

LOAD Statement

The LOAD statement identifies the program that is to be loaded into memory for subsequent execution. The LOAD statement is the first OCL statement of the set that defines a program. In addition, it must have a corresponding RUN statement that will execute the program.

Since RPG programs must be compiled and linked, the program specified in the LOAD statement must be a *load* module.

As an option, the library in which the program might be found may be specified:

Format
```
// LOAD program_name,library_name
```

Parameters

Two positional parameters are shown in the format of the LOAD statement:

1. *program_name* specifies the name of the program loaded into memory for subsequent execution. This parameter identifies a *load module* stored in a library.

   It should be noted that the program_name bears no relationship to the procedure name that executes the program. However, in order to identify which procedures run specific programs, the same name is normally used for both. In addition, a character is added to the end to distinguish the program from the procedure. In our example, we named the program EM401R, with the R standing for RPG program. The procedure, on the other hand, was identified with the same name, with its last character being a P to denote *procedure* (e.g., EM401P).

2. *library_name* is an *optional* parameter that specifies a library name where the operating system will search for the program. If this parameter is omitted, the current library is searched for the program.

Example   `// LOAD EM401R,EMPELIBR`

In this example, the program EM401R located in library EMPELIBR is loaded into storage.

If EMPELIBR was the current library, however, the following LOAD statement would perform the same function:

`// LOAD EM401R`

The FILE Statement

The FILE statement specifies file management parameters. For each disk file used by a program a FILE statement is required.

FILE statements must be placed between the LOAD statement and its associated RUN statement.

Here, we consider the format of the FILE statement and some of its optional parameters:

Format

```
// FILE NAME-logical_file_name,LABEL-physical_file_name
         ,RECORDS|BLOCKS-number
         ,RETAIN-(S|J|T)
         ,LOCATION-A1|A2|A3|A4
         ,DISP-NEW|OLD|SHR
```

Parameters

NAME-logical_file_name

The logical file name is the name of the file specified in the File Description and Input Specifications of the RPG program. This logical file identified in the program is a description of how the actual physical file stored on disk is viewed.

NAME, which is a keyword parameter, is the only parameter required for the FILE statement. In our example, shown in Figure A.3, FILEIN is the name of the file identified within the RPG program.

LABEL-physical_file_name

This is the label or file name assigned to the actual physical file stored on disk and listed in the VTOC (Volume Table of Contents). VTOC is the name given to the table of contents or directory of a direct storage device.

This file name may differ from the name referenced in the RPG program. If so, this parameter is required in order that the physical file stored on disk can be associated with the logical file identified in the program. If this parameter is omitted, the file label defaults to the logical file name specified with the NAME parameter.

In our example (Figure A.3), the logical file identified in the program is called FILEIN, whereas on disk the name of the actual physical file is called E.EM001. Thus, both the NAME parameter and the LABEL parameter are required. The two parameters work together in order to link the logical file (FILEIN) described in the RPG program with the physical file E.EM001 stored on disk.

(RECORDS|BLOCKS)-number

This parameter, used when a file is being created, uses either the RECORDS option or the BLOCKS option.

> The RECORDS option specifies the number of *records* to be allocated to the file.
>
> The BLOCKS option specifies the number of *blocks* to be allocated to the file.

When a file is created, either a RECORDS or BLOCKS parameter, but not both, may be specified.

RETAIN-(T|J|S)

This parameter indicates the retention status for the file. Before describing the options available for this parameter let us consider two new terms.

A *job* is all the control language statements required to complete a defined task such as calculation of the weekly payroll or calculation of the new inventories for the parts file. A job may require *more than one* program to complete the task. The individual programs that are required to complete the job are called *job steps*.

The following three options are available for the RETAIN parameter:

> RETAIN-S specifies a scratch file that exists for the one job step (one program). The file is automatically deleted after the job step is completed.
>
> RETAIN-J specifies a job file. This specification is similar to a scratch file except that the file is not automatically deleted until all job steps are completed and the job ends.
>
> RETAIN-T specifies a temporary file. This specification indicates a file that may (1) be used by several jobs, (2) be recreated, or (3) be referred to by specifying RETAIN-S, RETAIN-T, or RETAIN-J.

LOCATION-A1|A2|A3|A4

This indicates the disk placement of the file, as in A1, A2, A3, or A4. For example, the parameter LOCATION-A2 indicates that the disk file is found on drive A2. The default value is A1.

DISP-(NEW|OLD|SHR)

DISP-NEW specifies that a new file is being created. DISP-OLD specifies that the file is an existing file that can be recreated. When a program is creating a new file and a file exists on disk with the same name, the existing file is destroyed by the newly created file.

For example, assume a program that is run monthly produces a summary disk file that will eventually be used as input to another application. Each month when this program is run it is possible that the file created from the previous month is still on the disk. If so, DISP-OLD could be specified as a parameter for this file so that the newly created file will replace last month's existing file.

DISP-SHR specifies that the file is an existing file that can be accessed by more than one program at a time.

Suppose two programs, for example, are executing simultaneously and both programs use the same file. If DISP *is not* SHR, the second program to access the file will stop executing temporarily until the first program is completed and the file is then available.

In order for two programs to access the same file, DISP-SHR must be specified on the FILE statement for both programs.

RUN Statement

The RUN statement initiates the execution of the program loaded into memory by the associated LOAD statement.

A RUN statement must be the last statement in the set of procedure statements for a program.

Format

```
// RUN
```

Example   To LOAD and RUN a program called EM401R:

```
// LOAD EM401R
   .
   .
   .
// RUN
```

Printing on Nonstandard Forms

Sometimes specific applications that produce printed output need to change default printer settings. For example, the number of lines per inch (LPI), the number of characters per inch (CPI), or the number of copies to be printed may be changed in order to produce specific printed output. These values and additional values may be changed for a printed report using an OCL PRINTER statement.

PRINTER Statement

The PRINTER statement controls output of a printer file created by a program.

The PRINTER statement, if used, must appear between the LOAD statement and its associated RUN statement.

Format

```
// PRINTER NAME-file_name
           ,LINES-lines_per_page
           ,FORMSNO-forms_number
           ,ALIGN-YES or NO
           ,SPOOL-YES or NO
           ,LPI-4|6|8
           ,CPI-10|15
           ,COPIES -number_of_copies; Default-1
```

Parameters
NAME-file_name

This specifies the file name the program uses to refer to the printer file.

LINES-lines_per_page

The LINES parameter specifies the number of lines per page. The maximum value is 112. If this parameter is *not* specified, a default value of 66 lines per page is used.

FORMSNO-forms_number

This specifies the forms number of the printer forms to be used for printed output from the job. For example, if payroll checks for hourly employees are identified by the forms number PCHR, then the parameter FORMSNO-PCHR could be used. The operating system would then signal the operator to change the printer forms to hourly payroll checks.

The forms number can be any combination of up to 4 characters except for some special characters. We recommend that only alphabetic characters and numbers be used.

ALIGN-YES or NO

When special nonstandard forms are used, it may be necessary to give the operator an opportunity to align the forms in the printer before the actual printing begins.

ALIGN-YES specifies that the operator is to be given the opportunity to align the forms before the actual printout begins.

ALIGN-NO means that the operator will not be given the opportunity to align the forms before printing begins. ALIGN-NO is the default if this parameter is omitted.

LPI-(4|6|8)

The lines per inch (LPI) parameter specifies the number of lines per inch that the output report file will use. The report may be printed using 4, 6, or 8 lines per inch. For example, the parameter LPI-8 will cause the output report to print at 8 lines per inch.

CPI-(10|15)

The characters per inch (CPI) parameter specifies the number of characters per inch that will print horizontally on a line. For example, to print a report in compressed mode, the parameter CPI-15 could be specified.

COPIES-number-of-copies

The COPIES parameter specifies the number of copies of a printer file that are to be printed. For example, if three copies of a report are required, the parameter COPIES-3 would be specified. The default value for this parameter is 1.

Creating New Files

Another OCL procedure that is often used is the BLDFILE procedure.

BLDFILE Procedure
The **BLDFILE procedure** is used to create a disk file that contains no data. Once created, the file can be referenced as an existing file by subsequent programs. These programs can then add, change, or delete records in this file.

The format of the BLDFILE procedure contains several positional parameters:

Format
```
BLDFILE file_name,file_type,allot,file size,
   record_length,alternate_drive_location,retention,
   key_offset,key_length,delete_capable,duplicate_keys
```

Besides the above format, a *prompt screen* may be used to enter the nec-

Figure A.4
Example of a prompt screen for
entering BLDFILE parameters.

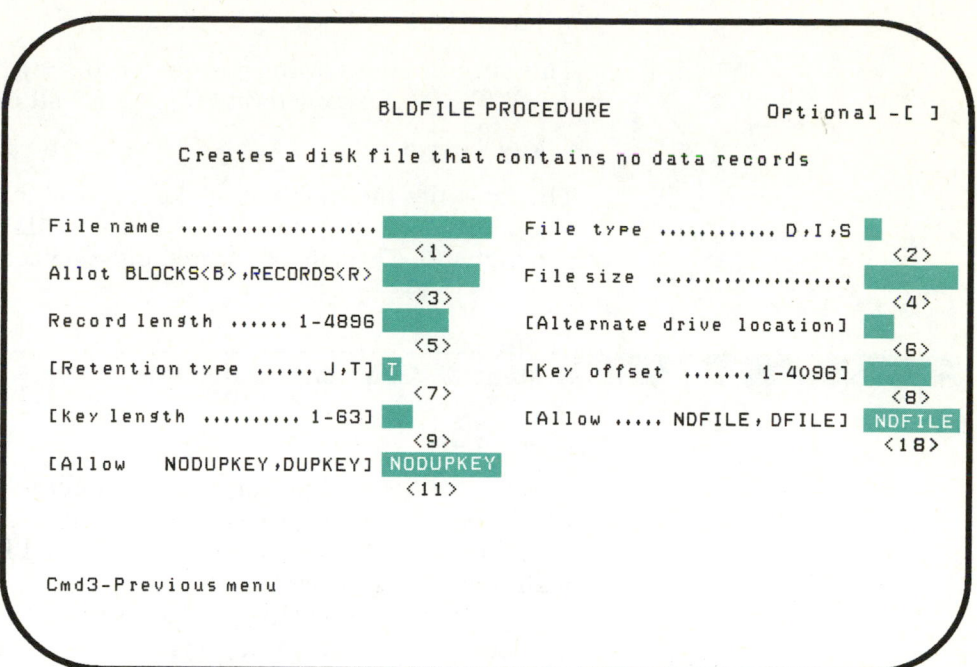

essary parameters (see Figure A.4). The prompt screen is displayed if the
BLDFILE procedure is entered with missing or incorrect parameters.

Parameters

file_name

This specifies the name of the file to be created.

file_type

D specifies that a direct file is to be created. I specifies that an indexed file is to
be created. S specifies that a sequential file is to be created.

allot BLOCKS(B),RECORDS(R)

BLOCKS or B specifies that file space is to be allocated by blocks.
RECORDS or R specifies that file space is to be allocated by records.

file_size

This specifies the size of the file to be created. The size is specified in records
or blocks and is determined by the allocation parameter.

record_length

This specifies the length of the record in bytes. The length may be a number
from 1 through 4096.

alternate_drive_location

This specifies an alternate drive on which files are to be built. Drive location
designations of the form A1, A2, A3, or A4 may be specified.

retention

The values J or T may be specified. The value T is normally used, which
indicates that the file is a resident file and will be used by several programs.

key_offset

This specifies the starting position of the key field within the record of an indexed file. This parameter is required for all indexed files.

key_length

This specifies the length of the key field within the record of an indexed file. The key_length is required if an indexed file is being created (I specified in parameter 2). The value indicated must be between 1 and 63.

System/38 Command Language

System 38

Entering the Source Program into the System

After you have written your RPG program on the specification forms, you must enter the source program into source files in the system. You can normally enter it interactively by using the Source Entry Utility (SEU) of the Interactive Data Base Utilities Licensed Program (IDU).

When you have identified your source program as RPG, you can enter the CRTSRC (Create Source) command to call SEU.

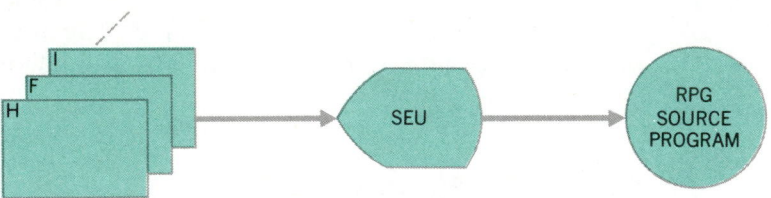

SEU has special display screen formats supplied by RPG that correspond to the RPG specification forms to help you enter your RPG source program specifications. You can enter specifications position-by-position or you can enter a specification field-by-field. Figure A.5 shows a display screen format, the relationship between the headings on the specifications form and the labels on the display screen, and where you can enter specifications on the display screen.

If you specify the APP (QSEURPG) parameter on the CRTSRC command, SEU invokes an RPG syntax checker that checks each specification line for errors as you enter it. The RPG syntax checker checks each position of the specification line for valid entries; it checks that all field, indicator, and operation code names are valid; it checks that the proper fields are specified for each operation code (for example, the arithmetic operations must have a Result Field entry); and it checks that literals are specified correctly. If a position contains an invalid entry, an error message is displayed that allows you to correct the error. The syntax checker cannot detect logic or relational errors between two or more statements (for example, if a subroutine SR200 is missing for an EXSR SR200 operation). These errors are detected by the RPG compiler when you compile your program. The RPG syntax checker also skips fields that are designated as skip fields and enters predefined constants (for example, C on the display screen format for Calculation Specifications).

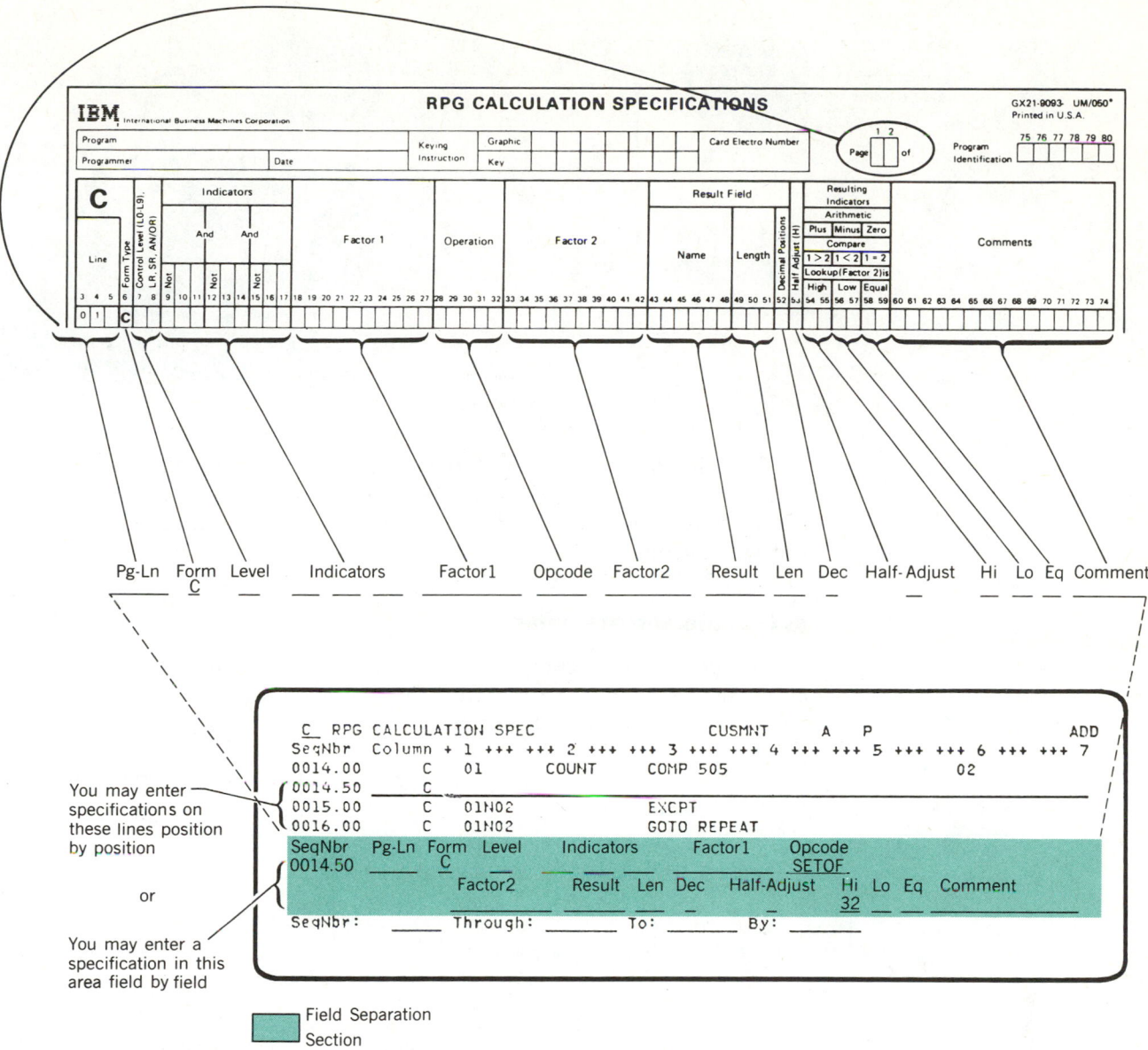

Figure A.5
Relationships between Calculation Specifications and display screen format.

Compiling the Source Program

After you have entered the source program into the system, you need to compile the source program. This process of compilation is done by the RPG compiler, which is part of the RPG III Licensed Program. If externally described files are used by the program, the control program facility, which is the system support program, provides information about the files to the compiled program. The compiler is invoked to create an executable RPG program and a listing:

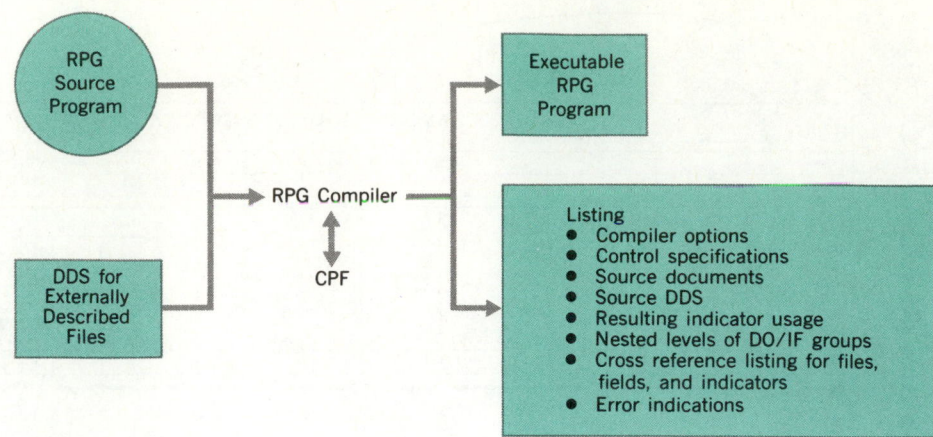

The compiler syntax checks the RPG source program line-by-line and the interrelationships between the lines. For example, it checks that all field names are defined and, if a field is multiply defined, that each definition has the same attributes.

RPG Command Statement

To compile an RPG source program into an executable program, you must enter the CRTRPGPGM (Create RPG Program) command that invokes the RPG compiler. The command is valid in batch and interactive jobs, and in CL programs. The command syntax is as follows (the defaults are underlined):

The description of the parameters follows. The defaults are explained first and are underlined:

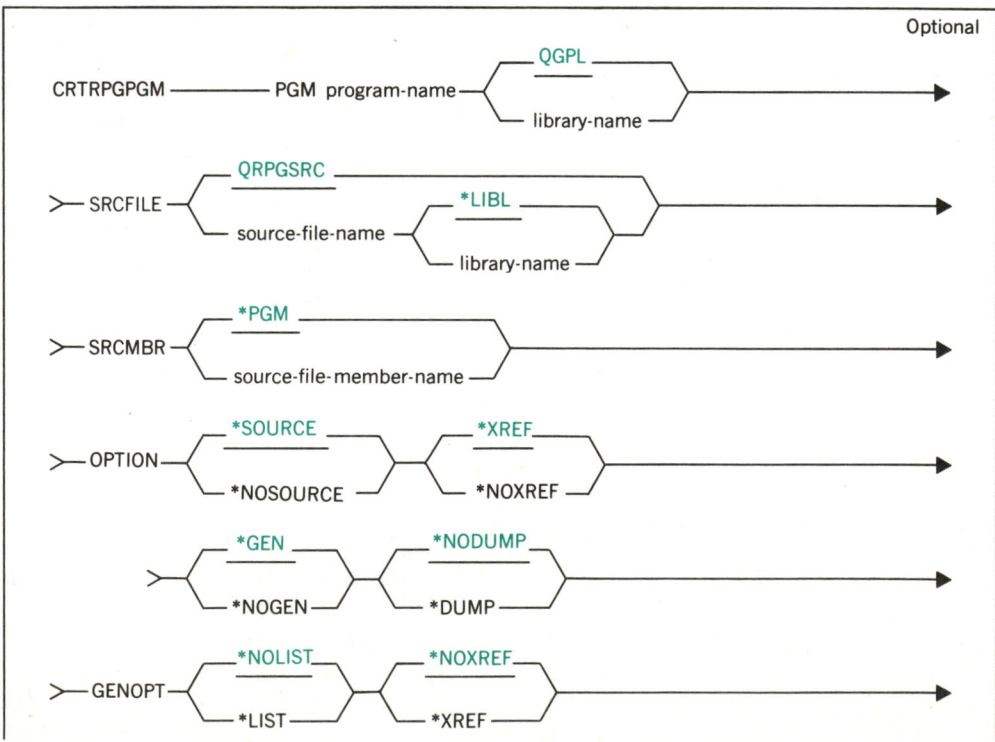

```
              *NOPATCH          *NODUMP
          ┌──────────────┐ ┌──────────────┐
          │              │ │              │
          └── *PATCH ─────┘ └── *DUMP ─────┘────────────────────►

              *QSYSPRT
          ┌──────────────┐
>── PRTFILE ┤              │
          │          *LIBL
          └── file-name ─┬──────────────┐
                         │              │
                         └── library-name ┘──────────────────────►

              *USER                          *NORMAL
          ┌──────────┐                   ┌──────────────┐
>── USRPRF ┤          ├── PUBAUT ─────────┤── *ALL ──────┤────────►
          └── *OWNER ─┘                   └── *NONE ─────┘

              *BLANK
          ┌──────────────┐
>── TEXT ──┤              │
          └── 'text' ────┘────────────────────────────────────────►
```

PGM *parameter.*   Specifies the qualified name by which the compiled RPG program can be known and the library in which the compiled program is to be located. The program name can also be entered in positions 75 through 80 of the control specification. However, a program name coded on the PGM parameter overrides an entry in positions 75 through 80 of the control specification. If a program name is not provided on the PGM parameter or in positions 75 through 80 of the control specification, the default name is RPGOBJ.

QGPL: Name of the temporary library in which the created program is stored if no library name is specified.

library name: Specifies the name of the library in which the created program is stored.

SRCFILE *parameter.*   Specifies the name of the source file that contains the RPG source to be compiled.

QRPGSRC: Specifies that the IBM-supplied source file, QRPGSRC, contains the RPG source to be compiled.

qualified-source-file-name: Enter the qualified name of the source file that contains the RPG source to be compiled. If no library qualifier is given, *LIBL is used to find the file.

SRCMBR *parameter.*   Specifies the name of the member of the source file that contains the RPG source to be compiled. This parameter is specified only when SRCFILE is a database file.

*PGM: The RPG source to be compiled is in the member of the source file that has the same name as that specified for the compiled program in the PGM parameter.

source-file-member-name: Enter the name of the member that contains the RPG source.

OPTION *parameter.*   Specifies whether the following options are to be written on the compiler listing when the RPG source is compiled.

*SOURCE: Source input and diagnostic listings are written.

*NOSOURCE: No source input or diagnostic listings are written.

*XREF: A cross-reference listing is written for variable data item references in the source data.

*NOXREF: No cross-reference listing is written for variable data item references in the source data.

*GEN: An executable program is generated after compilation time.

*NOGEN: No executable program is generated after compilation time.

*NODUMP: The compiler does not dump all data areas.

*DUMP: The compiler dumps all data areas.

GENOPT *parameter.* Specifies whether the following options are to be in effect during program creation.

*NOLIST: No source input or generated output (along with any messages) are written.

*LIST: The source input and generated output (along with any messages) are written.

*NOXREF: No cross-reference listing is written for all objects defined in the source input.

*XREF: A cross-reference listing is written for all objects defined in the source input.

*NOPATCH: No space is to be reserved in the compiled program for a program patch area.

*PATCH: Space is to be reserved in the compiled program for a program patch area. The size of the patch area is based on the size of the generated program.

*NODUMP: The compiler does not dump all data areas.

*DUMP: The compiler dumps all data areas.

PRTFILE *parameter.* Specifies the file name that the program uses to refer to the printer file.

*QSYSPRT: Specifies that the IBM-supplied file, QSYSPRT, receives printer output.

qualified-file-name: Specifies the file name to receive printer output.

USRPRF *parameter.* Specifies under which user security profile the compiled RPG program is to execute. The user profile of either the program owner or the program user determines what storage resources, scheduling priority, and operational rights are used to execute the program.

*USER: The compiled RPG program executes under the program user's security profile.

*OWNER: The compiled RPG program executes under the program owner's user security profile.

PUBAUT *parameter.* Specifies what authority the public users (all users not specifically authorized by name) have for the program and its description. The different levels of authority are described in the *CPF Programmer's Guide.*

`*NORMAL`: The public has only operational authority for the program. Any user can execute the program, but cannot change or debug it.

`*ALL`: The public has all levels of authority for the program.

`*NONE`: No user, other than the program owner, can use the program, unless the owner authorizes specific levels of authority to users by name in the `GRTOBJAUT` (Grant Object Authority) command. (For information on the `GRTOBJAUT` command, see the *CPF Reference Manual—Control Language.*)

TEXT *parameter.* Lets the user enter text that briefly describes the program and its function. For example, the `DSPOBJD` (Display Object Description) command can be used to display text. (For information on the `DSPOBJD` command and other ways to enter text see the *CPF Reference Manual—Control Language.*)

`*BLANK`: No text is specified.

'text': The text that briefly describes the program and its function can be a maximum of 5Ø characters in length and must be enclosed in apostrophes. The apostrophes are not part of the 5Ø-character string.

Appendix B

Complete RPG Logic Cycle

Figure B.1 represents the complete RPG Logic Cycle.

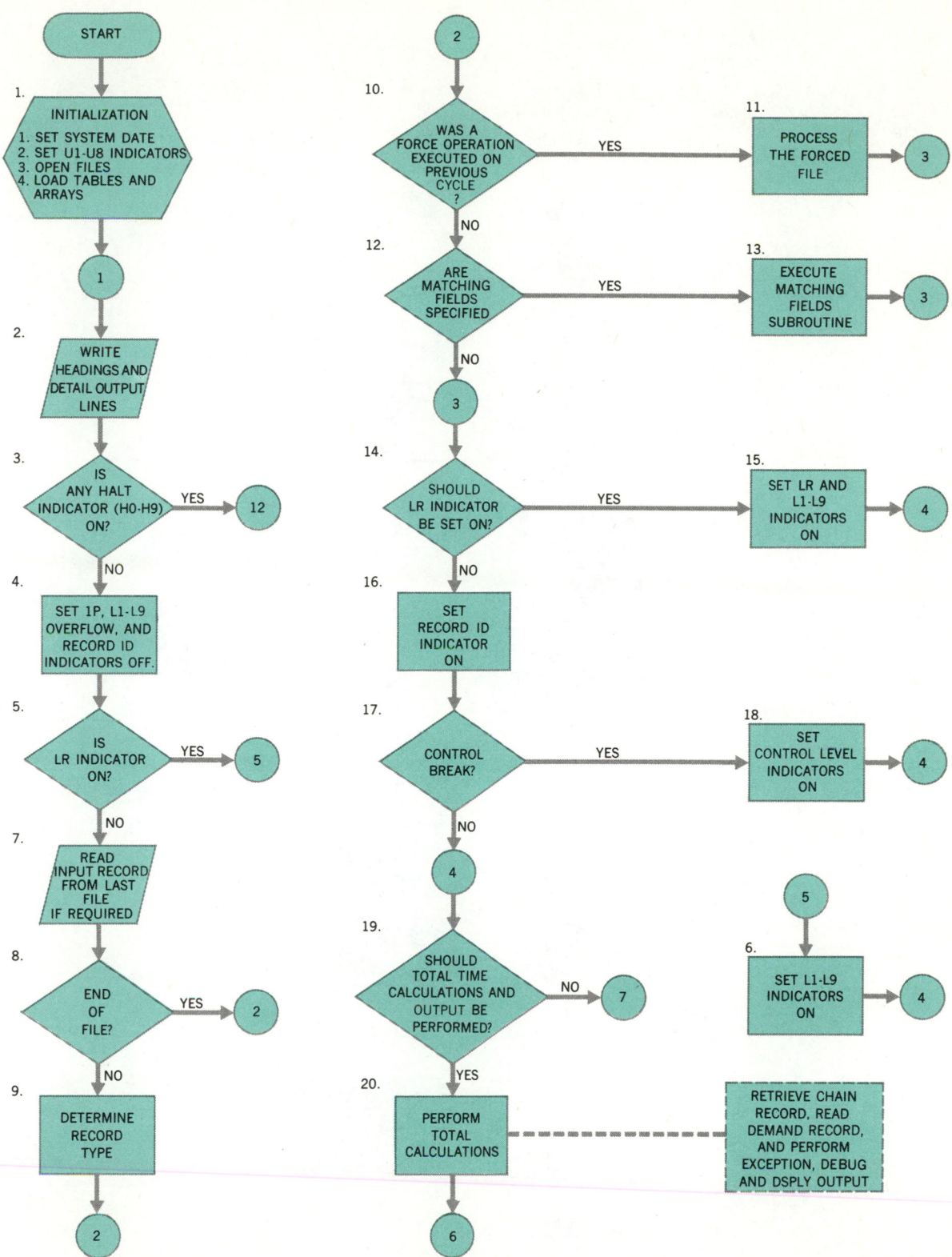

Figure B.1
The complete RPG Logic
Cycle.

(continued on next page)

Figure B.1
(continued)

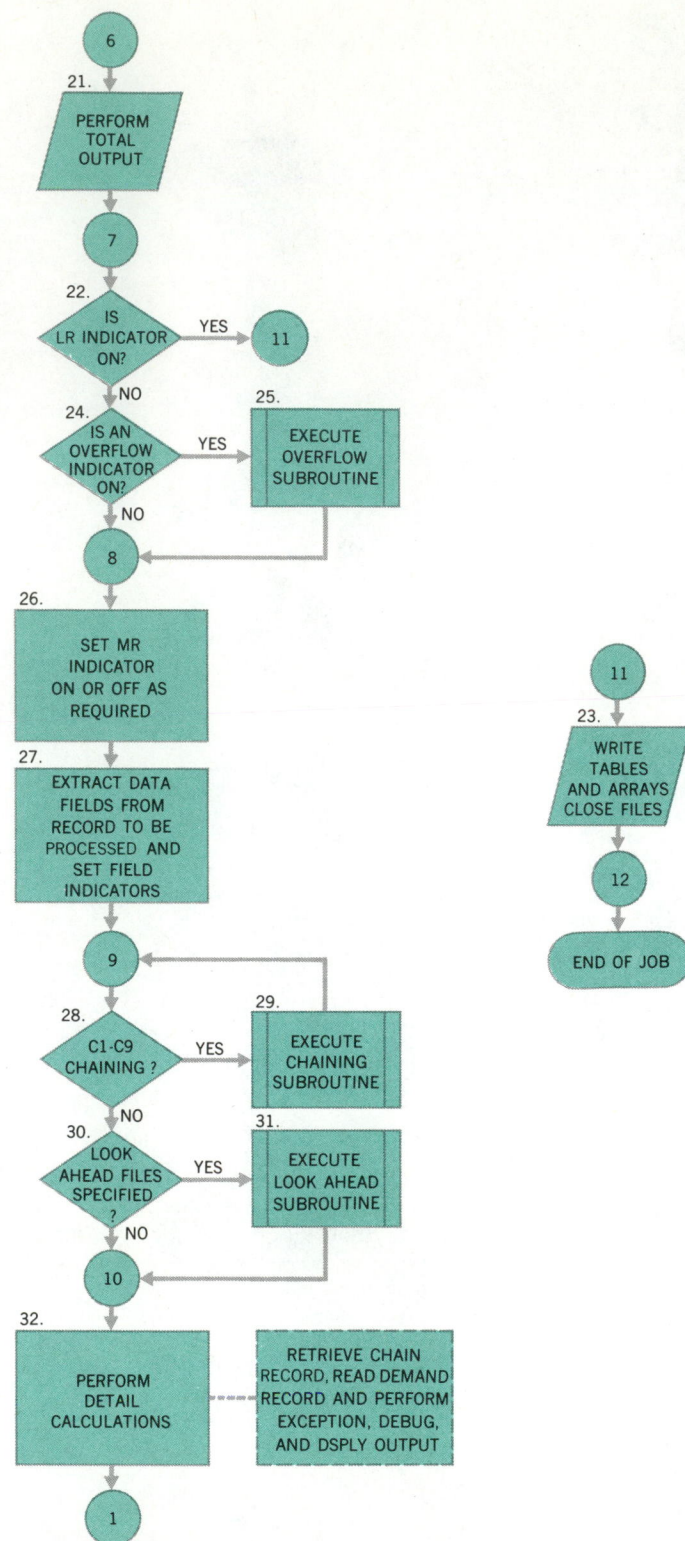

Glossary

Access time.   The time it takes to read a disk record into storage or write a disk record from storage.

ADD.   An RPG operation that adds data to a Result Field.

Address Out Sort.   Used to produce an ADDROUT file, which is a record address file. Contrast with **Tagalong Sort.**

ADDROUT (Address Out) file.   A record address file produced as a result of an Address Out Sort; it is organized sequentially and used to process records from another file; it contains relative record numbers of the records in the file to be sorted.

Alphabetic field.   A data field that can only contain letters and/or blanks.

Alphameric field.   See **alphanumeric field.**

Alphanumeric field.   A data field that can contain any combination of letters, digits, or special characters.

Alternate key.   An option that allows an indexed file to be created with and accessed by more than one identifying key.

Alternating arrays.   Consist of two parallel arrays usually having the same number of elements.

Array.   A series of elements with similar characteristics that are stored as one unit. Each element can be accessed with the use of an index.

ASCII code.   A common code for representing data; an acronym for *A*merican *Stan*-dard *C*ode for *I*nformation *I*nterchange.

Audit trail.   See **control listing.**

Batch processing.   The processing of records in groups or batches, usually at fixed intervals.

BEGSR.   Must be the first statement of a subroutine, thus serving as its entry point.

Blank after.   An output specification that initializes a numeric field with zeros or an alphanumeric field with blanks after that field has been used for output.

Blocking.   Combining several logical records into one physical record to conserve space on a magnetic disk.

Blocking factor.   The number of logical records in each physical block of data on a disk. See **blocking.**

Byte.   The representation of a character by eight bits. Each byte of storage can generally hold one character. See **packed data** for the exception.

CABxx (Compare and Branch) operation.   Used to permanently transfer control to another point in the program as a result of a comparison; a form of GOTO.

Calculation Specifications form.   An RPG coding form used to indicate the type of processing to be performed.

CALL operation.   Transfers control from the program currently being executed to the program specified in Factor 2.

Called module.   When a subroutine is accessed by the main procedure in an RPG program, the subroutine is referred to as the called module.

Calling module.   When a procedure accesses a subroutine, that procedure is referred to as the calling module.

CASE (CASxx) operation.   An RPG operation used when there are numerous paths to be followed depending on the contents of a given field.

Case structure.   A logical control structure used to compare the contents of two fields or literals and select or execute one of several routines as a result of that comparison.

CHAIN.   An RPG operation used to access an indexed file randomly.

Character.   A letter, digit, or special symbol representing the smallest unit of data.

Character field.   A field that can contain any combination of letters, digits, and special characters as $, %, @, or &.

Class test.   A data validation procedure used to ensure that input is entered in the appropriate data format, that is, numeric, alphabetic, or alphanumeric.

CLOSE.   An RPG operation that closes and releases a file from the program and deactivates the device assigned to the file.

Coded field test.   A type of field in which a code is used to designate data; for example, 'M' may be a code to designate 'Married' in a Marital Status field; keeps record formats shorter and more manageable.

Collating sequence.   The hierarchy of characters. For EBCDIC computers, for example, the collating sequence is ƁABC . . . ZØ123 . . . 9, going from low to high.

Combined file.   Allows an RPG program to read records from or write records to the workstation device.

Comment.   A word or statement in a program that serves as documentation rather than as instructions to the compiler.

COMP.   An RPG operation used to determine if one field is less than, equal to, or greater than another field.

Compile time array or table.   An array or table in which the data is compiled with the source program and becomes a permanent part of the object program. Contrast with **pre-execution time array or table.**

Compiler.   The special program that translates a source program into an object program.

Condition code.   Set equal to high, low, or equal when a comparison is made.

Conditional branch.   A branch, or transfer, that occurs in a program or flowchart only when a particular condition is met.

Conditional statement.   Statements executed only when the condition specified by the relational operator has been satisfied.

Conditioning.   The use of indicators to control when calculations or output operations are to be performed.

Constant.   A fixed value that is part of a program; this value does not change during the execution of the program. Same as **literal.**

Continuous form.   The output form generally produced by a computer printer. Although a continuous form can be separated into individual sheets, it is fed through the printer in one continuous sheet to increase speed and facilitate processing.

Control and File Description Specifications form.   An RPG coding form that indicates the system requirements and describes the files used in the program.

Control break.   When data is processed so that the contents of a key field controls the calculations and printing to be performed, this is referred to as control break processing. Typically, a change in the contents of a key field causes output to be produced and a new control group to be accumulated.

Control field.   A key field used to control the processing of data. Typically, when the contents of the control field change from one record to another, output is generated and new totals are accumulated.

Control language commands.   Used by programmers to communicate directly with the operating system.

Control listing.   A computer-produced report used for control or checking purposes; typically includes (1) identifying information about all input records processed by the computer, (2) any errors encountered, and (3) a total of records processed.

Control program facility (RPG III).   The system support program that provides many functions that are fully integrated in the system. These functions include database management, message handling, and job control.

Control total. A total of an amount field is accumulated for all records with the same control field.

COPY statement. Used to insert into a program a series of prewritten RPG source statements.

Counter. A field used to count the number of occurrences of a specific event.

Create program. A program designed to create a master file; when a new system is implemented, primary attention is given to data validation and edit routines in the create program.

Cursor. A symbol, such as a blinking square or a question mark, that indicates where on a screen the next character will be entered.

Data structure. Allows the programmer to define an area in storage and then subdivide that area into fields, called subfields.

Data validation. Techniques used to minimize the risk of input errors by checking input, as far as possible, before processing it.

Data verification. The editing of input data to detect errors before the data is processed.

Database. When a company maintains one single, common set of data that can be accessed by individual departments, this is referred to as a database. One database is much more efficient than having each department maintain its own files, which would result in frequent duplication of effort and lack of proper control and integration.

Date field. See **UDATE.**

Debug. To correct errors in a program.

Default. An assumption made by the computer in the absence of specific coding.

DELET. An RPG operation that deletes a record from a file; can be used only with a file specified as an update file.

Demand file. A file that serves as either an input, update, or special file and that is read sequentially.

Desk check. To correct errors in a program by manually verifying coding, even before the program is compiled.

Detail calculation (RPG Cycle). A calculation that is performed each time an input record is read.

Detail output. Output that is printed or produced for each input record read.

Detail printing. The printing of an output record from each input record.

Detail report. A report that generates one or more lines of output for each input record read; it requires more computer time than other reports and tends to be the most costly type of output. Contrast with **exception report** and **group report.**

Detail time. An operation in the RPG program cycle in which calculation and output operations are performed for each record read.

Diagnostic. A compile-time message that identifies RPG specification errors. All rule violations will be listed as diagnostics.

Direct access. The method of processing data independent of the actual location of that data. Contrast with **sequential access.** The term **random access** is sometimes used in place of direct access.

Direct file. A type of file where disk records are accessed by converting a key field, through some arithmetic calculation, to an actual address that typically identifies the surface and track or cylinder number.

Display Control (S) Specification. Used to define the characteristics of a display format used in an interactive RPG program.

Display Screen Layout Sheet. A tool used to plan display formats and exchanges between the user and an interactive computer program.

DIVIDE operation. An RPG operation that divides Factor 1 by Factor 2 and places the quotient in the Result Field.

DO . . . group (RPG III). A series of operations that are executed one or more times depending on the parameters specified. A DO operation and an END operation are the delimiters for a DO group. See **looping.**

Documentation. The set of records used to explain in detail how the program operates and what it is intended to accomplish.

DOUxx/END.　The DO Until operation; executes a group of instructions until a specified condition is met.

DOWxx/END.　The DO While operation; it indicates the execution of a group of operations as long as the condition specified in the relational operator (xx) is true.

Dynamic array.　An array created during execution time.

Dynamic processing.　A method of combining both random and sequential access in the same program. First, an indexed file is accessed randomly to locate the initial record wanted. It is then accessed sequentially from that point on.

EBCDIC.　See **Extended Binary Coded Decimal Interchange Code.**

Edit code.　A number or letter used on the Output form to indicate the type of editing that should be performed. Types of editing include zero suppression and printing of dollar signs.

Edit procedure.　The process of verifying that data entered into the computer is relatively error-free. Editing operations minimize computer-produced errors.

Elementary item.　A data field that is not further subdivided.

END (RPG III).　The last statement in a DO . . . group.

End-of-file (EOF).　The condition reached when there are no more input records to be read.

ENDSR.　Must be the last statement of a subroutine, thus serving to terminate the subroutine.

Entry point.　The beginning point of a routine to be branched to from other points in the program; specified by use of the TAG operation.

Exception output.　The writing of a number of similar or identical records at the time calculations are being performed.

Exception report.　The printing of only that output that does not fall within established guidelines.

EXCPT operation.　Allows records to be written at the time calculations are being performed, which is not the usual time for printing using the standard RPG Fixed Logic Cycle.

Execution.　The running of a program with data.

EXFMT operation.　Used with WORKSTN files; performs a combined WRITE followed by a READ operation to the workstation file.

EXSR.　Operation used to execute an internal subroutine from anywhere in a program.

Extended Binary Coded Decimal Interchange Code (EBCDIC).　A common computer code used to represent characters.

Extension and Line Counter Specifications form.　An RPG coding form used to provide information about (1) arrays and tables used in a program and (2) the number of lines to be printed on forms.

External subroutine.　A subroutine not part of a program that is called in from a library of functions or routines.

Externally defined file.　Used with RPG III and RPG/400 programs; means that the record description for the file is not defined as part of the program; the compiler obtains these descriptions at compilation time and includes them in the RPG source program.

Factor 1.　The first value specified on an RPG Calculation form in positions 18 to 27.

Factor 2.　The second value specified on an RPG Calculation form in position 33 to 42.

Field.　A group of consecutive positions used to represent a unit of data such as NAME or SALARY.

Field Definition (D) Specifications.　Used to define the characteristics of each element that will appear on a display format used in an interactive RPG program.

Figurative constant.　An RPG word, such as *BLANK, *BLANKS, *ZERO, or *ZEROS, where the word denotes the actual value.

File.　A collection of individual records that are treated as one unit. A payroll file, for example, refers to a company's complete collection of employee records.

File Description Specifications form.　The RPG coding form that defines and describes the files used in the program.

File maintenance procedure.　See **update procedure.**

File update.   The process of making a file current.

First page (1P) indicator.   Used to print headings; the 1P indicator is automatically turned on at the beginning of the program cycle and then turned off after the heading lines print.

Fixed-length record.   Used to describe a file in which all records are the same length.

Floating dollar sign.   A dollar sign that prints directly to the left of the first significant digit; the dollar sign is said to "float" with the field.

Flowchart.   A pictorial representation of the logic to be used in a program or a system.

Format load member.   Used to store screen formats that are compiled separately from an RPG program.

Full Procedural file.   A file that may be accessed both sequentially and randomly; a more powerful version of the Demand file feature.

GOTO.   An unconditional branch instruction; when the instruction is encountered, the program will automatically transfer control to some other point in the program.

GOTO-less programming.   Another term for **structured programming.** Such programming enables each module to function as a stand-alone entity and avoids branches or GOTO instructions.

Group indicate.   The printing of control information for only the first record of a group of records containing identical control information.

Group item.   A data field that is further subdivided; a major field consisting of minor fields.

Group report (printing).   Reports that print totals that can sometimes provide the user with enough information so that detail reports are not necessary.

Half-adjust.   A method of rounding off a number by determining whether the low-order digit is less than five. If it is less than five, then the last digit is truncated; if the low-order digit is five or more, then one is added to the next position. Thus, 12.75, for example, half adjusted to one decimal place becomes 12.8.

Halt indicator (H0).   An indicator that will terminate a program if a record is found out of sequence during a sequential file update.

Halt indicator (H1–H9).   An indicator that will terminate a program if set on; H1–H9 indicators either are automatically set by the computer or can be turned on by the programmer when a certain unacceptable condition occurs.

Hash total.   A control total consisting of the sum of numbers in a field such as ACCTNO that would not otherwise be summed.

Heading.   A constant printed on the top of each page of a report identifying the information on the page.

Hierarchy chart.   A planning tool for specifying the relationships among modules in a program; another term for hierarchy chart is structure chart or visual table of contents (VTOC); a tool used to depict top-down logic.

High-level language.   A symbolic programming language that requires compilation; it is easier to code than a low-level language but is more difficult to translate since it is English-like and not machine-like.

High-order position.   The left-most, or most significant, character in a field.

High-order truncation.   When a receiving field does not have enough integer positions to hold a result, the high-order or most significant digit is truncated or lost. This is referred to as high-order truncation and should be avoided.

IF-THEN-ELSE structure.   This is a technique used to represent a test for a specific condition; it is a pseudocode representation for depicting logical control procedures.

IFxx/ELSE/END.   An RPG operation that permits execution of an instruction or series of instructions depending on the result of a comparison of fields or literals.

Implied decimal point.   When a decimal point does not actually appear in a numeric field but the number is assumed to have a decimal point, we say that the decimal point is implied.

Index (for an array).   Used to indicate which element in an array is to be accessed.

Index (for an indexed file).   Used to indicate where each record is physically located.

Indexed file.   A file with an index that indicates where each record is physically located in a disk file.

Indicator.   A two-digit or two-character entry used to indicate when specific operations are to be performed. An indicator may be a control level indicator, field indicator, first page indicator, last record indicator, overflow indicator, record identifying indicator, or resulting indicator.

Infinite loop.   An error condition in which a program would continue performing a module indefinitely or until time has run out for the program.

Input.   The data that is entered into a computer system.

Input Specifications form.   An RPG coding form that describes the records and fields to be processed as input.

Interactive processing.   See **on-line processing.**

Interactive workstation.   A terminal used for inquiry-response purposes.

Internal subroutine.   A series of instructions within a program that is executed by a calling module. An internal subroutine may be executed from several different points in a program.

Iteration.   A logical control structure for indicating the repeated execution of a routine or routines.

Key field.   A field that uniquely defines a record within a file. A key field on a payroll file, for example, may be Social Security number.

Key file.   See **index (for an indexed file).**

Last Record (LR) indicator.   An indicator that is turned on after the last record has been processed. This indicator is commonly used to condition calculation and output operations to be performed at the end of a job.

Level indicator (L1–L9).   An indicator that is turned on when there is a change in a control field; commonly used to condition group indicators for group or summary printing.

Limit test.   A data validation procedure used to ensure that a field does not exceed a specified limit.

Line Counter Specifications form.   An RPG coding form used to indicate or override the system defaults regarding length of printed forms and the number of lines to be printed.

Linkage editor.   A program used to link object modules together into one executable load module.

Literal.   A constant that is used by a program but that remains unchanged during processing. Same as **constant.**

Load module.   An executable program that normally consists of object modules that have been linked together by a linkage editor program.

Logic error.   A logic error occurs when a sequence of programming steps is not executed properly; it is caused by incorrect sequencing of program instructions or misunderstanding of the problem or the logic flow.

Logical control structure.   The ways in which instructions in a program may be executed.

Logical record.   A tape or disk record that is to be processed as an individual unit; logical records are commonly grouped into physical records or blocks to maximize the efficient use of the tape or disk.

LOKUP.   An RPG operation that causes a search to be made for a specific element in a table or array.

Loop.   A series of programming steps that are executed a fixed number of times; when a specific condition occurs, control is transferred outside the loop.

Low-order position.   The rightmost or least significant position in a field.

Low-order truncation.   When a receiving field does not have enough decimal positions to accommodate a result, the least significant or low-order decimal position is truncated.

LR indicator.   See **Last Record indicator.**

Machine language.   The machine's own code; a program written in machine language requires no translation process.

Master file.   A major classification of data, containing records for a given application. Companies typically have payroll files, accounts receivable files, inventory files, and so forth. Contrast with **database.**

Menu. A technique used for interactive processing; the user is offered various options from which to select the procedures or routines required.

Missing data test. A validation procedure used to verify the presence of data in a field.

Module. A series of instructions treated as a unit by the program. It is considered good programming form to include a series of modules in a program that makes it easier to debug and understand the logic.

MOVE. An RPG operation that transmits data from one area of storage to another. Data is moved from right to left.

MOVEA. An RPG operation that can be used to move (1) a single alphanumeric field to an array and (2) several array elements to a single field.

MOVEL. An RPG operation that moves data from one area of storage to another; transmission begins from the leftmost position and proceeds to the rightmost position.

Multiple-level control break. A series of control fields (minor, intermediate, and major) determine what calculations are to be performed and what output is to be produced.

MULT. An RPG operation that multiplies Factor 1 by Factor 2 and places the product in the Result Field.

MVR. An RPG operation that moves the remainder of a division operation into the field specified in the Result Field.

Nested conditional. A conditional in which an IF operation itself can contain additional IF operations.

Nonnumeric field. A field that contains alphanumeric data.

Not (N) entry. An entry used to specify that the absence of an indicator is to signal an operation.

Numeric field. A field consisting of digits 0–9 with decimal alignment specified; a field that is typically used in an arithmetic operation.

Numeric literal. A constant consisting of digits 0–9, a decimal point, and a + or − sign.

Object module. The output from the compiler; see **object program.**

Object program. A machine-language equivalent of a source program. Object programs are the only ones that can be executed without being translated first.

Off-line operation. Entering data on a computer that is not connected to the main CPU; a type of data entry for future batch processing.

On-line processing. Refers to a system that provides immediate access to files, processes data immediately when it is entered, and always keeps files current.

OPEN. An RPG operation that opens the file specified in Factor 2 and makes it available for processing.

Output. The information produced by a computer system.

Output indicator. An indicator used to define the conditions under which an output operation is to be performed.

Output Specifications form. An RPG coding form used to describe the format of fields in an output record and to indicate when a record is to be produced.

Overflow (OF) indicator. An indicator used to determine when the end of a page has been reached; used to print headings on the top of a new page.

Packed data. Each byte within a field contains two numeric digits rather than one. The right-most byte, however, includes a sign and thus contains only one digit. Thus +123 in packed form would be represented in *two* bytes as $\boxed{12\mid 3+}$. Contrast with **zoned decimal format.**

PAGE. A reserved word used to instruct the computer to print page numbers on printed output.

Page overflow. See **overflow (OF) indicator.**

Parallel tables. See **related tables.**

Pointer. A field containing the location (actual physical disk address) of a record in an indexed file; the record is identified by a key field.

Pre-execution time array or table. An array or table that is loaded at the same time as the source program, that is, before actual execution of the program begins. Contrast with **compile time array or table.**

Preprinted form.   A form that can contain computer-produced output but that enters a computer system with heading and identifying information already imprinted.

Primary file.   The main file from which a program first reads records.

Primary key.   A key field that uniquely identifies each record in an indexed file.

Printer Spacing Chart.   A tool used to map out the proper spacing of output in a printed report.

Processing within limits.   See **dynamic processing.**

Program.   A series of instructions that enables a computer to read input data, process it, and convert it to output.

Program walkthrough.   A technique used to follow the logic in a program by stepping through each sequence of steps manually before actually running the program. This technique saves computer time and helps to minimize logic errors.

Programmer.   The computer professional who writes the set of instructions to convert input to output.

Prompt.   A request for information or response from a user. A prompt is typically displayed on a CRT. In order for the program to proceed, the user must respond to the prompt by keying in the appropriate characters.

Pseudocode.   This tool specifically depicts the logic flow of a structured program. It is a planning tool that uses a code similar to a program code for depicting logic. It is used for applications that have complex logical control procedures where a structured approach is most useful.

Quotient.   The result of dividing a dividend (in Factor 1) by a divisor (in Factor 2).

Random access.   See **direct access.**

Range test.   A data validation procedure to determine if a field has a value that falls within preestablished guidelines.

READ.   An RPG operation that reads the next record from a Demand file or a Full Procedural file.

Read/write head.   The part of a magnetic tape or magnetic disk drive that enables the device to read magnetic data or to record magnetic data, depending on the application.

Record.   A set of related fields treated as a unit. A payroll record on magnetic disk, for example, contains fields relating to a particular employee such as Social Security number, name, salary, and address.

Record format.   The description of the records in an externally described RPG III file.

Record identifying code.   Characters placed in a record to identify it to the system are designated with the use of a record identifying code.

Record identifying indicator.   An indicator that identifies the type of record being processed during the current program cycle.

Related tables.   Two or more tables that are related to one another. For an entry in one table, there is a corresponding entry in another table.

Relative file.   A file that uses a key field in each record for directly determining the location of each record.

Relative record number.   A method of numbering records from the beginning of a direct or relative file. Each record in the file is given a relative record number based on its location from the beginning of the file.

Report heading.   A line of output that provides identifying information such as a report name, page number, and date that defines the report to the user.

Result Field.   A field specified on the Calculation form that will contain the outcome or result of an arithmetic operation.

Resulting indicator.   An indicator that signals the result of a calculation, such as whether the result is plus, minus, or zero; a resulting indicator can also be used for determining whether a given field is greater than, less than, or equal to another field.

Rounding numeric fields.   See **Half-adjust.**

Routine.   A series of instructions that performs a specific operation or procedure.

RPG.   A high-level program generator; an acronym for *Report Program Generator*; most suited for printing reports and producing output files.

RPG coding sheet.   One of several specification forms used in RPG; each has space for 80 columns of information per line.

RPG Logic Cycle. The default sequence in which RPG performs all operations; not directly under the programmer's control.

Running total. A field that keeps track of a total as it is being accumulated.

Search argument. Factor 1 in a LOKUP instruction.

Secondary file. Any file other than the primary file used when multiple input files are required.

Selection. A logical control structure that performs operations if a given condition is met and can perform other operations if the condition is not met. Sometimes called **IF-THEN-ELSE** logical control structure.

Sequence. A logical control structure in which a series of instructions are executed in the order in which they appear.

Sequence test. A data validation technique used to determine whether input records are in proper sequence, ascending or descending, based on the control or key field.

Sequential access. A method of processing records in a file in sequence, starting with the record that is physically located at the beginning of the file and proceeding sequentially through the file.

Sequential file. A file in which records are processed in sequence as they appear on the file; to access a record in ACCTNO sequence on a sequential file, for example, begin with the first ACCTNO, proceed to the next, and so on.

Sequential processing. The method of processing records in the order in which they are located in a file.

SETLL. An RPG operation used to position the record pointer at the first record to be read; this is done before an indexed file can be accessed sequentially.

SETOF. An RPG operation used to turn off indicators.

SETON. An RPG operation used to turn on indicators.

SEU (Source Entry Utility). The most widely used line-editor in the RPG environment.

Single-entry table. A table that simply consists of a series of entries such as a table of out-of-stock part numbers.

Single-level control break. When one control field is used to condition calculation and printing operations.

Sizing fields. Determining the number of integer and decimal digits required in a field that will be used for storing the result of an arithmetic operation.

Sort Utility. A sort program typically supplied along with the operating system to sort records into a particular sequence before reading them.

SORTA. An RPG operation used to sort the elements of an array into either ascending or descending order.

Source program. A program written in a symbolic programming language; source programs must be translated into machine language before they can be executed.

Specifications form. RPG coding form.

Static array. Defined and described at compile time or pre-execution time.

Structure chart. See **hierarchy chart.**

Structured programming. An efficient programming technique that can facilitate the processing of programs in all languages; referred to as GOTO-less or modular programming.

Subprogram. An independent module that is external to the main program.

Subroutine. A series of steps that can be executed from anywhere in a program. See **external subroutine** and **internal subroutine.**

Subscript. See **index (for an array).**

SUB. An RPG operation that subtracts data from a field.

Summary printing. See **group report.**

Switch. A field established in a program to identify a particular condition within the program, such as an error condition.

Symbolic programming language. The writing of a program in an English-like language. Symbolic programs must be translated into machine language before they can be executed.

Syntax error. Any programming rules that have been violated will cause the computer to print an error message during the program translation phase. See **diagnostic.**

System integrity. Maintaining the reliability of a system by validating transaction data before it is used to update a master file.

Table. A list of related data items not part of a program that is stored in consecutive locations within main storage and may be accessed or referenced by an RPG program. See **related tables** and **single-entry table**.

TAG. Provides a name to which the program can branch; that is, it represents an entry point of a routine to be branched to.

Tagalong Sort. Produces a new sequential output file after selecting and sorting records from an input file. Contrast with an **Address Out Sort**.

Test data. Data created by a programmer to test the logic in a program; test data should include every condition that is to be processed by the program.

TESTN. An RPG operation that tests to determine if a field is numeric.

Top-down approach. An approach to programming where each module is written in sequence, with the first being the most significant module.

Total operation. A calculation or output operation that is performed only after a control group of records has been processed or at the end of the program.

Total time. The part of the RPG program cycle in which calculations or output specified for a group of records is performed. Total time operations are conditioned by control level indicators L1–L9.

Transaction file. A file that contains changes to be incorporated in a master file. A master file is updated with transaction records.

Transaction processing. A form of interactive processing that allows a user to input data and complete a transaction immediately. The associated files are updated immediately.

Truncation. See **high-order truncation** and **low-order truncation**.

Two-dimensional array. A type of array that has a row and column format.

UDATE. The RPG specification for obtaining the date of the run specified as mm/dd/yy.

Unconditional branch. A branch, or transfer, in a program or flowchart that occurs regardless of any existing condition.

UPDAT. An RPG operation that modifies or changes the last record read from an update file.

Update procedure. The process of making a file of data current.

User. The individual who will actually use the output from a computer run.

User-friendly. A form of processing designed to facilitate processing by a user who may not be very familiar with computers. Instructions and output are clear and easy to read and interpret.

Variable-length record. The term used to describe a file in which records are of different sizes.

Visual Table of Contents (VTOC). See **hierarchy chart**.

Walkthrough. See **program walkthrough**.

WORKSTN file processing. RPG programs that are written for interactive applications and that refer to the display screen component as a workstation (WORKSTN).

XFOOT. An RPG operation that is used for summing elements in an array.

Z-ADD. An RPG operation used for initializing a Result Field with zeros and then adding the contents of another field to it.

Zero suppression. The elimination of leading zeros in a report. For example, 0026 becomes 26 when zero suppressed.

Zoned decimal format. Representation of data so that one byte contains a character consisting of both a zone and digit portion.

Z-SUB. An RPG operation used primarily to change the sign of a field.

INDEX

RPG CONTROL AND FILE DESCRIPTION SPECIFICATIONS

Program				Keying Instruction	Graphic					Card Electro Number		Page	1 2 of	Program Identification	75 76 77 78 79 80
Programmer		Date			Key										

Control Specifications

For the valid entries for a system, refer to the RPG reference manual for that system.

H	Line	Form Type	Size to Compile	Object Output	Listing Options	Size to Execute	Debug	Reserved	Currency Symbol	Date Format	Date Edit	Inverted Print	Reserved	Number of Print Positions	Alternate Collating Sequence	Reserved	Inquiry	Reserved	Sign Handling	1 P Forms Position	Indicator Setting	File Translation	Punch MFCU Zeros	Nonprint Characters	Reserved	Table Load Halt	Shared I/O	Field Print	Formatted Dump	RPG to RPG II Conversion	Number of Formats	S/3 Conversion	Subprogram	CICS/DL/I	Transparent Literal																
	3 4 5	6	7 8 9	10	11	12 13 14	15	16 17	18	19	20	21	22	23 24 25	26	27 28 29 30 31 32 33 34 35 36	37	38 39	40	41	42 43	44	45	46	47	48	49	50	51	52 53	54	55	56	57	58 59 60 61 62 63 64 65 66 67 68 69 70 71 72 73 74																
0 1		H																																																		

File Description Specifications

For the valid entries for a system, refer to the RPG reference manual for that system.

F	Line	Form Type	Filename	I/O/U/C/D	P/S/C/R/T/D/F	E	F/V/S/M/D/E	Block Length	Record Length / External Record Name	L/R	A/P/I/K	I/X/D/T/R/ or 2			Extension Code E/L	Device	Symbolic Device	Labels S/N/E/M	K	Name of Label Exit / Continuation Lines Option	Extent Exit for DAM / Storage Index / Entry	A/U	R/U/N	File Condition U1–U8, UC
	3 4 5	6	7 8 9 10 11 12 13 14	15	16 17	18	19	20 21 22 23	24 25 26 27 28 29 30 31 32 33 34 35 36 37 38	39	40	41 42 43 44 45 46			39	40 41 42 43 44 45 46	47 48 49 50 51 52	53	54 55 56 57 58 59 60 61 62 63 64 65	66	67 68 69 70	71 72 73 74			
0 2		F																						
0 3		F																						
0 4		F																						
0 5		F																						
0 6		F																						
0 7		F																						
0 8		F																						
0 9		F																						
1 0		F																						
		F																						
		F																						

RPG INPUT SPECIFICATIONS

| Program | | | | Keying Instruction | Graphic | | | | | Card Electro Number | | Page | 1 2 | of ___ | Program Identification | 75 76 77 78 79 80 |
| Programmer | | Date | | | Key | | | | | | | | | | | |

I	Form Type	Filename or Record Name		Sequence	Number (1/N), E	Option (O), U, S	Record Identifying Indicator, **, or DS	External Field Name / Record Identification Codes													Stacker Select	P/B/L/R	Field Location			Decimal Positions	RPG Field Name	Control Level (L1–L9)	Matching Fields or Chaining Fields	Field Record Relation	Field Indicators				
								1			2			3						From	To						Plus	Minus	Zero or Blank				
Line		Data Structure Name	O R / A N D					Position	Not (N)	C/Z/D	Character	Position	Not (N)	C/Z/D	Character	Position	Not (N)	C/Z/D	Character			Occurs n Times	Length										
3 4 5	6	7 8 9 10 11 12 13	14 15 16		17	18	19 20	21 22 23 24	25	26	27	28 29 30 31	32	33	34	35 36 37 38	39	40	41	42	43	44 45 46 47	48 49 50 51	52	53 54 55 56 57 58	59 60	61 62	63 64	65 66	67 68	69 70	71 72 73 74
0 1	I																															
0 2	I																															
0 3	I																															
0 4	I																															
0 5	I																															
0 6	I																															
0 7	I																															
0 8	I																															
0 9	I																															
1 0	I																															
1 1	I																															
1 2	I																															
1 3	I																															
1 4	I																															
1 5	I																															
1 6	I																															
1 7	I																															
1 8	I																															
1 9	I																															
2 0	I																															
	I																															
	I																															
	I																															
	I																															
	I																															

RPG EXTENSION AND LINE COUNTER SPECIFICATIONS

Program				Keying Instruction	Graphic					Card Electro Number		Page	1 2	of	Program Identification	75 76 77 78 79 80
Programmer		Date			Key											

Extension Specifications

E		Record Sequence of the Chaining File					To Filename	Table or Array Name	Number of Entries Per Record	Number of Entries Per Table or Array	Length of Entry	P/B/L/R	Decimal Positions	Sequence (A/D)	Table or Array Name (Alternating Format)	Length of Entry	P/B/L/R	Decimal Positions	Sequence (A/D)	Comments
Line	Form Type		Number of the Chaining Field																	
				From Filename																
3 4 5	6	7 8	9 10	11 12 13 14 15 16 17 18	19 20 21 22 23 24 25 26		27 28 29 30 31 32	33 34 35	36 37 38 39	40 41 42	43	44	45	46 47 48 49 50 51	52 53 54	55	56	57	58 59 60 61 62 63 64 65 66 67 68 69 70 71 72 73 74
0 1	E																			
0 2	E																			
0 3	E																			
0 4	E																			
0 5	E																			
0 6	E																			
0 7	E																			
0 8	E																			
	E																			
	E																			

Line Counter Specifications

L			1		2		3		4		5		6		7		8		9		10		11		12	
Line	Form Type	Filename	Line Number	FL or Channel Number	Line Number	OL or Channel Number	Line Number	Channel Number	Line Number	Channel Number	Line Number	Channel Number	Line Number	Channel Number	Line Number	Channel Number	Line Number	Channel Number	Line Number	Channel Number	Line Number	Channel Number	Line Number	Channel Number	Line Number	Channel Number
3 4 5	6	7 8 9 10 11 12 13 14	15 16 17	18 19	20 21 22	23 24	25 26 27	28 29	30 31 32	33 34	35 36 37	38 39	40 41 42	43 44	45 46 47	48 49	50 51 52	53 54	55 56 57	58 59	60 61 62	63 64	65 66 67	68 69	70 71 72	73 74
1 1	L																									
1 2	L																									
	L																									

*Number of sheets per pad may vary slightly.

RPG EXTENSION AND LINE COUNTER SPECIFICATIONS

Program

Programmer

Date

Keying Instruction

Graphic

Key

Card Electro Number

Page ___ of ___

Program Identification   75 76 77 78 79 80

1 2

Extension Specifications

E			Record Sequence of the Chaining File		To Filename	Table or Array Name	Number of Entries Per Record	Number of Entries Per Table or Array	Length of Entry	P/B/L/R	Decimal Positions	Sequence (A/D)	Table or Array Name (Alternating Format)	Length of Entry	P/B/L/R	Decimal Positions	Sequence (A/D)	Comments
	Line	Form Type	Number of the Chaining Field															
			From Filename															
3 4 5	6	7 8	9 10 11 12 13 14 15 16 17 18	19 20 21 22 23 24 25 26	27 28 29 30 31 32	33 34 35	36 37 38 39	40 41 42	43	44	45	46 47 48 49 50 51	52 53 54	55	56	57	58 59 60 61 62 63 64 65 66 67 68 69 70 71 72 73 74	
0 1	E																	
0 2	E																	
0 3	E																	
0 4	E																	
0 5	E																	
0 6	E																	
0 7	E																	
0 8	E																	
	E																	
	E																	

Line Counter Specifications

L			Filename	1		2		3		4		5		6		7		8		9		10		11		12	
	Line	Form Type		Line Number	FL or Channel Number	Line Number	OL or Channel Number	Line Number	Channel Number	Line Number	Channel Number	Line Number	Channel Number	Line Number	Channel Number	Line Number	Channel Number	Line Number	Channel Number	Line Number	Channel Number	Line Number	Channel Number	Line Number	Channel Number	Line Number	Channel Number
3 4 5	6	7 8 9 10 11 12 13 14		15 16 17	18 19	20 21 22	23 24	25 26 27	28 29	30 31 32	33 34	35 36 37	38 39	40 41 42	43 44	45 46 47	48 49	50 51 52	53 54	55 56 57	58 59	60 61 62	63 64	65 66 67	68 69	70 71 72	73 74
1 1	L																										
1 2	L																										
	L																										

*Number of sheets per pad may vary slightly.

Program				Keying Instruction	Graphic						Card Electro Number		Page	1 2	of ___	Program Identification	75 76 77 78 79 80
Programmer		Date			Key												

I		Filename or Record Name		Sequence	Number (1/N), E	Option (O), U, S	Record Identifying Indicator, ** , or DS	External Field Name / Record Identification Codes												Stacker Select	P/B/L/R	Field Location				Decimal Positions	RPG Field Name	Control Level (L1–L9)	Matching Fields or Chaining Fields	Field Record Relation	Field Indicators			
								1				2				3						From		To							Plus	Minus	Zero or Blank	
Line	Form Type							Position	Not (N)	C/Z/D	Character	Position	Not (N)	C/Z/D	Character	Position	Not (N)	C/Z/D	Character			Data Structure												
		Data Structure Name	O R / A N D																			Occurs n Times		Length										
3 4 5	6	7 8 9 10 11 12 13	14 15 16		17	18	19 20	21 22 23 24	25	26	27	28 29 30 31	32	33	34	35 36 37 38	39	40	41	42	43	44 45 46 47		48 49 50 51	52	53 54 55 56 57 58	59 60	61 62	63 64	65 66	67 68	69 70	71 72 73 74
0 1	I																																
0 2	I																																
0 3	I																																
0 4	I																																
0 5	I																																
0 6	I																																
0 7	I																																
0 8	I																																
0 9	I																																
1 0	I																																
1 1	I																																
1 2	I																																
1 3	I																																
1 4	I																																
1 5	I																																
1 6	I																																
1 7	I																																
1 8	I																																
1 9	I																																
2 0	I																																
	I																																
	I																																
	I																																
	I																																
	I																																

RPG OUTPUT SPECIFICATIONS

O		Filename or Record Name	Type (H/D/T/E)	Stkr #/Fetch (F)	Space		Skip		Output Indicators					Field Name or EXCPT Name	Edit Codes	B/A/C/1 – 9/R	End Position in Output Record	P/B/L/R	Commas	Zero Balances to Print	No Sign	CR	–	X = Remove Plus Sign Y = Date Field Edit Z = Zero Suppress	5 – 9 = User Defined
				R	Before	After	Before	After		And		And							Yes	Yes	1	A	J		
				D	E	L													Yes	No	2	B	K		
				A	D	D													No	Yes	3	C	L		
Line	Form Type			O R A N D					Not		Not		Not	*Auto					No	No	4	D	M		
3 4 5	6	7 8 9 10 11 12 13	14	15 16	17 18		19 20 21 22		23 24 25	26	27 28 29	30	31	32 33 34 35 36 37	38	39	40 41 42 43	44	Constant or Edit Word						

Line	Form
1	O
2	O
3	O
4	O
5	O
6	O
7	O
8	O
9	O
0	O
1	O
2	O
3	O
4	O
5	O
6	O
7	O
8	O
9	O
0	O
	O
	O
	O
	O
	O

RPG CALCULATION SPECIFICATIONS

Program		Keying Instruction	Graphic						Card Electro Number		Page		of		Program Identification	75 76 77 78 79 80
Programmer	Date		Key													

C			Indicators							Factor 1	Operation	Factor 2		Result Field				Resulting Indicators			Comments
				And		And								Name	Length	Decimal Positions	Half Adjust (H)	Arithmetic / Plus / Minus / Zero			
Line	Form Type	Control Level (L0 – L9, LR, SR, AN/OR)	Not		Not		Not											Compare 1>2 / 1<2 / 1=2			
																		Lookup (Factor 2) is			
																		High	Low	Equal	
3 4 5	6	7 8	9	10 11	12 13	14	15 16	17	18 19 20 21 22 23 24 25 26 27	28 29 30 31 32	33 34 35 36 37 38 39 40 41 42	43 44 45 46 47 48	49 50 51	52	53	54 55	56 57	58 59	60 61 62 63 64 65 66 67 68 69 70 71 72 73 74
0 1	C																				
0 2	C																				
0 3	C																				
0 4	C																				
0 5	C																				
0 6	C																				
0 7	C																				
0 8	C																				
0 9	C																				
1 0	C																				
1 1	C																				
1 2	C																				
1 3	C																				
1 4	C																				
1 5	C																				
1 6	C																				
1 7	C																				
1 8	C																				
1 9	C																				
2 0	C																				
	C																				
	C																				
	C																				
	C																				
	C																				

RPG CALCULATION SPECIFICATIONS

Program			Keying	Graphic						Card Electro Number			Page	1 2	of	Program Identification	75 76 77 78 79 80
Programmer		Date	Instruction	Key													

C	Form Type	Control Level (L0 – L9, LR, SR, AN/OR)	Indicators									Factor 1	Operation	Factor 2	Result Field				Resulting Indicators					Comments
				And		And									Name	Length	Decimal Positions	Half Adjust (H)	Arithmetic					
			Not		Not		Not												Plus	Minus	Zero			
																			Compare					
																			1 > 2	1 < 2	1 = 2			
																			Lookup (Factor 2) is					
Line																			High	Low	Equal			
3 4 5	6	7 8	9 10 11		12 13 14		15 16 17					18 19 20 21 22 23 24 25 26 27	28 29 30 31 32	33 34 35 36 37 38 39 40 41 42	43 44 45 46 47 48	49 50 51	52	53	54 55	56 57	58 59	60 61 62 63 64 65 66 67 68 69 70 71 72 73 74		
0 1	C																							
0 2	C																							
0 3	C																							
0 4	C																							
0 5	C																							
0 6	C																							
0 7	C																							
0 8	C																							
0 9	C																							
1 0	C																							
1 1	C																							
1 2	C																							
1 3	C																							
1 4	C																							
1 5	C																							
1 6	C																							
1 7	C																							
1 8	C																							
1 9	C																							
2 0	C																							
	C																							
	C																							
	C																							
	C																							
	C																							

RPG OUTPUT SPECIFICATIONS

Program		Keying Instruction	Graphic						Card Electro Number		Page	1 2	of	Program Identification	75 76 77 78 79 80
Programmer	Date		Key												

O		Filename or Record Name	Type (H/D/T/E)	Stkr #/Fetch (F)	Space		Skip		Output Indicators			Field Name or EXCPT Name	Edit Codes	B/A/C/1 – 9/R	End Position in Output Record	P/B/L/R	Commas	Zero Balances to Print	No Sign	CR	–	X = Remove Plus Sign / Y = Date Field Edit / Z = Zero Suppress	5 – 9 = User Defined
	Line	Form Type			R	Before	After	After	And	And							Yes / Yes / No / No	Yes / No / Yes / No	1 / 2 / 3 / 4	A / B / C / D	J / K / L / M		
					O R / A N D	D E A	L D D	Before	Not	Not	Not	*Auto					Constant or Edit Word						

Column ruler: 3 4 5 | 6 | 7 8 9 10 11 12 13 | 14 | 15 | 16 | 17 | 18 | 19 20 21 22 | 23 24 25 | 26 | 27 28 | 29 30 31 | 32 33 34 35 36 37 | 38 | 39 | 40 41 42 43 | 44 | 45 46 47 48 49 50 51 52 53 54 55 56 57 58 59 60 61 62 63 64 65 66 67 68 69 70 | 71 72 73 74

Line	Form Type
0 1	O
0 2	O
0 3	O
0 4	O
0 5	O
0 6	O
0 7	O
0 8	O
0 9	O
1 0	O
1 1	O
1 2	O
1 3	O
1 4	O
1 5	O
1 6	O
1 7	O
1 8	O
1 9	O
2 0	O
	O
	O
	O
	O
	O